For Reference

Not to be taken from this room

THE LINGUISTICS ENCYCLOPEDIA, SECOND EDITION

THE LINGUISTICS ENCYCLOPEDIA, SECOND EDITION

Edited by Kirsten Malmkjær

London and New York

2-13-2003
ww
$/50 00

First published 1991
by Routledge
11 New Fetter Lane, London EC4P 4EE

Simultaneously published in the USA and Canada
by Routledge
29 West 35th Street, New York, NY 10001

First published in paperback 1995
Reprinted 1996

Second edition 2002

Routledge is an imprint of the Taylor & Francis Group

Selection and editorial matter © 1991, 2002 Kirsten Malmkjær.
Individual entries © the authors

Typeset in 10/12 Times by Graphicraft Limited, Hong Kong
Printed and bound in Great Britain by TJ International Ltd, Padstow, Cornwall

All rights reserved. No part of this book may be reprinted or reproduced or
utilized in any form or by any electronic, mechanical, or other means, now
known or hereafter invented, including photocopying and recording, or in any
information storage or retrieval system, without permission in writing from the publishers.

British Library Cataloguing-in-Publication Data
A catalogue record for this book is available from the British Library

Library of Congress Cataloging-in-Publication Data
A catalogue record for this book has been requested

ISBN 0–415–22209–5

For John Sinclair

Contents

List of entries

Preface

You are reading something, or listening to a lecture, or taking part in a conversation about language. You notice an unfamiliar term, or realize that you don't know enough about what is being said to understand. At this point, you should seek out this encyclopedia. Strategies for the use of encyclopedias differ, but this one is designed to allow you to proceed in one of three ways:

- You can consult the index at the back of the book, where you will find the term or subject in question appearing in its alphabetically determined place, with a page reference, or several, which will tell you where in the main body of the work it is defined, described and/or discussed.
- If you are looking for a major field of linguistic study, you can consult the List of entries immediately before this Preface.
- You can simply dive into the body of the work.

The entries are designed to be informative and easy to access. They do not provide as much information as you will find in a full book on any given topic, but they contain sufficient information to enable you to understand the basics, and to decide whether you need more. Each entry ends by listing some suggestions for further reading, and draws on many more works than those listed as further reading. These are mentioned in the text by author and year of publication, and a full reference can

be found in the Bibliography at the end of the book. Almost all the entries contain cross-references to other entries.

This book has lived through ten successful years. However, no work of reference to a developing discipline can remain at its cutting edge unless it, too, absorbs these developments. So, in this second edition of *The Linguistics Encyclopedia*, all but a very few entries – mostly those dealing with historical matters – have been extensively revised to take account of new developments in the fields they cover. The material on grammars has been rearranged, and there are brand-new entries on applied linguistics, cognitive linguistics, contrastive linguistics and cross-linguistic studies, and forensic linguistics. In addition, there is a comprehensive, new Introduction to the discipline, written by Tony Howatt from Edinburgh University, a leading authority on the history of linguistics.

This volume demonstrates the many-faceted face of linguistics and the new Introduction provides a view of its history. But it is likely that people have taken a theoretical interest in language for much longer than the timespan covered there. Having language is probably concomitant with wondering about language, and so – if there is one thing that sets linguistics apart from other disciplines – it is the fact that its subject matter must be used in the description. There is no metalanguage for language that is not translatable into language, and a metalanguage is, in any case, also a language. According to some, language is literally all there is. According to others, it reflects, more or less adequately, what there is. What seems certain is that we use it prolifically in creating and changing our momentary values, and that, in seeking to understand language, we are seeking to understand the cornerstone of the human mentality.

Kirsten Malmkjær
Cambridge, 2000

Key to contributors

T.A.	Tsutomu Akamatsu	C.H.	Christopher Hookway
J.M.A.	James M. Anderson	A.P.R.H.	Tony Howatt
C.B.	Colin Baker	R.F.I.	Robert F. Ilson
J.P.B.	James P. Blevins	A.J.	Adam Jaworski
J.B.	Jacques Bourquin	C.-W.K.	Chin-W. Kim
D.C.B.	David C. Brazil	J.P.L.	James P. Lantolf
E.K.B.	E. Keith Brown	G.N.L.	Geoffrey N. Leech
R.A.C.	Ronald A. Carter	D.G.L.	David G. Lockwood
R.C.	Richard Cauldwell	M.J.McC.	Michael J. McCarthy
R.M.C.	R. Malcolm Coulthard	M.K.C.MacM.	Michael K.C.
N.C.	Nikolas Coupland		MacMahon
R.D.	René Dirven	M.M.	Molly Mack
T.D.-E.	Tony Dudley-Evans	K.M.	Kirsten Malmkjær
S.E.	Susan Edwards	M.Nk	Mark Newbrook
N.F.	Norman Fairclough	F.J.N.	Frederick J. Newmeyer
E.F.-J.	Eli Fischer-Jørgensen	M.Nn	Margaret Newton
W.A.F.	William A. Foley	T.P.	Teresa Parodi
R.F.	Roger Fowler	A.M.R.	Allan M. Ramsay
A.F.	Anthony Fox	W.S.-Y.W.	William S.-Y. Wang
M.A.G.	Michael A. Garman	J.N.W.	John N. Williams

Notes on contributors

Tsutomu Akamatsu studied Modern Languages at Tokyo University of Foreign Studies, Phonetics at the University of London and General Linguistics at the University of Paris. He earned his Ph.D. from the University of Leeds, where he is a lecturer in the Department of Linguistics and Phonetics. He is a member of the Société Internationale de Linguistique Fonctionnelle (SILF) and has published more than a hundred articles in linguistics journals. His other publications include *The Theory of Neutralization and the Archiphoneme in Functional Phonology* (1988), *Essentials of Functional Phonology* (1992), *Japanese Phonetics: Theory and Practice* (1997) and *Japanese Phonology: A Functional Approach* (2000).

James M. Anderson holds a first degree in Spanish and received his Ph.D. in Linguistics from the University of Washington, Seattle, USA, in 1963. He taught Linguistics at the University of Calgary, Alberta, Canada, from 1968 and became a tenured Professor there in 1970. He was appointed Professor Emeritus on his retirement in 1988. In addition to some forty articles and papers, his publications include *Structural Aspect of Language Change* (1973) and *Ancient Languages of the Hispanic Peninsula* (1988). He co-edited *Readings in Romance Linguistics* (1972). He was President of the Rocky Mountain Linguistics Society in 1982.

Colin Baker obtained a first class honours degree in Educational Studies and a subsequent Ph.D. in Social Psychology from the University of Wales. He holds a Personal Chair at the University of Wales, and is currently Professor of Education at the University of Wales, Bangor, and Director of Research Centre Wales. His books include: *Aspects of Bilingualism in Wales* (1985), *Key Issues in Bilingualism and Bilingual Education* (1988), *Attitudes and Language* (1992), *Foundations of Bilingual Education and Bilingualism* (1993, second edition 1996), *A Parents' and Teachers' Guide to Bilingualism* (1995, second edition 2000), *The Encyclopedia of Bilingualism and Bilingual Education* (with S.P. Jones, 1998) and *The Care and Education of Young Bilinguals: An Introduction for Professionals* (2000).

James P. Blevins received his Ph.D. from the University of Massachusetts, Amherst, in 1990. He currently teaches in the Research Centre for English and Applied Linguistics at the University of Cambridge. His research interests include syntax, morphosyntax, computational linguistics and the history of linguistics.

Jacques Bourquin, Docteur ès sciences, Docteur ès lettres, is Professor of French Linguistics at the University of Franche-Comté, Besançon, France. He has written a thesis entitled 'La Dérivation suffixale (théorie et enseignement) au XIXe siècle', plus several articles on the problem of reading, and on the epistemology of linguistics.

David C. Brazil was Senior Lecturer in English at the College of Further Education, Worcester, UK, from 1966 till 1975, when he became a Senior Research Fellow on the SSRC project 'Discourse intonation' at the University of Birmingham, UK, led by Malcolm Coulthard. He received his Ph.D. from the University of Birmingham in 1978 and lectured there until his early retirement in 1986, which he spent teaching and lecturing in many parts of the world. His main publications are *Discourse Intonation and Language Teaching* (1981) and *The Communicative Value of Intonation in English* (1985). David Brazil died in September 1995.

E. Keith Brown received his Ph.D. from the University of Edinburgh, UK, in 1972. He has lectured in Ghana, Edinburgh, Essex (where he was Research Professor in Linguistics) and Cambridge. He has held visiting appointments in Toronto, Stirling, Heidelberg, Vienna and Düsseldorf, and his lecture tours have taken him to Germany, Poland, Bulgaria, Iran and Japan. His major publications include *Linguistics Today* (1984) and (with J.E. Miller) *Syntax: A Linguistic Introduction to Sentence Structure* (1980), *Syntax: Generative Grammar* (1982), *A Concise Encyclopedia of Syntactic Theories* (1996) and *A Concise Encyclopedia of Grammatical Categories* (1999).

Ronald A. Carter is Professor of Modern English Language in the School of English Studies at the University of Nottingham, UK. His publications include *Language and Literature: A Reader in Stylistics* (1982), *The Web of Words* (with teacher's book, 1987), *Vocabulary: Applied Linguistic Perspectives* (1987, second edition 1998), *Vocabulary and Language Teaching* (with M. McCarthy, 1988), *Seeing Through Language* (with Walter Nash, 1990), *Exploring Spoken English*

(with M. McCarthy, 1997), *The Routledge History of Literature in English: Britain and Ireland* (with John McRae, 1997, second edition 2001), *Investigating English Discourse* (1997), *Exploring Grammar in Context* (with Rebecca Hughes and Michael McCarthy, 2000), *Standard Spoken English: Common Language, Creative Discourse* (2001), *The Cambridge Grammar of English* (with Michael McCarthy, 2002), as well as a number of edited volumes and numerous research papers. He is the editor of six book series and his research activities range from empirical classroom investigations of the relationship between language awareness and language teaching to a multi-million-word, corpus-based analysis of spoken English.

Richard Cauldwell is a lecturer in the Department of English at the University of Birmingham, UK. His Ph.D. concerned the intonation of Philip Larkin's poetry readings. He is now interested in developing models of spontaneous speech for teacher training and teaching listening.

R. Malcolm Coulthard is Professor of English Language and Linguistics at the University of Birmingham, where he has been for the whole of his academic career. He is best known for his work on the analysis of spoken discourse, published in *Towards an Analysis of Discourse* (1975), *An Introduction to Discourse Analysis*, (1977, new edition 1985) and *Advances in Spoken Discourse Analysis* (1992). In the late 1980s, he became involved in the field of forensic linguistics and was elected Chairman of the establishing committee of the International Association of Forensic Linguists. He is the founding joint editor of the journal *Forensic Linguistics: The International Journal of Speech, Language and the Law*. He has been consulted as an expert witness in over 120 cases, including the high-profile Birmingham Six, Derek Bentley and Bridgewater Four appeals.

Nikolas Coupland is Professor and Director of the Centre for Language and Communication Research at Cardiff University, Wales, UK. He is, with Allan Bell, founding editor of the *Journal of Sociolinguistics*. He has published books and more than 100 articles on dialect stylistics, the socio-linguistics of ageing, accommodation theory, sociolinguistics and social theory, metalanguage and the social psychology of language.

René Dirven studied Germanic Philology at the Catholic University of Leuven from 1952 till 1956, and taught in the secondary-school sector until 1958, when he became a lecturer in two Brussels training colleges. In 1965, he was appointed to a lectureship in the Higher Institute for Translators and Interpreters Marie Haps in Brussels. He obtained his Ph.D. in Germanic Philology in 1971 and was appointed Professor in English Linguistics at the University of Trier, Germany, in 1972. Here he set up the Linguistic Agency University Trier (LAUD), organizing annual linguistic symposia and publishing linguistic pre-prints. In 1985 he was offered a full professorship at the University of Duisburg, Germany, where he stayed till 1995, when he retired from teaching. As Professor Emeritus, he continues his research and work in international projects and organizations such as LAUD, LICCA (Languages in Contact and Conflict in Africa) and Icla (International Association of Cognitive Linguists), of which he was President from 1995 till 1997. The group project EUROPILL, which aims at producing introductions to language and linguistics in the most important European languages, was completed in 2000, and a Cognitive English Grammar and a project in electronic bibliographies, E-Bib, was begun. René Dirven's publications include (with Wolf Paprotté) *The Ubiquity of Metaphor: Metaphor in Language and Thought* (1985), (with V. Fried) *Functionalism in Linguistics* (1987) and *Fillmore's Case*

Grammar: A Reader (1987), (ed.) *A User's Grammar of English: Word, Sentence, Text, Interaction* (1989), *Metonymy and Metaphor: Different Mental Strategies of Conceptualisation* (1993), *Metaphor and Nation: Metaphors Afrikaners Live by* (1994), (with Johan Vanprys) *Current Approaches to the Lexicon* (1995) and (with Marjolijn Verspoor) *Cognitive Exploration of Language and Linguistics* (1998).

Tony Dudley-Evans is Senior Lecturer in the English for International Students Unit at the University of Birmingham. He is co-editor of *English for Specific Purposes: An International Journal* and author, with Maggie Jo St John, of *Developments in ESP: A Multidisciplinary Approach* (1998). He has a second career as a promoter of contemporary jazz in Birmingham.

Susan Edwards is a lecturer in the Department of Linguistic Science at the University of Reading and a qualified speech and language therapist. Her publications cover a variety of topics in language pathology, including aphasia. She is co-author (with Fletcher, Garman, Hughes, Letts and Sinka) of *The Reynell Developmental Language Scales* (1997) and co-author, with Rondal, of *Language in Mental Retardation* (1997). She is part of the development team for a new test of aphasia (with Bastiaanse and Rispen), *The Verb and Sentence Test*. She is on the editorial board of *Aphasiology* and the *Asia Pacific Journal of Speech Language and Hearing*.

Norman Fairclough is Professor of Language in Social Life at Lancaster University, UK. His publications include *Language and Power* (1989), *Discourse and Social Change* (1992), *Critical Discourse Analysis* (1995), *Media Discourse* (1995), (with Lilie Chouliaraki) *Discourse in Late Modernity* (1999), *New Labour, New Language?* (2000). The focus of his current research is language in the new capitalism.

Eli Fischer-Jørgensen was Professor of Phonetics at the University of Copenhagen from 1966 to 1981, and was appointed Professor Emeritus on her retirement. In addition to about seventy article publications on phonological problems, and several Danish language volumes, her publications include *Trends in Phonological Theory* (1975) and *25 Years' Phonological Comments* (1979). She was Chair of the Linguistics Circle of Copenhagen, 1968–72, and has served on the editorial boards of several journals devoted to phonetics. In 1979 she presided over the Ninth International Congress of the Phonetic Sciences, held in Copenhagen. She received honorary doctorates from the Universities of Åhus and Lund in 1978.

William A. Foley received his Ph.D. from the University of California, Berkeley. He taught for twelve years at the Australian National University, and now holds the Chair of Linguistics at the University of Sydney, Australia. He is especially interested in the languages of the islands of Melanesia, particularly the Papuan languages of New Guinea, about which he wrote a volume for the Cambridge University Press 'Language Survey' series. His other interests include semantically and pragmatically based approaches to grammatical theory, and their application to the grammatical description of the languages of the Pacific and anthropological linguistics, a field for which he has published a major survey work with Blackwell.

Roger Fowler was Professor of English and Linguistics at the University of East Anglia, Norwich, UK. His numerous publications in the field of critical linguistics include *Literature as Social Discourse* (1981), *Linguistic Criticism* (1986), *Language in the News* (1991) and, with R. Hodge, G. Kress and T. Trew, *Language and Control* (1979). He died in 1999.

Anthony Fox holds a Ph.D. from the University of Edinburgh. He is Senior Lecturer in the Department of Linguistics and Phonetics at the University of Leeds, UK, where he has been Head of Department since 1989. He has published four books: *German Intonation* (1984), *The Structure of German* (1990), *Linguistic Reconstruction* (1995) and *Prosodic Features and Prosodic Structure* (2000). His research and publications have been mainly devoted to intonation and other suprasegmental features, especially from a typological point of view.

Michael A. Garman is a lecturer in the Department of Linguistic Science at the University of Reading, UK.

Christopher Hookway has been Professor of Philosophy at the University of Sheffield, UK, since 1995, having previously taught at the University of Birmingham. His publications include *Peirce* (1985), *Quine: Language, Experience and Reality* (1988), *Scepticism* (1990) and *Truth, Rationality, and Pragmatism* (2000). He has edited *Minds, Machines and Evolution* (1984) and, with Donald Peterson, *Philosophy and Cognitive Science* (1993). His research interests are epistemology, American pragmatism, and the philosophy of language.

Tony Howatt was born in Sheffield and educated in Yorkshire and Scotland, graduating with an MA (Edinburgh) in 1958. He taught English as a Foreign Language in Spain and Germany and, after gaining a distinction in the Diploma in Applied Linguistics (also Edinburgh) in 1962–3, he took up a research and development post with Kursverksamheten vid Stockholms Universitet. He returned to a lectureship in applied linguistics at Edinburgh in 1965, becoming a senior lecturer in the early 1980s. He retired in 1999, but continues to serve as Honorary Fellow. His early publications were teaching materials for

English as a foreign language, including *Weltsprache Englisch* (with Hans G. Hoffmann, 1962) and *A Modern Course in Business English* (with John Webb and Michael Knight, 1966), but his best-known work is *A History of English Language Teaching* (1984). He has also made contributions to journals, encyclopedias, etc., mainly in the field of historical studies in language teaching and applied linguistics.

Robert F. Ilson is an Honorary Research Fellow of University College London, UK, and sometime Associate Director of the Survey of English Usage which is based there. He has been editor of the *International Journal of Lexicography* and the *Bulletin of the European Association for Lexicography*. He has been convenor of the Commission on Lexicography and Lexicology of the International Association for Applied Linguistics.

Adam Jaworski is Senior Lecturer at the Centre for Language and Communication Research at Cardiff University, Wales, UK. He has published five books and numerous articles and book chapters on various topics in sociolinguistics including non-verbal communication, political discourse, casual conversation and literary pragmatics.

Chin-W. Kim received his Ph.D. in Linguistics from the University of California, Los Angeles, USA, in 1966. He is Professor and Head of Linguistics, Speech and Hearing Sciences, and English as an International Language at the University of Illinois at Urbana-Champaign, USA. He authored a paper entitled 'A theory of aspiration' in *Phonetica* in 1970 and contributed the entries 'Experimental phonetics' in W.O. Dingwall's *Survey of Linguistic Science* (1978) and 'Representation and derivation of tone' in D.L. Goyvaerts' *Phonology in the 80s* (1981). His fields of specialization are phonetics, phonology and Korean linguistics.

James P. Lantolf is Professor of Spanish and Applied Linguistics and Director of the Center for Language Acquisition at the Pennsylvania State University. He has been on the faculty of Cornell University, the University of Delaware and the University of Texas at San Antonio. He was co-editor of *Applied Linguistics* 1993–98 and continues to serve on its editorial panel. He also serves on the editorial boards of *The Modern Language Journal* and *Spanish Applied Linguistics*. He has been Visiting Professor at the University of Melbourne, the University of Nottingham, the University of Rome (*La Sapienza*), and the University of Kassel, as well as *Language Learning* Visiting Scholar at the University of Auckland. His research focuses on sociocultural theory and second language learning. Among his publications are *Vygotskian Approaches to Second Language Research* (co-edited with Gabriela Appel, 1994) and *Sociocultural Theory and Second Language Learning*, an edited volume (2000).

Geoffrey N. Leech is Research Professor of English Linguistics at Lancaster University, UK. He is co-author of *A Comprehensive Grammar of the English Language* (1985), based on the Survey of English Usage based at University College London. He has also written books and articles in the areas of stylistics, semantics and pragmatics; notably, *A Linguistic Guide to English Poetry* (1969), *Semantics: the study of Meaning* (2nd edition 1981) and *Principles of Pragmatics* (1983). In recent years, his research interests have focused on the computational analysis of English, using computer corpora. He was a member of the groups that compiled and annotated the Lancaster–Oslo–Bergen Corpus (LOB) and the British National Corpus (BNC). He is co-author of a large-scale corpus-based grammar of English: D. Biber *et al.*, *The Longman Grammar of Spoken and Written English* (1999).

David G. Lockwood received his Ph.D. from the University of Michigan (Ann Arbor), USA, in 1966. He has taught at Michigan State University since then, and has been a Professor there since 1975. In addition to numerous articles, his publications include *Introduction to Stratificational Linguistics* (1972), *Readings in Stratificational Linguistics* (which he co-edited, 1973) and *Morphological Analysis and Description: A Realizational Approach* (1993). His teaching specialities are stratificational grammar and phonology, problem-oriented courses in phonology, morphology, syntax and historical linguistics, structure of Russian, and comparative Slavic linguistics.

Michael J. McCarthy is Professor of Applied Linguistics at the University of Nottingham, UK. He has published widely in the field of English language teaching, co-authoring *Vocabulary and Language Teaching* (with R.A. Carter, 1988). *Vocabulary* was published in 1990, *Discourse Analysis for Language Teachers* in 1991 and *Spoken Language and Applied Linguistics* in 1998. He holds a Ph.D. (Cantab) in Spanish, and his current research interests are in corpora of spoken language, discourse analysis and vocabulary.

Michael K.C. MacMahon is Professor of Phonetics in the Department of English Language at the University of Glasgow, UK. He holds a Ph.D. on British neuro-linguistics in the nineteenth century, and his publications have dealt with aspects of phonetics, dialectology and neurolinguistics.

Molly Mack received her Ph.D. in Linguistics from Brown University, USA. She is an Associate Professor in the Department of Linguistics at the University of Illinois at Urbana-Champaign, USA. Her research interests are in speech perception and production, the psycholinguistic and neurolinguistic aspects of bilingualism, and age-related effects upon the acquisition of dual-language phonetic systems in bilinguals. As Resident Associate in the Center for Advanced Study at the University of Illinois, she has co-organized and led an interdisciplinary faculty seminar and national conference on the topic of the relationship between the mind, brain and language. Her publications include 'From the Ancients to axial slices: a historical perspective on the role of neuroscience in linguistic science' (2001) and the co-edited volume (with Marie T. Banich, 2001), *Mind, Brain and Language: Multidisciplinary Perspectives*.

Kirsten Malmkjær was lecturer in Modern English Language and MA course tutor at the University of Birmingham from 1985 until 1989, when she moved to the Research Centre for English and Applied Linguistics, the University of Cambridge. She directed the Centre's M.Phil in English and Applied Linguistics until April 1999, when she was appointed Professor of Translation Studies and Head of the Centre for Research in Translation at Middlesex University, UK.

Mark Newbrook received his Ph.D. in Linguistics from the University of Reading, UK, in 1982. He has taught linguistics in Singapore (1982–85), Hong Kong (1986–89) and Western Australia (1990), before taking up his post as Senior Lecturer in Linguistics at Monash University in Melbourne. His publications include *Sociolinguistic Reflexes of Dialect Interference in West Wirral* (1986), *Aspects of the Syntax of Educated Singaporean English*, (ed. and main author, 1987), *Hong Kong English and Standard English: A Guide for Students and Teachers* (1991), *English is an Asian Language* (ed., 1999), plus many articles on variation in contemporary English and latterly on 'Skeptical linguistics'.

Frederick J. Newmeyer received a Ph.D. from the University of Illinois in 1969. He is Professor in the Department of

Linguistics at the University of Washington, USA. He is editor-in-chief of *Linguistics: The Cambridge Survey* (1988), and author of *English Aspectual Verbs* (1975), *Linguistic Theory in America* (1980), *Grammatical Theory: Its Limits and its Possibilities* (1983), *Politics of Linguistics* (1986) and *Language Form and Language Function* (1998). His interests are syntactic theory and the history of linguistics.

Margaret Newton holds the UK's first Ph.D. on dyslexia. She is Director of the Aston House Consultancy and Dyslexia Trust in Worcester, UK, an independent charitable organization, which continues the clinical and research work in dyslexia and the programme of dyslexia diagnosis, assessment and advice that Dr Newton and her colleagues began at the University of Aston in Birmingham, UK, in 1967. The team developed the diagnostic instruments known as the Aston Index and the Aston Portfolio of teaching techniques, and prepared the Aston Videotapes on Dyslexia.

Teresa Parodi holds a Ph.D. from the University of Düsseldorf (Germany). She is a Senior Research Associate in the University of Cambridge, Research Centre for English and Applied Linguistics. Her research interests focus on first and second language acquisition of syntax and morphology. Her publications include *Der Erwerb funktionaler Kategorien im Deutschen* (1998) and *Models of Inflection* (co-edited with R. Fabri and A. Ortmann, 1998).

Allan M. Ramsay is Professor of Formal Linguistics in the Department of Computation at UMIST, UK. He previously held a Chair in Artificial Intelligence at University College Dublin, and before that was a lecturer in AI at the University of Sussex. He is the author of *Formal Methods in AI* (1991) and *The Logical Structure of English* (Taylor & Francis, 1990). His research interests include the application of reasoning and planning techniques within language processing and the development of algorithms for dealing with languages with free word order.

William S.-Y. Wang received his Ph.D. from the University of Michigan, USA, in 1960. From 1966 till 1994 he was Professor of Linguistics at the University of California at Berkeley, USA, and Director of the Project on Linguistic Analysis. Since 1973, he has been editor of the *Journal of Chinese Linguistics*. He is an Academician of Academia Sinica in Taiwan, and the founding president of the International Association of Chinese Linguistics. Since 1995, he has held the Chair in Language Engineering at the City University of Hong Kong.

John N. Williams graduated in Psychology at the University of Durham in 1981 and went on to do doctoral research at the MRC Applied Psychology Unit, Cambridge. His Ph.D. in psychology, which concerned semantic processing during spoken language comprehension, was awarded by the University of Cambridge in 1985. He spent two years as a post-doctoral researcher at the University of Padova, Italy, examining semantic processing and word recognition. He worked as an English language assistant at the University of Florence for one year before taking up his post as Assistant Director of Research at the Research Centre for English and Applied Linguistics, University of Cambridge, where he teaches courses on psycholinguistics and language learning. His research interests include the cognitive mechanisms of second language learning, and syntactic processing in the second language.

Acknowledgements

The great majority of the work involved in the first edition of this encyclopedia took place in the School of English at the University of Birmingham. My colleagues there were a constant source of inspiration, support and encouragement. My debt to them is implicit in a number of entries in this work, but I want to make explicit my gratitude to the following one-time or present members of the English Language Research team: Mona Baker, the late David Brazil, Deirdre Burton, Malcolm Coulthard, Flo Davies, Tony Dudley-Evans, Harold Fish, Ann and Martin Hewings, Michael Hoey, Diane Houghton, Tim Johns, Chris Kennedy, Philip King, Murray Knowles, Paul Lennon, Mike McCarthy, Charles Owen and John Sinclair. When it came to the second edition, I turned again to many of these good friends for help, and I am grateful to Tony Dudley-Evans for updating the entry on genre analysis, and to a new Birmingham colleague, Richard Cauldwell, for updating the entry originally written by the late David Brazil.

Between the first and second editions of this encyclopedia, linguistics also experienced the loss of Roger Fowler; I am very grateful indeed to Norman Fairclough for bringing Roger Fowler's Critical Linguistics entry up to date.

By the time the first edition saw the light of day, I had moved on to the Research Centre for English and Applied Linguistics at the University of Cambridge. My colleagues there, Jim Blevins, Gillian and Keith Brown, Teresa Parodi, Sue Sentance, Ianthi Tsimpli and John Williams, helped me to discover new perspectives on a number of topics. John Williams advised me on the entries on psycholinguistics and language acquisition for the first edition, and I was delighted when he agreed to take on the psycholinguistics entry as his own for this edition; that Teresa Parodi agreed to update the entries on language acquisition and morphology; and that Jim Blevins agreed to take on the revision of a substantial part of the material on grammar.

All of the editing for the second edition has taken place after my move to Middlesex University. I am extremely grateful to the Dean of the School of Humanities and Cultural Studies there, Gabrielle Parker, for the patience she has shown as other projects, more central to my work at Middlesex, got delayed while this one was completed.

A number of students at Birmingham and Cambridge have been exposed in one way or another to versions or drafts of some of the entries. I should like to thank them all for their patience and reactions; in particular, I am grateful to Martha Shiro, Amy Tsui and Deborah Anderson for their helpful comments.

It goes without saying that I am very grateful indeed to the contributors themselves, all of whom had busy schedules, but who were, in spite of this, always ready to read and reread their entries during the editing stage. I should particularly like to thank Tsutomu Akamatsu, who worked tirelessly and with great kindness to help me from the planning stage and throughout the editing process of the first edition. Tsutomu Akamatsu, James Anderson, Gillian Brown, Eve Clark, David Crystal, Janet Dean Fodor, Michael Garman, Tim Johns, Chin-W. Kim, George Lakoff, Bertil Malmberg, Keith Mitchell, Maggie-Jo St John, Bertil Sonesson, Peter Trudgill and George Yule provided valuable guidance in the choice of contributors.

I am grateful to Bernard Comrie for advice on the entries on language typology and language universals, and to the anonymous readers who gave advice on how the second edition could be made an improvement on the first. I hope they find it so, even though I have not been able to incorporate every one of their suggestions. Of course, the faults that remain are my sole responsibility.

This encyclopedia was the brainchild of Wendy Morris, then Linguistics Editor at Routledge. Without her encouragement and guidance, I could not have contemplated taking on such a major commitment. I am grateful to her, to Steve, Poul and Stuart, who also believed the book would see the light one day, and to Jonathan Price of Routledge for his help in the later stages of editing the first edition. The second edition has been greatly speeded on its way by the help and encouragement of Louisa Semlyen, Ruth Bourne and Katharine Jacobson at Routledge.

David, Tomas, Amy and Nils have lived with this project through all our life together, providing the most delightful distractions and keeping everything in perspective. I could not wish for a better context.

K.M.

Permissions

In the entry on the INTERNATIONAL PHONETIC ALPHABET, the three versions of the alphabet are reproduced by kind permission of the International Phonetic Association.

In the entry on ACOUSTIC PHONETICS, Figures 9 and 14 are reprinted with permission of the publishers from *A Course in Phonetics*, 2nd edition, by Peter Ladefoged, © 1982 Harcourt Brace Jovanovich, Inc. Figure 10 in the same entry is reprinted with permission of the Journal of the Acoustical Society of America.

Introduction

As the present encyclopedia shows, linguistics today encompasses a wide range of component disciplines and associated activities, all of which use the name to announce their commitment to the serious study of language and languages. This (relatively recent) expansion of linguistics means we need to focus on the core of the subject and how it emerged from its nineteenth-century origins as 'the science of language', a phrase which is still taken as a gloss on modern linguistics though not all linguists find it equally congenial.

The roots of linguistics

While the nineteenth century is a reasonably well-motivated starting point for modern linguistics, the roots of serious language study lie deep in the past. The development of fully linguistic (i.e. post-pictographic) writing systems entailed not only a conscious awareness of linguistic processes but also an account of how they worked. Only in this way could the knowledge have been preserved and passed on to succeeding generations. This would locate the source of linguistic studies in the literate civilizations of antiquity – Mesopotamia, north India and China, Egypt, etc. – and it was in India that one of the earliest of the great traditions of linguistic scholarship was founded leading to **Panini's grammar of Sanskrit** in the first millennium BC (see Cardona 1990/1994). At much the same time, the Greeks embarked on the codification of

their language in a long series of works culminating in the **Techne grammatike of Dionysius Thrax** (*c*. 100 BC) (see Matthews 1990/1994).

The full story of 'grammar' would take too long to tell, but in its Latin guise it was the bedrock of Western schooling until the secularization of education in the eighteenth-century Enlightenment encouraged the creation of vernacular grammars, providing for the needs of an increasingly literate society. Latin grammars had been designed to teach the subject as a foreign language and they therefore adopted a highly normative approach. The unthinking transfer of this prescriptivism to the teaching of the mother tongue resulted in a species of simplistic, Latin-based 'school grammars', which tended to tarnish the reputation of traditional grammar as a whole.

The need to improve language pedagogy was one motivation for the reorientation of linguistic studies in Europe in the early nineteenth century, but so too was the renewal of contact with other traditions, most importantly that of the **Sanskrit** scholars whose objectivity and sharpness of focus on the linguistic (rather than literary) aspects of the subject seemed to accord with contemporary intellectual trends influenced by the methods and procedures of the natural sciences. The example of the Swedish botanist **Carl Linnaeus** (1707–78) in classifying the plant world had greatly impressed the eighteenth century, and geology was another science that seemed to offer language an appropriate model, particularly as it had a historical dimension that suited the intellectual climate of the time (e.g. Whitney 1875: 195). In fact the nineteenth century represented a synthesis between a sober demand for meticulous scientific research and a romantic desire to 'return to national roots' fired by revolutions in America and France and by the disintegration of the classical tradition in the arts and sciences.

A commitment to rigour was at the heart of the new linguistic sciences, including the close observation and careful collection of the 'facts', meticulous record-keeping and the exercise of objective judgement in the processes of classification, accountability to the wider scientific community through the dissemination of findings, etc. More significant, however, was the intellectual conviction that language was subject to the kind of 'general laws' that were the hallmark of the natural sciences. Arguments such as these increased as the young science (still known as 'philology' – 'linguistics' came later) moved decisively into comparative studies from the early 1820s onwards, applying notions such as sound change in the investigation of, for example, 'language families', a line of research influenced by the interest in the biological sciences kindled *inter alia* by the appearance of **Charles Darwin**'s *Origin of Species* in 1859.

Then quite suddenly in the 1870s the argument turned much sharper. A group of young German scholars in Leipzig – the so-called **Junggrammatiker (Neogrammarians**, initially a term of abuse) – challenged the contemporary establishment by announcing that their scientific claims convinced nobody. In particular, the sound-change laws were not scientific in any serious sense unless they aimed at generalizations that were water-tight and exceptionless. In addition, linguistic evidence should be derived from spoken language sources, not merely written inscriptions, and suitable informants

could be found among the speakers of non-standard dialects whose speech had not been 'corrupted' by education in the standard language. There was a hint of romanticism in this suggestion, but it was also noted positively by **Ferdinand de Saussure** (1857–1913), a young student at Leipzig at the height of the Junggrammatiker furore, and repeated in the opening chapter of his posthumous **Cours de linguistique générale** (1916), namely that a language should not be seen 'as an organism developing of its own accord but . . . as a product of the collective mind of a linguistic community' (Saussure 1916/1983: 5).

In 1876, Saussure (who had moved into philological studies from physics and chemistry) was poised to become the most highly respected philological scholar of his time. In 1906–7, with a major academic career behind him and still only 50 years of age, he gave a series of lectures in his home university of Geneva, to which he had returned in 1891 after ten years as a professor in Paris. He repeated the course twice more, ending in 1911. In their eventual published form these lectures effectively transformed nineteenth-century **historical and comparative philology** into the twentieth-century discipline of contemporary linguistics. They were to be Saussure's last academic achievement – two years later he died of cancer aged 56, leaving no manuscript or lecture notes. His Geneva colleagues and students collaborated in a complex editorial project to bring his work to the outside world with the publication of the *Cours* in Paris in 1916. Through this extraordinary chain of events, Saussure became known as the 'founding father' of modern linguistics. We shall look at his ideas again below.

Three phases of development in twentieth-century linguistics

Twentieth-century linguistics can be divided into two main phases: a phase of emergence

Phase 1: The emergence of modern linguistics (1911–33)

1911	Saussure's third (final) lecture series in Geneva
	Boas's 'Introduction' to *Handbook of American Indian Languages*
1912	Daniel Jones becomes Head of Department of Phonetics, University of London
1913	Death of Saussure (1857–1913)
1914	Bloomfield's *Introduction to the Study of Language*
1916	Saussure's *Cours de linguistique générale*
1921	Sapir's *Language*
1924	Linguistic Society of America founded
1925	First volume of the journal, *Language*
1928	First International Congress of Linguists (The Hague)
1932	First International Congress of Phonetic Sciences (Amsterdam)
1933	Bloomfield's *Language*

Phase 2: A time of transition (*c.* 1925–60)

1923	Malinowski's 'The problem of meaning in primitive languages'
1926	Linguistic Circle of Prague founded
1938	Death of Trubetzkoy (1890–1938)
1939	Trubetzkoy's *Grundzüge der Phonologie*
	Death of Sapir (1884–1939)
1941	Death of Whorf (1897–1941)
1942	Death of Boas (1858–1942)
1944	J.R. Firth becomes Professor of General Linguistics, University of London
1949	Death of Bloomfield (1887–1949)
1951	Harris's *Methods in Structural Linguistics*
1953	Weinreich's *Languages in Contact*
1956	Jakobson and Halle's *Fundamentals of Language*
1957	Chomsky's *Syntactic Structures*

Phase 3: The expansion and diversification of linguistics (since 1960)

1961	Halliday's 'Categories of the theory of grammar'
1963	Greenberg's *Universals of Language*
1965	Chomsky's *Aspects of the Theory of Syntax*
1966	Labov's *The Social Stratification of English in New York City*
1973	Halliday's *Explorations in the Functions of Language*
1978	Halliday's *Language as Social Semiotic*
1981	Chomsky's *Lectures on Government and Binding*
1985	Halliday's *Introduction to Functional Grammar*
1986	Chomsky's *Knowledge of Language*
1995	Chomsky's *The Minimalist Program*

Figure 1 Three phases of development in twentieth-century linguistics: a chronology

lasting until the late 1920s or early 1930s, and a later phase of expansion and diversification triggered by the general expansion of higher education after 1960. Between them was a period of transition, which affected the subject differently in Europe and America (see Figure 1).

Phase 1: The emergence of modern linguistics (1911–33)

Five principles of modern linguistics

As we have seen, modern linguistics was founded by the leading philologist of his day towards the end of his academic career. Saussure was no young Turk setting out to break the mould; he was the recognized elder statesman whose greatness lay in his ability to identify and preserve what his profession had achieved in the nineteenth century while at the same time setting it on a completely new course for the future. He did not get everything right (perhaps this explains his decision to scrap his lecture notes), but after Saussure linguistics could never be the same. We shall look at his specific proposals later. First we need to summarize the basic principles behind his transformation of '**philology**' into '**linguistics**'.

Linguistics is the scientific study of language for its own sake
The stress on science was not new, though its interpretation varied with time and context. What was important for Saussure was the focus on language for its own sake (philology never really gave up its links with the study of texts).

Linguistics is not prescriptive
For Saussure this was an obvious preliminary to a definition of linguistic science. It was perhaps more central to American linguistics, with its more practical orientation.

Spoken language is the primary object of study
The spoken language principle was already strongly held in phonetic and (some) philological circles, but Saussure's emphasis on it is quite explicit ('the spoken word alone constitutes [the object of study in linguistics]' (Saussure 1916/1983: 24–5). However, he was also prepared to be practical – written texts might be the only materials available.

Linguistics is an autonomous discipline
As a new science, linguistics had to fight off the claims of other more powerful disciplines, such as psychology, philosophy and anthropology. The first principle (the

study of language 'for its own sake') was very significant in this context – as was the last, the synchronic principle.

Synchronic studies of language at a specific point in time take precedence over diachronic (historical) studies
For Saussure this was the principle that revolutionized linguistics – 'it is absolute and admits no compromise' (Saussure 1916/ 1983: 83). It was, so to speak, the Rubicon philology could not cross. It also opened the way to the central (structural) point of his theory; namely, that 'the linguist must take the study of linguistic structure as his primary concern, and relate all other manifestations of language to it' (Saussure 1916/ 1983: 9). We shall discuss what he meant by 'linguistic structure' later.

The beginnings of American linguistics

By a curious coincidence of timing modern linguistics can be said to have emerged in the same year on both sides of the Atlantic. 1911 was not only the year of Saussure's final lecture series at Geneva; it was also the year in which the first part of the official *Handbook of American Indian Languages* was published in Washington. The Introduction by Franz Boas (1858–1942) came to be seen as a major milestone for the subject in the United States.

Unlike European linguistics, with its emphasis on theory, American priorities were firmly practical. The Amerindian project was a large-scale study designed to cover the whole field before too many of the languages involved became extinct, and it was led by an anthropologist who could claim expertise in the new linguistic sciences. The basic message of his famous Introduction was: respect for the data and the generalizations that could be drawn from it, provided the proper procedures were followed in a disciplined manner.

The project became a kind of rite of passage for all the major linguists of the time, and it also provided a clear perimeter fence that distinguished the **linguist** from the **philologist** – though there were significant individuals like Leonard Bloomfield (1887–1949) who were equally at home in both environments. In his first book (Bloomfield 1914), published after a study visit to Germany, his philological interests were still strong, though he called his subject 'linguistics', a term which (following Whitney 1875) the Americans (unlike the British; cf. Bolling 1929) accepted without difficulty. Although Boas and Bloomfield published their early work before Saussure, their general approach, following consciously in the footsteps of Whitney (1867, 1875), was consistent with the five principles listed above. In the context of the autonomy issue, Bloomfield's prefatory note is particularly instructive: 'I hope that this essay may help to introduce students of philosophy, psychology, ethnology, philology and other related subjects to a juster acquaintance with matters of language' (Bloomfield 1914: vi).

The other young scholar of importance in America was Edward Sapir (1884–1939) who, like Boas, was an anthroplogist with a consuming interest in language. In *Language*, published in 1921 and written in typically elegant prose, Sapir made the most extensive statement yet on the new approach to language study, introducing for the first time notions such as the significance of formal linguistic patterning which were to become increasingly influential. He also emphasized the independence of form and function: 'we cannot but conclude that linguistic form may and should be studied as types of patterning, apart from the associated functions' (Sapir 1921: 60).

Soon there were the first signs of successful institutionalization. The Linguistic Society of America (LSA) was inaugurated in December 1924, with its 'house journal' *Language* appearing the following year (though it was a long time before articles on linguistics formed more than a minority

of the contents (Matthews 1993: 10–11)). Back in Europe, a group of followers of Saussure established the Prague Linguistic Circle in 1926, the membership of which eventually included major figures in the subsequent history of the subject: Roman Jakobson, for instance, and Prince Nikolai Trubetzkoy. In 1928 the first International Congress of Linguists was held in The Hague, and the first in the Phonetic Sciences in Amsterdam in 1932. Finally, with the appearance of Bloomfield's massive second book, also called *Language* (1933), there could no longer be any doubt: linguistics had arrived, though it comes as a bit of a shock to note that, among the 264 founder members of the LSA in 1924, only 2 could claim to hold an academic post explicitly linked to the subject (one being Bloomfield).

Before moving to Phase 2, we should take a brief look at linguistics in Britain. For centuries the English have always been good at the same two linguistic things: phonetics and lexicography, and both were riding high in the late nineteenth century. It was not difficult, for instance, to claim scientific status for **phonetics** and it also had considerable potential for practical application: in language pedagogy, for instance, medicine, or the new technology of sound recording (Thomas Edison's phonograph appeared in 1877). **Lexicography** benefited from the nineteenth-century obsession with history, which provided the basis for the huge project that dominated England as the American Indian project dominated America; namely the *Oxford English Dictionary*. While phonetics counted as part of linguistics in the broad sense, the dictionary project is much more doubtful. It was essentially an exercise in philology. Where the new linguistic sciences had some influence was in the interest in **dialectology**; which was given plenty of house room in the *Transactions of the Philological Society* from the 1840s onwards. But there was no British equivalent of W.D. Whitney to lead the transition from **philology** to modern linguistics. The leadership role in England fell to **phonetics** (see Firth 1946/1957a) and therefore to Henry Sweet (1845–1912) – the man who 'taught phonetics to Europe' (Onions 1921: 519), but who was also very protective of traditional philological studies in which he had a formidable (and enduring) reputation. He passed the phonetics torch to Daniel Jones (1881–1967) and the subject was accorded the status of an academic department at London University as early as 1912. By 1921 there was a Chair, with Jones as the obvious appointee; general linguistics had to wait another twenty-three years for a similar honour.

The history of the term 'linguistics' in Britain is instructive in this context. Sweet avoided it, preferring his home-made term **'living philology'** (e.g. Sweet 1884: 593, 1899: 1). Jones had little need for it, since most of his work was closely tied to phonetic data, and general 'linguistic' matters were not seen as pressing, though his language teaching colleague Harold Palmer used it as the title of a course he gave at the School of Oriental Studies (Smith 1999: 62). Oxbridge preferred not to recognize its existence at all: C.K. Ogden, for instance, possibly the nearest Oxbridge had to a linguist before 1945, only used the word in *The Meaning of Meaning* (with I.A. Richards, 1923) when translating from other languages (even using 'linguistic' as a noun on two occasions) or when introducing Malinowski, who contributed a famous Supplement. Bolling (1929) tells us that the British establishment tried (unsuccessfully) to persuade the Americans that 'philology' was the right label (Bolling 1929). Whitney's early groundwork in the United States had borne fruit.

Phase 2: A time of transition (c. 1925–60)

Modern linguistics emerged at much the same time in Europe and the USA, and the postwar revival started around 1960 for both, but the intervening years were very different in the two continents. In America structural linguistics, or descriptive linguistics as it came to be known, grew in size and extent throughout the inter-war period until it suddenly and unexpectedly lost its leadership in the 1940s, initiating a period of transition before Chomsky's 'generative enterprise' took centre stage in the 1960s. Saussurean linguistics, on the other hand, had no leader and change began as soon as the ideas had been assimilated in Europe after World War I.

As it stood, Saussure's *Cours* had little to say about the practical description of particular languages, and it was partly to fill this gap that the **Linguistic Circle of Prague** was founded in 1926. Phonology was the first – but not the only – focus of the Circle's work, which rapidly developed a personality of its own, adopting a strongly functional interpretation of linguistics. **Functionalism** was also the mark of André Martinet in Paris in the late 1930s before internment during the war and ten years in America, and, in a rather different sense, function was a central component of Louis Hjelmslev's theory of **glossematics** published in Copenhagen in 1943, though it was little known until an English translation appeared in 1953. Finally, there was London, where linguistics (as distinct from phonetics) began in a small way with a contribution by the anthropologist Bronislaw Malinowski in 1923. Although superficially reminiscent of the role of Boas and Sapir in America, Malinowski's work led the subject in an entirely different direction – away from the structural properties of sentences and their parts, and towards the functional values of texts (especially spoken texts) and their role in social life. London under J.R. Firth in the 1940s and 1950s effected a new synthesis that combined the 'micro' traditions of English phonetics/phonology with the textual traditions of Malinowski and later also Prague, within Malinowski's anthropological framework known as 'the context of situation' (see p. xxxix). It might have been a rather mixed assortment, but under the influence of Firth's student M.A.K. Halliday it was forged into a powerful model that genuinely sought to establish a fertile union between form and function within a general theory of language in a social context ('social semiotic', to use Halliday's phrase (1978)). With Halliday, the long transition from Saussurean structuralism was complete.

The American story is more traumatic. After a long period of growth between the wars, structural-descriptive linguistics was deprived of all its leading founder members within a few years. Sapir died from a heart condition in 1939 aged 55; Whorf from cancer in 1941 aged only 44; Boas in 1942 (he was already an elderly man); and Bloomfield himself through a stroke, which effectively removed him from the profession in 1947 at the age of 60 (he died in 1949). The next generation, delayed somewhat by the war anyway, was not ready to take over and Bloomfield's colleagues and followers, who had not expected the role of leadership to be thrust upon them, understandably held back from any overt move to step into his shoes. Under such circumstances, new initiatives were bound to come from the edges rather than the mainstream, and one of the successful new departures of the 1950s was **applied linguistics** in both language pedagogy (Charles C. Fries) and mission work (e.g. Eugene Nida and Kenneth Pike of the **Summer Institutes**).

The linguists left behind in 1950 (Bernard Bloch, for instance, George L. Trager, Charles F. Hockett and Zellig S. Harris) have since become known collectively as '**post-Bloomfieldians**' in acknowledgement of their decision to carry on with the work Bloomfield had initiated, but the practical effect (see Matthews 1993 for details) was inevitably to extend the technicalities of structural analysis rather than rethink the approach. However, Harris, in some ways the most influential of the group, produced

the idea that brought this unsought-for and somewhat unhappy transitional interlude to an end: **transformational grammar**. By the 1960s, in the hands of Harris's former student Noam Chomsky, it had become **transformational-generative grammar (TG)** and was well on the way to re-creating the energies of the inter-war years.

Phase 3: the expansion and diversification of linguistics (since 1960)

From around 1960, linguistics in both Europe and the United States began to benefit from the expansion of higher education following the postwar economic recovery: new departments were opened, research programmes initiated, posts created, and so on. It was a lively time and the subject itself attracted a large number of young people, including those at the top with the new ideas – scholars like Noam Chomsky in the United States and M.A.K. Halliday in Britain (later Australia).

The chronology in Figure 1 offers only a short list of texts under the present heading, but this does not reflect a lack of activity (rather, the reverse). So much was being done that only a very few publications stood out as marking a major new departure. In addition, all the important works since 1960 are listed under individual entries elsewhere in this encyclopedia.

The unifying theme of structuralism which had maintained a broad transatlantic consensus before the war evaporated fast in the early 1960s, and by 1970 it had vanished, leaving two contrasting approaches to the subject, both descended from different branches of the structuralist 'family tree'. One (Chomskyan **generativism**) was fathered directly by American structuralism, and the other (**functionalism**) had more complex parental origins, but there was no doubt that the line went back to Saussure in the end.

The details of this contrast will emerge later, but some of the key features can be

sketched quickly here. Generativism typically idealizes the data and employs it in the
pursuit of an increasingly powerful theory
of language acquisition and its role in
understanding the human mind. There is no
interest in the 'real world' here; language
is the realm of (largely silent) cognition.
For many people, however, this is a world
of great allure that affords the kind of
excitement that 'frontiers of knowledge'
have always generated. The functionalist
alternative refuses to idealize language; it
is located in a world of real events affecting the lives of everybody in one way or
another. This has a special attraction for
those who are concerned to understand, and
perhaps influence – even control – the
power that language has in the conduct of
everyday life. It is an approach that places
a high value on respect for authentic language data and in recent years it has been
able to match the technological gloss that
used to be a generativist preserve by developing massive computer-based corpora on
the basis of which to judge the status of
linguistic generalizations. The functionalists
use words like 'scientific', individual' and
'cognitive' less often than their generativist
rivals, and words like 'human', 'social' and
'relationship' more frequently. For the fore-
seeable future, there is no possible consensus; eventually, there will be a synthesis
because they both inhabit the same world.
But not yet.

Rivalries between approaches should not
be allowed to mask the fact that modern
linguistics is not defined solely by its
'mainstreams' but also by its breadth of
coverage. Three initiatives, also dating from
the 1960s, deserve particular prominence
(and are dealt with in their own right in the
encyclopedia) but there are, no doubt, many
more.

The **descriptivist tradition** – the respect
for language diversity, the meticulous collection and classification of appropriate
data, and the commitment to language in
the real world – lost its mainstream status

in the 1960s, but it lived on, for instance,
in the research, associated with figures like
Joseph Greenberg (e.g. Greenberg 1963),
that focuses on patterns of similarity among
apparently diverse languages, associations in
the data that would lend support to a theory
of universals, not in the sense that 'all languages have such-and-such-a-feature', but
that the spread of variation is narrower than
it may appear to be. Greenberg's results
continue to excite useful controversy.

A second major development in America
was a direct challenge to the emergence of
mainstream generativism. Known from the
1950s as **sociolinguistics**, it gathered considerable momentum in the 1960s, building
to some extent on the past work of Sapir
and Uriel Weinreich (1953), but also introducing a wholly new range of concerns into
modern linguistic studies: the processes of
language change, for instance, and language
variation have been important themes,
along with the linguistic consequences of
human communication. It is impossible
to identify specific 'leaders', but important
contributors would have to include William
Labov, John Gumperz, Dell Hymes and
Joshua Fishman.

If sociolinguistics can be said to complement generativism, then in principle
psycholinguistics, the third major development of post-1960 linguistics, should complement the rather low priority that theories
of language learning and acquisition tend
to have in a functionalist context. However, this attempt at symmetry is probably
misguided, since psychology has never been
'neutral' with regard to linguistics (in the
late nineteenth century, for instance, it was
seen as the greatest threat to the autonomy
of the new subject). In its behaviourist guise
it underpinned Bloomfield's structuralism
and in its cognitivist manifestation has been
central to generativism – so much so that,
on at least one occasion, Chomsky himself
has appeared to accept the overlordship
of cognitive psychology. In fact for its
adherents the attraction of modern psycho-

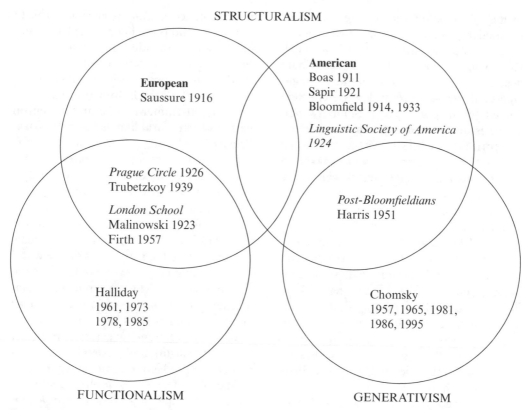

STRUCTURALISM

European
Saussure 1916

American
Boas 1911
Sapir 1921
Bloomfield 1914, 1933

*Linguistic Society of America
1924*

Prague Circle 1926
Trubetzkoy 1939

London School
Malinowski 1923
Firth 1957

Post-Bloomfieldians
Harris 1951

Halliday
1961, 1973
1978, 1985

Chomsky
1957, 1965, 1981,
1986, 1995

FUNCTIONALISM   GENERATIVISM

Figure 2 Trends in modern linguistics: a 'map of the world'

linguistics consists in its links with the new cognitive sciences.

Trends in modern linguistics: a 'map of the world'

Figure 2 shows the three 'mainstream' approaches to linguistics in the twentieth century: structuralism, functionalism and generativism. However, it does not show examples of 'crossover' links, nor does it include subdisciplines outside the mainstream (sociolinguistics, psycholinguistics, etc.).

Structuralism

Structuralism in linguistics has two interpretations: one derived from Saussure, and the other from the American school founded by Boas.

The Saussurean model

In his *Cours de linguistique générale* Saussure famously compared language to chess, pointing out that the design of the pieces and their names are structurally irrelevant: they can take any form agreed between the participants provided only that each side starts with sixteen pieces divided into six contrasting categories, with the correct number of units in each category. The game may then proceed according to a system of agreed rules known to each player. This analogy demonstrates clearly the distinction between the surface phenomenon of 'a game' and the underlying system of categories and the rules for their deployment which together constitute 'chess'. Perhaps the most important point Saussure wanted to make is that each component of the system is defined by reference to its distinctive place in the system: change one element and the entire system is affected. Removing the bishop, for instance, would destroy 'chess', but a different game might emerge if the new bishop-less system were agreed by all participants. Similarly, language is an arbitrary system of rules and categories that works by virtue of a 'social contract' tacitly accepted by all speakers, a socially sustained agreement to call a rose 'a rose'.

Given the chess analogy, we can understand why Saussure's first step towards a theory of language is to draw a basic distinction between instances of language in use (**parole**) and the underlying language system (**langue**) (the French terms have no exact equivalents in English and typically remain untranslated in accounts of Saussure's work). Linguistic structure lies at the heart of langue and is the primary concern of linguistics (cf. Saussure 1916/ 1974/1983: chapter 3).

Saussure goes on to characterize langue as a 'social fact', that is a socially sanctioned system of signs each of which represents a conventionalized ('arbitrary') fusion of sound (the **signifier**) and meaning (the **signified**). Since the significance of a sign derives from its relationships with other signs in the system, it has no meaning 'on its own'. The meaning of the signifier *house* in English, for instance, is that it contrasts with *flat*, *tower-block*, etc., etc., and each language determines its system of contrasts in a different way. The same is true *mutatis mutandis* for sounds: /p/ is a significant sound in English because it contrasts with /b/, /f/, etc. What is important is the total system, not the component 'bits'.

Langue is not, however, merely a bundle of signs; it is a structured system of relations organized in terms of two contrasting axes. The first is a 'horizontal' (**syntagmatic**) axis along which signs are combined into sequences. Saussure declined to call these sequences 'sentences', since for him a sentence was an instance of parole (a unit that would probably be called an 'utterance' today). In addition, each point in the sequence represents a (more or less tightly constrained) choice of alternatives on a 'vertical' ('**associative**') axis. This two-dimensional framework became a central feature of structural linguistics (with '**paradigmatic**' replacing the term 'associative').

The final point of importance in this thumbnail sketch of a complex work is Saussure's emphatic rejection of the notion that language is a nomenclature, i.e. a set of labels for pre-existing categories 'in the real world'. Quite the opposite – linguistic systems impose their structures on the world and each language 'sees the outside world' in a unique way. This does not mean that speakers are 'prisoners' of their linguistic categories, but it does mean that all languages are different (a cardinal principle of structuralism) and a special effort is needed to understand the categories of a new one. The *Cours* itself provides an excellent example in the resistance of *langue* and *parole* to translation into English.

The lack of a translation for many years meant that the reception of Saussure's work in the anglophone world was rather slow, though Bloomfield himself was an early reviewer in America (Bloomfield 1923), acknowledging that Saussure had 'given us the theoretical basis for a science of human speech', but noting also that he differed from Saussure 'chiefly in basing my analysis on the sentence rather than on the word' (Bloomfield 1923: 319). This was to become a major point of difference between Saussurean and American linguistics, including Chomsky (1964: 23f.).

American structuralism

In writing his Introduction to the *Handbook of American Indian Languages*, Franz Boas aimed to produce a scientific study as free from prejudice and preconception as possible and dedicated to an objective and positive approach to the practical work in hand.

Being an anthropologist, Boas began with a warning against simplistic notions purporting to link language, race and culture, each of which must be studied independently before connections are proposed. From there he turned to language and the first instance of the most emblematic of structuralist themes: respect the data and let it speak for itself. He answered the contemporary prejudice that 'primitive peoples don't pronounce accurately' by pointing out that listeners impose their own sound system on others and then complain they cannot understand. The first task of linguistics was to provide objectively accurate phonetic descriptions on the principle that 'every single language has a definite and limited group of sounds' (1911: 12). Later this was to become **the phoneme principle**.

Other basic principles included:

- All languages are different: 'in a discussion of the characteristics of various languages, different fundamental categories will be found' (1911: 39). Boas provides a memorable set of examples which must have come as a shock to readers used only to the predictabilities of a few Indo-European languages.
- 'Give each language its proper place' (1911: 39), i.e. do not impose preconceived categories on the data – including categories derived from other Indian languages.
- The sentence is the basic unit of language: 'since all speech is intended to serve for the communication of ideas, the natural unit of expression is the sentence' (1911: 23).

Already the positivist, data-led ground rules of American structuralism had been laid; much later Bloomfield picked up the same themes in a famous structuralist dictum, 'the only useful generalizations about language are inductive generalizations' (Bloomfield 1935: 20).

The next significant step came in Sapir's *Language* (1921), where for the first time the discussion is couched in structural terms and Sapir introduces the concept of formal patterning, a notion he went on to explore in more detail in his later work.

Sapir's (1921) wholly integrated approach to language, culture and social life was later somewhat modified by the ideas of Benjamin Lee Whorf (1897–1941) – in the so-called '**Sapir–Whorf Hypothesis**'. In an extreme form the hypothesis claimed that the human mind could not escape from the cognitive constraints of specific linguistic systems, but there were weaker and perhaps more convincing versions. What the idea really needed was a long-term research programme, but the early deaths of both Sapir (1939) and Whorf (1941) left a legacy of unfinished business (see Lee 1996 for a recent comment).

Finally came Bloomfield's *Language* (1933), probably the major classic of the period, yet difficult to assess because it plays more than one tune. As Matthews puts it: 'one of the marvellous things about Bloomfield's *Language* is the way in which it reconciled so much that was the established wisdom in the discipline . . . with so much that was strikingly new' (Matthews 1993: 11).

This was the book that taught linguistics to America. It marked a crucial watershed: before *Language*, linguistics might have been absorbed into traditional academia once the Amerindian project was completed; after it, however, this could not have happened. The subject had earned and deserved its autonomy.

Language is no descriptivist manual (Bloomfield wrote one later (see Bloomfield 1942)). It is a hugely well-informed and detailed account of the whole field of linguistics, traditional and modern, but it is better known now for what its later opponents have criticized rather than for what it set out to do in its own day. This is particularly true of its approach to **meaning**.

As is well known, Bloomfield accepted the arguments of **behaviourism**, including the principle that scientific enquiry required overt, observable evidence. This committed him to a situational theory of meaning ('we have defined the meaning of a linguistic form as the situation in which the speaker utters it and the response which it calls forth in the hearer' (Bloomfield 1935: 139)), which he illustrated in a lengthy anecdote about 'Jack and Jill' (1935: chapter 2). In summary form, Jack gets Jill an apple off a tree as the (apparent) consequence of Jill speaking to him (presumably she asked for it). This approach to meaning proved very influential in foreign language pedagogy for a long time, but as a serious contribution to linguistic theory it will not do. Even in the – heavily manipulated – Jack and Jill story, which puts the situational approach in the best possible light, it is still impossible to know what Jill actually said. Bloomfield's need for scientific consistency had led him up an intellectual cul-de-sac, and he tried a different tack. This time he maintained that the only way of reaching a scientific definition of meaning was to obtain the relevant scientific knowledge (e.g. defining salt in terms of chemistry (Bloomfield 1935: 139)). Finally, he gave up – 'any utterance can be fully described in terms of lexical and grammatical forms; we must remember only that the meaning cannot be defined in terms of our science' (1935: 167) – and continued with his book. Unfortunately, the long-term effect of this weakness made his followers nervous of the topic, encouraging the belief that meaning had to be 'kept out' of scientific linguistic procedures.

It is interesting to speculate whether Bloomfield would have modified his 'mechanistic' views on meaning if he had not died prematurely in 1949 (it is not impossible: he had changed his mind before). What happened in practice, however, was an even more determined effort by his successors (the '**post-Bloomfieldians**') to extend the practical analytic procedures of descriptive linguistics (for details see Matthews 1993). Bloomfield's teachings stressed the importance of formal features and mechanical (i.e. 'objective') techniques. The outcome was an approach known as '**distributional analysis**', in which categories were established by systematically testing the data in all possible structural environments (its distribution) through techniques like substitution. Using meaning and 'mixing levels of analysis' were forbidden. This 'bottom-up' approach had its strengths, but eventually it could go no further. Higher-level grammatical units could never be 'discovered' in this way, as the postwar generation (particularly Noam Chomsky (b. 1928)) argued.

Generativism

Generativism is associated so closely with Noam Chomsky that it is often referred to (despite his disapproval) as '**the Chomskyan revolution**'. However, as Lyons (1991: 162ff.) and others have stressed, it is important to draw a distinction between transformational-generative grammar and the broader views and beliefs that characterize the so-called 'generative enterprise'. Acceptance of the former does not necessarily entail commitment to the latter.

Transformational grammar (**TG**) first emerged in the early 1950s in the work of the leading 'post-Bloomfieldian' Zellig S. Harris, Chomsky's supervisor at Pennsylvania, and was the central focus of his Ph.D. (1955), entitled 'Transformational Analysis'. The basic notion was that sentence types, e.g. actives and passives, were systematically related to each other. This was a commonplace of traditional grammar but rejected by structuralism because of the dependence on meaning. From these beginnings Chomsky devised a theory of so-called '**kernel sentences**' (sentences without transformations (active, declarative, etc.)), which could be described in terms of a set of **phrase-structure rules**, plus a set of **trans-**

formation rules, in order to '**generate**' – i.e. provide structural descriptions for – the non-kernel derivatives (passive, interrogative, etc.). This model was the basis for his first major publication, *Syntactic Structures* (1957).

Chomsky's revival of the concept of 'rules' was predictably controversial. In their attack on traditional grammar, the structuralists had made a special point of replacing 'rules' with 'patterns' and 'structures' that emerged from close involvement with the data. The term 'rules' may have reminded people of old school grammars, but there is nothing prescriptive about saying, for instance, that sentences in English consist of a noun phrase followed by a verb phrase (e.g. *the dog* followed by *chased the cat*). The rule, which Chomsky formalized to look something like S → NP VP, is in effect a theory of English sentence structure which can be challenged empirically. More generally, Chomsky maintained that scientific linguistics had to start from theory, like any other science and the procedures for handling data offered by the structuralists would not do. Nor were these procedures as modestly practical as they appeared to be. Their ultimate aim was to 'discover' the grammar of the language under analysis – an aim which Chomsky dismissed as an impossible dream. Linguistic theory in his view should adopt a more limited and conventional goal; namely, to provide ways of choosing between alternative descriptions (e.g. between three possible candidate analyses of our example sentence: *the dog/chased the cat* or *the dog chased/the cat* or *the dog/chased/the cat*).

In 1957, Chomsky's linguistic and psychological views were kept separate, but in 1959 there was more than a hint of what was to come when he published a fiercely hostile review of *Verbal Behavior* by the leading behaviourist psychologist of the day B.F. Skinner, the subtext of which was a further criticism of the methods and procedures of structural linguistics which, as we have seen, had been heavily influenced by behaviourist thinking – particularly in the crucial area of meaning.

In 1965 Chomsky dropped the 'kernel sentence' notion in a major reworking of his model, which introduced a revolutionary new concept to the theory of syntax: a distinction between underlying ('**deep**') **structure** and '**surface structure**', the two interrelated by **transformations**, allowing active and passive sentences, for example, to have the same deep structure but two different transformational histories producing two different surface structures. Published as *Aspects of the Theory of Syntax*, this became known as the '**standard theory**'. In practice, however, the model soon showed itself to be cumbersome and insufficiently sensitive to the needs of languages other than English. Chomsky and his colleagues made substantial revisions during the 1970s to create the '**extended standard theory**'. The old phrase-structure rules were largely replaced by a more flexible syntactic process known as '**X-bar theory**'. The deep/surface distinction was preserved along with transformations, but in a heavily modified form, and there were also new features, all tending towards greater simplicity. The revised model (called **Government and Binding (GB)**, later **Principles and Parameters (P&P)**) appeared in 1981 and gave the whole 'generativist enterprise' a new lease of life. Since then there have been further simplifying changes resulting in **The Minimalist Program** of the 1990s.

Chomsky's work has always been motivated by a single goal: to explain human **language acquisition**. Many of the changes mentioned above were expressly designed to help account for the acquisition process by offering simpler procedures in tune with the innate capacities of the acquirer. The reintroduction of '**innate ideas**' has been Chomsky's most far-reaching and controversial proposition. The key notion is that human language acquisition cannot be explained by any theory of social learning. It is too powerful and universal for that: there are no exceptions and no unexplained failures. Chomsky's response has been to postulate the existence in each human of what he calls '**universal grammar**' (**UG**), a set of genetically determined principles that define the nature of language and determine the course of acquisition. It has nothing to do with the specifics of particular languages, which are acquired through contact with data in the environment.

The final outcome of the acquisition process is a system of (tacit) knowledge ('**competence**' is Chomsky's term) that can be put to use in social communication, private thought, expression, and so on, activities that Chomsky categorizes as 'language **performance**'. The **competence/performance distinction** (first put forward in *Aspects* in 1965) is reminiscent of Saussure's **langue/parole contrast**, but the choice of terms is psychological, not linguistic. 'Competence' seems an odd synonym for 'knowledge' (Chomsky himself has agreed), but 'performance' is an effective label, though typically described in rather negative terms, as the source of memory limitations, distractions, shifts of attention and errors of various kinds that prevent the true reflection of underlying competence. Like langue for Saussure, competence is the ultimate focus of linguistic theory, which is defined by Chomsky in his most famous quotation as being 'concerned primarily with an ideal speaker-listener, in a completely homogenous speech-community, who knows its language perfectly and is unaffected by [performance limitations]' (1965: 3). How the ideal speaker-listener interacts with the actual language acquirer has been at the heart of the Chomskyan research programme since 1965.

Functionalism

While generativism reformulated structuralism without changing fundamentals such as the centrality of the sentence, functionalism transformed it by restoring an aspect of linguistic organization that had been set on one side by the emphasis on form. Form and function (in at least one of its many guises) have long been traditional partners in the business of accounting for language and its use, form being concerned with the establishment of categories and function with the relations between them. In an English sentence like *The cat caught the mouse*, for example, *the cat* and *the mouse* have the same form (noun phrases) – but different functions: *The cat* functions as the subject of the sentence and *the mouse* as the object of the verb. '**Function**' can be extended to cover notional distinctions: the cat, being animate, functions as the **agent** of the catching, while the mouse is the one affected by the catching (functions as the '**patient**').

Functionalism is, however, even broader than this and it can be said to have had two godparents, both European: (i) the **Linguistic Circle of Prague** (1926–39), including Vilém Mathesius (1882–1945), Roman Jakobson (1896–1982) and Prince Nikolai S. Trubetzkoy (1890–1938), and (ii) the linguists of the so-called '**London School**', beginning with Bronislaw Malinowski (1884–1942) in 1923.

The Linguistic Circle of Prague (1926–39)
The principal aim of the linguists of the Prague Circle was to explore Saussurean structuralism and make proposals for its extension. Their best-known work is Trubetzkoy's *Grundzüge der Phonologie* (*Principles of Phonology*), an account of phonology published posthumously in Prague through the good offices of Jakobson in 1939. Following Saussure, Trubetzkoy was the first to distinguish systematically between **phonetics** (**parole**) and **phonology** (**langue**), placing the distinction in a functional context: 'phonology of necessity is concerned with the linguistic function of the sounds of language, while

phonetics deals with their phenomenalistic aspect without regard to function' (Trubetzkoy 1939/1969: 12), the best-known instance of this principle being the phoneme and its contrastive function in distinguishing between different words, e.g. *pin* and *tin* in English. The characterization of the phoneme itself as a 'bundle of distinctive features' also derived from Prague and was taken to America by Jakobson in 1942 and incorporated in publications with Morris Halle and others, including *Fundamentals of Language* (1956).

At the other end of the scale so to speak was the functional approach to text introduced by Karl Bühler (a philosopher colleague of Trubetzkoy's at Vienna University), who proposed a threefold classification which distinguished between a central **'representational' function** concerned with the content of the text, together with a contrasting pair of functions: **'expressive'** relating to the speaker/writer and **'conative'** to the listener/reader. Bühler's was the first of many such schemes which later influenced both Jakobson and Halliday. In the former case, Bühler's framework turned up in a much-extended form in Jakobson's famous contribution to a conference on stylistics in the late 1950s (Jakobson 1960).

Somewhere between the micro-functions of sentence components and the macro-functions of textual design, the Prague School (particularly Mathesius himself) founded an important line of research which came to be known as **'functional sentence perspective'** (**FSP**), aimed at identifying systematic relationships between linguistic units and features of text structure. It was specifically concerned with the way in which successive sentences in texts are constructed in order to reflect the developing pattern of information: what is **'new information'** (**rheme**) in one sentence, for instance, becomes **'given information'** (**theme**) in a later one and each language has its own way of signalling these relationships.

Functional linguistics in Britain

As we have already seen, the main British contribution to scientific language study focused on phonetics, a success that was recognized institutionally at University College London (UCL) in 1912. The founding of the School of Oriental Studies (SOS) in 1916 expanded the range of expertise in the linguistic sciences considerably and it was intended that the School should do for the languages of the British Empire what the Americans were doing for Amerindian languages, and this was the case to some extent. In addition, Bronislaw Malinowski, an anthropologist with an interest in language from the London School of Economics, established a working relationship with J.R. Firth (1890–1960), a senior member of staff at the School from the late 1920s and (from 1944) the first Professor of General Linguistics in the UK.

Malinowski's work in the Trobriand Islands led him to develop a functional repertoire of text types, with special reference to spoken language in pre-literate societies (Malinowski 1923). His principal theoretical contribution to the subject was a notion that became closely associated with London linguistics: the **context of situation**, without knowledge of which he argued no coherent account of the meaning of spoken utterances was possible. In a detailed example based on a narrative describing the return home of a canoe, a key phrase literally translatable as 'we paddle in place' could only be understood properly as 'we arrived' if you knew that paddles replaced oars in the shallow water near the shore, i.e. the context of situation imposed a meaning on the text that in isolation it did not possess. For Malinowski – and for Firthians in general – this interdependence between contextual meaning and linguistic form was crucial.

Writing in 1950, Firth expanded the notion of 'context of situation' into a schematic construct, as he called it (Firth

1950/1957b), and one of the major themes that he drew from it was the importance of language variation in context, an idea that later became known as '**register**'. In fact the investigation of 'meaning' in all its manifestations is at the heart of Firth's work, but it was only with Halliday (from 1961 onwards) that the crucial interrelationship between meaning and its linguistic realization began to find a systematic foundation.

Halliday's contribution to late twentieth-century linguistics is immensely generous. His publications range over the entire field of language study from formal syntax to the teaching of reading in the most versatile display of talent and inspiration the subject has yet encountered. As a consequence, it is impossible to summarize his contribution with any justice, except perhaps to emphasize one or two major themes. The first is his insistence, following Firth, that language must be studied in an integrated, unified manner without the intervention of a **langue/parole distinction** (cf. Firth 1950/1957b: 180–1). Instead, linguistics must study language as 'part of the social process' (Firth 1950/1957b: 181) or as '**social semiotic**' (Halliday 1978). More specifically, the linguist must attempt to make explicit and systematic statements on the choices people make within the linguistic systems at their disposal ('**textual function**') in response to their social ('**interpersonal function**') and cognitive ('**ideational function**') needs. The three functions (or '**metafunctions**') provide the basic architecture of the approach within which the key concept is the network (or system) of choices. Taken together, these features explain the use of '**systemic-functional linguistics**' as the name for his approach.

As he says in his *Introduction to Functional Grammar* (1985/1994: xvi–xvii), his early work concentrated on the importance of meaning in language, since he believed the current stress on formal syntax was undervaluing it, but later his emphasis shifted as he felt that the formal properties

of language were being neglected in a rush for meaning. The interdependence between the two is the bedrock principle of his work. Of particular importance in this context is his joint publication with Hasan, *Cohesion in English* (1976), and his support for the tradition of discourse analysis associated with J.M. Sinclair and M. Coulthard. The details of functionalist linguistics are covered elsewhere in the encyclopedia.

Two macro-themes

Two themes have played a powerful role in the history of linguistics over the past 150 or so years. Both have to do with the implications of major methodological decisions and their theoretical implications.

The first of these themes relates to the imposition of a basic distinction between linguistic systems and language-in-use: Saussure's **langue/parole distinction** is the original one, but Chomsky's **competence/performance contrast** is drawn in much the same place on the map. It could also be said that Bloomfieldian structuralism tacitly operated a **system/use distinction** in the search for 'patterns'. At the outset, it seems a convenient way of coping with the scope of the material, if nothing more. However, before long the theory-laden abstract 'sister' (langue, competence, system, etc.) has moved centre stage and her ordinary, everyday, 'real-world' sibling is marginalized. In 1875, Whitney said something rather powerful that may well still be relevant:

> not one item of any existing tongue is ever uttered except by the will of the utterer; not one is produced, not one that has been produced or acquired is changed, except by causes residing in the human will, consisting in human needs and preferences and economies.

Where has this gone? (cf. Joseph 1994).

Finally, it is appropriate to finish with a restatement of Saussure's basic aims for linguistics which reflect the second macro-theme of recent linguistic history: the contrast between **diversity** and **universality**. This was recognized by Sapir in 1921: 'There is no more striking general fact about language than its universality' and 'scarcely less impressive than the universality of speech is its almost incredible diversity' (1921: 22–3); and by Saussure in 1916, in a statement of basic aims which is out of date on specifics, but entirely relevant in its general thrust:

The aims of linguistics will be:

(a) to describe all known languages and record their history. This involves tracing the history of language families and, as far as possible, reconstructing the parent languages of each family;

(b) to determine the forces operating permanently and universally in all languages, and to formulate general laws which account for all particular linguistic phenomena historically attested;

(c) to delimit and define linguistics itself.
(Saussure 1916/1983: 6)

A.P.R.H.

Suggestions for further reading

Joseph, J.E. (1994) 'Twentieth-century linguistics: overview of trends', in R.E. Asher, (editor-in-chief) *The Encyclopedia of Language and Linguistics* vol. 9, Oxford: Pergamon.

Matthews, P.H. (1993) *Grammatical Theory in the United States from Bloomfield to Chomsky* (Cambridge Studies in Linguistics, no. 67), Cambridge: Cambridge University Press.

Morpurgo Davies, A. (1998) in G. Lepschy (ed.) *History of Linguistics* vol. 4, London: Longman.

Acoustic phonetics

Acoustic phonetics deals with the properties of sound as represented in variations of air pressure. A sound, whether its source is articulation of a word or an exploding cannon ball, disturbs the surrounding air molecules at equilibrium, much as a shove by a person in a crowded bus disturbs the standing passengers. The sensation of these air pressure variations as picked up by our hearing mechanisms and decoded in the brain constitutes what we call **sound** (see also AUDITORY PHONETICS). The question whether there was a sound when a tree fell in a jungle is therefore a moot one; there definitely were air-molecule variations generated by the fall of the tree but, unless there was an ear to register them, there was no sound.

The analogy between air molecules and bus passengers above is rather misleading, though, since the movements of the molecules are rapid and regular: rapid in the sense that they **oscillate** at the rate of hundreds and thousands of times per second, and regular in the sense that the oscillation takes the form of a swing or a pendulum. That is, a disturbed air molecule oscillates much as a pushed pendulum swings back and forth.

Let us now compare air molecules to a pendulum. Due to gravity, a pushed pendulum will stop after travelling a certain distance, depending on the force of the push; will then begin to return to the original rest position, but, instead of stopping at this position, will pass it to the opposite direction due to inertia; will stop after travelling about the same distance as the initial displacement; again will try to return to the initial rest position; but will again pass this point to the other direction, etc., until the original energy completely dissipates and the pendulum comes to a full stop.

Imagine now that attached at the end of the pendulum is a pencil and that a strip of paper in contact with the pencil is being pulled at a uniform speed. One can imagine that the pendulum will draw a wavy line on the paper, a line that is very regular in its ups and downs. If we disregard for the moment the effect of gravity, each cycle, one complete back-and-forth movement of the pendulum, would be exactly the same as the next cycle. Now if we plot the position of the pendulum, the distance of displacement from the original rest position, against time, then we will have Figure 1, in which the y-ordinate represents the distance of displacement and the x-abscissa the time, both units representing arbitrary units. Since a wave form such as the one given in Figure 1 is generatable with the sine function in trigonometry, it is called a **sine wave** or a **sinusoidal wave**. Such a wave can tell us several things.

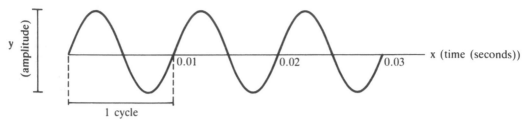

Figure 1 A sine wave whose cycle is one-hundredth of a second, thus having the frequency of 100 Hz

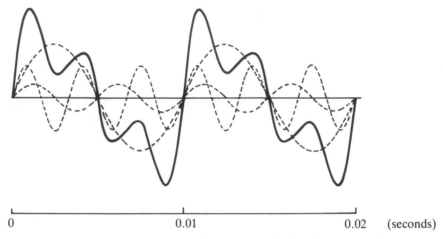

Figure 2 A complex wave formed with a combination of 100 Hz, 200 Hz and 300 Hz component waves

First, the shorter the duration of a cycle, the greater (the more frequent) the number of such cycles in a given unit of time. For example, a cycle having the duration of one hundredth of a second would have a frequency of 100 cycles per second (**cps**). This unit is now represented as **Hz** (named after a German physicist, Heinrich Hertz, 1857–94). A male speaking voice has on average 100–150 Hz, while a woman's voice is twice as high. The note A above middle C is fixed at 440 Hz.

Second, since the y-axis represents the distance of displacement of a pendulum from the rest position, the higher the peak of the wave, the greater the displacement. This is called **amplitude**, and translates into the degree of loudness of a sound. The unit here is **dB** (decibel, in honour of Alexander Graham Bell, 1847–1922). A normal con-versation has a value of 50–60 dB, a whisper half this value, and rock music about twice the value (110–20 dB). However, since the dB scale is logarithmic, doubling a dB value represents sound intensity which is ten times greater.

In nature, sounds that generate sinusoidal waves are not common. Well-designed tuning forks, whistles, sirens are some examples. Most sounds in nature have complex wave forms. This can be illustrated in the following way. Suppose that we add three waves together having the frequencies of 100 Hz, 200 Hz and 300 Hz, with the amplitude of x, y and z, respectively, as in Figure 2. What would be the resulting wave form? If we liken the situation to three people pushing a pendulum in the same direction, the first person pushing it with the force z at every beat, the second person

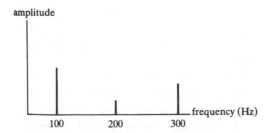

Figure 3 A line spectrum

with the force y at every second beat, and the third person with the force x at every third beat, then the position of the pendulum at any given moment would be equal to the displacement, which is the sum of the forces x, y and z. This is also what happens when the simultaneous wave forms having different frequencies and amplitudes are added together. In Figure 2, the dark unbroken line is the resulting complex wave.

Again, there are a few things to be noted here. First, note that the recurrence of the complex wave is at the same frequency as the highest common factor of the component frequencies, i.e. 100 Hz. This is called **fundamental frequency**. Note, secondly, that the frequencies of the component waves are whole-number multiples of the fundamental frequency. They are called **harmonics** or **overtones**. An **octave** is a relation between two harmonics whose frequencies are either twice or one half of the other.

There is another way to represent the frequency and amplitude of the component waves, more succinct and legible than Figure 2; namely by transposing them into a graph as in Figure 3. Since the component waves are represented in terms of lines, a graph like Figure 3 is called **line spectrum**.

Recall that the frequencies of the component waves in Figure 2 are all whole-number multiples of the lowest frequency. What if the component waves do not have such a property; that is, what if the frequencies are closer to one another, say, 90 Hz, 100 Hz and 110 Hz? The complex wave that these component waves generate is shown in Figure 4.

Compared to Figure 2, the amplitude of the complex wave of Figure 4 decays rapidly. This is called **damping**. It turns out that the more the number of component waves whose frequencies are close to one another, the more rapid the rate of damping. Try now to represent such a wave in a line spectrum, a wave whose component waves have frequencies, say 91 Hz, 92 Hz, 93 Hz, etc. to 110 Hz. We can do this as in Figure 5.

What if we add more component waves between any two lines in Figure 5, say ten or twenty more? Try as we might by sharpening our pencils, it would be impossible to draw in all the components. It would be unnecessary also if we take the 'roof' formed by the lines as the envelope of the

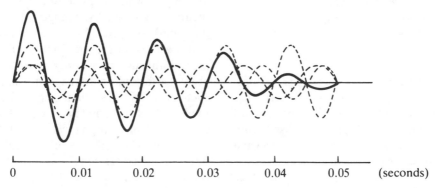

Figure 4 A 'decaying' complex wave formed with a combination of 90 Hz, 100 Hz and 110 Hz component waves

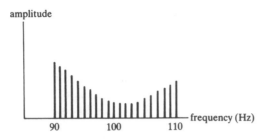

Figure 5 A line spectrum showing relative amplitudes and frequencies from 90, 91, 92 . . . to 110 Hz of the component waves

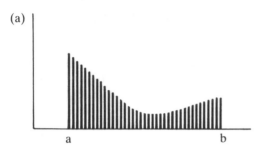

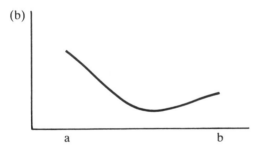

Figure 6 (a) A line spectrum with an infinite number of component waves whose frequencies range from a to b; (b) An envelope spectrum which is an equivalent of the line spectrum in Figure 6a

amplitude under which there is a component wave at that frequency with that amplitude, as in Figure 6. To contrast with the line spectrum in Figure 3, the spectrum in Figure 6b is called **envelope spectrum** or simply **spectrum**.

What is the significance of the difference in the two kinds of spectrum, Figure 3 and Figure 6b? It turns out that, if we divide

sound into two kinds, **melody** and **noise**, melody has regular, recurrent wave forms, while noise has irregular non-recurrent wave forms.

Before turning to speech acoustics, it is worth noting that every object, when struck, vibrates at a certain 'built-in' frequency. This frequency, called **natural resonance frequency**, is dependent upon the object's size, density, material, etc. But in general, the larger the size, the lower the frequency (compare a tuba with a trumpet, a bass cello with a violin, or longer piano strings with shorter ones) and the more tense or compact the material, the higher the frequency (compare glass with carpet, and consider how one tunes a guitar or a violin).

Acoustics of speech

Vowels

A pair of vocal folds can be likened to a pair of hands or wood blocks clapping each other. As such, the sound it generates is, strictly speaking, a noise. This noise, however, is modified as it travels through the pharyngeal and oral (sometimes nasal) cavities, much as the sound generated by a vibrating reed in an oboe or a clarinet is modified. Thus what comes out of the mouth is not the same as the pure unmodified vocal tone. And, to extend the analogy, just as the pitch of a wind instrument is regulated by changing the effective length or size of the resonating tube with various stops, the quality of sounds passing through the supraglottal cavities is regulated by changing the cavity sizes with such 'stops' as the tongue, the velum and the lips. It is immediately obvious that one cannot articulate the vowels [i], [ɑ] and [u] without varying the size of the oral cavity (see also ARTICULATORY PHONETICS). What does this mean acoustically?

For the sake of illustration, let us assume that a tube consisting of the joined oral and

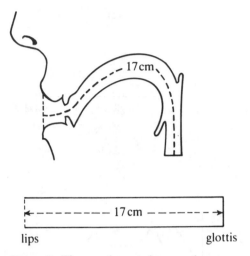

Figure 7 The vocal-tract shape and an idealized tube model of the tract for the most neutral vowel

pharyngeal cavities is a resonating acoustic tube, much like an organ pipe. The most uniform 'pipe' or tube one can assume is the one formed when producing the neutral vowel [ə] (see Figure 7). Without going into much detail, the natural resonance frequency of such a tube can be calculated with the following formula:

$$f = (2n - 1)\frac{v}{4l}$$

Where f = frequency, v = velocity of sound and l = length of the vocal tract

Since v is 340 m per second, and l is 17 centimetres in an average male, f is about 500 Hz when $n = 1$, 1500 Hz when $n = 2$, 2500 Hz when $n = 3$, etc. What this means is that, given a vocal tract which is about 17 centimetres long, forming the most neutral tract shape usually assumed for the schwa vowel [ə], the **white noise** (the vocal-fold excitation) at one end will be modified in such a way that there will be resonance peaks at every 1000 Hz, beginning at 500 Hz. These resonance peaks are called **formants**.

It is easy to imagine that a change in the size and shape of a resonating acoustic tube results in the change of resonance frequencies of the tube. For the purpose of speech acoustics, it is convenient to regard the vocal tract as consisting of two connected tubes, one front and the other back, with the velic area as the joint. Viewed in this way, vowel [i] has the narrow front (oral) tube and the wide back tube, while [ɑ] is its mirror image, i.e. [ɑ] has the wide front tube but the narrow back tube. On the other hand, [u] has the narrow area ('the bottle neck') in the middle (at the joint) and, with lip rounding, at the very front as well. The vocal-tract shapes, the idealized tube shapes and the resulting acoustic spectrum of these three vowels are as illustrated in Figure 8. The formant frequencies of all other vowels would fall somewhere between or inside an approximate triangle formed by the three 'extreme' vowels. The frequencies of the first three formants of eight American English vowels are given in Table 1.

Table 1 can be graphically represented as Figure 9 (adapted from Ladefoged 1993: 193). A few things may be observed from this figure:

- F1 rises progressively from [i] to [ɑ], then drops to [u];
- F2 decreases progressively from [i] to [u];
- In general, F3 hovers around 2500 Hz.

From this it is tempting to speculate that F1 is inversely correlated with the tongue height, or the size of the oral cavity, and that F2 is correlated with the tongue advancement, or the size of the pharyngeal cavity. While this is roughly true, Ladefoged feels that there is a better correlation between the degree of backness and the distance between the first two formants (i.e., F2–F1), since in this way there is a better match between the traditional articulatory vowel chart and the formant chart with F1 plotted against F2, as shown in Figure 10 (from Ladefoged 1993: 179).

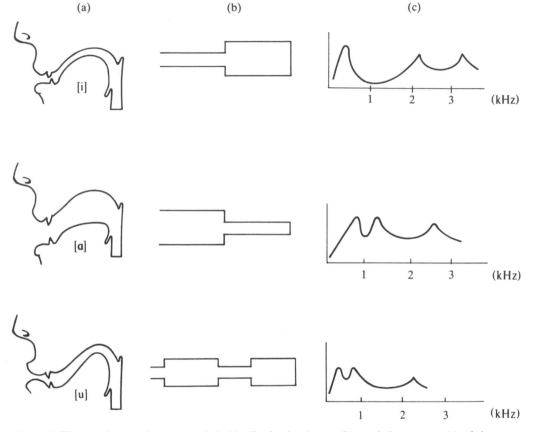

Figure 8 The vocal-tract shapes (a), their idealized tube shapes (b), and the spectra (c) of the three vowels [i], [ɑ] and [u]

Table 1 The frequencies of the first three formants in eight American English vowels

	[i]	[ɪ]	[ɛ]	[æ]	[ɑ]	[ɔ]	[ʊ]	[u]
F1	280	400	550	690	710	590	450	310
F2	2250	1920	1770	1660	1100	880	1030	870
F3	2890	2560	2490	2490	2540	2540	2380	2250

Consonants

The acoustics of consonants is much more complicated than that of vowels, and here one can talk only in terms of generalities.

It is customary to divide consonants into **sonorants** (nasals, liquids, glides) and **obstruents** (plosives, fricatives, affricates). The former are characterized by vowel-like acoustic qualities by virtue of the fact that they have an unbroken and fairly unconstricted resonating tube. The vocal tract for nasals, for example, can be schematically represented as a reversed letter F, shown in Figure 11.

The open nasal tract, functioning as a resonating acoustic tube, generates its own resonance frequencies, known as **nasal formants**, which are in general discontinuous with vowel formants. Different lengths

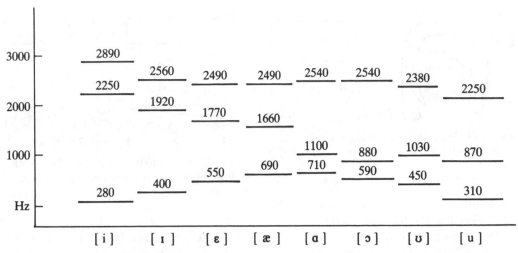

Figure 9 The frequencies of the first three formants in eight American English vowels

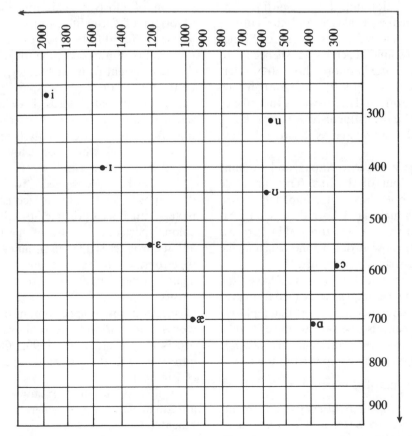

Figure 10 A formant chart showing the frequency of the first formant on the vertical axis plotted against the distance between the frequencies of the first and second formants on the horizontal axis for the eight American English vowels in Figure 9

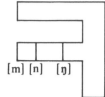

Figure 11 The vocal-tract shape and the idealized tube shape for nasal consonants [m], [n] and [ŋ]

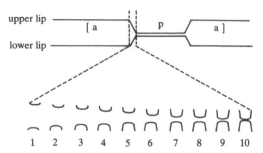

Figure 12 A schematic diagram of the closing of lips in [apa], its progression slowed down in ten steps

of the middle tube, i.e. the oral tract, would be responsible for different nasals.

The acoustic structure of obstruents is radically different, for obstruents are characterized by either the complete obstruction of the airflow in the vocal tract or a narrow constriction impeding the airflow. The former creates a silence and the latter a turbulent airstream (a hissing noise). Silence means no sound. Then how is silence heard at all and, furthermore, how are different silences, e.g. [p], [t], [k], distinguished from each other? The answer is that silence is heard and distinguished by its effect on the adjacent vowel, as illustrated in the following.

Assume a sequence [apa], and examine the behaviour of the lips. They are wide open for both [a]s, but completely closed for [p]. Though rapid, both the opening and closing of the lips is a time-taking process and, if we slow it down, one can imagine the process shown in Figure 12.

Now, as we have seen, vowels have their own resonance frequencies, called formants. A closed tube, such as the one that a plosive assumes, can also be said to have its own resonance frequency, although it is inaudible because no energy escapes from the closed tube (for what it is worth, it is $\frac{v}{2l}$). If we take the resonance frequency (i.e. formant) of the vowel to be x, and the resonance frequency of the plosive to be y, then the closing and opening of the lips can be seen to be, acoustically speaking, a transition

from x to y and then from y to x. It is this formant transition towards and from the assumed value of the consonant's resonance frequency that is responsible for the perception of plosives. This imagined place of origin of formant transitions is called **locus**. As for different places of plosives, the lengths of a closed tube for [p], [t] and [k] are different from each other; so would be the loci of these plosives; and so would be the transitional patterns. They are shown schematically in Figure 13. It can be seen that all formants rise rapidly from plosive to vowel in [pa], while higher formants fall in [ta], but converge in [ka].

A machine designed to analyse/decompose sound into its acoustic parameters, much as a prism splits light into its colour spectrum, is called a **spectrograph**, and its product is a **spectrogram**. A normal spectrogram shows frequency (ordinate) against time (abscissa), with relative intensity indicated by degrees of darkness of spectrogram. A spectrogram of English words *bab*, *dad* and *gag* is shown in Figure 14 (from Ladefoged 1993: 200). Compare this with the schematic spectrogram of Figure 13.

In addition to the formant transitions, a noise in the spectrum generated by a turbulent airstream characterizes fricatives and affricates. This noise may vary in its frequency range, intensity and duration depending upon the location and manner

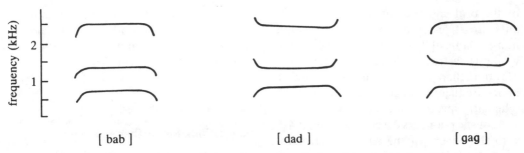

[bab]   [dad]   [gag]

Figure 13 A schematic spectrogram of the words [bab], [dad] and [gag], showing different patterns of transitions of upper formants for different places of articulation. Compare this with the real spectrogram in Figure 14

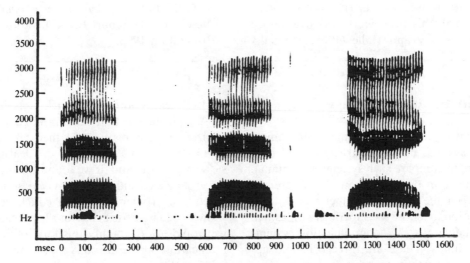

Figure 14 A spectrogram of the words [bab], [dad] and [gag]. Compare with Figure 13

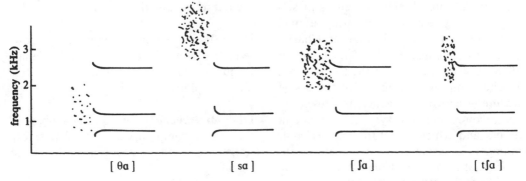

[θɑ]   [sɑ]   [ʃɑ]   [tʃɑ]

Figure 15 A schematic spectrogram showing different fricatives. Note that the difference between [θ] and sibilants is in the noise intensity; in the noise frequency between [s] and [ʃ]; and in the noise duration between [ʃ] and [tʃ]

of the oral constriction. In general, sibilants are stronger in noise intensity than non-sibilants ([f], [θ], [h] – [h] being the weakest); affricates have a shorter noise duration than fricatives; and [s] is higher in its frequency range than [ʃ]. See the schematic spectrograms in Figure 15.

Acoustic phonetics developed in the 1940s with the advent of the age of electronics, and provided a foundation for the theory of distinctive features of Jakobson and Halle (Jakobson *et al.* 1951) (see DISTINCTIVE FEATURES), which in turn formed the basis of generative phonology in the 1950s and 1960s (see GENERATIVE PHONOLOGY). Although this framework was overhauled by Chomsky and Halle (1968: especially chapter 7), acoustic phonetics is still an indispensable tool both in instrumental phonetic research and in validation of aspects of phonological theories.

C.-W.K.

Suggestions for further reading

Fry, D.B. (1979) *The Physics of Speech*, Cambridge: Cambridge University Press.
Ladefoged, P. (1962) *Elements of Acoustic Phonetics*, Chicago: University of Chicago Press; 2nd edition 1996.
——(1975/1993) *A Course in Phonetics*, New York: Harcourt Brace Jovanovich; 3rd edition 1993.

Animals and language

Linguists' interest in animal communication systems has been largely fuelled by a desire to compare such systems with human language in order to show the differences between the two, and sometimes, by implication, to show the superiority of human language over the communication systems of animals. There are three principal approaches to this comparison.

The design feature approach

One of the most famous attempts at setting up a system for comparing animal and human language is that of Charles Hockett (1960; also Hockett and Altmann 1968). For the purpose of the comparison, Hockett employs the notion of the **design feature** – a property which is present in some communication systems and not in others and which therefore enables communication systems to be classified into those that have a particular design feature and those that do not. Hockett lists sixteen such design features of human language; namely:

DF1   **Vocal-Auditory Channel**: it is in a sense coincidental that human language is realized through this channel; there are non-vocal sign systems for use by the deaf (see SIGN LANGUAGE) and, if we found that apes, for instance, could use non-vocal sounds to engage in what we could conclusively show to be linguistic behaviour (see below), we would not disqualify this kind of communication on the grounds that it was not vocal-auditory.

DF2   **Broadcast Transmission and Directional Reception**: this is a consequence of the nature of sound.

DF3   **Rapid Fading**: again as a consequence of the nature of sound, human language does not 'hover in the air', but 'fades' rapidly.

DF4   **Interchangeability**: adult members of the speech community are interchangeably transmitters and receivers of the linguistic signal.

DF5   **Complete Feedback**: the speaker hears everything of what s/he says.

DF6   **Specialization**: linguistic signals are specialized in the sense that their only true function is to convey the linguistic message.

DF7   **Semanticity**: linguistic signs are connected to elements and features of the world.

DF8   **Arbitrariness**: there is no **iconicity**, or physical resemblance, between a linguistic sign and the element or feature of the world to which it is connected (except in the very rare instances of **onomatopoeia**: those linguistic signs which sound like what they represent, as in *tick-tock* for the sound a clock makes or *bow-wow* for the sound a dog makes; but even here languages differ – in Danish, the clock says *tik-tak* and the dog *vov-vov* – so some arbitrariness is still involved). An iconic system is more limited than an arbitrary one, because it can only refer to things and situations that can be imitated.

DF9   **Discreteness**: the messages a language is able to convey are not arranged along a continuum, but are discrete of each other. Had they been continuous, the system would have had to be iconic (compare bee-dancing, described below); a discrete system can be either iconic or arbitrary.

DF10   **Displacement**: language can be used to talk about things that are remote in time and place from the interlocutors. A system without displacement could not be used to talk about the past or the future, to write fiction, to plan, speculate, or form hypotheses.

DF11   **Openness**: language allows for the making and interpretation of infinitely many new messages. Its grammatical patterning allows us to make new messages by blending old ones, analogizing from old ones, or transforming old ones. Second, in new contexts, old linguistic forms can take on new meanings, as when *hardware* was taken over for use in computer

terminology, or as in the case of figurative language use.

DF12   **Tradition**: the conventions and (at least surface) structure of any one language are learned rather than inherited.

DF13   **Duality of Patterning**: every language has a pattern of minimal meaningless elements (phonemes), which combine with each other to form patterns of meaningful elements (morphemes). This duality goes right 'up' through the system: Morphemes combine to form a further layer of meaningful patterning in the lexis, items of which form meaningful phrases, etc.

DF14   **Prevarication**: the ability to lie. This feature is crucially dependent on displacement.

DF15   **Reflexiveness**: with language, we can communicate about language. In other words, language can function as its own **metalanguage**.

DF16   **Learnability**: a speaker of one human language can learn another.

Armed with this list, we can examine animal communication systems to see whether or not they possess all or some of the design features listed. In the discussion, I shall ignore the first three design features, since, as indicated above, they are incidental to human language.

It is only possible here to provide rough sketches of the communication systems of two non-human species – the stickleback and the honey bee. The communication systems of these two species are popular examples among linguists because of their respective simplicity and complexity.

Further details of the communicative and other behaviour of sticklebacks can be found in Tinbergen (1972). Male sticklebacks display a composite visual sign in the breeding season: their eyes go turquoise, their backs go green, and their undersides go bright red. Each male builds an algae tunnel nest and tries to get pregnant females to lay their eggs in it. The males are very aggressive towards each other during this time, but friendly towards pregnant females, who go a silvery grey colour. Tinbergen wished to discover whether the visual displays influenced the stickleback's behaviour during the breeding season and, if so, to isolate those aspects of the visual display which caused the males to attack each other but to court the females. The male sticklebacks were kept in tanks on the window ledge of Tinbergen's laboratory, and he noticed that whenever the mail van (which was bright red) passed the window, the fish became agitated and behaved aggressively. This made Tinbergen suspect that it was the red colour of their underside which caused the male fish to attack each other, whereas the grey of the females attracted them. He tried and tested this hypothesis by presenting the male sticklebacks with wax models of various shapes and colours: they always reacted favourably to grey and with aggression to red; shape was unimportant.

So it seems that, for male sticklebacks, there are two meaningful signs: red and grey. Only having two signs in one's communication system need not be restrictive – consider what can be achieved with the binary system. However, the effectiveness of the binary system arises largely from its Duality of Patterning, a feature noticeably lacking in the stickleback system. In fact, the only design features which the stickleback system seems to share with human language are Discreteness, Arbitrariness and Semanticity: males and females signal differently, so there is no Interchangeability. Presumably, the fish do not perceive the colour of their own undersides, so there is no Complete Feedback. The signals have a direct biological (as opposed to a purely communicative) function, so there is no Specialization. The signal is linked to the

bodily state of the fish in the here and now, so there is no Displacement. The fish do not appear to make new messages, so there is no Openness. The signalling is not learned, but biologically determined, so there is no Tradition. The link with the state of the fish's body prevents Prevarication. The fish does not signal about the signal, so there is no Reflexiveness. As male and female stickleback cannot learn to use each other's signals, there seems to be no Learnability.

Compared to the communication system of sticklebacks, the worker honey bee's system appears to be the epitome of sophistication, and was deciphered by the Austrian naturalist Karl von Frisch (1967). A simplified account of the system might go something like this: a bee that has located a food source will return to the hive and inform its colleagues of the discovery by dancing to them. If the food source is more than 50 metres away from the hive, the bee dances in a figure of eight, a dance called the **waggle-dance**. The length of the straight runs of this dance, up the long lines of the figure eight, called the **waggle-run**, is proportionate to the distance between the hive and the food source, and during the waggle-run the dancer shakes its tail with a vigour which is in proportion to the richness of the food source. The frequency with which the bee dances also indicates distance: a bee returning from a food source 100 metres from the hive dances 10 times every 15 seconds, while a bee returning from 2000 metres away dances only 5 times every 15 seconds. The direction of the food source is given by the orientation of the waggle-run. If the food source is less than 50 metres away from the hive, direction is not indicated, and the bee dances a **round dance**, which is more lively the richer the food source.

Bee dancing has Arbitrariness, Displacement and Openness of the type that allows for infinitely many messages to be created, although not of the type that allows for making new messages of old – bees probably only ever dance about food, not about food as a symbol of anything else. As far as the workers are concerned, the system also has Interchangeability, and, in so far as the bee is aware of what it is doing, the system has Complete Feedback, Specialization, and Semanticity. It does not have Discreteness; bee dancing is a continuous system because of the proportionality of the signal to richness and distance of the food source. It is doubtful whether one would want to claim Tradition for it, and it has no Duality of Patterning. Nor do bees appear to engage in Prevarication, and there seems to be no Reflexiveness in the system. Finally, other bees do not learn to dance like the worker honey bee, so there is no Learnability.

The functional approach

The examples above illustrate how Hockett's method might be employed in the comparison of animal and human communication systems. However, there is some doubt about the usefulness of this approach. First, if one begins by defining language in terms of *human* language, it could be argued that other systems are put at a disadvantage from the start. Second, with the possible exception of Reflexivity, it is possible to find a researcher willing to declare that some animal communication system or other possesses it (Ristau 1996/ 1999: 648), and it is difficult to decide, in the case of any definition that relies on a listing of properties, exactly how many of these we would want a given phenomenon to possess before we would be prepared to admit it to the class of things covered by the definition. Finally (Lieberman 1977: 6):

> Defining language in terms of the properties of human language is fruitless, because we do not know what they really are. Even if we knew the complete inventory of properties that characterize

human language we probably would not want to limit the term 'language' to communication systems that had all of these properties. . . . The operational definition of language is functional rather than taxonomic. It is a productive definition insofar as it encourages questions about what animals can do with their communication systems and the relation of these particular systems to human language.

As far as we know, the functions of animal communication systems are limited to the following:

- food – telling others that there is food, where it is, competing for it, begging for it when young
- alarm/warning
- territorial claims
- recognition and greeting
- reproduction
- grouping
- comforting
- indication of emotional state.

Almost all animals emit sounds or make gestures in connection with some of these functions. But humans habitually talk about numerous other subjects – arguably, language has many more, and much more complex, functions than animal communication systems (in so far as we understand the functions of the latter). The question is, then, whether this multifunctionality of human language *vis-à-vis* animal communication systems arises because humans are further along the evolutionary path than animals, and have, therefore, developed far more complex social groupings than animals, which (in turn) make increasingly complex demands for a communication system to serve many more and more complex functions (the functionalist explanation); or whether human language is, in fact, unique to humans and, as such, dependent on a faculty of the human mind reserved for humans alone. The testing ground for this question has been experiments intended to teach higher primates to use human language.

Approaches involving teaching animals to 'speak'

There is a long tradition of attempting to teach human language to higher primates, in particular to chimpanzees. Most of these studies have involved chimpanzees reared in a human home or human-home-like environment, since it is in such an environment that most humans learn to speak. One early study, however, involved not a home-reared chimpanzee, but a performing one (Witmer 1909; see Fouts and Rigby 1977). The chimpanzee in question, Peter, was employed in Philadelphia's Keith Theatre, where the psychologist Witmer met him. Peter was then between 4 and 6 years old and had received two and a half years of training for his theatrical work. Witmer took Peter for intelligence tests at the Psychological Clinic in Philadelphia and found him capable of carrying out simple reasoning tasks easily – unlocking doors, opening boxes and hammering nails in – but apparently he did not display any particular aptitude for writing. He could say *mama*, although unwillingly and with difficulty, having severe problems with vowels; however, it took him only a few minutes to learn to say /p/, and Witmer comments:

> If a child without language were brought to me and on the first trial had learned to articulate the sound 'p' as readily as Peter did, I should express the opinion that he could be taught most of the elements of articulate language within six months' time.

Witmer also noticed that, although Peter could not speak, he understood words, and he thought that Peter would probably be able to learn to associate symbols with objects; several later experiments have confirmed that chimpanzees can indeed learn this associative connection (see below). Early on, however, the focus was on teaching chimpanzees to speak. Three more or less unsuccessful attempts at this involved the chimpanzees Joni, Gua and Viki.

Joni was raised and observed by N. Kohts and her family between 1913 and 1916, when he was between 18 months and 4 years old. The study was not published until 1935, because Kohts was saving her notes on Joni for comparison with notes on the behaviour of her own child, Roody, between 1925 and 1929, when he was of the same age as Joni had been during the study involving him. Kohts did not specifically train Joni to speak, because she wanted to see if he would do so as relatively spontaneously as a human child does; but the only sounds he produced were those that young chimpanzees normally produce, from which Kohts concluded that his intellectual capacities were different in kind from those of humans.

Gua was a $7^{1}/_{2}$-month-old chimpanzee adopted by W. and L. Kellogg, who had a son, Donald, of the same age as Gua. Gua and Donald lived in the same surroundings and were given the same treatment during the nine months of Gua's stay with the family. But, while Donald made the normal babbling sounds of a human infant, Gua restricted herself to the barking, screeching and crying noises of a young chimpanzee (Kellogg and Kellogg 1967).

Keith and Catherine Hayes' experiment with the chimpanzee Viki met with more success, relatively speaking. The Hayes took Viki into their home when she was just a few days old and treated her as much as possible like a human child – Viki stayed with the Hayes for six years and learned to articulate four words, *mama*, *papa*, *cup* and *up*, with difficulty, in a hoarse voice, and often in inappropriate contexts, so that it was unclear whether she understood their meanings (Hayes and Hayes 1952).

By 1968, there was conclusive evidence that human speech is not, in fact, a suitable medium of communication for chimpanzees, for both behavioural and anatomical reasons (Lieberman 1968; Gardner and Gardner 1971). This means that there is no more justification for claiming that a chimpanzee cannot learn language because it cannot learn to speak than one would have for claiming that a fish cannot learn to move because it cannot learn to walk – the fish simply has no legs; the chimpanzee simply does not have the appropriate voice box.

Since chimpanzees in the wild use a form of gestural communication system naturally, the Gardners – whose experiment with Washoe is probably the most famous chimpanzee language experiment of them all – chose to exploit this ability, and taught Washoe to communicate using American Sign Language (ASL), a language widely used in the United States by the deaf. It consists of gestures made by the arms, hands and fingers, and the signs made are analogous to spoken words used in conformity with syntax (see further SIGN LANGUAGE). Project Washoe ran from June 1966 until October 1970 at the University of Nevada in Reno. During this time Washoe learned to use over 130 signs correctly, but considerable controversy has arisen over the question of whether this impressive lexical store is merely an extended list of referential signs similar to, for example, the warning calls made by very many species of birds and monkeys (see e.g. Seyfarth and Cheney 1986, and Seyfarth *et al.* 1980a, 1980b, on the alarm calls of vervet monkeys), or whether it should be considered a restricted sample of human language. The issue here is whether chimpanzees can be said to have shown an ability to acquire syntax.

The question of syntax

The reason that syntax acquisition seems to most linguists to be crucial to the question of whether a chimpanzee's achievements in learning to employ features of human language can be described as language acquisition is of course that linguists generally believe that syntax is the most crucially defining feature of human language – that all human languages are basically cut to the same syntactic pattern, that this pattern defines human language and that the mental faculty on the basis of which the pattern develops is uniquely human (see e.g. Chomsky 1972a). In each human, this mental faculty, called the **Language Acquisition Device**, begins life in an initial state, the theory of which is known as **Universal Grammar (UG)**, and ends in a steady state theorized as '**grammar**' (Chomsky 1995: 4). UG determines the '**principles**' or possible forms of human language and the '**parameters**' within which they can vary (Chomsky 1981), and the rate and route of development from the initial to the steady state of human language are largely genetically determined (the typology of the language to be acquired also plays a part, however).

Washoe was between 8 and 14 months old when the Gardners bought her from a trader; they assumed that she was born in the wild and had lived with her natural mother for several months until she was captured. The Gardners kept her in a caravan in their back garden, and anyone who came into contact with her used only ASL in her presence, both to communicate with her and with other humans. Since Washoe was never left alone except when she was asleep, she was the subject of a total immersion in ASL, just as a human child would be immersed in whatever was the language of the community around it, and the Gardners claim that her acquisition pattern was like that of a child learning ASL, beginning with manual babbling, which was gradually replaced by true signing. She began to combine signs into sentences when she was between 18 and 24 months, during the tenth month of the experiment, and her early two-word combinations resembled those of children in subject matter. It appeared that a chimpanzee had finally learnt some rudimentary language.

Two other chimpanzee experiments tended to confirm this ability of chimpanzees. In one, a 6-year-old chimpanzee, Sarah, was taught to communicate using pieces of plastic of different shapes and colours to stand for words. The system was invented, and the experiment carried out by, Premack and Premack (1972), who claimed that Sarah learned a vocabulary of around 130 terms, which she used correctly between 75 and 80 per cent of the time; her ability resembled that of a 2-year-old child (1972: 99).

The second experiment involved teaching the chimpanzee, Lana, to read from a computer screen and to communicate with the computer. It took her six months to learn to read characters off the screen, to complete incomplete sentences, and to reject sentences that were grammatically incorrect. This experiment was held to confirm that chimpanzees can understand and use syntax (Rumbaugh et al. 1973).

However, doubt was cast on this conclusion by Herbert Terrace (1979), who worked with a chimpanzee called Nim Chimpsky. Nim was taught ASL like Washoe had been, but in controlled laboratory conditions. He appeared to display an acquisition pattern and ability very similar to those of Washoe, but Terrace claims that careful study of the video recordings of Nim's behaviour, and of Washoe's, shows that neither animal is in fact using language like a human does, but merely imitatively.

In response, Gardner and Gardner (1978) and Gardner (1981) have argued that, whereas this might have been true of Nim, who was treated as a research animal and investigated by researchers who were not all fluent in ASL, it was not true of Washoe, who was home-reared (Yule 1985: 30):

The Gardners have stressed the need for a domestic environment. . . . Their most recent project involves a number of chimpanzees, Moja, Pili, Tatu and Dar, being raised together from birth in a domestic environment with a number of human companions who naturally use sign language. They report that these chimpanzees, beginning earlier than Washoe, are acquiring sign language much faster.

Most claims for syntactic ability on the part of chimpanzees are made on the basis of the chimpanzees' apparent ability to observe word order rules, because the chimpanzees' utterances are usually too short (four signs at most, with longer utterances consisting of repeated strings) for any more complex syntax to be involved (Ristau 1996/1999: 651). However, Savage-Rumbaugh et al. (1993) claim that their Bonobo chimpanzee (*Pan paniscus*), Kanzi, displays receptive syntactic abilities comparable to those of a 2-year-old child. Kanzi and the child, Alia, were tested for comprehension of the same set of spoken (as opposed to signed) English sentences, and both had 'acquired' the ability to comprehend them in the course of normal socialization (as opposed to through specific training or coaching). The experiment was carefully controlled: neither Kanzi nor Alia were able to see the experimenter who gave them instructions, and the human assessors of their responses were unable to hear the instructions. The test sentences included instructions to put one item into another, to act on an item with another item, to give or show a person (or toy) an item, moving items to or from places and making toys interact, all of which involve complex syntax, and some of the sentences involved multiple actions (Ristau 1996/1999: 651–2). Although none of the sentences involved such complexities as recursion, passive voice or the subjunctive mood, Ristau concludes that 'sensitivity to simple, arbitrary ordering rules has been established' (1996/1999: 653).

K.M.

Suggestions for further reading

Aitchison, J. (1998) *The Articulate Mammal: An Introduction to Psycholinguistics*, 4th edition, London: Routledge.

Ristau, C.A. (1996/1999) 'Animal language and cognition projects', in A. Lock and C.R. Peters (eds) *Handbook of Human Symbolic Evolution*, Oxford: Blackwell Publishers; 1st edition 1996, Oxford: Oxford University Press.

Sebeok, T.A. (ed.) (1977) *How Animals Communicate*, Bloomington and London: Indiana University Press.

Aphasia

Aphasia is the loss or partial loss of normal language abilities as a result of damage to cortical and/or sub-cortical brain tissue. A strict use of **aphasia** (meaning 'total loss') vs **dysphasia** (meaning 'partial loss') is sometimes followed, but the terms **aphasia** and, rather less commonly, **dysphasia** are most often used for any degree of loss. The term 'normal language abilities' takes account of variation within adult speakers and these variations may arise because of a number of factors, including chronological age and level of education, so that there is not a single norm for all. There is increasing research in this area but we still lack large-scale normative studies that would enable us to define 'normal'. When considering individual variations it is important to recognize that language in old age may differ in subtle ways from language used by healthy, younger adults. There may be increasing difficulty with word-finding, with the access of nouns especially affected. If these changes are considered within 'normal variation', then it follows that the term 'aphasia' is not usually applied to normal language changes associated with age. The term **language abilities** within the definition requires some interpretation. Traditional approaches within aphasiology have emphasized a fundamental distinction between 'speech' and 'language' abilities, and hence disorders, and it is worth noting that these terms still have clinical value even though the nature of the distinction is not, from a linguistic viewpoint, as fundamental as the tradition believed.

A clinician describing a patient as having speech and language difficulties is using these terms to denote articulatory and grammatical-semantic levels of disorder; but the strict adherence to this distinction by theoretical aphasiologists has led to problems in defining the boundary of **aphasia** (disorders of 'language' in the non-speech sense). **Aphasia** is seen as a condition that is essentially separate from **dysarthria**, although the two conditions may co-occur. (**Dysarthria** may have a structural or neural origin. Neurological lesions associated with dysarthria result in some weakness or poor co-ordination of muscles and structures of the vocal tract (see LANGUAGE PATHOLOGY AND NEUROLINGUISTICS).) Within this approach, the status of **dyspraxia**, a condition that may accompany aphasia, has proved difficult and controversial: it is characterized by impaired control and timing of the implementation of speech.

There are other problems in delineating the boundaries of aphasia. Impairment of particular or general intellectual functions that may be present with the language disorder may be seen as part of the aphasic disorder. Here, terms such as **acalculia** (impaired manipulation of number concepts) imply that these stand outside aphasia, although such conditions receive consideration in the aphasia literature. The difficulty in such cases derives straightforwardly from our lack of knowledge concerning the boundary between meaning as expressed in language and non-linguistic knowledge systems.

A further issue arises when alternative media of language behaviour are considered, the most important being those involved in reading and writing: terms such as **agraphia** and **alexia** suggest that aphasia is restricted to spoken-language abilities, but most researchers and clinicians regard reading and writing performance as forming part of the total picture of an acquired language disorder.

Finally, the presence of some significant 'pathology' is a useful defining notion. Advances in scanning techniques have substantially increased our knowledge of the relationship between location of lesions and type of aphasia. In broad terms, investigations have confirmed the conclusions of the nineteenth-century neuro-anatomists; namely that aphasia arises from damage to the peri-Sylvian area of the dominant cortical hemisphere. The relationship between site of lesion and type of aphasia or the language-brain area correlates are less clear.

The usually encountered causes, and resulting types, of brain damage in aphasia are: vascular disease, that is, problems in the blood supply – embolism, thrombosis or haemorrhage; tumour; trauma, i.e. external source of injury, as with gunshot wounds or road-traffic accidents; infection, leading to infarct   atrophied brain tissue – compression, rupture and micro-organic invasion of brain cells. '**Cardio-vascular accidents**' or **CVA** – frequently referred to as '**strokes**' – are the single most common cause in most non-military situations, with thrombosis and embolism resulting in infarcts, and haemorrhage in compression of brain tissue.

Determining the precise extent and location of the damage is not at all easy in many cases. Differences of about 1cm can be significant for establishing an association with impairment to specific language functions, so the precision called for in establishing neurolinguistic correlations is of a high order. Further, typical infarcts may border on zones of softened cortical and subcortical tissue, whose functional integrity is hard to determine. Direct inspection of damaged areas is only available either during surgery or at autopsy – and the bulk of stroke cases in hospitals do not undergo surgery. Indirect examination techniques include: bedside neurological-function examination, to determine, from the overall pattern of sensory-motor functions, where the lesion is likely to have occurred; instrumental investigations such as **electroencephalography** (**EEG**) and **regional blood flow** (**rCBF**), in which sensors are placed over the scalp in order to record patterns of activity in the brain; and more recent techniques of scanning. There are two main types of scanning – structural, which includes **computerized axial tomography** (**CAT**) and **magnetic resonance imaging** (**MRI**); and functional neuro-imaging, such as **single-photon emission computed tomography** (**SPECT**), **positron emission tomography** (**PET**) and **functional magnetic resonance imaging** (**fMRI**). Scanning procedures are much more precise than the use of scalp sensors, but the scanning methods used have particular strengths and weaknesses; some methods are more sensitive than others to different types of damage.

Because of the difficulties, expense and uncertainties of lesion-location attempts, most aphasic patients are classified into syndromes on the basis of clinical rather than neurological-location criteria. Thus, while **Broca's area** (see LANGUAGE PATHOLOGY AND NEUROLINGUISTICS) is definable in neuroanatomical terms, some cases of **Broca's aphasia** may be classified as such on the basis of their symptoms, rather than by site of lesion, although patients are increasingly scanned as part of the routine clinical examination. Broca's aphasia exists as a clinical entity but the diagnosis is not necessarily dependent on lesion site, and it is in this sense that most of the major syndromes that we shall now consider are usually understood.

The following discussion of syndromes is based on a neoclassical taxonomy. Aphasiologists working within this framework have a general agreement about the major syndromes although there may be some difference in terminology. It should be noted, however, that there is by no means a universal acceptance of this framework or, indeed, any syndromic framework, and some aphasiologists (especially those in clinical practice) reject the syndromic framework.

Anomic aphasia or **Anomia**: the *symptom* of anomia, or word-finding difficulty, is frequently found in other syndromes, where it may be subclassified further, e.g. into word-production anomia, word-selection anomia, and different types of specific anomia, depending on which word classes, e.g. verbs vs nouns, are most severely affected. As a syndrome, anomia is recognized by a marked difficulty with word retrieval, fluent speech and normal or mildly impaired comprehension. It is frequently a syndrome that results from alleviation of symptoms present in some other syndrome – a sort of 'recovery syndrome'. It accounts for around one third of a broad aphasic population, and is by far the mildest sort of aphasia. Anomic lesion sites tend to lie in the area of the lower parietal lobe, close to the junction with the temporal lobe (see LANGUAGE PATHOLOGY AND NEUROLINGUISTICS for illustration).

Global aphasia: at the other end of the scale of severity, this syndrome accounts for around one sixth of a general aphasic population, and is characterized by impairment of all testable language functions. Global aphasia is the most disabling kind of aphasic syndrome. Although there may be only residual language functioning, patients with this type of aphasia are frequently alert, aware of their surroundings and able to have limited communication by using gesture and facial expression. It is frequently found in acute cases of brain damage, and may be followed by uneven patterns of alleviation of certain symptoms, resulting in a case-history shift from this syndrome to another, non-global type. Global aphasia lesions tend to be distributed over the areas of the frontal, parietal and temporal lobes that border the Rolandic and Sylvian fissures demarcating these areas.

Broca's aphasia: this may arise as global aphasia ameliorates in respect of comprehension abilities, or as a distinct syndrome from the outset. It has about the same incidence as global aphasia, but is less severe. Speech articulation is non-fluent and effortful, with many simplifications of consonant clusters and some substitutions. A component syndrome of **agrammatism** has been recognized, involving impairment of closed-class grammatical morphemes (see MORPHOLOGY), selective difficulties with verbs over nouns, and reduction in the variety of syntactic patterns. Fluent control of stereotypic utterances such as *Oh I don't know!* may provide striking contrast with spontaneous productive attempts, and may also be employed by **Broca's aphasics** in ways that suggest that they know what they want to say but lack the means to structure their output appropriately. It is possible that their degree of intact comprehension abilities may be overestimated by the unwary. Although people with Broca's aphasia may appear to have good comprehension in conversation, when tested some problems with comprehension may be revealed. Comprehension may be better for concrete referential rather than abstract relational terms. More specific comprehension problems are associated with agrammatism. **Agrammatism** is characterized by the same output problems as seen in Broca's aphasia but, additionally, it has come to be recognized that it involves problems of comprehension. The specific comprehension problems of **agrammatic speakers** involve sentences that have non-canonical structure and/or where the meaning of the sentence cannot be obtained through lexical semantics alone. Typically people with agrammatism can understand reversible active declarative sentences better than reversible passives, and subject clefts better than object cleft sentences. Various theories have been proposed to explain these phenomena and, despite considerable debate, there is still no one accepted explanation. **Broca's lesions** are generally found in the lower frontal lobe, just anterior to the Rolandic fissure that divides the frontal and parietal lobes.

Wernicke's aphasia: like **Broca's aphasia**, this is another classic syndrome, described by a pioneering nineteenth-century aphasiologist (see LANGUAGE PATHOLOGY AND NEUROLINGUISTICS), and it provides in many ways a complementary pattern to that of Broca's aphasia. Spontaneous speech production is fluent, though marked by numerous sound substitutions (**phonemic paraphasias**), word-form errors (**verbal paraphasias**) and nonce-forms (neologisms), and abnormal grammatical sequences (paragrammatisms). Identifiable words in the fluent output tend to be referentially vague, with much use of general proforms and stereotyped social phrases. Although, classically, these speakers are considered to have a lexical-semantic deficit rather than a syntactic deficit, there is growing evidence that there are problems with certain aspects of grammar. Inflectional errors occur, there may be errors in the use of determiners and pronouns, and some fluent aphasic speakers use a smaller proportion of complex sentences compared with normal speakers. There appears to be little self-monitoring ability – the patient may not be aware that what s/he says is hard to interpret, and may not be able to stop when asked to. Comprehension of what others say is severely impaired. Lesion sites are generally in the upper surface of the temporal lobe, close to and often involving the auditory cortex, and sometimes extending to the parietal lobe.

Broca's and **Wernicke's syndromes** provide cardinal points for the delineation of four other types of aphasia, which all involve an impaired ability to transfer the results of processing in one area of the cortex to another.

In **conduction aphasia**, a sub-cortical lesion of restricted extent is supposed to be responsible for interfering with sub-cortical pathways, the arcuate fasciculus, running from Wernicke's area to Broca's area, i.e. carrying the results of semantic processing to the speech-output control area. This results in fluent speech output, with Wernicke-type characteristics, together with relatively good comprehension, but severely impaired repetition abilities.

Transcortical motor aphasia is thought to involve an impaired connection between Broca's area and surrounding frontal-lobe association areas; as a result, spontaneous speech control is non-fluent and agrammatic, but connectors into Broca's area from the temporal-parietal auditory-comprehension areas are relatively spared, leading to better repetition abilities than are found in Broca's aphasia.

Transcortical sensory aphasia looks similar to Wernicke's aphasia in respect of fluent spontaneous output, with many paraphasias and paragrammatisms; but here again the impairment seems to involve the connections between the auditory cortex and the surrounding association areas, leading to a situation which may be described as compulsive repetition or **echolalia**. Note the contrast with Wernicke's aphasia, where the patient seems not to attend to what is said to him/her; in transcortical sensory aphasia, what is said is faithfully retained and repeated, though without apparent comprehension.

Finally, **mixed transcortical aphasia** is defined as the simultaneous disconnection of both the speech-output control centre and the speech-perception centre from surrounding areas of cortex, so that these central production and perception abilities are effectively cut off from the interpretative processes of the rest of the cortex; for this reason, mixed transcortical aphasia is often referred to as the **isolation syndrome**.

It should be stressed that these are highly simplified and idealized thumbnail sketches of the major categories of acquired language disorders. They serve as cardinal points within a descriptive clinical framework, in relation to which the particular difficulties found with individual patients may be located. There is increasing awareness of the extent to which individual differences exist within broad classification categories such as **Broca's** and **Wernicke's aphasia**, and it may be that the days are past when the approach to aphasiology in terms of syndromes can continue to yield benefits.

One alternative is to consider the presenting symptoms in more detail. In this connection, there is growing awareness in aphasiology of the need for (and the potential of) more refined assessment of naturalistic language performance, as opposed to the highly constrained types of behaviour elicited in the standardized test batteries. Linguistic and psycholinguistic studies of normal adult conversational behaviour are important in this respect, including such aspects as turn-taking (see DISCOURSE ANALYSIS AND CONVERSATION ANALYSIS), eye-gaze, and non-verbal gestures (see KINESICS), as well as normal non-fluency – filled pauses, part- and whole-word repetitions, back-trackings, false starts – and normal types and incidence of errors, including syntactic misformulations, incomplete utterances, and word-selection errors (see PSYCHOLINGUISTICS). These normative data, and the types of theories they support, provide an indispensable foundation for the appropriate assessment of aphasic conversational attempts.

The assessment of comprehension in naturalistic contexts is likewise of major importance; although it is possible for normal language users to understand words and constructions that are presented in isolation, and to compare aphasics' attempts on the same basis, there is reason to believe that this is essentially a metalinguistic skill that may bear little relation to the sorts of language demands that are made on the aphasic outside the assessment situation. In the typical situation of utterance, the specifically linguistic input (the acoustic signal) is accompanied by other types of auditory and visual input, deriving from the speaker and from the environment, and these inputs interact in complex ways. Furthermore, there is reason to believe that attentional factors play an important role in language understanding, and that these are difficult to engage in tasks and situations where language forms are being used in simulated rather than real acts of communication. Attempts have been made to devise 'communicative' assessment procedures, but much work remains to be done in refining these.

Developments in clinical aphasiology have seen the rejection of the syndromic approach and focus of study has been on single-word production. Here, a simple, single-word processing model adapted from cognitive neuropsychology is applied to production and comprehension using the notion of stages. These stages are represented visually as a series of boxes and connecting arrows, and the loci of damage is assumed to affect one or more of the 'stages'. In fact, the model does not account for language *per se*, but for isolated single words. Furthermore, the model best accounts for the production and comprehension of highly imageable nouns. As such, it has helped researchers and clinicians differentiate between different types of some word-retrieval problems; although, as we have seen above, word-retrieval problems, although pervasive in aphasia, are only part of the language deficit.

S.E.

Suggestions for further reading

Bastiaanse, R. and Grodzinsky, Y. (eds) (2000) *Psycholinguistic Aspects of Aphasia*, London: Whurr.

Davis, G.A. (2000) *Aphasiology: Disorders and Clinical Practice*, Boston, MA: Allyn and Bacon.

Goodglass, H. (1993) *Understanding Aphasia*, San Diego: Academic Press.

Lesser, R. and Milroy, L. (1993) *Linguistics and Aphasia*, London: Longman.

Applied linguistics

Perhaps no other field in either the humanities or the social sciences has experienced as much debate and discussion in coming to terms with its self-image as has **applied linguistics**. The term was coined more or less simultaneously in the United States and in Britain in the latter half of the 1950s. In 1956, the University of Edinburgh established the School of Applied Linguistics under the direction of J.C. Catford, and in 1957 the Center for Applied Linguistics was founded in Washington, DC, directed by Charles Ferguson (Strevens 1992: 14). While the two organizations differed in scope, both shared the general aim of promoting and enhancing the teaching of the English language around the world. Thus, from the outset, applied linguistics was a field not only related to the teaching and learning of language, but to the teaching and learning of a specific language – English. Over the course of its (more than) thirty-year history, however, the field has not only grown to encompass the teaching and learning of languages other than English, but it has also broadened its vision to include more than language teaching and learning. Rampton (1995b: 234), for instance, contends that the British School of applied linguistics is shifting away from traditional concerns with pedagogy, linguistics and psychology, and towards a more general interest in social phenomena. In fact, there appears to be a general consensus among those who consider themselves to be applied linguists that, in addition to its traditional base, the field now encompasses such areas as language policy and language planning, lexicography and lexicology, speech therapy, multilingual and language contact studies, language assessment, second language acquisition, literacy, forensic linguistics, and some would even include (although not uncontroversially) stylistics, genre studies, discourse analysis, sociolinguistics, language socialization, **conversation analysis** and translation and interpreting (see Grabe and Kaplan 1992).

The field counts a number of internationally recognized journals among its publishing organs, including *Applied Linguistics*, the *Annual Review of Applied Linguistics*, the *International Review of Applied Linguistics* and the *International Journal of Applied Linguistics*. These journals, among others, espouse editorial policies that have paralleled the expansion of the field and regularly publish articles in many of the areas listed above. Other journals, such as *Language Learning*, *Studies in Second Language Acquisition*, *Second Language Research* and the *Modern Language Journal*, have maintained their focus on empirical and, to a lesser extent, theoretical studies, relating to the acquisition and teaching of languages beyond the first. At least two journals focus primarily on the teaching and learning of English (*TESOL Quarterly* and *English Language Teaching Journal*), and at least one journal, *Spanish Applied Linguistics*, founded in 1997, is exclusively dedicated to acquisition research on a language other than English. Still others are concerned with specific domains, such as *Language Testing* and the *Journal of Second Language Writing*. Another sign of the robustness of the field is the increasing number of monograph and book-length volumes published by important academic and commercial presses, including Oxford University Press, Cambridge University Press, Blackwell, Routledge, Edward Arnold, Pearson, John Benjamins, Kluwer, Lawrence Erlbaum, Elsevier and Ablex. Attendance at conferences such as those sponsored by the American, British, German and Spanish Associations for Applied Linguistics, as well as the International Association of Applied Linguistics, continues to increase. There has also been remarkable growth in the number of universities around the world offering graduate degrees in applied linguistics.

Despite its prosperity, the field continues to be nagged by a lack of agreement on the precise nature of applied linguistics as an academic discipline and on how it relates to other domains of linguistics. What, for example, are the fundamental statements around which the field coheres? What precisely is applied in applied linguistics? Is there a theoretical component to applied linguistics or is it only a practical discipline?

The early Edinburgh School considered applied linguists to be consumers rather than producers of linguistic theory. The task of applied linguistic activity was to interpret the findings of linguistic research on how languages are learned and used, in order to inform language teaching (Corder 1973: 10). In arguing for an expanded understanding of the domain of applied linguistics to include not just language teaching but also stylistics, language disabilities and translation, Crystal (1980) proposed that, not only could the findings of linguistic research be made relevant to these areas, but so could its theories and research methods.

As applied linguistics expanded its interests beyond the domain of language teaching, it became apparent that disciplines other than linguistics would need to be drawn on in order to develop in-depth understandings and solutions to real-world

language problems. Eventually, Widdowson, a disciple of the Edinburgh School, proposed an important distinction between *applied linguistics* and *linguistics applied*. The latter concept is closer to the original understanding of the term 'applied linguistics'; that is, it assumes that language-based real-world problems can be solved exclusively through the application of linguistic theory, methods and findings (Widdowson 1980). The former term recognizes that, while linguistics offers important insights and solutions to language problems, and continues to form the core of applied linguistics, research from other disciplines, such as psychology, anthropology, sociology (and perhaps even philosophy and literary research), can also profitably be brought to bear on these problems. In fact, according to Widdowson (2000a, 2000b), there is good reason to reject the understanding of applied linguistics as linguistics applied, since most language-based problems cannot reasonably be solved through the application of linguistic principles alone. According to Widdowson, the applied linguist serves as a mediator between linguistics and language teaching in order to convert the abstract findings of linguistic research into knowledge that is useful for pedagogical practices (Widdowson 2000a: 28). This perspective, then, seems to mirror the earlier 'applied linguists as consumer' interpretation proposed by Corder. Unlike Corder, however, Widdowson recognizes the necessity for applied linguistics to draw on disciplines outside of linguistics in order to develop its insights and recommendations.

One reason for drawing a distinction between applied linguistics and linguistics applied is the worry that, as linguistics itself expands the domain of its own research interests beyond theorizing about autonomous and abstract grammatical systems to recognition of the relevance of context for language use and language learning, the narrow interpretation of applied linguistics as linguistics applied could well make redundant the work of applied linguists (Widdowson 2000a). Furthermore, the need for applied linguistics to draw on disciplines outside of linguistics means that, unlike linguistics proper, it is a genuinely interdisciplinary field. Spolsky (1980: 73) argues that a more appropriate way to mark the distinction between applied linguistics and linguistics proper is to recognize that the former is a 'relevant linguistics', while the latter believes there is merit in the autonomous study of language as an object in itself divorced from any real-world use.

Another matter of some controversy concerns the brand of linguistics that should inform the activities of applied linguists. Widdowson (2000a: 29–30), for example, argues that generative theory is relevant to language teaching, but it is not the task of the theoretician to demonstrate its relevance. The applied linguist, as the mediator between theory and practice, is charged with the responsibility of realizing this task. Widdowson contends, for example, that Chomsky's rejection of language learning as habit formation, and recognition that acquisition is a 'cognitive and creative process' in which learners infer possible grammars on the basis of input and biologically determined constraints, has had a major impact on language teaching practice. While learners most certainly draw inferences based on what they hear and see in their linguistic surroundings, it is not at all clear, despite a good deal of research, that their inferences are constrained in the ways predicted by generative theory. What is more, Chomsky's understanding of 'creativity' is quite technical in nature and does not reflect the kind of creativity that others, such as Harris (1981), Bakhtin (1981) or Kramsch (1995), recognize as genuine linguistic creativity (i.e. the ability to create new meanings and forms, especially in the domain of metaphor), and it is this latter kind of creativity that might in

the long run be more relevant to the language learning process.

Grabe (1992) proposes that, in addition to generative research, applied linguists draw upon work in three other lines of linguistic research: functional and typological theories as seen in the work of Halliday, Chafe, Givon, Comrie and Greenberg; anthropological linguistics and sociolinguistics, represented in the research of Labov, Hymes, Ochs, Gumperz, Fishman and the Milroys; and research which results in descriptive grammars based on corpus linguistic analyses (see CORPORA). Interestingly, this latter type of research is criticized by Widdowson (2000a: 24) as too narrow in scope because its focus is on what is done rather than on what is known – although it has to be added that Widdowson sees some relevance for corpus linguistics, since it is at least able to reflect a partial view of how language is deployed in the real world.

What agreement has been achieved seems to point to applied linguistics as a field whose scope of interest is the development of solutions to language-based problems in the real world. To realize its goal, it draws on theoretical, methodological and empirical research from a wide array of disciplines, including (but not limited to) linguistics. One problem with perspective, however, is that it is not clear that all of the work that refers to itself as applied linguistics can legitimately be seen as entailing solutions to real-world problems. For instance, some of the leading journals in applied linguistics publish articles on genre studies, discourse analysis and sociolinguistics that are potentially of interest to applied linguists, but in and of themselves do not purport to solve real-world language problems. The same can be said of the programmes of the important international conferences in the field. The argument could be made that this type of research, while not really applied in nature, is at least relevant to applied linguistics, and therefore could be included within its domain.

But this same argument can be made for work in linguistics proper; yet it is not likely that such research would find its way into the field's journals or conferences. Where, then, are we to draw the line? If we draw it too broadly, everything could be included within applied linguistics; if we draw it too narrowly, some of the areas that have been traditionally included under the umbrella of applied linguistics would be left out. If applied linguistics does not stay focused on solving real-world language-based problems, then it might eventually be taken over by linguistics itself, as the parent discipline is no longer content with analysis of language as an autonomous object but has become increasingly interested in contexualized language learning and use (Widdowson 2000a). Yet, if the problem-solving focus is to be the distinguishing feature of applied linguistics, we might even question whether an area such as second language acquisition research should be legitimately included in applied linguistics. Some SLA researchers, especially those working within the framework of **Universal Grammar**, have in fact claimed that their project is not about solving real-world problems and might better be situated within the domain of theoretical linguistics. This argument is not without merit, as such research can be construed as an attempt to explore whether or not the same constraints that operate in first language acquisition also hold for languages acquired later in life. This is not to suggest that SLA research is not relevant to applied linguistics, but it does point to the complexities entailed in deciding whether a particular research programme meets the criteria for inclusion within applied linguistics.

In laying the foundation for linguistics as the science of languages, Saussure proposed that if linguistics was to operate as a legitimate scientific enterprise it would be necessary to overlook how people actually use and learn languages in their life-world.

He thus created the illusion of language as an autonomous object, akin to the objects of the physical universe, so it could be studied in accordance with the principles of scientific enquiry (see Crowley 1996). This viewpoint has dominated much of the research in linguistics to the present day. Kaplan (1980a: 64) believes, however, that despite an assumption that applied linguistic research adheres to the principles of scientific investigation, applied linguists might, on occasion, have to sacrifice allegiance to these principles in their commitment to find solutions to language-based human problems. Kaplan (1980a: 63) contends that for this reason applied linguists are 'the most humanistic breed of linguists'. Perhaps, then, applied linguistics would be more appropriately situated alongside literary, historical and even some branches of psychological research as a human, rather than as a social, science (see Polkinghorne 1988).

Even though a humanistic applied linguistics manages to bring people back into the picture, it continues to foreground language over people as its proper object of study. Another way to conceptualize applied linguistics is as the human science that is interested in the theoretical, as well as empirical, study of people as linguistic beings. Applied linguistics, according to this view, investigates how people come to participate linguistically with other people in communities of practice and how they mediate their activities within these communities. It also seeks to uncover and understand the sources and consequences of problems that arise when people experience difficulties fully participating in communities of practice and attempts to help people develop ways of overcoming such difficulties. It also undertakes to understand the ways in which people succeed or fail in their attempts to participate in new communities of practice, and it seeks to develop appropriate means to assist them in their efforts. All of this clearly distinguishes applied linguistics from linguistics proper, which has as its object of study language, not people.

J.P.L.

Suggestions for further reading

Annual Review of Applied Linguistics (2000) 20.

Grabe, W. and Kaplan, R. (eds) (1992) *Introduction to Applied Linguistics*, Reading, MA: Addison Wesley.

Rampton, B. (1995b) 'Politics and change in research in applied linguistics', *Applied Linguistics* 16: 231–56.

Widdowson, H. (2000b) 'On the limitation of linguistics applied', *Applied Linguistics* 21: 2–25.

Articulatory phonetics

Introduction

Articulatory phonetics, sometimes alternatively called **physiological phonetics**, is a sub-branch of phonetics concerned with the study of the articulation of speech sounds. **Speech sounds** are produced through various interactions of **speech organs** acting on either an **egressive** (i.e. outgoing) or an **ingressive** (i.e. incoming) airstream. Such articulation of speech sounds is unique to human beings (*homo loquens*, 'speaking human').

The term **articulation** refers to the division of an egressive or ingressive airstream, with or without vocal vibration, into distinct sound entities through the above-mentioned interaction of speech organs. The concept of articulation in phonetics has evolved in such a way that present-day phoneticians use expressions like 'articulating/the articulation of such and such a speech sound' as practically equivalent to 'pronouncing/the pronunciation of a speech sound as a distinct entity', and the term 'articulation' will be used in this technical sense in what follows.

In articulatory phonetics a speech sound is primarily considered and presented as a discrete entity so that the replacement of one speech sound by another in an identical phonetic context is regarded as possible, at least in theory. However, phoneticians are also well aware that, in the vast majority of cases, speech sounds occur in sequential combination in connected speech, with the result that they partially blend into each other in such a way that the conception of speech sounds as discrete entities is unsatisfactory. Consequently, in articulatory phonetics, speech sounds are normally first presented as discrete entities showing how they are each articulated, and then as less than discrete entities showing how they articulatorily affect each other in the speech chain.

Speech organs

The human physiological organs which are employed for the articulation of speech sounds and which are hence called **speech organs** or **vocal organs** all have a more basically biological function than that of allowing for verbal communication by means of speech. Thus the teeth are used for chewing food; the tongue serves to push food around during chewing and then to carry it towards the food-passage into which it is swallowed; the lungs are used for breathing; the vocal folds function as a valve to prevent the accidental entry of foreign bodies into the windpipe; if foreign bodies are about to enter the windpipe, the vocal folds quickly close before being pushed open again by an egressive airstream which at the same time blows the foreign bodies upwards; in other words, what happens in this case is a cough. The vocal folds also assist muscular effort of the arms and the abdomen; the vocal folds close to create a hermetic air-filled chamber below them, and this helps the muscles of the arms or the abdomen to be made rigid. The use of these biological organs for the purpose of articulating speech sounds is another property unique to human beings.

In the articulation of speech sounds, the speech organs function as follows. A well-coordinated action of the **diaphragm** (the muscle separating the lungs from the stomach) and of the **intercostal muscles** situated between the ribs causes air to be drawn into, or be pushed out of, the **lungs** through the **trachea** or **windpipe**, which is a tube consisting of cartilaginous rings, the top of which forms the base of the larynx.

The **larynx**, the front of which is indirectly observable from outside and is popularly known as the Adam's apple, houses the two **vocal folds**, also known as **vocal lips**, **vocal bands** or **vocal c(h)ords**. The whole of the larynx can be moved upward – in pronouncing an **ejective** sound like [p'] – or downward – in pronouncing an implosive sound like [ɓ] – (see the INTERNATIONAL PHONETIC ALPHABET for information on phonetic symbols).

The vocal folds are fixed on the front–back axis in a horizontal direction, hinged together at the front end while being mobile sideways in two opposite directions at the back end, where they are mounted on the arytenoid cartilages, which are also mobile. The vocal folds can thus be brought close together in such a way that their inner edges, which lightly touch each other, are set into vibration by an egressive or ingressive airstream as it rushes through between them. There is then said to be **vocal vibration** or **glottal vibration**, or simply **voice**, and speech sounds articulated with vocal vibration are said to be **voiced** (e.g. [b z v]). The vocal folds can be made to approach each other in such a way that air passing through them

causes **friction** without, however, causing vocal vibration; this happens in the case of [h]. Also, the vocal folds can be kept wide apart from each other (as in quiet breathing) so that air passes freely between them in either direction, causing neither glottal friction nor vocal vibration; speech sounds articulated with the vocal folds thus wide apart are said to be **voiceless** (e.g., [p s f]). Furthermore, the vocal folds can be brought tightly together to form a firm contact so that no air can pass through them either inwards or outwards: the only speech sound produced when this posture of the vocal folds is assumed and then released is the **glottal plosive**, also popularly known as the **glottal stop**, i.e. [ʔ]. The space between the vocal folds is known as the **glottis**, so that the above-mentioned four different postures of the vocal folds may be viewed as representing four different states of the glottis; they are among the most important in normal speech, though other states of the glottis are possible, including those for breathy or murmured speech and creaky or laryngealized speech.

The area in which the speech organs above the larynx are situated is generally referred to as the **vocal tract**. It consists of three cavities: **pharyngeal** or **pharyngal**, **nasal** and **oral**. The pharyngeal cavity is also known as the pharynx. These three cavities function as **resonators**, in that a tiny voiced sound originating from the vocal folds is amplified while passing through them. The shapes of the pharyngeal and oral cavities are variously changeable, while that of the nasal cavity is unalterable.

The pharyngeal cavity is bounded by the larynx at the bottom, by the pharyngeal wall at the back, by the root of the tongue at the front, and by the area of bifurcation into the nasal and oral cavities at the top. Apart from functioning as a resonator, the pharynx is responsible for producing **pharyngeal sounds** – to be exact, **pharyngeal fricatives** – with or without vocal vibration, i.e. [ʕ] or [ħ], in the articulation of which the root of the tongue is drawn backwards to narrow the pharynx.

The nasal cavity, which is larger than the pharyngeal or oral cavity, extends from the nostrils backwards and downwards to where the nasal cavity and the oral cavity meet. The nasal cavity can be closed off from the two other cavities or can remain open to them, depending on whether the movable **soft palate** or **velum** (see below) is raised, in which case there is said to be a **velic closure**, or lowered, in which case there is said to be a **velic opening**. Any speech sound articulated in such a way that the egressive airstream issues outwards through the nasal cavity is a **nasal sound** or a **nasalized sound**, as the case may be. On the one hand, a **nasal consonant** is produced if the air meets total obstruction at a given point in the oral cavity (e.g. [n]), or between the lips ([m]). On the other hand, a **nasalized vowel** such as [õ] is produced if the air is at the same time allowed to issue out freely through the oral cavity as well.

The oral cavity extends from where the front teeth lie to the end of the roof of the mouth at the top, and the end of the tongue at the bottom. The lips form the orifice to the oral cavity. It is in the oral cavity that further speech organs are situated, which will be examined below. Various interactions between these speech organs in the oral cavity, with or without the involvement of the lips, and with or without vocal vibration, and with or without the involvement of the nasal cavity, give rise to a number of different **manners** and **places of articulation**, which are associated with a number of different speech sounds, oral or nasal (or nasalized).

Figure 1 shows the different speech organs found in the oral cavity, and the lips. The **lips** are obviously the easiest to observe from outside. They can be brought together to form a firm contact, or separated well apart from each other, or made to touch or approach each other lightly in such a way that audible friction may or may not occur as air passes between them. They can also be spread, or can assume a neutral unrounded posture, or can be rounded.

The teeth are next easiest to observe, particularly the upper and lower front teeth. There are of course other teeth further towards the back, including the molars, which are also important in articulating some speech sounds.

What is sometimes called the **roof of the mouth** is what phoneticians refer to as the **teeth ridge** and the **palate**. It consists of the following: (1) the front end (convex to the tongue) which is known as the **teeth ridge** or the **alveolar ridge**; (2) the hard (concave) immovable part which is known as the **hard palate**; (3) the soft (also concave) mucous part capable of up-and-down movement known as the **soft palate** or **velum**; and (4) the pendent fleshy tip at the end of the soft palate, which is known as the **uvula**.

The **tongue** plays a prominent role in the articulation of speech sounds in the oral cavity. It is particularly versatile in the movements it is capable of making, in the speed with which it can move, and the shapes it is capable of assuming. For the purpose of describing various speech sounds articulated in the oral cavity, phoneticians conveniently divide the tongue into various parts in such a way that there is some correlation between the division of the tongue and that of the roof of the mouth. Thus, as well as (1) the **tip** or **apex** of the tongue, we have (2) the **blade**, i.e. that part of the tongue which, when the tongue is lying at rest (this state of the tongue also applies to (3) and (4) below), faces the upper teeth ridge, (3) the **front**, i.e. that part of the tongue which faces the hard palate, and (4) the **back**, i.e. that part of the tongue which faces the soft palate. Notice that the above-mentioned division of the tongue does not include what one might call the middle or the centre of the tongue, which corresponds to the area consisting of the

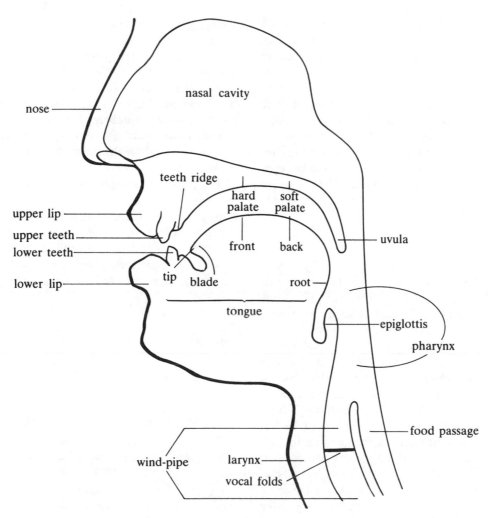

Figure 1 Speech organs

posterior part of the front of the tongue and the anterior part of the back of the tongue and whose recognition is implied in phoneticians' general practice of talking about central vowels or centralization of certain vowels.

Before speech sounds are articulated due to the intervention of various speech organs such as have been mentioned above, movement of an airstream is required; this airstream is then variously modified by speech organs into speech sounds.

There are three types of airstream mechanism. First, there is the **pulmonic airstream mechanism**. This is initiated by the lungs, and in normal speech the airstream is egressive – that is, the air is pushed out from the lungs. **Vowels** and many of the **consonants** require this type of airstream mechanism. Second, there is the **velaric airstream mechanism**. This is initiated by **velar closure**, i.e. the closure between the back part of the tongue and the soft palate, and the airstream is always ingressive. **Clicks** require this type of airstream mechanism. Third, there is the **glottalic airstream mechanism**. This is initiated by the glottis, which may be firmly or loosely closed, and the airstream is either egressive or ingressive. **Ejectives** (egressive) and **implosives** (ingressive) require this type of airstream mechanism, the firmly closed glottis for the former and the loosely closed glottis for the latter. Certain combinations of two of these types of airstream mechanism also occur.

In classifying speech sounds from the articulatory point of view, phoneticians frequently operate with the division between vowels and consonants. The so-called **semivowels** (e.g. [j w ɥ]) are, articulatorily speaking, vowels.

Vowels

Vowels are speech sounds in whose articulation: (1) the highest part of the tongue, which varies, is located within a certain zone in the oral cavity, which may be described as the **vowel area** (cf. the cardinal vowels discussed below); and (2) the egressive airstream from the lungs issues into the open air without meeting any closure or such constriction as would cause audible friction in the oral cavity or the pharyngeal cavity. Note that the occurrence of audible friction between the vocal folds, i.e. voice or vocal vibration, does not disqualify sounds as vowels provided there occurs at the same time no closure or constriction in any of the above-mentioned cavities. Many phoneticians assume a vowel to be voiced by definition; others consider that some languages have voiceless vowels – indeed it is possible to argue that [h] in English is a voiceless vowel. The soft palate, when raised (cf. velic closure), prevents the airstream from entering the nasal cavity, and oral vowels are produced, e.g. [i]; but when lowered, the soft palate allows the airstream to enter the nasal cavity as well as the oral cavity, and nasalized vowels result, e.g. [õ].

In describing a vowel from the point of view of articulatory phonetics, many phoneticians customarily make use of a certain auditory-articulatory reference system in terms of which any vowel of any

language may be described. The auditory-articulatory reference system in question is the **cardinal vowel system** devised by the English phonetician, Daniel Jones (1881–1967). The cardinal vowel system consists, as shown in Figure 2, of eight **primary** cardinal vowels, numbered from 1 to 8, and ten **secondary** cardinal vowels, numbered from 9 to 18; all of these eighteen cardinal vowels are oral vowels.

The primary cardinal vowels are posited in such a way that no. 1, [i], is articulated with the front of the tongue as high and front as possible consistent with its being a vowel – i.e. without becoming a consonant by producing audible friction; no. 5, [ɑ], is articulated with the back of

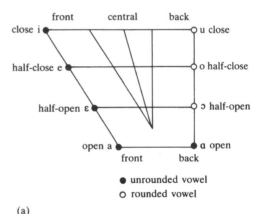

(a)

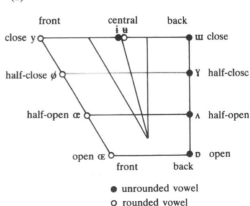

(b)

Figure 2 (a) Primary cardinal vowels (b) Secondary cardinal vowels

the tongue as low and back as possible consistent with its being a vowel; nos 2, 3 and 4, [e ɛ a], are so articulated as to form an auditory equidistance between each two adjacent vowels from no. 1 to no. 5; nos 6, 7 and 8, [ɔ o u], are so articulated as to continue the auditory equidistance, with no. 8 being articulated with the back of the tongue as high and back as possible consistent with its being a vowel. Nos 1, 2, 3, 4 and 5 are articulated with the lips unrounded, and nos 6, 7 and 8 with the lips rounded.

The secondary cardinal vowels are posited in such a way that nos 9 to 16, [y ø œ Œ ɒ ʌ ɣ w], correspond to the same points as nos 1 to 8, respectively, except for the posture of the lips in terms of rounded and unrounded. Nos 17 and 18, [ɨ ʉ], are articulated with the central part of the tongue as high as possible consistent with their being vowels; the former is unrounded and the latter rounded. Thus, by connecting the highest points of the tongue in the articulation of all the cardinal vowels, we can conceive of what may be referred to as the **vowel area**.

Use of the cardinal vowel system enables phoneticians to specify a vowel of any given language with regard to the following: (1) the height of the part of the tongue that is the closest to the palate, the reference points being close, half-close, half-open, open; (2) the part of the tongue on the front–back axis which is the closest to the palate, the reference points being front, central, back; and (3) the posture of the lips, rounded or unrounded. In addition, phoneticians specify the posture, raised or lowered, of the soft palate; that is, whether the vowel is oral or nasalized.

Monophthongs are vowels in the articulation of which the tongue all but maintains its posture and position, thereby maintaining practically the same vowel quality throughout, e.g. the vowels in the English words *raw*, *too*, etc. On the other hand, **diphthongs** are vowels in the articulation of which the tongue starts with the position for one vowel quality and moves towards the position for another vowel within one syllable, e.g. the vowels in the English words *no*, *buy*, etc.

Consonants

Consonants are speech sounds in the articulation of which the egressive or ingressive airstream encounters either a closure or a constriction which may or may not cause audible friction. Consonants may be classified according to the **manner of articulation** on the one hand and according to the **place of articulation** on the other. According to the various manners of articulation, consonants are classified into (1) plosives, (2) fricatives, (3) affricates, (4) approximants, (5) nasals, (6) rolls, (7) flaps, (8) ejectives, (9) implosives and (10) clicks. Note that this classification is only one of different possible ones current among phoneticians.

1   A **plosive** is a sound in whose articulation the airstream meets a closure made by a firm contact between two speech organs, which prevents the airstream from issuing beyond the point of the closure. The closure is then quickly released, but since a complete (if brief) stopping of the airstream has taken place, the sound is considered to be **non-continuant**. Some examples of plosives are [p d ʔ]. The release of a plosive may be incomplete in certain sequences of plosives or of plosives followed by homorganic affricates (see below). In English, for example, [k] in *actor* is incompletely released, while in French [k] in *acteur* is completely released; similarly, [t] in *what change* in English and the second [t] in *toute table* in French are not released.

2   A **fricative** is a sound in whose articulation the airstream meets a narrowing between two speech organs and causes audible friction as it passes through this narrowing – a close approximation – in the vocal tract. Some examples of fricatives are [f z h], which are **central fricatives**, and [ɬ],

which is a **lateral fricative**. In the articulation of a central fricative, the egressive air issues out along the median line in the oral cavity, while in that of a lateral fricative it issues out from one or both sides of the tongue.

3   An **affricate** is a sound in whose articulation the closure made by two speech organs for a plosive is slowly and partially released, with the result that what is known in phonetics as a **homorganic fricative** immediately follows. In this sense, an affricate combines the characteristic of a plosive and that of a fricative; the term **homorganic** is used in phonetics to indicate that a certain consonant is articulated in the same place in the vocal tract as another consonant articulated in a different manner. Some examples of affricates are [tɪ dɪ ʧ ʤ], which are sequences of homorganically pronounced plosives and fricatives.

4   An **approximant** is a sound in whose articulation the airstream flows continuously, while two speech organs approach each other without touching; that is, the two speech organs are in **open approximation**. Consequently, there is no audible friction – the sound is **frictionless**. Approximants, which correspond to what the IPA (see the INTERNATIONAL PHONETIC ALPHABET) formerly called **frictionless continuants** and **semivowels**, are by definition any speech sounds so articulated as to be just below **friction limit**; that is, just short of producing audible friction between two speech organs. Approximants are subdivided into **lateral approximants** and **median approximants**. Examples of lateral approximants include [l l ʎ], in the case of which the two speech organs which are said to approach each other are the side(s) of the tongue and the side(s) of the teeth ridge. Some examples of median approximants are [ʋ ɹ j w ʁ].

One particular type of speech sound which the IPA only partially recognizes but which should be fully recognized as median approximants are the speech sounds to which some refer as **spirants** and which are

quite distinct from fricatives. The sounds correspond to the letters *b*, *d* and *g* in – for example, *haber*, *nada* and *agua* in Spanish – in the articulation of which, in normal allegro speech, there occurs no audible friction. These spirants are often symbolized by ƀ, đ and g respectively, although these symbols are not recognized by the IPA. Note also that any close and 'closish' vowels, situated along or near the axis between the cardinal vowels nos 1 and 8, or nos 9 and 16, may justifiably be said to be approximants when they function as the so-called semivowels. Approximants thus make up a category of heterogeneous speech sounds, including (as they do) certain of the vowels. There are divergent identifications of some approximants on the part of individual phoneticians.

5   A **nasal** is a sound in whose articulation the egressive airstream meets obstruction at a given point in the oral cavity and is channelled into the nasal cavity – the soft palate being lowered – through which it issues out. Some examples of nasals are [m n ŋ].

6   A **roll** or **trill** is a sound in whose articulation one speech organ strikes several times against the other rapidly, e.g. [r].

7   A **flap** or **tap** is a sound in whose articulation one speech organ strikes against the other just once, i.e. [r].

8   An **ejective** is a sound in whose articulation a contact or constriction made by two speech organs at a given point in the oral cavity is released as the closed glottis is suddenly raised and pushes the compressed air in the mouth outwards, e.g. [p' s' ts'], and the air issues out as the oral closure is suddenly released. An ejective can thus be a **plosive**, a **fricative** or an **affricate**.

9   An **implosive** is a sound in whose articulation a contact made by two speech organs in the oral cavity is released as air rushes in from outside. This is made possible by a sudden lowering of the loosely closed glottis, e.g. [ɓ], and the air then rushes further inwards as the oral closure

is released. An implosive is thus a **plosive** as well.

10   A **click** is a sound in whose articulation a contact between two speech organs is made at a relatively forward part in the oral cavity at the same time as the closure made between the back of the tongue and the soft palate – velar closure – is released. As a result air rushes in as the back of the tongue slides backwards on the soft palate, e.g. [ʇ]. A click is a plosive or a lateral as well.

Consonants may also be classified according to various **places of articulation**. The major places of articulation are as follows: (1) **bilabial**, i.e. both lips, as in [p]; (2) **labio-dental**, i.e. the lower lip and the upper front teeth, as in [f]; (3) **apico-dental**, i.e. the tip of the tongue and the upper front teeth, or the tip of the tongue placed between the upper and lower front teeth, as in [θ]; (4) **apico-alveolar**, i.e. the tip of the tongue and the teeth ridge, as in [t]; (5) **blade-alveolar**, i.e. the blade of the tongue and the teeth ridge, as in [s]; (6) **apico-post-alveolar**, i.e. the tip of the tongue and the back part of the teeth ridge, as in [ɹ]; (7) **palatal**, i.e. the front of the tongue and the hard palate, as in [c]; (8) **alveolo-palatal**, i.e. the front of the tongue, the hard palate and the teeth ridge, as in [ɕ]; (9) **palato-alveolar**, i.e. the tip and blade of the tongue, the back part of the teeth ridge, and the hard palate, as in [ʃ]; (10) **retroflex**, i.e. the curled-up tip of the tongue and the hard palate, as in [ʂ]; (11) **velar**, i.e. the back of the tongue and the soft palate, as in [k]; (12) **uvular**, i.e. the uvula and the back of the tongue, as in [q]; (13) **pharyngeal**, i.e. the root of the tongue and the pharyngeal wall, as in [ʕ]; and (14) **glottal**, i.e. the vocal folds, as in [h].

Thus, for example, [p] is described as the voiceless bilabial plosive, [z] as the voiced blade-alveolar fricative, [ʧ] as the voiceless palato-alveolar affricate, [ŋ] as the voiced velar nasal, [ʎ] as the voiced palatal lateral approximant, [ʋ] as the voiced labio-dental approximant, [ɾ] as the voiced alveolar flap or tap, [r] as the voiced alveolar roll or trill, [p'] as the voiceless bilabial ejective, [ɓ] as the voiced bilabial implosive and [ǀ] as the voiceless dental click.

Assimilation

It was mentioned above that speech sounds, when occurring in connected speech, partially blend into each other. Some phoneticians talk about **combinatory phonetics** in this connection. There are a number of such combinatory articulatory phenomena, but we shall concentrate on just one, known as **assimilation**. Assimilation is said to occur when a speech sound undergoes a change in articulation in connected speech, becoming more like another immediately (or otherwise) adjacent sound. In English, for example, when [m] is replaced by [ɱ] before [f] or [v] – as in *comfort* or *circumvent* in an allegro pronunciation – its bilabiality changes into labio-dentality, and the pronunciation becomes ['kʌɱfət] or [ˌsəːkɱ'vent]. In French, the voicelessness of [s] as in the word *tasse* is changed into voicedness, thus [s̬] (the diacritic mark ˬ signifies voicing), in normal pronunciation of e.g. *tasse de thé*, without [s̬] being identical to [z] all the same: [tɑs̬dəte] ≠ [tɑz də te]. In English, the voice of [m] in e.g. *mall* is either partially or completely lost in e.g. *small* under the influence of the voicelessness of [s] preceding it, producing [sm̥ɔːl] (the diacritic mark ̥ signifies devoicing).

An assimilation in which the following sound affects the preceding sound, as in *comfort*, *circumvent*, *tasse de thé* is said to be regressive in nature and is therefore called **regressive assimilation**; an assimilation in which the preceding sound affects the following sound, as in *small*, is said to be progressive in nature and is therefore called **progressive assimilation**. Assimilation of these kinds relates to the question of what is called an **allophone** of a **phoneme** (see PHONEMICS) and to the question of a realization of a phoneme or an **archiphoneme** (see FUNCTIONAL PHONOLOGY).

Segmentals and suprasegmentals

What we have seen above concerns speech sounds to which phoneticians often refer as **segmental units**, or **segmentals** for short, since they are phonetic units that occur sequentially. In languages there are also what phoneticians refer to as **suprasegmental units** (or **suprasegmentals**), which are associated in their occurrence with stretches of segmentals and therefore are coterminous with them. They may be in other cases associated in their occurrence with single segments but ultimately have implications on multiple segments. **Intonation** and **stress** are among the better-known suprasegmentals (see INTONATION). Another well-known segmental is **duration**: a segmental may be relatively long, i.e. a long sound (e.g. [iː] in *beet* [biːt] in English; [tː] in *itta* [itːa] 'he/she/it/they went' in Japanese), or relatively short, i.e. a short sound (e.g. [ɪ] in *bit* [bɪt] in English; [t] in

ita [ita] 'he/she/it/they was/were (here, there, etc.)' in Japanese).

Finally, **tones** that characterize **tone languages** are, physically speaking, comparable to intonation but are assigned ultimately to **morphemes**, i.e. to the smallest linguistic units endowed with meaning (see TONE LANGUAGES). Therefore, tones are, linguistically, comparable to phonemes and archiphonemes (see FUNCTIONAL PHONOLOGY), whose function it is to distinguish between morphemes, rather than be comparable to intonation. However, every language, be it tonal or not, has intonation.

T.A.

Suggestions for further reading

Abercrombie, D. (1967) *Elements of General Phonetics*, Edinburgh: Edinburgh University Press: chapters 2, 4, 8, 9 and 10.

Ladefoged, P. (1982) *A Course in Phonetics*, 2nd edition, New York: Harcourt Brace Jovanovich: chapters 1, 6, 7, 9 and 10.

O'Connor, J.D. (1973) *Phonetics*, Harmondsworth: Penguin: chapter 2.

Artificial Intelligence

Introduction

Any discussion of the relations between **Artificial Intelligence** (AI) and linguistics needs to start with a brief review of what AI actually is. This is no place to attempt a definition of AI, but we do need some rough guidelines.

Just about the only characterization of AI that would meet with universal acceptance is that it involves trying to make machines do tasks which are normally seen as requiring intelligence (whatever 'intelligence' might turn out to be). There are countless refinements of this characterization: what sort of machines we want to consider; how

we decide what tasks require intelligence; and so on. For the current discussion, the most important question concerns the *reasons why* we want to make machines do such tasks. Among all its other dichotomies, AI has always been split between people who want to make machines do tasks that require intelligence because they want more useful machines, and people who want to do it because they see it as a way of exploring how humans do such tasks. We will call the two approaches the **engineering approach** and the **cognitive-science approach** respectively.

The techniques required for the two approaches are not always very different. For many of the tasks that engineering AI wants solutions to, the only systems we know about that can perform them are humans, so that – at least initially – the obvious way to design them is to try to mimic what we know about humans. For many of the tasks that cognitive-science AI wants solutions to, the evidence on how humans do them is too hard to interpret to enable us to construct computational models, so the only approach is to try to design solutions from scratch and then see how well they fit what we know about humans. The main visible difference between the two approaches is in their criteria for success: an engineer would be delighted to have created something that outperformed a person; a cognitive scientist would regard it as a failure (or as meaningless – how, for instance, could you be 'better' at using language than a person?).

Natural language processing vs computational linguistics

The distinction between the two approaches is as marked in AI work on language as in any other area. Language has been a major topic of AI research ever since people first thought that there might be some point in the discipline at all. As far as the engineering view of AI is concerned, the initial focus on language was on **machine translation**, since **translation** was viewed (with typical arrogance) as a mundane and easily mechanizable task. When it became apparent that this was not so, the focus switched to the use of language to enable people who were not explicitly trained in computer programming to make use of computers anyway – tasks such as interpreting and answering database queries, entering facts and rules into expert systems, and so on.

Much of this work took the view that, for constrained tasks of this kind, systems that could deal with **sublanguages** would suffice. It is possible to argue with this view. Conversing in a language which looks a bit like your native tongue, but which differs from it in ways which are not made clear, may be more difficult and irritating than

having to learn an entirely new but very simple and explicit language. Whether or not users will be happier with a system that speaks a fragment of some natural language than with a formal language, it is clear that much work in engineering AI differs from work in traditional linguistics by virtue of the emphasis on sublanguages.

The cognitive-science view, on the other hand, is concerned with very much the same phenomena as traditional linguistics, and its theories are couched in very similar terms. The main divergences between this sort of AI work on language and work within other branches of linguistics concerns the degree of precision required, and the constraint that theories must pay attention to the possibility of being used in programs. The need to see how to compute with your theory of language led to the comparative neglect of standard transformational approaches in AI (see below), and thence to the emergence of competing theories of grammar which have now percolated back into linguistics as such.

As in all of AI, the two approaches feed off each other whilst retaining rather different flavours, and especially rather different criteria for success. The terms **computational linguistics (CL)** and **natural language processing (NLP)** are widely used for the cognitive-science and engineering viewpoints respectively, with the term **language engineering** expressing even more clearly the application-oriented nature of some work in the field. The discussion below will indicate, where possible, which way particular theories are best viewed, but it must be emphasized that they are highly interdependent: successful ideas from one are likely to influence work in the other; the failure of an idea in one is likely to lead to its rejection in the other.

History of AI work on natural language

AI work on natural language is now as fragmented as linguistics as a whole, though along different divisions. To understand the theories being used in AI, and to relate them to other work in linguistics, we need to see where they came from and how they fit into the overall framework. Therefore the discussion of particular concepts and theories will be preceded by a brief overview of the history of AI work in the field.

In the beginning: machine translation

The earliest work on language within AI was concerned with machine translation (Weaver 1955). The early approach to this task took the view that the only differences between languages were between their vocabularies and between the permitted word orders. Machine translation, then, was going to be just a matter of looking in a dictionary for appropriate words in the target language to translate the words in the source text, and then reorder the output so it fitted the word order rules of the target language. The systems that resulted from this simple-minded approach appeared to be almost worse than useless, largely because of the degree of lexical ambiguity of a non-trivial subset of a natural language. Trying to deal with lexical ambiguity by including translations of each possible interpretation of each word led to the generation of text that contained so many options that it was virtually meaningless.

The superficial inadequacies of these systems, probably accompanied by overenthusiastic sales pitches by their developers, led in 1966 to a highly critical report from the American National Academy of Sciences and to a general loss of enthusiasm. Ironically, one of the earliest of these systems did remain funded, and eventually turned into what probably remains the most effective real machine-translation system, **SYSTRAN** (which is now available as the on-line translation system **BabelFish**). Furthermore, the 'transfer' approach to machine translation that underlies the massive EEC-funded **EUROTRA** project

probably owes more to the early word-for-word approach than is usually made apparent.

Speech processing

Another group of early optimists, funded largely by the US advanced research-projects agency ARPA (later DARPA – Defense Advanced Research-Project Agency), attempted the task of producing systems capable of processing speech. Some of these systems more or less met their proclaimed targets of processing normal connected speech, over a restricted domain and with a 1000-word vocabulary, with less than 10 per cent error. Descendants of these systems are now available as everyday tools (dictation machines, interfaces to telephone help services, etc.), alongside prototypes for more advanced applications such as 'interpreting telephony' (see, for instance, the German **VERBMOBIL** project (Kay et al. 1994)). At present, such systems either use a very restricted vocabulary and syntax, with applications which tightly constrain the range of possible interpretations and dialogue moves; or they require a fairly extensive training session with their intended users. One of the main changes in computational approaches to language over the past ten years has been the increasing use of statistical information and machine learning techniques (see below). This is particularly important for tasks involving speech, where the raw signal tends to be highly degraded, and varies considerably from speaker to speaker. In such situations, a 'language model' which estimates the likelihood of competing interpretations, using information about co-occurrence sets (N-grams) and other conditional probabilities, is invaluable.

Question answering

Other early workers attempted to build systems that could accumulate facts and answer questions about them. Most of these did very little analysis of the linguistic structure of the texts they were dealing with. The emphasis was on the sort of processing which goes on after the basic meaning has been extracted. Weizenbaum's (1966) **ELIZA** program, which simply permutes and echoes whatever the user types at it, is probably the best known of these systems. **ELIZA** does less work than almost any other well-known computer program, since all it does is recognize key words and patterns in the input and place them in predefined slots in output schemas (after suitable permutations, such as switching *you* to *me*).

The other programs of this period did little more syntactic processing, but did at least do some work on the patterns that they extracted. A reasonable example is Bobrow's (1968) program for solving algebra problems like the following:

> If the number of customers Tom gets is twice the square of 20 per cent of the number of advertisements he runs, and the number of advertisements he runs is 45, what is the number of customers Tom gets?

This appears to be in English, albeit rather stilted English. Bobrow's program processed it by doing simple pattern matching to get it into a form which was suitable for his equation-solving program. It is hard to say whether what Bobrow was doing was really language processing, or whether his achievement was more in the field of equation solving. It is clear that his program would have made no progress whatsoever with the following problem:

> If the number of customers Tom gets is twice the square of 20 per cent of the number of advertisements he runs, and he runs 45 advertisements, how many customers does he get?

The other pattern-matching programs of this time were equally frail in the face of the real complexity of natural language. It seems fair to say that the main progress made by these programs was in inference, not in language processing. The main lesson for language processing was that pattern matching was not enough – what was needed was proper linguistic theory.

Linguistic theory

The apparent failure of the early work made AI researchers realize that they needed a more adequate theory of language. As is far too often the case with AI work, there was already a substantial body of research on the required properties of language which had been ignored in the initial enthusiasm for writing programs. Towards the end of the 1960s, people actually went away and read the existing linguistic literature to find out what was known and what was believed, and what they might learn for their next generation of programs. Simultaneously, it was realized that NLP systems would need to draw on substantial amounts of general knowledge about the world in order to determine the meanings in context of words, phrases, and even entire discourses. Work in the late 1960s and early 1970s concentrated on finding computationally tractable versions of existing theories of grammar, and on developing schemes of meaning representation. These latter are required both to enable the integration of the specifically linguistic part of an NLP system with the sort of knowledge required for disambiguation and interpretation in context, and actually to link the NLP system to some other program which had information a user might want to access.

Syntactic theory

It was rapidly found that the dominant theory of syntax at that time, the extended standard (EST) version of transformational grammar (TG) did not lend itself easily to computational treatment. There is a long gap between Friedman's (1969, 1971) system for experimenting with putative transformations to see whether they generate all and only the required forms, and Stabler's (1987) attempt to combine unification grammar and government and binding theory, and during this time TG had virtually no direct representation within CL. The major threads in syntactic theory in CL for most of this time were the following: (1) the use of adaptations of Fillmore's (1968) case grammar; (2) attempts to do without an explicit grammar at all; and (3) attempts to extend the power of phrase-structure grammar by incorporating mechanisms from programming languages.

Case grammar
Case grammar started out as an attempt to explain some apparent syntactic anomalies: why, for instance, the sentences *John is cooking* and *Mary is cooking* can be collapsed to a single sentence *John and Mary are cooking*, whereas *John is cooking* and *The meat is cooking* cannot be collapsed to *John and the meat are cooking*; and why *She opened the door with a key* can be contracted to *The key opened the door* and *The door opened*, but not to *The key opened*. Within linguistics it remained an interesting, but essentially minor, theory. Within CL, and especially NLP, it became for a while more or less dominant.

The reason for this appears to be that the semantic roles that were invoked to explain the given phenomena mapped extremely directly on to the sorts of role that were already being discussed as the basis of techniques for meaning representation. The roles in case grammar could be interpreted directly as arcs in a **semantic network**, a graphical encoding of a set of relations between entities. Bruce (1975) provides an overview of a number of NLP systems employing some variant of case grammar. As the weakness of semantic-network representations becomes more apparent, it

seems that case grammar is becoming less significant for AI, but its influence has not disappeared entirely.

Grammarless systems
It may seem odd to include a subsection on systems which do without grammar within a section called 'Syntactic theory'. It would be unrealistic, however, to leave it out. To take the view that there *is* no syntactic level in language processing is to take a very strong view indeed as to what rules are required for the description of syntactic structure in NLP – none at all. The main proponents of this view, the **Yale School** based around Roger Schank, argue that whatever information is encoded in the organization of language can be extracted directly without building an intermediate representation.

It is not, in fact, all that easy to see what their claim really amounts to. Common sense tells us that they cannot entirely ignore the structure of the text they are processing, since if they did, their systems would come up with identical interpretations for *The lion beat the unicorn all round the town* and *Town lion unicorn round all the the the beat*; which they do not, and just as well too – we would hardly be very impressed by an NLP system which could not tell the difference between these two. Furthermore, one of the core programs in the substantial suite they have developed is Riesbeck's (1978) **conceptual analyser**. This program makes explicit mention of syntactic categories like 'noun' and 'determiner' in order to segment the text and extract the relations between the concepts represented by the words in the text – exactly what we always regarded as the task of syntactic analysis. We could weaken their claim to say that, by building the semantic representation by direct analysis of the relations of individual words in the input text, they avoid constructing an unnecessary intermediate set of structures. This, however, fails to provide any serious contrast with theories like **Montague grammar** (Dowty *et al.* 1981), **generalized phrase-structure grammar (GPSG)** (Gazdar *et al.* 1985) and **head-driven phrase-structure grammar (HPSG)** (Pollard and Sag 1994; Sag and Wasow 1999). These theories contain extremely complex and specific rules about permissible configurations of structures, of the sort that the Yale School seems to avow. They also, however, contain very straightforward mappings between syntactic rules and rules for semantic interpretation, so that any structure built up using them can equally easily be seen as semantic and syntactic.

Phrase-structure grammar and programs
For most of the 1970s the main example of this third approach was Woods' (1970, 1973) **augmented transition network (ATN)** formalism, which incorporated virtually unchanged the basic operations of the programming language LISP. Many very successful systems were developed using this formalism, but it had comparatively little effect on linguistics as a whole because the choice of the operations from LISP seemed to have very little explanatory power. ATNs work quite well, but they do not seem to capture any significant properties of language.

More recent work using notions from the logic programming language **PROLOG** seems to have had a wider effect. This is presumably because of PROLOG's status as an attempt to mechanize the rules of logic, which are themselves attempts to capture the universal rules of valid inference. These grammars use the PROLOG operation of **unification**, a complex pattern-matching operation, to capture phenomena such as agreement, subcategorization and long-distance dependency, rather than using the more standard programming operations of variable assignment and access.

The first such **unification grammar** was Pereira and Warren's (1980) **definite clause grammar (DCG)**. This was simply an attempt to capitalize on the facilities which came for free with PROLOG, without any very strongly held views on whether language was really like this or not. Since then, however, variants of unification seem to have taken over grammatical theory. **Generalized phrase-structure grammar** (Gazdar *et al.* 1985), **lexical-functional grammar** (Bresnan and Kaplan 1982), **functional-unification grammar** (Kay 1985), **restricted-logic grammar** (Stabler 1987) – the list seems to be growing daily. More recent grammatical formalisms such as **HPSG** (Pollard and Sag 1994; Sag and Wasow 1999), make use of extended unification algorithms which have been designed explicitly for use within linguistic frameworks, with more emphasis on providing appropriate expressive power and less on raw computational speed (Kasper and Rounds 1986; Gazdar *et al.* 1988). Unlike DCG, these later formalisms are generally defended in wider terms than their suitability for computer implementation, though at the same time they all respect the need to consider processing issues. This seemed, in the late 1980s, one of the most significant contributions of AI/NLP to general linguistic theory – a growing consensus on the general form of syntactic rules, which emerged initially from the AI literature but later came to be taken seriously within non-computational linguistics.

Syntactic processing

As well as choosing an appropriate syntactic theory, it was necessary to construct programs that could apply the theory, either to analyse the structure of input texts or to generate well-formed output texts. The development of **parsing algorithms**, i.e. programs for doing syntactic analysis, became an area of intense activity. The debate initially concentrated on whether it was better to apply rules **top-down**, making guesses about the structure of the text and testing these by matching them against the words that were actually present, or **bottom-up**, inspecting the text and trying to find rules that would explain its structure. In each of these approaches, there are times when the system has to make a blind choice among different possible rules, since there is generally not enough information available to guide it directly to the right answer. The simplest way of dealing with this is to use **chronological backtracking**; in other words, whenever you make a choice, remember what the alternatives were, and when you get stuck go back to the last choice-point, which still has unexplored alternatives, and try one of these.

It rapidly became apparent that, although this worked to some extent, systems that did this kind of naive backtracking tended to throw away useful things they had done as well as mistakes. To see this, consider the sentence *I can see the woman you were talking to coming up the path*. Most systems would realise that *see* often occurs as a simple transitive verb, so that the initial sequence *I can see the woman you were talking to* would be analysed as a complete sentence bracketed something like:

$$[[I]_{NP} [can see [the woman you were talking to]_{NP}]_{VP}]_S$$

The fact that there was some text left over would indicate that there was a mistake somewhere, and after further exploration an analysis more like the following might be made:

$$[[I]_{NP} [can see [[the woman you were talking to]_{NP} [coming up the path]_{VP}]_S]_{VP}]_S$$

It is hard to see how you could avoid having to explore the two alternatives. What should be avoidable is having to reanalyse the string *the woman you were talking to* as an NP simply because its initial analysis occurred during the exploration of a dead-end.

There were two major reactions to this problem. The first involved keeping a record of structures that had been successfully constructed, so that any attempts to repeat work that had already been done could be detected and the results of the previous round could be used immediately. This notion of a **well-formed substring table** (Earley 1970) was later developed to include structures which were currently being constructed, as well as ones that had been completed, in Kay's (1986) **active chart**. The other approach to dealing with these problems was to try to write the rules of the grammar in such a way that mistaken hypotheses simply did not get explored. The grammar developed by Marcus (1980) was designed so that a parser using it would be able to delay making decisions about what to do next until it had the information it needed to make the right choice. Riesbeck (1978) designed a system that would directly extract the information embodied in the syntactic structure, rather than building an explicit representation of the structure and then trying to interpret its significance. This approach at least partly sidesteps the issue of redoing work that has been done previously.

Meaning representation

AI has largely accepted from linguistics the view that language processing requires analysis at various levels. It has not, however, taken over the exact details of what each level is about. In particular, the AI view of semantics is very different from the linguistic treatment. It is inappropriate – and probably dangerous – at this point to try to give a characterization of the subject matter of semantics within linguistics (see SEMANTICS). But, whatever it is, it is not the same as the need of AI systems to link the language they are processing to the other information they have access to, in order to respond appropriately.

We have already seen this in the discussion of early question-answering systems. Much of what purported to be language processing turned out there to be manipulations of the system's own knowledge – of how to solve algebra problems, or of the statistics of the last year's baseball games, or whatever. This is entirely appropriate. Probably the biggest single lesson linguistics will learn from AI is that you have to integrate the linguistic component of your model with the rest of its knowledge.

The easiest way to do this seems to be to have some form of internal **interlingua**, some representation language within which all the system's knowledge can be expressed. The nature of this interlingua depends on what the system actually knows. There have been three major proposals for representation languages: logic, programming languages, and semantic primitives. There are, of course, a wide variety of notations for these, and there is some degree of overlap, but the division does reflect genuinely different approaches to the question of internal representation.

Logic
Logic, in various guises, has long been used as a language for analysing the semantics of natural languages. It has also been widely recommended, for instance by Charniak and McDermott (1985), as a good general-purpose representation language for AI systems. It is therefore no surprise to see it being proposed as the language NLP systems should use as the interlingua that connects them to the rest of the system of which they are a part.

There are two major traditions of using logic as the representation language in NLP systems. First, the widely used **semantic network** representation can easily be seen as a way of implementing a subset of the first-order logic (FOL) (see FORMAL LOGIC AND MODAL LOGIC) so as to facilitate certain types of inference. A semantic network is an implementation technique for recording a set of two-place relations between individuals as a labelled directed graph. As an example, we could represent some of the meaning of *John loves Mary* as the following set of relations:

agent(loving, John)
object(loving, Mary)

we could then represent these as a semantic network as follows:

```
              agent              object
John   ---------> loving <--------- Mary
```

N-place relations can be recorded by splitting them into collections of two-place relations. It is fairly easy to show that their expressive power is equivalent to that of a subset of FOL, but the internal representation as a network of pointers can make it easier to perform operations such as finding out all the relations a particular individual enters into. Semantic networks frequently contain pointers which contain information about class hierarchies, since this is both useful and particularly amenable to processing within graphical representations.

Semantic networks have a long history within NLP, with Sowa's (1984) conceptual graphs providing a widely used general framework, with explicit connections to FOL. There has often been a connection between the use of case grammar as a grammatical formalism and semantic networks as a representation language. In particular, the relations that are represented in the network are often just the roles implied by the grammar. There is, however, no necessary link between the two theories. An alternative is to use the main verb of the sentence being interpreted as the label on an arc between its subject and object, though this can be awkward in the case of intransitive verbs, where there is no object to put at the far end of the arc and, in the case of bitransitive verbs or verbs with adjuncts, since there is no obvious place to put the extra items.

The other use of logic as a representation language has followed more directly from work within formal semantics (see FORMAL SEMANTICS). The semantic theories associated with grammatical theories like GPSG and UCG descend directly from work by logicians and philosophers of language on questions of logical relationships between sentences. The key to this strand of work is Montague's demonstration that you can construct formal paraphrases of natural language sentences, for some fragments of natural language, purely on the basis of the syntactic structure of the sentence and the meanings of the words that it can contain (Dowty *et al.* 1981). Attempting to obey the **principle of compositionality**, which states that 'the meaning of the whole is determined by the meaning of the parts and their mode of combination', led to a substantial body of work where detailed, accurate formal paraphrases are obtained from natural language utterances. There are, of course, numerous problems with this work, not least that it turns out to be almost impossible to obey the principle rigidly. The structure of natural language utterances **underdetermines** their meanings: a great deal of effort has gone into developing logics that are underdetermined in the same way that natural language semantics seems to be, and into looking for algorithms that help choose between alternative readings.

At the same time, it has become apparent that the meanings of natural language utterances have to be somehow situated in the context in which they are produced. Again a range of logics and semantic frameworks, such as situation semantics (Barwise and Perry 1983), dynamic semantics (Groenendijk and Stokhof 1991) and discourse representation theory (DRT) (Kamp 1984), have been developed. These theories share a general outlook that upgrades the role of the discourse context in semantic analyses: they differ substantially in detail, but many of the general principles remain the same.

At various points this work has shown that FOL is not in fact rich enough to express all the distinctions which can be made in natural language, and that more powerful formalisms such as modal logic and intensional logic may be needed. It has also become apparent that if you want to *do* something with your formal paraphrase – to treat it as a question to be answered, or an instruction to be obeyed – then you will have to be able to link it up to your general knowledge, and to the task you are currently undertaking. To be successful in this, you need two things:

- You need to have the relevant knowledge encoded in the same logical formalism as you are using for your semantics. This is a massive task: in some sense, it is the whole of AI. The CYC project (Lenat and Guha 1990) made a valiant effort in this direction, but it is clear that there are technical and conceptual problems to overcome, in addition to the problem of finding the required manpower.
- You need an inference engine that can manipulate all this information. Recent advances in theorem proving have opened the way for experiments in this area, and a number of interesting systems that exploit modern inference engines have been reported.

Procedural semantics
Just as with the inclusion of notions from programming languages in grammatical formalisms, the fact that the meaning representation is to be used by a computer has led a number of researchers to try to use a programming language as their representation language.

Winograd's (1972) program, **SHRDLU**, is perhaps the best-known example of this. Winograd realized that a hearer is not normally thought of just as a passive receiver of information. In any normal dialogue, the speaker expects the hearer to *do* something as a result of processing what they are told. If they are asked a question, they are expected to answer it; if they are given an order, they are expected to carry it out; if they are told a fact, they are expected to remember it. Since the languages that are used to get computers to do things are programming languages, it seemed reasonable to require the interpretation to be expressed in a programming language, as a command to find the answer to a question, or to perform an action, or to assert something in a database, as appropriate.

Winograd used a special-purpose programming language called **MICRO-PLANNER** (Hewitt 1971) for this **procedural semantics**. Norman *et al.* (1975) used the standard programming language **LISP** for their implementation of this idea. With the development of **PROLOG** as a language with alternative readings as either a version of FOL or an executable programming language, the distinction between using logic and using procedural semantics has become rather blurred, as can be seen in, for instance, **CHAT-80** (Warren and Pereira 1982).

Semantic primitives
Any representation language has **primitives** – that is, terms which are basic, or taken as given, because it is not possible to define all the terms in any vocabulary in terms of each other without introducing unexplained circularities. The choice of a programming language for the representation language provides one way out of the problem, since the semantics of this language as a programming language will define the semantics of the primitives. An alternative solution is to try to find some set of terms which can be taken as the real primitives of human thought, and try to base everything on these.

The major proponents of this notion are, again, the Yale School led by Roger Schank. Schank's (1972) theory of **conceptual dependency (CD)** is an attempt to find a minimal set of primitives which can be used for the interpretation of all natural language texts. Schank motivates the development of his theory with the argument that any two sentences that would be judged by a native speaker to have the same meaning should have identical representations, and illustrates this by requiring that *John loves Mary* should have the same meaning as *Mary is loved by John*. CD is a brave attempt to find a manageable set of primitives which will support this argument. However, many linguists would not agree that any two sentences which differ in form can be identical in meaning.

The number of primitives in CD has fluctuated slightly as the theory has developed, but is remarkably stable when compared to the range of cases and roles that have been suggested in all the variants on case grammar. One reasonably representative version of the theory has eleven primitive actions, a set of roles such as **instrument** and **object**, as in case grammar, and a notion of causal connection.

These actions have been widely reported (e.g. in Charniak and McDermott 1985), and I will not go into details here. One thing I will note is that at first sight they seem remarkably biased towards human beings, with the action of **SPEAKing**, i.e. making a string of sounds of a language, having roughly the same status as **PTRANSing**, or moving an object from one place to another. Careful consideration, however, shows that if there is anything at all in the theory then this sort of claim is one of its more significant consequences. Furthermore, their analysis does seem to work for a non-trivial subset of the language. The emphasis on human activities is perhaps less surprising when we realize that most of what humans talk about is things that humans do.

CD is not the only AI theory based on semantic primitives. Most others make weaker claims about the status of their primitives. Wilks' (1978) theory of **preference semantics**, for instance, used quite a large set of primitives (a hundred or more) as the basis for disambiguation of word senses in a translation program. This set of primitives is offered as a useful tool for this task, but very little is said about either their psychological reality or about whether or not they are a minimal set even for the task in hand.

In many theories the presence of primitives is left unremarked: theories deriving from Montague semantics, for instance, simply permit the presence of uninterpreted elements of the vocabulary without any explanation at all. Pustejovsky (1991) and others have tried to take a more flexible approach to lexical semantics, aiming to cope with the way that words seem to shift their meanings from context. To take an example from Pustejovsky, consider the following pair of sentences:

(1) John baked a cake.
(2) John baked a potato.

In (1), the action of *baking* involves a transformation of one set of materials (eggs, flour . . .) into a single, hopefully pleasant tasting, object. In (2), however, all that happens is that the state of a single item which existed both before and after the event took place is changed. Do we say that *bake* is an ambiguous lexical item? Surely not. But if it is not, then how can it describe such different processes?

There are a number of explanations of the way that lexical items shift their meanings in this way. Pustejovsky (1991) and Moens and Steedman (1988) argue for a process of coercion of the meaning of an item away from its normal interpretation. Ramsay (1994) attempts to explain this phenomenon as an emergent property of the inference process. There is, at least, a widespread recognition that you cannot just write down something which purports to be the 'meaning' of a word and hope that it will stay unchanged just where you put it.

Beyond the sentence

NLP systems have always recognized that dealing with individual sentences was only part of the task. Processing larger texts requires research on at least two further topics: linguistic and structural properties of connected discourses, and the use of background knowledge.

Discourse processing
As soon as we move to connected discourses, we meet a collection of problems which simply did not present themselves when we were just considering isolated sentences. Some of them concern the problem of interpreting the individual sentences that make up the discourse, in particular the problem of determining referents for pronouns. Others concern the placing of each sentence in relation to the others: is it an elaboration, or an example, or a summary, or a change of topic (compare TEXT LINGUISTICS). Progress on these topics was fairly slow so long as people concentrated on systems for interpreting language. A few heuristics for pronoun dereferencing were developed, and there were some experiments on **story grammars** (e.g. Rumelhart 1975), but generally not much was achieved. This seems to be because it is possible to get at least some information out of a connected text even when its overall structure is not really understood, so that people were not really aware that there was a lot more there that they could have been getting.

The situation changed radically when serious attempts were made to get computers to *generate* connected texts. It soon became apparent that if you misuse cues about the structure of your text, then human readers become confused. For instance, the use of pronouns in *John likes fish; he hates meat* and *Mary likes fish; Jane hates it* enables us to track the topic of the two texts – *John* in the first, *fish* in the second. Failure to use them, as in *John likes fish; John hates meat* and *Mary likes fish; Jane hates fish*, leads to confusion, since we have no clues to tell us what we are really being told about. Systems for comprehension of text which had no idea about topic and focus could cope with either example, so long as they had some vague heuristics about pronoun dereferencing. But systems that are to generate coherent text must have a more adequate understanding of what is going on. Work by Appelt (1985) and McKeown (1985) on language generation, and by Webber (1983) and Grosz and Sidner (1986), represents some progress in these areas. Much of this work has now coalesced around **centring theory** (Grosz *et al.* 1995), which provides a unified, and fairly successful, account of the way that discourses are structured around themes, which shift backwards and forwards as the discourse progresses.

This work also draws on the notion of language as rational, planned behaviour. This idea, which stems originally from suggestions by Wittgenstein (1953/1968) and from Searle's (1969) work on speech acts (see SPEECH-ACT THEORY), was originally introduced into AI approaches to language by Allen and Perrault (1980) and Cohen and Perrault (1979). The idea here was to characterize complete utterances as actions which could be described in terms of their preconditions and effects. This characterization would enable connected texts and dialogues to be understood. Using existing AI theories of planning (Fikes and Nilsson 1971), a speech act could be planned as just another act on the way to realizing the speaker's overall goal and, perhaps more interestingly, such an act could be interpreted by trying to work out what goal the speaker could have that might be furthered by the act. There are many problems with this approach, not least the sheer difficulty of recognizing another's plan simply by reasoning forwards from their actions, but it certainly seems like a fruitful area for further research.

Background knowledge
In addition to needing an analysis of the functional structure of connected texts, we also clearly need to access substantial amounts of general knowledge. We need this both for interpreting texts in which a lot of background information is left unstated, and for generating texts which will leave out enough for a human reader to find them tolerable. Although it is again well known that we need such background knowledge, comparatively little work has been done on providing it. This must be at least partly because no one has ever really had the resources to compile the sort of knowledge base that would be required for effective testing of theories about how to use it.

The only substantial attempt to do something about it comes again from the Yale School. Schank and Abelson (1977) developed the notion of a **script**, namely a summary of the events that constitute some stereotyped social situation. Scripts can be used in both the comprehension and generation of stories about such situations. Schank and Abelson argue that to tell a story for which both speaker and hearer have a shared script, all the speaker has to do is to provide the hearer with enough information to invoke the right script and instantiate its parameters, and then state those events in the current instance that *differ* from what is in the script.

There is a lot that seems right about this, not least that it explains the feeling of frustration that we experience when someone insists on spelling out all the details of a story when all we want is the bare bones plus anything unusual. Quite a number of programs based on it have been developed (Lehnert 1978; Wilensky 1978), showing that it is not just appealing but that it may also have practical applications. There is, however, still a substantial set of problems with it. Outstanding among these are the question of how we acquire and manage the many hundreds of thousands of scripts that we would need in order to cope with the range of stories that we do seem able to cope with, and the problems of mutual knowledge that arise when the speaker and hearer are trying to co-ordinate their view of the script that is currently in use. Schank (1982) makes an informal, if plausible, attempt to discuss the first of these problems; the second is a problem for all theories, of how to organize connected discourse to reflect the social processes that underlie language use.

Machine learning

Artificial Intelligence is concerned with providing computational models of a range of cognitive abilities – not just language, but also vision, reasoning, game playing, etc. Most AI work in these areas has little relation to language processing (though the discussion of semantics above does remark on the increasing importance of inference processes in the construction of meaning representations). Machine learning, however, has begun to play a very prominent role in computational approaches to language.

Machine learning is a very broad topic, and much work in the area has had little impact on language processing. There are, however, two approaches to machine learning which have changed the way that AI/CL researchers have approached language – namely **neural nets** and **stochastic learning**.

Neural nets are configurations of very simple computing devices, called **perceptrons**, which can compute weighted combinations of input features in order to determine what class a particular item belongs to. Perceptrons are rather like highly idealized neurons. When large numbers of them are connected together, they can be made to perform interesting computations. Researchers have investigated such devices since the very early days of AI, partly because of the attraction of working with computing systems that seem to share at least some of the properties of the cells that make up the brain, but more importantly because they can be made to *learn*. The original learning algorithm for perceptrons

was shown to have very severe limitations (Minsky and Papert 1969), and it was not until the development in the late 1970s of the **backpropagation algorithm** (Rumelhart *et al*. 1988) for complex networks of perceptrons that work in the area recovered from Minsky and Papert's result.

Neural networks have been applied to a number of language-oriented tasks, but it has proved very difficult to encode the notion of 'structure' in a neural network, and especially difficult to deal with recursion. Consequently, the main applications of neural networks in language processing have been in areas such as lexical disambiguation (where sets of properties of the other words in a sentence can be used as inputs to the network) and the acquisition of morphological rules (which are largely local, and hence can be encoded on a finite vector). Neural network approaches to syntax and semantics have been less successful, though a number of systems have been developed which attempt to acquire grammatical knowledge from examples, and then to apply that knowledge robustly to real data.

The *appeal* of neural nets lies in their apparent similarity to the 'computing devices' in the brain. Their *success*, on the other hand, arises because they extract statistical regularities from data which is not amenable to more orthodox statistical tests. There are, however, a number of other statistical techniques which can be applied to language-oriented tasks. There has been a growing trend towards approaching language processing as an essentially probabilistic activity.

This trend is taking AI/CL away from orthodox linguistics, but it is a trend that linguistics cannot afford to ignore. In particular, the use of **hidden Markov models** (finite state automata with transition probabilities inferred from statistical analyses of large corpora) and of models based on conditional probabilities have transformed the effectiveness of grammar induction algorithms, and have led to practical systems for retrieving and classifying documents for various purposes. Search engines for the World Wide Web, systems for automatically selecting and summarizing documents, email filtering systems, and so on, all depend on these statistical properties of language. The existence of large (100 million words and upwards) corpora, often automatically tagged for part of speech, have made it possible to apply statistical methods that would have been unthinkable a few years ago. The success of such systems will inevitably have an impact on linguistics in general. It is likely that statistical analyses will always be dependent on a sound underlying linguistic theory, but it is increasingly true that linguistic theories that ignore the importance of the statistical properties of language will be seen as flawed, and as

unlikely to be useful in language *engineering*, no matter how attractive they seem as language *science*.

A.M.R.

Suggestions for further reading

Allen, J.F. (1987) *Natural Language Processing*, Amsterdam: John Benjamins.
Grosz, B.J., Sparck Jones, K. and Webber, B.L. (1986) *Readings in Natural Language Processing*, Los Altos: Morgan Kaufman.
Reilly, R. and Sharkey, N.E. (1992) *Connectionist Approaches to Language Processing*, Hove: Lawrence Erlbaum Associates.
Sparck Jones, K. and Wilks, Y. (1983) *Automatic Natural Language Parsing*, Chichester: Ellis Horwood.

Artificial languages

An **artificial language** is one that has been created for some specific purpose or reason, as opposed to a **natural language**, such as those spoken by most speech communities around the world, which is normally thought of as having evolved along with its speech community, and for which it is not possible to find some ultimate source of creation. The machine codes and various programming languages we use with computers (see ARTIFICIAL INTELLIGENCE) and the languages of logic (see FORMAL LOGIC AND MODAL LOGIC) are all artificial languages, but will not be dealt with in this entry, which is devoted, rather, to those artificial languages which have been developed for general use in attempts to provide 'a neutral tongue acceptable to all' (Large 1985: vii). The best-known such language is probably **Esperanto**, which was one hundred years old in 1987. In that year, the United Nations estimated that Esperanto was spoken by 8 million people, from 130

countries. There were around 38,000 items of literature in Esperanto in the Esperanto library at Holland Park, London, which is the largest in the world, and the Esperanto Parliamentary Group at Westminster numbered 240 MPs. The *Linguist* (26(1) (winter) 1987: 8) lists the following further facts as evidence for the success of the language as an international medium of communication:

> Radio Peking broadcasts four half hour programmes in it each day, British Telecom recognise it as a clear language for telegrams, Dutch telephone booths have explanations for the Esperanto-speaking foreigner, it is available under the Duke of Edinburgh Award Scheme, and the Wales Tourist Board have begun issuing travel brochures in it. . . . Liverpool University has recently appointed a Lecturer in Esperanto, and the Dutch Government has given the computer firm BSO a grant of £3 million to develop a machine translation programme with

Esperanto as the bridge, or intermediate language.

Before one rushes off to take lessons, however, it is worth knowing that there are around 300 million native speakers of varieties of English around the world, and that almost as many people use it as an additional language. In 1975, English was the official language of twenty-one nations and one of the languages of government, education, broadcasting and publication in a further sixteen countries (Bailey and Görlach 1982: preface).

Nevertheless, Esperanto is the most successful outcome of the Artificial Language Movement (Large 1985), which began seriously in the seventeenth century with the efforts of Francis Bacon (among others) to develop a written language composed of **real characters**, symbols which represented concepts in a way that could be understood universally because they were pictorial (as he wrongly supposed that Chinese characters and Egyptian Hieroglyphics were; see WRITING SYSTEMS). Such a language would not only be universal, but would also reflect nature accurately, a major concern in that age of scientific endeavour, and it would be free of ambiguities, so that ideas could be expressed clearly in it. It would, however, require considerable powers of memory, since large numbers of characters would have to be remembered if the language was to be of general use, and interest in universal-language projects such as Bacon's (of which Large 1985 gives a comprehensive overview) faded during the eighteenth century.

The creation of a universal language came to be seen as a serious proposition again with the invention of **Volapük** in the late nineteenth century. Volapük was created by a German parish priest, Monsignor Johann Martin Schleyer (1832–1912), who was, according to Large (1985: 64), reputed to have 'some familiarity with more than 50 languages'. Schleyer thought that all natural languages were defective because their grammars were irrational and irregular, and his aim was to develop a language that would be simple to learn, grammatically regular, and in which thought could be clearly and adequately expressed. Its vocabulary consisted of **radicals** derived mainly from English words, with some adaptation of words from German, French, Spanish and Italian. The radicals were derived from the source words according to a number of rules. For instance, the letter *h* was excluded, and *r* almost totally eliminated because Schleyer thought that it was difficult to pronounce for Chinese, old people and children; all radicals had to begin and end with a consonant; as far as possible, consonants and vowels should alternate in radicals. According to these rules, the English words *moon, knowledge, speak, world, tooth* and *friend* become the Volapük radicals *mun, nol, pük, vol, tut* and *flen*. Nouns had four cases and two numbers, providing case and number endings as in the following example:

	Singular	Plural
Nominative	*vol*	*vols*
Genitive	*vola*	*volas*
Dative	*vole*	*voles*
Accusative	*voli*	*volis*

The compound *volapük* can thus be seen to be formed from the genitive of *vol* 'world' and *pük* 'speak' (meaning 'language').

It is possible to argue that Volapük has a masculine bias, in so far as the male term, for instance *blod* ('brother'), is taken as the norm from which feminine variations are formed by means of the prefix *ji-*; thus *jiblod*, 'sister'. Adjectives are formed by adding the suffix *-ik*. Verbs have one regular conjugation, and voice and tense are indicated by prefixes, while mood, person and personal pronouns are indicated by suffixes. Word-building rules include using the suffix *-av* to indicate a science and the suffix *-alto* indicate spiritual or abstract concepts. Large (1985: 67) charts the growth of Volapük as follows:

The Volapük movement experienced a spectacular growth, spreading rapidly from Germany into Austria, France and the Low Countries, and thence to the far-flung corners of the globe. By 1889 there were some 283 societies or clubs scattered throughout the world as far away as Sydney and San Francisco, 1,600 holders of the Volapük diploma and an estimated one million Volapükists (at least according to their own estimates; one-fifth of this figure is a more realistic number). Over 300 textbooks on the language had been published and 25 journals were devoted to Volapük, seven being entirely published in the language. The First Volapük International Congress, held in Friedrichshafen in August 1884, was conducted in German . . . as was the Second Congress in Munich (1887), but the Third International Congress, held in Paris in 1889, was completed exclusively in Volapük.

Subsequently, however, enthusiasm for the language as a possible universal medium of communication declined. The grammar, although regular, was complicated, offering several thousands of different forms of verbs, and because of the strict rules for deriving vocabulary from other languages the words were often difficult or impossible to recognize, so the vocabulary simply had to be memorized. Therefore, the language was not one which non-experts or enthusiasts would find easy to appropriate, and attempts to simplify it were met with hostility by Schleyer. The controversy generated by the simplification issue within the movement led to its rapid decline, so that by the time of Schleyer's death in 1912 the rival artificial language, **Esperanto**, had many more followers than Volapük, and had even won over large numbers of former Volapükists.

Esperanto was created by the Polish polyglot (Russian, French, German, Latin, Greek, English, Hebrew, Yiddish and Polish, according to Large 1985: 71) Ludwick Lazarus Zamenhof (1859–1917), who was by profession a medical doctor. His language was called **Lingvo Internacia** when first published in 1887, but this name was soon displaced by the author's pseudonym, Doctor Esperanto. Zamenhof thought that Volapük was too complicated to learn, and his familiarity with English convinced him that grammatical complexity such as that which Volapük displayed in spite of its regularity, was not a necessary feature of a universal language.

Esperanto has only sixteen grammatical rules (listed in Large 1985: appendix 1) and its vocabulary is based largely on Romance languages and Latin. Like all living languages, Esperanto is able to adapt to changes in its environment, since it is highly receptive to new words, which, if they can be made to conform to Esperanto orthography, are simply taken over from their source; if they cannot easily be made to conform to Esperanto orthography or compounded from existing Esperanto roots, new words will be created. All nouns end with *o*, adjectives with *a* and adverbs with *e*. Plurals end with *j* (/ɪ/). Use of affixes to common roots provides for further regularities of word formation, and ensures that families of words can be created from a relatively small stock of roots – 16,000 in the most comprehensive dictionary of Esperanto, *La Plena ilustrita vortaro*. From these roots ten times as many words can be formed. The Esperanto alphabet has twenty-three consonants and five vowels, each of which has one sound only, so that spelling and pronunciation are broadly phonological.

Zamenhof's aim in developing Esperanto was to provide an international language: 'one that could be adopted by all nations and be the common property of the whole world, without belonging in any way to any existing nationality' (quoted from Dr Esperanto 1889, in Large 1985: 72). Such a language would have to be easy to learn and must be a viable intermediary for international communication.

While many Esperantists feel that the language conforms to these requirements, it has been criticized for its use of circumflexed letters, which makes writing and typing difficult, and because its words are not easily recognizable by those familiar with the natural language words from which they are derived. The latter criticism is one which has been levelled at most artificial languages (see Large 1985: chapters 2–4), and is serious, since difficulty in recognizing roots will mean that they have to be learned anew, and this, in turn, is a serious obstacle to universal spread of the language. It is also possible to argue that Esperanto is not, in fact, suitable as a truly universal language, because it is too Eurocentric to appeal to speakers of, for instance, Asian languages.

A less well-known artificial language, still in fairly wide use, is **Ido**, which resembles Esperanto in many ways (Large 1985: 134):

> The Idists organised their first World Congress in 1912, held in Vienna. The movement increased in strength during the inter-war period, only to be set back again by the Second World War. Today, it manages to maintain a tenuous foothold in several European countries, North America, and a few other scattered outposts. In Britain the International Language (Ido) Society of Great Britain promotes the language in various ways. It organises courses, particularly of the correspondence variety, publishes a journal, *Ido-Vivo*, three times per year and convenes annual meetings. Nevertheless, membership remains very small. Such national associations in turn are affiliated to La Uniono por la Linguo Internaciona (Ido), which publishes its own journal, *Progreso*, and organises international conferences.

Dissatisfaction with Ido led to the publication in 1922 of **Occidental** by Edgar von Wahl (or de Wahl). Occidental was conceived as a language for use in the Western world alone. Its vocabulary is 'largely made up from "international" roots found in the chief Romance languages of Western Europe, or from Latin roots when no such common form could be found' (Large 1985: 141).

The first artificial language to be published by a professional linguist was Otto Jespersen's **Novial**, which based its vocabulary largely on Ido and its grammar largely on Occidental. Novial became one of the six candidates for an international language which were considered by the **International Auxiliary Language Association (IALA)**, founded in 1924 with financial support from the Rockefeller Foundation and the Vanderbilt family. The other five languages receiving consideration were Esperanto, Esperanto II (a revised version of Esperanto), Ido, Occidental and Latino sine flexione. By 1945, however, the IALA had come to the conclusion that, rather than select one of these languages, the common base underlying them all should serve as the starting point for an auxiliary language whose vocabulary would be such that most educated speakers of a European language would be able to read it and understand its spoken form with no previous training (Large 1985: 147):

> In order to identify this international vocabulary, the IALA looked at the chief members of the Anglo-Romanic group: English, French, Italian, and Spanish-Portuguese. If a word occurred in one of these four 'control languages' it was adopted at once. . . . If a word could not be found in at least three of the control languages, then German and Russian were also consulted.

The resultant language is known as **Interlingua** (Large 1985: 150):

> The grammar of Interlingua is essentially romanic, and not unlike Edgar de Wahi's Occidental. It is intended to be as

simple as possible whilst still remaining compatible with pan-occidental usage. Any grammatical feature which one of Interlingua's contributing languages has eliminated should not be included; neither should any grammatical feature be excluded which is to be found in all the contributing languages. . . . Interlingua has no genders, personal endings for verbs or declensions of nouns. It does include, however, a de-finite and indefinite article, a distinctive plural for nouns, and different endings to distinguish between different verbal tenses. . . . As regards pronunciation, it is virtually that of ecclesiastical Latin.

Interlingua is intended primarily for scientific communication, and within this field it made good progress for a time, but has now been superseded as an international language of science by English.

Other artificial languages invented in the twentieth century include **Eurolengo**, intended as a means of communication for use in business and tourism, and **Glosa**, which is intended to function as an international auxiliary language.

It is unlikely that any invented language will ever succeed as a universal means of communication. It requires special effort to learn a new language, and any such new language would be closer to some of the world's languages than to others. Those people most likely to need to communicate internationally are also quite likely to know one or more foreign languages, and when no common language is available to prospective communicators, translators and interpreters are used. Official international communication, in institutions like the United Nations, proceeds via translators and interpreters, to allow all speakers ease of communication in their own language.

Since a number of natural languages, including English, already function as international means of communication and, given the availability of increasingly well-qualified translators and interpreters, it is probable that the pursuit of artificial languages will remain a minority occupation.

K.M.

Suggestions for further reading

Large, A. (1985) *The Artificial Language Movement*, Oxford: Basil Blackwell.

Auditory phonetics

Definition

Auditory phonetics is that branch of phonetics concerned with the perception of speech sounds. It thus entails the study of the relationships between speech stimuli and a listener's responses to such stimuli as mediated by mechanisms of the peripheral and central auditory systems, including certain cortical areas of the brain (see LANGUAGE PATHOLOGY AND NEUROLINGUISTICS). It is distinct from **articulatory phonetics**, which involves the study of the ways in which speech sounds are produced by the vocal organs (see ARTICULATORY PHONETICS), and from **acoustic phonetics**, which involves the analysis of the speech signal primarily by means of instrumentation (see ACOUSTIC PHONETICS). In fact, however, issues in auditory phonetics are often explored with reference to articulatory and acoustic phonetics, and there may be no clear distinction made by some speech-perception researchers between aspects of acoustic and auditory phonetics, due to the fact that the two fields are so closely related.

Mechanisms involved in speech perception

Auditory perception of the sounds of speech requires that a listener receive, integrate and process highly complex acoustic stimuli which contain information ranging from relatively low to relatively high frequencies at varying intensities. Young adults can perceive sounds whose frequencies range from about 20 Hz (Hertz), i.e. 20 cycles per second, to about 20 kHz (kilo-Hertz), i.e. 20,000 cycles per second. However, this entire range is not utilized in the production of natural speech sounds; hence the effective perceptual range is much smaller. Likewise, the dynamic range of the human auditory system is extremely large – about 150 dB (decibels); that is, if the smallest amount of intensity required to detect a sound were represented as a unit of 1, the largest amount tolerable before the ear sustained damage would be 10^{15}. Needless to say, this full dynamic range is not utilized in normal speech perception.

Many of the principles concerning how acoustic stimuli are converted from sound-pressure waves into meaningful units of speech have been formulated and tested empirically since Helmholtz (1821–94) set forth his theories of hearing well over a century ago (Helmholtz 1869). Much of the data obtained have come from psychometric, psycholinguistic and neurolinguistic studies of humans and from physiological experiments with animals. A description of the various scaling techniques and experimental procedures utilized in studies of auditory perception is beyond the scope of the present discussion, but the major findings that have been obtained by means of such techniques and procedures will be presented.

The fundamentals of auditory phonetics can best be understood by first viewing the role of the major physiological mechanisms involved in hearing with reference to the peripheral auditory system, including the ear and the auditory nerve, and the central nervous system, including certain areas of the brain. The combined role of these systems is to receive, transduce, encode, transmit and process an acoustic signal. Although a detailed discussion of the acoustic properties of a signal would deal with, at least, frequency, intensity, duration and phase, the focus of the present discussion will be on frequency – perhaps the most thoroughly studied parameter and the one most relevant to a discussion of auditory phonetics.

The **ear** is divided into three anatomically distinct components; namely the outer, middle and inner ear, as represented in Figure 1.

The **outer ear** includes the **pinna** and the **external meatus** – the visible cartilaginous structures – and the **external auditory canal**, which terminates at the **tympanic membrane** or **eardrum**. The outer ear 'collects' auditory signals which arrive as sound waves or chang-ing acoustic pressures propagated through the surrounding medium, usually air. The outer ear also serves as protection for the delicate middle ear, provides some amplification and assists in sound localization, i.e. in determining where a sound originates.

The **middle ear** is bounded on one side by the tympanic membrane and on the other by a bony wall containing the **cochlea** of the inner ear. In addition to the tympanic membrane, the middle ear contains three **ossicles**; these are the **malleus**, **incus** and **stapes**, a set of three tiny interconnected bones extending in a chain from the tympanic membrane to the **oval window** of the cochlea. The tympanic membrane vibrates in response to the sound waves impinging upon it; the ossicles greatly amplify these vibratory patterns by transferring pressure from a greater area, the tympanic membrane, to a much smaller one, the footplate of the stapes attached to the oval window of the cochlea.

The **inner ear** contains the **vestibule**, the **semicircular canals** – which primarily affect

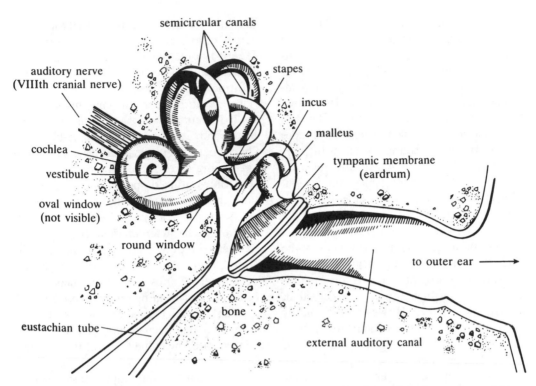

semicircular canals

auditory nerve
(VIIIth cranial nerve)

stapes

incus

malleus

cochlea

tympanic membrane
(eardrum)

vestibule

oval window
(not visible)

round window

to outer ear ⟶

eustachian tube

bone

external auditory canal

Figure 1 If the outer ear were depicted, it would appear at the far right of the figure. It would be the anterior portion of the ear, i.e. as it appears when viewed from the front. Note that, although the cochlea appears to be a discrete object, it is actually a coiled passage located within the bone of the skull. Ligaments of the ossicles are not shown.

balance – and the **cochlea**, a small coiled passage of decreasing diameter. Running the length of the cochlea are the **scala tympani** and **scala vestibuli**, two fluid-filled canals which are separated from the fluid-filled **scala media** or **cochlear duct**. The vibratory patterns of sound-pressure waves, are transferred into hydraulic pressure waves, which travel through the scala vestibuli and scala tympani and from the base to the apex of the scala media.

One surface of the scala media contains a layer of fibres called the **basilar membrane**. This tapered membrane is narrow and taut at its base in the larger vestibular end of the cochlea, and wide and flaccid at its terminus or apex in the smaller apical portion of the cochlea. On one surface of the basilar membrane is the **organ of Corti**, which contains thousands of inner and outer hair cells, each supporting a number of **cilia** or hairs. When the basilar membrane is displaced in response to the travelling waves propagating throughout it, the **tectorial membrane** near the outer edge of the organ of Corti also moves. It is believed that the shearing effect of the motion of these two membranes stimulates the cilia of the hair cells, thereby triggering a neural response in the auditory-receptor cells. These cells, in turn, relay electrochemical impulses to a fibre bundle called the **auditory nerve**, or the **VIIIth cranial nerve**. Information about the spatial representation of frequencies on the basilar membrane is preserved in the auditory nerve, which is thus said to have **tonotopic organization**.

The precise nature of the information received on the basilar membrane and encoded in the auditory nerve has been a matter of much investigation. The fact that the basilar membrane changes in width and rigidity throughout its length means that the amplitudes of pressure waves peak at specific **loci** or places on the membrane. Hence, the peak amplitudes of low-frequency sounds occur at the wider and more flaccid apex while the peak amplitudes of high-frequency sounds occur at the narrower and tauter base, which can, however, also respond to low-frequency stimulation. This was demonstrated in a series of experiments conducted by von Békésy in the 1930s and 1940s (see von Békésy 1960).

This finding gave rise to one version of the **place** or **spatial theory of perception**, in which the tonotopic organization of information on the basilar membrane is preserved in the auditory nerve. However, this theory does not adequately account for certain perceptual phenomena (Sachs and Young 1979). It does not, for example, account for the perception of very low-frequency sounds or the existence of extremely small **j.n.d.**'s (just noticeable differences) obtained in **pure-tone experiments**, i.e. experiments which test listeners' ability to detect differences in the frequency of sounds whose wave forms are smooth and simple, rather than complex. In addition, it seems unable to account for the fact that the fundamental frequency of a complex tone can be perceived even if it is not present in the stimulus (Schouten 1940). Moreover, it has been observed that, for frequencies of about 3–4 kHz or less, auditory-nerve fibres discharge at a rate proportional to the period of the stimulus. To explain such phenomena, researchers have proposed various versions of a **periodicity** or **temporal theory**. Such a theory is based upon the premise that temporal properties, such as the duration of a pitch period, are utilized to form the psychophysical percept of a stimulus. More recently, an **integrated theory**, **average localized synchronous response** (**ALSR**), has been proposed (Young and Sachs 1979; Shamma 1985). Such a theory maintains

that information about the spatial tonotopic organization of the basilar membrane is retained, but synchronous rate information is viewed as the carrier of spectral information.

In addition, careful and highly controlled neurophysical experiments have been conducted to measure single-fibre discharge patterns in the auditory nerve of the cat (Kiang *et al.* 1965). These studies have sometimes utilized speech-like stimuli and have demonstrated a relationship between the phonetic features of the stimuli and the fibre's **characteristic frequency**, i.e. that frequency requiring the least intensity in stimulation to increase the discharge rate of a neuron above its spontaneous rate of firing. For example, in response to two-formant vowel (see ACOUSTIC PHONETICS) stimuli, it has been found that activity is concentrated near the formant frequencies, suggesting that phonetic categories are based, at least in part, upon basic properties of the peripheral auditory system (e.g. Delgutte and Kiang 1984). This finding has received support from non-invasive behaviourally based animal studies (Kuhl and Miller 1975; Sinnott and Brown 1997).

From the auditory nerve, auditory information begins its ascent to the cortex of the brain by way of a series of highly complex interconnections and routes from one 'relay station' or area to another. These interconnections and routes may be understood in general outline in the description below of the **afferent** or ascending pathway. In the description, the **nuclei** referred to are groups of nerve cell bodies. In addition to the afferent pathway, there is also an **efferent** or descending pathway (which will not be described here), which appears to have an inhibitory or moderating function.

A highly simplified description of the conduction path from auditory nerve to cortex is as follows: the auditory nerve of each ear contains about 30,000 nerve fibres, which terminate in the **cochlear nucleus** of the lower brainstem. From the cochlear nucleus, some fibres ascend ipsilaterally (i.e. on the same side) to the **olivary complex**, then to the **inferior colliculus** of the midbrain via the **lateral lemniscus**. From here, fibres originate which proceed to the **medial geniculate body** of the **thalamus** and finally to the **ipsilateral auditory cortex** in the temporal lobe. Other fibres ascend contralaterally (i.e. on the opposite side) to the **accessory olive** and to the **superior olive**. They then follow a path similar (but not identical) to the one just described. In addition, other fibres originating at the cochlear nucleus proceed directly to the **contralateral dorsal nucleus**, while still others do so by way of the **ipsilateral accessory superior olive** (Harrison and Howe 1974; Yost and Nielsen 1977; Nauta and Fiertag 1979).

At the **synapses**, where information is transmitted from neuron to neuron along the route described, there is increasing complexity as well as transformation of the signal. The 30,000 fibres of the two auditory nerves feed into about a million subcortical neurons in the auditory cortex (Worden 1971; Warren 1982). In addition, at each synapse, the input is transformed (recoded) so that it can be understood at higher levels of the system (Webster 1995). It is thus not appropriate to consider the route an auditory input follows as a simple pathway, or the synaptic junctions as mere relay stations.

The **auditory cortex**, like the auditory nerve, is characterized by tonotopic organization. Moreover, certain of its neurons exhibit differential sensitivity to specific stimuli. For example, some are responsive only to an increase in frequency while others are responsive only to a decrease. These findings are analogous to those obtained in studies of the mammalian visual system (Hubel and Wiesel 1968) and they suggest that auditory-feature detectors subserve higher-order mechanisms of phonetic perception.

The auditory cortex alone cannot convert speech stimuli into meaningful units of language. Further processing must occur in an adjacent area in the temporal lobe known as **Wernicke's area**. This is graphically demonstrated by the fact that damage to this area usually results in deficits in speech perception. This language area is not present in both hemispheres and, for about 95 per cent of all right-handed adults, it and other language areas, e.g. **Broca's area**, are localized to the left hemisphere (see also APHASIA and LANGUAGE PATHOLOGY AND NEUROLINGUISTICS).

In the 1960s and 1970s, a non-invasive technique known as the **dichotic-listening test** was widely used to determine the relationship between the properties of speech sounds and the extent to which they are left- or right-lateralized in the brain. In this test, competing stimuli are presented simultaneously to both ears. For most right-handed subjects, right-ear accuracy is generally greater than left-ear accuracy for some speech stimuli, possibly because contralateral connections between the peripheral auditory and central nervous systems are stronger than the ipsilateral ones – at least when competing stimuli are presented – so that a right-ear advantage is interpreted as reflecting left-hemisphere dominance. In recent years, the reliability and validity of dichotic-listening test results have been questioned. Still, a pattern of left-hemisphere dominance for speech has been observed in sodium amytal (Wada) tests and measures of brain-wave activity, in split-brain and aphasic (see APHASIA) patients (Springer and Deutsch 1993), and in studies using brain-scanning techniques, such as positron emission tomography (PET) and functional magnetic resonance imaging (fMRI) (Fiez *et al.* 1996; Schlosser *et al.* 1998).

However, the finding of left-hemispheric dominance for speech has only emerged for certain types of speech stimuli. For example, while plosive consonants (see ARTICULATORY PHONETICS) yield a right-ear advantage in dichotic-listening tasks, vowels do not (Shankweiler and Studdert-Kennedy 1967). Moreover, suprasegmental information, such as fundamental frequency (FO), experienced subjectively as **pitch**, may or may not be mediated by the left hemisphere depending upon its linguistic status; that is, depending upon whether or not it carries linguistic information (Van Lancker and Fromkin 1973; Blumstein and Cooper 1974; Belin *et al.* 2000). This suggests that it is not necessarily the inherent properties of the stimuli which determine laterality effects, but the nature of the tasks to be performed as well as the status of the stimuli in the listener's perceptual system. And some researchers have asserted that the role of the left neocortex in speech processing has been overestimated and have found that the right hemisphere and subcortical structures also play an important role (Zatorre *et al.* 1992; Lieberman 2000).

Clearly, the relationship between the acoustic/phonetic properties of speech and its processing in the brain is complex. In attempting to understand this relationship, it is also important to make a distinction between the acoustic or auditory properties of speech, which are pre- or alinguistic, and the phonetic properties of speech, which are linguistic (Pisoni 1973). The difference is not always readily apparent, and the task is further complicated by the fact that what may be perceived as acoustic in one language may be perceived as phonetic in another. Various languages often utilize different perceptually salient cues, and these differences have measurable behavioural consequences (Caramazza *et al.* 1973; Cutler *et al.* 1986; Mack 1982, 1988, 1989).

Selected issues in auditory phonetics

One recurrent theme in auditory phonetics revolves around the question 'Is speech special?' In other words, is speech perception essentially akin to the perception of other acoustically complex stimuli, or is it somehow unique? Several sources of evid-

ence are often invoked in discussions of this issue. First, it is apparent that the frequencies used in producing speech are among those to which the human auditory system is most sensitive, and certain spectral and temporal features of speech stimuli correspond to those to which the mammalian auditory system is highly sensitive (Kiang 1980; Stevens 1981; Lieberman 1998). This suggests a close relationship between the sounds that humans are capable of producing and those that the auditory system most accurately perceives. Indeed, experiments with prelinguistic infants have revealed that linguistic experience is not a necessary condition for the perception of some speech properties such as those involved in place and manner of articulation (Eimas *et al.* 1971; Kuhl 1979; Werker 1995).

Other evidence is based upon what has been termed **categorical perception**. It has repeatedly been shown that a continuum of certain types of speech stimuli differing with respect to only one or two features is not perceived in a continuous manner. Categorical perception can be summarized in the simple sentence 'Subjects can discriminate no better than they can label.' That is, if subjects are presented with a continuum in which all stimuli differ in some specific and equivalent way, and if those subjects are required to label each stimulus heard, they will divide the continuum into only those two or three categories, such as /d–t/ or /b–d–g/, over which the continuum ranges. If these subjects are also presented with pairs of stimuli from the same continuum in a discrimination task, they do not report that members of *all* acoustically dissimilar pairs are different, even though they actually are. Rather, subjects report as different only those pair members which fall, in the continuum, in that region in which their responses switch from one category to another in the labelling task. It has been argued that non-speech stimuli, such as colours and tones, are not perceived categorically; hence the special status of categorical perception of speech. However, not all speech stimuli demonstrate equally strong categorical effects, with vowel perception being less categorical than stop-consonant perception (Fry *et al.* 1962; Schouten and van Hessen 1992).

Another source of evidence for the claim that speech is special may be found in **normalization**. The formant frequencies of speech give sounds their spectral identity and are a direct function of the size and shape of the vocal tract which produces them. Hence, the frequencies which specify an [e] (as in the vowel in *bake*) produced by a child are quite unlike those which specify an [e] produced by an adult male (Peterson and Barney 1952). None the less, both sounds are perceived as representations of the same sound unit. A process of normalization must take place if this perceptual equivalence is to occur. It has been hypothesized that a listener 'derives' the size of the vocal tract which could have produced the sound by means of a calibration procedure in which certain vowels such as /i/ or /u/ are used in the internal specification of the appropriate phonetic categories (Lieberman 1984). If this type of normalization occurs, it does so extremely rapidly and without conscious mediation by the listener.

The above-cited topics – the match of the perceptual system to the production system, infant speech perception, categorical perception and normalization – have often been interpreted as evidence that speech is special. But some linguists maintain that speech is *not* special, but rather that it is simply one highly elaborated system based upon a complex of productive and perceptual mechanisms which underlie other abilities, and even other sensory modalities, and which are thus not unique to speech.

Two other important issues involved in auditory perception are **segmentation** and **invariance**. Attempts to grapple with these issues have given rise to several major theories of relevance to auditory phonetics.

It is well known that speech is highly encoded; that is, phonetic units in a word are not simply strung together, intact and in sequence, like beads on a string. In fact, speech sounds are **smeared** or time-compressed as a result, in part, of co-articulation. The encoded nature of the speech signal makes it a highly efficient and rapid form of communication, yet it also results in the production of phonetic segments which differ, in context, slightly to substantially from the 'same' segments produced in isolation.

Closely related to the issue of segmentation is the notion of **invariance**. Various hypotheses have been proposed to account for the fact that, although given phonetic segments may be acoustically dissimilar, they are responded to perceptually as if they were identical, i.e. as if they were instantiations of the same phonetic unit. For example, the word-initial [d] in *deed* is acoustically distinct from [d] in *do*: in [di] the second-formant transition rises, while in [du] it falls. Further, in [di] the second-formant transition may start at a frequency nearly 1000 Hz higher than does the second-formant transition in [du]. Yet both syllable-initial consonants are considered to be the same unit, /d/ – in traditional terminology, the same **phoneme** (see PHONEMICS). The size and salience of the invariant unit has been a matter of considerable debate, as has its level of abstractness and generalizability (Liberman *et al.* 1952; Stevens and Blumstein 1978; Kewley-Port 1983; Mack and Blumstein 1983; Suomi 1993).

Attempts to relate an acoustic signal to a listener's internal and presumably abstract representation of speech have given rise to various theories of speech perception. One of these, the **motor theory**, was developed in the 1960s. This theory related a listener's knowledge of his/her production to perception, and it was hypothesized that a listener interprets the afferent auditory signal in terms of the efferent motor commands required for its production (Liberman et al. 1967). Essentially, the activity of the listener's own neuromuscular system was believed to serve as reference for perception. A related theory, **analysis-by-synthesis**, was somewhat more complex (Stevens 1960; Halle and Stevens 1962). Here, the auditory signal is analysed in terms of distinctive features, and rules for production are generated. Hypotheses about these rules are utilized to construct an internal 'synthesized' pattern of phonetic segments which is compared to the acoustic input and is then accepted or rejected. In the 1980s, some espoused the **event approach**, which was based upon a 'direct-realist perspective'. In this case the problems of segmentation and invariance were minimized, for it was not presumed that a 'distorted' acoustic stimulus was mapped on to an idealized abstract phonetic unit (Fowler 1986).

These and other related theories have been termed **strong gestural approaches**, in distinction to **strong auditory approaches**, in which the relevant properties of a speech signal are believed to be based upon their acoustic or auditory properties (Kingston and Diehl 1994). A gestural approach can account for the fact that an articulatory target may vary but still yield an invariant percept, as in the case of vowels (Ladefoged et al. 1972; Nearey 1980). More recently it has been claimed that a strong version of either approach is inappropriate, as revealed in the **double-weak theory** proposed by Nearey (1997). This is based upon pattern-recognition techniques and the direct mapping of speech cues on to phoneme-sized units. In short, the 1970s and 1980s witnessed a flourishing of perceptual models (see Klatt 1989 for a review): many drew heavily upon issues in artificial intelligence (Klatt 1980; Reddy 1980) and on **connectionist** and **stochastic** (probabilistic) models derived from work in computational linguistics, and many have continued to do so into the new millennium.

Recent research in auditory phonetics has dealt with talker-specific effects (Nygaard and Pisoni 1998), perception in naturalistic listening conditions (Kewley-Port and Zheng 1999), age-based differences in the response to acoustic cues and sound categories (Werker 1995; Jusczyk 1997; Mack et al. in progress), and the cross-language processing of phonetic units by bilinguals (Best and Strange 1992; Mack 1992; Flege et al. 1999). New conceptual approaches to speech processing have also emerged, such as the **speech learning model** (Flege 1992, 1995) and the **native language magnet model** (Kuhl 1992, 1994). These models, combined with further-refined theories and increasingly sophisticated analytic tools in neurobiology, are providing valuable information about how a 'simple' acoustic signal is transformed into a complex meaningful linguistic unit. In this way, light is being shed on issues still to be resolved in auditory phonetics.

M.M.

Suggestions for further reading

Johnson, K. (1997) *Acoustic and Auditory Phonetics*, Cambridge: Blackwell Publishers.

Lieberman, P. and Blumstein, S.E. (1988) *Speech Physiology, Speech Perception, and Acoustic Phonetics*, Cambridge: Cambridge University Press.

Moore, B.C.J. (1997) *An Introduction to the Psychology of Hearing*, 4th edition, London: Academic Press.

B

Behaviourist linguistics

The psychological theory known as **behaviourism** was founded by J.B. Watson (1924). Its main tenet is that everything which some refer to as mental activity (including language use) can be explained in terms of **habits**, or patterns of **stimulus** and **response**, built up through **conditioning**. As these patterns of behaviour – an organism's **output** – and the conditioning through which they become formed – the **input** to the organism – are observable phenomena, behaviourism accorded well with the strong current of empiricism that swept the scientific communities in the USA and Britain early in the twentieth century.

In linguistics, one of the finest examples of the empiricist/behaviourist tradition is Leonard Bloomfield's *Language* (1933/1935), although the most rigorous application of behaviourist theory to the study of language is probably *Verbal Behavior* (1957), by Burrhus Frederic Skinner, one of the most famous behaviourist psychologists of the twentieth century. This book was severely criticized by Chomsky (1959).

In *Language*, Bloomfield insists that a scientific theory of language must reject all data that are not directly observable or physically measurable. A scientific theory should be able to make predictions, but Bloomfield points out that (1935: 33):

We could foretell a person's actions (for instance, whether a certain stimulus will lead him to speak, and, if so, the exact words he will utter) only if we knew the exact structure of his body at that moment, or, what comes to the same thing, if we knew the exact make-up of his organism at some early stage – say at birth or before – and then had a record of every change in that organism, including every stimulus that had ever affected the organism.

Language, according to Bloomfield, is a type of substitute for action. In his famous story, with translations into behaviourese of the main events, of Jack and Jill (1935: 22–7), in which Jill, being hungry ('that is, some of her muscles were contracting, and some fluids were being secreted, especially in her stomach'), asks Jack to fetch her an apple which she sees ('the light waves reflected from the red apple struck her eyes') on a tree, Bloomfield explains that Jill's hunger is a primary stimulus, S, which, had Jill been speechless, would have led to a response, R, consisting of her fetching the apple herself, had she been capable of so doing. Having language, however, Jill is able to make 'a few small movements in her throat and mouth, which produced a little noise'. This noise, Jill's words to Jack, is a substitute response, r, which now acts as a substitute stimulus, s, for Jack, who carries out the response, R. So *'Language enables one person to make a reaction (R) when another person has the stimulus* (S)', and instead of the simple sequence of events

$$S \longrightarrow R$$

we have the more complex

$$S \longrightarrow r \ldots\ldots\ldots s \longrightarrow R$$

and Jill gets her apple. But, again, this course of events depends on the entire life history of Jack and Jill (1935: 23):

> If Jill were bashful or if she had had bad experiences of Jack, she might be hungry and see the apple and still say nothing; if Jack were ill disposed toward her, he might not fetch her the apple, even though she asked for it. The occurrence of speech (and, as we shall see, the wording of it) and the whole course of practical events before and after it, depend upon the entire life-history of the speaker and of the hearer.

The speech event has the meaning it has by virtue of its connection with the practical events with which it is connected. So (Bloomfield 1935: 139):

> In order to give a scientifically accurate definition of meaning for every form of a language, we should have to have a scientifically accurate knowledge of everything in the speaker's world. The actual extent of human knowledge is very small, compared to this. We can define the meaning of a speech-form accurately when this meaning has to do with some matter of which we possess scientific knowledge. We can define the meaning of minerals, for example, as when we know that the ordinary meaning of the English word *salt* is 'sodium chloride (NaCl)', and we can define the names of plants and animals by means of the technical terms of botany or zoology, but we have no precise way of defining words like love or hate, which concern

situations that have not been accurately classified – and these latter are in the great majority.

Bloomfield therefore advocated leaving semantics, the study of meaning, well alone 'until human knowledge advances very far beyond its present state' (1935: 140), advice which was heeded by both Zellig Harris and his pupil, Noam Chomsky – at least in the latter's early work; and Bloomfield and his followers concentrated instead on developing appropriate discovery procedures for the more easily observable aspects of language, such as its sounds and structures (see HISTORY OF GRAMMAR).

Skinner (1957), in contrast to Bloomfield, claims that it is possible to tackle linguistic meaning without recourse to the internal structure and life histories of speakers. His main aim is to provide what he calls a 'functional analysis' of verbal behaviour, by which he means an identification of the variables that control this behaviour, and a specification of how they interact to determine a particular verbal response. He describes these variables purely in terms of such notions as **stimulus**, **reinforcement**, **deprivation** and **response**, and he makes four basic claims:

1 Language behaviour can be accounted for in a way that is in principle no different from the behaviour of rats in laboratory conditions.
2 Language behaviour can be explained in terms of observable events, without reference to the internal structure of the organism.
3 This descriptive system is superior to others because its terms can be defined with reference to experimental operations.
4 So it is able to deal with semantics in a scientific way.

Skinner divides the responses of animals into two main categories:

● **Respondents**, which are purely reflex responses to particular stimuli; things like shutting your eyes if a bright light is shone at them, or kicking if your knee is hit in a particular spot by a small hammer. Clearly, these are not central to learning theory, and Skinner's research is concentrated on the second category.

- **Operants**, which is behaviour for which no particular obvious stimulation can initially be discovered, but which, it turns out, is susceptible to manipulation by the researcher.

A rat placed in a box will engage in **random operant behaviour**: it will run about in (what appears to the researcher to be) an unsystematic fashion, randomly pressing its nose against parts of the box. If the box contains a bar which, when pressed, releases a food pellet into a tray, then the chances are that the rat will sooner or later press this bar and obtain a food pellet during its random operant behaviour and, if the rat is hungry, suffers **deprivation**, then it is likely to try pressing the bar again to obtain more food.

In Skinner's terms, the rat's pressing the bar is now becoming a conditioned **operant**, no longer random; the event consisting of the release of the food pellet is a **reinforcing event**, the food pellet itself being the **reinforcer**. The reinforcing event will increase the **strength** of the bar-pressing operant; the strength of an operant is measured in terms of the rate of response during extinction: that is, the researcher will have observed and estimated the average number of times during a certain interval that the rat would randomly press the bar before it was adjusted to release food; s/he will then estimate the average number of times that the rat will press the bar once the rat has been conditioned to expect food when pressing; next, s/he will adjust the bar so that food is no longer released when the bar is pressed; the strength of the operant is defined in terms of how long it takes the rat to revert to its preconditioned rate of bar-pressing. The rate of the bar-pressing operant is affected by another variable,

drive, which is defined in terms of hours of deprivation – in the case of the rat and the food pellet, hours of food deprivation.

A box such as the one just described is often called a **Skinner box**. It can be constructed in such a way that a food pellet will only be released when a light is flashing; eventually, the rat will learn this, and only press the bar when the light is flashing. In this case, the flashing light is called the **occasion for the emission of the response**, the response is called a **discriminated operant**, and what the rat has learned is called **stimulus discrimination**. If the box is so constructed that the rat only gets a food pellet after pressing for a specific length of time, then the rat will learn to press the bar for the required length of time, and what has been learned in such a case is called **response differentiation**.

Skinner (1957) now goes about applying something very like this apparatus to human verbal behaviour, which he defines as *behaviour reinforced through the mediation of other persons*, listeners, whose responses mediate the responses of the speaker. The hearers' responses have been conditioned precisely in order to reinforce the behaviour of the speakers. Chomsky (1959) strongly objects to the implication here that parents teach their children to speak just so that the children can, in turn, reinforce the parents' speech.

Further, Skinner suggests that children learn by imitation, although, since there is no innate tendency to imitate (nothing being innate, according to Skinner's brand of behaviourism), parents will initially respond in a reinforcing manner to random sound production on the child's part. Some of the sounds the child makes during random behaviour (not unlike the rat's random pressing of parts of the box) happen to sound like the sounds the parents make, and only these will be reinforced by the parents. Chomsky objects that children do not imitate the deep voices of their fathers, so that Skinner is using 'imitation' in a selective way, and that, in any case, he does not pay sufficient attention to the part played by the child in the language acquisition process.

Skinner calls utterances **verbal operants**, and classifies them according to their relationship with discriminated stimulus, reinforcements and other verbal responses.

A **mand** (question, command, request, threat, etc.) is a verbal operant in which the response is reinforced by a characteristic consequence and is therefore under the functional control of relevant conditions of deprivation or aversive stimulation. Chomsky suggests that this definition cannot account for cases more complex than those as simple as *Pass the salt*, when it might be appropriate to say that the speaker suffers salt deprivation. As soon as we come to utterances like *Give me the book*, *Take me for a ride*, *Let me fix it*, etc., it becomes highly questionable whether we can decide which kind of deprivation is at issue and what the required number of hours of deprivation might be.

Further, Chomsky points to the absurdity of the theory in its attempt to deal with threats in terms of the notion of aversive control. According to Skinner, if a person has a history of appropriate reinforcement, which means that if, in the past, a certain response was followed by the withdrawal of a threat of injury, or certain events have been followed by injury, then such events are **conditioned aversive stimuli**. A person would therefore have to have had a previous history of being killed before being likely to respond appropriately to a threat like *Your money or your life*. No one has a past history of being killed. But an utterance will only be made if there is another person who mediates it, so no one should ever be inclined to utter threats like *Your money or your life*. Yet people do. And, in general, speakers are not fortunate enough always to have their mands appropriately reinforced – that is, we do not invariably get what we want.

Skinner is aware of this problem, and sets up a second category of mand, the **magical mand**, which is meant to cover cases in which speakers simply describe whatever reinforcement would be appropriate to whatever state of deprivation or aversive stimulation in which they may find themselves. See below for Chomsky's comment on this type of mand.

Skinner's second main category of verbal operant is the **tact**, defined as a verbal operant in which a response of a given kind is evoked or strengthened by a particular object or event or property thereof. Some tacts are under the control of private stimuli. For instance, *There was an elephant at the zoo* is a response to current stimuli that include events within the speaker, and this is clearly a problem for a theory that claims to avoid a Bloomfieldian position that takes account of speaker-internal events.

Responses to prior verbal stimuli are of two kinds: **echoic operants**, which cover cases of immediate imitation; and **intraverbal operants**, histories of pairings of verbal responses, which are meant to cover responses like *Four* to the stimulus *Two plus two*, and *Paris* to *The capital of France*, and also most of the facts of history and science, all translation and paraphrase, plus reports of things seen, heard and remembered.

Finally, Skinner deals with syntax in terms of responses called **autoclitics**. A sentence is a set of key responses to objects (nouns), actions (verbs) and properties (adjectives and adverbs) on a skeletal frame. Chomsky's objection to this is that more is involved in making sentences than fitting words into frames. For example, *Struggling artists can be a nuisance* and *Marking papers can be a nuisance* fit the same frame, but have radically different sentence structures. Skinner's theory cannot account for such differences.

Chomsky's (1959) overall criticism of Skinner's application of his learning theory to human verbal behaviour is that, while the notions described above are very well defined for experiments in the laboratory, it is difficult to apply them to real-life human behaviour.

First, the researcher in the laboratory can predict what a rat's response to a particular stimulation will be; that is, the stimulation is known by the researcher *before* the response is emitted. But, in the case of a verbal response, a tact, such as *Dutch* to a painting, which Skinner claims to be under the control of subtle properties of the painting, such response prediction seems to be illusory. For, says Chomsky, suppose that someone says *Clashes with the wallpaper*, or *I thought you liked abstract art*, or *Never saw it before*, or *Hanging too low*, or whatever else – then Skinner would have to explain that, in each case, the response was under the control of some different property of the painting, but the property could only be determined *after* the response was known. So the theory is no longer predictive.

Second, while the terms used for the rat experiments may have clear definitions, it is unclear that these hold when transferred to the verbal behaviour of humans. Skinner claims that proper nouns are controlled by a specific person or thing – this would mean that the likelihood that a speaker would utter the full name of some other person would be increased when s/he was faced with that person, and this is not necessarily the case. And it is certainly not the case that one goes around uttering one's own name all the time, yet this, again, would seem to be predicted by the theory. In fact, it looks as if, in this case, Skinner is merely using the term 'control' as a substitute for the traditional semantic terms

'refers to' or 'denotes'. So Skinner's claim to have surpassed traditional semantic theories does not seem to hold water.

Similarly, it seems that, in the case of Skinner's category of magical mands, where (according to Skinner) speakers describe the reinforcement appropriate to their state of deprivation, speakers are, in fact, simply asking for what they want. But, as Chomsky points out, no new objectivity is added to the description of verbal behaviour by replacing *X wants Y* with *X is deprived of Y*. All in all, Chomsky shows that the terms from experimental psychology do not retain their strict definitions in *Verbal Behavior*, but take on the full vagueness of ordinary language, and Skinner cannot be said to have justified his claims for the strictly behaviourist account of human language use.

K.M.

Suggestions for further reading

Bloomfield, L. (1933/1935) *Language*, New York: Holt, Rinehart and Winston; revised edition 1935, London: George Allen and Unwin.

Chomsky, N. (1959) 'A review of B.F. Skinner's *Verbal Behavior*', *Language* 35(1): 26–58; reprinted in J. Fodor and J.J. Katz (eds) (1964) *The Structure of Language: Readings in the Philosophy of Language*, Englewood Cliffs, NJ: Prentice Hall, and L.A. Jakobovits and M.S. Miron (1967) *Readings in the Philosophy of Language*, Englewood Cliffs, NJ: Prentice Hall.

Lyons, J. (1981) *Language and Linguistics: An Introduction*, Cambridge: Cambridge University Press: sections 7.4, 8.2.

Bilingualism and multilingualism

Introduction

Bilingualism and **multilingualism** are frequent phenomena in almost every country of the world. Current estimates are that between 50 per cent and 70 per cent of the world's population are bilingual or multilingual – depending partly on how a 'bilingual' is defined (see below) and the complex relationship between languages and dialects.

A person's ability in two languages was once predominant in characterizations of bilinguals. For example, Bloomfield (1933: 55) specified bilingualism as the 'native-like control of two languages'. Very few bilinguals are equally proficient in both languages and tend to use their languages for different purposes in different contexts and with different people. **Balanced bilingualism** is rare in individuals and is more of an idealized concept.

Recent characterizations of bilinguals have moved from ability to use of languages – for example, portraying the different purposes of dual language use, codeswitching behaviours, parental strategies in raising bilingual children, and the economic/social/cultural/religious/educational and political use of bilingualism. This discussion is continued later, since bilingual usage can be individual but also at the societal level. Such an individual/societal distinction has led to different linguistic, psychological, neurological, sociolinguistic, cultural and political research and theory. We begin with individual bilingualism – the realm of linguists, and psychologists in particular.

Individual bilingualism

Inexactness in defining individual bilingualism is apparent in providing simple answers to the following questions: (1) at what point does a second language learner become a bilingual? (2) If someone has ability in a language but does not use it, is s/he a bilingual? (3) How do the four language skills (understanding, speaking, reading and writing) relate to classification of who is a bilingual or not? (4) Do multilinguals have the same or different proficiency and usage profiles as bilinguals? (5) Since ability in, and use of, two languages varies over time, how stable are bilinguals in their language repertoire? Each question shows that there are no simple classifications; just multitudinous shades of colour among bilinguals (for a full discussion of these issues, see Baker and Jones 1998).

However, the following central issues help clarify the concept of individual bilingualism.

- The difference between ability in language and use of language is usually referred to as the difference between **degree** (proficiency or competence in a language) and **function** (use of two languages). An individual's proficiency in each language will typically vary across the four language competences of speaking, listening, reading and writing. A person who understands a second language well, in its spoken and/or written form, but does not speak or write it well is termed a **passive bilingual**, or is said to have **receptive competence** in a second language. In contrast, a person who speaks and/or writes in both languages is termed an **active bilingual**.
- Few bilinguals are equally competent in both languages, with one language often the **dominant language**. However, the dominant language can change across time, context and function. It is not always the first or native language of the bilingual (e.g. immigrants who need to operate almost solely in the host country's dominant language). Thus degree and function are not separate.
- Bilinguals do not usually possess the same proficiency as monolingual speakers in either of their languages. Levels of

proficiency in a language relate, in part, to which **domains** that language is used in (e.g. family, work, school, religion, mass media usage) and how often the language is used. **Communicative competence** in one of a bilingual's two languages is usually stronger in some domains than in others. This partly explains why many bilinguals are not expert at interpretation and translation, as most do not have identical lexical knowledge in both languages.

- A distinction between a **second language learner** and a bilingual is arbitrary and artificial. There are multiple series of dimensions, such that classification is dependent on self- and other attribution as much as ability in languages; that is, labels can be dependent on perception as much as proficiency. Any language learner is an incipient bilingual. Any bilingual is/was a language learner.

- A much-contested type of bilingual is a 'semilingual' or '**double semilingual**', regarded as having 'insufficient' proficiency in either language. Such a person is considered to possess a small vocabulary and incorrect grammar, consciously thinks about language production, is stilted and uncreative with both languages, and finds it difficult to think and express emotions in either language – particularly when monolinguals are seen as the benchmark.

The concept of double semilingualism among bilinguals has received much criticism (e.g. Skutnabb-Kangas 1981). This label fails to take account of the situational nature in the use of two (or more) languages. For example, one language may be fluently used in the extended family and networks of friends, but does not have the register needed for school work or a profession. A second language may thus be proficiently used at school or in the workplace, but rarely at home. When a person has a low level of proficiency in both languages (a rare occurrence), this is usually a result of social and economic circumstances and does not relate to any limits of a bilingual's linguistic or cognitive potential. Thus the danger of the term 'semilingualism' is that it locates the origins of underdevelopment in the individual rather than in external, societal factors that co-exist with bilingualism.

This portrayal of bilinguals as double semilinguals symbolizes that, until recently, bilinguals have often been wrongly portrayed negatively (e.g. as having a split identity, or cognitive deficits). Part of this is political (e.g. prejudice against immigrants; majority language groups asserting their greater power, status and economic ascendancy; those in power wanting social and political cohesion around monolingualism and monoculturalism).

However, the portrayal of bilinguals varies internationally. In some countries (e.g. India, parts of Africa and Asia), it is normal and expected to be **multilingual** (e.g. in a national language, an international language and one or more local languages). In other countries, bilinguals are typically **immigrants** and seen as causing economic, social and cultural challenges to the dominant majority. Where **indigenous language minorities** exist (e.g. the Basques in Spain, the Maori in New Zealand, the Welsh speakers in Wales), more recognition has sometimes been accorded to such groups following the movement away from nationalism in favour of the 'ethnic revival' (Fishman 1999). With both immigrant and indigenous minorities, the term 'minority' is decreasingly defined in terms of smaller numbers in the population and increasingly as a language of low prestige and low in power relative to the majority language. This indicates that bilinguals are most frequently found in lower status groups, although there are also increasing numbers of 'elite' bilinguals – those who use two or more majority languages (e.g. German and English) as internationalism increases.

Grosjean (1985) suggests two contrasting views of bilinguals: one about separation, the other about 'wholeness'. The **fractional view** of bilinguals sees the individual as two monolinguals in one person. For example, if English is the second language, scores on English tests will often be compared against native monolingual anglophone norms.

One consequence of the fractional view is to limit the definition of bilingualism to those who are approximately equally fluent in both languages, with proficiency comparable to a monolingual. If that competence does not exist in both languages, especially in the majority language, then bilinguals may be denigrated and classed as inferior. In the United States, for example, children of language minority families are often classified as LEP (Limited English Proficient). The monolingual is seen as normal, and the bilingual as an exception or oddity. This monolingual view often wrongly predicts negative consequences in cognitive processing, because of the perceived potential confusion between two underdeveloped languages (C. Baker 1996). This reflects a current reality in that many bilinguals feel themselves insufficiently competent in one or both of their languages compared with monolinguals, accepting and reinforcing the monolingual view of bilinguals. A bilingual may apologize to monolinguals for not speaking their language as well as they do.

Yet the bilingual is a **complete linguistic entity**, an integrated whole. Thus Grosjean (1994) presents an alternative and positive '**holistic view**'. In athletics, could we fairly judge a sprinter or high-jumper against a hurdler? The sprinter and high-jumper concentrate on excellence in one event. The hurdler develops two different skills, trying to combine a high standard in both. The hurdler will be unable to sprint as fast as the sprinter or jump as high as the high-jumper. This is not to say that the hurdler is an inferior athlete to the other two; any such comparison makes little sense.

Comparing the language proficiency of a monolingual with a bilingual's dual or multiple language proficiency is similarly seen as unjust (Grosjean 1994).

Yet the political reality is that bilinguals are measured and compared by reference to monolinguals in many countries. When someone learns English as a second language, should that competence in English be measured against monolinguals rather than other bilinguals? In countries like the United States, where first-language Spanish-speaking children have to compete against monolingual English speakers in an English-language job market, a politically dominant view is that they should face the same English assessments in school. In Australia, most of Canada, the United States and the UK, dominant English-speaking politicians and administrators will usually not accept a different approach or standard of assessment (one for monolinguals, another for bilinguals).

The fractional and holistic viewpoints parallel an ongoing and unresolved debate about the representation and storage of language in the bilingual brain. One dated conception is that there were **coordinate bilinguals** (who had two separate systems for their two languages), **compound bilinguals** (who had one integrated system for their two languages) and **subordinate bilinguals**. Language learners were often conceived as subordinate bilinguals who filter their second language through the first language (e.g. interpret words in the second language through the first language). There is little evidence to support this triple classification and the distinctions are generally regarded as too simplistic. Similarly, there is little confirmation as to whether bilinguals **store** their languages separately, interdependently or have three stores (first language, second language, concepts) (Grosjean 1994).

Some children acquire two first languages from birth. This is often called **simultaneous bilingualism** or 'bilingualism as a first language', as different from **consecutive, sequential** or **successive bilingualism**, which results from the initial acquisition of a mother tongue plus informal or formal second language learning in later years. This distinction hides some conceptual simplicity in certain much-used terms. For example, the term '**first language**' is used in different, overlapping ways, and can mean: the first language learned; the stronger language; the 'mother tongue', the language most used. **Mother tongue** is also used ambiguously. It variously means: the language learned from the mother; the first language learned, irrespective of 'from whom'; the stronger language at any time of life; the 'mother tongue' of the area or country (e.g. Irish in Ireland); the language most used by a person; the language to which a person has the more positive attitude and affection.

Multilingualism

The word 'bilingual' also serves as an umbrella term for the many people who have varying degrees of proficiency in three or more languages. In many parts of the Indian, African and Asian continents, several languages co-exist, and large sections of the population speak two or more languages. In such countries, individual multilingualism is often the result of a process of industrial development, political unification, modernization, urbanization and greater contact between different local communities. Many individuals speak one or more local languages, as well as another indigenous language, which has become the medium of communication between different ethnic groups or speech communities. Such individuals may also speak a colonial or international language such as English, French or Spanish. This latter language is often the vehicle of education, bureaucracy and privilege.

In many Western countries, individual monolingualism rather than multilingualism has been the desired norm (e.g. France, England, United States, the old USSR). This has often been the result of a drive towards political and national unification, which required the establishment of an official language or languages to be used in education, work and public life. However, in Western countries where there are indigenous minorities (e.g. the Catalans and Basques in Spain) or many immigrants (e.g. Canada), bilingualism and multilingualism are often present. In the Asian communities of Britain and Canada, some individuals are trilingual: in their 'heritage language', in another Asian language often associated with literacy (such as Urdu or Hindi), and in English. In addition, a Moslem child will learn Arabic, the language of the Koran and the Mosque.

Multilingualism also occurs among individuals who do not live in a multilingual community. Families can be trilingual when the husband and wife each speak different languages to their children, which are themselves different from the majority language of the country of residence. A person can also learn multiple languages at school or university, at work, or in leisure hours. The motives for such language learning include personal enrichment, travel, educational betterment and employment advantages. Such '**elite multilingualism**' is usually voluntary and planned, frequently bringing economic, educational and social advantages. Both **integrative** and **instrumental** motivations may be at work. It is more widespread in countries where the native tongue is not an international, high-prestige language; in such countries, the inhabitants may be particularly conscious of the economic, employment and travel value of multilingualism.

Many mainland European children learn two languages in school, such as English, German or French, as well as being fluent in their home language, for example, Finnish, Swedish, Danish, Luxembourgish or Dutch. In parts of Scandinavia, many people seem particularly successful in trilingualism. The economic, employment and travel value of speaking several languages is a major explanation of this Scandinavian multilingual accomplishment, aided by school systems that place a relatively high premium on classroom language learning.

Individual multilingualism is thus possible, non-problematic and potentially valuable (V.J. Cook 1992). Human beings have the brain capacity to learn and retain several languages. However, different languages serve **different purposes** for most multilingual people. The individual typically does not possess the same level or type of proficiency in each language. In Morocco, a native Berber speaker may also be fluent in colloquial Moroccan Arabic but not be literate in either Berber or Moroccan Arabic. This Berber speaker will be educated in modern standard Arabic and use it for writing and formal purposes. Classical Arabic is the language of the mosque, used for prayers and to read the Koran. Many Moroccans also have some knowledge of French, the former colonial language.

Languages within a multilingual individual tend to **develop** or **decay** over time. One or two of them may become stronger, another may weaken. This is even truer of multilinguals than of bilinguals (Edwards 1994). As opportunities for practice vary and motivations change, so may language dominance. Few individuals live in a situation that allows regular use of their three or more languages over a lifetime. The co-existence of multiple languages will shift within an individual or family, according to religious, cultural, social, economic, political and community pressures. A person's languages are surrounded by 'market forces', external manipulation and internal motivations, honest advice and active hostility.

Codeswitching

Codeswitching is a change of language within a conversation, most often when bilinguals are with other bilinguals. Bilinguals often operate along a dimension from monolingual speech acts to frequent codeswitching with similar bilinguals, with many possibilities between these two. Codeswitching can also be used to mark relationships, signalling status and situation, deference and intimacy. These behaviours will now be considered in more detail.

When conversing, bilinguals consciously, or more frequently subconsciously, select the conversational language. This selected language is called the **base**, **recipient** or **matrix language**. Codeswitching occurs when items from another language are introduced into the base language. The 'other' language is called the **donor** or **embedded language**. Codeswitching can occur in large blocks of speech, between or within 'sentences', even involving single words or phrases. It may occur between a base language and more than one donor language in multilinguals (Myers-Scotton 1992, 1998).

Monolinguals who hear bilinguals codeswitch may view it negatively, believing it shows a deficit in mastery of both languages. Bilinguals themselves may be defensive or apologetic, and attribute codeswitching to careless language habits. However, it is a valuable, rational and rule-bound linguistic strategy. There is usually purpose and logic in changing languages.

Various terms have been used to describe switches between languages in bilingual conversation. **Codemixing** is sometimes used to describe changes at the word level, when one or two words change in a sentence. A mixed-language sentence, such as *Leo un magazine* ('I read a magazine'), is an example. In contrast, '*Come to the table, bwyd yn barod*' ('food is ready'), might be called codeswitching; the first phrase is in English, the second in Welsh. However, 'codeswitching' is now generally used for any switch within the course of a single conversation, whether at the level of word, sentence or blocks of speech.

Language borrowing indicates foreign loan words or phrases that have become an integral and permanent part of the recipient language. *Le weekend* in French, and *der Computer* in German are examples. All languages borrow words or phrases from others with which they come in contact. Codeswitching may often be the first step in this process. As these elements are widely used, they become accepted and perceived as part of the recipient language. Some linguists have tried to distinguish between 'nonce borrowings' (one-time borrowings, as in codeswitching) and established borrowings. Myers-Scotton (1992) argues against distinctions between codeswitches and loans, as they form a continuum rather than two distinct and separate entities.

Grosjean (1992) distinguishes between the 'monolingual mode', when bilinguals use one language with monolingual speakers of that language, and the 'bilingual mode', when bilinguals are together and have the option of codeswitching. In the 'monolingual mode' bilinguals may occasionally mix languages. Often the dominant language influences the less dominant. Such influence was called **interference**, although the term **transfer** is sometimes preferred.

Grosjean (1992) distinguishes between **static** and **dynamic interference**. Static interference describes the relatively permanent influence of one of the bilingual's languages on the other. Accent, intonation and the pronunciation of individual sounds are common areas where static interference may be present. A native German speaker speaking English with German intonation may pronounce various sounds in a 'German' way, such as hardening soft consonants at the end of words (*haf* for *have*, *goot* instead of *good*). Dynamic interference recognizes that features from one language are transferred temporarily into the other. This can occur in syntax, phonology or vocabulary, and in both written and spoken language. For example, an English speaker with some competence in French may show dynamic interference by using the word *librairie* to mean 'library', whereas it actually means 'bookshop'.

Many bilinguals find the term 'interference' negative and pejorative, revealing a monolingual, 'fractional' perspective. Switching between languages may serve to convey thoughts and ideas in the most personally efficient manner. A person may realize that the listener understands such switching. According to Grosjean (1992), when bilinguals interact among themselves they are in the **bilingual language mode**, where both languages are activated and the resources of both are available.

In many bilingual situations throughout the world, codeswitching between two languages has become the norm. Among Wolof–French bilinguals in Dakar, the capital of Senegal, there is continuous, acceptable mixing of the two languages (Swigart 1992). A similar pattern is found in India, where there is a relatively stable use of codeswitching between Hindi and English. Swigart (1992) argues that in such cases codeswitching is unmarked and lacks the stylistic or sociological significance of marked codeswitching. Rather, it is a general marker of belonging to a mixed group with a multiple identity. From a linguistic and grammatical point of view, such stable codeswitching should not be analysed in terms of donor or recipient language, but in its own terms as a third code or language.

'Hinglish' (Hindi–English), 'Spanglish' (Spanish–English), 'Tex-Mex' (Texan–Mexican) and 'Wenglish' (Welsh–English) are often used derogatorily to describe standardized and accepted language borrowing within a particular community. Some Puerto Rican communities in New York use a relatively stable 'Spanglish'. However, in other bilingual communities, strict separation of languages can be the acceptable norm, for political, cultural or social reasons. In cases of power conflict between ethnic groups, language may be a prime marker of separate **identity**. Code-switching is then unacceptable.

Treffers-Daller (1992) illustrates how French–Flemish codeswitching in Brussels, the Belgian capital, was acceptable to the older bilingual generation, who identified with both the French and Flemish groups. It has become less acceptable, however, among younger Belgians, because of the gradual polarization of the Walloon and Flemish ethnic groups. Similarly, French–English codeswitching is unacceptable among some Canadian francophone groups, because of their power and ethnic-identity struggle with anglophones.

Tanzania illustrates the reverse situation. English, the colonial language, was marginalized for many years after independence in 1964, while Swahili was promoted as the national language. Although older Tanzanians still associate English with colonization and do not favour code-switching, it has become more widespread among young Tanzanians, as English has become the fashionable medium of Anglo-American culture.

The uses of codeswitching

Social and psychological factors, rather than linguistic ones, trigger codeswitching. Codeswitches have a variety of **purposes and aims** and change according to who is talking, the topic, and the context of the conversation (Baker and Jones 1998; Myers-Scotton 1993).

- Codeswitches may be used to *emphasize* a particular word or phrase or its central function in a sentence.
- When a speaker does not know a word or phrase in one language, another language may be *substituted*. This often happens because bilinguals use different languages in different domains of their lives. An adult may codeswitch to discuss work, because the technical terms associated with work are only known in that language.

- Bilinguals may switch languages to express a concept *without an equivalent* in the culture of the other language. A French–English bilingual living in Britain may use words like *pub* and *bingo hall* in French, because these words have no French equivalent. As previously stated such words and phrases are called 'loans' or 'borrowings' when they become established and in frequent use in the other language. However, there is no clear distinction between a codeswitch and a borrowing.
- Codeswitching may *reinforce* a request. For example, a teacher repeats a command to emphasize it: '*Taisez-vous, les enfants!* Be quiet, children!' In a majority/minority language situation, the majority language may emphasize authority. A Spanish-speaking mother in San Francisco may use English with her children for short commands like 'Stop it! Don't do that!', and then return to Spanish.
- Repetition of a phrase or passage in another language may also *clarify* a point. Some teachers explain a concept in one language then explain it again in another, believing that repetition adds reinforcement of learning and aids understanding.
- Codeswitching may *communicate friendship* or family bonding. Moving from the common majority language to a home or minority language both the speaker and listener understand well may communicate common identity and friendship. Also, the use of the listener's stronger language may indicate deference.
- In relating an earlier conversation, the speaker may report it in the language(s) used. Two people may be speaking Punjabi. When one reports a previous conversation with an English speaker, the conversation is *reported authentically* in English, as it occurred.
- Codeswitching is a way of *interjecting* into a conversation. A person attempting to break into a conversation may introduce

a different language. Changing languages may signal interruption, with the message 'I would like to join this conversation.'

- Codeswitching may ease tension and inject humour into a conversation. If committee discussions become tense, the use of a second language can signal a change in the 'tune being played'. Just as in an orchestra, where different instruments in a composition may signal a *change of mood* and pace, a language switch may indicate a change of mood within the conversation.
- Codeswitching often reflects a *change of attitude* or *relationship*. When two people meet, they may use the common majority language. As the conversation proceeds, and roles, status and ethnic identity are revealed, a change to a regional language may indicate the crossing of boundaries. A codeswitch signals lessening of social distance, with growing solidarity and rapport.
- Conversely, a change from minority language or dialect to majority language may indicate the speaker's wish to elevate status, *create a distance* from the listener, or establish a more formal, business relationship.
- Codeswitching can also *exclude people* from a conversation. When travelling on the subway (metro, underground), two people may switch from English to their minority language to talk about private matters.
- In some situations, codeswitching occurs regularly when certain *topics* are introduced. For example, Spanish–English bilinguals in the southwestern United States regularly switch to English to discuss money; this reflects the fact that English is the language of commerce and often the dominant language of the mathematics curriculum.

Familiarity, projected status, the ethos of the context and the perceived linguistic skills of the listeners affect the nature and process of codeswitching. Codeswitching is not 'just' linguistic; it indicates *important social and power relationships*.

Bilingual children and families

The future of the world's approximately 6000 languages, which are declining rapidly in number are tied closely to family influence. Unless families reproduce minority languages at home, then bilingual (diglossic) communities are in danger of fast diminution. Language transmission in the family is an essential but insufficient condition for language preservation.

The term **bilingual family** encompasses an almost infinite variety of situations and is difficult to define simply. Each bilingual family has its own patterns of intrafamilial language and in relation to the local community. A profile of such families involves: the language(s) spoken between parents, by the parent(s) to the children, by the children to the parent(s), between the children, the language(s) spoken or understood by the nearby extended family and the local community or network of friends, the language of education and religious observance, the official or majority language(s) of the state or country, and the family's geographical stability or mobility. These factors influence the nature and level of bilingualism within an individual family. They also indicate the difficulty of neatly categorizing bilingual families, illustrated below:

- Bilingualism is not always home-grown. A bilingual or multilingual family may speak more than one language, but use only one language (often a minority language) at home, while acquiring the dominant language of the community outside the home.
- Not every individual in a bilingual family is bilingual. One parent may be bilingual and decide to speak a native language to the children, while the other parent may only speak the dominant

language of the local community, as in a UK family with a Bengali-speaking mother and monolingual English-speaking father.

- Monolingual parents may have bilingual children, while bilingual parents may raise monolinguals. Many first-generation immigrants develop a limited command of the majority language of the host country; their children learn the majority language at school and on the streets. Alternatively, parents who speak one language of a country may have their children educated in a second majority language, or a heritage minority language. For example, in Canada, many anglophone parents choose French-immersion education so their children may benefit from bilingualism in both Canadian majority languages.

- Minority-language parents may have negative attitudes toward their language and raise their children in the majority language. Many immigrant families progress from monolingualism in the minority language to bilingualism in both majority and minority languages, then monolingualism in the majority language within a few generations. Sometimes termed **three-generational shift**, this happened with many immigrants to the United States in the nineteenth and early twentieth centuries and continues to occur in many parts of the world today.

- There may be different degrees of bilingualism within families. Within bilingual families, language dominance and competence may vary among members and over time. Where parents speak a minority language to their children, and where the school and community share the dominant, majority language, the children may have only passive competence in the minority language. In immigrant communities, parents may have only limited command of the majority language, while

children eventually become dominant in it. Moving to another area or country or switching to a minority (or majority) language school for the children may mean a change in the family language balance.

Types of family bilingualism

Harding and Riley (1986) and Romaine (1995) outline a variety of types of family bilingualism based on parental language strategies in raising children bilingually. One of the most covered in the literature is the **'one person, one language' family**. The parents have different native languages, one the dominant community language. The parents each speak their own language to the child from birth. Literature on child bilingualism praises this strategy as an effective path to bilingualism, believing that the child keeps the two languages separate, with relatively little codeswitching. DeHouwer (1995) has loosened this orthodoxy, arguing that complete separation is an ideal rather than a reality, and that case histories show that when one parent uses both languages the child still communicates effectively in both. Discrete episodes in one language before using the other, and correction when there is unacceptable language mixing, allow separation of a child's language.

Other types of bilingual family vary around the following dimensions: whether the parents speak the same or different languages to the child; whether those languages are majority or minority languages; whether one is the dominant community language, or whether the child learns the dominant language outside the home, particularly through education. Most 'types' assume a stable bilingual environment and a commitment to bilingualism. However, in many families, bilingualism is in a state of development or decline, often reflecting the state of bilingualism in the wider speech community.

Simultaneous bilingualism

Until recently, a three-stage model of early childhood bilingual development was accepted as accurate. This model, originating from Volterra and Taeschner (1978) portrays the young bilingual mixing two languages, then moving to partial, and finally full, separation. A thorough review by DeHouwer (1995) finds little basis for the three-stage model, as children as young as 2 years old separate their languages rather than mixing them. Similarly, Paradis and Genesee (1996) have shown that the French and English grammars of 2- and 3-year-olds in Canada are acquired separately and autonomously. While Quay's study (1994) was based on only one case, that child had equivalent terms for objects, events and processes in both Spanish and English from the beginning of speech; that is, from about the age of 1.

Young children learning two languages simultaneously follow much the *same pattern* as monolinguals. First, they assemble a vocabulary of elements from both, but usually with only one label for each concept, taken from one language; later, they separate vocabularies, using equivalent terms in each language, but combining grammatical rules of both.

The pace of language development does not differ significantly in average bilingual and monolingual children. They utter their first words around the same age (approximately at 1 year). During a bilingual child's early years, progress may be slower, with two vocabularies and language systems to acquire instead of one. However, by the age of 4 or 5, many bilinguals catch up with their counterparts in one of their languages.

The **societal context** where children are raised is likely to have an effect on language life within the person. In a **submersion** or **transitional bilingual situation**, the introduction of a second language detracts from the child's developing skills in the first language. The second language is acquired at the expense of the first language, the first language skills fail to develop properly, yet the child struggles to acquire the second language skills needed to cope in the classroom.

Some children survive and succeed in this subtractive environment. For many others, this situation initiates a pattern of failure throughout their school career. Current research (see Cummins 2000) suggests that minority-language children succeed better when they are taught initially through their home language. Here the child's skills are valued and built upon. Later, when the majority language is gradually introduced, the academic skills and knowledge acquired through the first language transfer easily to the second.

For majority-language children, the situation is different. Some parents, wishing their children to become bilingual, send them to **dual-language schools**, where two languages are used to teach content (e.g. mathematics, social studies), or to a **heritage language school**, where teaching is mostly through the medium of a minority language. Majority-language children usually cope well in the curriculum in a second language. Their home language and culture have status and prestige and will not be supplanted.

Bilingual education

Bilingual education would seem to describe a situation where two languages are used in a school. However, 'bilingual education' is a simple label for a diverse phenomenon. One important distinction is between a school where there are bilingual children and a school that promotes bilingualism. In many schools throughout the world, there are bilingual and multilingual children. Yet the aim of the school may be to ensure that children develop in one language only.

For example, a child may come to school speaking a minority language fluently but not the majority language. The school may aim to make that child fluent and literate in the majority language only, with integration and assimilation of that child into mainstream society in mind.

Such 'weak' forms of bilingual education aim for a transition from the home culture and language to the majority culture and language. 'Weak' bilingual education occurs when children are only allowed to use their home language in the curriculum for a short period, with a transition to education solely through majority language. 'Strong' bilingual education occurs when both languages are used in school to promote bilingualism and biliteracy. For example, in **heritage language schools**, children may receive much of their instruction in the home language, with the majority language being used to transmit 20 per cent to 90 per cent of the curriculum. Alternatively, a child from a majority-language background may go to an **immersion school** (e.g. Canada, Finland), dual-language school (USA) or a mainstream bilingual school and learn through a second majority (or minority) language.

'Bilingual education' is a term that includes not only 'weak' and 'strong' forms but also trilingual and multilingual schools, where three or more languages are used (e.g. in the European Schools Movement, or Luxembourgish–German–French education in Luxembourg, or Hebrew–English–French in Canada, or Basque–Spanish–English in the Basque Country).

Societal bilingualism

Bilinguals typically live in **networks**, **communities** and **societies**, which take on particular social characteristics. The distinction between **additive** and **subtractive** **bilingualism** indicates that bilingual communities differ. When the addition of a second language and culture is unlikely to replace or displace the first language and culture, the bilingual situation is additive. English-speaking North Americans who learn French or Spanish will not lose English, but gain a second language and parts of its culture. The 'value-added' benefits are social and economic, as well as linguistic and cultural. Positive attitudes about bilingualism may also result.

In contrast, the learning of a majority second language may undermine a minority first language and culture, thus creating a **subtractive** situation (e.g. many Asians in the UK and Latinos in the United States). Immigrants may experience pressure to use the dominant language and feel embarrassed to use the home language. When the second language is prestigious and powerful, used exclusively in education and employment, while the minority language is perceived as low in status and value, there is subtraction, with the potential loss of the second language.

With little or no pressure to replace or reduce a first language, the acquisition of a second language and culture occurs as an **additive** form of bilingualism, with a positive self-concept as a component. When the second language and culture are acquired with pressure to replace or demote the first, as with immigrants, a **subtractive** form occurs, related to a less positive self-concept, loss of cultural identity, possible alienation and assimilation. There is also the danger of failure in education and finding work.

Diglossia

'Bilingualism' typically serves to describe an individual's two languages. When the focus changes to two-language varieties co-existing in society, a common term is **diglossia** (Ferguson 1959; J. Fishman 1980; Schiffman 1998). In practice, a community is unlikely to use both language varieties for the same purposes. It is more likely for one variety to serve in certain situations and functions, and the other to be used in others. A language community may use its heritage, minority language in the home, for devotions and in social activity. The majority language may serve at work, in education and in the mass media.

Ferguson (1959) first defined diglossia as the use of two divergent varieties of the same language for different societal functions. Joshua Fishman (1980) extended the idea to two languages existing side by side within a geographical area. In both situations, different languages or varieties may serve varied purposes and be used in different situations with the low (L) variety, or minority language, more frequent in informal, personal situations and the high (H), majority language in formal, official communication contexts.

Different contexts usually make one language more prestigious than the other. Because the majority language is used for prestigious functions, it may seem superior, more elegant and more cultured, the door to both educational and economic success. On the other hand, the low variety is often restricted to interpersonal, domestic functions, and may seem inferior, inadequate and low class.

Diglossia and bilingualism

Joshua Fishman (1980) combines the terms 'bilingualism' and 'diglossia' to characterize four language situations where bilingualism and diglossia may exist with or without each other. The first situation is where most people use both the high language variety and the low language variety, but for a separate set of functions; this tends to lead to relatively stable bilingualism. The second situation is diglossia without bilingualism, with two languages within a particular region. One group of people will speak one language, another group a different language. In some cases, the ruling power group will speak the high variety, with the larger (less powerful) group speaking only

the low variety. Fluent bilingual speakers of both languages may be the exception rather than the rule, as in colonial situations.

The third situation is where most people will be bilingual and will not restrict one language to a specific set of functions. Either language may be used for almost any purpose. Joshua Fishman (1980) regards such communities as unstable, suggesting that one language will, in the future, become more powerful and have increasing purpose and domain control. The other language may decrease in its functions and decay in status and usage. The fourth situation is where there is neither bilingualism nor diglossia; that is, where monolingualism is the norm (e.g. Cuba and the Dominican Republic, where the indigenous languages were eradicated and where there is little in-migration).

A problem with **diglossia** is that the reasons for the distribution of two or more languages across domains are left unexplained. A full understanding of a diglossic situation requires an historical analysis of socioeconomic, sociocultural development within geographical areas; that is, by itself diglossia and the concept of the domains are in danger of providing descriptions rather than explanations – a static picture rather than an evolutionary explanation, where differences in power and histories of political change are hidden.

C.B.

Suggestions for further reading

Baker, C. and Jones, S.P. (1998) *The Encyclopedia of Bilingualism and Bilingual Education*, Clevedon: Multilingual Matters.

Cummins, J. (2000) *Language, Power and Pedagogy: Bilingual Children in the Crossfire*, Clevedon: Multilingual Matters.

Romaine, S. (1995) *Bilingualism*, 2nd edition, Oxford: Basil Blackwell.

C

Cognitive linguistics[1]

Introduction: a new paradigm in linguistics

Cognitive linguistics, which was developed in the late 1970s, sees language as an interactive part of the cognitive abilities of the human mind such as perception, memory, attention, emotion, reasoning, etc. It is opposed to the traditional approach to language, which is rooted in the Aristotelian belief in classical definitions of categories, in objectivist realism (the existence of a mind-independent reality), and in the possibility of stating absolute truths. Cognitive linguistics, in contrast, adopts a **phenomenological approach** as its philosophical basis (Lakoff and Johnson 1980: 181, 1999) – all individuals have an intentional relationship to the world and their access to the world or their consciousness is realized by their bodily experiences of that world (Geeraerts 1985: 355).

Second, cognitive linguistics is opposed to Saussurean and second-generation structuralist axioms, especially **dichotomies** such as *langue* vs *parole*, synchrony vs diachrony, syntax vs semantics, lexis vs grammar, etc. The claim of the arbitrariness of the linguistic sign is replaced by a search for **motivation** and iconic principles of linguistic organization. Third, cognitive linguistics is opposed to **generative linguistics** (see GENERATIVE GRAMMAR), which sees language as an autonomous system, detached in principle from any other type of knowledge, especially **encyclopedic knowledge**. Cognitive linguistics, in contrast, holds that there is no clear-cut distinction between linguistic knowledge and encyclopedic knowledge (Haiman 1980). As Goldberg (1995: 5) puts it, 'knowledge of language is knowledge'.

Cognitive linguistics and functionalism

Cognitive linguistics belongs to the **functionalist tradition**. Although Saussure (1916/1974) saw linguistics as part of semiology or **semiotics**, he mainly emphasized one semiotic principle, **symbolicity**, as the organizing principle of linguistic structure. In a more balanced semiotic view of language (e.g. Haiman 1985, 1986) the two other, more perceptually and experientially based, semiotic principles (i.e. iconicity and indexicality) are also shown to be important. The organizing **principle of iconicity**, which functions partly as one of the many direct manifestations of the interaction between perception and language, becomes visible in three subprinciples of linguistic organization. First, the **principle of sequential order** – The order of the phenomena in our perceived or conceived world is reflected at all levels of linguistic structure. At discourse level,

Caesar's wording *'Veni, vidi, vici'* reflects the temporal succession of these historical events. The same holds in advertising slogans such as *Eye it, try it, buy it*. The second iconic principle of organization is the **principle of proximity**, or **distance**. What belongs together conceptually tends to stay together syntactically, and vice versa. The order in the adjective sequence *a large purple satin coverlet* reflects the primacy of material over colour over size in the intrinsic nature of artefacts. The **principle of quantity** (more form = more meaning) is dictated by functional factors such as politeness, demands of informativity, rhetoric, etc. All this means that extralinguistic factors and knowledge of them may have a direct bearing on linguistic structure.

Prototype theory and categorization

The **Aristotelian** belief in **classical definitions** for categories assumes that all members of a category, e.g. *fruit*, share some **essential feature(s)**, that all category members have equivalent status as members, and that **category boundaries** are clear-cut. Suppose that for the category *fruit*, characteristics such as *sweet*, *soft* and *having seeds* are **necessary and sufficient features**. In this case, several types of fruit would remain outside the category: lemons (which are not sweet), avocados (which are not necessarily soft) and bananas (which have no visible seeds). Strawberries are more like rhubarb because both grow on the ground, not on bushes or trees. Are they fruits? Why is a strawberry a fruit, while rhubarb is not? All this **fuzziness** within or between categories points to a **prototype view** of categorization (Rosch 1973, 1977b, 1978; Berlin and Kay 1969; Geeraerts 1989), which holds that categories do not reflect 'objective' assemblies of features; rather, they are approximations consisting of clear, central or 'prototypical' members such as *apples*, *pears* and *oranges* for *fruit*, and less central or even marginal members such as *avocados*, *lemons* and

strawberries. Hence, members of a category do not have equivalent status, and category boundaries are not clear-cut (*nuts* grow on trees, but do not share any of the three basic features). Categories are to some extent also based on '**family resemblances**', as Wittgenstein (1953/1968) showed for the German category *Spiele*, 'games'. There is also **psychological evidence** for prototype effects in categorization. Statements about central members are processed far more quickly than statements about marginal members, and reasoning about any category is based on what is known about good examples of the category (Rosch 1978).

Polysemy and radial networks

In linguistic theorizing there is a huge cleft between monosemist and polysemist views of the lexicon. Generative linguists (e.g. Bierwisch and Schreuder 1992) tend to subscribe to a **monosemist** view, according to which words have only one basic meaning and the different applications to various entities in the world are managed via an **interface** between language and thought (cf. Taylor 1995b). This may work nicely for words for **artefactual entities**, such as *university*: a university can be categorized as a building, a place of learning, a period in a person's life, etc. But things are far more complicated in the case of the words for natural entities, such as *fruit*. In its prototypical use, *fruit*$_1$ refers to 'something such as an apple, banana, or strawberry that grows on a tree or other plant and tastes sweet' (*Longman Dictionary of Current English*). In this sense we can oppose *fruit*$_1$ to *vegetables*, e.g. *fresh fruit and vegetables*. But in a technical sense, *fruit*$_2$ is 'the part of a plant, bush, or tree that contains the seeds (*Longman Dictionary of Current English*). In this sense, *potatoes* and all other root crop are fruits. Obviously, these two senses of one word are mutually exclusive. *Fruit*$_2$ is an instance of **specialization**, but the basic polysemy of lexical items does not end here. Each lexical item may undergo four different cognitive processes of **meaning extension**, i.e. **generalization**, specialization, **metaphor** and **metonymy**. *Fruit₃* is an instance of generalization and means 'all the natural things that the earth produces such as fruit, vegetables or minerals' (*Longman Dictionary of Current English*). **Metaphorical extension** applies to *fruit₄* as in *the fruits of one's work*, meaning 'the good results from working very hard' (*Longman Dictionary of Current English*). The four senses of *fruit* are systematically related by the various cognitive processes discussed so far: *fruit₁* is the prototypical sense; *fruit₂* is a more specific term, though only applicable to anything carrying or counting as seeds, hence also to grains, nuts, roots, tubes, etc.; *fruit₃* is a more abstract generalization, including minerals; *fruit₄* applies metaphorically to the abstract domain of the results of human endeavour. These four senses are clearly interrelated and can be represented in a **radial network** (see Dirven and Verspoor 1998: 33ff.), in which the conceptual links between the senses of a term are revealed.

Metaphor and the conceptual leap

The human perceptual system is based on a number of **pre-conceptual**, most of all spatial, **image schemata**, which enable us to react to and manipulate the world. They include sensory-motor and visual schemata such as motion, containment, surface, contact, support, blockage, verticality, proximity-distance, etc. and, as the human mind and language develop, they serve as the basis for categorizing the physical world and, by a **metaphoric leap**, the abstract world as well (Johnson 1987). Lakoff and Johnson (1980) claim that metaphors are not merely a matter of language, but just as much a matter of thought. The **metaphorical mind** seizes upon the world of spatial and concrete categories, and by means of metaphor, applies these concepts

to less concrete, abstract entities such as emotion, time, event structure, causality, etc. For example, we tend to understand the emotion of anger in terms of the **conceptual metaphor**, HOT FLUID IN A CONTAINER, which may be expressed in various **linguistic metaphors**, e.g. *My blood was boiling, He was seething with anger, He blew his top*. Time is experienced as A MOVING OBJECT (*The years flew by*) or as A BOUNDED REGION FOR A MOVING OBSERVER (*We are coming up to Christmas*). The complex **event structure metaphor** consists of various subtypes such as states, changes, causes, actions, purposes, means, difficulties. All of these are conceptualized in spatial **image schemata**: STATES ARE LOCATIONS (*be in doubt*), CHANGE OF STATE IS MOTION, e.g. CHANGE OF LOCATION (*get into trouble*); ACTION IS SELF-PROPELLED MOTION, PURPOSES (OF ACTION) ARE DESTINATIONS, MEANS ARE PATHS (TO DESTINATIONS) and DIFFICULTIES ARE IMPEDIMENTS TO MOTION. Lakoff's claim is that such basic conceptual metaphors may well be **universal**, since human **bodily experience** is basically the same all over the world. This claim receives substantial support in Ning Yu (1998), who shows that the three domains of emotion, time and event structure are conceptualized both in English and Chinese by means of the same conceptual metaphors.

Embodied realism

Cognitive linguistics, as Lakoff, Johnson and many others see it, is a challenge to traditional Western thought from Aristotle to Descartes, as well as many philosophical assumptions and linguistic theories such as Chomsky's **generative grammar** (see GENERATIVE GRAMMAR). Traditional thought is based on **objectivist realism**, for which 'true knowledge of the external world can only be achieved if the system of symbols we use in thinking can accurately represent the external world' (Lakoff 1987a: 183). The alternative view of the world is **embodied realism**. In the **phenomenological** tradition, this theory holds that 'human language and thought are structured by, and bound to, an embodied experience' (Lakoff and Johnson 1999: 233). Perceptual, especially spatial, experience paves the way for categorization, and these concrete categories are mapped by the process of metaphor onto abstract thought. It does not come as a surprise, then, that most domains of life, including religion and science, philosophy and metaphysics, are conceptualized at a metaphorical level. This **aptness for metaphor** does not 'belittle' scientists, since metaphoric theories 'can have **literal entailments**' (Lakoff and Johnson 1999: 91), which make predictions in the form of generalizations or natural laws. These non-metaphorical predictions can always be verified or falsified. A typical example is neuroscience, where most statements are made in terms of the **circuitry metaphor**, which invokes physical circuits for the conceptualization of ion channels and glial cells (Lakoff and Johnson 1999: 103). It is through the **converging evidence** from many different experiments that scientists achieve stable results, in the same way that we deal with real things in everyday life on the basis of **intersubjective experience**.

The relation of grammar to cognition

Lakoff and Johnson mainly concentrate on abstract categorization and reasoning, and less on grammatical processes. As a highly abstract symbolic system, the grammar of a language is even more intimately linked with, and subject to, general cognitive processes than the lexical system. Talmy (1978, 1988a, 1988b) shows that the structure of grammar is related to principles of **gestalt perception**, one of which states that the perception of an overall shape comes about by dividing the perceptual field into a more prominent **figure** and a less salient **ground**, against which the figure moves, is moved or stands out otherwise. Talmy applies the perceptual principle of **figure/ground**

alignment to complex sentences and shows that the main clause typically functions as figure and the subordinate clause as ground. Langacker (see 'Cognitive grammar in operation' below) applies this principle to linguistic structuring at all levels (see also Lakoff 1977). Probing into the relation of grammar to cognition, Talmy (1988b) treats the relations between lexicon, grammar and cognition in terms of a building metaphor. Whereas the lexicon can be compared to the single bricks of a building, the grammar is 'the **conceptual framework** or, imagistically, a skeletal structure or scaffolding for the **conceptual material** that is lexically specified' (Talmy 1988b: 165). The lexicon contains **content words** and reflects the tens of thousands of individual phenomena as single, conceptual categories, whereas the grammar develops more abstract, **schematic categories**. Thus the **schematic meaning** of the plural morpheme – that is, a meaning applying to all possible contexts – is the notion of 'multiplexity'. This is found not only with count nouns (*cups*), but also with abstract nouns (*fears*, *misgivings*), uncountable nouns (*ashes*, *waters*) or event nouns (*the silences between the two lovers*). The concept 'multiplex' is not limited to nouns and the plural morpheme, but can also be found with iterative verb forms, as in *He was hitting her*. Thus, whereas the lexicon diversifies the conceptual world more and more, the grammar synthetizes under one common denominator quite different manifestations of 'more than one', be it concrete entities, abstract entities, uncountable phenomena, or events. In this way grammatical 'structuring is necessary for a disparate quantity of contentful material to be able to cohere in any sensible way and hence to be amenable to simultaneous **cognizing** as a Gestalt' (Talmy 1988b: 196). Still, lexical and grammatical specifications are to be seen along a continuum ranging from content categories to schematic categories, which (like all categories) are by definition equal in nature.

Cognitive grammar in operation

According to Langacker (1995: 4), all linguistic meaning resides in **conceptualization**. All conceptual entities are either **things** like *book* or *linguistics*, or **relations** like *about* or *know*. They are joined to each other in **relationships** like *a book about linguistics* or *I know that book*. A linguistic expression (be it word, phrase, sentence or text) always imposes a **construal** on some body of conceptual content. When describing a conceived situation, a speaker must make choices as to the **scope**, i.e. which aspects of the situation are to be included, and as to the **perspective** adopted on the situation. Perspective involves three components. First, it involves the choice of a **vantage point**, from which one looks at the situation. Second, it involves the choice between an **objective** or **subjective** construal. An objective construal is an explicit setting of the scene, e.g. the adverb *before now* defines the time reference point objectively as the speech act time (now). A subjective construal, in contrast, only implies a speaker-dependent reference point, as in the case of the past tense in *I saw him*. Third, perspective involves the choice of a **direction of mental scanning**, as in the opposition between *The roof slopes steeply upward* and *The roof slopes steeply downward*. The **cognizer/speaker** selects things and relations in accordance with these cognitive processes, and **assembles** them into larger composite wholes such as relationships, clauses, sentences and texts. Not only clauses, but also things and relationships, are structured as **gestalts**, consisting of figure and ground. In the case of things, the figure/ground components are a **profile** and a conceptual **base**. Thus, for *strawberry*, the ground or conceptual base is the domain of a *strawberry plant* with roots, leaves and fruit, and *strawberry* profiles the fruit. A **relationship** like *the strawberry on the plate* consists of the relation *on* and the two **participants**, *strawberry* and *plate*. The relation *on*

profiles contact or support with a surface in the domain of space. The figure/ground alignment holds between the first participant *strawberry* as a **trajector** – even though it does not move – and the second participant, *plate*, as the **landmark**. Expressions that profile things are, prototypically, nouns, pronouns, determiners and higher-order expressions such as a full noun phrase; verbs typically profile temporal relations or processes, whereas prepositions, adjectives, and non-finite verbs profile **atemporal relations**.

These simple expressions can be assembled into complex expressions by grammatical patterns or **constructions**. A typical construction consists of two **components** that are **integrated** both semantically and phonologically. Such a **composite** structure, e.g. *the strawberry on my neighbour's plate* depends on **correspondences** between the sub-parts of the two components, i.e. *strawberry on X*, and *my neighbour's plate*. The corresponding entities *X* and *plate* are superimposed, i.e. their specifications are merged to form the composite structure. The figure/ground relation is also operative in the process of **grounding** the conceived situation in the **speech event**, comprising the **speech act**, its participants (speaker and hearer) and speech-act time. The speech event serves as the ground, and the linguistic expression communicated as the figure. The grounding of situations is achieved by means of the tense system for temporal relationships and by the determiner system for referential relations (see further Langacker 1987, 1991a, 1991b, 1999).

Construction grammar

Langacker (1991b: 8) characterizes the difference between his cognitive grammar and 'construction grammar' as follows: whereas cognitive grammar considers constructions to be reducible 'to symbolic relationships', construction grammar assumes that 'grammatical classes and other constructs are still thought of as a separate level of organization'. Lakoff (1987: 467, 538), Goldberg (1995, 1996), Fillmore (1990), Kay and Fillmore (1999) and many others have pointed to the existence of **gestalt-like patterns** or 'established configurations', which are both simpler to produce and also have meaning relations between the composing parts above their ad hoc composition. According to Goldberg (1995: 4), such patterns or **constructions** 'carry meanings independently of the words in the sentence'. A few instances of very frequently used constructions are the transitive construction, the intransitive construction, the passive construction, the ditransitive construction or double-object construction (Goldberg 1992); less frequent, but still common, are the middle construction (*This book sells well*), the incredulity response construction (*What? Him write a novel?!*), the *let-alone* construction (Fillmore et al. 1988), etc. The middle construction is a special case of the intransitive construction, such as *The book fell down*, which combines at least four semantic relations beyond the assembly of constituent parts. First, the verb is often a transitive verb (like *sell*), but used intransitively. Second, the subject *book* goes beyond the semantic value of a non-agentive intransitive in that it has some special properties that 'enable' what is denoted by the predicate, *sell well* (Yoshimura 1998: 279). Third, unlike the intransitive construction, which may take all possible tenses, the middle construction prototypically occurs in the simple present, suggesting a kind of genericness. Fourth, the middle construction requires an adverbial or other modifier specifying the manner of what the predicate denotes. According to Taylor (1998: 21), constructions are thus **schemata** which have to be characterized by criteria such as the **configuration of the parts**, the contribution of the parts to the overall meaning of the construction, and the semantic, pragmatic and discourse value of the construction (the middle construction is especially favoured

in advertising). In a nutshell, the semantic relation of 'property' does not come from the assembly of *book* with *sell*, but it originates from the gestalt of the construction as a whole. In other words, constructions are instantiated by linguistic expressions that 'inherit' their (more) abstract relations from the higher **sanctioning construction**. Thus, the middle construction need not only use what would be a direct object in a transitive construction (*sell a book*), but it can, though marginally, also have a locative as in the following bookseller's exchange: '*Where shall we put the new travel book?*' – '*Well, the corner shop window sells very well.*' Obviously, we can observe prototypicality effects in this construction too, demonstrating that we witness the impact of the same very general cognitive principles at all levels of linguistic structure.

Mental spaces

Cognitive linguistics is not only a lexicogrammatical theory of language; it also embraces the whole of language functions and structure, including pragmatic and discourse dimensions. In discourse, various knowledge frames, linguistic or non-linguistic, are invoked, which Fauconnier (1985/1994) called **mental spaces**. Each utterance, even each content word, in discourse reflects and evokes a **mental representation** of some situation. For the encoding and interpretation of mental representations we draw not only on the linguistic expression, but also on the speech situation, and on encyclopedic knowledge, often called **world knowledge**. Each utterance is based in a mental space which is the speaker's **perspective** and possibly shared by other participants in the speech event. This is the **base space** (space 0). In base space we can open new spaces as illustrated in a much-discussed example *I dreamt I was Marilyn Monroe and kissed me*. Here *I dreamt* is part of the base space, and the verb *dream* is a **space-builder** opening a **new space** (space 1), an imagined world, in which the second *I* (*was Marilyn Monroe*) is no longer identical with the first *I* (*dreamt*) in the base space, but is part of a new knowledge frame in which Marilyn Monroe is not kissing herself, but the speaker, i.e. the *I* in the base space. **Mental space theory** started out as a cognitive alternative to solve many of the referential problems left unsolved by logic-oriented trends in generative linguistics, but has, in the work of Fauconnier (1997) and Fauconnier and Sweetser (1996), developed into an encompassing cognitive theory of discourse and **discourse management**. In the development of the ongoing discourse, speaker(s) and hearer(s) have to keep track of all the mental spaces opened up and can at any time go back to any of them to elaborate them further.

R.D.

Note

1 I wish to thank Günter Radden and Ad Foolen for their highly valuable suggestions about the form and contents of this presentation.

Suggestions for further reading

Dirven, R. and Verspoor, M. (eds) (1998) *Cognitive Exploration of Language and Linguistics*, Amsterdam: John Benjamins.
Janssen, Th. and Redeker, G. (eds) (1999) *Cognitive Linguistics: Foundations, Scope, and Methodology* (Cognitive Linguistics Research, no. 15), Berlin and New York: Mouton.
Ungerer, F. and Schmid, H.-J. (1996) *An Introduction to Cognitive Linguistics*, London: Longman.

Contrastive linguistics and cross-linguistic studies

The Contrastive Analysis Hypothesis

'Cross-linguistic studies' is the term most commonly used to describe work in the tradition that originates in **contrastive linguistics**. Contrastive linguistic studies (e.g. Lado 1957) compares the phonological, lexical and grammatical systems of languages with a view to predicting difficulties which might face native speakers of one language trying to learn another. The belief was, as Robins puts it, that (1964/1989: 413) 'there have to be somewhat differently constructed teaching grammars for students according to the principal typological differences of their own languages, since these to a large extent determine the sort of errors, in pronunciation and grammar, to which they are most prone'. Wardhaugh (1970) refers to this as the strong version of the **Contrastive Analysis Hypothesis**.

The influence of the first language on the learning of a second is generally referred to as **transfer**. Transfer may be benevolent in the sense of helping the learner, in which case it is often referred to as **positive transfer**, or it may be malevolent, in the sense of hindering the learning of the new language. In the latter case it is often called **interference** or **negative transfer**. For example, if a lexical item in the new language closely resembles one in the native language, the learner may transfer their understanding of the term's meaning to the new language, and this may be helpful to them in the learning process. However, the strategy may backfire in the case of **false friends**, terms in two languages which are phonologically and graphologically similar (**cognates**), but have more or less subtly different meanings. For example, the Danish term *aktuel* means 'current', not 'actual', and a learner who suggests that the class discuss some actual problems may be considered insulting rather than helpful. The double-edged nature of

L1 influences on L2 learning was noted by such giants in the history of foreign language teaching as Sweet (1899/1964: 54ff.) and Palmer (1917/1968: 33ff.), but it was in the 1950s that the influence of the mother tongue on second language learners became a major issue in language teaching theory, boosted by the publication of Weinreich (1953/1968), Lado (1957) and Haugen (1953). In the US interest waned in the 1970s, whereas in Europe it survived albeit with an emphasis on a weaker version of the Contrastive Analysis Hypothesis. According to this weaker version, *differences* between languages (Ringbom 1987: 47, quoting Wardhaugh 1970: 126) do not 'predict difficulty; it "requires of the linguist only that he use the best linguistic knowledge available to him in order to account for observed difficulties in second language learning"'.

Error analysis

This weak version of the hypothesis switches the emphasis from prediction of difficulty to observation of difficulty, which is then explained with reference to contrastive analysis. In other words, the emphasis switched to a primary focus on the analysis of learner errors, **error analysis** (see e.g. Richards 1974). Much error analysis, however, especially in the US, did not regard the L1 as influential at all, or regarded its influence as minimal, on learner errors (e.g. Dulay and Burt 1972, 1973, 1974a, 1974b, 1974c). Instead, the learning process and the learner's active part in it were placed in focus, and the new concept of **interlanguage** became central in theorizing about second language learning.

Interlanguage

The notion of an interlanguage was first broached by Nemser (1961/1971) and Briere (1964/1968), but it is best known through the work of Larry Selinker (1972, 1992,

1996). It arises from the observation that learners often produce structures that exist neither in their first language nor in the language they are learning and which (it seems) no native speaker of any language ever produces (Selinker 1996: 97).

Interlanguage competence is of three types: **fossilized competence**, **functional competence** and **transitional competence** (Selinker 1996: 97). The notion of fossilized competence derives from Corder (see Selinker 1996: 98). The idea is that many L2 learners appear to reach a plateau in their learning, ceasing to improve any further. On their way there, they pass through a number of stages, which are therefore transitional. Some learners achieve competence in restricted domains only, enabling them to use the new language mainly for specific purposes, and it is this kind of competence that Selinker refers to as 'functional competence' – the notion appeared originally in Jain (1969, 1974).

In Selinker's work (1996) the idea of L1 influence remains in his claim that there is firm evidence that L2 learners' preferred learning strategy is the search for **interlingual identifications**, a notion derived from Weinreich (1953/1968) (Selinker 1996: 97).

Cross-linguistic research

In work by Kellerman and Sharwood-Smith (1986) the notion of language transfer is renamed **cross-linguistic influence**, probably coincidentally along with a shift in nomenclature among people with a more direct pedagogical interest in the comparison of languages away from 'contrastive linguistics' to **cross-linguistic research**. In the more directly theoretically minded branch of the study of relationships between the learning of various languages by people having various native tongues, the focus has generally speaking shifted towards clarification of the role in **L2 acquisition** of **UG** (see LANGUAGE ACQUISITION and the studies collected in Brown *et al.* 1996).

Research in this new contrastive linguistics is typically carried out using large machine-readable corpora of texts in two or more languages. The texts may either be sets of pairs of original and translation, or sets of texts originally written in the languages but of the same genre. Corpora whose uses have been extensively described include the **English–Norwegian Parallel Corpus** held at the universities of Oslo and Bergen, Norway, the **English–Swedish Parallel Corpus** held at Lund University, Sweden, and the **Danish–English–French Corpus in Contract Law** held at Aarhus Business School, Denmark (see Aijmer *et al.* 1996; Johansson and Oksefjell 1998).

Linguists working in this paradigm investigate aspects of language well beyond the traditional areas of phonology, lexis and syntax, such as the pragmatics and the rhetorical structure of texts, including texts such as telephone calls and business negotiations (Aijmer and Altenberg 1996: 11). A particularly helpful corpus

for pedagogical purposes is Granger's machine-readable **International Corpus of Learner English**, situated at Louvan-la-Neuve, Belgium (see Granger 1996).

K.M.

Suggestions for further reading

Johansson, S. and Oksefjell, S. (eds) (1998) *Corpora and Cross-Linguistic Research: Theory, Method, and Case Studies*, Amsterdam and Atlanta, GA: Rodopi.

Richards, J.C. (ed.) (1974) *Error Analysis: Perspectives on Second Language Acquisition*, Harlow, Essex: Longman.

Robinett, B.W. and Schachter, J. (eds) (1983) *Second Language Learning: Contrastive Analysis and Related Aspects*, Ann Arbor: University of Michigan Press.

Selinker, L. (1992) *Rediscovering Interlanguage*, London: Longman.

Corpora

At its most general, a corpus (plural *corpora*) may be defined as a body or collection of linguistic data for use in scholarship and research. Since the early 1960s, interest has increasingly focused on **computer corpora** or **machine-readable corpora**, which are the main subject of this entry. However, in the first three sections I shall begin by considering the place in linguistic research of corpora in general, whether machine-readable or not. In the remaining sections I shall consider why computer corpora have been compiled or collected; what are their functions and their limitations; what are their applications, more particularly, their use in **natural language processing** (**NLP**). This entry will illustrate the field of computer corpora only by reference to corpora of Modern

English (cf. CONTRASTIVE LINGUISTICS AND CROSS-LINGUISTIC STUDIES).

Corpora in an historical perspective

In traditional linguistic scholarship, particularly on **dead languages** (languages which are no longer used as an everyday means of communication in a speech community), the corpus of available textual data, however limited or fragmentary, was the foundation on which scholarship was built. Later, particularly in the first half of the twentieth century, corpora assumed importance in the transcription and analysis of extant, but previously unwritten or unstudied, languages, such as the Amerindian languages studied by linguists such as Franz Boas (1911) and the generation of American linguists who succeeded him.

The urgent task of analysing and classifying the unwritten languages of the world has continued up to the present day. But this development was particularly important for setting the scene for the key role of the corpus in American structural linguistics in the work of Bloomfield (1933/1935) and the post-Bloomfieldians (see Harris 1951: 12ff.) for whom the corpus was not merely an indispensable practical tool, but the *sine qua non* of scientific description. This era saw a shift from the closed corpus of a dead language – necessarily the only first-hand source of data – to a closed and finite corpus of a **living language** (a language in use as the means of communication in a speech community), where the lack of access to unlimited textual data is a practical restriction, rather than a restriction of principle. Another shift is from the written textual data of a dead language to the spoken textual data of a living and heretofore unwritten language. If we associate the terms 'text' and 'corpus', as tradition dictates, with written sources, this tradition must give way to a contrasting emphasis, in the post-Bloomfieldian era, on the primacy of spoken texts and spoken corpora.

However, a complete reversal of the post-Bloomfieldians' reliance on corpora was effected by the revolution in linguistic thought inaugurated by Chomsky. Chomsky saw the finite spoken corpus as an inadequate and degenerate observational basis for the description of the infinite generative capacity of natural languages, and speaker intuitions replaced the corpus as the sole reliable source of data about the language. It was in this unfavourable climate of opinion that the compilation of a systematically organized computer corpus – the first of its kind – was undertaken in the USA. The **Brown University Corpus of American English** (known as **Brown Corpus**, and consisting of approximately 1,000,000 text words) was compiled under the direction of Francis and Kučera in 1961–64 (see Francis and Kučera 1964; also Francis 1979). It contained 500 written text samples of *c*. 2000 words each, drawn from a systematic range of publications in the USA during 1961. Since that time, machine-readable corpora have gradually established themselves as resources for varied research purposes.

The justification for corpora in linguistics

It is necessary, in view of the influential Chomskyan rejection of corpus data, to consider in what ways corpora (whether computerized or not) contribute to linguistic research. The following are six arguments against the Chomskyan view.

1 The opposition between the all-sufficient corpus of the post-Bloomfieldian linguist and the all-sufficient intuitions of the generative linguist is a false opposition, overlooking consideration of reasonable intermediate positions. Recent corpus users have accepted that corpora, in supplying first-hand textual data, cannot be meaningfully analysed without the intuition and interpretative skill of the analyst, using knowledge *of* the language (*qua* native speaker or proficient non-native speaker) and knowledge *about* the language (*qua* linguist). In other words, corpus use is seen as a question of corpus *plus* intuition, rather than of corpus *versus* intuition.

2 The generativist's reliance on the native speaker's intuition begs a question about the analysis of language by proficient non-native speakers. In so far as such analysts have unreliable intuitions about what is possible in a language, their need for corpus evidence is greater than that of a native speaker. It is thus no accident that corpus studies of English have flourished in countries where a tradition of English linguistics is particularly strong, but where English is not a native language; such as Belgium, The Netherlands, Norway, Sweden.

3 The distinction between competence and performance, a cornerstone of Chomsky's rationalist linguistics, has been increasingly challenged since the 1950s, especially through the development of branches of linguistics for which detailed evidence of performance is arguably essential, such as sociolinguistics, psycholinguistics, pragmatics and discourse analysis. To these may be added developments in **applied linguistics**, where it has become clear that studies of how language *is used*, both by native speakers and by learners, are relevant inputs to the study of language *learning*.

4 The generative linguist's reliance on 'intuition' has required the postulation of an 'ideal native speaker/hearer' and in practice of an invariant variety of the language in question (see Chomsky 1965). But research in sociolinguistics has highlighted the variability of the competences of different native speakers belonging to different social groupings, and even the dialectal variability of a single native speaker's language. As soon as the non-uniformity of the language is accepted as normal, it is evident that native speakers' knowledge of their language, as a social or cultural phenomenon, is incomplete, whether considered in terms of dialect or in terms of register (e.g. British native speakers of English obviously have unreliable intuitions about American usage, or about scientific or legal usage in their own country). Hence corpus studies that range over different varieties reveal facts which are not accessible from intuition alone. (Good examples have been provided by various corpus-based studies of the English modal auxiliaries, notably Coates 1983; here corpus analysis reveals an unexpectedly wide range of variation between spoken and written English, and between British and American English.)

5 Studies of corpora also bring to the attention an abundance of examples which cannot be neatly accommodated by intuition-based generalizations or categories. These cannot be dismissed as performance errors (see Sampson 1987: 17–20): rather, they invite analysis in terms of non-deterministic theories of language, accommodating **prototypes** (Rosch and Mervis 1975; Lakoff 1982), **gradience** (Bolinger 1961; Quirk *et al.* 1985: 90) or **fuzzy categories** (Coates 1983). From the viewpoint of such theories, it is the linguist's intuition that is suspect, since the linguist who relies on intuition is likely to find clear-cut, prototypical examples to support a given generalization or, in contrast, to find unrealistic counter-examples for which a corpus would provide no authentic support. Thus intuition may be seen not as a clear mirror of competence, but a distorting mirror, when it is used as the only resource for the linguistic facts to be analysed.

6 We turn finally to an argument applicable specifically to computer corpora. The goal of natural language processing (NLP) by computer must reasonably include the requirement that any text to be processed should not be pre-selected by linguistic criteria, but should be unrestricted, such that any sample of naturally occurring English should be capable of analysis. Although this ambitious goal is well beyond the capabilities of present NLP systems in such complex tasks as machine translation, it motivates the increasingly indispensable use of computer corpora in computational linguistics (see ARTIFICIAL INTELLIGENCE), and shows that this branch of linguistics, like others mentioned in (3) above, cannot neglect the detailed study of performance, in the form of authentic textual data.

Limitations of corpora

On the other hand, corpora have clear limitations. The Brown Corpus (see above) illustrates two kinds of limitation general to corpus linguistics.

First there is a limitation of size. Even though the million words of the Brown Corpus seem, at first blush, impressive, they represent only a minute sample of the written texts published in the USA in 1961, let alone of a theoretically conceivable 'ideal corpus' of all texts, written and spoken, in (Modern) English.

The second limitation, already implied, is a limitation of language variety. In the defining criteria of the Brown Corpus, 'written English' proclaims a limitation of medium; 'American English', one of geographical provenance; and '1961', a third limitation of historical period. In addition to those limitations, the Brown Corpus, by the detailed principles of its selection, includes certain registers (journalism, for example) but excludes others (such as poetry). Hence, any study of Modern English based on the Brown Corpus must be accompanied by a caveat that the results cannot be generalized, without hazard, to varieties of the language excluded from its terms of reference.

Similarly, the limitation of corpus size means that samples provided in the corpus may be statistically inadequate to permit generalization to other samples of the same kind. While the size of the Brown Corpus may be considered adequate for the study of common features (e.g. punctuation marks, some affixes, common grammatical constructions), it is manifestly inadequate as a resource for (for example) lexicography, since the corpus contains only *c.* 50,000 word types, of which *c.* 50 per cent occur only once in the corpus. (By contrast, the more recent corpus known as the Bank of English, compiled under the leadership of John Sinclair, consists of over 300 million words.)

To some extent, however, the generalizability of findings from one corpus to another is itself a matter of empirical study. The list of the fifty most common words in the Brown Corpus is replicated almost exactly in corresponding corpora of British English (the **Lancaster–Oslo/Bergen Corpus** – known as the **LOB Corpus**) and of New Zealand English (the **Wellington Corpus**); see Kennedy (1998: 98–9). In this very limited respect, therefore, these three corpora are virtually equivalent samples. As more corpora representing different language varieties are compared, it will become evident how far a sample may be regarded as representative of the language as a whole, or of some variety of it. Carroll (1971) has implemented a statistical measure of representativeness *within* a corpus (a function of frequency and dispersion), and this may again, with caution, be extended to approximate measures of representativeness for the language as a whole.

Why should a corpus be machine-readable?

The advantages of a machine-readable corpus (also termed an **electronic corpus**) over a corpus stored, in the traditional way, on paper derive from capabilities of automatic processing and automatic transmission.

Automatic processing subsumes operations which vary from the simple and obvious, such as sorting the words of a text into alphabetical order, to complex and specialized operations such as **parsing** (syntactic analysis). The computer's advantage over a human analyst is that it can perform such operations with great speed, as well as accurately and consistently. Thus the computer can, in practice, accomplish tasks of text manipulation which could scarcely be attempted by even large numbers of (trained) human beings.

Automatic transmission includes transferring a text either locally (e.g. from a computer's storage to an output device such as a VDU or a printer), or remotely to other installations – either via a direct electronic link or through the mediation of a portable storage device, such as a CD-ROM. Thus, technically, a corpus can be 'published' in the sense of being copied and made available to a user, in any part of the world, who has access to the necessary computer resources. In the present era of inexpensive but powerful computers and storage devices, the computer corpus is becoming a everyday resource for a large body of users – not only for research, but for applications in areas such as education, lexicography and language engineering. Technical availability, however, does not mean availability in a legal or practical sense – see 'Availability limitations' in the next section.

Computer corpora of modern English: data capture and availability

What is available?

Focusing on English, we may now consider some of the existing computer corpora, in addition to the Brown Corpus, in order to gain an impression of the extent of linguistic coverage which has been achieved.

The LOB Corpus mentioned above (see Johansson *et al.* 1978) is a corpus of printed British English compiled in order to match as closely as possible the Brown Corpus of American English. Its size and principles of selection are virtually the same as those of the Brown Corpus.

The **London–Lund Corpus** (Svartvik *et al.* 1982) is a corpus of *c.* 500,000 words of spoken English, transcribed in detailed prosodic notation, and constituting spoken texts of the **Survey of English Usage Corpus** compiled at London University under the direction of Randolph Quirk (see Quirk 1960; Quirk and Svartvik 1979). The London–Lund Corpus (1978) was computerized at Lund University, Sweden, under the direction of Jan Svartvik.

Starting with the early (American) Brown Corpus and its British equivalent, the LOB Corpus, a set of corpora following the same design has proliferated, including corpora of Indian, Australian and New Zealand English. Of particular interest are two corpora compiled at Freiburg, and known familiarly as the Frown and FLOB Corpora, which consist of text samples dating from 1991; these match the Brown and LOB corpora respectively, and permit a diachronic comparison over the thirty-year period separating the two pairs of corpora. Another ongoing project, the International Corpus of English, initiated by Sidney Greenbaum in the late 1980s, aims to build and annotate matching corpora from around eighteen English-speaking countries and regions throughout the world. Each corpus consists of a million words of spoken and written data (see Greenbaum 1996).

Much larger than these are the British National Corpus (or BNC – http://info.ox.ac.uk/bnc/) and the already-mentioned Bank of English, 'megacorpora', which have been compiled primarily for lexicography but have many other uses. Another vigorous initiative has been the development of historical and dialectal corpora of English, centred at the University of Helsinki. Corpora of spoken English have also proliferated, beginning with the London–Lund Corpus and now including many more specialist and regional corpora, such as the Corpus of London Teenage English (COLT) – see Haselrud and Stenström (1995).

Seventeen of the smaller corpora of varied types are available on a CD-ROM as the ICAME Collection of English Language Corpora, available at a reasonable cost from the HIT Centre, University of Bergen, Norway (http://www.hit.uib.no/icame/). The Linguistic Data Consortium (LDC; http://www.ldc.upenn.edu/) based at the University of Pennsylvania is another corpus provider, distributing data from a large and growing archive of corpus resources of different kinds, primarily for the language engineering community. Details of all these corpora can be found not only at relevant Web sites, but also in introductory books such as McEnery and Wilson (1996), Kennedy (1998) and

Biber *et al.* (1998). Demonstration material from the Bank of English corpus is available on-line from the COBUILD Direct Web site (http:/titania.cobuild.collins.co.uk/direct_demo.html), and a similar service is available for the BNC.

This selective list only represents the tip of the iceberg, in that there exist more specialized corpora, both for English and for other languages – e.g. corpora of children's language (see the CHILDES Database – http://childes.psy.cmu.edu) – and many corpora are currently in the process of compilation. In fact, since the Brown Corpus came into being in the early 1960s, possibilities of **data capture**, i.e. of obtaining texts in machine-readable form, have increased astronomically. The Brown and LOB corpora had to be compiled by **manual data capture**: texts had to be laboriously keyboarded and corrected by a human operator using an input device such as a card punch or (later) a terminal. But in the 1970s and 1980s the development of computer typesetting and word processing has meant that vast quantities of machine-readable text have come into existence as a by-product of commercial text-processing technologies. This may be termed **automatic data capture**, other sources of which are the World Wide Web and the use of **scanners** (or **OCRs**): machines that can scan a printed or typewritten text and automatically convert it into machine-readable form. With such resources, it is now possible for an individual to build a corpus for personal research purposes.

Automatic data capture means that, in principle, corpora of unlimited size can be created. There is a consequential move away from the idea of a fixed, closed corpus towards data capture as an open-ended, ongoing process.

Availability limitations

In three respects, however, the above account paints too optimistic a picture of the current computer corpus availability. First, the technical problems of data capture for research are considerable – but must be ignored here.

Second, automatic data capture is limited to written text, and is likely to remain so for some time to come. Spoken texts must first be transcribed into written form, which means a continuing deficit of spoken (in comparison with written) corpus data.

Third, machine-readable texts are subject to copyright and other proprietary restrictions, which impose strong constraints on their availability for research. Many corpora can be made available for purposes of academic research only (i.e. not for commercial or industrial exploitation). Other corpora or text collections are subject to stronger restrictions, and of the many corpora that have been automatically compiled, most are available (if at all) only through agreement or negotiation with their compilers and/or copyright holders.

Linguistically annotated corpora

To put ourselves in the position of a linguist using a computer corpus, we may initially imagine someone who wishes to investigate the use of the English word *big* (say, as part of a comparison of *big* and *large*). The task of the computer in this case is most naturally seen as that of producing a list (perhaps a sample list) of occurrences of *big* in a given corpus, together with sufficient context to enable the researcher to interpret examples in terms of their syntactic, semantic or pragmatic determinants. This is part of what is provided by search tools such as WordSmith (Scott 1996). A **KWIC concordance** is a particularly convenient form of data display, in which each token of the target word (*big*) is placed in the middle of a line of text, with the remainder of the line filled with its preceding and following context.

Typically, a set of characters at the beginning or end of the line specifies the **location** of the given occurrence in the corpus. Elements of the **mark-up**, i.e. the encoding of features of the orthographic format of the corpus, may be displayed to the user, or else hidden from view. A concordance is one of the simplest yet most powerful devices for retrieving information from a corpus. But it also illustrates a limitation of any corpus stored in the normal orthographic form. If the word to be investigated had been (for example) *little*, the concordance would have listed all the occurrences of *little*, whether as an adverb, a determiner, a pronoun or an adjective, so the investigator would have had to sort the occurrences manually in order to identify those instances of *little* relevant to a comparison with *big*. Another type of difficulty would have arisen if the investigator had wanted to study *come* and *go*: here several different concordance listings would have been necessary, to find all morphological forms (*comes*, *came*, *coming*, etc.) of the same verb.

This illustrates a general problem: that information which is not stored in orthographic form in the 'raw' corpus cannot be retrieved in a simple or useful way. An answer to this problem is to build in further information, by producing linguistically analysed or annotated versions of the corpus. A valuable stage in the **annotation** of a corpus is **grammatical tagging**; that is, the attachment of a grammatical **tag** or **word-class label** to each word it contains. The result is a grammatically tagged corpus.

A number of corpora (e.g. Brown, LOB and the BNC) are available in grammatically tagged versions. Although manual tagging is possible in principle, in practice the tagging of a sizeable corpus is feasible only if done automatically, by a computer program or suite of programs known as a **tagger**. This ensures not only speed, but consistency of tagging practice. The tagging of the BNC (using a set of around 60 grammatical tags) was undertaken by a system which achieved 96–7 per cent success (see Garside *et al.* 1997: chapters 2

and 9), increasing to 98 per cent in the latest version. Where a tagger makes mistakes, these should preferably be corrected by hand – a mammoth task so far only undertaken for a two-million-word sample of the BNC.

Grammatical tagging is only part of a larger enterprise, the **syntactic analysis** (or **parsing**) of a corpus. This is being undertaken at various centres and, although at present no completely parsed version of any of the corpora mentioned above is available, substantial parts of the Brown and LOB corpora have been parsed (Sampson 1995; Garside and Leech 1987). An important initiative in corpus parsing is Marcus's **Penn Treebank Project** – ftp://ftp.cis.upenn.edu/pub/treebank/doc/manual/ – as is the constraint grammar parser developed at Helsinki (Carlsson *et al.* 1995), which has been applied to a large part of the Bank of English, for in-house use. The British incarnation of the International Corpus of English (known as ICE-GB) is available in parsed form on CD-ROM (Wallis *et al.* 2000). From a parsed corpus or subcorpus it is possible to retrieve information (for example, in the form of a structurally defined concordance query) about more abstract grammatical properties which cannot be specified in terms of words or word classes – for example, types of phrases or clauses.

There is no reason why the annotation of a corpus should be restricted to grammatical analysis. Research is well advanced, for example, in the tagging of semantic classes, of speech acts (see SPEECH-ACT THEORY), and of discourse features such as pronoun anaphora (see TEXT LINGUISTICS): these can be undertaken manually, automatically or by a combination of manual and automatic methods. Annotation of a wide range of linguistic features in the LOB and London–Lund corpora has been undertaken by Biber *et al.* (1988) in a large-scale investigation of stylistic variation in spoken and written English.

Data resources such as frequency lists

A corpus can also be processed in order to produce derived databases, or data resources, of various kinds. The simplest example is the production of word-frequency lists (e.g. Carroll *et al.* 1971; Johansson and Hofland 1989), a task now routinely performed by search tools such as WordSmith (see above). With a tagged corpus, it is possible to automate the production of frequency lists which are **lemmatized**; that is, where different grammatical forms of the same word (or **lemma**) are listed under one entry, as in a standard dictionary (Johansson and Hofland 1989 provide such lists for the LOB Corpus).

As more annotation of corpora is undertaken, further types of derived data resources become available, e.g. corpus-derived lexicons, probabilistic grammars and collocation dictionaries.

Applications of corpus-based research

Apart from applications in linguistic research *per se,* the following practical applications may be mentioned.

Lexicography

Corpus-derived frequency lists and (more especially) concordances have established themselves as basic tools for the lexicographer. For example, KWIC concordances of the Birmingham Collection (a predecessor of the Bank of English) were systematically used in the compilation of the *Collins COBUILD English Language Dictionary* (COBUILD 1987). While the *COBUILD Dictionary* was something of a landmark publication, other dictionary publishers have since invested heavily in building and maintaining such resources: for example, the BNC has been used for the dictionaries of Oxford University Press, Longman and Chambers, the three publishers who contributed to its compilation.

Language teaching

Applications to the educational sphere are likely to develop more rapidly in the future, as cheaper and more powerful hardware comes within the range of educational budgets. The use of concordances as language-learning tools has been a major interest in **computer-assisted language learning** (**CALL**; see Johns 1994; Wichmann *et al.* 1997). In language-teaching and -learning research, the development of specialized corpora (see Kennedy 1998: 33–45) of, say, spoken English and technical and scientific Englishes are having obvious applications to English language teaching, while the value of corpora for interlanguage research (e.g. corpora of learners' English, corpora of learners' errors) has been demonstrated through initiatives such as the establishment of an **International Corpus of Learner English** (**ICLE**; see Granger 1996).

Translation

Another fast-developing field of application is the use of corpora as aids to (the teaching of) translation, or as tools for machine or machine-aided translation, and as sources for establishing the special nature of translated text. Corpora of texts and their translations exist for a number of language pairs: for example, a 60-million-word corpus of parallel English and French versions of the *Canadian Hansard* (proceedings of the Canadian Parliament) was used experimentally in the early 1990s to develop a new kind of corpus-based automatic-translation technique. The compilation was of a corpus including texts from a number of languages translated into English, together with a comparable (in terms of size and text type) corpus of texts originally written in English, intended for comparison aimed at establishing whether there are features specific to translated texts. It was begun by Baker in the early 1990s (see M. Baker 1993, 1995, 1996) and continues, with initially promising results (Laviosa-Braithwaite

1996). For recent developments in cross-linguistic corpus-based research, see Johansson and Oksefjell (1998), and for explicitly translational uses of corpora, see *Meta* 43(4) (December).

Speech processing

Machine translation is one example of the application of corpora for what computer scientists term **natural language processing** or **language technology**. In addition to machine translation, a major research goal for NLP is **speech processing**; that is, the development of computer systems capable of outputting automatically produced speech from written input (**speech synthesis**), or converting speech input into written form (**speech recognition**).

Although speech synthesizers have been available for some years, their output remains an imperfect imitation of natural speech, and in order to produce high-quality speech with appropriate features of connected speech (such as stress, vowel reduction and intonation), a key tool is a corpus of spoken texts, including a version with detailed prosodic transcription. Two projects on these lines are those described in Altenberg (1987) and Knowles *et al.* (1996).

Speech *recognition* is more difficult but, again, systems which perform recognition on a large vocabulary are now commercially available. Research is still, however, a long way from the ultimate goal – a computer system that will accurately recognize continuous speech using unrestricted vocabulary.

The problem is that acoustic processing can accomplish with sufficient accuracy only part of the task of speech recognition: the ambiguities of the spoken signal mean that a speech recognizer must incorporate a **language model**, predicting the most likely sequence of words from a set of sequences of candidate words left undecided by acoustic analysis. Thus the speech recognizer must incorporate sufficient 'knowledge' of the language to enable the most likely sequence of candidate words to be chosen. This knowledge of the language must include, at a basic collocational level, the knowledge that, say, the sequence *a little extra effort* is more likely than *a tickle extra effort*, or that *deaf ears* is more likely than *deaf years.* At a more abstract level, a language model may incorporate likelihoods of word-class sequences (grammatical-tagging information), likelihoods of syntactic structures (parsing information) or likelihoods of semantic dependencies (semantic information). To obtain accurate statistical estimates, very large quantities of textual data have to be analysed automatically. In effect, a corpus-based approach is essential.

The most challenging area of research in speech and language technology today is probably that of **spoken dialogue systems**, designed to enable interactive communication to take place between human and machine, or between human and human, with a machine as intermediary. Not only speech processing but all levels of natural language processing may be simultaneously required, if a computer is to simulate the behaviour of a human interlocutor. Here, as elsewhere, the corpus turns out to be an essential tool: we cannot build a machine to mimic human dialogue behaviour, unless dialogue behaviour has first been modelled in detail, through the analysis of corpora of real dialogue (see Gibbon *et al.* 1998).

Conclusion

The research paradigm for speech recognition, as mentioned above, is probabilistic, and this is likely to remain a dominant feature of corpus-based NLP. The strength of the corpus-based methodology is that it trains a computer to deal with unrestricted text input. Although any corpus, however large, is finite, a probabilistic system can use this as a basis for predicting the nature of previously unencountered text. The negative side of this approach is that the system is fallible: hence one focus of current research is the synergy of probabilistic and rule-driven techniques, which will hopefully add greater accuracy to the robustness of statistical models.

Returning to the discussion in the first section, we may observe in the methodology of recent corpus linguistics an ironic resemblance to the pre-Chomskyan corpus-based paradigm of post-Bloomfieldian American linguistics. Whereas Chomsky, emphasizing competence at the expense of performance, rejected the significance of probabilities, the 'language engineering' approach is unashamedly probabilistic, using a sophistication of the Markov process probabilistic model of language which was summarily rejected by Chomsky in the early pages of his *Syntactic Structures* (1957).

Such probabilistic methods, tending to use the minimum degree of linguistic knowledge compatible with achieving a practical end, may be regarded as simplistic and psychologically unrealistic by adherents of mainstream linguistics. But their relative success suggests that the computer's superhuman ability to process quantitatively very large bodies of text can compensate, to a considerable degree, for a lack of the more 'intelligent' levels of linguistic knowledge used in human language processing. At least, this research programme illustrates supremely the fact that computer corpora have promising applications totally unforeseen by their early compilers.

G.N.L.

Suggestions for further reading

Biber, D., Conrad, S. and Reppen, R. (1998) *Corpus Linguistics: Investigating Language Structure and Use*, Cambridge: Cambridge University Press.

Garside, R., Leech, G. and McEnery, T. (eds) (1997) *Corpus Annotation: Linguistic Information from Computer Text Corpora*, London: Longman.

Kennedy, G. (1998) *An Introduction to Corpus Linguistics*, London: Longman.

McEnery, A. and Wilson, A. (1996) *Corpus Linguistics*, Edinburgh: Edinburgh University Press.

Creoles and pidgins

A **pidgin** is a language which has arisen by a process of mixing a simplified form of a language spoken by people who travelled and colonized extensively (such as English, French, Spanish, Portuguese and Dutch), with a simplified form of a language of the people with whom they interacted repeatedly. Such languages often develop near main shipping and trading routes (Trudgill 1974b: 166, 169–70):

English-based pidgins were formerly found in North America, at both ends of the slave trade in Africa and the Caribbean, in New Zealand and in China. They are still found in Australia, West Africa, the Solomon Islands . . . and in New Guinea. . . . (Not all pidgin languages have arisen in this way, though. Kituba, which is derived from Kikongo, a Bantu language, is a pidgin widely used in western Zaire and adjoining areas. And Fanagolo, which is based on Zulu, is a pidgin spoken in South Africa and adjoining countries, particularly in the mines. There are several other indigenous pidgins in Africa and elsewhere.)

(See further Holm 1988: xvi–xix, for comprehensive maps of areas using pidgin and creole languages.) Pidgins also arose when

Africans who did not share a language were working together on plantations and chose to communicate using what they could glean of the colonizer/slave-owner's language, to which they added elements of their own native languages.

For second and subsequent generation users, pidgins may become a mother tongue, a **creole**; (Holm 1988: 6) 'a language which has a jargon or a pidgin in its ancestry; it is spoken natively by an entire speech community, often one whose ancestors were displaced geographically so that their ties with their original language and sociocultural identity were partly broken'. Examples of creoles include Sranan, an English-based creole spoken in coastal areas of Surinam (Trudgill 1974b: 170), and the English-based West Indian creoles used mainly by people of African origin in the Caribbean (Sutcliffe 1984: 219). Non-English-based creoles derived from other European languages include French-based creoles spoken in, among other places, Haiti, Trinidad, Grenada, French Guiana, Mauritius, the Seychelles, and some parts of Louisiana. There are also creoles based on Portuguese and Spanish (Trudgill 1974b: 170). A pidgin may become creolized at any stage of its development (see below).

Some generally fairly limited, anecdotal accounts of creoles and pidgins were written by travellers, administrators and missionaries as long ago as the early sixteenth century. Although some early reports were written with the explicit aim of teaching Europeans something about the structure of a pidgin or creole so that they could use it to communicate with its speakers (Romaine 1988: 7), the serious study of creoles and pidgins began with Schuchardt's series of papers on creole studies, *Kreolische Studien*, published in the 1880s (Schuchardt 1882, 1883), and Schuchardt (1842–1927) is regarded by many as the founding father of pidgin and creole linguistics (Romaine 1988: 4).

However, creoles and pidgins tended to be regarded as merely inferior, corrupt versions of donor languages (Romaine 1988: 6), and the study of them did not gain generally perceived respectability until 1959, when the first international conference on creole language studies was held in Jamaica by a group of scholars who recognized themselves as **creolists** (DeCamp 1971a), and the proceedings published (Le Page 1961). Growing interest in the relationship between American Black English and pidgin and creole English also helped establish the discipline as a proper academic concern, and the publication in 1966 of the first undergraduate textbook on pidgins and creoles (Hall 1966) greatly helped to secure its place (Holm 1988: 55). A second conference was held in Jamaica in 1968 (Hymes 1971b), and since then conferences on pidgin and creole linguistics have been held regularly.

In the development of a pidgin language, the **superstrate language** typically provides most of the vocabulary. The superstrate language will commonly be that of the socially, economically and/or politically dominant group, and will be considered the language that is being pidginized, so that a pidgin is often referred to as, for instance, Pidgin English or Pidgin French. The other language or languages involved are referred to as the **substrate language(s)**. The pidgin tends to retain many of the grammatical features of the substrate language(s). In spite of the fact that pidgins thus arise as two or more languages are mixed, so that speakers of any one of these languages may perceive the pidgin as a debased form of their own language (an attitude clearly expressed by the superstrate-language-speaking authors of many early studies), it is important to note that it is now generally agreed among scholars of pidgin languages that they have a structure of their own which is independent of both the substrate and superstrate languages involved in the original contact (Romaine 1988: 13).

Linguistic characteristics of pidgins and creoles

It is impossible to give a comprehensive overview of all the linguistic characteristics of creoles and pidgins here, but see Holm (1988) for a full account.

Phonology

In general, languages in contact build on those sounds they have in common. Therefore, phonemes that are common throughout the world's languages are more likely to occur in pidgin and creole languages than those phonemes that occur in only very few of the world's languages. Thus /d/ or /m/, for instance, are more common in pidgins and creoles than /ð/ and /θ/. However, the actual pronunciation, or phonetic realization, of the phonemes frequently varies according to speakers' first languages, and during the creolization process (see below) pronunciation will tend towards the pronunciation used by the group whose children are using the language natively rather than towards the superstrate language pronunciation. In addition, if contact with the substrate language(s) is maintained and/or superstrate contact is lost early in the development of a creole, it tends to contain phonemes only found in the substrate language. In addition, the sound systems of pidgins and creoles are subject to the general patterns of phonological change which can be found throughout the world's languages (Holm 1988: 107).

Creoles often retain pronunciations which are no longer retained in the source language. For instance (Holm 1988: 75):

> Miskito Coast CE [Creole English] retains the /aɪ/ diphthong that was current in polite eighteenth-century British speech in words like *bail* 'boil' and *jain* 'join'; this sound became /ɔɪ/ in standard English after about 1800. This makes the creole word for 'lawyer' homophonous with standard English *liar* (but there is no confusion since the latter takes the dialectal form *liard* analogous to *criard* 'crier' and *stinkard* 'stinker' – cf. standard *drunkard*.

Lexis

Since the early contact situations which produced pidgins revolved around trade, work and administration, since most of the items and concepts involved were European, and since the Europeans involved were more powerful socially, economically and politically, the vocabulary of early pidgins was mainly based on European languages and was limited to that required for trade, administration and giving orders. Consequently, pidgins have rather smaller vocabularies than natural languages, but this tends to be compensated for by **multifunctionality** (one word to many syntactic uses), **polysemy** (one word to many meanings) and **circumlocution** (phrase instead of single word) (Holm 1988: 73), so that the semantic system need not be impoverished, certainly not in the later stages of the development of the language (Hall 1972: 143):

> the vocabularies of pidgins and creoles manifest extensive shifts in meaning. Many of these changes are the result of the inevitable broadening of reference involved in pidginization. If a given semantic field has to be covered by a few words rather than many, each word must of course signify a wider range of phenomena. Two pidgin examples out of many: CPE [Chinese Pidgin English] *spit* means 'eject matter from the mouth', by both spitting and vomiting; MPE [Melanesian Pidgin English/Tok Pisin] *gras* means anything that grows, blade-like, out of a surface', as in *gras bilong hed* 'hair', *gras bilong maus* 'moustache', *gras bilong fes* 'beard'.

As Romaine (1988: 36) points out, the restricted vocabularies of pidgins lead to a high degree of **transparency** in pidgin compounds; that is, the meaning of a compound can often be worked out on the basis of the meanings of the terms that make up the compound. However, **semantic broadening**, which takes place when a term takes on new meanings while still retaining its original meaning, can create confusion for the uninitiated. Thus, in most English creoles, *tea* has broadened in meaning to refer to any hot drink, so that '*coffee-tea* is used throughout the Anglophone Caribbean, including Guyana where Berbice CD [Creole Dutch] speakers use the term *kofitel*. . . . In Lesser Antillean CF [Creole French] "hot cocoa" is *dite kako* (cf. F *du thé* "some tea")' (Holm 1988: 101).

Any gaps in the vocabulary of a pidgin in the early stages of development will be filled in through borrowing or circumlocution. Later, however, at the stage which Mühlhäusler (1986) refers to as **stable** (see below), a pidgin will often have set formulae for describing new concepts. He cites the use in Hiri Motu, an Australian pidgin, of the formula O-V-*gauna* to express that something is a thing for doing something to an object, as in (1986: 171):

Hiri Motu	Gloss	Translation
kuku ania gauna	'smoke eat thing'	pipe
lahi gabua gauna	'fire burn thing'	match
traka abiaisi gauna	'truck raise thing'	jack
godo abia gauna	'voice take thing'	tape recorder

Syntax

A stable pidgin can also use grammatical categories to distinguish between meanings, as in the case of the Tok Pisin aspect marker of completion, *pinis* (1986: 171).

Pidgins and creoles tend to have little or no inflectional morphology (see MORPHO-LOGY, though see Holm 1988: 95–6, for some examples of inflection in creoles), and are often characterized by shifts in morpheme boundaries, so that an English word with plural inflection, for instance *ants*, becomes a morpheme with either plural or singular meaning. In French-based creoles, the article often becomes agglutinated, as in Haitian Creole French, where *moon* is *lalin*, from French *la lune*, 'the moon' (Holm 1988: 97). The general lack in pidgins of bound morphemes greatly facilitates change of, or increase in, the syntactic functions of words (Holm 1988: 103):

Category changes found in Miskito Coast Creole include nouns from adjectives ('He catch *crazy*' 'He became psychotic'), from adverbs ('*afterwards*' 'leftovers'), and from prepositions ('He come from *out*,' i.e. 'from abroad'). Verbs can come from nouns ('He *advantage* her,' i.e. 'took advantage of') as well as adjectives ('She *jealousing* him,' i.e. 'making him jealous').

Romaine (1988: 27–8) notes that agreement markers are dropped in pidgins if they are redundant:

For example, in the following English sentence, plurality is indicated in the noun and its modifier as well as in verb agreement in the third person singular present tense: *Six men come* (cf *One man comes*). The equivalent utterances in Tok Pisin show no variation in the verb form or the noun: *Sikspela man i kam/Wanpela man i kam*. Thus there is a tendency for each grammatical morpheme to be expressed only once in an utterance, and for that morpheme to be expressed by a single form.

Mühlhäusler (1986: 158–9) points out that the pronoun system of a pidgin is typically reduced, as in Chinese Pidgin English which has three pronouns, first, second and third person, but no number distinctions. Most pidgin pronoun systems are not marked for gender or case (Romaine 1988: 27).

Creoles contain a large number of syntactic features which are not found in the European languages that supply much of their vocabularies. Most of them rely on free rather than inflectional morphemes to convey grammatical information, so that typically the verb phrase, for instance, uses particles to indicate tense and aspect, and although these often have the form of auxiliary verbs from the lexical-source language, semantically and syntactically they resemble the substrate language's preverbal tense and aspect markers. If there are no such markers, the simple form of the verb refers to whichever time is specified earlier in the discourse, or by the general context (Holm 1988: 144–50). Studies of creole verb phrases in general have demonstrated the structural similarities of creoles and their structural independence of their superstrate languages, but (Holm 1988: 174)

> it was comparative studies of the creoles' various words for 'be' that unequivocally demonstrated that the creoles were not merely simplified forms of European languages. These studies showed that the creoles were in certain respects more complex than their lexical-source languages in that they made some grammatical and semantic distinctions not made in the European languages. . . . [They] often use quite different words for 'be' depending on whether the following element is a noun phrase, an adjective, or an indication of location.

In addition, a 'highlighter be' exists, the function of which is to bring the following words into focus rather like extra stress on a word in English or like introducing it with *it's* as in *It's Jane who lives here* (*not Elizabeth*) (Holm 1988: 179).

Serial verbs – that is, a series of two or more verbs which are not joined by a conjunction such as *and* or by a complemetizer such as *to*, and which share a subject – are also a common feature of creoles. These often function as adverbs and prepositions in European languages, to indicate (1) directionality, as in Jamaican Creole English, *ron go lef im*, 'run go leave him', meaning 'run away from him'; or (2) instrumentality, as in Ndjuka, *a teke nefi koti a meti*, 'he took knife cut the meat', meaning 'he cut the meat with a knife'. In addition, serial 'give' can be used to mean 'to' or 'for', and serial 'say' can be used to mean 'that' when introducing a quotation or a that-sentence. Serial 'pass'/'surpass'/'exceed' can be used to indicate comparison. Similar construction types are found in many African languages (Holm 1988: 183–90).

The origin of pidgins

One of the most important theories to surface at the first conference on pidgin and creole linguistics in Jamaica in 1959 (see above) was the idea that all or most pidgins or creoles could be traced back to one common source, a Portuguese-based pidgin developed in the fifteenth century in Africa, which was later **relexified**, translated word for word, into the pidgins with other European bases which gave rise to modern creoles. This theory is known as the theory of **monogenesis** (one origin) or **relexification**, and it originates in its modern form in Whinnom's (1956) observation of the strong similarities in terms of vocabulary and structure between Philippine Creole Spanish and Ternate (Indonesian) Creole Portuguese. He hypothesized that a seventeenth-century pidgin version of the latter, itself possibly an imitation of the Mediterranean lingua franca, Sabir, had been transported to the Philippines.

Others noted that many of the features of Philippine Creole Spanish were also present in Caribbean creoles, in Chinese Pidgin English and in Tok Pisin, but that these had been relexified (Taylor 1959, 1960; Thompson 1961; Stewart 1962a; Whinnom 1956; Voorhoeve 1973). Stewart (1962a) pointed out that, while speakers from opposite ends of the Caribbean were able to converse in their French-based creoles, neither would easily be able to converse with a French speaker. So, whereas the similarity of vocabulary could account for some mutual intelligibility, it was in fact syntactic similarity which was the more important factor, and this syntactic similarity pointed to a common origin for the French-based creoles.

In contrast to the monogenesis theory, Hall (1962) argued that pidgins would arise spontaneously wherever and whenever a need for a language of minimal communication arose, and that these could then be creolized. This view is known as the theory of **polygenesis** (multiple origin), and it found support in DeCamp's (1971a: 24) argument that there are 'certain pidgins and creoles which clearly developed without any direct Portuguese influence'. In fact, few creolists would argue for a pure monogenesis theory, but most accept that a certain amount of relexification is an important element in the development of pidgins and creoles, particularly when closely related lexicons, such as Creole Spanish and Creole Portuguese, are involved (Holm 1988: 51–2).

The development of pidgins and creoles

A particularly interesting and provocative explanation for the development and characteristics of creoles has been offered by Bickerton (1974, 1977, 1979, 1981, 1984b), who argues (1984b: 173) 'in favor of a **language bioprogram hypothesis** (henceforth **LBH**) that suggests that the infrastructure of language is specified at least as narrowly as Chomsky has claimed'. The arguments for LBH are drawn from Bickerton's observations about the way in which a creole language develops from a pidgin which is in an early stage of development (1984b: 173):

> The LBH claims that the innovative aspects of creole grammar are inventions

on the part of the first generation of children who have a pidgin as their linguistic input, rather than features transmitted from preexisting languages. The LBH claims, further, that such innovations show a degree of similarity, across wide variety in linguistic background, that is too great to be attributed to chance. Finally, the LBH claims that the most cogent explanation of this similarity is that it derives from the structure of a species-specific program for language, genetically coded and expressed, in ways still largely mysterious, in the structures and modes of operation of the human brain.

The data Bickerton uses to support his hypothesis shows early-stage pidgin to lack any consistent means of marking tense, aspect and modality, to have no consistent system of anaphora, no complex sentences, no systematic way of distinguishing case relations, and variable word order (1984b: 175). Children faced with this type of input impose ways of realizing the missing features, but they do not borrow these realizations from the language which is dominant in their environment, nor from the substrate language(s), and Bickerton concludes that 'the LBH or some variant thereof seems inescapable . . . [and] the LBH carries profound implications for the study of language in general, and for the study of language acquisition and language origins in particular' (1984b: 184).

Bickerton claims (1984b: 178) that the evidence he cites shows the similarities in creoles to arise from 'a single substantive grammar consisting of a very restricted set of categories and processes, which . . . constitute part, or all, of the human species-specific capacity for syntax'. He leans towards the view that the single, substantive grammar does, in fact, constitute *all* of universal grammar, and he thinks that this view is supported by Slobin's (1977, 1982, 1984) notion of a **basic child grammar**, a grammar which is generated by a set of innate operating principles which children use to analyse linguistic input (cf. LANGUAGE ACQUISITION). But Bickerton (1984b: 185) claims that these operating procedures 'fall out from the bioprogram grammar': a child receiving only pidgin input will simply not have enough data for the operating principles alone to work on. In addition, Slobin's work shows that young children consistently violate the rules of their input language, and these violations are consistent with the rules Bickerton proposes for the bioprogram *and* with surface forms found in creoles (1984b: 185).

A number of commentators dispute the reliability of Bickerton's data. For example, Goodman (1984: 193) points out that Bickerton bases his argument entirely on data provided by a number of elderly Japanese, Korean and Filipino immigrants who arrived in Hawaii between 1907 and 1930. At this time, however, it is probable that a pidgin had already developed for use between English seamen and native Hawaiians (Clark 1979). This pidgin was historically linked both to other Pacific pidgin Englishes and to Chinese Pidgin English, with which it shared certain vocabulary and grammatical features. Consequently, it cannot be assumed that 'the pidgin as spoken by 20th-century immigrants from Japan, Korea and the Philippines is in any way characteristic of the incipient stage of Hawaiian Creole English' (Goodman 1984: 193). Goodman (1984: 194) argues that 'many widespread features of creole languages can be accounted for on the basis of similar structures in either the target or the substratal languages coupled with certain universal processes of selection in the context of language contact'. In his response to these arguments, however, Bickerton (1984a) questions the data which Goodman draws on in suggesting that a pidgin already existed in Hawaii when the subjects of Bickerton's study arrived there.

Maratsos (1984: 200) suggests that, judging from Bickerton's data, the input the creole speakers were presented with was too impoverished for them to have developed the creole. The creole, he notices, contains features of English vocabulary and syntax not found in the pidgin, so the creole speakers must have had access to linguistic sources other than the pidgin, and some relexification is likely to have been involved. Again, Bickerton (1984a: 215) counter-questions Maratsos' data.

Lightfoot (1984: 198) and Woolford (1984: 211) both point out that it is, in fact, extremely difficult to establish exactly what input creole speakers in the past may have had from their pidgin and from other sources, and what grammars they arrived at. Furthermore, comparable evidence from early stages of the formation of other pidgins and creoles would be required in order to evaluate Bickerton's claims for Hawaian Creole English, but little evidence of this nature is available (Romaine 1988: 309). Nevertheless, because of the implications for linguistics of Bickerton's hypothesis (if it is correct), his work has had a profound effect on the study of creoles (Holm 1988: 65).

As mentioned above, the creoles that concern Bickerton have arisen from pidgins which are at an early stage of development. The idea of developmental stages through which pidgins and creoles pass – a kind of life-cycle of pidgins and creoles – was present in Schuchardt's work, but found prominence in Hall (1962; Romaine 1988: 115). It has been developed by Todd (1974: 53–69), who distinguishes four phases of the **creolization process**: marginal contact; period of nativization; influence from the dominant language; and the post-creole continuum.

Mühlhäusler (1986: 22) points out that there are, in fact, two factors involved in the development of, and changes in, pidgins and creoles: development or expansion from jargon, through stabilized pidgin

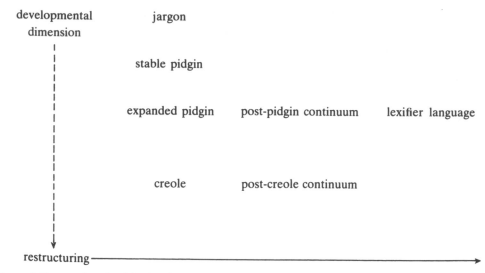

Figure 1 Factors involved in development and change in pidgins and creoles

and expanded pidgin, to creole; and restructuring of either a stabilized pidgin or a creole, through post-pidgin or post-creole, to superimposed language. Restructuring occurs as a result of contact with other languages and does not affect the overall power of the linguistic system; therefore the varieties on this continuum are roughly equal in terms of linguistic complexity. On the developmental continuum, however, the varieties differ in terms of linguistic complexity and in terms of overall referential and non-referential power. He depicts the contrast as shown in Figure 1 (1986: 11).

The notion of a continuum was first borrowed from traditional dialectology (see DIALECTOLOGY) and applied to the gradation of varieties between creole and standard English in the Caribbean by DeCamp (1961; Holm 1988: 55). These varieties are known as **mesolects**. The languages on the left of the mesolects in Figure 1 are called **basilects** and their related standard lexifier languages are called **acrolects**.

The early **jargon** phase is characterized by great variation in different speakers' versions of the jargon, a simple sound system, one- or two-word sentences and a very limited vocabulary (Romaine 1988: 117), with some simple grammar to allow for longer utterances added later (Mühlhäusler 1986: 52). The jargon is used only in restricted contexts, such as trade and recruitment of labour.

In a **stable-pidgin** stage, speakers have arrived at a shared system of rules governing linguistic correctness, so that individual variation is diminished. The process of stabilization of a pidgin is generally characterized by **grammaticalization**, whereby autonomous words become grammatical markers. According to Mühlhäusler (1986), the stabilization stage in the pidgin or creole life-cycle is particularly important, because it is at this stage that the future shape of the language is determined.

An **expanded pidgin** has a complex grammar and a developing word-formation component, and the new constructions are added to the existing simpler grammar in an orderly fashion (Mühlhäusler 1986: 177). It is spoken faster than its precursor, and is used in almost all areas of life (Romaine 1988: 138). Expanded pidgins only arise in linguistically highly heterogeneous areas and typically accompany increased geographic mobility and intertribal contact due to colonial policies. Examples include West African Pidgin English, Tok Pisin (which also exists in creolized varieties), recent varieties of Hiri Motu, Bislama, Solomon Island Pidgin, Sango, and some varieties of Torres Straits Broken (Mühlhäusler 1986: 177):

> The importance of expanded pidgins to linguistic research is twofold. First, they illustrate the capacity of adults to drastically restructure existing linguistic systems; secondly, they call into question such dichotomies as first and second, primary and secondary, native and non-native language.

A creole may arise from a jargon, a stable pidgin or an expanded pidgin. Since these differ in the respects broadly outlined above, the degree of repair needed before they can function as adequate first languages for their speakers is also different. A **creolized jargon** will have undergone repair at all the linguistic levels, to bring about natural phonological, syntactic, semantic and pragmatic systems. In the case of a **creolized stable pidgin**, pragmatic rules will have been arrived at, and the systems already at play in the stable pidgin will have been developed. A creolized extended pidgin differs from its basilect mainly in its stylistic and pragmatic potential (Romaine 1988: 155).

According to Foley (1988), Tok Pisin has undergone two kinds of creolization: urban and rural. An urban environment in Papua New Guinea is highly diverse linguistically, so that the only language an urban child will typically have in common with its peers tends to be Tok Pisin. In rural parts of Papua New Guinea, particularly in the Sepik region, Tok Pisin has been perceived as a high-prestige language offering access to the outside world since at least as long ago as the 1930s (Mead 1931), and parents are therefore very eager that their children, particularly boys, should use

it. Foley (1988) suggests that this parental encouragement of the use of Tok Pisin, together with the fact that the native languages of many communities have very complex morphologies so that bilingual children find it easier to use Tok Pisin, has led to complete creolization of Tok Pisin and the disappearance of a number of the vernaculars.

Once a creole is in existence, it may, according to DeCamp (1971b): continue almost without change, as appears to be the case for Haitian Creole; become extinct; evolve further into a normal language; gradually merge with its acrolect through a process known as **decreolization**. During this process, a creole continuum of varieties between the creole and acrolect will emerge (Holm 1988: 52):

> A creole continuum can evolve in situations in which a creole coexists with its lexical source language and there is social motivation for creole speakers to acquire the standard, so that the speech of individuals takes on features of the latter – or avoids features of the former – to varying degrees. These varieties can be seen as forming a continuum from those farthest from the standard to those closest to it.

Mühlhäusler (1986: 237) defines a **post-pidgin** or **post-creole** variety as

> a pidgin or creole which, after a period of relative linguistic independence, has come under renewed vigorous influence from its original lexifier language, involving the restructuring and/or replacement of earlier lexicon and grammar in favour of patterns from the superimposed 'target' language.

African-American Vernacular English and British Jamaican Creole are often considered post-creole varieties (see, for example, Rickford 1998; Sutcliffe 1992).

K.M.

Suggestions for further reading

Holm, J.A. (1988) *Pidgins and Creoles*, vol. 1, *Theory and Structure*, Cambridge: Cambridge University Press.

Mühlhäusler, P. (1986) *Pidgin and Creole Linguistics*, Oxford: Basil Blackwell.

Romaine, S. (1988) *Pidgin and Creole Languages*, London and New York: Longman.

Critical linguistics/critical discourse analysis

The term **critical linguistics** was first used in its currently accepted sense in 1979, as the title of the synoptic and programmatic concluding chapter of *Language and Control* by Fowler, Hodge, Kress and Trew, a group of colleagues at that time working at the University of East Anglia, Norwich. The label (or, increasingly, **critical discourse analysis** or **CDA**) is now used by increasing numbers of social scientists – particularly sociologists, political scientists, students of the media and sociolinguists – to designate analytic work on real texts of the kind advocated and illustrated in that book.

Critical linguistics is a socially directed application of linguistic analysis, using chiefly concepts and methods associated with the 'systemic-functional' linguistics developed by M.A.K. Halliday (see FUNCTIONALIST LINGUISTICS; SYSTEMIC-FUNCTIONAL GRAMMAR); its basic claims are that all linguistic usage encodes ideological patterns or discursive structures which *mediate* representations of the world in language; that different usages (e.g. different sociolinguistic varieties or lexical choices or syntactic paraphrases) encode different ideologies, resulting from their different situations and purposes; and that by these means language works as a social practice – it is not, as traditional linguistics claims, a transparent medium for communication about an objective world, nor is it a reflection of a stable social structure, but it promulgates a set of versions of reality and thereby works as a constantly operative part of social processes.

Critical linguistics proposes that analysis using appropriate linguistic tools, and referring to relevant historical and social contexts, can bring ideology (normally hidden through the habitualization of discourse) to the surface for inspection. In this way, critical linguistics can shed light on social and political processes. Promising revelation through an analytic technique – indeed, quite a simple set of tools – critical linguistics has been welcomed by a variety of workers concerned with discourse.

But it must also be conceded that the model is controversial. It is faulted by its critics within the academic institution of linguistics because it challenges some central established principles in the dominant schools of the subject; and by others, including people sympathetic to the aims of the venture, because it employs some notoriously difficult concepts such as 'ideology' and 'function' and is still in the process of clarifying them. And, less rationally, critical linguistics is resisted in some quarters because its practitioners have made no bones about their socialist motives and have doggedly subjected the dominant discourses of authoritarianism, capitalism and militarism to linguistic critique.

Note, however, that the words 'critical' and 'critique' do not essentially carry the negative connotations of carping and complaint that seem to inhabit their popular usage – 'You're always being critical... Why can't you be constructive for once?' 'Critical' linguistics is simply a linguistics that seeks to understand the relationships between ideas and their social conditions of possible existence (see Connerton 1976: Introduction).

To say that critical linguistics is 'an application of linguistic analysis' is to offer too superficial a characterization. Two qualifications need to be entered at this point. First, critical linguistics is not an automatic hermeneutic procedure that would allow one to identify linguistic structure (passive voice, say) and read off ideological or social significance from it. There is no invariant relationship between textual structure and its social meanings – the latter are dependent on the contexts in which the former occurs and the purposes for which it is used. Passives have quite different discourse functions in scientific writing and in newspaper headlines (and a variety of functions within each of these, particularly the latter). In fact, the critical linguist cannot have any idea of the discursive meaning of a piece of language unless s/he possesses rich and accurate intuitions and understanding of context, function and relevant social relations. Then the analysis will be plausible to the extent that this understanding of context is made explicit, and documented. It is necessary to insist that critical linguistics is an *historical* discipline, which requires high standards of documentation and argumentation. It has to be admitted that early work within this model tended to be cavalier about these historical requirements, choosing familiar types of contemporary texts and relying on the analyst's and her/his reader's intuitions to vouch for the suggested interpretation.

The second reason why we need to elaborate on 'an application of linguistic analysis' is that not any model of linguistic analysis will do the job: only a model with some very specific assumptions and procedures can be the basis for critical linguistics. This observation is perhaps surprising in view of the methodological pluralism of critical linguists. Believing, rightly, that any element of linguistic structure, from phonemes to semantic schemata, can carry ideological significance, practitioners have been happy to borrow 'modality' from

Halliday, 'transformation' from Chomsky, 'speech act' from Searle, all in the course of one analysis. The point is that different models are good at describing different aspects of linguistic structure, and it would be absurd to spurn the insights that colleagues working in various frameworks have made available.

Some basic assumptions of critical linguistics may now be listed. It will be evident that the major inspiration behind the model is the 'functional' linguistics of M.A.K. Halliday, and that the critical model is in several ways crucially at odds with mainstream linguistics both in its traditional and its contemporary modes. Other intellectual sources for critical linguistics, more prominent in recent years as scholars have worked to make the model less 'narrowly linguistic', more integrated with general theories of society and ideology, include French psychoanalytic, structuralist and poststructuralist theories for their accounts of discourse, intertextuality and the subject (see Kress 1985; Threadgold 1986).

The **functional** approach: Halliday (1970: 142) claims that 'The particular form taken by the grammatical system of language is closely related to the social and personal needs that language is required to serve.' This is diametrically opposed to the Chomskyan assertion that linguistic form is a chance selection from the universal structural possibilities that are genetically present in, and available to, each infant. It is, of course, quite likely that what counts as a human language is formally constrained in the way Chomsky suggests, and that some structures may be universally present because of biological reasons. The theory of **natural semantics**, for example, gives plausible arguments to the effect that concepts like 'red', 'circle' and 'up' are lexicalized in all languages studied, or can be easily learned through made-up words, because they reflect the natural biological characteristics of human beings (colour vision, vertical posture, etc.). But such explanations can account for only a minute portion of the vocabulary of a language. If we think about a selection of other words – say *AIDS, macho, interface, privatization* – it will be immediately clear that, to say anything interesting about these words, we need to refer to their social origins and uses. As for syntax, the interesting questions for the critical linguist concern the social functions of variation rather than the universal biological constraints on possible structures.

Halliday brings the functional theory closer to the details of language by proposing three **metafunctions**: the ideational, the interpersonal and the textual. The **ideational function** is crucial to the theory of critical linguistics. This relates to traditional conceptions of language, since Halliday admits that it is about the expression of content. A disabling defect of conventional theories of representation was that 'content', the world being communicated about, was supposed to be a fixed objective reality represented neutrally through the transparent medium of language. Halliday, however (who refers to Whorf; see LINGUISTIC RELATIVITY), affirms that language 'lends structure to experience'. The ideational component, through structural mechanisms such as lexical categorization, transitivity, co-ordination, constitutes a structured grid through which a speaker's (that is to say, a society's, a text's, a register's) view of the world is mediated. Ideational structure has a dialectical relationship with social structure (see below), both reflecting it and influencing it. This element of grammar has so far been the chief interest of critical linguists, who have found in it the linguistic key to the notion that a text, under social pressures, offers a mediated, partial, interpretation of the objective reality of which it claims to speak.

Ideational structure is, then, neither an autonomous structure within language (as, for example, the structure of the lexicon would be in generative linguistics), nor a predetermined reflection of a fixed reality, but an arbitrary, variable version of the world, which can be understood only in relation to social contexts and purposes. Critical linguistics is still in the process of clarifying the nature of the concept and its contextual relations. The meanings in some sense pre-exist language, yet language is their primary mode of materialization and management. Think about *AIDS* – the word is an acronymic label for a medical condition (acquired immune deficiency syndrome, caused by a virus transmitted through blood, semen and vaginal fluid, and thus easily transmitted during sexual intercourse), which existed before the label was devised. The acronym became very current in the 1980s – its never being out of the news being a handy implement for managing public consciousness, the focus for discourses on morality, on education, on medical resources. AIDS is not simply a physical condition in some individuals; it is also (helped by language) a concept in society, part of our way of perceiving and judging the contemporary situation.

Halliday's notion of **language as social semiotic** (see Halliday 1978) – simultaneously socially derived and having socially instrumental meanings – is one way of understanding these relationships; it is, for example, the model being investigated by recent Australian linguistic critics and semioticians such as Threadgold and Thibault, who find the original critical-linguistic model too closely preoccupied with linguistic structure. The East Anglians, as the authors of *Language and Control* and their associates have come to be called, foregrounded the term **ideology**: see Kress and Hodge (1979), or Trew's chapters in *Language and Control* (Fowler *et al.* 1979), where he speaks cautiously of 'theory or ideology' and has in mind a Foucauldian conception of **discourse**.

The term *ideology* has too many misleading senses and reverberations to be discussed in detail here, but at least one should say that it is to be understood in a positive, not a negative, sense. By 'ideology' critical linguists do not mean a set of ideas which are false, beliefs which betray a 'distorted consciousness' and are therefore politically undesirable. More pertinent is a neutral kind of definition that relates to the ways in which people order and justify their lives: 'the sum of the ways in which people both live and represent to themselves their relationship to the conditions of their existence' (Belsey 1980: 42). Compare Kress's use of the much more manageable word 'discourse' (following Foucault) in an effort to understand the social nature of meanings (Kress 1985: 67):

> Discourses are systematically-organised sets of statements which give expression to the meanings and values of an institution. Beyond that, they define, describe and delimit what it is possible to say and not possible to say . . . with respect to the area of concern of that institution, whether marginally or centrally.

A priority in critical linguistics is to agree on some ways of formally analysing or representing these 'sets of statements'. Available models exist in discourse analysis, structuralism and psychology: for example, the 'general propositions' of Labov and Fanshel, Grice's 'conventional implicatures', Barthes's 'referential code' and, most promisingly, the various kinds of 'schemata', such as Minsky's 'frames', that have been proposed in cognitive psychology.

The form of the title of Kress's book (1985), which because of our preconceptions may be perceived as cumbersome, is meant to capture another principle of critical linguistics: we must resist theorizing 'language' and 'society' as separate entities. The discourse of the institution of linguistics puts great pressure on us to do so, as can be seen from dichotomous book titles such as *Language and Society*, *Language and Social Context*, *Language and Social Behaviour*.

Conventional sociolinguistics (e.g. Labov, Trudgill) presents 'language' and 'society' as two independent phenomena which can be separately described and quantified; variations in language (e.g. whether /r/ occurs or does not occur after a vowel and before a consonant, and with what frequency) can be observed to *correlate* with variations in society (e.g. socioeconomic class, sex, age).

But 'correlation', like 'reflection', is too weak an account of the relationship. Sociolinguistic variation is to be regarded as functional rather than merely fortuitous. This can already be seen in Labov's and Trudgill's own studies: hypercorrection and hypocorrection, for instance, do not simply reflect subjects' social situations, but they express an intention to use language to change their situations. In such cases language can be seen as an intervention in social processes. Critical linguistics invites a view of language which makes 'intervention' a general principle: language is a **social practice**, one of the mechanisms through which society reproduces and regulates itself. Thus language is 'in' rather than 'alongside' society. It is the aim of critical linguistics to understand these dialectical processes, both as a theoretical understanding that involves a redefinition of linguistics, and also as a matter of practical analysis, the close reading of discourse within history (R.F.).

The term 'critical discourse analysis' is now increasingly used in preference to 'critical linguistics'. The terminological change reflects an increasing interdisciplinarity, an increasing concern to connect critical language analysis with the concerns of social theory and social scientific research. This development is linked with a focus on social change, and with change in language and other forms of semiosis as a significant dimension of social change (Fairclough 1992b).

Critical discourse analysis draws upon a variety of theoretical sources, including

Marxist-based critical theory, and post-structuralist and postmodernist theory. While the contemporary emphasis on 'discourse' has largely been inspired by the latter, critical discourse analysts have also followed contemporary critical theorists who attempt to redefine and renew critical theory through an engagement with and selective appropriation of poststructuralist and postmodern positions, for instance in giving greater emphasis to social difference and the contingency and openness of the social (Chouliaraki and Fairclough 1999).

At the same time, there is an increasing tendency explicitly to link work in critical discourse analysis with social research and theorizing on change in contemporary social life (e.g. the work of Jürgen Habermas, Pierre Bourdieu and Basil Bernstein). There is a case for arguing that contemporary social change based upon the shift to a new 'global' economic order entails a greater salience for language and other forms of semiosis in social life (e.g. the 'knowledge-based' economy is also a discourse-based economy, in which a crucial part is played by the production and circulation of especially expert discourses and their operationalization in new practices and technologies). This suggests that critical discourse analysis can make an important contribution to research on changing social life, and growing interest in CDA in areas such as urban studies, public policy research and development studies suggests that this potential is being recognized.

In focusing upon change in discourse as part of wider social change, CDA has drawn upon Bakhtinian views of language, and especially ideas of intertextuality and interdiscursivity. These provide the basis for analysis of texts and interactions which focuses upon shifting articulations of genres, discourses and styles, which on the one hand are realized linguistically in heterogeneities of form and meaning, and on the other hand can be seen as the linguistic/ semiotic 'moment' (in a dialectical theory of discourse) of ongoing social change.

But there are a number of different approaches within critical discourse analysis, partly reflecting different research topics, but also theoretical differences (*Discourse and Society* 1993; Fairclough and Wodak 1998; van Dijk 1993; Wodak 1996). For instance, van Dijk's socio-cognitive approach to discourse has emphasized the cognitive interface between discourse structures and social structures, in his empirical work on racism and his more recent theoretical work on ideology. Wodak's discourse-historical approach, also applied most notably in studies of racist and anti-Semitic discourse, is particularly oriented to locating discourse within its socio-historical background.

N.F.

Suggestions for further reading

Chilton, P. (ed.) (1985) *Language and the Nuclear Arms Debate: Nukespeak Today*, London and Dover, NH: Frances Pinter.

Chouliaraki, L. and Fairclough, N. (1999) *Discourse in Late Modernity: Rethinking Critical Discourse Analysis*, Edinburgh: Edinburgh University Press.

Discourse and Society (1993) 4(2) (special issue on critical discourse analysis).

Fairclough, N. (1992a) *Discourse and Social Change*, Cambridge: Polity Press.

—— and Wodak, R. (1997) 'Critical discourse analysis', in T. van Dijk (ed.) *Discourse as Social Interaction*, London: Sage.

Fowler, R., Hodge, R., Kress, G. and Trew, T. (1979) *Language and Control*, London: Routledge & Kegan Paul.

Kress, G. (1985) *Linguistic Processes in Sociocultural Practice*, Geelong, Australia: Deakin University Press; 2nd edition 1989, Oxford: Oxford University Press.

Threadgold, T. (1986) 'Semiotics – ideology – language', in T. Threadgold, E.A. Grosz, G. Kress and M.A.K. Halliday (eds) *Semiotics, Ideology, Language* (Sydney Studies in Society and Culture, no. 3), Sydney: Sydney Association for Studies in Society and Culture: 15–60.

van Dijk, T. (1993) *Discourse and Elite Racism*, London: Sage.

Wodak, R. (1996) *Disorders of Discourse*, London: Longman.

D

Dialectology

Introduction

Dialectology is the study of dialects – both descriptive and theoretical – and those engaged in this study are known as **dialectologists**. Interpreting the term 'dialect' broadly to mean 'variety of language' (but see below), this means that it is concerned with analysing and describing related language varieties, particularly in respect of their salient differences and similarities. It is also concerned with developing theoretical frameworks for such analysis and description, and for arriving at generalizations and explanatory hypotheses about the nature of linguistic differentiation and variation.

Like most branches of linguistics, dialectology began to assume its modern form in the nineteenth century. It was, however, preceded by a long and widespread tradition of **folk linguistics** – anecdotal and somewhat unsystematic discussion of regionalisms and variation in usage. This tradition has continued, with the result that dialectology (in common with the study of grammar) has to deal with both theoretical and practical issues in respect of which folk-linguistic concepts and beliefs have had, and continue to have, considerable currency. It is therefore important to distinguish at the outset between the views and definitions adopted by academic dialectologists and those espoused by lay commentators.

Most crucially, the key term 'dialect' itself has various non-technical meanings. Some of these are mutually incompatible and most of them are also implicated in partisan, often negative, attitudes to non-standard speech; these meanings are usually rejected or seriously modified by dialectologists.

- In popular usage, the term **dialect** usually refers to a geographical variety of a language, e.g., (the) Lancashire dialect (of English). Dialectologists, however, have increasingly used the term to refer to any user-defined variety; that is, any variety associated with speakers of a given type, whether geographically or otherwise defined, e.g. members of a given social class, males/females, people of shared ethnic background, etc. One can thus speak of a 'middle-class dialect', 'working-class dialect', etc., where 'dialect' must be distinguished from register (see FUNCTIONALIST LINGUISTICS). Further, the speech of any individual or homogeneous group can be characterized on many dimensions relating to different non-linguistic factors – different characterizations will be relevant for different purposes, and two or more dimensions may be combined in the characterization (e.g. 'middle-class Lancashire dialect').

The amount of emphasis placed on particular non-linguistic features of this kind has varied from period to period, and from school to school. **Generativist** work on language variation has, in addition, used the term 'dialect' to refer to any variety or variety feature not shared by all speakers of a language, whether or not use of such a feature correlates with any non-linguistic factor; in cases where there is no such correlation, one may speak of **randomly distributed dialects**.

- Forms of speech which are, or are believed to be, unwritten, unstandardized, and/or associated with groups lacking in prestige, formal education, etc., or culturally subordinated to other groups, are often described as **dialects**, by contrast with standardized, prestigious varieties (described as 'languages'). For instance, in popular usage, 'rural Yorkshire dialect' may be contrasted with 'the English language', and 'the dialects of Southern India' with 'the Tamil language'; linguists, however, would tend to make the distinction between the first terms in each pair and 'Standard English' and 'Classical or Standard Tamil' respectively. Most dialectologists hold that there is no correlation between linguistic type or structure and suitability for adoption as a standard, written or prestigious variety, and regard this distinction as placing undue weight on these essentially accidental social properties of varieties; although they would accept that prolonged and marked differences of status can affect structure and, in particular, speakers' perceptions of the relevant varieties and their ability to intuit accurately about them. Dialectologists would thus avoid using the terms 'dialect' and 'language' in this way, and most would describe standard varieties as being dialects to the same degree as non-standard varieties, despite their differences in status.
- Dialects are also often perceived as individually discrete units, collectively comprising the equally discrete languages of which they are dialects. This interpretation of the distinction is in fact incompatible with that outlined above – according to which languages and dialects are of necessity separate entities – but both are sometimes held simultaneously, often without any real synthesis; for instance, Chinese speakers, especially in Southeast Asia, tend to think of Mandarin both as 'the Chinese language' and as one variety of it, although with a special status, and to think of the 'dialects', such as Hokkien, as dialects of Chinese, but also as separate from and inferior to Mandarin in its guise as Chinese. In contrast, dialectologists would argue that neither dialects nor even languages themselves are really discrete. Dialects can be distinguished only in terms of differences in particular variable features, but these are liable to display differently situated boundaries (isoglosses; see below); in any event, close to a boundary, geographical or social, there is much fluctuation even within the usage of individual speakers. Furthermore, the transition between two languages which are geographical neighbours, particularly when they are genetically related languages (see HISTORICAL LINGUISTICS) or have been subject to prolonged contact, is, again, gradual, piecemeal and massively variable (e.g. Dutch and German). Attempts to use such criteria as mutual intelligibility in order to determine the location of the boundaries between languages therefore founder on serious objections. The distinction between dialect and language, and hence this kind of definition of dialect, cannot, it seems, be sustained in any rigorous interpretation. Both terms are therefore often used merely as shorthand expressions for any 'bundles' of variant forms that are sufficiently large/ closely associated, and have roughly coinciding boundaries.

Other popular terms are also used differently by dialectologists. The well-known term **accent** is generally used in the field in the strict sense of a variety differing relevantly from others only in phonological respects, not in grammar or lexis. There is some dispute as to just how 'phonological respects' should be defined for this purpose; thus some unpredictable phonological differences such as that between standard /brɪʤ/ and Yorkshire dialect /brɪg/ would traditionally be regarded as accent differences only, but are now regarded, by some scholars, as so gross that they must count as differences in dialect. However, a clear case of accent difference only might involve an American speaker who pronounces the *r* in *car*, and an English speaker who does not; whereas the difference between American *underpass* and British *subway* is one of dialect proper. Similarly, the term **vernacular**, with a variety of popular meanings, has also been used in the literature in a more technical sense. For instance, 'vernacular' may be used non-technically to refer to the current local language of a region as opposed to, e.g. classical or liturgical languages, or more generally to 'popular usage' of an informal, not to say uneducated, kind. It has been used more technically in the field, to refer to the most casual style of speech produced by speakers or, more specifically, by the least standardized speakers.

Review of the development of the subject over the last century

Nineteenth-century dialectology was predominantly geographical – linguistic thought was not then socially oriented – and developed along with the related disciplines of phonetics and historical linguistics (descriptive and theoretical), most notably in Germany in the period after 1876. It rapidly spread to other areas, and in the United Kingdom the two major pioneering works appeared in 1889 (Ellis) and 1905 (Wright), the latter being associated with the English Dialect Society, founded in 1873. Concern with the history of the relevant forms encouraged a general historical bias: interest in the origin in medieval languages of contemporary forms perceived in isolation, rather than in their contemporary patterning. The description of current usage was in any case hampered by the absence of any structuralist theory, most obviously phoneme theory.

For various reasons, to be outlined below, the subject was slow to assimilate structuralist ideas once these were developed, and this and the historical bias continued to affect the field until relatively recently. Treatment of phonology has suffered particularly badly from these constraints, though the focus on phonetic facts for their own sake has sometimes been regarded subsequently as more helpful than premature or theory-laden guesses at the underlying system.

Another early focus of interest, also now generally abandoned, was the search for **pure** dialect, i.e. the supposedly regular and systematic form of speech produced by those remote from standardizing influences. This was sought both with a view to recording it before it vanished in the face of modern developments in transport, education, media, etc. and in the belief that it was of greater theoretical interest than more mainstream usage, which was thought corrupt. The ensuing methodology involved the deliberate selection of **norms** – non-mobile, old, rural males, mostly uneducated – regardless of whether such speakers were really representative of their communities' current usage. As a result of changed attitudes to these and other issues, theoretical and methodological priorities are nowadays rather different, and older works – as well as being difficult to interpret – are widely perceived as unhelpful in approach and presentation, despite their undoubted usefulness in terms of tracing recent historical developments. This affects work researched as recently as the 1960s and some material published during the 1970s and early 1980s. A gradual shift of interest from phonology, lexis and morphology to syntax – part of a general trend in linguistics – also reduces the relevance of older publications.

German scholars such as Georg Wenker and Ferdinand Wrede pioneered the concept of a dialect atlas in the 1870s (see also LANGUAGE SURVEYS). They developed extensive frameworks for fieldwork methodology and analysis, but were hindered by the sheer scale and time-consuming nature of such enterprises, and many of the results of their work were never published. The German method concentrated on indirect postal surveys, aimed at wide geographical coverage and at the elicitation, through amateur fieldworkers acting in a voluntary capacity, of dialect versions of standard lexical, grammatical and phonological features.

Jules Gilliéron, who took on the task of surveying French dialects in 1897, employed the alternative direct approach, involving face-to-face interviews using a single, trained fieldworker. He thereby reduced the coverage severely, but obtained more complete and more reliable results in each locality. Major surveys of the Italian-speaking area of Europe and, later, of North American regions (Kenyon 1930; Thomas 1958; Kurath and McDavid 1961, among many others; see Baugh and Cable 1978: 368–9 for an extensive list) were carried out by scholars trained in this tradition, although multiple fieldworkers gradually became the norm. The Survey of English Dialects, developed by Eugen Dieth and Harold Orton and run from Leeds University, also used this method, and the form of questionnaire adopted in that study has been widely imitated in more traditional works on specific dialect areas.

Other surveys, such as the ongoing Linguistic Survey of Scotland, have employed both types of technique. Smaller-scale studies have continued to select approaches according to their own requirements and resources, and it is now generally accepted that each method has its advantages and drawbacks (e.g. indirect methods work much better for lexis, direct for phonology).

Atlases and more specific findings based on these surveys have often been used in support of positions adopted relative to contemporary theoretical issues. In particular, the early work was interpreted both by adherents and opponents of the **Neogrammarian Principle** (see HISTORICAL LINGUISTICS) as supporting their respective views. This issue has now been largely superseded, but current disputes within variation theory (see below) are conducted using similar evidence. Much often depends on the method of presentation chosen; where maps are used, for instance, a favourite device has been the **isogloss**, a line on the map supposedly dividing from each other areas where different variant forms occur. Isoglosses represent, of course, considerable idealizations, especially where non-geographical factors are not taken into account, and some of the debates on their significance depend heavily on the amount of information reduced to a single line in each case, and on the internal complexity of this information. The same applies to the statistical presentations of recent **urban dialectology** (Labov 1966).

The rise of **structural linguistics** in the early twentieth century had relatively little impact on dialectology at first, owing to the ensuing separation of synchronic and diachronic studies, and dialectology's links with the diachronic side. As a result, emphasis on synchronic systems (phoneme inventory, etc.; see PHONEMICS) did not become usual in dialect studies until the 1950s. Studies commenced before this time are typically not informed by these notions, which were at first much more current in American than in European dialectological circles (though see LANGUAGE SURVEYS on the **Linguistic Survey of Scotland**).

The rejuvenation of the subject proceeded at a rapid pace from around 1960, and some structuralist tenets were themselves quickly challenged, in particular the tendency to dismiss **residual variability** in a dialect (that is, variability which still remains to be explained after a full analysis in terms of intralinguistic conditioning factors) as **free variation**. Whether this occurred across a community or within the speech of an individual, it was revealed to be highly structured and often predictable, to some extent, statistically at least, in terms of intralinguistic constraints and also the effects of non-linguistic factors.

Further changes were prompted by the criticisms made by sociologically aware commentators such as Pickford (1956). This led to a reappraisal of research methodology, including both informant selection and interview design and technique. After a series of publications in the field of structural dialectology in the mid- to late 1950s (Weinreich 1954; Moulton 1960), the 1960s saw the development of a new tradition based on attempts to obtain more natural usage than that typical of questionnaire responses, on statistically sound sampling of the relevant populations and on generativist formalism and concepts. William Labov pioneered this type of work in the USA, starting in the early 1960s.

Since then the new urban dialectology movement, which has concentrated largely on the hitherto-neglected dialects of cities, has developed in many forms both in the USA and elsewhere, including the United Kingdom and the rest of Europe. Many of Labov's original ideas have been, in turn, seriously modified by himself and by others, though the early work in the tradition, including Peter Trudgill's (1974a) influential emulation of Labov's New York City study in Norwich, UK, did follow Labov closely. In the USA, and to some extent elsewhere, formalization of the numerical aspects of variation was pursued during the 1970s (Cedergren and Sankoff 1974),

and a rival tradition of analysis developed under the influence of Bailey (1973) and Bickerton (1971), describing itself as the **dynamic paradigm**, in contrast with Labov's **quantitative paradigm**. This tradition differed sharply from Labovian ideas on such issues as the range of possible forms of dialect grammars, the scope of the variation to be found in rigorously defined combinations of environments such as one speaker in one style (the **inherent-variation debate**), and the relationship between variation and change. For instance, advocates of the dynamic paradigm claimed, against Labov's position, that, if all relevant linguistic and non-linguistic factors are taken into account, there is *no* remaining variability (inherent variation) – unless change is actually in progress at the relevant point in the system – and that any such variability is in fact an effect, rather than a partial cause, of change. The studies conducted within the dynamic paradigm were, at least at first, mainly concerned with **post-creole continua** (see CREOLES AND PIDGINS), and it is possible to argue that in these situations the facts are typically very different: the dynamic paradigm, positing as it does a smaller range of possible patterns, is more successful in modelling situations of this kind, where the structure of the variability present often seems to be simpler than in the areas studied by Labov and other adherents of his position.

Other studies, conducted in areas where the pattern of **norms** (forms perceived as suitable for emulation) is much more complex than in New York City, have produced results leading their authors to reject many of Labov's views, in particular his views on attitudinal factors and their consequences for informant behaviour. The best known such studies have been carried out in northern Britain, most notably in Belfast by the Milroys (commencing around 1980), who have also extended changes in methodology originally made by Labov himself – there has been a move away from formal interviews towards attempts to obtain still more natural usage and a renewed interest in fieldwork technique (see FIELD METHODS) and the role of the interviewer or observer. In addition, the 1980s and 1990s saw the development of 'interactionist' models and analyses of linguistic variability, in which mere correlation of linguistic and non-linguistic phenomena has a more marginal role and may indeed be seen as unduly deterministic; the focus is upon the active role of conversational participants (or indeed of monologuers) in constructing their identities (often collaboratively) through the culturally significant choices they make from the range of variants available. There has also been much discussion of the concept of the vernacular and of its theoretical significance. Associated with both these developments has been a tendency (pioneered especially by Suzanne Romaine) to criticize as oversimplified the more general assumptions harboured in the Labovian tradition about the relative significance of various non-linguistic factors and the structure of variation. An early attempt to remedy these problems had previously been made by those responsible for the Tyneside Linguistic Survey, a long-term project based in Newcastle, UK.

More recent dialectological work of all kinds has also been marked by the ever more extensive use of computers (including computerized methods of analysis of variation such as Sankoff's VARBRUL program) and a concern with the reliability of statistics and with the examination of a wide range of non-linguistic factors. But, despite all these and other innovations, the debt of all workers in this field to Labov remains and is widely acknowledged.

Generative dialectology was another development of the 1960s; it is concerned neither with data collection nor with explanation of patterns of usage, but, rather, with providing formal descriptions of variation – mostly phonological – within some form of the generativist paradigm. The subject is closely linked with generative phonology (and syntax) and with applications of these techniques of analysis to historical phenomena and, true to this tradition, it has displayed a tendency to posit recapitulation of historical developments in the minds of current speakers. For instance, the events of the **Great Vowel Shift** (see HISTORICAL LINGUISTICS), by which the long monophthongs of English shifted one 'notch' in tongue height in early modern times, are recapitulated in the derivation of the relevant words, as posited in this tradition – the **underlying representations** preserve pre-shift relationships.

In the best studies, the evidence for this sort of procedure has been synchronic and independent of the known history of the forms. Within its limited goals, generative dialectology has been successful – Newton's (1972) work on Modern Greek dialects stands out – but the interest of dialectologists as such seems to have moved elsewhere, and generative dialectology has increasingly been practised by generativists themselves rather than within the field. Its failure to offer explanations, its conceptualizing of dialect features as invariant within each discrete 'dialect' and its asocial approach have not endeared it to empiricist dialectologists or theoretical sociolinguists.

Since the mid- to late 1960s, many young scholars have, however, found the new urban dialectological enterprise attractive – in part, perhaps, because it is openly concerned with widely spoken, modern varieties, rather than with obsolescent and obscure forms of speech, and because this leads it to findings of unprecedented practical relevance. Dialect differences, resulting misunderstandings and sheer prejudice are important factors for the success and failure of educational systems and programmes, and views of all kinds on how these problems should be addressed are frequently espoused with great vigour, both by linguists and teachers and by members of the general public. It is clear that the vastly increased amount of information about the linguistic facts that is now available ought to form part of the basis for any discussion of these issues. Trudgill (1975) and others have repeatedly used these facts to suggest that certain educational policies – those which can be seen to be based on folk-linguistic attitudes and which are hostile to non-standard usage – should be radically revised (see also LANGUAGE AND EDUCATION).

Another attraction of the field for young scholars lies in its theoretical orientation. There is a marked contrast with the heavily descriptive flavour of much earlier dialect study, the findings of which seem to many to be excessively concerned with minutiae lacking in general relevance – particularly in the area of lexis. As mentioned above, urban dialectologists have engaged in intense theoretical debate within their own field, and their work has also led to a renewal of theoretical activity within historical linguistics, itself experiencing a considerable revival. However, the early adherence of the Labovian tradition to the dominant generativist paradigm of the time has been replaced by a more eclectic, often sceptical, approach to current synchronic linguistic theory, and to an increasingly voiced belief that the synchronic/diachronic distinction has itself been interpreted too rigorously.

Moreover, the application to linguistics of findings in theoretical human geography has led to a fresh attack on specifically geographical aspects of variation and diffusion, and to the rediscovery of much fascinating data collected earlier. One of the best instances of this has been the **geolinguistic** work of Trudgill and others during the 1980s and 1990s on the diffusion of innovations from urban centres such as London, Chicago and centres in Norway. Despite problems of methodology and interpretation (see above), comparison of older and newer findings is frequently highly illuminating and, even where only current data are available, techniques for the study of the diffusion of forms and ensuing patterns are being developed. In addition, purely descriptive studies, now more sophisticated in character than the earlier studies, continue to be undertaken.

M.Nk

Suggestions for further reading

Chambers, J.K. and Trudgill, P. (1980) *Dialectology*, Cambridge: Cambridge University Press; 2nd edition 1998.
Petyt, K.M. (1980) *The Study of Dialect*, London: Audré Deutsch.
Trudgill, P. (1990) *The Dialects of England*, Oxford: Basil Blackwell.

Discourse analysis and conversation analysis

Discourse analysis

Discourse has become a core concept across the humanities and social sciences, well beyond the discipline of linguistics itself. The origins of discourse analysis are to be found not only in linguistics and the philosophy of language, but also in social anthropology and theoretical sociology. The unifying insight is that discourse organizes important aspects of our social lives, whether in the moment-to-moment social interchanges of everyday talk or, more abstractly, in the beliefs, understandings and principles ('discourses') that structure our lives. Discourse analysis is therefore the multi-layered attempt to observe, unravel and critique these acts of construction. The theoretical position it adopts can itself be called '**constructivist**' because it makes the radical claim that the realities we take to define our social circumstances, and our selves within them, are the product of linguistic processes (Shotter and Gergen 1989).

The term 'discourse analysis' was first employed by Zellig Harris as the name for 'a method for the analysis of connected speech (or writing)' (Harris 1952: 1), for 'continuing descriptive linguistics beyond the limits of a single sentence at a time' and for 'correlating "culture" and language' (Harris 1952: 2), and some early studies approached well-defined speech events, such as classroom interaction and doctor – patient interviews, with particular grammatical models in mind. For example, Sinclair and Coulthard (1975) used a system of analysis based on the 1961 version of Halliday's grammar (see SYSTEMIC-FUNCTIONAL GRAMMAR) to analyse teacher–pupil interaction in order to begin to answer such questions as (Sinclair and Coulthard 1975: 4):

> how are successive utterances related; who controls the discourse; how does he do it; how, if at all, do other participants take control; how do the roles of speaker and listener pass from one participant to another; how are new topics introduced and old ones ended; what linguistic evidence is there for discourse units larger than the utterance?

See Coulthard (1977/1985) for examples of studies in this tradition.

In a more sociologically oriented tradition of discourse analysis, the theoretical work of Foucault (1972, 1977) and of Pêcheux (1982) has been influential in introducing a link between discourse and ideology. Pêcheux stresses how any one particular discourse or 'discursive formation' stands, at the level of social organization, in conflict with other discourses. He gives us a theory of how societies are organized through their ideological struggles, and how particular groups (e.g. social-class groups or gender groups) will be either more or less privileged in their access to particular discourse networks.

Critical discourse analysis has combined both these traditions by applying the ideologically charged interpretations to the analysis of textual data (see CRITICAL LINGUISTICS/CRITICAL DISCOURSE ANALYSIS). Some of this work is concerned with analysing the changes taking place in contemporary life, at least in the world's most affluent and 'developed' societies. Here, social life and its language have qualities distinguishing them quite markedly from those of the 'modern' industrial, pre-World War II period. Discourse analysts investigate the discursive shifts that mark the transition into '**Late**' or '**High Modernity**' (Giddens 1991) – what is more generally referred to as **postmodernity**. Fairclough (1992b, 1995) refers to parts of this phenomenon as the 'technologization' and 'consumerization' of discourse in **post-Fordist societies** (since the beginning of mass production of motor cars and similar industrial developments). Critical discourse analysis offers a means of exposing or deconstructing the social practices that constitute 'social structure' and what we might call the conventional meaning structures of social life. It is a sort of forensic activity, with a libertarian political slant. The motivation for doing this sort of discourse analysis is very often a concern about the opaque patterns of social inequality and the perpetuation of power relationships, either between individuals or between social groups, difficult though it is to prejudge moral correctness in many cases.

A cornerstone of discourse analysis is the conviction that language is both a product and a producer of the values and beliefs of the society in which it operates. Thus, the construction of any message designed to represent some reality necessarily entails decisions about which aspects of that reality to include, and then about how to arrange them. Each of the selections made in the construction of a message carries its share of these ingrained values, so that the reality represented is simultaneously socially constructed (Hodge and Kress 1993; Fowler *et al.* 1979; van Dijk 1993; Chouliaraki and Fairclough 1999). In this sense, critical discourse analysis follows, broadly, the Whorfian position on the influence of language on thought and perception of reality (see below, and see LINGUISTIC RELATIVITY).

An influential strand of sociological research on discourse is found in the work of Goffman and his notions of 'self-presentation' and 'the interaction order' (1959, 1967). Goffman argues that interactants engage in conversation as a form of social action (and indeed performance), which, to use his favourite theatrical metaphor, is used to create a specific 'dramatic effect' (Goffman 1959: 252–3). Communication is, in this view, a reflexive and even a ritualized process, which allows its participants to construct and project desirable versions of their identities, enacted in a succession of performances targeted at specific audiences. Because of the interdependence of social actors in talk, the behaviour of one participant defines and constructs social relations and the identities of other members of the group. Thus, **emergent social meaning** is an intrinsic quality of interaction, and people's **social** (**gender**, **ethnic**, **age**, and other) **identities** are multiple and dynamic (changeable in the course of interaction). This is a line of investigation developed in intercultural settings by Gumperz (e.g. Gumperz 1982).

Cognitive approaches to discourse

Cognitive approaches to discourse are influenced by work in cognitive linguistics and pragmatics (see COGNITIVE LINGUISTICS; PRAGMATICS). The philosopher H.P. Grice (1975/1999) proposed a model of communication based on the notion of **the co-operative principle**, i.e. the collaborative efforts of rational participants in directing conversation towards attaining a common

goal. By observing the co-operative principle the participants follow a number of specific **conversational maxims**, such as *be informative*, *be truthful*, *be relevant* and *be clear*. When the maxims are adhered to, meaning is produced in an unambiguous, direct way. However, most meaning in discursive interaction is *implied*, and this is a process where participants assume that the co-operative principle is being observed but one of the maxims is violated.

The approach to communication proposed by Sperber and Wilson (1986) makes Grice's *be relevant* maxim central to explaining how information is processed in discourse. Their **relevance theory** (see PRAGMATICS) assumes that linguistic communication is based on **ostension** and **inference**, which can be described as the communicator's manifestation of what s/he means through a linguistic code and the audience's interpretation of the utterance, respectively. Inferential comprehension of the communicator's ostensive behaviour relies on deductive processing of any new information presented in the context of old information. This derivation of new information is spontaneous, automatic and unconscious, and gives rise to certain **contextual effects** in the **cognitive environment** of the audience. The occurrence of contextual effects, such as **contextual implications**, **contradictions** and **strengthening**, is a necessary condition for relevance. The relation between contextual effects and relevance is that, other things being equal, 'the greater the contextual effects, the greater the relevance' (Sperber and Wilson 1986: 119). In other words, an assumption which has no contextual effects at some particular moment of talk is irrelevant, because processing this assumption does not change the old context.

A second factor in assessing the degree of relevance of an assumption is the processing effort necessary for the achievement of contextual effects. It is a negative factor, which means that, other things being equal, 'the greater the processing effort, the lower the relevance' (Sperber and Wilson 1986: 124). The theory holds that, in communication, speaking partners first assume the relevance of an assumption and then select a context in which relevance will be maximized (it is not the case that context is determined first and then the relevance of a stimulus assessed). Sperber and Wilson also say that, of all the assumptions that a phenomenon can make manifest to an individual, only some will actually catch her/his attention. Others will be filtered out at a sub-attentive level. These phenomena, which have some bearing on the central thought processes, draw the attention of an individual and make assumptions and inferences appear at a conceptual level. Thus, they define the **relevance** of a phenomenon as follows (Sperber and Wilson 1986: 153):

> [A] phenomenon is relevant to an individual to the extent that the contextual effects achieved when it is optimally processed are large. . . .

> [A] phenomenon is relevant to an individual to the extent that the effort required to process it optimally is small.

Owing to its cognitive orientation and its initial interest in information processing, relevance theory has been largely concerned with the referential function of language (rather than social or relational functions).

Another link between language and cognition was made in the early decades of the twentieth century by Sapir and Whorf in their research on **linguistic relativity** – the so-called **Sapir–Whorf hypothesis** (e.g. Whorf 1939/1941/1956/1997; Gumperz and Levinson 1996; see LINGUISTIC RELATIVITY). One of Whorf's key observations that transfers directly into the domain of discourse analysis is that a language or an utterance form can unite demonstrably different aspects of reality by giving them similar linguistic treatment, what Whorf calls the process of **linguistic analogy**. Linguistic analogy allows or encourages us to treat diverse experience as 'the same'. A famous example in the area of vocabulary is the word 'empty' in the expression *empty gasoline drums*. As Whorf points out, the word 'empty' commonly implies a void or absence, and conjures up associations of 'absence of threat' or 'safety'. It is as if this expression steers us into treating 'empty gasoline drums' as lacking danger, when they are in fact unusually dangerous. Language used to shape cognitive structures can be referred to as *the cognitive appropriation of linguistic analogies*.

Similarly, cognitive linguists have proposed that the type of language people use has direct influence on their thought. This position is most clearly manifested in the well-known work of Lakoff and Johnson (1980) on metaphor. For example, they argue that such metaphors as 'Time is money' (e.g. You're *wasting* my time) or 'Argument is war' (e.g. I *demolished* his argument) are ways of 'seeing' the world and conceptualizing one category (e.g. *argument*) in terms of another (e.g. *war*), precisely because of the conventionalized and subconscious use of metaphors (see COGNITIVE LINGUISTICS; METAPHOR).

A third strand of cognitive discourse analysis, strongly influenced by **cognitive science** (cognitive psychology, cognitive linguistics and Artificial Intelligence; see PSYCHOLINGUISTICS; COGNITIVE LINGUISTICS; ARTIFICIAL INTELLIGENCE), is exemplified by Werth's work on **text worlds**, 'conceptual scenarios' which participants in language events must build in order to make sense of the utterances involved. Text worlds contain information about time, place and interactants, derived from the **world-building elements** of the discourse (deictic and referential elements; Werth 1999: 180) and from the **function-advancing propositions** of the discourse, each of which is 'a non-deictic expression which functions, for the most part, as part of the motivation for setting up a text world in the first place: it tells the story, it prosecutes the argument' (Werth 1999: 190).

Conversation analysis

The origins and much of current practice in conversation analysis (**CA**) reside in the sociological approach to language and communication known as **ethnomethodology** (Garfinkel 1974). Ethnomethodology means studying the link between what social actors 'do' in interaction and what they 'know' about interaction. Social structure is a form of order, and that order is partly achieved through talk, which is itself structured and orderly. Social actors have common-sense knowledge about what it is they are doing interactionally in performing specific activities and in jointly achieving communicative coherence. Making this knowledge about ordinary, everyday affairs explicit, and in this way finding an understanding of how society is organized and how it functions, is ethnomethodology's main concern (Garfinkel 1967; Turner 1974; Heritage 1984).

Following this line of enquiry, CA views language as a form of social action and aims, in particular, to discover and describe how the organization of social interaction makes manifest and reinforces the structures of social organization and social institutions (Boden and Zimmerman 1991; Drew and Heritage 1992). Hutchby and Wooffitt (1998: 14), who point out that the title 'talk in interaction' is now generally preferred to the designation 'conversation', define CA as follows:

> CA is the study of *recorded, naturally occurring talk-in-interaction*. . . . Principally it is to discover how participants understand and respond to one another in their turns at talk, with a central focus being on how sequences of interaction are generated. To put it another way, the objective of CA is to uncover the tacit reasoning procedures and sociolinguistic competencies underlying the production and interpretation of talk in organized sequences of interaction.

As this statement implies, the emphasis in CA, in contrast to earlier ethnomethodological concerns, has shifted away from the patterns of 'knowing' *per se* towards discovering the **structures of talk** that produce and reproduce patterns of social action. At least, structures of talk are studied as the best evidence of social actors' practical knowledge about them.

One central CA concept is **preference**, the idea that, at specific points in conversation, certain types of utterances will be more favoured than others (e.g. the socially preferred response to an invitation is acceptance, not rejection). Other conversational features which CA has focused on include: **openings and closings of conversations**; **adjacency pairs** (i.e. paired utterances of the type **summons–answer**, **greeting–greeting**, **compliment–compliment response**, etc.); **topic management** and **topic shift**; **conversational repairs**; **showing agreement and disagreement**; introducing **bad news** and processes of **troubles-telling**; (probably most centrally) mechanisms of **turn-taking**.

In their seminal paper, Sacks *et al.* (1974) suggested a list of guiding principles for the organization of turn-taking in conversation (in English). They observed that the central principle that speakers follow in taking turns is to avoid gaps and overlaps in conversation. Although gaps do of course occur, they are brief. Another common feature of conversational turns is that, usually, one party speaks at a time. In order to facilitate turn-taking, which usually takes place in 'the transition relevance places' (Sacks *et al.* 1974), speakers observe a number of conventionalized principles. For example, speakers follow well-established scripts, as in service encounters, in which speaker roles are clearly delineated. They fill in appropriate 'slots' in discourse structure, e.g. second-part utterances in adjacency pairs, and they anticipate completion of an utterance on the basis of a perceived completion of a grammatical unit (a clause or a sentence). Speakers themselves may signal their willingness to give up the floor in favour of another speaker (who can be 'nominated' by current speaker only). They can do this by directing their gaze towards the next speaker and by employing characteristic gesturing patterns synchronizing with the final words. They may alter pitch, speak more softly, lengthen the last syllable or use stereotyped discourse markers (e.g. *you know* or *sort of thing*).

A.J. and N.C.

Suggestions for further reading

Cobley, P. (ed.) (1996) *The Communication Theory Reader*, London: Routledge.

Gumperz, J.J. (ed.) (1982) *Language and Social Identity*, Cambridge: Cambridge University Press.

Jaworski, A. and Coupland, N. (eds) (1999) *The Discourse Reader*, London: Routledge.

Lee, D. (1992) *Competing Discourses*, London: Longman.

Schiffrin, D. (1994) *Approaches to Discourse*, Oxford: Blackwell Publishers.

Distinctive features

Introduction

Distinctive features have their origin in the theory of phonological oppositions developed by the Prague School (see Trubetzkoy 1939/1969). In this theory, words of a language are differentiated by oppositions between phonemes, and the phonemes themselves are kept apart by their **distinctive features** – phonetic properties such as 'voice', 'nasality', etc. These features are grouped phonetically into a variety of types, and the oppositions between the phonemes are also classified 'logically' in a number of different ways, according to the nature of the features concerned (see further FUNCTIONAL PHONOLOGY; PHONEMICS).

The theory of distinctive features was elaborated and radically transformed by Roman Jakobson (1896–1982), especially in the 1940s. For classical Prague School theory, features were merely dimensions along which oppositions between phonemes may be classified; Jakobson made the features themselves, rather than indivisible phonemes, the basic units of phonology, and further developed the theory of their nature and role, attempting to make it simpler, more rigorous and more general.

The acoustic character of features

Unlike the majority of phonological theories, which have taken articulatory parameters as the basis for phonetic description, Jakobson's theory characterizes features primarily in acoustic or auditory terms. The motivation for this is to be found in the act of communication which, according to Jakobson, depends on the possession of a common linguistic code by both speaker and hearer, and this can only be found in the sound which passes between them, rather than in the articulation of the speaker. Jakobson collaborated with the Swedish acoustic phonetician Gunnar Fant in the investigation of acoustic aspects of oppositions (cf. Jakobson *et al.* 1951), using the recently developed sound spectrograph, and was thus able to devise a set of acoustic or auditory labels for features, such as 'grave', 'strident', 'flat', etc., each defined primarily in terms of its acoustic properties, and only secondarily in terms of the articulatory mechanisms involved.

The use of acoustic features allows a number of generalizations which are more difficult to achieve in articulatory terms (see ARTICULATORY PHONETICS). The same set of features may be used for consonants and for vowels; for example, back and front vowels are distinguished by the same feature, 'grave' vs 'acute', as velar and palatal consonants. The same feature 'grave' may be used to group together labial and velar consonants on account of their 'dark' quality and oppose them to both dentals and palatals.

In later revisions of the set of features by Chomsky and Halle (1968), this original acoustic character of the features was abandoned in favour of articulatory definition, which is felt to be more in keeping with the speaker orientation of generative phonology (see GENERATIVE PHONOLOGY).

The binary nature of feature oppositions

An important and controversial aspect of Jakobson's theory is that feature oppositions are binary: they can only have two values, '+' or '−', representing the presence or the absence of the property in question. In Prague School theory, oppositions may be 'bilateral' or 'multilateral', according to whether there are two or more than two phonemes arranged along a single dimension, and they may also be 'privative' or 'gradual', according to whether the phonemes are distinguished by the presence versus the absence, or by more versus less of a feature. But by allowing only binary features with '+' or '−', Jakobson treats all oppositions as, in effect, 'bilateral' and 'privative'. This is justified by an appeal to the linguistic code; although it is true that many phonetic distinctions are of a 'more-or-less' kind, the code itself allows only an 'either–or' classification. With oppositions, the only relevant question is 'Does this phoneme have this feature or not?', to which the answer can only be 'Yes' or 'No'. Thus 'the dichotomous scale is the pivotal principle of . . . linguistic structure. The code imposes it on the sound' (Jakobson *et al.* 1951: 9).

One consequence of this is that, where more than two phonemes are arranged along a single phonetic parameter or classificatory dimension, more than one distinctive feature must be used. A system involving three vowel heights – 'high', 'mid' and 'low', for example – must be described in terms of the two oppositions: [+compact] vs [−compact] and [+diffuse] vs [−diffuse]; 'high' vowels are [−compact] and [+diffuse], 'low' vowels are [+compact] and [−diffuse], while 'mid' vowels are [−compact] and [−diffuse].

Binary values have remained a fundamental principle of distinctive features in more recent applications of the theory, though with some reservations. In terms of generative phonology, Chomsky and Halle (1968) note that features have two functions: a phonetic function, in which they serve to define physical properties, and a classificatory function, in which they represent distinctive oppositions. They suggest that features must be binary only in their classificatory function, while in their phonetic function they may be multi-valued.

The 'relational' character of features

The feature values are 'relational', i.e. '+' is positive only in relation to '−'. Each feature thus represents not an absolute property, but a relative one. This allows the same contrast to be located at different points on a scale. For example, in Danish there is a 'strong' versus 'weak' opposition which in initial position is found between a pair such as /t/ vs /d/, but which in final position is contained in the pair /d/ vs /ð/. Though the same sound may be found on different sides of the opposition in each case, it can be treated as the same opposition, since the first phoneme is 'stronger' *in relation to* the second in both cases. Despite this relational character, however, Jakobson maintains that distinctive features are actual phonetic properties of the sounds, and not merely abstract labels, since 'strength' in this sense is a definable phonetic property even if the terms of the opposition may be located at variable points along the scale. The feature itself remains invariant, the variation in its physical manifestation being non-distinctive.

The universal character of features

A major aim for Jakobson is the identification of a universal set of features that may be drawn on by all languages, even though not all will necessarily be found in every language. Thus he establishes a set of only twelve features. This means that some of the features used must cover a wide phonetic range, a notorious example being [+flat]: [+flat] phonemes are characterized as having 'a downward shift or weakening of some of their upper frequency components' (Jakobson and Halle 1956: 31), but in practice this feature is used to distinguish 'rounded' from 'unrounded', 'uvular' from 'velar', and *r* from *l*, as well as 'pharyngealized', 'velarized' and 'retroflex' sounds from sounds which lack these properties.

Many criticisms have been made of the original features and the way in which they were used. In their revision of Jakobson's feature framework, Chomsky and Halle (1968) extend the set considerably, arguing that Jakobson was 'too radical' in attempting to account for the oppositions of all the languages of the world in terms of just twelve features. Their framework breaks down a number of Jakobson's features into several different oppositions as well as adding many more; they provide, for example, special features for clicks, which in Jakobson's framework were covered by other features. Other scholars (e.g. Ladefoged 1971) have proposed further revisions of the set of features.

The hierarchical structure of oppositions

Not all features are of equal significance in the languages of the world; some features are dependent on others, in the sense that they can only occur in a language if certain other features are also present. This allows **implicational universals**, e.g. if a language has feature B it must also have feature A.

Jakobson supports this point with evidence from language acquisition and aphasia (see Jakobson 1941). If a feature B can only occur in a language when another feature A is also present, then it follows that feature A must be acquired before feature B, and in aphasic conditions when control of oppositions is impaired, feature B will inevitably be lost before feature A. Thus, 'the development of the oral resonance features in child language presents a whole chain of successive acquisitions interlinked by laws of implication' (Jakobson and Halle 1956: 41).

Redundancy

The features utilized in specific languages are also not of equal significance; some are predictable from others. For example, in English all nasals are voiced, hence any phoneme which is [+nasal] must also be [+voice]. In the specification of phonemes, features which are predictable in this way, and which are therefore not distinctive, are termed **redundant**. In English, then, [+voice] is redundant for [+nasal] phonemes.

Redundancy of specific features is not universal, but depends on the system in question. For example, front unrounded vowels of the sort [i] and back rounded sounds of the sort [u] are found in English, German and Turkish, but the status of the feature [+flat], i.e. rounded, is different in each case. Rounding is redundant for both types of high vowels in English, since the rounding is predictable from the frontness or backness of the vowel. In German, where there are rounded as well as unrounded front vowels, rounding is predictable and therefore redundant only for the back vowels. In Turkish, which has both rounded and unrounded front and back vowels, rounding is redundant for neither front nor back vowels.

Table 1 Two feature matrices for *dog*

	(a)			(b)		
	/d/	/ɒ/	/g/	/d/	/ɒ/	/g/
vocalic	−	+	−	−	+	−
consonantal	+	−	+	+	−	+
compact	−	+	+	−	+	+
grave	−	+	+	−	+	+
flat	−	+	−	0	0	0
nasal	−	−	−	0	0	0
tense	−	−	−	−	−	−
continuant	−	+	−	−	0	−
strident	−	−	−	0	0	−
voice	+	+	+	0	0	0

Table 2

	Vocalic	Consonantal
V = vowel	+	−
C = 'true' consonant	−	+
L = 'liquid' (*l*, *r*)	+	+
H = 'glide' (*h*, *w*, *j*)	−	−

Table 3

	(a)				(b)			
	C	C	L	V	C	C	L	V
vocalic	−	−	+	+	−	−	0	0
consonantal	+	+	+	−	+	0	+	0

Table 1 gives two feature matrices for the English word *dog*, one (a) fully specified, the other (b) with redundant feature values marked by 0. Since there is no opposition between [+flat] (rounded) and [−flat] (unrounded) consonants in English, and since [+grave] (back) vowels are all rounded, the specification of the feature 'flat' is unnecessary. Similarly, all [+nasal] consonants are [+continuant], hence [−continuant] consonants must be [−nasal]; there are also no nasal vowels in English, hence [−nasal] is redundant for the vowel. All vowels are [+continuant], and all non-tense phonemes are [+voice], while neither vowels nor [−compact], [−continuant] consonants can be [+strident]. All these restrictions are reflected in the 0 specifications in the matrix.

Redundancy also applies in sequences. If a phoneme with feature A must always be followed by a phoneme with feature B, then the latter feature is predictable, and therefore redundant, for the second phoneme. For example, English has /spin/ but not */sbin/: voiced plosives are not permitted after /s/. Hence the feature [−voice] is redundant for /p/ in this context.

As a further illustration, consider the possible beginnings of English syllables. If phonemes are divided into major classes using the features [vocalic] and [consonantal], we obtain the four classes of Table 2.

English syllables can only begin with: V, CV, LV, HV, CCV, CLV or CCLV. There are thus three constraints on sequences:

1 a [−vocalic] phoneme must be [+consonantal] after C.
2 CC must be followed by a [+vocalic] phoneme.
3 L must be followed by V.

Hence the sequence CCLV, which is fully specified for these features in Table 3 (a), can be represented as in Table 3 (b).

Natural classes and the evaluation measure

The assignment of features to individual phonemes is not arbitrary, but is intended to reflect **natural classes** of sounds. In terms of feature theory, a natural class is any group of phonemes which has fewer feature specifications than the total required for any one phoneme. Thus, as the class becomes more general, the number of features required decreases. For example,

/p/	[−compact], [+grave], [+tense], [−continuant]
/p, t, k/	[+tense], [−continuant]
/p, t, k, b, d, g/	[−continuant]

On the other hand, any set of phonemes which does not constitute a natural class, e.g. /p/, /s/, /a/, cannot be grouped together using a smaller number of features than is needed for any one of them.

This principle, together with that of redundancy, means that features are able to achieve generalizations which are not possible in the case of phonemes. The more general a description is, the smaller will be the number of features that are required. This allows the use of an evaluation measure, a **simplicity metric**, for descriptions, based on the number of features used.

In order to ensure that the description is also evaluated in terms of 'naturalness', Chomsky and Halle (1968) reintroduce the notion of **markedness**. Trubetzkoy (1939/1969) used this concept; the **marked term** of an opposition was for him that phoneme which possessed the feature, as opposed to that which did not. Chomsky and Halle extend the notion so that the unmarked value of a feature can be '+' or '−', according to universal conventions. Thus, the phonological matrices include 'u' and 'm' as well as '+' and '−' and there are rules to interpret these as '+' or '−', as appropriate. For evaluation, only 'm' is taken into account, hence '0' is unnecessary. This proposal was not, however, widely accepted.

The phonetic content of the features

The set of features required and the phonetic characteristics ascribed to them have been, and continue to be, subject to change. Jakobson's original twelve features, with an approximate articulatory description in terms of International Phonetic Alphabet (IPA) categories, are:

- *vocalic/non-vocalic* (vowels and liquids vs consonants and glides)
- *consonantal/non-consonantal* (consonants and liquids vs vowels and glides)
- *compact/diffuse* (vowels: open vs close; consonants: back vs front)

- *grave/acute* (vowels: back vs front; consonants: labial and velar vs dental and palatal)
- *flat/plain* (rounded vs unrounded; uvular vs velar; *r* vs *l*; pharyngealized, velarized and retroflex vs plain)
- *sharp/plain* (palatalized vs non-palatalized)
- *nasal/oral*
- *continuant/interrupted* (continuant vs stop)
- *tense/lax* (vowels: long vs short; consonants: fortis vs lenis)
- *checked/unchecked* (glottalized vs non-glottalized)
- *strident/mellow* (affricates and fricatives: alveolar vs dental, post-alveolar vs palatal, labiodental vs bilabial)
- *voiced/voiceless*

The feature framework of Chomsky and Halle is very complex, but the most important differences from Jakobson, apart from the use of articulatory rather than acoustic features, are:

- Use of the feature **sonorant** vs **obstruent** in addition to vocalic and consonantal. Vowels, glides, nasals, and liquids are [+sonorant]; the rest are [−sonorant].
- Use of the features **anterior, coronal, high, back** and **low** in place of 'compact', 'grave', 'sharp', and some uses of 'flat'; other uses of 'flat' are catered for by other features, e.g. **round**.

For place of articulation, the main differences between the two frameworks are given in Table 4.

Later developments

In the 1970s, generative phonology (see GENERATIVE PHONOLOGY) was more concerned with rule systems than with features, and generally assumed Chomsky and Halle's framework with only minor modifications and additions. The rise in the 1980s of **non-linear** generative phonology, however, brought renewed interest in the nature of phonological representations and

Table 4

IPA category	Jakobson		Chomsky and Halle	
bilabial	grave	diffuse	anterior	///////
labio-dental	grave	diffuse	anterior	///////
dental	acute	diffuse	anterior	coronal
alveolar	acute	diffuse	anterior	coronal
post-alveolar	acute	compact	///////	coronal
palatal	acute	compact	///////	high
velar	grave	compact	back	high
uvular	grave	compact	back	///////
pharyngeal	grave	compact	back	low

new developments in feature theory, particularly in the field of **feature geometry** (see Clements 1985; Clements and Hume 1995). In the approach of Jakobson or Chomsky and Halle, features are essentially independent properties of individual phonemes or segments; in non-linear, and especially **autosegmental**, phonology they are represented separately from segments, as independent 'tiers' linked to segmental 'timing slots'. It is claimed that these tiers are arranged hierarchically, so that individual feature tiers may be grouped together under, for example, 'place' and 'manner' tiers, these being dominated by a 'supralaryngeal' tier. 'Supralaryngeal' and 'laryngeal' tiers are in turn dominated by a 'root' tier. Such an arrangement of feature tiers, which is justified by the fact that features behave as classes in phonological processes such as assimilation, can no longer be represented as a two-dimensional matrix.

A.F.

Suggestions for further reading

Baltaxe, C.A.M. (1978) *Foundations of Distinctive Feature Theory*, Baltimore: University Park Press.

Chomsky, N. and Halle, M. (1968) *The Sound Pattern of English*, New York: Harper and Row.

Jakobson, R. and Halle, M. (1956) *Fundamentals of Language*, The Hague: Mouton.

Dyslexia

The Greek term *dys-lexia* means 'a difficulty with words and linguistic processes'. Since the 1930s, it has increasingly been used to describe an extreme difficulty in acquiring the fundamental skills of written language in otherwise ordinarily functioning people. The difficulty leads to failure and underachievement in reading, spelling and prose writing, in spite of ordinary educational opportunities. It is also marked by epiphenomena such as; the disordering of letter and sound patterns; reversals and confusions in spoken and written language; poor fluency and sequencing abilities; short-term memory difficulties for symbolic series; disturbances in time judgements; directional and orientation confusions and the failure to develop asymmetric functions; disturbances in grapho-motor fluency; and a general inability to recognize linguistic patterns, e.g. syllables, rhyme, alliteration, linguistic rhythm, stress and prosody. Money (1981: 16) describes these symptoms as 'a pattern of signs which appear in contiguity', and Miles (1983) describes the syndrome as a 'pattern of difficulties'.

In some cases, dyslexia appears to be related to a more general difficulty with language patterning – i.e. to speed and fluency capacity in *spoken* language in early developmental years and sometimes of possible familial and constitutional nature. In many cases, however, the dyslexia phenomenon can be 'elective' – i.e. mainly observed in written language.

Dyslexia was defined by the World Federation of Neurology, 1968, as 'a language disorder in children who, despite conventional classroom experience, fail to attain language skills of reading, writing and spelling commensurate with their intellectual abilities'. The United States Office of Education describes the difficulty as 'a disorder in one or more of the basic psychological processes involved in understanding or using language' (Newton 1977). Newton (1977) writes: 'dyslexia appears to occur in all countries where universal literacy is sought by the use of a sequential, alphabetic/phonetic symbol-system of written language'. Tarnapol and Tarnapol (1976) found that forty-three developed countries recognized a specific learning phenomenon of 'reading' failure, and that they variously used the terms 'dyslexia', 'reading difficulties' or 'specific learning difficulties' to describe it. Estimates of the incidence of dyslexia vary from 4 per cent

to 25 per cent of populations in societies where a phonetic alphabet is used, the variation probably depending on the severity of the condition. However, it has been postulated in the 1980s that 10 per cent of children in the UK and USA can enter formal education with the pattern of difficulties described above. A brief definition of the term is 'A specific difficulty in acquiring literacy and fluency in alphabetic/phonetic scripts' (Newton *et al.* 1985). The difficulty appears independent of intelligence, emotional state, socioeconomic status and cultural background.

Research from world sources indicates that the phenomenon, although manifested in educational failure, is linked to neurology and neuropsychology – involving differential specialization in the central nervous system itself, i.e. it is postulated that intrinsic developmental patterns of central-nervous-system functioning could be linked to literacy difficulties. Masland (1981) suggests that dyslexia may represent a difference in brain organization, and Newton (1984) refers to the phenomenon as 'differences in information-processing in the central nervous system'. These postulates of links between language and the brain have arisen from a long history of neurological and clinical observations.

These observations range from the first reference to a dominant hemisphere of the brain for language by Broca (1865), a French neurologist (see LANGUAGE PATHOLOGY AND NEUROLINGUISTICS), to the first use of the term **word blindness** by Kussmaul (1877), a German internist; the term 'dyslexia' was first used by Professor Berlin of Stuttgart in 1887 as an alternative to 'word blindness'. In 1892, Professor Déjérine of Paris found that in the brains of stroke patients with attendant dyslexia, the damage tended to be located in the posterior-temporal region in the left cerebral hemisphere, where the parietal and occipital lobes meet. The specialists mentioned above were in the main working with traumatized patients who suffered disturbances of spoken and written language. However, from 1895, James Hinshelwood, a Glasgow eye surgeon, published in the *Lancet* and the *British Medical Journal* a series of articles describing a similar disorder, but not apparently caused by brain injury. He described the phenomenon as (Hinshelwood 1917: 16):

> a *constitutional* defect occurring in children with otherwise normal and undamaged brains, characterized by a disability in learning to read so great that it is manifestly due to pathological conditions and where the attempts to teach the child by ordinary methods have failed.

Following upon Hinshelwood's seminal work in this field, the notion of a developmental dyslexia was accepted by a number of medical and psychological authorities. These include the eminent American neurologist Samuel Orton, who (in 1937), described the underlying features of dyslexia as difficulties in acquiring series and in looking 'at random', associating the occurrence with unstable patterns of individual laterality. He related such patterns to hemispheric control of functions, and referred to the problem as one of 'lacking cerebral dominance'. The neurological conception of dyslexia may be summed up in Skydgaard's brief definition (1942), 'A primary constitutional reading disability which may occur electively', or at greater length in Critchley (1964: 5):

> Within the heterogeneous community of poor readers, there exists a specific syndrome wherein particular difficulty exists in learning the conventional meaning of a verbal symbol and of associating the sound with the symbol in appropriate fashion. Such cases are marked by their gravity and purity. They are 'grave' in that the difficulty transcends the more common backwardness in reading and the prognosis is more serious unless some special steps are taken in educational

therapy. They are 'pure' in that the victims are free from mental defect, serious primary neurotic traits and all gross neurological deficits. This syndrome of developmental dyslexia is of constitutional and not of environmental origin and is often – perhaps even always – genetically determined. It is independent of the factor of intelligence and consequently may appear in children of normal IQ while standing out conspicuously in those who are in the above average brackets. The syndrome occurs more often in boys. The difficulty in learning to read is not due to peripheral visual anomalies but represents a higher level defect – an asymbolia. As an asymbolia, the problem in dyslexia lies in the normal 'flash' or global identification of a word as a whole, as a symbolic entity. Still further, the dyslexic also experiences a difficulty – though of a lesser degree – in synthesising the word itself out of its component letter units.

Since then, many eminent scientists have sought understanding in the patterns of links between sensory, motor, perceptual, linguistic and directional mechanisms of the two hemispheres of the brain. It would appear from their studies that language, symbolic order, analytic, timing and discrete skills are processed in the left hemisphere of the brain in most people, whereas global, visuo-spatial and design skills have a pre-eminence in the right hemisphere in most people. The above localization of function would be the constellation for the right-dominant (right-handed) individual, whereas the left or ambilateral individual could have these skills subserved at random in either or both hemispheres. In relating such organizations of brain function to motor and language performance, Dimond and Beaumont (1974) report on the negative findings of the relationship between left-handedness and reading disabilities, and yet a positive relationship between reading disabilities and mixed lateral prefer- ence. They conclude that reading difficul- ties could be associated with indeterminate lateral preference, but not with clearly established left-preference. Zangwill (1971) refers to the complex relationship between left-handedness and right or left brain for language. Birch (1962) has postulated a **theory of hierarchical unevenness** in develop- ment, i.e. between auditory, visual, motor, perceptual and linguistic mechanisms, caus- ing inconsistency and confusion in language perception.

Cerebral dominance is viewed by some researchers more as a decision-processing system that is responsible for bringing order to our various mental activities and their final cognitive path. In this view, as expressed by Dimond and Beaumont (1974), the term refers to the cerebral control system that institutes order in a chaotic cognitive space. It involves itself in language, but at the same time it is a superordinate system that is independent of the natural language mechanism *per se*. Similarly, Gazzaniga (1974: 413) writes: 'It is the orchestration of these processes in a finely tuned way that is the task of the dominant mechanism, and without it being formally established, serious cognitive dys- function may result.' Other researchers have linked findings from cognitive psychology to the dyslexia phenomenon. Miles and his team at Bangor University have postulated that lexical-encoding difficulties could be at the root of dyslexia; they compare access to **verbal-labelling strategies** between good and poor readers and spellers. The dyslexic population seem much poorer at using such linguistic facilitation (Pavlides 1981).

Following upon these neurological and neuropsychological observations on the nature of information processing in the central nervous system, other intriguing findings emerge. Clinical and psychological observation reveals that dyslexic persons are often superior in the so-called right- hemisphere skills, i.e. in skills which require basic aptitudes in spatial perception and integration. Dyslexic persons often succeed in the areas of art, architecture, engineer- ing, photography, mechanics, technology, science, medicine, athletics, music, design and craft. Some also succeed in math- ematics, but there is also an overlap in percentages of cases between dyslexia and mathematical difficulties. The above would indicate probabilities of inherent differences in patterns of human central-nervous- system development. As a result of these differences, one could expect differential problems in acquisition of various human skills. The dyslexia phenomenon, therefore, could be regarded as the outcome of such eventualities of personal development.

In addition to these more ordinary variations of individual differences *vis-à-vis* written language, clinical observation also reveals a second group of potential dyslexic learners. This group is characterized by pre- and postnatal trauma and developmental anomalies which lead to the dyslexic pattern of difficulties, exacerbated by distractibility, hyperactivity, the 'clumsy-child syndrome', and the more organic motor and language difficulties. Children in this group often have visuo-spatial problems; grapho-motor difficulties resulting in poor handwrit- ing; visual discrimination and sequencing anomalies; and perceptuo-motor difficulties. There can be overlap between the devel- opmental, constitutional group and the so-called traumatized group, resulting in a considerable number of children entering school at the age of 5 with grave potential literacy problems.

John Marshall, of the Radcliffe Infirmary in Oxford, and Max Coltheart of London University, have made intensive studies of **acquired dyslexia** in brain-traumatized patients, and have sought to establish a rational taxonomy, grouping patients on the basis of their particularly outstanding characteristics (see Coltheart *et al.* 1987). An information-processing model has been used as a basis for much of their work.

Attempts have also been made to make analogous comparisons with developmental dyslexia. The term 'deep dyslexia' is also used by such researchers to designate the nature of acquired dyslexia.

Since the mid-1940s, however, educationists, educational psychologists and sociologists have been investigating the problem of school-learning failure in terms of psychogenic and environmental factors. Their standpoint has been that educational difficulties in the main derive from various combinations of extrinsic conditions – socioeconomic factors; emotional states and maladjustment due to trauma; and inadequate standards and methods of teaching. Intrinsic causations, such as poor general underlying ability, i.e. 'intelligence', and/or general retardation of speech development, such as aphasic conditions (see APHASIA), have also been considered, as have physical handicaps such as defective sight and hearing. The terms learning disabilities, specific learning disabilities and reading disabilities have been used to describe severe underfunctioning in reading, writing and spelling. In the main, remedial techniques have been linked to diagnoses of the above factors. UK educational policy especially has, on the whole, favoured diagnosis of learning difficulties in the above psychogenic and environmental areas; and educational psychologists, educationists, etc. have been reluctant to ascribe underachievement in school to patterns of inherent difficulties related to the more neuropsychological aetiologies. The situation has been a contentious one; and the somewhat rigid stand often taken by educational specialists would appear to have frustrated attempts by many families, scientists, psychologists and neuropsychologists to provide help based upon appropriate understanding and diagnosis.

However, from the early 1960s in the UK, and somewhat earlier in the USA and some mid-European countries, a number of psychologists, neuropsychologists and neurologists began to observe the pattern of difficulties described above. While the terms strephosymbolia, congenital-alexia, legasthernia, word amblyopia, typholexia, amnesia visualis verbalis, analphabetia partialis, bradylexia and script blindness have been used by various specialists and scientists in the field as synonyms for dyslexia, the latter term has been adopted by many as a scientific, neutral and definitive term for the observed phenomena – pinpointing the central issue of language involvement. The use of this term, with its emphasis on developmental, linguistic, and symbolic factors and constitutional issues, has resulted in a continuing programme of research and clinical observation, which has yielded new insights into human learning, on the one hand, and probable differences in learning, on the other. A central feature has been the role of the left hemisphere of the brain in perceptual, linguistic, ordering, analytic and sequencing mechanisms – all of which, it is hypothesized, are needed for success in encoding alphabetic/phonetic scripts, and for the integration of such activities with other essential right-hemisphere and interhemisphere transmissions. The Harvard team in the USA is especially renowned for its seminal work in this field (see, for instance, Duffy et al. 1980; Masland 1981; Geschwind 1982). Many psychologists and a growing number of teachers now acknowledge the usefulness of the word 'dyslexia' as a specific term to describe a specific phenomenon.

Further clinical observation and research appears to have established different kinds of subgroups of difficulty within the total universe of dyslexia. Because of the complex nature of linguistic tasks, and the number of different mechanisms involved, aspects of the pattern of difficulties can differ with the individual. For example, the phonological aspects of linguistic ordering can be the problem for some, whereas the visual route to reading, and/or graphomotor disturbances, can cause the confusion in others. Indeed, some learners can experience difficulties in all mechanisms, causing overwhelming confusion of the alphabetic/phonetic script in the earliest days of school. In the ability to recognize an individual's own pattern lies the most critical issue of preparing and planning appropriate remedial-teaching techniques.

Since the 1930s, effort has been directed internationally to the development of teaching techniques for dyslexic persons. The basic need is to establish a kind of **mediational teaching** in which the crucial elements of written language are highlighted in such a way that a child who would not automatically perceive them (and their linkages) can do so. The responsibility of teaching is to present the linguistic signal in such a way that the child's own associative systems can be used to make sense of the structures and meaning of written language. Skilful teaching, which can lead to effective learning, needs to be based, therefore, upon the appropriate diagnosis and assessment, leading to the identification of individual needs. The key issue appears to be the provision in all first and primary schools of approved diagnostic and assessment measures for the earliest recognition of a child's pattern of learning, and the inclusion in teacher training of such techniques. For example, does a child best process information in a pictorial and spatial manner? If so, the use of pictograms, visual-recognition games, colour-coded materials, videotapes, computer-aided programs, and the emphasis on pattern in visual discrimination, can all serve to provide the initial groundwork for perceiving the nature of the task. If, however, a child is better on the phonological route, teaching proceeds through sound patterns – rhymes, doggerel, repetition, blending techniques, games and recitations – concentrating on simple, regular consonant–vowel–consonant arrays. In both systems, the teaching materials will be linked to a child's own world of experience, its spoken vocabulary, its love of stories, jingles and

fun. Research constantly shows that 'teaching to the strength' is the most effective way forward. Once a child is over the threshold of meaningful perceptions helped by teaching based on this rule, then the business of linking the various sound–symbol–graphomotor essentials can proceed. The phrase 'creating order in a chaotic cognitive space' can have real, practical meaning for the teacher.

Apart from the mediational aspects of teaching and its use of mnemonic systems to provide the necessary associative links, other essential techniques would include emphasis on rules and regularities, and the need for constant, repetitive reinforcement in a number of novel and interesting ways. Motivation becomes a prime factor in view of the very difficult nature of the task for the young learner, and effective teaching therefore relies upon the constant use of stimulating, lively and interesting material.

Remediation is one key area of understanding, but the other critical responsibility for education is the creation of opportunities for the special aptitudes (as listed above) of dyslexic persons. Since the 1930s, a number of lay, independent research and teaching bodies have arisen, which attempt to ameliorate the educational situation of the dyslexic learner. In the United Kingdom, these include the **British Dyslexia Association**, the **Dyslexia Institute**, the **Helen Arkell Dyslexia Centre** and. the **Aston University Study, Research and Clinical Practice**. In the USA, the **ACLD (Association for Child Learning Difficulties)** and the **Orton Society** are two prestigious bodies whose activities have led to recognition and amelioration of dyslexia difficulties. Much research has centred around the stress-reaction patterns and acute anxieties which have been observed clinically over many years in dyslexic persons. The responsibility of education, therefore, would be to ensure good personal development, self-concept and self-confidence in the young learners by appropriate recognition of skills and abilities other than those of written language. The implications for curriculum development in secondary and tertiary education, especially, would lead to a 'positive approach to dyslexia', as described in a number of scientific and educational publications (see, for instance, *Bulletins of the Orton Society* 1960, 1968, 1969 and 1970; Kershaw 1974; and Newton *et al.* 1985). Dyslexia difficulties can overwhelm the whole of education and life itself, if not appropriately recognized; and, concomitant with the growth of scientific research into and understanding of the dyslexia phenomenon since the 1930s, a number of lay independent pressure groups have arisen, which attempt to ameliorate the situation of the dyslexic learner.

Often beginning as parental pressure groups, these bodies have established their own professional responsibilities, diagnoses, teaching and teacher-training activities. Combined with the continuing efforts of universities, medical and paramedical authorities, and educational institutes, their efforts have resulted in increasing the understanding of dyslexia and the implications for statutory education and universal literacy.

During the final decades of the twentieth century, in the UK, a number of informed specialist and independent schools for dyslexic pupils were established and a growing number of specialist teachers were appointed in Local Education Authority schools.

Postgraduate courses for qualified teachers have been set in train in a number of universities specializing in the dyslexia phenomenon, and a well-established RSA Diploma course exists to educate and train specialists for both advisory and classroom teaching. Awareness of Specific Developmental Dyslexia has been heightened by media presentations and press coverage, and academic research into the nature and diagnosis of dyslexia is carried out in a number of UK universities. In addition, prestigious research into the neurological aspects of the phenomenon takes place in both European and American universities and medical centres.

In the UK, the 1981 and 1988 Education Acts represent a move forward in the recognition of and provision for this specific educational need. However, even in the twenty-first century concern can still be expressed for the many thousands of young people whose education and life opportunities will depend on the findings of science, the open and professional attitudes of educationalists, and the sponsorship and goodwill of governments in promoting understanding and appropriate provision for the specific patterns of difficulties that is dyslexia.

M.Nn.

Suggestions for further reading

Newton, M.J., Thompson, M.E. and Richards, I.L. (1979) *Readings in Dyslexia* (Learning Development Aids Series), Wisbech, Cambridgeshire: Bemrose.

Pavlides, G.T. (1981) *Dyslexia Research and Its Application to Education*, Chichester: John Wiley and Sons.

Reid, G. (1999) *Dyslexia – A Practitioner's Handbook*, 2nd edition, Edinburgh: Moray House.

Thompson, M.E. (1984) *Developmental Dyslexia*, London: Edward Arnold.

Vellutino, F.R. (1979) *Dyslexia: Theory and Research*, London: MIT Press.

F

Field methods

In this entry I will be discussing procedures used to collect information about the language of a traditional community, with a view to producing a grammar of that language. I will not be treating here the methods needed to gather material for a sociolinguistic study of language-internal variation (see LANGUAGE SURVEYS), nor those for investigating the acquisition of native language by children (see LANGUAGE ACQUISITION). The best source on the procedures of linguistic fieldwork remains Samarin (1967), but chapter 7 of Nida (1946) is also a very good summary and is strongly recommended. Much of the outline of elicitation procedures presented herein was learned from Nida.

The ideal way to study the language of a traditional community is *in situ*, living within the village, learning as much of the social customs of the people as possible. It is very important to understand something about the social contexts in which the language is used, for in many languages these will directly affect aspects of its structure. The only way these contexts can be learned and properly appreciated is by living in an environment where the language is used constantly, i.e. the village community. Further, it is very important, if the time available is sufficient, for the linguist actually to learn to speak the language. The best way to do this, of course, is to live in the village, where one is surrounded by the language in constant use. This is not to say that valuable work cannot be done without a speaking knowledge – many good descriptive studies have come from the pen of linguists who could not fluently speak the language under description. None the less, there will be many aspects of the language which may only be properly understood (or, indeed, discovered) if the linguist possesses a speaking knowledge.

Living in the village may put the linguistic investigator under severe psychological and physical stress, often described as **culture shock**. S/he has to come to terms with possibly very different local concepts of proper social behaviour, hygiene and time from her/his own, and particular difficulty may arise from the fact that traditional people's conceptualization of privacy is often very different from that of European-based cultures. The 'goldfish-bowl' existence that this implies for investigators, even when performing intimate functions, can be very stressful. Readable and thoroughly entertaining accounts of the rigours (and joys!) of fieldwork are provided in Bowen (1964) and Barley (1983). These are written by two anthropologists about their experiences in West Africa, but their descriptions are generalizable to fieldwork situations in traditional communities anywhere in the world. The best way to combat culture shock is with knowledge, for understanding of the local people's conceptualizations of behaviour and the world will ultimately lead to appreciation. In order to gain this knowledge and appreciation, a linguistic fieldworker needs to be something of an amateur anthropologist, using the same skills in gaining access to a people's cultural conceptualizations. Two very good manuals of anthropological techniques in fieldwork are Agar (1980) and Georges and Jones (1980).

Also before undertaking the project, the fieldworker must be very clear about what s/he intends to accomplish, for her/himself but, equally importantly, for the community whose language is to be studied. In most parts of the world where traditional communities exist today, the governments of the country concerned will require the fieldworker, typically a North American or a European, to apply for a research visa. This visa application will necessarily entail a fairly detailed description of what the fieldworker wishes to accomplish with the project and, on the basis of this, the government will either approve or reject the application. It is important that the fieldworker be aware of the political implications of all this. In many countries, traditional communities are at a severe social and economic disadvantage with respect to the modernizing elites of the central government, who, of course, give permission for the project to commence. The possible motives of these elites must always be borne in mind; they may view the fieldworker and the project as a useful tool for introducing modernizing ideologies and the breaking down of the conservatism of the traditional social order. If the fieldworker is to be a pawn of government policy, it is best to be aware of it and act accordingly.

Assuming the blessing of a central government with the best possible will towards the traditional community, the question then arises of the fieldworker's own respon-sibilities towards that community. S/he will be living with them, and they will be opening their lives and language to her/him, offering information about their cultural and linguistic conceptualizations, ideas which define them uniquely as human beings, as selves. On a personal level the fieldworker will form close friendships with people in the village, and it goes without saying that the kind of reciprocal social responsibilities that form the basis of true friendship in Australia, Europe, North America and elsewhere will apply here as well. But beyond that, and on a professional level, the fieldworker must seek to help the local people in ways that they can understand and appreciate. What types of cultural or linguistic projects they would like done, s/he must endeavour to accomplish.

On arriving in the village, the fieldworker can begin the proper task of learning the language. To do so, of course, will require one or more persons to serve as language teachers or **informants**. Social conditions will commonly constrain who can serve as an informant. For example, in many traditional communities it would be considered improper for the informant to be the opposite sex to the fieldworker. If the fieldworker is male, this can present special problems, for the men may commonly work away from the village during the day, in their gardens or the forest; he may then have to work with elderly, physically incapacitated men, but this is often a great boon, for elderly people usually possess the most detailed and accurate language information. On the other hand, constraints like this can be quite frustrating. It has been my experience in New Guinea that elderly women actually are the most knowledgeable about their native language, but because of cultural mores they are not possible informants for a male linguist. The best fieldworkers would seem to be a male and female team.

Even with such social constraints, it is quite likely that a range of people are available as potential informants. In selecting her/his primary informant(s), the fieldworker should look for someone who has a good command of the intermediate **contact language** (in very few areas today is monolingual fieldwork necessary, so I will ignore this possibility), who is keen to teach the language and enthusiastic about the project, and who has an outgoing, communicative personality. It is, of course, crucial that the informant be intelligent, but mental agility may not be immediately apparent to the culturally naive fieldworker because of the different ways this is expressed in various cultures. After a few weeks, however, the suitability and degree of mental alertness of the informant will become clear to the fieldworker, and if s/he is dissatisfied, or if another obviously more qualified candidate presents her/himself, then a switch should be made, provided this will be an acceptable act in that culture. In some societies such a change would be a terrible social rebuff to the informant, and in such cases it is imperative that fieldworkers be sure about the suitability of someone as an informant before taking her/him on in the first place.

Having tied down an informant, the fieldworker is ready to initiate studying the language. By this point s/he has heard the language spoken around her/him, perhaps for several days, but is unlikely to have made much headway, for long unbroken chains of discourse are simply too difficult to process at the beginning. The first task the fieldworker faces is to master the sound system of the language, to learn the system of phonemes and allophones (see PHONEMICS). Only with this solid foundation can s/he go on to control the morphology and the syntax.

The best way to learn the phonology is with simple words. The fieldworker should draw up a list of basic words, perhaps 200–500 items, in the intermediate contact language of elicitation, in order to elicit the vernacular equivalents. The words should largely be nouns, with pronouns and a few basic adjectives, adverbs and numerals included, because nouns are usually morphologically simpler than verbs and hence easier to record and analyse at the outset.

The nouns used should be those belonging to basic vocabulary, such as body parts, kin terms, household and local cultural objects, local animals and important plants, and geographical and natural objects. The fieldworker should say the word in the eliciting language, which will prompt the informant to provide the vernacular equivalent. The informant should say this twice, after which the fieldworker will attempt to repeat it. The informant will say if the attempt was correct or not. If correct, the fieldworker should then record the form in phonetic transcription in her/his field notebook. If incorrect, the informant should articulate it again, with the fieldworker then attempting to repeat it. This can go on two or three times, but in no case should the informant be expected to provide more than five repetitions. If the form is simply too difficult, go on to the next one and come back to it later. After transcribing about fifty words or so, the fieldworker should record these on tape for later, more detailed work. The fieldworker will pronounce the word in the eliciting language, after which the informant will say the vernacular equivalent two or three times, with a two-second pause between each repetition.

Following some basic mastery of the phonology, the fieldworker is ready to tackle the morphology. Some languages, such as those of Southeast Asia, have little or no morphology, so what the fieldworker will actually get when trying to elicit morphology will be basic syntactic patterns of the noun and verb phrase. Both morphology and syntax ultimately need to be studied as they are used in actual spontaneous discourse in the language. Only in textual discourse will the natural morphological and syntactic patterns of the language emerge. However, at this stage, with just a basic knowledge of the phonology, the fieldworker is in no position to start transcribing complete narrative or conversational texts. S/he is simply too ignorant of the basic building blocks of the language to make any sense of the running discourse of texts. Hence, it is crucial at this stage that the fieldworker do some basic elicitation work in the morphological and syntactic patterns of the language in order to construct a picture of its fundamental units and constructions.

It is important to remember that data collected at this stage are highly constrained and may give a quite artificial view of the language. A description of a language should *never* be based principally on elicited data, for these may reflect the contrived situation of the eliciting session or even more likely the morphological and syntactic patterns of the contact language of elicitation. The primary data for a description must be the natural spontaneous data of narrative and conversational texts, collected in a variety of contexts.

Bearing in mind the contrived nature of elicited data, the fieldworker proceeds to study the morphology of the language. In most languages nouns are simpler morphologically than verbs, so it is judicious to begin with them. Nouns are typically inflected morphologically for number, gender, possession and case, but case is predominantly a feature of clause-level grammar and will not show up contrastively in lists of nouns. A language need not have these inflectional categories (for example, Indonesian nouns lack all of them), or they may have others (noun classes in some Papuan languages or in Bantu languages), but these can be regarded as a good starting point.

The fieldworker should proceed to elicit basic noun stems in these inflectional categories. S/he already has the word for *eye* so s/he asks for *two eyes* (this will give the dual form if the language has a distinct dual category. S/he already has *house*, so asks

for *many houses*. As always, the fieldworker should repeat what the informant has said to ensure that s/he has it correctly, before writing it down. If one gets distinct inflectional forms for *man* vs *woman* and *boy* vs *girl*, this suggests a gender distinction operating in the language, and further elicitation exploring this will be warranted. Possessed nominals should be elicited using pronominal possessors: *my eye, your eye . . . my eyes, your eyes*, etc. One should try a couple of dozen or so basic words in different semantic categories for their possessed forms. If they all inflect according to the same pattern, the linguist can assume the language is regular. Differences in inflection among nouns indicate complications and most probably a system of noun classes.

Now the fieldworker is ready to turn to that more complex category – verbs. S/he should first elicit some verb forms in the simple present or present continuous, e.g. *she walks* or *she is walking*. The third-person singular form should be chosen for elicitation, as it is likely to cause the least confusion. First and second persons often get hopelessly garbled in translation, so that an elicited *I am hearing* often as not comes back as *you are hearing* and vice versa. The fieldworker should choose verbs denoting simple, easily perceived, events like *walk*, *hit*, *run*, *jump*, *eat*, *sleep*, *stand*, *sing*, *talk*, etc. S/he should use a mixture of intransitive and transitive verbs to investigate whether these have significant differences, but should be aware that the native language may require the expression of an object with transitive verbs, so if a recurring particle seems to be associated with the elicited transitive verb forms, it is quite possibly just this.

Having got some basic verb forms, the fieldworker is now ready to fill out the paradigms. Verbs are commonly inflected for tense, aspect, mood, voice and agreement for subject and object. Many languages lack some of these – for example, Thai marks its verbs only for aspect and mood (tense is not a category in Thai grammar), and even these are indicated by independent words, not bound morphemes. Other languages have additional verbal inflectional categories. Yimas, of New Guinea, inflects verbs for all five (tense, aspect, mood, voice and agreement), as well as others, such as direction or location of the action. Languages like Yimas have such morphologically complex verb forms, with so many inflectional categories and distinctions, that a fieldworker could never hope to discover all of them through early elicitation. Rather, many will crop up only when working with texts and will be the target of later, more informed, elicitation. At this early stage the fieldworker is only concerned with getting an overview of the verbal morphology.

The fieldworker needs to get paradigms of both intransitive and transitive verbs in a few tenses. It is suggested that s/he elicit verbs in the simple present (*she walks/is walking*), past (*he walked*), and future tenses (*she will walk*). Many languages have much more complex tense systems than this (Yimas, for example, has seven distinct tenses), but the fieldworker is in no position at this stage to cope with the subtleties of meaning that the different forms may encode. Rather, s/he should confine her/himself to the relatively straightforward system of present, past and future, without assuming that all these may be true tense distinctions (future, for example, may be a mood). S/he should elicit paradigms for intransitive verbs (*I walk, you walk*, etc.) and transitive verbs (*I hit you, I hit him, I hit them . . . you hit me, you hit him, you hit us*, etc.) in all possible combinations of person and number for both subject and object, bearing in mind the common confusion and switch in first and second persons. The paradigms for intransitive and transitive verbs should be elicited in all three tenses and then in the negated forms for all three. The fieldworker may well notice systematic

differences between the inflections for intransitive and transitive verbs; not uncommonly, for example, the agreement affix for the subject of an intransitive verb will be quite different from that of a transitive verb, as in so-called **ergative–absolutive** languages (Yimas is of this type).

With a basic idea of the morphology of the two principal parts of speech – nouns and verbs – the fieldworker is ready to undertake a preliminary study of the syntax. Simple clauses should be formed by combining a noun with an intransitive verb, such as:

(1) The woman is cooking.
(2) The tree fell down.
(3) The child is sleeping.
(4) The old man will die.
(5) The boys will go tomorrow.
etc.

Similar sentences with two nouns and a transitive verb can be elicited:

(1) The woman is cooking meat.
(2) The man cut down the tree.
(3) The child sees the house.
(4) The old man will eat meat.
(5) The boys hit the ball.
etc.

Various combinations of nouns and verbs should be tried, to see if these are linked to systematic structural differences in the clause. Different choices of verb may reveal case distinctions – for example, in some languages, the subject of *see* is in the dative case, but the subject of *hit* is in the nominative. Similar differences may show up in the case of the object. Also, different nouns with the same verbs may be responsible for different agreement affixes. This is because the nouns belong to different noun classes, and the verbal affixes vary for noun class: Yimas and the Bantu languages work this way. A syntactic-elicitation procedure like this will often provide information about word order of constituents within clauses, but this must be treated with suspicion. The word order of the clausal constituents of the elicited vernacular example may simply reflect that of the prompting language of elicitation, especially if the word order of the vernacular language is rather free. For example, a linguist studying a language of Indonesia using English as the eliciting language rather consistently got Subject–Verb–Object (SVO) word order in the elicited examples and concluded that the language under investigation was also an SVO language. But, as later studies have proved, the basic word order of the language is actually quite free and, if any order is more basic, it is that with the verb in initial position, i.e. VSO or VOS.

If interference from the language of elicitation is a problem with clause-level syntax, it is much more of a problem with complex sentence constructions. Here the actual structure of the vernacular language can be disguised and highly distorted if the fieldworker relies heavily on elicited material for her/his description. Some constructions which are very common in everyday language usage may be rare or fail to show up at all in elicited material. For example, in Yimas, **serial-verb constructions** (see CREOLES AND PIDGINS) are extremely common, both in narrative texts and conversations, yet if one tries to elicit them using Tok Pisin equivalents, one is rarely successful. What one does get is a sentence consisting of conjoined clauses, essentially the structure of the Tok Pisin prompt. The prompted Yimas translation is a grammatical sentence in the language, but it is not the natural or spontaneous way of expressing it.

Thus, the proper materials for the study of complex sentences and other syntactic phenomena are texts. A **text** is a body of language behaviour generated continuously over a period by the informant and recognized as an integrated whole. The texts the fieldworker is initially concerned with are conversations and narratives. Other types of texts, such as songs, poems and other forms of oral literature, are likely to be far too difficult at first, with many archaic and conventionalized forms, as well as those arising from poetic licence, and should only be approached at an advanced state of research, when the fieldworker's understanding of the grammar of the language is well developed.

Conversations, too, are likely to prove somewhat difficult because of their speed, the presence of multiple speakers, and reduced colloquial speech forms. However, they are a very important source of information on these phonologically reduced forms, as well as context-based uses of pronouns and deictics, so, difficult or not, they must be studied. It is prudent, though, to delay analysing conversations until a number of the more straightforward narrative texts have been transcribed and analysed.

Narrative texts are of two types: personal experiences of the informant or her/his acquaintances; and traditional myths and legends. The latter are the most popular form of texts with linguistic fieldworkers and are unquestionably a goldmine of information, but they are, in fact, more difficult to work with than the former, for their very status as myths sanctioned by tradition means that their form may be rather conventionalized and hence less indicative of the actual productive use of the language in everyday life.

Texts should be collected in the following way. A complete text is first recorded on tape. If it is a narrative, a translation by the informant in the contact elicitation language should also be recorded immediately following the vernacular version – this will prove useful later in analytical work. The text then needs to be transcribed. In the early stages of work it will be extremely difficult for the fieldworker to transcribe directly from the tape; her/his knowledge of the language is simply insufficient. Further, the informant is still present, so it is advantageous to make the best use of this fact. The most productive way to proceed is to play back a section of the recorded text (around five to ten seconds, at this stage) and get the informant to repeat that. It is important to check that the informant repeats what is on the tape (they often use this as an opportunity to edit their performance) – one does not want the recorded and transcribed versions of the text to differ significantly, although it is wise to note down the changes the informant *does* try to make, for later reference. The fieldworker then repeats what the informant has said and, if the informant says the repetition is correct, writes down this section of the text. If the repetition is incorrect, the whole procedure begins again. Once this section of the text has been correctly transcribed, the linguist can proceed to the next section, and so on, until the whole text is transcribed. By following this procedure with a number of texts, both narratives and conversations, a large corpus of material in the vernacular can be collected. Once the fieldworker's knowledge of, and fluency in, the language is up to it, s/he should be able to transcribe directly from the tape, without section-by-section repetitions by the informant.

A crucial step in field procedures is the analysis and expansion of textual material. Immediately after transcribing a complete text, the fieldworker should set about analysing it. In the early stages this will be difficult, as word boundaries will be hard to ascertain, and many words and morphemes will be unknown. Isolatable words should be presented to the informant for glossing, but bound morphemes will not succumb to this treatment; the best the linguist can hope for is a glossing of the entire word containing the morpheme. However, with a gradually enlarging corpus, things will become clearer. Recurring morphological particles can be noted along with the translations of the words containing them. By collecting enough examples of these, it should be possible to establish the form and function of the bound morpheme. Commonly, important bound and free mor-

phemes are not glossed by the informant, and the function of these can usually only be ascertained by carefully examining the contexts in which they occur.

A very important role of texts is in the basis for supplementary elicitation. Many morphemes and construction types will come to the fieldworker's attention for the first time in transcribed texts. S/he can use these examples as the basis for collecting further data so that enough material is available to describe the morpheme or construction. For example, I first became aware of the existence of embedded nominalized complements in Yimas from their sporadic occurrences in texts. I used the examples from the texts, but substituted various components such as the nouns and verbs involved, to generate a corpus of complements more or less different in form. This allowed me to be more precise in my description of their forms and functions.

This entry might have conveyed the impression that linguistic fieldwork consists largely of tedious drudgery, and I do not deny that it has its mechanical side. However, to describe a language from scratch, to sort out and put the pieces together, is a tremendously exciting intellectual exploration, like doing an immense crossword puzzle. And to live closely with a people still following a traditional lifestyle, who share their language and their lives with you, offers opportunities for personal growth (for the fieldworker and the village community!) and creative understanding that can hardly be matched in any other area.

W.A.F.

Suggestions for further reading

Nida, E.A. (1946) *Morphology: The Descriptive Analysis of Words*, Ann Arbor: University of Michigan Press, chapter 7.
Samarin, W. (1967) *Field Linguistics*, New York: Holt, Rinehart and Winston.

Finite-state (Markov process) grammar

Finite-state grammars are known within mathematics as **finite-state Markov processes**, and a model of this type is used by Hockett (1955) to model the 'single uniqueness' of human beings among other animals, namely 'the possession of speech' (1955: 3). The model represents language in terms of block diagrams or control-flow charts as used in electrical engineering, and Hockett explains that 'in the present state of knowledge of neuro-physiology, there is no guarantee that the units we posit do exist inside a human skin' (1955: 4), so that the model is not physiological: rather, it is a type of 'as if' mode, which can be explicated in the following two ways: humans, as users of language, operate *as if* they contained apparatus functionally comparable to that we are about to describe; an engineer, given not just the rough specifications presented below but also a vast amount of detailed statistical information of the kind we could work out if we had to, could build something from hardware which would speak, and understand speech, as humans do.

Hockett's model may thus be considered as a model of the human language faculty. It contains a **grammatic headquarters (GHQ)**, which emits a flow of morphemes. This constitutes the input to the **phoneme source**, the output of which is a flow of phonemes constructed according to a code. This latter flow is the input to the **speech transmitter**, which converts it to a **continuous speech signal**. Finally, a language user has a **speech receiver**, whence speech signals follow a converse route back to the GHQ. It is the GHQ that is of interest here, since it is the seat of the finite-state grammar. Hockett imagines that (1955: 7):

> G.H.Q. can be in any of a very large number of different *states*. At any given moment it is necessarily in one of these

states. Associated with each state is an array of probabilities for the emission of the various morphemes of the language. ... When some morpheme is actually emitted, G.H.Q. shifts to a new state. Which state the new one is depends, in a *determinate way* (not just probabilistically), on both the preceding state and on what morpheme has actually been emitted. ... [A] specific combination of preceding state ... and actually emitted morpheme ... results always in the same next state.

Such a grammar is referred to by Chomsky (1957: 6) as a 'very simple communication theoretic model of language', according to which (1957: 20) a speaker producing a sentence

> begins in the initial state, produces the first word of the sentence, thereby switching into a second state which limits the choice of the second word, etc. Each state through which he passes represents the grammatical restrictions that limit the choice of the next point in the utterance.

Chomsky (1957: 19) produces the following **state diagram**:

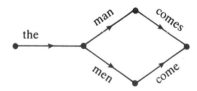

By adding **loops** to a grammar of this kind,

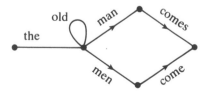

it can become able to produce an indefinite number of sentences, and will thus satisfy one of the requirements grammars must meet: the requirement that the grammar generate an infinite number of sentences from the finite linguistic material the language provides. At the end of the sentence, the 'final state' will have been reached.

Another requirement that grammars of natural languages must meet is that they must be able to generate *all* of the possible sentences of the language, and Chomsky argues convincingly that no finite-state grammar will be able to meet this condition, since no natural language is a finite-state language. The finite-state model assumes that language is linear; it assumes that a sentence can be analysed as a string of items in immediate succession. Therefore, it is incapable of accounting for cases of **embedding**; that is, for cases in which one string of items 'breaks up' the regular succession of items within another string, as in *The woman who saw you was angry*, where the sentence *who saw you* breaks up the sentence *the woman was angry*. Chomsky provides the following examples (1957: 22):

(1) If S_1, then S_2
(2) Either S_3, or S_4
(3) The man who said that S_5 is arriving today

where 'S' stands for any declarative sentence. A finite-state grammar would have no way of accounting for the selection of one particular embedded sentence, or for the links of dependence which determine the selection of *then* rather than *or* in (1) and the selection of *or* rather than *then* in (2). So Hockett's claims that a finite-state grammar can be perceived as a model of

the human speech capacity, and that one state predicts the following state, are not justified. Humans are able to generate structures containing embedded sentences, and there are many selections which are made by speakers of natural language which a finite-state grammar could not predict.

In the model's favour, however, it can be said that *spoken* language, at least, does reach hearers in a linear way with one word following the next in immediate succession. It should also be pointed out (see Lyons 1977a: 55) that the mathematical communication theory, **information theory**, which has developed since 1945 is highly sophisticated:

Chomsky did not prove, or claim to prove, that 'information theory' as such was irrelevant to the investigation of language, but merely that if it were applied on the assumption of 'word-by-word' and 'left to right' generation, it could not handle some of the constructions in English.

K.M.

Suggestions for further reading

Chomsky, N. (1957) *Syntactic Structures*, The Hague, Mouton, chapter 3.
Kimball, J.P. (1973) *The Formal Theory of Grammar*, Englewood Cliffs, NJ: Prentice Hall, chapter 2.
Lyons, J. (1977a) *Chomsky*, 2nd edition, Glasgow: Fontana Collins, chapter 5.

Forensic linguistics

In 1968, Jan Svartvik published *The Evans Statements: A Case for Forensic Linguistics*, in which he demonstrated that disputed parts of a series of statements which had been dictated by Timothy Evans to police officers, and which incriminated him in the murder of his wife, had a grammatical style measurably different from that of uncontested parts of the statements. A new discipline was born . . .

For the purpose of this entry I will take **forensic linguistics** in its widest possible meaning, embracing all descriptions of language undertaken for the purpose of assisting courts and thus will (contentiously) subsume forensic handwriting analysis and forensic phonetics under this general label. Forensic linguists help courts to answer three questions about a text – What does it say? What does it mean? Who wrote/typed/authored it?

What does the text say?

For the phonetician, this may be a question of decoding a few crucial phrases, words or even single syllables – indeed, more than one case has depended on the placement of tonic stress or the discrimination of a single phoneme. When a recording is of poor quality, the non-expert may hear one thing, while the expert (with a trained ear and with the help of sophisticated equipment, which can enhance the quality of the recording) may perceive something entirely different. In one case an indistinct word, in a clandestine recording of a man later accused of manufacturing the designer drug Ecstasy, was crucially misheard by a police transcriber as the contextually plausible 'hallucinogenic':

> but if it's as you say it's *hallucinogenic*, it's in a Sigma catalogue

whereas what he actually said was

> but if it's as you say it's *German*, it's in a Sigma catalogue

In another case, a West Indian accused of murder was transcribed as saying that he got on to a train and then 'shot a man to kill'; in fact, what he said was the innocuous and contextually much more likely 'showed a man ticket'.

For the handwriting expert, providing the court with an opinion on what a text said was traditionally a question of decipher-ing handwriting that was illegible to the layman. In the past fifteen years, however, a machine called by the acronym ESDA (Electro-Static Detection Apparatus) has become an indispensable additional tool

through which the expert often discovers new evidence, rather than simply analyses existing evidence (see Davis 1994). Essenti-ally this machine allows the user to read the indentations created by someone writing on a sheet of paper resting at the time on the sheet being examined. Thus, if a writer were using a block or pile of paper while writing – as would typically happen during police statement taking – each sheet would carry an indentation record of what had been written on the immediately preced-ing sheet. It was ESDA evidence that led directly to the disbanding of the West Midlands Serious Crime Squad, when a dis-puted page of a supposedly contemporan-eous handwritten record of an interview was shown to have imprinted on it an ear-lier and uncontentious version of the same page, which had apparently been rewritten to include two incriminating utterances. Similarly, the three surviving members of the Bridgewater Four were released within twenty-four hours when an ESDA analysis revealed evidence of a forged confession whose existence the police had denied.

What does (part of) a text mean?

A significant number of texts are produced by lawyers specifically for communication with a lay audience – contracts, health warnings, the police caution, etc. By their very nature such texts have inherent prob-lems in that, on the one hand, they are designed to be legally unchallengable but, on the other hand, that very fact may make them at best opaque and at times incom-prehensible to their intended readers.

Forensic linguists work on such texts for two purposes. Sometimes they are asked to give a professional opinion when a dispute about meaning goes to court – for example, in one case a man was refused a payout on a sickness insurance policy because it was said that he had lied when, in completing a health insurance proposal form he replied 'No' to the following question:

Have you any impairments? . . . Loss of
sight or hearing? . . . Loss of
arm or leg? . . . Are you crippled or
deformed? . . . If so explain. . . .

The insurance company asserted that he did
indeed have 'impairments' on the grounds
that 'he was overweight, had a high choles-
terol level and occasional backaches', even
though they did not dispute his assertion
that none of these conditions had ever
caused him to take any time off work. In
her evidence in support of the claimant,
the linguist focused on the vagueness of
the word 'impairment', and argued that any
'co-operative reader' would reasonably
infer that, given the phrases that followed,
the word 'impairment' in this question
was being used to mean a relatively severe
and incapacitating physical condition and
that therefore the man had indeed answered
'No' 'appropriately and in good conscience'
(Prince 1981: 2). The court ruled against
the insurance company. Other such cases
involve questions of what does and does not
constitute a warning, particularly when it
is a short text written on a cigarette packet.

In the majority of cases, however, courts
do not call on and, indeed, often explicitly
forbid the use of the expertise of linguists,
because deciding on and defining the meaning of words and phrases is an integral part
of the work of courts – according to Pearce
(1974), up to 40 per cent of cases require a
ruling on the meaning of an expression.
In the famous 1950s English case, when
Derek Bentley was convicted of the murder of a policeman although he was under
arrest at the time the policeman was shot,
the lawyers debated the meaning of the
utterance 'Let him have it, Chris' disputing
whether it meant 'Shoot him' (which incriminated him in the murder) or 'Give it
[the gun] to him [the policeman]' (which
were grounds for mitigation).

Sometimes there is no legal dispute,
but a perceived communication problem.
Forensic linguists have been involved in
evaluating the communicative problems
of texts like temporary restraining orders,
jury instructions, the police caution and its
American equivalent, the Miranda Warning, and then suggesting ways in which these
texts can be modified to express better the
originally intended meaning. Forensic linguists have also campaigned for the right
of non-native speakers to have interpreters,
in order to ensure that they understand
what is being said to them and that what
they themselves say to the court in return
accurately conveys what they mean.

Who is the author?

Much of the work of the handwriting expert
is concerned with forged handwriting –
often on wills – where the little-known fact
that it is possible to differentiate normal-
speed from slower handwriting assumes
great importance. Recent pure research into
the differences between left- and right-
handed writing, between male and female
writers, and between European hands, also
has obvious forensic applications.

Forensic phoneticians are sometimes
called on to identify the accent of an unknown voice making obscene or threatening phone calls or ransom demands. More
often, they are asked to compare tape-
recorded samples of known voices with
samples of an unknown and sometimes disguised voice. A few forensic phoneticians
still work only by ear, but the majority
now use sophisticated computer programs,
which, among other facilities, offer real-
time analysis and the accurate visual comparison of spectrographic prints through a
split-screen presentation. In addition, the
phonetician may be asked to offer an opinion on whether a tape has been interfered
with either physically or instrumentally,
whether it is an original or a copy, and on
which machine it was originally recorded.

A current research concern of forensic
phoneticians is with 'voice line-ups'. The
problem is the design of a method which

gives a victim who thinks s/he can accurately recall the voice of the criminal a fair chance of matching this audio memory with audio recordings of the suspect voice(s). Related research questions are concerned with a speaker's necessary level of competence in a foreign language before s/he is able to begin to distinguish voices at all, and how competent s/he needs to be in order to be as successful as native speakers.

The forensic linguist is concerned with the unknown or disputed authorship of written texts. In cases where there are no suspects – for example, some threatening letters and hate mail – the linguist may be asked to discover linguistic clues suggesting the nationality, regional or social origins or educational level of the author/scribe/typist.

Usually, however, there is non-linguistic evidence, which significantly reduces the number of potential authors – in the case of suspect suicide notes, typically to only two. In such cases the linguist will usually have access to samples of other texts produced by the candidate author(s) and will be looking for distinctive lexical, grammatical and orthographic choices, as well as layout preferences. The major problem for the linguist is that s/he needs substantially more data than does the phonetician or handwriting expert, while most of the texts are distressingly short. Naturally, the task is made considerably easier if there are a number of non-standard features – the example below is unfortunately not typical.

> ... I hope you appreciate that i am enable to give my true idenity as this would ultimately jeopardize my position. ...
> ... have so far deened it unnecessary to investegate these issus. ...

Nevertheless, intending writers of anonymous letters are advised to make good use of the spelling- and grammar-checking facilities of the word-processing package!

There have, in the past, been many cases where an accused has claimed that the police had (in part or entirely) fabricated interview and/or statement records – British readers will recall the cases of Derek Bentley, the Bridgewater Four and the Birmingham Six. Nowadays, in order to avoid the possibility of fabrication, interactions between the police and the accused are routinely tape-recorded in many countries. In looking at such disputed records of statements the linguist has a battery of available tests and tools. In the Derek Bentley case, for instance, it was possible to derive evidence of usage from the Bank of English corpus in order to demonstrate that one grammatical feature in the language attributed to Bentley – the use and positioning of the word *then* – was in fact typical of the register of police report-writing. In this same case, evidence from both narrative analysis and research into the textual use of negatives was used to support Bentley's claim that his statement was, at least in part, the product of question-and-answer exchanges converted into monologue. In the Bridgewater Four case, evidence about the uniqueness of utterance and the nature of cohesion between and within question–answer sequences was used to support a claim that an interview record had been fabricated.

In the main, investigations into authorship attribution use existing linguistic tools in a forensic context. However, in one area –that concerned with plagiarized text – new computerized tools are being developed and new knowledge about individual style and the creation of text is being generated. Recently, increased access to word-processing facilities linked with an explosion in the use of the World Wide Web have made it much easier for students in particular to 'borrow' text and insert it seamlessly into their own text. The simultaneous explosion in student numbers means that only computer-assisted techniques can hope to cope with this problem. There already exists software for the automatic detection of student plagiarism when they are borrowing from fellow students (Woolls and Coulthard 1998). Now the search is on for style measures that will work on short texts and can therefore discover inconsistencies in essays which are partially plagiarized, or which consist of extracts from various sources sewn together. To complement this there will also be a need for sophisticated keyword analysis to provide the lexical input into Web searches to discover the source of the alien text.

Forensic linguistics continues to push back the frontiers of knowledge.

R.M.C.

Suggestions for further reading

Baldwin, J. and French, J. (1990) *Forensic Phonetics*, London: Pinter.
Forensic Linguistics, The International Journal of Speech, Language and the Law.
Gibbons, J. (ed.) (1994) *Language and the Law*, London: Longman.

Formal grammar

Formal grammars are associated with linguistic models that have a mathematical structure and a particularly abstract view of the nature of linguistic study. They came to prominence in linguistic theory through the early work of Noam Chomsky and perhaps for this reason are sometimes, though quite wrongly, associated exclusively with his school of linguistics. It is nevertheless appropriate to start with a quotation from Chomsky (1975a: 5):

> A language L is understood to be a set (in general infinite) of finite strings of symbols drawn from a finite 'alphabet.' Each such string is a sentence of L. . . . A grammar of L is a system of rules that specifies the set of sentences of L and assigns to each sentence a structural description. The structural description of a sentence S constitutes, in principle, a full account of the elements of S and their organization. . . . The notion 'grammar' is to be defined in general linguistic theory in such a way that, given a grammar G, the language generated by G and its structure are explicitly determined by general principles of linguistic theory.

This quotation raises a number of issues. The first and most general is that a language can be understood to consist of an infinite set of sentences and the grammar of that language to be the finite system of rules that describes the structure of any member of this infinite set of sentences. This view is closely related to the notion of a **competence grammar**: a grammar that models a speaker's knowledge of her/his language and reflects her/his **productive** or **creative** capacity to construct and understand infinitely many sentences of the language, including those that s/he has never previously encountered. I shall assume this position in what follows.

A second, more formal, issue is that the grammar of a particular language should be conceived of as a set of rules formalized in terms of some set of mathematical principles, which will not only account for, or **generate**, the strings of words that constitute the sentences of the language but will also assign to each sentence an appropriate grammatical description. The ability of a grammar simply to generate the sentences of the language is its **weak generative capacity**; its ability to associate each sentence with an appropriate grammatical description is its **strong generative capacity**.

A third issue concerns the universal nature of the principles that constrain possible grammars for any language, and hence define the bounds within which the grammar of any particular language will be cast. Here we shall be concerned with two interrelated questions. The first is a formal matter and concerns the nature of the constraints on the form of the rules of the grammar. A properly formal approach to this question would be formulated in mathematical terms: I will, however, limit myself to an informal outline of the issues involved and invite the reader interested in the formal issues to consult Gazdar (1987) and Wall (1972). The second is a substantive matter and concerns the nature of the linguistic principles that constrain the 'appropriate grammatical description' mentioned above. Since linguistic principles tend to vary from theory to theory, and indeed can change over time within one theory, it is perhaps hardly surprising that the establishment of the 'correct' grammar can be a matter of controversy.

To put some flesh on these observations, consider a simple example involving the analysis of a single sentence: *The cat sat on the mat*. We will make the simplifying assumption that words are the smallest unit that a grammar deals with, so, for example, although it is obvious that *sat*, as the past tense form of the verb SIT, is capable of

further analysis, we will treat it as a unit of analysis. A more detailed account would need to discuss the grammar of the word. Given this simplification, the analysis shown in Figure 1 is largely uncontroversial, and we will suppose that this deliberately minimal account is the appropriate grammatical description mentioned above.

The analysis identifies the words as the smallest relevant units, and displays information about their **lexical categorization** (*the* is an article, *mat* is a noun, etc.). It also shows the **constituent structure** of the sentence, what are and what are not held to be proper sub-parts of the sentence, and assigns each constituent recognized to a particular **category** (*the cat* is a noun phrase, *on the mat* is a prepositional phrase, and so on). Implicitly it also denies categorial status to other possible groupings of words; *sat on*, for example, is not a constituent at all.

A simple grammar that will generate this sentence and its grammatical description is:

Syntax
  S   → NP VP
  NP → Art N
  VP → V[l] PP
  PP → Prep NP

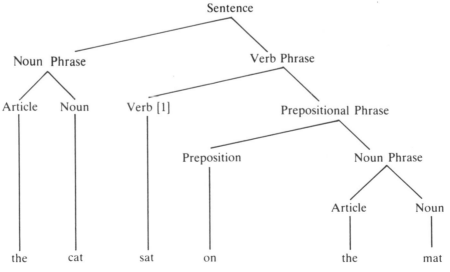

Figure 1

Lexicon
cat	N
mat	N
on	Prep
sat	V[1]
the	Art

(S = Sentence; NP = Noun Phrase; VP = Verb Phrase; Art = Article; N = Noun; V[1] = Verb of subclass [1]; PP = Prepositional Phrase; Prep = Preposition.)

Simple though this grammar is, it is formulated in accordance with some general principles. The most general of these is that a grammar consists of a number of distinct **components**. In this case there are two: a **syntax**, which defines permissible constituent structures; and a lexicon, which lists the words in the language and the lexical class to which each belongs. The syntax rules are themselves constrained along the following lines:

1 All rules are of the form A → B C.
2 → is to be interpreted as 'has the constituents'.
3 A rule may contain only one category on the left-hand side of →.
4 A rule may contain one or more categories (including further instances of the initial symbol 'S') on the right-hand side of →.
5 Categories introduced on the right-hand side of → are ordered with respect to each other.
6 'S' is the **initial symbol**; i.e. the derivation of any sentence must start with this symbol.
7 When the left-hand side of a rule is a phrasal category, the right-hand side of the rule must contain the corresponding lexical category, e.g. an NP must have an N as one of its constituents (and may have other categories – Det, say).
8 The lexical categories N, V, P, Det, etc. are the **terminal vocabulary**; i.e. these symbols terminate a derivation and cannot themselves be further developed in the syntax.

9 The lexical categories may be augmented to indicate the membership of some subclass of the category; e.g. in the example above, the category V is differentiated into V[l] (*lay*, *sat*), to distinguish it from V[2], V[3]), etc. (to which we will come).
10 The lexicon must be formulated in such a way that each word is assigned to one of the permissible lexical categories listed in 7.

The grammar can be easily extended. We could extend the lexicon:

a	Art
dog	N
under	Prep
lay	V[1]

We can add more rules to the syntax. For instance, *sat* and *lay* require to be followed by a PP – *The cat lay under the table* – but cannot be directly followed by an NP (**The cat lay the mouse*) or by a sentence (**The cat lay that the man chased the mouse*). They are characterized as V[1], i.e. verbs of subclass 1. By contrast, a verb like *caught* requires a following NP: *The cat caught the mouse* but not **the cat caught under the table* or **the cat caught that the mouse lay under the table*. We will characterize these as V[2]. The verb *said* is different again: it requires a following sentence: *The man said that the cat caught the mouse* but not either **the man said the cat* or **the boy said under the table*. We will label it as a member of V[3]. To accommodate these different grammatical subclasses of verb, we can add the following rules:

VP → V[2] NP
VP → V[3] S

This will entail additional vocabulary:

caught	V[2]
chased	V[2]
said	V[3]
thought	V[3]

This slightly enlarged grammar is capable of generating large numbers of sentences. It is true that they will exhibit a boringly limited range of syntactic structures and the difference between them will largely be lexical, but they will nevertheless be different. And with a modest number of additional rules of syntax and a few more lexical items, the number of distinct sentences the grammar will be capable of generating will become very substantial. Indeed, since the grammar contains the recursive rule VP → V[3] S, the formal power of the grammar is infinite.

This being the case, two things follow. The first is that the notion of **generative** must be understood to relate to the abstract capacity of the grammar to recognize a sentence as a member of the set of sentences it generates, rather than to a capacity to physically produce any particular sentence, or indeed physically recognize some particular sentence as a member of the set of sentences it can generate. The second is that the grammar is in itself neutral as to production and recognition. A mathematical analogy is appropriate. Suppose we had a rule to generate even numbers. It should be clear that in a literal sense the rule could not actually produce all the even numbers: since there are infinitely many of them, the task would be never-ending. It could, however, be the basis of an algorithm that could be used to produce an arbitrary even number as an example, or to check whether an arbitrary number is or is not an even number. In a comparable fashion we can construct an algorithm that will use a generative grammar in the construction of sentences together with their analyses, or the analysis of a particular sentence to see if it belongs to the set of sentences generated by the grammar. There are many ways of performing either task, so the set of rules which follow are merely exemplificatory. To produce sentences and assign them analyses of the kind shown in Figure 1, we could construct a **sentence generator** along the following lines:

1 Start with the initial symbol S.
2 Until all the category symbols are members of the terminal vocabulary (i.e. the lexical category symbols), repeat: for any category symbol that is not a member of the terminal vocabulary, select a rule from the syntax which has this symbol as the left-hand constituent and develop whatever structure the rule specifies.
3 Develop each lexical category symbol with a word from the lexicon of the relevant category.
4 Stop when all the items are words.

To check whether a sentence is generated by the grammar and offer an analysis, we could construct a parser along these lines:

1 Identify the lexical category of each word.
2 Repeat: for any category symbol or sequence of category symbols select a rule of the grammar in which these occur as the right-hand constituents of a rule and show them as constituents of the symbol on the left-hand side of the rule.
3 Stop when all the category symbols are constituents of S.

Let us now relate this simple account to the issues with which we began. With respect to the first issue, the productive capacity of a grammar, even the simple grammar illustrated can account for large numbers of sentences, particularly since it contains the **recursive** rule VP ≃ V[3] S, and the grammar can readily be extended. The second issue was concerned with the potential of an explicit rule system to derive the actual sentences of the language and to associate them with a grammatical description: given suitable generators and parsers, our rules can do this. The final issue is more contentious. Our grammar is indeed couched in terms of a set of principles of the sort that might be construed as universal principles of grammar design. Such principles can be formulated in mathematical terms. As to whether our grammar, as stated, also captures appropriate linguistic universals – this is clearly a matter that depends on what these are considered to be. The principles of constituent structure illustrated are not particularly controversial, but different theories may place other constraints.

E.K.B.

Suggestions for further reading

Chomsky, N. (1975a) *The Logical Structure of Linguistic Theory*, New York: Plenum Press.

Gazdar, G. (1987) 'Generative grammar', in J. Lyons, R. Coates, M. Deuchar and G. Gazdar (eds) *New Horizons in Linguistics*, vol. 2, Harmondsworth: Penguin.

Lyons, J. (1970) 'Generative syntax', in J. Lyons (ed.) *New Horizons in Linguistics*, Harmondsworth: Penguin.

Wall, R. (1972) *Introduction to Mathematical Linguistics*, Englewood Cliffs, NJ: Prentice Hall.

Formal logic and modal logic

Introduction

Logic studies the structure of arguments, and is primarily concerned with testing arguments for correctness or **validity**. An argument is **valid** if the premises cannot be true without the conclusion also being true: the conclusion **follows from** the premises. Since the time of Aristotle, validity has been studied by listing patterns or forms of argument all of whose instances are valid. Thus, the form:

Premise   All *A* is *B*.
Premise   *C* is *A*,
Conclusion so *C* is *B*.

is manifested in distinct arguments such as:

All men are mortal.
Socrates is a man,
so Socrates is mortal.

All Frenchmen are Europeans.
De Gaulle was a Frenchman,
so de Gaulle was European.

A third example clarifies the notion of validity:

All men are immortal.
Socrates is a man,
so Socrates is immortal.

Although the conclusion of this argument (*Socrates is immortal*) is false, the argument is valid: one of the premises (*All men are immortal*) is also false, but we can easily see that if both premises were true, the conclusion would have to be true as well.

There are good arguments which are not valid in this sense. Consider the argument:

All of the crows I have observed so far have been black.
I have no reason to think I have observed an unrepresentative sample of crows,
so all crows are black.

Both of the premises of this argument could be true while the conclusion was false. Such **inductive** arguments are central to the growth of scientific knowledge of the world. But **formal logic** is not concerned with inductive arguments; it is concerned with **deductive** validity, with arguments which meet the stricter standard of correctness described above (see Skyrms 1975, for a survey of work in inductive logic).

Logically valid arguments are often described as **formally valid**: if an argument is valid, then any argument of the same form is valid. This means that logicians are not concerned with arguments which depend upon the meanings of particular descriptive terms, such as:

Peter is a bachelor, so Peter is unmarried.

Rather, they are concerned solely with arguments that are valid in virtue of their logical or grammatical structure; they are concerned with features of structure that are signalled by the presence of so-called **logical words**: **connectives**, like *not*, *and*, *or*, *if . . . then . . .* ; **quantifiers** like *all*, *some*, and so on. We can represent the **logical form** of an argument by replacing all the expressions in it other than logical words and particles by variables, as in the example in the opening paragraph. The logical form of the example in the present paragraph can be expressed:

a is *F*, so *a* is *G*.

We see that the argument is not logically valid because it shares this form with the blatantly invalid

John is a husband, so John is a woman.

To explain why Peter's being unmarried follows from his being a bachelor, we must appeal to the meanings of particular non-logical words like *bachelor* and *married*; it cannot be explained solely by reference to the functioning of logical words.

I have described logic as concerned with the validity of arguments. It is sometimes described as concerned with a particular body of truths, the logical truths. These are statements whose truth depends solely upon the presence of logical words in them. For example:

Either London is a city or it is not the case that London is a city.

This is claimed to be true by virtue of its logical form: any statement of the form

Either *P* or it is not the case that *P*.

is true and is an illustration of the **law of excluded middle**, i.e. there is no third intermediate possibility.

The two descriptions of logic are not in competition. Corresponding to any valid argument, there is a conditional statement, i.e. an 'if . . . then . . .' statement, which is a logical truth. For example:

If all men are mortal and Socrates is a man,
then Socrates is mortal.

The Aristotelian approach to logic held sway until the late nineteenth century, when Gottlob Frege (1848–1925), Charles Peirce (1839–1914) and others developed new insights into the formal structure of arguments which illuminated complex inferences that had previously proved difficult to describe systematically. Philosophers normally hold that understanding a sentence requires at least some capacity to identify which of the arguments that the sentence can occur in are valid. Someone who did not see that *Socrates is mortal* follows from the premises *Socrates is a man* and *All men are mortal* would put into question her/his understanding of those sentences. In that case, the formal structures revealed by logicians are relevant to the semantic analysis of language. It should be noted, however, that until recently many logicians have believed that natural languages were logically incoherent and have not viewed their work as a contribution to natural language semantics. The motivation for the revitalization of logic just referred to was the search for foundations for mathematics rather than the understanding of natural language. I shall describe the most important systems of modern logic, which reflect the insights of Frege, Peirce, Bertrand Russell (1872–1970) and their followers.

Logicians study validity in a variety of ways and, unfortunately, use a wide variety of more or less equivalent notations. It is important to distinguish syntactic from semantic approaches. The former studies proof, claiming that an argument is valid if a standard kind of proof can be found which derives the conclusion from the premises. It describes rules of inference that may be used in these proofs and, sometimes, specifies axioms that may be introduced as additional premises in such proofs. This enables us to characterize an indefinite class of formally valid arguments through a finite list of rules and axioms. Semantic approaches to logic rest upon accounts of the truth conditions of sentences and the contributions that logical words make to them. An argument is shown to be valid when it is seen that it is not possible for the premises to be true while the conclusion is false (see FORMAL SEMANTICS). Semantic approaches often involve looking for **counterexamples**: arguments of the same form as the argument under examination, which actually have true premises and a false conclusion (see, for example, Hodges 1977, which develops the system of **truth trees** or **semantic tableaux**, which provides rules for testing arguments in this way).

Propositional calculus

The logical properties of **negation, conjunction, disjunction** and **implication** are studied within the **propositional** or **sentential calculus**. These notions are formally represented by connectives or operators, expressions which form complex sentences out of other sentences. *And*, for example, forms the complex sentence

Frege is a logician and Russell is a logician.

out of the two shorter sentences *Frege is a logician* and *Russell is a logician*. Logicians often speak of those sentence parts which can themselves be assessed as true or false as sentences; hence, the displayed sentence 'contains' the simpler sentences *Frege is a logician* and *Russell is a logician*. Similarly, *It is not the case that . . .* forms a complex sentence out of one simpler one. If A and B represent places that can be taken by complete sentences, a typical notation for the propositional calculus is:

$\neg A$ It is not the case that A
$A \vee B$ A or B
$A \mathbin{\&} B$ A and B
$A \rightarrow B$ If A then B

Complex sentences can be constructed in this way:

$(A \vee \neg B) \rightarrow$ If either A or it is
$(C \mathbin{\&} (B \rightarrow \neg D))$ not the case that B, then both C and if B then it is not the case that D.

The propositional calculus studies the logical properties of sentences built up using these logical notions.

Logicians treat these connectives as **truth functional**. We can evaluate utterances of indicative sentences by establishing whether what was said was **true** or **false**: these are the two **truth values** recognized by standard systems of logic. In the use of natural language, the truth value of a sentence can depend upon the context of its utterance: this is most evident in context-sensitive aspects of language like tense and the use of personal pronouns. Classical systems of logic abstract from this relativity to context and assume that they are dealing with sentences which have determinate truth values that do not vary with context. This allows logical laws to be formulated more simply and does not impede the evaluation of arguments in practice. Below, I shall indicate how logical systems can be enhanced to allow for context-sensitivity.

When a sentence is constructed from other sentences using such expressions, the truth value of the resulting sentence depends only upon the truth values of the sentences from which it is made. Thus, whatever the meaning of the sentence negated in a sentence of the form $\neg A$, the resulting sentence is true if the original sentence is false; and false if it is true. Similarly, a conjunction is true so long as each conjunct is true; and a disjunction is true so long as at least one disjunct is true. These relationships are expressed in **truth tables** (see Table 1). The two left-hand columns in Table 1 express the different possible combinations of truth values for A and B, and the other columns indicate the truth

Table 1 Truth tables

A	B	¬A	A & B	A ∨ B	A → B
t	t	f	t	t	t
t	f	f	f	t	f
f	t	t	f	t	t
f	f	t	f	f	t

values the complex sentences have in those circumstances.

Systems of propositional calculus provide rules for the evaluation of arguments which reflect the meanings the logical words receive according to this interpretation. A straightforward method of evaluation is to compute the truth values the premises and the conclusion must have in each of the possible situations, and then inspect the result to determine whether there are any situations in which the premises are true and the conclusion is false. This method can become cumbersome when complex arguments are considered, and other methods (such as truth trees) can be easier to apply.

The propositional calculus serves as a core for the more complex systems we shall consider: most arguments involve kinds of logical complexity which the propositional calculus does not reveal. Some claim that it is oversimple in other ways, too. They deny that logical words of natural languages are truth functional, or claim that to account for phenomena involving, for example, vagueness, we must admit that there are more than just two truth values, some statements having a third, intermediate, value between truth and falsity. Philosophers and logicians developed the notion of **implicature** partly to defend the logician's account of these logical words. They claim that phenomena which suggest that *and* or *not* are not truth functional reflect implicatures that attach to the expressions, rather than central logical properties (see PRAGMATICS). However, many philosophers would agree that this

is insufficient to rescue the truth-functional analysis of *if . . . then . . .* , with its implausible consequence that any indicative conditional sentence with a false antecedent is true. Such criticisms would not disturb those logicians who denied that they were contributing to natural-language semantics. They would hold it a virtue of their system that their pristine simplicity avoids the awkward complexities of natural languages and provides a precise notation for scientific and mathematical purposes.

Predicate calculus

Within the propositional calculus, we are concerned with arguments whose structure is laid bare by breaking sentences down into elements which are themselves complete sentences. Many arguments reflect aspects of logical structure which are not revealed through such analyses. The **predicate calculus** takes account of the logical significance of aspects of sub-sentential structure. It enables us to understand arguments whose validity turns on the significance of *some* and *all*, such as:

> John is brave.
> If someone is brave, then everyone is happy.
> so John is happy.

Aristotelian logic, mentioned above, described some of the logical properties of quantifiers like *some* and *all*. However, it was inadequate, largely because it did not apply straightforwardly to arguments that involve multiple quantification – sentences containing more than one interlocking quantifier. We need to understand why the following argument is valid, and also to see why the premise and conclusion differ in meaning:

> There is a logician who is admired by all philosophers.
> so Every philosopher admires some logician or other.

We shall now look at how sentences are analysed in the predicate calculus.

'John is brave' is composed of expressions of two sorts. *John* is a **name** or **singular term**, and *( ) is brave* is a **predicate**. The predicate contains a gap which is filled by a singular term to form the sentence. *Wittgenstein admired Frege* is similarly composed of predicates and singular terms. However, *( ) admired ( )* is a **two-place** or **dyadic** predicate or **relational expression**: it has two gaps which must be filled in order to obtain a complete sentence. There are also triadic predicates, such as *( ) gives ( ) to ( )*, and there may even be expressions with more than three places. Following Frege, predicates are referred to as 'incomplete expressions', because they contain gaps that must be filled before a complete sentence is obtained. Predicates are normally represented by big letters, and the names that complete them are often written after them, normally using small letters. Thus, the examples in this paragraph could be written:

Bj.
Awf (or wAf).
Gabc.

Combining this notation with that of the propositional calculus, we can symbolize

If Wittgenstein is a philosopher then Wittgenstein admires Frege.

thus:

Pw → wAf.

We can introduce the logical behaviour of quantifiers by noticing that the sentence

All philosophers admire Frege.

can receive a rather clumsy paraphrase:

Everything is such that if it is a philosopher then it admires Frege.

Similarly,

Someone is brave.

can be paraphrased:

Something is such that it is brave.

In order to regiment such sentences, we must use the **variables** x, y, etc. to express the pronoun *it*, as well as the **constants** that we have already introduced.

Everything is such that $(Px \rightarrow Axf)$
Something is such that (Bx)

And the relation between these variables and the quantifiers is made explicit when we regiment *Everything is such that* by '$\forall x$'; and *Something is such that* by '$\exists x$':

$\forall x\ (Px \rightarrow Axf)$
$\exists x\ (Bx)$

'$\forall$' is called the **universal quantifier**, '$\exists$' the **existential quantifier**. Our sample argument can then be expressed:

$\exists x\ (Lx\ \&\ \forall y\ (Py \rightarrow Ayx))$.
so $\forall y\ (Py \rightarrow \exists x\ (Lx\ \&\ Ayx))$.

The different variables 'keep track' of which quantifier 'binds' the variables in question.

Compare the two sentences:

Someone loves everyone.
Everyone is loved by someone.

These appear to have different meanings – although some readers may hear an ambiguity in the first. The notation of the predicate calculus helps us to see that the difference in question is a **scope distinction**. The former is naturally expressed:

$\exists x \forall y\ (xLy)$.

and the latter as:

$\forall y \exists x\ (xLy)$.

In the first case it is asserted that some individual has the property of loving everyone: the universal quantifier falls within the scope of the existential quantifier. In the second case, it is asserted that every individual has the property of being loved by at least one person – there is no suggestion, in this case, that it is the same person who loves every individual. The universal quantifier has **wide scope**, and the existential quantifier has **narrow scope**. The second statement follows logically from the first. But the first does not follow logically from the second.

> Some car in the car park is not green.
> It is not the case that some car in the car park is green.

reflects the scope difference between:

> $\exists x ((Cx \ \& \ Px) \ \& \ \neg Gx)$
> $\neg \exists x ((Cx \ \& \ Px) \ \& \ Gx)$

The former asserts that the car park contains at least one non-green car; the second asserts simply that it does not contain any green cars. If the car park is empty, the first is false and the second is true. In the first sentence, the negation sign falls within the scope of the quantifier; in the second case, the scope relation is reversed.

Tense logic and modal logic

While the logic I have described above may be adequate for expressing the statements of mathematics and (a controversial claim) natural science, many of the statements of natural language have greater logical complexity. There are many extensions of this logical system that attempt to account for the validity of a wider range of arguments. Tense logic studies arguments which involve tensed statements. In order to simplify a highly complex subject, I shall discuss only propositional tense logic, which results from introducing tense into the propositional calculus. This is normally done by adding tense operators to the list of logical connectives. Syntactically, 'It was the case that' and 'It will be the case that' ('P' and 'F') are of the same category as negation. The following are well-formed expressions of tense logic:

> PA.   It was the case that A.
> $\neg FPA$.   It is not the case that it will be the case that it was the case that A.

These operators are not truth functional: the present truth value of a sentence occupying the place marked by A tells us nothing about the truth value of either PA or FA. However, a number of fundamental logical principles of tense logic can be formulated which govern our tensed reasoning. For example, if a statement A is true, it follows that:

> PFA.
> FPA.

Moreover, if it will be the case that it will be the case that A, then it will be the case that A:

> $FFA \rightarrow FA$.

More complex examples can be found, too. If

> $PA \ \& \ PB$.

it follows that:

> $(P \ (A \ \& \ B)) \lor (P \ (PA \ \& \ B)) \lor (P \ (A \ \& \ PB))$

There is a variety of systems of tense logic, which offers interesting insights into the interplay of tense and quantification, and which augments these tense operators by studying the complex logical behaviour of temporal indexicals like *now* (see McCarthur 1976: chapters 1 and 2).

Modal logic was the first extension of classical logic to be developed, initially through the work of C.I. Lewis (see Lewis 1918). Like tense logic, it adds non-truth-functional operators to the simpler logical systems; in modal logic, these operators express the concepts of possibility and necessity. The concept of possibility is involved in assertions such as:

> It is possible that it will rain tomorrow.
> It might rain tomorrow.
> It could rain tomorrow.

Necessity is involved in claims like:

> Necessarily bachelors are unmarried.
> A vixen must be a fox.

Other expressions express these modal notions too.

Just as tense logic formalizes temporal talk by introducing tense operators, so modal logic employs two operators, 'L' and 'M', which correspond to 'It is necessarily the case that' and 'It is possibly the case that', respectively. The sentences displayed above would be understood as having the forms 'M*A*' and 'L*A*' respectively. There is an enormous variety of systems of modal logic, and rather little consensus about which of them capture the logical behaviour of modal terms from ordinary English. Some of the problems concern the interplay of modal operators and quantifiers. Others arise out of kinds of sentences which are very rarely encountered in ordinary conversation – those which involve several modal operators, some falling within the scope of others. To take a simple example: if 'L' is a sentential operator like negation, then it seems that a sentence of the form 'LLL*A*' must be well formed. However, we have very few intuitions about the logical behaviour of sentences which assert that it is necessarily the case that it is necessarily the case that it is necessarily the case that vixens are foxes. Only philosophers concerned about the metaphysics of modality are likely to be interested in whether such statements are true and in what can be inferred from them.

Some principles of inference involving modal notions are uncontroversial. Logicians in general accept as valid the following inference patterns:

L*A*, so *A*.

For example: vixens are necessarily foxes, so vixens are foxes. If something is necessarily true then, *a fortiori*, it is true.

A, so M*A*.

For example, if it is true that it will rain tomorrow, then it is true that it might rain tomorrow; if today is Wednesday, then today might be Wednesday. In general,

whatever is actually the case is possible. Moreover, there is little dispute that necessity and possibility are interdefinable. 'It is necessarily the case that *A*' means the same as 'It is not possible that it is not the case that *A*'; and 'It is possible that *A*' means the same as 'It is not necessarily the case that it is not the case that *A*'. Once one tries to move beyond these uncontroversial logical principles, however, the position is much more complex. There is a large number of distinct systems of modal logic, all of which have received close study by logicians. There is still controversy over which of these correctly capture the inferential properties of sentences about possibility and necessity expressed in English.

The extensions of the standard systems of logic are not exhausted by those alluded to here. **Deontic logic** is the logic of obligation and permission: it studies the logical behaviour of sentences involving words like *ought* and *may*. There is also a large body of work on the logic of subjective or counterfactual conditionals. Consider a claim such as:

If the door had been locked, the house would not have been burgled.

Although this is of a conditional form, the conditional in question is plainly not truth functional. If we substitute for the antecedent (the first clause in the conditional) another sentence with the same truth value, this can make a difference to the truth value of the whole sentence. For example:

If the window had been left open, the house would not have been burgled.

Like the statements studied in modal logic, such statements appear to be concerned with other possibilities. The first claim is concerned with what would have been the case had the possibility of our locking the door actually been realized (see Lewis 1973).

Progress in both modal logic and the logic of these subjunctive conditionals has resulted in the development of **possible-world semantics** by Saul Kripke and a number of other logicians (see, for example, Kripke 1963). This work, which is discussed in the article in this volume on FORMAL SEMANTICS, has led many philosophers and linguists to find in the work of formal logicians materials which can reveal the semantic structures of the sentences of a natural language.

C.H.

Suggestions for further reading

There are many introductory logic textbooks; the following illustrate contrasting approaches:

Guttenplan, S. (1997) *The Languages of Logic*, Oxford: Blackwell Publishers.
Hodges, W. (1977) *Logic*, Harmondsworth: Penguin.
Useful introductions to tense logic and modal logic are:
Chellas, B. (1980) *Modal Logic*, Cambridge: Cambridge University Press.
McCarthur, R. (1976) *Tense Logic*, Dordrecht: Reidel.
McCawley, J.D. (1981) *Everything That Linguists Have Always Wanted to Know About Logic . . . But Were Ashamed to Ask*, Oxford: Basil Blackwell.

Formal semantics

Introduction

Inspired by the work of Alfred Tarski (1901–83) during the 1920s and 1930s, logicians have developed sophisticated semantic treatments of a wide variety of systems of formal logic (see FORMAL LOGIC AND MODAL LOGIC). Since the l960s, as these semantic treatments have been extended to tense logic, modal logic and a variety of other systems simulating more of the expressions employed in a natural language, many linguists and philosophers have seen the prospect of a systematic treatment of the semantics of natural languages. Richard Montague, David Lewis, Max Cresswell, Donald Davidson and others have attempted to use these techniques to develop semantic theories for natural languages.

Underlying this work is the idea that the meanings of sentences are linked to their **truth conditions**; we understand a sentence when we know what would have to be the case for it to be true, and a semantic theory elaborates this knowledge. Moreover, the truth conditions of sentences are grounded in referential properties of the parts of those sentences in systematic ways. Tarski's contribution was to make use of techniques from set theory (see SET THEORY) in order to state what the primitive expressions of a language refer to, and in order to display the dependence of the truth conditions of the sentence as a whole upon these relations of reference.

Throughout, **true** is understood as a metalinguistic predicate. In general, the **object language** is the language under study; for example, our object language is English if we study the semantics of sentences of English. The **metalanguage** is the language we use to talk about the object language. 'True' belongs to the language we use in making our study, i.e. the metalanguage. Moreover, the primitive notion of **truth** is assumed to be **language-relative**, as in:

'Snow is white' is a true sentence of English.
'La neige est blanche' is a true sentence of French.

We shall use **TL** to stand for the predicate '. . . is a true sentence of L'. The task is to construct a theory which enables us to specify the circumstances under which individual sentences of a given language are true. It will yield theorems of the form:

S is TL if, and only if, *p*.

For example:

'La neige est blanche' is True(French) if, and only if, snow is white.

The interest of the theory lies in the way in which it derives these statements of truth conditions from claims about the semantic properties of the parts of sentences and about the semantic significance of the ways in which sentence parts are combined into grammatical wholes.

There are alternative approaches to the task of constructing such a semantic theory, and there is no space here to consider all of the controversies that arise. In the space available, I shall develop a semantic theory for a formal language which mirrors some of the logical complexities of a natural language. The language will contain the connectives and quantifiers employed in the predicate calculus and also include some tense operators and modal operators (see FORMAL LOGIC AND MODAL LOGIC).

A simple language

First we consider a language L_1, which contains no quantifiers, tense operators or modal operators. It contains three names, 'a', 'b' and 'c'; three **monadic** (one-place) predicates, 'F', 'G' and 'H', and the **dyadic** (two-place) relational expression 'R' (see FORMAL LOGIC AND MODAL LOGIC). It also contains the standard logical connectives of propositional logic: '&', '¬', '∨' and '→'.

The grammatical sentences of this language thus include the following:

Fa, Hb, Ga, Gc, Rab, Gb & Rbb, Ha ∨ (Ha & ¬Rbc).

We need to specify the truth conditions of all of these sentences together with the others that can be formulated within L_1.

We first specify the **referents** of the names; that is, we say who the bearers of the names are – which objects in the world the names stand for:

(la) ref(a) = Caesar
ref(b) = Brutus
ref(c) = Cassius

We then specify the **extensions** of the predicate expressions; that is, we say what property qualifies an object for having the predicate ascribed to it:

(lb) ext(F) = {*x*: *x* is a Roman}
ext(G) = {*x*: *x* is a Greek}
ext(H) = {*x*: *x* is an emperor}
ext(R) = {<*x*,*y*>: *x* killed *y*}

We then state:

(2) If a sentence is of the form *Pn*, then it is TL if, and only if, ref(*n*) ∈ ext(*P*).
If a sentence is of the form *Rnm*, then it is TL if and only if <ref(*n*), ref(*m*)> ∈ ext(*R*).

(see SET THEORY for the meaning of ∈). It is easy to see that the following specifications of truth conditions follow from these statements:

Fa is TL_1 if, and only if, Caesar is a Roman.
Rbc is TL_1 if, and only if Brutus killed Cassius.

and so on. We have constructed an elementary semantic theory for part of our elementary language.

It is easy to extend this to include sentential connectives:

(3) A sentence of the form *A&B* is TL_1 if, and only if, *A* is TL_1 and *B* is TL_1.
A sentence of the form ¬*A* is TL_1 if, and only if, *A* is not TL_1.

and so on. Relying upon such axioms, we can derive a statement of the TL_1 conditions of any sentence of our simple language.

The conditions listed under (1) specify semantic properties of sub-sentential expressions: names and predicates. Those under (2) explain the truth conditions of the simplest sentences in terms of the semantic properties of these sub-sentential

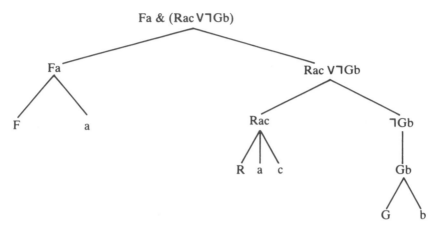

Figure 1

expressions. Finally, those in (3) concern the semantic roles of expressions which are used to construct complex sentences out of these simple ones. I mentioned that L_1 was a rather simple language, and we can now notice an important aspect of this simplicity. Consider the sentence 'Fa & (Rac ∨ Gb)'. We can represent the way in which this sentence is built out of its elements with a tree diagram (Figure 1).

The conditions in (1) state the semantic properties of expressions in the bottom nodes of the tree: those in (2) concern how the truth conditions of the next higher nodes are determined by these bottom semantic properties. All the higher nodes are explained by the conditions in (3). It is a feature of this language that, apart from the sub-sentential expressions at the bottom level, every expression of the tree has a **truth value**. It is true or false, and this is exploited in the conditions for explaining the truth conditions for complex sentences. We must now turn to a language which does not share this feature.

Quantifiers

L_2 is obtained from L_1 by adding universal and existential quantifiers ('∀' and '∃') together with a stock of individual variables, 'x', 'y', 'z', etc., as in formal logic (see

FORMAL LOGIC AND MODAL LOGIC). The grammatical sentences of L_2 include all the grammatical sentences of L_1 together with such expressions as:

$$\exists x Fx, \ \exists x \forall y \ Rxy, \ \forall z(Hz \ \& \ \exists x \ Rzx).$$

The tree diagram in Figure 2 displays the structure of the last of these. Such sentences are less straightforward than those discussed above. First, it is unclear what the semantic properties of variables are: they do not refer to specific objects, as names do. Second, the expressions 'Hz', 'Rzx' '$\exists x \ Rzx$' and '$Hz \ \& \ \exists x \ Rzx$' contain **free variables**, variables which are not bound by quantifiers. It is hard to see how such expressions can be understood as having definite truth

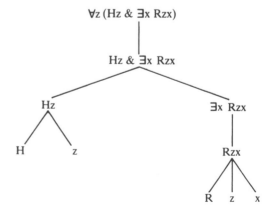

Figure 2

values. If that is the case, then we need a different vocabulary for explaining the semantic properties of some of the intermediate expressions in the tree. Furthermore, if these expressions do lack truth values, the condition we specified for '&', which was cast in terms of 'truth', cannot be correct: 'Hz & ∃x Rzx' is built out of such expressions and, indeed, is one itself.

First, we can specify a set D: this is the **domain** or **universe of discourse** – it contains everything that we are talking about when we use the language. The intuitive approach to quantification is clear. '∃xFx' is a true sentence of L$_2$ if at least one object in D belongs to the extension of 'F'; '∃x ∃y Rxy' is true so long as at least one pair of objects in D belongs to the extension of 'R'; '∀x Gx' is true if every object in D belongs to the extension of 'G'. The difficulties in the way of developing this idea emerge when we try to explain the truth conditions of sentences which involve more than one quantifier, such as '∃x ∀y Rxy', and those which contain connectives occurring within the scope of quantifiers, like '∀z (Hz & ∃x Rxz)'. The following is just one way to meet these difficulties. The strategy is to abandon the task of specifying truth conditions for sentences *directly*. Rather, we introduce a more primitive semantic notion of **satisfaction**, and then we define 'truth' in terms of satisfaction.

The problems to be faced here are largely technical, and it is not possible to go into the mathematical details here. However, it is possible to introduce some of the underlying concepts involved. Although variables do not refer to things as names or demonstrative expressions do, we can always (quite arbitrarily) allocate objects from the universe of discourse to the different variables. We shall call the result of doing this an **assignment** – it assigns values to all of the variables. It is evident that many different assignments could be constructed allocating different objects to the variables employed in the language.

We say that one of these assignments **satisfies** an open sentence if we should obtain a true sentence were we to replace the variables by names of the objects that the assignment allocates to them. For example, consider the open sentence

x is a city.

An assignment which allocated London to the variable 'x' would satisfy this open sentence, since *London is a city* is true. However, an assignment which allocated Brutus or the moon to this variable would not satisfy it. This close connection between satisfaction and truth should make it clear that an assignment will satisfy a **disjunctive** (*or*) sentence only if it satisfies at least one of the **disjuncts** (clauses held together by *or*). It will satisfy a **conjunctive** (*and*) sentence only if it satisfies both of the **conjuncts** (clauses held together by *and*).

We can then reformulate our statement of the truth conditions of simple quantified sentences. The existentially quantified sentence '∃x Fx' is true so long as at least one assignment satisfies the open sentence 'Fx'. If there is an assignment which allocates London to x, then at least one assignment satisfies 'x is a city'; so 'Something is a city' is true. In similar vein, '∀x Fx' is true if every assignment satisfies 'Fx'. So far, this simply appears to be a complicated restatement of the truth conditions for quantified sentences described above. The importance of the approach through satisfaction, as well as the mathematical complexity, emerges when we turn to sentences involving more than one quantifier. Consider the sentence *Someone admires all logicians*. Its logical form can be expressed:

∃x ∀y(Ly → xAy).

Under what circumstances would that be true?

As a first step, we can see that it is true so long as at least one assignment satisfies the open sentence:

∀y(Ly → xAy).

But when does an assignment satisfy an open sentence containing a universal quantifier? We cannot say that every assignment must satisfy 'Ly → xAy': that will be true only if *everybody* admires every logician, and so does not capture the truth conditions of the sentence that interests us. Rather, we have to say that an assignment satisfies our universally quantified open sentence so long as every assignment that agrees with it in what it allocates to 'x' satisfies 'Ly → xAy'. Our sentence is true so long as a large number of assignments satisfy 'Ly → xAy' which have the following properties:

1 Each one allocates the same object to 'x'.
2 Every member of the universe of discourse is assigned to 'y' by at least one of them.

This provides only an illustration of the use that is made of the concept of satisfaction in formal semantics. More complete, and more rigorous, treatments can be found in the works referred to in the suggestions for further reading. It illustrates how truth-conditional semantics can be extended beyond the fragment of a language where all of the sub-sentential expressions occurring in sentences have either truth values, references or extensions.

Tense and modality

I shall now briefly indicate how the semantic apparatus is extended to apply to L$_2$T and L$_2$TM: these are L$_2$ supplemented with tense operators and modal operators respectively (see FORMAL LOGIC AND MODAL LOGIC). L$_2$T contains the tense operators 'P' (*it was the case that . . .*) and 'F' (*it will be the case that . . .*). L$_2$M contains the modal operators 'L' (*necessarily*) and 'M' (*possibly*). In order to avoid forbidding complexity, we shall ignore problems that arise when we combine tense or modality with quantification. This means that we shall be able to consider the truth conditions of sentences without explaining these in terms of conditions of satisfaction.

Tensed language introduces the possibility that what is true when uttered at one time may be false when uttered at other times. Hence the truth predicate we need in our metalanguage if we are to describe the truth conditions of tensed sentences involves the idea of a sentence being true at a time:

'It is raining' is a true sentence of English at noon on 1 January 1991.

Similarly, we shall talk of expressions being satisfied by assignments at certain times and not at others. We can introduce a set T of moments: we order the members of T using the relational expression '<': '$t_1 < t_2$' means that t_1 (a member of T) is earlier than t_2. Unless time is in some way circular, this relation will be transitive, asymmetric and irreflexive (see SET THEORY).

We shall also have to introduce more complexity into our extensions for predicates and relations. A car may be red at one time, and then be painted blue, so it does not unequivocally belong to the extension of 'red'. The extension of 'red' will be a set of ordered pairs, each pair consisting of an object and a time: $<a, t_3>$ will belong to the extension of 'red' if object a was red at time t_3. (Alternatively, we could retain a set of objects as the extension of 'red' and insist that a predicate will have a different extension at different times.) Similarly, the extension of the relation 'loves' will be a set of ordered triples, comprising two individuals and a time such that the first individual loved the second individual at that time.

The idea behind the semantics for tense is straightforward. 'PA' is true at a time if 'A' is true at some earlier time: 'FA' is true at a time if 'A' is true at a later time. More formally:

'PA' is true at t_n if, and only if, $\exists t_m$ ($t_m < t_n$ & 'A' is true at t_m)
'FA' is true at t_n if, and only if, $\exists t_m$ ($t_n < t_m$ & 'A' is true at t_m)

On this basis, we can account for the truth conditions of complex tensed sentences, especially when quantification is introduced.

The semantics for modality is analogous to that for tense. We can all conceive that the world might have been very different from the way it actually is: there are countless 'ways the world could have been'. Many sentences will have different truth values in these **different possible** worlds. Just as we have seen that the truth value of a sentence can vary from time to time, so it can vary from possible world to possible world. We make use of a set W of possible worlds, whose members, $w_1, w_2, \ldots w_n, \ldots$, include the actual world together with many others that are 'merely' possible. Just as tensed discourse led us to recognize that we should only talk of the truth value of a sentence at a time, so modal discourse leads us to relativize truth to a world:

S is a true sentence of L at t in w.

The intuitive idea is again straightforward. 'MA' is true in a world w if 'A' is true in at least one possible world, but not necessarily w itself. Once again we may have to adjust the semantic values of predicates: the extension of 'red' is extended into a set of ordered triples, which will serve as its **intension**. Each triple will consist in an object, a time and a world. $<o, t_n, w_n>$ belongs to the extension of 'red' if object o is red at time t_n in world w_n. Statements of truth conditions are again relativized:

'Fa' is true at t_n in w_n if, and only if, $<\text{ref}(a), t_n, w_n>$ belongs to the extension of 'F'.
'LA' is true at t_n in w_n if, and only if, 'A' is true at t_n in every world. etc.

There is a large number of systems of modal logic and tense logic that have been described and studied in the literature. For example, systems of tense logic vary according to their conception of the members of the set of moments T, and of the relation between moments '<'. Thus, there are systems which describe the structure of discrete time and others which assume that

time is densely ordered; other systems allow for circular time or for the possibility that time branches. Modal logicians usually define a relation on the class of worlds which is analogous to '<'. This is often called an **accessibility relation** or an **alternativeness relation**. If we express this relation 'R', then the truth conditions of sentences involving modal operators are expressed:

'LA' is true at t_n in w_n if, and only if, A is true at t_n in every world w_m such that $w_n R w_m$,
'MA' is true at t_n in w_n if, and only if, there is a world w_m such that $w_n R w_m$, and 'A' is true in w_m.

This relation has no natural expression corresponding to the reading of '<' as 'earlier than'. However, examination of the structure of the class of a world in this way has yielded insights into the understanding of sentences involving several iterated modal operators. Chellas (1980) or Hughes and Cresswell (1968) provide detailed introductions to the use of these techniques in studying the semantics of modal logics.

Many logicians have been occupied with extending this framework to account for a much larger fragment of English. The literature contains explorations of the semantics of adjectives and adverbs, the semantics of **subjunctive conditionals**, words like *ought* and *may*, and sentences involving mental-state words such as *believes* and *desires*.

C.H.

Suggestions for further reading

Bridge, J. (1977) *Beginning Model Theory*, Oxford: Oxford University Press.

Dowty, D.R., Wall, R.E. and Peters, S. (1981) *Introduction to Montague Semantics*, Dordrecht: Reidel.

Lewis, D. (1970/1983) 'General semantics', *Synthese* 22: 18–67; reprinted 1983, in *Philosophical Papers*, vol. 1, New York and Oxford: Oxford University Press.

Functional phonology

By **functional phonology** is normally meant the phonological theory predominantly associated with the Russian, Nikolaj Sergeyevich Trubetzkoy (1890–1938). This theory is also known as **Prague School phonology**, and there exists a fair amount of literature on the subject. Much less has been written in English about the functional phonological theory developed by the Frenchman André Martinet (1908–99) and his associates. Both streams of functional phonology are founded on linguistic functionalism (see FUNCTION-ALIST LINGUISTICS) and have much in common, but also significant divergences on some fundamental theoretical points.

Functionalists study phonic elements from the points of view of the various functions they fulfil in a given language. They identify and order these functions hierarchically. Some of the better-known functions are the following:

- The **representative function**, whereby speakers inform listeners of whatever extralinguistic facts or states they are talking about. This corresponds to what the Austrian psychologist-linguist, Karl Bühler (1879–1963) – a member of the Prague Linguistic Circle – calls *Darstellungsfunktion*.
- The **indexical** or expressive function (Bühler's *Kundgabefunktion* or *Ausdrucks-funktion*), whereby information is revealed to the listener about various aspects of the speaker. For example, British speakers who consistently use in their pronunciation of *mate* a monophthongal vowel (e.g. [e:], which is very close to cardinal vowel no. 2 – see ARTICUL-ATORY PHONETICS), instead of the corresponding diphthongal vowel ([ei]) thereby reveal that their geographical provenance is northern England or Scotland. A speaker of Chukchi of northeastern Asia who pronounces [ʧ] reveals himself as an adult male, while another

Chukchi speaker who pronounces [ts] in its place shows her/himself as an adult female or a child. The indexical function may further impart information about the speaker's socioeconomic status, occupation, degrees of formal education, etc.
- The **appellative** or **conative function** (Bühler's *Appellfunktion*), which serves to provoke well-definable impressions or feelings in the listener. For example, an imperative tone in which a military order is given by a superior officer urges soldiers to undertake a certain action. Or, a specific intonation with which an utterance is made may have the effect of inducing the listener to carry out or not to carry out a certain act.
- The **distinctive function**. This is a function which derives directly from the concept of opposition and, in the case of phonological analysis, from the concept of phonological opposition. It is the function by virtue of which linguistic forms are opposed to, or differentiated from, each other. The minimal linguistic form that is meaningful, or the minimal significant unit, is known as a **moneme**, which consists of the association between a **signifier** (vocal expression) and a **signified** (semantic content). For example, in English, *bet* and *bit* are monemes whose signifiers and signifieds are, respectively, /bet/ and 'bet', and /bɪt/ and 'bit'. Two further examples of monemes are *spell* and *smell*, whose signifiers and signifieds are, respectively, /s p–be l/ (where /p–b/ is an **archiphoneme** – see below) and 'spell', and /smel/ and 'smell'. The members of the former pair are phonologically distinguished by virtue of the opposition between /e/ in bet and /ɪ/in bit, and those of the latter pair by virtue of the opposition between /p–b/ and /m/. Conventionally, the letters enclosed by two diagonal lines stand for sequentially minimal distinctive units which may be phonemes (e.g. /b/ above) or archiphonemes (e.g. /p–b/ above). We say that a phoneme or

an archiphoneme fulfils the distinctive function. Similarly, in a tone language (see TONE LANGUAGES), each of the tones fulfils the distinctive function, so that, for example, /˜ma/ 'mother' and /´ma/ 'hemp' in Mandarin Chinese are phonologically differentiated from each other by virtue of the opposition between /˜/ (a high level tone) and /´/ (a high rise from a mid-high level). Of course, a tone language also possesses phonemes and archiphonemes, so that, for example, /˜ma/ and /˜ta/, 'it, he, she', are differentiated from each other by virtue of the opposition between /m/ and /t/, while /şi-y/ 'teacher' and /şu/ 'book' are distinguished from each other by virtue of the opposition between /i–y/ and /u/. Note that a phoneme, an archiphoneme, a tone or an **architone** has no meaning. The distinctive function is an indispensable phonological function in any given language.

- The **contrastive function** (Martinet's *fonction contrastive*, Trubetzkoy's *kulminative Funktion*), which enables the listener to analyse a spoken chain into a series of significant units like monemes, words, phrases, etc. Accent in a language functions contrastively by bringing into prominence one, and only one, syllable in what is called an accentual unit. Since an accentual unit is in many languages (e.g. Polish, Spanish, Russian, Italian) what is commonly referred to as a word, the listener automatically analyses a spoken chain into a series of words. However, in such a language as German, which allows cumulative compounding in word formation, a compound word may consist of a number of elements, each of which bears accent. To consider just one example, in the German word *Kleiderpflegeanstalt* ('valet service'), each element (*Kleider-*, *-pflege-*, *-anstalt*) receives accent, but with a hierarchy in the strength of the accent, so that the accent in *Kleider-* is the strongest, that in *-anstalt* less strong, and that in *-pflege-* the least strong. What is meant by

the term contrastive is that the accented syllable contrasts with (stands out in relation to) the unaccented syllable(s) and thus characterizes the accentual unit as a whole.

- The **demarcative** or **delimitative function**, which is fulfilled in such a way that the boundary between significant units is indicated. For example, in German, the phoneme sequence /nm/ reveals a boundary as existing between /n/ and /m/, since in this language no word either begins or ends with /nm/. The word *unmöglich* is a case in point, *un* being one significant unit (here a moneme) and *möglich* another significant unit (here a combination of monemes). In Tamil, to consider another language, an aspirated voiceless plosive occurs in word-initial position only. Consider, for example, *talai* [tʰ] 'head', *pontu* [-ḍ-] 'hole', *katu* [-ð-] 'ear'. The three different sounds are all realizations of one and the same phoneme [t̪]. The occurrence of the aspirated voiceless plosive in this language therefore indicates the boundary between the word which begins with it and the preceding word. Another example of a phonic feature functioning demarcatively is a fixed accent, i.e. an accent whose place in the accentual unit is always fixed in relation to (as the case may be) the beginning or end of the accentual unit. A fixed accent functions not only contrastively but also demarcatively. Accent in Swahili always falls on the last but one syllable of the accentual unit which corresponds to a word, so that the occurrence of the accent shows that the following word begins with the second syllable after the accented syllable. Likewise, accent in Finnish, which is a fixed accent always falling on the initial syllable of the accentual unit that corresponds to a word, reveals that the word boundary occurs between the accented syllable and the preceding syllable. Of course, a free accent (i.e. one which is not fixed) can only function contrastively and not demarcatively as well.

- The **expressive function**, whereby speakers convey to listeners their state of mind (real or feigned) without resorting to the use of an additional moneme or monemes. For example, a speaker of English may say *That tree is eNNNormous*, overlengthening /n/ and employing an exaggerated high fall pitch over *-nor-*, instead of saying *That tree is absolutely enormous* or *That tree is tremendously enormous*, employing the additional monemes *absolute* and *ly*, or *tremendous* and *ly*. The specific suprasegmental phonic elements just mentioned fulfil the expressive function in that they indicate the speakers' admiration, surprise, etc. at the size of the tree in question. It should be noted in this connection that intonation pre-eminently fulfils the expressive function in which pitch phenomena are exploited expressively, i.e. speakers express definiteness or lack of definiteness, certainty or uncertainty, etc. in their minds about what they predicate.

The above are some major functions of phonic elements (there are other, minor, ones) that are identified in various languages. They are all recognized as major functions, but it is possible to establish a hierarchy of functions in terms of their relative importance from a functional point of view. For example, Trubetzkoy (1939/ 1969: 28) says that the distinctive function is indispensable and far more important than the culminative and deliminative functions, which are expedient but dispensable; all functionalists agree with him on this point.

It has been pointed out (see above) that the distinctive function derives directly from the concept of phonological opposition and that the distinctive function is fulfilled by a phoneme, an archiphoneme, a tone or an architone. As mentioned above, the distinctive function is considered to be by far the most important function, and in what follows we shall be exclusively concerned with some aspects of functional phonology that are relevant to this function.

It is crucial to understand that, in functional phonology, the concept of **phonological opposition** is primary, while the concept of the **phoneme** is secondary; without a phonological opposition, phonemes are inconceivable and inadmissible; the concept of the phoneme derives its validity from the fact that phonemes are members of a phonological opposition. The concept of phonological opposition is thus at the centre of functional phonology.

A **phoneme** or an **archiphoneme** is a sum of **phonologically relevant features** – relevant features, for short – which themselves fulfil the distinctive function. (Relevant features should not be confused with distinctive features as employed in generative phonology – see DISTINCTIVE FEATURES.) For example, the English monemes *bark* and *mark*, or *park* and *mark*, are distinguished from each other by virtue of the opposition between /b/ and /m/, or between /p/ and /m/. Furthermore, /b/ and /m/, or /p/ and /m/, are distinguished from each other because of the opposition between the relevant features 'non-nasal' and 'nasal'. An opposition between phonemes, between phonemes and archiphonemes, between archiphonemes, between relevant features, or between tones, between tones and architones, or between architones, is said to be a **phonological opposition**. The inventory of the distinctive units of a given language comprises the phonemes and the archiphonemes, and the tones and architones (if any) as well, in the case of a tone language. A phoneme or an archiphoneme is realized by sounds, generally referred to as **variants** or **realizations**, each of which possesses the phonologically relevant phonic features that characterize the phoneme or the archiphoneme concerned, plus phonologically irrelevant features. The same is true of realizations of a tone, except that these are pitches. Variants too are identified in terms of their functions, so that the functionalist talks about, for example, **combinatory variants** (variants associated with specific phonetic contexts in which they occur), **individual variants** (variants endowed with the indexical function), **stylistic variants** (variants indicative of different styles of speech), etc. These variants are also hierarchically identified according to their different functions in the phonology of a given language.

The **phonemes** and the **archiphonemes** of a given language are identified at the same time as mutually different sums of relevant features in terms of which they are definable, by means of the **commutation test**. In order to perform the commutation test, the functionalist chooses from within a corpus of data a certain number of **commutative series** which are associated with different phonetic contexts and each of which consists of a series of monemes, arranged in a parallel order, whose signifiers differ minimally from each other by the difference of a single segment at a corresponding point while the rest are identical.

Let us suppose that functionalists have at their disposal a corpus of English data. Let us also suppose that they have selected the following commutative series: commutative series 1, associated with the phonetic context [-ɪn], consisting of *pin, bin, tin, din, sin, zinn(ia), fin, vin(cible)*, etc.; commutative series 2, associated with the phonetic context [mæ], consisting of *map, Mab, mat, mad, mass, Maz(da), maf(ia), mav(erick)*, etc.; commutative series 3, associated with the phonetic context [ʌ-ə], consisting of *upper, (r)ubber, utter, udder, (t)usser, (b)uzzer, (s)uffer, (c)over*, etc. More commutative series are, of course, available, but the three we have chosen will suffice to illustrate the commutation test here.

As functionalists go on to consider more and more different commutative series, a point of diminishing return is reached fairly soon. In commutative series 1 above, we can see that [p] is differentiated from [b], [t], [d], [s], [z], [f], [v], etc., and that in commutative series 2, [p] is differentiated from [b], [t], [d], [s], [z], [f], [v], etc.: the phonetic differences between these segments are similarly minimal across the different commutative series. It will also be seen that, for example, [p] in commutative series 1 differs from [m] in the same series by the same phonetic difference that distinguishes [p] in commutative series 2 from [m] in that series, and furthermore, [p] in commutative series 3 from [m] in that series. The phonetic difference consists in the opposition between non-nasality (in [p]) and nasality (in [m]). Comparison between [p] and [t] in all three commutative series reveals bilabiality ascribable to [p] and apicality ascribable to [t].

Similarly, comparison between [p] and [b] in all three commutative series reveals voicelessness ascribable to [p] and voicedness ascribable to [b]. The latter phonetic difference needs some clarification, which will be provided below when the internal structure of a relevant feature is explained.

On the basis of this commutation test, functionalists identify, among other relevant features, the relevant features 'non-nasal', 'bilabial' and 'voiceless', the sum of which constitutes the phoneme /p/. Similarly, the sum of 'non-nasal', 'bilabial' and 'voiced' constitutes the phoneme /b/; the sum of 'non-nasal', 'apical' and 'voiceless' constitutes the phoneme /t/; the sum of 'non-nasal', 'apical' and 'voiced' constitutes the phoneme /d/; and so on. What have been referred to above as [p]s in the different commutative series are realizations of one and the same phoneme, /p/. Likewise, other segments are realizations of other given phonemes.

If functionalists identify [b]s (correctly, [b̥]s, i.e. devoiced) in commutative series 1 and 2 as realizations of the same phoneme (/b/) whose realization is [b] (voiced) in commutative series 3, rather than as a realization of a different phoneme (/p/) whose realizations in all three commutative series are voiceless ([p] or [p]), this is *not* because of phonetic similarity or orthography or functionalists' linguistic consciousness but because of the identical proportional relation of distinction that exists between [b]s and other segments in each of the different commutative series. The principle of the commutation test fundamentally and closely resembles that of the theory of the **micro-phoneme** and the **macro-phoneme** proposed in 1935 by the American linguist, William Freeman Twaddell (1906–82).

A **relevant feature** is identified in the course of the commutation test performed on a corpus of data obtained from a given language under phonological analysis. Unlike **distinctive features**, with which generative phonology operates (see DISTINCTIVE FEATURES), there is no universal framework of relevant features set up *a priori*. Furthermore, the **internal structure** of a relevant feature is a complex of multiple nondissociable distinctive phonic features, some of which may be present in some phonetic contexts while others may not be present in other phonetic contexts. Here lies a difference between a relevant feature on the one hand and a distinctive feature *à la* generative phonology on the other, since the latter refers to a single phonic feature. Yet another difference is that a relevant feature is not **binary**, while a distinctive feature in generative phonology always is. Thus, for example, the relevant features 'nasal' (as in /m/) and 'non-nasal' (as in /p/ and /b/) in English consonant phonemes which are opposed to each other are two different relevant features, and should never be confused with [+nasal] and [–nasal] as used in generative phonology, where they are seen as deriving from the single distinctive feature [nasal]. It goes without saying that, for example, the relevant features 'bilabial' (as in /p/), 'apical' (as in /t/), 'velar' as in /k/), etc., in English consonant phonemes which are opposed to each other, are not binary.

We shall now look in some detail at the question of the **internal structure** of a relevant feature. For example, the relevant feature 'bilabial' in English consists of not only the bilabial closure, but also all the other concomitant physiological phenomena occurring in the oral and pharyngeal cavities. To consider another example, the relevant feature 'voiced' (in, e.g. /b/) in English is a complex of glottal vibration, a relatively lax muscular tension in the supraglottal vocal tract and all the other concomitantly occurring physiological phenomena when, for example /b/ is opposed to /p/, /d/ is opposed to /t/, /z/ is opposed to /s/, and so on. Glottal vibration is partially or entirely absent when /b/, /d/, /z/, etc. occur in post-pausal or prepausal position (e.g., in *bark*, *cab*, etc.), but this does not change 'voiced' into 'voiceless' nor does it give primacy to the phonic feature **fortis** (i.e. relatively great muscular tension), which is opposed to the phonic feature **lenis**, over voicelessness, or even to the exclusion of voicelessness.

Such absence of a certain phonic feature is dictated by a particular phonetic context in which the relevant feature occurs, for the voicedness does occur in all those different phonic contexts that are favourable to voicing – say, in intervocalic position. A relevant feature in a given language is identified, in spite of any minor variation observed in terms of the presence or absence of some of its multiple non-dissociable distinctive phonic features, as a unitary entity which phonologically functions as a single global unit in opposition to another, or other, relevant feature(s) in the same language, which also function(s) phonologically as (a) single global unit(s). The term **non-dissociable**, used in definitionally characterizing the relevant feature, is therefore to be taken in this particular sense and not in the sense of 'constant'. It may be the case that the common base of the member phonemes of a phonological opposition in a given language is *not* found in any other phoneme(s) of the same language. For example, in English, /m/ (defined as 'bilabial nasal'), /n/ ('apical nasal') and /ŋ/ ('velar nasal') share the common base, 'nasal', which is not found in any other phoneme(s) of this language. In such a case, the phonemes are said to be in an exclusive relation; that is, the common base is exclusive to the phonemes in question. Some functionalists suggest the term 'exclusive opposition' to designate conveniently this type of phonological opposition, whose member phonemes are in an exclusive relation. An exclusive opposition is of particular importance in functional phonology, as we shall see below.

On the other hand, it may be the case that the common base of the member phonemes of a phonological opposition in a given language *is* found in another, or other, phoneme(s) of the same language. For example, again in English, /p/ ('voiceless bilabial non-nasal') and /t/ ('voiceless apical non-nasal') share the common base 'voiceless non-nasal' which is also found in /k/ ('voiceless velar non-nasal') of this language. In such a case, /p/ and /t/ are said to be in a **non-exclusive relation**, and some functionalists suggest the term **non-exclusive opposition** to designate conveniently this type of phonological opposition, whose member phonemes are in a non-exclusive relation.

The common base of the phonemes of an exclusive opposition – provided that it is **neutralizable** (see below) – (but not of a non-exclusive opposition) is the **archiphoneme**, which may be defined as the sum of the relevant features of the (two or more) phonemes of an exclusive opposition.

An exclusive opposition may or may not be a **neutralizable opposition**. However, a neutralizable opposition is bound to be an exclusive opposition; it is never a non-exclusive opposition. This brings us to the concept of **neutralization**, which may be illustrated as follows. In English, /m/–/n/–/ŋ/ (that is, the opposition between /m/, /n/ and /ŋ/), is operative in, say, moneme-final position (cf. *rum* vs *run* vs *rung*). It

is, however, not operative, e.g. moneme-medially before /k/ (cf. *anchor*) or /g/ (cf. *anger*), that is, there is no possibility of having /m/–/n/–/ŋ/ in such a position. According to functionalists, /m/–/n/–/ŋ/, which is operative in moneme-final position (the position of relevance for this phonological opposition), is neutralized in the position describable as 'moneme-medially before /k/ or /g/' (the position of neutralization for this phonological opposition). This neutralization results from the fact that the opposition between the relevant features 'bilabial' (in /m/), 'apical' (in /n/) and 'velar' (in /ŋ/), which is valid in moneme-final position, is cancelled (note, not 'neutralized') moneme-medially before /k/ or /g/. What is phonologically valid in the latter position is the common base of /m/, /n/ and /ŋ/, which is none other than the archiphoneme /m–n–ŋ/, definable as 'nasal'.

/m/–/n/–/ŋ/ in English is, then, said to be a neutralizable opposition which is operative in the **position of relevance** but is neutralized in the **position of neutralization**. Since the relevant feature 'nasal', which alone characterizes the archiphoneme /m–n–ŋ/, is not found in any other phoneme in English, the opposition /m/–/n/–/ŋ/ is, of course, an exclusive opposition. The phonic feature of velarity, which characterizes the realization (i.e. [ŋ] in ['æŋka] or ['æŋga]) of this archiphoneme, is not part of its phonological characteristics; rather, the occurrence of velarity in its realization is merely dictated by the fact that /k/ or /g/ which follows the archiphoneme is phonologically velar.

The concept of neutralization presented above is largely in line with Martinet and his associates' phonological analysis. In contrast, Trubetzkoyan phonological analysis is incapable of accounting for the neutralization of /m/–/n/–/ŋ/ monememedially before /k/ or /g/ in English, for Trubetzkoy always presents a phonological opposition as consisting of two (and not more than two) phonemes, and operating with other phonological concepts compatible with such a concept of phonological opposition. His presentation of various types of phonological opposition (bilateral, multilateral; proportional, isolated; privative, gradual, equipollent; constant, neutralizable) is always such that a phonological opposition is formed by two phonemes. (See Trubetzkoy 1939/1969: 67–83, for a detailed explanation of these types of phonological opposition.)

In a case where a neutralizable opposition happens to be a phonological opposition consisting of two phonemes, Trubetzkoy accounts for its neutralization in the following way. For instance, in German, /t/–/d/, which is a bilateral opposition operative in, say, moneme-initial prevocalic position (cf. *Tank, Dank*), is neutralized in moneme-final position (cf. *und, freund(lich)*), where only the archiphoneme is valid and is 'represented' by the unmarked member of the opposition (/t/? [t]?). The phonetic or phonological status of the **archiphoneme representative** is a moot point over which there exists disagreement even among functionalists. As is evident from Trubetzkoy's use of the notion of the **mark** and the associated notions of **marked** and **unmarked**, a neutralizable opposition is supposed to be a privative opposition formed by the marked and the unmarked phonemes.

Martinet and the majority (if not all) of his associates give much the same account of the neutralization of such an exclusive opposition consisting of two phonemes, except that they generally do not resort to the concept of bilateral opposition and to the concept of the archiphoneme representative. It should be noted in passing that a few functionalists do not operate with the notions of the mark, marked and unmarked in their account of any neutralization (see Akamatsu 1988: chapter 11).

However, it is important to note that functionalists' concept of neutralization is an inevitable consequence of their prior belief in the concept of phonological opposition.

It should be mentioned in this connection that some functionalists (see Vachek 1966: 62; Buyssens 1972a, 1972b) have abandoned the concept of the archiphoneme while claiming to operate with the concept of neutralization, a stance which has come under fire from other functionalists. The debate on this issue can be pursued through the writings of Akamatsu, Buyssens and Vion in issues of *La Linguistique* from 1972 to 1977. It is also discussed in Davidsen-Nielsen (1978) and in Akamatsu (1988; 1992).

Finally, a few words are in order about the concepts of the **mark**, **marked** and **unmarked**, and the concept of **correlation**. Most functionalists consider that one of the two phonemes of a privative opposition possesses the mark and hence is marked, while the other phoneme lacks it and hence is unmarked. Thus, with regard to /d/–/t/ in English, for example, /d/ is said to possess the mark (i.e. voice) and is marked, while /t/ is said to lack it and is hence unmarked. Some functionalists disagree with this idea (see Akamatsu 1988: chapter 11).

A **correlation** consists of a series of bilateral privative proportional oppositions and involves the concept of the mark. For example, a partial phonological system like

p   t   k
b   d   g

is a simple correlation wherein /p/ and /b/, /t/ and /d/ and /k/ and /g/ are said to be correlative pairs; /p/, /t/ and /k/ are said to be unmarked while /b/, /d/ and /g/ are said to be marked, the mark of correlation being voice. Furthermore, for example, a partial phonological system like

p   t   k
b   d   g
m   n   ŋ

is a **bundle of correlations** wherein, in addition to the above-mentioned simple correlation with voice as the mark, there is a further correlation whose mark is nasality, which separates /p t k b d g/, on the one hand, and /m n ŋ/, on the other, from each other, so that the former group of phonemes is said to be unmarked and the latter marked.

T.A.

Suggestions for further reading

Akamatsu, T. (1992) *Essentials of Functional Phonology*, Louvain-la-Neuve:

Peeters, particularly chapters 3–6 and chapter 9.

Martinet, A. (1964) *Elements of General Linguistics*, London: Faber and Faber, particularly chapters 1–3.

Trubetzkoy, N.S. (1939/1969) *Principles of Phonology*, trans. C.A.M. Baltaxe, Berkeley and Los Angeles: University of California Press, particularly chapters 1, 3, 5 and 6, and part 2.

Functionalist linguistics

Functionalism in linguistics arises from the concerns of Vilém Mathesius (1882–1945), a teacher at the Caroline University in Prague, who in 1911 published an article, 'On the potentiality of the phenomena of language' (English translation in Vachek 1964), in which he calls for a non-historical approach to the study of language. Some of the linguists who shared his concerns, including the Russian, Roman Osipovich Jakobson (1896–1982), and who became known as the **Prague School Linguists**, met in Prague for regular discussions between 1926 and 1945, but the Prague School also included linguists not based in Czechoslovakia (Sampson 1980: 103), such as the Russian, Nikolaj Sergeyevich Trubetzkoy (1890–1938) (see FUNCTIONAL PHONOLOGY). More recently, functionalism has come to be associated with the British linguist Michael Alexander Kirkwood Halliday (b. 1925) and his followers.

It was the belief of the Prague School linguists that 'the phonological, grammatical and semantic structures of a language are determined by the functions they have to perform in the societies in which they operate' (Lyons 1981: 224), and the notions of **theme**, **rheme** and **functional sentence perspective**, which are still much in evidence in Halliday's work (see especially Halliday 1985/1994), originate in Mathesius's work (Sampson 1980: 104).

J.R. Firth (1890–1960), who became the first professor of Linguistics in England, took what was best in structuralism and functionalism and blended it with insights provided by the anthropologist Bronislaw Malinowski (1884–1942). Because both Firth and Malinowski were based in London, they and their followers, including Halliday and R.A. Hudson (b. 1939), are sometimes referred to as the **London School** (Sampson 1980: chapter 9).

Malinowski carried out extensive fieldwork in the Trobriand Islands and argues that language is not a self-contained system – the extreme structuralist view – but is *entirely* dependent on the society in which it is used (in itself also an extreme view). He maintains that language is thus dependent on its society in two senses:

1 A language evolves in response to the specific demands of the society in which it is used.
2 Its use is entirely context-dependent: 'utterance and situation are bound up inextricably with each other and the context of situation is indispensable for the understanding of the words' (Malinowski 1923).

He maintains (Sampson 1980: 225):

that a European, suddenly plunged into a Trobriand community and given a word-by-word translation of the Trobrianders' utterances, would be no nearer understanding them than if the utterances remained untranslated – the utterances become comprehensible only in the context of the whole way of life of which they form part.

He distinguishes the immediate **context of utterance** from a general and generalizable **context of situation**, and argues that we must study meaning with reference to an analysis of the functions of language in any given culture. For example, in one Polynesian society Malinowski studied, he distinguished three major functions:

- The **pragmatic function** – language as a form of action
- The **magical function** – language as a means of control over the environment
- The **narrative function** – language as a storehouse filled with useful and necessary information preserving historical accounts

Malinowski is perhaps best known, however, for his notion of **phatic communion**. By this, he means speech which serves the function of creating or maintaining 'bonds of sentiment' (Sampson 1980: 224) between speakers (Malinowski 1923: 315); English examples would include idle chat about the weather, and phrases like *How are you?*

In connection with the idea of context of situation and the idea of function as explanatory terms in linguistics, Firth points out that if the meaning of linguistic items is dependent on cultural context, we need to establish a set of categories which link linguistic material with cultural context. Thus, the following categories are necessary in any description of linguistic events (1950/1957b: 182):

A. The relevant features of participants: persons, personalities.
   (i) The verbal action of the participants.
   (ii) The non-verbal action of the participants.
B. The relevant objects.
C. The effect of the verbal action.

According to Firth, the notion that 'meaning is function in context' needs formal definition so that it can be used as a principle throughout the theory; both the smallest and the largest items must be describable in these terms.

To achieve this formal definition, Firth uses a Saussurean notion of system, though his use of the term is more rigorous than Saussure's. Firth's **system** is an enumerated set of choices in a specific context. Any item will have two types of context: the context of other possible choices in the system, and the context in which the system itself occurs. The choices made in the systems will be functionally determined.

Halliday works within a highly explicit systemic theory which is clearly Firthian, but more fully elaborated, and the grammars written by scholars in the Hallidayan tradition are, therefore, often called **systemic grammars** (see SYSTEMIC-FUNCTIONAL GRAMMAR). When accounting for how language is used, for the choices speakers make, however, Halliday prefers to talk of **functional grammar**; as he puts it (1970: 141):

> The nature of language is closely related to . . . the functions it has to serve. In the most concrete terms, these functions are specific to a culture: the use of language to organize fishing expeditions in the Trobriand Islands, described half a century ago by Malinowski, has no parallel in our own society. But underlying such specific instances of language use, are more general functions which are common to all cultures. We do not all go on fishing expeditions; however, we all use language as a means of organizing other people, and directing their behaviour.

This quotation both shows the influence from Malinowski and hints at how Halliday generalizes the notion of function in order that it may become more widely applicable as an explanatory term.

Halliday's theory of language is organized around two very basic and common-sense observations: that language is part of the social semiotic, and that people talk to each other. The theory of language is part of an overall theory of social interaction, and from such a perspective it is obvious that a language must be seen as more than a set of sentences, as it is for Chomsky. Rather, language will be seen as text, or **discourse** – the exchange of meanings in interpersonal contexts. The creativity of language is situated in this exchange. A Hallidayan grammar is therefore a grammar of meaningful choices rather than of formal rules.

By saying that language is part of the **social semiotic**, Halliday means that the whole of the culture is meaningful, is constructed out of a series of systems of signs. Language is one of these systems – a particularly important one, because most of the other systems are learned through, and translatable into, language, and because it *reflects* aspects of the situations in which it occurs.

As a social system, language is subject to two types of variation: variation according to *user*, and variation according to *use*. The first type of variation is in accent and dialect (see DIALECTOLOGY), and it does not, in principle, entail any variation in meaning. Different dialects, are, in principle, different ways of saying the same thing, and dialectal linguistic variation reflects the social order basically in terms of geography. Variation according to *use* (**register variation**), however, produces variation in meaning. A **register** is what you are speaking at a particular time, and is determined by what you and others – and which others – are doing there and then; that is, by the nature of the ongoing social activity. Register variation therefore reflects the social order in the special sense of the variety of social processes. The notion of register is a notion required to relate the functions of language (see below) to those aspects of the situation in which it is being used that are the relevant

aspects for us to include under the notion of **speech situation** or **context**. According to Halliday, the relevant aspects of the situation are what he calls, respectively, **field**, **tenor** and **mode**.

The **field of discourse** is *what is going on* – the social action, which has a meaning as such in the social system. Typically, it is a complex act in some ordered configuration, in which the text is playing some part. It includes 'subject matter' as one aspect of what is going on.

The **tenor of discourse** relates to *who is taking part* in the social action. It includes the role structure into which the participants in the discourse fit; that is, socially meaningful participant relationships, whether these are permanent attributes of the participants – mother–child – or whether they are role relationships that are specific to the situation – doctor–patient. Actual speech roles are also included, and these may be created through the exchange of verbal meanings: through the exchange itself, it will become clear, for instance, who, at any particular time, is **knower** and **non-knower** (Berry 1981) with regard to any particular subject matter of the discourse.

The **mode of discourse** deals with the role that the text or language itself is playing in the situation at hand. It refers to the particular status that is assigned to the text within the situation and to its symbolic organization. A text will have a function in relation to the social action and the role structure (plea, reprimand, informing); it will be transmitted through some channel (writing, speech); and it will have a particular rhetorical mode (formal, casual).

It is now possible to determine the general principles governing the way in which these semiotic aspects of the situation are reflected in texts. Each linguistically relevant situational component will tend to determine choices in one of the three semantic components that language comprises, by virtue of being the system through which we talk to each other.

Since it is the means whereby we talk to each other, language has two major functions. It is a means of *reflecting on things* – that is, it has an **ideational function** – and it is a means of *acting* on things. But, of course, the only 'things' it is possible to act on symbolically (and language is a symbolic system) are *people* (and some animals, perhaps), so the second function of language is called the **interpersonal function**.

Finally, language has the function which enables the other two functions to operate; namely, that which represents the language user's text-forming potential. This is called the **textual function**, and 'it is through the options in this component that the speaker is enabled to make what he says operational in context, as distinct from being merely citational, like lists of words in a dictionary, or sentences in a grammar book' (Halliday 1975: 17).

As indicated in the quotation just given, for each of the functions that language has for its users there is a correspondent component of the semantic system of language from which choices are made somewhat as follows:

The **field of discourse** – what is going on – will tend to determine choices in the **ideational component** of the language, among classes of things, qualities, quantities, times, places and in the transitivity system (see SYSTEMIC-FUNCTIONAL GRAMMAR).

The **tenor of discourse** – who is taking part – will tend to determine choices in the **interpersonal systems** of mood, modality, person and key; and in intensity, evaluation and comment.

The **mode of discourse** – the part the text is playing – will tend to determine choices in the **textual component** of language, in the system of voice, among cohesive patterns, information structures and in choice of theme. The concept of genre, too, is an aspect of what Halliday sees as mode.

But exactly *what* choices are made is subject to variation according to two further factors. Reference to these factors – register and code – must be made in the explanation of the relationship between language and situation.

Register means that concept of text variety which allows us to make sensible predictions about the kind of language which will occur in a given situation – that is, in association with a particular field, tenor and mode. Register is (Halliday 1978: 111) 'the configuration of semantic resources that the member of a culture typically associates with a situation type'. However, members of different (sub)cultures will differ as to which text type they tend to associate with which situation type, and differences of this supralinguistic, socio-semiotic type are explained in terms of Bernstein's (1971) notion of the **code** (see LANGUAGE AND EDUCATION), which acts as a filter through which the culture is transmitted to a child.

It is important to remember that the interpersonal, ideational and textual functions mentioned here are the **macrofunctions** of the semantic system of language; they are the functions that Halliday thinks of as universal. In addition, of course, language serves a number of **microfunctions** for its users, such as asking for things, making commands, etc., but the proper heading under which to consider these is that of speech-act theory (see SPEECH-ACT THEORY).

K.M.

Suggestions for further reading

Halliday, M.A.K. (1978) *Language as Social Semiotic*, London: Edward Arnold.

Sampson, G. (1980) *Schools of Linguistics. Competition and Evolution*, London: Hutchinson, chapters 5 and 9.

G

Generative grammar

This article is about the body of work which owes its original inspiration to the insights of **Noam Chomsky** in the mid-1950s and has been continually revivified by his insight up to the present. It has become one of the most influential syntactic theories of the twentieth century and, although by no means all practising linguists adhere to its principles and results, none can ignore them. Since its inception there have been huge developments in the theory and reactions to it have often been violent. In the mid-1960s work on the developing theory of 'Transformational Generative Grammar' (TG) was perhaps coherent enough for one to be able to talk of a school of 'transformational' linguistics. This has not been possible for many years. Many who grew up within the model have gone on to develop theories of their own, often in reaction to the current work of Chomsky, and even among those who would describe themselves as generative linguists there is considerable divergence. That having been said, many linguists adhere to some version of a grammar that owes its intellectual genesis to one or other of the continually developing models offered by Chomsky. This entry is organized into four sections, based loosely around some of his more influential publications: *Syntactic Structures* (1957); 'Standard Theory', developing from *Aspects of the Theory of Syntax* (1965);

'Principles and Parameters', the theory developing out of *Lectures on Government and Binding* (1981) and *Barriers* (1986a); and some of Chomsky's most recent ideas, stimulated by *The Minimalist Program* (1995).

Syntactic structures

When *Syntactic Structures* was published in 1957, the position it took on the nature of linguistic activity was sufficiently at odds with that of the prevailing orthodoxy that it was appropriate to refer to it as revolutionary. The first chapter declared that grammar was an autonomous system, independent of the study of the use of language in situations, and of semantics, and furthermore that it should be formalized as a system of rules that generates an infinite set of sentences.

This approach contrasted sharply with the (then) fashionable orthodoxy that believed that the application of appropriate procedures to a corpus of data would yield a grammatical description. Chomsky rejected the use of a corpus, proposing instead that the empirical adequacy of a grammar should not be judged by whether it accounted for some finite body of observable data but by whether it could generate an infinite number of grammatical sentences and in doing so account for certain types of intuitive judgements that native speakers have about their language. Among these judgements are **grammaticality** judgements: that is, that a string of words, particularly a novel string, is or is not a well-formed sentence; that certain sentences are **ambiguous**, i.e. that a single sentence can have more than one interpretation; that distinct sentences can **paraphrase** each other, i.e. that distinct sentences can, in particular respects, have identical interpretations; that certain sentence types (affirmative and negative, declarative and interrogative, etc.) can be systematically related to each other, and so forth. Judgements of this kind, it is claimed, constitute what speakers know about their language, and in addition to being able to generate all the grammatical sentences of the language a grammar should also account for this knowledge.

It was mentioned above that Chomsky proposed that grammar should be considered as an autonomous system, independent of semantic or phonological systems, though, of course, bearing a relation to them. Furthermore, he proposed that the syntax itself should consist of a number of distinct but related levels, each of which is characterized by distinct rule types and bears a particular part of the descriptive burden. We shall look briefly at the two most important components in a syntactic structures model: the phrase-structure component and the transformational component.

The **phrase-structure (PS)** component consists of a set of phrase-structure (PS) rules which formalize some of the traditional insights of **constituent-structure** analysis. Consider, for example, the following set of rules, adapted from Chomsky (1957: 26 and 111; items in curly brackets, { }, are alternatives, e.g. Number is either sing(ular) or pl(ural)).

Sentence → NP + VP
NP → T + N + Number   NP (noun phrase); T (articles, etc.)
Number → {sing, pl}   sing(ular) or pl(ural)

VP → Verb + NP
Verb → Aux + V
Aux → Tense   simplified to cover only a marker of Tense
Tense → {pres, past}   pres(ent) or past

Each rule is an instruction to rewrite the symbol on the left of the arrow as the symbol or symbols on the right of it: informally, it can be construed as 'the category on the left of the arrow has the constituent(s) specified on the right of the arrow, and in the order shown'.

The phrase-structure component will need to be supplemented by a **lexicon**, a list of the lexemes of the language, each one characterized with its lexical category (that MAN and BALL are nouns, that HIT is a verb, and so on) with information about their subcategorization (that HIT is a transitive verb and so on), and with information about its pronunciation and its sense.

Using these phrase-structure rules and a rule that inserts lexical items into the appropriately labelled nodes, a derivation from this grammar can then be represented by the **tree** shown in Figure 1 (adapted from Chomsky 1957: 27).

We will refer to lexicalized structures generated by the PS rules as **underlying structures**. One small reason should be immediately apparent: the postulated underlying structure shown in Figure 1 is characterized by a degree of abstraction. The NPs are analysed as containing a marker of number, and the analysis of the verb form *hit* as a past tense form is shown by postulating the item 'Tense', preceding the verb itself. None of these items has an overt realization in the actually occurring form of the sentence, its **syntactic surface structure**. We will see the reason for these analyses below.

PS rules of this kind can be elaborated to capture certain basic facts about the grammar of English, or indeed any other language. They capture relations of **con-**

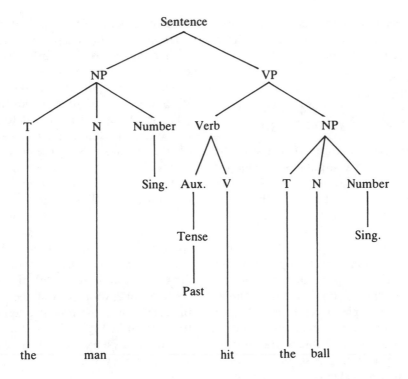

Figure 1

stituency and **order**. Strings like *the man, the ball* and *hit the ball* are **proper constituents** of the sentence, whereas a string like *man hit* is not. In English, articles are ordered before nouns within noun phrases; the verb precedes its object within the VP and the subject precedes the VP. They can also be used to capture facts about **functional relations** like subject, object, and main verb – the **subject** is the NP **daughter** of the Sentence **node**, the object is the NP daughter of the VP and **sister** of the main verb, and the **main verb** is a daughter of the VP, which is itself a sister of the subject. (A node is the daughter of the node immediately above it, which **dominates** it, as shown by the 'branches' of the tree. Sister nodes share a dominating node.) As we have noted, information about the **subcategorization** of lexical items (that HIT is a **transitive verb** and so requires to be followed by an NP) is to be found in the associated lexicon.

The **transformational component** consists of rules which perform a variety of functions. We will be interested in three: first, rules which relate particular sentence types to each other, as active sentences to their passive counterparts; second, a set of rules that accounts for morphological operations of various kinds, like number agreement between subject and verb; finally, those rules that are responsible for generating complex sentences.

A **transformational rule** is a rule that maps one syntactic-analysis tree into another. If PS rules can be informally thought of as instructions to build up structures like those in Figure 1, then a transformational rule can be informally thought of as an instruction to change one structure into another. A rule that takes one structure as input and outputs another structure, will obviously need two parts: a **structural analysis (SA)** specifying the input, the structure to which the rule applies; and a **structural change (SC)** specifying what the output structure will be. A double-shafted arrow is often used to signify a transformational rather than a PS rule. A version of the Passive transformation (modified from Chomsky 1957: 112) is:

Passive (optional)
SA: NP – Aux – V – NP
SC: Xl – X2 – X3 – X4 $\Rightarrow$ X4 – X2 + ($_{\text{pass}}$BE + *en*) – X3 – ($_{\text{pp}}$by – Xl)

The structure in Figure 1 can indeed be analysed as the SA stipulates: it contains the string NP – Aux – V – NP, so it can thus be subjected to the rule yielding the derived structure shown in Figure 2.

Early transformational grammars assumed a rule like the passive transformation to be a complex unitary operation and this may well reflect the native speaker's intuition of the matter. The rule is, however, a very complex operation and from a formal point of view can be broken down into a number of **elementary transformations**, each performing a single operation, **adjoining**, **moving**, **deleting** or **copying** a con-

stituent. Several of these operations can be exemplified in the passive transformation: *by* is adjoined to the subject NP *the man* to create a new piece of structure, the PP (prepositional phrase) *by the man*; this PP is then moved to final position in the VP; the object NP is moved to the front of the sentence and adjoined as a daughter of the topmost Sentence node; a new passive auxiliary is introduced, and so forth. Perhaps the most compelling reason for considering Passive to be a series of small operations rather than one complex one is that, while it may be possible to specify exactly the structural change for each of the component operations, it is far from clear how to do this for a very complex operation. Given the version of the rule above, just how the derived structure shown in Figure 2 was constructed is actually a mystery, yet a formal grammar should be very precise on matters of this kind.

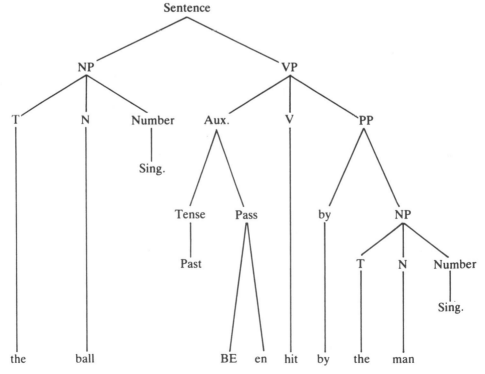

Figure 2

At this point there is a conflict between an intuition that 'construction types' should be matched as wholes, and the formal operation of grammatical rules, which would prefer to atomize complex operations. In the earliest transformational work the preference was to follow traditional intuitions and to relate construction types as wholes to one another, but this leads to prodigious formal difficulties and later work takes the opposite approach, as we shall see, and construction types are atomized into their component elementary transformations. It should also be noted that the transformation is marked as 'optional'. This is for the obvious reason that not all sentences are passive sentences. Comparable transformations, often also complex and invariably also optional, were proposed to derive interrogatives from declaratives, negatives from affirmatives, and so on. Combinations of these operations will derive more complex structures like interrogative, negative passives, and so forth. The insight that operations of this kind encapsulates is that of **sentence-relatedness**.

The second set of transformations mentioned above were those concerned with morphological operations – the agreement rules of English are an example – and with word formation in general, of which past tense formation is an example. The traditional account of **number agreement** is that the main verb must agree in number with the subject, an insight that can be captured straightforwardly by a transformation. Given that subject and main verb can be identified in structural terms in the kind of way noted above, we need a rule that uses this structural information to copy a marker of number from the subject NP into the verb group. There is, however, a little bit more to it than that, since we need to be sure that the number marker on the verb group occurs in the right place, which is the tensed element within the verb group, whether this is an auxiliary verb (*is/are walking*, *has/have walked*) or the main verb itself (*walk/walks*). This can be ensured by copying the number marker into the tense constituent itself. The effect of such an operation is shown in Figure 3.

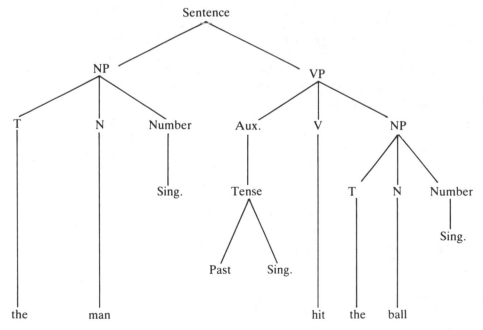

Figure 3

Before pursuing this matter further we should briefly consider how tense is marked. In English, the marker of past tense in verbs is most frequently a suffix, *-ed*, on the verb stem: *walk-s* (present) vs *walk-ed* (past). In this respect our example, *hit*, is an **irregular** past tense formation, and we will come to that in due course. However, in our grammar and in the analysis displayed in Figure 1, the fact that *hit* is analysed as a 'past tense verb' is shown by a constituent labelled 'Tense' positioned before rather than after the verb stem.

This apparently curious analysis is in fact rather ingenious, since it captures several important regularities in the formation rules for tensed verb groups in English. First, tense is invariably realized on the initial constituent of the verb group, irrespective of whether this is an auxiliary (*is/was walking*, *has/had walked*, etc.) or the main verb itself (*walks/walked*). Second, whereas the auxiliaries are optional constituents of the verb group, all finite sentences must be tensed. Making tense obligatory at the beginning of the verb group captures this fact. The correct surface position of the actual tense marker can be ensured by proposing a rule that positions the tense marker as a suffix on whatever immediately follows it in the final derivation, and indeed such a transformation, later called **affix hopping**, was proposed in *Syntactic Structures*. It should be clear that this rule will also account for the position of the marker of number agreement: if it is copied into the tense marker, then where the tense marker goes, so does the number marker. The reader can easily imagine the effect of affix hopping on the structure in Figure 3.

Consider, finally, the analysis of the passive. This introduces a passive auxiliary, 'BE + *en*', as the final constituent in the string of auxiliaries: 'Aux' in the SA (Structural Analysis) will include whatever auxiliaries there are in the active sentence, so the stipulation 'Aux + pass' will get the

ordering right; BE recognizes the fact that the passive auxiliary is indeed a form of BE; *en* recognizes the fact that the verb that follows the passive auxiliary always does so as a passive participle. Now, if *en*, like tense, is defined as an affix, affix hopping will ensure the correct surface facts. The reader can see that if the number agreement rule and affix hopping are applied to the structure in Figure 2, the resultant sentence will be *The ball was hit by the man*. It will be clear that, whereas the sentence-relating rules, like Passive, are optional, the morphological rules will generally need to be obligatory.

We have only examined a part of the extremely complex formation rules for the English verb group, but it must be clear that a few simple but powerful rules can both generate the correct sequence of forms and exclude ungrammatical ones, while at the same time capturing important generalizations about the structure of the language. It is worth mentioning that the elegance and insightfulness of this account was instantly recognized, and this was an important factor in ensuring the initial success of the transformational way of looking at syntax.

The structure that emerges after the operation of all the transformations is known as the **syntactic surface structure**. This will then need to go off to the morpho-phonemic and phonological components to receive its final phonological form. The rules in these components need not detain us, but it is perhaps worth noting that a complete description will clearly need a set of morphophonemic rules to specify the shapes of word forms. So, for example, there will need to be rules of the kind:

HIT + past → *hit* (the past tense form of *hit*)

HIT + *en* → *hit* (the passive participle of *hit*)

MAN + pl → *men* (the plural form of *man*)

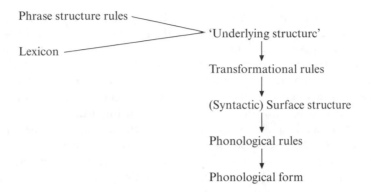

Phrase structure rules

Lexicon

'Underlying structure'

Transformational rules

(Syntactic) Surface structure

Phonological rules

Phonological form

Figure 4

to accommodate irregular morphology, followed by others of the kind:

WALK → *walk*
past   → *-ed* (the past marker for regular verbs)

to accommodate regular morphology. The kinds of rules that are at issue should be clear and need not detain us further.

It will be helpful at this point to summarize the overall structure of the model as it applies to simple sentences, and this is shown in Figure 4.

Within this model all sentences will have two levels of syntactic description: an underlying structure created by the PS rules, and a surface structure resulting from the operation of the transformations. Several things follow from this.

Perhaps most significant is that it draws particular attention to the fact that language is a complex structural organization. All the rules we have looked at work on structures, or subparts of structures, either developing them or modifying them. This **structure dependence** of the rules of language is held by all models of transformational grammar to be one of the characterizing features of human language.

Another such feature is that the relationship between underlying and surface structure enables us to capture many of the generalizations mentioned in the opening paragraphs. Thus, a paraphrase relation

between superficially distinct sentences – such as, for example, an active sentence and the corresponding passive – arises from the fact that both derive from the same underlying structure. By contrast, an ambiguous sentence arises when a transformational derivation collapses distinct underlying structures on to a single surface structure.

Finally we may mention that this description allows us to identify a special class of sentences, **kernel sentences**, that have traditionally been recognized as of particular interest: simple active, declarative, affirmative sentences. The distinguishing feature of kernel sentences is that they are those sentences derived with the absolute minimum of transformational machinery, the obligatory transformations alone. As we have seen, the obligatory transformations are in essence those that account for number agreement, the surface ordering of markers of tense, and similar 'housekeeping' operations. Other sentences – questions, negatives and the like – will undergo, in addition, one or more of the optional structure-changing operations.

The third group of transformations mentioned was those responsible for the generation of **complex sentences**, sentences which themselves contain sentences, or sentence-like structures as constituents: for example, ($_{s1}$*Kim said* ($_{s2}$*that his mother expected him* ($_{s3}$*to tell John* ($_{s4}$*that . . .* , where the various embedded sentences are identified as S1, S2, and so forth. This process is clearly very productive. In *Syntactic Structures*, the embedding operation is performed by a distinct set of transformations called **generalized transformations**, which take as input two sentence structures, and yield as output a single structure with one sentence embedded into the other. The problem in general is obviously an important one, but the particular solution adopted in *Syntactic Structures* was extraordinarily complicated, led to considerable formal difficulties, and was soon abandoned, so we will not pursue the matter here. It will be clear that the outline offered above says nothing about the generation of complex sentences.

There are two final remarks to be made about this model. The first has to do with the relationship between syntax and semantics. In *Syntactic Structures*, Chomsky is at pains to stress the autonomy of syntax, in particular with regard to semantics. He does, however, draw attention to the fact that a description of a language must have the means to discuss the relation between syntax and semantics, and points out that in this respect kernel sentences have a privileged part to play, since, if kernel sentences are in some sense 'basic' sentences, an understanding of how they are understood is the key to understanding how sentences in general are understood. How later versions of the theory come to terms with this insight (again, a rather traditional insight), we will see.

The second remark has to do with Chomsky's interest in language as a formal system of rules and the fact that this led him to explore the mathematical properties of various kinds of formal grammar. The immediate spur to this investigation was the claim that PS rules alone were inadequate to describe the range of structures found in a natural language. It was claimed, for example, that some structures found in natural language are literally impossible to generate with PS rules; this is particularly the case where potentially infinite nested

dependencies are at issue (e.g. if$_1$, if$_2$ . . . then$_2$ then$_1$). There are some kinds of structures that can be generated using PS rules, but the description is clumsy and lacks generality (e.g. the rules for number agreement or the formation rules for auxiliary verbs in English).

While it may be possible to generate particular sentence types, it is not possible to relate them to each other formally in the grammar, which means that certain of the kinds of insight (especially those about sentence relatedness, etc.) mentioned above cannot be captured in PS grammar alone. Furthermore, it is impossible to generate certain occurring structures without also generating certain non-occurring structures. Many of these alleged inadequacies of PS rules have subsequently turned out not to be sustainable. Chomsky's work on formal grammar, however, remains of importance since the investigation of the mathematical properties of grammars provoked by *Syntactic Structures* remains an important field of investigation both in linguistics and in related disciplines, notably computer science, artificial intelligence and cognitive science. Chomsky's answer to the inadequacies of PS rules was to supplement a phrase-structure grammar with another, more powerful, kind of rule, the transformation. Interestingly, considering the amount of attention paid to the formal properties of PS rules, *Syntactic Structures* contains no discussion of the mathematical properties of transformational rules. This, as we shall see, was soon a source of trouble.

Syntactic Structures triggered an intensive research programme: we only have space to look at a few aspects of this. Of the new syntactic machinery the powerful tool of different levels of structure related by transformations was particularly beguiling, since transformations appeared to offer a means of explaining the often amazingly complex relationships between the form of sentences and their understanding. An early and influential contribution was Lees' (1960/1963) transformational account of the formation and understanding of nominal forms. For example, the superficially similar *talking machine, eating apple* or *washing machine* differ in the kinds of relationships between the various parts: subject–verb, as in *the machine talks*; verb–object as in *NP eats the apple*; and verb–object of preposition, as in *NP washes NP in a machine*. Data of this kind seemed cut out for a transformational account: the various forms must be derived from different underlying structures (this accounts for the different interpretations) by transformational routes that have destroyed that structure (this accounts for the identical surface structures). A superficially appealing conclusion.

In syntax, intensive work on the structure of complex sentences eventually showed that it was possible to discard the unwieldy machinery of generalized transformations. A straightforward example will show the kind of thing that was at issue: in a *Syntactic Structures* type of grammar, the generation of relative clauses involved taking two sentences – say, *The cat died* and *We loved the cat* – and embedding one in the other with whatever consequent changes were necessary to yield *The cat that we loved died*. Instead of taking two sentences, it was suggested that the NP could be developed by a rule of the kind NP → Art N S, and permitting the S node to recycle through the rules. In this way an underlying structure could contain within itself a series of embedded sentences requiring only transformational machinery to tidy up the surface forms. Given this approach, the old optional generalized transformations responsible for the various embedding operations now become obligatory, being triggered by an appropriate underlying structure.

Another line of research looked at the derivation of different simple sentence types: for example, in *Syntactic Structures*, negative sentences would have been derived by an optional transformation inserting a negative element into an affirmative kernel. It was proposed that instead the underlying structure could contain an optional abstract negative **marker**, S → (neg) NP + VP. Now the transformational rule can be triggered by this marker to produce the appropriate negative sentence structure. A similar move is open to interrogative sentences: S → (Qu) NP + VP and, once again, the abstract interrogative marker triggers the interrogative transformation. As before, what was formerly an optional operation now becomes obligatory, conditional on the presence of the abstract marker.

As proposals of this kind increased, they began to have profound implications for the structure of the grammar. A small consequence was the demise of the notion of the kernel sentence. Kernel sentences, it will be recalled, were active, affirmative, declarative simple sentences derived by the application of obligatory transformations alone: the disappearance of a significant distinction between obligatory and optional transformations described above sounded the death knell for the kernel sentence. A more profound result was that the incorporation into underlying structures of more and more markers, like the negative and interrogative markers mentioned above, led to underlying structures becoming increasingly abstract. This in turn led to a requirement for ever-more-substantial transformational machinery to relate it to surface structures. And the explosion in the number of transformations created problems of controlling the way they operate and interact with each other; the formal implications of this are largely a 'theory-internal' problem. An interesting consequence was the exploration of an increasingly wide variety of syntactic facts, and the discovery of a range of syntactic problems that still defy proper description.

Perhaps the most profound consequence, however, was that the new ideas opened up the possibility of an interesting rapprochement between semantics and grammar.

Consider, for example, the interpretation of a negative sentence. One way of thinking of this is to suppose that understanding a negative sentence depends on the application of negation to the understanding of the corresponding affirmative sentence. In a *Syntactic Structures* model, formalizing this procedure would require access to the underlying structure, to acquire an understanding of the kernel, and also a history of the transformational derivation of the sentence, to know whether the optional negative transformation has applied. However, if we suppose that there is a negative marker in the underlying structure itself and that this triggers off the application of the negative transformation, then all that is necessary for the semantic interpretation is already in the underlying structure, and can be read directly off it. The transformation would have no effect on the meaning, but be simply an automatic operation serving only to trigger off operations which would make the necessary surface adjustments. Katz and Postal (1964) proposed just this.

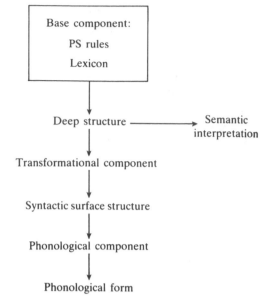

Figure 5

Standard Theory

The modifications outlined at the end of the previous section were incorporated into Chomsky's *Aspects of the Theory of Syntax* (1965). In its day this was an enormously influential model, the basis for an explosion of research and expounded in a wide variety of student textbooks – so much so that it became known as the **Standard Theory**.

The structure proposed by the theory is more overtly modular than before, with different types of rules gathered into 'components' related to each other as set out in Figure 5. The PS rules (which look after particular basic syntactic relations and the distribution of lexical items in deep structures) and the lexicon (which contains category and subcategory information about lexical items) become the base

component. A deep structure, which is the output of this component, is passed on the one hand to a semantic interpretation and on the other through the transformational rules to become a syntactic surface structure and subsequently a phonological form.

At the beginning of *Aspects*, Chomsky defines the task of linguistic theory as

> to develop an account of linguistic universals that on the one hand will not be falsified by the actual diversity of languages and, on the other hand, will be sufficiently rich and explicit to account for the rapidity and uniformity of language learning and the remarkable complexity and range of the generative grammars that are the product of language learning. (Chomsky 1965: 27–8)

The research programme this defines focuses on the explanatory power of the grammar in so far as it bears on a set of questions related to the way grammar might reveal general properties of the human mind. What, if any, are the universal properties of language? What is the possible range of variation within human languages?

What is the nature of the innate knowledge a child must bring to bear on the acquisition of language? How is grammar involved in adult language processing?

In the *Aspects* model, the answer to these questions seemed to lie in transformations, which is doubtless why the model was popularly referred to as TG (transformational grammar). More and more were proposed, and as the number rose they began to raise a number of technical problems, so much so that within a few years it became apparent that the transformation was too powerful a tool and the transformation itself became a major source of difficulty. A typical dilemma, for example, was the question of whether transformations should be ordered, and if so by what principles. At the time, the matter spawned miles of print, but ordering eventually proved to be an internal difficulty created by the structure of the theory rather than anything to do with any property of language itself, and the mountain of technical literature is now only of historical interest. However, it should be said that, although this eventually proved to be an unfruitful line of research, the investigation was not in vain, because in the course of the research a quite extraordinary amount was discovered about the grammar of English and other languages, much of it still awaiting a satisfactory explanation.

A more serious problem concerned the explanatory power of the transformation itself. We have already observed that, although in *Syntactic Structures* Chomsky was very concerned to explore the mathematical properties of PS rules, little attention was devoted to the mathematical power of transformations. Once the mathematical properties of this kind of rule were explored, it became clear that a grammar with transformations has the formal properties of a **universal Turing machine** – in other words, they are such a powerful tool that they can explain nothing except that language can be described in terms of some set of rules. An obvious effect of this unwelcome result was to see whether the power of the transformational component could be constrained so that it could, after all, do some useful explanatory work. An early, and still influential, line of research was inaugurated by Ross (1968).

To illustrate what was at issue, consider the formation rules for questions. From the earliest days, transformational grammarians postulated that a **wh-interrogative sentence** is derived by a **movement rule** from a deep structure resembling that of the corresponding declarative. So, for example, and disregarding the inversion and the appearance of a form of *do*, a sentence like *What did Bertie give – to Catherine?* would be derived from a deep structure of the form *Bertie gave 'wh' to Catherine* (the dash in the derived sentence indicates the site from which the *wh*-word has been extracted). **Wh-movement** can also extract *wh*-words from within embedded sentences, and apparently from an unlimited depth: *What did Albert say Bertie gave – to Catherine?*, *What did Zeno declare that Albert had said that Bertie gave – to Catherine?*, and so forth. The rule is, however, not entirely unconstrained. For example, if the constituent sentence is itself interrogative, then extraction cannot take place: *Albert asked whether Bertie gave a book to Catherine*, but not **What did Albert ask whether Bertie gave – to Catherine?* In Ross's terms, certain constructions form **islands** (the example shows a *wh*-island) and the transformational rule must be restricted from extracting constituents from islands. **Island constraints** turn out both to be quite general and to occur in many languages. An obvious question, then, is this: Are island constraints a property of universal grammar and, if so, how are they to be formulated? Investigations to discover the properties of islands gradually focused on the notion of **bounding**: an attempt to identify what configurations of constituents constitute a **barrier** to movement. We will return to this in the next section.

Another line of research suggested that a movement transformation should leave a **trace** of the moved constituent in the **extraction site**: in these terms, our example above would be: *What did Albert say Bertie gave 't' to Catherine?* The full implications of this proposal will become apparent in the next section. Immediately, we will observe that the proposal offers another way of constraining transformations: we can allow the rule to apply freely and then apply a set of **filters** to weed out ill-formed structures. So, for example, we could allow unrestricted movement (even out of islands) and then have a filter to detect illegal traces and mark offending sentences as ungrammatical. In other words, instead of constraining the operation of the transformation itself, we can scan the output of the operation to check its legality.

Yet another approach to restricting the power of transformations suggested that the range of operations they could perform should be severely limited. Emonds (1976) proposed a **structure-preserving constraint**. In essence, the proposal was that a transformation should be able neither to create nor destroy structure (structure-preserving), but only to move lexical material around within already established structures. This entailed several radical innovations. First, no structure created by a transformation can be different from a structure that the PS rules themselves might create. Second, if lexical material is to move, there must be somewhere to move it to. Between them these constraints ensure that the deep structure must have some lexicalized nodes (to provide the material to move) and some empty nodes (to provide places for the lexical material to move to).

Consider the effect on the passive. The deep structure will have to look like this: *NP(empty) – was – hit – the ball (by – the man)*, and a rule of NP movement will move the object NP, *the ball*, into the empty subject position. The surface structure will then be: *The ball – was – hit – (by*

the man). At first blush this may all seem a little odd, but we shall see in the next section that the proposal has some interesting consequences.

One consequence we can immediately notice: there is a move away from highly abstract deep structures. In fact, deep and surface structures become almost mirrors of each other, differing substantially only in the distribution of lexical items. Indeed, given a structure-preserving constraint and traced movement rules, the deep structure can always be reconstructed from the surface structure – this was by no means the case in the early days after *Aspects*. A further consequence of this development was to force attention once more on to the nature of PS rules. A consequence of this was the development of a more restrictive theory of phrase structure known as **X-bar syntax**, which we turn to in the next section.

We have seen that one way of restricting the power of transformations is to constrain them. A more drastic way is, of course, to abolish them altogether. This was indeed the fate of many. A natural question follows: What happens to the generalizations that the transformation purported to capture? The answer was that many transformational operations transferred themselves from the grammar to the lexicon. In both *Syntactic Structures* and *Aspects*, the lexicon was more or less a word list, and a repository of exceptions. Gradually it came to have a more central role. It came to be seen that the kinds of operation that Lees (1960/1963) had proposed for nominalizations were ill sorted as syntactic operations and more appropriately considered as lexical rules, hence most appropriately situated in the lexicon itself. Furthermore, rules involving the redistribution of the arguments of the verb within a simple sentence also came to be seen as lexical rather than syntactic rules.

Consider, for example, the rule of **Dative movement**. This was supposed to relate pairs of sentences like *John gave a book to Mary* and *John gave Mary a book* – the transformation deleting *to* and moving the NP following it to a position immediately after the verb. The problem for this as a general transformation is that it is in fact heavily constrained: there are some verbs which permit the first form but not the second (*They transmitted the enemy propaganda*) and others that permit the second but not the first (*John asked a question to Mary*). The constraints appear to be lexical rather than grammatical and hence perhaps better situated in the lexicon than in the grammar. The appropriate lexical rule would state that, for appropriate verbs, if they occur in the environment 'NP1 – NP2 to NP3', they can also occur in the environment 'NP – NP3 NP2'.

Note that this line of argument can be extended to the passive: there are some verbs, like *resemble*, that do not typically occur in the passive, and others, like *rumour*, that hardly occur in the active. A lexical derivation for the passive would say in effect that appropriate verbs that occur in the environment 'NP1 – NP2' can also occur in the passive participle form in the environment 'NP was – NP2 (by NP1)'. This, of course, is the very structure I discussed above.

We have seen that in the years following *Aspects* the various modules of the grammar have developed into specialist components, each with a particular kind of rule and each dealing with a part of the derivation of a sentence: the phrase-structure component looks after particular basic syntactic relations and the distribution of lexical items in deep structure; the lexicon looks after word-formation rules; the transformational component is reduced so that the only substantial transformations left are very general movement operations, themselves heavily constrained.

Principles and Parameters

Chomsky's (1981) *Lectures on Government and Binding*, and work which followed over the next few years, pulled these changes together into a model that is generally referred to under the label 'Principles and Parameters' (P&P). This model revisits the concerns of a 'universal grammar' outlined in the quotation from *Aspects* at the beginning of the previous section: that it should be able to accommodate the facts of any natural language, help towards an explanation of child language acquisition, etc., is often referred to as 'universal grammar' (UG), and it is clearly more suitable for this purpose.

It is more modular than its predecessors, a sentence now being assigned a description at each of four levels of description. The levels are in many ways similar to those proposed in Standard Theory, and clearly develop from them, but their internal structure is further elaborated and the relationships between the levels (as shown in Figure 6) is rearranged. The principal organizational difference is that, whereas in the Standard Theory the derivation bifurcated at D-structure – one path leading to a

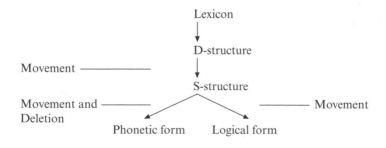

Figure 6

semantic interpretation and the other through the transformational component to a syntactic surface structure and thence to a phonetic form – this time the bifurcation into Logical and Phonetic form is at S-structure. Some of the reasons for this change will have become apparent in the preceding discussion.

The structures generated at the various levels are constrained by a set of theories (X-bar, Theta, Government, Binding, Bounding and Case), each of which is associated with one or more **principles**, which define syntactic relations and regulate the various levels and the relations between them, and a set of **parameters**, which define the range of variation a particular principle permits in different languages.

Structures are formulated as the familiar syntactic trees, the possible configurations being defined according to the principles of **X-bar theory**, which defines the nature and type of syntactic relationships in tree structures, and **theta theory**, which deals with the functional relationships between a predicate and its arguments. Both, as we shall see, are constrained by the lexicon.

The central notion of X-bar theory is that each of the major lexical categories (Noun, Verb, Preposition, Adjective) is a 'head' and will 'project' a phrasal node of the same category as itself (noun: noun phrase, verb: verb phrase, etc.). An ongoing question was whether other categories also projected phrasal categories – we shall

see examples shortly. The phrasal category is the 'maximal projection' of the head. There may in addition be a number of intermediate categories. So, for example, English NPs have structures like that shown in Figure 7.

The noun *discussion* is the head. The PP *about linguistics* is its 'complement'; the *AP interesting* is an adjunct, modifying its sister N1, and the determiner *an* is the specifier of the phrase. (The AP and PP projections are not expanded here for reasons of space.) Complement is an important relationship for several reasons. Heads are 'subcategorized' by their complements – a relationship most clearly seen with verb heads (intransitive verbs (*John laughed*) have no complement, transitive verbs (*John kicked the ball*) must have an NP complement, di-transitive verbs (*John gave Mary a ball*) have two NP complements and so on) and subcategorization of this kind can readily be applied to the other major categories. Subcategorization information of this sort is, of course, recorded in the lexicon. We can use this relationship to define the grammatical relation 'Object of the verb': it is an NP complement. (The relation 'Subject of the sentence' we come to below.) Furthermore, heads assign a theta role to their complements, a notion that will be explicated when we discuss theta theory below. In X-bar trees, complements are represented as sisters of the head dominated by the intermediate category X1 (read

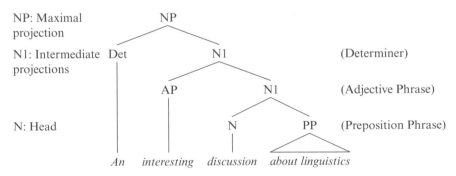

Figure 7

as 'X bar') – X1 can be thought of as a constituent that is intermediate between the head and the phrase. Specifier is also an important relationship since it is the locus for grammatical categories characteristic of the phrase in question – in the NP determiners, articles and the like – and frequently it must agree in number with the head (c.f. *this* (sg) *man* (sg); *these* (pl) *men* (pl)). In X-bar trees specifiers are represented as daughters of the head and sisters to an X1. Adjuncts are daughters of an X1 and sisters of another X1; adjuncts in the NP are adjectives, relative clauses and similar modifiers; in the VP, they are adverbs. These observations could be formulated as a set of principles: the head projects an X1, which may also dominate a phrasal category as complement, and so on.

These principles can also applied to the D-structure of the sentence itself. This is illustrated in outline in Figure 8 (for reasons of space, details of several of the phrasal projections are suppressed, including X1 categories not relevant to the argument).

We can use the figure to ask this question: If the noun is the head of the noun phrase, the verb of the verb phrase, etc., what is the head of the sentence? P&P offers two answers. One answer is that the head is a marker of the 'mood' status of the sentence, whether it is declarative, interrogative, etc. In simple declarative sentences there is,

of course, no mood marker in English, but it is argued that the 'complementizer' *that* which occurs in embedded declaratives, as in *I think [**that** the cat caught the mouse]* is in fact an overt declarative marker, just as the complementizer *whether* is an interrogative marker: *I wonder [**whether** the cat caught the mouse]*. Now if the complementizer is a head, we may suppose that, like other heads, it projects a phrasal category, let us call it CP. Suppose, finally, that simple declarative sentences have an abstract marker of their mood status, then we can have a representation like that of Figure 8. A further advantage is now that the Specifier of the C node can serve as the landing site for fronted *wh*-words in interrogative sentences (*What did the cat catch?*) and the fronted *wh*-word certainly seems to be an overt marker of interrogative mood. The second answer is that the head is the tense marker, and a tense marker is obligatory in simple sentences. If we call the category of the tense marker I or Infl (for Inflection – and tense is characteristically marked as an inflection of some kind on the first verb in the verb group), then it too will project a phrasal category, this time IP. This analysis too is shown in Figure 8. Note that we can use this configuration to define the grammatical relation 'Subject of the sentence': it is the NP that is specifier of the IP. We noted earlier that the Specifier node is the locus for grammatical information for its particular phrasal projection; here we have seen the SpecC as the site for fronted *wh*-words, and SpecI as the grammatical subject.

In the initial section we noted that PS grammars captured relations of constituency (or dominance) and order. X-bar theory captures notions of dominance and in addition gives a configurational definition to the relationships outlined in the previous paragraph – it can be argued that such relations are indeed universal. It does not, however, determine the order of constituents, which is well known to vary from

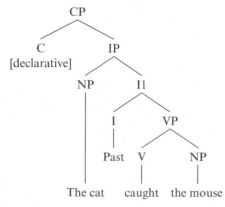

Figure 8

language to language: in English adjectives usually precede their noun heads, in French they typically follow; in the English VP the verb is followed by its complements, English is a SVO language; in Japanese the complements precede the verb, Japanese is a SOV language. In both languages order is defined with respect to the head. These variations between languages are handled by the **word order parameter**. The way the parameter is set for any particular language is then an empirical matter for the language learner (head first in Japanese; head last in English). What the X-bar principles do is define constituency and dominance; what the parameter does is to define the range of permissible word order variations. A particular language can be thought of as choosing some position in the **syntactic space** defined by the interaction of the principles and the parameter.

Before turning to theta theory, we should note the pivotal role in all this of the lexicon. As we have seen, information on sub-categorization is associated with items in the lexicon. It will record that, say, CATCH is a transitive verb, and it might do so in an entry which contained, *inter alia*, information like this: CATCH; V; –NP (i.e. that CATCH is a verb and that it occurs with an NP sister). There is now a real sense in which, given this lexical information and the X-bar principles enunciated above, CATCH can 'project' the relevant partial structure shown in Figure 8. Lexical items will also have semantic information, for our immediate purposes, in the case of a verb, some account of its 'predicate argument' structure (the verb being the predicate and its subject, object, etc. its arguments). For CATCH, we need to know that it is associated with an agent as subject ('the catcher') and a patient as object ('the caught').

Theta theory is concerned with predicate argument structure: a predicate is said to take the relevant information from the lexicon and **assign** a **theta role** to each of its syntactic arguments. One of the principles

associated with theta theory is the **theta criterion**: this says that each argument of the verb receives one and only one theta role and each theta role is assigned to one and only one argument. The theta criterion thus ensures that a verb will be associated with just the right number of lexical arguments. So, for example, with CATCH the theta criterion will ensure that it occurs with two lexical NPs and that **agent** and **patient** are assigned correctly to its subject and object. A further principle of theta theory is the **Projection principle**: the theta-marking properties of a lexical item must be represented, or projected, at each syntactic level: D-structure, S-structure and logical form. This has a number of profound effects. One is that there can be no rules deleting or inserting items that have a semantic interpretation – in effect, transformations will be limited to movement rules. A second is that the D-structure will have the possibility of generating NP nodes that are unfilled by lexical material and these will provide 'landing sites' for movement rules, in accordance with the structure-preserving principle introduced at the end of the previous section. Suppose, for example, that we derive the passive, as suggested at the end of the previous section, from a deep structure of the form 'NP1 – was – Passive Participle –NP2 (by NP3)'. Theta theory will ensure that the verb assigns at a maximum two theta roles – patient to NP2, and agent (if it is chosen) to NP3 – and so only two of the NPs can be lexicalized. In a passive sentence, NP1 will receive no theta role, but will be the site for the patient NP to move to – how and why it does that, we will come to.

As a further example, consider a verb like SEEM. The lexicon must record that SEEM has a proposition, a sentence, as an argument but is associated with no lexical NP arguments and so assigns no theta roles. In a sentence like *It seems that the cat caught the mouse*, the lexical NPs (*cat* and *mouse*) receive their theta roles from

a D-structure: ($_s$ e + tns seem ($_s$ that the cat
   + tns catch the mouse))
   (pleonastic *it* inserted)
b S-structure: ($_s$ it + tns seem ($_s$ that the cat
   + tns catch the mouse))
c LF: (seem, (catch (the cat, the mouse))
d PF: It seemed that the cat caught the mouse

Figure 9

CATCH in the subordinate clause. What
then of *it*? The traditional description
would have it as a **dummy** subject: dummy
because it has no semantics (you cannot,
for example, ask *What seems that the cat
caught the mouse?*), which we can interpret
as having no theta relation to SEEM. The
deep structure will then have the general
form shown in Figure 9(a). By the theta
criterion, the subject of SEEM cannot be a
lexical NP but both the subject and object
of CATCH must be lexical. *It* will be
supplied between D- and S-structure. *It* is
supplied because English sentences require
tensed verbs (shown by the marking '+ tns')
to have grammatical subjects; how this
comes about we will discover when we turn
to case theory shortly. The Projection principle ensures that the theta properties of
predicates are projected at each syntactic
level: D-structure, S-structure (9b) and
logical form. In the schematic representation, a form of predicate calculus (which
should be self-explanatory) is used to represent the logical form.

I will discuss another example involving
SEEM below.

At this point we should return to examine transformations again. As before,
D-structure provides a structural description of a sentence. D-structure is related
to S-structure by transformation, as are PF
and LF to S-structure. The notion of transformation is, however, much restricted.
Between D- and S-structure, and between
S-structure and LF, the theta criterion and
the Projection principle forbid the insertion
or deletion of meaningful elements. The
means we are left with are only Movement

transformations, and this is expressed as
the extremely general rule 'move alpha'
in essence, 'move anything'. This may seem
to be an extraordinarily relaxed approach
to movement, but it is in reality severely
controlled by the various subtheories. In
effect, movement is restricted to lexical
material moving from one node to another
(empty) node, leaving an empty category
behind marked with a trace, to which it is
'bound' (i.e. co-referential, shown by marking with the same subscript). Movement
rules have the potential for moving an item
very far from its deep structure position:
*[What$_i$ [t$_i$ was caught t$_i$ by the cat]]: [What$_i$
[did you say [t$_i$ [t$_i$ was caught t$_i$ by the
cat]]]]*. However, movement is in fact
constrained by the fact that an item and
its immediate trace cannot be too far away
and, as we saw from the discussion of
'islands' in the previous section, there are
some boundaries that cannot be crossed
at all. Movements like this are **chained**.
A chain will show where an item started
its journey, where it finished its journey,
and all its intermediate stopping places
and all these positions will be subject to
checking. **Bounding theory** defines these
restrictions.

Central to all these subtheories is **Government theory** (note that 'Government' is
part of the title of Chomsky's 1981 book
with which we began this section). Government involves the relationship between a
governor and a governed. The governor
controls the governed, a relationship that
can, but need not, be overtly marked by
the morphology. The notion is an old one
– in traditional grammar verbs and prepositions were said to govern their complements
in a particular case. In English, they govern
object pronouns in the objective case: *saw
me (*I); to me (*I)*. The relationship can
be given a configurational definition: within
a maximal projection a head will govern
its complement. In P&P the definition is
extended so that it covers other relationships we have thus far considered, and will

come to later, in more detail. It is extended to cover the relationship between a specifier and its head: this will subsume many agreement phenomena, as, for example, subject–verb agreement: in Figure 8, the head, I(nfl), the tensed inflection, can be defined to govern its specifier, the subject NP, in the nominative case (*I (*me) saw the mouse*). In theta theory, which we looked at earlier, theta assignors will govern the items to which they assign theta roles. Government can also be extended to regulate movement rules in that it is defined to cover the distribution of traces, formalized by the 'empty category principle', which declares that all traces must be properly governed, and the 'minimality condition', which restricts the distance between a governor and what it governs.

Government is also central to **Case theory**. This regulates the distribution of phonetically realized NPs by assigning **abstract case** to them. **Case** is assigned by a set of **case assignors** to the constituents they govern. We have assumed that V, Prep and Infl(+ tns) are case assignors: Infl(+ tns) assigning nominative case to the NP it governs (the subject, reflecting the fact that tensed sentences require subject expressions); V assigning oblique case to the NP it governs (the object) and Prep also assigning oblique case to the NP it governs. These definitions can now be associated with a **Case filter**, a checking device that will declare a sentence to be ungrammatical if it contains an NP containing phonetic material but assigned no case or, vice versa, an empty NP which is assigned case but contains no phonetic material. In effect, case theory will require, *inter alia*, the positions of grammatical subject in a finite sentence and object to be filled with lexical material. The phrase **phonetic material** is used to cover not only lexical NPs but also items like the dummy *it* associated with *seems*. The reader is invited to check this with the derivations shown in outline in Figure 9.

We are now in a position to sharpen up our notions of D-structure, S-structure and the relationship between them: **D-structure** is the level at which theta positions must be filled by lexical material. At this level verbs must be associated with the correct number of arguments: if active *catch* is associated with fewer than two NPs, or if *seem* is associated with any NP, then the theta criterion will rule the structure as ill formed. Transformations may then move material into empty nodes, and in appropriate cases a dummy *it* will be supplied. Case theory will then check the final distribution of lexical items, both moved and unmoved, and if material is found where it ought not to be, or if there is no material where some should be, the sentence will be marked as ill formed.

The matter can be illustrated by another example involving *seem*. Consider the sentence *The cat seemed to catch the mouse*. If we are to be consistent with our own account of theta theory, the distribution of lexical material in the D-structure and the logical form assigned to the sentence must be the same as that assigned to *It seemed that the cat caught the mouse*, shown in Figure 9. These similarities are recorded in the derivation shown in Figure 10. The differences between the two sentences are due to the fact that the constituent sentence in our first example is finite and tensed (*that the cat caught the mouse*), whereas in the second sentence it is non-finite, and hence untensed (*to catch the mouse*): this difference is recorded in the D-structure below by the notation + tns (finite, tensed)

a D-structure: ($_s$ e + tns seem ($_s$ the cat − tns catch the mouse))
   (move the cat into the empty subject position)
b S-structure: ($_s$ the cat$_1$ + tns seem ($_s$ e$_1'$ − tns catch the mouse))
c LF: (seem, (catch (the cat, the mouse))
d PF: The cat seemed 'e' to catch the mouse

Figure 10

or – tns (non-finite, untensed). We saw above that + tns was a governing category and governed an NP in the nominative case: suppose now that – tns is not a governor; as such, it will not assign case: this reflects the traditional view that infinitives cannot have subjects. Now, according to the theory, lexical material must be given case: this it can only acquire by moving into the position of subject of *seem* where, being governed by + tns, it will, as required, acquire case. Move alpha produces a situation where the chain created by movement will, as required, ensure that the chain with the lexical NP *the cat* has one theta role (*the cat* is assigned agent as subject of *catch*: the subject of *seem* has no theta role) and one case (*the cat* acquires nom(inative) case from + tns in the main clause, but no case from – tns in the constituent clause). Similarly, the lexical NP *the mouse* gets oblique case as object of *catch* and is assigned the theta role of theme. The reader is invited to work out why strings like *It seemed the cat to catch the dog*, *The cat seemed caught the dog*, etc. are ill formed.

Binding theory is concerned with the syntactic domains in which NPs can or cannot be construed as **coreferential**. If we suppose that all NPs are assigned a **referential index**, then coreference can be shown by marking NPs with the same index and **non-coreference** by marking them with different indices. An NP with an index distinct from all other NPs is said to be **free**; an NP which has the same index as another is said to be **bound**. An NP must be either free or bound within a particular **domain**. Thus, for example, in $John_1$ *likes* $himself_1$, the reflexive pronoun, *himself*, must be bound by some other NP within its domain, in this case the subject NP *John* – this is shown in the subscripting. In $John_1$ *likes* $Mary_2$, the full lexical NPs *John* and *Mary* cannot be coreferential, and this is shown by assigning them different indices. The relevant domain for the binding of reflexive pronouns in English is, informally

speaking, the simple sentence, but different languages are able to select domains differently. Binding theory is concerned with the categories that must be bound and free and with defining the domain in which binding takes place; another area of grammar in which languages differ or, in terms of government and binding (GB) theory, set their **parameters** differentially.

We appear to have come a long way from *Syntactic Structures*, and in some senses this is indeed the case. In others, however, the thirty-four years since its publication have shown a remarkably consistent purpose. Details of grammatical organization have clearly changed and developed and the general architecture of the theory has changed. But in many ways the goals set out in the first sentences of the introduction to *Syntactic Structures* remain (Chomsky 1957: 11). Universal grammar, child language acquisition and language understanding still motivate the investigation, but the machinery is now more subtly adapted to the task since there are now many interacting components, each of which can be fine-tuned.

The Minimalist Program

In a series of papers from the late 1980s Chomsky returned to re-examine some of the fundamental principles of generative grammar. We shall look at two: the first is the recurrent issue of the number and nature of the levels of representation, the relationships between them and the way these levels are justified; the second is the nature of the rules required in a derivation. The two issues are, as always, intertwined.

We have seen that the levels of representation identified in the P&P model and the relationship between them are as shown in Figure 6. The levels and the relationships between them proposed in minimalism is shown in Figure 11: LF and PF remain, but DS and SS disappear: we will return to SPELL OUT below. The claim is that LF

Figure 11

and PF can be 'externally motivated': they are the 'interfaces' between, respectively, the cognitive systems relating to language production and understanding, and the articulation/auditory production systems. By contrast, DS and SS could only be motivated by considerations purely internal to the linguistic model and hence have no psychological reality or justification.

For reasons of space we shall concern ourselves only with LF (although the kind of issues we will look at apply *pari passu* to PF) and will concentrate on 'grammatical' categories, like tense, number, gender, case and the like.

Let us first return to Figure 11. In Principles and Parameters, a D-structure is constructed according to the lexical properties of particular items, constrained by the structures that are permitted by the principles of X-bar theory. Suppose, however, that we were to construct an analysis tree simply by selecting items randomly from the lexicon and seeing if they 'fit together' or merge to form a larger item, either because of lexical properties of their own or because of general principles governing the merge operation. Suppose, for example, a random selection

from the lexicon produced the words *into*, *sing* and *cats*; there is no way these could merge successfully to produce a well-formed sentence and consequently at spell out a derivation would 'crash'. On the other hand, suppose we selected *he*, *is* and *singing*: the lexical properties of the progressive auxiliary form of BE requires it to have an -*ing* verb form as its complement and those of SING allow it to be used intransitively. These properties allow *is* and *singing* to merge successfully. A general property of Merge requires a tensed verb, like *is*, to have a subject with which it agrees in number: *he* satisfies these requirements so *he* can merge with *is singing* and be spelled out as the acceptable sentence *he is singing*.

To see in a bit more detail what is involved, let us suppose our example sentence has an analysis as in Figure 12. As a comparatively recent development, minimalism has not yet settled down to a generally agreed form of representation and in the discussion we will largely follow the representation developed in Radford (1997).

As we have assumed, each of the words is characterized in the lexicon as belonging to a particular lexeme: *is* is a form of BE, for example, and each is characterized by a set of features representing the 'grammatical categories' of the word concerned (there will also, of course, be information about the sense of the item concerned, its pronunciation and so on, but we are not concerning

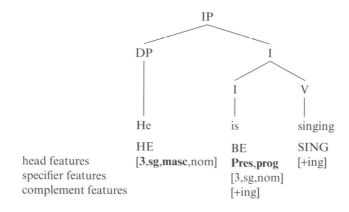

Figure 12

ourselves with these here). In Figure 12 the features are divided into three subsets. Head features are those particularly important for the interpretation of the word form concerned: *he* is the third person singular masculine, nominative (subject) form of the pronoun; *is* is the present progressive form of the verb BE, and *singing* is the present participle (*-ing*) form of the verb SING. Complement features indicate the form of the constituent which is to be the complement of the item in question: progressive BE requires to be followed by the present participle, so BE is marked with the complement feature [+ ing]; SING here is intransitive and has no complement. Specifier features indicate agreement properties: English requires a tensed verb to agree in person and number with its subject, which must furthermore be in the nominative case if it is a pronoun to be (and, recall from the previous section, the subject of a finite verb in the specifier position with respect to the verb of which it is subject).

Now, some of the features in Figure 12 contribute to the semantic interpretation of the sentence: we need to know that *he* is the third person masculine singular form of the pronoun (as opposed to, say, *she* or *they*); and *is* is the present progressive form of BE (as opposed to, say, the past form *was*). Features of this kind are 'interpretable' to LF in the sense that they contribute to the semantic interpretation, and hence can be externally motivated: if we had any of the other forms in brackets in the previous sentence, we would have a different interpretation (*she was singing*, say). To distinguish them, interpretable features are emboldened in Figure 12. By contrast, the other features – while they are clearly necessary for grammatical well-formedness – do not contribute to semantic interpretation. Thus, for example, the agreement features on *is* merely reflect the relevant features of the subject and do not themselves add to the interpretation; similarly, the fact that SING is in the present participle form is a formal consequence of its being the complement of BE and contributes nothing to the interpretation. Neither **She be singing* nor **he is sing* are well formed in Standard English and, in so far as they are comprehensible, they do not have different semantic interpretations from the example sentence. Features of this kind then are not 'interpretable'. The claim is that, since LF interfaces with the cognitive system, it should contain only interpretable features – this is formulated as the 'principle of full interpretation'.

Now, if LF is to have only interpretable features, then we must have a derivation whereby the uninterpretable features necessary for grammatical well-formedness are eliminated in the process of derivation, leaving only the interpretable features to reach LF. This is done by a process of 'checking': items are examined pair by pair and uninterpretable features are eliminated if they can be checked off against a matching feature. If the matching feature is interpretable, then it will remain and the uninterpretable feature is eliminated; if both are uninterpretable, then both will be eliminated. Applied to our example, this will yield:

	HE	BE	SING
head features	[**3,sg,masc,** ~~nom~~]	**Pres,prog**	[+ ~~ing~~]
specifier features		[~~3,sg,nom~~]	
complement features		[+ ~~ing~~]	

Since this contains only interpretable features the derivation survives after SPELL OUT. By contrast, a structure like that shown in Figure 13

will, after checking, yield:

	HE	BE	SING
head features	[**3,sg,masc,** ~~nom~~]	**Pres,prog**	[+ ~~ing~~]
specifier features		[2,sg,~~nom~~]	
complement features		[+ ~~ing~~]	

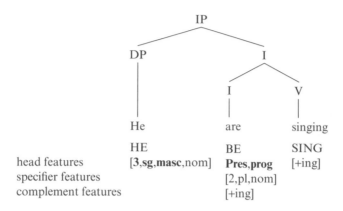

head features
specifier features
complement features

Figure 13

This derivation contains uninterpretable features; consequently, following the principle of full interpretation, it will 'crash' at SPELL OUT.

We started this section by observing that DS and SS disappear, and it can now be seen how this is so. The structure in Figure 12 derives from selecting and merging lexical items: unlike a D-structure, it has no particular status with respect to semantic interpretation, grammatical well-formedness or the like. SPELL OUT is not like SS: in Principles and Parameters SS is a level at which certain properties are determined (typically, case assignment or binding, or both), by contrast, SPELL OUT is not a level but a procedure that can in principle occur at any stage in a derivation, and will either lead to a successful derivation or to a derivation crashing. The discussion also casts some light on the second issue raised at the beginning of this section – the nature of the rules required in a derivation. We have only had the space to examine a few simple sentences: more complex sentences will require the familiar movement rules, but this time, instead of constraining them by a web of general restrictions, they will be constrained by highly local configurational considerations. The intention is to make the grammatical machinery as spare (minimal) as possible and only use that which can be justified as required by the nature of the cognitive systems that are under investigation.

E.K.B

Suggestions for further reading

Atkinson, M. (1996) 'Generative grammar', in K. Brown and J. Miller (eds) *A Concise Encyclopaedia of Syntactic Theories*, Oxford: Pergamon Press.

Freidin (1996) 'Generative grammar: Principles and Parameters', in K. Brown and J. Miller *A Concise Encyclopaedia of Syntactic Theories*, Oxford: Pergamon Press.

Newmeyer, F.J. (1980/1986) *Linguistic Theory in America: The First Quarter Century of Transformational Generative Grammar*, New York and London: Academic Press; 2nd edition 1986.

Radford, A. (1988) *Transformational Grammar*, Cambridge: Cambridge University Press. (A student's introduction to Principles and Parameters.)

—— (1997) *Syntactic Theory and the Structure of English: A Minimalist Approach*, Cambridge: Cambridge University Press. (A student's introduction to the Minimalist Program.)

Generative phonology

Introduction

Generative phonology (GP) is the theory, or theories, of phonology adopted within the framework of generative grammar (see GENERATIVE GRAMMAR). Originating in the late 1950s, principally in work by Halle and Chomsky (Chomsky *et al.* 1956; Halle 1959), it developed during the 1960s to reach a standard form in Chomsky and Halle's *The Sound Pattern of English* (1968) (henceforth *SPE*). Much of the work in the 1970s derived from *SPE* in an attempt to overcome the difficulties posed by this framework, and by the late 1970s the theory had fragmented into a number of competing models. The 1980s saw more of a consensus, particularly with the development of **non-linear** phonology, while the rise (in the 1990s) of **optimality theory** has again radically transformed the theory.

The standard model

The *SPE* model of phonology adopts the framework of Chomsky's (1965) **Standard Theory** of generative grammar, in which a central syntactic component enumerates abstract 'deep' structures which underlie the meaning, and which are related to actual 'surface' structures by means of transformations. Within this model, the role of the phonological component is to interpret such surface structures, assigning to them an appropriate pronunciation, and thus accounting for the speaker's competence in this area of the language.

The surface structures which constitute the input to the phonological rules are represented as a string of 'formatives' (morphemes) and a labelled syntactic bracketing. The phonological rules convert such a structure into a phonetic representation, expressed in terms of a universal set of phonetic features.

In addition to phonological rules, we require a **lexicon**, a listing of those features of the formatives, including phonological attributes, which are not derivable by rule. Since formatives are subject to a variety of phonological processes in specific contexts, their lexical representation must be in the most general form from which the individual realizations can be derived. It will thus be morphophonemic (see MORPHOLOGY). For example, the German words *Rad* and *Rat*, both pronounced [ra:t], will have different lexical representations, since inflected forms such as *Rades* [ra:dəs] and *Rates* [ra:təs] are pronounced differently. In this case *Rad* can be given a lexical representation with a final /d/, since the [t] is derivable by general rule.

Although the segments of lexical representations are comparable to morphophonemes, Halle (1959, 1962) demonstrated that there is not necessarily any intermediate level, corresponding to the phoneme, between such representations and the phonetic representation. Thus in Russian there are pairs of voiced and voiceless 'obstruent' phonemes, i.e. plosives, affricates and fricatives, and voiceless obstruents are regularly replaced by voiced ones when followed by a voiced obstruent; thus, [mok l,ɨ] but [mog bɨ]. The same rule applies to /ʧ/ – [doʧl,i] but [doʤbi], though [ʤ] is not phonemically different from [ʧ]. This rule is a single process, but to incorporate a phonemic level would involve breaking it into two, since it would need to apply both to derive the phonemes and to derive the allophones. Hence, the phoneme has no place in the GP framework; phonemic transcriptions are, according to Chomsky and Halle, merely 'regularized phonetic representations', while 'complementary distribution', the fundamental criterion of phonemic analysis, is 'devoid of any theoretical significance' (Chomsky 1964: 93).

Since the lexical representation is intended to contain only non-predictable information, it will take the form of redundancy-free feature matrices in which predictable features are unspecified. Since, however, redundant features may be required for the operation of phonological rules, these features must be inserted by a set of conventions, **redundancy rules** or **morpheme structure rules**, which express in indirect form the constraints on segment types and morpheme structures in the language concerned. These rules, together with rules to eliminate superfluous structure, etc., are called **readjustment rules**, and they will apply before the application of the phonological rules proper.

The rules of the phonological component thus operate on fully specified feature matrices constituting the **phonological**, or **underlying**, representation. These rules are of the form:

$$A \rightarrow B/ C \_\_\_ D$$

where A is the feature matrix of the affected segment(s), and B the resulting matrix; C and D represent the context, ___ being the position of the affected segment(s) A. In the Standard Theory these rules are in part ordered so as to apply in a fixed sequence. Thus, from English /k/ we can derive [s] and [ʃ]: *electric* [k], *electricity* [s] and *electrician* [ʃ]; but since [ʃ] is also derived from [s] in, e.g. *racial*, cf. *race*, the [ʃ] of *electrician* is best derived by two ordered rules: /k/ → [s], [s] → [ʃ].

The application of rules may be constrained by grammatical factors. Thus the rules for English stress depend on whether the word is a noun or a verb: '*import* vs *im'port*, while the realization of German /x/ as [x] or [ç] in words such as *Kuchen* [kuːxən] ('cake') and *Kuhchen* [kuːçən] ('little cow') depends on the morphological structure of the words, which can be represented as /kuːxən/ and /kuː + xçən/ respectively. There is therefore no need for the phonemic 'separation of levels', nor for 'juncture phonemes' (see PHONEMICS).

A special case of the relationship between syntax and phonology is the **cyclical application of rules**, where some sets of rules may reapply to progressively larger morphological or syntactic domains. In the description of English stress, which takes up a large part of *SPE*, the different stress patterns of *blackboard eraser* and *black board-eraser* follow the cyclical application of the stress rules. If these expressions have different structures, with different bracketing of constituents, then a cyclical procedure whereby rules apply within the brackets, after which the innermost brackets are deleted and the rules apply again, will achieve the desired results. On each cycle, primary stress is assigned, automatically reducing other levels by 1:

	[[[black]	[board]]	[eraser]]
Cycle 1	[1]	[1]	[1]
Cycle 2	[1	2]	–
Cycle 3	[1	3	2]

	[[black]	[[board]	[eraser]]]
Cycle 1	[1]	[1]	[1]
Cycle 2	–	[1	2]
Cycle 3	[2	1	3]

The rules are intended to capture significant generalizations, and a measure of this is the simplicity of the rules themselves. In a number of cases special formal devices are necessary to ensure that more general rules are also simpler. For example, assimilation is a very general process in which feature values of adjacent segments agree, but this would normally involve listing all combinations of features in the rules, e.g.:

$$[- \text{syll}] \rightarrow \left\{ \begin{array}{l} \begin{bmatrix} + \text{ant} \\ - \text{cor} \end{bmatrix} / \_\_\_ \begin{bmatrix} + \text{ant} \\ - \text{cor} \end{bmatrix} \\ \begin{bmatrix} + \text{ant} \\ + \text{cor} \end{bmatrix} / \_\_\_ \begin{bmatrix} + \text{ant} \\ + \text{cor} \end{bmatrix} \end{array} \right\}$$

etc.

A simpler statement can be achieved by using 'Greek letter variables', e.g. [αanterior], where 'α' must have the same value ('+' or '–') for the two segments involved, e.g.

$$[- \text{syll}] \rightarrow \begin{bmatrix} \alpha \text{ant} \\ \beta \text{cor} \end{bmatrix} / \_\_\_ \begin{bmatrix} \alpha \text{ant} \\ \beta \text{cor} \end{bmatrix}$$

Problems and solutions

The *SPE* framework offered a new and often insightful way of describing phonological phenomena, and it was applied to a variety of languages. But it became clear that unconstrained application of the above principles can lead to excessively abstract phonological representations and insufficiently motivated rules. Consider the description of nasalization in French (Schane 1968). French nasal vowels can be derived from non-nasal vowels followed by nasal consonants: /bɔn/ → [bɔ̃]; this process, involving a nasalization rule followed by a nasal consonant deletion rule, applies in final position and before a consonant, but not before vowels, e.g. *ami* [ami] – or in the feminine, e.g. *bonne* [bɔn]. If we assume that feminine forms have an underlying /ə/, i.e. /bɔnə/, which prevents the application of the nasalization rules, followed by a further rule deleting the [ə], then the feminine is no longer an exception, and the rules can apply more generally.

Thus the application of rules can be manipulated by means of a suitably abstract phonological representation, in which segments are included whose sole purpose is to prevent or facilitate the application of rules. This procedure can easily be abused to give underlying forms which, though apparently well motivated in terms of formal adequacy, may be counterintuitive and quite spurious. For example, the rules of *SPE* predict that stress will not fall on the final syllable of an English verb if it contains a lax or short vowel followed by only a single consonant. The word *caress* [kəˈres] appears to be an exception, but it can be made regular with a phonological representation containing a double final consonant, and with a rule of **degemination** to eliminate the superfluous consonant after the stress rules have applied. Similar considerations motivate representations such as /eklipse/ and /giraffe/. The problem is not that such representations are necessarily incorrect – though most generative phonologists assumed that they are – but rather that the theory offers no way of distinguishing between legitimate and illegitimate abstractions in such representations.

Many different proposals were made to solve these problems, and to reduce the arbitrariness and abstractness of phonological representations and rules. In *SPE*, Chomsky and Halle themselves (1968: chapter 9) proposed the use of **universal marking conventions** to maximize naturalness of segments. Under their proposal, feature values in lexical representations may be in terms of 'u' (unmarked) and 'm' (marked) instead of '+' and '–', these being interpreted as '+' or '–' according to universal principles. However, this approach found little favour. Other proposals involved constraints on underlying representations or rules, but the problem with all such proposals is that they tend to be too strong, ruling out legitimate as well as illegitimate abstractions.

For example, to avoid underlying forms which are too remote from phonetic reality, we might propose that the underlying form of a formative should be identical with the alternant which appears in isolation. But this is clearly unsatisfactory, since the forms of German *Rat* and *Rad* cited above can only be predicted from the inflected stem. Or we might require the underlying form to be identical with one of its phonetic manifestations; however, none of the stems of, for example, the set of words *photograph*, *photography* and *photographic* could serve as the underlying form of the others, since all have reduced vowels from which the full vowels of the others cannot be predicted. Similarly, constraints were proposed on **absolute neutralization**, in which an underlying contrast is posited which is never manifested on the surface, and on the use of phonological features, such as the double consonants of the above English examples, merely to 'trigger' or to inhibit the appropriate rules. But, again, cases were adduced where such devices seem justified. Thus all the proposals suffer from the drawback that they are often as arbitrary as the phenomena they purport to eliminate.

Another factor contributing to the power of generative phonology is **rule ordering**. Ordering relations among rules are either **intrinsic**, that is, dictated by the form of the rules themselves, or **extrinsic**, that is, specifically imposed on the grammar. The latter fall into a number of types. In view of the power that ordering gives to the grammar, some phonologists sought to impose restrictions on permissible orderings, and some, e.g. Koutsoudas *et al.* (1974), argued for the complete prohibition of extrinsic ordering, requiring all rules to be either intrinsically ordered or to apply simultaneously.

By the late 1970s, some of these principles had been included in a range of alternative theories (see Dinnsen 1979) which claimed to overcome the difficulties posed by the *SPE* framework, particularly by imposing a variety of constraints on phonological representations, rules or rule ordering. An important requirement made by a number of phonologists was that phonological descriptions must not only provide adequate descriptions, but must also be **natural**, and some theories explicitly adopted the label **natural phonology**. The theory of Stampe (1969, 1973; cf. Donegan and Stampe 1979), for example, argues that speakers of all languages are susceptible to universal **natural processes** – for example, rules of assimilation or word-final devoicing – which will thus form a part of the grammars of all languages, unless speakers learn to suppress them. The problem here is to determine which rules belong to this category. The theory of **natural generative phonology** of Vennemann and Hooper (see Hooper 1976) is perhaps the most constrained of all, disallowing all non-intrinsic ordering and imposing further restrictions such as the **True Generalization Condition**, which prohibits the positing of any phonological rule which is apparently contradicted by surface forms. There could not, for example, be a rule voicing intervocalic consonants if voiceless consonants can occur intervocalically in phonetic forms of the language.

Non-linear phonology

Although these various alternative theories claimed to offer solutions to the problems of the *SPE* framework, and a number of them won a following, the 1980s saw the rise of a new trend, eclipsing most of the proposals and providing a set of more unified approaches. This new orientation addressed another weakness of *SPE* generative phonology – its linearity.

In the *SPE* framework, the phonological representation of a sentence takes the form of a linear sequence of segments and boundaries. The boundaries reflect a hierarchical syntactic structure, but the phonological segments themselves are in purely linear order. Although many phonological rules can be adequately stated in terms of such an order, a linear representation is less appropriate for **suprasegmental** features such as stress and tone. Two influential approaches which adopt a more structured, non-linear approach are autosegmental phonology and metrical phonology.

Autosegmental phonology (Goldsmith 1976) began as a theory of tone. In the *SPE* framework, the purely segmental representations, which do not even recognize the syllable as a unit, imply that tones are specified as features of vowels. This becomes difficult, however, if (as in some approaches) **contour** tones, i.e. rises and falls, are regarded as sequences of pitch levels, since two successive features must be assigned to the same vowel. Furthermore, in many tone languages, particularly those of Africa, the number of tones is not always the same as the number of vowels, since more than one tone may occur on a given syllable, and tones may 'spread' to adjacent syllables (see TONE LANGUAGES). This is solved in the autosegmental framework by regarding the tones not as features of the vowels but as a separate, autonomous level, or **tier** of representation, related to the segments by rules of **association**, e.g.:

L H L
| | ∧
u y a l i m a

A universal set of **well-formedness conditions** is proposed to determine the permissible associations, as well as rules which operate on the tonal tier itself. In later work, other phenomena, such as vowel harmony (Clements 1976) and nasalization (e.g. Hyman 1982), have been given a similar treatment.

Metrical phonology began as an interpretation of the stress rules of the *SPE* framework (see Liberman 1975; Liberman and Prince 1977), in which it was shown that the various stress levels could be derived from a hierarchically ordered arrangement of **strong** and **weak** nodes. Such a hierarchy results in a **metrical grid** from which the stress levels of individual syllables can be read off, e.g.:

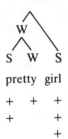

pretty girl

+ + +
+   +
    +

This theory, too, has been extended into other areas, such as syllable structure (Kahn 1976), and even into tonal structure, which in some cases can be shown to involve hierarchical organization. Later versions of the theory (e.g. Halle and Vergnaud 1987; Hayes 1995) have been particularly concerned with the typology of stress systems, and have been very influential.

A number of other theories have also developed within the generative framework, one of the most important of which is **lexical phonology** (Mohanan 1986). Deriving from generative work on morphology, this approach develops the cyclical principles of *SPE* in ways which integrate phonological and morphological processes. The theory of **prosodic phonology** (Nespor and Vogel 1986) develops a view of prosodic structure comprising a hierarchy of prosodic units; **moraic phonology** (Hayes 1989) incorporates the classical quantitative unit of the **mora** in order to account for length and syllable weight.

The phonological representations assumed in these theories are very different from those of the *SPE* model, and their introduction involves a shift of focus away from discussions of such issues as abstractness or rule ordering, and from the appropriate formalisms, towards an exploration of the structural complexities of such representations. Nevertheless, many of the original principles of generative phonology, such as the postulation of an abstract underlying phonological structure related by rules to a phonetic representation, are not abandoned.

Optimality Theory

The most dynamic development since non-linear phonology is **Optimality Theory** (OT). This was first presented in the early 1990s in unpublished work by Prince, Smolensky and McCarthy (Prince and Smolensky 1993; McCarthy and Prince 1993b). Much of the literature was at first available only on the World Wide Web at the Rutgers Optimality Archive (http://roa.rutgers.edu), but the theory has since become more widely known and influential. While maintaining the distinction between underlying and surface representations ('inputs' and 'outputs'), it has abandoned much of the apparatus of the *SPE* model, including phonological rules, which are replaced by **constraints**.

The theory starts from the existence of limitations on the phonetic form of words. These include universal principles ('every language has vowels'), language-specific restrictions ('Hawaian has no voiced obstruents') and general 'markedness' tendencies ('oral vowels are preferred to nasal vowels'). In OT, all such restrictions and preferences are incorporated into a set of constraints which differ from earlier constraints in a number of important ways. First, they are **universal**, and thus apply to all languages. Since, however, languages are subject to them in different degrees, they are **violable**. Differences between languages are the result of different **ranking** of the constraints. Forms may violate constraints, but only in order to comply with higher-ranking ones.

Constraints are broadly of two types, **markedness** constraints and **faithfulness** constraints. For example, the marked nature of voiced obstruents and their tendency not to occur in syllable-final position are reflected in the markedness constraints *VOICED-OBSTR (voiced obstruents are not allowed) and *VOICED-CODA (voiced obstruents do not occur in syllable-final position), where '*' indicates a negative constraint. The preference for CV syllables reflects the constraints ONSET (all syllables have onsets) and NO-CODA (syllables do not have codas). These constraints are assumed to exist in all languages, but whether or not they are violated depends on their ranking relative to other constraints. Faithfulness constraints cater mostly for the relationship between the underlying input forms and the phonetic output. They include **maximality** constraints, which specify that features of the input should be preserved in the output, and thus prohibit deletion; **dependence** constraints, which specify that every element of the output should correspond to the input, and thus prohibit epenthesis; and **identity** constraints, which ensure the preservation of feature values. The constraint IDENT-IO(voice), for example, stipulates that the voicing of the output sounds should be identical to that of the input.

These constraints are ranked differently in different languages. Since Hawaiian disallows voiced obstruents, it ranks *VOICED-OBSTR higher than faithfulness constraints. Since final voiced obstruents are not tolerated in German, faithfulness to the input is here outranked by *VOICED-CODA, though as it maintains voiced obstruents in initial position the faithfulness constraint IDENT-IO(voice) dominates *VOICED-OBSTR. English remains faithful to the input, but thereby violates both of these markedness constraints, which are hence lower-ranking. Thus, the different ranking of constraints provides a means of distinguishing different language types (a 'factorial' typology).

The model assumes a formal mechanism with a number of functions. Candidate output forms are generated from the input by a function GEN and submitted to CON, the set of constraints. Since the constraints filter out the ineligible forms, the number of candidates is in principle unlimited (the 'richness of the base'), though the input forms themselves are constrained by the principle of 'lexicon optimization', which requires that the input form be the one which involves the smallest number of constraint violations in the output. The function EVAL evaluates the candidate forms in terms of the constraints so as to identify the optimal form.

This operation is conventionally displayed in a **tableau**. The input form is placed at the top left and the relevant constraints form the column headings, in order of ranking in the language concerned. The possible candidate output forms are ranged down the left column. Violations are indicated by '*' in the relevant box. Where this violation is 'fatal', disqualifying the candidate from further consideration, this is indicated by '!'. The optimal candidate – the one which violates only lower-ranking constraints – is marked by '☞'.

In the following tableau for German *bund* ([bunt]), only candidates with the possible combinations of voiced and voiceless obstruents have been included. Since German ranks *VOICED-CODA higher than the faithfulness constraint IDENT-IO(voice), outputs (b) and (c), with a final voiced obstruent, fatally violate the former; (a), (c) and (d), which contain a voiceless obstruent, violate IDENT-IO (voice), since the input form has only voiced obstruents, but this is only fatal in initial position, in forms (c) and (d). All the forms except (c) contain a voiced obstruent, but *VOICED-OBSTR ranks lower than the other constraints and its violation is not fatal. As a result, form (a) emerges as the optimal or most 'harmonic' form, even though it violates these two constraints. The shaded boxes are those which are irrelevant, given the application of higher-ranking constraints.

/bund/	*VOICED-CODA	IDENT-IO(voice)	*VOICED-OBSTR
(a) ☞ [bunt]		*	*
(b) [bund]	*!		**
(c) [punt]		*!*	
(d) [pund]	*!	*!	⁎

In a similar way, in languages which allow only CV syllable structure, and which delete input codas and insert epenthetic consonants in order to maintain this, ONSET and NO-CODA are ranked higher than the faithfulness constraints MAX-IO and DEP-IO. In the following tableau, given the input form /-VC-/ (which may arise, for example, through morphological processes), the maximally faithful output [VC] fatally violates both ONSET and NO-CODA. The deletion of the coda and the insertion of an onset consonant violate MAX-IO and DEP-IO, respectively, but these rank lower, and [CV] emerges as the optimal form. In this way, the theory claims to capture universal principles of markedness and provide a typology of languages more satisfactorily than a rule-based theory.

/-VC-/	ONSET	NO-CODA	MAX-IO	DEP-IO
(a) [V]	*!		*	
(b) [VC]	*!	*!		
(c) ☞ [CV]			*	*
(d) [CVC]		*!		*

A.F.

Suggestions for further reading

Chomsky, N. and Halle, M. (1968) *The Sound Pattern of English*, New York: Harper and Row.

Durand, J. (1990) *Generative and Non-Linear Phonology*, London: Longman.

Goldsmith, J. (1989) *Autosegmental and Metrical Phonology*, Oxford: Blackwell Publishers.

Kager, R. (1999) *Optimality Theory*, Cambridge: Cambridge University Press.

Kenstowicz, M. (1994) *Phonology in Generative Grammar*, Oxford: Basil Blackwell.

Roca, I. (1994) *Generative Phonology*, London: Routledge.

Generative semantics

Generative semantics was an important framework for syntactic analysis within generative grammar in the late 1960s and early 1970s. This approach, whose leading figures were George Lakoff, James McCawley, Paul Postal and John R. Ross, at first posed a successful challenge to Chomsky's 'interpretive semantics' (see INTERPRETIVE SEMANTICS): indeed, around 1970 probably the great majority of generative grammarians

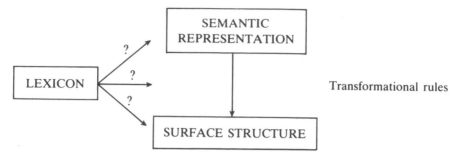

Figure 1

claimed allegiance to it. However, its relative importance had begun to decline by around 1973 or 1974, and today it has all but ceased to exist.

The leading idea of generative semantics is that there is no principled distinction between syntactic processes and semantic processes. This notion was accompanied by a number of subsidiary hypotheses: first, that the purely syntactic level of 'deep structure' posited in Chomsky's 1965 book *Aspects of the Theory of Syntax* (*Aspects*) (see GENERATIVE GRAMMAR) cannot exist; second, that the initial representations of derivations are logical representations which are identical from language to language (the **universal-base hypothesis**); third, all aspects of meaning are representable in phrase-marker form. In other words, the derivation of a sentence is a direct transformational mapping from semantics to surface structure. Figure 1 represents the initial (Chomsky 1967) generative-semantic model.

In its initial stages, generative semantics did not question the major assumptions of Chomsky's *Aspects* theory; indeed, it attempted to carry them through to their logical conclusion. For example, Chomsky had written that 'the syntactic component of a grammar must specify, for each sentence, a *deep structure* that determines its semantic representation' (1965: 16). Since in the late 1960s little elaborative work was

done to specify any interpretive mechanisms by which the deep structure might be mapped on to meaning, Lakoff and others took the word 'determines' in its most literal sense, and simply equated the two levels. Along the same lines, Chomsky's (tentative) hypothesis that selectional restrictions were to be stated at deep structure also led to that level's being conflated with semantic representation. Since sentences such as (1a) and (1b), for example, share several selectional properties – the possible subjects of *sell* are identical to the possible objects of *from* and so on – it was reasoned that the two sentences had to share deep structures. But, if such were the case, generative semanticists reasoned, then that deep structure would have to be so close to the semantic representation of the two sentences that it would be pointless to distinguish the two levels.

(1) (a) Mary sold the book to John.
    (b) John bought the book from Mary.

As Figure 1 indicates, the question of how and where lexical items entered the derivation was a topic of controversy in generative semantics. McCawley (1968) dealt with this problem by treating lexical entries themselves as structured composites of semantic material (the theory of **lexical decomposition**), and thus offered (2) as the entry for *kill*:

(2)

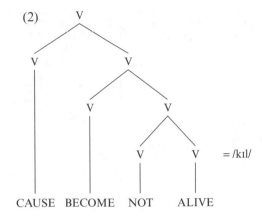

CAUSE   BECOME   NOT   ALIVE

$= /\text{k}\scriptstyle\text{I}\textstyle\text{l}/$

After the transformational rules had created a substructure in the derivation that matched the structure of a lexical entry, the phonological matrix of that entry would be insertable into the derivation. McCawley hesitantly suggested that lexical-insertion transformations might apply in a block after the application of the cyclic rules; however, generative semanticists never did agree on the locus of lexical insertion, nor even whether it occurred at some independently definable level at all.

Generative semanticists realized that their rejection of the level of deep structure would be little more than word-playing if the transformational mapping from semantic representation to surface structure turned out to be characterized by a major break before the application of the familiar cyclic rules – particularly if the natural location for the insertion of lexical items was precisely at this break. They therefore constructed a number of arguments to show that no such break existed. The most compelling were moulded after Morris Halle's classic argument against the structuralist phoneme (Halle 1959) (see GENERATIVE PHONOLOGY). Paralleling Halle's style of argumentation, generative semanticists attempted to show that the existence of a level of deep structure distinct from semantic representation would demand that the same generalization be stated twice, once in the syntax and once in the semantics (see Postal 1970).

Since a simple transformational mapping from semantics to the surface entails that no transformation can change meaning, any examples that tended to show that such rules were meaning-changing presented a profound challenge to generative semantics. Yet such examples had long been known to exist; for example, passive sentences containing multiple quantifiers differ in meaning from their corresponding actives. The scope differences between (3a) and (3b), for example, seem to suggest that Passive is a meaning-changing transformation:

(3) (a) Many men read few books.
     (b) Few books were read by many men.

The solution to this problem put forward by Lakoff (1971a) was to supplement the strict transformational derivation with another type of rule – a **global rule** – which has the ability to state generalizations between derivationally non-adjacent phrase markers. Examples (3a–b) were handled by a global rule that says that if one logical element has wider scope than another in semantic representation, then it must precede it in surface structure. This proposal had the virtue of allowing both the hypothesis that transformations are meaning-preserving and the hypothesis that the deepest syntactic level is semantic representation to be technically maintained.

Soon many examples of other types of processes were found which could not be stated in strict transformational terms, but seemed instead to involve global relations. These involved presupposition, case assignment and contractions, among other phenomena. For a comprehensive account of global rules, see Lakoff (1970).

In the late 1960s, the generative semanticists began to realize that, as deep structure was pushed back, the inventory of syntactic categories became more and more reduced.

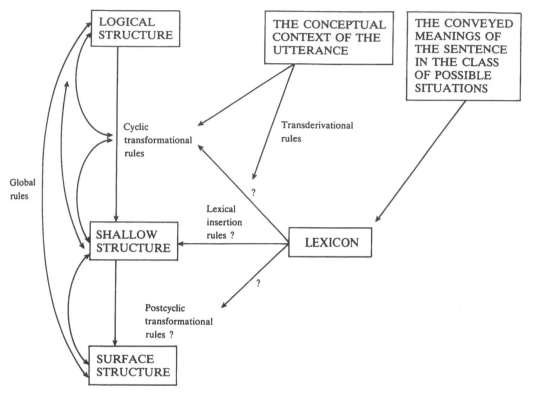

Figure 2

And those remaining categories bore a close correspondence to the categories of symbolic logic (see FORMAL LOGIC AND MODAL LOGIC). The three categories whose existence generative semanticists were certain of in this period – sentence, noun phrase and verb – seemed to correspond directly to the proposition, argument and predicate of logic. Logical connectives were incorporated into the class of predicates, as were quantifiers. This was an exhilarating discovery for generative semanticists and indicated to them more than anything else that they were on the right track. For, now, the deepest level of representation had a 'natural' language-independent basis, rooted in what Boole (1854) had called 'The Laws of Thought'. What is more, syntactic work in languages other than English was leading to the same three basic categories for all languages. The

universal base hypothesis, not surprisingly, was seen as one of the most attractive features of generative semantics.

The development of generative semantics in the early 1970s was marked by a continuous elaboration and enrichment of the theoretical devices that it employed in grammatical description. By 1972, George Lakoff's conception of grammatical organization appeared as in Figure 2 (an oversimplified diagram based on the discussion in Lakoff 1974).

This elaboration was necessitated by the steady expansion of the type of phenomena that generative semanticists felt required a 'grammatical' treatment. As the scope of formal grammar expanded, so did the number of formal devices and their power. Arguments motivating such devices invariably took the following form:

(4) (a) Phenomenon P has in the past been considered to be simply 'pragmatic'; that is, part of performance and hence not requiring treatment within formal grammar.

(b) But P is reflected both in morpheme distribution and in the 'grammaticality' judgements that speakers are able to provide.

(c) If anything is the task of the grammarian, it is the explanation of native-speaker judgements and the distribution of morphemes in a language. Therefore, P must be handled in the grammar.

(d) But the grammatical devices now available are insufficient for this task. Therefore, new devices of greater power must be added.

John R. Ross (1970) and Jerrold Sadock (1974) were the first to argue that what in the past had been considered to be 'pragmatic' phenomena were amenable to grammatical treatment. Both linguists, for example, argued that the type of speech act (see SPEECH-ACT THEORY) a sentence represents should be encoded directly in its semantic representation, i.e. its underlying syntactic structure. Analogously, George Lakoff (1971b) arrived at the conclusion that a speaker's beliefs about the world needed to be encoded into syntactic structure, on the basis of the attempt to account syntactically for judgements such as the following, which he explicitly regarded as 'grammaticality' judgements:

(5) (a)   John told Mary that she was ugly and then she insulted him.

(b) *John told Mary that she was beautiful and then she insulted him.

He also argued that, in order to provide a full account of the possible antecedents of anaphoric expressions, even deductive reasoning had to enter into grammatical description (1971c). As Lakoff pointed out, the antecedent of *too* in (6), 'the mayor is honest', is not present in the logical structure of the sentence, but must be deduced from it and its associated presupposition, 'Republicans are honest':

(6) The mayor is a Republican and the used-car dealer is honest too.

The deduction, then, was to be performed in the grammar itself.

Finally, Lakoff (1973) concluded that the graded nature of speaker judgements falsifies the notion that sentences should be either generated, i.e. be considered 'grammatical', or not generated, i.e. be treated as 'ungrammatical'. Lakoff suggested instead that a mechanism be devised to assign grammaticality *to a certain degree*. The particulars of **fuzzy grammar**, as it was called, were explored primarily in a series of papers by John R. Ross (see especially Ross 1973).

Not surprisingly, as the class of 'grammatical' phenomena increased, the competence–performance dichotomy became correspondingly cloudy. George Lakoff made it explicit that the domain of grammatical theory was no less than the domain of linguistics itself. Grammar, for Lakoff, was to

specify the *conditions* under which sentences can be *appropriately* used . . . One thing that one might ask is whether there is anything that does *not* enter into rules of grammar. For example, there are certain concepts from the study of social interaction that are part of grammar, e.g. relative social status, politeness, formality, etc. Even such an abstract notion as *free goods* enters into rules of grammar. Free goods are things (including information) that everyone in a group has a right to.

(Lakoff 1974: 159–61; italics in original)

Since it is hard to imagine what might not affect the appropriateness of an utterance in actual discourse, the generative-semantic programme with great rapidity moved from the task of grammar construction to that of observing language in its external setting. By the mid-1970s, most generative semanticists had ceased proposing explicit grammatical rules altogether. The idea that any conceivable phenomenon might influence such rules made doing so a thorough impracticality.

As noted above, generative semantics had collapsed well before the end of the 1970s. To a great extent, this was because its opponents were able to show that its assumptions led to a too complicated account of the phenomenon under analysis. For example, interpretivists showed that the purported reduction by generative semantics of the inventory of syntactic categories to three was illusory. As they pointed out, there is a difference between nouns, verbs, adjectives, adverbs, quantifiers, prepositions and so on in surface structure, regardless of what is needed at the most underlying level. Hence, generative semantics would need to posit special transformations to create derived categories, i.e. categories other than verb, sentence and noun phrase. Along the same lines, generative semantics never really succeeded in accounting for the primary function of the renounced level of deep structure – the specification of morpheme order. As most syntacticians soon realized, the order of articles, adjectives, negatives, numerals, nouns and noun complements within a noun phrase is not predictable, or even statable, on semantic grounds. How, then, *could* generative semantics state morpheme order? Only, it seemed, by supplementing the transformational rules with a close-to-the-surface filter that functioned to mimic the phrase-structure rules of a theory with the level of deep structure. Thus, despite its rhetorical abandonment of deep structure, generative semantics would end up slipping that level in through the back door.

The interpretive account of 'global' phenomena, as well, came to be preferred over the generative-semantic treatment. In general, the former involved co-indexing mechanisms, such as traces, that codified one stage of a derivation for reference by a later stage. In one sense, such mechanisms were simply formalizations of the global rules they were intended to replace. Nevertheless, since they involved the most minimal extensions of already existing theoretical devices, solutions involving them, it seemed, could be achieved without increasing the power of the theory. Co-indexing approaches came to be more and more favoured over global approaches since they enabled the phenomenon under investigation to be concretized and, in many cases, pointed the way to a principled solution.

Finally, by the end of the decade, virtually nobody accepted the generative-semantic attempt to handle all pragmatic phenomena grammatically. The mid- and late 1970s saw an accelerating number of papers and books which cast into doubt the possibility of one homogeneous syntax–semantics–pragmatics and its consequent abandonment of the competence–performance distinction.

While the weight of the interpretivist counterattack was a major component of the demise of generative semantics, it was not the deciding factor. In fact, it is not unfair to say that generative semantics destroyed itself. Its internal dynamic led it irrevocably to content itself with mere descriptions of grammatical phenomena, instead of attempting explanations of them.

The dynamic that led generative semantics to abandon explanation flowed from its practice of regarding any speaker judgement and any fact about morpheme distribution as a *de facto* matter for grammatical analysis. Attributing the same theoretical weight to each and every fact about language had disastrous consequences. Since the number of facts is, of course, absolutely overwhelming, simply *describing* the incredible complexities of language became the all-consuming task, with formal explanation postponed to some future date. To students entering theoretical linguistics in the mid-1970s, who were increasingly trained in the sciences, mathematics and philosophy, the generative-semantic position on theory construction and formalization was anathema. It is hardly surprising that they found little of interest in this model.

At the same time that interpretivists were pointing out the syntactic limitations of generative semantics, that framework was co-opted from the opposite direction by sociolinguistics. Sociolinguists looked with amazement at the generative-semantic programme of attempting to treat societal phenomena in a framework originally designed to handle such sentence-level properties as morpheme order and vowel alternations. They found no difficulty in convincing those generative semanticists most committed to studying language in its social context to drop whatever lingering pretence they still might have of doing a grammatical analysis, and to approach the subject matter instead from the traditional perspective of the social sciences.

While generative semantics is now no longer regarded as a viable model of grammar, there are innumerable ways in which it has left its mark on its successors. Most importantly, its view that sentences must at one level have a representation in a formalism isomorphic to that of symbolic logic is now widely accepted by interpretivists, and in particular by Chomsky. It was generative semanticists who first undertook an intensive investigation of syntactic phenomena which defied formalization by means

of transformational rules as they were then understood, and led to the plethora of mechanisms such as **indexing devices**, **traces** and **filters**, which are now part of the interpretivists' theoretical store. Even the idea of lexical decomposition, for which generative semanticists were much scorned, has turned up in the semantic theories of several interpretivists. Furthermore, many proposals originally mooted by generative semanticists, such as the non-existence of extrinsic rule ordering, post-cyclic lexical insertion, and treating anaphoric pronouns as bound variables, have since appeared in the interpretivist literature.

Finally, the important initial studies that generative semantics inspired on the logical and sub-logical properties of lexical items, on speech acts, both direct and indirect, and on the more general pragmatic aspects of language, are becoming more and more appreciated as linguistic theory is finally developing the means to incorporate them. The wealth of information and interesting generalizations they contain have barely begun to be tapped by current researchers.

F.J.N.

Suggestions for further reading

McCawley, J. (1976) *Grammar and Meaning*, New York: Academic Press.
Newmeyer, F. (1980/1986) *Linguistic Theory in America: The First Quarter Century of Transformational Generative Grammar*, New York and London: Academic Press; 2nd edition 1986; especially chapters 4 and 5.

Genre analysis

Genre analysis is an important area within English for Specific Purposes (ESP)-orientated studies (but see also STYLISTICS).

The first use of the term in relation to ESP is Swales (1981), who refers to it as 'a system of analysis that is able to reveal something of the patterns of organisation of a "genre" and the language used to express those patterns'.

A general definition of genre might explain that a **genre** is a text or discourse type which is recognized as such by its users by its characteristic features of style or form, which will be specifiable through stylistic and text-linguistic/discourse analysis, and/or by the particular function of texts belonging to the genre (see RHETORIC, STYLISTICS, TEXT LINGUISTICS and DISCOURSE ANALYSIS AND CONVERSATION ANALYSIS; see Miller 1984 for a thorough discussion of the notion and definition of genre). Swales provides a more specific definition of genre:

> A genre comprises a class of communicative events, the members of which serve some set of communicative purposes. These purposes are recognized by the expert members of the parent discourse community, and thereby constitute the rationale for the genre. This rationale shapes the schematic structure of the discourse and influences and constrains choice of content and style.
>
> (Swales 1990: 58)

This definition seems to create a more 'technical' sense of genre, limiting its field of reference to those communicative events for which it is possible to perceive a fairly specific function for the event. This would be difficult to do with communicative events such as a lyric poem or a casual conversation. Swales (1981) lists as 'classic attempts at genre analysis in Applied Linguistics literature' studies of doctor–patient interactions in casualty wards (Candlin *et al.* 1978), of technical displays (Hutchinson 1978), of dictated post-operative surgical reports (Pettinari 1981) and of the investigation of qualifying statements in legal documents (Bhatia 1981). Swales (1990) argues that genre analysis should be concerned with the differences between, for example, medical journal editorials and medical journal articles, which are part of the same register, but constitute different genres, and he also mentions in this context the

differences between legislative prose, legal textbooks and legal case reports.

Genre analysis is not, however, principally concerned with the classification of genres, but with the investigation of regularities of communicative purpose and language form in genres that can inform ESP materials for writing and teaching. Swales' own work has focused on the academic article, and in particular on the article introduction. In Swales (1990), he sets out his **Creating a Research Space (CARS) model** for the pattern of organization of the article introduction. This consists of three main moves each of which has a number of steps. The full CARS model is:

Move 1	*Establishing a Territory*
Step 1	Claiming centrality and/or
Step 2	Making topic generalizations and/or
Step 3	Reviewing items of previous research
Move 2	*Establishing a Niche*
Step 1A	Counterclaiming or
Step 1B	Indicating a gap or
Step 1C	Question raising or
Step 1D	Continuing a tradition
Move 3	*Occupying a Niche*
Step 1A	Outlining purposes or
Step 1B	Announcing present research
Step 2	Announcing principal findings
Step 3	Indicating research article (RA) structure

This model (originally presented by Swales 1981 in a rather different form, with four moves) has had considerable influence on the development of genre analysis and on the teaching of academic writing within English for Academic Purposes (EAP). It is the first detailed example of move analysis, an approach to text analysis which Skelton (1994) defines in the following way:

> Move structure analysis tentatively assigns a function to a stretch of written or spoken text, identifies that function with one, or a set of exponents which signal its presence, and seeks to establish whether or not the pattern identified is a general pattern, by reference to similar texts.

Following the initial work on the Introduction, work in the area of move analysis has concentrated on other sections of the article and on related sections in the Masters or Ph.D. thesis or dissertation. A move analysis approach has also been used for the analysis of other sections of the research article, such as the abstract (Salager-Meyer 1990), the Methods section (Wood 1982), the Results section (Brett 1994; Williams 1999), the Discussion section (Belanger 1982; Dudley-Evans 1994), and also for the analysis of dissertations (Hopkins and Dudley-Evans 1988).

The model for the Discussion section proposed by Dudley-Evans (1994) has nine moves:

Move 1   Information move
Move 2   Statement of result
Move 3   Finding
Move 4   (Un)expected outcome
Move 5   Reference to previous research
Move 6   Explanation
Move 7   Claim
Move 8   Limitation
Move 9   Recommendation

Writers will not necessarily use all these moves in a Discussion section, but will make their points or build their argument through the appropriate selection of the moves and ordering them into **cycles**.

Genre analysis has mostly been concerned with written academic texts, but its methods are equally relevant to the analysis of texts in business, professional and occupational contexts (English for Occupational Purposes or EOP). Bhatia (1993: 45–75) looked at two types of business letter which he calls **promotional genres** – the **sales promotion** letter and the **job application** letter. His conclusion is that the two types of letter follow a very similar pattern of moves and therefore constitute one genre:

	Sales promotion letter	*Job application letter*
Move 1	Establishing credentials	Establishing credentials
Move 2	Introducing the offer	Introducing the candidature
Move 3	Offering incentives	Offering incentives
Move 4	Enclosing documents	Enclosing documents
Move 5	Soliciting response	Soliciting response
Move 6	Using pressure tactics	Using pressure tactics
Move 7	Ending politely	Ending politely

Bhatia (1993: 118) also suggests a four-move pattern for the structure of legal cases:

Move 1   Identifying the case
Move 2   Establishing the facts of the case
Move 3   Arguing the case
　　　　　3.1 stating the history of the case
　　　　　3.2 presenting arguments
　　　　　3.3 deriving *ratio decidendi* (the principle of law that the judge wishes to set down for application to future cases of a similar description)
Move 4   Pronouncing judgement

Genre analysis is also applicable to spoken text, though the difficulty of obtaining data has meant that much less analysis has been done into oral genres. Charles' analysis of business sales negotiations is an excellent example of what is possible when spoken data has been collected (Charles 1996).

All the research findings reported above have been concerned with texts and moves. The early research under the heading of genre analysis was of this kind, but in recent years (particularly in the USA) genre studies have focused rather more on the discourse communities that use and create genres. Swales' most recent book (Swales 1998) does not include detailed move analysis, but rather describes in detail three discourse communities located in one building at the University of Michigan, and uses what he names **textography** (ethnography with a linguistic focus) to show the role that particular texts play in the activities of those discourse communities. Berkenkotter and Huckin (1995: 2–3) argue that early genre analysis tended to reify genres and see them as linguistic abstractions. They suggest 'case research with insiders' to analyse the ways in which writers or speakers use their knowledge of genre and of the expectations of the discourse community they belong to in a strategic manner to participate successfully in the activities of a discipline or a profession.

This consideration of the context in which genres are created and used by the discourse community has added an extra, very useful, dimension to genre studies and their value in ESP work. Studies that draw on the work of sociologists of science and studies of the workplace (e.g. Myers 1989; Bazerman and Paradis 1991) have shown how 'local' discourse communities may adapt the genres they use to meet their specific communicative needs. Many genres are dynamic in that they develop or die in response to changes in society and in particular workplace or academic situations. Smart (1993) argues that the ESP teacher working within a particular situation can play an important role in helping professionals understand the tension between the convenience of following a formula or model in writing and the need to adapt the model to suit their particular rhetorical purposes. The study of change in genres has led to the growth of a specific research area investigating the ways in which key genres such as the research article have reflected change in particular disciplines over a specified period of time. Atkinson (1992), for example, showed how articles published in the *Edinburgh Medical Journal* between 1735 and 1985 have adjusted to developments in the nature of the medical profession.

More text-based research has, none the less, continued to be reported. The development of computer-based corpora has enabled researchers to look more closely and in greater detail at lexical features of genres and provided the possibility to make more detailed analyses of moves.

T.D.-E.

Suggestions for further reading

Berkenkotter, C. and Huckin, T. (1995) *Genre Knowledge in Disciplinary Communication: Cognition/Culture/Power*, Hillsdale, NJ: Lawrence Erlbaum Associates.

Bhatia, V.K. (1993) *Analysing Genre*, London: Longman.

Swales, J.M. (1990) *Genre Analysis: English in Academic and Research Settings*, Cambridge: Cambridge University Press.

Glossematics

Introduction

Glossematics is a structural linguistic theory developed in the 1930s by the two Danish linguists, Louis Hjelmslev (1899–1965) and Hans Jørgen Uldall (1907–57).

Hjelmslev had a broad background in comparative and general linguistics. He had studied under Holger Pedersen, whom he succeeded to the Chair of Comparative Philology at the University of Copenhagen in 1937. In 1928 he published *Principes de grammaire générale*, which contains many of the ideas which were later developed further in his glossematic theory, above all the attempt to establish a general grammar in which the categories were defined formally on the basis of their syntagmatic relations. In 1935 he published *La Catégorie des cas I*, presenting a semantic analysis of the category of case.

Uldall had studied phonetics under Daniel Jones and anthropology under Franz Boas, and had felt a strong need for a new linguistic approach when trying to describe American-Indian languages. He spent the years 1933–9 in Denmark, during which period he and Hjelmslev, in very close co-operation, developed the glossematic theory. In 1939 they were approaching a final version, but during the years of the war, which Uldall spent abroad working for the British Council, their co-operation was interrupted, and it was not until 1951–2 that they had an opportunity to work together again.

In the meantime, Hjelmslev had published an introduction to the theory, *Omkring sprogteoriens grundlæggelse* (1943a), which was published in English in 1953 under the title *Prolegomena to a Theory of Language*. In 1951–2, Uldall wrote the first part (*General Theory*) of what was planned to be their common work, *Outline of Glossematics*, but this first part was not published until 1957. It contains a general introduction, largely in agreement with the *Prolegomena*, but more comprehensible, and a description of a glossematic algebra, meant to be applicable not only to linguistics, but to the humanities in general. The plan had been that Hjelmslev should write the second part, containing the glossematic procedures with all rules and definitions.

However, during the long years of separation, Uldall had come to new conclusions on various points, whereas Hjelmslev on the whole had stuck to the old version of their theory. Some of the differences were due to the fact that Uldall was concerned with fieldwork (see FIELD METHODS), whereas Hjelmslev was more interested in the

description of well-known languages. Moreover, he found the algebra constructed by Uldall unnecessarily complicated for the purposes of linguistics. Hjelmslev therefore found it difficult to proceed from Uldall's algebraic system and hesitated to write the second part (see Fischer-Jørgensen 1967b). After a while, he decided to return to a simpler algebra used in earlier versions of the theory and to base the second part on the summary he had written in 1941 and revised in 1943. However, illness prevented him from fulfilling this plan. The summary was translated and edited by Francis Whitfield in 1975 under the title *Résumé of a Theory of Language*. This book consists of several hundred definitions and rules with no supporting examples.

An easier access to glossematics are Hjelmslev's many papers on various aspects of the theory, most of which are published in the two volumes of collected articles, *Essais linguistiques* (1959a) and *Essais linguistiques II* (1973a). The papers, 'Structural analysis of language' (1947) and 'A causerie on linguistic theory' (written in 1941, in Hjelmslev 1973b), may be recommended as relatively easy introductions to the theory. But the most essential papers are 'Essai d'une théorie des morphèmes' (1938), describing the grammatical inflectional categories on the basis of glossematic functions, and 'La stratification du langage' (1954 and 1959), which contains some revisions of the theory. However, the most important and widely read and commentated glossematic publication is *Omkring sprogteoriens grundlæggelse* (*OSG*) (1943a). (Page numbers refer to *OSG*, because the two editions (1953 and 1961) of the English translation have different page numbers, while both indicating the page numbers of *OSG*.) The shorter book, *Sproget* (1963), translated as *Language* (1970), is not a description of glossematic theory, but a general introduction to linguistics. Several of the chapters, however, show strong traces of glossematics. As short and easy introductions written by other linguists, one may mention Martinet (1946), Malmberg (1964: 140–57) and Whitfield (1954).

General character of glossematic theory

The goal of glossematics is to establish linguistics as an exact science on an **immanent** basis. In *OSG*, Hjelmslev states that it is in the nature of language to be a means to an end, and therefore to be overlooked. It is this peculiarity of language which has led scholars to describe it as 'a conglomerate of non-linguistic (e.g. physical, physiological, psychological, logical, sociological) phenomena', rather than as 'a self-sufficient totality, a structure *sui generis*'. This, however, is what the linguist should attempt to do (*OSG*: 7). Glossematics is 'a linguistic theory that will discover and formulate premises of such a linguistics, establish its methods, and indicate its paths' (*OSG*: 8). 'Theory' in this connection does not mean a system of hypotheses, but 'an arbitrary and at the same time appropriate system of premises and definitions' (*OSG*: 14).

Behind the linguistic **process** (text), the linguist should seek a **system**, through which the process can be analysed as composed of a limited number of elements that constantly recur in various combinations (*OSG*: 10). For this purpose, it is necessary to establish a procedural method where each operation depends on those preceding it, and where everything is defined. The only concepts necessary to, but not defined within, the theory are a few, such as 'description', 'dependence' and 'presence', which are defined in epistemology. But before setting up the procedure, the linguistic theoretician must undertake a preliminary investigation of those objects which people agree to call languages, and attempt to find out which properties are common to such objects. These properties are then generalized as defining the objects to which the theory shall be applicable. For all objects

of the nature premised in the definition, a general calculus is set up, in which all conceivable cases are foreseen, and which may therefore form the basis of language typology. The calculus itself is a purely deductive system independent of any experience. By virtue of this independence, the theory can be characterized as **arbitrary**, but by virtue of the premises introduced on the basis of the preliminary experience it can be characterized as **appropriate** (*OSG*: 14). In his endeavour to establish linguistics as an exact science, Hjelmslev is inspired by formal logic, but his theory is not fully formalized, and he does not stick to logical functions, but has chosen those functions which he found adequate for the description of language.

The glossematic concept of language

OSG is mainly concerned with the preconditions of the theory; that is, with the features which, according to the preliminary investigations, characterize a **language**.

In his view of the nature of language, Hjelmslev is strongly influenced by Saussure (1916/1974/1983). Like Saussure, Hjelmslev considers language to be a sign structure, a **semiotic system**. Corresponding to Saussure's signifier and signified, Hjelmslev speaks of **sign expression** and **sign content**; and **expression** and **content** are described as the two planes of language (*OSG*: 44ff.). It is a characteristic feature of glossematics that content and expression are regarded as completely parallel entities to be analysed by means of the same procedures, leading to analogous categories. At the same time, however, it is emphasized that the two planes are not conformal. A given sign content is not structured in the same way as the corresponding sign expression, and they cannot be divided into corresponding constituents or **figurae**, as Hjelmslev calls them. Whereas, for example, the Latin sign expression *-us* in *dominus* can be analysed into the expression figurae *u* and *s*, the corresponding sign content is analysed into 'nominative', 'masculine' and 'singular', of which none corresponds specifically to *u* or *s*. In the same way the expression *ram* can be analysed into *r*, *a* and *m*, and the corresponding content into 'he' and 'sheep', but *r*, *a* and *m* do not correspond to any of these content elements.

From the point of view of its purpose, then, language is first and foremost a sign system; but from the point of view of its internal structure, it is a system of figurae that can be used to construct signs. If there is conformity between content and expression, i.e. structural identity, there is no need to distinguish between the two planes. Hjelmslev calls such one-plane systems **symbolic systems** (for example, the game of chess); two-plane structures are called **semiotics**. A natural language is a semiotic into which all other semiotics can be translated, but the glossematic theory is meant to be applicable not only to (natural) languages but to all semiotic systems (*OSG*: 90–7). It is worth pointing out that the terminology I have used above is that used in the English, Italian and Spanish translations of *OSG*, and in the *Résumé*. In the Danish original, the terminology is different, and this terminology has been retained in the French and German translations, although the German gives references to the English terminology. Since this has caused a certain amount of confusion, the correspondences are presented here:

Version of OSG	Terminology	
Original Danish	*sprog*	*dagligsprog*
French	*langue*	*langue naturelle*
German	*Sprache*	*Alltagssprache*
English and Résumé	*semiotic*	*language*
Italian	*semiotica*	*lingua*
Spanish	*semiotica*	*lengua*

Content and expression must be analysed separately, but with constant regard to the interplay between them; namely, the function between sign expression and sign content. Replacement of one sign expression, e.g. *ram*, by another, e.g. *ewe*, normally results in another sign content; conversely, the replacement of one sign content, e.g. 'male sheep', by another, e.g. 'female sheep', brings about another sign expression. Parts of signs (figurae) may be replaced in the same way, e.g. /a/ by /ɪ/ in the frame /r–m/, leading to the new sign content 'edge', or 'male' by 'female' in the sign content 'male sheep', resulting in the new sign expression *ewe*. The smallest parts reached by the given procedure and whose replacement may bring about a change in the opposite plane are called **taxemes**. (In the expression plane, the level of taxemes corresponds roughly to that of phonemes.) For this replacement test, glossematics coined the term **commutation test**, which is now widely used. This test has, of course, also been applied by other linguists, e.g. the Prague School linguists, but it is characteristic of glossematics that it stresses the fact that the test may take its point of departure in any of the two planes, as illustrated in the examples above. By means of the commutation test, a limited number of commutable elements, **invariants**, is reached in both planes (*OSG*: 66–7).

It happens that the commutation test gives a negative result in some well-defined positions for elements which have been found to be invariant in other positions. In this case, glossematics uses the traditional term **syncretism**. In Latin, for instance, there is syncretism between the content elements 'dative' and 'ablative' in masculine and neuter singular of the first declension, e.g. *domino*; and in German, there is syncretism between the expression taxemes /p t k/ and /b d g/ in final position – *Rad* and *Rat* are both pronounced [raːt] – whereas medially there is commutation – [raːdə], [raːtə] (in the Prague School, syncretism in the expression is called **neutralization**).

Syncretisms may be manifested in two ways: as **implications** or as **fusions**. When the manifestation is identical with one or more members entering into the syncretism, but not with all, it is called an **implication** – in German, for instance, the syncretism /t/d/ is manifested by [t]. Otherwise, it is called a **fusion** – in Danish there is syncretism between /p/ and /b/ in final position, manifested optionally by [p] or [b], or by something in between. **Latency** is seen as syncretism with zero – in French *petit* [pti], there is syncretism between /t/ and zero. When a syncretism is manifested by an implication – that is, by one of its members – this member is called the **extensive** member of the opposition and the other is called the **intensive** member – thus in German /t/ is extensive and /d/ is intensive. This distinction is related to, but not identical with, the Prague distinction between **unmarked** and **marked** members (see FUNCTIONAL PHONOLOGY).

Like Saussure, Hjelmslev also distinguishes between **form** and **substance**, and this distinction is basic in glossematics. But, in contradistinction to Saussure, who sets up one form between two substances, sound and meaning, Hjelmslev operates with two forms, an expression form and a content form. Since the two planes are not conformal, each must be described on the basis of its own form. Form comprises all paradigmatic and syntagmatic functions and the terminal points of these functions, i.e. **elements** and **categories**.

In addition to form and substance, Hjelmslev introduces a third concept, **purport** (French *matière* – the Danish term, rather misleadingly, is *mening*, 'meaning'), which refers to sounds and meanings apart from the way in which they are formed linguistically, whereas substance designates linguistically formed purport. It may be formed differently by various sciences like physics or psychology. An example of purport in the content is the colour spectrum. It may be formed differently as content substance of the signs designating colours in different languages – that is, the numbers of colours distinguished and the delimitations between them may be different. As an example of expression purport, one may mention glottal closure or stricture, which may be substance for a consonant in one language and for a prosody or a boundary signal in other languages. (In *OSG*, *substans* is sometimes used for *mening* – e.g. *OSG*: 69–70 – this is corrected in the second edition of the English translation.)

The function between form and substance is called **manifestation**. A given form is said to be manifested by a given substance. Form is the primary object of the linguistic description, and differences between languages are mainly differences of form.

Form is also called **schema**, and in *OSG* usage is almost synonymous with substance. But sometimes, such as in the paper 'Langue et parole' (1943b), Hjelmslev draws a distinction between schema, norm and usage. In this case 'norm' refers to the admissible manifestations, based on the mutual delimitation between the units, e.g. *r* as a vibrant distinguished from *l*, whereas usage refers to the manifestations actually used in the language, e.g. [r] as a tongue-tip vibrant. 'Norm' and 'usage' correspond to Coseriu's (1952) 'system' and 'norm' respectively; the phonemes of the Prague School, which are defined by distinctive features (see DISTINCTIVE FEATURES), belong to Hjelmslev's norm.

According to *OSG*, the **relation between form and substance** is a unilateral dependence, since substance presupposes form, but not vice versa. That substance presupposes form simply follows from the definition of substance as formed purport, but the claim that form does not presuppose substance is more problematic. It is evident that the calculus of possible languages can be a purely formal calculus and that it is possible to reconstruct a language, e.g. Proto-Indo-

European, without attaching any substance to it (see HISTORICAL LINGUISTICS). But when concrete living languages are involved, it seems fairly obvious that both form and substance must be there. However, Hjelmslev argues that there may be several substances (e.g. speech and writing) attached to the same form, so that the form is independent of any specific substance. It is also said (e.g. in *OSG*: 71) that the description of substance presupposes the description of form, but not vice versa. This is, however, not possible in the preliminary descriptions, but only in the glossematic procedure seen as a final control. In the paper 'La Stratification du langage' (1954), it is stated explicitly that substance has to be taken into account in the operations of communication and identification (see also Fischer-Jørgensen 1967a).

'La Stratification du langage', which resulted from the discussions between Hjelmslev and Uldall in 1951–2, brings in certain revisions. First, content substance, content form, expression form and expression substance are called the four **strata of language**, and a distinction is made between **intrastratal** (**intrinsic**) and **interstratal** (**extrinsic**) functions. **Schema** covers the intrinsic functions in the two form strata, whereas **norm**, **usage** and **speech act** cover interstratal (extrinsic) functions. Usage is no longer used synonymously with substance; the sign function is said to belong to usage – new signs may be formed at any moment – and figurae result from an intrastratal (intrinsic) analysis of each stratum. The sign function is, however, still considered to be a basic linguistic function. It is not quite clear what is meant by an intrinsic analysis of the substance strata. The paper seems to contain some concessions to Uldall's points of view in *Outline*, volume 1, written in 1951–2, views which have not been fully incorporated into Hjelmslev's own theory.

Second, a distinction is made between three **levels of substance** – the **apperceptive** level (Uldall's 'body of opinion'), the **sociobiological** level; and the **physical** level – and these three levels are ranked with the apperceptive level as primary. This represents progress compared to Hjelmslev's rather more physicalistic description of substance in *OSG*.

Substance plays a greater role in *La Stratification* (1954) than in *OSG*, although it appears clearly from *OSG* that Hjelmslev never meant to exclude substance from linguistics; he merely considers form to be its primary object. According to *OSG*, a detailed description of substance is undertaken in **metasemiology**; that is, a metasemiotic which has the linguist's descriptive language (also called a **semiology**) as its object language. In semiology, the ultimate irreducible variants of language – sounds, for instance – are minimal signs, and in metasemiology these units must be further analysed (see *OSG*: 108).

The description of style belongs to the so-called **connotative semiotics**.

On the whole, Hjelmslev sets up a comprehensive system of semiotics and metasemiotics (see *OSG*: 101ff.; Hjelmslev 1975: xviii; Rastier 1985).

The glossematic procedure

An important feature of glossematics is the claim that a formal description of a language must begin with an explicit analysis of texts by means of a constantly continued partition according to strict procedural rules. Such a continued partition is called a **deduction** (a somewhat uncommon use of this term). The functions registered in the analysis are of three types: **determination**, or unilateral presupposition; **interdependence**, or mutual presupposition; and **constellation**, or compatibility without any presupposition. These three functions have special names according to their occurrence in syntagmatics or paradigmatics (sequence or system). In syntagmatics, they are called **selection**, **solidarity** and **combination**; in paradigmatics, **specification**, **complement-arity** and **autonomy**, respectively. This very simple and general system of functions requires the different stages of the analysis to be kept apart, so that a particular function may be specified both by its type and by the stage to which it belongs. This procedure thus involves a hierarchical structure.

The analysis is guided by some general principles, of which the most important is the so-called **empirical principle** ('empirical' is used here in an unusual sense). This principle says that the description shall be free of contradiction (self-consistent), exhaustive and as simple as possible, the first requirement taking precedence over the second, and the second over the third (*OSG*: 12). It is not quite clear whether Hjelmslev wants to apply the empirical principle both to the general calculus and to the description of actual languages. It is particularly in the interpretation of simplicity that glossematics differs from other forms of structural linguistics. According to glossematics, the simplest possible description is the one that leads to the smallest number of minimal elements, while the demand for exhaustiveness implies that as many categories and functions as possible must be registered. A principle of generalization (*OSG*: 63) prevents arbitrary reduction of the number of elements.

Before stating the functions in an actual case, it is necessary to undertake **catalysis**; that is, to interpolate an entity which is implied in the context. In German *guten Morgen!*, for example, a verb (i.e. a syncretism of all possible verbs) is catalysed as a necessary prerequisite for the accusative (*OSG*: 84).

After the syntagmatic deduction is completed, a paradigmatic deduction is undertaken in which the language is articulated into categories. The paradigmatic deduction is followed by a synthesis. It is a characteristic feature of glossematics that analogous categories are set up for content and ex-pression; Figure 1 gives an example of the parallelism.

It should be kept in mind that in glossematic terminology, **morphemes** are inflectional categories, like case, person, etc., seen as content elements. **Verbal morphemes**, like tense, are considered to characterize the whole utterance, not just the verbal theme.

The definitions of the categories are based on syntagmatic relations, the same definitions applying to content and expression. But, for the categories exemplified in Figure 1, the definitions differ between earlier and more recent glossematic papers. In the recent version, **exponents** are defined as entering into a particular type of **government**, which establishes an utterance and is called **direction**, and **intense** and **extense** exponents are distinguished on the basis of their mutual relations (see Hjelmslev 1951). A unit comprising both constituents and exponents is called a **syntagm**. The minimal syntagm within expression is the syllable; within content, the **noun**.

The requirement that all categories should be defined by syntagmatic functions means that in the content analysis no separation is made between morphology and syntax. Both word classes, which (according to glossematics) are classes of content constituents or **pleremes**, and grammatical classes, classes of **morphemes**, are defined by their syntagmatic functions. The nominal and verbal morphemes are further divided into **homonexual** and **heteronexual** morphemes, according to relations within and across the boundaries of a **nexus** (which roughly equals a clause). Case, for instance, is a homonexual intense morpheme category, whereas mood is an extense morpheme category which can be either homonexual or heteronexual (Hjelmslev 1938).

Vowels and consonants are arranged in categories according to the possibilities for their combination within the central and marginal parts of the syllable, respectively.

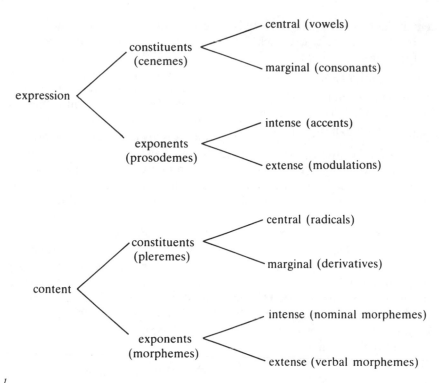

Figure 1

Since the principle of simplicity requires a minimal inventory of taxemes, a glossematic analysis often goes further in reduction of the inventory than other forms of analysis. Single sounds may be interpreted as clusters – e.g. long vowels as clusters of identical short vowels, Danish [p] as /b + h/, etc.; and formal syllable boundaries may be used to reduce the inventory, e.g. German [s] and [z] may be reduced to one taxeme by positing a syllable boundary after [s] in *reissen* [raisən] /rais-ən/ and before [z] in *reisen* [raizən] /rais-ən/ – by generalization from initial [z-] and final [-s] (e.g. *so* and *das*).

The inventory of sign expressions is also reduced as much as possible. This is accomplished by means of an **ideal notation**, in which syncretisms (including latencies) are resolved. Thus German *lieb–liebe* [liːp–liːbə] is in **actualized notation** /liːp/b–liːbə/, but in ideal notation /liːp–liːbə/, and French *petit–petite* [pti–ptit] is in ideal notation /pətit–pətitə/, where the stem is the same in masculine and feminine and the feminine ending is /ə/. The glossematic ideal notation is closely related to underlying forms in generative phonology (see GENERATIVE PHONOLOGY), but ordered rules are not used in glossematics.

Expression taxemes (vowels and consonants) are not analysed further into distinctive features, an analysis which is considered to belong to pure substance, but – both in content and in expression – taxemes within each category are arranged into dimensions in such a way that there is a minimal number of dimensional elements. These dimensional elements are called **glossemes**. The demand for a minimal number of glossemes being absolute, 6 taxemes are always arranged as 2 × 3, and 10 as 2 × 5, etc. Since the number of dimensions is thus fixed irrespective of the language involved, this is called a universal **analysis**. But the placement of the taxemes within the system is language-specific since it is governed by syncretisms, where such are found. If, for instance, a language has syncretism between *p/b*, *t/d* and *k/g*, with $\begin{smallmatrix} p\,t\,k \\ b\,d\,g \end{smallmatrix}$ appearing in the position where the commutation is suspended (i.e. it is an implication), then $\begin{smallmatrix} p\,t\,k \\ b\,d\,g \end{smallmatrix}$ will be placed in a two-dimensional array, /p t k/ as the extensive members, and /b d g/ as the corresponding intensive members. In cases where formal criteria are lacking, affinity to substance may be taken into account.

Members of grammatical categories like case (i.e. nominative, accusative, etc.) are subjected to a similar analysis. Hjelmslev's system of participative oppositions is described in his book on case (1935: 111–26; but note that in this pre-glossematic work he starts from semantics, not from formal facts like syncretisms). Each dimension may contain from two to seven members, so the oppositions need not be binary.

A characteristic feature of glossematics is the claim that the analysis of content should be continued below the Sign level, not only in the case of grammatical endings like Latin *-us*, but also in the case of themes. Hjelmslev draws a parallel between the analysis of expression units like *sl-* and *fl-*, and content units like 'ram' and 'ewe', which may be analysed into 'he-sheep' and 'she-sheep' (*OSG*: 62–5) by means of commutation. This is evidently feasible for small closed inventories like prepositions, modal verbs, restricted semantic categories of nouns like terms for family relations, etc., but it seems an almost impossible task to reduce the whole inventory of nouns to a restricted number of content figurae, and Hjelmslev gives no further indications concerning the method of analysis. All his examples are analyses of signs (e.g. *ram–ewe–bull–cow*, or *father–mother–brother–sister*), but in the paper 'La Stratification du language' (1954), it is said that the analysis in figurae should be undertaken intrinsically in each stratum. This can, how-

ever, only be meant as a final control analysis of what has already been found by means of the commutation test, for commutation is an interstratal function operating with signs and parts of signs. Another problem is the statement in 'Stratification' that the sign function belongs to usage and that it is always possible to form new signs. Thus, if the content form has to be different in different languages, it must be based on different possibilities of combination between the figurae and different types of relation between them within and beyond the sign, and it must be possible to distinguish between accidental gaps and systematic gaps in the sign inventory. There are thus many unsolved problems in this analysis (for discussions, see, for example, Fischer-Jørgensen 1967a; Rischel 1976; Stati 1985).

The influence of glossematics

Applications of glossematics to actual languages are very rare. This is probably due partly to the rather forbidding terminology, which has been exemplified only sporadically above, and partly to the fact that, except for some fragments in scattered papers, the analytical procedure itself and the definitions were not published until 1975, and only in the form of a condensed summary (the *Résumé*) without any examples. A few applications can, however, be mentioned, such as Alarcos Llorach's description of Spanish (1951), Børge Andersen's analysis of a Danish dialect (1959) and Una Canger's (1969) unpublished thesis on Mam. Knud Togeby's analysis of French (1951) is strongly influenced by glossematics, but also by American structuralism.

Glossematics has, however, been eagerly discussed, particularly in the Linguistic Circle of Copenhagen, and although there is no glossematic school as such, a whole generation of Danish linguists has been more or less influenced by Hjelmslev's general ideas about language and by his demand for a stringent method and definitions of the terms employed.

Outside Denmark, glossematics was often discussed in the years following the publication of *OSG*, and particularly after the publication of Whitfield's English translation, by E. Coseriu (1954) and B. Malmberg (1964 and other publications), for example. It has further had a strong influence on the theories of Sidney Lamb (1966) (see STRATIFICATIONAL LINGUISTICS) and S.K. Šaumjan (1962). In the 1960s, the interest in glossematics was overshadowed by the success of transformational grammar, but from the end of the 1960s and, particularly, in the 1980s, there has been a renewed interest in glossematics, not only in the young generation of Danish linguists, but also outside Denmark, particularly in France and in southern Europe, especially Italy and Spain. Special volumes of the periodicals *Langages* (1967) and *Il Protagora* (1985) have been devoted to glossematics, and treatises concerned particularly with glossematics have been published (e.g. Caputo 1986).

This renewed interest is not in the first place concerned with the glossematic procedures or definitions of linguistic categories, which were the main subjects of discussion in the Linguistic Circle in Hjelmslev's lifetime (see, for example, *Recherches structurales 1949* and *Bulletin du Cercle Linguistique de Copenhague 1941–5*), but mainly with Hjelmslev's general ideas on content and expression, form and substance, and his system of semiotics and metasemiotics – that is, with the epistemological implications of the theory. Moreover, Hjelmslev's demand for a structural analysis of the content has inspired the French school of semantics (see, for example, Greimas 1966), and the problem of levels in the substance described in 'La Stratification du langage' (1954) has also been taken up.

In this connection, many translations of glossematic works into various languages have been undertaken. Thus glossematics is still a source of inspiration for linguists, semanticists and philosophers.

E.F.-J.

Suggestions for further reading

Hjelmslev, L. (1948) 'Structural analysis of language', *Studia Linguistica*: 69–78; reprinted in L. Hjelmslev (1959) *Essais linguistiques: Travaux du Cercle Linguistique de Copenhague*, vol. 12, Copenhagen: Nordisk Sprog-og Kulturforlag.
—— (1973b) 'A causerie on linguistic theory', in L. Hjelmslev *Essais linguistiques II: Travaux du Cercle Linguistique de Copenhague*, vol. 14, trans. C. Hendriksen, Copenhagen: Nordisk Sprog-og Kulturforlag.
Malmberg, B. (1964) *New Trends in Linguistics* (Bibliotheca Linguistica, no. 1), Stockholm: Bibliotheca Linguistica.
Whitfield, F.J. (1954) 'Glossematics', in A. Martinet and U. Weinreich (eds) *Linguistics Today: Publication on the Occasion of Columbia University Bicentennial*, New York: Linguistic Circle of New York.

Historical linguistics

Introduction

From a practical point of view, **historical linguists** map the world's languages, determine their relationships, and with the use of written documentation, fit extinct languages of the past into the jigsaw puzzle of the world's complex pattern of linguistic distribution.

From a theoretical perspective, the practitioner may be interested in the nature of linguistic change itself; that is, how and why languages change, and the underlying forces and processes which shape, mould and direct modifications. Of paramount concern is the notion of **language universals**, which shed light on the linguistic behaviour of the species. Such universals may reflect tendencies in language to change towards preferable types of sound patterns, syllabic structures and even syntactic arrangements. Such universals may relate to physiological and cognitive parameters inherent in the organism in a form of marked and unmarked features of language. The historian must also identify the various influences that disrupt these tendencies with varying degrees of intensity related to the degree and nature of external contacts and internal conflicts.

Perhaps the greatest achievement of the forces at work in evolutionary biology has been the development of natural human language, and historical linguistic studies are important for our understanding of this complex behaviour. Only through such studies can we account for many of the social and cultural aspects of language and certain innate linguistic propensities of human kind. In its structural, social and biological complexity, and its relationships to other forms of communication, human language can only be fully understood when we know how it responds to internal and external stimuli.

Historical background

Antiquity and the middle ages

The foundations for historical linguistic studies in the West were laid down by the ancient Greeks, whose philosophical studies incorporated speculation on the nature of their language. The highest degree of sophistication was reached among the scholars of Alexandria during Hellenistic times. In **etymology** – in the ancient Greek sense, 'the true meaning of the word' – they debated whether or not the names of things arose due to the natural attributes of the objects in question or were founded by convention, and a large part of the dialogue of Plato's *Cratylus* is devoted to this subject. The Greeks also discussed the nature of language in terms of a **pattern (analogy)** or its absence (**anomaly**), and formulated statements concerning the various **parts of speech** (see also HISTORY OF GRAMMAR; RHETORIC; STYLISTICS).

The embryonic science of language initiated by the Greeks was passed on to the Romans, whose linguistic studies on Latin were in general the application of Greek thought, controversies and grammatical categories. Like the Greeks, the Romans were aware of word changes in both form and meaning from earlier texts but no significant headway was made in the study of etymology. Latin and Greek grammar were studied throughout the Middle Ages primarily from a pedagogical point of view.

The Renaissance

With the advent of the Renaissance, language studies underwent a change as both local and non-Indo-European languages came under linguistic scrutiny. As trade routes opened up to the East and explorers ranged the lands of the New World, data on exotic languages began to accumulate and stimulate the imagination. Once vernacular languages were deemed worthy of study and the world's diversity in linguistic structures was recognized, language studies turned to universal linguistic concepts and to the idea of **universal grammar** as expressed, for example, in the work of the **Port-Royal** grammarians of the seventeenth century (see PORT-ROYAL GRAMMAR). These concepts of French rationalists were somewhat at odds with the English empiricists, who fostered descriptive phonetics and the grammatical uniqueness of languages.

An important trend in the seventeenth century was the effort to compare and classify languages in accordance with their resemblances. The study of etymology also gained momentum, but words were still derived from other languages haphazardly, by rearranging the letters, especially those of Hebrew (thought by many to have been the original language).

The eighteenth century

Early in the eighteenth century, comparative and historical linguistics gained more consistency. For instance, J. Ludolf in 1702 stated that affinities between languages must be based on grammatical resemblances rather than vocabulary, and among vocabulary correspondences the emphasis should be on simple words such as those which describe parts of the body. In a paper published in 1710, Leibnitz maintained that no known historical language is the source of the world's languages since they must be derived from a **proto-speech**. He also attempted to establish language classifications and toyed with the idea of a universal alphabet for all languages (see Robins 1967).

During the eighteenth century, the gathering of information proceeded as specimens of more and more languages were added to the repertoire. Attention also turned to speculation on the **origin of language**, especially in the works of Hobbes, Rousseau, Burnett (Lord Monboddo), Condillac and Herder. The subject had been treated before as early as the ancient Egyptians, but now it took on more substance in relation to supposed universals of language and its global diversity. The fundamental historical study of language can be said to have begun in earnest at this time through efforts to compare and classify languages in accordance with their origins, hypothetical or otherwise. The crowning achievement in the latter part of the eighteenth century came with the discovery that the Sanskrit language of ancient India was related to the languages of Europe and to Latin and Greek.

Sanskrit

The first known reference in the West to Sanskrit occurred at the end of the sixteenth century when F. Sassetti wrote home to his native Italy about the *lingua Sanscruta* and some of its resemblances to Italian. Others, too, such as B. Schulze and Père Coerdoux made similar observations on the resemblance of Sanskrit to Latin and European languages. The importance of these relationships came to the fore in 1786, however, when Sir William Jones, a judge in the English colonial administration, announced to the Royal Asiatic Society in Calcutta that Sanskrit, Greek, Latin, Gothic and Celtic were seemingly from the same origin, which perhaps no longer existed. In his words (in Lehmann 1967: 15):

> The Sanskrit language, whatever be its antiquity, is of a wonderful structure; more perfect than the Greek, more copious than the Latin, and more exquisitely refined than either, yet bearing to both of them a stronger affinity, both in the roots of verbs and in the forms of grammar, than could possibly have been produced by accident; so strong indeed, that no philologer could examine them all three, without believing them to have sprung from some common source which, perhaps, no longer exists: there is a reason, though not quite so forcible, for supposing that both the Gothic and the Celtic, though blended with a very different idiom, had the same origin with the Sanskrit; and the Old Persian might be added to the same family.

Interest in the discovery mounted and, early in the nineteenth century, Sanskrit was being studied in the West. Sanskrit philological studies were initiated in Germany by W. von Schlegel about the time the first Sanskrit grammar in English was published. The linguistic study of this language set in motion the comparison of Sanskrit with languages of Europe, forming the first period in the growth of historical linguistics and setting **comparative linguistics** on a firm footing. Meanwhile, systematic etymological studies helped clarify and cement the family ties of the Indo-European languages.

Indian linguistic tradition

Ancient Indian grammarians were centuries ahead of their European counterparts in language studies, and from their best-known scholar, Pānini – whose studies (still extant) date back to the second half of the first millennium BC – we see brilliant independent linguistic scholarship in both theory and practice.

As far as is known, the inspiration for Sanskrit studies in India stemmed from the desire to preserve religious ritual and the orally transmitted texts of the earlier **Vedic** period (1200–1000 BC) from phonetic, grammatical and semantic erosion. **Pānini's Sanskrit grammar**, the *Astadhyayi* or 'Eight Books', was a grammarian's grammar and not designed for pedagogical purposes. Phonetic description in this and other, later, Indian works were not matched in the West until at least the seventeenth century. Nor were they equalled in grammatical analysis which involved ordered rules of word formation and extreme economy of statement. For example, a finished product such as *abhavat* 'he, she was', from a root form *bhu* 'to be', may be seen to pass through successive representations in an ordered sequence.

The identification of **roots** and **affixes** in ancient Sanskrit grammar inspired the concept of the morpheme in modern analysis, aided by the studies of Arabic and Hebrew, breaking away from the **Thrax–Priscian word and paradigm pedagogical model** of early Greek and Latin language studies.

The impact of Sanskrit on the West

The introduction of Sanskrit and its subsequent study in Europe was a prime inducement to **comparative-historical linguistics**. It came at an auspicious time: from Dante on, various but sporadic attempts had been made to shed light on relationships between languages and their historical developments and the time was right for more cohesive views of historical studies. It is generally accepted that the nineteenth century is the era *par excellence* of comparative-historical linguistics – a century in which most of the linguistic efforts were devoted to this subject, led (in the main) by German scholarship.

The nineteenth century

A few of the best-known historical linguists of the early nineteenth century are the Dane, Rasmus Rask, and the Germans, Franz Bopp and Jacob Grimm. With these scholars comparative-historical linguistic studies of Indo-European languages had a definite beginning.

In his book *Über die Sprache und Weisheit der Inder*, published in 1808, Friedrich von Schlegel (1772–1829) used the term *vergleichende Grammatik* 'comparative grammar', and in 1816 Bopp published a work comparing the verbal conjugations of Sanskrit, Persian, Latin, Greek and German. After adding Celtic and Albanian, he called these the **Indo-European family of languages**. Bopp has often been considered the father of Indo-European linguistics.

Rask (1787–1832) wrote the first systematic grammars of Old Norse and Old English and, in 1818, he published a comparative grammar outlining the **Scandinavian languages**, noting their relationships to one another. Through comparisons of word forms, he brought order into historical relationships, matching a letter of one language to a letter in another, so that regularity of change could be observed.

Jacob Grimm (1785–1863), a contemporary of Bopp (1791–1867), restricted his studies to the **Germanic family**, paying special attention to **Gothic** due to its historical value (having been committed to writing in the fourth century). This endeavour allowed him to see more clearly than anyone before him the systematic nature of **sound change**. Within the framework of comparative Germanic, he made the first statements on

the nature of **umlaut** (see below) and **ablaut**, or, as it is sometimes called, **vowel gradation** (as found, for example, in German *sprechen*, *sprach*, *gesprochen*), and developed, more fully than Rask, the notion of *Lautverschiebung*, or **sound shift**, which became the first law in linguistics and which has been referred to as Grimm's Law, or the **First Germanic Sound Shift**.

The work, published in 1822 and entitled *Deutsche Grammatik*, contained general statements about similarities between Germanic obstruents – i.e. plosives, affricates and fricatives – and their equivalents in other languages. Using the old terms of Greek grammar where T = *tenuis* (p, t, k), M = *media* (b, d, g) and A = *aspirate* (f, θ, x), he noted

Proto Indo-European = Germanic

T	A
M	T
A	M

A modern tabulation of his conclusions would appear as:

Indo-European	>	*Germanic*
p		f
t		θ
k		x

Indo-European	>	*Germanic*
b		p
d		t
g		k

Indo-European	>	*Germanic*
bh		b
dh		d
gh		g

J.H. Bredsdorff (1790–1841), a disciple of Rask, tried to explain the causes of **language change** in 1821 (Bredsdorff 1821/1886). He considered such factors as mishearing, misunderstanding, misrecollection, imperfection of speech organs, indolence, the tendency towards analogy, the desire to be distinct, the need for expressing new ideas, and influences from foreign languages.

Some of his ideas are still viable today. For instance, it is recognized that the tendency towards **analogy**, speakers' desire for uniformity, for regular patterns, causes language to become more rather than less regular in syntax and phonology. Colloquial speech – which popular, though rarely expert, opinion often classifies as **indolent** – can also eventually result in changes in pronunciation, spelling, grammatical patterning and the semantic system. The influence from foreign languages is clearly observable when new words enter a language and become absorbed in its grammar and pronunciation system, as when *pizza* receives the English plural form *pizzas*, or when *weekend* is pronounced as beginning with /v/ in Danish and is given the plural ending -*er*. This often results in the ability of speakers of a language to express a new idea or name a new thing – pizzas were at one time unfamiliar in Britain, and at one time Danish did not have a word that could express the conceptualization of the weekend as a whole. Similarly, new inventions often result in the need for new terminology, as when the advent of computers led to the coinage of the term *software* by analogy with *hardware*, which was itself borrowed from another sphere, namely that of the traditional hardware store, selling things like nails, glue, string and various tools.

In the mid-nineteenth century, one of the most influential linguists, August Schleicher (1821–68), set about reconstructing the hypothetical parent language from which most European languages were derived – the **proto-language** (see below). He also devised the *Stammbaumtheorie* or **genealogical family-tree model** of the **Indo-European languages** (see below). He worked out a typological classification of languages based on the work of his predecessors in which he viewed languages as isolating, agglutinating and inflectional (see LANGUAGE TYPOLOGY). On a more philosophical level, he brought to linguistics three important concepts mostly rejected today but which at the time stimulated much discussion and work in the discipline; namely: that language is a natural organism; that it evolves naturally in the Darwinian sense; and that language depends on the physiology and minds of people (that is, it has racial connotations). In short, he stimulated a new and different approach to language study – a **biological approach**.

The work of Schleicher represents a culmination of the first phase of historical linguistics in the nineteenth century. In the second half of the century the discipline of linguistics became more cosmopolitan as scholars in countries other than Germany began seriously to investigate linguistic problems. Germany, however, remained the centre of linguistic attention throughout the century.

In 1863, Hermann Grassmann, a pioneer in internal reconstruction (see below), devised a phonetic law based on observations of the Indo-European languages, showing why correspondences established by Grimm did not always work. His **Law of the Aspirates** demonstrated that, when an Indo-European word had two aspirated sounds (see ARTICULATORY PHONETICS) in the same syllable, one (usually the first) underwent de-aspiration. For example, Sanskrit *ba-bhú-va* 'he has become' < **bha-bhū́-va* shows the reduplicated syllable of the root reduced through loss of aspiration (the asterisk indicates that the form is reconstructed).

This exception to Grimm's Law, where Sanskrit [b] corresponds to Germanic [b] and not to [bh], then, proved to be a law itself.

In 1875, still another phonetic law was proposed by Karl Verner (1846–96). This succeeded in accounting for other exceptions to Grimm's statements by showing that the place of the Indo-European accent was a factor in the regularity of the correspondences. For example, Indo-European [t] in [*pθtĕ́r] > [ð] [faðar] in Germanic; not [θ], as might be expected. The accent later shifted in Germanic to the first syllable.

In his *Corsi di Glottologia*, published in Florence in 1870, Graziadio Ascoli (1829–1907) demonstrated by comparative methods that [k-] in certain places became [ʃ-] in Sanskrit. Compare the word for 'one hundred':

Latin	*centum*
Greek	*hekaton*
Old Irish	*cet*
Sanskrit	*çata*
Germanic	*hundred*

The discovery that [k] remains in some Indo-European languages but became [ʃ] in Sanskrit ended the belief that Sanskrit was the oldest and closest language to the proto-form or parent language. Further investigation would reveal that this change [k > ʃ] occurred before a front vowel, in this case [e], which later merged with [a] in Sanskrit.

The formulation of sound laws, which appeared to be systematic and regular to the extent that exceptions seemed to be laws themselves, gave rise to one of the most important and controversial theories in historical linguistics, promulgated in the doctrine of the Neogrammarians or *Junggrammatiker*.

The Neogrammarians

Inspired in 1868 by the ideas of Wilhelm Scherer (1841–86) who, in his book on the history of the German language (Scherer 1868), advocated fixed laws in sound change, the Neogrammarian movement soon dominated linguistic enquiry. To account for situations where phonetic laws were not upheld by the data, Scherer looked to **analogy** (see above) as the explanation for change. The chief representatives of the movement – Brugmann, Osthoff, Delbrück, Wackernagel, Paul and Leskien – held that phonetic laws were similar to laws of nature of the physical sciences in their consistency of operation. In 1878, in the first volume of a journal edited by Brugmann (1849–1919) and Osthoff (1847–1909), *Morphologische Untersuchungen*, they delineated the Neogrammarian doctrine and the special designation *junggrammatische Richtung* ('Neogrammarian School of Thought'). The crux of their doctrine was, as Osthoff put it: 'sound-laws work with a blind necessity and all discrepancies to these laws were the workings of analogy'. Centred around the University of Leipzig, the Neogrammarians saw in sound change the application of laws of a mechanical nature opposed by the psychological process of the speakers towards regularization of forms resulting in analogically irregular sound changes.

The Neogrammarian doctrine did not go unopposed. For example, the psychologist Wilhelm Wundt (1832–1920) found fault with their views relating to psychological aspects of language. In addition, Hugo Schuchardt (1842–1927) of the University of Graz published an article in 1885 on the sound laws in which he considered language change to be due to a mixing process both within and outside language. Similarly, Ascoli attributed much of the process of language change to a theory proposed by him called the **Substratum Theory**, in which languages were influenced by a mixture of populations (see below).

The twentieth century

The first decade of the twentieth century saw a shift away from German domination of linguistic science with the work of Ferdinand de Saussure (1857–1913) of the University of Geneva. His view of language as a system of arbitrary signs in opposition to one another, his distinction between language and speech, and his separation of descriptive linguistics and historical linguistics into two defined spheres of interest, earned him the reputation of one of the founders of structural linguistics (see Introduction).

From this time on, the field of **descriptive linguistics** developed rapidly while historical linguistics and comparative studies lost their pre-eminence.

Today, among the disciplines that make up the broad field of linguistics (descriptive, historical, sociological, psychological, etc.), historical linguistics, from once being the embodiment of the discipline, has become another branch of the multivaried area of investigation. Twentieth-century advancements in historical-comparative language studies have been on the practical side, with the collection of data and reformulation of previous work. On the theoretical side, much has come from advancements in descriptive linguistics and other branches of the discipline – for example, from structural concepts such as the phoneme, and refinements in phonetics, to more stringent application of ordered rules and underlying structures, statistical methods and their relationship to language change and language universals.

Principles, methods, objectives and data of historical linguistics

Certain principles in the field of historical linguistic enquiry are taken as axiomatic; for example,

- All languages are in a continual process of change.
- All languages are subject to the same kind of modifying influences.
- Language change is regular and systematic, allowing for unhindered communication among speakers.
- Linguistic and social factors are interrelated in language change.
- Language systems tend toward as-yet-unspecified states of economy and redundancy.

A linguistic change or state not attested in known languages would be suspect if posited for an earlier stage through reconstruction. A phonological change, for example,

of the type /b/ > /k/ between vowels, runs counter to empirical linguistic facts. Similarly, no system of consonants in any known language consists entirely of voiced fricatives (see ARTICULATORY PHONETICS). Any reconstruction that ignored this observation and posited only voiced fricatives would be highly suspect.

The **diachronic study** of language may be approached by comparing one or more languages at different stages in their histories. **Synchronic** or **descriptive** studies underlie historical investigations inasmuch as an analysis of a language or a part thereof at period *A* can then be compared to a descriptive study at period *B*. For example, an investigation of English at the time of Chaucer, and another of Modern English, would reveal a number of differences. Similarly, a descriptive statement of Latin and one of Modern French would disclose very different systems in phonology and morphosyntax. The **historical linguist** attempts to classify these differences and to explicate the manner and means by which they came about.

When the various historical facts of a language are discovered, the investigator might then establish general rules based on the data. These rules will demonstrate in more succinct form the manner in which the language changed and how it differs from other related languages.

Rules of change may be written in several ways: [t] > [d]/V__V states that the sound [t] becomes [d] in the environment between vowels. Such rules can also be stated in **feature specification**:

$$\begin{bmatrix} +\text{consonantal} \\ +\text{plosive} \\ +\text{coronal} \\ +\text{anterior} \\ -\text{voiced} \end{bmatrix} \rightarrow [+\text{voiced}]/[+\text{vocalic}]\_\_[+\text{vocalic}]$$

As is often the case, an entire class of sounds – for example, [p t k] – behave in an identical manner and, instead of different rules for each, one rule suffices:

$$\begin{bmatrix} +\text{consonantal} \\ +\text{plosive} \\ -\text{voiced} \end{bmatrix} \rightarrow [+\text{voiced}]/ \\ [+\text{vocalic}]\_\_[+\text{vocalic}]$$

If we were to compare Latin and Italian, we would find such words as:

Latin	Italian	
noctem	*notte*	'night'
octo	*otto*	'eight'
lactem	*latte*	'milk'
factum	*fatto*	'fact'
lectum	*letto*	'bed'

In these examples, and others that could be added, we discover that Latin [k] (e.g. in [noktem]) became Italian [t] in the environment before [t]. This assimilatory change is a general rule in Italian and can be stated as: [k] > [t]/__ [t], or it can be stated in feature specifications. The rule helps account for the differences between Latin and Italian, and between Italian and other Romance languages, where a different set of rules apply to give, say, Spanish *noche* [nóʧe] and French *nuit* [nyɪ].

Objectives of the practitioners of historical linguistics vary. Excluding here language changes resulting from evolutionary or maturation processes of developing neuroanatomical structures of *Homo sapiens*, some historical linguists are concerned with phonological, morphological, syntactic and semantic changes that occur in languages over a given period of time, to acquire an understanding of the mechanisms underlying the modifications and to seek explanations for them. Answers to these questions also bear on the nature of the species and may be sought within cognitive and physiological parameters which govern the behaviour of the species.

Through historical studies some linguists may be more concerned with reconstruction and comparison of languages to arrive at historical relationships indicating common origins of languages, which allow them to be grouped into families. The geographical distribution of families is of paramount importance in our understanding of migrations and settlement patterns over the surface of the earth.

Sociological aspects of language change encompassing questions of dialect, style, prestige, taboos, changes in social behaviour, technology, and even individual needs to be different, are also important considerations in the understanding of cultural associations and ultimately human behaviour.

The changes that languages undergo make up the data for historical linguistics which are themselves generally transmitted by and derived from written documentation or reconstructed from the languages in question if such records are not available.

In cases where the underlying language of the documentation is known, such as Old English, Latin and Sanskrit, the investigator must try to determine the orthoepic features of the language through knowledge of the writing system employed, through commentary on the language by contemporary authors, by rhyme, and by the pronunciation of the descendent languages.

In dealing with primary written sources inscribed in an unknown language, the investigator must decipher the texts in order to gain a clear view of the underlying linguistic structure. The performance of this task must take into account the kind of writing system used, the direction of writing, and the phonetic basis underlying the orthographic signs. Morphemes and morpheme boundaries must be determined, syntactic features assessed, and semantic properties determined.

Philology

The forerunner of historical linguistics, **philological studies**, is concerned with language and culture. The term is generally used to denote the study of literary monuments or inscriptions to ascertain the cultural features of an ancient civilization. **Classical philology** continues the activities of the ancient Greeks and Alexandrians who delved into the already old texts of their ancestors. The philological tradition sank to a low ebb during the Middle Ages, but with the rediscovery of classical antiquity in the Renaissance the discipline again prospered. Philological endeavours were given further impetus in the early nineteenth century as Sanskrit literature became available in the West. Historical linguistics was known as **comparative philology** until about the time of August Schleicher, who, because of his pure language work, preferred to be called a *Glottiker* – that is, a **linguist**.

Phonological change

Regularity of sound change

(For explanation of the phonetic terms in this and the following sections, see ARTICULATORY PHONETICS.)

The sounds of a language are affected over the course of time by modifications that tend to be regular and systematic, in that the changes have a propensity to apply in the same manner to all relevant environments. The reflexes of the Latin vowel [a], for example, demonstrate this principle.

Latin [a] regularly became French [ɛ], as in the following words:

Latin	French	
marem	mer	[mɛʁ]
fabam	fève	[fɛv]
patrem	père	[pɛʁ]
labram	lèvre	[lɛvʁ]

This change of Latin [a] to French [ɛ] occurred when [a] was accented and free; that is, in an open syllable, as in [má-rem].

The accented Latin vowel [a] in an open syllable, but followed by a nasal, resulted in [ɛ̃]:

Latin	French	
manum	main	[mɛ̃]
panem	pain	[pɛ̃]
planum	plain	[plɛ̃]
famen	faim	[fɛ̃]

Cases where Latin [a] became French [a], while they may at first glance appear to have been exceptions to the above rule, were in fact the result of another regular sound change in which accented [a] behaved predictably in a closed environment, that is, in a closed syllable or one blocked by a consonant, as in [pár-te], [vák-ká], etc. Compare:

Latin	French	
partem	part	[paʁ]
vaccam	vache	[vaʃ]
carrum	char	[ʃaʁ]
cattum	chat	[ʃa]

When Latin [a] was closed by a nasal consonant, the result was a nasal [ã] as in:

Latin	French	
campu	champ	[ʃã]
grande	grand	[grã]
annu	an	[ã]
manicam (manca)	manche	[mãʃ]

Since the environment dictated the phonological change, the conditions of the modifications can be established along the following lines (where o = syllable boundary):

$$[a] > \begin{cases} [\varepsilon]/ \_\_ \text{ o con.} \\ [\varepsilon]/ \_\_ \text{ o con. + nasal} \\ [a]/ \_\_ \text{ con. o} \\ [\tilde{a}]/ \_\_ \text{ con. o + nasal} \end{cases}$$

This general rule requires clarification based on further environmental factors that regularly affect the vowel [a]. For example:

alterum	autre	[otʁ]
valet	vaut	[vo]

where [a] plus [l] become [au] and subsequently reduces to [o].

Beginning in the period of Late Old French, the vowel [ɛ] (from [a]) underwent a further change to become [e] when the syllable became open through the loss of a final consonant, cf.:

clavem	> clé	[kle]
pratum	> pré	[pre]

When [a] was unaccented, it underwent another set of changes which resulted in [ə] or [a] as in:

camisam	> chemise	[ʃəmiːz]
amicum	> ami	[ami]

The treatment of [a] in the above examples is intended to be indicative of the kind of regularity found in phonological change but is not meant to be exhaustive.

Phonological processes

The mechanisms by which phonological modifications occur entail changes in the features of a sound (e.g. voiceless, voiced, plosive, fricative) or the addition, loss or movement of sound segments. Many such changes are of an anticipatory nature whereby a modification takes place under the influence of a following sound; for example, the **assimilation** of [k] > [t]/ __ [t] in Latin octo [okto] to Italian otto is of this type, in which the feature velar is changed to dental before a following dental sound. Compare:

[k]	[t]
voiceless	voiceless
plosive	plosive
velar	dental

Other processes of this type include **nasalization**, as in Latin bonum to Portuguese bom [bõ], where a non-nasal vowel acquires the nasality of a following nasal consonant.

Often a velar consonant becomes a palatal consonant under the influence of a following front vowel that pulls the highest point of the tongue from the velar forward into the palatal zone, as in Old English kin [kɪn] and Modern English chin [tʃɪn], or Latin centum [kentum] and Italian cento [tʃɛnto].

A specific kind of assimilation, referred to as **sonorization**, involves the voicing of voiceless consonants and appears to be motivated primarily by voiced surroundings. For example, voiceless [p], [t] and [k] become [b], [d] and [g] in the environment between vowels, as in the following examples:

Latin	Spanish		
cupa	cuba ['kúba]	[p]	> [b]
vita	vida ['bida]	[t]	> [d]
amica	amiga [a'miga]	[k]	> [g]

Assimilation may take place over syllable boundaries, as occurs through the process of **umlaut**, or, as it is sometimes called, **mutation**. The Proto-Germanic form [*musiz] gave Old English [mɪːs] (Modern English mice), when the vowel in the first syllable was drawn forward through the influence of the front vowel in the second syllable. Similarly, Latin feci gave rise to Spanish hice when the influence of the Latin vowel [i] raised [e] to [i] through assimilation. Final [i] subsequently lowered to [e]. Compare also Latin veni and Spanish vine.

The opposite of assimilation, **dissimilation**, modifies a segment so that it becomes less like another, often neighbouring segment, in the word. Dissimilation is less frequent than assimilation in the known histories of the world's languages. The conditioning factor may be juxtaposed to the sound which undergoes change, or it may operate at a distance. The first case is illustrated by Latin luminosum, which became Spanish lumbroso where, after the loss of unaccented [i], the resultant cluster [mn] dissimilated to [mr] and subsequently became [mbr]. The nasal [n], by losing its nasal quality and changing to [r], became less like [m]. The second case is illustrated by Latin arbor, which became Spanish arbol by changing [r] to [l] under the influence of the preceding [r].

The addition of a segment into a particular environment of the word, epenthesis, is essentially a form of anticipation of a following sound and may involve either consonants or vowels. The Old English word glimsian through the insertion of an epenthetic [p] in the environment [m__s] gave rise to Modern English *glimpse*. The inserted sound agrees with the preceding [m] in place of articulation (bilabial) and with the following [s] in manner of articulation (voiceless). Compare Old English *timr* and Modern English *timber*, and Old English *ganra*, Modern *gander*.

Basque speakers borrowed a number of words from late Latin but lacked certain consonant clusters found in the lending language. Vowels were inserted in the borrowed words to make them more compatible to the Basque system of phonological distribution, which, for example, tended to avoid sequences of plosive plus [r]; compare:

Latin	*Basque*	
[krus]	[guruts]	'cross'
[libru]	[libiru]	'book'

The addition of a word-initial segment generally applied to facilitate the pronunciation of an initial consonant cluster is a process referred to as **prothesis**; for example,

Latin	*Spanish*
schola [skola]	*escuela* [eskwela]
stella [stela]	*estrella* [estreʎa]

Sounds are subject to deletion. The two most common processes of segment deletion are **apocope** and **syncope**, which are especially common in environments after accented syllables. In word-final position, apocope has been common in the history of many languages including French. Compare:

Latin	*French*
cane [kane]	*chien* [ʃjɛ̃]
caru [karu]	*cher* [ʃɛʁ]

Consonantal loss in word-final position is also common among many languages. Again, we see in French the deletion of consonants in forms such as Latin *pratu* > French *pré*.

Other word positions are also vulnerable to deletion of segments; Old and Middle English employed the cluster [kn-] as in *knight*, *knot*, *knee*. The [k] was lost in the transition period to Modern English.

The loss of a word-medial vowel, or syncope, occurs in English in words such as *vegetable* ['vɛdʒtəbl̩], where the unaccented second syllable lost the vocalic segment. The process does not commonly occur in English, however, but appears much more readily in the Romance languages.

Latin	*Spanish*	*French*
viride	*verde*	*vert*
lepore	*liebre*	*lièvre*
calidu	*caldo*	*chaud*

A change in the relative position of sounds, probably caused by a kind of anticipation, is referred to as **metathesis**. Adjacent sounds may be affected, as in the West Saxon dialect of Old English, where [ks] became [sk] in words such as *axian* > ask. Sounds separated by some phonetic distance may also undergo metathesis as, for example, popular Latin *mirac(u)lu* became Spanish *milagro* through the transposition of [l] and [r].

A number of other processes are often at work in language change. Stated briefly, some further changes that affect consonants are:

aspiration	[t]	>	[tʰ]
affrication	[t]	>	[ts]
labialization	[t]	>	[tʷ]
prenasalization	[t]	>	[nt]
glottalization	[t]	>	[t']
velarization	[t]	>	[ɫ]
rhotacization	[z]	>	[r]

or the opposite – de-aspiration, de-affrication, etc.

Further processes observed among vocalic segments are:

{ raising	[e]	>	[i]
{ lowering	[i]	>	[e]
{ fronting	[o]	>	[e]
{ backing	[e]	>	[o]
{ rounding	[i]	>	[u]
{ unrounding	[u]	>	[i]

lengthening	[a]	>	[aː]
shortening	[aː]	>	[a]
diphthongization	[e]	>	[ie]
monophthongization	[ie]	>	[e]

An entire syllable may undergo loss, a process called **haplology**, cf. Latin *stipipendium* > *stipendium*.

Phonetic and phonological change

As we have seen, phonemes develop variants in accordance with environmental conditions and are the result of influences exercised through phonetic processes such as assimilation. We know, for example, that English vowels have nasalized variants preceding nasal consonants, as in the word *can't*, but not in other environments, compare *cat* – phonetically (US) [kʰæ̃ːnt], [kʰæt]. These phonetic changes have no impact on the overall phonological system, since the variation is conditioned and predictable, affecting only the distribution of allophones (see PHONEMICS).

Sound changes that result in an increase or reduction in the number of phonemes in a language, or lead to the replacement of phonemes by others, are generally brought about by **splits** or **mergers**. A change in which several phonemes are replaced in a systematic way is called a shift, which also may be partial or complete:

1 split

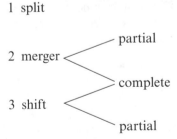

2 merger

3 shift

If, in English, nasal consonants were to disappear, the form *can't* would be represented phonetically as [kʰæt] and would, in fact, contrast with *cat* as /kæt/, /kæt/, with the distinguishing feature of nasal versus non-nasal vowel. What was once a phonetic

feature of the language, through the loss of the nasal consonant, would then become a phonemic feature brought about by phonological split. Something similar to this occurred in French, where nasal and non-nasal vowels distinguish meaning:

Latin	*French*		
bonus	> /bõ/	*bon*	'good'
bellus	> /bo/	*beau*	'pretty, handsome'

At some stage in the history of English, allophonic conditioning led to the development of a velar nasal [ŋ] before a velar plosive through assimilation. In the course of Middle English, the voiced velar plosive disappeared in word-final position after the nasal consonant, as in the words *young* or *sing*. The velar nasal allophone of /n/, then, became a separate phoneme, as attested by such minimal pairs (see PHONEMICS) as

| sin | /sin/ |
| sing | /siŋ/ |

A phoneme may also split into multiple forms as attested in French. Compare

$$/k/ \quad > \quad \begin{matrix} k/\_w \\ s/\_ \begin{bmatrix} i \\ e \end{bmatrix} \\ s/\_a \end{matrix}$$

Latin — *French*

in such words as

quando	>	*quand*	/kâ/	'when'
centum	>	*cent*	/sã/	'hundred'
campus	>	*champ*	/ʃã/	'field'

Phonological split may also result in merger in which no new phonemes are created in the language. In some dialects of English, for example, /t/ split into [t] and [d] in certain environments and [d] merged with the phoneme /d/ already in the language. This was the case where *latter* /lætə/ became homophonous with *ladder* /lædə/ and *bitter* with *bidder*.

Mergers may be **partial** or **complete**. If merger is complete, there is a net reduction in the number of phonemes in the language. Such is the case in some varieties of Cockney, a non-standard dialect of London, where the two dental fricatives /θ/ and /ð/ have merged completely with /f/ and /v/ respectively. Hence, *thin* /θin/ is pronounced /fin/ and *bathe* /beɪð/ is pronounced /beɪv/. Four phonemes were reduced to two:

/f/   /θ/   >   /f/
/v/   /ð/   >   /v/

In Black English pronunciation in the United States, /θ/ merges partially with /f/, i.e. /θ/ > /f/ in all positions except word-initial. The form *with* is articulated as /wɪf/ but the word *thing* retains /θ/ as in /θɪŋ/ or /θæŋ/.

When a series of phonemes is systematically modified, such as /p/, /t/, /k/, > /b/, /d/, /g/, we may consider a shift to have occurred. A shift may be **partial**, in as much as all the allophones of the phoneme do not participate in it, or it may be **complete**, when they do. The modification of long vowels in Late Middle English known as the **Great English Vowel Shift** (see below) left no residue and appears to have been complete. The **First Germanic Consonant Shift**, in which /p/, /t/, /k/ > /f/, /θ/, /x/, however, left some of the voiceless plosives unaffected in specific environments, such as after /s/. Compare, for example, Latin *est* and German *ist* and see above.

Phonological processes that lead to allophonic variation and subsequent new phonemes generally occur one step at a time. The change of Latin /k/ to French /ʃ/, for example, in words such as *cane* /kane/ to *chien* /ʃjẽ/, did not do so directly, but instead entailed two changes:

/k/ voiceless > /tʃ/ voiceless > /ʃ/ voiceless
      plosive   plosive   fricative
      velar   palatal   palatal

Phonological change usually takes place within the range of allophonic variation which varies by one feature. A phoneme /k/ might have allophones [t] or [x] differing by one phonological feature, but not

generally an allophone /ʃ/ differing by two features. A change to /ʃ/ could be the result of either of the two allophones serving as intermediaries:

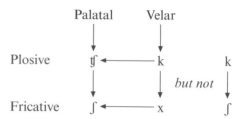

Non-phonologically motivated sound change

Many phonological changes are not conditioned by the surrounding environments but are motivated by other factors relating to external forces, such as substratum influences, internal forces inherent in the structural paradigmatic make-up of the language and, as is often the case, by unknown factors whose influences, obscured by time, are no longer recoverable. The **First Germanic Consonant Shift**, for example, occurred at a time in which there were no written records for the Germanic languages and under unknown circumstances.

A major change in the history of English vowels took place at the end of the Middle English period (sixteenth century), in which the long tense vowels underwent a regular modification without the apparent assistance of an environmental stimulus. The modification is referred to as the **Great English Vowel Shift**.

Middle English	*Early Modern English*	
[miːs]	[mays]	'mice'
[muːs]	[maws]	'mouse'
[geːs]	[giːs]	'geese'
[goːs]	[guːs]	'goose'
[brɛːken]	[breːk]	'break'
[brɔːken]	[broːk]	'broke'
[naːm]	[neːm]	'name'

The vocalic movement upward in which the high vowels diphthongized can be shown schematically as:

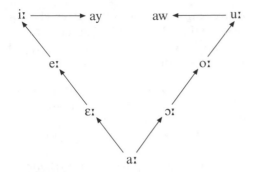

An upward pressure was also exerted on the back vowels of the Gallo-Roman language in about the ninth century during the evolution from Latin to French, and the high back vowel from Latin [uː] which had become [u] then shifted to [y].

Gallo-Roman Free Accented Vowels

i   y ◄——————————— u

     ei   ou

        iɛ   uɔ

                   ɛ   ɔ

mūrum → [muːrə]   → *mur* [myːʁ]
dūrum → [duːrə]   → *dur* [dyːʁ]
lūna → [luːnə]   → *lune* [lyːn]

Note [u] → [y] regardless of environmental position, where explanations other than those involving conditioned change must be sought. One plausible interpretation of the event, based on paradigmatic considerations, suggests that, with the reduction of Latin [au] → [ɔ] (*aurum* → *or* [ɔr]) which occurred prior to the change [u] → [y], the margin of tolerance, i.e. the physical space, between back vowels was not sufficient. The monophthongization of [au] consequently forced upward pressure on the back vowels, and [u], the closest vowel, could go no closer and palatalized.

The plosive and fricative consonantal structure of Early Old French of the ele-

venth and twelfth centuries consisted of the phonetic inventory and relationships

		Labial	Dental	Pre-palatal
Plosives	vl	p	t	ts
	vd	b	d	dz
		Palatal	Velar	
	vl	ʧ	k	
	vd	ʤ	g	
Fricatives	vl	f	s	
	vd	v	z	

(vl = voiceless; vd = voiced)

During the thirteenth century, the affricated palatal sounds ceased to be plosives and became fricatives:

ć	[ts]	→	s
ż	[dz]	→	z
č	[ʧ]	→	ʃ
ǧ	[ʤ]	→	ʒ

The result of these changes was a later Old French system of consonantal sounds as follows:

```
p   t        k
b   d        g
f   s    ʃ
v   z    ʒ
```

The rationale for these changes has been sought in a tendency to reduce the overcrowded palatal zone and a leaning towards symmetry by reducing the five orders (labials, dentals, etc.) to four in accordance with the four series of plosives and fricatives.

In other attempts to explain phonological modifications which fall outside the realm of conditioned change, the notion of **substratum influence** has often been invoked. Certain words in Spanish, for example, developed an [h] (which became φ in the modern language), where Latin had [f].

Latin	Spanish		
filium	*hijo*	[ixo]	'son'
fabam	*haba*	[áɓa]	'bean'
folia	*hoja*	[óxa]	'leaf'
feminam	*hembra*	[émbra]	'female'
fumum	*humo*	[úmo]	'smoke'

As the replacement of Latin [f] by [h] began in the north of the peninsula, where the Basques were in contact with Hispano-Roman speakers, and because Basque had no [f] sound, the notion has been put forward that Basque speakers, upon learning the Hispano-Roman language, substituted their closest sound. According to this view, this sound was [ph] which became [h]. Those words not affected (cf. Latin *florem*, which became Spanish *flor*) are excused from the change on the basis of other criteria such as learned influences.

Diffusion of language change

Besides the study of mechanisms and processes of language change, the historical linguist may also be concerned with how changes spread throughout a speech community. The vocabulary of a language may be modified by **lexical diffusion** in which a change begins in one or several words and gradually spreads throughout the relevant portions of the lexicon. One such ongoing change can be seen in words such as *present*, which can be used as either a verb or a noun. At one time all such words were accented on the second syllable regardless of their status as noun or verb. In the period that gave rise to Modern English (sixteenth century), words such as *rebel*, *outlaw* and *record* began to be pronounced with the accent on the first syllable when they were used as nouns. Over the next few centuries more and more words followed the same pattern, cf. *récess* and *recéss*, *áffix* and *affíx*. The diffusion process is still in progress, however, as indicated by the fact that many English speakers say *addréss* for both noun and verb and others use *áddress* as the noun and *addréss* for the verb. There are still many words that have as yet not been affected by the change, compare *repórt*, *mistáke* and *suppórt*.

Not all changes are processed through the gradual steps of lexical diffusion. Some changes affect all words in a given class at the same time. In some Andalusian dialects of Spanish, the phoneme /s/ has developed an allophone [h] in syllable-final position:

Standard pronunciation	Andalusian
[dos]	[doh]
[es]	[eh]
[mas]	[mah]

The change is regular and systematic, affecting all instances of syllable-final /s/ in the speech patterns of the individuals who adopt this dialect.

Along with linguistic diffusion of change throughout the lexicon of the language, the linguist may also take into account diffusion of change throughout the speech community. A given speech modification begins in the speech habits of one or several individuals and spreads (if it spreads at all) to an ever-increasing number of people. Whether or not diffusion occurs may depend on the relative prestige of the people who initiate the change and their influence on the speech population. If the prestige factor is high, there is a good chance that the innovation will be imitated by others. The loss of postvocalic /r/ in some eastern dialects of the United States was due to a change that originated in England and was brought to the New World by immigrants. Similarly, the adoption of the sound /θ/ in southern Spain (where no such sound existed) by speakers of the Andalusian dialect is due to their imitation of Castilian Spanish, the prestige dialect of Madrid and its surroundings.

Morphological and syntactical change

Effects of sound change on morphology

The effect of phonological change on aspects of morphology is evident in the restructuring of the plural forms in some English words:

	Germanic	Old English	Modern English
Sing	*mūs	mūs	[maʊs] 'mouse'
Pl	*mūsi	mīs	[maɪs] 'mice'
Sing	*fōt	fōt	[fʊt] 'foot'
Pl	*fōti	fēt	[fiːt] 'feet'

In these and examples like them, the process of **umlaut** or **mutation** operated to change the stem vowel [uː] > [iː] and [oː] > [eː] through the fronting influence of a following close front [i] which then disappeared. Subsequently, [iː] > [ai] and [eː] > [iː] (see above).

The influence of sound change on the morphological structures may also be seen in the Old English system of nominal forms whose suffixes marked case and gender. Compare the Old English masculine noun *hund* 'dog'.

Old English

	Singular	Plural
Nom	hund	hund-as
Acc	hund	hund-as
Gen	hund-es	hund-a
Dat	hund-e	hund-um

Other nouns belonged to either masculine, feminine or neuter types distinguished on the basis of case endings, e.g. feminine *gief* 'gift' declined along the lines of *gief-u* in the nominative singular, *gief-e* in the accusative singular, etc.

Through phonological change, the case and gender distinctions of Old English were lost. By the fifteenth century, the /m/ of the dative plural suffix had been effaced and unaccented vowels of the case endings had been reduced to /ə/.

Middle English

	Singular	Plural
Nom	hund	hund-əs
Acc	hund	hund-əs
Gen	hund-əs	hund-ə
Dat	hund-ə	hund-ə

Previous distinctions between dative singular and dative plural, genitive singular and nominative plural, and so on, disappeared.

The distinction between singular and plural forms in Middle English was preserved by the continuance of the phoneme /s/, which survived also to mark the genitive singular forms. A genitive plural /s/ was added by analogy with the singular. The loss of case endings also obliterated the gender distinctions that were found among Old English forms. Sound change further modified the internal structure of morphemes such as *hund*, subject to the result of the Great English Vowel Shift, which diphthongized /u/ to /au/ and resulted in:

Present-day English

Singular		Plural	
hound	/haund/	hounds	/haundz/
hound's	/haundz/	hounds'	/haundz/

Classical Latin contained six cases, which were reduced in the popular Latin speech of the Empire, and finally disappeared altogether in the Romance languages, with the exception of Romanian.

Increasing stress patterns in Popular Latin gradually neutralized the differences between long and short vowels by creating long vowels in accented syllables and short vowels in unaccented syllables regardless of the original arrangement. With the concomitant loss of final -m in the accusative, the nominative, vocative, accusative and ablative forms merged. The genitive and dative conformed to the rest of the pattern by analogy.

As in English, the loss of the case system brought on a more extensive and frequent use of prepositions and a more rigid word order to designate the relationships formerly employed by case functions.

	Classical Latin	Popular Latin	French
Sing			
Nom	*porta*	*porta*	*la porte*
Voc	*porta*	*porta*	*la porte*
Acc	*portam*	*porta*	*la porte*
Gen	*portae*	*de porta*	*de la porte*
Dat	*portae*	*ad porta*	*à la porte*
Abl	*portā*	*cum porta*	*avec la porte*

Word order, prepositions and articles

As long as relationships within a sentence were signalled by case endings, the meaning of the sentence was unambiguous. Compare the following Latin sentences.

Poeta puellam amat
Puellam poeta amat   'The poet loves
Poeta amat puellam   the girl'
Puellam amat poeta

With the loss of case endings such as the accusative marker [m], subject and object would have become indistinguishable.

*Poeta puella amat
*Puella poeta amat

Fixed word order came into play, in which the subject preceded the verb and the object followed:

Poeta ama puella

This word order has persisted into the Romance languages, accompanied by the use of articles, and in Spanish by a preposition, *a*, to indicate personalized objects:

French   *Le poète aime la jeune fille*
Spanish   *El poeta ama a la muchacha*
Italian   *Il poeta ama la ragazza*

More extensive use of prepositions also became an important factor in signalling subject, object and verb relationships:

Latin   *Puella rosam poetae in porta videt*
French   *La jeune fille voit la rose du poète à la porte*
Spanish   *La muchacha ve la rosa del poeta en la puerta.*

The changing phonological conditions in the Latin of the Empire also had a profound effect on verbal forms. For example, compare Latin and French:

Latin	Old French	French
Sing		
1 *cantō*	*chant(e)* [ʃãnt(ə)]	*chante* [ʃãt]
2 *cantas*	*chantes* [ʃãntəs]	*chantes* [ʃãt]
3 *cantat*	*chante* [ʃãntə]	*chante* [ʃãt]

The first person singular [o] was lost, as were final consonants, and final unaccented vowels were weakened to [ə]. In the first person singular an analogical [e] was added by the fourteenth century.

The merger of verb forms in the French paradigm through phonological change necessitated some manner of differentiating them according to person and entailed the obligatory use of subject pronouns.

je chante
tu chantes
il chante

As the verb forms were clearly distinguishable in Latin by the endings, there was no need to employ subject pronouns except in special cases, as is still the case in languages such as Spanish and Italian:

	Spanish	Italian
1	*canto*	*canto*
2	*cantas*	*canti*
3	*canta*	*canta*

Not unlike phonological change, morphological changes proceed on a regular and systematic basis. The Latin **synthetic future**, for example, *cantabo* 'I will sing', disappeared in all forms and was replaced by a new **periphrastic future**; for example, *cantare habeo* > *chanterai* [ʃãtre].

Analogical change

The effects of phonological change may be offset by analogical formations that regularize forms on the basis of others in the paradigm. An example in Old English is the word for *son*.

	Singular		Plural	
Nom	*sunu*	'son'	*suna*	'sons'
Acc	*sunu*		*suna*	
Dat	*suna*		*sunum*	
Gen	*suna*		*suna*	

The plural forms had no [s] but the word became *sons* by analogy with other words that did make the plural with *s*, such as *bāt* (nom. sing.) and *bãtas* (nom. plur.) which became *boat* and *boats* respectively.

As discussed earlier, accented [á] in Latin became [ɛ] in French, as we see again in the following paradigm.

Singular	Latin	Old French	French
1	*ámo*	*aim(e)*	*aime* [ɛm]
2	*ámas*	*aimes*	*aimes* [ɛm]
3	*ámat*	*aime*	*aime* [ɛm]
Plural			
1	*amámus*	*amons*	*aimons* [ɛmõ]
2	*amátis*	*amez*	*aimez* [ɛme]
3	*ámant*	*aiment*	*aiment* [ɛm]

These forms undergo regular phonological change into Old French, in which initial accented [a] became [ɛ] but remained as [a] in the first and second person plural, where it was in unaccented position. This led to an irregular paradigm. During the transition from Old French to Modern French, however, the paradigm was regularized through analogy with the singular and third person plural forms resulting in an irregular phonological development. Similarly, an orthographic *e* (cf. also *chante*) was added to the first person singular to conform with the rest of the paradigm.

When phonological change threatens to eliminate a well-entrenched grammatical category such as, for instance, singular and plural in Indo-European languages, adjustments may occur that preserve the category (albeit in a new phonological form).

The loss of syllable- and word-final [s] in some dialects of Andalusian Spanish, for example, also swept away the earlier plural marker in [s]. For example, compare:

Castilian		Andalusian (Eastern)	
Singular	Plural	Singular	Plural
libro	*libros*	*libro*	*librɔ*
gato	*gatos*	*gato*	*gatɔ*
madre	*madres*	*madre*	*madrɛ*
bote	*botes*	*bote*	*botɛ*

In compensation for the loss of the plural indicator [s], the final vowel of the word opened (lowered a degree), to indicate plurality.

Morphological differentiation was also a factor in the modifications of the second person singular of the verb *to be* in the Romance languages. The distinction of second and third person in popular Latin was threatened by the loss of word-final /-t/; compare:

Latin	*sum*	
	es	> *es*
	est	> *es(t)*

The various Romance languages resorted to different strategies to maintain the distinction between the second and third persons singular. French distinguished them on the basis of pronouns which were obligatory in the language; Spanish borrowed a form from another part of the grammar no longer needed, namely the disappearing synthetic future; and Italian resorted to analogy of the second person with that of the first person by adding /s-/. For example, compare:

French	Spanish	Italian
je suis	*soy*	*sono*
tu es [ɛ]	*eres*	*sei*
il est [ɛ]	*es*	*è*

Some syntactic changes appear to be unmotivated by modifications in the phonological or morphological component of the grammar. In Old and Middle English, an inversion rule relating to the formation of Yes/No questions could apply to all verbs – for example, *They speak the truth* and *Speak they the truth?* During the sixteenth and seventeenth centuries, the rule changed to apply to a more limited set of verbs, those that function as auxiliaries. Disregarding the fact that the verbs *be* and *have* undergo an inversion even when they do not perform as auxiliaries, and ignoring here the emergence of the auxiliary verb *do*, the change can be shown as follows:

Old	They speak	→	Speak they?
construction	They can speak	→	Can they speak?
New	They speak	→	xxx
construction	They can speak	→	Can they speak?

Historical linguistics has only in recent years begun to investigate syntactic change in a systematic manner in conjunction with syntactic developments in the field of synchronic studies.

Lexical and semantic change

Besides changes in the grammar of language, modifications also occur in the vocabulary, both in the stock of words (**lexical change**) and in their meanings (**semantic change**). Words may be added or lost in conjunction with cultural changes. The many hundreds of words that once dealt with astrology, when the art of divination based on the stars and their supposed influence on human affairs was more in vogue, have largely disappeared from the world's languages, while large numbers of new words related to technological developments are constantly revitalizing their vocabularies.

Some of the word-formation processes by which lexical changes occur in English are:

Process	*Examples*
compounding	sailboat, bigmouth
derivation	uglification, finalize
borrowings	yacht (Dutch), pogrom (Russian)
acronyms	UNESCO, RADAR
blends	smoke + fog > smog, motor + hotel > motel
abbreviations	*op. cit.*, *ibid.*, Ms
doublets	person, parson
back formations	typewrite < typewriter, burgle < burglar
echoic forms and inventions	miaow, moo, splash, ping
clipping	prof *for* professor, phone *for* telephone

proper names	sandwich < Earl of Sandwich (1718–92), boycott < Charles Boycott (1832–97)

Changes in the meanings of words constantly occur in all natural languages and revolve around three general principles: **semantic broadening**, that is, from the particular to the general, e.g. *holy day* > *holiday*, Old English *dogge*, a specific breed > *dog*; **semantic narrowing**, from the general to the particular, e.g. Old English *mete* 'food' > *meat*, a specific food, i.e. flesh, Old English *steorfan* 'to die' > *starve*; shifts in meaning, e.g. *lust* used to mean 'pleasure', *immoral* 'not customary', *silly* 'happy, blessed', *lewd* 'ignorant', and so on.

The etymological meaning of a word may help to determine its current meaning. English words such as *television* or *telephone* can be deduced from their earlier Greek and Latin meanings with respect to the components (*tele* 'at a distance', *vision* 'see', *phone* 'sound'). Such is not always the case, however. Borrowed words as well as native forms may undergo semantic change so that etymological knowledge of a word may not be sufficient to assess its meaning. Compare the following:

English	*Latin*	
dilapidated	*lapis*	'stone'
eradicate	*radix*	'root'
sinister	*sinister*	'left'
virtue	*vir*	'man'

From the origin of *dilapidated*, it might be thought that it referred only to stone structures; *eradicate*, only to roots, *sinister*; to left-handed people; and *virtue*, only to men.

Words, then, do not have immutable meanings that exist apart from context. They tend to wander away from earlier meanings and their semantic values are not necessarily clear from historical knowledge of the word.

Changes in the material culture, sometimes called **referent change**, have an effect on the meaning of a word – as is the case of the English word *pen*, which once meant 'feather' from an even earlier *pet* 'to fly'. This name was appropriated when quills were used for writing but remained when pens were no longer feathers. Similarly, the word *paper* is no longer associated with the papyrus plant of its origin.

Social and psychological aspects of language change

Language change often comes about through the social phenomena of **taboos**, **metaphor** and **folk etymologies**. The avoidance of particular words for social reasons seems to occur in all languages and **euphemisms** arise in their place. For instance, instead of *dies* one may use the expression *passes away*, which seems less severe and more sympathetic. Or one *goes to the bathroom* instead of the *toilet*, but does not expect to take a bath – even dogs and cats may go to the bathroom in North America. Elderly people are *senior citizens* and the poor are *underprivileged*. Like all social phenomena, taboos change with time and viewpoint. In Victorian England the use of the word *leg* was considered indiscreet, even when referring to a piano.

Taboos may even cause the loss of a word, as in the classical Indo-European case of the word for 'bear'. A comparison of this word in various Indo-European languages yields:

Latin	*ursus*	Old Church Slavonic	*medvedi*
Greek	*arktos*	English	*bear*
Sanskrit	*ṛkṣah*	German	*Bär*

The presumed Indo-European ancestor of Latin, Greek and Sanskrit was **arktos*. Avoidance of the term is thought to have occurred in the northern Indo-European regions, where the bear was prevalent, and another name, (employed, perhaps, not to offend it), was substituted in the form of **ber-* 'brown'; that is, 'the brown one'. In Slavic the name invoked was *medv-*, from Indo-European **madhu* 'honey' and **ed* 'to eat', that is, 'honey eater'.

Taboo words may also account for seeming irregularities in phonological change. The name of the Spanish town of Mérida, for example, did not undergo the usual syncope of the post-tonic vowel as did other Spanish words of the *veride > verde* type, presumably because the result would have been *Merda* 'dung', a word that would have inspired little civic pride.

Unaccustomed morphological shapes in a given language are often replaced by more familiar ones through a process of **reinterpretation**. Loan words are readily subject to this process, as they are often unfamiliar or unanalysable in the adopting language. Reinterpretation of forms is generally referred to as **folk etymology**. One example involves the Middle English word *schamfast*, which meant in Old English 'modest'; that is, 'firm in modesty'. To make the word more familiar, the form *fast* was changed to *face* and the word came to be *shamefaced*. Middle English *berfrey* 'tower', with nothing to do with bell, has become *belfry* and associated with a *bell tower*. Words may change their shapes due to popular misanalysis, such as Middle English *napron*, which was misconstrued as *an apron* and became *apron*. Similarly, Middle English *nadder* became *adder*.

Among other characteristics of variation or style in language that may lead to semantic change (metonymy, synecdoche, hyperbole, emphasis, etc.), **metaphor**, a kind of semantic analogy, appears to be one of the most important aspects of linguistic behaviour. It involves a semantic transfer through a similarity in sense perceptions. Expressions already existent in the language are often usurped, giving rise to new meanings for old words – for example, *a galaxy of beauties*, *skyscraper*. Transfer of meanings from one sensory faculty to another occurs in such phrases as *loud colours*, *sweet music*, *cold reception*, and so on.

Linguistic borrowing

When a community of speakers incorporates some linguistic element into its language from another language, **linguistic borrowing** occurs. Such transferences are most common in the realm of vocabulary, where words may come and disappear with little consequence for the rest of the grammar. The borrowing language may incorporate some cultural item or idea and the name along with it from some external source; for example, Hungarian *goulash* and Mexican Spanish *enchilada* were taken into English through borrowings, and the words *llama* and *wigwam* were derived from American Indian languages.

When words are borrowed, they are generally made to conform to the sound patterns of the borrowing language. The German word *Bach* [bax] which contained a voiceless velar fricative [x], a sound lacking in most English dialects, was incorporated into English as [bɑːk]. English speakers adopted the pronunciation with [k] as the nearest equivalent to German [x]. In Turkish, a word may not begin with a sound [s] plus a plosive consonant. If such a word is borrowed, Turkish speakers added a prothetic [i] to break up the troublesome cluster. English *scotch* became Turkish [iskoʃ] and French *station* appears in Turkish as [istasjon]. Latin loan words in Basque encountered a similar kind of reconditioning: Latin *rege* became Basque *errege*, in that Basque words did not contain a word-initial [r-].

Only in relatively rare instances are sounds or sequences of sounds alien to the adopting language borrowed. The word-initial consonant cluster [kn-] does not occur in native English words, having been reduced to [n] in the past and persisting only in the orthography, but the word *knesset* 'parliament', from Hebrew has been taken over intact.

Borrowing is one of the primary forces behind changes in the lexicon of many languages. In English, its effects have been substantial, as is particularly evident in the extent to which the common language was influenced by Norman French, which brought hundreds of words into the language relating to every aspect of social and economic spheres, e.g.

> *Government and social order*: religion, sermon, prayer, faith, divine
> *Law*: justice, crime, judge, verdict, sentence
> *Arts*: art, music, painting, poet, grammar
> *Cuisine*: venison, salad, boil, supper, dinner

For the historical linguist, borrowings often supply evidence of cultural contacts where vocabulary items cannot be accounted for by other means. The ancient Greeks, for example, acquired a few words such as *basileus* 'king' and *plinthos* 'brick', non-Indo-European words from presumably a pre-Indo-European substratum language of the Hellenic Peninsula along with certain non-Indo-European suffixes such as *-enai* in *Athenai*.

Onomastic forms, especially those relating to **toponyms** such as names of rivers, towns and regions, are especially resistant to change and are often taken over by a new culture from an older one. Compare, for example, *Thames*, *Dover* and *Cornwall*, incorporated into Old English from Celtic, and American and Canadian geographical names such as *Utah*, *Skookumchuck* and Lake *Minnewanka*.

A sampling of the broad range of sources that have contributed to the English lexicon are: *bandana* < Hindustani; *gimmick* < German; *igloo* < Inuktitut (Eskimo); *kamikaze* < Japanese; *ukulele* < Hawaiian; *zebra* < Bantu; *canyon* < Spanish; *henna* < Arabic; *dengue* < Swahili; *lilac* < Persian; *xylophone* < Greek; *rocket* < Italian; *nougat* < Provençal; *yen* < Chinese; and many others.

The social contexts in which linguistic borrowing occurs have often been referred to as the **substratum**, **adstratum** and **super-stratum**. When a community of speakers learns a new language which has been superimposed upon them, as would have been the case when Latin was spread to the provinces of Spain or Gaul, and carry traces of their native language into the new language, we have what is commonly called **substratum influence**. The French numerical system partially reflecting multiples of twenty, for example, seems to have been retained from the Celtic languages spoken in Gaul prior to the Roman occupation; that is, from the Celtic substratum. **Adstratum influence** refers to linguistic borrowing across cultural and linguistic boundaries as would be found, for example, between French and Spanish, or French and Italian or German. Many words for items not found in the cultures of English colonists in America were borrowed from the local Indians under adstratum conditions such as *chipmunk* and *opossum*. Influences emanating from the **superstratum** are those in which linguistic traits are carried over to the native or local language of a region as the speakers of a superimposed language give up their speech and adopt the vernacular already spoken in the area. Such would have been the case when the French invaders of England gradually acquired English, bringing into the English language a number of French terms.

The degree of borrowing from language to language or dialect to dialect is related to the perceived prestige of the lending speech. Romans, great admirers of the Greeks, borrowed many words from this source, while the German tribes in contact with the Romans took up many Latin words. English borrowed greatly from French after the Norman Conquest, when the French aristocracy were the overlords of England.

While borrowing across linguistic boundaries is primarily a matter of vocabulary, other features of language may also be taken over by a borrowing language. It has been suggested that the employment of the preposition *of* plus a noun phrase to express possession in English, e.g. *the tail of the cat* versus *the cat's tail*, resulted from French influence: *la queue du chat*. In parts of France adjoining Germany, the adjective has come to precede the noun, unlike normal French word order. This is due to German influence, e.g. *la voiture rouge* has become *la rouge voiture* (cf. German *das rote Auto*).

Sometimes only the meaning of a foreign word or expression is borrowed and the word or words are translated in the borrowing. Such conditions are referred to as **loan translations**. The English expression *lightning war* is a borrowing from German *Blitzkrieg*. The word *telephone* was taken into German as a loan translation in the form of *Fernsprecher*, combining the elements *fern* 'distant' and *Sprecher* 'speaker'.

Language reconstruction

The systematic comparison of two or more languages may lead to an understanding of the relationship between them and whether or not they descended from a common parent language. The most reliable criterion for this kind of genetic relationship is the existence of systematic phonetic congruences coupled with semantic similarities. Since the relationship between form and meaning of words in any language is arbitrary, and since sound change is reflected regularly throughout the vocabulary of a given language, concordances between related languages, or lack of them, become discernible through comparisons. Languages that are genetically related show a number of **cognates** – that is, related words in different languages from a common source, with ordered differences.

When the existence of a relationship has been determined, the investigator may then wish to reconstruct the earlier form of the languages, or the common parent, referred to as the proto-language, in order to extend the knowledge of the language in question back in time, often even before written documentation. Reconstruction makes use of two broad strategies: the phoneme that occurs in the largest number of cognate forms is the most likely candidate for reconstruction in the proto-language; and the changes from the proto-language into the observable data of the languages in question are only plausible in the sense that such changes can be observed in languages currently spoken.

A phoneme that occurs in the majority of the languages under consideration but nevertheless cannot be accounted for in the daughter language by a transition from the proto-language based on sound linguistic principles, should not be posited in the proto-form. For example, if a majority of languages had the sound [ʧ] and a minority contained [k] in both cases before the vowel [i], one would reconstruct the phoneme /k/ and not /ʧ/, by virtue of the fact that /k/ before /i/ has often been seen to become /ʧ/, while the reverse never seems to occur.

All things being equal, it may still not be reliable to use the statistical method. Given the following languages

Sanskrit	*bharami*	bh-
Greek	*phero*	ph-
Gothic	*baira*	b-
English	*bear*	b-
Armenian	*berem*	b-

the predominance of [b-] suggests that it is the most likely candidate for the **proto-sound**. On the other hand, assuming that the simplest description is the best one and that phonological change occurs one step at a time, we might note that, given the various possibilities,

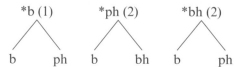

changes (1) and (2) require at least two steps to derive one of the reflexes ([b] > [p] >

[ph], [ph] > [p] > [b]), while change (3) requires only one step, that is, loss of aspiration and voiced to voiceless. The sound [bh-] appears to be the logical candidate for the proto-sound. Further enquiry would also show that Gothic and English reflect a common stage with [b-]. The predominance of [b-] in three of the five languages is then somewhat deceptive in terms of comparative reconstruction.

If we compare the words for *foot* in the Indo-European languages,

Latin	*pēs*
Greek	*pous*
Sanskrit	*pad-*
Old High German	*fuoz*
Old English	*fōt*
Church Slavonic	*noga*

we could disregard the form *noga* as being from another source (actually, it once meant 'claw') and consider either *[p] or *[f] as the initial proto-sound. As the Germanic branch of Indo-European has [f] where other languages have [p], we deduce a shift from [p] to [f] in Germanic and posit the proto-sound as *[p].

Through examination of the vocabulary of other related languages of the Indo-European family, such as Umbrian *peři* 'foot', Lettish *peda* 'sole of foot', Church Slavonic *pesi* 'on foot', we could posit the proto-vowel as *[e].

Considerations in establishing the earlier form of the final consonant might come from the Latin genitive form *pedis*, from the Greek genitive *πodos*, Gothic and Old English *fōt* – among others. The proto-consonant in root-final position seems certain to have been a dental plosive ([t̪] or [d̪]). Noting that Germanic languages generally have [t] where other Indo-European languages (Latin, Greek, Sanskrit) have [d], compare Latin *decem*, Greek *deka*, Sanskrit *daça* and English *ten*, we might conclude that the proto-language had *[d], which became [t] in Germanic. The proto-word for *foot* can now be constituted as *[ped-], a non-attested hypothetical construct of the proto-language.

In reconstructing the phonological forms of an earlier language, the linguist will also be concerned with the possible motivating factors underlying the change as these will often give some insight into the direction of the modification and ultimately help to establish the proto-form. Among the following Romance words one can readily see the influence exerted by environmental conditions which led to modifications in some of the languages.

Spanish	Portuguese	Italian	
agudo	agudo	acuto	'acute'
amigo	amigo	amico	'friend'

The appearance of voiced plosives [b, d, g] in Spanish and Portuguese, contrasted with their voiceless counterparts in Italian, suggests that the voiced surrounding (between vowels) gave rise to the voiced consonants and that Italian represents a more conservative or older stage of the language. There is no motivation for the process to have occurred the other way around, with the voiced sounds becoming voiceless in voiced surroundings.

Some features of a proto-language are beyond recovery through reconstruction. The identification of proto-sounds or grammatical and syntactic characteristics of a parent unwritten language after complete loss through merger or other means in the descendent languages may simply not be reconstructable. Without written records of the period, we could not identify or reconstitute vowel quantity in proto-Romance (Latin) speech. The phonological distinctiveness of vowel quantity in Latin is obvious from such words as *dĭcō* 'I dedicate' and *dīcō* 'I say', but the modern descendent languages display no such oppositions in vowel quantity.

Similarly, the proto-language, Latin, had a system of **synthetic passive** forms, e.g. *amor, amaris, amatur*, etc., which left no trace in the Romance languages, where

analytic passives developed as in Spanish *soy amado* and French *je suis aimé* 'I am loved', in conjunction with the Latin verb *esse* 'to be' and the past participle of the main verb. Without written records, such constructions in the proto-language would remain virtually undetected.

While the **comparative method** is the most powerful model for reconstruction, another – the **internal method** – may be utilized when comparative information is not available, or when the goal is to reconstruct earlier forms of a single language. The primary assumption underlying internal reconstruction is that many events in the history of a language leave discernible traces in its design. An examination of these traces can lead to a reconstruction of linguistic processes of change and thus to a reconstructed form of the language prior to events which changed it. By way of example, we can look at a few related forms in Spanish from the point of view of internal methods.

[nótʃe]	*noche*	'night'	[nokturnál]	'nocturnal'
[óʧo]	*ocho*	'eight'	[oktagonál]	'octagonal'
[díʧo]	*dicho*	'said'	[dikta jón]	'dictation'

There is an alternation among these related words between [ʧ] ~ [kt] but no apparent motivation for a change such as [t] > [kt], while, on the other hand, [kt] > [ʧ] would not be unexpected. The [k] was pulled forward into the palatal zone by anticipation of [t] (assimilation) to become [j] and then the [t] was palatalized by the preceding [j], i.e. [kt] > [jt] > [ʧ].

We can now reconstruct the forms in [ʧ] as [kt]:

*nókte
*ókto
*díkto

The undeciphered ancient Iberian language of Spain's Mediterranean coasts, known only from inscriptions and so far related to no other language, contains the following lexical forms:

baite   baikar
baiti   bainybar
baitolo   baiturane

Since the sequences *kar* and *-nybar* appear in other words, they are assumed to be separate morphemes, compare *balkar*, *antalskar*.

This suggests an alternation between *bait* and *bai*, in which the forms (allomorphs) occur as follows:

bai   +   consonant
bait   +   vowel

or

bai   > bait/__vowel

We are now in a position to reconstruct *baikar* as an earlier form of **baitkar*, **baitnybar*, *baitturane.*

The reduction of the sequences **[-tk-]* to [-k-], **[tn] > [n], [tt] > [t]*, is in accordance with the phonotactics of Iberian, which does not display sequences of plosive plus consonant as part of the language.

The results of this method of internal reconstruction are not verifiable, however, unless corroborating evidence can be found. In this case, we note that Basque has a form *bait* which, when combined with *-gare* becomes *baikare*, similarly, *bait-nago > bainago*, *bait-du > baitu*, avoiding sequences alien to Basque and suggesting an affiliation between the two languages.

Linguistic palaeontology

The lack of cognate forms of a particular word in related languages may suggest that the earlier and common stage of the languages in question had no such word and linguistic differentiation occurred before such a word was needed to represent the relevant idea or cultural entity. For example, few words for metals are common to the Indo-European family of languages. This kind of information means to the practitioner of **linguistic palaeontology** that

words for these items were unknown in the proto-language, which, therefore, must have broken up during the period of pre-metal usage or Neolithic times. Conversely, the various cognates for names of trees such as 'beech' suggest that the word existed in the proto-speech and that the homeland of the speakers was located in the vicinity of these trees.

The lack of specific words in the parent language for grains and vegetables but many words for animals, both domestic and wild, alludes to a heavy reliance on meat. Words relating to the level of the family are abundant, but those indicating a higher social order or political structure are not evident. Information of this kind may be used to reconstruct the cultural ambience and the geographical location of the proto-speakers.

Pitfalls abound, however, in the study of linguistic palaeontology; besides the fact that words may change their reference (a *robin* in England is not the same species as a *robin* in the United States), they are also readily borrowed from language to language. The word *tobacco*, common to the Romance languages, could easily lead to the false conclusion that the Romans smoked. The word itself appears to have spread from Spanish and Portuguese to the other Romance languages at a much later time.

Genetic classification of language

A major result of historical and comparative linguistic investigation has been the mapping of the world's languages into families and subgroupings within these families. When a given language has been shown to belong within the folds of a particular grouping as defined by linguistic relationships indicating a common descent from an earlier proto-language, it is said to have been classified genetically. The most popular method for expressing genetic relationships is the family-tree diagram consisting of the parent language as the starting point and branches indicating the descended languages.

Genetic classification has shown that the vast majority of the languages currently spoken in Europe belong to one of four families: Indo-European, Uralic, Caucasian and Basque.

Indo-European

The Indo-European family extended from Europe to India and in recent times has spread over much of the globe, including North America, South Africa, Australia and New Zealand as well as a number of pockets around the world. It is the most thoroughly investigated and best-known family of languages today and is derived from a hypothetical parent called **Proto-Indo-European**, thought to have been spoken in the third millennium BC. Judging from the distribution of the various Indo-European languages, their migratory chronologies, and from archaeological evidence (Kurgan Culture), the parent language is thought to have been spoken in the region of southeastern Europe.

The major groupings of the Indo-European family of languages are shown below. The **Germanic** branch of Indo-European has been divided into three subgroups: East Germanic languages are now extinct but the best known is Gothic, for which written texts exist from the fourth century AD. The North Germanic or Scandinavian branch includes Icelandic, Norwegian, Swedish, Danish and Faroese. West Germanic contains German, Yiddish, Dutch, Flemish, Frisian, Afrikaans and English. Afrikaans is a descendant of Dutch spoken by the early white settlers of South Africa, the Boers. Frisian is spoken along the northern coast of the Netherlands, the northwestern coast of Germany and on the Frisian Islands. English is derived from the languages of the Angles, Saxons and Jutes, Germanic tribes of northern Germany and southern Denmark who began settling in England in the fifth century AD. Yiddish is an offshoot of German and in some estimations, basically a dialect of German.

The once-widespread **Celtic** languages, extending from the British Isles to the Anatolian peninsula are now generally extinct except for those surviving in the British Isles and Brittany. The continental Celtic languages are best known from Gaulish spoken in France, and Hispano-Celtic of Spain and Portugal which have bequeathed some documentation. The insular branch has been segmented into two groups – Brythonic and Goidelic – of which the former includes Welsh and Breton, and the latter Irish Gaelic and Scots Gaelic. Breton is an offshoot of now extinct Cornish, spoken in Cornwall up to the eighteenth century.

Prior to about the third century BC, linguistic relationships on the **Italic** peninsula are obscure, but clearly attested after this time as belonging to the Indo-European family are the two groups Oscan-Umbrian and Latin-Faliscan. Latin, in time, displaced the other languages on the peninsula and gave rise to the Romance group of languages.

Indo-European speakers entered the **Hellenic** peninsula apparently sometime early in the second millennium BC, and at a later time we can speak of two main groups: East Greek, called Attic-Ionic, the languages of Attica and much of Asia Minor, and West Greek. All modern Greek dialects except Tsakonian are descendants of Attic, the classical speech of Athens.

Proto-Indo-European

Germanic   Celtic   Italic   Hellenic   Tocharian   Batic   Slavic   Indo-Iranian   Albanian   Armenian   Anatolian

Tocharian was an Indo-European language recovered from manuscripts of the seventh and eighth centuries AD. It was once spoken in what is now Chinese Turkestan.

Lithuanian, Latvian (or Lettish) and the now extinct Old Prussian make up the **Baltic** languages, situated along the eastern coast of the Baltic Sea. Lithuanian contains an elaborate case system much like that established for the parent Indo-European language.

The **Slavic** branch of the Indo-European family is composed of three sub-branches: East, South and West Slavic. East Slavic consists of Russian, Ukrainian and Byelorussian, the latter spoken in the western USSR around Minsk, while South Slavic is composed of Bulgarian, Serbo-Croatian, Slovene and Macedonian, among others. The West Slavic branch includes Czech, Slovak, Polish and Sorbian (Lusatian).

The **Indo-Iranian** branch was carried to India and Iran and consisted of two main branches: Indic and Iranian. The former appeared as Sanskrit, which subsequently evolved into the various Indo-European languages of India and Pakistan, such as Hindi, Urdu, Bengali and Gujarati, while the latter evolved early into the Avestan and Old Persian dialects. Various Iranian languages are in use today and include Pastu, Persian, Kurdish and Ossetic, among others.

With an obscure line of descent from the proto-language, present-day **Albanian** is spoken in Albania and parts of Greece and Yugoslavia. Some see the language as an immediate descendant of the poorly known Illyrian, and others of the little-known Thracian languages. A third view posits an independent line from Proto-Indo-European.

Located in the Caucasus and northeastern Turkey, the **Armenian** language also continues a line of descent from the proto-language not yet agreed upon. Some scholars see it as a separate offshoot; others, as related to the poorly understood Phrygian language of ancient southeast Europe.

Indo-European migrations into the **Anatolian** peninsula gave rise to Hittite and the related Luwian and Palaic languages. The little-known Lydian and Lycian are also thought to have been related to Hittite, the latter as a continuation of Luwian. All are extinct.

There are many other extinct languages such as Illyrian, Thrachian, Ligurian, Sicil and Venetic, whose scanty documentation points to membership in the Indo-European family, but their affiliations are unclear.

Uralic

Consisting of about twenty languages, the Uralic family is spread out across the northern latitudes from Norway to Siberia. There are two major branches: Samoyedic and Finno-Ugric. The former is spoken in the USSR, the latter includes Hungarian, Finnish, Estonian and Lappish. They are primarily agglutinating languages (see LANGUAGE TYPOLOGY) with an extensive system of cases. The proto-language may have been spoken in the northern Ural mountains about 6000 BC. The earliest texts are from the twelfth century AD, a Hungarian funeral oration.

Caucasian

Spoken in the region of the Caucasus mountains between the Black and the Caspian seas, this family of about thirty-five languages may actually consist of two independent groups: North Caucasian and South Caucasian. The situation is still far from clear. The languages are characterized by glottalized consonants, complex consonant clusters and few vowels. The earliest texts are in Georgian, a South Caucasian language, and date back to the fifth century AD.

Asia

Language families indigenous to Asia are: Altaic, Sino-Tibetan, Austro-Asiatic and Dravidian.

The thirty-five to forty-five languages of the **Altaic** family comprise three main branches – Turkic, Tungusic and Mongolian – although some specialists include Japanese and Korean in this family. Geographically, these languages are found primarily in Turkey, the USSR, China and Mongolia (and perhaps Japan and Korea). The family is characterized by agglutinating structures and some languages by vowel harmony. The earliest Turkish texts, the Lokhon inscriptions, date from the eighth century AD.

Second only to Indo-European in number of speakers, the **Sino-Tibetan** family contains about 300 languages in two major branches: Tibeto-Burman and Sinitic (Chinese). The Sinitic branch encompasses northern and southern groups of languages. The principal language of the north is Mandarin, and those of the south are Cantonese and Wu. Tibeto-Burman languages are found in Tibet, India, Bangladesh and Burma. The region contains great linguistic diversity and, as yet, the overall linguistic picture is unclear. The languages are generally tonal (see TONE LANGUAGES).

The **Austro-Asiatic** family consists of about 150 languages, in two major groupings: Munda, which includes languages of central and northeast India; and the larger, Mon-Khmer group with Cambodian (Khmer), Vietnamese, and many others of Cambodia and Vietnam, Burma and southern China. These languages are characterized by complex vowel systems, and some (e.g. Vietnamese) by tones. The Mon-Khmer branch may have been a unified language in the second millennium BC. The earliest texts date to the sixth century AD.

Found mainly in southern India, there are about twenty-three **Dravidian** languages. The most important, in terms of number of speakers, are Telegu, Tamil, Kannada and Malayalam. Dravidian peoples appear to have been more widespread once, but were displaced southward during the Indo-European incursions into northern India.

The languages are commonly agglutinating and non-tonal, with an order of retroflex consonants and word-initial stress.

Africa

The number of distinct languages spoken throughout Africa is estimated at about 1000, all of which belong to one of the four language families: Afro-Asiatic, Niger-Kordofanian, Nilo-Saharan and Khoisan.

Afro-Asiatic, often referred to by its older name of Hamitic-Semitic, is a group of languages spoken mainly across the northern half of the continent and throughout the Middle East, and consists of about 250 languages divided into six primary branches: Egyptian, now extinct except for the limited use of its descendant, Coptic, in religious rituals; Cushitic languages of Ethiopia, the Sudan, Somalia and Kenya; Berber, once widespread across the northern regions of the continent but now primarily restricted to pockets of speakers in Morocco and Algeria; Chadic, spoken in the region of Lake Chad and distinguished from the other groups through the use of tones; Omotic, considered by some to be a branch of Cushitic; and Semitic, the branch responsible in large part for the displacement of the Egyptian and Berber branches, spoken throughout the Middle East, across North Africa and in Malta. The three best-known members of this branch are Arabic, Hebrew and Ambaric. Pharyngeal sounds and consonantal roots characterize many of the languages.

The **Niger-Kordofanian** language family covers much of the southern half of the African continent and embodies many more languages than Afro-Asiatic. Of the two main branches, Kordofanian and Niger-Congo, the latter consists of especially numerous sub-branches. The languages are typically tonal (except Swahili) and usually agglutinating in structure. Perhaps the best-known subgroup of Benue-Congo, itself a branch of Niger-Congo, is Bantu, which consists of over one hundred languages, including Swahili, Zulu and Kikuyu. Found primarily in East and Central Africa, the **Nilo-Saharan** family contains several subgroups and about 120 languages. They are generally tonal and nouns are often inflected for case. This family is still relatively unexplored. Some of the languages are Masai (Kenya), Nubian (Sudan) and Kanuri (Nigeria).

Squeezed by Bantu expansion from the north and European expansion from the south, **Khoisan** speakers of approximately fifteen languages are now pretty well restricted to areas around the Kalahari Desert. Hottentot is, perhaps, the most widely known of the Khoisan languages. This family, unlike any other, is characterized by clicks of various kinds which function as part of the consonantal system. A few neighbouring languages of the Bantu sub-branch, such as Zulu and Xhosa, have borrowed these clicks from the Khoisan languages. They are also characterized by tones and nasal vowels.

Oceania

It is estimated that throughout Oceania there are between 1000 and 1500 languages spoken today, which are believed to belong to one of three language families – **Indo-Pacific**, **Australian** and **Austro-Tai**.

Of the estimated 700-plus languages of the Indo-Pacific family, nearly all of them are found on the island of New Guinea and some of the neighbouring islands. There appear to be at least fourteen branches, but classification is still in its infancy.

Approximately 200 **Australian** languages are each spoken by at least a few Aborigines, and another sixty or so are extinct. Located predominantly in central Australia, north-central Arnhem Land and north-western Australia, they are characterized by simple vowel systems and case markings.

Spread out from Madagascar to Hawaii, the geographically enormous **Austro-Tai** family contains an estimated 550 languages in two major and remotely related subgroups: Kam-Tai and Austronesian, the latter also known as Malayo-Polynesian. There are about fifty languages of the former spoken in Thailand, Laos, Vietnam and China, and about 500 of the latter, including Malagasy (Madagascar), Bahasa Indonesia/Malaysia (Malay), Tagalog, Fijian, Tahitian, Maori and Hawaiian. The classification, however, remains controversial.

American-Indian languages

While many relationships remain unclear with regard to Amerindian languages in the northern hemisphere, the following families have been identified, to which most of the languages belong: Eskimo-Aleut, Algonquian (northeast USA and Canada), Athapaskan (Alaska, western Canada and southwestern USA), Salish (Pacific northwest), Wakashan (Vancouver Island), Siouan (Great Plains), Uto-Aztecan (Mexico), Muskogean (southeastern USA), Iroquoian (eastern USA), Yuman (Baja California), Mayan (Mexico and Guatemala). It is estimated that nearly 400 distinct languages were spoken in North America in pre-Columbian times, 300 of these north of Mexico. Today, about 200 survive north of Mexico, but many of these are near extinction.

Along with Indo-Pacific languages, South American linguistic relationships are the least documented in the world, and estimates run from 1000 to 2000 languages, although only about 600 are actually recorded and 120 of these are extinct. Three major South American families which account for most of the known languages have been posited: Andean-Equatorial, whose principal language is Quechua; Ge-Pano-Carib, extending from the Lesser Antilles to southern Argentina; and Macro-Chibchan, covering some of Central America, much of northern South America and parts of Brazil.

Some language isolates

In some cases, a single language has no known relationships with other languages and cannot be assigned to a family. When this occurs, the language in question is called an **isolate**. Some languages that have not been related to any other are Basque (spoken in northeastern Spain and southwestern France), Ainu (of northern Japan), Koutenay (British Columbia), Gilyak (Siberia), Taraskan (California) and Burushaski (spoken in Pakistan). There are also the extinct Sumerian, Iberian, Tartessian, and many other languages known only from inscriptional material.

J.M.A.

Suggestions for further reading

Anderson, J.M. (1973) *Structural Aspects of Language Change*, London: Longman.

Anttila, R. (1972) *An Introduction to Historical and Comparative Linguistics*, New York: Macmillan.

Arlotto, A. (1972) *Introduction to Historical Linguistics*, Boston, MA: University Press of America.

Bynon, T. (1977) *Historical Linguistics*, Cambridge: Cambridge University Press.

Lehmann, W.P. (1962) *Historical Linguistics: An Introduction*, New York: Holt, Rinehart and Winston.

—— (1967) *A Reader in Nineteenth-Century Historical Indo-European Linguistics*, Bloomington and London: Indiana University Press.

Lockwood, W.B. (1972) *A Panorama of Indo-European Languages*, London: Hutchinson.

Robins, R.H. (1967) *A Short History of Linguistics*, London: Longman.

Ruhlen, M. (1975) *A Guide to the Languages of the World*, Language Universals Project: Stanford University.

History of grammar

The grammars that concern linguists today have developed the basis of a long tradition of describing the structure of language which began, in the West at least, with the grammars written by classical Greek scholars, the Roman grammars largely derived from the Greek, the speculative work of the medievals, and the prescriptive approach of eighteenth-century grammarians (Dinneen 1967: 166; Allen and Widdowson 1975: 47). These early grammars also form the basis for many grammars in use in schools in both native- and foreign-language teaching. In particular, the adaptation of Greek grammar to Latin by Priscian (sixth century) has been influential.

Priscianus major and minor

Priscian's work is divided into eighteen books. The first sixteen, which the medievals called *Priscianus major*, deal with morphology, and the last two, *Priscianus minor*, deal with syntax. Here, Priscian defined eight parts of speech (see Dinneen 1967: 114–15):

1 The **noun** is a part of speech that assigns to each of its subjects, bodies, or things a common or proper quality.
2 The **verb** is a part of speech with tenses and moods, but without case [the noun is inflected for case], that signifies acting or being acted upon . . .
3 The **participles** are not explicitly defined, but it is stated that they should come in third place rightfully, since they share case with the noun and voice and tense with the verbs.
4 The **pronoun** is a part of speech that can substitute for the proper name of anyone and that indicates a definite person.

5 A **preposition** is an indeclinable part of speech that is put before others, either next to them or forming a composite with them. (This would include what we would distinguish as 'prepositions' and 'prefixes.')

6 The **adverb** is an indeclinable part of speech whose meaning is added to the verb.

7 The **interjection** is not explicitly defined, but is distinguished from an adverb, with which the Greeks identified it, by reason of the *syntactic independence it shows and because of its emotive meaning.*

8 The **conjunction** is an indeclinable part of speech that links other parts of speech, in company with which it has significance, by clarifying their meaning or relations.

It is easy to see that a variety of bases for classification are in operation here: for instance, the noun is defined on the basis of what it refers to, a semantic type of classification, and also on formal grounds – it is conjugated for case; similarly, the verb is formally defined as that class of item which is conjugated for tense and mood, but also in terms of what it signifies. Considering the grammar as a whole, Dinneen (1967: 118–23) demonstrates that it was in fact an insufficient and often incorrect description even of Latin, largely because Priscian underemphasizes formal features while overemphasizing meaning in the process of classification.

Medieval and Renaissance grammars

Priscian's grammar exerted a powerful influence on grammarians of the medieval period. It was adjusted in the twelfth century by Peter Helias, a teacher at the University of Paris, to take account of changes which the Latin language had undergone since Priscian's time, and also to take account of the new interest in Aristotelian logic of the period (Dinneen 1967: 128). The only formal advance made in Helias's commentary was a development of Priscian's original distinction between **substantival nouns** and **adjectival nouns**, which became the now familiar distinction between nouns and adjectives (Dinneen 1967: 132).

In addition to the notion of parts of speech, the Greeks developed most of the grammatical concepts we are familiar with today, such as **gender**, **inflection**, **voice**, **case**, **number**, **tense** and **mood**, and the Romans retained them. Since Latin was of the utmost importance in the medieval period in Europe, as the language of diplomacy, scholarship and religion (Lyons 1968: 14), Latin grammar became a fundamental ingredient of the school system, and later grammars of the different vernacular languages were modelled on Latin grammars. The earliest non-Latin grammars include a seventh-century grammar of Irish, a twelfth-century grammar of Icelandic and a thirteenth-century grammar of Provençal – but it was during the Renaissance that interest in the vernacular became really widespread, and the writing of grammars of the vernacular truly common (Lyons 1968: 17). One of the most famous Renaissance grammars is the *Grammaire générale et raisonnée* published in 1660 by the scholars of Port Royal (see PORT-ROYAL GRAMMAR).

Early grammars of English

Grammars of English became common in the eighteenth century; the most famous of these being Bishop Robert Lowth's *A Short Introduction to English Grammar* (1762) and Lindlay Murray's *English Grammar* (1795). These early English grammars were written by scholars steeped in the Latin tradition, who felt that a grammar should provide a set of rules for correct language use, where 'correct' meant according to the rules of the grammar of Latin. Such grammars are known as **prescriptive** or **normative**, and are often compared unfavourably with the **descriptive** grammars produced by linguists, whose main concern is with how a language *is* used, rather than with how some people think it *ought* to be used. Thus Palmer (1971: 14–26) shows that many of the rules of prescriptive grammars, derived from Latin, are unsuitable to English, and that the reasons commonly given for observing the rules are unsound.

Take the rule which says that *It is I* is correct and that *It is me* is incorrect. The sentence consists of a subject *It*, a predicator *is*, which is a form of the verb BE, and a complement, *I/me*. In the case of Latin sentences containing the Latin verb ESSE ('be'), there is a rule according to which the complement must be in the same case as the subject. So if the subject is in the nominative, *ego* 'I', say, or *tu* 'you', then the complement must also be in the nominative, and we get in a play by Plautus *Ego sum tu tu es ego* 'I am you, you are I/me.' The Latin case system and the rules for using it are then imposed on English: it is said that *I* is nominative, and *me* is accusative. But then, following the Latin rule, we clearly cannot allow *It is me*, since *it* is nominative and *me* accusative; therefore, *It is me* is ungrammatical. Palmer argues that this proof suffers from two defects, one being the virtual absence in modern English of a case system, and the other being the unjustified assumption that Latin should be a model for English; had a case language other than Latin been chosen as a model (French, *C'est moi* 'It is me'), the rule for BE might have been different; in other words, even among case languages the conventions governing the use of the various cases differ (as do the cases available in different languages), but English is not a case language anyway.

'Traditional grammar'

According to Palmer (1971: 26) the 'most notorious example' of a normative grammar within the last century is J.C. Nesfield's *Manual of English Grammar and Composition*, 'first published in 1898 and reprinted almost yearly after that and sold in huge quantities at home and abroad'. Palmer

(1971: 41–106) draws on this grammar as he deals in detail with the terminology of so-called 'traditional grammar', showing, also, how these terms have been used in modern linguistics. The terminology refers to **grammatical units**, such as words, phrases, clauses and sentences on the one hand, and to **categories**, such as gender, number, person, tense, mood, voice and case on the other hand.

In traditional grammars, the **word** is rarely defined; it is simply assumed that everyone knows what a word is (see MORPHOLOGY). The **sentence** is then defined as a combination of words, and the **parts of speech** as **classes** of words. As we have already seen above, the parts of speech can then be defined according to the kind of reference they have, and also according to how the words of the various classes take on various forms according to rules of **inflection**, and combine in various ways, according to the rules of **syntax**.

According to most traditional grammars, there are eight parts of speech, namely noun, pronoun, adjective, verb, preposition, conjunction, adverb and interjection. Nesfield defines the **noun** as (see Palmer 1971: 39) 'A word used for naming anything', where 'anything' may be a person, quality, action, feeling, collection, etc. The **pronoun** is a word used instead of a noun; an **adjective** qualifies a noun; a **verb** is a word used for saying something about something else (Palmer 1971: 59). The **preposition** is often said to be used to indicate directionality or place; and the **adverb**, to say something about the time, place and manner of that about which something is said by the verb. The **conjunction** links sentences or parts of them together, and the **interjection** is a word or group of words used as an exclamation.

The sentence, as well as being a combination of words, is also often defined by traditional grammarians as the expression of a complete thought, which it can only do if it contains both a subject and a predicate.

In the most basic subject–predicate sentence, the **subject** is that which the sentence is about, and the **predicate** is what says something about the subject; an example would be *John laughed*, where *John* is subject and *laughed* is predicate. Dividing sentences into their parts like this is called **parsing** in traditional grammar. Subject and predicate need not, however, consist of single words, but may consist of several words (Palmer 1971: 80–1):

In Nesfield, for instance, we are instructed to divide a sentence first into subject and predicate, then to divide the subject into nominative and its enlargement and finally its predicate into finite verb, completion and extension, the completion being either object or complement or both. For the [sentence] *The new master soon put the class into good order . . .* the analysis is [see the table below]:

1. Subject			*2. Predicate*		
Nominative or Equivalent	Enlargement	Finite verb	Completion		Extension
			Object	Complement	
master	(1) The			into good	
	(2) new	put	the class	order	soon

If what looks like a complete sentence appears as a part of something larger which also looks like a complete sentence, a traditional grammar will call the former a **clause**. Clauses are combined in two different ways to form sentences; they may either be **co-ordinated**, as when a number of clauses of equal standing or importance are joined together by *and* (*I wore a blue shirt and you wore a green dress*), or one clause may be **subordinate** to another, which is known as the **main clause**. Thus in *I wore a blue shirt while you wore a green dress*, *I wore a blue shirt* is the main clause to which the rest is subordinate. If the subordinate clause does not have a **finite verb** – that is, a verb which gives a time reference – in it, traditional grammars call it a **phrase**. In *I don't like you wearing that*, therefore, *you wearing that* is a phrase, not a clause, because *wearing* does not contain a time reference (as we can see if we try to change the time reference of the whole sentence from present to past, the change will occur in the main clause, *I didn't like*, while no change will occur in the phrase *you wearing that*).

Of the grammatical categories of traditional grammar, some are thought to be categories applicable to the noun, others to the verb, and the inflections which affect the forms of the words derive from the categories. The traditional categories and their definitions are (adapted from Palmer 1971: 834):

- *Gender* – **masculine, feminine** and **neuter** – a feature of nouns, associated with male, female and sexless things.
- *Number* – **singular** and **plural** – a feature of nouns and verbs, associated with one thing and more than one thing respectively.

- *Person* – **first**, **second** and **third** – classifies the pronouns and is a feature of verbs.
- *Tense*, **present**, **past** and **future** – a feature of verbs, giving them a time reference.
- *Mood*, **indicative** and **subjunctive** – a feature of the verb associated with statements of fact versus possibility, supposition, etc.
- *Voice* – **active** and **passive** – a feature of the verb, indicating whether the subject is the doer of the action or the recipient of it.
- *Case* – **nominative**, **vocative**, **accusative**, **genitive**, **dative** and **ablative** – a feature of the noun, largely functionally definable (nominative for mentioning the subject, vocative for exclaiming or calling, accusative for mentioning the object, genitive for indicating ownership, dative for indicating benefit, ablative for indicating direction or agenthood; these definitions are not watertight and there are variations within languages) and translatable as *boy* (subject), *O boy, boy* (object), *of a boy*, *to* or *for a boy*, *from* or *by a boy*.

Other categories are applicable to languages other than English, and it is doubtful whether all of those listed are, in fact, applicable to English. They are, however, the ones often retained in traditional grammars. The definitions are not obviously helpful, as Palmer (1971: 84–97) convincingly demonstrates. For instance, in most languages grammatical gender has little connection with biological sex – in French, the moon, which we must assume is sexless, is grammatically feminine (*la lune*) and, in German, a girl is grammatically neuter (*das Mädchen*). However, the terms for the categories recur in descriptive linguistics.

The grammatical categories restrict the forms of words through **concord** or **agreement** and through **government**. A verb has to agree with the noun which is its subject in person and number. In English this only affects the verb when the subject is the third person singular, except for the case of the verb TO BE. The concept of government is necessary in languages like Latin and German to account for the way in which certain prepositions and verbs determine the case of the noun. In English, however, the 'cases' are at most three – **genitive**, or **possessive**, which is indicated by *'s* or by the *of* construction (but where *of* does not alter the form of the noun following it); and, in the case of the pronouns only, **nominative** and **accusative**, *I/me*, *he/him*, *we/us*. These are not governed by verbs or prepositions, but by the grammatical function of the word in the clause, i.e. whether it is subject or object.

Case grammar

The notion of case has continued to play a role in grammar and was especially foregrounded by Fillmore (1966, 1968, 1969, 1971a, 1971b), who developed his **case grammar** in reaction to the neglect of the **functions** of linguistic items within transformational grammars as represented by, for instance, Chomsky (1965). These were unable to account for the functions of clause items as well as for their categories; they did not show, for instance, that expressions like *in the room*, *towards the moon*, *on the next day*, *in a careless way*, *with a sharp knife* and *by my brother*, which are of the category prepositional phrase, simultaneously indicate the functions, location, direction, time, manner, instrument and agent respectively (Fillmore 1968: 21). Fillmore suggested that this problem would be solved if the underlying syntactic structure of prepositional phrases were analysed as a sequence of a noun phrase and an associated prepositional case-marker, both dominated by a case symbol indicating the thematic role of that prepositional phrase (Newmeyer 1980/1986: 103).

Fillmore's argument is based on two assumptions: **the centrality of syntax** in the determination of case; and **the importance**

of covert categories. In traditional grammar, **case** is morphologically identified; that is, cases are identified through the forms taken by nouns, and only then explained by reference to the functions of the nouns within larger constructions. However, some of the rules governing the uses of the case system cannot be explained very clearly in functional terms; the use of one case after certain prepositions, and another after certain other prepositions, seems a fairly arbitrary matter. In addition, not all languages mark case on the surface as clearly as, for example, Latin and German. In English, for instance, the singular noun only alters its form in the genitive with the addition of *'s*, and the personal pronouns alone have *I–me–my*, etc. (Palmer 1971: 15, 96–7).

However, in a grammar which takes syntax as central, a **case relationship** will be defined with respect to the framework of the organization of the whole sentence from the start. Thus, the notion of case is intended to account for functional, semantic, deep-structure relations between the verb and the noun phrases associated with it, and not to account for surface-form changes in nouns. Indeed, there may not be any surface markers to indicate case, which is therefore a **covert category**, often only observable 'on the basis of selectional constraints and transformational possibilities' (Fillmore 1968: 3); they form 'a specific finite set'; and 'observations made about them will turn out to have considerable cross-linguistic validity' (Fillmore 1968: 5).

The term **case** is used to identify 'the underlying syntactic–semantic relationship', which is universal (Fillmore 1968: 24):

> the case notions comprise a set of universal, presumably innate concepts which identify certain types of judgements human beings are capable of making about the events that are going on around them, judgements about such

matters as who did it, who it happened to, and what got changed.

According to Fillmore (1968: 21), the notions of subject and predicate and of the division between them should be seen as surface phenomena only; a sentence consists of a proposition, a tenseless set of verb-case relationships, and a modality constituent consisting of such items as negation, tense, mood and aspect (Newmeyer 1980/1986: 105). Sentence (S) will therefore be rewritten Modality (M) + Proposition (P), and P will be rewritten as Proposition (P) + Verb (V) + one or more case categories (Fillmore 1968: 24). The case categories, which Fillmore sees as belonging to a particular language but taken from a universal list of meaningful relationships in which items in clauses may stand to each other, are listed as follows (1968: 24–5):

- **Agentive (A)**: the case of the typically animate perceived instigator of the action identified by the verb [*John opened the door*; *The door was opened by John*].
- **Instrumental (I)**: the case of the inanimate force or object causally involved in the action or state identified by the verb [*The key opened the door*; *John opened the door with the key*; *John used the key to open the door*].
- **Dative (D)**: the case of the animate being affected by the state or action identified by the verb [*John believed that he would win*; *We persuaded John that he would win*; *It was apparent to John that he would win*].
- **Factitive (F)**: the case of the object or being resulting from the action or state identified by the verb, or understood as a part of the meaning of the verb [Fillmore provides no example, but Platt 1971: 25 gives, for instance, *The man makes a wurley*].
- **Locative (L)**: the case which identifies the location or spatial orientation of the state or action identified by the verb [*Chicago is windy*; *It is windy in Chicago*].

- **Objective (O)**: the semantically most neutral case, the case of anything representable by a noun whose role in the action or state identified by the verb is identified by the semantic interpretation of the verb itself; conceivably the concept should be limited to things which are affected by the action or state identified by the verb. The term is not to be confused with the notion of direct object, nor with the name of the surface case synonymous with accusative [*The door opened*].

The examples provided make plain the mismatch between surface relations such as subject and object, and the Deep-structure cases.

Fillmore (1968: 26, 81) suggests that another two cases may need to be added to the list given above. One of these, **benefactive**, would be concerned with the perceived beneficiary of a state or an action, while dative need not imply benefit to anyone. The other, the **comitative**, would account for cases in which a preposition seems to have a comitative function similar to *and*, as in the following example, which Fillmore quotes from Jespersen (1924: 90): *He and his wife are coming/He is coming with his wife.*

Verbs are selected according to their case frames; that is, 'the case environment the sentence provides' (Fillmore 1968: 26). Thus (1988: 27):

> The verb *run*, for example, may be inserted into the frame [____A], . . . verbs like *remove* and *open* into [____O + A], verbs like *murder* and *terrorize* (that is, verbs requiring 'animate subject' and 'animate object') into [____D + A], verbs like *give* into [____O + D + A], and so on.

Nouns are marked for those features required by a particular case. Thus, any noun occurring in a phrase containing A and D must be [+animate].

The case frames will be abbreviated as **frame features** in the lexical entries for verbs. For *open*, for example, which can occur in the case frames [____O] (*The door opened*), [____O + A] (*John opened the door*), [____O + I] (*The wind opened the door*) and [____O + I + A] (*John opened the door with a chisel*), the frame feature will be represented as + [____O(I)(A)], where the parentheses indicate optional elements. In cases like that of the verb *kill*, where either an I or an A or both may be specified, linked parentheses are used (1968: 28): + [____D(I)A)].

The frame features impose a classification of the verbs of a language. These are, however, also distinguished from each other by their transformational properties (Fillmore 1968: 28–9):

> The most important variables here include (*a*) the choice of a particular NP to become the surface subject, or the surface object, wherever these choices are not determined by a general rule; (*b*) the choice of prepositions to go with each case element, where these are determined by idiosyncratic properties of the verb rather than by a general rule; and (*c*) other special transformational features, such as, for verbs taking S complements, the choice of specific complementizers (*that*, *-ing*, *for*, *to*, and so forth) and the later transformational treatment of these elements.

Fillmore claims that the frame-feature and transformational-property information which is provided by a theory that takes case as a basic category of deep structure, guarantees a simplification of the lexical entries of transformational grammar.

With the list of cases go lists of roles fulfilled by the things referred to by the linguistic items in the various cases. One such list, organized hierarchically, is presented in Fillmore (1971a: 42):

(a) AGENT   (e) SOURCE
(b) EXPERIENCER (f) GOAL
(c) INSTRUMENT   (g) LOCATION
(d) OBJECT   (h) TIME

The idea behind the hierarchy is that case information will allow predictions to be made about the surface structure of a sentence: if there is more than one noun phrase in a clause, then the one highest in the hierarchy will come first in the surface form of the clause, etc. This explains why *John opened the door* (AGENT, ACTION, OBJECT) is grammatical while *The door opened by John* (OBJECT, ACTION, AGENT) is not. Newmeyer (1980/1986: 104–5) mentions this type of syntactic benefit as a second kind of benefit. Fillmore claims that case grammar gains from taking case to be a primitive notion. A third claim is made for semantic benefit. Fillmore points out that the claim made in transformational-generative grammar, that deep structure is an adequate base for semantic interpretation, is false. Chomsky (1965) would deal with *the door* as, respectively, deep-structure subject and deep-structure object in the two sentences:

The door opened
John opened the door

Case grammar makes it clear that, in both cases, *the door* stands in the same semantic relation to the verb, namely OBJECT: '*Open* is a verb which takes an obligatory OBJECT and an optional AGENT and/or INSTRUMENT' (Newmeyer 1980/1986: 104, paraphrasing Fillmore 1969: 363–9).

As mentioned above, Fillmore (1968: 30–1) claims that entering the cases associated with verbs in the lexicon would lead to considerable simplification of it, since many pairs, such as *like* and *please*, differ only in their subject selection while sharing the same case frames, + [——O + E], in the case of *like* and *please*. However, transformationalists (Dougherty 1970; Chomsky 1972c; Mellema 1974) were quick, in their turn, to point to the problems involved in subject selection, the rules for which would seriously complicate the transformational component (see Newmeyer 1980/1986: 105–6).

Fillmore (1977) lists a number of criticisms of case grammar, and his answers to them. A major worry is that no linguist who has developed a grammar in which the notion of case figures has been able to arrive at a principled way of defining the cases, or of deciding how many cases there are, or of deciding when two cases have something in common as opposed to being simply variants of one case (Cruse 1973; compare the cases indentified by Fillmore with those listed by Halliday, for example, for which see SYSTEMIC-FUNCTIONAL GRAMMAR). For example, Huddleston (1970) points out that in *The wind opened the door*, *the wind* may be interpreted as having its own energy and hence as being AGENT, or as being merely a direct cause of the door opening, and hence as INSTRUMENT, or as having a role which is distinct from both AGENT and INSTRUMENT, called, perhaps, 'force'. On yet another view, a case feature 'cause' can be seen as a feature of both agent and instrument (Fillmore 1977: 71). Fillmore thinks that this problem may be explained with reference to the notions of perspective and of meaning being relativized to scenes (see above). The wind is brought into perspective in the clause and is thus a **nuclear element**. And (1977: 79–80) 'perspectivizing corresponds, in English, to determining the structuring of a clause in terms of the nuclear grammatical relations'.

The obvious attractions of case grammar include the clear semantic relevance of notions such as agency, causation, location, advantage to someone, etc. These are easily identifiable across languages, and are held by many psychologists to play an important part in child language acquisition. In addition, case grammar was instrumental in drawing the attention of an initially sceptical tradition of linguistic study to the importance of relating semantic cases or thematic roles to syntactic descriptions.

Early grammars in America

As mentioned in the section above, Fillmore's **case grammar** was developed in reaction to early transformational-generative grammars. Prior to the appearance of these, most work on grammar published in the USA in the 1940s and 1950s was heavily influenced by Leonard Bloomfield's book, *Language* (1933/1935), which is characterized by a strict **empiricism**. Bloomfield believed that, if linguistics was to be scientific, it must confine itself to statements about observables, and grammars in this tradition are 'discovered' through the performing of certain operations, called **discovery procedures**, performed on a corpus of data. The data consist of speech, so the first operation the grammarian will need to perform is a phonological analysis of the stream of sound into phonemes (see PHONEMICS).

During the second stage of observation-based analysis, the phonemes will be grouped into types of structure. The smallest recurrent sequences of phonemes are called **morphs**, and those morphs which are phonemically similar and which are in **complementary distribution**, i.e. have no contexts in common, are members of the same **morphemes** (see MORPHOLOGY). So when we look at language at this level, it consists of strings of morphemes. But morphemic information, since it can only be gained *after* phonemic information has been discovered, cannot be drawn on in the discovery of phonemic information, since then the account would be circular. This consideration gives rise to the principle that the levels of linguistic description must not be mixed and to a strict 'bottom-up' one-way ordering of linguistic descriptions.

Having discovered the morphemes of a language, the task of the linguist is to discover how the morphemes may be combined; that is, to write the grammar. According to Bloomfield (1933/1935: 184) words can occur as larger forms, arranged by **modulation**, **phonetic modification**, **selection** and **order**, and any such arrangement which is meaningful and recurrent is a **syntactic construction**. By **modulation**, Bloomfield means intonation and stress, and by **phonetic modification** he means the kind of phenomenon by which *do not* becomes *don't*, and *run* becomes *ran*. The problems with these concepts are discussed in Palmer (1971: 119–23; see also MORPHOLOGY). Here I shall only discuss the two really structural ways of making syntactic constructions – namely, selection and order.

Basically, what is at issue here is that in uttering a syntactic structure we select morphemes and place them in order. This ordering is clearly very important – it matters a great deal whether I say *Brutus killed Caesar* or *Caesar killed Brutus*. In Latin it would not matter, because the names would be inflected for case (see 'Traditional grammar' above). So it looks as if, in English, word ordering performs the same kind of function that the morphemes that are used to give the Latin case endings perform in Latin.

Selection of morphemes, and combinations of selections, is equally important, since when the same form is selected in combination with a variety of forms that differ from one another, the resultant forms are also different from one another. For instance, when a noun, *milk*, is combined with an adjective, *fresh*, the resultant combination, *fresh milk*, is different from the result of combining *milk* with the verb *drink*, *drink milk*. In the first case, we have a noun phrase; in the second, a sentence in the imperative mood. So by combining a selected morpheme or group of morphemes with other, different, morphemes the linguist is able to discover different **form classes** (Palmer 1971: 123): '*drink milk* is different from *fresh milk*, and as a result of this difference we can identify *drink* as a verb and *fresh* as an adjective'. Thus the principle of complementary distribution influences discovery procedures in syntactic analysis, too; albeit in a different way, as here morphemes are said to be of the same syntactic type if they are not in complementary distribution; that is, if they display **distributional equivalence** (i.e. if they occur in the same range of contexts). For instance, any morpheme that can occur before the plural {-s} morpheme is a noun (Newmeyer 1980/1986: 9).

The notion of the form class was developed by Fries (1952/1957), who described English as having four major form classes defined according to the kinds of frames words of a class could enter into, as follows (from Allen and Widdowson 1975: 53–4):

- Class 1 words fit into such frames as:
  (The) _____ was good
  (The) _____s were good
  (The) _____ remembered the _____
  (The) _____ went there
- Class 2 words fit the frames:
  (The) 1 _____ good
  (The) 1 _____ (the) 1
  (The) 1 _____ there
- Class 3 words fit the frames:
  (The) 1 is/was _____
  (The) _____ 1 is/was
- Class 4 words fit the frames:
  (The) 3 1 is/was _____
  (The) 1 2 (the) 1 _____
  (The) 1 2 there _____

The numerals in the examples refer to words of the respective classes.

Although the correspondence is not complete, it is clear that there is a large amount of overlap between Fries' classes and nouns, verbs, adjectives and adverbs respectively; similarly, Fries recognized fifteen groups of **function words**, corresponding roughly to articles, auxiliaries, prepositions and so on. However, the perceived advantage of Fries' classification was its distributional character.

Because of the emphasis on classes, this kind of grammar is often labelled **taxonomic**.

There are very few actual descriptive syntactic studies available from the post-Bloomfieldians, largely because the processes of arriving at them are lengthy; and what there is has largely had to bypass its own prescribed procedures, since no complete morphemic analysis was ever worked out for English (or for any other language). Wells' (1947) 'top-down' immediate constituent analysis has, however, been widely applied (see Immediate Constituent analysis below).

Tagmemics

The term **tagmeme** was used by Bloomfield (1933/1935) to stand for the smallest unit of grammatical form which has meaning. A tagmeme could consist of one or more **taxemes**, 'the smallest unit [of grammar] which distinguishes meanings, but which has no meaning itself' (Dinneen 1967: 264). The notion of the tagmeme was developed largely by Kenneth Lee Pike (1967, 1982; but see also Longacre 1964, 1968–9/1970, 1976, 1983) into a full-blown grammatical theory, called tagmemics, although the assumptions on which the theory is based are such that language cannot be viewed as a self-contained system and that linguistics, therefore, cannot be self-contained either, but must draw on insights from psychology, sociology, anthropology, and so on (Jones 1980: 78).

Tagmemics is based on four major assumptions (Waterhouse 1974: 5):

(1) Language is . . . a type of human behavior;
(2) as such, it must be looked at in the context of and in relation to human behavior as a whole;
(3) an adequate theory of language is applicable to other types of behavior as well, and to combinations of verbal and nonverbal behavior; thus, it is a unified theory;

(4) human behavior is structured, not random;

and on four postulates which are universals claimed to hold for all human behaviour (Jones 1980: 79–80):

(1) All purposive behaviour, including language, is divided into units.
(2) Units occur in context.
(3) Units are hierarchically arranged.
(4) Any item may be viewed from different perspectives.

A **unit** may have various physical forms. It may be distinguished from other units by its distinctive features and by its relationships with other units in a class, sequence or system. The distinctive unit of any behaviour is called the **behavioreme**, and the verbal behavioreme is the sentence (Waterhouse 1974: 27).

The **context** in which a unit occurs often conditions its form, and any unit must be analysed in its context. So, in the grammar, sentences must be analysed in the context of the discourse in which they occur, because the choice of a particular discourse type (narrative, scientific, etc.) affects the choice of the linguistic units of which the discourse is composed.

The notion of the **hierarchy** is a cornerstone of tagmemic theory. By hierarchy is meant a part–whole relationship in which smaller units occur as parts of larger ones. Language is viewed as having a trimodal structuring: phonology, grammar and reference. Reference includes pragmatics and much of speech-act theory, while semantics is found among the meaning features of phonology and grammar, and in various aspects of reference (Jones 1980: 89). The modes and their levels interlock because units at each level may either be composed of smaller units of the same level or units from another level; and they may enter larger units at the same level or units at another level. The structurally significant levels of the **grammatical hierarchy** include morpheme (root), morpheme cluster (stem),

word, phrase, clause, sentence, paragraph, monologue discourse, dialogue exchange and dialogue conversation (Jones 1980: 80).

The **perspectives** from which items may be viewed are the static perspective, the dynamic perspective and the relational perspective. From a **static** point of view, an item is a discrete, individual item or **particle**. A **dynamic** point of view focuses on the dynamics of items: the ways in which they overlap, blend and merge with each other, forming **waves**. The **relational** perspective focuses on the relationships between units in a system. A total set of relationships and of units in these relationships is called a **field**. Language may be described from each of these perspectives, and descriptions adopting the different perspectives complement but do not replace each other (Jones 1980: 79–80; Pike 1982: 19–30).

Tagmemics is sometimes called **slot and filler grammar**. The unit of grammar is the **tagmeme**. The tagmeme is the correlation of a specific grammatical function with the class of items which performs that function (Waterhouse 1974: 5). In other words, a tagmeme occurs in a particular place, or **slot**, in a sentence, where it fulfils a **function**, such as subject, predicate, head, modifier, which items of its **class** (noun, noun phrase, verb, verb phrase, adjective) are capable of fulfilling. Both slot and class must be represented in a tagmeme, because they represent different types of information, neither of which can be derived from the other: it is not possible to know from the fact that *student* is a noun which function it fulfils in any one of its possible occurrences. Thus, *student* is modifier in *the student employees* (Jones 1980: 81), but subject in *The student went to bed early*. It is simultaneously noun in both cases. Instead of providing two independent statements about a sentence – one dividing the sentence into minimal classified units such as noun phrases and verb phrases, and the other assigning grammatical functions like subject and predicator to these units – tagmemics offers an analysis into a sequence of tagmemes, each of which simultaneously provides information about an item's function in a larger structure, and about its class, which can fulfil that function (Crystal 19/81b: 213).

The view of the tagmeme as a correlation between class and function reflects Pike's objection to the extreme distributionalism of mainstream Bloomfieldians, which he refers to as an **etic**, or exterior, **view of language** (Waterhouse 1974: 6): 'The etic view has to do with universals, with typology, with observation from outside a system, as well as with the nature of initial field data, and with variant forms of an emic unit.' Such a view, he thinks, needs to be supplemented with an **emic** view, 'concerned with the contrastive, patterned system of a specific language or culture or universe of discourse, with the way a participant in a system sees that system, as well as with distinctions between contrastive units'.

The method of analysing data in terms of positions in stretches of text and the linguistic units which can be placed in these positions – a basic technique in code-breaking – is useful for describing hitherto unknown languages. This has been one of the main aims of the **Summer Institute of Linguistics**, which Pike founded and which trains translators and field linguists in tagmemics. Waterhouse (1974) contains a comprehensive survey of the languages to which tagmemic analysis has been applied (see also Pike 1970).

While Longacre continues to employ a two-feature tagmeme, Pike adopts a four-feature view of the tagmeme in his later writings. He adds to slot and class the features role and cohesion. Jones (1980: 81) symbolizes the four features as a four-cell array:

slot	class
role	cohesion

Role may be, for example, actor, undergoer (patient), benefactee and scope, which in-

cludes inner locative, goal and some experiencer (cf. 'Case grammar' above). **Cohesion** here is grammatical cohesion, cases in which 'the form or occurrence of one grammatical unit is affected by another grammatical unit in the language' (Jones 1980: 81). It includes such agreement features as number agreement in English and gender agreement in many Romance languages.

Tagmemes are the constituents of **syntagmemes**, also known as **patterns** or **constructions**. Some tagmemes are obligatory and are marked +, while optional tagmemes are marked –. In the four-cell notation, the intransitive clause *the farmer walks* would have two tagmemes – the first representing *the farmer*; the second, *walks* (Jones 1980: 82):

Intransitive Clause	= +	Subject	Noun Phrase
		Actor	Subject number >

	+	Predicate	Verb
		Statement	> Subject number
			> Intransitive >

The arrow-like symbols in the cohesion cells above indicate cohesion rules such as (Jones 1980: 83):

Subject number: the number of the subject governs the number of the predicate.
Intransitive: mutual requirement of subject (as actor) and predicate tagmeme.

If the arrow is to the right, the tagmeme is the governing source; if the arrow is to the left, the tagmeme is the governed target.

The analysis can be summarized in a string such as IndeDecITClRt = + S:NP + ITPred: ITVP, which can be read as 'Independent Declarative Intransitive Clause Root consisting of obligatory subject slot filled by a noun phrase, followed by an intransitive predicate slot filled by an obligatory intransitive verb phrase' (cf. Waterhouse 1974: 11; Pike 1982: 82). There are a limited number of construction types at each of the grammatical **ranks** of sentence, clause, phrase, word and morpheme (Allen and Widdowson 1975: 57), and in this respect tagmemics bears a close resemblance to scale and category grammar (see SYSTEMIC-FUNCTIONAL GRAMMAR).

Tagmemes are the essential units of tagmemic analysis. But just as phonemes can be analysed into smaller units, which are classifiable as allophones of the phonemes, tagmemes can be analysed into smaller, etic, units called **tagmas**, which are **allotagmas** of the tagmeme (Crystal 1985: 304).

The ultimate aim of tagmemics is to provide a theory which integrates lexical, grammatical and phonological information. This information is presented in terms of **matrices**, networks of intersecting dimensions of contrastive features (Waterhouse 1974: 40). However, the view of language as part of human behaviour necessitates a recognition that language cannot be strictly formalized. No representational system could accommodate all the relevant facts of language, and tagmemics seeks a balance between the need for generalizations about language, and the particularities and variations found in it. Therefore, tagmemics accepts various different modes of representation for different purposes, and does not insist that there must be only one correct grammar or linguistic theory (Jones 1980: 78–9).

Tagmemics differed from most of the grammars of the period during which it was developed in looking beyond the sentence to the total structure of a text, and Longacre's work in this area is particularly well-known. Longacre (1983: 3–6) claims that all monologue discourse can be classified according to four parameters: contingent temporal succession, agent orientation, projection and tension.

- **Contingent temporal succession** refers to a framework of temporal succession in which some, usually most, of the events in the discourse are contingent on previous events.
- **Agent orientation** refers to orientation towards agents with at least a partial identity of agent reference through the discourse.
- **Projection** refers to a situation or action which is contemplated, enjoined or anticipated, but not realized.
- **Tension** refers to the reflection in a discourse of a struggle or polarization of some sort. Most discourse types can realize tension, so this parameter is not used to distinguish types of discourse from each other.

The parameters of contingent temporal succession and agent orientation provide a four-way classification of discourse types, with projection providing a two-way subclassification within each, as shown in the following matrix (from Longacre 1983: 4):

	+ Ag-orientation	– Ag-orientation	
+ Contingent temporal succession	Narrative	Procedural	
	Prophecy	How-to-do-it	+ Proj
	Story	How-it-was-done	– Proj
– Contingent temporal succession	Behavioural	Expository	
	Hortatory Promissory	Budget proposal Futuristic essay	+ Proj
	Eulogy	Scientific paper	– Proj

Narrative discourse tells a type of story which involves contingent temporal succession and agent orientation. But the story may present its event as having already taken place, as in story and history, or as projected, as in prophecy.

Procedural discourse, which is about how to do or make something, also has contingent temporal succession, but it does not have agent orientation because it focuses on the actions involved in doing something rather than on the doer of the actions. Again, the projection parameter distinguishes two types of procedural discourse: after-the-fact accounts of how something was done, and before-the-fact accounts of how to do something.

Behavioural discourse, which deals with appropriate behaviour, has agent orientation, but does not have contingent temporal succession. There are two types: one which deals with behaviour which has already taken place, as in eulogy; and one which prescribes/proscribes future behaviour as in hortatory discourse and a campaign speech – making promises about future actions.

Expository discourse, which expounds a subject, has neither agent orientation nor contingent temporal succession. It may, however, concern something which already pertains, as in the case of a scientific paper, or it may deal with something projected, as in the case of a futuristic essay.

Each type of discourse may be embedded within examples of the other types, and each type contains **main line** material, in which the main line of development takes place, and **supportive** material, which includes everything else.

The characteristic types of linkage of units displayed by each type of discourse are reflections of their classification on the contingent temporal succession parameter. Thus narrative and procedural discourse are characterized by **chronological linkage** (*and then*, *after that*, etc.), while behavioural and expository discourse have logical linkage (*if–then*, *because*, etc.). The presence or absence in different text types of lines of **participant reference** reflect their classification on the agent orientation parameter. Lines of participant reference are present in narrative and behavioural discourse, but absent in procedural and expository discourse. The projection parameter is reflected in tense, aspect and voice characteristics (Longacre 1983: 6–7). For example, past tense characterizes the main line of narrative discourse; present or future tense characterize the main line of procedural discourse (1983: 14). Longacre also claims that different types of monologue discourse display characteristic initiating, closing and nuclear tagmemes and that each tends towards a particular paragraph and sentence type (see Waterhouse, 1974: 45–8; and cf. TEXT LINGUISTICS), but the most widely known aspect of his work on discourse is probably his view that narrative is structured in terms of Peak, Pre-peak and Post-peak episodes.

Peak may be marked by: change in tense and/or aspect; sudden absence of particles which have marked the event line of the story; disturbance of routine participant reference; **rhetorical underlining**, such as parallelism, paraphrase and tautologies (see STYLISTICS); concentration of participants (stage crowding); and a number of other stylistic effects (see Longacre 1983).

Immediate constituent analysis

While most work on grammar in the Bloomfieldian tradition is based on a 'bottom-up' approach to grammatical analysis – beginning with the smallest linguistic unit and showing how smaller units combine to form larger ones – **Immediate Constituent analysis** (henceforth **IC analysis**) begins with a sentence – say, *Poor John ran away* (Bloomfield 1933/1935: 161) – the immediate constituents of which are *poor John* and *ran away*, and works gradually down through its constituent parts until the smallest units that the grammar deals with, which will be the **ultimate constituents** of a sentence, are reached; it is a 'top-down' approach. Both approaches are solely concerned with the surface structures of language; that is, they deal only with the language that is physically manifest, whether written or spoken, and make no mention of underlying structures or categories of any kind. The constituents may be represented hierarchically in rectangular boxes (Allen and Widdowson 1975: 55):

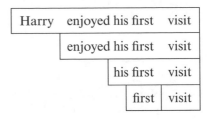

or in a Chinese box arrangement (Francis 1958; Allen and Widdowson 1975: 56):

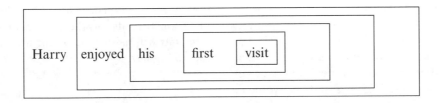

or lines between the constituents may be used (see Palmer 1971: 124).

A ||| young |||| man || with ||| a |||| paper | follow- ||| ed || the |||| girl ||| with |||| a ||||| blue ||||| dress.

Alternatively, parentheses can be used, either (as in Palmer 1971: 125), within the sentence:

(((A) ((young) (man))) ((with) ((a) (paper)))) (((follow) (ed)) (((the) (girl)) ((with) ((a) ((blue) (dress)))))))

or drawn below the sentence (Nida 1968; Allen and Widdowson 1975: 55–6). According to Palmer (1971: 125), however, the best way to show IC structure is to use a **tree diagram** similar to the sort also employed by generative grammarians and transformational-generative grammarians (see GENERATIVE GRAMMAR; FORMAL GRAMMAR).

The main theoretical issue involved in IC analysis is, of course, the justification of the division of a sentence into one set of constituents rather than another set. Why, for instance, do we class *a young man* and *with a paper* as constituents rather than *a young*, *man with a* and *paper*? The answer given by Bloomfield (1933/1935), Harris (1951) and other proponents of IC analysis was that the elements which are given constituent status are those which may be replaced in their environment by others of the same pattern *or* by a shorter sequence of morphemes. The technical term used for this substitution test is **expansion**.

Thus, in Palmer's sentence above, it is clear that *a young man with a paper* can be replaced by a single morpheme, like *he*, for example, while *a young man with a paper followed*, in contrast, would fail the substitution test. *He* here would obviously not be a suitable substitute for that part of the item constituted by *followed*; it would, however, be suitable as a substitute for any item of the kind that we might call a **noun phrase**, of whatever length; that is, for any item conforming to a specific pattern. Similarly, *followed the girl with a blue dress* can be replaced by a two-morpheme item like *sleeps*. A full analysis into ICs would give the tree shown below (Palmer 1971: 125).

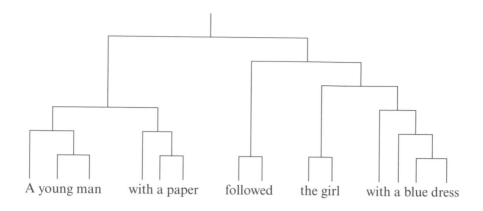

A young man   with a paper   followed   the girl   with a blue dress

Cutting sentences into their constituents can show up and distinguish ambiguities, as in the case of (Palmer 1971: 127) the ambiguous item *old men and women*, which may either refer to 'old men' and 'women of any age' or to 'old men' and 'old women'. The two different interpretations can be represented by two different tree structures:

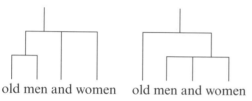

old men and women   old men and women

The type of expansion where the short item which can substitute for the longer item in the sentence is not actually part of that sentence item is called **exocentric expansion**. Another type, called **endocentric**, is more easily understood literally as expansion, since it works by the addition of more and more items to a head word in a group; for instance, *old men* above is an expansion of *men*, and further expansions would be *happy old men*, *the happy old men*, *the three happy old men*, *the three happy old men in the corner*, etc.

As the head word here, *men* is an item of the type normally classed as a noun, it would be reasonable to call it, and any expansion of it, a **noun group**, **noun phrase** or **nominal group**, and labelling items in grammatical terms clearly adds an extra, highly informative dimension to the division of sentences into constituents. Mere division into constituents of the ambiguous item *time flies* will neither show nor account for the ambiguity:

time flies

A labelled analysis, in contrast, would show that in one sense *time* is a noun and *flies* is a verb, while in the other sense *time* is a verb and *flies* a noun. The second sense allows for the joke (Palmer 1971: 132):

A: Time flies
B: I can't; they fly too fast

Labelled IC analysis is now commonly referred to as **phrase-structure grammar** – **scale and category grammar**, **tagmemics** and **stratificational grammar** are famous examples which go far beyond simple tree diagrams representing only sequential surface structure.

Pure IC, being developed by Bloomfield and his followers in the climate which then prevailed of strict empiricism, was meant to precede classification, but (Palmer 1971: 128)

> In actual fact a great deal of IC cutting can be seen to be dependent upon prior assumptions about the grammatical status of the elements. . . . For instance, even when we start with a sentence such

as *John worked* as the model for the analysis of *All the little children ran up the hill* we are assuming that both can be analysed in terms of the traditional categories of subject and predicate. This is implicit in the treatment of *All the little children* as an expansion of *John* and *ran up the hill* as an expansion of *worked.*

Of course, this fact does not prevent the notion of the immediate constituent from remaining very useful, and consequently drawn on frequently by contemporary grammarians; and IC, as conceived by Bloomfield (1933/1935), in spite of its shortcomings (see Palmer 1971), presented a great advantage over the haphazard 'methodology' of traditional grammatical classification and parsing.

K.M.

Suggestions for further reading

Dinneen, F.P. (1967) *An Introduction to General Linguistics*, New York: Holt, Rinehart and Winston.

Fillmore, C.J. (1968) 'The case for case', in E. Bach and R.T. Harms (eds) *Universals in Linguistic Theory*, New York: Holt, Rinehart and Winston.

—— (1977) 'The case for case reopened', in P. Cole and J.M. Sadock (eds), *Syntax and Semantics*, vol. 8, *Grammatical Relations*, New York: Academic Press.

Longacre, R.E. (1983) *The Grammar of Discourse*, New York and London, Plenum Press.

Newmeyer, F.J. (1980/1986) *Linguistic Theory in America: The First Quarter Century of Transformational Generative Grammar*, New York and London: Academic Press; 2nd edition 1986.

Palmer, F.R. (1971) *Grammar*, Harmondsworth: Penguin.

Pike, K.L. (1982) *Linguistic Concepts: An Introduction to Tagmemics*, Lincoln, NE and London: University of Nebraska Press.

Waterhouse, V.G. (1974) *The History and Development of Tagmemics*, The Hague and Paris: Mouton.

International phonetic alphabet

The **International Phonetic Alphabet (IPA)**
provides a means of symbolizing the segments and certain non-segmental features of
any language or accent, using a set of symbols
and diacritics drawn up by the **International
Phonetic Association** (also **IPA**). It is one of
a number of phonetic alphabets that have
been devised, but in terms of ease of use
and influence it is pre-eminent. Hundreds
of published works have employed it. It
is used throughout the world by a variety
of professionals concerned with different
aspects of speech, including phoneticians,
linguists, dialectologists, philologists, speech
scientists, speech and language therapists,
teachers of the deaf, language teachers and
devisers of orthographic systems.

Its origins lie in the alphabets used by
the forerunner of the IPA, the **Phonetic
Teachers' Association**, founded in 1886 in
Paris by Paul Passy (1859–1940). Since
then, a number of slightly differing versions of the Alphabet have been published
by the IPA. Three versions of the Alphabet
likely to be found in books, etc. on phonetics are 'Revised to 1951', 'Revised to 1979'
and 'Revised to 1993 (updated 1996)' – see
the reproductions in Figures 1–3. The latest version, 1993/1996, is based on a major
revision undertaken in 1989.

The guiding principles for the symbolization of sounds are set out in the *Handbook*
of the International Phonetic Association
(1999).

The aim of the Alphabet is to provide
the means for creating a *phonemic* transcription of speech; or, in the words of the
Association's first statement of its principles in 1888, 'there should be a separate
letter for each distinctive sound; that is,
for each sound which being used instead of
another, in the same language, can change
the meaning of a word'. Thus, the distinction between English *thin* and *sin* can be
indicated by the use of θ and s for the first
sound in each word. Often, however, the use
of symbols, with or without diacritics, can
provide an allophonic as well as a phonemic
(see PHONEMICS) notation. For example,
the labio-dental nasal in some English
pronunciations of the /m/ in *symphony* is
symbolized allophonically as [ɱ], since the
symbol exists for notating the phonemic
difference between that sound and [m]
in a language like Teke. Nevertheless, the
phonemic principle has sometimes been
set aside in order to allow the notation of
discernible allophonic differences within
a single phoneme. Thus, far greater use
is made in practice of the ɱ symbol for
notating the labio-dental nasal allophone of
/m/ or /n/ in languages like English, Italian
and Spanish than for showing a phonemic
contrast between /m/ and /ɱ/.

Since the Alphabet is designated as
phonetic, it has often been assumed that it

	Bi-labial	Labio-dental	Dental and Alveolar	Retroflex	Palato-alveolar	Alveolo-palatal	Palatal	Velar	Uvular	Pharyngeal	Glottal
Plosive	p b		t d	ʈ ɖ			c ɟ	k g	q ɢ		ʔ
Nasal	m	ɱ	n	ɳ			ɲ	ŋ	ɴ		
Lateral Fricative			ɬ ɮ								
Lateral Non-fricative			l	ɭ			ʎ				
Rolled			r						ʀ		
Flapped			ɾ	ɽ					ʀ		
Fricative	ɸ β	f v	θ ð s z ɹ	ʂ ʐ	ʃ ʒ	ɕ ʑ	ç ʝ	x ɣ	χ ʁ	ħ ʕ	h ɦ
Frictionless Continuants and Semi-vowels	w ɥ	ʋ	ɹ				j (ɥ)	(w)	ʁ		

CONSONANTS

	Front	Central	Back	
Close	i y	ɨ ʉ	ɯ u	(y ʉ u)
Half-close	e ø		ɤ o	(ø o)
Half-open	ɛ œ	ə ɜ	ʌ ɔ	(œ)
Open	a ɶ	a	ɑ ɒ	(ɒ)

VOWELS

(Secondary articulations are shown by symbols in brackets)

OTHER SOUNDS.—Palatalized consonants: ƫ, ɖ, etc.; palatalized ʃ, ʒ: ʆ, ʓ. Velarized or pharyngealized consonants: ɫ, d, z, etc. Ejective consonants (with simultaneous glottal stop): p', t', etc. Implosive voiced consonants: ɓ, ɗ, etc. ƈ fricative trill. ơ, ǫ (labialized θ, ð, or s, z). ʓ (labialized ʃ, ʒ). ʇ, ʖ, c, ʗ (clicks, Zulu c, q, x). ɺ (a sound between r and l). ŋ̍ Japanese syllabic nasal. ʩ (combination of x and ʃ). ʍ (voiceless w). ɪ, ʏ, ʊ (lowered varieties of i, y, u). ɐ (a variety of ə). o (a vowel between ø and o).

Affricates are normally represented by groups of two consonants (ts, tʃ, dʒ, etc.), but, when necessary, ligatures are used (ʦ, ʧ, ʤ, etc.), or the marks ‿ or ͡ (t͡s or t͡ʃ, etc.). c, ɟ may occasionally be used in place of tʃ, dʒ, and ʒ, ʑ for ts, dz. Aspirates plosives: ph, th, etc. r-coloured vowels: eɹ, aɹ, ɔɹ, etc., or eˑ, aˑ, ɔˑ, etc.; r-coloured ə: əɹ or əˑ or ɹ or ɑ or ɚ.

LENGTH, STRESS, PITCH.—ː (full length). ˑ (half length). ˈ (stress, placed at beginning of the stressed syllable). ˌ (secondary stress). ˉ (high level pitch); ˗ (low level); ˊ (high rising); ˏ (low rising); ˋ (high falling); ˎ (low falling); ˆ (rise-fall); ˇ (fall-rise).

MODIFIERS.— ˜ nasality. ˳ breath (l breathed ḷ. ˬ voice (ṣ = z). ʻ slight aspiration following p, t, etc. ˷ labialization (ŋ = labialized n). ˌ dental articulation (ṭ = dental t). ˴ palatalization (ż = ź). ˌ specially close vowel (ẹ = a very close e). ˓ specially open vowel (ẹ = a rather open e). ˔ tongue raised (e˔ or ẹ = e̝). ˕ tongue lowered (e˕ or ẹ = ɛ). ˖ tongue advanced (u˖ or ʉ = an advanced u, ṭ = ṱ). ˗ or ˗ (tongue retracted (i˗ or i̠, ṭ = alveolar t). ˮ lips more spread. Central vowels: ï (= ɨ), ü (= ʉ), ë (= ə˞), ö (= ɵ, ë, ö̈). ˌ (e.g. ŋ̍) syllabic consonant. ˯ consonantal vowel. ˒ variety of ʃ resembling s, etc.

Figure 1 The International Phonetic Alphabet (revised to 1951)

CONSONANTS (pulmonic air-stream mechanism)

	Bilabial	Labiodental	Dental, Alveolar, or Post-alveolar	Retroflex	Palato-alveolar	Palatal	Velar	Uvular	Labial-Palatal	Labial-Velar	Pharyngeal	Glottal
Nasal	m	ɱ	n	ɳ		ɲ	ŋ	ɴ				
Plosive	p b		t d	ʈ ɖ		c ɟ	k g	q ɢ		k͡p g͡b		ʔ
(Median) Fricative	ɸ β	f v	θ ð s z	ʂ ʐ	ʃ ʒ	ç ʝ	x ɣ	χ ʁ			ħ ʕ	h ɦ
(Median) Approximant		ʋ	ɹ	ɻ		j	ɰ		ɥ	w		
Lateral Fricative			ɬ ɮ									
Lateral (Approximant)			l	ɭ		ʎ	ʟ					
Trill			r					ʀ				
Tap or Flap			ɾ	ɽ				ʀ				
Ejective	p'		t'				k'					
Implosive	ɓ		ɗ				ɠ					
(Median) Click	ʘ		ʇ			ʗ						
Lateral Click			ʖ									

CONSONANTS (non-pulmonic air-stream mechanism)

DIACRITICS

- ˳ Voiceless n̥ d̥
- ˬ Voiced s̬ t̬
- ʰ Aspirated tʰ
- ⸴ Breathy-voiced b̤ a̤
- ˌ Dental t̪
- ˷ Labialized t̫
- ʲ Palatalized t̪
- ˗ Velarized or Pharyn- gealized t̴, ɫ
- ̩ Syllabic n̩ l̩
- ˶ or ˛ Simultaneous ʃ (but see also under the heading Affricates)
- ˄ or ⸜ Raised e˖, e̝, e̬ w
- ˅ or ⸝ Lowered e˕, e̞, e̞, ʁ
- ˖ Advanced u˖, u̟
- ˗ or ⸜ Retracted i̠, i-, t̠
- ¨ Centralized ë
- ˜ Nasalized ã
- ˞ ˞, ˞ r-coloured a˞
- ː Long aː
- ˑ Half-long aˑ
- ˘ Non-syllabic ŭ
- ˒ More rounded ɔ˒
- ˓ Less rounded y˓

OTHER SYMBOLS

- ɕ, ʑ Alveolo-palatal fricatives
- ʲ, ʒ Palatalized ʃ, ʒ
- ɺ Alveolar fricative trill
- ɺ Alveolar lateral flap
- ʄ Simultaneous ʃ and x
- ʃˢ Variety of ʃ resembling s, etc.
- ɨ = ɨ
- ʉ = ʊ
- ɜ = Variety of ə
- ɚ = r-coloured ə

STRESS, TONE (PITCH)

- ˈ stress, placed at beginning of stressed syllable:
- ˌ secondary stress:
- ˉ high level pitch, high tone:
- ˊ high rising:
- ˎ low level:
- ˏ low rising:
- ˋ high falling:
- ˴ low falling:
- ˇ rise-fall:
- ˆ fall-rise.

AFFRICATES can be written as digraphs, as ligatures, or with slur marks; thus ts, tʃ, dʒ: t͡s t͡ʃ d͡ʒ: t͡s t͡ʃ d͡ʒ. c, ɟ may occasionally be used for tʃ, dʒ.

VOWELS

	Front		Back
Close	i y	ɨ ʉ	ɯ u
Half-close	e ø		ɤ o
Half-open	ɛ œ		ʌ ɔ
Open	a œ		ɑ ɒ
	Unrounded		Rounded

Figure 2 The International Phonetic Alphabet (revised to 1979)

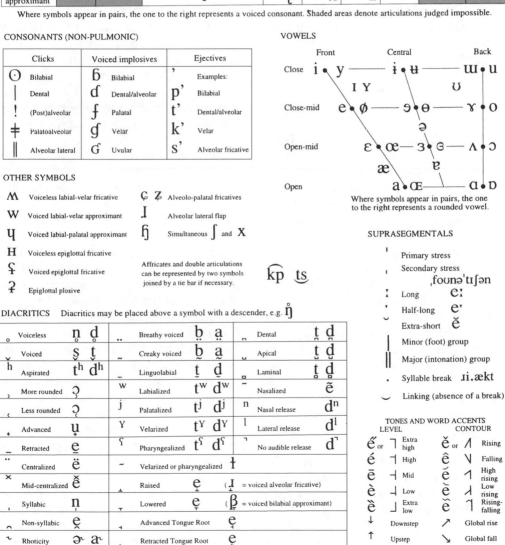

Figure 3 The International Phonetic Alphabet (revised to 1993, updated 1996)

should have the capacity to symbolize any human speech sound. This is not, nor has it ever been, its purpose, which is to facilitate the notation of phonemes in any of the world's 3000 or more languages. If such symbols (with or without diacritics) can also be used for an allophonic transcription (of whatever degree of phonetic narrowness), then this must be seen as a bonus.

There are many sounds which a human vocal tract can produce, but for which there are no IPA symbols – labio-dental plosives and alveolar approximants, for example. In such cases, an ad hoc method must be used by individual scholars for indicating such sounds. In due course, the IPA may decide to provide suitable symbols or diacritics.

It will be noticed that some 'cells' on the charts contain no symbols, and (on the 1993/1996 chart) some are shaded. There are two reasons for this: one, that, as far as is known, such a sound, even though it may be pronounceable, is not used as a separate phoneme in any language; and the other, that the sound is a physiological impossibility (e.g. a pharyngeal trill or a glottal lateral).

Almost all the symbols and diacritics are assigned specific, unambiguous articulatory or phonatory values. Thus, in the word *cease*, the /s/ at the beginning and at the end of the syllable are the same, and must therefore be written in the same way. This principle may lead to difficulties, however, in interpreting correctly the actual phonetic quality of an allophone. For example, the glottal plosive [ʔ], used by many speakers of English as an allophone of /t/ in certain phonological contexts, might be interpreted as alveolar rather than glottal from its phonemic symbolization as /t/. The use of the bracketing conventions – / / for phonemes, [ ] for allophones – could assist in resolving any ambiguity.

Where the same symbol is used for more than one sound (e.g. ʀ for the uvular tap as well as the uvular trill), the explanation lies either in the fact that no phonemic contrast exists between the sounds in question, or in the opinion of the IPA the contrast is

not sufficiently widespread in the world's languages to justify devising extra symbols.

The choice of symbols in the Alphabet is based as far as possible on the set of letters and punctuation marks of the Roman alphabet, with as few new characters as possible being used. A glance at any of the charts reveals that most of the symbols are either Roman or adjustments of Roman characters. For example, ɹ is a turned r, ɔ a turned c, ʕ a turned and modified question mark. Symbols from other alphabets have been introduced, for example θ and χ from Greek, but the typefaces have been adjusted so that they harmonize visually with the Roman characters. Only when the Roman alphabet has been exhausted have special, non-alphabetic characters been used: for example, ɞ for the open mid-central rounded vowel.

The 1993/1996 chart draws a distinction between two different types of consonants (pulmonic and non-pulmonic), vowels, 'other symbols' (i.e. other consonants), two sets of suprasegmental features and a series of diacritics. This arrangement is intended to reflect the practical requirements of the user.

For the symbolization of consonants, the traditional articulatory phonetic parameters of **place of articulation, manner of articulation** and **state of the glottis** are employed. The number of places of articulation varies: on the 1951 and 1993/1996 charts, there are eleven; on the 1979 chart, ten single places and two double places (labial-palatal and labial-velar). Voiceless sounds are placed towards the left-hand side of the 'cell', and voiced sounds towards the right. Alveolo-palatal on the 1951 chart is relegated to the category of 'other symbols' on the 1979 and 1993/1996 charts, although it has every right to be considered alongside palato-alveolar, etc., since it is needed in a phonemic notation of, for example, Polish.

Certain differences of terminology, especially for manners of articulation, are evident among the charts: cf. lateral non-fricative (1951) and lateral approximant (1979 and later), rolled (1951) and trill

(1979 and later), frictionless continuant and semi-vowel (1951) and approximant (1979 and later), etc. Non-pulmonic stop sounds (ejectives, implosives, clicks), which had been located under 'other sounds' in 1951, have their own rightful position amongst the consonants in 1979 and later. Other differences among the charts include the removal of certain symbols in 1979 (σ and ʔ, for example), a slightly different orientation of the central area of the vowel diagram, and the reintroduction of ɪ and ʊ as successors to ɩ and ɷ.

It is only in the symbolization of certain sounds that a consistent graphic principle can be noted. All the nasal symbols are constructed as variants of the letter 'n'; and all the retroflex symbols have a descender below the x-line which curls to the right. All the implosive symbols have a hook on top; and all ejectives have the apostrophe diacritic ' after the symbol.

For the transcription of disordered speech, a set of additional symbols and diacritics were made public in 1994: see *Handbook* (1999: 186–93). Even so, agreed notations are still lacking for certain other aspects of speech, particularly non-segmental features such as rhythm and voice qualities. In view of the emphasis on segmental phonemic notation in the Alphabet, however, such a gap is understandable.

A variety of IPA fonts are available for Macintosh and Windows computers. With the advent of a Unicode version of IPA symbols and diacritics, it will be possible to reproduce, both on screen and in print, the full set of IPA characters. A Braille version of the Alphabet exists.

The Alphabet may be written in two forms: either as handwritten approximations to the printed characters or in specially devised cursive forms. The IPA recommends the former. Examples of the latter can be found in the *Principles* (1949: 53).

Illustrations of the Alphabet for connected texts can be found in the specimens of twenty-nine languages included in the *Handbook*. All are accompanied by an explanation of the main phonological and phonetic features of the languages. Further illustrations can be found in the *Journal of the International Phonetic Association*.

A development of the Alphabet is **International Phonetic Spelling**, although it is little used nowadays. Its purpose is to provide an orthographic representation of a language such that the pronunciation and the spelling system are brought into closer line with each other. An example, taken from the *Principles*, is the spelling of the English clause *weak forms must generally be ignored* as 'wiik formz məst ʤenərali bi ignord'. International Phonetic Spelling, then, is an alternative, but more phonemically realistic, Roman-based reformed orthography. Examples of such an orthography for English, French, German and Sinhalese can be found in the *Principles* (1949: 51–2).

Another extension of the Association's Alphabet is **World Orthography**, which, like International Phonetic Spelling, is a means of providing hitherto unwritten languages with a writing system; see *Principles* (1949: 52). Its symbols are almost the same as those of the 1951 Alphabet.

M.K.C.MacM.

Suggestions for further reading

Abercrombie, D. (1967) *Elements of General Phonetics*, Edinburgh: Edinburgh University Press, pp. 111–32.

International Phonetic Association (1949) *The Principles of the International Phonetic Association*, University College London: International Phonetic Association.

—— (1999) *Handbook of the International Phonetic Association: A Guide to the Use of the International Phonetic Alphabet*, Cambridge: Cambridge University Press.

MacMahon, M.K.C. (1996) 'Phonetic notation', in P.T. Daniels and W. Bright (eds) *The World's Writing Systems*, New York: Oxford University Press, pp. 821–46.

Interpretive semantics

The label **interpretive semantics** describes any approach to generative grammar that assumes that rules of semantic interpretation apply to already generated syntactic structures. It was coined to contrast with **generative semantics** (see GENERATIVE SEMANTICS), which posits that semantic structures are directly generated, and then undergo a transformational mapping to surface structure. Confusingly, however, while 'generative semantics' is the name of a particular framework for grammatical analysis, 'interpretive semantics' is only the name for an approach to semantic rules *within* a set of historically related frameworks. Thus there has never been a comprehensive theoretical model of interpretive semantics as there has been of generative semantics.

After the collapse of generative semantics in the late 1970s, virtually all generative grammarians adopted the interpretive-semantic assumption that rules of interpretation apply to syntactic structures. Since the term no longer singles out one of a variety of distinct trends within the field, it has fallen into disuse.

Followers of interpretive semantics in the 1970s were commonly referred to simply as **interpretivists** as well as by the more cumbersome **interpretive semanticists**. A terminological shortening has been applied to the name for the approach itself: any theory that posited rules of semantic interpretation applying to syntactic structures is typically called an **interpretive theory**.

The earliest generative treatment of semantics, Katz and Fodor's (1963) paper 'The structure of a semantic theory', was an interpretive one. The goals they set for such a theory were to underlie all subsequent interpretive approaches to semantics and, indeed, have characterized the majority position of generative grammarians in general with respect to meaning. Most importantly, Katz and Fodor drew a sharp line between those aspects of sentence interpretation deriving from linguistic knowledge and those deriving from beliefs about the world; that is, they asserted the theoretical distinction between **semantics** and **pragmatics** (see SEMANTICS; PRAGMATICS).

Katz and Fodor motivated this dichotomy by pointing to sentences such as *Our store sells horse shoes* and *Our store sells alligator shoes*. As they pointed out, in actual usage, these sentences are not taken ambiguously – the former is typically interpreted as '. . . shoes for horses', the latter as '. . . . shoes from alligator skin'. However, they argued that it is not the job of a semantic theory to incorporate the purely cultural, possibly temporary, fact that shoes are made for horses, but not for alligators, and that shoes are made out of alligator skin, but not often out of horse hide (and, if they are, we call them 'leather shoes'). Semantic theory, then, would characterize both sentences as ambiguous – the only alternative, as they saw it, would be for such a theory to incorporate all of human culture and experience.

Katz and Fodor thus set the tone for subsequent work in interpretive semantics by assuming that the semantic component of the grammar has responsibility for accounting for the full range of possible interpretations of any sentence, regardless of how world knowledge might limit the number of interpretations actually assigned to an utterance by participants in a discourse.

Katz and Fodor also set a lower bound for their interpretive theory; namely, to describe and explain speakers' ability to determine the number and content of the readings of a sentence; to detect semantic anomalies; to decide on paraphrase relations between sentences; and, more vaguely, to mark 'every other semantic property that plays a role in this ability' (1963: 176).

The Katz/Fodor interpretive theory contains two components: the **dictionary**, later called the **lexicon** and the **projection rules**. The former contains, for each lexical item, a characterization of the role it plays in semantic interpretation. The latter determines how the structured combinations of lexical items assign a meaning to the sentence as a whole.

The dictionary entry for each item consists of a **grammatical portion** indicating the **syntactic category** to which it belongs, and a **semantic portion** containing **semantic markers**, **distinguishers** and **selectional restrictions**. The semantic markers and distinguishers each represent some aspect of the meaning of the item, roughly corresponding to **systematic** and **incidental** aspects, respectively. For example, the entry for *bachelor* contains markers such as (Human), (Male), (Young), and distinguishers such as [Who has never married] and [Who has the first or lowest academic degree]. Thus a Katz/Fodor lexical entry very much resembles the product of a componential analysis (see SEMANTICS; LEXIS AND LEXICOLOGY).

The first step in the interpretation of a sentence is the plugging in of the lexical items from the dictionary into the syntactically generated **phrase-marker** (see GENERATIVE GRAMMAR). After insertion, **projection rules** apply upwards from the bottom of the tree, amalgamating the readings of adjacent nodes to specify the reading of the node that immediately dominates them.

Since any lexical item might have more than one reading, if the projection rules were to apply in an unconstrained fashion, the number of readings of a node would simply be the product of the number of readings of those nodes which it dominates. However, the selectional restrictions forming part of the dictionary entry for each lexical item serve to limit the amalgamatory possibilities. For example, the entry for the verb *hit* in the Katz/Fodor framework contains a selectional restriction limiting its occurrence to objects with the marker (Physical Object). The sentence *The man hits the colourful ball* would thus be interpreted as meaning '. . . strikes the brightly coloured round object', but not as having the anomalous reading '. . . strikes the gala dance', since *dance* does not contain the marker (Physical Object).

In the years following the appearance of Katz and Fodor's work, the attention of interpretivists turned from the question of the character of the semantic rules to that of the syntactic level most relevant to their application.

An attractive solution to this problem was put forward in Katz and Postal's book, *An Integrated Theory of Linguistic Descriptions* (1964). They concluded that all information necessary for the application of the projection rules is present in the deep structure of the sentence or, alternatively stated, that transformational rules do not affect meaning. This conclusion became known simply as the **Katz–Postal Hypothesis**.

The Katz–Postal Hypothesis received support on several grounds. First, rules such as **Passive** distort the underlying grammatical relations of the sentence relations that quite plausibly affect its semantic interpretation. Hence, it seemed logical that the projection rules should apply to a level of structure that exists before the application of such rules, i.e. they should apply to deep structure. Second, it was typically the case that discontinuities were created by transformational rules (*look . . . up, have . . . en*, etc.) and never the case that a discontinuous underlying construction became continuous by the application of a transformation. Naturally, then, it made sense to interpret such constructions at an underlying level where their semantic unity is reflected by syntactic continuity. Finally, while there were many motivated examples of transformations which deleted elements contributing to the meaning of the sentence – the transformations forming imperatives and comparatives, for example – none had been proposed which inserted such elements. The rule which Chomsky (1957) had proposed to insert meaningless supportive *do* was typical in this respect. Again, this fact pointed to a deep-structure interpretation.

The hypothesis that deep structure is the sole input to the semantic rules dominated interpretive semantics for the next five years, and was incorporated as an underlying principle by its offshoot, generative semantics. Yet there were lingering doubts throughout this period that transformational rules were without semantic effect. Chomsky expressed these doubts in a footnote in *Aspects of the Theory of Syntax* (1965: 224), where he reiterated the feeling he had expressed in *Syntactic Structures* (1957) that *Everyone in the room knows at least two languages* and *At least two languages are known by everyone in the room* differ in meaning. Yet he considered that both interpretations might be 'latent' in each sentence. A couple of years later he gave his doubts even stronger voice, though he neither gave specific examples nor made specific proposals:

> In fact, I think that a reasonable explication of the term 'semantic interpretation' would lead to the conclusion that surface structure also contributed in a restricted but important way to semantic interpretation, but I will say no more about the matter here.
>
> (1967: 407)

In the last few years of the 1960s there was a great outpouring of examples from Chomsky and his students, which illustrated superficial levels of syntactic structure playing an important role in determining semantic interpretation. Taken as a whole, they seemed to indicate that any strong form of the Katz–Postal Hypothesis had to be false – everything needed for semantic interpretation was *not* present in the deep structure. And, while these facts might still allow one, legalistically, to maintain that transformations do not change meaning, the conclusion was inescapable that all of meaning is not determined before the application of the transformational rules For example, Jackendoff (1969) cited the contrast between (1a) and (1b) as evidence that passivization has semantic effects:

(1) (a) Many arrows did not hit the target
   (b) The target was not hit by many arrows

The scope of *many* appears wider than that of *not* in (1a), but narrower in (1b). Jackendoff also argued that the rule proposed in Klima (1964) to handle simple negation, which places the negative before the finite verb, is also meaning-changing. As he observed, (2a) and (2b) are not paraphrases; the negative in (2a) has wider scope than the quantifier, but the reverse is true in (2b):

(2) (a) Not much shrapnel hit the soldier
   (b) Much shrapnel did not hit the soldier

In fact, it appeared to be *generally* the case that the scope of logical elements such as quantifiers and negatives is determined by their respective order in surface structure. Thus, the scope of the word *only* in (3a) is the subject, *John*, while in (3b) it may be the whole verb phrase, or just the verb, or just the object, or just one subconstituent of the object:

(3) (a) Only John reads books on politics
   (b) John only reads books on politics

Observations like these led Chomsky, Jackendoff and others to propose rules taking surface structures as their input and deriving from those surface structures the representation of the scope of logical elements in the sentence. Nevertheless, it was clear that not *all* interpretation takes place on the surface. For example, in sentences (1a) and (1b), the semantic relation between *arrows*, *hit* and *target* is the same. Indeed, it appeared to be generally the case that the main propositional content of the sen-

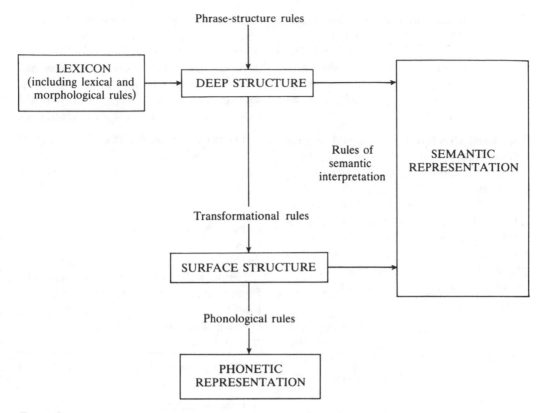

Phrase-structure rules

LEXICON
(including lexical and
morphological rules)

DEEP STRUCTURE

Rules of
semantic
interpretation

SEMANTIC
REPRESENTATION

Transformational rules

SURFACE STRUCTURE

Phonological rules

PHONETIC
REPRESENTATION

Figure 1

tence – the semantic relationship between the verb and its associated noun phrases and prepositional phrases – does not change under transformation. Hence, it made sense to continue to interpret this relationship at the level of deep structure.

By 1970, the term 'interpretive semantics' had come to be used most commonly to refer to the idea that interpretive rules apply to both deep and surface structures, rather than to deep structures alone. Nevertheless, Katz (1972) maintained only the latter approach to interpretive rules and, therefore, quite understandably, he continued to use the term 'interpretive semantics' to refer to his approach.

Figure 1 depicts the model that was posited by the great majority of interpretivists in the early 1970s. The most comprehensive treatment of the interpretive semantic rules in the early 1970s was Ray

Jackendoff's *Semantic Interpretation in Generative Grammar* (1972). For Jackendoff, as for interpretivists in general, there was no single formal object called a 'semantic representation'. Rather, different types of rules applying at different levels 'filled in' different aspects of the meaning. Jackendoff posited four distinct components of meaning, each of which was derived by a different set of interpretive rules:

(4) (a) *Functional structure* – the main propositional content of the sentence.

(b) *Modal structure* – the specification of the scope of logical elements such as negation and quantifiers, and of the referential properties of noun phrases.

(c) *The table of coreference* – the specification of which noun phrases in a sentence are understood as coreferential.

(d) *Focus and presupposition* – The designation of what information in the sentence is understood as new and what is understood as old.

Functional structure is determined by **projection rules** applying to deep structure. Thus, the semantic relationship between *hit*, *arrows* and *target* in (1a) and (1b) could be captured in part by rules such as (5a) and (5b), the former rule interpreting the deep-structure subject of both sentences as the semantic agent, and the latter rule interpreting the deep-structure object of both sentences as the semantic patient:

(5) (a) Interpret the animate deep-structure subject of a sentence as the semantic agent of the verb.

(b) Interpret the deep-structure direct object of a sentence as the semantic patient of the verb.

In **modal structure** are represented relationships such as those between *many* and *not* in (1a) and (1b). A rule such as (6) captures the generalization that the scope of the quantifier and the negative differs in these two sentences:

(6) If logical element A precedes logical element B in surface structure, then A is interpreted as having wider scope than B (where 'logical elements' include quantifiers, negatives and some modal auxiliaries).

Jackendoff's third semantic component is the **table of coreference**. Indeed, by 1970 all interpretive semanticists agreed that **interpretive rules** state the conditions under which anaphoric elements such as pronouns are understood as being coreferential with their antecedents. This represented a major departure from the work of the preceding decade, in which it was assumed that pronouns replace full noun phrases under identity with

another noun phrase by means of a transformational rule (see, for example, Lees and Klima 1963). In this earlier work, (7b) was derived from (7a) by means of a **pronominalization transformation** that replaced the second occurrence of *John* in (7a) by the pronoun *he* (the indices show coreference):

(7) (a) John$_i$ thinks that John$_i$ should win the prize

(b) John$_i$ thinks that he$_i$ should win the prize

However, by the end of the 1960s, it came to be accepted that such an approach faced insuperable difficulties. The most serious problem involved the analysis of the famous class of sentences discovered by Emmon Bach and Stanley Peters and therefore called **Bach–Peters sentences**, involving **crossing coreference**. An example from Bach (1970) is:

(8) [The man who deserves it$_j$]$_i$ will get [the prize he$_i$ desires]$_j$

If pronominalization were to be handled by a transformation that turned a full noun phrase into a pronoun, then sentence (8) would require a deep structure with an infinite number of embeddings, since each pronoun lies within the antecedent of the other:

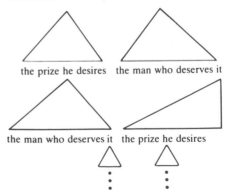

Interpretivists concluded from Bach–Peters sentences that infinite deep structures could be avoided only if definite pronouns were present in the deep structure, which, in turn, implied the existence of an interpretive rule to assign coreferentiality between those base-generated pronouns and the appropriate noun phrases. Such a rule was posited to apply to the surface structure of the sentence.

Finally, surface structure was also deemed the locus of the interpretation of such discourse-based notions as **focus** and **presupposition**. In support of this idea, Chomsky (1971) noted that focusable phrases are *surface structure* phrases. This point can be illustrated by the question in (10) and its natural responses (11a–c). In each case, the focused element is in a phrase that did not even exist at the level of deep structure, but rather was formed by the application of a transformational rule. Therefore the interpretation of focus and presupposition must take place at surface structure:

(10) Is John certain to win?
(11) (a) No, he is certain to *lose*.
    (b) No, he's likely not to be *nominated*.
    (c) No, the election won't ever *happen*.

While the Jackendovian model outlined above is the best-known 1970s representative of interpretive semantics, it proved to have a rather short life-span. In particular, by the end of the decade most generative grammarians had come to conclude that no rules of interpretation at all apply to the deep structure of the sentence. Chomsky (1975b) noted that, given the **trace theory** of movement rules (Chomsky 1973), information about the functional structure of the sentence is encoded on the **indexed traces** and carried through the derivation to surface structure. Hence, functional struc-

ture as well could be determined at that level. On the other hand, Brame (1976), Bresnan (1978) and others challenged the very existence of transformational rules and thus, by extension, of a level of deep structure distinct from surface structures. Given such a conclusion, then, necessarily all rules of semantic interpretation would apply to the surface.

The consensus by the end of the 1970s that semantic rules are interpretive rules applying to surface structure stripped the term 'interpretive semantics' of informational content. In its place, labels began to be used that referred to the distinctive aspects of the various models of grammatical analysis. Thus, the Chomskyan wing of interpretivism was commonly known as the **extended standard theory** (**EST**) or **trace theory**, which itself by the 1980s had developed into the **government–binding theory**. The rival interpretivist wing is now represented by such transformationless models as **lexical-functional grammar** (Bresnan 1982a) and **generalized phrase-structure grammar** (Gazdar *et al.* 1985).

F.J.N.

Suggestions for further reading

Chomsky, N. (1965) *Aspects of the Theory of Syntax*, Cambridge, MA: MIT Press.
—— (1972b) *Studies on Semantics in Generative Grammar*, The Hague: Mouton.
—— (1977) *Essays on Form and Interpretation*, New York: North Holland.
Newmeyer, F.J. (1980/1986) *Linguistic Theory in America: The First Quarter Century of Transformational Generative Grammar*, New York: Academic Press; 2nd edition 1986, especially chapters 4 and 6.

Intonation

Intonation is the term commonly used about variation in the pitch of a speaker's voice. In lay usage, it is often taken to include all such variation, and overall impressions of its effects are described variously in terms of characteristic 'tunes' or 'lilts', often with special reference to the speech of a particular individual or to that of a geographically defined group of speakers. As a technical term in linguistics, however, it usually has a more restricted application to those pitch phenomena which contribute to the meaning-defining resources of the language in question.

A distinction can be made between two types of language. In **tone languages** (see TONE LANGUAGES) such as Chinese, the choice of one pitch treatment rather than another serves to differentiate particular lexical items (as well as sometimes serving a suprasegmental function, as described below). In **intonation languages**, like English, it is said to have a **suprasegmental** function: the lexical content of any utterance is held to be already determined by other means (i.e. by its segmental composition), so that intonation has to be thought of as adding meaning of some other kind to stretches of speech which comprise more than one lexical item. Discovering what the stretches of speech are that bear those added meanings, and developing a conceptual framework to make explicit the particular contribution that intonation makes to meaning, are essential parts of the business of setting up systematic descriptions of the phenomenon.

It is fair to say that attempts to provide such intonational descriptions of particular languages have been rather less successful than those which relate to other aspects of linguistic organization like syntax and segmental phonology. Certainly the descriptive models that have been proposed have commanded less widespread assent. One general reason for this is doubtless the comparative recency of serious analytical interest in speech compared with the many centuries of scholarly preoccupation with written text. There are, however, two specific and closely related problems that could be said to have got in the way of progress.

The first derives from what is, in reality, a pre-theoretical definition of the phenomenon. The practice of starting with the nature of the speech signal as something susceptible to detailed physical analysis, and of proceeding on this basis to separate out pitch from other variables like **loudness** and **length** for individual attention, has tended to obscure the fact that simultaneous variation on all these parameters probably plays a part in our perception of all the functional oppositions whereby differences in intonational meaning are created. Moreover, a strong tradition which has encouraged making an initial separation between what have been referred to as **levels of pitch** and **levels of stress** has made it difficult to appreciate the essential features of the unified system in which they both work.

The difficulty of knowing just what physical features of the data to take note of, and of appreciating how those features combine as realizations of perceived linguistic contrasts, is necessarily bound up with the second of the two problems. This is the difficulty of setting up a working hypothesis about just how intonation can be said to contribute to meaning. An essential early step is to find a way of discounting those innumerable phonetic variables which do not enter into a language user's perception of a meaningfully contrastive event, and this depends upon there being some, at least provisional, agreement as to what those events are. It is well recognized that progress in the field of segmental phonology depended upon prior agreement as to what was in contrast with what. The elaboration of the notion of the **phoneme**, as an abstract, meaning-discriminating entity, which might be represented in performance by a whole range of phonetically different events, provided a means of incorporating that agreement into descriptive models. In the field of intonation, however, there has been – and there still remains – disagreement of a quite fundamental kind about how the contribution that intonation makes to meaning should be conceptualized.

While the common-sense perception of the 'word' as a carrier of a readily identifiable meaning provided a satisfactory start for setting up a working inventory of segmental phonemes, there is no comparable basis for determining if, and how, one intonation pattern is in opposition to another. Pre-theoretical judgements about the effects of intonation tend to be expressed in impressionistic terms, and commonly make reference to the attitudes, emotional nuances or special emphases that are judged to be superimposed upon what is being said.

A number of the descriptions that have been proposed have taken such judgements as their starting point and sought to systematize them. Among the better known are those of Kenneth Pike (1945) and O'Connor and Arnold (1961/1973). When the orientation is towards the needs of the language learner, the approach can be said to have the merit of providing characterizations of meaning that are comparatively accessible, precisely because they are grounded in common-sense apprehensions of what is going on. A weakness, even in the pedagogical context, is that the judgements are inevitably made about the attitudinal implications of a particular intonation pattern, produced on a particular occasion, in association with a particular combination of grammatical and lexical features. The meaning label, presented as the characterization of an attitude, turns out on inspection to refer as much to the lexis of the utterance and, more importantly perhaps, to the particular circumstances in which the utterance is assumed to have occurred, as it does to intonation.

This focus upon the purely local meanings of intonation in unique contexts seems unlikely to be helpful to anyone who wants to get access to the comparatively abstract component of meaning which the actual intonation pattern contributes. An unfortunate consequence of the attitudinal approach can easily be the highly specific pairings of one utterance with one intonation pattern. No insight is provided into the nature of the finite system of oppositions on which both successful learning and a satisfactory theoretical perspective could be said to depend.

Attempts to integrate intonation into the various theoretical models that are currently in use have been strongly conditioned by the central position given to sentential grammar. Linguists of the American structuralist school hoped that intonation would provide criteria for determining the grammatical structure of sentences. More generally, the task of handling intonation has been seen, essentially, as one of extending the mechanisms that have been postulated to account for regularities in the syntax of the unspoken sentence.

The relationship between intonation and grammar has been viewed in a number of different ways. At a comparatively unsophisticated level, it is easy to show that, in some cases, a sentence which is capable of two different interpretations, if presented simply as a written specimen, seems to lose its ambiguity when a particular intonation is supplied. On this basis it is possible to argue that intonation has a **grammatical function**, as the only perceptible differentiator of distinct grammatical structures. Not all intonational contrasts are easy to relate to grammatical differences, as these are usually understood, however. Neither can all sentences which are regarded as being structurally ambiguous be disambiguated by intonation. This apparently partial correspondence between the two features of the utterance has led some linguists to assign a **multifunctional** role to intonation, claiming that it sometimes indicates grammatical structure and sometimes does something else. Crystal's (1969) proposal, for instance, is that there is a continuum from what, in his terms, are the 'more linguistic' to the 'less linguistic' uses, where 'linguistic' seems to mean 'pertaining to sentence grammar'.

The concept of multifunctionalism is applied in a different way by Halliday (1967). The view of grammar as comprising three components, the **ideational**, the **interpersonal** and the **textual component** (see SYSTEMIC-FUNCTIONAL GRAMMAR; FUNCTIONALIST LINGUISTICS), provides a framework within which Halliday's rigorously defined theoretical position can be maintained. This is that all linguistic meaning is either lexical or grammatical. Except in some tone languages, therefore, meaning contrasts which are realized intonationally are to be treated as grammatical systems and integrated into the systemic network which relates all other contrasts to each other. The consequence of adopting this position is, naturally, to extend the scope of grammar beyond its usually assigned limits.

Within the interpersonal component fall some of the features that others have regarded as attitudinal. Of considerable importance is the fact that engagement with textual matters, by opening up the focus of interest to take in matters beyond the bounds of the sentence, makes it possible to show that some intonational meaning must be explained by reference to the overall organization of the discourse. The concept of **delicacy** is invoked to determine just which occurrences of the proposed intonational features are to be incorporated into the description: they are those which can be integrated into the grammar in its present state. While this gives a coherence to the description which is lacking from the multifunctional view, it has to be said that, in spite of the considerable complexity of the expository apparatus, it remains limited in its ability to account for the intonational features of naturally occurring speech.

Linguists working in the transformational-generative tradition have been strongly influenced by the work of Chomsky and Halle (1968) on the application of what are called **cyclical rules** to the distribution of stress (see GENERATIVE PHONOLOGY). The underlying contention of this work is that, if the syntactic rules that generate sentences are properly formulated, they will enable us to predict in advance the *normal* stress pattern of a sentence. The lexical items that are introduced into the sentence by the operation of transformational-generative type rules each has a rule-determined stress pattern. This pattern is then progressively modified in a way which can be consistently related to grammatical relationships holding among the components of the sentence.

There were problems in applying this approach as it was originally promulgated, and much attention was given to solving them, largely by revising the grammatical rule system on which the phonological end product was held to depend. The most consistent critic of this point of view and, by implication, of the work that has taken it for a starting point, is Bolinger (1985); for him, the relationship between grammar and intonation is 'casual' rather than 'causal'.

The concept of a **normal** or **neutral** intonation for any given sentence, which is crucial to the Chomsky and Halle approach, has had wide currency among linguists. Adopting it as part of a theory involves regarding such neutral realizations of the sentence as being in some generalizable sense in contrast with all other possible presentations.

Attempts to explicate the nature of this contrast have taken various forms. For some, versions which depart from the neutral form have some kind of added meaning: the neutral form is defined as the one which has no meaning not already present in the (unspoken) text. For others, the neutral form is the one which makes the least number of presuppositions. In less rigorously theoretical approaches, there is often an implication that the neutral version is statistically more likely to occur, or that it is the intonation pattern chosen when people read uncontextualized sentences aloud. There appears to be no evidence in support of either. Neither have we any reason to suppose that, by postulating a neutral–contrastive opposition in this way, we are any closer to achieving a detailed and workable characterization of intonational meaning.

A practical problem for the phonologist is the provision of transcription conventions which will make it possible to record intonation in written form. Early attempts, which sought to adapt the conventions of musical notation, overlooked the essentially phonemic nature of the phenomenon. The need to attend to a recurrent pattern of meaningful events rather than to all the incidental phonetic variation that accompanies it suggests that what is wanted is something of the same order of generality as a broad International Phonetic Script. The fact that no such analytical tool is in general use is obviously connected with the lack of consensus as to the function of intonation referred to above.

A well-canvassed discrepancy between an American predilection for 'levels' and a British preference for 'tunes' is only one aspect of the differences that exist concerning how the utterance should be divided into units for the purposes of describing its intonation. There is a rough similarity between the categories referred to in the literature as **sense units**, **breath groups**, **tone groups** and **contours**, but the similarities are deceptive; and the various ways of further segmenting into nucleus, head, tail, tonic, pre-tonic, etc. compound the differences. The important point is that, whether this is explicit or not, each formulation amounts to a starting assumption about how the underlying meaning system is organized.

An approach which takes the setting up of a tenable working account of that system as the essential first step is that which has come to be referred to as **Discourse Intonation** (Brazil 1985). In essence, the claim is that the communicative significance of intonation becomes accessible to investigation only when language is being used in the furtherance of some interactionally perceived purpose. The act of abstracting the sample sentence away from any context, and hence from any putative usefulness its production may have in the conduct of human affairs, isolates it from just those factors on which its intonational features depend. According to this, intonation is not to be regarded as a permanently attributable component of a sentence or of any other lexicogrammatical entity; it is rather one of the means whereby speakers both acknowledge and exploit the constantly changing state of understanding they share with a hearer or group of hearers. Its successful description depends, therefore, upon its being investigated in the context of a general theory of the organization of interactive discourse.

The stress patterns of words, as these are given (for instance) in dictionaries, provide a working template for the communicatively significant segment of discourse, the **tone unit**. Instead of being regarded as the elementary particles from which utterances are constructed, such citation forms are rather to be taken as the consequence of compressing all the features of the tone unit into a single word; in the atypical circumstances of speaking out a word merely to demonstrate its citation form, the word *is* the communicative unit.

In normal usage, however, the pattern is usually distributed over longer stretches of language. Thus, while the dictionary gives

^{2}after^{1}noon
^{1}evening

we commonly find, for instance,

^{2}afternoons and ^{1}evenings
^{2}evenings and after^{1}noons
^{2}saturday afternoons and ^{1}evenings

Afternoon, with what is often referred to as secondary stress (indicated as [2] in the above examples) followed by primary stress (indicated as [1]), and 'evening', with only primary stress, together represent the two subtypes of the tone unit. But instead of regarding these as exhibiting different degrees of 'stress', on a scale of difference which may have three, four or more such levels, the description highlights their functional significance.

This results in a recognition both of their functional similarity and their functional difference. They are similar in that, as prominent syllables and represented in transcripts thus

AFternoons and EVenings
EVenings and afterNOONS
SATurday afternoons and EVenings

they have the identical effect of assigning **selective** status to the word they belong to. They are different in that the so-called primary stress carries the principal phonetic evidence for what is perceived as a meaningful choice of **pitch movement**, or **tone**. The meaning component deriving from this latter choice attaches not to the word but to the complete tone unit. The class of syllables labelled **prominent**, therefore, includes, as a subclass, those with which **tone choice** is associated, the **tonic** syllables. To take the two kinds of event together as levels on a scale, and to include syllables which can be heard as having lesser degrees of 'stress', but which have no comparable function, is to obscure fundamental features of the way speech sound is organized to carry meaning.

The communicative value of **prominence** and **tone choice**, and of two other variables that are available in the tone unit, are all explicated by reference to the here-and-now state of speaker–hearer understanding. Co-operative behaviour is assumed on the part of both participants, so that speakers orientate towards a view of that state which they assume hearers share, and hearers, for their part, display a general willingness to go along with the assumption.

On this basis, an either/or distinction is made between words which, at the moment of utterance in the current interaction, represent a **selection** from a set of alternatives and are made **prominent**, and those for which the speaker assumes that there are currently no alternatives. The latter are made **non-prominent**. Thus, in a straightforward example, if meetings are known to take place on Saturdays, a response to

When is the meeting?

might be

on saturday afterNOON

But if meetings are known to take place in the afternoon, we might expect:

on SATurday afternoon

Generalization from simple examples like these to take in all the consequences of speakers' choices in the **prominent/non-prominent option** requires elaboration, at some length, of the notion of **existential value** (Brazil 1997), which is central to the discourse approach to intonation.

The significance of choice of **tone** is likewise related to the special state of convergence which is taken to characterize the relationship between speaker and hearer at a particular moment in time. The central choice here is between a **proclaiming tone**, which falls, and a **referring tone**, which rises. At its most general, this choice is associated with a projected assumption as to which of two aspects of the relationship is foregrounded for the duration of the tone unit.

Proclaiming tones present the content of the tone unit as if in the context of separateness of viewpoint, while referring tones locate it presumptively in a shared world. A fairly concrete example would be:

i'm going to a MEETing // on SATurday afterNOON

With referring tone in the first tone unit, and proclaiming tone in the second, the projected understanding would be that the hearer already knew that the speaker had a meeting to go to; what it was necessary to *tell* was when. If the tones were reversed, with proclaiming tone preceding referring tone, it would be a prior interest in what the speaker was going to do on Saturday afternoon that was taken for granted, and the fact that s/he was going to a meeting that was told. If both tone units were proclaimed, the speaker would be telling the hearer both what s/he was going to do and when s/he was going to do it.

Within each of the options, referring and proclaiming, there is a further choice of tone. A referring tone may be realized as either a **fall–rise** or a **rise**; and a proclaiming tone as either a **fall** or a **rise–fall**. Choice in these secondary systems depends upon the speaker's decision with respect to another aspect of the here-and-now state of the relationship. At any point in the progress of an interaction, it is possible to ascribe a **dominant** role to one of the participants. That is to say, one party or the other can be said to be exercising some kind of control over the way the interaction develops. On some occasions, like lessons, dominant status is assumed to be assigned by common consent for the duration of the interaction. On others, for instance during most social conversation, it is subject to constant negotiation and renegotiation. The second version of each of the pairs of tones serves to underline the speaker's temporary occupancy of dominant role. So the rising tone has the dual significance **referring + dominance**, and the rise–fall signifies **proclaiming + dominance**.

The set of meaningful variables associated with each consecutive tone unit is completed by two three-way choices, the most readily perceived phonetic correlate of which is **pitch level**. (Note that this is not to be confused with the **pitch movements**, or **glides**, which correlate with tone choice.)

The reference points for the identification of these variables are the prominent syllables, and the significance of each is once more explicated by reference to the immediate state of speaker–hearer understanding.

The first prominent syllable of each tone unit selects **high**, **mid** or **low key**. By selecting high key, the speaker can be said to attribute a certain expectation to the hearer and simultaneously to indicate that the content of the tone unit is contrary to that expectation. With low key, the expectation projected can be paraphrased roughly as that, in the light of what has gone before, the content of this tone unit will naturally follow. The mid-key choice attributes expectations of neither kind to the hearer.

The relevant pitch levels are recognized, not by reference to any absolute standard, but on a relative basis within the immediately surrounding discourse. The same is true of those which correlate with the other choice, **termination**. Provided there are two prominent syllables in the tone unit, pitch level at the second realizes **high**, **mid** or **low termination**. If there is only one prominent syllable in the tone unit, key and termination are selected simultaneously. Termination is the means whereby a speaker indicates certain expectations of her/his own about how the hearer will react to the content of the tone unit. Its function is closely related to that of key in that the responses expected are distinguished by the respondent's choice of key. Thus high termination anticipates high key, mid termination anticipates mid key, while with low termination the speaker signals no particular expectation of this sort.

This last consideration provides a basis for recognizing a further phonological unit, of potentially greater extent than the tone unit, the **pitch sequence**. A pitch sequence is a concatenation of one or more tone units which ends in low termination. Both on its own and in conjunction with special applications of the significance of key, the pitch sequence plays an important part in the larger-scale structuring of the discourse.

It will be noticed that the discourse model stops short of attempting to provide detailed phonetic prescriptions for the various meaningful features it postulates. This follows from the priority given to the meaning system. Useful investigation of just what hearers depend upon in their perception of one or other of those features is taken to be dependent upon prior recognition of how each fits into that system. It is to be expected that users will be tolerant of very considerable phonetic variation within the range that they will regard as realizations of the 'same' feature.

Variations in realization – which do not, however, affect the perception of oppositions within the system – seem likely to account for many of the so-called 'intonational' differences between dialects, and even among languages. The bulk of the systematic work carried out in intonation and related areas has concentrated upon English. There is a fairly common assumption that the intonation systems of different languages are radically different (Ladd 1996; Hirst and Di Cristo 1998): however, it is extremely difficult to compare like with like, because of inter-language differences such as word order. Only by applying a method of analysis which relates intonational choices functionally to what use speakers are making of the language can we hope to be in a position to compare like with like and to discover to what extent differences are differences of system and to what extent they are comparatively superficial matters of realization.

D.C.B. and R.C.

Suggestions for further reading

Brazil, D.C. (1997) *The Communicative Value of Intonation in English*, 2nd edition, Cambridge: Cambridge University Press.

Cruttenden, A. (1986/1997) *Intonation*, Cambridge: Cambridge University Press; 2nd edition 1997.

Halliday, M.A.K. (1985/1994) *An Introduction to Functional Grammar*, London: Edward Arnold; 2nd edition 1994.

Ladd, D.R. (1996) *Intonational Phonology*, Cambridge: Cambridge University Press.

Tench, P. (1996) *The Intonation Systems of English*, London: Cassell.

K

Kinesics

Kinesics is the technical term for what is normally known as **body language** – the systematic though possibly unconscious use of facial expressions, gestures and posture as components in speech situations. Although this visual system is important in so far as a large amount of information is often communicated by means of it, it is not usually held to fall within the scope of linguistics proper, which deals with specifically *linguistic* meaning, but rather to be part of the broader discipline of semiotics, which deals with signification in general (see SEMIOTICS). Nevertheless, it can be argued that it is not possible to provide adequate theories of naturally occurring conversation without paying attention to kinesics (Birdwhistell 1970), and the felt need to video-record, rather than simply sound-record conversations for study provides some support for this contention (see Gosling 1981b).

In addition, kinesics is of interests to linguists in so far as the theory and methodology of it has been consistently influenced by linguistics (Birdwhistell 1970; extract in Gumperz and Hymes 1986: 385). Thus Birdwhistell (1970) acknowledges his debt to structural linguistics, particularly to the model provided by Trager and Smith (1951), while Gosling (1981a, 1981b) works within the framework of functional linguis-

tics. Sapir (1927) refers to gestures as conforming to an elaborate and secret code that is 'written nowhere, known by none, and understood by all', and kineticists can be seen as attempting to unravel and write down this code.

Ekman and Friesen (1969) distinguish five major categories of kinesic behaviour (Gumperz and Hymes 1972/1986: 383; emphasis added):

> (1) **emblems**, non-verbal acts which have a direct verbal translation, i.e., greetings, gestures of assent, etc.; (2) **illustrators**, movements tied to speech which serve to illustrate the spoken word; (3) **affective** displays such as facial signs indicating happiness, surprise, fear, etc.; (4) **regulators**, acts which maintain and regulate the act of speaking; (5) **adaptors**, signs originally linked to bodily needs, such as brow wiping, lip biting, etc.

Both Birdwhistell and Gosling wish to exclude the first three of these categories from study, because, in Gosling's words, they are '*superimposed* on the basic communicative gestures which realise discourse functions' (1981b: 171). Adaptors are excluded because they do not appear to be used in a systematic way during speech events, so it is the regulators which form the centre of kinesic research.

Structural kinesics is based on the notion of the **kinesic juncture** (Birdwhistell 1970;

Table 1

Symbol	Term	Gross behavioral description
K#	Double cross	Inferior movement of body part followed by 'pause'. Terminates structural string.
K//	Double bar	Superior movement of body part followed by 'pause'. Terminates structural strings. . . .
K‡‡‡	Triple cross	Major shift in body activity (relative to customary performance). Normally terminates strings marked by two or more K#s or K//s. However, in certain instances K‡‡‡ may mark termination of a single item kinetic construction, e.g., in auditor response, may exclude further discussion or initiate subject or activity change.
K =	Hold	A portion of the body actively involved in construction performance projects an arrested position while other junctural activity continues in other body areas.
K/	Single bar	Projected held position, followed by 'pause'. Considerable idiosyncratic variation in performance; 'pause' may be momentary lag in shift from body part to body part in kinemorphic presentation or may involve full stop and hold of entire body projection activity.
K.	Tie	A continuation of movement, thus far isolated only in displacement of primary stress.

reprinted in Gumperz and Hymes 1972/1986: 393):

> The fact that streams of body behavior were segmented and connected by demonstrable behavioral shifts analogic to double cross, double bar and single bar junctures [see PHONEMICS] in the speech stream enhanced the research upon kinemorphology and freed kinesics from the atomistic amorphy of earlier studies dominated by 'gestures' and 'sign' language.

Birdwhistell provides the tentative table of kinemes of juncture shown in Table 1 (1970: 394).

In addition to the junctural kinemes, Birdwhistell isolates several stress kinemes which combine to form a set of suprasegmental kinemorphemes (1970: 399). However, he points out that it is not possible to establish an absolute relationship between kinetic stresses and junctures and linguistic stress and intonation patterns.

Birdwhistell's study referred to above is based on a two-party conversation, and it is interesting that his observation of the links between intonation and kinetics, and between linguistic and kinetic junctures, is confirmed in Gosling's (1981a, 1981b) analysis of a number of videotaped seminar discussions – that is, multiparty communicative events.

Gosling (1981b: 161) focuses on those 'recurrent features of non-vocal behaviour which . . . seem to be realisations of discourse function'. Kinetics is particularly important in the study of multiparty discourse, because in many discourse situations of this type, a speaker may address her/himself to any one or more of the other participants at any one time, so it is impossible from a sound recording alone to establish addresser–addressee relations (1981b: 162), and one loses important clues, such as the establishment of eye contact (1981b: 166), to how one speaker may select the next speaker, or to how an interactant may bid for a turn at speaking.

Gosling therefore argues that it would be useful to establish kinesics as a formal linguistics level, which would include 'all those meaningful gestures or sequences of gestures which realise interactive functions in face-to-face communicative situations' (1981b: 163); it is the function of **discourse kinesics** to isolate and describe these (1981b: 170). They include some changes in body posture and posture change accompanied by intent gaze at present speaker, both of which appear to be signals of a desire to speak next; Gosling calls these turn-claims (1981b: 173). During a speaker's turn, Gosling suggests that the following gestures are typically used by the speaker (1981b: 173–4; see also DISCOURSE ANALYSIS AND CONVERSATION ANALYSIS):

(a) a movement of body posture towards a mid-upright position, with head fairly raised at the start, oriented towards previous speaker;

(b) some movement of the dominant hand at some stage, either immediately prior to, or fairly soon after the start of the 'turn'.

(c) If the 'turn' is of some length, and becomes positively expository in nature, rather than being an extended reaction, there is a tendency to the formation of a 'box' with both hands (possibly associated with neutralisation of gaze, or loss of eye contact). It also seems a fairly strong rule that dominant hand gesture precedes both-hands 'box' in any turn. Towards the end of a natural turn (i.e. one that is not interrupted), the 'box', if there is one, tends to disappear, and hands move towards an 'at rest' position.

(d) Associated with (a) above is the intake of breath, either before a phonation, or very soon afterwards.

Gosling also makes observations about the possible functions of gaze in addition to its function as bid for a speaking turn or as next-speaker nomination. For instance, a speaker who frequently redirects her/his gaze appears to be seeking **feedback**, and if a speaker establishes eye contact with another person who, however, does not take up the offer of a turn at speaking, then the present speaker seems to take this as a signal that s/he may continue to speak (1981b: 174).

Although it is clear that some useful statements can be made about kinesic behaviour, and although no one would dispute the communicative import of such behaviour, kinesics is likely to remain a fairly peripheral area of linguistics, if it is included in that discipline at all, because of the great difficulties involved in providing fairly definitive statements about how non-vocal behaviour contributes to speech exchanges in a systematic way, and because it is difficult to perceive structure at the level of kinetic form.

K.M.

Suggestions for further reading

Abercrombie, D. (1968) 'Paralanguage', *British Journal of Disorders of Communication* 3: 55–9.

Birdwhistell, R.L. (1970) *Kinesics and Context: Essays on Body Motion Communication*, Philadelphia: University of Pennsylvania Press.

Gosling, J.N. (1981a) *Discourse Kinesics* (English Language Research Monograph, no. 10), University of Birmingham.

L

Language acquisition

Introduction

Language acquisition is the term commonly used to describe the process whereby children become speakers of their native language (first language acquisition) or children or adults become speakers of a second language (second language acquisition).

According to Campbell and Wales (1970), the earliest recorded study of first language acquisition was carried out by the German biologist Tiedemann (1787) as part of a general study of child development, and other important early studies include Charles Darwin's (1877) and Hippolyte Taine's (1877). However, 'it was in the superb, detailed study of the German physiologist Preyer (1882), who made detailed daily notes throughout the first three years of his son's development, that the study of child language found its true founding father' (Campbell and Wales 1970: 243).

Preyer's study falls within the period which Ingram (1989: 7) calls **the period of diary studies (1876–1926)**. As the name suggests, the preferred data-collection method during this period was the **parental diary**, in which a linguist or psychologist would record their own child's development. Few such studies were confined to the development of language alone;

Preyer, for example, makes notes on many aspects of development in addition to the linguistic, including motor development and musical awareness. The first published book to be devoted to the study of a child's language alone was C. and W. Stern's *Die Kindersprache* (1907; not available in English), and it is from this work that the notion of **stages** of language acquisition (see below) derives (Ingram 1989: 8–9). The diarists' main aim was to describe the child's language and other development, although some explanatory hypotheses were also made. These typically emphasized the child's 'genius' (Taine 1877: 258), an inbuilt language faculty which, according to Taine, enabled the child to adapt to the language which others presented it with, and which would, had no language been available already, have enabled a child to create one.

With the rising popularity of behaviourist psychology (see also BEHAVIOURIST LINGUISTICS) after World War I, **longitudinal** studies of individual children – studies charting the development of one child over a long period – came to be regarded as insufficient to establish what 'normal behaviour' amounted to. Different diaries described children at different intervals and concentrated on different features of their behaviour, so that it was impossible to make clear comparisons between subjects. Instead, **large-sample studies** were favoured, studies of large numbers of children all of the same age, being observed for the same length of time engaged in the same kind of behaviour. Several such studies, concentrating on several age groups, would provide evidence of what was normal behaviour at each particular age, and the results of the studies were carefully quantified. Environmental factors were carefully controlled, as behaviourism only took as scientifically valid statements about the influence of the environment on the child's development: hence, all the children in a given study would come from similar socioeconomic backgrounds, and each study would use the same numbers of boys and girls.

Ingram (1989: 11ff.) pinpoints the **period of large-sample studies** to 1926–57, the period beginning with M. Smith's (1926) study and ending with Templin's (1957) study. Studies carried out during this period concentrated mainly on vocabulary growth, mean sentence length and pronunciation. **Mean sentence length** (Nice 1925) was calculated by counting the number of words in each sentence a child produced and averaging them out. The results for these three areas for what were perceived as normal children (Smith 1926; McCarthy 1930; Wellman *et al.* 1931) were compared with those for twins (Day 1932; Davis 1937), gifted children (Fisher 1934) and lower-class children (Young 1941).

The publication of Templin's study, the largest of the period, took place in the year which also saw the publication of Noam Chomsky's *Syntactic Structures* (1957; see GENERATIVE GRAMMAR), which heralded the end of the reliance on pure empiricism and behaviourist psychology in linguistic studies (see BEHAVIOURIST LINGUISTICS). Chomsky's work and that of his followers highlighted the rule-governed nature of language, and a major focus of attention of many linguists working on language acquisition since then has been the acquisition of syntactic rules. From a post-Chomskyan vantage point, the large-sample studies seem

linguistically naive in their neglect of syntax, and of the interaction between linguistic units (Ingram 1989: 16): the information about the age at which particular auxiliary verbs or particular sounds are acquired do not reveal which grammatical or phonological rules are at work for an individual child. However, the need to establish norms, the need for careful selection of subjects and careful research design, and for measurement, still inform studies of language acquisition.

Ingram (1989: 21ff.) refers to the period from 1957 onward as **the period of longitudinal language sampling**. In typical studies of this kind (Braine 1963; Miller and Ervin 1964; Bloom 1970; Brown 1973), at least three carefully selected, talkative children, just beginning to use multi-word utterances, are visited and recorded at regular intervals by the researcher(s). Braine (1963) supplemented this methodology with diaries kept by the mothers of the children. A sample of three children is considered the minimum required if any statement about general features of acquisition is to be made (Ingram 1989: 21): 'if one is chosen, we do not know if the child is typical or not; if two, we do not know which of the two is typical and which is unusual; with three, we at least have a majority that can be used to make such a decision'.

Relation between child and adult competence

Researchers influenced by Chomsky's (1965) distinction between **competence** and **performance** – between the underlying ability which allows linguistic behaviour to take place and the behaviour itself – are not content simply to chart performance. Rather, the aim will be to arrive at statements concerning the state of the child's underlying linguistic competence at each stage of its development.

If the study of child language acquisition is to provide evidence for or against theories of adult grammar as well as insights into the child's progression towards it, the relationship between the child's grammar and that of the adult needs careful examination. While all approaches acknowledge differences between the child's and the adult system, the interpretation offered varies. The question is to what extent the child's system needs to be changed or restructured, and basically three answers can be given.

- **Strong continuity** (Weissenborn 1990; Poeppel and Wexler 1993; Hyams 1992, 1994, 1996) The child's system is basically identical to the adult one and differences relate not to the system as such, but to phonetics: some elements are not overtly realised. According to Hyams (1994: 45) children show evidence of syntactic operations at a stage when they fail to produce the lexical items which act as carriers of syntactic information. The fact that these elements typically lack referentiality or meaning could make them difficult to learn (see also Weissenborn 1992; Hyams 1996).
- **Weak continuity** Principles of Universal Grammar are available for the child at the onset of the acquisition process and guarantee that child grammars will fall within the borders of a natural language. The child's system, however, may deviate from the adult's: it may represent a subset of the adult system or be underspecified with respect to it. Structure-building approaches (e.g. Lebeaux 1988; Radford 1990; Guilfoyle and Noonan 1992; among others) identify mainly lexical heads in the child's language, but no projections of functional heads, i.e. of those heads which carry syntactic information such as AGR(eement) or T(ense). According to other researchers, however, this syntactic information is present but underspecified with respect to the adult system (Clahsen 1990; Clahsen *et al.* 1993/1994).
- **Discontinuity** At an early stage, the child's system is radically different from the adult's. Bickerton (1990) calls the initial system 'protolanguage' and claims that it has no proper linguistic characteristics – it consists of strings of words, as can be produced by trained chimpanzees – that is, principles of Universal Grammar have not yet emerged and children's grammars may fall outside the borders of possible natural languages.

A central question for discontinuity and weak continuity approaches is what brings about the change to the adult system. According to the **maturational theory of language acquisition** (Borer and Wexler 1987), principles of Universal Grammar are genetically programmed to become operational at different, determined stages, rather like other aspects of human development. This hypothesis accounts plausibly for the similar path of development for different individuals, but it fails to explain why children who are exposed to two languages from birth do not always develop both languages equally well; in some cases, one of the languages is stronger (Schlyter 1995).

An alternative explanation is the **Lexical Learning Approach** (Pinker 1984, 1989; Clahsen 1990), according to which grammar acquisition is driven by the learning of lexical items with their specifications, say, as mass noun or transitive verb with an agentive subject. For example, the lexical entry for *give* will specify three arguments, i.e. agent, theme and goal, realized as subject, direct object and indirect object respectively.

Sound perception and production

The first year of a child's life may be referred to as the **period of prelinguistic development** (Ingram 1989: 83ff.), since children do not normally begin to produce words until they are a year old. The main reason for studying prelinguistic development as part of a theory of child language acquisition is to try to establish which links, if any, there are between the prelinguistic period and the period of linguistic development.

While most parts of an infant's body need to grow and develop during its childhood, the inner ear is fully formed and fully grown at birth, and it is thought that infants in the womb are able to hear. Certainly, they are able within a few weeks of birth to discriminate human voices from other sounds, and by about two months they can distinguish angry from friendly voice qualities. Experiments have been devised using the **non-nutritive sucking technique** in which an infant is given a device to suck that measures the rate of sucking; a sound is played to the infant until the sucking rate stabilizes; the sound is changed; if the infant notices the sound change, the sucking rate will alter. Such experiments have shown that, as early as at one month, infants are able to distinguish voiced from unvoiced sound segments (Eimas *et al.* 1971), and by seven weeks they can distinguish intonation contours and places of articulation (Morse 1972; Clark and Clark 1977: 376–7). They also show perceptual constancy: they focus on a vowel or consonant and disregard incidental variation (Vihman 1996: 71). In the first six months of life, infants can accommodate to any language-specific selection from the universal set of phonetic categories. Changes towards the native language can be observed in the second half of the first year. It is still controversial how the shift towards the native language takes place. Some factors which may guide the infant in this process are according to Vihman (1996: 96) the affective value of the mother's voice and of the intonation patterns used in interaction with children, as well as growing familiarity with the prosody, the phonotactic structure and frequently occurring word forms.

This ability to discriminate human voice sound qualities does not, of course, amount to knowledge of human language: infants still need to learn which differences between sounds are meaningful in their language, which combinations of sounds are possible and which are not possible in their language, how to use intonation contours and much else besides. However, it does indicate that human infants are tuned in to human language from very early on in life.

Sound production

The only sounds a newborn baby makes, apart from possible sneezes, coughs, etc., are crying sounds. By three months old, the child will have added to these **cooing** sounds, composed of velar consonants and high vowels, while by six months, **babbling** sounds, composed of repeated syllables (*bababa*, *dadada*, *mamama*, etc.) have usually appeared. Vihman (1996: 118) observes that 'regressions' to apparently 'earlier' forms are observed together with changes in the child's capacity for sound production. So, for example, 'grunts' occur shortly before the emergence of reduplicated babbling as well as shortly before the use of words. Evidence for the influence of the language of the environment has been observed at around eight months for prosodic features, and around ten months for vowels and consonants. These findings suggest that a link between perceptual and articulatory processes develops in the second half of the first year (Vihman 1996: 119).

The changes in the child's vocalizations during the first year of its life are connected with gradual physiological changes in the child's speech apparatus, which does not begin to resemble its adult shape until the child is around six months old. Until then, the child's vocal tract resembles that of an adult chimpanzee (Lieberman 1975). The vocal tract and pharynx (see ARTICULATORY PHONETICS) are shorter than the adult's, and the tract is wider in relation to its length. Since the baby has no teeth, the oral cavity is also flatter than the adult's (Goldstein 1979). The tongue fills most of the oral cavity, and its movement is limited by this fact and by immaturity of its muscles. The infant has no cavity behind the back of the tongue, and its velum operates in such a way that breathing takes place primarily through the nose, not the mouth. This allows the baby to breathe while it is sucking, and causes its vocalizations to be highly nasalized and velarized.

Some people speak to babies and young children in a particular way known as **motherese**, **baby talk**, **care-taker speech** or **care-giver speech**. For many English speakers, this is characterized by (Kaye 1980) high pitch, a large range of frequencies, highly varied intonation, special words like *choo-choo* and *quack-quack*, short, grammatically simple utterances, repetition and restriction of topics to those relevant to the child's world. However, it is by no means the case that all English-speaking adults speak in this way to babies and young children; many employ normal pitch, frequency range, intonation patterns and vocabulary. It is probably true that most adults restrict topics when addressing babies and young children, but then all topics of all conversations are geared to the occasion and to the interactants.

Opinions vary on whether there is a connection between the babbling stage and the later acquisition of the adult sound system. According to the **continuity approach**, the babbling sounds are direct precursors of speech sounds proper, while according to the **discontinuity approach** there is no such direct relation (Clark and Clark 1977: 389). Mowrer (1960) has argued in favour of the continuity hypothesis that babbling contains all the sounds found in all human languages, but that through selective reinforcement by parents and others this sound repertoire is narrowed down to just those sounds present in the language the child is to acquire. Careful observation, however, shows that many sounds found in human languages are not found in babbling, and that some of the sounds that are found in babbling are those a child may have pro-

blems with when she/he starts to speak the adult language. Such findings cast doubt on the continuity hypothesis.

A pure **discontinuity approach**, however, fares little better than a pure continuity approach. One of its staunchest advocates is Jakobson (1968), according to whom there are two distinct sound production stages: the first is the babbling stage, during which the child makes a wide range of sounds which do not appear in any particular order and which do not, therefore, seem related to the child's subsequent development; during the second stage many of the sounds present in the first stage disappear either temporarily or permanently while the child is mastering the particular sound contrasts which are significant in the language it is acquiring. The problems with this approach are, first, that many children continue to babble for several months after the onset of speech (Menn 1976); second, many of the sound sequences of later words seem to be preferred during the babbling stage – as if being rehearsed, perhaps (Oller *et al.* 1976); finally, babbling seems often to carry intonation patterns of later speech, so that there seems to be continuity at least at the suprasegmental level (Halliday 1975; Menn 1976). Clark and Clark (1977: 390–1) believe that:

> Neither continuity nor discontinuity fully accounts for the facts. The relation between babbling and speech is probably an indirect one. For example, experience with babbling could be a necessary preliminary to gaining articulatory control of certain organs in the mouth and vocal tract. . . . If babbling simply provided exercise for the vocal apparatus, there would be little reason to expect any connection between the sounds produced in babbling and those produced later on. . . . Still, there is at least some discontinuity. Mastery of some phonetic segments only begins when children start to use their first words.

Acquisition of the lexicon

Early words are used at the same time as deictic gestures, grunts and **proto-words** – relatively stable vocal forms with a consistent but child-particular meaning (Vihman 1996: 147).

Vocabulary learning involves much more than storing a list of words. The mental lexicon is an active store in which lexical items are collected and organized and many lexicon models assume that not only words are stored but also inflectional material. Processing data, e.g. errors, indicate how lexical items are stored and processed. Different types of information have to be stored with a lexical item and constitute the lexical entry, including the following, using *cat* as an example:

* The **semantic representation**: +concrete, +animate, reference to a subgroup of 'animal'
* The lexical category or word class: noun
* Syntactic properties, e.g. gender in languages which mark it
* Morphological properties and internal structure, e.g. non-compound, regular plural
* The phonetic-phonological form, e.g. /kæt/, number of syllables, word stress

The child has to identify this information and store it in a lexical entry. When the child acquires a word they must grasp complex information and establish relations between new and already existing information. The existing structure of the lexicon has an influence on the way new lexical items are stored, but the acquisition of new lexical items also triggers a reorganization of the established links in the lexicon. Under this perspective it seems plausible to assume that the child's lexicon is not only smaller than the adult's, but also organized in a different way.

The first fifty words

The first words occur at the age of 10–18 months, and in the several months follow-ing the child acquires a vocabulary of 30–50 words. At this stage the lexicon grows slowly, at a rate of two or three words a week and the form and function of the first words differ from those of the adult language. With respect to form, the first words are usually phonologically simplified and, with respect to function, Clark (1993: 33) suggests that some of the first 10–20 words children produce only occur in certain contexts: a child might say 'car' only when seeing a car from the window but not when seeing toy cars or cars in other settings. However, not all words are context-bound; most of the early words are used appropriately in a variety of contexts to refer to objects (e.g. a car), individuals (e.g. a teddy) or situations.

After the child has acquired the first 50 words, and towards the end of the second year of age, new words are added to the existing vocabulary at a very fast pace, with several new words occurring daily. This stage is often known as the **vocabulary spurt**. Smith's (1926) subjects' average productive vocabulary was 22 words at 18 months, 118 words at 21 months, and 272 words at 2 years. According to Clark (1993) the vocabulary size of a 2-year-old varies between 50 and 500 words in production and the vocabulary a child is able to understand, its **receptive vocabulary**, is considerably larger.

Children adhere to what Clark (1993) calls the principle of conventionality in assuming that target words are those given by the speakers around them and in general do not make up sound strings and assign them their own meaning. They also appear to assume that each word form has a meaning different from that of other words and might avoid uses that overlap in meaning. Some of the early words may be **undergeneralized**, i.e. refer to a subset of a class only (e.g. 'dog' used only about poodles). In other cases they may be **overgeneralized** and apply to the members of the class distinguished in the adult language as well as to perceptually similar members of different classes (e.g. 'dog' for all walking animals, dogs, cats, and even birds on the ground). Such **overextensions** seem to be a communicative strategy at a stage when the productive vocabulary is limited, but children who overextend in production are often able to identify the appropriate referent for the more precise term (Clark 1993: 33ff.). For example, a child may be able to pick out the appropriate object in response to 'motorcycle', 'bike', 'truck', 'plane', but refer to them all as 'car' in production (Rescorla 1980: 328).

Grammatical word classes and bootstrapping hypotheses

The problem of identifying word classes in child language as well as the question of how children identify word classes has been subject to debate ever since the publication of Brown (1973). Recurrent ideas with respect to language acquisition are that children start by developing their grasp of semantic relations and only once these are in place can syntax develop. Syntax is felt to be too complex for a child.

According to Pinker's (1984) **semantic bootstrapping hypothesis**, children determine word classes on a semantic basis. Their semantic knowledge leads them then to discover the word classes associated with the semantic categories, even if there is no one-to-one correspondence between them. The **syntactic bootstrapping hypothesis** (Gleitman 1990), on the other hand, claims that syntactic information, e.g. the argument structure of a verb, can be used to derive the meaning of a word. This approach refers to a stage in which word classes are already acquired, whereas according to the semantic bootstrapping hypothesis the child uses semantic information in order to identify word classes. As Rothweiler and Meibauer (1999b: 15) point out, a problem for the semantic bootstrapping hypothesis is the fact that words can only be recognized

in a sentence as members of different classes and only then is it possible for children to see a link between word classes and semantic categories. (cf. also Behrens 1999).

Lexical representation and inflectional elements

For a long time studies on the acquisition of inflectional elements focused on the relation between morphological markings and syntactic representation, e.g. in subject–verb agreement. More recently, attention has also been paid to the lexical representation of inflectional elements and their acquisition. The status of regular and irregular inflection plays a central role here, as different approaches predict a different acquisitional course. It has been observed that children overgeneralize morphological markings, e.g. 'goed' for 'went'. In a connectionist approach (e.g. Rumelhart and McClelland 1986) no differences between regular and irregular morphology are assumed and both are represented in an associative network. Accordingly, there will be no difference in the way regular and irregular morphology are acquired; the observed overgeneralizations are claimed to follow from frequency of occurrence in the input. A dual-mechanism approach (Pinker and Prince 1992), on the other hand, assumes that regular morphology is driven by rules based on symbolic representations while irregular morphology is based on idiosyncratic lexical information. Regular morphology is used when no other information is available. As children in early acquisitional stages cannot resort to many stored forms, they overextend regular forms (Rothweiler and Meibauer 1999b: 24).

Syntactic development

The period between 6 and 12 months, during which children normally begin to comprehend words and produce single-unit utterances, is usually referred to as the **one-word** stage. Benedict (1979) shows that the gap between comprehension and production is usually very great at this time: a child may be able to understand about 100 words before it begins to produce words. By the time the child's vocabulary has grown to around 50 words s/he enters the so-called **two-word stage**. During the early stages of stringing more than two words together, many children's speech lacks grammatical inflections and function words, consisting of strings like 'cat drink milk' (Yule 1985: 141); this kind of language is known as **telegraphic speech** (Brown and Fraser 1963). Even if children are presented with full sentences to imitate, they tend to repeat the sentences in telegraphic form.

Many two-word utterances can be seen as instantiations of **pivot grammar** (Braine 1963). Braine (1963) observed a tendency for some words in children's utterances to be placed either at the beginning or at the end of the utterance. He calls these words pivots, as opposed to open-class words. Different children will experience different words in each class, but Braine's subject, Andrew's, pivot grammar contained the two-word combinations in Table 1.

Braine claims that the child will notice that certain open-class words always come after a pivot, while other open-class words always come before a pivot, and that this information allows the child to begin to distinguish different word classes among the open-class words. However, pivot grammar can only account for the utterances of a child who is at the very beginning of sentence use; even Braine's subject, Andrew, was at this stage also producing utterances consisting of a nominal plus an action word, modifier or personal-social word. It is clear that children soon move beyond such simple utterances as those which the pivot grammar would allow for.

In Braine's (1963) approach, the child's system seems to be quite different from the adult's. However, it is obvious that the child's system is more complex than simple strings of words and that it can be interpreted as the beginning of phrase structure.

In the one-word stage it is not always obvious which category the words produced by the child should be assigned to; for this reason Radford (1990) calls this period the 'acategorial stage'. In the two-word stage, on the other hand, syntactic categories such as nouns and verbs are used by the child in a systematic way. Verbs are used to predicate something of the nouns, as in the following examples (from Radford 1996: 44): 'baby talking' (Hayley 1 year; 8 months),

Table 1 A pivot grammar

Pivot-class word	Open-class word	Pivot-class word
all	broke; buttoned; clean; done; dressed; dry; fix; gone; messy; shut; through; wet	
I	see; shut; sit	
no	bed; down; fix; home; mama; more; pee; plug; water; wet	
see	baby; pretty; train	
more	car; cereal; cookie; fish; high; hot; juice; read; sing; toast; walk	
hi	Calico; mama; papa	
other	bib; bread; milk; pants; part; piece; pocket; shirt; shoe; side	
	boot; light; pants; shirt; shoe; water	off
	airplane; siren	by
	mail; mama	come

'daddy gone' (Paula 1;6). At this stage children do not use finite verbs (examples from Radford 1996: 54):

- the third person marking -*s* is missing in the relevant contexts: 'Paula play with ball' (Paula 1;6)
- auxiliaries are missing: 'baby talking' (Hayley 1;8), 'daddy gone' (Paula 1;6)
- Infinitival *to* is missing: 'want go out' (Daniel 1;10)

The generalization in the clause domain is that children's utterances at this stage contain projections of the lexical category V(erb) but not of the categories which carry syntactic information (functional categories) associated with it, such as AGR(eement) or T(ense). The lexical categories N(oun), A(djective) and P(reposition) are attested as well, but, as in the verbal domain, no syntactic information is associated with them (e.g. number for nouns).

The following is an X-bar representation of sentence structure, where V(erb)P(hrase) is a projection of the lexical category V and **F(initeness)P(hrase)** a projection of a functional category, i.e. a projection carrying syntactic information. 'Finiteness' is used here as a generic label; it is used as an example of a functional category without further specifying which one (e.g. AGReement, Tense).

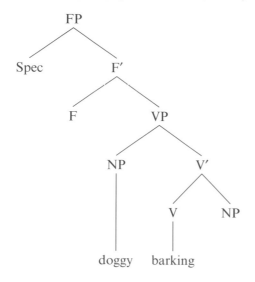

Under the assumption that child utterances consist only of projections of lexical categories, we expect to find lexical material which can be accommodated within the domain of a VP (Radford 1990; among others). In an underspecification approach (e.g. Clahsen 1990; Clahsen *et al.* 1993/ 1994; Hyams 1996), one or more functional projections are available but not fully specified as in the steady state.

Question and negative formation are among the most studied areas. Yule (1985: 144–5) isolates three stages for their acquisition. Stage I occurs between 18 and 26 months; stage II, between 22 and 30 months; and stage III, between 24 and 40 months. At the earliest stage, children form negatives by simply beginning the utterance with *no* or *not*. In stage II *don't* and *can't* begin to appear, and both these forms and *no* and *not* are placed in front of the verb instead of at the beginning of the utterance. The explanation for this acquisitional pattern is that in early utterances negation is either adjoined to VP or heads the underspecified functional projection. At a later stage, as projections for finite elements develop, finite verbs will occupy that position leaving the negation behind, as in *didn't* and *won't*.

Early questions are typically marked by rising intonation alone: 'Fraser water?' (Klima and Bellugi 1966: 200) is an example of a Yes/No question, 'Daddy go?' (Radford 1990: 123) an example of a *wh*-question. Auxiliaries or modals are not attested at this stage and nor are *wh*-words. When children start using *wh*-words, the inventory is limited and includes mainly *where, who, what*: 'where helicopter?' (Stefan 1;5, from Radford 1990: 125). These *wh*-words can be followed by -*s*, which can be interpreted as a cliticized realization of the copula: 'where's helicopter?' (Stefan 1;5, from Radford 1990: 125; see also Klima and Bellugi 1966: 201). These questions are initially formulaic. Evidence for this claim comes from (missing) agreement facts:

'what's these?' (Adam 2;2, from Radford 1990: 126).

Some authors (Klima and Bellugi 1966; Radford 1990) observe that children fail to understand *wh*-questions which include movement (from a position in the IP into the Spec(ifier)-C). An example is the following exchange (Klima and Bellugi 1966: 202):

Adult: what are you doing?
Child: no

This is taken as an indication that at this stage the projection which should host the moved element has not been developed in the child's system, and the sentence cannot be parsed by the child.

In the nominal domain, nouns and adjectives occur, but not determiners such as articles and possessives. Demonstratives occur on their own, but not together with a noun. This resembles the picture we observe in the verbal domain, in that elements carrying syntactic information are absent from early utterances.

Morphology development

Children normally begin to acquire grammatical morphemes at the age of around 2 years. Studies of the acquisition of grammatical morphemes go back to Berko (1958), who studied the acquisition by English-speaking children of plural -*s*, possessive -*s*, present tense -*s*, past tense -*ed*, progressive -*ing*, agentive -*er*, comparative -*er* and -*est*, and compounds. Berko worked with children aged between 4 and 7 years old, and she showed that 5- and 6-year-old children were able to add the appropriate grammatical suffixes to invented words when the words' grammatical class was clear from the context. Her experimental procedure has become known as the **wug procedure**, *wug* being one of the invented words used in the experiment.

This experiment and others like it may be used to argue for the hypothesis that children are 'tuned in', not only to the sounds of human language (see above) but also to its syntax, in the sense that they display 'a strong tendency . . . to analyse the formal aspects of the linguistic input' (Karmiloff-Smith 1987: 369). Karmiloff-Smith (1979) shows that French children determine gender by attending to word endings from about the age of 3, and Levy (1983) produces similar findings for Hebrew-speaking children.

The order in which morphemes are acquired has been studied for different languages (see, for example, Brown 1973 and many others). The order of acquisition of grammatical morphemes in English tends to be that -*ing* appears first, then the regular plural -*s*; irregular past tense forms are attested before the regular forms. The order observed is compatible with the assumptions of the structure-building approach to language acquisition (Radford 1990; Guilfoyle and Noonan 1992; among others) since the presence of -*ing* before third person -*s* or any past tense form would indicate that inflectional material associated with the functional categories AGReement and Tense are attested later.

The acquisition of the core grammar is finished very early, within the first three or four years. The process of acquisition of other parts of language (e.g. expanding the vocabulary, subtleties of use of tenses and moods and, in the languages which have them, rules of discourse) takes several years or goes on through an individual's life.

Second language acquisition

This section takes a brief look at the central questions concerning second language (L2) acquisition, mainly as to how it compares to first language (L1) acquisition. The central question in this domain is whether the acquisition process in second language acquisition is the same as the first time round or of a wholly different nature.

It is striking that, while everyone succeeds in becoming a competent speaker of her/his first language, this level of competence is usually not achieved by a second language speaker. The difference in developmental paths observed in first and second language acquisition is taken to be a further argument for the non-availability of UG in the latter (Meisel 1991). It is mainly these differences that have led researchers to assume that the acquisition processes involved in first and second language acquisition are different as well.

In the light of the assumption that Universal Grammar (UG) guides the acquisition of the first language, the observed differences in second language acquisition could be due to the fact that UG is no longer accessible. If this is the case, what does 'no longer' accessible mean? Does it mean after a certain point in time? Does it mean after one language has been learned? And what is the alternative to the UG guidance?

The biological notion of maturation leads to the assumption of a critical period for language acquisition, originally proposed by Lenneberg (1967) for first language acquisition. Based on hemispheric lateralization as an explanation, Lenneberg characterized the period between the ages of 6 and 13 as the critical period within which the acquisition of the first language should be activated, though these boundaries are no longer taken to be so strict. It is also claimed that there are different sensitive periods for different components of language. In Long's (1990) view, the critical period for phonology starts to decline around age 6, while it lasts until around age 15 for syntax and morphology.

What a critical period for second language acquisition means is subject of much debate. Some researchers (Bley-Vroman 1989; Schachter 1990) argue that the differences in achievement in first and second language acquisition indicate that UG is not available beyond puberty; otherwise, adult learners would reach a higher level of

proficiency in the second language. Others (e.g. White 1989; Schwartz and Sprouse 1994) argue that the innate knowledge that UG represents remains available after puberty and throughout an individual's life. The claim is based on the observation that L2 grammars at different developmental stages are natural languages.

Related questions concern the initial stage in second language acquisition and the role of the first language. Does the assumption that UG is accessible for those learning a second language entail that these speakers start from scratch just like children acquiring the first language? The debate about the role of the L1 tries to clarify not whether the L1 has any influence, since it is clear that there is some, but rather its extent.

According to the **Minimal Trees hypothesis** (Vainikka and Young-Scholten 1994), adult second language learners start off just with projections of lexical categories, similarly to children learning their L1. The speakers will build up their structure based on the L2 input and no significant influence from the L1 is expected. In contrast, other researchers (e.g. White 1992; Schwartz and Sprouse 1994; Eubank 1993/ 1994, 1996) claim that adults acquiring a second language have full access to Universal Grammar, both to principles of Universal Grammar and to language-specific parameters, so that the L1 specification can be reset to the values of the L2. There are different views about how much of the L1 is available in the L2 acquisition process: according to the **Full Access/Full Transfer hypothesis** (Schwartz and Sprouse 1994), the L1 with all its specifications constitutes the starting point in L2 acquisition. In **Weak Transfer approaches** (e.g. Eubank 1993/ 1994, 1996) grammatical properties of the L1 are assumed to be selectively transferred: syntactic properties transfer while morphology-driven information does not. It seems counterintuitive that adults, who have an L1 and 'know' about the structure of a language, would not make use of this knowledge and prefer instead to operate with a partial structure. In fact, evidence for *wh*-questions and for embedded clauses are found at the earliest stages of L2 acquisition, contrary to the evidence from children's data. This indicates that a more complex structure is available to adults learning a second language.

The account given above of how children learn the language of their speech community and how this process compares to second language acquisition has, of necessity, been limited in many ways, and the reader is encouraged to consult Goodluck (1991) and Ellis (1994) for a very thorough account of all of the issues and data involved.

T.P.

Suggestions for further reading

Brown, R. (1973) *A First Language: The Early Stages*, Cambridge, MA: Harvard University Press.

Ellis, R. (1994) *The Study of Second Language Acquisition*, Oxford: Oxford University Press.

Goodluck, H. (1991) *Language Acquisition: A Linguistic Introduction*, Oxford: Blackwell Publishers.

Language and education

There is no doubt that an individual's linguistic abilities affect her/his chances of success in the formal education system of her/his culture, since much of what takes place in that system is linguistically realized. Nor is there any doubt, however, that the relationship between language and educational success is complex. Stubbs (1983: 15) lists a number of pertinent questions:

> How, for example, is language related to learning? How is a child's language related, if at all, to his success or failure at school? Does it make sense to call some children's language 'restricted'? What kind of language do teachers and pupils use in the classroom? Does a child's dialect bear any relation to his or her educational ability? What is the significance of the fact that over a hundred languages are spoken in Britain? Should special educational provision be made for the very high concentrations of speakers of immigrant languages in several areas of the country?

One sad but well-established fact has done much to raise such and similar questions – this is that a working-class (WC) child in Britain has less chance of doing well in the school system than a middle-class (MC) child. It is also a fact that there are, typically, certain differences in the children's language (Stubbs 1983: 46). Faced with these two facts, it is tempting to draw the conclusion that the former is causally related to the latter. Two other possibilities, however, obtain (1983: 47): possibly there is no causal connection between the two facts which may both be caused by something else – a possibility that will not be explored in this entry – or they may be related, but only indirectly.

People who believe in a direct causal connection between the two facts typically draw more or less directly on the work of Basil Bernstein (1971) and his notions of **restricted** and **elaborated** linguistic **codes**. The early version of this theory, which Bernstein later modified considerably, but which, according to Stubbs (1983: 49), is the version which is best known and which has been most influential on certain educationalists, posits a direct relation between social class and linguistic codes (1983: 49):

> In the out-of-date version in which Bernstein's theories are most widely

known, the argument runs thus. There are two different kinds of language, *restricted* and *elaborated* code, which are broadly related to the social class of speakers. MC speakers are said to use both codes, but some WC speakers are said to have access only to restricted code, and this is said to affect the way such speakers can express themselves and form concepts. This is claimed to be particularly important in education, since schools are predicated upon elaborated code.

In other words, because elaborated code is used predominantly at school, and because the ability to use it is necessary for the formation of certain concepts which are important in the educational setting, a child with no access to elaborated code will be unable to succeed academically at school.

Elaborated code was said to be characterized by grammatical complexity and completeness; restricted code, by grammatical simplicity and incompleteness and much use of brief imperatives and interrogatives – restricted code was also said to be logically simpler than elaborated code. This gross oversimplification of Bernstein's fully developed theory has been discredited indirectly by Labov (1969; see below), but it led easily into the so-called myth of linguistic deprivation according to which speakers of non-standard English of any kind are deprived of appropriate linguistic stimulation in the home. The fault is thus seen to lie with the child who fails at school – the child fails because his or her language is inappropriate to the school situation, preventing him or her from forming the kinds of concepts necessary for academic success.

A less simplistic interpretation of Bernstein's work, however, suggests that the link between language and academic failure is indirect. Such an interpretation takes account of Bernstein's later version of the theory which includes considerations of contexts of socialization, of which there are four (reprint of extracts from Bernstein 1971, in Giglioli 1972: 170; emphasis added):

1 The **regulative** context – these are authority relationships where the child is made aware of the rules of the moral order and their various backings.
2 The **instructional** context, where the child learns about the objective nature of objects and persons, and acquires skills of various kinds.
3 The **imaginative** or **innovative** contexts, where the child is encouraged to experiment and re-create his world on his own terms, and in his own way.
4 The **interpersonal** context, where the child is made aware of affective states – his own, and others.

These are 'generalized situation types which have greatest significance for the child's socialization and for his interpretation of experience' (Halliday's foreword to Bernstein 1973). Halliday goes on to explain the indirect causation theory thus:

What Bernstein's work suggests is that there may be differences in the relative orientation of different social groups towards the various functions of language in given contexts, and towards the different areas of meaning that may be explored within a given function. Now if this is so, then when these differences manifest themselves in the contexts that are critical for the socialization process they may have a profound effect on the child's social learning; and therefore on his response to education, because built into the educational process are a number of assumptions and practices that reflect differentially not only the values but also the communication patterns and learning styles of different subcultures. As Bernstein has pointed out, not only does this tend to favour certain modes of learning over others, but it also creates for some children a continuity of cultures between home and school which it largely denies to others.

Such a view invites change in the school as much as in the pupils, and teaching programmes such as The Wigan Language Project (Mason 1988) are designed to effect just such a reciprocal change.

Halliday (1973) suggests that, of the child's seven models of language which arise from the functions that language has for the child, adults (including teachers) tend to have only the seventh, the **representational** model of language as a means of expressing propositions. Yet the **personal** function of language as a means of expressing one's own personality, and the **heuristic** function of language as a means of investigating reality and thus learning about things, are obviously crucially important at school. The child has been using both functions naturally within its own meaning group in its own environment, but (1973: 19) 'the ability to operate institutionally in the personal and heuristic modes is ... something that has to be learnt'.

Again, it is, then, possible to argue that some children enter school better equipped to operate institutionally with these two functions than other children because of the ways in which they have experienced language in the critical socializing contexts. Halliday advocates raising teachers' and other adults' awareness of what language is for the child. If the adult's focus is solely on the representational model of language, s/he will obviously be unlikely to be sensitive to the types of problems some children have in conforming to the educational institution's demands that the child employ the personal and heuristic functions in a particular way within it. Equally, if teaching materials are based solely on the representational model of language, they will fail to conform to what the child knows language to be, and the child will find it difficult to relate to such materials.

Labov's (1969, 1972a) studies of the language of black and Puerto Rican children in New York supports the theory that the relationship between language and academic failure is indirect, and that social context is a crucial factor in the explanation of the relationship (Stubbs 1983: 76–7):

A major finding of sociolinguistics is that the *social context* is the most powerful determinant of verbal behaviour. Fieldwork with Black children (e.g. Labov, 1969) has shown that they produce vivid, complex language in unstructured situations with friends, but may appear monosyllabic and defensive in asymmetrical classroom or test situations where an adult has power over them. Philips (1972) has found exactly the same with American Indian children: that they are expressive outside the classroom, but silent, reticent and defensive inside it with their White teachers.

Such research indicates that there is something about the school situation that prevents some children from benefiting appropriately from the education it offers them.

Labov also argues convincingly against the view that non-standard dialects are less 'logical' than standard dialects and that their speakers lack certain important concepts because their language denies them access to these concepts. Stubbs (1983: 68–9) succinctly explicates Labov's arguments on this matter as follows:

A criticism often raised against pupils' speech by teachers is that it is 'badly connected' and inexplicit. Teachers often feel this about Black English Vernacular (BEV) which has sentences like: 'he my brother' (SE [standard English]: 'he's my brother'). But there are many languages which do not use the verb *to be* in such sentences, for example Russian: 'on moj brat' (literally: 'he my brother'). .... It would be ludicrous to argue that a

Russian had a defective concept of existential relationships, just because of this detail in the grammar of his language. . . . A comparable example occurs with BEV forms like: 'He come yesterday' (SE: 'he came yesterday'). Failure to mark explicitly the past tense in the verb does not indicate a failure to perceive past time. It merely means that in BEV *come* is in the same class as verbs like *put* and *hit* in SE (cf. 'I always *put* it there, I *put* it there yesterday').

It is also easy to confuse logic and grammar. Many non-standard dialects of British and American English use double negatives such as: 'I don't know nothing' (SE: 'don't know anything'). It is sometimes said that such sentences are illogical on the grounds that if I *don't* know *nothing*, then I *do* know *something*. . . . Again, many languages use double negatives (e.g. French: 'je N'en sais RIEN'. Spanish: 'yo NO sabe [*sic*] NADA'). Again, these languages may be foreign, but they are not illogical just because they often use two participles to negativize a sentence.

A child's accent and dialect may, however, also indirectly affect her/his academic success even in cases where educators do not consciously hold any views about the access to concept formation of dialect speakers, or about the logic of the dialects; teachers may consciously or subconsciously react in a negative way to non-standard language forms, and may tend to consider non-standard speakers less intelligent than standard speakers. This will tend to affect the way in which they deal with the various children, and there is a good chance that a child who is not expected to do well will realize this and conform to the teacher's expectation. It is also the case that (Stubbs 1983: 86):

> Even if the teacher goes out of his way to accept the child's language as different but equally valuable, his own lan-

guage is likely to be noticeably different from the child's in the direction of the standard, prestige variety. And the child will be aware that the teacher's form of language is the one supported by institutional authority. Children may then be caught in a double bind. They may recognize that to get ahead they must adopt the teacher's style of language, but to do this will separate them from their friends. A nonstandard dialect may have low social prestige for schools, but serve the positive functions of displaying group loyalty for its speakers.

An obvious way to avoid imposing this dilemma on children would, of course, be for schools to stop giving institutional authority to the standard language. Schools could simply allow children to use any dialect and accent they wished in school. However, this solution is probably too simplistic, because it might result in more severe difficulties for the children later on; in society as a whole, dialect tolerance is minimal (Trudgill 1979/1983: 667) suggests the following compromise:

> the greatest dialect-related problem in the UK is the attitudes and prejudices many people hold toward nonstandard dialects. In the long term, it will probably be simpler to ease this problem by changing attitudes (as has already happened to some extent with accents) than by changing the linguistic habits of the majority of the population.
>
> In the short run, however, we have to acknowledge the existence of these attitudes and attempt to help children to overcome them. Clearly many jobs and opportunities for upward social mobility will be denied to those who are not able to use standard English. To act on these motives in school with some degree of success, however, it is important to recognize that the teaching of higher status accents and of spoken standard English in school is almost

certain to fail. Standard English is a dialect which is associated with a particular social group in British society and is therefore symbolic of it. Children will in most cases learn to speak this dialect only if they wish to become associated with this group and feel that they have a reasonable expectation of being able to do so. . . .

Writing, on the other hand, is a different matter. It is much easier to learn to write a new dialect than to learn to speak it, and in writing there is time for planning and checking back. Standard English, moreover, can be regarded as a dialect apart which is used in writing and whose use in written work does not necessarily commit one to allegiance to any particular social group.

In the 1980s, the question of how to deal with dialects in schools was largely overshadowed by that of how to accommodate those children whose home language is not English. The debate here centres on the notion of **mother-tongue teaching** – should a mother tongue other than English be taught in schools or should the language of the school be exclusively English?

It is obvious that it is easier to come to a decision in favour of the former option in areas where there are large numbers of children sharing one non-English mother tongue than in areas with children speaking many different non-English mother tongues. For instance, in certain parts of Wales, Welsh is the medium of education, with English being introduced at some stage as a second language in most schools because most of the children are Welsh speaking and because there is an active interest in the community in keeping the language, with its culture, alive (see Davies 1981).

In most areas of Britain, however, schools still regard English as the medium of education; here, one or more other languages may be used as media of instruc-tion early on because a child's learning process will obviously be severely hampered if it does not understand the language used in the school. In addition (Saifullah Kahn 1980: 79):

> It is also likely that this sudden switch to an environment that does not recognize and value the first language, its detachment from the home and the community life and the negative connotations related to minority status in the wider society, are bound to cause psychological stress, influence identity formation and thus affect educational achievement.

Furthermore, Skutnabb-Kangas and Toukomaa (1976) and Toukomaa and Skutnabb-Kangas (1977) have shown that Finnish-speaking children in Sweden learned Swedish more efficiently when given the opportunity to develop their native Finnish language at the same time. Their research suggests that unless a child is proficient in its first language it will not develop full proficiency in a second language. Although this research, and the considerations mentioned immediately above, suggest the desirability of mother-tongue teaching, there are many other issues to be considered, for which see Saifullah Kahn (1980).

K.M.

Suggestions for further reading

Spolsky, B. (ed.) (1999) *Concise Encyclopedia of Educational Linguistics*, Oxford: Pergamon.

Stubbs, M. (1986) *Educational Linguistics*, Oxford: Basil Blackwell.

—— and Hillier, H. (eds) (1983) *Readings on Language, Schools and Classrooms*, London and New York: Methuen.

Trudgill, P.J. (1975) *Accent, Dialect and the School*, London: Edward Arnold.

Language and gender

In this entry, the term **gender** refers to the socially constructed categories **male** and **female**, and *not* to such grammatical categories as 'masculine', 'feminine', 'neuter' or 'common'.

The study of language in relation to gender has two main foci. First, it has been observed by many linguists that men and women speak differently; and second, it has been observed by many feminists and by some linguists that men and women are spoken about differently, and it is often claimed that the language is discriminatory against women.

Differences in male and female language use

Differences in male and female language use began to be noticed at least as early as the seventeenth century in the societies visited by missionaries and explorers, and the interest these differences caused often led to claims that in some societies men and women spoke completely different languages. This, however, is an overstatement – what tends to happen to varying degrees in various societies is that the gender of a speaker will determine or increase the likelihood of choices of certain phonological, morphological, syntactic and lexical forms of a language while precluding or diminishing the likelihood of certain other choices (Coates 1986/1993: 35).

Coates (1986/1993: 35–40) and Smith (1985: 3–6) provide surveys of a number of studies detailing **gender-exclusive** differences; that is, cases in which certain linguistic forms are used only by one sex. Gender-exclusive differences do not exist in European languages. However, in European languages there are certain forms which tend to be preferred by women and other forms that are preferred more by men; the differences which appear because of such tendencies are known as **gender-**

preferential differences. The gender-exclusive/gender-preferential distinction probably reflects a distinction between societies in which gender roles are more strictly defined and societies in which they are less strictly defined (Coates 1986/1993: 40).

Early dialect studies provided little or no evidence of gender-preferentiality because early dialectologists tended to use elderly rural males as informants, so that little was known about how women spoke (see DIALECTOLOGY). However, with the advent of quantitative sociolinguistic studies (see LANGUAGE SURVEYS) which included female speakers, such as Trudgill's Norwich survey (1974a) and Labov's studies of language in New York (1971, 1972a, 1972b), it began to appear that female speakers tend to use more **prestige forms** than males. The pattern revealed by Labov's New York City study (1972a), Trudgill's Norwich survey (1972), Macaulay's study of Glasgow English (1977, 1978), Newbrook's study of West Wirral (1986), and Romaine's Edinburgh study (1978), is summed up by Coates (following Coates 1986/1993: 65–6):

1. In all styles, women tend to use fewer stigmatized forms than men.
2. In formal contexts, women seem to be more sensitive to prestige patterns than men.
3. Lower-middle-class women make major shifts in style; in the least formal style, they use a high proportion of the stigmatized variant, but in more formal styles, they correct their speech to correspond to that of the class above them.
4. Use of non-standard forms seems to be associated not only with working-class speakers, but also with *male* speakers.

Evidence of this kind seems to show that females are more sensitive to linguistic norms than males are, a conclusion strengthened by Trudgill's (1972, 1974a) self-evaluation test. Using tape-recordings, Trudgill played to his informants two or more pronunciations, more or less close to the **received pronunciation (RP)** (or standard) variant and to the non-standard Norwich variant respectively, and asked the informants to say which pronunciation was nearest their own. Then he compared the informants' answers with recordings of their own actual pronunciation. The test revealed that the females **over-reported** significantly, while the males **under-reported**, i.e. female informants thought their own pronunciation was closer to RP than it actually was, while male informants thought their own pronunciation was closer to the Norwich variant than it actually was. Assuming that what speakers *think* they do is what they would *like* to do, this shows that women want to use standard forms while men do not. For men, therefore, non-standard forms are prestigious, while for women, standard forms are prestigious. If it is further assumed that standard English has institutionalized prestige because it is the institutionalized norm, an assumption supported by research in social psychology (Coates 1986/1993: 75), then it is possible to argue further that standard English enjoys **overt prestige**, while non-standard forms enjoy **covert prestige**. Finally, it can be claimed 'that women are attracted by the norm of Standard English while men respond to the covert prestige of the vernacular' (Coates 1986/1993: 74).

At this point, it is appropriate to ask why this might be the case, and the typical explanation is that women, who occupy socially insecure positions, are seeking to appropriate some of the status attached to being an RP-speaker. This explanation is supported by Elyan *et al.*'s (1978) Lancashire study, which showed that women using RP were considered (Coates 1986/1993: 76)

> more fluent, intelligent, self-confident, adventurous, independent and *feminine* than women with a regional accent. In addition, RP-accented women were also rated as being more *masculine* (judges

had to rate each speaker for both masculinity and femininity on a nine-point scale). This may seem contradictory, but if masculinity and femininity are seen as two independent dimensions then individuals have the choice of both characteristics.

In other words, a woman speaking RP may have greater access to traditionally male territories (jobs, activities, etc.).

However, if it is accepted that, as much sociolinguistic research has shown, non-standard speech typically functions to maintain group identity, another explanation is possible; namely, that males tend to belong to close-knit groups while females tend not to. Males have greater access to membership of such groups than females, because they have greater access to work and to evening activities outside the home. Milroy's (1980/1987) comparative study of Ballymacarrett, and the Clonard and the Hammer (parts of Belfast, Northern Ireland) supports this explanation (Coates 1986/1993: 84–5):

> Ballymacarrett as a community differs from the other two: it suffers little from male unemployment. . . . The Hammer and the Clonard both had unemployment rates of around 35 per cent. . . . Men from these areas were forced to look for work outside the community, and also shared more in domestic tasks. . . . The women in these areas went out to work and, in the case of the young Clonard women, all worked together.

The young Clonard women used more non-standard forms than the young men. However, the study also showed that in the Hammer, where groups were less close-knit than they were in Ballymacarrett and Clonard (because of rehousing and unemployment), speakers – male and female – did not approximate more closely to standard English than speakers in the Clonard. Rather, there was 'a drift away from the focused vernacular norms of more tight-knit groups' (Coates 1986/1993: 92). Group solidarity therefore seems more influential in activating group speech patterns than a desire to achieve a certain norm with covert or overt prestige, and it appears to be too simplistic to explain the different speech patterns of men and women by suggesting that men and women aim for different norms. The speech patterns in question appear, rather, to reflect the social fact that men generally have greater access to group membership than women.

In addition to differences in syntax, morphology and pronunciation, men and women differ in terms of communicative strategies. When men and women converse, for instance, men tend to interrupt very frequently and are slow to provide supporting responses to women's speech turns (Zimmerman and West 1975). Women, on the other hand, use more facilitative tags (Lakoff 1975; Holmes 1984) than men; that is, tags which help a conversation to move along smoothly, and more Yes/No questions (Fishman 1980), which can, of course, also help to keep a conversation going.

Men also generally talk more than women (Bernard 1972; Swacker 1975; Eakins and Eakins 1978). This clearly contradicts the popular belief that women talk more than men, and Spender (1980) explains that the reason that it *seems* to us that women speak more than men, even though studies show that it is the other way round, is that men are *expected* by the culture in general to talk, while women are expected to remain silent. When women do talk, therefore, it is more noticeable than when men talk.

When women talk to each other, the term **gossip** is often used to describe their activity, and in popular parlance this term is negatively loaded (it is rarely said of a group of men that they are gossiping). In anthropology and sociolinguistics, however, no negative connotations are attached to the term *gossip*, which is used to refer to

'informal communication between members of a social group' (Coates 1986/1993: 115). Gossip has the important function of maintaining the group's unity, morals and values (D. Jones 1980), and contains all the features that characterize women's way of interacting in conversation. It is a form of interaction which increases and reflects solidarity and support, and in which expressions intended to reflect or gain power for a speaker have no place.

These gender-related differences in speech patterns are acquired by children as they learn to speak (Coates 1986/1993; chapter 7), just as other gender stereotypes (how boys should behave and how girls should behave) and cultural values in general are learned along with language (Halliday 1978: 9).

The definition through language of gender roles

As a major vehicle for the transmission of cultural beliefs and values, language may profoundly affect female–male relations. The attitudes transmitted through language may either help to reinforce the status quo, or they may be a factor in changing it. It is possible to argue that the belief that standard English has been transmitting since the eighteenth century is that males are the species and women the subspecies, thus making it appear natural than males should be dominant. The main aspect of English usage normally mentioned in support of this argument is the use of *man* and *he* as **generic terms**; that is, as terms referring to the entire species – to all of humankind. The argument is as follows (see Miller and Swift 1981: chapters 1, 2).

Use of *man* and the male pronouns as generics is usually justified on two grounds: it is an ancient rule of English grammar; and everybody knows that in generalizations, the male terms are meant to include females. Neither claim appears to stand up to scrutiny.

In Old English, *man* meant 'person' or 'human being', and was equally applicable to either sex. It is used in this way in *The Anglo-Saxon Chronicle*, where, for instance, Ercongota, the daughter of a seventh-century English king, is described as 'a wonderful man'. English at that time had *wer* for 'adult male' and *wif* for 'adult female'. The combined forms *waepman* and *wifman* meant, respectively, 'adult male person' and 'adult female person'. Over time, *wifman* evolved into *woman*, and *wif* narrowed in meaning to 'wife'. *Man* narrowed in meaning in replacing *wer* and *wæpman*. The change in the meaning of *man* from broad to narrower, is similar to the way in which *deor* and *heafon* have narrowed from meaning 'animal' and 'sky' to meaning 'deer' and 'heaven' with the importation to English of the words *animal* and *sky*.

Later writers, like William Caxton, Shakespeare and Chesterfield, used *they* to refer to the species: 'Each of them should . . . make themself ready' (Caxton); 'God send everyone their heart's desire' (Shakespeare); 'If a person is born of a gloomy temper . . . they cannot help it' (Chesterfield).

However, early grammars of Modern English were written in the sixteenth and seventeenth centuries and were intended for boys from wealthy families to prepare them for the study of Latin. They used masculine gender pronouns, not because they could refer to both sexes, but because males dominated the world of education and literacy. No early grammar book has as one of its rules any that says that masculine pronouns include females when used in general reference, and the usage only became a general rule in 1746 when John Kirkly made it the twenty-first of eighty-eight grammatical rules, on the grounds that the male pronoun was more comprehensive than the female.

Later grammarians added to this feeling the notion that the use of *they* violated rules of number agreement – a consideration which, as we have seen above, did not concern Shakespeare, and one which appears to make the unwarranted assumption that number agreement is more important than gender agreement. Finally, in 1850, an Act of Parliament made it a law that 'words importing the masculine gender shall be deemed and taken to include females'. The second argument in favour of the use of male forms as generics states that we all know this to be the case.

However, the evidence appears to suggest that the terms in question are **false generics**. If they were true generic terms, there should be nothing odd about sentences like *Man breastfeeds his young*, *Man suffers in childbirth* and *Diana Nyad became the first man to swim from the Bahamas to Florida*. Studies like that of Schneider and Hacker (1973) provide empirical evidence against *man* as a generic. They asked two groups of college students to select pictures from magazines and newspapers to illustrate a sociology textbook. One group were asked to find illustrations for headings like *Industrial man*, *Political man* and *Urban man*. The other group's headings were of the type *Industrial life*, *Political life* and *Urban life*. In a majority of cases, students of both sexes chose pictures of males to illustrate the titles including the term *man*, while choosing pictures including both sexes to illustrate the *life* titles. This shows that the term *man* is semantically loaded in favour of males; that is, it makes users think predominantly of males.

It is also odd, if we assume the generic status of the male forms, that *she* should nevertheless be used so often in generalizations about secretaries, nurses, primary-school teachers, babysitters, shoppers, childminders and cleaners – in fact, about just those workers who are most frequently female.

The effect of the use of the false generic is held to be that women are often being made invisible by the language; that is, the language has only a **negative semantic space** for women (Stanley 1977) – women are – MALE. As Graham (1975) argues, if you have a group C divided into two halves, A and B, then A and B can be equal members of C. But if you call the whole group A, one half A and the other half B, then the B half will be seen as deviant, the exception, the subspecies, the outsiders.

It is, furthermore, very easy to find evidence in support of the claim that, when women are seen through language, they are seen in an unfavourable light (cf. Spender 1980). Indeed, the term *woman* itself had negative connotations for most of the culture until the 1970s and retains these connotations in some groups in the early 1990s. The polite term, or **euphemism**, for a woman used to be (and in some circles it still is) *lady*, and there were (are) very clear rules for how a lady should behave and talk (see R. Lakoff 1975).

Some of these behavioural standards are reflected in linguistic usage; thus Stanley (1973) counts 220 English words for sexually promiscuous females and only 20 for sexually promiscuous males. This reveals some of the culture's general attitude to males and females – sexual vigour is seen as deviant in females; it is the male who is supposed to dominate in this field as in every other. The theory of maleness includes features such as courage, strength, toughness, vigour, rationality, while the theory of femaleness includes tenderness and emotionality. Consequently, it is not unusual to hear surprised statements to the effect that a female professional is able to combine her professional standing and ability with an undeniable femininity (it would be unlikely that anyone would remark on a man's ability to combine professionalism with masculinity). The language also still bears traces of the cultural norm of women as housewives and men as workers outside the home; thus *working wife* and *working mother* are, to say the least, more likely to occur than *working husband* and *working father*.

Finally, it is easy to dig up linguistic evidence to support the argument that those qualities which are assigned to males are held in higher esteem than those assigned to females. Thus it can be complimentary to call a girl a tomboy, but it can *never* be complimentary to call a boy a sissy (derivative of *sister*).

All this demonstrates the ways in which males and females are stereotyped within the culture, and the way in which language use can highlight stereotypical features. For those in favour of altering the status quo, the question then arises as to the degree to which a change in language use can assist in this endeavour. The answer one gives will depend on how one views the relationship between language and culture in general, but it is unlikely that either of two possible extremist answers are correct. One such answer is that altering language use will achieve nothing, because any alternative terms will simply be infiltrated with the prejudices inherent in the old terms. At the other extreme, the answer would be that a change in language use alone would result in a change in the culture's beliefs about men and women respectively.

What cannot be doubted is that a heightened awareness of how language works for men and women as it is used by them and about them cannot but help aid an awareness of how they are viewed by the culture, including, of course, by themselves. It cannot be denied, either, that newsreaders and newspaper reporters in the third millennium are less likely to use male pronouns and more likely to use *they* as a singular term than they were in the 1960s. (For further discussion of the relationship between language, thought and culture, see LINGUISTIC RELATIVITY; CRITICAL LINGUISTICS/CRITICAL DISCOURSE ANALYSIS; PHILOSOPHY OF LANGUAGE, DISCOURSE ANALYSIS AND CONVERSATION ANALYSIS, COGNITIVE LINGUISTICS; METAPHOR.)

K.M.

Suggestions for further reading

Cameron, D. (1992) *The Feminist Critique of Language*, London: Routledge.

Coates, J. (1986/1993) *Women, Men and Language: A Sociolinguistic Account of Gender Differences in Language*, London: Longman; 2nd edition 1993.

—— (1998) (ed.) *Language and Gender: A Reader*, Oxford: Blackwell Publishers.

Smith, P.M. (1985) *Language, the Sexes and Society*, Oxford: Basil Blackwell.

Tannen, D. (ed.) (1993) *Gender and Conversational Interaction*, New York and Oxford: Oxford University Press.

Language pathology and neurolinguistics

Language pathology is a convenient cover term for the study of all aspects of language disorders. As such, it includes the main disciplines involved; namely, medical science (especially neuroanatomy and physiology), psychology (especially neuropsychology and cognitive psychology), linguistics and education. It also covers all categories of disorder, including developmental as well as acquired disorders, disorders that are associated with other deficits, such as hearing impairment or structural abnormality (such as cleft palate) or mental handicap, as well as those that are 'pure' language disorders. It comprises disorders that can be characterized at all levels of language structure and function, from articulatory and auditory speech-signal processing to problems of meaning, and it includes all modalities of language use, in production and comprehension, as represented through such media as speech, writing and signing. Finally, it includes research and all aspects of intervention, from initial screening and diagnosis, through more extensive assessment procedures, to therapeutic management and remedial teaching.

Thus, many different professions are involved in the field of language pathology, including speech therapy (see SPEECH AND LANGUAGE THERAPY), normal and special education, clinical and educational psychology, aphasiology (see below and APHASIA),

paediatrics, ENT surgery and neurosurgery, audiology and linguistics.

Within this field, certain historical factors have made a lasting impression. The **medical** approach was an early influence in the characterization of certain aspects of language disorder, particularly in the field of **aphasiology**, which is concerned with acquired disorders associated with neurological damage. Within this approach people having language disorders are regarded as patients, and classification proceeds from the identification of symptoms to a diagnosis in terms of syndromes. **Syndromes** are symptom complexes which have a systematic internal relationship such that the presence of certain symptoms guarantees the presence or absence of certain others (see APHASIA).

A further characteristic of the medical approach is the categorization of language disorders in terms of their aetiology – thus developmental disorders may be linked to difficulties noted with the mother's pregnancy, the delivery, or subsequent childhood illness, such as otitis media or 'glue ear', while acquired disorders may be linked to the site of brain lesions, and the type of brain damage arising from either external sources – gunshot wounds yielding more focal destruction of brain tissue than 'closed head' injuries sustained in road traffic accidents for example – or by diseases such as tumour or degenerative conditions such as Parkinsonism.

The **psychological** approach has also had considerable influence. The tendency here has been coloured by the dominant tradition, but it is possible to discern a consistent emphasis on language as possibly the most accessible, subtle and complex form of overt human behaviour. Disorders in a complex system may provide valuable information on the properties of that system, both in the way that they arise – showing which parts of the system are vulnerable, and how far they may be selectively impaired – and in the sorts of compensatory processes that appear to take place.

A key feature of the behavioural approach has therefore been a concern with psychometric assessment of language functions in relation to other psychological capacities. The early assessments drew largely on intelligence tests, and focused attention on the link between language disorders and impaired psychological functions such as memory and perception. More modern aphasia test batteries, such as the **Boston Diagnostic Aphasia Examination** or the **Western Aphasia Battery**, still contain components that derive from this tradition, such as the requirement to perform simple calculations, and the matching of shapes (see APHASIA).

The **linguistic** approach is of more recent origin, based on the methods of structural linguistics developed most completely in the 1930s to 1950s, and on the subsequent trends that derive directly or indirectly from the work of Chomsky. Jakobson is generally regarded as the first to apply the concepts of linguistics to the field of language disorders – he sought a connection between the linguistic characteristics of various disorders and the traditional lesion sites associated with them. In essence, this was the first exercise in what has since become known as **neurolinguistics** (see below). His work was not followed up, however, and what is now referred to as representative of the linguistic approach is a research tradition that has rather distinct origins and characteristics.

The **clinical linguistic** approach may generally be described as one that treats a presenting language disorder as a phenomenon that can be described in linguistic terms, independently of factors such as aetiology and general psychological functions – phonetic, phonological, morphological, syntactic, lexical, semantic and pragmatic, to provide a fairly representative general inventory – and allows for the possibility that any particular case of a language disorder may involve a differential pattern of impairment across some or all of these levels. One implication of this view is the calling into question of the fundamental separation of 'speech' vs 'language' in the taxonomy of disorders.

The clinical linguistic approach clearly has much to contribute to the appropriate description and interpretation of language disorders, but there is a general problem regarding the psychological reality of linguistic descriptions and models. For this reason, it is necessary to supplement the clinical linguistic approach by one which attempts to identify the psycholinguistic structures and processes involved in language behaviour, in impaired as well as in normal contexts. This leads us to consider the field of **neurolinguistics**. This term appears frequently to be used for what are, essentially, psycholinguistic studies of neurologically based language disorders. But there is what may be regarded as a more strict interpretation of the term, now briefly reviewed here. **Neurolinguistics** is the study of the relationship between language and its neurological basis. It is convenient to distinguish three general orders of description in the study of language abilities: the linguistic, the psycholinguistic and the neurolinguistic. The first may be represented by the general descriptive approach that recognizes such levels of organization as the phonetic, the phonological, the morphological, the syntactic, the lexical and the semantic and pragmatic;

techniques of description at these levels, when applied to the field of language pathology, constitute what we have referred to above as **clinical linguistics**. Alternatively, a rather more integrated system of linguistic description may be attempted, such as is found in the generative tradition (see GENERATIVE GRAMMAR).

The second order of description is concerned with the evidence that reveals the nature of the linguistic structures and processes that are actually involved in the use of language – perceptual processes, information-processing strategies, memorial factors and motor-control processes.

The third order of description is concerned with the nature of the neurological operations involved in these psycholinguistic processes; with the structure and function of the auditory system and its associated elements; and with the neural basis for articulatory gestures, and so on.

It is not very easy to understand the relationship between such distinct orders of description, partly because information in all three is still so incomplete. It would be premature to conclude that linguistic properties 'reduce' to, or can be explained by, psycholinguistic properties, and that these in turn can be accounted for in terms of the properties of the neurological substrata of language. For example, it has been observed, within the transformational-syntax tradition, that a number of constraints on the privilege of occurrence of certain syntactic elements may be expressed as a general constraint on movement of such elements – hence a constraint of **subjacency** is proposed to the effect that no constituent may be moved across more than one **bounding node**, a node which acts as a constituent boundary (e.g. NP, S) at a time. The psycholinguistic evidence for the role of subjacency in facilitating the operation of human parsing operations is a controversial matter, however, and the status of subjacency from a strict neurological

perspective is currently difficult even to raise as an issue.

In what sense, then, can there be a neurolinguistics at present? There are two general answers to this question: the first lies in a general understanding of the neurological organization of language abilities (what might be called the **neurology of language**); the second is mainly found in the detailed study of language disorders where there is sufficient neurological evidence to allow for some interpretation of the linguistic and psycholinguistic characteristics of the disorder in neurological terms (see APHASIA).

An overview of the basic neurology of language may conveniently start with the articulatory system, which has four main components from the point of view of neurological involvement: (1) the **cortex** – the outer layer of so-called 'grey matter' in the brain – where initiating cells located primarily in the **motor strip** make connections with (2) long connecting fibres known as the **upper motor neurons**, which connect to control centres in the **basal ganglia**, **thalamus** and **cerebellum**, and terminate in relay stations in the **brainstem** and **spinal cord**; (3) the **lower motor neurons** which carry signals from the relay stations out to the muscles of the head, neck and chest regions; and finally (4) the muscles served by the lower motor neurons, and which are linked to a sensory feedback loop, to permit monitoring of motor control.

Starting with the first of these components, the relevant part of the cortex is located in the so-called **motor strip**, running anteriorly along the line of the fissures which serve to demarcate the **frontal lobe** in each hemisphere of the brain. Along this strip, the cells controlling muscles all over the body are organized systematically in such a fashion that those responsible for the lower limbs are located towards the top of the motor strip, while those innervating the muscles of the vocal tract are found at the bottom, close to the junction with the anterior part of the **temporal lobe**. The motor strip cells operate in conjunction with those of the immediately anterior portion of the frontal lobe, the **pre-motor cortex**, which is involved in certain controlling functions, and the **parietal lobe**, posterior to the frontal lobe, also contributes copiously to the upper motor neuron system that connects to the lower control centres.

The very rapid and precise movements of the speech organs require involvement not just of the motor cortex but sensory areas as well. The nervous system appears to function very broadly, therefore, in the control of speech output, through wide subcortical connections in each hemisphere. Each hemisphere is responsible for controlling the complete functioning of the oral tract musculature; thus both left and right sides of the tongue, for example, are controlled from each hemisphere. Such complex behaviour as speech requires consciously willed movements and semi-automatic and completely automatic control of sequences of movements, and it appears that all these aspects are represented in the signals carried by the upper motor neurons as they group together to pass down through the base of the brain. Some, the **cortico-bulbar neurons**, terminate in the brainstem, and others, the **cortico-spinal neurons**, pass down further into the spinal cord. Still other neurons connect to the basal ganglia and the thalamus; the cerebral cortex is thus able to influence this complex of structures, which in turn influences the brainstem and spinal cord relays.

As consciously willed movements become increasingly automatic, as in the development of speech patterns, they become part of the basal ganglia repertoire. There are both voluntary and postural inputs to the basal ganglia, allowing for the overriding of automatic sequences, and for the integration of information concerning the position of articulators relative to each other in the vocal tract. Part of the function of the cerebellum is bound up in the role of the thalamus and basal ganglia, to regulate postural reflexes and muscle tone – the resistance of muscles to movement.

The **reticular formation**, in the brainstem, is also involved in connections from the upper motor neurons, and appears to exert facilitating and inhibiting effects on certain types of slower-transmitting (or **gamma**) **neurons**, whose function is to help to control the operation of the fast-transmitting (or **alpha**) **fibres**, which are responsible for the movement of the main muscles. This control vs movement distinction is represented in both the upper and lower neuron systems. Most upper motor neurons diverge within the brainstem, carrying control from each hemisphere to each side of the oral tract.

The connection from the upper to the lower motor neurons marks the division between the **central** and **peripheral nervous systems**. Each lower motor neuron forms part of a **motor unit**, containing in addition the muscle that the lower motor alpha neuron innervates, an associated muscle **spindle**, and a slow-transmitting gamma neuron linked to the reticular formation and cerebellum via the upper/lower motor neuron relay. The spindle carries information on the state of the muscle – extended or contracted – which is used to regulate the innervation of the muscle via the fast-transmitting alpha neuron. The lower motor neurons that are involved in movements of the oral tract connect from relays in the **pons** and **medulla** in the brainstem, and are known anatomically as **cranial nerves** – those conventionally numbered as V, VII, X, XI and XII being the most important – and the **thoratic nerves**, numbered from I to XII, connect from the spinal cord to control the muscles of the ribcage and the abdomen, and thus serve to initiate and regulate the pulmonary airstream mechanism.

If we now pass quickly over the speech signal that is created by the movement of articulators and carried by resultant movement of air particles, we can pick up the process of neurological involvement in speech audition at the point where mechanically boosted signals in the 2–6 kHz speech frequency range are transported to neural impulses in the **organ of Corti**, lying along the **basilar membrane** in the inner ear (see also AUDITORY PHONETICS). The impulses take the form of very brief, all-or-none electrical activity, **action potentials**, travelling along the fibres of the **auditory nerve** from the **cochlea**. In ways that are still not completely understood, these action potentials carry frequency and amplitude information, as well as duration, to the **cochlea nuclei cells** in the medulla of the brainstem. These cells effectively extract critical features from the auditory nerve signal, by being selectively tuned to respond to different characteristics of the input.

Elsewhere in the medulla, important processing of temporal interactions occurs, which requires a contralateral blending of inputs from both ears. Some medullary neurons respond only to truly synchronous input from each ear, while others are tuned for critical intervals of asynchronous input. Such processing allows for accurate location of the speech signal source in space, and initiates appropriate orientation responses. Fibres from the medullary areas pass through the brainstem bilaterally, with links to the reticular formation and the cerebellum. The **reticular formation** is responsible for relaying sensory input and for readying the cortex as a whole for the arrival of this input. The **cerebellum**, while primarily associated with motor control, has a number of sensory inputs including the auditory and, like the reticular formation, has rich connections with the cortex.

Further complex intermixing of binaural input takes place in the neurons of the **inferior colliculus** in the **midbrain**, some of which are specialized for **ipsilateral** or for **contralateral** input. The major output from here is to an area of the thalamus represented bilaterally as the **medial geniculate body**. This has two-way connections with the cells of the **auditory cortex**, and is thus rather more than simply a further relay station in the auditory system. One of the problems in defining the functions of cells higher up the system is the extent to which their operation is dependent on such higher brain processes as attention, emotion, memory and so on. Likewise, the organization and function of cells in the auditory cortex is complex and difficult to determine. As in other sensory modalities, the relevant parts of the cortex are organized into a series of **projection fields**, or 'maps' of the relevant parts of the body, in this case the basilar membrane, with one field having primary function.

Thus far, we have not considered the way that language is organized within the brain itself, essentially between the auditory cortex and the motor speech cortex. Functionally, we can think of the cerebral cortex as consisting of four separate but interconnected areas – the frontal, the parietal, the temporal and the occipital lobes, with each of these lobes being represented in the left and right hemispheres (see Figure 1).

Within this structure, the auditory cortex is located on the upper surface of the temporal lobe in each hemisphere, close to the junction between the temporal, parietal and frontal lobes. This area is concerned, like the whole auditory system of which it forms a part, with all auditory processing, not just with speech. In most individuals, the left hemisphere is dominant, and this is linked to handedness – left-hemisphere dominance is particularly noticeable in right-handers. The implication of this for speech audition is that the auditory cortex in the left (i.e. normally dominant) hemisphere is more especially involved than the corresponding area on the right; and, because the majority of nerve fibres travel to the auditory cortex contralaterally, this leads to a typical **right-ear advantage** for

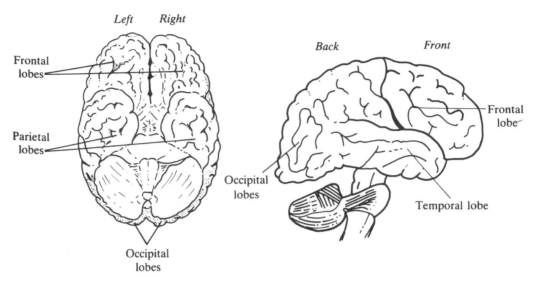

speech, particularly for stop consonants (see ARTICULATORY PHONETICS) that are maximally distinct. This phenomenon has been viewed as evidence for a specialized speech-perception centre in the left hemisphere, but it is not clear that this specialization is strictly for speech sounds alone.

As far as speech production is concerned, we have noted the area of the cerebral cortex which is represented bilaterally at the base of the so-called motor strip, close to the junction of the frontal, parietal and temporal lobes. This controls the musculature of the lips, tongue, velum, etc. (see ARTICULATORY PHONETICS) for both speech and non-speech activities such as blowing and swallowing. Again, the implication of cerebral dominance is that it is normally the left hemisphere that is most closely involved in speech functions, but the issue is not very clear. Generally, it appears that both hemispheres contribute to sensory feedback and motor-control functions in speech as well as non-speech oral-tract activities; the motor nerve fibres are routed from the cortex to the oral tract in bilateral fashion. Nevertheless, dominance is a left-hemisphere characteristic for speech, and it appears that the reason for this may

lie in an association between a specialized speech-control centre in the dominant hemisphere and the area of motor cortex devoted to the innervation of oral tract musculature. The function of such a specialized speech processor in production may be primarily bound up in the need for very rapid sequencing of the very precise articulatory movements in speech.

The evidence for hemispherically specialized speech control comes in the main from two remarkable sorts of surgical sources: silver electrode stimulation on the exposed brains of anesthetized but fully conscious patients in cases where precise mapping of the speech area is required prior to surgical intervention, and from so-called 'split brain' patients in whom the left and right hemispheres have been surgically sectioned, resulting in a situation where information that is made available only to the right hemisphere cannot be expressed in speech output, i.e. by the left hemisphere. Much information on the organization of language in the brain also comes from the study of brain-damaged patients, where, however, the evidence is frequently difficult to interpret as a result of problems in identifying the precise nature of the damage, and the effects of compensatory strategies (see APHASIA).

M.A.G.

Suggestions for further reading

Crystal, D. (1980) *An Introduction to Language Pathology*, London: Edward Arnold.

Espir, M.L.E. and Rose, F.C. (1983) *The Basic Neurology of Speech and Language*, 3rd edition, Oxford: Blackwell Scientific.

Perkins, W.H. and Kent, R.D. (1986) *Textbook of Functional Anatomy of Speech, Language, and Hearing*, San Diego: College-Hill.

Walsh, K.W. (1978) *Neuropsychology: A Clinical Approach*, Edinburgh: Churchill Livingstone.

Whitaker, H. and Whitaker, H.A. (eds) (1976) *Studies in Neurolinguistics* (Perspectives in Neurolinguistics and Psycholinguistics Series), vol. 1, New York: Academic Press.

Language surveys

The development of dialect studies during the late nineteenth century was greatly facilitated by the simultaneous development of a set of techniques for undertaking surveys of linguistic usage and of other variables associated with language (attitudinal, etc.). During the intervening century or so, a large body of literature on the mechanics and requirements of language surveys has built up, and a large number of surveys have been carried out: some dialectological, some more general; some micro- and some macrolinguistic in character. The depth and scope of coverage of these surveys has varied greatly, in terms of the range of aspects of the language(s) with which they have dealt, in terms of the geographical and social constraints placed on selection of speakers for the survey, and in terms of the density of sampling across each population surveyed. Early works in this tradition dealt predominantly with geographical dialects, mainly rural, of familiar European languages – often using very small and unrepresentative samples of informants (see also DIALECTOLOGY).

More recently, one of the effects of the increasing sophistication of dialectologists with respect to sampling technique and general research methodology has been the growth of a tendency to aim at coverage of entire populations, without any prior decision as to which types of variety or speaker are most relevant. Furthermore, surveys of varieties traditionally perceived as entire languages, either singly or in geographically associated groupings, have become more common. These vary in level of sophistication from the often crude, general questions on language which form part of many government censuses, etc., to highly detailed surveys of usage and other matters, both in immigrant communities in the West and (sometimes) across whole populations, including native speakers of indigenous languages. The main thrust of all these kinds of survey has typically been the investigation of actual usage, including bilingualism or bidialectism and the distribution of functions between the different languages or dialects spoken.

To some extent, it has been deemed possible to control certain aspects of the situation in which speech and/or comments on language are obtained, in particular formality, and thus to study the covariation of usage with such factors. This method has yielded much data of interest, though it must be applied with due caution: speakers and writers may have a range of culturally defined identities and orientations (e.g. age- or gender-based) which affect their conscious or unconscious situation-related choice of usage, and correlation *per se* is not always the best approach. (The same caveat applies to naive correlation of variable linguistic data with supposedly objective social characteristics of the speakers themselves.)

Much investigation of usage, however, has of necessity been carried out through indirect channels such as informants' self-reports, which naturally vary considerably in reliability and completeness. In recognition of this, and because of the inherent interest of this sort of material, techniques have been developed – particularly within the Labovian tradition of urban dialectology – for studying informants' opinions and beliefs about their own and others' usage, and also for examining their subjective reactions to usage of various kinds, their impressions of the facts regarding distribution of functions, etc.

In addition, one can obtain from actual data some evidence on the accuracy or otherwise of informants' intuitions about their own usage. Devices such as reading passages and blank-filling tests are frequently used, in addition to conversational sections intended to produce approximations to normal speech. Some such techniques have, of course, long been employed in more traditional studies where there has been less focus on obtaining spontaneous instances of phenomena.

In their interest in both usage itself and attitudes/beliefs concerning it, workers in this area typically differ both from the **descriptivist** tradition, with its tenet enjoining concentration on usage alone, and from the **generativist** tradition, in which intuitions have been allocated a central place and status in argumentation, and in which the possibility of major discrepancy between intuitions and the usage to which they relate has seldom been a focus of attention. Theoretical considerations have, however, seldom exercised survey workers as much as problems in methodology; they have been concerned largely with the accuracy of their descriptions for their own sake, or with practical implications of their findings.

The features shared by most language surveys are those fairly obviously associated with sampling, data collection and analysis. As a first step, the goals of the survey must be defined, i.e. what kind of material is desired (data *per se*, attitudes, etc.) and what the purpose is behind obtaining it – descriptive, theoretical, practical (e.g. remedial), etc. In the light of these considerations, the scope of the survey – the population to be sampled, the range and form of any questionnaire used, etc. – must be settled. Resources and theoretical/methodological persuasions will then yield a variety of decisions as to the means of approach to informants (direct, postal, etc.), the number of informants approached and the format used in selecting these, the number and background of fieldworkers used, etc.

The main survey will often be preceded by a pilot study – a small-scale, often less rigorous study, aimed at determining the relative importance of potential linguistic or non-linguistic variables, or at testing other features or aspects of the survey in advance – and by examination of all available background material, both linguistic and demographic (size, density, origin, distribution and character of human population).

After the survey itself has been carried out, the material obtained will be analysed in accordance with whatever paradigm has been adopted, and conclusions will be drawn. In some cases, these latter may involve modification of the paradigm. Any practical recommendations arising from the conclusions will then emerge. It will be seen that there is considerable scope for variation in the detailed character of such surveys, and the range of formats may best be illustrated by consideration of the most important groups of surveys, of all types, undertaken over the last century or so.

The German dialect survey of Wenker, Wrede and others (from 1876)

This pioneering survey was concerned strictly with rural non-standard dialects of German and coincided with the first studies of specific dialects, carried out in the same vein. Initially, the aims were descriptive, but the project was drawn into controversies of a theoretical nature arising from the much-publicized pronouncements of the **Junggrammatiker** (e.g., the **Neogrammarian Principle** – see HISTORICAL LINGUISTICS). Both adherents and opponents of the relevant tenets, which related to constraints on linguistic change, cited the findings in support of their divergent viewpoints.

Only actual data were collected – not evidence of beliefs, attitudes, etc. The survey eventually covered the entire European German Empire. Every village with a school was sampled; the method adopted was indirect, involving the mailing of a questionnaire to the schoolteacher at each location, with instructions about how it should be filled in. Approximately forty sentences were to be translated from Standard German into the local dialect, and pronunciation was to be indicated using the regular orthography as best the teachers could. The intention was to obtain information on the most specifically local forms, typically the most archaic; this reflects the nineteenth-century interest in supposedly pure speech (see also DIALECTOLOGY). However, the degree to which this was obtained is questionable, since teachers would vary a great deal in their ability to reproduce usage accurately, and the system adopted was obviously more suitable for syntax and morphology than for phonology. In addition, all nineteenth-century work on phonology was pre-structuralist, with only rare attempts at moving beyond surface phonetics to statements of systems.

Over 52,000 questionnaires were returned adequately completed, and the survey became based at the University of Marburg. The vast amount of data involved hindered the task of synthesis, and maps did not begin to appear until 1926, fifteen years after the death of Georg Wenker, the originator. Publication was sparse and the project was abandoned after eighty years in 1956. In 1939, 48,000 copies of a second questionnaire were received, and the results, mainly concerning lexis, were published between 1953 and 1978 (Wrede and Mitzka 1926–56; Mitzka and Schmidt 1953–78).

The French dialect survey of Gilliéron and Edmont (from 1897)

In France, concern developed during the 1880s at the apparently imminent demise of local dialect in the face of the advance of Standard French. Jules Gilliéron accepted the task of carrying out a survey of the relevant varieties, and, partly in view of the alleged urgency of his mission, adopted radically different techniques from those used in Germany – though he retained the German assumptions about the kind of speech/speaker to be examined, and also the German interest in contemporary issues in historical linguistics. He employed the direct method, i.e. on-the-spot investigation by a fieldworker. In order to increase the level of consistency, he used only one, trained fieldworker – the amateur dialectologist Edmond Edmont.

These decisions necessarily reduced dramatically the geographical density of the coverage – only 683 locations in mainland France and Corsica were investigated over a period of some fifteen years – but the amount of linguistic detail obtained for each locality, the reliability and consistency of the material, and the speed of analysis and publication (carried out while the survey was progressing, using material posted back to Gilliéron) were all vastly superior to the corresponding features of the German survey. Edmont used one or two informants in each locality, predominantly males lacking in formal education, and worked with a large questionnaire which in its final form elicited 1900 items from each informant. The resulting atlas appeared between 1902 and 1910 (Gilliéron and Edmont 1902–10).

Two of Gilliéron's students, Karl Jaberg and Jakob Jud, later produced a similar but improved format for their atlas of the Italian-speaking area of Europe (1928–40), and Jud, together with their chief fieldworker Paul Scheuermeier (himself a successful innovator in fieldwork methodology), had a decisive influence on the early stages of American survey work (see below).

The English dialect society

In 1870 W.A. Wright called for the founding of an English Dialect Society (*Notes and Queries* 1870; see Petyt 1980: 76), and the Society got underway in 1873 with W.W. Skeat as its Secretary and Director. Between 1873 and 1896 it published many volumes on English dialects, including bibliographies, reprinted and original glossaries, and dialect monographs of varying length and type.

The Society's aim was to produce a definitive dialect grammar and dictionary, and in 1895 Joseph Wright, a self-taught academic from Yorkshire who became Professor of Comparative Philology at Oxford, was appointed editor of both works. The Society was then disbanded, perceiving its task as having been completed. The dictionary was published in six volumes between 1898 and 1905 (Wright 1898–1905), with the grammar forming part of volume 6 and also appearing separately (Wright 1905). The Society's influence continued in the form of regional dialect societies.

American surveys of Kurath and others (from 1931)

A large number of scholars began to work on a projected linguistic atlas of the United States and Canada in 1931. Owing to the huge area to be covered, it was necessary to treat each region as a self-contained unit, and the key role was that of overall coordinator; Hans Kurath, who took up this position, also directed the first regional survey – that dealing with New England. This proceeded rapidly, partly assisted by the smaller distances and denser settlement patterns in that area, and provided a model for other regions. The amount of variability was typically small by comparison with that to be found in Europe, owing to the relatively recent occupation of North America by English speakers, but, particularly in the east, large quantities of interesting material on folk speech and other regionalized usage were collected. Prominent workers on the project have included Harold B. Allen, E. Bagby Atwood and Guy S. Lowman.

By this time, tape-recorders were becoming more readily available, to some extent circumventing the problem of the role of the fieldworker in interpreting and recording the responses – a problem which had become increasingly obvious as awareness of the different character of broad and narrow transcriptions (see PHONEMICS) grew. Now decisions could at least be made later and at greater leisure on the evidence of a recording. Other aspects of the work also represented advances on the European studies; attempts, albeit somewhat haphazard and simplistic by later standards, were made to examine informants of different social and educational levels, and also of different age ranges, since the organizers realized that 'broad' dialect of the type traditionally studied in Europe was of lesser importance in a North American context.

The project proceeded only slowly in later decades and, following the publication of the New England work (Kurath *et al.* 1939–43), no major volumes on other areas appeared until 1961 (Kurath and McDavid 1961). Under the influence of Allen further volumes continued to appear, but much work remains to be done for American dialectology.

The Survey of English Dialects (SED) (Dieth, Orton and others, from 1948)

After the winding up of the English Dialect Society, serious work on English dialects resumed only at a relatively late date. In the intervening period only regional dialect societies and various isolated academic investigations were in existence, but after World War II, Eugen Dieth, based in Zürich, Switzerland, suggested a general survey. Harold Orton, at Leeds, took up the role of organizer for England, and the **Linguistic Survey of Scotland** (see below) also began soon afterwards.

Despite Dieth's own enthusiasm for synchronic as opposed to purely historical issues, the form taken by the study as it developed was largely traditional. The focus was mainly on phonology and lexis, and in respect of the former the interest was predominantly diachronic, and the transcriptions used strictly phonetic (by intention) rather than phonemic. Furthermore, only informants of the standard European type (elderly uneducated males) were used, unless none was available. Some of the locations – though very few – were in this case urban, but the main focus was again on rural areas. An assortment of fieldworkers investigated 311 localities around 1015 miles (1600Km) apart between 1948 and 1961.

Some tape-recordings were made, but little use was made of these in analysis, and attempts were accordingly made, as in North America, to standardize the training of fieldworkers, though this enterprise was not totally successful. The questionnaire was highly structured, with various different types of question, e.g. naming, completing, converting (i.e. obtaining a variant on a construction). This aspect of the survey was the focus of considerable attention, and many subsequent studies of particular dialects used questionnaires based on the SED model.

As usual, the rate of publication was slow – an Introduction by Orton appeared in 1962, followed by four volumes of unprocessed responses sorted by regions (Orton and Dien 1962–71); there is a fairly clear bias towards northern areas in respect of accuracy and interest. After Orton's death in 1975, other workers continued the project and in 1978 a *Linguistic Atlas of England* appeared (Orton *et al.* 1978), synthesizing some of the most important findings in map form (expense prohibited the display of all the data in this form). Many articles and a number of books (see in particular Wakelin 1972) were based on SED data, and Leeds University continued as a centre of dialect studies under the aegis of Stanley Ellis. Attitudes to SED are at present ambivalent – the resurgence of interest in geographical issues and the desire for real-time material encourage use of the data, but for modern purposes it is often difficult to interpret and it is sometimes plainly wrong or misleading.

The Linguistic Survey of Scotland (LSS) (from 1949)

The LSS differs from the studies described above in a number of ways: it is broader in scope within its geographical bounds, dealing with Gaelic as well as English, and with any form of usage, in either language, found in or just outside Scotland, rather than with 'broad' dialect alone (hence 'linguistic' rather than 'dialect' in its title); it is more eclectic in its methodology, using varying approaches to suit different kinds of data; it is an ongoing study rather than a once-for-all project – since 1965, it has been a department in the Faculty of Arts at its home base, the University of Edinburgh; from the outset its focus has been on synchronic and structuralist issues rather than on the traditionally popular diachronic matters, and its more specific concerns have continued to alter in accordance with changes in linguistics as a whole. Important workers have included J.C. Catford, Trevor Hill, James Y. Mather, Angus McIntosh and Hans-Hennig Speitel.

The initial stages of the survey dealt with lexis, and were conducted by means of postal questionnaires (1951ff.) – over 2600 copies were returned in a usable state by the local teachers who had been asked to supervise their completion by suitable informants. Fieldwork of a more direct nature commenced in 1955, and over 250 localities have been investigated in this way, using trained interviewers working from a standardized questionnaire aimed at eliciting phonological and morphological information. Wherever possible, the main points of phonological systems were to be determined on the spot rather than in later analysis, a policy not favoured in the American surveys owing to its time-consuming nature and the resulting strain placed on informants.

Serious publication did not begin until 1975, but the *Linguistic Atlas of Scotland* (Mather and Speitel 1975ff.) appeared in three volumes. The Gaelic section of the survey lagged behind, but work in this area, and also on Scots and Scottish English, continues.

Surveys in the Labovian tradition (1965 and after)

Labov's seminal work in New England and New York City (see DIALECTOLOGY) prompted a number of studies, varying considerably in scope and type but all influenced by the central tenets of Labov's position: the need to focus on statistically valid samples of the relevant populations; to work with a structured interview or other

procedure designed to obtain speech at various levels of formality; to investigate intuitions and attitudes in addition to actual usage (not as a substitute for it). Some of these studies, such as the theoretically oriented **Tyneside Linguistic Survey** (Barbara Strang, John Pellowe, etc.) have persisted over long periods without producing widely circulated results; others have been completed rapidly by one or a few investigators and quickly publicized.

Labov's own study of New York City, published in 1966, established many of the precedents for such surveys. Around 100 informants were used, selected through a stratified random sample – a random sample was taken from each of several 'strata' of the population, established on the basis of factors known to be relevant to its structure – and the interview elicited two conversational styles and also included a reading passage, a word list, linguistic exercises aimed at obtaining subjective reactions to variant forms, and more anecdotal discussion of this sort of issue. Labov himself later organized a longer-term study of the usage of New York African Americans, employing less formal contexts of observation (Labov 1972a), and some subsequent work emulated and extended this feature of his work (e.g. Milroy 1980/1987).

Even before these developments, however, the classical Labovian paradigm had been used by others, in particular Roger Shuy and his colleagues in their Detroit survey (Shuy *et al.* 1968). This large-scale project was one of the first to examine grammatical variation quantitatively, and also refined considerably the Labovian classification of variables as perceived and evaluated by speakers. In addition, the Detroit team pioneered the use of computers in processing and storing data – techniques which have been vastly extended more recently – and also pursued educational implications of their findings, another aspect of this kind of work which has repeatedly featured in later studies.

Recent macrolinguistic surveys

The previous section dealt with surveys produced within a framework developed by practitioners of the new discipline of sociolinguistics, but **sociolinguistics** is, of course, by no means confined to Labovian urban dialectology. A quite different, macrolinguistic type of study also developed during the 1970s and 1980s, under the influence of sociolinguists. Studies of this latter kind seek, broadly speaking, to answer the question: Who speaks what, about what subjects, where, when, to whom, etc.? Some investigators have worked with second-hand data obtained from government censuses, etc., but more recently the need has been felt for more precise, theoretically sounder surveys carried out by experts.

One of the best-known such surveys is that carried out by the **Linguistic Minorities Project**, financed by the British Department of Education and Science. This project was concerned with the newer minority languages of the United Kingdom – those used by originally immigrant communities from Asia, the European continent and elsewhere. Earlier surveys (e.g. by the Inner London Education Authority in 1978; ILEA 1979) had revealed the complexity of the linguistic situation in the schools of London and other British cities, and in addition had increased awareness of the educational consequences of failure to develop positive policies to deal with the many minority languages involved. The Linguistic Minorities Project commenced operation in 1980 and conducted questionnaire-based studies in several cities, dealing mainly with school-age subjects. The questionnaires sought to establish: patterns of usage (fluency, frequency and domain of selection of each available language, etc.); nomenclature; literacy; attitudes (including attitudes to the use of the languages in education and to their possible status as examination subjects), etc. As a result of the findings of these studies, various educational programmes were instigated or altered in character, generally in the direction of providing more encouragement for and recognition of the home languages of students from immigrant/minority backgrounds.

Issues of this kind have also been examined in countries and communities where bilingualism/multilingualism is common and where the status and domain distribution of the various languages is different, e.g., in Wales (Council for the Welsh Language/Cyngor yr Iaith Gymraeg 1978) and Canada (Cauldwell 1982). There is still scope and need for many other such studies and for programmes (educational, planning in the media, etc.) based on their results.

M.Nk

Suggestions for further reading

Ferguson, C.A. and Heath, S.B. (eds) (1981) *Language in the USA*, Cambridge: Cambridge University Press.

Francis, W.N. (1983) *Dialectology*, London: Longman.

Trudgill, P.J. (ed.) (1984) *Language in the British Isles*, Cambridge: Cambridge University Press.

Language typology

Language typology is based on the assumption that (Greenberg 1974: 54–5)

the ways in which languages differ from each other are not entirely random, but show various types of dependencies among those properties of languages which are not invariant differences statable in terms of the 'type'. The construct of the 'type' is, as it were, interposed between the individual language in all its uniqueness and the unconditional or invariant features to be found in all languages.

The data provided by typological language studies show the limits within which languages can vary, and in so doing provide statements about the nature of language (Mallinson and Blake 1981: 6). Each language is not necessarily assigned to one class only. For example, in Sapir's (1921) morphological typology, languages are arranged on a comparative scale in regard to some properties, and in Greenberg (1954) such scales are made explicit by the provision of a metric with ten indices.

Since language typology is concerned with the historical comparison of languages, while genetic classification (see HISTORICAL LINGUISTICS) is historically determined, 'there is no contradiction in the fact that closely related languages might be separated in some particular typological classification, while languages only remotely or not at all related are classed together' (Greenberg 1974: 56). Nor is there any reason why 'a typological characteristic should not itself involve an historic fact about the language as long as no assumption is made that the properties found in the language are themselves historically connected' (1974: 56). For example, historicity is itself a criterion which distinguishes **natural** from **artificial languages** (see ARTIFICIAL LANGUAGES) such as Esperanto and Volapük (Stewart 1962b).

Greenberg (1974: 13, n.4) dates the first use of the word 'typology' in linguistic literature to the theses presented by the Prague School linguists to the First Congress of Slavonic Philologists held in 1928. Until then, classification of languages was largely **genetic**; that is, it was based on the development of languages from older source languages (see HISTORICAL LINGUISTICS), and the only extensively used typology was morphological classification of languages as approximating towards **ideal types**: isolating, agglutinating/agglutinative, inflecting/

flectional/fusional and polysynthetic/incorporating (although see Wundt 1900).

An ideal **isolating language** is one in which there is a one-to-one correspondence between words and morphemes. Comrie (1981/1989: 43) provides these examples from Vietnamese:

> *Khi tôi đến nhà bạn tôi,*
> when I   come house friend I
> *chúng tôi bắt đấu làm bài*
> PLURAL I   seize head do lesson
> 'When I came to my friend's house, we began to do lessons'

In addition to Vietnamese, Chinese and several other Southeast Asian languages are usually classified as close to isolating.

An **agglutinating** or **agglutinative language** is one which attaches separable affixes to roots (see MORPHOLOGY), so that there may be several morphemes in a word, but the boundaries between them are always clear. Each morpheme has a reasonably invariant shape, as the following example from Comrie (1981/1989: 44) demonstrates. The example shows the declension of the Turkish noun *adam* 'man':

	Singular	Plural
Nominative	*adam*	*adam-lar*
Accusative	*adam-ı*	*adam-lar-ı*
Genitive	*adam-ın*	*adam-lar-ın*
Dative	*adam-a*	*adam-lar-a*
Locative	*adam-da*	*adam-lar-da*
Ablative	*adam-dan*	*adam-lar-dan*

Hungarian and Japanese are also usually classified as close to agglutinating.

An **inflecting**, **flectional** or **fusional language** is one in which morphemes are represented by affixes, but in which it is difficult to assign morphemes precisely to the different parts of the affixes. For instance, in the Latin *Puellam bellam amo*, 'I love the beautiful girl', the *-am* ending on the noun and on the adjective marks the noun as feminine, singular and accusative, and the *-o* ending on the verb represents first person singular subject and present active indicative (Mallinson and Blake 1981: 20–1). Russian, Ancient Greek and Sanskrit are also inflecting.

A **polysynthetic** or **incorporating language** makes great use of affixation and often incorporates what English would represent with nouns and adverbs in that element which resembles a verb. Ireland (1989: 108) provides the following example from Inuktitut (Baffin Island Eskimo):

Tavva   *-guuq   ikpiarju(q)*
Then(suddenly) they say work-bag
-ku(t)- -Luni-
by   while she
tigualaka   *-mi*
swept up (in one motion) LOC (from)
-uk takanu-   *nga ikijaq-*
POSS that one there below her way out
tuq- Luni qaja(q)r- mun
she while kayak   towards
'Then suddenly, she swept up her work-bag from its place below her as she went out towards the kayak'

Other Inuit (Eskimo) languages and some American Indian languages are also polysynthetic.

Few languages fall clearly into one of these categories, and linguists working in this tradition have provided increasingly complex classification systems. For instance, Sapir (1921) provides three parameters – grammatical concepts, grammatical processes and firmness of affixation – with multiple values for each. According to Horne (1966), this gives rise to 2870 language types; that is, about half as many types as there are languages, and if typology aims to order linguistic variety then the value of such a system may be questioned. In addition, it is often difficult to establish word and morpheme boundaries, and even to arrive at a satisfactory definition of either phenomenon (see MORPHOLOGY), and these difficulties cause severe practical difficulties for morphological typology (see Comrie 1981/1989: 46–52 for a thorough discussion).

The Prague School linguists were primarily interested in typologizing languages on the basis of their phonology. Phonological typology is based on the different ways in which languages organize sounds into phonological systems and syllable structures (Robins 1964/1989: 370). Perhaps the best-known distinction here is that between tone languages and non-tonal languages. This distinction is drawn according to the function in the different languages of voice pitch: briefly, in **tone languages** pitch helps distinguish one word from another, while in non-tonal languages pitch does not have this function. Within tone languages, distinctions may be made between those whose tones are of contrasting levels and those in which rising and falling pitch is part of the tone system itself. Tone languages can also be typologized on the basis of the number of tones they contain and on the basis of the uses to which the tones are put (see, further, TONE LANGUAGES).

Languages also differ phonologically in terms of the kinds of syllable structure they permit. Every known language contains CV syllables (syllables composed of a consonant, C, followed by a vowel, V), but languages like English and German permit a high degree of consonant clustering at the beginning and end of syllables, whereas Fijian and Hawaiian do not. A **consonant cluster** consists of several consonants in succession, e.g. German *Angst*, English *scream*; the Danish versions of these two clusters come together in the compound, *angstskrig*, 'scream of fear', with six consonants in pronunciation, /aŋstskri/.

Since the middle of the twentieth century, typological research has mainly centred on syntax and has been closely linked with the study of language universals (see LANGUAGE UNIVERSALS). Some language universals are features present in all or an overwhelming majority of languages. Other universals are implicational: they state that if feature x is present in a language, then (it is highly likely that) feature y will also be present in that language. The interplay with typology can be seen in the selection of the features in terms of which universals are defined. For instance, many of Greenberg's (1966b) universals (see LANGUAGE UNIVERSALS) imply a typological analysis in terms of the order of subject (S), object (O) and verb (V).

S, O and V are, properly speaking, clause or sentence constituents, but typology involving them is normally referred to as **word-order typology**. Word-order typology also includes studies of the order of words or constituents within the noun phrase and of whether a language has prepositions or postpositions (see below).

The notion of a **basic word order** in terms of S, O and V is common to a large number of studies in grammatical language typology: languages are typologized on the basis of the order in which S, O and V typically occur in the simple sentences of the language. The most common basic word orders are SVO, as in English and French, and SOV, as in Japanese and Turkish. German has SVO in main clauses and SOV in subordinate clauses, and Robins (1964/1989) classes it as an SVO language. VSO, as in Welsh, is the next most common, but all of the six logically possible configurations – SOV, SVO, VSO, VOS, OVS, OSV – are, in fact, found: Malagasy (West Indonesian language of Malagasy, previously Madagascar) has VOS, and Hixkaryana (Carib language of northern Brazil) has OVS. There are also languages, such as Dyirbal (Australian language of north-eastern Queensland), that do not appear to have any basic word order. This, however, merely means that typology in terms of word order is limited to those languages that have a basic word order, just as tone-language typology is limited to tone languages.

The relative frequencies of the six possible orders is (Tomlin 1986: 3) SOV = SVO > VSO > VOS = OVS > OSV. Tomlin establishes this relative frequency on the basis of data from 1063 languages, and explains it on the basis of interaction among three principles: the Theme First Principle, the Verb–Object Bonding principle, and the Animated First Principle.

The **Theme First Principle** (**TFP**) says that thematic information – information which is particularly salient to the development of the discourse – is likely to come first in simple main clauses. The **Verb–Object Bonding** (**VOB**) principle says that in general the O of a transitive clause is more tightly bound to the V than to S. The **Animated First Principle** (**AFP**) states that in basic transitive clauses, the NP which is most animated will precede others. The more of these principles which a constituent order allows to be realized, the more frequent the order. The principles are explained as arising from the processes and limitations of human information-processing ability (see LANGUAGE UNIVERSALS).

Word order within the noun phrase concerns the relative order of adjective (A), noun (N), genitive (G) and relative clause (Rel). For A and N there are, obviously, two possible configurations, AN (English, Turkish) and NA (French, Welsh). Languages with basic order NA are more tolerant of exceptions (French – *le petit prince* 'the little prince' as opposed to *le tapis vert* 'the carpet green') than AN languages: in English, for instance, *the carpet green* is distinctly odd, and such constructions are only found in set expressions like *princess royal* and *court martial* and in some poetry (and even there they seem archaic).

There are three possible configurations for N and Rel. In English, for instance, N precedes Rel – *the potato that the man gave to the woman* – while in Turkish, Rel precedes N (Comrie 1981/1989: 90):

adam-ın kadin-a ver -diğ -i
man GEN woman DAT give NOM SUF his
patates
potato
'man's to the woman giving his potato', that is 'the that-the-man-gave-to-the-woman potato'.

The third possibility is that Rel is **circumnominal**; that is, it surrounds N. Comrie (1981/1989: 145) gives the following example from Bambara (a member of the Mande branch of the Niger-Congo languages, spoken in Senegal, Mali and Burkina Faso (Upper Volta)):

> *tyè*   *be*   *[n ye so min ye]*
> man the PRESENT I PAST house see
> *dyɔ*
> build
> 'The man is building the house that I saw.'

The part in square brackets is the relative clause in this construction, but it is a construction which can stand alone, in which case it would mean 'I saw the house.' So in relative clauses in Bambara, N is expressed in the relative clause in the usual form for a noun of that grammatical relation within a clause, and there is no expression of it in the main clause. Bambara has SOV basic order, and the relative clause functions as object in the main clause: 'The man is the house that I saw building.' It should be noted that there are languages which may not have any construction which could be called a relative clause at all (see Comrie 1981/1989: 144).

For G and N there are again two possible orders, GN and NG. English uses both: *the man's son* and *the son of the man*. French uses NG and Turkish GN.

Adpositional word order typology is concerned with whether a language uses mainly **prepositions** (Pr) or **postpositions** (Po). English uses Pr: *for the man*; whereas Turkish uses Po: *adam için* 'the man for'. Pr and Po are adpositions (Ap), Pr being a pre-N adposition and Po a post-N adposition; hence we can typologize languages as ApN (English) or NAp (Turkish). Estonian uses both orders and most Australian languages have neither Pr nor Po (Comrie 1981/1989: 91).

Word order typology is considered particularly important because although they are logically independent of each other, word order parameters such as those discussed above seem to correlate. For example, NAp appears to correlate with SOV, while ApN appears to correlate with VSO; ApN correlates with NG, NAp with GN; VSO correlates with NA; SOV + NG correlates with NA (Comrie 1981/1989: 92–3).

Grammatical typology also uses grammatical catagories such as case, gender, number and tense as bases for classification.

Over time, languages may change in type (Greenberg 1974: 64). For instance, languages without nasalized vowels may acquire them in the following way (1974: 66): 'A previously oral vowel becomes non-distinctively nasalized by a preceding or following nasal consonant. The nasal consonant, the former conditioning factor, is lost and the oral and nasal vowels are now in contrast.'

Another powerful demonstration of this change of typology over time is found in the phenomenon of the *Sprachbund*. When languages are in close geographical proximity, and their speakers interact freely with each other, it sometimes happens that even if the languages are not genetically related they come to share more features with each other than they share with other members of their language family. The study of this phenomenon is known as **areal typology**, and a group of languages which has become similar because of geographical proximity is known as a ***Sprachbund*** or **language union**.

Comrie (1981/1989: 204–5) suggests that the initial impetus to areal typology arose from the discovery that Modern Greek and Albanian (separate branches of Indo-European), Bulgarian and Macedonian (Slavonic), Romanian (Romance), and other languages all spoken in the Balkan area, have a number of features in common which they do not share with other languages to which they are more closely related genetically. All the languages are Indo-European, but they belong to different branches (see HISTORICAL LINGUISTICS), and the other languages in these branches do not exhibit the features which the Balkan *Sprachbund* exhibits. These include a wide range of shared lexical items, as one would expect of languages in close geographical proximity. But each language also possesses all or some of the following features: syncretism of genitive and dative case – the same form is used to indicate both the possessor and indirect object in noun phrases; postposed articles – the definite article follows the noun; and the loss of the infinitive – each language translates *Give me something to drink* with the structure 'give (to-)me that I-drink', in which the place of the infinitive is taken by a finite subordinate clause introduced by a conjunction (Comrie 1981/1989: 206):

Romanian	Bulgarian
dă-mi să beau	*daj mi da pija*
Albanian	Modern Greek
a-më të pi	*dós mu na pjó*

As Comrie (1981/1989: 209) goes on to point out, the phenomenon of typological change raises the question whether there are any constraints on language change. In fact, research reveals that there are a number of such constraints which are statable in the form of implicational universals such as (1981/1989: 210) 'a language will borrow non-nouns only if it also borrows nouns', 'a language will borrow affixes only if it also borrows lexical items from the same source'.

Main centres for research in language typology include Stanford University, the University of Southern California, the Department of Linguistics of the University of Cologne, Germany (Universalenprojekt), and the Leningrad section of the Linguistics Institute of the Academy of Sciences, Russia (Structural Typology Group).

It is usually languages as such which are typologized, but the word **typology** may also be applied to analyses of grammatical or other properties of languages, for example to Bloomfield's (1933/1935: 194–6) division of syntactic constructions into endocentric and exocentric types (Greenberg 1974: 14). An **endocentric** construction is one which is of the same form class as one of its constituents – for instance, *poor John* is of the same class (noun phrase) as *John*. An **exocentric** construction is one which is not of the same form class as any of its constituents – for instance, *John ran* is neither a noun phrase nor a verb phrase, but a sentence.

K.M.

Suggestions for further reading

Comrie, B. (1981/1989) *Language Universals and Linguistic Typology: Syntax and Morphology*, Oxford: Basil Blackwell; 2nd edition 1989.

Greenberg, J.H. (1974) *Language Typology: A Historical and Analytic Overview* (Janua Linguarum, Series Minor, no. 184), The Hague: Mouton.

Language universals

Introduction

The study of **language universals** is based on the premise that 'underlying the endless and fascinating idiosyncrasies of the world's languages there are uniformities of universal scope. Amid infinite diversity, all languages are, as it were, cut from the same pattern' (Greenberg *et al.* 1966: xv). The theory of language universals specifies which properties are necessary to human languages, which are possible, but not necessary, and which are impossible, so that (Comrie 1981/1989: 33–4) 'over all, the study of language universals aims to establish limits on variation within human language'. Since the study of linguistic typology (see LANGUAGE TYPOLOGY) is concerned with studying this variation, there is a strong link between the two disciplines. For example, the study of language universals can help set the parameters for typological research – if it is discovered that all languages have vowels (a language universal; see below), then it will not be fruitful to make the presence versus absence of vowels a basis for the typological classification of languages (Comrie 1981/1989: 38).

There are two main approaches to the study of language universals, one influenced by the work of Joseph Greenberg, and the second by the work of Noam Chomsky (Comrie 1981/1989: 2). The two approaches differ quite radically in terms of their attitude to evidence for and explanation of universals, and since the Chomskyan approach is the simplest in both respects I shall discuss it first.

The Chomskyan approach to universals

Linguists influenced by the early work of Noam Chomsky distinguished two kinds of universal, formal and substantive universals (Chomsky 1965). Some of these are features of all languages, while others represent a set of features from which each language selects a subset. For example, Jakobson's distinctive feature theory (see DISTINCTIVE FEATURES) provides a list of 15–20 features, for which it is claimed that (Comrie 1981/1989: 15)

> the phonological system of any arbitrary language will make use of no distinctive feature not contained in the list, although it is not necessary that any individual language should make use of the whole set (thus English does not make use of the feature Checked).

A **formal universal** is one which determines the form of the grammar – the components, rule types and the principles of rule interaction. A **substantive universal** refers to the content of the rules such as the categories

and bar levels of X-bar theory (see GENERATIVE GRAMMAR) (Hawkins 1988: 6).

One of the first universals to be established within this tradition, namely the universal 'all languages are structure dependent', is based on (Cook 1988: 2): 'the principle of **structure-dependency**, which asserts that knowledge of language relies on the structural relationships in the sentence rather than on the sequence of items'. It is obvious that English speakers' ability to form Yes/No questions, for instance, does not depend merely on knowledge that a word appearing at a certain place in a declarative clause must be moved to the front to form the interrogative. To form the question *Will the letter arrive tomorrow?*, for example, one needs to move the third word of the declarative, *The letter **will** arrive tomorrow*, while to form the question *Is this a dagger I see before me?* one needs to move the second word of the declarative, *This **is** a dagger I see before me.* What is crucial in question formation is a knowledge of syntactic categories: to be able to form English questions, it is necessary to recognize the class of auxiliary verbs, and to know that items of this class are put first in questions.

But even this knowledge is not sufficient to explain English speakers' ability to form questions involving relative clauses. In *The man who is tall is John*, the related question is formed by moving the second auxiliary, while in *John is the man who is tall*, the related question is formed by moving the first auxiliary. Knowing how to form questions in sentences with relative clauses involves knowing that it is the auxiliary in the main clause that has to be moved, and this involves a knowledge of structure. Similarly, in forming passives, one needs to move a phrase, not just a word in a particular place in the sequence, and this again implies a knowledge of structure, since without such knowledge the identification of phrases would be impossible (see, further, GENERATIVE GRAMMAR).

Universals established as transformational-generative grammar evolved include Chomsky's (1981, 1982) figurationality parameters (see GENERATIVE GRAMMAR) – for instance, the **head parameter** – which specifies the order of elements in a language. Any phrase will contain one element which is 'essential'. This element is called the **head** of the phrase (Cook 1988: 7). For instance, in the verb phrase, *liked him very much*, *liked* is the head. The head in English appears on the left of the rest of the phrase, while in Japanese, for instance, it appears on the right. The innate, universal, head parameter specifies that there are just these two possibilities, and that a language chooses one consistently; that is, 'a language has the heads on the same side in all its phrases' (Cook 1988: 9). Parameters reduce the variation between languages to just a few possibilities.

The Chomskyan tradition establishes its universals on the basis of careful, detailed analysis of one or a small number of languages. The surface structure of any language is explained with reference to certain highly abstract features which are shared by all languages because they are innate in humans.

Greenberg's approach to universals

The universals isolated in the Greenberg tradition tend to be established on the basis of data from a large, representative sample of the languages of the world (Greenberg *et al.* 1966: xvi). The ideal base for the study of language universals is all potential human languages. However, many extinct languages were not recorded, or not recorded in sufficient detail to provide usable data, and there is obviously no evidence available from any languages which might evolve in the future. Research must therefore be limited to the study of languages available for present observation, even though it is logically possible that these may turn out, at some distant point in the

future when quite different languages may have evolved, not to be at all representative of all of the possible kinds of language.

But even within this limit it is quite impractical to investigate and work with every single one of the world's languages, since it is estimated that there are around 4000 of these, so that research awaiting evidence from them all would be unlikely ever to get off the ground. Obviously, a selection of languages must be made, and it must be made in such a way that biasing is, as far as possible, avoided. In particular, it is necessary to ensure that the languages chosen represent a range of genetic language families (see HISTORICAL LINGUISTICS), since languages of the same family share a number of traits simply because these have been inherited from the parent language and *not* because the traits are universals.

Ideally, the sample should consist of one language from each of 478 **language groups** isolated by Bell (1978). Each group contains a set of genetically related languages which are separated from their common ancestor by 3500 years. In practice, however, samples are usually smaller, and those languages which have not been adequately described and whose speakers are not easily available to researchers are generally seriously underrepresented. Indo-European languages, for instance, tend to be overrepresented, while the languages of New Guinea and Amazonia are usually missing. Bias can also arise if a sample contains many languages from one geographical area, even if these represent different groups, because languages in geographical proximity tend to influence each other over time. Finally, bias may arise if languages of the same type (see LANGUAGE TYPOLOGY) predominate in a sample (Comrie 1981/ 1989: 10–12).

Greenberg (1966b) works with a sample of thirty languages: Basque, Serbian, Welsh, Norwegian, Modern Greek, Italian, Finnish (European), Yoruba, Nubian, Swahili, Fulani, Masai, Songhai, Berber (African),

Turkish, Hebrew, Burushaski, Hindi, Kannada, Japanese, Thai, Burmese, Malay (Asian), Maori, Loritja (Oceanic), Maya, Zapotec, Quechua, Chibcha and Guarani (American Indian). He proposes forty-five universals of the following three kinds.

I Word order universals
(S = subject, V = verb, O = object)

1 In declarative sentences with nominal subject and object, the dominant order is almost always one in which the subject precedes the object.
2 In languages with prepositions, the genitive almost always follows the governing noun, while in languages with postpositions it almost always precedes (Norwegian has both genitive orders).
3 Languages with dominant VSO order are almost always prepositional.
4 With overwhelmingly greater-than-chance frequency, languages with normal SOV order are postpositional.
5 If a language has dominant SOV order and the genitive follows the governing noun, then the adjective likewise follows the noun.
6 All languages with dominant VSO order have SVO as an alternative or as the only alternative basic order.
7 If, in a language with dominant SOV order, there is no alternative basic order, or only OSV as the alternative, then all adverbial modifiers of the verb likewise precede the verb.

II Syntactic universals

8 When a Yes/No question is differentiated from the corresponding assertion by an intonational pattern, the distinctive intonational features of these patterns are reckoned from the end of the sentence rather than from the beginning.
9 With much more than chance frequency, when question particles or affixes are specified in position by reference to the

sentence as a whole, if initial, such elements are found in prepositional languages and, if final, in postpositional.
10 Question particles or affixes, when specified in position by reference to a particular word in the sentence, almost always follow that word. Such particles do not occur in languages with dominant order VSO.
11 Inversion of statement order so that verb precedes subject occurs only in languages where the question word or phrase is normally initial. This same inversion occurs in Yes/No questions only if it also occurs in interrogative-word questions.
12 If a language has dominant order VSO in declarative sentences, it always puts interrogative words or phrases first in interrogative-word questions; if it has dominant order SOV in declarative sentences, there is never such an invariant rule.
13 If the nominal object always precedes the verb, then verb forms subordinate to the main verb also precede it.
14 In conditional statements, the conditional clause precedes the conclusion as the normal order in all languages.
15 In expressions of volition and purpose, a subordinate verbal form always follows the main verb as the normal order except in those languages in which the nominal object always precedes the verb.
16 In languages with dominant order VSO, an inflected auxiliary always precedes the main verb. In languages with dominant order SOV, an inflected auxiliary always follows the main verb.
17 With overwhelmingly more than chance frequency, languages with dominant order VSO have the adjective after the noun.
18 When the descriptive adjective precedes the noun, then the demonstrative and the numeral, with overwhelmingly more than chance frequency, do likewise.

19 When the general rule is that the descriptive adjective follows, there may be a minority of adjectives which usually precede, but when the general rule is that descriptive adjectives precede there are no exceptions.

20 When any or all of the items (demonstrative, numeral, and descriptive adjective) precede the noun, they are always found in that order. If they follow, the order is either the same or its exact opposite.

21 If some or all adverbs follow the adjective they modify, then the language is one in which the qualifying adjective follows the noun and the verb precedes its nominal object as the dominant order.

22 If, in comparisons of superiority, the only order, or one of the alternative orders, is standard-marker-adjective, then the language is postpositional. With over whelmingly more than chance frequency, if the only order is adjective-marker-standard, the language is prepositional.

23 If in apposition the proper noun usually precedes the common noun, then the language is one in which the governing noun precedes its dependent genitive. With much better than chance frequency, if the common noun usually precedes the proper noun, the dependent genitive precedes its governing noun.

24 If the relative expression precedes the noun either as the only construction or as an alternative construction, either the language is postpositional, or the adjective precedes the noun or both.

25 If the pronominal object follows the verb, so does the nominal object.

III Morphological universals

26 If a language has discontinuous affixes, it always has either prefixing or suffixing or both.

27 If a language is exclusively suffixing, it is postpositional; if it is exclusively prefixing, it is prepositional.

28 If both the derivation and inflection follow the root, the derivation is always between the root and the inflection.

29 If a language has inflection, it always has derivation.

30 If the verb has categories of person–number or if it has categories of gender, it always has tense–mode categories.

31 If either the subject or object noun agrees with the verb in gender, then the adjective always agrees with the noun in gender.

32 Whenever the verb agrees with a nominal subject or nominal object in gender, it also agrees in number.

33 When number agreement between the noun and verb is suspended and the rule is based on order, the case is always one in which the verb precedes and the verb is in the singular.

34 No language has a trial number unless it has a dual. No language has a dual unless it has a plural.

35 There is no language in which the plural does not have some non-zero allomorphs, whereas there are languages in which the singular is expressed only by zero. The dual and trial are almost never expressed only by zero.

36 If a language has the category of gender, it always has the category of number.

37 A language never has more gender categories in non-singular numbers than in the singular.

38 Where there is a case system, the only case which ever has zero allomorphs is the one which includes among its meanings that of the subject of the intransitive verb.

39 Where morphemes of both number and case are present and both follow or precede the noun base, the expression of number almost always comes between the noun base and the expression of case.

40 When the adjective follows the noun, the adjective expresses all the inflectional categories of the noun. In such cases

the noun may lack overt expression of one or all of these categories.

41 If in a language the verb follows both the nominal subject and nominal object as the dominant order, the language almost always has a case system.

42 All languages have pronominal categories involving at least three persons and two numbers.

43 If a language has gender categories in the noun, it has gender categories in the pronoun.

44 If a language has gender distinctions in the first person, it always has gender distinctions in the second or third person, or in both.

45 If there are gender distinctions in the plural of the pronoun, there are some gender distinctions in the singular also.

Although some universals, such as 'all languages have oral vowels' are **non-implicational** – they specify that a certain property is found in all languages without making reference to any other properties of language – it is evident from Greenberg's list that many other universals are **implicational** – they relate the presence of one property to the presence of some other property in such a way that if one property is present, then the other must also be present. Since for any two properties, p and q, it is logically possible that both may be present, that p may be present while q is not, that neither may be present, and that q may be present while p is not, we can see that an implicational universal delimits the logically possible combinations of linguistic properties – they specify that it is not the case that p can be present while q is not. It is only when all the other three possibilities are in fact manifest in some language(s) that there is any point in making an implicational universal claim. For instance, where p is 'nasalized vowels' and q is 'oral vowels', the claim 'if p then q' is empty, because, since all languages have oral vowels, the case where neither p nor q

are manifest does not obtain. Therefore, the non-implicational universal 'all languages have oral vowels', together with the statement 'nasalized vowels are possible', render the implicational universal superfluous (Comrie 1981/1989: 17–18).

Greenberg's list reproduced above also illustrates another parameter, in addition to the implicational/non-implicational parameter, along which universals may be classified; namely, the distinction between **absolute universals**, which are exceptionless, and **universal tendencies**, to which there are exceptions (Comrie 1981/1989: 19):

> This distinction is independent of that between implicational and non-implicational universals, giving over all a fourfold classification. There are absolute non-implicational universals, such as all languages have vowels. There are absolute implicational universals, such as if a language has first/second person reflexives, then it has third person reflexives. There are non-implicational tendencies, such as nearly all languages have nasal consonants (although some Salishan languages have no nasal consonants). Finally, there are implicational tendencies, such as if a language has SOV basic word order, it will probably have postpositions (but Persian, for instance, is SOV with prepositions).

In practice, given the constraints on research discussed above, it is often not possible to establish for certain whether a universal is absolute or just a strong tendency (Comrie 1981/1989: 20).

Hawkins (1988: 5) defines a **distributional** or **frequency universal** as one which states that languages of one type are more frequent than languages of another type. Distributional universals include 'the more similar the position of syntactic heads across phrasal categories, the more languages there are' and 'languages without self-embedded relative clauses are more frequent than those with'.

Linguists working in the Greenbergian tradition allow for variation in the explanation of the existence of the universals which they isolate: it is considered possible that some universals may require one type of explanation, while others may require explanation of another kind. For instance, some universals, such as the fact that all languages have at least three persons and two numbers, may be explained from the point of view of discourse pragmatics: they facilitate communication because they allow speakers to make referential distinctions which make communication more efficient (Hawkins 1988: 11). Comrie (1981/1989: 28) proposes a similar explanation of the fact that the existence of first or second person reflexive forms in a language implies the existence of third person reflexive forms:

> For each of the first and second persons, there is hardly ever ambiguity in a given context whether different instances of the corresponding pronoun are coreferential or not: in a given sentence, all instances of *I* are coreferential, as are usually all instances of *we* and all instances of *you*. In the third person, however, there is potentially a vast number of referents. Some languages say *I hit myself* and some say *I hit me*, but it is not possible to have both interpreted literally with a semantic difference of coreference. But if a language has both *he hit himself* and *he hit him* as possible sentences, then a semantically important distinction of coreference versus non-coreference can be made. Thus reflexivity is simply more important in the third person than in the first or second persons, and this is reflected in the implicational universal.

Other universals may be explained as resulting from constraints which one part of grammar imposes on other parts, or from constraints imposed by the level of meaning on the level of form. Keenan (1979, 1987)

argues for a **Meaning–Form Dependency Principle (MFDP)**, also known as the **Functional Dependency Principle**, which explains why, if in a language there is morphological agreement between, say, nouns and adjectives in (for instance) number and gender, it is always the adjective that agrees with the noun. He argues that this agreement restriction in the morphology arises from a semantic restriction which tends to cause any function category, such as adjective, to change its interpretation to accord with that of its argument, for instance a noun, while the interpretation of the noun is typically invariant with different modifying adjectives. For instance, *flat* has a different interpretation in *flat tyre*, *flat beer* and *flat road*, whereas *road* has the same interpretation in *flat road*, *dusty road* and *windy road* (Hawkins 1988: 8–9). The MFDP thus explains 'a Strong form of internal consistency within the grammar: a dependency in form . . . mirrors a dependency in meaning. That is, a universal morphological dependency follows from a semantic dependency.'

Some language universals may be explained by reference to the **processing demands** placed on language users by, for instance, memory constraints and by the relative ease or difficulty involved in processing certain structures in comprehension and production. For example, it is known that it is more difficult to process **centre-embedded relative clauses** (that is, relative clauses which come in the middle of the sentence) than it is to process **left-peripheral relative clauses** (relative clauses which come at the beginning of the sentence) or **right-peripheral relative clauses** (relative clauses which come at the end of the sentence). This may be because centre embedding requires the processor to interrupt the processing of the main clause in order to process the embedded clause. Thus, in *The man [that the boy kicked] ran away*, one has to interrupt the processing of *The man ran away* to process *that the boy kicked*.

This becomes increasingly difficult if more than one clause is embedded. Consider: *The man [that the boy [that the dog [that the cat [that the mouse hated] scratched] bit] kicked] ran away.*

Languages tend to avoid centre embedding, even though it is, as we have seen, a possible construction in English. But the general tendency to avoid it, and the difficulty in processing it when it does occur, might motivate the grammatical phenomenon of word correlation between verb position and relative-clause position (Comrie 1981/1989: 27):

> If a SOV language had postnominal relative clauses, then every single relative clause would be centre-embedded, occurring between its head noun and the verb. . . . Likewise, if a VSO language had prenominal relative clauses, then every single relative clause would be centre-embedded. The attested correlation means that at least some noun phrases are left-peripheral (in SOV languages) or right-peripheral (in VSO languages).

Certain properties of the human perceptual and cognitive apparatus are also relevant to the discussion of universals (Hawkins 1988: 15). For instance, Berlin and Kay (1969) have shown that if a language has a colour system at all, it will distinguish at least black and white. If it has three colours, the third will be red; if it has four, then the fourth will be either green or yellow; the fifth will be the other of green or yellow; the sixth will be blue; and the seventh brown. Kay and McDaniel (1978) point out that this universal feature can be explained by reference to the neural anatomy of the colour vision of humans.

As Hawkins (1988: 4) and Comrie (1981/1989: 23) both point out, there is no reason why one should not embrace both the Chomskyan and the Greenbergian approach and work toward a greater degree of precision in the kinds of explanation offered within each, since it is likely that natural languages are constrained by all of the phenomena mentioned. Each kind of explanation is likely to be able to provide elements which are necessary in a theory of universals, but it is unlikely that any one alone can produce a sufficient theory.

K.M.

Suggestion for further reading

Comrie, B. (1981/1989) *Language Universals and Linguistic Typology: Syntax and Morphology*, Oxford: Basil Blackwell; 2nd edition 1989.

Lexicography

What is a dictionary?

Lexicographers produce lexically-oriented reference works of several types, e.g. **dictionaries**, **thesauruses** and **glossaries**, but this article deals with their most typical product: dictionaries. A **lexicographic dictionary** is one that provides **lexically relevant information**, e.g. pronunciation and meaning, about **lexically relevant units**, e.g. words. These lexically relevant units are displayed in a **macrostructure** that is a succession of independent articles (**entries**), so ordered that any article may be found through an explicitly statable search procedure (an **algorithm**). The typical **dictionary algorithm**, alphabetical order, is based on the written form of the lexically relevant units rather than on their meaning, and the typical dictionary entry is **semasiological** – that is, going from name to notion. By contrast, the typical thesaurus entry is **onomasiological** – that is, going from notion to name.

Lexically relevant units in dictionaries

The best-known type of lexically relevant unit is the lexical unit. A **lexical unit** is a constituent unit of the **lexical system**, the **vocabulary**, of a language; and the best-known type of lexical unit is the **word** (see MORPHOLOGY). A lexical unit, a **lexeme**, is a set of units of form, **morphemes**, that represents a set of units of content, **sememes**. The morphemic representation of a lexical unit is realized in writing by one or more sets of **graphical units** or **graphemes**, such as letters, and in speech by one or more sets of **phonological units** or **phonemes** (see PHONEMICS). The relation between form and content can best be understood as a **correspondence** or **mapping**. Table 1 shows what mappings can occur.

As shown in Table 1, *encyclop(a)edia* and *'controversy/con'troversy* are one lexical unit apiece despite the variability of their morphemic representations in writing or in speech. In most dictionaries there would be a single entry for *controversy*, with two British English pronunciations, and a single entry for *encyclopaedia, encyclopedia*, here with two alphabetically adjacent spellings.

Since the macrostructure of dictionaries is based on the form of their lexically relevant units, most dictionaries would have a single entry each for *penicillin*, with one 'sense', and for the noun *crane*, with two 'senses'. About *bank*, however, dictionaries differ. Almost all would have separate entries for the **homographs** (see SEMANTICS) *¹bank* 'shore' and *²bank* 'financial institution' because of their different origins or **etymologies**: *¹bank* came into Middle English from Scandinavian, while *²bank* derives from French or Italian. As for the verb *bank*, some dictionaries would make it part of the entry for *²bank* on etymological grounds; other dictionaries would make it yet a third homograph: *³bank*.

Most dictionaries are willing to bring together in a single entry a set of lexical units that differ in meaning but have a common etymology and at least one common morphemic representation, especially when their syntactic use, shown by their part of speech (see HISTORY OF GRAMMAR), is the same.

However, certain modern French dictionaries, notably the Larousse *Dictionnaire du français contemporain* (*DFC*) and *Lexis*, impose additional restrictions on their entries. Each entry must have a single set of inflections and a single set of derivatives. A dictionary that applied this principle

Table 1 Form–content mappings

Mapping	Form	Content	Dictionary entries	Lexical units
One–one	*penicillin/*'peni'silin/	'drug x'	1	1
	encyclopaedia, encyclopedia	'reference book'	1	1
	controversy/'kontrəvəːsi, kən'trovəsi/	'dispute'	1	1
One–many	*crane/*'krein/	{'bird x' 'machine x'	1	1
	bank/'baŋk/	{'shore' 'financial institution' 'deposit or keep (money) in a bank	2 or 3	3
Many–one	*furze/*'fəːz/ *gorse/*'gɔːs/	'plant x'	2	2
Many–many	*toilet/*toilit/ *loo/*'luː/ *lavatory/*'lɑvatəri/	{'appliance x' 'site of appliance x'	3	6

to English would have to make two homographs of the verb *shine*: [1]*shine* (*shined*) and [2]*shine* (*shone*), and two homographs of the adjective *lame*, of which [1]*lame* 'crippled' would have the derivative *lameness* and [2]*lame* 'inadequate' would have the derivatives *lameness* and *lamely*.

The lexical units discussed so far have had the form of single words. However, dictionaries usually enter other types of lexical unit as well. These include the following:

1 Units 'below' the word: **bound morphemes** that help to form inflections, derivatives, and compounds: *pre-*, *-ing*, *-ly*, *-ness*, *Eur-*, *-o-*.

2 Units 'above' the word, such as:

a units consisting of parts of more than one word, i.e. **blends** and **initialisms** like *smog* (**sm**oke plus *fog*), *VIP*, *NATO*;

b units including more than one complete word, i.e. **compounds** and **idioms** like *blackbird, bank on, give up, night owl, hammer and tongs, at all, kick the bucket*. For such **multi-word combinations** to be considered true **multi-word lexical units** the convention is that their meanings should be more than the sum of the meanings of their components. Thus *night owl* is a lexical unit but *nocturnal owl* is not, and *kick the bucket* is a lexical unit when it means 'die' but not when it means 'strike the pail with one's foot'.

An important class of lexical units, some single-word, some multi-word, is the class of **proper names**, whether of real entities such as *Atlanta, Aristotle, Hood, Thomas* or of fictional entities, such as *Atlantis, Ajax* and *Robin Hood*. It can be argued that proper names, though they are lexical units, are lexical units of no language in particular, or of all languages. However, the same argument could be advanced with respect to many technical terms like *penicillin*.

Many dictionaries, e.g. monolingual dictionaries for native speakers, strive to limit their entries to lexical units, including or excluding the proper names of real entities. Other dictionaries, e.g. monolingual learners' dictionaries and bilingual dictionaries, enter lexically relevant units that are not lexical units. Thus a dictionary might enter **routine formulas** like *Many happy returns!* because their use is pragmatically restricted. An English–French dictionary might enter *rural policeman*, which is not a lexical unit of English, because its French translation, *garde champêtre*, is a lexical unit of French. Similarly, it might enter the phrase *beat a drum*, which is not a lexical unit of English, in order to show that its French translation *battre **du** tambour*, though not itself a lexical unit of French, is nevertheless not a word-for-word equivalent of its English counterpart either – *a* in English would be *une* or *un* in French.

Organization of the macro-structure

For anyone consulting or producing a dictionary, there are three questions immediately relevant to its macro-structure: Is the macro-structure single or multiple? Which units are main entries and which are subentries? What is the ordering of graphically similar units (**homologues**) and, in particular, graphically identical units (**homographs**)?

1 A dictionary may display all its lexically relevant units in a single A–Z list; alternatively, it may relegate certain types of unit (e.g. abbreviations, 'real' proper names) to appendices.

2 Dictionaries differ greatly in their main-entry policies. But here is a list of types of lexical unit going from those most likely to be main entries to those most likely to be subentries under one of their components: single morphemes (*furze, pre-*); blends (*smog*) and initialisms (*VIP, NATO*); noun compounds **written solid**, i.e. without a space between the

parts of the compound (*blackbird*); noun compounds **written open**, i.e. with a space between the parts of the compound (*night owl, hammer and sickle*); verb compounds (phrasal verbs like *give up*); non-verb compounds and idioms (*at all, hammer and tongs, in front of*); verb idioms (*kick the bucket*). In general, English-language dictionaries have a far higher proportion of main entries than dictionaries of other languages.

One important class of possible sub-entries is derivatives whose meaning is that of the sum of their parts, such as *lameness* from *lame* and *prewar* from *war*. By convention, such derivatives, unlike *nocturnal owl*, are regarded as lexical units despite their **semantic transparency**; that is, in spite of the fact that their meaning is easily understood on the basis of the meanings of the parts of which they are composed. Large dictionaries may make them main entries; many smaller dictionaries make them subentries to save space. However, such subentries are presented without explicit explanation of their meaning. Those formed by suffixation (*lameness*) are entered under their source (*lame*) as so-called **undefined run-ons**; those formed by prefixation (*pre-war*) are in English-language dictionaries typically listed in alphabetical order under the prefix, e.g. *pre-*; but in some dictionaries of other languages, e.g. those, like the Larousse *DFC* and *Lexis*, that homograph by derivational families, they appear out of alphabetical order under their sources, with cross-references to them from their proper alphabetical position in the macro-structure.

3 Graphically identical homologues (homographs, like ¹*bank n*, ²*bank n*, ³*bank v*) may be ordered historically – older before newer; by perceived frequency – more frequent before less frequent; or even by the alphabetical order of their part of speech – adjective before noun before verb. For graphically similar homologues, a variety of related algorithms may be used, such as lower-case before capital (*creole, Creole*), solid before spaced (*rundown, run down*), apostrophe before hyphen(s) (*o', -o-*) – or any of these rules may be reversed!

Lexically relevant information

Dictionaries provide any or all of the following types of lexically relevant information about the lexically relevant units they enter:

1 Information about the etymology, or origin, of the unit.

2 Information about the form of the unit, including spelling(s) and pronunciation(s).

3 Syntactic categorization and subcategorization. In the first instance this information is given by a part-of-speech label (*noun, verb*, etc.), but subcategorization can be supplied to any **delicacy** desired; that is, in finer and finer detail. Thus a lexical unit represented by the word-form *tell* may be categorized as *verb, verb transitive* (**tell** *the truth*), or *verb ditransitive* (**tell** *them the truth*).

4 Inflections. Thus, the entry for *tell* will show that its past and past participle are *told*.

5 Derivatives, especially if, like *lameness*, they are of the semantically transparent type that can qualify as undefined run-ons.

6 'Paradigmatic' information, such as **synonyms** (same meaning), **antonyms** (opposite meaning), **superordinates** (*crippled* is superordinate to one sense of *lame*), **converses** (like *buy* for *sell*), and even **paronyms** or **confusibles** (like *imply*

for *infer*). A special case of synonymy is presented by pairs like *launchpad/launching pad* or *music box/musical box*, which differ only by the presence or absence of an affix.

7 'Syntagmatic' information; that is, information about the use of the item in forming sentences. Some syntagmatic information is conveyed by the syntactic categorization mentioned above. Additional information may also be provided about complementation (*tell* them to leave vs *saw* them leave), collocation with specific words or types of words (*fond of* vs *fondness for*; the association of *capsize* with boats or ships), and selectional restrictions (such as that the verb *frighten* requires a direct object that is 'animate': *frightened* the child, but not **frightened* the stone).

8 'Analogical' information about the lexical field of which a given lexical unit is a part. Subsuming and perhaps transcending paradigmatic and syntagmatic information, analogical information is given sparingly by English-language dictionaries and thesauruses, but much more extensively by French dictionaries – especially those produced by Robert. An English-language 'alphabetical and analogical' dictionary *à la* Robert might at its entry for *horse* provide cross-references to types of horse (*mare, pony*), its colours (*bay, roan*), its parts (*hock, pastern*), its gaits (*trot, canter*), and other 'horsey' words (*saddle, jockey, gymkhana*).

9 'Diasystemic' information, indicating whether or not something belongs to the unmarked standard core of the language that can be used at all times and in all places and situations. According to Hausmann (1977: chapter 8), lexically relevant units can receive – typically by means of labels or usage notes – any

or all of the following types of diasystemic marking: **diachronic** (e.g. *archaic, neologism*); **diatopic** (e.g. *American English* for *elevator* 'lift', *British English* for *loo* and *lift*, 'elevator'); **diaintegrative** for foreign borrowings used in English (e.g. *German* for *Weltanschauung*); **diastratic** (e.g. *informal* for *loo, formal* for *perambulator*); **diaconnotative** (e.g. *from Webster's Tenth New Collegiate Dictionary (W10), often used disparagingly* for *dyke*); **diatechnical** (e.g. *law* for *tort, anatomy* for *clavicle*; **diafrequential** (e.g. *rare*); **dianormative** (e.g. *substandard* for *ain't*).

10 Explanation of use, meaning, and reference: see below.

The **domain** of the information provided by dictionaries may be a whole entry or part of an entry. Thus, at an entry for the noun *crane*, the domain of both its spelling and its pronunciation is both lexical units it represents ('bird' and 'machine'). But at an entry for the verb *shine*, dictionaries must show that the domain of its inflection *shined* is restricted to the meaning 'polish', while *shone* prevails elsewhere. And an entry for *colour/color* should show that for all the lexical units it represents, the spelling *color* is American English and the spelling *colour* is British English: here the diatopic marking applies to spelling alone.

Finally, lexicographers and dictionary users alike should bear the following in mind.

1 Information may be given covertly as well as overtly. Thus the absence of a diasystemic label indicates that a lexical unit belongs to the common core of the language, and the absence of inflections in the entry for a unit may show that the unit has none, but may also imply that its inflections are regular (or can be inferred from the inflections of its components).

2 Information of the same type may be given in more than one way. Thus the transitivity of a verb may be shown by its part-of-speech label (*v.t.*), by the form of its definition, and/or by examples of its use, as well as by special codes as in learners' dictionaries.

3 Dictionary information can help with both understanding language ('decoding') and producing language ('encoding'). Some dictionaries, e.g. learners' monolingual dictionaries and the native-language-to-foreign-language parts of bilingual dictionaries, emphasize their encoding function more than others, e.g. monolingual dictionaries for native speakers.

Dictionary explanations

Dictionaries may offer explanations of the use, meaning and reference of the lexically relevant units they enter. **Use** has to do with the syntactic and pragmatic functions of the unit; **meaning**, with the relation of the unit to other lexically relevant units; and **reference**, with the relation of the extralinguistic item named by the unit to other extralinguistic items.

1 Dictionaries use at least the following seven explanatory techniques, alone or in combination.

2 **Explanatory cross-reference** – as when *came* is explained as '*past of* come'.

3 **Illustration** – This includes pictures, tables and diagrams.

4 **Exemplification** – Thus for the noun *vow* the example *She* **made** *a vow* **to** *avenge her father's death* shows collocation with *make* and complementation by a *to*-infinitive, as well as reinforcing the notion that a vow is a solemn promise.

5 **Expansion** – For example, *VIP* is expanded to '*Very Important Person*', *NATO* to '*North Atlantic Treaty Organization*', or *smog* to '*smoke* plus *fog*'. Expansion is particularly appropriate for initialisms and blends, and functions as an etymology. When the expansion is sufficiently informative, it also functions as a definition, as in the case of *VIP* and *smog*. In the case of *NATO*, however, expansion is not sufficiently informative to tell the dictionary user anything about the membership and purpose of NATO.

6 **Discussion** – Here this is used in more or less its everyday sense to mean a discursive and at most semi-formalized technique that can present any of the types of lexically relevant information described above. A short discussion – a so-called **usage note** – can supplement or replace a label (e.g. 'often used disparagingly') or a definition. For example, at ¹*here adv*, *W10* explains the subentry *here goes* as follows: '– used interjectionally to express resolution or resignation esp. at the beginning of a difficult or unpleasant undertaking'. For lexical units serving as interjections or function words, discussion is often the explanatory technique of choice. A longer discussion in the form of a **synonym essay** or **usage essay** can present information too detailed to compress into examples and too loosely structured to be formalized as a definition.

7 **Definition** – This is a formalized paraphrase. The definition of a lexically relevant unit presupposes a delexicalization of the unit into its components; these components are then reassembled into another lexically relevant unit, and the content of this unit characterizes the meaning and reference of the **definiendum** – the item which is being defined – while its form instantiates the definiendum's use. For example, a lexical unit

represented by *bachelor* might be delex-icalized into the components 'male', 'adult', 'never been married', which are then reassembled into the lexically relev-ant noun phrase, 'man who has never been married'. The content of this de-finition characterizes the meaning and reference of the word *bachelor*, while the form of the definition – a countable noun phrase – instantiates the grammatical use of the word *bachelor* – a countable noun. Thus nouns are defined by noun phrases; verbs by verb phrases – which for transitive verbs may contain a slot for the direct object; adverbs, prepositions, adjectives and even some bound mor-phemes (see MORPHOLOGY) by phrases or clauses that can function in the same way as the definiendum.

Such standard dictionary definitions may be classified into:

a **definitions by synonym**, in which all the information is compressed into a single lexical unit (e.g. *gorgeous*: 'striking');
b **analytical definitions**, in which prim-ary syntactic, semantic, and refer-ential information is provided by one part of the definition, the **genus**, and secondary information by the rest, the **differentiae** (e.g. *gorgeous*: 'strikingly beautiful', where *beautiful* is the genus and *strikingly* is the differentia);
c **formulaic definitions**, in which primary semantic and referential information is provided by one part of the defin-ition, while the rest provides primary syntactic information together with secondary semantic and referential information (e.g. *gorgeous*: 'of/having/ that has striking beauty').

A single lexical unit may have more than one definition: these definitions may be linked by **parataxis** (appo-sition or asyndetic co-ordination, as in *gorgeous*: 'of striking beauty, stunning') or **hypo-taxis** (subordination, as in

gorgeous: 'of striking beauty; *specifically*, stunning').

Besides standard dictionary definitions, ordinary people, including lexicographers off duty, use definitions of other types, such as *'tired* is when you want to lie down'. Such **folk definitions** are used in some dictionaries for young children. For example, *The Charlie Brown Dictionary* has *hog*: 'When a male pig grows, he becomes a *hog*.' Non-standard definitions are also used in the *Collins COBUILD English Language Dictionary* (COBUILD 1987), which has *hog*: 'A *hog* is . . . a male pig that has been castrated.'

8 **Translation** – The process of definition yields a definition as its product. At the level of a whole text, the process of trans-lation likewise yields as its product a translation. But the translation of a lexically relevant unit need not yield a relexicalized translation of that unit. Sometimes, instead, it yields a definition, especially in the case of culture-specific items like *Scotch egg*, which Collins-Robert explains as *œuf dur enrobé de chair à saucisse*; sometimes a discussion, as for pragmatically restricted routine formulae from a very different culture; and some-times nothing at all, as when one lan-guage uses, for instance, a preposition (Spanish: *María vio a Clara*) in construc-tions in which another language uses none (English: *Maria saw Clara*).

Furthermore, the process of context-free lexical translation can produce trans-lation equivalents either at the level of lexical units, or at the level of their mor-phemic representation. Thus there is a difference between the superficially sim-ilar English–French equations *penicillin: pénicilline*, where one English lexical unit has been translated into one French lexical unit, and *crane noun:grue*, where an English representation of two lexical units has been translated into a French representation of two analogous lexical units. The first case is a translation of an English one–one lexical mapping into a French one–one lexical mapping; the second, a translation of an English one–many lexical mapping into a French one–many lexical mapping. However, both equations can be regarded as one–one mappings of a single 'translation unit' of English on to a single French translation equivalent.

Other possible mappings of source-language translation units on to target-language translation equivalents are:

Mapping	English translation unit(s)	French translation equivalent(s)
one–many	jacket (garment)	(of woman's suit) jaquette; (of man's suit) veston
many–one	bucket; pail	seau
many–many	furze; gorse	gênet(s) épineux; ajonc(s)

In these last three cases, the translation units have been lexical units (of English), and their translated explanations have been translation equivalents (of French) – that is, lexical units, too. But, as we have seen, neither translation units nor their translated explanations need be lexical units. All permutations and combinations occur in bilingual dictionaries: lexical unit–lexical unit (*penicillin: pénicilline*); lexical unit–non-lexical unit (*Scotch egg:œuf dur enrobé de chair à saucisse*); non-lexical unit–lexical unit (*rural policeman:garde champêtre*); non-lexical unit–non-lexical unit (*beat a drum: battre du tambour*). Unfortunately, most bilingual dictionaries do not distinguish consistently between those translation units and translated explanations that are lexical units and those that are not.

The example '*jacket* (garment)' above shows that when bilingual dictionaries deal with a single morphemic represent-ation of more than one lexical unit (e.g. *jacket noun 1*: 'garment x' *2*: 'skin of baked potato' . . .), they increasingly use various devices to show which lexical unit they are translating, and the example '(of woman's suit) *jaquette*' shows that they use similar devices to distinguish the domains of their translations. Such orientating devices can utilize any of the types of lexically relevant information listed above.

Whatever explanatory technique or techniques they use, dictionaries must order their explanations when a single article treats of more than one lexical unit and therefore requires more than one explanation. Such lexical units, or 'senses', may be ordered historically, by perceived frequency, by markedness (unmarked before diasystemically marked) or semantically ('basic' before 'derived', 'literal' before 'figurative'). However, semantic ordering may coexist with any of the other ordering principles, in which case semantically related senses are grouped together, and each such 'sense group' is placed according to its age, its frequency, or its markedness. The ordering of senses may or may not follow the same principles as the ordering of homologues in the macro-structure. Thus some dictionaries that order senses by frequency nevertheless order homographs historically.

Subentries such as run-ons and idioms are either collected at one place in the article – typically near the end – or scattered throughout it, each subentry going near the sense to which it is felt to be most closely related.

Lexicographic evidence

Lexicographers need to decide which lexically relevant units should be entered in a dictionary and what information should be given about them, and like investigators in other fields they use evidence gained from three overlapping processes of investigation; namely, **introspection**, **experiment**, and **observation**. Lexicographic observation may be of **primary sources**, i.e. authentic language in use (formerly written language only, but now sometimes recordings of spoken language also), or of **secondary sources**, i.e. existing dictionaries and grammars.

Moreover, introspection, observation, and experiment have come to be used not only to investigate language for lexicographic purposes, but also to investigate the use of dictionaries and, by market research, the wishes of dictionary users. Such investigations are undertaken not only to improve the form and content of dictionaries, but also for the commercial purpose of increasing their distribution.

The significance of dictionaries

Dictionaries are important as repositories of information about language and about social attitudes (for instance, ethnic slurs have been marked diaconnotatively for far longer than sexual slurs); as texts with relatively explicit and formalized conventions; and as the oldest and most widespread self-instructional learning aid. They have long enjoyed the favour of the general public, and commend themselves to the attention of anyone interested in language – both for what they *say*, and for what they *are*.

R.F.I.

Suggestions for further reading

Béjoint, H. (2000) *Modern Lexicography: An Introduction*, Oxford: Oxford University Press.

Benson, M. *et al.* (1986) *Lexicographic Description of English*, Amsterdam and Philadelphia: John Benjamins.

Ilson, R.F. (ed.) (1985) *Dictionaries, Lexicography and Language Learning*, Oxford: Pergamon Press, in association with the British Council.

Lexis and lexicology

Introduction

The study of **lexis** is the study of the vocabulary of languages in all its aspects: words and their meanings, how words relate to one another, how they may combine with one another, and the relationships between vocabulary and other areas of the description of languages (the phonology, morphology and syntax).

Lexical semantics

Central to the study of lexis is the question of word meaning. If the word is an identifiable unit of a language then it must be possible to isolate a core, stable meaning that enables its consistent use by a vast number of users in many contexts over long periods of time. Linguists have attempted to see the meaning of a word in terms of the features that compose it – its **componential features** – and the process of analysis of those features as **lexical composition**. Most important in this respect is the work of Katz and Fodor (1963). According to them, words are decomposable into primitive meanings and these **primitives** can be represented by **markers**. In addition, **distinguishers**, specific characteristics of the referents of words, serve to differentiate between different word senses. The description of a word in a dictionary must cover the wide range of senses that words can have: the dictionary entry is a 'characterization of *every* sense that a lexical item can bear in *any* sentence' (1963: 184). (See SEMANTICS for a diagram and exposition of Katz and Fodor's descriptive apparatus as this is employed to deal with the term *bachelor*.)

Another way of looking at the features of a word's meaning is **componential analysis (CA)**. CA breaks the word down into a list of the components present in its meaning; thus *man* can be ascribed the features +HUMAN +ADULT +MALE (Leech 1981: 90). Once again, the purpose of CA is to distinguish the meaning of a given word from that of any other word, but the features attached to a word will also identify it as belonging to a **field** or **domain** (Nida 1975: 339), which it shares with other words having common components. *Father, mother, son, sister, aunt*, etc. are united in having the components of HUMAN and KINSHIP in common (1975: 339). CA enables us to identify **synonyms**, i.e. words that have identical componential features, regardless of differences of register, and to ident ify anomalous combinations such as 'male woman' (Leech 1967: 21; see SEMANTICS).

But CA and the kind of labelling proposed by Katz and Fodor are open to criticism. Most powerful among early criticisms to appear was that of Bolinger, who showed that the two categories of marker and distinguisher could easily be collapsed, rendering the distinction questionable: the distinction anyway did not correspond to any clear division in natural language (1965b). Nor could such a theory easily cope with metaphor, or with the fact that much of natural-language meaning resides not only in words but in longer stretches of morphemes, or **frozen forms** (1965b).

Also important in the study of lexis is **semantic field theory**. Field theory holds that the meanings represented in the lexicon are interrelated, that they cluster together to form 'fields' of meaning, which in turn cluster into even larger fields until the entire language is encompassed. Thus *sprinting, trotting* and *jogging* cluster into a field of running, which in turn clusters with many other verbs into a larger field of human motion, and so on to a field of motion in general. Lehrer (1969) sums up the central feature of field theory: 'that vocabulary is organized into lexical or conceptual fields, and the items within each field are tightly structured with respect to each other'. This view goes back to Trier in the 1930s (see Lyons 1977b: 253; Lehrer 1974: 17), and the notion that the entire vocabulary can be divided and subdivided into interlinked fields underpins such works as *Roget's Thesaurus*.

Field theory can be used to illustrate language change: the way semantic space is carved up and realized in lexical items changes constantly; it can also be used in contrastive analysis of different languages (see Lehrer 1974) to illustrate how a given semantic area is subdivided similarly or differently in different languages. Languages often differ even in apparently quite basic lexical divisions, and fields such as temperature terms, kinship terms, colour terms, parts of the body and divisions of the animal and vegetable worlds will divide the semantic space differently and reflect this in the vocabulary items covering those fields. Lehrer (1969 and 1978) offers seminal applications of field theory to cooking terms and makes interesting generalizations concerning the formal properties of words that share common fields.

But Lehrer (1974) and Lyons (1977b) both see shortcomings in field theory. For one thing, words are not always sharply separated from one another in fields, and Lehrer suggests that Berlin and Kay's (1969) view, that there are **focal points**, or **prototypes** (Rosch 1973, 1977a; Rosch *et al.* 1976), within fields rather than clearly delineated boundaries between words, might capture better how lexical meaning is perceived. What is more, not all words are amenable to field analysis; even more fundamentally, perhaps, the relationship between actual words and the concepts they stand for – which can only be expressed in words – is not at all clear (Lehrer 1974:

17). Lyons' criticism overlaps with Lehrer's: both see as a weakness in field theory the fact that it fails to take into account the contribution to meaning of *syntagmatic* features (see STRUCTURALIST LINGUISTICS), concentrating as it does solely on paradigmatic relations (Lehrer 1969; Lyons 1977b: 261). Thus we cannot say much about the meaning of *bark* without reference to *dog*, or the colour *auburn* without mention of its restricted collocation with *hair* rather than *bicycle* or *door*.

Relations between items

Field theory raises the question of how vocabulary items are related to one another in terms of meaning. Lexical semanticists have devoted much attention to formulating basic relations between words; chief among such efforts have been Ullmann (1962), Lehrer (1974), Nida (1975), Lyons (1977b), Leech (1981) and Cruse (1986). Leech and Lyons discuss basic or **primitive** semantic relations, principally **synonymy**, **antonymy** and **hyponymy**. Ullmann (1962: 141) discusses synonymy and concludes that it is very rare that words are 100 per cent interchangeable. Words may share identical componential features but may still be distinguished along a variety of dimensions of actual use. He quotes Collinson's (1939) set of nine principles whereby words may be distinguished – these include literary and non-literary usage, neutrality versus marked evaluation, formal versus colloquial usage, etc. Taking usage into account conflicts with a purely componential view, which is only concerned with a word's inherent, abstract features.

Antonymy, or oppositeness, is also not an entirely straightforward matter. Leech (1981: 92) points out that possible 'opposites' to *woman* include *girl* and *man*. It is thus more correct to label *woman* as **incompatible** with *man*, *boy* and *girl* within its field. Lyons also uses incompatibility, referring to the relationship between words in sets such as flower names or names of the days of the week (1977b: 288). Further types of oppositeness distinguish between pairs such as *alive* and *dead* and *hot* and *cold*. The first pair are called by Lyons (1977b: 291) **ungradable**, and the latter pair by **gradable**: intermediate terms exist between *hot* and *cold*; namely, *warm*, *cool*, etc. Leech calls such gradables **polar oppositions** (1981: 100). Opposite terms such as *big* and *small* may even have other **intensified** terms at the polar extremes which represent a more complex set: *enormous* occupying a position beyond *big*, *tiny* beyond *small*; while other terms occupy the territory in between: *middle-sized*, *average*, *medium*. In such cases it seems that terms like *big* and *small* have a focal or **core** status (see Carter 1987). Gradable antonyms are relative in meaning, and their relativity is sociolinguistically determined (Lyons 1977b: 274; Leech 1981: 102).

Lyons (1977b: 274) prefers to keep the term *antonymy* for the gradable antonyms only and suggests **complementarity** as a description of the ungradables, **converseness** for the reversible relationship between terms such as *husband/wife*, *teacher/pupil*, where to say *A is B's husband* implies *B is A's wife*, and **directionality** for pairs such as *arrive/depart*, *come/go*. Directionality and converseness are given the more general heading **relative opposition** by Leech (1981: 102).

Hyponymy, the relation of inclusion, is dealt with by Lyons (1977b: 291–5) and, with new insight, by Cruse (1975, 1986). Hyponymous relations can be expressed by taxonomic tree diagrams, showing levels of generality and specificity and which words include which in their meaning. Thus a simple tree diagram for *car* showing its relations with its near neighbours might be:

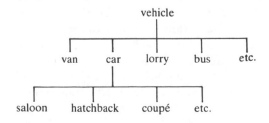

Vehicle is the **superordinate** term and *car* is a hyponym of it. *Van, car, lorry*, etc. are **cohyponyms**. *Car* is then, in its turn, superordinate to *saloon, hatchback, coupé*, etc. Hyponymy, as is evident, is one of the major organizing principles of thesauruses. Not all taxonomic-type relations, however, are true examples of hyponymy: part–whole relations such as *finger/hand* may be termed **meronymy** and Lyons (1977b: 293–301) points to a variety of types of **quasi-hyponymy**, which include sets such as *stroll/amble/plod*, etc. under the superordinate *walk*, and *round/square/oblong* under *shape* (where *shape* is not of the same grammatical class as the quasi-hyponyms). Cruse (1975) argues that many quasi-hyponymic relations in natural language cannot be explained at all in terms of entailment and should be seen as purely conventional arrangements of phenomena in the world. Thus *watches, ties, cameras and other presents* has no permanent implication that *If it is a tie, it is therefore a present* (cf. *If it is a rose, it is therefore a flower*).

The discussion of relations between the items in sets that realize semantic fields does not necessarily imply that all items behave in the same way. If we consider the gradable antonyms it is clear that one term of the pair usually operates as the **unmarked** term, i.e. the question *How long will the meeting be?* is heard as a neutral question concerning duration: *How short will the meeting be?* will be heard as **marked**, or else can only function where 'brevity' is already given in the context. Likewise, *How big is your house?* and *How wide is the room?* testify to the unmarked nature of *big* and *wide*. Among other incompatibles, one term can often double up as gender-marked – often, but not exclusively, male – and as gender-neutral. Lyons (1977b: 308) gives *dog* as an example, which can be used to refer to any dog, bitch or puppy, but which can also be used to differentiate gender, as in the question *Is it a dog or a bitch?* *Tiger, fox* and *pig* are other examples. *Dog*

can thus be said to be simultaneously superordinate to *bitch* and its co-hyponym.

Syntagmatic features

So far, the discussion of lexical relations has proceeded firmly within the domain of semantics and the types of meanings carried by paradigmatic relations. But a parallel, vigorous line of study, dominated by British linguists, concentrated its efforts during the mid- to late twentieth century on syntagmatic aspects of lexis. The seeds of this variety of lexical studies are found in the work of J.R. Firth, and it is the notion of **collocation** that is Firth's principal contribution to the field.

In contrast with the decontextualized, **theoretical dictionary** (Leech 1981: 207), which is the construct of decomposition, componential analysis and semantic relations, Firth is concerned with an 'abstraction at the syntagmatic level . . . not directly concerned with the conceptual or idea approach to the meaning of words' (1950/1957c: 196). He is concerned with the distribution of words in text, and how some occur predictably together more than others. One of the meanings of *night* is its collocation with *dark*, and vice versa: likewise, we can predict the restricted range of adjectives that commonly occur with *ass*: *silly, obstinate, stupid*, etc. (1950/1957b: 196).

Much of the impetus to Firth's work on collocation is provided by his concern with literary stylistics, where it is frequently necessary to recognize certain collocations as **a-normal** (1950/1957c: 196) in order to explain literary effect. Firth also gives a systematic classification of the collocational types with the verb *get* (1968: 20–3) and sees these as 'a basis for the highly complex statement necessary to define the forms of *get* in a dictionary' (1968: 20–3): this makes an interesting comparison with Katz and Fodor (1963), who were also preoccupied with the form an entry for a word in a dictionary might take (see above).

McIntosh (1961/1966) continued Firth's work on collocation and used the term **range** to describe the **tolerance of compatibility** between words. The range of an item is the list of its potential collocates: thus *molten* has a range that includes *metal/lava/lead*, etc., but not *postage*. The sentence *The molten postage feather scores a weather* violates the tolerance of compatibility of the words within it: despite our willingness to accommodate new and unusual collocations (e.g. in literary works), we cannot contextualize such an odd sentence. Yet range is not fossilized, and part of the creative process of language change is **range extension**, whereby a previously limited range is broadened to accommodate new concepts, thus *ware* (whose range included *hard*, *table* and *house*) now includes in modern English *soft* and *firm*, in computer jargon.

Firth's seminal ideas on collocation (1957b; see also 1957d: 11–13, 267) have since been developed by, among others, Mitchell (1958, 1971, 1975), Halliday (1966a), McIntosh (1961/1966), Sinclair (1966, 1987a) and Greenbaum (1970). Central among these studies are Halliday's and Sinclair's. Halliday (1966a) is concerned with two concepts: collocation and how this, in turn, defines membership of **lexical sets**. Halliday's paper is entitled 'Lexis as a linguistic level', and his purpose is to sketch out 'a lexical theory complementary to, but not part of, grammatical theory'. Firth had already, to a certain extent, separated lexical matters from semantics and grammar (1957b: 7–33); Halliday was now concerned to make that separation more complete. The many unresolved issues of language patterning left over when grammatical analysis, however thorough, was complete, could either be relegated to semantics or tackled at a **lexical level** of analysis, with the aim of making lexical statements at a greater level of generality than dictionaries do. As an example of the **lexicality** of collocation, Halliday compares the different collocability of *strong*

and *powerful*. The figure below shows the acceptability of *strong tea* but not of *strong car*, while *argument* collocates with both. Moreover, the relation is constant over a variety of grammatical configurations: *He argued strongly against . . .*; *the strength of his argument*; *This car has more power*, etc. So the lexical statement can operate independently of grammatical restrictions. *Strong, strength, strongly, strengthen* represent the 'scatter' of the same **lexical item**.

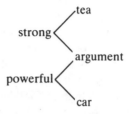

The lexical statement will not, however, remain independent but will ultimately be integrated with grammatical and other statements, a truly Firthian position. That *strong* and *powerful*, qua items, collocate with *argument* entitles them to enter into the same set. Each will also enter into different sets by virtue of their non-overlapping collocations with *tea* and *car*, respectively: item, set and collocation are **mutually defining** (1957b: 7–33).

Collocation and **set**, as terms in a lexical description, are analogous to **structure** and **system** in a grammatical theory (see SYSTEMIC-FUNCTIONAL GRAMMAR): the difference is that collocation is a relation of *probable* co-occurrence of items, and sets are **open-ended** (cf. the **closed** systems of grammar). The set is a 'grouping of items with like privilege of occurrence in collocation' (1957b: 7–33). Some items in the language will not be amenable to lexical statements of any real power or significance: *the*, for example, is a **weak collocator**, combining, potentially, with almost any common noun: *blond* is a **strong collocator**, restricted to *hair* and a few related words (*tresses*, *wig*, etc.). *The* is best left to the grammarian to describe: it occupies one end of the continuum running from grammatical to most lexical, while *blond* dwells at the other end.

Words can thus predict their own environment to a greater or lesser extent. Some items predict the certain occurrence of others: when such predictability is 100 per cent (e.g. *fro* always predicts *to and*, and *kith* always predicts *and kin*) we are justified in declaring the whole of the fixed occurrence to be a single lexical item.

The notion of collocation and lexical set can also have a bearing on decisions concerning polysemy and homonymy (see SEMANTICS). The occurrence of the word form *bank* in two different collocational environments (*river, trees, steep*, cf. *money, deposit, cheque*) suggests that *bank* is best described as a homonym. Likewise, noncognate word forms (e.g. *city* and *urban*) can be shown to have the same collocates, and therefore to belong to the same set.

The set can be demonstrated as a statistical reality. 2000 occurrences of the word *sun* might be examined in terms of what occurs three words either side of it. These 12,000 collocates might show a significant frequency of *bright/hot/shine/light*, etc. A similar operation on 2000 occurrences of *moon* might show *bright, shine* and *light* to be statistically significant. These match with the collocates of *sun* and thus delineate *bright, shine* and *light* as candidates for members of a set in which *moon* and *sun* occur. And so the process could repeat itself on masses of data, preferably some 20 million words of text, according to Halliday's reckoning.

Halliday's (1966a) work leans clearly towards data-based observations of lexical patterning, a field which Sinclair has since developed significantly. Sinclair (1966) also takes a Firthian approach to collocation and much of his argument agrees with Halliday, not least in his stressing that all text can be seen lexically as well as grammatically. Common function words are difficult to describe lexically and hardly attain the

status of independent lexical items; the same is true of common verbs such as *take, make* and *do*. Sinclair (1966) addressed some of the theoretical issues he later took up in the massive COBUILD project at the University of Birmingham where, under his direction, a vast corpus of 20 million words of text was stored on computer and analysed in depth (see also CORPORA). The most notable product of this research was the COBUILD (1987) dictionary, but many independent insights have emerged from the study of the corpus.

Chief among these new insights is the realization of the delicate relationship between sense and structure, that the different senses of an item are often paralleled by preferred structural configurations (see Sinclair 1987b). It is also clear that the facts of lexical combinability often defy even native-speaker introspection and, equally far-reaching, that much of natural language occurs in 'semi-preconstructed phrases that constitute single choices, even though they might appear to be analysable into segments' (Sinclair 1987a). This last remark expands the concept of the lexicon from being a collection of words into a huge repository of meaning, many of whose items span several words or whole phrases and clauses; such findings confirm Bolinger's views on the nature of the lexicon (1965b, 1976).

Two other names central to the British approach to lexis are Mitchell (1958, 1966, 1971, 1975) and Greenbaum (1970). Mitchell was essentially concerned with all kinds of syntagmatic delimitation (see Cruse 1986: chapter 2) and his work represents a unique blend of levels of analysis, a syntactico-lexical approach similar to that of Sinclair in the COBUILD project. Mitchell (1971) is of prime importance. He examines the delicate interrelation of syntax and lexis – configurations containing the same lexical morphemes do not necessarily mean the same when rearranged or inflected. For instance, the *hard* in *hard work* means something different from *hard* in *hard-working*. Equally, *goings-on* means something different from that which is *on-going*. Syntagmatic bonds between lexical items are also responsible for the unproductive characteristics of fixed collocations, or **bound collocations** as Cruse (1986: 41) calls them, and the lack of productivity of idioms. Mitchell (1971) notes as a characteristic of idioms the frequent grammatical generalizability of their structure (e.g. tournures such as *kick the bucket, see the light, hit the sack, bite the bullet*); Greenbaum (1970) also focuses on collocation 'in certain syntactic relationships' and concludes that limited, homogeneous grammatical classes – in his case, verb intensifiers – yield the most useful analytic results. The approach that treats collocation as a purely independent level Greenbaum calls **item-orientated**; an approach taking syntax and semantics into account is **integrated** (1970).

Multi-word lexical items

The neo-Firthian tradition, with its emphasis on syntagmatic aspects of lexis, has run parallel to, and cross-fertilized, traditional studies of idioms and other fixed stretches of language that constitute single, indivisible meanings and which display degrees of semantic transparency or opacity and degrees of syntactic productivity. **Idioms**, in the sense of fixed strings whose meanings are not retrievable from their parts have been described by Weinreich (1969), Makkai (1972, 1978) and Strässler (1982), who gives good coverage of little-known Soviet work. Additionally, a wide variety of other types of multi-word lexical units (Zgusta 1967) have come under scrutiny, such as **binominals** (Malkiel 1959), **conversational formulae** (Coulmas 1981) and **restricted collocations** (Cowie 1981). Bolinger (1976) and Sinclair (1987a) are also central to any study of multi-word units, both of them arguing for the need to see

idiomaticity and **analyticity** – the amenability of linguistic phenomena to be broken down into ever smaller analytic units – as equally important to language study. This idiomatic view of the lexicon shifts the emphasis irrevocably from seeing the word as the unit of the lexicon to the adoption of more eclectic units.

Lexis and discourse analysis

A growing area of interest has been the relationship between lexical choice and the organization of discourse. Halliday and Hasan's (1976/1989) description of cohesion in English includes a chapter on the lexical cohesion observable in texts over clause and sentence boundaries (see TEXT LINGUISTICS). Textual content may be repeated in identical lexical form or may be reiterated by use of synonymy, hyponymy or selections from the class of general nouns. Additionally, collocation occurs over sentence boundaries and creates chains of mutually collocating words in texts. Hasan (1984) revised the 1976 model, rejecting collocation as non-structural and adding antonymy and meronymy to the structural devices for reiteration. She also examined devices for creating localized or **instantial** lexical relations realized in individual texts.

Work has also concentrated on the role of a large number of text-organizing words which duplicate the work of conjunctions and sentence connectors in the signalling of textual relations between clauses and sentences and in the creation of larger patterns of discourse. Words such as *reason, means, result* and *effect* overtly indicate logical relations between clauses, such as temporality, causality, etc. Of importance here is work by Winter (1977; see TEXT LINGUISTICS).

In the study of spoken discourse, much interesting research has focused on marker words, which occur widely in large spoken corpora (e.g. Tottie and Bäcklund, 1986) and on the fixed formulae found in conversation (Coulmas 1979). McCarthy (1987, 1988) has reported on types of lexical cohesion, or **relexicalization**, in conversation, and has argued for its intimate relationships with phonological features. His work owes much to Brazil (1985), who redefines the concept of paradigmatic lexical choice within the real-time constraints of discourse production.

M.J.McC.

Suggestions for further reading

Bazell, C.E., Catford, J.C., Halliday, M.A.K. and Robins, R.H. (eds) (1966) *In Memory of J.R. Firth*, London: Longman. (Particularly the papers by Halliday, Sinclair and Mitchell.)

Cruse, D.A. (1986) *Lexical Semantics*, Cambridge: Cambridge University Press.

Lehrer, A. (1974) *Semantic Fields and Lexical Structure*, Amsterdam: North Holland.

Linguistic relativity

Linguistic relativity is the thesis (Gumperz and Levinson 1996: 1) 'that culture, *through* language, affects the way we think, especially perhaps our classification of the experienced world'. Versions of it have been ascribed to various scholars of earlier times (e.g. Roger Bacon 1220–92, Wilhelm von Humboldt 1767–1835), and one version is also implicit in Saussurean structuralism (1916): for if the value of an individual sign derives from its relationship to other signs in the system, and if all systems (languages) do not divide up their 'value space' identically between identical numbers of signs (and they do not), then there is certainly some arbitrariness involved in the linguistic grid overlaid on experience by any language. However, the most famous variant is without a doubt the **Sapir–Whorf Hypothesis**, so called after the American linguists Edward Sapir (1884–1939) and Benjamin Lee Whorf (1897–1941), both of whom were strongly influenced by Franz Boas (1858–1842).

At the turn of the twentieth century, many linguists in the USA were concerned to construct records of the American Indian languages before they disappeared as the Indians became more and more strongly influenced by white American society. Earlier, these languages had been investigated by linguists from Europe who had tended to impose on them grammatical descriptions based on the categories appropriate to their own Indo-European language. Boas (1911) criticizes this practice, insisting that it is the task of the linguist to discover, for each language under study, its own particular grammatical structure, and to develop descriptive categories appropriate to it.

Many languages do not display the kinds of distinction which European linguists might tend to take for granted, such as the singular/plural and past/present distinctions, but may instead display distinctions between categories quite new to European linguists. For example, Hockett (1958) describes the tense system of Hopi as divided into three:

- Timeless truths: *Mountains are high.*
- Known or presumed known happenings: *I saw him yesterday.*
- Events still in the realm of uncertainty: *He is coming tomorrow.*

So, whereas in English the speaker's attitude in terms of certainty or uncertainty about the propositional content of utterances is indicated in the modal system by means of the modal auxiliaries (*can, may, will, shall, should, ought, need,* etc.), in Hopi, the tense of the verb itself carries this information.

In the same vein, Hockett says of Menomini that it has a five-way modality contrast:

- Certainty
  /pɪʔw/:   he comes
                  he is coming
                  he came
- Rumour
  /pɪʔwen/:   he is said to be coming
                  it is said that he came
- Interrogative
  /pɪʔ/:   is he coming?
                  did he come?
- Positive, contrary to expectations
  /pɪɑsah/:   so he is coming after all
- Negative, contrary to expectations:
  /pɪɑpah/:   but he was going to come!

Hopi also has three words which function where English only has one binder, *that*. Consider:

(1) I see that it is new
(2) I see that it is red
(3) I hear that it is new
(4) I hear that it is red

In Hopi, (1) has one word for *that*, (2) another, and (3) and (4) yet another; this is because three different types of 'representation to consciousness' are involved. In (1), the newness of the object is inferred by the speaker from a number of visual clues and from the speaker's past experience; in (2), the redness of the object is directly received in consciousness through the speaker's vision; in (3) and (4), the redness and newness are both perceived directly via the speaker's faculty of hearing (Trudgill 1974b: 25–6).

It seems clear, then, that languages, through their grammatical structure and their lexis, do not all 'interpret' the world and experience in the same way. The question is whether and to what degree this linguistic difference effects differences in possibilities of conceptualization between cultures.

Sapir, who was taught by Boas at Columbia University from 1900, began his study of Amerindian languages with a field trip to the Wishram Indians in 1905. His experience of the Amerindian languages and culture convinced him that the connection between language and thought is direct, and the influence of language on thought decisive in determining ontology (the theory of reality) (Sapir 1929, in Mandelbaum 1949: 69):

> Human beings do not live in the objective world alone, nor alone in the world of social activity as ordinarily understood, but are very much at the mercy of the particular language which has become the medium of expression for their society. It is quite an illusion to imagine that one adjusts to reality essentially without the use of language and that language is merely an incidental means of solving specific problems of communication or reflection. The fact of the matter is that the 'real world' is to a large extent built up on the language habits of the group. No two languages are ever sufficiently similar to be considered as representing the same social reality. The worlds in which different societies live are distinct worlds, not merely the same world with different labels attached.

Whorf was initially trained as a chemical engineer and worked as a fire prevention officer, and it was during his work in that capacity that he became interested in the effect of the linguistic description of an event on the way in which people perceive the event (1939/1941/1956/1997; see also DISCOURSE ANALYSIS AND CONVERSATION ANALYSIS):

> Thus around a storage of what are called 'gasoline drums' . . . great care will be exercised; while around a storage of what are called 'empty gasoline drums', [behaviour] will tend to be different – careless, with little repression of smoking or of tossing cigarette stubs about. Yet the 'empty' drums are perhaps more dangerous, since they contain explosive vapor.

Whorf enrolled on Sapir's course on Amerindian linguistics at Yale University in 1931, and in 1932 Sapir obtained a grant for Whorf to carry out fieldwork among the Hopi Indians. He observed (1936) that, whereas the metaphysics underlying Western languages 'imposes' on their speakers the two 'cosmic forms', time – divided into past, present and future – and space – which is static, three-dimensional and infinite – Hopi leads its speakers to see the universe in terms of two different cosmic forms, the manifest (or objective) and the unmanifest (or subjective). The manifest is everything that is or has been accessible to the senses, whereas the un-manifest is everything in the future and everything that is present in the minds of people, animals, plants and things. Nevertheless, Whorf's work led him to formulate a weaker version of the thesis of linguistic relativity than that propounded by Sapir. Whorf's **principle of relativity** (1940, in Carroll 1956: 214) says merely that

> No individual is free to describe nature with absolute impartiality, but is constrained to certain modes of interpretation. . . . All observers are not led by the same physical evidence to the same picture of the universe, unless their linguistic backgrounds are similar, or can in some way be calibrated.

It is implicit in Whorf's writings that he thought that languages could, in general, in some way be 'calibrated' – he succeeds throughout in explaining in English the differences between it and the world view it embodies and other languages and the world views they embody. Obviously, exact translating between languages as different from each other as English and the American Indian languages which occupied Whorf might be very difficult, involving, more often than not, extensive paraphrasing in order to convey all the ontological particularities that Whorf and others have

noticed. Nonetheless, translating, in some sense, would be possible, and this possibility has indeed often been championed by linguists with an interest in translation. For example, Roman Jakobson proposes that (1959: 431–2):

> All cognitive experience and its classification is conveyable in any existing language. Whenever there is a deficiency, terminology can be qualified and amplified by loanwords or loan translations, by neologisms or semantic shifts, and, finally, by circumlocutions. . . . No lack of grammatical devices in the language translated into makes impossible a literal translation of the entire conceptual information contained in the original.

In support of such **universalism**, Wierzbicka (1996) argues that there exists a set of 'semantic primitives' or 'semantic primes' (1972: 3; 1996: 9 *et passim*), by which she means a fixed set of meaning components, which cannot be broken down into smaller meaning components, and which are universal in the sense that every language has a word for them. They include, among others: 'I; you; someone; something; where; when; big; small; good; bad; do; happen' (Wierzbicka 1996: 14).

A number of studies carried out in the 1980s and 1990s focus on the linguistic realization in different languages of the apparently universal category, deixis (see Gumperz and Levinson 1996); and Bowerman (1996: 149–50) argues that 'All languages make categorical distinctions among spatial configurations for the purpose of referring to them with relatively few expressions, such as the spatial prepositions', although what counts as a particular spatial relationship varies between languages.

Undoubtedly, the question of whether the apparent universality of fairly basic, low-level phenomena such as those just mentioned is enough to guarantee the possibility of cross-cultural conceptual compatibility will continue to exercise linguistic and philosophical imaginations. Gumperz and Levinson (1996) contains a number of studies of various cognitive and linguistic phenomena in support of both sides in the relativism/universalism debate. The philosophical aspects of the thesis of linguistic relativity and its connection with the notion of **ontological relativity** are further discussed in the entry on PHILOSOPHY OF LANGUAGE.

K.M.

Suggestions for further reading

Carroll, J.B. (ed.) (1956) *Language, Thought and Reality: Selected Writings of Benjamin Lee Whorf*, Cambridge, MA: MIT Press.

Gumperz, J.J. and Levinson, S.C. (1996) *Rethinking Linguistic Relativity*, Cambridge: Cambridge University Press.

Mandelbaum, D.G. (ed.) (1949) *Selected Writings of Edward Sapir in Language, Culture and Personality*, Berkeley and Los Angeles: University of California Press, and London: Cambridge University Press.

Metaphor

According to Eco (1984: 87), metaphor 'defies every encyclopedic entry'. Nevertheless, metaphor merits such an entry because, although sometimes seen as merely one among the different tropes (see STYLISTICS) available to a language user, it may equally be seen as a fundamental principle of all language use. It has even been claimed (Lakoff and Johnson 1980: 3) that 'our ordinary conceptual system, in terms of which we both think and act, is fundamentally metaphorical in nature'. It should be pointed out, however, that even researchers taking a view of metaphor very much opposed to this would agree about the importance to linguistic theory of the phenomenon of metaphor. Thus Sadock (1979), according to whom metaphor falls outside linguistics proper because it has non-linguistic parallels while linguistics should be confined to the study of the uniquely linguistic aspects of human communication (1979: 46), believes, in spite of this, that an understanding of metaphor is important for linguists because 'figurative language is one of the most productive sources of linguistic change' and 'Most lexical items [are] dead metaphors' (1979: 48).

Lakoff and Johnson's book presents the most extreme form of **constructivism**, one of the two broad categories into which theories of metaphor may fall, the other

being **non-constructivism** (Ortony 1979b: 2). According to constructivism, 'the objective world is not directly accessible, but is constructed on the basis of the constraining influences of human knowledge and language'; on this view, metaphor may be seen as instrumental in *creating* reality, and the distinction between literal and figurative, including metaphorical, language tends to break down. Constructivists tend, in fact, not to distinguish metaphors from other tropes, and to take what Ortony (1979b: 4) terms a **macroscopic** view of metaphor: it is held that metaphors at sentence level are symptomatic of underlying systems of metaphor, or metaphoric models. These systems, or models, may be expressed in a sentence-level metaphor, for instance *Argument is war* (Lakoff and Johnson 1980: 4). This underlying metaphor, or **metaphorical concept**, as Lakoff and Johnson call it, gives rise to expressions like *Your claims are indefensible, He shot down all of my arguments*, etc. from which the researcher can 'read off' the underlying metaphor.

According to non-constructivism, reality exists independently of human knowledge and language, and can be 'precisely described through the medium of language' (Ortony 1979b: 1). The language used for describing reality precisely is literal language which is clearly distinguishable from tropes such as metaphors, which are at best ornamental, and at worst, misleading.

Non-constructivist writers on metaphor tend to take a **microscopic** view (1979b: 4), studying individual, sentence-level metaphors each of which they see as independent of others, rather than as part of any metaphorical system.

The identification and classification of metaphors have been the subjects of much discussion. According to many writers, for instance Beardsley (1967) and Searle (1979), the criterion for identifying a metaphor is that, taken literally, the metaphorical utterance would be plainly false. Black (1979: 35), however, points out that:

> An obvious objection is that this test, so far as it fits, will apply equally to such other tropes as oxymoron or hyperbole, so that it would at best certify the presence of some figurative statement, but not necessarily a metaphor. A more serious objection is that authentic metaphors need not manifest the invoked controversion, though many of them do. Suppose I counter the conversational remark, 'As we know, man is a wolf . . .' by saying, 'Oh, no, man is not a wolf but an ostrich.' In context, 'Man is not a wolf' is as metaphorical as its opposite, yet it clearly fails the controversion test. The point is easy to generalize: The negation of any metaphorical statement can itself be a metaphorical statement and hence possibly true if taken literally. Nor need the examples be confined to such negatives. When we say, 'He does indeed live in a glass house,' of a man who actually lives in a house made of glass, nothing prevents us from using the sentence to make a metaphorical statement.

Black is of the opinion that there is no infallible test for discriminating the metaphorical from the literal; he claims, rather unhelpfully, it may be thought (1979: 356), that we recognize a metaphor because, on the one hand, we know what a metaphor is and, on the other hand, we judge that a metaphorical reading is preferable to a literal reading.

The broadest division of metaphors is that which distinguishes **dead** from **live** metaphors. A dead metaphor is an expression like *leg of a table/chair*, which is in very common use and in the case of which we no longer think of the use of *leg* as metaphorical. Idioms such as *kick the bucket* can, in the case of many, be presumed to have begun life as metaphors (see Sadock 1979: 48). A live metaphor is one which is new, or relatively new, or which has not become part of everyday linguistic usage, so that we know when hearing it that a metaphor has been used. Of this division, Black (1979: 26) says that it 'is no more helpful than, say, treating a corpse as a special case of a person: a so-called dead metaphor is not a metaphor at all, but merely an expression that no longer has a pregnant metaphorical use'. Instead, he proposes to distinguish, among live metaphors, to which he refers as **active**, between **strong** and **weak** metaphors. This distinction depends on two aspects of metaphors – their **emphasis** and their **resonance** (1979: 267):

> A metaphorical utterance is *emphatic* . . . to the degree that its producer will allow no variation upon or substitution for the words used. . . . Emphatic metaphors are intended to be dwelt upon for the sake of their unstated implications. . . . Some metaphors, even famous ones, barely lend themselves to implicative elaboration, while others, perhaps less interesting, prove relatively rich in background implications. For want of a better label, I shall call metaphorical utterances that support a high degree of implicative elaboration *resonant.*

A strong metaphor is one which is both emphatic and resonant.

Within the two broad categories of theory described above, a number of explicit theories of metaphor are discernible. One of the oldest of these is the Aristotelian

comparison view, according to which a metaphor is an implicit **simile**, an implicit statement of comparison. Thus *my love is like a red, red rose* is a simile: the presence in it of *like* marks it explicitly as a comparison between my love and a red red rose; however, *my love is a red red rose* is a metaphor differing from the simile in that the comparison is left implicit. Richards (1936) called the subject of the metaphor (in this case, *my love*) the **topic** or **tenor**, and the terms in which the tenor was being described (in this case, *a red red rose*) the **vehicle**. The basis on which topic and vehicle could be thus put together he called the **ground**. So, on a comparison theory of metaphor, the similarity between the two terms in the metaphor would provide the ground for the comparison. The comparison view of metaphor is a special case of what is known as the **substitution** view, according to which a metaphor can be interchanged with a literal utterance; this view will always be open to the objection that if a literal statement could have been used just as well as the metaphor, it is difficult to explain why anyone should wish to use a metaphor at all. It is at this point that it is usually claimed that the metaphor is used for solely ornamental reasons.

According to Richards' own **tensive** theory of metaphor, the success of a metaphor depends on the **tension** or apparent incompatibility between topic and vehicle – an incompatibility which a successful metaphor shows to be only apparent. Richard's tensive view remains an aspect of Black's **interaction** view, but is most clearly developed by Sternberg *et al.* (1979).

The interaction view of metaphor may be summarized as follows (from Black 1979: 28–9):

1 A metaphorical statement has two distinct subjects, the primary and the secondary subject.
2 The secondary subject is to be regarded as a system rather than an individual thing.
3 The metaphorical utterance works by projecting upon the primary subject a set of associated implications, comprised in the implicative complex, that are predicable of the secondary subject.
4 The maker of a metaphorical statement selects, emphasizes, suppresses, and organizes features of the primary subject by applying to it statements isomorphic with the members of the secondary subject's implicative complex.
5 In the context of a particular metaphorical statement, the two subjects interact in the following ways: (a) the presence of the primary subject incites the hearer to select some of the secondary subject's properties; and (b) invites him or her to construct a parallel implication-complex that can fit the primary subject; and (c) reciprocally induces parallel changes in the secondary subject.

At times, the metaphor will change the relationships between the primary and secondary subjects and, in so doing, it will generate new knowledge and insight (1979: 37); as such, metaphors are creative, they are **cognitive instruments** 'indispensable for perceiving connections that, once perceived, are *then* truly present . . . Some metaphors enable us to see aspects of reality that the metaphor's production helps to constitute' (1979: 39). A metaphor can show us how things are in the same way as do 'charts and maps, graphs and pictorial diagrams, photographs and realistic paintings, and above all models' (1979: 41). All of these devices are correct or incorrect representations, or appropriate or inappropriate, rather than plainly true or false. Boyd (1979) takes this idea further, claiming that metaphors can *constitute* scientific theories.

It follows from a view such as Black's that metaphors can highlight certain aspects of a phenomenon while hiding others. For example, the metaphor of argument as war creates a focus on the conflict of opinions involved, while hiding another aspect;

namely, the fact that the parties to the argument are both giving some of their time, a valuable commodity, and might even be doing so in order to reach an agreement, that is, for a co-operative purpose (Lakoff and Johnson 1980: chapter 3).

Searle (1979: 100) takes interaction theories to task for failing to distinguish between sentence and utterance meaning, having himself described metaphor as a case in which speaker meaning and sentence meaning come apart but are related to each other in a principled way (1979: 93). Metaphor is always a property of the utterance meaning, never of the sentence meaning; rather, a sentence can be *used* to utter a metaphor (or to make a literal statement, or an ironical statement or an indirect speech act; see SPEECH-ACT THEORY) (1979: 96). The user of a sentence to make a metaphor *says metaphorically* that S is P, but means *S is R* (1979: 113); that is, the metaphor can be given a literal paraphrase, albeit (possibly) a poor one. In spite of the extensive list of strategies and principles for determining that a metaphor has been uttered that Searle provides, he can be accused of failing to show how a hearer – having decided that a sentence is not being used literally, because, taken literally, it would be false – is then able to decide that the sentence is being used metaphorically rather than ironically or as an indirect speech act (Morgan 1979: 143–4). Morgan's own suggestion is that the purpose of making a metaphor is to convey emotionality and that hearers/readers recognize this (1979: 149).

Cohen (1979: 65–6) challenges Searle's view that metaphors are properties of utterance meaning rather than of sentence meaning on the grounds that, whereas speech acts (properly described as an aspect of utterance rather than sentence meaning) are overridden in indirect speech, metaphors are not; thus both *The boy next door is a ball of fire* and *Tom said that the boy next door is a ball of fire* can only be understood

by someone who understands the metaphor – the metaphor is therefore still a feature of the indirect speech. But in the case of *I am sorry* and *Tom said that he was sorry*, only the former retains its status of apology; so a speech act is not retained when passing from direct to indirect speech:

> Arguably, therefore, metaphorical meaning inheres in sentences, not just in speech acts. This point is a very serious difficulty for anyone, like Searle . . . who wants to construe metaphor solely in terms of speaker's meaning – the meaning of the utterance rather than of the sentence uttered.

According to Rumelhart (1979) the distinction between literal and figurative language, and consequently between utterance and sentence meaning, is in itself suspect. He argues (1979: 80–1) that the processes of comprehension of non-literal speech form the basis of our linguistic competence. This can be seen by considering the way in which a child learns its first language (1979: 79–80):

> Presumably, a child learns a lexical item with respect to some particular domain of reference that in no way exhausts the set of situations to which the word can be correctly applied. In this domain of original use, some of the features of the situation presumably are relevant, and others presumably are not. Normally speaking, the process of language comprehension and production for a young child not fully familiar with the conventional range of application of a term must proceed through a process of fitting the aspects of the current situation into the closest lexical concept already available. Often this will conform with the conventional application of the term and it will therefore appear that the child is using the bit of language 'literally'. Just as often, the child will apply the concepts in a nonstandard way and

appear to generate 'nonliteral' or 'metaphorical' speech. Thus, for example, if the term 'open' is learned in the context of (say) a child's mouth being open, and then it is applied to a door or a window, the child will appear merely to be demonstrating an understanding of the term. On the other hand, if the child uses the term 'open' to mean 'turn on' (as with a television set or a light) the child will be perceived as having produced a metaphor. Yet the process of applying words to situations is much the same in the two cases – namely that of finding the best word or concept to communicate the idea in mind. For the child the pro-

duction of literal and nonliteral speech may involve *exactly* the same processes.

K.M.

Suggestions for further reading

Goatley, A. (1997) *The Language of Metaphors*, London: Routledge.
Kreitman, N. (1999) *The Roots of Metaphor: A Multidisciplinary Study in Aesthetics*, Aldershot: Ashgate.
Ortony, A. (ed.) (1979a/1993) *Metaphor and Thought*, Cambridge: Cambridge University Press; 2nd edition 1993.

Morphology

Background and basic terms

While **syntax** is concerned with how words arrange themselves into constructions, **morphology** is concerned with the forms of words themselves. The term has been used by linguists for over a century, although opinions have varied as to precise definitions of the subject area and scope. Interest in classifying language families across the world in the nineteenth century (see HISTORICAL LINGUISTICS) led to the study of how languages were differently structured both in broad and narrower ways, from the general laws of structure to the study of significant elements such as prefixes and inflections (see Farrar 1870: 160; Lloyd 1896). In the twentieth century the field narrowed to the study of the internal structure of words, but definitions still vary in detail (see Bloomfield 1933/1935: 207; Nida 1946: 1; Matthews 1974/1991: 3, as important main sources and, for an overview, Molino 1985).

Most linguists agree that morphology is the study of the *meaningful* parts of words, but there have broadly been two ways of

looking at the overall role played by these meaningful parts of words in language. One way has been to play down the status of the word itself and to look at the role of its parts in the overall syntax; the other has been to focus on the word as a central unit.

Whichever way is chosen, all linguists agree that, within words, meaningful elements can be perceived. Thus in the English word *watched*, two elements of meaning are present: WATCH plus PAST TENSE. WATCH and PAST TENSE are generally called **morphemes**. In the word *pens*, two morphemes, PEN and PLURAL, are present. A word such as *unhelpful* has three morphemes: NEGATIVE + HELP + ADJECTIVE. But terms such as NEGATIVE, PLURAL and ADJECTIVE are abstract; they are not real forms. The real forms that represent them (*in-*, *-s* and *-ful*) are therefore usually called **morphs** (see Hockett 1947). We can represent the examples thus:

Words	*Morphs*	*Morphemes*
watched	watch-ed	WATCH + PAST
pens	pen-s	PEN + PLURAL
unhelpful	un-help-ful	NEGATIVE + HELP + ADJECTIVE

In theories where the word is an important unit, morphology therefore becomes the description of 'morphemes and their patterns of occurrence within the word' (Allerton 1979: 47). In the American structuralist tradition interest lay more in the morpheme as the basic unit in syntax rather than in its role within the word; Harris (1946), for example, recognized only 'morphemes and sequences of morphemes' and eschewed the word as a unit of description. While this sidesteps the problem of defining the word, the morpheme itself has also presented difficulties of definition and identification. Bloomfield (1926) describes the morpheme as 'a recurrent (meaningful) form which cannot in turn be analyzed into smaller recurrent (meaningful) forms. Hence any unanalyzable word or formative is a morpheme'. The problem is – what is *meaningful*?

What is more, recurrent forms in themselves are also problematic. Nida (1946: 79) said that morphemes are recognized by 'different partial resemblances between expressions', which enables us to identify a common morpheme PAST in *sailed, landed* and *watched*, and a common morpheme SAIL in *sails, sailing, sailor, sail* and *sailed*. PAST and SAIL are both meaningful and are established by noting the recurrent pieces of word forms (Robins 1980: 155), in this case the morphs written as *-ed* and *sail*. However, the following examples from English show that there are serious problems with this approach (after Allerton 1979: 49–50):

(1) disarrange, disorganize,
(2) discern, discuss,
(3) dismay, disgruntle,
(4) disappoint, disclose.

Group 1 are clearly *morpheme + morpheme* words (they contain recurrent *and* meaningful parts). Group 2 cannot be analysed into parts and so represent single morphemes. Group 3 seem to have some sense of 'disturbance of a state' in their *dis-* element,

but the parts *-may* and *-gruntle* can then only be labelled as **unique morphemes** in that they do not reoccur elsewhere. Group 4 looks superficially like group 1, but the parts *-appoint* and *-close* bear no meaningful relation to the morphemes APPOINT and CLOSE, which appear elsewhere as separate words. Group 4 therefore contains **pseudomorphemes**.

Bloomfield (1933/1935: 244) had also noted what he called **phonetic-semantic resemblances** between recurrent parts of words which occur in very limited sets and yet do not seem to have any specifiable meaning nor any meaning at all beyond the limited set, for example:

/ð/   *in* this, that, then, there
/n/   *in* not, neither, no, never
/fl/   *in* flash, flicker, flame, flare
/sn/   *in* sniff, snort, snore, snot

Firth (1930/1964: 184) called such words **phonaesthemes** and their study **phonaesthetics**. Marchand (1969: chapter 7), who examines this phenomenon in great detail, calls it **phonetic symbolism**.

Other problems in labelling morphemes include variations of meaning within a single recurrent form (Bazell 1949), which is evident in the English element *-er* in *leader* ('one who leads'), *recorder* (not 'one who records' in the phrase *to play the recorder*; see Allerton 1979: 226), and meaningfully related forms that have no phonetic resemblance (e.g. *go/went, city/urban*). The problems are basically those of trying to relate forms and meanings, and morphologists have never fully resolved them. Bolinger (1948) calls the morpheme 'scarcely easier to pin down than a word' and sees one of the main problems as being the separation of **etymology**, which is the study of how present-day words came to be formed in the past, and the description of the structure of words. Thus **diachronic morphology** will be interested in the elements that originally built words such as *disease* and *away*, words which to the vast majority of present-day

English speakers would consist of a single morpheme each.

Bolinger, and after him Haas (1960), also recognized the difficulty of trying to identify morphemes on purely formal (distributional) grounds: for how does one separate the *cat* in *pussycat* from *cat* in *cattle*, or the *re-* in *recall* and *religion*? Bolinger's solution is that the morpheme be rather pragmatically defined as what the majority of speakers can recognize as one, or as the smallest element that can enter into *new* combinations (i.e. that an element must be **productive**). This enables us to dispense with 'meaning' and concentrate on 'a measurable fact, the recurring appearance in new environments' (Bolinger 1965a: 187; see also Marchand 1969: 2ff.). This approach certainly clears away niggling difficulties such as any apparent relationship between the word *stand* and its purely formal recurrence in *understand* and *withstand* (which form their past like *stand*, but have no obvious present-day connection and are not part of a productive set) (see Makkai 1978); it also rules out the *cran* of *cranberry* from having the status of a morpheme. But problems remain: a cranberry *is* opposed in meaning to a strawberry or a loganberry, and so the elements preceding *-berry* certainly have some 'significance'.

One solution is to see morphemes as only having true significance in relation to the words they appear in and so to make the word absolutely central to morphology. Such an approach is seen in Aronoff (1976: 10). Whatever the case, there do seem to be strong arguments for separating **synchronic** from **diachronic** studies (see INTRODUCTION), for without such a separation, the difficulties become insurmountable. To rescue the morpheme as a manageable unit it is also clear that neither form nor meaning alone are entirely reliable but must be wed in a compromise. The arbitrariness of meaning will persist in providing inconsistencies such as *selection* (act of selecting/things selected) compared with *election* (act of electing/*people elected) (Matthews 1974/1991: 50–1), but linguists continue to seek statements that will express underlying meanings for apparently unrelated forms (e.g. Bybee 1985: 4; Booij 1986). It will generally be the case, though, that morphemes will be identified by an accumulation of formal and semantic criteria. Such criteria can be seen in operation in Nida's (1946) principle for identifying morphemes (see also Spencer 1991: 4ff.; Olu Tomori 1977: 25ff., for a summary and discussion).

However, the morpheme will often be recognized by semantic and distributional criteria without its form being identical. A clear example is the formation of plurals in English. If we compare the final elements in *hands* [z], *cats* [s] and *matches* [z], we can observe a common meaning (PLURAL), a common distribution (distinct from that of the present-tense *-s* of verbs, such as *sees*, *writes*, etc.) and phonological resemblances. So, just as the sound [ɫ] in *bottle* does not contrast in *meaning* anywhere in English with the sound [l] in *lamp*, nor does [hændz] ever contrast with a word [hændɪz]; and just as we talk of the **phoneme** /l/ being realized by two **allophones** (see PHONEMICS), so the **morpheme** PLURAL is realized by different **allomorphs** (/-z/, /-s/ and /-ɪz/). Similarly, the English PAST morpheme has its allomorphs in the different realizations of *-ed* in *hooked* /t/, *raised* /d/, and *landed* /ɪd/.

Another way of looking at allomorphs is to say that the allomorphs of the English morpheme PLURAL alternate between /s/, /z/ and /ɪz/ and that these are three different **alternants** (see Matthews 1974/1991: 85ff.). Alternation is usually studied in terms of the type of conditioning that brings it about. For instance, the English PLURAL allomorphs mentioned are **phonologically conditioned**: they follow the same rules as the allomorphs of present tense third person singular *-s* and the *'s* possessive (Bloomfield 1933/1935: 211). Whether a past participle ends in *-en* or *-ed*, however, is not determined by phonology and is thus said to be **morphologically conditioned**.

But the notion of allomorphs and alternation raises a further problem. *Sheep* can be singular or plural, and *put* is the present, past or past participle of the verb. To overcome this difficulty, some linguists have proposed the existence of a **zero morph** (written ɸ). Then, in the case of English plurals, ɸ would be one allomorph of the morpheme PLURAL, alternating with /s/, /z/ and /ɪz/. Likewise ɸ would be an allomorph of PAST, alternating with /t/, /d/ and /ɪd/. Nida (1946: 3) justifies this approach by saying that the absence of an ending in verbs like *hit* and *cut* is 'structurally as distinctive as the presence of one', but other linguists have seriously challenged the viability of ɸ as a linguistic element. Haas (1960) calls zero allomorphs 'ghostly components' and Matthews (1974/1991: 117) says incisively that 'one cannot examine one's data and determine the "distribution" of "zero"'.

Not only this, but it does not solve the problem of the existence of other plurals such as *man/men* and *foot/feet*, or past tenses such as *drink/drank* and *sing/sang*. An alternative, therefore, is to talk of **morphological processes**, whereby the individual elements (e.g. MAN + PLURAL) interact to form a unified product, *men*, and are in no way obliged to represent the segments as a **sequence** of morphemes (Matthews 1974/1991: 122–3). This approach enables the analyst to dispense with the notion of allomorphs and to dispense with ɸ: HIT + PAST simply interact to give the unified form *hit*, while SING + PAST interact to produce *sang*.

Morphemes and the morphs that represent them are, however, clearly of different types. In the word *repainted*, the morph *paint* can stand alone as a word and is therefore a **free morph**; *re* and *-ed* cannot stand alone and are therefore **bound morphs**. Another distinction is often made between **lexical morphs** – morphs such as *head*, *line*,

-ist and *de-*, which can be used in the creation of new words (e.g. *headline*, *economist*, *depopulate*) – and **grammatical morphs**, those that simply represent grammatical categories such as person, tense, number, definiteness, etc.

Lexical morphs which are *not* of the kind *-ist* and *de-* but which form the 'core' of a word (Olu Tomori 1977: 32), such as *help* in *unhelpful* or *build* in *rebuild*, are known as **roots**. The root is that part of the word which is left when all the **affixes** – that is, all the morphs that have been added to it, whether before or after it (such as *de-*, *-er*, *-ist*, *-ing*, *-ed*, etc.) – are taken away. The root is obviously central to the building of new words, but not all roots can stand as free words: In the series *dentist*, *dental*, *dentures*, there is certainly a root to which various morphs are added to produce nouns and adjectives, but there is no free morph *dent* which represents the morpheme OF THE TEETH. So some roots are **bound** (*econom-*, as in *economist*, *economy*, *economic* is another example). Allerton (1979: 213) sums up this complex relationship between free and bound, lexical and grammatical morphemes, and roots and affixes. Affixes are divided into **prefixes**, occurring at the beginnings of words, and **suffixes**, occurring at the end of words. **Infixes**, morphs inserted within other morphs, also exist in some languages; in English it is possible to use them in semi-standardized terms like *abso-bloody-lutely*.

Not all linguists agree precisely on the definition of the term **root** (Matthews 1974/1991: 39–40 has a different view; Malkiel 1978 prefers to talk of **primitives**), but for most purposes it may be conveniently thought of as the core or unanalysable centre of a word.

The scope of morphology

The different approaches to identifying morphemes and to the relationships between morphemes and words are reflections of different major trends in linguistics during the twentieth century, but most linguists are in agreement on the type of phenomena morphology is concerned with. A sample of English words will illustrate these areas:

(5) locates, locating, located
(6) location, locative, dislocate
(7) earache, workload, time-bomb

In group 5, the suffixes realize morphemes such as PRESENT, PAST, PRESENT PARTICIPLE, etc. but do not change the nature of *locate* as a verb; morphemes such as PRESENT, PAST, PLURAL, THIRD PERSON and so on, are called **inflectional morphemes**. **Inflection** is a major category of morphology (see Matthews 1972). Group 6 adds bound morphs to *locate* which change its word class and enable us to **derive** new words (an adjective, a noun and a verb with opposite meaning). The process of adding bound morphs to create new words of the same or different word classes (see below) is called **derivation**. Group 7 shows examples of words which are made by combining two free roots (e.g. *ear + ache*). This is called **composition** or **compounding** and *earache*, *workload* and *time-bomb* are compounds. Groups 6 and 7 are different from 5, then, in that they enable new words to be formed; they are examples of word formation, and the scope of morphology may be represented in the following way (see Bauer 1983: 34):

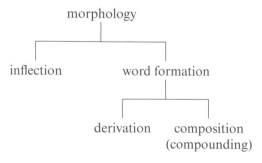

Inflection

Bloomfield (1933/1935: 222) referred to inflection as the outer layer of the morphol-ogy of word forms, and derivation as the inner layer. A simple example to illustrate what he meant by this is that the natural morphemic segmentation of the word form *stewardesses* is as in (8), not as in (9) below:

(8) stewardess + es
(9) *steward + esses

In other words, inflections are added when all derivational and compositional processes are already complete. The plural forms of *motorbike* and *painter* are *motorbikes* and *painters*, not *motorsbike* and *paintser*. Inflections such as tense, number, person, etc. will be attached to ready-made stems. Stems are the forms to which inflections may be added, but which may already have derivational affixes. Examples of stems are *repaint* (which can yield *repaints*, *repainted*, etc.) and *computerize* (which can give *computerized*, *computerizing*, etc.). Again, not all linguists agree on the use of these terms. The various terms can be related by the following example of some possible forms of the root *paint*:

root	*paint*
affixes	(re-)paint(-ed)
stem	repaint(-ed)
morphs	re-paint-ed
morphemes	AGAIN-PAINT-PAST

Inflectional categories such as tense, voice and number play an important role in syntax and are called **morphosyntactic categories**, since they affect both the words around them and the words within which they occur (see Matthews 1974/1991: 66). Inflectional morphemes are very productive: the third person singular present tense -*s* can be attached to any new English verb; the same cannot necessarily be said about derivational affixes (we can say *rework* and *dismissive* but not *rebe* or *wantive*, for example). Inflectional morphemes are semantically more regular than derivational ones; meaning will remain constant across a wide distributional range. Inflections create full conjugations and declensions for verbs and nouns; unlike derivations, they usually do not produce 'gaps': whereas the past inflectional morph *-ed* can be attached to any of the verbs *arrive*, *dispose*, *approve* and *improve* in English, only the first three form nouns with the *-al* suffix.

Word formation

There is broad, but not complete, agreement as to how the field of word formation should be divided up. Marchand (1969: 2) distinguishes between formation involving 'full linguistic signs', i.e. compounding, prefixation, suffixation, derivation by the zero morph, and back-formation (see below); and formations not involving full linguistic signs, which include expressive symbolism (e.g. Firth's **phonaesthemes**, see above), blending, clipping and word manufacturing (see below for definitions of these terms). Adams (1973: chapter 10) adds acronyms to clippings, and both Adams (1973) and Bauer (1983) separate off the class of 'neoclassical compounds' (items such as *television* and *astronaut*), whereas Marchand (1969) subsumes many of the initial morphs of neoclassical formations under the general heading of prefixes. While there are undoubtedly hazy border areas, the general distinction between derivation and composition (compounding) holds good.

Derivation

Derivation is the reverse of the coin of inflection. Like inflection, it consists in adding to a root or stem an affix or affixes (the root is also sometimes called the **unmarked base form** and the affixed form the **marked form**; see Adams 1973: 12). But, while new inflections occur only very slowly over time, new derivational affixes seem to occur from time to time, principally in that speakers use elements of words that are not established as affixes in a way that makes them

like established, productive ones (e.g. English *sputnik*, *beatnik*, *refusenik*; *alcoholic*, *workaholic*, *radioholic*; see Adams 1973: 139 for further examples). Matthews (1984) gives a good summary of the arguments concerned in the separation of inflection from derivation.

Derivational affixes function not to express morphosyntactic categories but to make new words. They are somewhat erratic in meaning and distribution: the suffix *-al* that creates nouns from verbs such as *arrive* and *dispose* forms adjectives from the nouns *brute* and *option*. What is more, whereas *nasal* means 'of the nose', *brutal* means 'like a brute' and *optional* means that something '*is* an option'. Derivational affixes vary in their productivity: English nouns ending in *-hood* are few and new ones are unlikely, as are adjectives with the negative prefix *ig-* (e.g. *ignoble*) or the suffix *-ose* (*jocose*, *verbose*) (see Kastovsky 1986), but the *-ist* in *communist* is fully productive, as is the *-ize* verb-forming morph (*computerize*, *centralize*). Within derivation, the distinction is often made between **class-maintaining** and **class-changing processes**. Class-changing produces a new word in a different word class – e.g. *computer* (noun) – *computerize* (verb) – , while class-maintaining produces a new word but does not change the class – e.g. *child* (noun) – *childhood* (noun) – (but see Bauer 1983: 31–2 for arguments against the distinction). Equally important is the phenomenon of conversion where a word changes word class without any affixation, e.g. *a hoover* (noun) – *to hoover* (verb); *a service* (noun) – *to service* (verb) (see also Bolinger and Sears 1981: 65); Malkiel (1978) calls this **internal derivation**.

Composition (compounding)

Marchand (1969: 11) talks of compounding as occurring when two or more words combine into a morphological unit, and Adams (1979: 30) refers to the combination 'of two free forms, or words that have an otherwise independent existence'. Examples of compounds are *blackmail, bathroom, skyscraper* and *gearbox*. They function to all intents and purposes like single words: if the room where I have my bath is old it is an *old bathroom*, not a **bath old room*. Like single words they will be spoken with only one primary stress, and any inflectional suffixes will occur at the end of the whole unit (*bathrooms*, not **bathsroom*). They occupy full, single, grammatical slots in sentences, unlike idioms, which can be a whole clause (Bolinger and Sears 1981: 62). Compounds may contain more than two free roots (e.g. *wastepaper basket*) and in some languages (e.g. Germanic ones) may contain in excess of half a dozen free roots (see Scalise 1984: 34 for examples). Compounds may be formed with elements from any word class but, in English at least, noun + noun compounds are the most common and are very productive; verb + verb compounds are few in English.

The following are examples of noun compounds in English according to the form classes of their components, following Bauer (1983) (for other approaches to classification, see Bauer 1983: 202):

noun + noun	bookshelf	football
verb + noun	pickpocket	killjoy
noun + verb	nosebleed	moonshine
adjective + noun	software	slowcoach
particle + noun	in-crowd	aftertaste
verb + particle	clawback	dropout
phrase compounds	gin-and-tonic	forget-me-not

These all function as nouns. Similar constructions can function as verbs. Some combinations are rare, for example, verb + verb functioning overall as a verb: *to freeze-dry* is a recent occurrence, but the same type (verb + verb) functioning as an adjective seems more productive: Bauer (1983: 211–12) gives *go-go* (*dancer*), *stop–go* (*economics*) and *pass–fail* (*test*) as examples.

Compounds are often divided into four semantic types: **endocentric**, **exocentric**, **appositional** and **dvandva** (see Bauer 1983:

30–1). Where the second element is the grammatical head word and the first a modifier, as in *wristwatch* (where *wrist* modifies *watch*), the compound is **endocentric**. Endocentric compounds are **hyponyms** (see SEMANTICS) of the head word. Where hyponymy of this kind does not exist, as in *scapegoat*, which is a kind of person, not a kind of goat, the compound is **exocentric** (the term **bahuvrihi** is also used for this type). Where the hyponymy is **bidirectional**, as in *sofa-bed*, which is a kind of sofa and/ or a kind of bed, or *clock-radio*, which is a kind of clock and/or a kind of radio, these are known as **appositional compounds**. Where compound elements name separate entities neither of which is a hyponym of the other and either of which might seem to be the grammatical head word, then these are **dvandva** or **copulative compounds**, as in names such as *Slater-Walker*, *Austin-Rover* or *Alsace-Lorraine*.

The type of compounds referred to as **neoclassical compounds** take elements, usually from Greek or Latin, and make words in a way that often resembles derivation but which needs to be kept distinct, for often such elements can combine with each other without any other root being present, and are therefore acting like roots themselves. It is for this reason that they may be considered as similar to compounds. Examples are *anglophile* (cf. *hibernophile*, *francophile*, etc.), *telephone* (*television*, *telegram*), *astronaut* (*cosmonaut*), *biocrat*. *Anglophile* belongs to a medial -*o* type, which includes *sphero-cylindrical*, *sociopolitical*, *physico-chemical*, etc. (see Adams 1973: 132).

Other word-formation types

Back-formation occurs when a suffix (or a morph perceived as a suffix) is removed from a complex word; *lecher* – *to lech*, or *liaison* – *to liaise* are recent English examples; Malkiel (1978) has interesting examples from old Provençal and Modern

French. Malkiel (1978) also gives examples of **clipping**, which can involve deletion of initial morphemes or final word-segments: *lab*(*oratory*), (*aero*)*plane*, (*tele*)*phone*, etc. are examples. Blends are another interesting type of formation, where normally initial and terminal segments of two words are joined together to create a new word; for example, *brunch* (*breakfast* + *lunch*). English examples include *selectorate* (*selectors* + *electorate*), *chunnel* (*channel* + *tunnel*), *fantabulous* (*fantastic* + *fabulous*). Cannon (1986), who provides an excellent description of blends, sees them as popular but often short-lived.

Acronyms, words formed from the initial letters of a fixed phrase or title, are also popular and often equally short-lived. English examples are *quango* (quasi-autonomous non-governmental organization), *misty* (more ideologically sound than you); established acronyms include *NATO*, *SALT* (strategic arms limitation talks) and *radar*. **Word manufacture**, the invention of completely new morphs, is rare in comparison to the kinds of word formation described above. One example often cited is *kodak*. Equally, some words appear whose origin is unknown or unclear (the OED attests *gazump* from the 1920s onwards with no etymological information) and literary works often contain one-off inventions (see Bauer 1983: 239 for some examples).

Word-formation processes are variably productive but constantly in operation to expand the lexicon as new meanings emerge, social and technological change takes place, and individuals create new forms. Recently, the advent of computers has given English items like *software* and *firmware*, and an extended meaning of *hardware*, plus a host of other terms. A survey in the London *Observer* newspaper (23 March 1987: 51) of the professional jargon of young City professionals, included compounds such as *Chinese wall*, *concert party*, *dawn raid*, *marzipan set* and *white knight*, all with specific meanings within the world of financial dealing, as well as clever acronyms such as *oink* (one income, no kids) and *dinky* (dual income, no kids yet).

Morphophonology (or morphonology or morphophonemics)

Morphophonology in its broadest sense is the study of the phonological structure of morphemes (the permitted combinations of phonemes within morphemes in any given language; see Vachek 1933), the phonemic variation which morphemes undergo in combination with one another (e.g. *hoof/hooves* in English), and the study of alternation series (e.g. recurrent changes in phonemes before certain suffixes in English: *electric* → *electricity*, *plastic* → *plasticity*; *malice* → *malicious*, *pretence* → *pretentious*; see Trubetzkoy 1931). Such changes are from one **phoneme** to another, not just between allophones (see also Trubetzkoy 1929).

The study of such changes is carried out within a morphological framework. Swadesh (1934) points out that the /f/ in *leaf* and the /f/ in *cuff* are phonemically the same but morphologically distinct in that their plurals are formed in /v/ and /f/ respectively. This latter fact can be represented by a morphophonemic symbol /F/, which would represent /v/ before /z/ plural and /f/ elsewhere (Harris 1942; see also Lass 1984: 57–8).

The broad areas covered by morphophonemics in Trubetzkoy's terms have been successively narrowed and rebroadened in linguistics over the years (see Kilbury 1976, for a detailed survey). Hockett (1947) concentrates on 'differences in the phonemic shape of alternants of morphemes' in his definition of morphophonemics, rather than on the phonemic structure of morphemes themselves. Wells (1949) takes a similar line. Hockett (1950) later returns to a broader definition, which 'subsumes every phase of the phonemic shape of morphemes', and later still gives morphophonemics a central place in the description of language (1958: 137). One of the problems in studying the phonemic composition of alternants is the separation of those alternants whose phonemes differ purely because of phonological rules, those which differ purely on lexicogrammatical grounds and those which might be seen as most narrowly morphophonologically determined (see Matthews 1974/1991: 213, for a critique of these distinctions).

Central to the study of alternation is the notion of **sandhi**, which comes from a Sanskrit word meaning 'joining' (see Andersen 1986: 1–8 for a general definition). Sandhi rules attempt to account for the phonological modification of forms joined to one another. A distinction is usually drawn between **external sandhi**, which occurs across word boundaries, and **internal sandhi**, which occurs within word boundaries (see Matthews 1974/1991: 111). Matthews gives an example of a sandhi rule for ancient Greek: 'any voiced consonant is unvoiced when an s (or other voiceless consonant) follows it'; this rule is realized in, for example, the forms *aigos* (genitive) – *aiks* (nominative) (1974/1991: 102). Lass (1984: 69) locates the principal domain of sandhi as the interface between phonology and syntax; it is concerned with processes at the margins of words in syntactic configurations or at the margins of morphemes in syntactically motivated contexts. Sandhi rules form an important part of morphophonemic description. Andersen (1986) contains accounts of sandhi phenomena in European languages.

Over the years, much debate has taken place on the overall status of morphophonology in linguistic description. Chomsky's (1951) thesis on modern Hebrew sees the morphophonological statements of a language as the third stage in the generation of sentences from the basic syntactic statements to the final sequence of phones (Chomsky 1979: 3–4) (see GENERATIVE GRAMMAR), and Hockett (1958: 135–42)

makes morphophonemics centrally important but not independent; it is, rather, an interlevel between grammar and phonology. Chomsky and Halle (1968: 11) reject the term 'morphophonology' altogether and deal with matters such as alternation under the umbrella of phonology (1968: 178ff.). The debate has resurfaced within modular approaches to linguistics and is represented in Dressler (1985), whose view is that morphophonology mediates between morphology and phonology without being a basic level in itself. Zwicky's (1986) work illustrates the interaction of independent modular components; his Shape Component, which contains the lexicon itself together with rules for inflectional and for derivational morphology, is a separate grammar module that regulates the distribution of allomorphs such as English *a/an*. However, contemporary theories differ from pre-generative structuralism in that the idea of an independent morphophonemic level has been discarded.

Morphology: schools and trends

Three general approaches may be discerned within structuralist morphology; these are usually known as **word and paradigm**, **item and process** and **item and arrangement**. In addition, the debates on morphology within the general framework of generative grammar must be mentioned.

Word and paradigm

This is the approach to morphology many will be familiar with from school-book descriptions of Latin grammar and the grammar of some modern European languages. Word and paradigm (WP) has a long-established history, going back to ancient classical grammars. In this approach, the word is central and is the fundamental unit in grammar. WP retains a basic distinction between morphology and syntax: morphology is concerned with the formation of words and syntax with the structure of sentences. Central, therefore, to WP is the establishment of the word as an independent, stable unit. Robins (1959) offers convincing criteria for words and argues that WP is an extremely useful model in the description of languages. Word forms sharing a common root or base are grouped into one or more paradigms (e.g. the conjugations of the different tenses of the Latin verb *amo*). Paradigm categories include such things as number in English, case in Latin, or gender in French. Paradigms are primarily used for inflectional morphemes; derivational ones can be set out in this way but they tend to be less regular and symmetrical.

WP is particularly useful in describing fusional features in languages; using the word as the central unit avoids the problems of 'locating' individual morphosyntactic categories in particular morphs, especially where several may be simultaneously fused in one word element (e.g. Latin *amabis*, where tense, mood, voice, number and person cannot be separated sequentially). Matthews (1974/1991: 226) points out that exponents of morphosyntactic categories may extend throughout a word form, overlapping each other where necessary. He also illustrates, with reference to Spanish verbs, how identical forms appear in different paradigms and can only be meaningfully understood in relation to the other members of their paradigm. Thus the systematic reversal of inflectional endings to indicate mood in -*ar* and -*er* verbs in Spanish, e.g. *compra* (indicative) *compre* (subjunctive), compared with *come* (indicative) – *coma* (subjunctive) can only be captured fully within the paradigm (1974/1991: 137ff.; see also Molino 1985).

WP avoids the morphophonological problems that beset other approaches and can also dispense with the zero morph, since morphosyntactic features are exhibited in the word form as a whole. In general, WP may be seen to be a model which has great usefulness in linguistic description, although it may be of less use in describing certain types of language.

Item and process

The item and process (IP) model, as its name suggests, relates items to one another by reference to morphological processes. Thus *took* is related to *take* by a process of vowel change. IP considers the morpheme, not the word, to be the basic unit of grammar and, therefore, the morphology/syntax division is negated. In IP, each morpheme has an underlying form, to which processes are applied. This underlying form will sometimes be the most widely distributed allomorph; thus in Latin *rex*, *regis*, *regi*, *regem*, etc. [ks] occurs only in nominative singular, suggesting *reg-* as the underlying form (Lass 1984: 64; see also Allerton 1979: 223).

In IP, labels such as 'plural' become an operation rather than a form (Molino 1985). Processes include affixation, alternation of consonants and/or vowels (e.g. *sing/sang*), reduplication (e.g. Malay plurals: *guru-guru* 'teachers'), compounding, and stress differences (e.g. *récord/recórd*) (Robins 1959). Matthews (1974/1991: 226) exemplifies how generative grammarians have included processes in descriptions of lexical entries, to activate features such as vowel change when certain morphemes are present (e.g. English *goose* + plural *geese*). IP, like WP, has great value as a model of analysis; it can do much to explain word forms but, as with WP, it cannot account for all features of all languages.

Item and arrangement

Hockett (1954) contrasts IP and IA (item and arrangement) sharply, and Robins (1959) suggests that WP should be considered as something separate, not opposed to IP and IA in the way that IP and IA are opposed to one another. IA sees the word as a linear sequence of morphs which can be segmented. Thus a sentence such as *the wheel/s turn/ed rapid/ly* would be straightforwardly segmented as shown. Again, the morpheme is the fundamental unit. IA talks simply of items and 'the arrangements in which they occur relative to each other in utterances – appending statements to cover phonemic shapes which appear in any occurrent combination' (Hockett 1954).

IA is associated with structural formalism and the systematization that followed from Bloomfield. In his comparison of IA and IP, Hockett illustrates the contrast in the two approaches to linguistic forms: for IP, forms are either **simple** or **derived**; a **simple form** is a root, a **derived form** is an 'underlying form to which a process has been applied'. In IA, a form is either **simple** or **composite**; a **simple form** is a morpheme and a **composite form** 'consists of two or more immediate constituents standing in a construction'. IA encountered many problems in description, not least how to handle alternation, but its value lay in its rigorous, synchronic approach to unknown languages and its formalism. Its goal was to describe the totality of attested and possible sequences of the language using discrete minimal units established by distributional criteria (Molino 1985).

WP, IP and IA have different domains of usefulness and no one model can serve all purposes. All three leave certain areas unresolved, and the best features of each are undoubtedly essential in any full description of a language.

Morphology and generative grammar

The place of morphology within a generative framework has been the subject of much debate since the late 1950s. Early transformational grammarians continued the structuralist tradition of blurring the morphology/syntax division. Chomsky (1957: 32) viewed syntax as the grammatical sequences of morphemes of a language. In general, morphology was not held to be a separate field of study (see Aronoff 1976: 4; Scalise 1984: ix). Phonology and syntax were the central components of grammatical description. Lees (1960/1963) is a key document of the approach that attempts to explain word-formation processes in terms of syntactic transformations. A compound such as *manservant* was seen to incorporate the sentence *The servant is a man*; this sentence by transformation generates the compound (Lees 1960/1963: 119). Such a description is naturally highly problematic, especially when confronted with the idiosyncrasies of derived and compound words.

Chomsky (1970) saw an opposition between this **transformationalist view** and the **lexicalist view**, which transferred to the lexicon proper the rules of derivation and compounding. In the **lexicalist view**, the rules of word formation are rules for generating words which may be stored in the dictionary. Halle (1973) sees the dictionary as a set of morphemes plus a set of word-formation mechanisms; word formation occurs entirely within the lexicon. The growing importance of the lexicon and the debate on the status of word formation meant the steady re-emergence of morphology as a separate area of study. From the 1970s on, important works on morphology have been produced within the generative framework. Different perspectives on morphology will be illustrated in what follows.

In the mid-1970s interest grew in natural morphology and in lexical phonology and morphology, lexical phonology for short. **Natural morphology** is an approach which looks for natural universals over a wide range of languages with regard to **morphotactic** (the way morphemes are joined) and morphosyntactic tendencies. The trend is summarized by Dressler (1986). **Lexical**

phonology regards the lexicon as the central component of grammar, which contains rules of word formation and phonology as well as the idiosyncratic properties of words and morphemes. The word-formation rules of the morphology are paired with phonological rules at various levels or **strata**, and the output of each set of word-formation rules is submitted to the phonological rules on the same stratum to produce a word. The lexicon is therefore the output of the morphological and phonological rules of the different strata put together (Kiparsky 1982a; see further Pulleyblank 1986; Katamba 1989: chapter 12). Kiparsky also introduced the **Elsewhere Condition**, which states how rules apply. Rules A and B in the same component apply disjunctively to a form, provided that '(i) the structural description of A (the special rule) properly includes the structural description of B (the general rule); (ii) the result of applying A to φ is distinct from the result of applying B to φ. In that case, A is applied first, and, if it takes effect, then B is not applied' (Kiparsky 1982a: 136f). The Elsewhere Condition thus ensures that the more specific rule will be applied first.

Anderson's (1982, 1986, 1988, 1992) **Extended Word and Paradigm model** takes the word and paradigm approach as starting point. Paradigms have an important place in this system. They are generated by morpholexical rules that specify how morphosyntactic categories are spelled out in phonological form. Anderson gives up the notion of morpheme in inflectional morphology in favour of binary morphosyntactic features, such as [+me] and [−me]. [+me] characterizes a first person form and [+you] a second person form, while third person is specified as [−me], [−you]. Morpholexical rules take the feature specification and provide the actual surface form. Stems are provided by the lexicon, by other morpholexical rules or by the output of phonological rules applying to an earlier stage in the derivation (Spencer 1991: 216). Rules

are disjunctively ordered and presuppose Kiparsky's Elsewhere Condition, so that when more than one rule could be applied it is the more specific that wins out. This makes it unnecessary to specify independently how rules are ordered.

In Anderson's system, morphemes are processes or rules and in this it differs from approaches such as Selkirk, Williams or Lieber, which view morphemes as stored in the lexicon and related by rules.

Williams (1981) attempts to break down the inflection/derivation distinction with regard to word formation, as does Selkirk (1982), who clearly places derivation, compounding and inflection within a morphological component of the grammar (but see also Anderson 1982).

For Lieber (1980), as for Williams (1981), morphology is basically a property of the lexicon, a lexical approach that excludes word formation by syntactic means. In Lieber's approach morphemes are listed in the lexicon with information on their syntactic category. In the case of affixes a subcategorization frame indicates which category they should be attached to. Subcategorization frames are strictly local: morphemes can only relate to sisters (the Adjacency condition; Siegel 1977). The plural affix -z, for example, has the following subcategorization frame:

z: [[N] _]; [N; +plural]

Inflectional and derivational affixes are treated in the same way. According to Lieber there are no purely morphological differences between both types of affixes. Stems hosting the affixes do not distinguish between them. Spencer (1991: 204) illustrates this with the irregular plural stem allomorph of English *house*, /hauz/, which is also the verb stem allomorph *to house*.

Another lexicalist approach to morphology is di Sciullo and Williams' (1987). These authors see syntax and morphology as entirely separate domains, so that syntactic rules cannot influence morphological processes. Important for their approach is the distinction between several ways of understanding the notion of 'word'. Di Sciullo and Williams (1987) distinguish 'word' as a morphological object, as a syntactic atom and as 'listeme'. Linguistic objects which do not have the form or the meaning 'specified by the recursive definitions of the objects of the language' (Di Sciullo and Williams 1987: 3) have to be memorized by the speakers and listed in the lexicon; they are called **listemes**. Morphemes form **morphological objects** by the processes of affixation and compounding (Di Sciullo and Williams 1987: 46). **Syntactic atoms** are the syntactic units of the language and because of their atomicity syntactic rules are unable to analyse their subcomponents.

Lexicalist approaches like those mentioned above contrast strongly with approaches that observe the morphology–syntax interface from a syntactical standpoint (Baker, Marantz, Halle and Marantz, among others). An example of such an approach is Baker's **incorporation theory**, a radically syntactic approach to morphology. In this approach, most aspects of morphology are seen as consequences of syntactic operations (a characteristic Baker shares with Marantz). Baker regards valency-changing operations as cases of incorporation of lexical categories into a lexical head via syntactic movement. The host element is in most cases the lexical verb; the incorporated element heads its own lexical projection. The following illustration of possessor incorporation is taken from Spencer (1991: 275). (1a) and (1b) are represented in (2) and (3) respectively. (3) shows how the original direct object is incorporated into the verb, thus forming the compound verb *spear-stole*. The possessor NP plays now the role of the object subcategorized by the new compound verb.

(1) (a) Dick stole Tom's spear
    (b) Dick spear-stole Tom

(2)

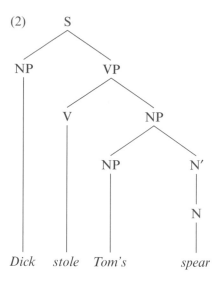

(3)

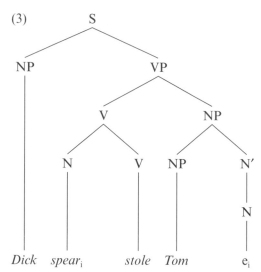

The idea of incorporation is applied to different phenomena such as causatives, applicatives, anti-passives and passives.

An argument for the syntactic nature of incorporation is the fact that it observes the **Head Movement Constraint** (Travis 1984). According to this constraint, a head can only move to the head position in the next highest phrase in the structure, i.e. to the head that governs its projection. This amounts to stating that a lexical item such as a verb will only incorporate a word it properly governs. Furthermore the Head Movement Constraint accounts both for allowed cases of incorporation (noun incorporation, applicatives, anti-passives, passives) as well as for disallowed ones.

In Baker's perspective, productive morphological processes mirror syntax, providing evidence for the syntactic nature of morphological operations. In this spirit he formulates the Mirror Principle, which claims that the order of morphological operations as seen in the order of affixes mirrors the order of syntactical operations.

However, Baker's approach does not cover the morphological aspect of the morphology–syntax interface. Some valency-changing operations cannot be accounted for in this framework, either. Spencer (1991: 296) mentions as an example the case of verbs formed from other verbs by prefixation, e.g. the productive use of *out-* to form transitive verbs from intransitive ones (*grow – outgrow*).

In the Chomskyan framework similarities and differences between languages are accounted for by **Principles** and **Parameters**. Similarities among languages are assumed to be due to inviolable principles of **Universal Grammar**. The range of variation possible – for example, in word order – is determined by parameters. A different approach is offered by **Optimality theory**, which was developed in the 1990s and introduced in Prince and Smolensky (1993) and McCarthy and Prince (1993a). The theory includes two basic claims:

a Universal Grammar is a set of violable constraints,
b Language-specific grammars rank these constraints in language-specific ways.

Constraints define what is universal, while constraint violations characterize markedness and variation. Two formal mechanisms, **GEN** and **EVAL**, regulate the relation between input and output. GEN (for generator) creates linguistic objects, EVAL (evaluator) checks the language-specific ranking of constraints (called **CON**) and selects the best candidate for a given input from those produced by GEN (Russell 1997).

Optimality theory has been influential mainly in phonology. In a morphological analysis, it provides a way of dealing with morpheme ordering and with mappings between syntactic and morphological categories.

In addition to the approaches presented here, a number of other models exist. The reader is referred to Spencer (1991) for detailed accounts and to Lapointe *et al.* (1998) for first-hand discussions of the relation of morphology to phonology and syntax.

M.J.McC, revised by T.P.

Suggestions for further reading

Bauer, L. (1983) *English Word-Formation*, Cambridge: Cambridge University Press.
Matthews, P.H. (1974/1991) *Morphology*, Cambridge: Cambridge University Press.
Spencer, A. (1991) *Morphological Theory: An Introduction to Word Structure in Generative Grammar*, Oxford: Basil Blackwell.

N

Non-transformational grammar

The class of non-transformational generative grammars comprises frameworks that share many of the broad goals espoused in early transformational work (e.g. Chomsky 1957) but use different devices to pursue these goals. This class of grammars can be divided into three principal subclasses. The family of **feature-based** approaches, also known variously as 'unification-based', 'constraint-based' or 'description-based' grammars, makes essential use of complex-valued features in the analysis of local and non-local dependencies. **Generalized Phrase-Structure Grammar**, **Head-driven Phrase Structure Grammar** and **Lexical Functional Grammar** are among the most important members of this class. There are two basic varieties of **relational** approaches – **Relational Grammar** and **Arc Pair Grammar** – which both accord primacy to grammatical relations and relation-changing rules. The class of **categorial** approaches uses flexible category analyses and highly schematic rules to combine expressions that often do not correspond to syntactic constituents in other approaches. Categorial approaches fall into three main groups: versions of the **Lambek calculus**, **Combinatory Categorial Grammars**, and offshoots of **Montague Grammar**.

This entry identifies the distinctive characteristics that broadly define the three primary subclasses and summarizes some significant properties and insights of individual frameworks.

Feature-Based Grammars

It is customary to divide feature-based grammars into 'tools' and 'theories'. The class of tools includes versions of the **PATR** formalism (Shieber 1986), along with approaches, such as **Functional Unification Grammar** (Kay 1979), which have mainly provided a basis for **grammar implementations**. While theories such as **Generalized Phrase-Structure Grammar** (GPSG), **Head-driven Phrase-Structure Grammar** (HPSG) and **Lexical-Functional Grammar** (LFG) have also been successfully implemented, these formalisms provide a more general framework for theoretical analysis.

A distinguishing property of this class of formalisms is the use of complex feature values to regulate grammatical dependencies that are attributed to constituent structure displacements in transformational accounts. The analysis of **subject–verb agreement** provides a useful illustration. The subject agreement demands of an English verb such as *walks* may be expressed by assigning *walks* a complex-valued SUBJ(ECT) feature which contains the features that represent third person and singular number. In a simple feature system, these might be [PERS 3RD] and [NUM SG].

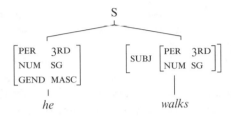

Figure 1 Subject-verb agreement

Agreement between the 3sg verb *walks* and the 3sg subject *he* in Figure 1 is then keyed to a non-directional requirement that the SUBJ features associated with the verb must be 'compatible' with the grammatical features of its syntactic subject. The execution details of this analysis vary slightly across approaches, though in all accounts the conditions that determine subject verb agreement refer to the features introduced by the subject and verb, not to the elements *walks* and *he*. It is the ability to refer to such features, independently of the expressions on which they are introduced, that permits feature-based approaches to dispense with the constituent-structure displacements that induce the 'flow' of feature information in transformational accounts.

Grammatical compatibility is usually determined 'destructively' in feature-based approaches. What this means in the present case is that the SUBJ features of the verb phrase are directly amalgamated or **unified** with the features of the syntactic subject. The result of combining two sets of compatible features is a single feature structure that contains the information from both. Unifying the features of *he* with the SUBJ features of *walks* yields a structure that just preserves the features of *he*, because these features already contain the SUBJ features of *walks*. If the input features are incompatible, unification is said to 'fail', in virtue of the fact that no consistent structure can contain conflicting values for a single feature 'path'. (The possibility of failure distinguishes unification from the formally similar set union operation.) The central

role of unification in GPSG, LFG and HPSG underlies the now largely deprecated term 'unification-based grammars'.

Feature structure unification or, equivalently, structure sharing, retains a key role in most feature-based frameworks. It is nevertheless important to realize that the 'constructive' strategy of determining compatibility by actually combining the features of input structures does not in any way require a fully 'destructive' mechanism that overwrites the inputs in the process. To regulate agreement in Figure 1, we must combine the SUBJ features of *walks* and the features of its syntactic subject. It is, of course, more efficient to merge the original inputs than it is to copy their feature information and amalgamate it in another location, e.g. on the common S mother in Figure 1. Yet there is evidence that this efficiency incurs a significant descriptive cost in coordinate structures and other environments in which a single element is subject to multiple compatibility demands. The fact that such elements may satisfy incompatible demands suggests that, in at least some cases, valence and concord demands must be regulated by the non-destructive or semi-destructive mechanism suggested in recent accounts (Dalrymple and Kaplan 2000; Blevins to appear).

Another general issue concerns the symmetrical or non-directional character of operations such as unification. This is widely viewed as a virtue, as order-independent formalisms fit particularly well with incremental models of comprehension or production. Nevertheless, it remains to be seen whether symmetrical operations can provide illuminating analyses of all of the cases that motivate the traditional distinction between agreement 'controllers' and 'targets' (Corbett 1991).

Generalized Phrase-Structure Grammar

Although the descriptive potential of complex syntactic features is set out clearly by Harman (1963), this potential was not fully realized until the emergence of GPSG nearly twenty years later. A decisive step in the development of GPSG – and non-transformational approaches generally – was the demonstration in Gazdar (1981) that any non-local dependency that could be described in terms of transformational 'movement' rules could also be described by a local mechanism that 'passes' the features of a dislocated element successively from daughters to mothers in a phrase-structure tree. This demonstration effectively refuted longstanding claims that transformational devices were necessary for the description of non-local dependencies. The intervening decades have seen the development of a range of other non-transformational strategies (see, e.g., the discussion of **domain union**, **functional uncertainty** and **function composition** below), as well as a general recognition that derivational structure is not an intrinsic property of natural languages or of the language faculty, but rather a purely contingent property of transformational approaches.

Yet, with the benefit of hindsight, the success of the GPSG analysis of unbounded dependencies can be seen as something of a blessing and a curse. On the positive side, the discovery that **phrase-structure grammars** could define structural descriptions isomorphic to those attributed to transformational devices threw open a number of issues that many linguists had taken to be settled. On the negative side, the successful use of features to mimic the effects of 'movement' rules encouraged two somewhat conservative tendencies in later GPSG work. The first was a tendency to push feature-based strategies into areas where they did not provide an illuminating analysis. The second was a tendency to use features to 'emulate' existing transformational analyses.

GPSG treatments of co-ordination display the first tendency, while analyses of passivization illustrate the second. GPSG accounts of co-ordinate structures squarely address the problems posed by cases of unlike constituent co-ordination, such as *Max is a Guardian reader and passionate about penal reform*. In this example, the noun phrase *a Guardian reader* appears to be conjoined with the adjective phrase *passionate about penal reform*, violating the widely assumed constraint that conjuncts must be of the same category. The solution developed within GPSG assigns a co-ordinate mother the **generalization** of the features of its conjunct daughters, so that *a Guardian reader and passionate about penal reform* is assigned the features from each conjunct that do not conflict with the other conjunct. GPSG accounts acknowledge that this account does not extend to cases of non-constituent co-ordination, and subsequent work suggests that a generalization-based account also does not apply correctly to verbs with unlike valence demands. At an even more basic level, one might question the grounds for treating *a Guardian reader and passionate about penal reform* as a constituent in the first place. While the precise analysis of these constructions remains a matter of dispute, it is generally accepted that the solution is not likely to lie in an innovative strategy for combining the features associated with unlike conjuncts or non-constituent sequences.

By pushing a feature-based strategy to its limits, GPSG analyses of co-ordination can be seen to obtain a useful, if somewhat negative, result. GPSG treatments of passivization in terms of **meta-rules** are perhaps best regarded in much the same way. These accounts demonstrate that the structure-to-structure mapping invoked in transformational analyses can be mimicked by a meta-rule that maps phrase-structure rules that introduce active VPs onto derived rules that introduce detransitivized passive VPs. Yet, by reimplementing the transformational analysis, GPSG accounts inherit the weaknesses of this analysis, while exposing limitations of a standard phrase-structure formalism. As LFG accounts in particular have shown, passivization is a lexical – indeed, derivational – process, which is most insightfully expressed by analyses that relate entries, rather than structures or syntactic rules. This type of analysis is unavailable in a standard phrase-structure grammar, which represents the lexicon implicitly in the rules that rewrite preterminals. GPSG extends this conception by introducing entries that are cross-indexed with rules, though these entries still do not carry the information required for a lexicalist analysis of the passive.

GPSG accounts are arguably most successful in cases where they address a traditional issue or present an essentially new approach. For example, the GPSG **head feature convention** (or **principle**) illustrates how complex features yield an insightful treatment of traditional notions like 'endocentricity'. This principle requires that a syntactic head and the phrase that it heads must have the same values for the various 'head' features that represent part of speech and syntactically relevant inflectional properties. The inclusion of inflectional features contrasts with versions of **X-bar theory** in which part of speech features are, without any explicit justification, singled out as the only head features. In GPSG, the features of a finite clause may be inherited from a finite verb on the assumption that clauses are endocentric verbal projections. In transformational accounts, the distribution of tense features must again involve recourse to a movement rule.

The definitive presentation of GPSG in Gazdar *et al.* (1985) displays some of the other insights developed in this framework, along with the attendant formal complications. A significant feature of later versions of GPSG is the decomposition of standard **phrase-structure rules** into separate **immediate dominance** (ID) and **linear precedence** (LP) constraints. This division of labour permits an elegant and often highly general description of various types of word order patterns and word order. To take just one example, the relatively free ordering of a verb and its complements in a language like Russian may be described by introducing no rule that imposes a relative order on these elements. However, the usefulness of the structure/order dissociation is severely constrained by the desire to keep the GPSG formalism within the class of **context-free grammars**. One consequence of this meta-theoretical constraint is that precedence rules must have the same domain as dominance rules and thus may not order non-siblings. This entails that the free ordering of a verb and a VP-external subject in Russian cannot be attributed simply to the lack of an applicable linear constraint. Although **liberation meta-rules** were proposed to telescope a set of rules and define essentially flat constituent structures, the use of these rules undercuts the motivation for the original structure/order division. The descriptive challenge posed by free constituent order languages was not met in a satisfactory way until the advent of **linearization grammars** in HPSG (see below).

As is generally the case with feature-based approaches, GPSG accounts are explicitly – often painstakingly – formalized. The difficulties that this formalization may present to contemporary readers reflect a genuine tension between the simple architecture and complex 'control structure' of GPSG. At one level, a GPSG can be viewed as a set of constraints, interpreted uniformly as 'tree licensing conditions'. Dominance rules license tree structure, precedence rules dictate the relative order of siblings, and feature constraints determine the distribution of features on non-terminal nodes. Yet this straightforward conception is complicated in GPSG by the numerous types of feature conditions and their often intricate interactions. A general source of complications is the default interpretation of conditions, such as **feature specification defaults** or, indeed, the **head feature convention**. This aspect of GPSG has not been taken up directly in other syntactic approaches, though defaults appear in a different guise in recent **optimality extensions of LFG**.

Head-driven Phrase-Structure Grammar

HPSG is in certain respects a direct descendant of GPSG. However, it also includes features of Head Grammars (Pollard 1984), along with properties of categorial grammars and systems of feature logic. The two book-length expositions of HPSG, Pollard and Sag (1987, 1994), outline a general sign-based conception that integrates these diverse influences.

HPSG incorporates a number of evident improvements over GPSG. Foremost among these is a 'description-based' perspective that clarifies some of the representational issues that remained unresolved in GPSG. Like LFG, HPSG proceeds from a fundamental distinction between **(feature structure) descriptions**, which are sets of grammatical constraints, and the **feature structures** that actually model the expressions of a language. This distinction is clearly illustrated by the treatment of lexical entries, which are not viewed as structures, but rather as descriptions of lexical structures. Descriptions in HPSG are represented as standard **attribute-value matrices** (AVMs), similar to the bracketed 'feature bundles' familiar from phonological analyses. Structures are rarely exhibited in HPSG accounts, though they are conventionally depicted as directed acyclic graphs. The correspondence between descriptions and the structures that they describe is defined in terms of a standard satisfaction relation, as in **model-theoretic semantic** approaches. The structures that satisfy a description must, at the very least, preserve all of the information in the description, and also identify all of the values that are specified as token-identical in the description.

The interpretation of the basic HPSG formalism is thus relatively straightforward, as is the interpretation of feature distribution constraints. A distinctive aspect of HPSG is the assumption that structures are **typed**, and that types may be organized into general **type hierarchies**, in which properties may be inherited from general types to their subtypes. For example, the general type *sign* contains the subtypes *word* and *phrase*. Features common to all signs, i.e. the fact that they are associated with a phonological form, are associated with the type *sign* and inherited down to its subtypes. The properties that distinguish words from phrases are in turn associated with the corresponding subtypes. A general strategy of type-based inheritance achieves considerable concision, while eliminating some of the vagaries of the heterogeneous feature distribution conditions in GPSG. To take a simple example, the open-class categories 'noun', 'verb' and 'adjective' are represented by the *head* subtypes *noun*, *verb* and *adjective*. Properties that are only distinctive for a particular part of speech may be associated with the appropriate subtype. The features that represent tense/aspect properties or distinguish infinitives from participles are associated with the *verb* type and thereby restricted to verbs and their projections. Declensional features like case may likewise be associated with nouns and/or adjectives. Current models of HPSG extend the use of type inheritance to classes of construction types (Sag 1997). The **feature declarations** that are directly associated with a given type or inherited from a more general type then represent the features for which that type may – and in current versions of HSPG must – be specified.

Moreover, it is possible to introduce a qualified notion of 'default' within this kind of type hierarchy. HPSG type hierarchies make use of multiple inheritance, meaning that a given type may inherit properties from different general types. This permits a maximally general cross-classification and avoids the need to introduce the same properties at different points in a hierarchy. However, multiple

(a) $\begin{bmatrix} \text{PHON } book \\ \text{CAT} \begin{bmatrix} \text{HEAD } & noun \\ \text{SUBCAT } <> \end{bmatrix} \end{bmatrix}$

(b) $\begin{bmatrix} \text{CAT} \begin{bmatrix} \text{HEAD } & noun \\ \text{SUBCAT } <> \end{bmatrix} \end{bmatrix}$
$|$
$book$

Figure 2 Lexical signs in HPSG

inheritance also raises an issue of consistency, since different general types may introduce conflicting properties. Multiple inheritance systems usually address this issue by assigning a relative priority to general types, so that one type may 'outrank' or 'take precedence over' another type. In cases of conflict, the inheritance of properties from a higher-ranking type may then pre-empt the inheritance from a lower-ranking type. Controlling the inheritance of properties in this way provides an 'off-line' default mechanism that expresses a limited notion of defeasibility, while retaining a standard non-default interpretation of the constraints themselves.

In addition to these largely technical improvements, the neo-Saussurean perspective adopted in HPSG permits a highly flexible treatment of the relation between form and features. The form associated with a *sign* is represented as the value of a PHON(OLOGY) attribute, rather than by a terminal or sequence of terminals, as in other approaches. This difference is illustrated by the descriptions of the noun *book* in Figure 2 (the SUBCAT-(EGORISATION) feature is described below).

While these alternatives may look rather like notational variants, the description in Figure 2(a) implicitly supports the feature–form mapping characteristic of word and paradigm (WP) models of morphology (Anderson 1992; Stump 2001). At the lexical level, a sign-based system provides the formal prerequisites for morphological analyses in which a given form is said to 'spell out' or 'realize' a particular feature combination. Further, as Ackermann and Webelhuth (1998) argue at some length, this **exponence-based** conception extends

straightforwardly to a range of periphrastic constructions in which multiple words may realize a notion like 'perfect' or 'passive'.

At the level of phrasal analysis, the introduction of a *marker* type reconstructs the distinction that Hockett (1958) draws between the **immediate constituents** (ICs) of a construction, and formatives that merely serve to identify or 'mark' the construction. There is a direct parallel between the WP treatment of *-s* in *books* as a marker of plurality, rather than a morphological constituent proper, and the HPSG treatment of complementizers and co-ordinating conjunctions as markers of subordination and co-ordination, respectively, rather than defective 'functional' heads. The HPSG formalism likewise permits, in principle, a description of non-biunique patterns of exponence. To turn to a construction discussed by Hockett 1958, iterative co-ordinate structures, in which a co-ordinating conjunction is repeated before or after each conjunct, may be treated as a case of 'extended exponence' (Matthews 1974/1991) where the distinct occurrences of the conjunction collectively 'spell out' or 'realize' the features that represent the notion 'co-ordinate category'.

In sum, the simple representational shift illustrated in Figure 2 avoids a commitment to the rigid 'item and arrangement' perspective that many generative approaches have uncritically inherited from their structuralist predecessors. The basic design of HPSG also frees analyses from other, similarly anachronistic, assumptions.

Linearization-based accounts of word order variation provide perhaps the most striking illustration. The form associated with a node in a phrase-structure tree is standardly defined as the concatenation

(a)

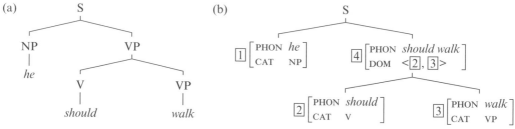

Figure 3 Linearization of order domains

of the terminals dominated by that node. Thus the tree in Figure 3(a) represents the sentence *He should walk.* On the conventional assumption that sister nodes are strictly ordered, it is not possible to interleave constituents that occur at different levels. In particular, there is no way to assign the subject–predicate structure in Figure 3(a) to the corresponding question *Should he walk?* This is precisely the sort of word order alternation that American structuralists took to justify discontinuous IC analyses and which motivated non-concatenative 'wrap' operations in Head Grammars and Montague Gram-mar. Linearization-based models of HPSG (Reape 1993; Kathol 2000) develop a general approach to this phenomenon in terms of independent **word order domains**. In the default case, the DOM(AIN) of a phrase is just a list containing its daughters, so that the form or 'yield' of the phrase is defined in much the same way as for a phrase-structure tree. However, by allowing daughters to pass up their DOM values to their mother, linearization grammars also make it possible to interleave or 'shuffle' non-siblings. The intuition underlying these approaches can be illustrated with reference to Figure 3(b). To simplify this illustration, DOM values are assumed to be lists of signs, as in Reape (1993). The boxed integer 'tags' in Figure 3(b) represent token identity and indicate that the DOM value of the VP contains its actual V and NP daughters. Precedence constraints apply to DOM elements, determining a sequence whose

order defines the relative order of PHON elements.

The yield of the S in Figure 3(b) thus depends on how its DOM list is defined. If this list contains the daughters of S, [1] and [4], it will only be possible to concatenate *he*, the yield of the subject daughter, to the yield of the predicate, i.e. the entire string *should walk*. However, if the VP in Figure 3(b) instead passes up its own DOM value, the DOM value of the S will contain the elements [1], [2] and [3]. This expanded domain 'unions' the subject into the domain of the predicate. Precedence constraints that place the head initially in this domain will determine the list <[2], [1], [3]>. Concatenating the yields of these elements produces the 'inverted' order *should he walk*.

The dissociation of structure and order illustrated in Figure 3(b) likewise accommodates the free ordering of a subject and VP-internal object in Russian, which was identified above as a problem that defied analysis in GPSG. While these cases are both extremely local, linearization approaches provide a general mechanism for describing constituency-neutral ordering variation. Reape (1993) and Kathol (2000) present analyses of the ordering freedom characteristic of the *Mittelfeld* in German, while recent extensions extend a linearization approach to cases of scrambling (Donohue and Sag 1999) and extraction (Penn 1999). Linearization accounts thus permit a simple and uniform treatment of hierarchical structure within HPSG, avoiding the spurious structural variation char-

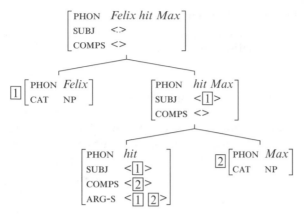

Figure 4 Valence and argument structure in HPSG

acteristic of transformational and some categorical approaches. Yet the introduction of word order domains also potentially undermines the feature-based technology for handling word order variation, including the feature-based account of unbounded dependencies.

An aspect of HPSG that reflects the influence of categorial approaches is the treatment of valence. The initial version of HPSG in Pollard and Sag (1987) introduced a single SUBCAT feature that consolidated all of the subcategorized arguments of a head. Pollard and Sag (1994) subsequently distinguished separate SUBJ(ECT) and COMP(LEMENT)S lists, while retaining an argument structure list, ARG-S, as a lexical counterpart of the SUBCAT list. Some current versions of HPSG add a further DEP(ENDENT)S list to integrate grammatical dependants that are neither subjects nor complements.

A significant difference between argument structure and valence features is that the elements of SUBJ and COMPS lists are removed or 'cancelled' as syntactic arguments are encountered. Thus the transitive verb *hit* begins with the singleton SUBJ list and singleton COMPS lists in Figure 4, which each contain an element from the ARG-S list. The VP *hit Max* retains a singleton SUBJ list, but has an empty COMPS list, signifying that it does not select any further complements. The S *Felix hit Max* has both an empty SUBJ and COMPS list, signalling that it is fully 'saturated'.

The tags on the syntactic subject and object in Figure 4 indicate that the features of these arguments are shared or, in effect, unified with the corresponding valence elements. The flow of feature information represented in Figure 4 highlights the strongly 'head-driven' nature of some versions of HPSG. The head in Figure 4 functions as the ultimate repository of the grammatical information in this sentence, since the features of the verb and its arguments are consolidated in the ARG-S value. In contrast, the projections of the verb become progressively less informative as elements are popped off their valence lists. The 'head-directed' flow in Figure 4 thus represents the transitivity of a head, while tightly restricting access to information about 'cancelled' arguments.

In addition to the properties discussed above, HPSG signs also represent constituent structure in terms of DAUGHTERS attributes. It is nevertheless common for HPSG analyses to be expressed informally as annotated tree structures, as in Figure 3(b) and Figure 4. Semantic and pragmatic information is also expressed via CONTENT and CONTEXT attributes. Yet the empirical consequences of bundling this disparate information together in a single data structure are not always obvious. The non-syntactic properties in signs rarely show significant interactions with grammatical processes, such as subcategorization. Agreement features, which HPSG accounts introduce as part of the CONTENT, are an exception, though these features are more traditionally regarded as syntactic.

Lexical-Functional Grammar

In some regards, LFG straddles the classes of feature-based and relational approaches. On the one hand, the lexicalist and description-based framework outlined in Kaplan and Bresnan (1982) is close to the perspective subsequently adopted in HPSG, though there is also a number of significant respects in which these approaches diverge. At the same time, the analyses developed in Bresnan (1982a) and subsequent work show an affinity with relational accounts, both in the importance they attach to grammatical functions and in their comparatively broad typological coverage.

LFG exhibits a clean formal architecture, with well-defined interfaces between levels of representation. A unique aspect of LFG is the separation between **c(onstituent)-structures**, which represent category and ordering information, and **f(unctional)-structures**, which represent the features that represent valence properties and feed semantic interpretation. The c-structure in Figure 5(a) and the f-structure in Figure 5(b) express the analysis assigned to *Felix hit Max*.

The functional annotations in Figure 5(a) define the correspondence between c-structure nodes and their f-structure counterparts in Figure 5(b). The equation '↑ = ↓' expresses the LFG counterpart of the **head feature principle** by associating the V, VP and S nodes with the same f-structure in Figure 5(b). This shared f-structure is the complete or 'outermost' f-structure in Figure 5(b). The equations 'SUBJ' and 'OBJ' unify the properties of the syntactic subject and object in Figure 5(a) into the values of the SUBJ and OBJ attributes in Figure 5(b).

The structures in Figure 5 are defined by annotated phrase-structure rules in conjunction with the lexical entries for the items *Felix*, *hit* and *Max*. The rules in Figure 6(a) determine the tree in Figure 6(a). The entry in Figure 6(b) likewise represents the properties of the verb *hit*.

The category symbol 'V' specifies the preterminal mother of *hit* in Figure 5(a). The functional equations in Figure 6(b) are both satisfied by the f-structure in Figure 5(b). The TENSE feature specified in Figure 6(b) is obviously present in Figure 5(b), as is the PRED value. The LFG **completeness** and **coherence** conditions, which are keyed to PRED features,

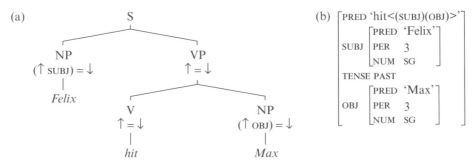

Figure 5 LFG c-structure and f-structure analysis

(a) S $\rightarrow$ $\begin{array}{cc} \text{NP} & \text{VP} \\ (\uparrow \text{SUBJ}) = \downarrow & \uparrow = \downarrow \end{array}$ (b) *hit*: V, ($\uparrow$ TENSE) = PAST

$\quad$ VP $\rightarrow$ $\begin{array}{cc} \text{V} & \text{NP} \\ \uparrow = \downarrow & (\uparrow \text{OBJ}) = \downarrow \end{array}$ ($\uparrow$ PRED) = 'hit <(SUBJ)(OBJ)>'

Figure 6 Annotated phrase structure rules and lexical entry

are also satisfied in Figure 5(b). Informally, an f-structure is **complete** if it contains all of the grammatical functions governed by its predicate and **coherent** if all of its governable grammatical functions are governed by its predicate. Governable functions are essentially those that can be selected by a predicate. The functions governed by the predicate 'hit <(SUBJ)(OBJ)>' are just SUBJ and OBJ. Since exactly these functions are present in Figure 5(b), the f-structure is complete and coherent.

The analyses in Figure 5 highlight some important contrasts with GPSG and HPSG. One unfortunate notational difference concerns the interpretation of AVMs. HPSG accounts use AVMs as a convenient graphical representation of descriptions, i.e. as sets of constraints. LFG interprets AVMs like Figure 5(b) as structures that provide the solution to a set of constraints.

The role of annotated phrase-structure rules in LFG reflects a more substantive difference. The separation of order and structure in GPSG and HPSG reflects an interest in unbundling the different types of information expressed by phrase-structure rules. The addition of functional annotations moves in precisely the opposite direction, by incorporating a further sort of information into phrase-structure rules. The use of an augmented phrase-structure formalism has a number of formal advantages, though it also severely constrains the role of constituency relations. Thus in interleaved constructions, such as Germanic cross-serial dependencies, a verb and its complements cannot form a syntactic constituent. Instead, these elements are introduced on parallel c-structure 'spines' and only associated in the corresponding

f-structure. The c-structures proposed for cross-serial dependencies in Bresnan *et al.* (1982) exhibit other remarkable properties, including verb phrases that consist entirely of noun and prepositional phrases. The patently expedient nature of these c-structures clearly signals the diminished importance of constituent structure in LFG.

Indeed, LFG c-structures are in many respects closer to the derivational structures of a categorial grammar than to the part–whole structures represented by **IC analyses**. Much as derivational structures are essentially by-products, produced in the course of deriving semantic representations, c-structures are the by-product of deriving f-structures in LFG. In versions of LFG that introduce a notion of **functional precedence** (Bresnan 1995; Kaplan and Zaenen 1995), c-structures do not even retain their original role as the unique locus of ordering relations and constraints.

The centrality of grammatical functions is another distinctive property of LFG, one which has contributed to highly influential analyses of relation-changing rules. Beginning with the analysis of the passive in Bresnan (1982b), LFG accounts have succeeded not only in establishing the viability of lexicalist analyses, but often in showing the essential correctness of such analyses. The influence of these analyses is perhaps most obvious in the treatment of passivization and other lexical rules in HPSG (Pollard and Sag 1987). The structure-neutral analyses proposed in relational approaches likewise strongly suggest a lexical reinterpretation. Moreover, the ultimately lexical basis of relation-changing rules is also tacitly conceded in transformational accounts that invoke a morphological operation to

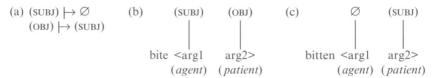

Figure 7 Passivisation by lexical rule

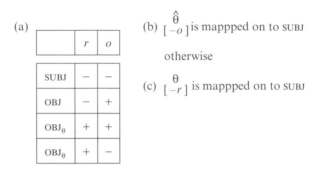

(b) $[\hat{\theta}_{-o}]$ is mappped on to SUBJ

otherwise

(c) $[\theta_{-r}]$ is mappped on to SUBJ

Figure 8 Argument classification and subject mapping principles

detransitivize a verb by 'absorbing' its case or thematic properties.

While the locus of relation-changing rules has remained constant in LFG, the form of these rules has undergone significant changes. This evolution is reflected in the contrast between the treatments of passive represented in Figures 7–9. Figure 7 summarizes the analysis in Bresnan (1982b), while Figure 9 outlines the lexical mapping approach of Bresnan and Kanerva (1989).

The form for *bite* in Figure 7(b) identifies the mapping between argument structure, thematic structure and grammatical functions characteristic of a transitive verb. The rule in Figure 7(a) applies to this lexical form, and defines the derived form in Figure 7(c). The first operation in Figure 7(a) suppresses arg1, which is lexically associated with the agent role, by reassigning arg1 the null grammatical function '∅'. This determines a 'short' passive in which the agent is not realized. The second operation in Figure 7(b) 'promotes' arg2 by reassigning it the SUBJ function.

Given the completeness and coherence conditions, the form in Figure 7(c) deter-

mines an f-structure whose only governed function is a SUBJ which is associated with the patient role. The alternation between the forms in Figure 7(b) and (c) thus expresses the relation between active sentences such as *Cecilia bit Ross*, and corresponding passives such as *Ross was bitten*. More recent work in LFG has refined this analysis in the context of what is known as **lexical mapping theory** (LMT). The main prerequisites of LMT are set out in Figure 8.

The features [*r(estricted)*] and [*o(bjective)*] cross-classify the governable grammatical functions in Figure 8(a). These features then guide the mapping principles in Figure 8(b) and (c), which link up the subject with a semantic role. The role $\hat{\theta}$ designates the highest thematic role of a predicate, which is usually taken to be defined with reference to a universal thematic hierarchy. The principle in Figure 8(b) associates the highest role with the SUBJ function. If the highest role is not available, the principle in Figure 8(c) maps an unrestricted role on to the SUBJ.

The configuration in Figure 9(a) represents the LMT counterpart of the lexical

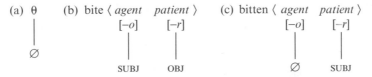

Figure 9 Passive via thematic suppression

rule in Figure 9(b). This mapping associates $\hat{\theta}$ to the null function $\varnothing$, thereby pre-empting the principles in Figure 8 and determining the contrast between the argument structures in Figure 9.

The active structure in Figure 9(b) conforms to the principle in Figure 8(b), as the SUBJ is mapped on to the highest role, the agent role. In the passive structure in Figure (c), the agent is 'suppressed' or unavailable by virtue of its association to $\varnothing$. Hence the SUBJ is linked to the unrestricted patient role, in conformance with the mapping principle in Figure 8(c).

The LMT account in Figure 9 differs from the lexical rule analysis in two main respects. First, the LMT analysis uses monotonic (albeit conditionalized) mapping principles, in place of non-monotonic attribute changes. More strikingly, suppression does not refer to subjects, but instead targets the highest thematic role. This shift implicitly rejects the traditional view, developed in greatest detail in relational approaches, that passivization is restricted to verbs that select subjects.

These assumptions must of course be understood in the context of the larger LMT programme, and its ambitious goal of mapping out the correspondences between grammatical functions and lexical semantics. Nevertheless, one can question whether either of the revisions incorporated in the LMT analysis contributes to an improved treatment of passives. It is, for example, not altogether clear why monotonicity should be regarded as a desirable property of derivational rules, given that derivational processes are to a great degree defined by their non-monotonic, feature-changing,

character. The benefits of a thematic role-based notion of suppression are similarly open to question. The rationale for this change rests on a number of prima facie cases of passives of **unaccusative** predicates (discussed in more detail in connection with relational approaches, below). Since unaccusative predicates, by definition, have no subject to target, a subject-sensitive passive rule cannot apply correctly to these cases. Yet the existing literature hardly considers the alternative, advocated by Postal (1986), that these cases involve impersonal rather than passive constructions, and thus are not directly relevant. Moreover, even a cursory examination of some of the 'passive' constructions in question suggests that they are equally problematic for role-based accounts. For example, the celebrated Lithuanian passive freely applies to 'weather' verbs (Ambrazas 1997), which are not standardly associated either with subjects or with thematic roles.

Contemporary work takes LFG in a number of different directions. One line of research involves incremental, carefully formalized, extensions to the original LFG formalism. Typical of this work is the f-structure treatment of extraction in terms of **functional uncertainty** (Kaplan and Maxwell 1995). In effect, this device identifies a dislocated TOPIC function with an *in situ* grammatical function GF by means of a regular expression of the form '($\uparrow$ TOPIC) = ($\uparrow$ COMP* GF)'. A separate line of research explores more radical extensions that integrate ideas from **Optimality theory**. Bresnan (2000) provides a good point of entry into this literature.

Relational Grammar

Relational grammar (RG) was initially developed in the mid-1970s by David Perlmutter and Paul Postal as a relation-based alternative to the highly configurational transformational accounts of that period. The three volumes of *Studies in Relational Grammar* (Perlmutter 1983; Perlmutter and Rosen 1984; Postal and Joseph 1990) provide a good survey of work in RG until the late 1980s, and display the descriptive detail and typological breadth that is typical of much of the work in this tradition. The insights developed in this framework have been highly influential and have often been directly integrated into other frameworks. The range of phenomena analysed within RG likewise provides a useful empirical 'test suite' for the validation of other approaches.

RG incorporates two distinctive claims. The first is that grammatical relations are primitive constructs that cannot be defined in terms of phrase-structure configurations, morphological case, thematic roles, or any other properties. RG recognizes two classes of grammatical relations. The core relations are referred to as **terms** and designated by integers. Subjects are designated as '1s', direct objects as '2s', and indirect objects as '3s'. Term relations correspond to the elements of an ARG-S list in HPSG or unrestricted functions in LFG. There is also a distinguished non-term relation, the **chômeur** relation, which is assigned to an element that becomes 'unemployed' by the advancement of another. This relation has no direct counterpart in non-relational approaches.

The second basic claim is that grammatical systems are intrinsically multistratal, consisting of multiple syntactic levels at which expressions may be assigned distinct grammatical relations. Strata are subject to a variety of wellformedness conditions, usually stated in the form of 'laws'. Among the important laws are the **Stratal Uniqueness Law**, which allows at most one subject, object and indirect object; the **Final 1 Law**, which requires a subject in the final stratum; and the **Motivated Chômage Law**, which prevents elements from 'spontaneously' becoming chômeurs.

Grammatical descriptions in RG take the form of **relational networks** that represent the relations associated with an expression at different strata. The network associated with *Cecilia bit Ross* in Figure 10(a) illustrates the limiting case in which there is no change in relations. The arc labelled 'P' identifies the verb *bit* as the predicate of the clause. The '1 arc' likewise identifies *Cecilia* as the subject (i.e. the 1) while the '2 arc' similarly identifies *Ross* as the direct object.

Changes within a relational network provide a general format for expressing relation-changing processes such as passivization or causativization. These changes fall into two basic classes: **advancements**, which assign an element a higher-ranking

(a)

(b)

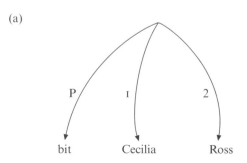
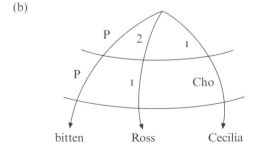

Figure 10 Active and passive relational networks

relation, and **demotions**, which assign a lower-ranking relation. For example, passive is analysed as a case of a $2 \to 1$ advancement, in which an initial object becomes a final subject, thereby forcing the initial subject into chômage. This view of the passive is represented in the analysis of *Ross was bitten by Cecilia* in Figure 10(b).

In the initial stratum at the top of Figure 10(b), *Cecilia* and *Ross* bear the same grammatical relations as in the active clause in Figure 10(a). In the second and final stratum, *Ross* is advanced to subject, represented by the fact that it 'heads' the '1 arc'. Given the Stratal Uniqueness Law, *Cecilia* cannot also remain a 1 and thus must become a chômeur, heading the 'Cho arc'.

The multistratal perspective illustrated in this treatment of the passive also underlies the **unaccusative hypothesis** (UH), which represents one of the lasting contributions of RG. In effect, the UH subclassifies predicates according to the initial grammatical relation associated with their subjects. Predicates whose final subjects are also initial subjects are termed **unergative**. The transitive verb *bit* in Figure 10(a) is unergative, as are intransitive verbs like *telephone* or *ski*. In contrast, predicates whose final subjects are initial non-subjects are termed **unaccusative**. This class is canonically taken to include intransitives like *exist*, *vanish*, *disappear*, *melt*, *faint*, etc. RG accounts also extend this class to include semi-transitive predicates such as *last* and *weigh*.

The networks in Figure 11 illustrate the advancement of non-subjects in initially unaccusative clauses. In the intransitive structure in Figure 11(a), representing *The manuscript vanished*, *the manuscript* is the direct object in the initial stratum and is advanced to subject in the final stratum. In Figure 11(b), representing *The concert lasted an hour*, *the concert* is analysed as an initial oblique, which heads the oblique GR_x arc in the initial stratum. This oblique is advanced to subject in the final stratum, while *an hour* is an object in both strata (Perlmutter and Postal 1984).

A striking property of unaccusative predicates is their resistance to passivisation. Neither *last* nor *weigh* may be passivized in English, and the counterparts of *vanish* or *exist* tend to resist passivization in languages that may otherwise form passives of intransitive verbs. Perlmutter and Postal took the robustness of this pattern as evidence of a universal constraint on advancement. Their 1-Advancement Exclusiveness Law (1AEX) had the effect of barring multiple advancements to subject in a single clause. Passives of unaccusative would violate the 1AEX, by virtue of the fact that they would involve both unaccusative and passive advancement in a single clause.

As mentioned in connection with the LMT treatment of passive in LFG, the factual basis of the 1AEX has subsequently come under scrutiny. Even if we were to assume that the putative counterexamples are not misanalysed, the observation that unaccusatives

(a)

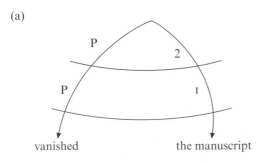

(b)

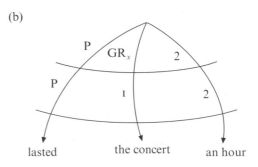

Figure 11 Unaccusative advancement

resist passivization describes a highly pervasive pattern. This pattern would seem to call for some principled explanation.

One particular alternative, raised but subsequently rejected in the RG literature, is worth reviewing for the insight it lends to this framework. The naive reader might at first wonder why the 1AEX is needed at all in RG. If passivization demotes initial subjects to chômeurs, and only unergative predicates have initial subjects, surely it follows directly that there can be no passives of unaccusatives? Further, as noted by Comrie (1977), an analysis along these lines applies to personal and impersonal passives, yielding a simple and uniform treatment of passive constructions.

Alas, however, this account runs foul of the Motivated Chômage Law (MCL), since the initial subject of an intransitive must go into chômage 'spontaneously', not as the result of an antecedent advancement to subject. One might have expected this conflict to lead to a reassessment of the MCL, along with other laws, such as the Final 1 Law, which disallows genuinely impersonal (i.e. subjectless) constructions. Instead, Permutter and Postal mounted a spirited and ultimately successful defence of the MCL. The arguments advanced in support of the MCL featured a number of ingenious and innovative strategies, including the advancement of invisible 'dummy' objects to force subjects of unergative intransitives into chômage. However, the defence of the MCL was something of a pyrrhic victory.

The MCL and Final 1 Law were upheld, and with them an intrinsically promotional treatment of the passive. Yet this orthodoxy was maintained at great cost. A general and largely theory-neutral treatment of passives was discarded, at a time when most competing approaches were only beginning to register the existence of impersonal passives. The analyses adopted in RG to preserve the MCL also contributed to the alienation of linguists, such as Comrie, who were sympathetic to the goals of RG, but were more interested in broad-based description and analysis than in the interactions of increasingly theory-internal relational laws.

The treatment of passivization and unaccusativity in RG illustrates a tendency within this framework to express fundamental, theory-neutral, insights in terms of a highly idiosyncratic and often inscrutable system of formal laws and principles. This tendency reaches its apogee in the closely related Arc Pair Grammar (APG) framework (Johnson and Postal 1980). APG shows more attention to formal detail than RG, facilitating comparisons with other non-transformational approaches. For example, the notion of 'overlapping arcs' proposed in Johnson and Postal (1980) corresponds quite closely to structure sharing in HPSG, and to the identity implicated in functional control in LFG. APG analyses likewise provide a distinctive perspective on issues of broad relevance, as in the case of the impersonal re-analysis of the passive constructions in Postal (1986). Unfortunately, these analyses tend to be formulated in an extremely uncompromising fashion, confronting the reader with an often impenetrable thicket of definitions and examples, illustrated or, at any rate, accompanied by, whimsically labelled and exotically annotated diagrams.

Nevertheless, the range of analyses developed in RG and APG provide a sustained argument for an intrinsically relational and multistratal perspective. This perspective also casts interesting light on the goals and methods of more structurally oriented approaches. For example, the transformational claim that constructions are mere 'epiphenomena' or 'taxonomic artifacts' (Chomsky 1995) makes perfect sense from the standpoint of RG. If the essential properties of constructions are indeed relational, it is only to be expected that analyses that make almost exclusive reference to features of form and arrangement will never yield a unified account of passive constructions.

Conversely, the lexicalist orientation of other non-transformational approaches suggests a basis for the strikingly non-structural character of RG analyses. Although these analyses are quite explicitly presented as syntactic, they conspicuously suppress all but the most superficial features of form and arrangement. In effect, the properties just suffice to associate the elements in a relational network with expressions in the clause it represents. One might of course regard RG as merely underspecified or incomplete in these regards. However, a more principled explanation can be obtained by reinterpreting RG as a covert theory of lexical alternations, in which grammatical relations are associated with the argument positions specified by a predicate, rather than with the syntactic arguments that ultimately fill those positions. The lack of configurational properties then follows from the fact that such properties are simply not defined in the lexical entries of predicates.

The strata in RG can likewise be associated with the lexical levels or strata assumed by nearly all approaches to morphology. A standard distinction between derivational stems and inflectional words provides morphological counterparts of initial and final strata. Where there is evidence for intermediate strata, these can be imported from approaches that recognize further lexical levels. Multistratalism thus does not require the notion of a syntactic derivation, and the derivational interpretation of RG is perhaps best regarded as a legacy of its transformational origins.

Categorial Grammar

Categorial grammars are in some respects the most venerable systems of formal analysis, deriving originally from the proposals of Ajdukiewicz (1935), particularly as these were developed in Bar-Hillel (1953) and Lambek (1961). A central feature of categorial systems is the assignment of expressions to **functor** and **argument** categories, and the use of a general rule of function application to combine functors with their arguments. Ajdukiewicz postulated two basic categories – 'sentence' and 'name'. All functor categories are non-basic, defined ultimately in terms of basic categories. Intransitive verbs or verb phrases are assigned the functor category s/n, denoting a function that applies to a name and yields a sentence. A transitive verb is likewise assigned the category, denoting a function that applies to a name to yield an intransitive verb phrase.

The combination of functors and arguments is sanctioned by highly general rules. The formulation of these rules depends on the interpretation of the slash '/' used to represent functor categories, a notational point on which there is no general consensus across different approaches. To facilitate the comparison of alternatives, this entry adopts the convention '$result/argument$', in which arguments occur uniformly to the right of the slash and results to the left. This convention is followed by the category s/n, in which the name n is the argument and s is the result. The general rules of function application in Figure 12 allow a result x to be derived from the combination of a functor x/y with its argument, y occurring in either order.

For the sake of illustration, let us assign *Cecilia* and *Ross* the category n, *walks* the category s/n, and *bit* the category $(s/n)/n$. Then *Ross walks* will be of category s, the result of combining the functor *walks* with the argument *Ross*. The expression *bit Ross* will be of category s/n, the result of combining the $(s/n)/n$ functor *bit* with *Ross*. Combining this functor with the argument

(a) $x/y \ y \Rightarrow x$ rightward or 'forward' application

(b) $y \ x/y \Rightarrow x$ leftward or 'backward' application

Figure 12 Rules of function application

Cecilia yields the result *Cecilia bit Ross*, which is again of category *s*. These examples highlight one of the sources of complex slash notations. The simple convention adopted here does not specify the relative order of functors and arguments and thus fails to represent the fact that English verbs generally precede their objects and follow their subjects in declarative clauses.

There is a transparent correspondence between simple categorial systems and standard **phrase-structure grammars**. As a consequence, categorial grammars were for a while regarded as notational variants of phrase-structure systems, and thought to suffer from the same descriptive limitations ascribed to standard phrase-structure systems. However, the various extended categorial formalisms have clarified some distinctive aspects of categorial systems and analyses. Reflecting their roots in logic and mathematics, categorial grammars represent a distinctively deductive approach to linguistic analysis. The derivation of a sentence is, in effect, a proof, in which lexical category assignments serve as premises and function application rules sanction the inference of a result. Although similar sorts of remarks apply, in a general way, to phrase-structure systems, the deductive structure of these systems plays no grammatical role. The grammatically significant output of a phrase-structure system consists of the trees that are defined, directly or indirectly, by its phrase-structure rules. In contrast, there is no 'native' notion of constituency defined by categorial systems, and it is often the inferential structure of such systems that is of primary importance.

This is especially true of the Lambek Calculus (Moortgat 1988; Morrill 1994), which represents one of the purest deductive systems applied to the task of linguistic description. Of particular importance in this system are rules that permit the inference of higher-order functors. The **type-raising** rule in Figure 13(a) raises an expression of any category *x* into a higher-order functor,

(a) $x \Rightarrow y/(y/x)$ type raising or 'lifting'
(b) $x/y \Rightarrow (z/x)/(z/y)$ division or 'Geach's rule'

Figure 13 Category inference rules

which applies to an argument of category x/y and yields a result of category *y*. The rule of **division** in Figure 13(b) likewise divides the elements of a functor by a common category *z*.

To clarify the effect of such rules, let us apply type raising to the expression *Ross*, substituting *s* for *y* in Figure 13(a). Since *Ross* is initially assigned the category *n*, the raised functor is of category $s/(s/n)$, a functor from intransitive verbs to sentences. This analysis permits an alternative derivation of the sentence *Ross walks* in which *Ross* is the functor and *walks* is its argument. Moreover, *walks* can also undergo type raising, yielding the higher-order function $s/(s/(s/n))$. This functor applies to type-raised arguments like *Ross* and restores the function–argument relations determined by the original category assignments. The process of categorial 'ratcheting' can be continued indefinitely, yielding an infinite number of derivations of the sentence *Ross walks*. This property of categorial systems with flexible type-assignment rules is sometimes termed the 'spurious ambiguity' problem, since there is no semantic difference between analyses.

Nevertheless, higher-order types may permit new combinations, notably in conjunction with rules of **function composition**. The rules in Figure 14 allow two functors *f* and *g* to form a composed functor, *f∘g*, which applies to the argument of *g* and yields the result of *f*.

The interaction of type raising and composition is explored most systematically in

(a) $x/y \ y/z \Rightarrow x/z$ rightward or 'forward' composition
(b) $y/z \ x/y \Rightarrow x/z$ leftward or 'backward' composition

Figure 14 Rules of function composition

Combinatory Categorial Grammar (Steedman 1996), in which these devices form the basis of a variable-free treatment of extraction. The basic idea is that a chain of composed functors can 'pass along' information about an extracted element. This analysis can be illustrated with reference to the embedded question in *I wonder* [*who Cecilia has bitten*]. Let us first assign *bitten* the transitive verb category *(s/n)/n*, and provisionally assign the auxiliary *has* the category *(s/n)/(s/n)*, denoting a function from verb phrases to verb phrases. The function application rules in Figure 12 provide no means of combining these elements with the Cecilia. However, if *Cecilia* is assigned the raised type category *s/(s/n)*, Figure 14(a) will sanction the composed functor *Cecilia has*, which is also of category *s/(s/n)*. This functor can in turn compose with *bitten*, yielding the functor *Cecilia has bitten*. This functor is of category *s/n*, i.e. a sentence with a missing argument. By combining type raising and composition in this way it is possible to propagate information about a missing element across an unbounded domain, to the point at which its 'filler' – *who*, in this case – occurs.

This simple example illustrates the important point that categorial derivations may contain sequences that do not correspond directly to units in constituency-based grammars, though analogues of composition are employed in some versions of HPSG. A rather different departure from standard models of constituency is characteristic of the syntactic component of Montague Grammars. In contrast to the rigidly concatenative Lambek and Combinatory systems, the syntactic fragments developed within the Montague tradition (Bach 1980; Dowty 1982; Jacobson 1987) propose non-concatenative 'wrap' operations to describe syntactically discontinuous constructions. For example, wrap operations permit an analysis of the verb–particle construction *put the rabbit out*, in which the object *the rabbit* is interposed between the parts of a complex transitive verb, *put out*. Similar analyses are applied to resultatives, ditransitives and various other constructions that, in one way or another, resist analysis in terms of a rigidly continuous syntactic description.

These analyses exploit a general distinction between syntactic rules and the combinatory operations that they perform. The function application rules in Figure 12 concatenate adjacent functors and arguments, though they could just as well be formulated to attach an argument to the head of a complex functor. The categorial effect of the rule would be the same; only the form of the derived expression would change. Although this distinction is of considerable linguistic interest, it is largely independent of the core deductive properties of categorial systems. Hence, contemporary categorial approaches have tended to standardize on Lambek or Combinatory systems. On the other hand, the contrast between rules and operations corresponds to an important distinction between dominance and precedence constraints in GPSG and HPSG. Hence it is in linearization approaches that one sees the clearest development of syntactic insights from Montague Grammar.

General remarks

Space constraints preclude a comprehensive discussion or even an exhaustive list of related approaches. Nevertheless, it is appropriate to mention a couple of frameworks that are of particular relevance to those described above. **Tree Adjoining Grammars** (**TAGs**; Joshi and Schabes 1996) introduce a distinction between initial and auxiliary trees that effectively isolates the recursive component of a phrase-structure grammar. In addition to their use for primary description and analysis, TAGs provide a 'normal form' for investigating other grammar formalisms. For example, the formal properties of 'weakly context sensitive' formalisms, such as Head Grammars or Combinatory Categorial Grammars, can often be determined by translating or 'compiling' these formalisms into a corresponding TAG whose properties have been or can be established. Models of Construction Grammar (Kay and Filmore 1999) can also be seen to complement other constraint-based approaches, though in a more empirical way, by supplying fine-grained lexical analyses that extend high-level descriptions of possible constructions or construction inventories.

The literature on nontransformational approaches now includes basic text books for each of they major feature-based grammars (Borsley 1996, Sag and Wasow 1999, Bresnan 2001), along with overviews (Sells 1985) and compilations (Borsley and Börjars (to appear)). These sources provide a useful entry point for linguists looking to investigate this family of approaches.

J.P.B.

Suggestions for further reading

Borsley, R.D. (1996) *Modern Phrase Structure Grammar*, Oxford: Blackwell Publishers.

—— and Börjars, K. (eds) (to appear) *Nontransformational Grammar*, Oxford: Blackwell Publishers.

Bresnan, J. (2001) *Lexical-Functional Syntax*, Oxford: Blackwell Publishers.

Sag, I.A. and Wasow, T. (1999) *Syntactic Theory: A Formal Introduction*, Stanford, CA: CSLI Publications.

Sells, P. (1985) *Lectures on Contemporary Syntactic Theories*, Stanford, CA: CSLI Publications.

Origin of language

Until the early 1990s, linguists tended to approach the question of the origin of language with caution, because they felt that it was not possible to provide any reliable evidence on the matter. The mood changed in 1990 with the publication of an issue of the journal *Behavioral and Brain Sciences* (volume 13), which carried a paper by Pinker and Bloom, together with peer commentaries, suggesting that the evolution of language was no more mysterious than the evolution of any other human trait or characteristic, and that the primary failure of research in the field was one of synthesis of the available evidence (Pinker and Bloom 1990: 727; Aitchison 1996/2000: viii).

This evidence includes fossil evidence from which the constitution of the vocal tract and brains of earlier hominids may be deduced, and archaeological evidence for the construction and use of tools, phenomena thought to rely on similar cognitive faculties as those which are required for language use. It may, even, be thought to include findings of so-called **remote reconstruction** of **primordial language** (Foster 1996/1999; see below).

While there is little doubt that human language is built on a biological base that is present in other primates (Lieberman 1984: 324), most linguists will readily agree that, although animals obviously have communication systems which are, in the case of many, highly sophisticated (see ANIMALS AND LANGUAGE), only humans have language proper; the question is why, how and when this unique system developed in humans.

To cast light on this, it can be helpful to speculate on what Hurford (1999: 178–83) terms '**preadaptations**' for language – cognitive, social and physiological.

Preadaptive bases for human language

Cognitive

A language-using creature needs an ability to link non-iconic symbols (such as words) to things through **reference** and **denotation** (see PHILOSOPHY OF LANGUAGE). According to Bickerton (1990), there may have been a precursor to the type of language spoken by humans today, which was available to the less highly developed precursors of *Homo sapiens*, *Homo erectus*. Bickerton calls this kind of language **proto-language**, though with a sense not to be confused with that given to this term in HISTORICAL LINGUISTICS, where it denotes the hypothetical parent languages of today's language families, reconstructed on the basis of assumptions about language change. Bickerton's proto-language is, rather, a simple system of lexical items and simple rules for stringing these together, but devoid of the complex syntactic rules characteristic of the languages we know today. This language could be used for referring to things and very basic relationships between them, but it would not have enabled its users to perform the many, far more complex, operations which members of *Homo sapiens* are able to perform with theirs (Hurford 1999: 174–5).

A language-using individual needs a **theory of mind**. An ability to imagine what goes on in the minds of others is a prerequisite for comprehending their utterances because comprehending another person's utterances essentially involves assuming that by saying so-and-so the other person *intended* (i.e. had it in mind) to make me understand such-and-such (see PHILOSOPHY OF LANGUAGE; PRAGMATICS).

Social

Possibly the large size of **human social groupings** encouraged the use of a symbolic system. Chase (1999: 36–7) argues that cultural symbolism is essential to the cohesion of large social systems in which individual members may only interact directly on single occasions and in which, as Hurford (1999: 182) points out, other forms of bonding practices, such as physical grooming, are simply not viable means of establishing group identity.

Physiological

It is a truism that the human **brain** is the basis of all forms of human cognition and that it is necessary for language. According to Lieberman (1984: 16–17) the brain has evolved through gradual elaboration of the central nervous system, and seems to be built up of the same neural components as the brains of other animals. However, the human brain distinguishes itself in terms of its size relative to the size of the human body. In all mammals, brain and body sizes correlate positively, but in primates the

brain is heavier in relation to body size than in other mammals. In *Homo sapiens*, this deviation is the greatest (Campbell 1996/1999: 44): the average weight of a human brain is 1300 grammes, which makes it about three times as large as the average brain of our nearest relation, the chimpanzee, and one third as large again as the brain of our immediate ancestor, *Homo erectus* (Gibson 1996/1999: 409; Aitchison 1996/2000: 85).

While the **larynx is** adapted for phonation at the expense of respiratory efficiency in all primates (Lieberman 1984: 324), the human **vocal tract** displays certain differences from that of any other animal. Some of these are very much to our disadvantage; for instance (Darwin 1859/1964: 191), 'every particle of food and drink which we swallow has to pass over the orifice of the trachea, with some risk of falling into the lungs'. Newborn humans do not share this disadvantage: until a baby is around three months old, it is able to breathe and drink at the same time, because its airway for breathing runs from the nose through the larynx and trachea into the lungs; the larynx is elevated in such a way that fluids can pass either side of it and enter the pharynx and oesophagus behind the larynx, but cannot fall into the larynx and trachea to choke the baby. The vocal tract of a newborn human baby is virtually identical to that of an adult chimpanzee; in fact, the ability to elevate the larynx to form an airway through the nose to the lungs that is sealed from the mouth is one that the human newborn shares with all other mammals, young and old, and Lieberman (1984: 274–9) proposes that these animals have retained the **standard-plan supralaryngeal airway** from which the supralaryngeal vocal tract of modern humans has evolved. The standard-plan tract is also straighter than the adult human's and the lower jaw is relatively long compared with its height. There is more room for teeth, and the tongue is long and thin and lies wholly inside the mouth. The process of evolution from such a tract to that of modern adult humans involves a recession of the jaws. As this took place without a reduction in tongue size, the tongue became curved and pushed the larynx down to lie opposite the fourth, fifth and sixth vertebrae in the neck (these are numbered from the top down).

The situation of the curved 'fat', agile human tongue in the human vocal tracts undoubtedly facilitates the production of the sounds of human language. But being sound-based is accidental to human language and is not a defining feature of it (see ANIMALS AND LANGUAGE; SIGN LANGUAGE), and the importance of the human vocal tract as a pre-adaptive basis for human language is unclear (Hurford 1999: 183): 'If we were capable of articulating fewer phonemes, we would have to use longer words.'

What is rarely in dispute among linguists is the importance of syntax in the definition of human language, and Lieberman (1984: 35) notes **serial motor control** as a necessary condition for the development of syntax:

> The neural mechanisms that first evolved to facilitate motor control now also structure language and cognition. The rules of syntax, for example, may reflect a generalization of the automatized schema that first evolved in animals for motor control in tasks like respiration and walking. In other words . . . the formal rules of Chomsky's 'fixed nucleus' are ultimately related to the way that lizards wiggle their tails.

The connection between the wriggling tails of lizards and human syntax lies in the notion of automatization; both motor activity and the use of syntax are rule-governed behaviour, and automatization ensures that rule-governed behaviour takes place precisely and quickly (Lieberman 1984: 57–9). Lieberman proposes that neural mechanisms which evolved to facili-

tate the automatization of motor activity were gradually generalized and channelled towards a new evolving function; namely, human syntactic ability (1984: 67). This suggestion is consistent with evidence that children's linguistic ability develops in tandem with their sensory-motor development (Piaget 1980), with Kimura's (1979) finding that motoric speech deficit in aphasics always occurs together with other motoric deficits, and with Bradshaw and Nettleton's (1981) suggestion that the functional asymmetry of the human brain (see LANGUAGE PATHOLOGY AND NEUROLINGUISTICS) follows from adaptations for the neural control of precise, sequential patterns of motor control in humans (Lieberman 1984: 68–9).

From preadaptation to realisation

It will come as no surprise that opinions vary about what was required for language to develop once its preconditions existed. Bickerton (1998) subscribes to what Hurford (1999: 180) calls a '**Big bang theory**' of the move from proto-language to language: language emerged following a sudden connection in the brain between referential skills and agency recognition (awareness of who did what to whom), which allowed for syntax (**theta roles**; see GENERATIVE GRAMMAR) to emerge.

Others seek for **evolutionary continuity explanations**. Lieberman (1984: 17) believes that humans uniquely possess a set of peripheral neural mechanisms which are comparatively recent add-ons to the basic cognitive computer and which are interposed between it and the mechanisms that humans have available to transmit and receive information. The specialized input–output functions are localized, but feed into the central, general-purpose distributed computer.

In contrast, Gibson, who subscribes to the view that the human brain distinguishes itself from other mammalian brains in terms of size alone, looks to develop a model of how quantitative changes in neural structures could result in the expansion of apelike capacities into modern linguistic skills (Gibson 1988, 1996/1999). Gibson compares ape and human tool use and their ability to work with stretches of discourse. While apes can use tools, they cannot use tools in combination, and they 'do not make tools which require the mental capacity to envision the end-result of numerous sequential steps'; wild chimpanzees use sticks and stones as tools, but do not combine them to make, for example, a spear or a hammer, and although apes can string together around three to four words (see ANIMALS AND LANGUAGE), they seem devoid of advanced grammatical abilities (Gibson: 1996/1999: 420–1). Gibson concludes that 'the expansion of the human brain was among the most fundamental of all evolutionary advances' and went along with 'ever-increasing *abilities* to organize large quantities of information into complex linguistic and cognitive constructions' (1996/1999: 421). However, it needs to be stressed that, although it is compelling to see a correlation between brain size and tool and language use as evidence of a causal-enabling relationship between the two, we do not yet have any knowledge *that* or *how* such a relationship might in fact function (see Holloway 1996/1999: 89).

When?

Most researchers now agree that humans (*Homo sapiens*) evolved about 140,000 years ago in Africa (Stringer and McKie 1996) and that it was in *Homo sapiens* that a language like ours was born. According to Gibson (1996/1999: 421), fossil records indicate that the brain reached its modern size in the Neanderthalers, who are archaic forms of *Homo sapiens*. Subsequently, however, changes took place in the shape of the cranium, and possibly in the proportions of the brain; in particular, it is possible that the frontal lobes increased in size. If so,

she believes, 'modern neurological capacities may not have been reached until the appearance of *Homo sapiens sapiens*' (1996/1999: 422). Archaeological finds of tools support this assumption, and Gibson concludes that language 'emerged gradually over a three-million year period and that the cognitive skills necessary for complex modern languages were finally achieved some time between 100 000 and 35 000 years ago' (1996/1999: 422).

How?

Of course, it is unlikely that language arose as a complete and fully formed system with all of the functions and features that characterize human languages as we know them. There are two basic hypotheses about the development of the system: one based on sound and one based on gesture. The former needs to explain the move from gesture to vocalization, the latter obviously does not.

The sound-based model of language development

The nineteenth-century Oxford philologist Max Müller (1891) famously and disparagingly labelled some of the accounts that were proposed in his day of how language developed on the basis of sound (Hewes 1996/1999: 576, 583):

- The 'bow-wow theory', according to which onomatopoeia was the basis of human language development (Herder 1891/1966). Since only a very minor part of language can be construed as onomatopoeic, this theory is generally discredited by linguists.
- The 'yo-he-ho theory', according to which speech evolved on the basis of co-operative work songs or chants (Noiré 1877/1917). There is no evidence whatsoever for this theory in what we know

of the life of early hominids, who seem unlikely to have engaged in activities that required synchronized muscular effort of the kind that tends to encourage work chants (Hewes 1996/1999: 584).

- The 'pooh-pooh theory', according to which spoken language arose from emotion-based, expletive noises; this theory was held by, among others, Rousseau, but has been discredited by research showing that emotional cries in both humans and animals involve cortical areas remote from those involved in speech (Lenneberg 1967; Lieberman 1984; Hewes 1996/1999: 583–4).
- The 'ding-dong theory', according to which spoken language arose from psychic resonances between sound combinations and natural objects; this theory was favoured by Müller himself.

None of these theories has any basis in fact. It is possible, however, that language arose as an elaboration of already existing call systems such as those used by higher primates and other mammals for basic social communication and for warning others of the approach of predators, for example (see ANIMALS AND LANGUAGE). The argument for this position relies on similarities between humans and apes in language-related cognitive abilities, with certain additional refinements in humans. According to Steklis and Raleigh (1979: 301–5, in Hewes 1996/1999: 591), apes and human share cross-modal perception and propositional symbol use, which may therefore be inferred to have been present in the earliest hominids. The vocal tract differences between humans and higher primates (see above) do not prevent the production of speech-like sounds by the animals, who also display some neocortical control of their vocal apparatus. Steklis and Raleigh conclude that 'primordial speech emerged in the earliest phases of human evolution and was unlikely to have been preceded by a gestural language

system' (1979: 304–5, in Hewes 1996/1999: 591).

The gesture-based account of language development

A gesture-based account receives support from archaeological evidence, which suggests that early tool makers were right-handed and therefore had left-dominant brain lateralization (Hewes 1996/1999: 584):

> If the earliest language or proto-language had been gestural rather than vocal, it could well be that its subsequent striking left-lateralization resulted from language's having been a function tacked on to the kinds of precise manipulations involved in the predominantly right-handed making and using of tools.

The reason why vocal language eventually took over might then be that gesturing would interfere with work, whereas vocalizations did not (Hewes 1996/1999: 584) and that it is possible to be more explicit and to communicate in finer detail by means of speech than by means of gesture (note that a gestural communication system is not the same as the sign languages used by the deaf, which are every bit as detailed and capable of fine discriminations in meanings as spoken languages; see SIGN LANGUAGE). This account of the movement from gesture to sound is more likely than an earlier account developed by Rae (1862) and elaborated by Wallace (1895) (Hewes 1996/1999: 583), according to which words arose from attempts to mirror hand and finger gestures by the use of the vocal tract. This account is somewhat unlikely given the significant differences in the ranges and types of movement that can be made by the two body spheres. It does, however, have something in common with a more sophisticated account of mouth-gesturing, which stands somewhat intermediate between a gesture-based and a sound-based account of human language origin.

An intermediate account

According to Foster (1996/1999) a sound-based system arose not from earlier call systems, but on the basis of analogy with movements within the physical world, such as the rising and setting of the sun, and of the human body, such as throwing things, embracing and offering food, which were mirrored by the vocal apparatus. Such an account has something in common with the **mouth-gesture account** of Rae and Wallace, but is not based on the pre-existence of a well-developed gestural system.

According to Foster (1996/1999: 763) it is possible, by a method of **remote reconstruction** similar to the methods employed by historical linguists, to arrive at accounts of the parent languages of current human language families (see HISTORICAL LINGUISTICS) to reconstruct far further back than they do, to the very origins of the first human language (or languages – Foster believes in one origin, but her method does not rely on this).

By this method, Foster isolates a set of highly abstract meanings associated with certain groups of sounds and deriving from the shaping and movement of the vocal tract in producing them. These sounds 'were originally . . . highly motivated analogical symbols, or *phememes*' (1996/1999: 763). These earliest beginnings of language were (1996/1999: 771):

visibly apprehended movements made towards the front of the mouth: sharp sounds, [p] and [t] (probably with protruding lips and tongue respectively), and more internally produced soft, or nasal, sounds, [m] and [n]. The sharp sounds mimicked striking, outward motion, and thrust. The soft sounds mimicked internally satisfying events such as eating, sexual gratification, and embracing. . . . Theoretically, in the beginning, [m] and [n] were *allophemes* of the same *phememe* with the abstract meaning of 'internal, inward, enclosure' . . . [and] [p] and [t] were *allophemes* of a *phememe* meaning 'outside, outward, thrust'.

Foster hypothesizes that with each advance in civilization finer and more precisely specified discriminations in meanings emerged to serve the advance.

K.M.

Suggestions for further reading

Aitchison, J. (1996/2000) *The Seeds of Speech: Language Origin and Language Evolution*, Cambridge: Cambridge University Press; 1st edition 1996, Canto edition 2000.

Lock, A. and Peters, C.R. (eds) (1996/1999) *Handbook of Human Symbolic Evolution*, Oxford: Blackwell Publishers; 1st edition 1996, Oxford: Oxford University Press.

P

Philosophy of language

Introduction

Grayling (1982: 173–5) distinguishes between the **linguistic philosophers**, whose interest is in solving complex philosophical problems by examining the use of certain terms in the language, and **philosophers of language**, whose interest is in the connection between the linguistic and the non-linguistic – between language and the world. This connection is held by philosophers of language to be crucial to the development of a **theory of meaning**, and this is their central concern. The philosophy of language is also known as philosophical **semantics** (cf. SEMANTICS).

The ideational theory of meaning

Let us begin by examining a very early theory of meaning, one that assumes meaning is attached to, but separable from words, because it originates elsewhere; namely, in the mind in the form of ideas. This theory was developed by the British empiricist philosopher John Locke (1632–1704), and is commonly known as the **ideational theory of meaning**. Locke (1690/1977: book 3; chapter 2) writes:

> 1. *Words are sensible Signs, necessary for Communication.* Man, though he have great variety of thoughts, and such from

which others as well as himself might receive profit and delight; yet they are all within his own breast, invisible and hidden from others, nor can of themselves be made to appear. The comfort and advantage of society not being to be had without communication of thoughts, it was necessary that man should find some external sensible signs, whereof those invisible ideas, which his thoughts are made up of, might be known to others. For this purpose nothing was so fit, either for plenty of quickness, as those articulate sounds, which with so much ease and variety he found himself able to make. Thus we may conceive how *words*, which were by nature so well adapted to that purpose, came to be made use of by men as the signs of their ideas; not by any natural connexion that there is between particular sounds and certain ideas, for then there would be but one language amongst all men; but by a voluntary imposition, whereby such a word is made arbitrarily the mark of such an idea. The use, then, of words, is to be sensible marks of ideas; and the ideas they stand for are their proper and immediate signification.

The theory underpinning Locke's view is, then, that language is an instrument for reporting thought, and that thought consists of successions of ideas in consciousness. As these ideas are private, we need a system of intersubjectively available sounds and marks, so connected to ideas that the proper use of them by one person will arouse the appropriate idea in another person's mind.

A major problem with this theory is that it does not explain how we can discover what the proper use of a word is. Ideas are private, so how can I know that when I use a word to stand for an idea of mine, the idea that that word evokes in your mind is like my idea? I cannot have your idea, and you cannot have mine, so how is it possible for us to check that our theory of meaning is correct? This problem is not solved by trying to clarify the notion of 'idea', or by reformulating the theory in such a way that 'idea' is replaced with the term, 'concept'; *any* referent posited in speakers' minds is going to be affected by the problem. In Locke's theory, God acts as guarantor of sameness of meaning (see Locke 1690/1977: book 3; chapter 1); but, as Peirce (1868) among others has pointed out, to say that 'God makes it so' is not the type of explanation we typically seek in the sciences, whether natural or human.

A further difficulty with Locke's view is that it assumes that meaning existed before its linguistic expression in the form of thoughts in the mind. But, as Grayling puts it (1982: 186–7):

It is arguable whether thought and language are independent of one another. How could thought above a rudimentary level be possible without language? This is not an easy issue to unravel, but certain observations would appear to be pertinent. For one thing, it is somewhat implausible to think that prelinguistic man may have enjoyed a fairly rich thought-life, and invented language to report and communicate it only when the social demand for language became pressing. Philosophical speculation either way on this matter would constitute

a priori anthropology at its worst, of course, but it seems clear that anything like systematic thought requires linguistic ability to make it possible. A caveman's ability to mull over features of his environment and his experience of it, in some way which was fruitful of his having opinions about it, seems incredible unless a means of thinking 'articulately' is imputed to him. The net effect of the 'private language' debate, instigated by some of Wittgenstein's remarks in the *Philosophical Investigations*, strongly suggests that language (this 'articulateness') could not be an enterprise wholly private to some individual, but must be, and therefore must have started out as, a shared and public enterprise.

Moreover, it appears on reflection plausible to say that the richer the language, the greater the possibility its users have for thinking discriminatively about the world. An heuristic set of considerations in support of this thought might go as follows. Consider two men walking through a wood, one of whom is an expert botanist with the name of every tree and shrub at his fingertips, and a command of much floral knowledge. The other man, by contrast, enjoys as much ignorance of botany as his companion enjoys knowledge, so that his experience of the wood is, on the whole, one of a barely differentiated mass of wood and leaf. Plainly, possession of the botanical language, and all that went into learning it, makes the first man's experience of the wood a great deal richer, more finely differentiated, and significant, *qua* experience of the wood as a wood, than is the second man's experience of it. Of course the second man, despite his botanical ignorance, might have poetic, or, more generally, aesthetic experiences arising from his woodland walk, which leave the first man's scientific experience in, as we say, the shade; but the point at issue here is the relevance of their relative commands of the language specific to making their experience of the wood *qua* wood more and less finely discriminative respectively.

So much is merely speculative. It does however show that the question whether language and thought are independent is more likely to merit a negative than an affirmative answer, in whatever way one is to spell out the reasons for giving the negative answer.

The argument from Wittgenstein's *Philosophical Investigations* (1953/1968), the **private-language argument**, merits further comment. By a **private language**, Wittgenstein means 'sounds which no one else understands, but which I "appear to understand"' (1953/ 1968: 169), and his argument is directed against the view according to which such a language is private in the sense that no one else could learn it because of the private nature of its referents. So when he says 'private language' he means a language which is necessarily unteachable – as Locke's ideational language would be because one person could not teach it to another by showing that other person the idea that a word stood for.

Any such private, necessarily unteachable language would have to be about sense data, entities very like Locke's ideas in many respects, and it could have no links with physical objects, since it would then be possible to use these links as **teaching links** – it would be possible to use them to teach the language to others. So a word in a private language would have to get its meaning by being correlated with a private sensation – otherwise, the language would not be private. Because of the private nature of the sensation that was the meaning of the word, the meaning of the word could not be taught to somebody else.

Pears presents Wittgenstein's argument against the idea that such a language could exist, as follows (1971: 159). Suppose you were trying to use such a language; then

there would be for any given statement that you might make only two possibilities: either you would be under the impression that it was true, or you would be under the impression that it was false. Neither of these two possibilities would subdivide into two further cases, the case in which your impression was correct, and the case in which your impression was incorrect. For since your statements would have been cut off from their teaching links, there would be no possible check on the correctness of your impressions. But it is an essential feature of any language that there should be effective rules which a person using the language can follow and know that he is following. Yet in the circumstances described there would be no difference between your being under the correct impression that you were following a rule and your being under the incorrect impression that you were following a rule, or, at least, there would be no detectable difference even for you. So there would be no effective rules in this so-called 'language'. Anything you said would do. Therefore, it would not really be a language, and what prevented it from being a language would be the thing that prevented it, indeed the only thing that could prevent it from being teachable. Therefore, there cannot be a necessarily unteachable language.

Most present-day philosophy of language could be seen to be concerned in some way or other with the nature of what might serve as 'teaching links' and, obviously, reference to things in the world (which appear to be there for the sharing) seems a very useful teaching aid. We shall now turn to theories of meaning concerned with the nature of reference from language to items in the world.

Sense and reference

Let us assume that words mean by referring to objects and states in the world. Until the end of the nineteenth century, it was generally thought that the relationship of words to things was one of what might be called **primitive reference**, as expressed by Russell (1903: 47): 'Words have meaning, in the simple sense that they are symbols that stand for something other than themselves.' The meaning of a word *is* the object it stands for – words are labels we put on things, and the things are the meanings of the words. Then names and definite descriptions will stand for objects, while verbs, adjectives, adverbs and prepositions will stand for properties of, and relationships between, objects. In addition, there would be **syncategorematic** words, function words, which get their meaning 'in context' – there being, for instance, no ifs and buts in the world for *if* and *but* to refer to.

In the case of general terms, we can say that they refer to classes of things; so whereas *that cow* and *the cow over there* will refer to a particular cow, *cows* and *the cow*, as in *The cow is a mammal* will refer to the class of all cows; this class is the **extension** of the term *cow*. Exactly how a speaker is supposed to be able to refer to the class of all the cows there are, ever have been and ever will be, when using the general term, is one of the problems involved in the theory of primitive reference.

Some semanticists prefer to reserve the term **reference** for what speakers do: by their use of words, speakers **refer** to things, but the thing referred to is the **denotation** of a word. So words denote, and speakers refer. I shall not draw this distinction in the following.

According to the theory of primitive reference, then, the sentence *Socrates flies* gets its meaning in the following way: *Socrates* means by referring to Socrates; *flies* means by referring to the action of flying; *Socrates flies* says of the man Socrates that he has the property of flying – that is, it says of Socrates that he **satisfies** the predicate *flies*. So the sentence names a state of affairs in the world, or refers to a state of affairs in the world, which is handy, since we can then check up on the accuracy of the sentence by seeing whether the state of affairs referred to in it actually obtains in the world: we can identify the referent of *Socrates* and check to see whether he is flying.

There are three insoluble problems inherent in this theory:

• How can true identity statements be informative?
• How can statements whose parts lack reference be meaningful?
• How can there be negative existential statements?

These questions cannot be answered from the standpoint of a theory of primitive reference; and since there are true, informative, identity statements, such as *The morning star is the evening star*, and since there are meaningful statements whose parts lack reference such as *The present king of France is bald*, and since there are negative existential statements such as *Unicorns do not exist*, the theory of primitive reference cannot be correct. This was demonstrated by Gottlob Frege, who showed in his article 'On sense and reference' (1892/1977c) how the first two questions could be answered; he dealt with the third question in two articles, 'On concept and object' (1892/1977b) and 'Function and concept' (1891/1977a).

The first problem is this: if the meaning of a word is its reference, then understanding meaning can amount to no more than knowing the reference. Therefore, it should not be possible for any true identity statements to convey new information; $a = b$ should be as immediately obvious to anyone who understood it as $a = a$ is, because understanding a and understanding b would simply amount to knowing their references. If we knew their references, we would know that the reference of a was the same as the referencc of *b*, so that no new information would be being conveyed to us in a sentence like *a* = *b*.

However, many such true identity statements do, in fact, convey new information; for instance, that the morning star is the evening star was an astronomical discovery, and by no means a truism. Consequently, there must be more to understanding the meaning of a term than knowing what it refers to, and Frege suggested that, in addition to that for which a sign stood, 'the reference of the sign', there was also connected with the sign 'a sense of the sign, wherein the mode of representation is contained'. Then (1892/1977c: 57), 'the reference of "evening star" would be the same as that of "morning star" but not the sense'.

Sense is the identifying sound or sign by means of which an object is picked out – it is a kind of verbal pointing; and understanding meaning amounts to knowing that this particular object is at this particular time being picked out by this particular sense. So (1892/1977c: p. 61): 'A proper name (word, sign, sign combination, expression) *expresses* its sense, *stands for* or *designates* its reference.'

The new information in a true statement of identity amounts, then, to the information that one and the same referent can be picked out by means of the different senses. The circumstance that *the morning star* stands for the same as that for which *the evening star* stands, is not just a fact concerning relationships within language, but is also a fact about the relationship between language and the world, and the identity relation does not hold between the senses, but between objects referred to by the senses. Things are not the meanings of words; meaning amounts, rather, to the knowledge that a particular sense stands for a particular reference.

It is now also possible to solve the second question, concerning expressions that have no reference. These need not now be taken as meaningless for lack of reference; instead their meaning will reside in their sense alone: *The present king of France* is not meaningless just because it lacks reference, since it still has sense. Frege thought that it was a fault of natural language that it allowed a place for reference-lacking expressions – in a logically perfect language, every expression would have a sense – and he posited the fall-back reference 0 for reference-lacking natural-language expressions. Such lack of confidence in natural language is not likely to endear a philosopher to linguists.

While it may seem fairly obvious that objects are going to serve as references for names and definite descriptions, it is less obvious what should serve this function for whole sentences. What is the reference for *I am going home now*? Is it, perhaps, the fact in the world consisting of me going home now? If so, then the reference of *You are going home in two hours* would have to be the fact in the world consisting of you going home in two hours. Facts of this kind are clearly not such nice referents as objects are, and the world would be rather crowded with them. But, worst of all, adopting this type of strategy could tell us nothing of the way in which word meaning contributes to sentence meaning; that is, it could not account for sentence structure.

In fact, Frege extended his theory to take in whole sentences in the following manner: we know that keeping the references of the parts of a sentence stable, we can refer to them by means of different senses. What, now, is to count as the sense of a whole sentence? Take the two sentences:

(1) The morning star is a body illuminated by the sun
(2) The evening star is a body illuminated by the sun

Here, the senses expressed by the nominal groups that are the grammatical subjects in the sentences differ from each other while their references remain the same. Because the senses differ, one person might believe one of the sentences, but not the other (1892/1977c: 62): 'anybody who did not know that the evening star is the morning star might hold the one to be true, the other false'. This indicates that the two sentences express different *thoughts*; the **sense** of a whole sentence, then, is the thought expressed in the sentence. We now need something which will serve as the *reference* for whole sentences.

Frege points out that, in the case of declarative sentences, we are never satisfied with just knowing which thought they express; we want to know, in addition, whether the sentences are *true*. He says (1892/1977c: 63):

> it is the striving for truth that drives us always to advance from the sense to the reference. . . . We are therefore driven into accepting the *truth value* of a sentence as constituting its reference. By the truth value of a sentence I understand the circumstance that it is true or false.

And, indeed, we can see that this circumstance remains stable in sentences (1) and (2) above when their senses are different; if (1) is true, so is (2).

Frege's full picture of linguistic meaning so far is, then, that the **sense** of a sentence is the thought it expresses, and this depends on the senses of its parts. The **reference** of a whole sentence is its truth value, and this, again, depends on the references of the parts of the sentences – for if we were to replace *the morning star* or *the evening star* in the two sentences with senses which picked out a different reference, then the sentence which resulted might well have a different truth value. Frege is thus the first philosopher of language to provide an account of semantic *structure*. The account is **truth-functional**, in that it says how the truth value of a whole sentence is a **function** of – is dependent on – the references of its parts.

Consequently, there are going to be sentences which have no truth value because some of their parts fail to refer. The sentence

The present king of France is bald

will have no truth value, because part of it, *the present king of France*, has no reference. But the sentence is not therefore meaningless – it still has its sense (and the fall-back reference 0).

We have now seen how Frege deals with the first two problems that a theory of primitive reference was incapable of solving. His solution to the third problem, of how there can be negative existential statements, is more difficult to understand, but it is interesting in that it involves an **ontology**, a theory of what there is in the world – of the fundamental nature of reality. The world, according to Frege, consists of complete entities, **objects**, and incomplete (or unsaturated) entities, **concepts**. To this distinction in the realm of the non-linguistic, the realm of reference, corresponds another in the realm of the linguistic, the realm of sense; namely, the distinction between **names** (including definite descriptions) and **predicates**. Objects exist in the realm of reference as the references for names, and concepts exist in the realm of reference as the references for predicates. The concepts, although they are incomplete entities, *do exist*; their existence, their being, consists in having some objects falling under them and others not falling under them.

They can be compared to mathematical functions: the function of squaring, for instance, exists – it is a function we can recognize as the same again every time we apply it, although we will apply it to different arguments. And every time we apply it to an argument, we obtain a **value**. The square of two, for instance, is the value four. We can represent the function of squaring: $(\ )^2$, and we can represent the number two with the numeral, 2. We can see that the sign for the function is incomplete or unsaturated, but that we can complete it by inserting 2, the sign for the number in the empty brackets giving $(2)^2$. The value for this is four, represented by the numeral 4, and we can write $(2)^2 = 4$. In other words, $(2)^2$ has the same referent as 4 does – they appear to be different senses by means of which the referent, four, can be picked out; and just as *the morning star is the evening star* has a truth value, namely true, so does $(2)^2 = 4$; and, again, if we change one of the senses in the mathematical expression for another with a different sense, we may get a different truth value, while keeping the references stable and changing the senses will not produce such an alteration of truth value.

The comparison with mathematical functions is important, because in his argument Frege needs to show that just as it is possible to apply one mathematical function to another – we can, say, work out the square root of the square on four – there are linguistic expressions which are **second-order predicates**, and Frege insists that existence is one of them. The problem now concerning Frege is that there can be true negative existential statements like *Unicorns do not exist*. According to the primitive theory of reference, this statement ought to be a contradiction because, having said *unicorns*, unicorns would have been labelled, so they must exist.

But, quite apart from this problem, existence had puzzled philosophers for a long time. Consider the sentences (following Moore 1936):

(3) Some tame tigers growl and some do not

(4) Some tame tigers exist and some do not

While (3) seems perfectly acceptable, (4) is very odd indeed, and it looks as if existence is not a predicate that functions like other predicates in the language. On Frege's theory, we can say that the oddity resides in the fact that sentence (4) looks as if it is saying of some objects that they do not exist, while it is not, in fact, possible for objects not to exist. If they are objects, then they exist. However, recall that it is possible for *concepts* not to be realized – indeed, their very being consists in being or not being realized by having objects falling under them. So, if there are second-order concepts, which have other concepts, rather than objects, falling under them, and if existence is one of these, then *exists* can still count as a predicate.

But a problem remains. For in sentences like

(5) Homer did not exist

(6) Unicorns do not exist

Homer and *unicorns* are names, and names stand for objects. But we have just decided that existence ought to be predicated, not of objects, but of other concepts. So Frege is forced, once again, to say that natural language is somehow defective: it obscures the fact that existence is a second-order concept taking other concepts as arguments. In (5) and (6) above, *did/do not exist* is completed with names. But Frege says that this surface structure hides an underlying logical structure something like:

Predicate	*Predicate*
(7) There was not	a man called Homer
(8) There are not	things called unicorns

In these cases, the second predicates are first-order predicates, and the first ones represent the second-order predicate, existence, whose being is assured by having some first-order predicates falling under it and others not falling under it. So existential statements, although they look like statements about objects, are in fact statements about concepts, and they say that a particular concept is or is not realized.

Once again, though, Frege has alienated himself from a good section of the linguistic community by judging natural language defective. Nevertheless, his influence on linguistic semantics has been enormous; the whole enterprise of studying sense relations (see SEMANTICS) derives from his distinction between sense and reference, and he was instrumental in the development of propositional calculus, on which linguistic semanticists also draw; it was Frege who succeeded in taming terms such as *all, every, some* and *no*, which the theory of primitive reference had had great difficulties with. A sentence like *All men are mortal* was seen as a simple proposition about men, which was, however, conceptually complex, the complexity having to do with our inability to conceive, in using it, of all the men there are, ever have been and ever will be. On Frege's theory, this sentence hides a complex proposition: *For all x, if x is a man, then x is mortal*, and this simply means that the proposition *if x is a man, then x is mortal* holds universally. There is therefore no longer any problem about the way in which *all* modifies the way in which *men* refers to the class of men. The **logical constants**, *all, some, any* and *no*, are simply part of the metalanguage we use for talking about propositions.

Frege also made what Dummett (1973) has called the most important philosophical statement ever made; namely, that it is only as they occur in sentences that words have meaning. And, as Davidson (1967: 22) adds, he might well have continued 'that only in the context of the language does a sentence (and therefore a word) have meaning'. Many linguists would be prepared to embrace him for this statement alone.

Logical positivism

In spite of his great achievements, however, problems were soon perceived in the Fregean picture of linguistic meaning. Logicians found it difficult to accept that there could be statements that did not have truth values, because it is one of the founding principles of logical systems that a proposition is either true or false. Furthermore, Frege's theory proved inconsistent with the logician's truth table for *or*, '$\vee$' (see FORMAL LOGIC AND MODAL LOGIC):

P	Q	P $\vee$ Q
T	T	T
T	F	T
F	T	T
F	F	F

According to Frege's theory, any sentence some of whose parts fail to refer is going to lack truth value. So the sentence

Either she does not have a cat *or* her cat eats mice

will lack a truth value if she has no cat – because the sentence part *her cat* will fail to refer. But, according to the truth table, the sentence is true, because, as she has no cat, the first disjunct is true.

Finally, Davidson (1967: 20) indicates a further weakness. Frege says that a sentence whose parts lack reference is not therefore meaningless, because it will still have its sense. But if we are enquiring after the meaning of the reference-lacking *the present king of France*, it is singularly unhelpful to be told that it is *the present king of France*, the sense. Yet, since there is no reference, this is all the answer we could be given.

Faced with such problems, a group of philosophers known as the logical positivists of the Vienna Circle tried to amend Frege's theory in such a way as to retain its strengths while removing its weaknesses. They began by trying to provide a consistent and satisfactory theory of meaning for at least a limited number of natural language sentences. Which set is specified in Alfred Ayer's (1936/1971: 48) **criterion of meaningfulness**, known as the **verification principle**:

A sentence is factually significant to any given person, if, and only if, he knows how to verify the proposition which it purports to express – that is, if he knows what observations would lead him, under certain conditions, to accept the proposition as being true, or reject it as being false.

Unverifiable sentences were said to be concerned with 'metaphysics', and not to be factually significant. Thus *God exists* is not a factually significant sentence, and nor is *God does not exist*; factually insignificant sentences may well be of great importance to some people, of course, but the logical positivists did not see them as falling within that part of the language that their philosophy should centre on.

Unfortunately, it soon became clear that very few sentences would, in fact, qualify as factually significant, so the relevant set of sentences for logical positivism to concern itself with became disappearingly small. For instance, the general laws of science, which are of the form 'All . . .' are not factually significant, since they are in principle unverifiable: you can never be sure you have examined all instances of something. History also falls by the wayside, because present observation cannot be used to verify statements about the past. And what of the verification principle itself? How can that be verified? If it cannot be verified, it itself seems factually insignificant.

For a time, it seemed that the verification principle could be verified through Moritz Schlick's (1936) **verification theory of meaning**. This is a theory of what meaning *is*, while Ayer's principle is a statement about what it is for someone to understand meaning. According to the verification theory of meaning, *the meaning of a proposition is its method of verification*. If this is true, then the verification principle is also true; for if the meaning of a proposition *is* the way in which it is verified, then to know that meaning one must know how to go about verifying it.

Schlick's theory is interesting in that it makes meaning into a *method*, rather than taking it to be an entity of some kind which attaches to words or sentences. He spells out the method: 'Stating the meaning of a sentence amounts to stating the rules according to which it is to be used, and this is the same as stating the way in which it can be verified (or falsified).' He thought that there were certain sentences called **protocol sentences**, which consist in incorrigible reports of direct observation, and which therefore do not need to be further verified. These would provide 'unshakable points of contact between knowledge and reality' and all other factually significant sentences could be derived from them. Since protocol sentences are immediately observably true or false, it is possible to specify exactly the circumstances under which they are true, and these circumstances constitute the **truth conditions** for the sentences. Schlick's protocol sentences are essentially similar to Carnap's (1928) **meaning postulates** and Wittgenstein's (1921/1974) **elementary sentences**.

Such proposals are open to the challenge that we do not have direct access to the basic stuff of the universe because all observation is theory-laden. We bring our already formed theories about what we are observing to our observations which are therefore never objective. This objection is made forcefully by Quine (1960: chapter 2) (see below). Austin's speech-act theory was developed in reaction to the lack of progress in the philosophy of language caused by the problems involved in logical positivism (see SPEECH-ACT THEORY). The notion of truth conditions has, however, remained with many philosophers of language (see below), linguistic semanticists and pragmaticists.

The indeterminacy of translation

Quine's (1960: 2) objection to projects like that of the logical positivists is, briefly, that statements are never verifiable or falsifiable in isolation, and that it is impossible to find the truth conditions for individual sentences, because the totality of our beliefs about how the world is gets in the way. It is not possible to separate belief from linguistic meaning, because we do not have any access to the world independent of our beliefs about what the world is like. He argues as follows.

Imagine a linguist who is trying to interpret the language of a hitherto unknown people of a culture very different to the linguist's own. It is a friendly people, and they do their best (as far as we can tell) to assist the linguist in her or his endeavour. The linguist has chosen a native informant.

The linguist sees a rabbit running by, and the informant points to it saying '*Gavagai*'. The linguist writes in her or his notebook, '*Gavagai* means *Rabbit/Lo! A rabbit*'. S/he will test this hypothesis against the possibility that *Gavagai* might, instead, mean *White*, or *Animal*, or *Furry creature*, by checking the informant's reaction to a suggested '*Gavagai*' in the presence of other white things, other animals, and other furry creatures – it being assumed that the linguist has been able to ascertain what counts as assent and dissent in the culture. If assent is only obtained in the presence of rabbits, then the linguist will take the hypothesis as confirmed, and assume that *Gavagai* does, indeed, mean *Rabbit*.

Although this example is supposed to illustrate a philosophical argument, the method presented is in fact a fair outline of that used by linguists engaged in field study, except that Quine's example is meant to deal with **radical translation** – with the case of a completely unknown language spoken by a people which has not previously been in contact with any other – whereas most linguists are now fortunate enough to be able to rely on informants with whom they share at least a working knowledge of some language, either that of the linguist or a third language (see FIELD METHODS).

Quine calls every possible event or state of affairs in the world which will prompt the informant to assent to *Gavagai* the term's **positive stimulus meaning**, and he calls every event or state of affairs in the world which will prompt the informant to dissent from *Gavagai* the term's **negative**

stimulus meaning. The two sets of events and states of affairs together make up the term's **stimulus meaning**. Since the stimulus meaning for any term covers all events and states of affairs, the stimulus meaning of each linguistic term is related to every other in a Saussurean manner (see INTRODUCTION), except that reference to concepts has been replaced with reference to situation.

But Quine now puts a serious objection in the way of the linguist's project, and in the way of any verification/falsification theory of meaning. He points out that, even when apparent stimulus synonymy has been established between two terms such as *Gavagai* and *Rabbit*, there is no guarantee that assent or dissent to their use is in fact prompted by the same *experience* (1960: 51–2):

> For, consider 'gavagai'. Who knows but that the objects to which this term applies are not rabbits after all, but mere stages, or brief temporal segments, of rabbits. In either event, the stimulus situations that prompt assent to 'Gavagai' would be the same as for 'Rabbit'. Or perhaps the objects to which 'gavagai' applies are all and sundry undetached parts of rabbits; again the stimulus meaning would register no difference. When from the sameness of stimulus meanings of 'Gavagai' and 'Rabbit' the linguist leaps to the conclusion that a gavagai is a whole enduring rabbit, he is just taking for granted that the native is enough like us to have a brief general term for rabbits and no brief general term for rabbit stages or parts.

Our theory of nature, then, is always and inevitably underdetermined by all possible 'evidence' – indeed, there is no real evidence of what somebody else's theory of nature is. This argument can equally well be used for speakers of the 'same' language – I do not have access to your experience of what we both call rabbits any more than I have to the experience of the informant in Quine's story. But this means that truth conditions are not available, so no theory of meaning can be set up in reliance on them, and interpretation of the speech of another is always radically indeterminate. What is, in my opinion, the most important development in modern philosophy of language, still in the Fregean tradition, has developed in an attempt to show that Quine's pessimism is unwarranted.

Radical interpretation

Quine's argument shows that it is probable that any theory of meaning which begins by looking for truth conditions for individual terms or sentences will fail; such truth conditions are simply not evidence which is plausibly available to an interpreter. But suppose now that we give up the search for those bits of the world which provide stimulus for speakers to assent to or dissent from sentences and that, instead of beginning our account with truth conditions for individual terms or sentences, we begin by seeing truth as (Davidson 1973: 134) 'a single property which attaches, or fails to attach, to utterances, while each utterance has its own interpretation'. That is, we could, perhaps, try initially to keep truth independent of the interpretation of individual utterances; we could see truth, not as a property of sentences, but as an attitude, the attitude of **holding an utterance true**, which is attached to speakers, rather than to their words. It is an attitude, furthermore, which it is not unreasonable to suppose that speakers adopt towards their own utterances a good deal of the time, even if we have not the faintest idea what truths they see themselves as expressing.

We are then no longer concerned to find some criterion for checking whether a sentence is true or not – which would depend on our already knowing what its truth conditions might be. Rather, we are assuming that a speaker whose words we do not understand sees her/himself as expressing

some truth or other. The question is how this evidence can be used to support a theory of meaning. Perhaps we could proceed as follows: we observe that a speaker, Kurt, who belongs to a speech community which we call German, has a tendency to utter '*Es regnet*' when it is raining near him. We could take this as evidence for the statement (Davidson 1973: 135): ' "Es regnet" is true-in-German when spoken by x at time t if and only if it is raining near x at t.'

We have now used the case of Kurt to make a statement which is supposed to hold for every member of the German speech community, so we must gather more evidence, by observing other speakers and trying out *Es regnet* on them in various circumstances, rather like Quine's linguist did in the case of the rabbit. Of course, we are assuming that German speakers are sufficiently like ourselves to hold true that it is raining if and only if it is in fact raining, and Quine's suggestion was that this assumption was unjustified. But perhaps it is not (Davidson 1973: 137):

> The methodological advice to interpret in a way that optimizes agreement should not be conceived as resting on a charitable assumption about human intelligence that might turn out to be false. If we cannot find a way to interpret the utterances and other behaviour of a creature as revealing a set of beliefs largely consistent and true by our own standards, we have no reason to count that creature as rational, as having beliefs or as saying anything.

Davidson is sometimes accused of arrogant Eurocentricity because of statements such as the above. But the theory is, of course, meant to work both ways – a person from the most remote culture compared to ours is supposed to be able to make use of the theory to make sense of us, just as we are supposed to be able to make sense of her/him.

The statement suggests that the moment one person tries to interpret the utterances of another, the assumption of sameness – at least at a very basic level – has already been made. If no such assumption is made, no attempt at interpretation will be made either, but any attempt at interpretation carries with it the sameness assumption. This contention is borne out by the facts: we do tend to ascribe more meaningful behaviour to things according to their similarity to ourselves – we are more likely to suggest that our neighbour is making meaningful noises than we are to suggest that our dog is doing so; but we are more likely to suggest that the dog is making meaningful noises than we are to suggest that our apple tree is signalling intentionally to us.

The theory of meaning which Davidson advocates, known as the theory of **radical interpretation**, provides a method and a conception of what meaning is which allows us to make sense of the linguistic and other behaviour of other persons, and to see how their use of certain utterances relates to their use of certain other utterances. It is important to be aware that the notion of truth with which Davidson operates is not a **correspondence theory of truth**: sentences are not made true or false because their parts correspond to bits of the world. Rather, stretches of language are taken by speakers to be appropriate to the ongoing situation. References for parts of utterances are worked out on the basis, in principle, of an understanding of the language as a whole, and the theory can accommodate variance in reference with variance in situation (see Davidson 1986). Reference is not a concept we need to use to set up the theory in the first place: it is not the place at which there is direct contact between linguistic theory and events, actions and objects. On this account, meaning is not an entity or property of an entity; it is a relation between (at least) a speaker, a time, a state of affairs and an utterance. We have, therefore, a theory of meaning compatible with many empirically based twentieth-century linguistic research projects in areas like, for instance, sociolinguistics, functional grammar, intonation, discourse analysis and text linguistics, and critical linguistics.

K.M.

Suggestions for further reading

Evnine, S. (1991) *Donald Davidson*, Stanford: Stanford University Press.
Grayling, A.C. (1982) *An Introduction to Philosophical Logic*, Brighton, Sussex: Harvester Press.
Wright, C. and Hale, R. (eds) (1999) *A Companion to the Philosophy of Language*, Oxford: Blackwell Publishers.

Phonemics

Phonemics is the study of phonemes in their various aspects, i.e. their establishment, description, occurrence, arrangement, etc. Phonemes fall under two categories, **segmental** or **linear** phonemes and **suprasegmental** or **non-linear** phonemes – these will be explained below. The term 'phonemics', with the above-mentioned sense attached to it, was widely used in the heyday of post-Bloomfieldian linguistics in America, in particular from the 1930s to the 1950s, and continues to be used by present-day post-Bloomfieldians. Note in this connection that Leonard Bloomfield (1887–1949) himself used the term 'phonology', not 'phonemics', and talked about **primary phonemes** and **secondary phonemes** while using the adjectival form 'phonemic' elsewhere. The term 'phonology', not 'phonemics', is generally used by contemporary linguists of other schools.

However, it should be noted that to take phonology simplistically as a synonym of phonemics may not be appropriate for at least two reasons. On the one hand, there exists a group of scholars who talk about phonology without recognizing, still less operating with, phonemes, be they segmental or suprasegmental; these are **prosodists** (see PROSODIC PHONOLOGY) and **generativists** (see GENERATIVE PHONOLOGY; DISTINCTIVE FEATURES). On the other hand, an English phonetician, Daniel Jones (1881–1967), developed a theory of phonemes wherein he talked about phonemes *tout court*, but neither 'segmental' or 'primary' phonemes nor 'suprasegmental' or 'secondary' phonemes. He did not recognize and practically never mentioned either phonemics or phonology.

Jones manifested an ambivalent attitude towards post-Bloomfieldian suprasegmental phonemes in that, on the one hand, he disagreed with the American practice of referring to suprasegmentals in terms of 'phonemes' but, on the other hand, he talked about **chronemes**, **stronemes** and **tonemes** conceived along the same line as phonemes. Jones' followers largely did not (and do not) subscribe to his chronemes and stronemes. Jones insisted that what post-Bloomfieldians called phonemics formed part of phonetics and refused to recognize a separate discipline called phonemics. Given this rather complex situation, we shall look, in what follows, mainly at post-Bloomfieldian phonemics and Daniel Jones' phoneme theory.

The first and most important task in phonemics, both for post-Bloomfieldians and Jones, is to establish the phonemes of a given language. To do this, they analyze phonetic data according to certain well-defined procedures.

Post-Bloomfieldians operate with the notions of **contrastive** and **non-contrastive**, which originally stem from the concept of **distribution** but are ultimately coloured by semantic implications. Sounds which occur in an identical context are said to be in **contrastive distribution,** or to be contrastive with respect to each other, or to contrast with each other. Such sounds are said to be **allophones** of different phonemes. For example, [pʰ] and [m], which occur in an identical context in the English words *pit* and *mitt*, are allophones of two different phonemes, /p/ and /m/. (It is customary to enclose symbols for phonemes by diagonal lines, and symbols for allophones in square brackets.)

However, this analytical principle does not work in all cases. For example [p⁼] (unaspirated), [p˺] (unreleased), [ʔp] (pre-glottalized), etc., which occur in an identical context in, say, the English word *sip*, and which are therefore in contrastive distribution, are nevertheless not allophones of different phonemes, i.e. /p⁼/, /p˺/, /ʔp/, etc., but allophones of one and the same phoneme /p/ in English. The allophones in this example are said to be in **free variation** and therefore to be **free variants**.

But how can one conclude that in the one case the sounds in question belong to different phonemes and in the other case the sounds in question belong to one and the same phoneme? The explanation commonly proffered is that, in English, while exchanging [p] for [m] in the context /-ɪt/ produces a change in the meaning of the word, exchanging the above-mentioned allophones of /p/ for each other in the same context does not alter the meaning of the word, but are merely variant pronunciations of the word-final phoneme /p/.

Notice that, in this explanation, recourse is had to semantic considerations or meaning despite the fact that some post-Bloomfieldians, including Bernard Bloch (1907–65), Charles Francis Hockett (b. 1916) and Zellig Sabbetai Harris (1909–92), avowedly refuse to operate with **meaning in phonemic analysis**. These post-Bloomfieldians have gone beyond their master who, while warning about the difficulty of dealing with meaning, did not exclude the possibility of recourse to meaning in either phonemics, which he called phonology, or in linguistics in general. They have therefore attempted to devise, if not always successfully or altogether consistently, such a series of analytical procedures in phonemic analysis as are primarily founded on distributional criteria. Their avoidance, at least in principle, if not always in practice, of meaning in phonemic analysis relates to their insistence that analysis at one linguistic level should be conducted independently of analysis at any other level; semantic considerations should therefore only operate in analysis at the morphemic and semantic levels of a language.

However, a few post-Bloomfieldians, most notably Kenneth Lee Pike (1912–2000), strongly claim that it is not only desirable but necessary to take meaning into account in phonemic analysis. It is not surprising in view of these facts that one should find in much post-Bloomfieldian phonemics literature that, apart from its original distributional implications, 'contrastiveness' is presented as almost equal to **distinctiveness**, i.e. capable of differentiating words. This has given rise to post-Bloomfieldians' general use of the term 'contrast' as a synonym of the functionalists' term opposition (see FUNCTIONAL PHONOLOGY); functionalists distinguish between opposition, which relates to paradigmatic relation, and **contrast**, which relates to syntagmatic relation (see PROSODIC PHONOLOGY).

Sounds which do not occur in an identical context are said to be in **non-contrastive distribution**. There are two subtypes. The first subtype is the following. If one of two or more sounds occurs in a context to the exclusion of other sound(s), i.e. in a context in which the other sound(s) never occur(s), they are said to be in **complementary distribution** or in **mutual exclusiveness**. For example, [h] and [ŋ] in English, as in *hat* and *ring*, are not only in non-contrastive distribution but also in complementary distribution since [h] never occurs in English

in word-final position and [ŋ] never in word-initial position. Although, to post-Bloomfieldians, the occurrence of sounds in complementary distribution is a prerequisite to these sounds being allophones of one and the same phoneme, this is not the sole condition. The other necessary condition to be met is the **criterion of phonetic similarity**; that is to say, the sounds in complementary distribution must be phonetically similar to each other for them to be regarded as allophones of one and the same phoneme. This latter condition is not met in the example of [h] and [ŋ], which are consequently considered to belong to separate phonemes. One example in which both conditions are met is that of [b] in, for example, *robin* and [b̥] in, for example, *hub*, which are not only in complementary distribution but phonetically similar to each other (the diacritic mark ̥ in [b̥] signifies devoicing).

The second subtype of non-contrastive distribution is the following. The sounds in question occur in **partial complementation**, i.e. they occur in contrastive distribution in some contexts where they are allophones of different phonemes, but occur elsewhere in non-contrastive distribution or, more precisely, in complementary distribution. The reference to this type of non-contrastive distribution within an explanation of the second subtype of non-contrastive distribution may be somewhat confusing but is inevitable, given the analytical procedures which are importantly, if not exclusively, based on the criterion of distribution adopted by the majority of post-Bloomfieldians. For want of an appropriate example in English, let us consider the occurrence of [ɾ], the alveolar tap, and [r], the alveolar trill (see ARTICULATORY PHONETICS), in Spanish, which are in partial complementation. [ɾ] and [r] occur in contrastive distribution in intervocalic position, i.e. between two vowels (cf. *caro* ['kaɾo], *carro* ['karo]), but in non-contrastive-distribution-cum-complementary-distribution in, say, word-initial position and word-final position (cf. *rojo* ['roxo], *hablar* [a'ƀlaɾ]). In the context where [r] and [ɾ] occur in contrastive distribution, they are considered as an allophone of /r/ and an allophone of /ɾ/, respectively; notice that this analysis involves recourse to meaning. In the contexts where they occur in non-contrastive-distribution-cum-complementary-distribution, [r] and [ɾ] are not considered as allophones of one and the same phoneme but an allophone of /ɾ/ and an allophone of /r/, respectively, on the strength of the post-Bloomfieldian axiomatic principle of 'once a phoneme, always a phoneme' (see further below). In such a case, different analyses are given by functionalists or prosodists. Thus, so far as post-Bloomfieldians are concerned, the fact of sounds occurring in complementary distribution does not in itself necessarily lead to the conclusion that they are allophones of the same phoneme. (Compare this conclusion with the one shown in the case of the first subtype.)

The analytical procedures whereby post-Bloomfieldians establish phonemes will be seen to be compatible with their concept of the phoneme as a class of phonetically similar and complementarily distributed sounds, i.e. the criteria of phonetic similarity and complementary distribution, these sounds being generally referred to as allophones of a phoneme. Further criteria are mentioned by post-Bloomfieldians, but the above-mentioned two are of crucial importance. This concept of the phoneme is, as we shall see further below, strikingly comparable to Jones'. Note that this concept does not accommodate those allophones which occur in free variation. Some post-Bloomfieldians, however, do accommodate such allophones in their definition of the phoneme, in which case recourse to meaning is inevitably involved.

Through the analytical procedures mentioned above, post-Bloomfieldians will establish for the phonemic system of English, for example, /k/ as a class of allophones which occur in complementary distribution, these allophones being: [kʰ], which is aspirated, as in *key*; [k˭], which is unaspirated, as in *pucker*; [k̚], which is unreleased, as in *luck*; [k̟], which is fronted, as in *keel*; [k̠], which is backed, as in *cool*; [k], which is neutral, as in *cur*; etc. These allophones are considered to be phonetically similar to each other. Likewise, post-Bloomfieldians establish the other consonantal phonemes and the vowel phonemes of English, or of any other language they analyze.

There is no uniform descriptive designation for each of these phonemes in the practice of post-Bloomfieldians, who variously use articulatory features to describe them, so that /p/ may be described as the voiceless bilabial plosive, and /k/ as the voiceless velar plosive, /i/, as in *feet*, as the front high, /ɒ/ as in *hot*, as the central low, etc. (see ARTICULATORY PHONETICS for keys to these descriptions).

To post-Bloomfieldians, and also to Jones, whose theory will be explained further below, a **phoneme** is the minimum phonemic unit that is not further analyzable into smaller units susceptible of concomitant occurrence. In other words, a phoneme is a block that cannot be broken down into smaller parts; it is the smallest element relevant to phonemic analysis. Therefore, the above-cited articulatory terms should be taken not as referring to subcomponents of a phoneme, but rather as convenient mnemonic tags derived from the study of how the sounds are produced by the speech organs.

Where there appear to be two alternative phonemic analyses according to which, for example, the phonetically complex consonants, as in *church* and *judge*, may be considered as either complex phonemes, i.e. /tʃ/and /dʒ/ respectively, or simple phonemes, i.e. /č/ and /ǰ/, respectively, post-Bloomfieldians tend to be guided by the principle of establishing as economic an inventory of phonemes as possible and therefore opt for the latter analysis.

Post-Bloomfieldians conduct their phonemic analysis with an axiomatic principle often dubbed 'once a phoneme, always a phoneme', by which is meant that once a given sound has been identified in a context as an allophone of a phoneme, the same sound occurring in any other context must also be considered as an allophone of this same phoneme and not of any other phoneme. To use the Spanish example mentioned above, [r] has been identified as an allophone of /r/ (cf. *carro*), as this sound is in contrast with [ɾ], which has been identified as an allophone of /ɾ/ (cf. *caro*). It so happens that [r] occurs in a different context (cf. *rojo*) and [ɾ] in a still different context (cf. *hablar*). Post-Bloomfieldians do not hesitate to consider the first as an allophone of /r/ and the second as an allophone of /ɾ/ by invoking the principle of 'once a phoneme, always a phoneme'.

At first sight, there appears to be an exception to this principle. For example, [ɾ] is considered an allophone of /t/ that occurs in, say, intervocalic position, e.g. *Betty* /'beti/ ['beɾi], but may also occur as an allophone of /r/ after [θ], cf. *three* [θɾiː]. However, the two [ɾ]s are regarded as allophones of two different phonemes, i.e. /t/ and /r/, without violating the axiomatic principle, because they are said to occur in 'separate' phonetic contexts – one intervocalic, the other not – and consequently to occur in **partial overlapping** when one takes into account other contexts in which they both occur, i.e. in contrastive distribution.

Investigation into the occurrence and arrangement of phonemes is of distributional concern to post-Bloomfieldians. The phonemes of a language are specified with regard to their occurrence or non-occurrence in specific contexts such as **syllable-initial**, **-medial**, or **-final position**, or **word-initial**, **-medial**, or **-final position**, etc. For example, in English, /p/ occurs in all the positions just mentioned (cf. *pea*, *apt*, *cap*, *packet*, *upper*, *ketchup*), while /ʒ/ occurs mainly in word-medial position (cf.

measure), but rarely occurs in word-initial position (cf. *genre*), or in word-final position (cf. *garage*). /iː/, as in *see*, occurs in all the above-mentioned positions (cf. *eat*, *feet*, *tree*), whereas /æ/, as in *rat*, occurs syllable- or word-initially (cf. *at*), and syllable- or word-medially (cf. *mat*), but never syllable- or word-finally.

Post-Bloomfieldians say that, in the contexts where a given phoneme does not occur, the phoneme is defectively distributed, hence the term **defective distribution**. It is important for post-Bloomfieldians to determine which phoneme, /p/ or /b/, in English is considered to occur after /s/ in, for example, *spit* – /spit/ or /sbit/? – since this has implications for the distributional statement about /p/ or /b/. For a different analysis on the part of functionalists, see FUNCTIONAL PHONOLOGY. The study of the distribution of phonemes can be extended to cases of clusters of phonemes; for example, in English, the cluster /mp/ is disallowed and therefore defectively distributed in syllable- or word-initial position, but is allowed in syllable- or word-final position as in *hamp*, or across morpheme boundaries, as in *impossible*.

Related to the study of the distribution of phonemes is **phonotactics**, which is the study of the permitted or non-permitted arrangements or sequences of phonemes in a given language. For example, among the permitted consonant clusters in English are the following: /spl-/, as in *spleen*; /skl-/, as in *sclerotic*; /spr-/, as in *spring*; /skr-/, as in *screw*. Note that these clusters are permitted in word-initial position only, and that /stl/ is disallowed. Further examples are /pl-/, as in *play*, /-pl-/, as in *steeply*, and /-pl/, as in *apple*; /kl-/ as in *clear*, /-kl-/, as in *anklet*, and /-kl/, as in *knuckle*; /-tl-/, as in *atlas*, and /-tl/, as in *little*. Note that /tl-/ is disallowed. Many other permitted clusters of consonant phonemes could be cited. It will have been noted that some of the permitted clusters are occurrent in certain contexts only. And it goes without saying that many theoretically possible consonant clusters are non-occurrent in English; for example, no English word begins with /zv-/.

The kind of phonemes we have seen above are referred to as **segmental** or **linear phonemes**, simply because they occur sequentially. A speech chain can be segmented into a series of such phonemes; for example, *box* /bɒks/, is a sequence of four segmental phonemes, /b/, /ɒ/, /k/ and /s/. Post-Bloomfieldians operate with what they call **suprasegmental phonemes** as well, such as

- **stress phonemes**, of which there are four: **strong** = ´, **reduced strong** = ^, **medium** = `, **weak** = ∅, i.e. zero, hence no diacritic mark: all four are illustrated in *elevàtor-ôperàtor*;
- **pitch phonemes**, of which there are also four: **low** (1), **mid** (2), **high** (3), **extra-high** (4), illustrated in:

He	killed	a	rat	but	George	killed	a	bird
1	3		2–4	1	4	1		4–1

- **juncture phonemes**, of which there are at least three: **external open**, **internal close**, **internal open**, illustrated in *nitrate*, which has external open junctures before /n/ and after the second /t/ and internal close junctures between /n/, /ai/, /t/, /r/, /ei/ and /t/, and in *night-rate*, which has external open junctures and internal close junctures as in *nitrate* except that it has an internal open juncture between the first /t/ and /r/ instead of an internal close juncture. An internal open juncture is customarily indicated as /+/, hence an alternative name **plus juncture**.

Some, not all, post-Bloomfieldians operate with three additional junctures, i.e. /‖/, called **double bar**, /#/, **double cross** and /|/, **single bar**. These are used in reference to intonational directions, i.e. **upturn**, **downturn** and **level** (= neither upturn nor downturn), respectively. Suprasegmental phonemes are said not to be linearly placed

but to occur **spread over**, or **superimposed on**, a segmental phoneme or phonemes, but this is obviously not the case with juncture phonemes though their effects themselves are phonetically manifested over segmental phonemes adjacent to the juncture phonemes.

Daniel Jones maintained that the phoneme is a phonetic conception, and rejected the separation of phonemics from phonetics, asserting that the two are part and parcel of a single science called phonetics. His use of the term 'phonemic', as in 'phonemic grouping' and other expressions, pertains to the phoneme, not to phonemics, a term which he does not use for his own phoneme theory. It is neither clear nor certain how much the latter benefited from the former. Jones' phoneme theory was intended for various practical purposes, including foreign pronunciation teaching and devising of orthographies, not for theoretical purposes. He excluded any reference to meaning in his so-called **physical definition** of a phoneme as a family of phonetically similar and complementarily distributed sounds – which he called **members** or **allophones** of phonemes – within a word in an idiolect. Jones meant by an **idiolect** here 'the speech of one individual pronouncing in a definite and consistent style'.

This concept of the phoneme is strikingly similar to (if not identical in detail with) that entertained by post-Bloomfieldians, who apply other criteria as well. Like post-Bloomfieldians, Jones admitted recourse to meaning as an expedient to establishing the phonemes of a language. He said that sounds occurring in an identical context belong necessarily to different phonemes and that it is phonemes which distinguish different words, not allophones of the same phoneme. He opined that a phoneme is what is stated in his definition of it and what a phoneme does is to distinguish words. Note, as Jones himself stressed, that it is a necessary corollary of his definition of the phoneme that different sounds occurring in an identical context must be members of different phonemes. A pair of words which are distinguished from each other through a difference between two phonemes, and through that difference alone, are known as a **minimal pair**. For example, *met* and *net* in English constitute a minimal pair since they are distinguished from each other only through the difference between /m/ in *met* and /n/ in *net.*

Unlike post-Bloomfieldians, Jones neither talked about nor operated with 'contrastive (distribution)' or 'non-contrastive (distribution)'. Jones' concept of the phoneme fails, like that of many post-Bloomfieldians', to accommodate those allophones that occur in free variation; such allophones are presumably accounted for by Jones through recourse to the concept of the **variphone**, i.e. a sound susceptible of being pronounced differently and erratically in an identical context without the speaker being aware of it, which Jones proposed in 1932 at an early stage in the development of his phoneme theory (Jones 1932: 23). For the concept of variphone, see Jones (1950).

Like post-Bloomfieldians, Jones took it as axiomatic that a given sound cannot be assigned to more than one phoneme, although, unlike post-Bloomfieldians, he admitted a few exceptions. Thus, for example, Jones considered [ŋ] in, say, *ink* as a member of /ŋ/, which will have been established in, say, *rung* /rʌŋ/. He therefore rejected any analysis which considered [ŋ] as being a member of /n/ occurring before /k/, as in *ink*, or before /ɡ/, as in *hunger.* Post-Bloomfieldians will agree with Jones' analysis here.

Jones worked on **suprasegmentals**, which he called **sound attributes**, with the same analytical principle that he applied to segmentals considered in terms of phonemes and allophones, and talked about **tonemes**, a term which he coined in 1921 (see Jones 1957: 12–13; Fudge 1973: 26) – Pike in America independently invented it in the early 1940s (Pike 1948) – and **allotones**,

and **chronemes** and **allochrones**, though he showed considerable reservations about **stronemes** and **allostrones**. Yet he was ultimately against considering suprasegmental phonemes *à la* post-Bloomfieldianism and even preferred the term **signeme**, proposed by Dennis Ward (b. 1924) (see Jones 1957: 20; Fudge 1973: 32) to designate any phonetic feature, segmental or otherwise, that contributes to meaning difference, cf. the concept of significance = distinctiveness; thus, **signemes of phone** (= phonemes), **signemes of length**, **signemes of stress**, **signemes of pitch** and **signemes of juncture**. The term 'signeme' has not caught on, however.

Jones's study of **intonation** is vastly different from that of post-Bloomfieldians. Unlike them, he does not operate with a fixed number of pitches or pitch phonemes. This is obvious by merely looking at his representation of intonation, which uses a graphic transcription with a stave of three horizontal lines – the top and bottom lines represent the upper and lower limits of the speaker's voice range, and the middle one an intermediate pitch level. Unstressed syllables are indicated with small dots placed at appropriate pitch levels, while stressed syllables are indicated with large dots, which are placed at appropriate pitch levels and are accompanied with curves if the stressed syllables have either a rising, a falling, a rising-falling or a falling-rising intonation. A specimen of his intonation transcription is shown below.

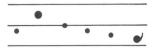

We did what we were told.

Jones himself and his followers frequently omit the middle line.

In the matter of transcription, it should be noted that Jones adopted from Henry Sweet (1845–1912), and used, two different types of transcription – **broad transcription**, in which the symbols stand for phonemes (though Sweet himself did not use the term 'phoneme'), and **narrow transcription**, in which the symbols stand for allophones or members of phonemes. Jones also used the expressions **phonemic transcription** and **allophonic transcription**.

Jones' followers continue to work on the phoneme theory inherited from him with no major modifications.

T.A.

Suggestions for further reading

Bloch, B. and Trager, G.L. (1942) *Outline of Linguistic Analysis*, Baltimore: Linguistic Society of America, chapter 3.

Hill, A.A. (1958) *Introduction to Linguistic Structures: From Sound to Sentence in English*, New York: Harcourt Brace Jovanovich, chapters 2–6.

Jones, D. (1950) *The Phoneme: Its Nature and Use*, Cambridge: Heffer, 2nd edition 1962, 3rd edition 1967.

Port-Royal grammar

The editions of the text

The real title of what has become popularly known as **Port-Royal grammar** is 'A general and reasoned Grammar containing the foundations of the art of speaking explained in a clear and natural way, the reasons for what is common to all languages and the main inferences that can be found between them etc.'

After its first publication in Paris in 1660, it was published again with successive additions in 1664, 1676, 1679 and 1709. In 1754, the French grammarian Duclos added to the text of 1676 'Remarks' that were regularly reprinted in later editions (1768, 1783, etc.). Moreover, the 1803 edition is preceded by an 'Essay on the origin and progress of the French language' by Petitot. In the editions of 1830 (Delalain, Paris) and 1845 (Loquin, Paris), the *Logic or the Art of Thinking* by Arnauld and Nicole (1662) is published together with the grammar. The grammar also represents volume 41 of the *Works of Antoine Arnaud gent* (Paris, 1780). More recently, H.E. Brekle has published a critical edition (Stuttgart, 1966); the edition of 1845 has been reprinted with an historical introduction by A. Bailly (Slatkine, Geneva, 1968) and the 1830 edition with an introduction by M. Foucault (Paulet, Paris, 1969).

The authors

The authors, Antoine Arnauld (1612–94) and Claude Lancelot (1628–95) are both linked to the Jansenist movement, whose devotees lived at the Abbey of Port-Royal des Champs, near Paris. Antoine Arnauld, a theologian and logician, was one of the leaders of the movement and, with Nicole, wrote the logic. Lancelot, a scholar and teacher, master of several languages, and author of handbooks for learners of Latin (1644), Greek (1655), Italian and Spanish (1660), was the chief architect of the transformations in teaching carried out over a twenty-year period in Port-Royal's renowned 'Petites Ecoles'. Although it is impossible to determine exactly the contribution of each author, it seems reasonable to assume that the knowledge of former doctrines and grammatical studies and mastery of languages came from Lancelot, and that Arnauld contributed his powerful intellect and his capacity for marshalling a mass of data.

The grammar and the logic

The grammar belongs to the rationalist current of thought already visible in the works of Scaliger (*De Causis linguae latinae*, 1540), Ramus (about 1560), Sanctius (*Minerva*, 1587), and Scioppius

(*Grammatica philosophica*, 1628). It is deeply influenced by René Descartes (1596–1650). In its second edition, the grammar includes an address to the readers informing them of the publication of *The Logic or the Art of Thinking* by Arnauld and P. Nicole, a work 'based on the same principles' which 'can be extremely useful to explain and demonstrate several of the questions raised in the Grammar'. The logic, which underwent several successive changes until 1683, includes several chapters (vol. II, chapters 1 and 2) reproduced almost literally from the grammar. Other chapters study in detail problems that had been dealt with cursorily or simply alluded to in the grammar. It is necessary to compare the two works – the second one often casts further light on the ideas on language in the first work – bearing in mind, however, that the successive emendations may have altered the unity of the doctrine on certain questions.

The difference in purposes of the two works must also be taken into account. The grammar deals with only three of the four 'operations of the mind' considered as essential at the time – to conceive, to judge, to reason and to order – stating that 'All philosophers teach that there are three operations of the mind: to conceive, to judge, to reason' (II, 1). Although the authors acknowledge that 'exercising our will can be considered as one mode of thinking' distinct from simple affirmation, they study it only in connection with the different ways of expressing it – optative, potential, imperative forms – in the chapter on verbal modes (II, 6). The logic shows even more reticence, as it avoids any allusion to the expression of the will. Out of the three remaining operations, the grammar leaves out the third one, reasoning, as being only 'an extension of the second one': 'To reason is to make use of two judgements to form a third' (II, 1). Therefore, reasoning is studied in the logic, which returns to the ideas developed in the grammar merely

to deal, in the third and fourth parts, with different ways of reasoning and the methods that enable one to judge correctly and to reach the truth. The chapters of the logic that deal, more exhaustively, with compound propositions are not a mere complement to the grammar, even though they seem to be so, but a study of reasoning, whose aim, as the examples analysed show, is apologetic and which should be situated in the context of the doctrinal conflicts and the metaphysical controversies in which the 'Messieurs' of Port-Royal were involved. As many commentators have pointed out (see, for instance, Chevalier 1968; Donzé 1971), the grammar, limiting its study to the problems of conceiving and judging, is a grammar of the single proposition. It lays down very firmly the simple sentence as the central linguistic unit of discourse. This idea influenced grammarians for more than two centuries.

Contents

The grammar is composed of two parts. The first part, comprising six chapters, deals with words as sounds and with the graphic signs that serve to describe them. The second, which is more developed, deals, in twenty-four chapters, with 'the principles and reasons on which the diverse forms of the meaning of words are based'. The general plan follows the traditional pattern in studying successively spelling (vol. I, chapters 1–2), prosody (I, 3–4), analogy (II, 2–23) and syntax (II, 24). The original feature of the grammar is a new distribution of the parts of speech and a justification of the procedure in a central chapter (II, 1) that expounds the underlying principles of the plan followed. The second part studies in succession 'nouns, substantives and adjectives', including numbers, genders and cases (chs 2–6), articles (7), pronouns (8), especially relatives (9–10), prepositions (11), adverbs (12), verbs (13), together with the problems of person and number (14), tense

(15), mood (16), infinitive (17), 'adjectival verbs' (18), impersonal verbs (19), participles (20), gerunds and supines (21), the auxiliary verbs in non-classical languages (22). Chapter 23 deals with conjunctions and interjections; the last chapter (24) deals with syntax from the double point of view of agreement and word order.

This plan, which may surprise the modern reader, is very coherent when we consider its underlying principles, which illuminate the authors' methods and their claim to have written a general and reasoned grammar. It seems that this was the first time a grammar had put forward such a claim. Unlike the grammars written by the Renaissance humanists, whose painstaking efforts to forge the description of modern languages from that of Latin remained for the main part centred on a morphological description, the grammar of Port-Royal was explicitly presented as applicable to all languages since it was based on an analysis of mental processes. Even though the authors started from an analysis of languages familiar to them – most of the examples being taken from Latin and French – their analysis was not based on morphology, but on the relationships between ideas and conceptual patterns on the one hand, and the words and discursive forms that serve to express them on the other. Beyond the diversity apparent in individual languages, they tried to find out 'the reasons for what all languages have in common, and for the main differences that can be found between them'. Their aim was to explain the fundamental and universal principles which formed 'the basis of the art of speech': 'The diversity of the words making up discourse' depends on (II, 1)

> what goes on in our minds . . . we cannot understand correctly the different kinds of meaning contained in words unless we have first a clear notion of what goes on in our thoughts, since words were invented only in order to express thoughts.

The theory of the sign

Thus the grammar stated again explicitly the theory of the word defined as a sign: 'one can define words as distinct articulated sounds that man has turned into signs in order to signify his thoughts' (II, 1). Yet the concept of the sign, however fundamental, was not developed in the grammar; it was in the logic, and this only in 1684, that a general theory of the sign was sketched out (Log. I, 4):

> When we consider a certain object as a mere representation of another, the idea we form of this object is that of a sign, and this first object is called a sign. This is how we usually consider maps and pictures. Thus the sign contains two ideas, first the idea of the thing which represents, second the idea of the thing represented; and its nature consists in giving rise to the second idea through the first one.

What makes up the 'nature' of the sign is therefore as much the very representation involved in it as the power of representation that it possesses. It operates on the mind not only as a symbolic representation, but also as directly endowed with the power of representing. 'Between the sign and its content, there is no intermediate element, nor any opacity' (Foucault 1966: 80). Hence, the question of the meaning of the linguistic sign does not arise, and the grammar includes no theory of meaning or of the word as a meaningful unit. Sounds are used by human beings as symbols of the representations of things as given by the mind. On the other hand, they are the creation of human beings – institutional signs as opposed to natural signs (see SEMIOTICS). As such, even though their capacity of representation is due to the Almighty's power at work in human minds, they have no inherent compulsory characteristics. In this respect, the theory foreshadows Saussure's theory of the arbitrary relationship between signified and signifier (see INTRODUCTION).

The two kinds of signs

The original feature of the grammar is that it makes a distinction between two sorts of linguistic signs according to whether they signify the 'objects' of our thoughts or their 'form and manner'. The first sort included nouns, articles, pronouns, participles, prepositions and adverbs. The second sort corresponds to verbs, 'conjunctions' and interjections. 'Conjunctions' include the particles that serve to express 'conjunctions, disjunctions and other similar operations'; that is to say co-ordinating conjunctions, *and*, *or*, *therefore*, the subordinating conjunction *if*, the Latin interrogative particle *ne* and the negative particle *non*. These two kinds of words correspond to the universal mental patterns underlying the production of discourse and made apparent in the two operations studied by the grammar: the conception of ideas and the bringing together of two conceived terms.

Conception is 'simply the way our minds look at things in a purely intellectual and abstract manner, as when I consider existence, duration, thought, or God, or with concrete images, as when I picture a square, a circle, a dog, a horse' (II, 1), or it may be 'simply the view we have of the things that come across our minds' (Log. Foreword). Notice that the grammar gives no definition of ideas, although this concept was at the heart of the controversies aroused by Descartes' philosophy, in which Arnauld took part. According to the logic, ideas are 'all that is present in our minds when we can say with certainty that we conceive a thing' (Log. I, 1). Like Descartes, Arnauld identifies thought and conscience, as well as will and thought. Ideas must be understood as 'all that is conceived immediately by one's mind': notions, concepts, feelings: 'all the operations of will, understanding, imagination and the senses' (Descartes; see Dominicy 1984: 36).

To judge is 'to state that a thing that we conceive is thus, or is not thus: for instance, once I have conceived what the earth is and what roundness is, I state that the earth is round' (Gram. II, 1). Here again Arnauld was borrowing from Descartes who said that in judgement we should distinguish 'matter' and 'form' and therefore judgement should be seen as resulting from a joint operation of understanding and will. While the authors placed particular emphasis on judgement, they did not neglect the other forms or manners of thinking: 'one must also include conjunctions, disjunctions and other similar operations of our minds and all other movements of our souls like desires, commands, questions etc.' (II, 1). However, judgement is the fundamental operation by which thinking usually takes place, for 'men seldom speak merely to express what they conceive, but nearly always to express the judgements they form about the things they conceive' (ibid.).

The example given above became the canon of affirmation and proposition. For if the underlying structure of 'what goes on in our thinking' seems to be outside the field of grammar, the transition to the grammatical domain is achieved through an equation, presented as absolutely obvious, between judgement, i.e. affirmation, and the proposition (II, 1):

> the judgement that we form of things, as for instance when I say, the earth is round, is a proposition; therefore, any proposition is neccessarily made up of two terms: one is called the subject about which we make an affirmation: the earth; and the other called the attribute which is what we affirm: round, and in addition the link between the two terms: is.

The significance of the example chosen to illustrate the identification of judgement with its spoken or written expression must be clarified. It is an inclusive judgement whose enunciation entails non-explicit features, all of which are not equally important. It is not obligatory for the proposition to include only simple terms and a single affirmation, which would make it comparable to the basic sentence of generative grammar (see GENERATIVE GRAMMAR), as can be seen in chapter I, 9 of the logic that deals with the relative pronoun and 'incidental' clauses that we shall study below. The presence of the subject attribute and, as a corollary, of the linking copula *is* is, however, imperative. It is linked with the theory of the verb (II, 13).

The verb

The grammar rejects the definition given by Aristotle, according to whom the verb signifies actions and passions – and this is no more than an interpretation of the attribute – and by Scaliger, according to whom the verb signifies what is passing, as opposed to the noun, which signifies what is permanent. Instead, the grammar defined the verb as

> a word whose main use is to signify affirmation, that is to say, to point out that the discourse in which this word is used is the discourse of a man who does not only conceive things, but also judges and affirms them.

The phrase 'main use' helps to distinguish affirmation from 'other movements of the soul, like wishes, requests, commands, etc.' that can also be expressed by the verb, but only through a change of inflection and mode; that is to say, by introduction of supplementary marks. The verb can also include the idea of subject, for instance in the Latin utterance *sum homo*, '*I am human*', where *sum* does not only contain the affirmation, but also contains the meaning of the *ego*, 'I' pronoun. The idea of subject itself can be combined with that of attribute: *vivo = I am alive*. Moreover, the verb can include an 'indication of time'. But the person, number and time are only the 'principal incidentals' which are added to the verb's essential meaning.

There are two categories of verbs. The one archetypal verb, which marks affirmation and nothing else, is the verb *to be*: 'Only the verb to be, which is called substantival, has preserved this simple character', and even then 'it has preserved it only in the third person of the present tense, and in certain occurrences' (II, 13). The other verbs, called 'adjectival verbs', contain, in addition to affirmation, the meaning of an attribute. *Petrus vivit*, *Peter lives* are equivalent to *Peter is alive*. Every verb can thus be reduced to a paraphrase which equates its participle to the adjectival attribute.

The idea of this paraphrase, presented as universally applicable, belonged to an old tradition in grammar. The paraphrase is not purely grammatical and very often it cannot be used in real discourse. It is halfway between logic and grammar, and it represents a form of logical relationship which can be formalized through a procedure of theoretical grammatical transformation. Thus, the notion of affirmation is organically linked with the verb which embodies at the same time 'the relationship that our minds set up between the two terms of a proposition'; that is to say, the inclusion of the idea of attribute within the idea of subject. Inclusion belongs to the logic of ideas. It is connected with the axiomatic conditions of categorical propositions and can be expounded in terms of comprehension and extension (Pariente 1985: 265). It appears that setting up a relationship also entails the acceptance of inclusion, 'the relationship that we set up in our minds', and this gives it an illocutionary (see SPEECH-ACT THEORY) character. It is in this respect that the verb differs (II, 13)

> from those few nouns that also signify affirmation such as affirmans, affirmatio,

because they signify it only in so far as it has become the object of our thinking, through a mental reflection, and thus they do not indicate that the person who makes use of these words is affirming, but only that he conceives an affirmation.

Simple and complex propositions

However, the definition of the proposition raises a number of problems when it comes to analysing more complex utterances than the minimal sentence used to illustrate it in the grammar. It is on this question that we find the most important changes in the successive editions of the grammar and the logic. Nowhere does the grammar really expound the concept of grammatical subordination and it deals with complex sentences only with reference to the relative pronoun (II, 9), to the interpretation of the Latin *quod*, the French conjunction *que* (which is in fact connected with the relative) of the Latin infinitive proposition and indirect interrogative propositions introduced by *si* in French and *an* in Latin (II, 17). The chapter devoted to the relative pronoun refers the reader back to the logic which deals with 'complex sentences'.

The 'simple proposition' includes only one judgement, and therefore only one subject and only one attribute: 'God is good.' When the utterance contains several subjects to which is applied a single attribute, or several attributes applied to one subject, the proposition is said to be 'compound' (Log. II, 5) for it contains several judgements: 'Life and death are within the power of language', 'Alexander was the most generous of Kings and the conqueror of Darius.' But the single subject or attribute can be expressed by a complex term and in this case the proposition may itself be either simple or complex, depending on the logical interpretation of the term used.

According to the grammar, when complexity is manifested by the 'union of two terms', one of which is governed by the other – as, for instance, when two substantives are linked by the preposition *of*, or, in English, the possessive case – 'this union of several terms in the subject and the attribute is such that the proposition may nevertheless be considered as simple, as it contains only one judgement or affirmation': 'Achilles' valour was the cause of the fall of Troy'.

Complexity, on the other hand, can occur in the linking of a single subject or attribute with a term or syntagm which can be interpreted from a logical point of view as expressing a first judgement distinct from the global one expressed by the subject and attribute and, so to speak, included within the latter. This is what happens with propositions introduced by a relative pronoun (Log. II, 5):

> There are several propositions which have properly speaking only one subject and one attribute, but whose subject or attribute is a complex term, containing other propositions which we may call 'incidental' and which are only parts of the subject or the attribute, as they are linked by the relative pronoun who, which, whose function is to join several propositions, so that they together form one single proposition.

The grammar emphasized the innovative nature of its interpretation of the relative, according to which 'the proposition in which it appears (which may be called incidental) can belong to the subject or to the attribute of another proposition which may be called the main proposition' (II, 9). It will be noticed that the term 'main' is applied to the whole, whereas subsequent practice applied the term differently. But the authors considered an adjectival term directly related to the noun as equivalent to an incidental proposition, so that the complex proposition may very well contain no incidental proposition expressed grammatically: 'these types of propositions whose subject or attribute are composed of several terms contain, in our minds at least, several judgements which can be turned into as many propositions'. Thus 'Invisible God created the visible world' is the equivalent of 'God, who is invisible, created the world, which is visible.'

It is this passage, among others, that Chomsky (1966: 34) interprets in terms of deep structure and surface structure to present the Port-Royal grammar as a forerunner of transformational-generative grammar (see GENERATIVE GRAMMAR), a presentation which has been severely criticized by other writers (see, for instance, Pariente 1985: chapters 1 and 2). Therefore, it is the logical interpretation of the complex term which tells us whether it contains a judgement distinct from – and included in – the global judgement, and whether one can find several propositions in the 'main' proposition, which is also called 'whole' (Gr. II, 9) or 'total' (Log. II, 6). But the effect of the assimilation of judgement with proposition, 'this judgement is also called proposition' (Log. II, 3), is that the two terms are used sometimes to mean different things and sometimes to mean the same thing. The result is to produce some terminological uncertainty: 'When I say invisible God created the visible world, three judgements are formed in my mind, which are contained in this proposition . . .' 'Now these propositions are often present in my mind, without being expressed in words' (Gram. II. 9). The logic (II, 5) points out that incidental propositions 'are propositions only very imperfectly . . . or are not so much propositions that are made at the time as propositions that have been made before; as a consequence, all one does is to conceive them, as if they were merely ideas'.

The influence of the grammar

The theory of the sign, of the proposition and of the verb have been presented here as the most important parts in the grammar because of their decisive influence in the development of grammar and of the philosophy of language. In returning to a mentalistic viewpoint presented as universal and using theoretical tools at once powerful and simple, the Port-Royal grammar was the starting point of the current of thought in general grammar which was to prevail, with some changes, until the middle of the nineteenth century. The theoreticians of the eighteenth century developed their ideas in reference to it, very often to refute or modify particular aspects of it. But the grammar had a powerful influence in establishing the proposition as the central unit of grammatical study.

The fact that it was written in French, twenty-three years after Descartes' *Discours de la méthode*, also contributed to French being viewed as a language to be studied in the same way as classical languages were studied, and as a language which could carry the weight of philosophical speculation, and whose clarity is derived from the 'natural order'. Finally, it was through its influence that the idea that a reasoned knowledge may facilitate language learning became widespread.

J.B.

Suggestions for further reading

Dominicy, M. (1984) *La Naissance de la grammaire moderne*, Brussels: Márdaga.
Donzé, R. (1971) *La Grammaire générale et raisonnée de Port Royal*, 2nd edition, Berne: A. Francke.
Pariente, J.C. (1985) *L'Analyse du langage à Port-Royal*, Paris: Editions Minuit.

Pragmatics

Introduction

Pragmatics may be defined as the study of the principles which govern language in use. Since the discipline's inception in the work of Grice (see below) and in the so-called natural language philosophy of Austin (see SPEECH-ACT THEORY), its scope has widened considerably, and many scholars now consider it to include a number of phenomena which are also of interest in, or which were originally considered the province of, other areas of language study. In this encyclopedia, some of these phenomena have entries of their own and others are covered in other entries. For example, discourse and conversation analysis, which Mey (1993) discusses under the heading 'Macropragmatics' has an entry of its own and most of what he treats, under the same overall heading, as 'Social pragmatics' is covered here (in the entries on CRITICAL LINGUISTICS/CRITICAL DISCOURSE ANALYSIS; LANGUAGE AND EDUCATION; LINGUISTIC RELATIVITY; SOCIOLINGUISTICS). Speech-act theory is similarly covered in an entry of its own, and deixis is covered in the entry on SEMANTICS.

Grice on conversational implicature

The theory of conversational implicature was first presented by Grice in a series of William James lectures at Harvard University in 1967. Its overriding aim is to show that there are no divergences between the meanings of the formal logical devices, $\neg$, $\&$, $\vee$, $\rightarrow$, $\forall$, $\exists$ and $\int$, on the one hand, and their natural language counterparts, *not*, *and*, *or*, *if–then*, *all*, *some* and *the* on the other hand. Divergences may appear to exist as follows (see also FORMAL LOGIC AND MODAL LOGIC):

Not

In logic, the negator works in such a way that if $\neg p$ is true, then p is false and vice versa; but in natural language, there seem to be many cases in which this is not so. For instance, it may not be true that James is not happy, but this does not guarantee the truth of the statement *James is happy*; James could simply be in a mental state somewhere in between happy and not happy.

And

In logic, *P & Q* is true in exactly the same circumstances as *Q & P*. But in natural language, *Jane got up and fell down* is not necessarily true in the same circumstances as *Jane fell down and got up*.

Or

Natural language users of *or* appear, at the very least, to have a different type of interest when using the word from that of logicians. In logic, *The book is in the library or the book is in the bookshop* is true, and is legitimately confirmable, if one of the disjuncts is true. But if someone asked me whether the book was in the bookshop or in the library, and I replied *yes*, thus confirming the truth of the whole disjunction, it is likely that my interlocutor would get annoyed, because in natural language what is normally at issue is *which* of the disjuncts is true.

If–then

In logic, $P \rightarrow Q$ does not imply that Q is true as a consequence of P being true; indeed, even if P is false, the conditional as a whole will be true as long as Q is true. But in natural language, if I say *If Charles is English then he is brave*, people will take me to mean that Charles' bravery is a consequence of his being English.

All and some

In logic, the truth of $\exists x(Fx)$ need not in any way conflict with the truth of $\forall x(Fx)$.

But in natural language, if I say *Some students pass their exams*, I will normally be understood to mean that not all students pass their exams.

The

Many logicians hold that if *the* appears in a definite description, then the phenomenon being referred to by whatever *the* modifies must exist and be unique. So, in logic, *The restaurant on the Bristol Road is excellent* would be taken to mean that there is one and only one restaurant on the Bristol Road, and that it is excellent. This is not the case in natural language, and anyone to whom I made the statement in question might well ask *Which restaurant do you mean?*

So, in all these cases, it is tempting to suggest that the formal logical devices do not, in fact, have natural language counterparts at all – that their meaning is radically different from the meaning of those natural language items which just happen to look like translations of the formal logical items.

To show that this suggestion is unwarranted, Grice draws a distinction between what is **said** and what is *conventionally implicated*. A logician and a natural language user *say* exactly the same, but it is a convention of natural language not shared by logic that the use of the words we are concerned with has certain implications in addition to what they say: *and* normally implicates one particular order of succession, *or* normally implicates exclusion of one of the disjuncts; *if–then* normally implicates consequentiality between antecedent and consequent, and so on. We can see that implicature cannot be part of what is being *said*, by considering the fact that it can be cancelled out. I can say *A happened and B happened, but not in that order*, where *but not in that order* obviously cancels out the implication of succession of *and*.

To illustrate what is meant by implicature, and to show that it is quite distinct from what is said, Grice introduces a third notion, namely **non-conventional implicature**. This differs from conventional implicature in that it is very obviously distinct from what is being said. Grice (1975: 43) gives an example:

> A and B are talking about a mutual friend, C, who is now working in a bank. A asks B how C is getting on in his job, and B replies, *Oh quite well I think; he likes his colleagues, and he hasn't been to prison yet.*

Whatever is implicated here obviously depends on many fact about A, B, C, and their life histories, and is thus in no sense *conventionally* implicated.

There is, however, a subclass of non-conventional implicature which has aspects of conventionality in it, and it is this class of implicature which has been so influential in pragmatic theory – it is what Grice calls **conversational implicature**. Conversational implicature is *essentially connected* with certain *general features of discourse*, and these general features of discourse arise from the fact that, if our talk exchanges are to be rational, they must consist of utterances which are in some way connected to each other. What guarantees this connection is called the **Co-operative Principle**: make your contribution such as is required, at the stage at which it occurs, by the accepted purpose or direction of the talk exchange in which you are engaged.

In order to comply with this principle, speakers need to follow a number of subprinciples, which fall into four categories – of quantity, quality, relation and manner:

I **Maxims of quantity** (which relate to the amount of information to be provided):

1 Make your contribution as informative as is required for the current purposes of the exchange.

2 Do not make your contribution more informative than is required.

II **Maxims of quality**
Supermaxim: Try to make your contribution one that is true.

More specifically:

1 Do not say what you believe to be false.
2 Do not say that for which you lack adequate evidence.

III **Maxim of relation**: be relevant. (Grice is, of course, aware of the difficulty of deciding what is relevant when; see below for a discussion of Sperber and Wilson's (1986/1995) approach to the question of relevance.)

IV **Maxims of manner** (which concern not so much *what* is said, but *how* it is said):

Supermaxim: Be perspicuous.

More specifically:

1 Avoid obscurity.
2 Avoid ambiguity.
3 Be brief (avoid unnecessary prolixity).
4 Be orderly.

And there may be others.

A participant in a talk exchange may fail to fulfil a maxim in a number of ways:

1 S/he may **violate** it, in which case s/he will be likely to mislead.
2 S/he may **opt out** of observing the principle by saying things like *I don't want to talk about it*.
3 There may be a **conflict of maxims**: you cannot be as informative as is required if you do not have adequate evidence.
4 S/he may blatantly **flout** a maxim.

When a maxim is being flouted while it is still clear that the Co-operative Principle is being observed, the hearer will supply whatever implicature is necessary to reinstate the maxim and, when conversational implicature is generated in this way, Grice says that a maxim is being **exploited**.

The data the hearer relies on to work out the implicature include:

1 The conventional meaning of the words used, and the referents of referring expressions (see PHILOSOPHY OF LANGUAGE).
2 The Co-operative Principle and its maxims.
3 The co-text and context.
4 Background knowledge.
5 The supposition that all participants suppose that all relevant items falling under 1–4 are available to them all.

Conversational implicature must possess five features:

1 It can be **cancelled**, since it depends on the Co-operative Principle being observed, and it is possible to opt out of observing it. You can simply add *I don't mean to imply . . .*
2 It is **non-detachable** from what is being said. If the same thing is being said in a different way, then the same implicature will attach to both manners of expression: the same implicature of 'having failed to achieve something' which attaches to the expression, *I tried to do it*, will also attach to the paraphrases, *I attempted to do it* and *I endeavoured to do it*.
3 It is not part of the meaning of the expression, since if it were, it could not be cancelled, but is, rather, dependent on the prior knowledge of that meaning.
4 It is not carried by what is said – the meaning – but by the saying of what is said – by the **speech act**, not by the propositional content (see SPEECH-ACT THEORY).
5 It is **indeterminate**: there are often several possible implicatures – though the types of data mentioned above will, of course, help hearers determine the most likely implicature.

Although Grice states his maxims as if the purpose of talk exchanges was always simply the effective exchange of information, he is, naturally, aware that there are many other reasons for engaging in conversation, and that other maxims, principles and concerns may influence the ways in which people conduct themselves in conversation, and we shall see below how later research in pragmatics has added to the basis provided by Grice. His schema works well for cases of information exchange. To give an example, if A has sent B out to buy milk and bread, and, on B's return, A enquires, *Did you get the shopping?*, then, if B replies, *Well, I got the milk*, B will either have been too informative (if one assumes that all that might have been required would have been *yes* or *no*), or not informative enough (if one assumes that a full statement of exactly what was bought was required). Since a maxim of quantity has thus been flouted, A will supply the implicature that no bread was obtained by B, and the maxim will be reinstated.

Reactions to 'Logic and conversation'

I am going to deal with two important reaction to Grice's theory. One tries to expand his system by providing more and more, and more and more finely discriminated maxims and principles and which introduces the hugely important topic of politeness (Leech 1983), and one (Sperber and Wilson 1986/1995), which tries to operate with just one of Grice's maxims, that of relevance.

The proliferation of principles

Leech approaches pragmatics 'by way of the thesis that communication is problem-solving' (1983: x–xi, 1):

A speaker *qua* communicator, has to solve the problem: 'given that I want to bring about such-and-such a result in the hearer's consciousness, what is the best way to accomplish this aim by using language?' For the hearer, there is another kind of problem to solve: 'Given that the speaker said such-and-such, what did the speaker mean me to understand by that?'

Although the Co-operative Principle (CP) provides a hearer's perspective on indirectness – that is, it offers an explanation of how hearers detect and interpret speaker indirectness – it fails to provide a speaker's perspective, an explanation of why the speaker chooses to be indirect instead of simply saying exactly what they mean. What explains this is, according to Leech, a Principle of Politeness (PP) (1983: 80), which has two modes of expressions, one negative, the other positive (1983: 81):

> PP neg: 'Minimize (other things being equal) the expression of impolite beliefs.'
> PP pos: 'Maximize (other things being equal) the expression of polite beliefs.'

Consider example (1):

(1) A: We'll all miss Bill and Agatha, won't we?
   B: Well, we'll all miss Bill.

This example breaks Grice's maxim of quantity, and we can explain why by suggesting that B neglects to mention explicitly that we won't miss Agatha out of politeness.

In example (2), the maxim of relation is broken:

(2) Parent: Someone's eaten the icing off the cake.
   Child: It wasn't me.

The parent is being polite in not directly accusing the child of eating the icing, but the child responds to the implicature of the parent's utterance, which is what makes it relevant.

So in both these cases, an exploitation of CP maxims involves PP at a deeper level of interpretation.

PP can also outweigh CP so that Quality is sacrificed, as in the case of white lies, and it helps in explaining another of Leech's principles, the Irony Principle (IP): 'If you must cause offense, at least do so in a way which doesn't overtly conflict with PP, but allows the hearer to arrive at the offensive point of your remark indirectly, by way of implicature.'

Leech deduces a number of additional principles to explain more stylistic aspects of expression: to account for hyperbole, he (1983: 146) suggests an Interest Principle; euphemism and understatement are explained by the Polyanna Principle: 'people prefer to look on the bright side rather than the dark side' (1983: 147); in addition, he lists a Clarity Principle, an Economy Principle and an Expressivity Principle. Clearly, in any account in which the number of principles is increased, the generalizability of each individual principle will decrease. Each principle will be applicable to fewer instances, and the account as a whole will become increasing complex. Perhaps partly for this reason, the second reaction to Grice's theory which we shall discuss here has achieved wider approbation than Leech's.

Relevance theory

In their development of Grice's theory, Sperber and Wilson (1986/1995) begin by pointing out that, in order for one human being to communicate with another at all, it must become clear to the other that the first wants to communicate with them. In order to achieve this, the first engages in **ostensive behaviour**, behaviour that makes manifest an intention to communicate something. Once a hearer has recognized that such behaviour is being engaged in, they can begin to try to work out what information it might be that the speaker

intends to communicate. Sperber and Wilson's contention is that only the principle of relevance is required for the hearer to be able to do this. Sperber and Wilson do not discuss how ostension is recognized; they assume that humans simply recognize ostension when they see it. Once ostensive behaviour *has* been recognized, though, it provides the hearer with a 'guarantee of relevance'; that is, a guarantee that whatever the person who has engaged in the behaviour may intend to get the other to know will be relevant (1986/1995: 50): 'It implies such a guarantee because humans automatically turn their attention to what seems most relevant to them.' So there is a 'principle of relevance', according to which (1986/1995: 260) 'Every act of ostensive communication communicates a presumption of its own optimal relevance.'

In other words, anyone trying to communicate with someone else thereby provides the other person with a guarantee that whatever it is they are trying to tell them will be relevant, and that their mode of expressing it is the mode of expression that provides optimal relevance. The onus is on the speaker to be relevant to the hearer.

This principle is sufficient grounds for the hearer to be able to work out what the intention behind the ostension is: it is the most relevant one to her/him. So we do not need the rest of the Gricean principles. Relevance suffices to account for both the working out of what is said as such and for what is implied, and can also explain why speakers leave some information implicit. A speaker aiming for optimal relevance, as a speaker should, will always leave implicit everything a hearer can be trusted to supply with less effort than would be needed to process the information if it were made explicit (1986/1995: 218).

What is relevant to a given person depends on that person's so-called 'cognitive environment'. When someone is trying to communicate with you, they are trying to alter your cognitive environment, but they will only be able to do that if what they are saying to you is relevant. So the speaker needs to make a number of assumptions about what the hearer's cognitive environment might be.

A person's cognitive environment is the set of facts that that person has manifest to her/him. For a fact to be manifest to an individual at a certain time means that the individual is capable at that time of representing it mentally and accepting its representation as true or probably true.

There are three kinds of information that a speaker (S) might be trying to impart to a hearer (H), but only one type will be processed by (H). The account is of subliminal processing; all that it described happens before information reaches consciousness. Thus Sperber and Wilson (1987: 701) write:

> In the second chapter of *Relevance*, we outline a model of the main inferential abilities involved in verbal comprehension. This model is concerned with only one type of inferential process . . . which, we claim, takes place automatically and unconsciously during comprehension. We do not discuss conscious reasoning, which sometimes plays a role in comprehension; we merely suggest how unconscious inference may be exploited in conscious reasoning.

Old information, information that is already available to (H), will not be worth processing, unless (H) needs it for a particular cognitive task, and did not have it immediately manifest. Then, to have (S) remind (H) of it can provide easier access to it for (H) than (H)'s own effort to recall it. But in the normal course of events, if (S) tells (H) something (H) already knows, (H) will not process it.

Other information might be not only news to (H), but also completely unconnected to anything (H) knows already. All (H) can do with this is take it on board as entirely isolated – that is, as irrelevant to anything (H) is already aware of – and doing this is too much effort for no benefit.

However, there is a third kind of information (S) might impart to (H); namely, information that is new, but connected with information (H) already has manifest in her/his cognitive environment. It is connected in the sense that the new information, together with information already available, can be used as premises in an inferential process which will provide further new information – information which could not have been inferred without this combination of old and new premises.

When the processing of new information gives rise to such an effect of multiplication of information, it is relevant. And, the greater the multiplication effect, the greater the relevance, provided that the working out of the effects is not too costly in terms of effort.

So the more new assumptions the new information (together with (H)'s existing assumptions) allows (H) to derive, the more relevant it is to (H).

Each new assumption is a conclusion of an inferential process of which previously formed assumptions are premises. This process involves (1986/1995: 85) 'a set of deductive rules which are spontaneously brought to bear in the deductive processing of information'.

This deductive processing proceeds according to the rules of logic (see FORMAL LOGIC AND MODAL LOGIC), except that to avoid the generation of interminable, trivial conclusions by processes like 'and introduction', 'or introduction' or 'double negation', Sperber and Wilson (1986/1995: 97) suggest that 'the human deductive device has access only to elimination rules and yields only non-trivial conclusions' or implications, where

> A set of assumptions {P} *logically and non-trivially implies* an assumption Q if

and only if, when {P} is the set of initial theses in a deduction involving only elimination rules, Q belongs to the set of final theses.

An assumption is composed of a set of concepts. The form into which the concepts are arranged to form the assumption is the assumption's logical form (1986/1995: 86):

> Each concept consists of a label, or address, which performs two different and complementary functions. First, it appears as an address in memory, a heading under which various types of information can be stored and retrieved. Second, it may appear as a constituent of a logical form, to whose presence the deductive rules may be sensitive.

The information held in memory for a concept is of three kinds: logical, encyclopedic and lexical. A logical entry (1986/1995: 86): 'consists of a set of deductive rules which apply to logical forms of which that concept is a constituent'. It also includes (Sperber and Wilson 1987: 702) 'rules of concept logic which determine deductions from "he ran" to "he moved," from "the glass is red" to "the glass is coloured"'.

The encyclopedic entry (1986/1995: 86) 'contains information about . . . the objects, events, or properties that instantiate it' and the lexical entry 'contains information about . . . the word or phrase of natural language' that expresses the concept, sense, intention. So (1986/1995: 86), 'A conceptual address is . . . a point of access to the logical, encyclopaedic and linguistic information which may be needed in the processing of logical forms containing that address.'

What we have is a human deductive device which explicates the content of any set of assumptions submitted to it, and our interest is in the effect of combining old with new, connected information. This combination is called a contextualization of the new information, the context being, obviously, the old information.

So in this account, a **context** is a psychological construct, a subset of the hearer's assumptions about the world. Each new utterance requires a slightly different context for its interpretation. This contextualization may yield conclusions not derivable from either the new or the old information alone, and such conclusions are called the contextual implications of the new information in the context of the old information. Then (1986/1995: 108), 'A central function of the deductive device is then to derive, spontaneously, automatically and unconsciously, the contextual implications of any newly presented information in a context of old information.' These contextual implications are contextual effects, and relevance is characterized in terms of the amount of contextual effect gained relative to the degree of processing effort expended. The concepts of relevance can therefore be defined in terms of its two so-called extent conditions (1986/1995: 125):

> *Relevance*
> *Extent condition 1*: an assumption is relevant in a context to the extent that its contextual effects in this context are large.
> *Extent condition 2*: an assumption is relevant in a context to the extent that the effort required to process it in this context is small.

Sperber and Wilson (1987: 703) assume that 'the mind assesses its own efforts and their effects by monitoring physio-chemical changes in the brain'.

The context – that is, the manifest assumptions that are to join up with the new information in the deductive process – is itself selected through consideration of relevance (1986/1995: 141). The mind spontaneously provides the context, given a new piece of information, that will yield most effects for least processing effort for that piece of information.

Every assumption that arises from the inference process has a certain strength which results from its processing history. Information derived from clear perception is very strong, information provided by someone you trust is too, information provided by a crook is not, and the strength of conclusions arrived at by deduction depends on the strengths of the premises used in the deduction.

There are three kinds of contextual effect derivable from the processing of new information in the context of old information. First, there are new assumptions. Second, there is strengthening of old assumptions. Third, there is the elimination of old assumptions in favour of new, stronger assumptions, which contradict the old ones.

Any linguistic stimulus a mind receives (1987: 704) 'triggers an automatic process of decoding'. This produces semantic representations in the shape of logical forms. The logical forms do not surface to consciousness, but act as assumption schemata, which are made into propositional forms through inferential completion. Each propositional form determines 'a single proposition' and tentatively identifies 'the intended explicit content of the utterance. This explicit content alone has contextual effects and is therefore worthy of conscious attention.'

Completing the logical form involves disambiguation, reference assignment and enrichment of the selected schema, all of which they suggest is done using the criterion of optimal relevance (1987: 705).

Sperber and Wilson's proposals have generated considerable interest (see the Postface to the second edition of *Relevance* for a list of work in the tradition; 1986/ 1995: 255–6), and it certainly provides a provocative account of the Eureka-phenomena involved in language use – of what may be going on in the subconscious mind *before* conscious working out sets in and, during it, in the phase just before a conclusion hits us, after we have set out our premises. Nevertheless, there is a good deal of interest also in explicating conscious aspects of language use, including speakers' exploitation of politeness phenomena.

The theory of politeness

Leech

As we saw above, Leech (1983) invokes politeness in his explanation of indirectness in linguistic interaction. The theory of politeness he presents involves reference to the notions of cost and benefit, and directness versus indirectness. He provides the following example to illustrate the cost–benefit scale and its relationship to the scale of politeness (1983: 107):

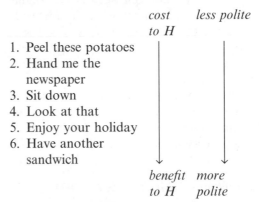

1. Peel these potatoes
2. Hand me the newspaper
3. Sit down
4. Look at that
5. Enjoy your holiday
6. Have another sandwich

The scale is intended to illustrate that the level of impoliteness of an utterance in the imperative form increases in tandem with the inconvenience that acting on it would impose on the hearer; and that it decreases in tandem with the amount of benefit a hearer might derive from acting on it. Notice also that, in speech-act theoretical terms, we would probably want to classify the utterances at the top of the scale (most impolite) as orders and those lower down as suggestions, benedictions and offers (see SPEECH-ACT THEORY).

Clearly, what is relevant to the scale of cost and benefit is the propositional content of an utterance. Leech's second scale, of directness/indirectness, has more to do with the form of an expression, since here, as his example shows, the propositional content can remain stable while the degree of politeness varies with the form of expression (1983: 108):

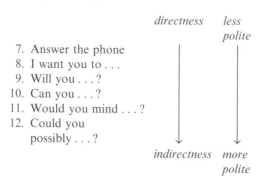

	directness	*less polite*
7. Answer the phone		
8. I want you to ...		
9. Will you ...?		
10. Can you ...?		
11. Would you mind ...?		
12. Could you possibly ...?		
	indirectness	*more polite*

This schema is interesting descriptively, and Leech's overriding purpose is to explain why people are indirect, which he does with reference to their desire to be polite. For a more encompassing theory of politeness as such, however, we need to look to an account grounded less in linguistics proper than in an ethnomethodological interest in the function of politeness phenomena in social groups and for the individuals who compose such social groups.

Brown and Levinson (1978/1987)

Brown and Levinson regard politeness phenomena as 'universal principles of human interaction' (Gumperz' preface to Brown and Levinson 1978/1987: xiii), although the expression of politeness may, of course, differ from society to society and also between groups within society.

Brown and Levinson (1978/1987: 59–60) summarize the universal principles which underlie politeness as follows.

There is in every speech community a Model Person (MP), who speaks its language fluently, and has will, rationality and face. Rationality enables the model person to reason from ends to the means that will achieve them, and **Face** is (1978/1987: 61–2):

> the public self-image that every [competent adult] member [of a society] wants to claim for himself, consisting in two related aspects:

(a) negative face: basic claim to territories, personal preserves, rights to non-distraction – i.e. to freedom of action and freedom from imposition. The want that one's actions be unimpeded by others.

(b) positive face: the positive consistent self-image or 'personality' (crucially including the desire that this self-image be appreciated and approved of) claimed by interactants. The want that one's wants be desirable to at least some others.

The politeness principles are (1978/1987: 59–60):

(i) All MPs have **positive** and **negative face** and are rational agents.

(ii) Because face is only preservable by the actions of others, it is generally to the mutual benefit of MPs to maintain each other's face.

(iii) Some acts are intrinsically face-threatening acts (FTAs). [This is the kernel of this account of politeness: politeness comes in because these intrinsically FTAs require softening; see Brown and Levinson (1978/1987: 24)]

(iv) Unless S's want to do an FTA with maximum efficiency is greater than S's want to preserve H's (or S's) face, S will want to minimize the face threat of the FTA.

(v) Given the following set of strategies, which offer payoffs of increasingly minimized risk, the more an act threatens S's or H's face, the more S will want to choose a higher-numbered strategy.

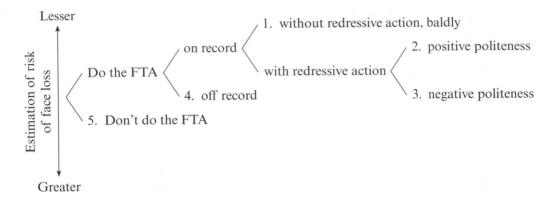

(vi) Since i–v are mutually known to all MPs, they will not choose a strategy less risky than necessary, as this may be seen as an indication that the FTA is more threatening than it actually is.

To be on record means that the intention of doing an act is made mutually known, as when someone says, for example, 'I'd like one of those cakes.' To be off record means that the act can be seen as done with more than one unambiguously attributable intention. For instance, if I compliment someone on something they have, it can be taken as a request that they give it to me, e.g. 'Those cakes look nice.' Doing an act baldly, without redress, means using the clearest, most distinct form: 'Give me a cake!' Redressive action is any action that 'gives face' to H by counteracting the potential face damage of FTA by modifying it, or adding to it, so as to indicate that no face-threat is intended or desired. This redressive action takes one of two forms, depending on which aspect of face that is being threatened (1978/1987: 70):

Positive politeness is oriented toward the positive face of H, towards H's wants and desires ('Would you like to give me one of those cakes?'), whereas **negative politeness** is oriented toward H's negative face, H's desire to remain unimpeded ('Would it trouble you to give me one of those cakes?'). Conventionalized indirectness results from the natural tension in negative politeness between the desire to go on record so that one can be seen as 'paying face', and the desire to go off record to avoid imposing.

The major linguistic realizations of politeness strategies include forms of address, honorifics and indirect speech acts (see SPEECH-ACT THEORY).

There are three sociological factors that determine the level of politeness S will use to address H: relative power of H over S; the social distance between S and H; and the ranking of the imposition involved in doing the FTA (1978/1987: 15).

Intercultural variation in the expression of politeness has been investigated by many scholars intrigued by Brown and Levinson's claim that politeness phenomena are universal (see Blum-Kulka 1983, 1987; Wierzbicka 1985; Matsumoto 1988, 1989; Hwang 1990; Gu 1990; and Sifianou 1992). As Saeed (1997: 220) puts it, 'the overall conclusion about a universal system is unclear'. It seems that researchers' willingness to concede universality decreases according to the degree of conventionalization of expressions of deference in the societies they investigate, and this is not surprising. If there are strict rules for showing deference, observance of these rules absolve speakers to a significant extent from having to prevent face-threat. But, the universality question aside, studies of the kind listed demonstrate the wide variation that prevails in modes of expressing politeness, and in community members' understanding about when to take politeness into consideration.

K.M.

Suggestions for further reading

Levinson, S.C. (1983) *Pragmatics*, Cambridge: Cambridge University Press.
Mey, J.L. (1993) *Pragmatics: An Introduction*, Oxford: Basil Blackwell.
Yule, G. (1996) *Pragmatics*, Oxford: Oxford University Press.

Prosodic phonology

Prosodic phonology, alternatively referred to as **prosodic analysis**, arose as a reaction against what proponents of prosodic phonology sometimes dub **phonemic phonology**, i.e. **phonemics** (see PHONEMICS), which operates with phonemes. In this sense as well as in certain other senses, prosodists' negative attitude extends also to functional phonology (see FUNCTIONAL PHONOLOGY). Prosodic phonologists reject the notion of the phoneme altogether, asserting that the phoneme has no existence in a language itself and is merely one of the convenient categories to which some linguists resort in order to present the linguistic data they analyse. Prosodists' objection to the phoneme arises out of their belief that it has been developed for transcriptional purposes so that phoneme theory is closely associated with phonetic transcription and the devising of orthographies, rather than with serious phonological analysis.

Instead of operating with the phoneme, prosodic phonology operates with the **phonematic unit** – not to be confused with phonemes of any kind – and with **prosody**, terms which will be explained below. Prosodic analysis is also sometimes referred to as **Firthian phonology** or **London School phonology** because it originated with John Rupert Firth (1890–1960), Britain's first Professor of Linguistics, who taught at the University of London, especially at the School of Oriental and African Studies. Prosodic phonology was conceived by Firth in the mid-1930s and subsequently developed by him. Firth's followers have put his prosodic theory into practice in their phonological analyses of, mainly, Southeast Asian and African languages (see Palmer 1970).

Prosodic phonology is best characterized in terms of the concepts and entities which **prosodists** entertain and work with in their attempt to distinguish themselves as far as possible from 'phonemicists'.

Prosodists operate with the notions of **system** and **structure**. The former relates to the concept of **paradigmatic relation**, and the latter to the concept of **syntagmatic relation**, two concepts commonly ascribed to the Swiss linguist Ferdinand de Saussure (1857–1913). Prosodists often use the following diagram to indicate the concepts of system and structure:

$$
\begin{array}{c}
\text{S} \\
\text{Y} \\
\text{S} \\
\text{S T R U C T U R E} \\
\text{E} \\
\text{M}
\end{array}
$$

Linguistic units function in terms of the interaction between system and structure. In so far as linguistic units follow and precede one another, they form sequential syntagmatic structural relations with each other. Simultaneously, they form paradigmatic relations with each other, since a linguistic unit is significantly, i.e. differentially, replaceable with another or others at that specific place in the structure, where all of the mutually replaceable linguistic units form a system (see also INTRODUCTION). Prosodic phonology attaches primary importance to syntagmatic relation, and secondary importance to paradigmatic relation, and consequently highlights those phonetic features which are relevant to structure, i.e. prosody, which is a non-segmental unit. Prosodists are of the view that phonemicists attach excessive importance to paradigmatic relation at the expense of syntagmatic relation and are preoccupied with **segmentation**, which is consistent with their operating with phonemes.

Prosodists operate with different kinds of prosody. First, a prosody may be a phonetic feature specifiable by dint of its occurrence over a certain stretch of structure and consequently characterizing the whole of such a structure. A **sentence prosody**, such as **intonation**, is one which occurs over the whole of a spoken sentence. The phonetic feature (**lip-)unroundedness**, which occurs over the whole of, for example, the English word *teeth*, and the phonetic feature (**lip-)roundedness** which occurs over the whole of, for example, the English word *tooth*, are both **word prosodies**. A **tone** (see TONE LANGUAGES), which is a prosody that occurs over a single syllable, e.g. in the Mandarin Chinese word for 'mother', ⁻*ma*, is a **syllable prosody**.

Second, a prosody may be a phonetic feature occurring at a particular place in a structure, rather than over a certain stretch of a structure, but which has ultimate relevance to a certain stretch of the structure. For example, the phonetic feature **aspiration** (= a puff of air) in the pronunciation of a Tamil voiceless plosive consonant, e.g. [pʰ], occurs in word-initial position only – the **focus of relevance** – never in word-medial or word-final position. Ultimately, however, its **domain of relevance** is the whole word in the sense that the aspiration characterizes the pertinent word as a whole. In Czech, accent falls on the initial syllable of a polysyllabic word, at least in principle,

and characterizes the whole word, though its incidence is localized on the initial syllable.

Third, a prosody may be a phonetic feature which shows the demarcation between consecutive structures. Such a prosody is often referred to as a **junction prosody**. For example, aspiration accompanying a voiceless plosive consonant in Tamil, or accent on the initial syllable in Czech mentioned above, have additionally the function of indicating the demarcation between words. To give yet another example, the glottal plosive [ʔ] in German is a prosody which reveals the demarcation between morphemes in cases where morphemes begin with accented vowels, e.g. *wir haben ein Auto* [. . . ʔain ˈʔauto . . .]; *ich verachte ihm* [. . . fɛrˈʔaxtə . . .].

Fourth, a prosody may be a phonetic feature which is linked to, and which is therefore an exponent of, a grammatical or lexical category. Such a prosody is often referred to as a **diagnostic prosody**. For example, [z] in *rows* as in *rows of chairs* is a phonetic exponent of the grammatical category of number, plural in this case; this is not the case with [z] in *rose*. [ð] is a phonetic exponent of the lexical category of **deixis**, which encompasses that group of deictic or demonstrative words whose referents are things, persons, places, times, etc., including *this, those, there, then*, etc; this is not the case with [ð] in *gather* or *either*. This last-mentioned type of prosody is obviously different from the others in that, for one thing, it does not characterize any particular stretch of structure and, for another, it involves a non-phonological factor, namely grammar or lexis in these examples. Note, however, that the involvement of non-phonological levels is not only admitted but recommended in prosodic analysis because of its principles of poly-systemicness and context, which will be explained below.

In prosodic phonology, prosodists first abstract all the prosodies, starting with that prosody whose domain of relevance is the most extensive, i.e. intonation. However, it would seem perfectly valid to start with a prosody whose domain is even more extensive; that is, a prosody which characterizes a whole speech. For example, nasality may characterize some people's speech throughout, while, in the case of speakers of a foreign language, elements from their own language may pervade their pronunciation of the foreign language. Abstraction of prosodies is carried on until there are no more phonetic features which characterize structures.

What remains when all the prosodies have been abstracted are the phonological units which prosodists call **phonematic units**. These are – unlike prosodies – **segmental**, hence linear, units, which are considered as being placed at particular points in the structure. A phonematic unit may be simply V (= vowel) or C (= consonant), or a phonetic feature like 'open' or 'close', if the phonematic unit happens to be vocalic.

To demonstrate how prosodic analysis is performed, we shall look at a few examples. Given the English word *tooth* [tuːθ], the prosodist abstracts the phonetic feature (lip-)roundedness which is manifested over the whole word: note that not only [uː] but also [t] and [θ] are rounded through assimilation (see ARTICULATORY PHONETICS) and this is precisely what the prosodist first wishes to abstract as a prosody. This prosody may be presented as **w prosody**, where 'w' refers to (lip-)roundedness. What remains are the phonematic units which the prosodist will present as **CVC** (consonant-vowel-consonant). The actual specification of a phonematic unit in terms of its phonetic components is neither important nor obligatory in prosodic phonology, so that it is not considered necessary to state which CVC are in question. Given the English word *teeth* [tiːθ], the prosodist abstracts as a prosody the phonetic feature (lip-)unroundedness, which runs throughout this word, and presents this prosody as

y prosody. What remains of this word after y prosody has been abstracted are the same phonematic units as we have seen above, i.e. CVC.

The prosodic analysis of the two English words *tooth* and *teeth* will be presented notationally as ^{w}CVC and ^{y}CVC, or $^w\overline{CVC}$ and $^y\overline{CVC}$. Note that the analysis did not start with segmentation, i.e. paradigmatically, into a series of phonemes, but with the abstraction of certain prosodies together with the identification of a structure, in this case a whole word, explicitly indicated by superimposed horizontal lines in one of the types of notation given above, the domain of relevance being words in these cases. Thus the two words in question, *tooth* and *teeth*, possess identical phonematic units, i.e. CVC, and differ from each other in that one of the words has w prosody and the other y prosody.

Another example of prosodic analysis that is frequently cited by prosodists is the following: Turkish possesses eight vowels which may be presented as: [i y e ø ɯ u a o]. These vowels may be represented in the following fashion:

[i y ɯ u]
[e ø a o]

Four prosodies, i.e. **front (f)**, **back (b)**, **rounded (r)** and **unrounded (u)**, can be appropriately abstracted from these eight vowels. This leaves two phonematic units: a relatively high (i.e. close) vowel (**H**) and a relatively low (i.e. open) vowel (**L**). The result of the analysis can be shown as follows:

[i] = ^{fu}H   [y] = ^{fr}H   [ɯ] = ^{bu}H   [u] = ^{br}H
[e] = ^{fu}L   [ø] = ^{fr}L   [a] = ^{bu}L   [o] = ^{br}L

Given a few Turkish words as examples, e.g. *el* ('hand'), *göz* ('eye'), *bas* ('head') and *kol* ('arm'), prosodic phonology will yield the following analysis (the corresponding phonemic analysis is added for comparison):

^{fu}Ll ^{fr}gLz ^{bu}bLs ^{br}kLl
(/el/   /gøz/   /bas/   /kol/)

It so happens that there occurs in Turkish what is called **vowel harmony**, whereby a given prosody which occurs in the initial syllable of a polysyllabic word prevails throughout the rest of the syllable(s), so that, for example, *elim* 'my hand' begins with [e] which, as has been seen above, possesses the prosodies of front (f) and unrounded (u), which prosodies also occur in [i] in the other syllable of this word. We shall see how *elim* 'my hand', *gözüm* 'my eye', *basim* 'my head' and *kolum* 'my arm' are analyzed in prosodic phonology (the corresponding phonemic analysis will again be added for comparison):

^{fu}LlHm ^{fr}gLzHm ^{bu}bLsHm ^{br}kLlHm
(/elim/   /gøzym/   /basɯm/   /kolum/)

It will be seen that, in prosodic analysis, the Turkish morpheme denoting 'first person singular possessive', corresponding to *my* in English, is expressed in terms of an identical form, i.e. Hm, throughout, even though the initial vowel sounds in the above-cited Turkish words are different, i.e. [e ø a o], as reflected in the corresponding different vowel phonemes yielded in the phonemic analysis (/e ø a o/), hence the mutually different forms (/im ym ɯ um/) for the Turkish morpheme corresponding to the English word *my* in phonemic analysis.

Another characteristic of prosodic phonology is the **principle of polysystemicness**. This principle is intimately connected with the principle of context, as we shall see below. By **polysystemicness** – as opposed to **monosystemicness**, which prosodists attribute to phonemic phonology – is meant that units operating at a given place in a structure are independent of those operating at another given place in the structure; in other words, the sets of units operating in different places in the structure should not be identified with each other. This applies, prosodists emphasize, even to cases where a physically identical sound is found in different places in the structure. For example, in English, [m] occurring in word-initial position where there exists what Firth called an **alternance** between [m] and [n] – e.g. *mice*, *nice* – cannot be identified with [m] occurring in word-final position where there exists an alternance between [m], [n] and [ŋ] – e.g. *rum*, *run*, *rung*. Furthermore, [m] occurring in word-medial position where there is also an alternance between [m], [n] and [ŋ] – e.g. *simmer*, *sinner*, *singer* – is not to be identified with [m] in word-final position any more than with [m] in word-initial position. It is evident that the contexts involved are different in terms of different places in the structure.

Actually, the principle of polysystemicness is further linked to that of context which, according to prosodists, operates at every linguistic level, including the phonological. This means that, to return to an example earlier adduced, [z] in *rows*, for example, which is an exponent of the grammatical category of number – plural, in this case – is considered to be a separate unit from [z] in, say, *rose*, which is not an exponent of this grammatical category. The two [z]s in question belong ultimately to different contexts in this sense, and should therefore not be identified with each other, though their phonetic context, i.e. word-final position, is the same. Moreover, [z] of *rows*, the verb, as in *he rows a boat*, which denotes third person singular present indicative, is not to be identified with [z] of *rows*, the noun. [ð] in *this* and [ð] in *father* are similarly non-identical. To give yet another example, none of the sounds in *display*, the noun, are to be identified with any of the sounds in *display*, the verb, even if a given sound in the former is physically identical with its corresponding sound in the latter: the two words are associated with different grammatical categories, i.e. noun and verb, and are consequently considered to occur in different contexts and should not be identified with each other.

It follows that the concept of **place** in prosodic phonology should be understood not narrowly in the sense of a place in a physically (i.e. phonetically) identifiable structure, but broadly in the sense that a place is associated with a particular system, the structure in question being phonetic or grammatical or syntactic or morphological or lexical or whatever, as the case may be. The implication of all this is that prosodists are first and foremost interested in seeking out **meanings** which they believe permeate through all domains of a language. In prosodic phonology, an attempt is made to identify meanings ascribable to sounds in a speech chain: this, in prosodists' view, justifies ascribing a meaning directly to a sound itself (cf. [z] in *rows* as a noun or as a verb).

The principle of polysystemicness and that of context inevitably multiply the units identified in different places in structures, or contexts, but without alarming prosodists. They believe that this multiplication is justified in prosodic phonology so long as phonological analysis is carried out according to principles compatible with prosodic phonology. The oft-quoted dictum, attributable to Antoine Meillet (1866–1936), a disciple of Saussure, that '*une langue est un système où tout se tient*' ('a language is a system in which everything holds together'), is irrelevant and unacceptable to prosodists because this conception of a language would be associated with the principle of monosystemicness to which prosodists are opposed. To prosodists, a language is a group of disparate and isolated subsystems which do not come together in a single global system.

T.A.

Suggestions for further reading

Palmer, F.R. (ed.) (1970) *Prosodic Analysis*, London: Oxford University Press.
Robins, R.H. (1964/1989) *General Linguistics: An Introductory Survey*, London: Longmans; 4th edition 1989, section 4.4, 'Prosodic phonology'.

Psycholinguistics

Psycholinguistics is a discipline in which the insights of linguistics and psychology are brought to bear on the study of the cognitive aspects of language understanding and production. One of the earliest psychological accounts of language was Wundt's *Die Sprache* (1900), which is essentially a psychological interpretation of the linguistic work of the Junggrammatiker (see HISTORICAL LINGUISTICS). However, the strongly empiricist and anti-mentalist attitude to science which dominated both linguistics and psychology during the first half of the twentieth century (see BEHAVIOURIST LINGUISTICS) inhibited theorizing about mental processes involved in linguistic behaviour, and it was not until the late 1950s and early 1960s that the work of Noam Chomsky (see GENERATIVE GRAMMAR) provided a climate of thought in which the discipline could flourish.

The main impetus for psycholinguistic research in the 1960s was the wish to explore the **psychological reality** of grammars produced by linguists; that is, to try to show that these in some way mirrored what went on in speakers' and hearers' minds. The two most famous controversies within this framework were produced by the **derivational theory of complexity** (DTC), according to which a sentence would be more difficult to process the further removed its surface structure was from its deep structure, and the theory of the **autonomy of syntactic processing**, according to which the syntactic analysis of sentences constitutes an independent stage in their perception. There is now general agreement that DTC is false (Garnham 1985: 71–4) and the grammars which produced it have, in any case, been superseded (see GENERATIVE GRAMMAR).

There has also been a general shift within psycholinguistics during the 1970s and 1980s away from models that take grammar as their starting point towards more psychologically based models. The question of whether syntactic processing is carried out independently of, or is interrelated with, other processes has not been decisively answered. It is an aspect of a more general disagreement about whether language is processed in a series of autonomous stages by autonomous components unaffected by each other, or whether there is interaction between levels of processing. The latter view became the more popular during the 1980s.

According to Clark and Clark (1977), psycholinguistics includes the study of children's acquisition of language. Many linguists would agree that both first and other language learning and also linguistic disabilities are the province of psycholinguistics (though see Garnham 1985: Preface), according to whom they are specialist areas, rather than central topics for psycholinguistics). In this volume, language acquisition and linguistic disabilities are treated in entries of their own (see LANGUAGE ACQUISITION; APHASIA; LANGUAGE PATHOLOGY AND NEUROLINGUISTICS). Artificial intelligence may also be regarded as an area of psycholinguistics, but in this encyclopedia it has its own entry (see ARTIFICIAL INTELLIGENCE). The psycholinguistic research that will be reviewed in this entry falls within the study of language from the perspective of cognitive psychology.

The cognitive approach

Three main questions lie at the heart of psycholinguistic research within the cognitive tradition.

- What mental representations are retrieved and created in the course of language processing, and what is their structure? This is the point of closest contact between cognitive psychology and linguistics. However, since (as mentioned above) early research failed to verify the psychological reality of transformational grammar, rather little research has directly addressed this question.

- What are the processes, or algorithms, by which one representation is transformed into another? Progress on this question has been largely confined to lower levels of processing, such as word recognition and word production, and has been dominated by interactive activation (McClelland and Rumelhart 1981) and connectionist models (Rumelhart and McClelland 1986).

- What is the overall processing architecture? According to the **modularity hypothesis** (Fodor 1983; Forster 1979), different aspects of language processing, such as word recognition and syntax, are encapsulated in distinct modules. 'First pass' processing of the input proceeds in a serial, bottom-up, fashion; each module takes as input the output of the preceding module. Modules do not have access to information outside of their domain of operations (e.g. the syntactic processing module has no access to semantic information). In contrast, according to the interactionist position (McClelland 1987), while there might be distinct representational domains (e.g. of phonological and orthographic word forms, syntax, semantics), these all interact with each other during processing. Processing occurs in 'cascade', such that higher levels of processing can influence lower levels, even before processing at the lower levels is complete.

Where possible, these aspects of the cognitive research agenda will be individually addressed in each of the core areas of psycholinguistic research covered here: visual and spoken word recognition, reading and phonology, accessing meaning, syntactic processing, and general comprehension processes. Finally, research on language production is discussed.

Visual and spoken word recognition

'Word recognition' refers to a process of perceptual categorization whereby input is matched to a known word form in memory. Different representations are assumed to be contacted by written and spoken input (referred to as written and spoken input 'logogens' by Morton 1979). Once such a representation has been contacted, it can then be used to access more information about the word; namely, its pronunciation or spelling, or its semantic and syntactic properties. Before considering these aspects of what is sometimes referred to as 'lexical access', research on word recognition as such will be discussed.

Processing

A basic principle underlying models of word recognition since Morton's **logogen model of word recognition** (Morton 1969) is that an input pattern simultaneously activates multiple lexical representations according to their degree of match with the input (although serial search models do not make this assumption – see Becker 1979; Forster 1976). McClelland and Rumelhart (1981) proposed a model of word recognition that adopted this idea and made additional assumptions about how simultaneously active representations compete and interact. Their model was an early example of the class of 'Interactive Activation' models which have come to be highly influential in many areas of psycholinguistics, and which could be regarded as the forerunners of **neural network**, or **connectionist**, models.

McClelland and Rumelhart's (1981) model assumes three levels of representation: visual features, letters and words (these representational assumptions are not crit-

ical, since it is the nature of the way they interact in processing which is crucial for present purposes). Activation of units at each level is determined by the degree of activation they receive from the bottom up (i.e. their degree of match to the units active at the preceding level, and ultimately the input) and also from the top down (since units pass activation down to units at the preceding level that are compatible with them). Crucially, processing at any one level does not have to be complete before higher-level representations can become active. Combined with the assumption of top-down activation, the result is what is often referred to as 'cascade' processing. Another important aspect of these kinds of model is that processing within levels is 'competitive' because units at the same level represent mutually exclusive hypotheses. McClelland and Rumelhart formalized this model mathematically, and were able successfully to simulate data from experiments on humans, such as the 'word superiority' effect on letter perception (letters are easier to perceive in words than in consonant strings). More recently, Johnson and Pugh (1994) tested one counter-intuitive prediction of Interactive Activation models: the more similar a word is to other words, the harder it will be to recognize (the less visually distinctive a word is, the greater the competition between word-level hypotheses). Johnson and Pugh (1994) confirmed this prediction, and interpreted the results within a more detailed model of visual word recognition than McClelland and Rumelhart's, but one which followed broadly similar principles. However, whether orthographic similarity to other words has inhibitory or facilitatory effects may depend upon task demands (Balota, Paul and Spieler 1999: 24–8).

Models which assume activation of multiple hypotheses have dominated work on spoken word recognition. The **TRACE model** (McClelland and Elman 1986) postulates feature-, phoneme- and word-level units which interact in a similar fashion to the feature, letter and word units in the McClelland and Rumelhart (1981) model of visual word recognition. In contrast, Marslen-Wilson's **cohort model** (1987, 1989) stresses the activation of multiple word-level hypotheses, but does not postulate an intermediate phoneme layer of representation, and rules out a top-down flow of activation from lexical to sub-lexical representations. Despite these differences, one important implication of both of these models is that a spoken word can be recognized at the point at which the acoustic information uniquely specifies a single word in the listener's lexicon, which will often be prior to the actual acoustic offset of the word (see Marslen-Wilson 1989 for a review of supporting evidence, and Bard *et al.* 1988 for evidence that because of problems of segmentation this is not always the case in continuous speech). Both models also stress the importance of lexical constraints for dealing with variability in the acoustic signal. In TRACE this is because of top-down activation from lexical to phoneme (and ultimately feature) units. There is considerable evidence for lexical effects on phoneme perception (Ganong 1980; Marslen-Wilson and Welsh 1978; Samuel 1997), although whether such effects imply top-down activation is disputed (Norris 1993; Pitt and McQueen 1998).

Architecture

In the case of visual and spoken-word recognition, the debate between modular and interactionist positions has centred on the question of whether semantic context influences word recognition. The interactionist position predicts that it should, because semantic context provides just another source of top-down activation which then percolates down to lower levels. According to the modular position it cannot, because semantic information can have no effect on the operation of the word

recognition module. There is considerable evidence for semantic context effects on visual word recognition tasks, but there has been much debate over whether these effects are actually due to facilitation of the word recognition process itself, as opposed to other processes which contribute to task performance (Neely 1991). Semantic context effects tend to be very weak or entirely absent when tasks are used which might be assumed to tap recognition most directly, e.g. speeded word reading (Forster 1981; Hodgson 1991; Lupker 1984) or fixation times (Balota *et al.* 1985). However, larger context effects can be obtained when the word is made more difficult to read (Williams 1996), or at low levels of reading ability (see Stanovich 1990 for a review). The latter results tend to support an interactive activation, or cascade, approach, and are consistent with the view that meaning interacts with the recognition process (see Balota *et al.* 1991 for a review). However, from the modularist perspective, effects of 'semantic' context can be attributed to direct associative/collocational connections between lexical entries, and hence do not violate the assumption that semantic information influences recognition. In view of this, some research has attempted to distinguish truly semantic and associative/collocational context effects, and found that indeed associative effects are stronger than semantic effects (Lupker 1984; Shelton and Martin 1992; Thompson-Schill *et al.* 1998; Williams 1996). This suggests that there is some representational distinction between collocational and semantic relationships. Semantic context effects have also been demonstrated in spoken word recognition, although accounts of this effect differ in the Cohort and TRACE models (see Marslen-Wilson 1989 for a review).

Representation

There has been debate over whether models of spoken word recognition require a distinct level of phonemic representation (as in TRACE). Marslen-Wilson (1999; Marslen-Wilson and Warren 1994) argues that lexical representations are specified in terms of distinctive features rather than phonemes. Following the theory of '**radical underspecification**' (**SPE**), he suggests that, while the distinctive features present in the signal are indeed represented pre-lexically, the lexical entries to which they are matched are abstract in the sense that they specify only non-default values of non-redundant distinctive features. This view permits a more parsimonious account of simplification phenomena, co-articulation and assimilation than is possible in TRACE.

Other researchers have argued that, in order to ease the problem of segmenting continuous speech into words, the lexical access process may utilize units of representation which are larger than the phoneme. Mehler *et al.* (1981) propose that French listeners segment the input into syllables prior to lexical access. However, Cutler and colleagues have argued that English listeners utilize full-quality strong syllables (see Cutler 1989 for a review). If segmentation strategies are language-specific, then it becomes interesting to consider the case of bilinguals, an issue explored in Cutler *et al.* (1992).

With regard to morphology, there is clearly a tension between listing complex forms as unique lexical entries (i.e. disregarding morphology in the process of lexical access) and decomposing words into their constituent morphemes prior to lexical access. While the former might seem necessary for opaque derivations and compounds (e.g. *re-strain*, *butter-fly*), the latter might be an economical means of dealing with inflections and transparent derivations and compounds (e.g. *mis-judge*, *space-walk*). Current models favour a dynamic interaction between these two kinds of representation, very much in the spirit of interactive activation models (Caramazza *et al.* 1988). Working from the perspective of spoken

word recognition, Marslen-Wilson *et al.* (1994) provide evidence that morphological structure is only lexically represented for transparent forms, access being via a shared stem morpheme (see also Marslen-Wilson 1999 for a brief review).

Reading and phonology

Once a written or spoken form as been categorized as an instance of a known word, further information about that word can then be retrieved. In the case of written words, there has been a good deal of debate over the way in which phonology is derived, and the role that this might play in accessing meaning and general comprehension.

Representation

With regard to the issue of deriving phonology from orthography, there is good evidence to suggest that a distinction can be drawn between knowledge of the rules relating orthography and phonology (grapheme–phoneme conversion rules, Coltheart *et al.* 1993), and lexically represented pronunciation. Rules seem to be needed to account for the ability to read novel words, while rote storage is necessary to read irregular words. Some people suffering from acquired dyslexia (after brain damage) (see DYSLEXIA) are able to read novel words, but tend to produce regular pronunciations of irregular words. This so-called '**surface dyslexic**' syndrome (Coltheart *et al.* 1983) can be explained in terms of damage to the lexical system, and over-reliance on a rule system. In contrast, '**phonological dyslexics**' (Funnell 1983) and '**deep dyslexics**' (Marshall and Newcombe 1980) make errors reading novel words, but can read even irregular words correctly (deep dyslexics also make semantic errors, e.g. reading *dinner* as *food*). These patients appear to have problems with the rule system (and an additional problem accessing meaning in the case of deep dyslexics).

Architecture

Even if one were to draw a representational distinction between lexical and rule-based routes to phonology – that is, between rote and rule – there remains the issue of how distinct these are in processing terms. There is considerable evidence that in non-brain-damaged individuals, these two types of knowledge are in dynamic interaction. Glushko (1979) showed that pronouncing nonsense words is affected by whether there are competing lexical analogies (e.g. *heaf* is relatively difficult to read aloud because of conflicting analogies with regular words like *leaf* and irregular words like *deaf*). This demonstrates an effect of lexically represented pronunciations on reading non-words. Similar effects have been obtained for reading regular known words, for example *beard* is relatively difficult because of competition from irregular analogies such as *heard* (Jared 1997; Jared *et al.* 1990).

Process

Coltheart *et al.* (1993) explain the interaction between lexical and rule-based systems in word reading by using an interactive activation framework that preserves the representational distinction between these two types of knowledge. However, a more radical approach is to conflate lexical and rule knowledge within one representational system, and to see rule knowledge as an emergent property of lexical knowledge. Novel words are then read through an essentially analogical process, as suggested by Glushko (1979). This is one area where **connectionist**, or **neural network models**, have been relatively successful (Plaut *et al.* 1996; Seidenberg and McClelland 1989). These are self-organizing systems which are 'taught' the pronunciations of a sample of English words, varying in frequency and regularity. Their performance on 'reading' these words, and the pronunciations they produce for novel words, are then com-

pared with human data. They demonstrate that it is possible for rule-like behaviour to emerge from a system which is only taught relationships between individual words and pronunciations (see Chater and Christiansen 1999 for an introduction to connectionist approaches to language processing). Furthermore, it is claimed that, when 'damaged', these systems can simulate certain dyslexic syndromes (Plaut 1997; Plaut *et al.* 1996). The assumption that it is possible to conflate lexical and rule knowledge has, as one might expect, been hotly debated, especially with reference to past tense morphology (see Chater and Christiansen 1999 for a connectionist perspective, and Clahsen 1999 for an opposing view).

Another strand of research on phonological processing of written language has addressed the role of phonology in accessing meaning. On the one hand, it has been argued that visually presented words access meaning directly (Coltheart 1978), while other researchers have made the strong claim that visual words only access meaning via phonology (Lukatela and Turvey 1994; Van Orden and Goldinger 1994; Van Orden *et al.* 1988). It must be stressed that the latter view relates to the unconscious and automatic use of phonology, and not to the subjective experience of phonology in silent reading. Jared and Seidenberg (1991) provide evidence for a middle position in which high-frequency words are read directly, but phonology plays a role in reading low-frequency words.

Whereas arguments for the involvement of phonology in accessing meaning are plausible in the case of alphabetic writing systems, one might expect that in non-alphabetic writing systems there would be a direct pathway between visual form and meaning. However, Perfetti and Zhang (1995) found evidence for rapid activation of phonology even from Chinese characters, and on this basis argued for a universal phonological principle. On the other hand, Zhou and Marslen-Wilson (1999) showed that only when Chinese characters contain phonetic radicals does meaning access appear to be phonologically mediated. For characters containing no such radicals, meaning appeared to be activated directly from the visual form. Evidence for similar effects in Japanese Kanji is provided by Wydell *et al.* (1993).

With regard to phenomenally experienced phonology, there is general agreement that this is used as the means of storing verbal material in short-term memory (Baddeley 1990). However, whether this form of representation plays a role in language comprehension is not clear, since even patients with severely impaired phonological short-term memory can show unimpaired language comprehension. Gathercole and Baddeley (1993) suggest that only when sentences are long and syntactically complex will phonological encoding contribute to the comprehension process.

Accessing meaning

Regardless of the route by which lexical representations of meaning are accessed, there remains the question of the form that those representations take (a representational issue) and how context influences what aspects of word meaning are activated (an architectural issue).

Architecture

Homonyms have provided a popular testing ground for evaluating modular versus interactive processing architectures. Early research suggested that when an ambiguous word such as *bug* is recognized, it immediately activates both of its meanings, regardless of the context, but in under a second only the contextually appropriate meaning is still active (Swinney 1979). Seidenberg *et al.* (1982) showed that this effect is particularly strong for noun–verb ambiguities such as *box*, and that selection of the appropriate meaning occurs within 0.2 seconds of

the word's offset. These findings have been interpreted as strong support for a modular view of language processing (Fodor 1983; Pinker 1994). However, Tabossi (1988) found that the subordinate (i.e. less frequent) meaning of a homonym does not become active in a strongly biasing irrelevant context, although it does in a more weakly biasing context. Rayner and Pacht (1994) found that a dominant meaning becomes active even in a very strongly biasing irrelevant context. From his review of the conflicting results in this area, Simpson (1995) concludes that meaning access is affected by meaning dominance and the strength of contextual bias. This is more consistent with an interactive than a modular processing architecture (see McClelland 1987 for the development of this point in relation to ambiguity research).

Representation

Early research on the representation of word meaning was concerned with **prototype effects** (see Aitchison 1987 for a review). It was discovered that people find it quite natural to make judgements about 'goodness' of category membership (for example, they will judge that an apple is a 'better' fruit than a fig). It was argued that concepts like 'fruit' cannot therefore be represented as a strict definition, but must instead be represented as a prototype which captures the central tendency, or family resemblance structure of the category (Rosch 1975; Smith and Medin 1981). However, Armstrong *et al.* (1983) found that people are also able to produce graded category membership judgements for concepts which are perfectly well defined, such as 'odd number' or 'female'. On this basis it seems more plausible to see prototype effects as a consequence of the way in which semantic information is accessed and used in a judgement task, rather than a direct reflection of underlying representations. Armstrong *et al.* (1983) drew a distinction between an 'identification function' and a 'conceptual core', where the former refers to a heuristic procedure used to make categorizations, and the latter to a core definition of the concept (see also Johnson-Laird 1987). According to Lakoff (1987b) prototype effects reflect underlying 'cognitive models' of a domain, and Barsalou (1985, 1987) argues that prototypicality judgements can be driven by 'ideals' which can be constructed on an ad hoc basis to form context-specific categories (e.g. foods to eat on a diet).

Some work on meaning access during sentence processing has attempted to distinguish different types of semantic information in terms of time course of activation. Properties of a word have been distinguished in terms of dominance, or centrality (i.e. the ease with which they come to mind when people are asked to write down the features of a concept). It has been found that central properties (e.g. 'music' for *piano*) are active regardless of the context, whereas in an irrelevant context peripheral properties (e.g. 'heavy' for *piano*) fail to become active at all (Greenspan 1986) or are rapidly suppressed (Whitney *et al.* (1985). Where these results differ from those obtained with homonyms is that the activation of central properties appears to persist even in seemingly irrelevant contexts. Barsalou (1982) distinguished context-dependent and context-independent properties, and found that the latter persist into the final interpretation of the sentence (e.g. the property of bank 'where money is kept' is as available after reading *The bank was robbed by three bandits* as after reading *The bank had been built three years ago*). Williams (1992) extended this line of investigation to polysemous adjectives, finding that 'central' aspects of an adjective's meaning (e.g. *firm* as in 'solid' as opposed to 'strict') remain active even in an irrelevant context. Other work has drawn a distinction between functional and perceptual aspects of word meaning. Some studies found that perceptual properties are accessed before

functional properties, while more recent work has found that, at least for words referring to artefacts, functional properties (e.g. 'shoot' for *rifle*) become active before perceptual properties (Moss and Gaskell 1999). Moss and Gaskell (1999) also review research showing that functional properties are particularly resistant to loss in brain-damaged patients, and suggest that functional properties are at the core of concepts for artifacts.

Syntax

Architecture

As in the case of meaning access, the debate over the modularity of syntactic processing has focused on the resolution of ambiguity – in this case, syntactic ambiguity – and whether the initial syntactic analysis of a sentence is affected by semantic and discourse factors. A modular position has been advocated by Frazier and colleagues (see Frazier 1987 for a review). On this view, a syntactic processing module takes as input the words of a sentence and, on the basis of their grammatical category, and only their grammatical category, constructs a single phrase marker (see Forster 1979 for an earlier expression of this hypothesis). Although there is no commitment to a specific parsing mechanism (see the section on process below), it is assumed that the parser operates in a highly incremental fashion; that is, by constructing the phrase marker on a word-by-word basis. One consequence of this assumption (which has amply been supported by experimental evidence, see below) is that the processor will often find itself with a choice as to how to attach the incoming word to the current phrase marker. For example, after receiving *The spy saw the cop with the . . .* , the processor will know that the word *the* indicates that a noun phrase should be opened. But where should this be attached to the phrase marker of the preceding fragment? Should it be attached to the verb phrase (*saw*) or to the object noun phrase (*the cop*)? Frazier (1987) proposed that the processor deals with these kinds of local syntactic ambiguity by applying structurally defined preferences; namely, the principle of **minimal attachment** (posit the fewest number of nodes) and **late closure** (attach an incoming word into the structure currently being built). In this example, the principle of minimal attachment dictates that the upcoming noun phrase should be attached to the verb phrase, since this involves postulating fewer nodes. Rayner *et al.* (1983) showed that, should this sentence continue with the word *revolver*, reading times in this region are slower than if it continued with *binoculars*. This, they argue, is because *revolver* is initially attached to the verb phrase, so the thematic processor attempts to interpret it as an instrument of seeing and, on realizing that this is implausible, requests an alternative parse from the syntactic processor. When the processor's initial parsing decisions are erroneous in this way, the reader is said to have been 'garden pathed'. In fact, the Frazier model has come to be referred to as the **Garden Path model**.

The Garden Path model has received support from a number of other experiments. Because the garden path effects that have been examined are often extremely local, and pass unnoticed by the reader, sensitive methodologies are necessary in order to record momentary slow-downs in reading. Usually eye-movement tracking (see Rayner and Pollatsek 1989 for background to this technique) or self-paced word-by-word reading have been employed. Ferreira and Henderson (1990) compared these two techniques and obtained similar results, although Spivey-Knowlton *et al.* (1995) provide evidence that under single-word presentation conditions the absence of information from peripheral vision has consequences for parsing. Examples of experiments which have supported the

Garden Path model are Mitchell (1987), who showed that the parser's initial decisions respect late closure and ignore subcategorization information, and Britt *et al.* (1992), who showed that the difficulty of reduced relatives, which is predicted by minimal attachment (e.g. *The coffee spilled on the rug was difficult to conceal*), is not eased by what was considered to be a supportive discourse context (one which refers to both coffee on a rug and scratches on a table). For other examples, see Mitchell (1994).

The interactive position makes the prediction that there should be circumstances in which parsing decisions are affected by thematic, semantic, and even discourse factors. Over recent years, evidence has accumulated for this position. Taraban and McClelland (1988) replicated the reading time differences for pairs like *The spy saw the cop with the revolver/binoculars* previously obtained by Rayner *et al.* (1983), but then showed that the difference in reading times between verb phrase and noun phrase attachments was reversed for pairs like *The couple admired the house with a friend/garden*, where the non-minimally attached *garden* led to faster reading times. They suggest that parsing preferences are a product of general expectancies based on world knowledge. Trueswell *et al.* (1994) found evidence for more specific preferences based on how well a noun fulfils alternative thematic roles at the point of ambiguity. Altmann and Steedman (1988) showed effects of discourse context on the prepositional phrase attachments. For example, the phrase *with the new lock* is non-minimally attached in *The burglar blew open the safe with the new lock* but it was found to be relatively easy to read in a context in which there was a safe with a new lock and a safe with an old lock. They suggested that parsing decisions are influenced by what they called the 'principle of referential support', rather than the purely structural principles proposed by the Garden Path model. In a similar vein, Spivey-Knowlton *et al.* (1995) found evidence of discourse context effects on processing reduced relatives. However, Britt (1994) found evidence that there are circumstances in which the effect of referential support for a prepositional phrase is overcome by what is presumably a stronger preference derived from the thematic structure of the verb (specifically in the case of verbs like *put*, which obligatorily take three arguments). For example, the prepositional phrase *on the battle* in *He put the book on the battle on to the chair* is difficult to read even in a referentially supportive context in which there are two books, but this difficulty disappears if the verb *dropped* (for which a locative phrase is optional) is used instead. These results suggest that decisions about how to attach incoming words are based on an interaction between different types of constraint, and there is no architectural barrier that prevents different information sources interacting.

Process

In the light of the mounting evidence for an interactive view of sentence processing, MacDonald *et al.* (1994) suggest that syntactic decisions are the result of a process of constraint satisfaction, where the constraints come from a variety of sources, and have varying strengths (for a critique, see Frazier 1995). Any particular input string will activate competing hypotheses in a number of domains, and the reader's task is to arrive at an interpretation that is consistent with hypotheses across domains (much as is the case in **Interactive Activation models of word recognition**). Take, for example, the input string *The workers lifted. . . .* The morphology of the verb *lifted* is ambiguous between past tense and past participle. However, *lifted* is more frequent in the past tense, and thus more strongly activated. In the domain of syntax, this fragment will activate two phrase-structure representations, one a main clause and one

a reduced relative. Presumably the main clause structure is the more frequently encountered, and hence the most strongly activated. There are two possible argument structures for *lifted*, one in which the subject is agent and one in which the subject is theme. The assignment of the subject (*workers*) to the agent role is more plausible, and hence the most strongly activated. Just as in other interactive activation models, hypotheses in different domains mutually support each other, while hypotheses within the same domain are in competition. In the present example, the most highly active hypotheses at all levels support each other, leading to a very strong preference for the main clause interpretation. If the sentence were to continue *The workers lifted by . . .*, only the activation of the syntactic structure for the reduced relative would be increased, although this might still be temporarily overridden by the biases at other levels. However, given that the goal of the system is to achieve compatibility at all levels, the activation of options in the other domains will eventually be brought into alignment. Furthermore, there may be other factors which support the reduced relative – such as plausibility (as in *The bricks lifted*), discourse context (two groups of workers which need to be distinguished) or the frequency of the past participle form of the verb (e.g. *The workers examined . . .*, where *examined* is more frequent as a past participle form). Trueswell (1996) has provided evidence that indeed the frequency of the past participle versus past tense form of the verb is critical in determining the ease of processing-reduced relative structures. Garnsey *et al.* (1997) explored the effects of putting different information sources into conflict, and McRae *et al.* (1998) obtained a good fit between human reading data and a computer instantiation of the constraint-based approach. In this latter study, corpora were used to establish frequencies of different morphological forms and syntactic structures, and rating studies measured thematic preferences.

Other models of parsing have aimed to be much more specific about the way that syntactic structures are computed, and in doing so have made more of an appeal to linguistic theory. Pritchett (1992) developed a model of parsing based on **Principles and Parameters** theory (see GENERATIVE GRAMMAR), which assumes that all of the principles of **Universal Grammar** are satisfied at each moment during parsing. In particular, the parser seeks to satisfy the theta criterion (i.e. assign each noun phrase a thematic role) at every point in processing. Ambiguities arise when alternative thematic roles are available for a noun phrase, and the processor selects the one which entails the lowest processing cost. This model differs from the Garden Path model in its emphasis on thematic processing. A radically different approach is taken by Pickering and Barry (1991), who develop a theory of parsing which does not depend on a phrase-structure grammar, or on empty categories (which are central to the Principles and Parameters theory). They employ an incremental version of **Categorial Grammar** (see NON-TRANSFORMATIONAL GRAMMAR) in which each word contains information about how it can be combined with other words, and parsing consists of determining whether the representations of adjacent words can be collapsed together. Since this model makes specific claims about the nature of syntactic representations, the evidence relating to it is dealt with in the following section. For a discussion of other parsing models, see Crocker (1999).

Representation

Rather little psycholinguistic work has addressed the issue of the psychological reality of specific theories of syntactic structure. Most work has been carried out in relation to empty categories, as posited by **Principles and Parameters** theory (see GENERATIVE GRAMMAR), and particularly **wh-trace**. Even though wh-traces are invisible surface markers of movement operations, it has been claimed that they have detectable effects on sentence processing. Frazier and Clifton (1989) proposed that the parser posits a wh-trace at every structural position that is consistent with the grammar (which they dubbed the '**Filler-Driven**' strategy). Compelling evidence for this was obtained by Stowe (1986), who found that Garden Path effects occur when a potential trace position is not realized, as after *bring* in *My brother wanted to know who Ruth will bring us home to at Christmas* (i.e. the reader initially posits a trace after *bring*, which is coindexed with *who* and is forced to reanalyse when *us* is encountered). Stowe *et al.* (1991) and Hickok *et al.* (1992) showed that a potential gap is postulated even when the resulting interpretation would be implausible. For example, in *Which bucket did the movie director from Hollywood persuade Bill to push?*, Hickok *et al.* (1992) found evidence for reactivation of the wh-filler, *bucket*, at the potential, but implausible, trace position immediately after *persuade*.

The above experiments could be interpreted as providing evidence for the psychological reality of wh-traces, and of the particular approach to syntax on which they depend (see Fodor 1989 for an elaboration of this line of argument). On the other hand, Pickering and colleagues (Pickering and Barry 1991; Pickering 1994; Traxler and Pickering 1996) argue that an '**immediate association**' between a verb and a wh-filler can be accomplished by a parsing mechanism which does not appeal to traces at all (i.e. one based on Categorial Grammar). For example, Traxler and Pickering (1996) showed that there are circumstances under which a thematic role is assigned even before a so-called trace position has been encountered (as shown by a reaction to the implausibility of *That's the garage with which the heartless killer shot the hapless man* *yesterday afternoon* even at the verb *shot*). However, Clahsen and Featherston (1999) argue that, since all of the above experiments examined processing immediately following the verb, effects of traces cannot be distinguished from those of thematic analysis. By performing experiments in German, they show that reactivation of the wh-filler can occur at other sentence positions, and argue that their data can only be explained by assuming wh-traces, as proposed by Principles and Parameters theory.

General comprehension

According to the **modularity hypothesis**, once a syntactic structure and thematic roles have been assigned, the construction of a full interpretation of a sentence lies in the domain of central, domain general, processes which have access to world knowledge. For this reason, processing architecture ceases to be an issue when these higher-level aspects of comprehension are considered. Early research in this area was concerned with the kind of representations which are formed as the products of the comprehension process, exploring people's memory for sentences or short texts. Theories of processing are less developed than for lower-level aspects of language and, as Gernsbacher and Foertsch (1999) remark, are so similar in spirit that they are difficult to distinguish empirically. Here we will focus on the issue of representation.

Researchers have attempted to distinguish three different types of memory representation for text or discourse: **surface memory**, **propositional memory** and **situation/mental models**. Jarvella (1971) found that people's memory for the precise wording and syntactic form of what they have heard (i.e. surface memory) is remarkably short-lived, and shows sharp drop-offs at major constituent boundaries. This could be because as soon as deeper representations have been formed, surface information is purged from memory (see also Anderson

and Paulson 1977). More recent work has also emphasized that short-term recall of sentences is achieved more through a process of regeneration from a conceptual representation than through simply reading off a verbatim record of what was read or heard (Lombardi and Potter 1992; Potter and Lombardi 1990), although how the accuracy and apparent verbatimness of short-term recall is to be accounted for on this view remains an issue (Lee and Williams 1997). Also, it should be noted that Keenan *et al.* (1977) found that long-term **verbatim memory** can occur for utterances that are of what they refer to as **high interactional content**; that is, utterances that convey wit, humour, sarcasm or personal criticism. By and large, though, for utterances of more neutral content there is very rapid loss of surface information.

What form do these deeper levels of representation take? A common proposal is that they should be described in terms of **propositional structures**. Ratcliff and McKoon (1978) provide an elegant demonstration of how, even under conditions where accurate recall of the content of utterances would be difficult, the underlying representation of their propositional structure can implicitly influence a reaction-time task. Kintsch *et al.* (1975) explored the way in which reading time and recall patterns are determined by the propositional structure of texts, showing for instance that recall accuracy is affected by the degree of interconnectedness of arguments, and that the recall of certain aspects of texts is affected by their hierarchical position in the propositional structure. It must be noted, however, that this research employed texts that were generated from a prior propositional analysis, and so whether analyses derived from naturally occurring texts would make the same predictions is not clear (see also Brown and Yule 1983: 106–16 for criticisms of this approach).

Propositional representations do not exhaust the meaning that people are able to derive from text. They capture thematic relations, and make clear the co-reference relations between terms (e.g. the relationship between an anaphoric expression and its antecedent). But they do not encode reference or the inferences that readers make in order to arrive at a full understanding. To capture this kind of representation, researchers have referred to a '**situation model**' (Kintsch 1988) or '**mental model**' (Johnson-Laird 1983). The former term will be adopted here. This level represents the content of text or discourse as a state of affairs in the real, or a possible, world. Bransford *et al.* (1972) were among the first to highlight the importance of this level of representation as constituting what is commonly thought of as '**understanding**'. They tested people on passages which were perfectly cohesive in propositional terms, but which in the absence of an appropriate title did not produce any sense of understanding. Much of the work on this approach has focused on spatial descriptions. For example, Bransford *et al.* (1972) found that after reading *The frog sat on a log. The fish swam under the log* (mixed in with a large number of other mini-texts), readers will later mistakenly judge that they actually read the sentence *The fish swam under the frog*. Since the content of this test sentence does not correspond to a proposition that was presented, it must have been inferred through the construction of a more analogical form of representation. In addition to language of this type, Johnson-Laird (1983) has applied a mental models approach to logical inference. This approach to comprehension lays great emphasis on the role of background knowledge in supporting the process of constructing a situation model. A useful discussion of the relationship between the situation model and background knowledge is provided by Sanford and Garrod (1981) (see also Garrod and Sanford 1990) who distinguish the elements of the discourse that are represented by tokens in the situation

model, which they refer to as being in 'explicit focus', and background knowledge that is in an active state, or as being in 'implicit focus'. One function of background knowledge is to provide roles for entities mentioned in the discourse. In terms of **schema theory** (Schank and Abelson 1977) these are provided by 'slots' in active schemata. For example, Sanford and Garrod (1981) describe experiments which show that, while there are certainly cases where definite reference to a previously unmentioned entity is infelicitous, if a role for that entity is available as part of active background information, then comprehension is unproblematic (e.g. *the clothes* in *Mary dressed the baby. The clothes were made of pink wool*). They also make the important point that, when a token is introduced into explicit focus, it merely points to a slot or role in an active schema, but other information associated with that role does not necessarily become incorporated into the situation model itself (hence the infelicity of *the material* in *Mary dressed the baby. The material was made of pink wool*). This restriction on the content that is represented in the situation model is important in relation to inferencing, as will be discussed shortly.

More recently, a mental models approach has been applied to the process of **anaphor resolution** (see Garnham 1999; Garnham and Oakhill 1992). For example, Oakhill *et al.* (1992) demonstrated the lack of cost in interpreting texts such as *Last night we went to hear a new jazz band. They played for nearly six hours*, where *jazz band* is routinely interpreted as the antecedent of *they* despite a lack of number agreement. Presumably this is because, at the level of the situation model, *jazz band* is represented by a number of discrete elements (standing for the players). The ease of interpretation suggests that anaphoric expressions seek antecedents in the situation model, rather than the text itself. However, Williams (1993) provided evidence that, for repeated noun anaphors, the surface form of the text may still play a mediating role in determining how the situation model is accessed. On the other hand, pronouns may access the situation model more directly (Cloitre and Bever 1988).

The dominance of the situation model in comprehension has been highlighted by Barton and Sanford (1993) (see also Sanford 1999; Sanford and Garrod 1995) who explored the so-called **Moses Illusion**: the tendency for people to answer the question, 'How many animals of each sort did Moses put on the ark?' with 'Two'. They suggest that this is because words that even vaguely fit supporting background knowledge only receive a shallow semantic analysis that is just sufficient to support construction of a situation model. Perrig and Kintsch (1985) showed that the nature of the situation model that the reader constructs may be affected by the nature of the text, and be subject to individual differences. Schmalhofer and Glavanov (1986) also demonstrated the effect of task demands, and found greater evidence for construction of a situation model when the task emphasized understanding for learning, and more evidence for construction of propositional representations when participants were merely told to summarize the text. Thus, whereas the propositional level of representation may capture the minimum that a person should have extracted from a text in order to support further comprehension processes, the content of the situation model is more variable.

In an attempt to separate out automatic and voluntary aspects of higher-level comprehension processes, a good deal of research has focused on whether there are certain classes of inference that are made spontaneously and automatically, whereas other types of inference are more optional. McKoon and Ratcliff (1992) propose a '**Minimalist Hypothesis**', according to which 'only two classes of inference, those based on easily available information and those required for local coherence, are encoded during reading, unless a reader adopts special goals or strategies'. In the first case, information that is strongly associated to words in the text triggers an elaborative inference. For example, McKoon and Ratcliff (1989) showed that when people read *The housewife was learning to be a seamstress and needed practice so she got out the skirt she was making and threaded her needle*, they spontaneously activate the concept 'sew' (a similar effect was also obtained by O'Brien *et al.* 1986). This appears to be an elaborative inference, but one that may be triggered through strong associations with the words in the text (in actual fact, as in much of this type of work, the methodologies only show that a concept is active, and not that a particular inference was actually made). More interesting are the second type of inference, those required for local coherence. These include **anaphoric inferences** and **thematic role assignments** (which here have been assumed necessary for construction of a propositional representation) and what Graesser *et al.* (1994) refer to as '**causal antecedent' inferences**. The latter concern an effort to understand the immediate causes of an event mentioned in the text. For example, Potts *et al.* (1988) found that after reading . . . *the husband threw the delicate porcelain vase against the wall. It cost him well over one hundred dollars to replace the vase*, there was evidence of activation of the concept 'broke' (implying that they had inferred that the vase broke), whereas this concept was not active after reading . . . *the husband threw the delicate porcelain vase against the wall. He had been feeling angry for weeks, but had refused to seek help*. Only in the former case is it necessary to infer that the vase broke in order to understand the rest of the text. Similarly, McKoon and Ratcliff (1989) showed that the concept 'dead' was not active after reading *The director and the cameraman were ready to shoot close-ups when suddenly the actress fell from the* *fourteenth storey*, presumably because there is nothing that requires the reader to infer that the actress died. McKoon and Ratcliff (1989) take this result as evidence against the '**constructivist' approach** originally advocated by Bransford *et al.* (1972) and taken up later in the mental/situation model approach. They argue that 'A mental model of a text such as *"the actress fell from the 14th stor[e]y"* should include the inference that she died. It would not be reasonable from the mental model point of view to leave her suspended in mid air'. However, as Glenberg *et al.* (1994) point out, mental models do not have to be complete representations of real situations; they can be highly schematic. This **schematic approach to mental models** is also consistent with the line taken by Garrod and Sanford (1990). Evidence against elaborative inferences is not evidence against situation models.

The Minimalist Hypothesis has come under attack for concentrating too much upon local coherence. Graesser *et al.* (1994) argue that inferences that are required for global coherence are spontaneously drawn as well. These concern the 'superordinate goal' of a character, the moral of the passage, and the emotional reactions of characters (see Graesser *et al.* 1994 for a review of the evidence). Other research has investigated whether readers spontaneously infer a specific exemplar of a superordinate category, for example that *vehicle* may refer to a car in the sentence *The reporter went to the vehicle to look for the papers* (Whitney 1986). Both Whitney (1986) and O'Brien *et al.* (1986) found evidence that such inferences are only made spontaneously when the superordinate term is foregrounded, for example in *The vehicle contained the papers that the reporter was looking for*. This points to the importance of discourse factors in determining what inferences are made spontaneously, making it difficult to maintain a strict minimalist position.

Language production

Only a brief overview of work on language production will be provided here. The reader is directed to Levelt (1989) for a comprehensive review of all aspects of the production process, and to Levelt *et al.* (1999) for a more up-to-date review of work on single-word production.

Representations

It is generally agreed that the process of producing a word can be separated into two stages. The first, **lexicalization**, concerns choosing the word that best matches the intended message (as represented at a conceptual level), and the second, form retrieval, concerns accessing and assembling the phonological information that is required to articulate the word. Note that the notion of lexicalization, as used above, implies the existence of abstract lexical representations, which mediate between concepts and word forms. These intermediate representations have been referred to as lemmas, and are also assumed to contain syntactic information associated with the word. Evidence suggesting the existence of lemmas comes from **tip-of-the-tongue (TOT) states** (Brown 1991), where it is possible for people to have the sensation that they know the word for a particular concept that they want to express (equivalent to having accessed a lemma) but are unable to retrieve its form. Vigliocco *et al.* (1997) showed that when speakers of Italian are in TOT states they can report the gender of the word even when they are unable to supply any phonological information, providing support for the idea that syntactic information is associated with the lemma. Levelt *et al.* (1999) provide further arguments for positing a lemma level of representation. However, this assumption has been contested by Caramazza and Miozzo (1997) on the basis of data from tip-of-the-tongue experiments and aphasics (but see Levelt *et al.* 1999: 66, for a response).

There has also been debate over whether the conceptual representations which are input to the production process should be specified in terms of sets of primitive features or in terms of lexical concepts which bear a one-to-one relationship to lemmas. Levelt *et al.* (1999) favour the non-decompositional approach on both theoretical and empirical grounds. They argue that 'lexical concepts form the terminal vocabulary of the speaker's message construction' (1999: 8). This implies that a good deal of language-specific conceptual processing needs to be done to package the intended message in such a way that it can be fed to the production process; what Slobin (1996) referred to as 'thinking for speaking'.

At the level of form retrieval, there is convincing evidence that the phonological form of a word is not simply retrieved as a whole unit, but rather that it is constructed, or 'spelled out', by inserting sub-syllabic units into syllabic frames (Levelt 1989; Levelt *et al.* 1999). **Speech error data** have traditionally provided the strongest evidence for this assumption. When sounds exchange between two words, they invariably occupy the same position in the syllable structure of the word, as for example in *mell wade* (exchange of onsets from *well made*), *bud beggs* (exchange of syllable nuclei from *bed bugs*), *god to seen* (exchange of codas in *gone to seed*). Although it may seem inefficient to construct the form of words when those forms are already lexically represented, Levelt *et al.* (1999) point out that this is necessary to cope with the fact that, in continuous speech, syllabification does not always respect lexical boundaries; that is, the syllable structure of words in citation form does not always correspond to their syllable structure in continuous speech. As regards the types of unit which fill the slots in syllabic frames, the fact that exchanges of phonological features can also occur (as in the voicing exchange which underlies *glear plue sky* for *clear blue sky*) suggests that abstract,

and possibly underspecified, phonological representations are involved.

It is generally assumed that the formulation processes underlying sentence production can be divided into two stages (Garrett 1990). In the first stage, the intended message is used to select relevant lemmas, and these are inserted into a representation of the functional argument structure of the sentence to form what Garrett refers to as the 'functional level representation'. Speech errors such as *This spring has a seat in it* (for *This seat has a spring in it*), where the exchanged words are of the same grammatical category, can be interpreted as errors in the assignment of words to slots in the functional level representation. In the second stage, syntactic encoding procedures generate a syntactic planning frame which contains slots for the content words specified in the functional representation. These slots also carry diacritic markers for tense and number, and so on. The phonological forms of the relevant lemmas are then inserted into the relevant slots in the planning frame. This explains why, when words exchange, they are appropriately inflected for the position they occupy in the syntactic structure (as in *I'd hear one if I knew* it for *I'd know one if I heard it*). Kempen and Hoenkamp (1987) present a model of sentence production which respects these general distinctions, while stressing the incremental nature of sentence production.

Process and architecture

The two main models of the production of single words are Dell's (1986) **Interactive Activation model** and Levelt *et al.*'s (1999) **WEAVER model**. There are two main differences between these models. First, Dell allows information to flow bidirectionally between levels (as in the McClelland and Rumelhart 1981 model of word recognition), whereas Levelt *et al.* only allow activation to flow from higher to lower levels in a feed-forward network. Second, whereas Dell achieves the binding between phonemes and structural positions through control of timing, Levelt *et al.*'s model achieves this through a checking operation. However, both models assume that there is competition between lemmas in lexical selection, consistent with evidence obtained by Wheeldon and Monsell (1994), as well as picture–word interference studies such as those reported by Schreifers *et al.* (1990). The latter studied the effects of auditorily presented distracter words on picture naming times, and found that semantically related distracters (e.g. *goat* for a picture of a sheep) produced interference (slower picture naming times) if they occurred just prior to presentation of the picture. The distracter word can be thought of as increasing the activation of a lemma that competes for selection with that corresponding to the target picture. However, whereas the Dell model allows competing, but not selected, lemmas also to activate their phonological form, the Levelt *et al.* model does not, because they assume a more serial processing architecture. Peterson and Savoy (1998) and Jescheniak and Schreifers (1997) have found evidence for phonological activation of non-selected lemmas, provided they are synonyms of the picture name (e.g. *soda* interferes with production of *couch*), a result which supports the interactive activation model (although see Levelt *et al.* 1999 for discussion). Another feature of the interactive activation approach is that, once a lemma has activated phonological representations, these can then back-activate lemmas of similar-sounding words. This assumption permits an elegant explanation of the higher-than-chance incidence of speech errors, where the produced word is both semantically and phonologically related to the intended word (e.g. *rat* for *cat*). The phonological form of *cat* activates the lemmas for phonologically similar words such as *rat*, *bat*, *mat* and so on, but, since the *rat* lemma is already partially active because it is similar to the

intended message, it has a greater probability of being produced than the others. However, Levelt *et al.* (1999) argue that there may be alternative explanations for the prevalence of mixed errors. For example, a self-monitoring mechanism (the properties of which are described by Levelt (1989)) might be less likely to detect, and prevent, a speech error that is broadly related to the context.

The debate over the appropriate processing architecture for word production continues, but it is worth noting that this mirrors that between interactive activation models of spoken-word recognition (McClelland and Elman 1986) and the Cohort Model (Marslen-Wilson 1989), in that, while the former permits activation from the lexical level to filter down to sublexical levels of representation in recognition, the latter only permits an upward flow of activation from lower to higher levels. At the same time, both of these models of spoken-word recognition stress multiple activation and competition between representational elements. This is a general theme which as we have seen runs through work on visual word recognition, word reading, syntactic processing and language production, and reflects the dominant way of thinking about psychological processes in modern psycholinguistics.

J.N.W.

Suggestions for further reading

Garrod, S. and Pickering, M. (1999) *Language Processing*, Hove: Psychology Press.

Gernsbacher, M.A. (1994) *Handbook of Psycholinguistics*, San Diego: Academic Press.

Harley, T.A. (1995) *The Psychology of Language: From Data to Theory*, Hove: Psychology Press.

Levelt, P. (1989) *Speaking: From Intention to Articulation*, Cambridge, MA: MIT Press.

R

Rhetoric

Introduction

In ancient Greece, a **rhetor** was a speaker skilled in addressing the law courts and large gatherings of people in order to persuade, and **rhetoric** originates from the theory or study of how, by means of what linguistic devices, a speaker or writer (since speeches are typically written) might best achieve this aim. Rhetoric is still studied as a subject in its own right in American universities, although the emphasis on persuasion occasionally gives way to one on appropriate expression in and organization of composition (though the two are, of course, not mutually exclusive). For instance, Baker (1973) provides chapters on thesis, structure, paragraphs, evidence, writing good sentences, correcting bad sentences, punctuation, words, the research paper, and appendices on a writer's grammar, spelling and capitalization, and a glossary of usage. On the other hand, Skwire (1985: 1) advises his intended student readers: *'Whenever possible, think of your writing as a form of persuasion'* (italics in original).

Rhetoric does not figure as a named course on the curricula of British universities, but students are, of course, still taught how to produce the type of essay appropriate to their subject. In addition, there are aspects of all discourse studies, such as stylistics, conversational analysis, discourse analysis, text linguistics, contrastive rhetoric (see below) and critical linguistics, which might be seen as falling under rhetoric; certainly, all these subject areas have their roots in it. Finally, 'rhetoric' remained a technical term in literary critical theory in the twentieth century, with Richards (1936: 23) defining it as the 'study of verbal understanding and misunderstanding' and Booth (1961: preface) calling it the study of 'the author's means of controlling his readers'.

Background and development

The best-known ancient rhetorician is probably Aristotle (384–322 BC), who developed his theory of prose style in his *Rhetoric*, and that of poetic style in *Poetics*. However, Aristotle built on a fairly long tradition of interest in effective language use. The earliest surviving formalized manifestation of this interest is the Sicilian Corax's handbook of rhetoric. Together with Tisias, Corax drew up a teachable system and set of rules for dealing with questions arising during civil lawsuits which Sicilian citizens returning to Sicily after the expulsion of the Tyrants (467 BC) instigated in order to reclaim their property. Corax's handbook deals chiefly with the **structure** of a speech, which he saw as divisible into three or five parts. A three-part speech would contain: the **exordium**, in which the situation would be described; the **arguments**, both constructive and refutative; and an **epilogue**, summing up what had gone before and drawing conclusions. A five-part speech would contain in addition a **narrative** after the exordium, and **auxiliaries**, which were subsidiary aids to the speech.

Tisias taught Gorgias of Leontini (*c.* 483–375 BC), whose main interest was in style rather than subject matter of a speech, and whose emphasis was therefore on ornamental, poetic diction, using unusual compounds, figures of speech, and symmetrical patterns of clauses and longer stretches of speech, which give a metre-like quality to his prose.

It is fairly obvious that it is possible to speak effectively and persuasively without speaking truthfully, and the sophist Protagoras (*c.* 485–415 BC) explicitly taught his pupils, who were fee-paying, to argue cases from opposing points of view, and also how to make a weak case appear stronger. Some of the Platonic dialogues, in particular the *Gorgias*, criticize this activity for providing merely a means to instil in an audience certain **beliefs**, which may be true or false, rather than a way to **knowledge** of the truth. Aristotle, however, points out that all good and useful things, with the exception of virtue itself, may be abused; the fault lies not in the thing itself, but in those who abuse it. The Platonic objection to rhetoric survives in the popular definition of rhetoric as unnecessarily flowery language, employed to mislead or to avoid answering a question straightforwardly.

Aristotle's *Rhetoric* was written about 330 BC and is divided into three books. The first deals with the nature of rhetorical proofs, the second with the nature of psychological proofs, and the third with style and arrangement. I shall only deal with the latter in detail here, since it is questions of style and arrangement which chiefly occupy present-day linguists; all references to the

Rhetoric are to the J.H. Freese translation in the Loeb Classical Library series (London, William Heinemann, 1926).

In Book I (1.2), rhetoric is defined as 'the faculty of discovering the possible means of persuasion in reference to any subject whatever'. It falls within the province of dialectic, since it is concerned with matters of common knowledge rather than with any particular science and, since a rhetorical proof is a type of syllogism, the **enthymeme**. It differs from dialectic, however, in that an enthymeme deals with the uncertain domain of human actions and events in the real world, whereas a logical syllogism deals with certainties. Nevertheless, since the form of enthymeme and syllogism are identical, skill in syllogistic reasoning is invaluable for a rhetorician. In addition to enthymeme, a rhetorician may use **examples** drawn either from things that have actually taken place, or from her/his own imagination.

In Book III (I.1), Aristotle points out that 'it is not sufficient to know what one ought to say, but one must also know how to say it'. He is of the opinion that a distinction must be drawn between poetic style (which he deals with in the *Poetics*) and prose style. Poetic style, such as that of *Gorgias*, is inappropriate to prose because it is artificial and 'that which is natural persuades, but the artificial does not' (III.II.4). Prose should be clear and should not differ too much from everyday talk: 'if a speaker manages well, there will be something "foreign" about his speech, while possibly the art may not be detected, and his meaning will be clear' (III.II.6). Metaphor and simile are the chief means of achieving foreignness and clarity, but they must not be too far-fetched, and they should be 'derived from what is beautiful either in sound, or in signification, or to sight, or to some other sense' (III.II.13). In addition, a prose writer or speaker may use epithets (adjectives) and diminutives (e.g. *cloaklet* for *cloak*), but again, 'one must be careful to observe the due mean in their use' (III.II.25).

The due mean lies between poetic style and what Aristotle calls frigidity of style. Frigidity of style arises from four causes: the use of compounds, strange words, too many or overlong or unnecessary epithets, and metaphors and similes that are inappropriate because they are ridiculous, too dignified or too far-fetched.

According to Aristotle, 'that which is written should be easy to read or easy to utter' (III.V.6). This ease will depend on what Aristotle terms **purity**. Purity, he says, is the foundation of style, and it depends on five rules. The first is to make proper use of connecting particles; the second is to employ special, not generic terms; the third is to avoid using ambiguous terms; the fourth is to keep the genders (masculine, feminine and neuter) distinct; and the fifth is to observe the number system. Obviously, the fourth rule would not apply to English, which does not have grammatical gender, but the fifth would, since English has a distinction between singular and plural.

The style of prose should not be **continuous**, by which is meant 'that which has no end in itself and only stops when the sense is complete. It is unpleasant, because it is endless, for all wish to have the end in sight' (III.IX.2). Rather, the style should be **periodic**, where by period is meant 'a sentence that has a beginning and end in itself and a magnitude that can be easily grasped' (III.IX.3). Much of what Aristotle has to say about style is not directly relevant to modern English, since it is based on the sound patterns and grammatical structure of ancient Greek, and since the contexts and subject matters which largely determine appropriateness of style are no longer applicable. Interestingly, however, the **arrangement** of the speech is not so far removed from the conventions of many genres of modern English writing – in particular, polemical academic articles (see GENRE ANALYSIS) and political speeches.

Aristotle points out that a speech must have two parts, because 'it is necessary to state the subject, and then to prove it' (III.XIII.1). The first part is therefore called the **statement of the case**, and the second, the **proof**. In addition to these, he allows that there may be an **exordium** at the beginning and an **epilogue** at the end, both of which are merely aids to memory. Any refutation of an opponent that there may be is part of the proof, and so is comparison for the purpose of amplifying one's own argument.

In the exordium, 'the speaker should say at once whatever he likes, give the key-note and then attach the main subject' (III.XIV.1), which is to be approached in the statement of the case, or **narrative**. The statements of the case may consist of clearing oneself of disagreeable suspicion; contesting disputed points; excusing oneself by 'saying that it was a case of error, misfortune, or necessity' (III.XV.3); counterattacking the accuser; appealing to previous cases; attacking slander; and many more. Proofs concern four types of disputed points – namely facts, harm done, degree of harm done and justification. Proofs are most effective if they are refutative of an opponent's position rather then merely demonstrative of one's own position. After all an opponent's or opponents' positions have been refuted, one can state one's own case. Finally, in the epilogue, one does four things in each of its four parts: dispose the hearer favourably towards oneself and unfavourably towards the adversary; amplify and depreciate; excite the emotions of the hearer; and recapitulate.

The Greek and Roman tradition of rhetoric influences our views of writing and speaking (see 'Contrastive rhetoric' below) via its place as one of the seven liberal arts on the medieval school curriculum, and readers may consult Howes (1961) and Bailey (1965) for examples of the writings on rhetoric from Aristotle to Joos, and Love and Payne (1969) for a number of influential articles on rhetoric written during the 1950s and 1960s. In particular, it is interesting to note a persistent interest in defining different styles appropriate for different purposes, as this relates directly to modern theories of non-regionally defined (non-dialectal) linguistic variation.

Thus Quintilian (*c.* 35–100) in *Institutio Oratoria* differentiates, with subdivisions possible in finer and finer detail, three correct styles of speaking: plain, grand or forcible, and intermediate or florid. **Plain style** is for purposes of instruction. **Intermediate style** is for charming or conciliating an audience – it will make more use of metaphor and digressions and will 'be neat in rhythm and pleasing in its reflexions; its flow, however, will be gentle, like that of a river whose waters are clear, but overshadowed by the green banks on either side'. **Grand style** is for moving an audience, and is likened to 'some great torrent that rolls down rocks . . . and carves out its banks for itself'. It is exalted by amplification and rises 'even to hyperbole' (i.e. overstatement) (Bailey 1965: 102–3).

According to Joos (1961), writing much later, there are five styles:

- **Frozen**, which is 'a style for print and for declamation . . . defined by the absence of authoritative intonation . . . as also by the fact that the reader or hearer is not permitted to cross-question the author'. It is a style 'for people who are to remain social strangers' (Bailey 1965: 297–8).
- **Formal style**, which is 'designed to inform' (Bailey 1965: 296) and which is characterized by detachment and cohesion. It differs from consultative style in disallowing audience participation.
- **Consultative style**, the two defining features of which are (a) that the speaker supplies background information (b) while the hearer participates continuously. 'Because of these two features, consultative style is our norm for coming to terms with strangers – people who speak our

language but whose personal stock of information may be different' (Bailey 1965: 290).
- **Casual style**, which is used with friends and acquaintances, when background information does not need to be supplied since it is already shared. Its two defining features are ellipsis and slang.
- **Intimate style** which excludes public information.

The interest in features of situational context as a major stylistic variable, which is evident in Joos, was present from the beginning of rhetorical study; Aristotle emphasizes that a speaker must be aware of which type of audience s/he is addressing, and that her/his style must vary accordingly. When, in the 1950s and 1960s the term **stylistics** began to gain currency (see STYLISTICS), the term 'rhetoric' tended to be retained by writers concentrating mainly on structural features of texts, excluding situational context. There are two major trends which retain the term 'rhetoric' in their designations, and which will therefore be dealt with briefly in this entry. One of these trends is known as **generative rhetoric**; the other, as **contrastive rhetoric**.

Generative rhetoric

Generative rhetoric developed under the influence of Noam Chomsky (see GENERATIVE GRAMMAR) in the late 1950s and 1960s. It stands in opposition to what Ohmann (1959: 1) calls the **organicist position**, according to which a difference in form always entails a difference in meaning. Chomsky had insisted that one common underlying deep structure was shared by, for instance, a sentence in the active voice, like *The cat ate the mouse*, and another sentence in the passive voice, such as *The mouse was eaten by the cat*. And, since it seemed to generative rhetoricians that the concept of style could only make sense on the assumption that the same thing could be said in different forms, i.e. that one meaning could be expressed using different styles of expression, the new grammar appeared to them to offer the first valid theoretical foundation for stylistic analysis. Generative rhetoric took over the transformationalists' framework for dealing with sentences. Thus Katz and Foder (1963) claim that

> except for a few types of cases, discourse can be treated as a single sentence in isolation by regarding sentence boundaries as sentential connectives. As a matter of fact, this is the natural treatment. In the great majority of cases, the sentence break in discourse is simply *and*-conjunction. (In others, it is *but*, *for*, *or*, and so on.)

In addition, it is possible to see the agents and states and processes of the agents of whole texts (whether or not it is seen as a single sentence) as surface realizations of deep-structure nouns and verbs. The framework for sentences of transformational grammar (TG) is displayed in the following way by Fowler (1977: 28):

> a **sentence** has a **surface structure**
> formed by **transformations** of a
> **semantic deep structure** consisting of a
> **modality** component plus a **propositional**
> component
> the latter based on a
> **predicate** attended by one or more **nouns**
> in different **roles**

As Fowler points out, a theory that narrative plot can be reduced to a series of stock nouns and verbs – easily interpreted as constituting a deep structure of the narrative – had already been developed by the French structuralists, largely based on Propp's analyses of Russian folk tales. According to Propp (1928/1958), the nouns are realized as characters such as **hero**, **dispatcher**, **villain**, **helper**, **donor**, **sought-for person**, **false hero**, and the verbs as functions of these, such as **absentation**, **reconnaissance**,

trickery, **departure**, **provision** or **receipt of a magical agent**, **pursuit** (see Fowler 1977: 29). Although these categories are probably specific to the folk tale, it is not difficult to see how texts in general may be reduced to sequences of verbs and nouns representing agents and states and actions of them. When we summarize a text, we report the sequences of events (verbs) undergone by the agents (nouns). In moving to look at the structure of whole texts, generative rhetoric has developed into what is often known as **text linguistics** (see TEXT LINGUISTICS). It should, however, be noted that TG has also been employed for the purpose of carrying out stylistic analysis (its methods are discussed in more detail in the entry in this volume on STYLISTICS; (see also CRITICAL LINGUISTICS/CRITICAL DISCOURSE ANALYSIS).

Contrastive rhetoric

The discipline of **contrastive rhetoric** is based on the notion, propounded by Sapir and Whorf in the first half of the twentieth century, that the different grammars of different languages reflect differences in the habitual patterns of thought of their speakers (see LINGUISTIC RELATIVITY). Linguists working on contrastive rhetoric, such as Diane Houghton in Britain and Robert Kaplan in the USA, employ a modified version of this hypothesis, according to which each culture at any particular time adheres to certain 'canons of taste' (Kaplan 1966: 2), which determine a popular notion of how argument ought to be structured. This popular notion is called a discourse rhetoric. Thus, for instance (Houghton and Hoey 1982: 9),

> the English language and its related thought patterns derive from the Greco-Roman tradition, modified by medieval European and later western thinkers. At the macrodiscourse level this produces what Kaplan calls a dominant linear paragraph organization which, in

an expository paragraph, typically begins with a topic statement followed by a series of subdivisions of the topic statement, each supported by example and illustration. A central idea thus developed is related to every other idea in the essay and used as a proof or argument. . . . Conversely, other languages show a different, less linear or non-linear organization at the macro-level, and Kaplan attempts to prove this by a mixture of analysis of texts from other languages, and by identification of non-linear patterns in the work of non-native speakers writing formal essays in English. He concludes that such students need specific help in learning to write appropriately in English, and gives examples of specimen materials designed for this purpose.

The notion of intercultural rhetorical differences and the problems associated with it are discussed by Houghton (1980), who also gives an account of a variety of studies in the area.

K.M.

Suggestions for further reading

Bailey, D. (ed.) (1965) *Essays on Rhetoric*, New York: Oxford University Press.

Burton, G. (1996–2001) *The Forest of Rhetoric: Silva Rhetoricae*, Humanities. byu.edu/Rhetoric/silva.HTM

Connor, U.M. (1996) *Contrastive Rhetoric: Cross-cultural Aspects of Second-language Writing*, Cambridge: Cambridge University Press.

Howes, R.F. (ed.) (1961) *Historical Studies of Rhetoric and Rhetoricians*, Ithaca, NY: Cornell University Press.

Love, G. and Payne, M. (1969) *Contemporary Essays on Style: Rhetoric, Linguistics, and Criticism*, Glenville, IL: Scott, Foresman and Co.

S

Semantics

Introduction

Semantics is the study of linguistic meaning, and is the area of linguistics which is closest to the philosophy of language. The main difference between the linguist's and the philosopher's way of dealing with the question of meaning is that the linguist tends to concentrate on the way in which meaning operates in language, while the philosopher is more interested in the nature of meaning itself – in particular, in the relationship between the linguistic and the non-linguistic. Since the 1980s, however, linguists have become increasingly interested in the phenomenon of **deixis** – the way in which participants in linguistic encounters relate what they say to the time, place and participants in the discourse; in other words, in exactly the relationship between language and what it is about that has long exercised philosophers of language (see PHILOSOPHY OF LANGUAGE).

Unfortunately, it is not easy to endow the term 'meaning' with the type of precise definition we may feel that the term for the grammarian's topic of investigation, 'structure', is capable of. We are fairly clear about what structure is – it is the way in which various pieces of something are put together. Every time, in whatever connection, the term 'structure' is used in English, we know that it has this same type of meaning – it has to do with how something is put together to form a whole. A body has structure; a car's engine has structure; a molecule has structure. But the term 'meaning' and its associates, 'mean', 'means', etc. are used in a variety of ways in naturally occurring English. Lyons (1977b: 1–2) and Palmer (1981: 3) between them offer examples like the following:

(1) I didn't mean to drop the brick on your foot
(2) She meant to become a solicitor
(3) He means well, but he always makes a mess of things

In each of these cases, what seems to be at issue is a person's intentions to do something; cases like these are not examples of the sense of 'meaning' we are interested in as semanticists. Nor are cases like

(4) Her life lost all meaning with the disappearance of the cat
(5) Money means nothing to a true sportsman

where the topic seems to be what is of importance to someone. In neither type of case is the term 'meaning' being used with reference to any linguistic aspect of the situation.

Compare these to the following:

(6) Those black clouds mean rain
(7) Those spots mean chickenpox

Again, no linguistic aspects are essentially involved in the relationships set up between features of the two situations. But they differ from the previous five situations in that it is possible here to perceive a relationship of **signification** between black clouds, on the one hand, and rain on the other, and between spots and chickenpox. Cases like these, therefore, fall under **semiotics**, the study of signs and signification (see SEMIOTICS), but they are too general to be studied in semantics, where it is *linguistic* meaning in particular which is of interest.

Now compare these cases with

(8) The red light means 'stop'

Here we are beginning to approach more closely what we want, because in this case a linguistic expression, the quoted word 'stop', is part of the subject matter of the utterance. In addition, there is no natural connection between a red light and the word *stop* as there is between clouds and rain and spots and chickenpox. The red light gets its meaning purely by convention among humans, and is a case of **non-natural meaning** (Grice 1957). Linguists (and philosophers of language), as opposed to semioticians, are interested only in non-natural meaning.

The traffic-light case is very like cases of dictionary definition, where the meaning of one term is given by other terms. In such cases, the terms 'meaning' and 'means' are used to say things like

(9) What is the meaning of 'semantics'?
(10) *Bachelor* means 'unmarried man'
(11) *Ungkarl* means 'bachelor'
(12) *Rot* means 'rød'

Clearly the study of this type of meaning falls within semantics, because the theory of linguistic meaning must explain the relationships between the various parts of language and languages. But it is insufficient in and for itself to constitute the subject matter of the discipline. Consider case (12) and, by implication, cases (11) and

(10). To a monolingual English speaker enquiring after the meaning of the German word *rot*, a reply like (12) would be of no use at all. To such a speaker enquiring after the meaning of the Danish word *ungkarl*, a reply like (11) would be useful only if s/he already knew what *bachelor* meant. And (10) is illuminating only to someone who already knows the meaning of one of the terms given.

In other words, dictionary definitions are circular – all the terms in a dictionary are defined by other terms in the dictionary (unless illustrations are used). Definitions like these say what terms *mean the same as*. Semanticists in general wish to break out of the definition circularity; they want, so to speak, to be able to remove the quotation marks from one of the terms in the definition, to gain an extralinguistic foothold – something which can function as the semantic coin.

There is one further usage of 'meaning' in English which ought to be mentioned here:

(13) He never means what he says
(14) She never says what she means

In these cases, an opposition is set up between what a speaker means and what her/his words mean. Cases of this kind are covered in detail in the entry on SPEECH-ACT THEORY, but it is worth mentioning here that if it is true that speakers can mean something other than their words seem to suggest, and if we are able to discover this, then we must, first, have a reasonably good grasp of the meaning of the words; otherwise we could hardly come to feel that their meaning was inappropriate in some cases.

Sense relations

Let us begin by seeing how far it is possible to get in semantics by concentrating on relationships between words. Several such relationships can be set up, and we can, in addition, discover relationships between sentences. Such relationships are commonly known as **sense relations** (see LEXIS AND LEXICOLOGY).

On the assumption that we understand how negation works, it will seem obvious to anybody that if a proposition, *P*, is true, then its negation, *it is not the case that P*, which we shall symbolize as ¬P, must be false. When two propositions stand in this relationship to each other, we say that the sentences expressing them **contradict** each other. We can also apply this knowledge of how negation works to a study of predicates. It is possible to produce two sentences that are contradictions of each other by simply negating the predicate of a sentence in another, otherwise identical, sentence. For instance, if *Thomas is a tank engine* is true, then *Thomas is not a tank engine* is false. Of course, the opposite holds as well – if an un-negated sentence is false, then its negation will be true. Any predicate will behave in this way when negated in one of two otherwise identical simple sentences; a fact which is, in itself not terribly exciting.

However, it seems that there are pairs of terms in natural language which behave in just the same way as predicates and their negations with respect to the ways in which they affect the truth and falsity of sentences in which they are used. Consider:

male – female
dead – alive
true – untrue
true – false
married – unmarried

It seems that if *Kim is male* is true, then *Kim is female* is as definitely and obviously false as *Kim is not male* would be; and if it is true that Kim is not male, then it must also be true that Kim is female. But, of course, the predicates *is male* and *is female* can only operate in this way if the individual of whom they are predicated is one of which it makes sense to say that it is

male or female. If Kim is a stone, then it does not follow from the fact that Kim is not male that Kim is female. Stones, houses, tables, and so on do not fall within the **semantic field** of gendered things.

However, within specific, appropriately delineated, semantic fields, we can call predicate pairs like those above **binary** or **complementary antonyms**. These produce sentences which are contradictions of each other when one of the pair is substituted for the other in a sentence. Linguistically, we can distinguish two ways in which the contrast between two antonyms may be realized, as the list above shows: either the graphological (and phonological) form of each member of the pair is distinct from that of the other, or they share a form but one member has a prefix such as *un-*. When there are distinct forms, we call the contrast **equipollent contrast**; when the basic form is shared and a prefix added to one member of the pair, we talk of **privative contrast**.

True binary antonyms such as the ones I have listed are, in principle, ungradable: something is either alive or dead, either male or female, either married or unmarried. One thing cannot be more dead than another, more male than another, more married than another, and so on. So when these terms appear in a simple subject–predicate sentence, the sentence has a very special relationship with a restricted set of other sentences. If

Socrates is dead

is true, then

Socrates is alive

is false

Socrates is not alive

is true, and

Socrates is not dead

is false. From the truth or falsity of any one of the sentences in the set, we can **infer** the truth or falsity of each of the other three; the truth or falsity of any one of them is **entailed** by the truth or falsity of any one of the others. **Entailment**, like **contradiction**, discussed above, is a relationship that may obtain between sentences, in virtue of the relationships between some of the terms used in the sentences.

Some sentences are true and false in a special way:

Anyone dead is dead
Anyone alive is alive

are **tautologies**, **tautologically true**, **necessarily true**, **logically true**, **true in all possible worlds**, **true a priori**, **truths of reason**; we can see immediately that they are true. Correspondingly,

Anyone dead is not dead
Anyone alive is not alive

are **contradictions**, **necessarily false**, **logically false**, **false in all possible worlds**, **false a priori**; we can see immediately that they are false. In contrast,

Anyone alive is not dead
Anyone dead is not alive

are true by virtue of the sense relations between the predicates in them and

Anyone dead is alive
Anyone alive is dead

are false by virtue of the sense relations between the predicates in them. These are called **analytic truths** and **analytic falsehoods**.

Most sentences, of course, are dependent on the state of the world for their truth and falsehood; for instance, *Socrates is dead* is true because of how things are in the world, and *Socrates is alive* is false because of the way things are in the world. Such sentences are true or false **contingently**, **synthetically**, **a posteriori**.

So far, the binary antonyms we have dealt with have been ungradable. Other pairs, such as

fast – slow
high – low
sweet – sour

are applicable to things in a more-or-less manner. These are called **gradable binary antonyms**, and we can recognize them by the fact that they can be modified by *very* and *how*. It is quite coincidental that there are no linguistic realizations of the stages intermediate between the pairs of terms. In some cases, indeed, some of the intermediate stages are realized, as in the case of

hot – warm – cool – cold

These, and the gradable binary antonyms, can be modelled as being situated at opposite ends of a continuum. As far as their effect on sentences in which they occur as predicates is concerned, they behave like the members of sets of **mutually exclusive** or **incompatible** terms, terms from semantic fields like 'days of the week', 'months of the year', 'animals', and so on. They differ in their effects on sentences from binary antonyms in that we cannot infer from the falsehood of a sentence containing one of the predicates from a field the truth of another sentence differing from the first only in containing one of the other predicates. We cannot infer from the fact that *It is Monday* is false the truth of any particular one of the other possibilities – though we will know that one of them must be true; the point is that we do not know *which* one. We can, of course, infer from the truth of any one of the sentences – say, *It is Sunday* – the falsehood of all the others.

So far, we have confined discussion to one-place predicates (see SET THEORY), and thus to sentences containing one predicate and one referring term. When we start looking at two-place predicates, we shall be dealing with sentences containing one predicate and two referring terms. It is then possible to identify some properties that such predicates have, by looking at the forms of relationship between the referring terms that are set up by means of the predicate which links them. Some two-place predicates, for example, are **symmetric**; we know that if

a is married to b

then

b is married to a

We shall say of any predicate, R, which satisfies the formulation (see FORMAL LOGIC AND MODAL LOGIC),

$$\forall x \forall y \ (xRy \rightarrow yRx)$$

that is, 'for all x and for all y if x stands in relation R to y, then y stands in relation R to x', that it is symmetric.

Other predicates are **transitive**. We know that if

a is in front of b

and

b is in front of c

then

a is in front of c

We shall say of any predicate that satisfies the formulation

$$\forall x \forall y \forall z \ ((xRy \ \& \ yRz) \rightarrow (xRz))$$

that is, 'for all x and for all y and for all z, if x stands in relation R to y, and y stands in relation R to z, then x stands in relation R to z', that it is transitive.

Some two-place predicates are such that the relation they set up between the individuals in the sentence indicates that another, converse relation also holds between those individuals. Thus, we know that if

a is a parent of b

then

b is a child of a

We shall say of any pair of predicates which satisfy the formulation

$$\forall x \forall y \ (xRy \rightarrow yR'x)$$

that is, 'for all x and for all y, if x stands in relation R to y, then y stands in relation R' to x', that they are converse or **relational opposites** of each other.

Two predicates are said to be **synonymous** when it is impossible to alter the truth value of a sentence containing one of them by substituting it for the other (there are problems with this definition, but we shall not address them; see Quine 1951/1961). The relation of synonymy has quite a complex logical form, in so far as specifying it involves saying not only that 'all Fs are Gs' but also that 'all Gs are Fs'; not only are all bachelors unmarried men, but in addition, all unmarried men are bachelors. So two predicates, P and R, are synonymous if they satisfy the formulation

$$\forall x \ ((Px \rightarrow Rx) \ \& \ (Rx \rightarrow Px))$$

That is, 'for all x, if x is P then x is R, and if x is R then x is P'.

If only one of the conjuncts in the proposition above holds, then we have a relationship of **hyponymy** between the two predicates. If a particular semantic field has a name, then that name is a **superordinate term** with respect to all the terms for the items that are contained in the field in question, and these terms will all be hyponyms of the superordinate term. In relation to each other, they are **co-hyponyms**. So *animal* is the superordinate term for terms like *lion*, *tiger*, *horse*, *dog*, *cat* and so on, and all of these are co-hyponyms of each other. There are hierarchies of hyponyms; for instance, *plant* is a superordinate term having as hyponyms, at one level, *tree*, *flower*, *bush*, *vegetable*. These terms are themselves superordinate with respect to other terms. For instance, *flower* is a superordinate term having as its own hyponyms *tulip*, *rose*, *violet*, etc.; but these are also hyponyms of *plant*. Generally speaking, when the relationship of hyponymy holds between two English nouns, *x* and *y*, it is possible to state the relationship in terms of the formulation x is a kind of y

The logical form of the hyponymy relationship is

$$\forall x \, (Fx \rightarrow Gx)$$

If we are trying to set up a systematic theory of meaning for a language, then the hyponymy relationship is clearly going to be one of the most useful sense relations. If we could start with some very basic term, B, and place it in a universally quantified proposition:

$$\forall x \, (Bx \rightarrow Cx)$$

where C is either an equally basic or slightly more complex term, and if we could then place C in a similar proposition with another term, D, etc., then we could eventually build up a systematic account of the meanings of a large number of the terms in our language. Alternatively, we could start with the most general term we can think of, and then work our way down to the most particular terms in our language, terms which we might think of as being in direct contact with the world. In either case, the problem is going to lie in establishing what the most simple, particular terms are, how they are connected to the world, and what aspects of the world they are connected to. The componential theory of meaning tries to break terms down to their component parts in this manner, and will be examined below.

There are some predicates in the language which can be used to express more than one proposition; these are the **ambiguous** predicates. Ambiguity is a property of predicates which will affect sentences in such a way that those sentences in which the predicates are used will be capable of two quite different interpretations. For example, *James was looking carefully at the coach* has an interpretation under which James is observing a large vehicle and another under which he is observing a person.

Ambiguous words or phrases have more than one extension (set of things they denote) and these extensions comprise quite different things or phenomena. This means that an ambiguous sentence has more than one potential set of quite different, unrelated truth conditions at any one time that it is being used (Quine 1960: 131). Usually properly ambiguous words or phrases will be given one entry for each of their extensions in a dictionary. For instance, there will typically be individual entries for each of the meanings of *coach*, *trunk*, *fall* and *lift*.

If ambiguity pertains to both the spoken and written form of a term, as in the case of *bank*, the term is said to be **homonymous**. If ambiguity pertains to the spoken form only, the two differently written forms are said to be **homophones**: *site–sight*; *rite–right*; *there–their*. If, on the other hand, terms are only ambiguous when written down, they are said to be **homographs**. An example would be *lead*, which may denote either a dog's lead or the metal, lead.

An ambiguous predicate such as *is light* may produce a sentence which is at once clearly true and clearly false, when predicated of an object. For example, if we predicate *is light* of a dark feather, then the sentence *this feather is light* is clearly true in the weight sense of *light*, and clearly false in the colour sense. Sometimes the ambiguity of a word is resolved by the rest of a sentence that contains it; thus *light* is generally taken to mean *not heavy* when followed by *as a feather*. When the ambiguity of a term infects the containing sentence, as in *our mothers bore us*, it can sometimes be resolved by the surrounding discourse (Quine 1960: 129).

There are some types of word that are systematically ambiguous. For example, some verbal nouns display systematic ambiguity between process and product. The form *utterance* can cause much disquiet in linguistics because it is ambiguous between the act of uttering and the utterance thereby produced. The form *assignment* can be used to refer to the act of assigning or to the thing assigned; *arrangement* to the act of arranging or to the things arranged; *shopping* can refer to the act of shopping or to the things bought. Other verbal nouns display ambiguity between action and custom, as in *skater*, which can refer to one who is skating now (and therefore has to be awake, for instance), or to one who often skates (but may at this very moment be asleep) (Quine 1960: 130).

The examples discussed so far have been examples of **lexical** ambiguity. However, we also often encounter what is known as **structural** ambiguity, as in *the chicken is ready to eat, visiting relatives can be a nuisance* (attributable to Chomsky) and *the police were ordered to stop drinking after midnight* (probably first used by Halliday). The different meanings of such sentences can usually be explicated by syntactic analysis.

Now, it is a fact that what looks ambiguous on paper rarely functions ambiguously in context; but it is another fact that almost any linguistic item can be used in many ways and with many functions. For this reason, it is useful to try to keep the notion of **ambiguity** apart from another property of terms, which we might prefer to call **vagueness**. Ambiguity can then be reserved for terms that have the potential, on each occasion of their use, to be both quite clearly true of what they are predicated of, and clearly false of what they are predicated of. Vague terms, on the other hand, might be said to be 'dubiously applicable to marginal objects' (Quine 1960: 129).

It is not clear, for instance, exactly how far down the spectrum towards yellow or up towards blue a thing can be and still count as green. So *green* is vague. Nor may it be clear when muddy water becomes wet mud. So *water* and *mud* are vague. It is not always clear whether something is a wood or a forest, so *wood* and *forest* are vague. It is not clear how wide or long or deep a waterway has to be to be a river rather than a stream, or a stream rather than a ditch. So *river* and *stream* and *ditch* are vague.

Furthermore, personal perception can play a part here: to someone from China, for instance, the English rivers, such as the Cam, might seem ditch-like (I am indebted to Huang Ai-Feng for this insight).

There can also be vagueness as to where items begin and end. For any mountain, for example, it is unclear where those parts of the world begin where you can be and justifiably say that you are standing on the mountain.

Some terms actually display vagueness on both counts. They can be vague both because there are marginal cases, and in terms of where their individual referents begin and end. Take the term *person*, for instance. When does x become a person? At conception? Or not until it is severed from its mother? Or at some point in between? This is the marginal-case problem. The problem of the borderline around a 'person' surfaces in the case of ingestion and digestion. When does food become part of the person – or of any organism, for that matter? (Quine 1960: 126).

Vagueness can also be said to obtain when it is unclear which of a number of possible relationships or characteristics a speaker might be intending to refer to by a term on a particular mention. Take, for example, *John's book*. The possessive/genitive here might be intended to indicate that the book in question belongs to John, was written by John, is being read by John, or has just been mentioned by John. In the case of *she has good legs*, *good* may be meant to indicate that the legs are beautiful or that they are strong or even, given a particular outlook on the world, that they are quite unremarkable. In the case of *John hit Bill*, *hit* may be being used to indicate different ways of hitting – e.g. with a flat hand, with a fist, with a club, and so on (see Kempson 1977: chapter 8).

So, most lexical items are, if not exactly strictly and systematically ambiguous, then subject to great variation in use. This can mean that the systematicity of sense relationships may seem under threat: if there is this great variation according to context and use, what kind of reality are we to suggest that sense relations have?

In fact, the circumstance that pairs of words do not always and invariably instantiate certain sense relations should not be taken as an invalidation of the theory of sense relations any more than we would expect grammatical theory to be invalidated by the fact that, e.g., no particular word always and invariably functions as, say, a noun modifier, or by the fact that we can understand e.e. cummings' poetry. What is important is our ability to make sense of discourse by means of our awareness of the possibility that (almost any pairs of) words may at various points in the discourse be placed in the types of sense relations discussed in linguistic semantics. Research into both spoken and written discourse clearly shows that we have this ability and that we use it to make sense of the discourse. The relationships may be exactly the stable phenomena which enable us to navigate with some success over the fluid vocabulary.

Componential analysis

The notion that there are some basic **meaning components** which make up the meanings of more complex terms is meant to offer a framework for handling sense relations when these are, in fact, interpreted as stable relations between particular words. Recall that we were forced above to import a notion of semantic fields before we could begin to suggest that natural language terms were capable of realizing logical relations and forms. Clearly, we must then give some justification for setting up these semantic fields in the way that we do: there must be something that all those things that we call animals have in common, something which all those things that we call tigers have in common, etc., and these features would be named by the terms that are the meaning components of **componential analysis**.

If we have these basic components, we can also avoid the problems caused by the fact that not all languages cut up the world in the same way. Many of the relationships named by natural language terms, even biological relationships, are differently realized in different languages. For instance, the relationship between cousins, biological as it may be, is not realizable in Danish by one predicate only, as it is in English. In Danish it is necessary to specify the biological gender of the cousin, too: a male cousin is a *fætter*, while a female cousin is a *kusine*. So the predicate *is a cousin of* does not exist in Danish in a form that covers both male and female cousins, and it looks as if natural language terms like *cousin, father, mother, uncle, aunt* are not basic enough to define the relationships that obtain between people, even though these relationships are universal because biological. What we seem to require is a set of **language-independent terms**, standing for the basic components of phenomena, which can be used to define the terms that are actually used in natural languages. In most English-language books on semantics, these language-independent terms are, in fact, given English forms, such as MALE and FEMALE, but it is important to note that they could, in principle, be presented as numbers or letters, say, or any kind of mark at all.

For cases like those under consideration at present, four biological relationships in which people stand to each other suggest themselves: **generation, gender, lineage, related through** (compare Palmer 1981, who does not include the fourth relationship which is, however, necessary to cope with some terms in Danish). We shall symbolize generation with the letter G, and specify which generation we are talking about by means of numbers. If *ego* is generation 0, G0, then *father* would be generation G1, *grandfather* G2, *child* G −1, etc. The gender would be two, *male* and *female*, M and F, and lineage would be of three kinds:

Table 1

Natural-language term	Generation	Sex	Lineage	Related through
mother	1	F	D	
father	1	M	D	
daughter	−1	F	D	
son	−1	M	D	
uncle	1	M	A	
aunt	1	F	A	
cousin	0	M/F	A	
kusine	0	F	A	
fætter	0	M	A	
brother	0	M	C	
sister	0	F	C	
sibling	0	M/F	C	
grandmother	2	F	D	
grandfather	2	M	D	
grandparent	2	M/F	D	
bedstemor	2	F	D	
bedstefar	2	M	D	
morfar	2	M	D	mother
mormor	2	F	D	mother
farfar	2	M	D	father
farmor	2	F	D	father

direct (child in relation to parent), D; ablineal (cousin in relation to cousin), A; co-lineal (sibling in relation to sibling), C. Related through is either mother or father, which must therefore be defined before this third category can be employed. We can now define precisely every term for a family relationship in any language by drawing up a grid like that in Table 1. Outside of grids, components are usually listed thus: *man*: +HUMAN +ADULT +MALE.

An interesting application of componential analysis is that proposed by Katz and Fodor (1963), in their attempt to account for those aspects of speakers' linguistic knowledge which transformational-generative grammar could not account for at the time. This included the knowledge:

- That identical structures can have different meanings. The grammar would assign identical structures to *the cat bit the woman* and *the dog bit the man*, and

could give no account of speakers' understanding of the differences between the expressions.

- That different structures can have identical meanings. *The cat ate the mouse* means the same as *the mouse was eaten by the cat*; yet the grammar would describe their structure differently.

- The disambiguation by parts of sentences of other parts which are non-structurally ambiguous. *The bill is large* is disambiguated if followed by *but need not be paid*.

- **Semantic anomaly**: *My typewriter has bad intentions* is perfectly formed from a structural point of view, but speakers consider it abnormal in meaning.

They classify each linguistic item syntactically with **syntactic markers**, and semantically with **semantic markers** and **distinguishers**. The semantic markers are meant to reflect **systematic** relations between an item and the rest of the vocabulary of a language,

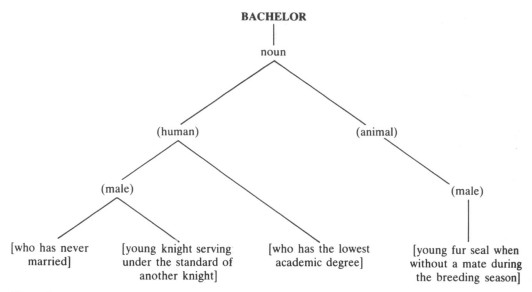

Figure 1

while distinguishers reflect what is **idiosyn-cratic** about the meaning of the term in question. A definition of the different meanings of *bachelor* would look like Figure 1 (syntactic markers are not bracketed; semantic markers are in round brackets; distinguishers are in square brackets).

The lines connecting the terms here are called 'paths'. If two terms have all their paths in common, they will be synonymous. If a term has more than one path leading from it, it is ambiguous, with one path for each possible meaning. The theory explains disambiguation as a case where all but one path for an item are precluded by other material in the sentence, and semantic anomaly as a case where every path for an item is precluded by other material in the sentence. For example, in *my typewriter has bad intentions*, *intentions* will be marked +ANIMATE, while *typewriter* will be marked –ANIMATE.

Katz and Fodor explicitly disregard setting as a source of speakers' understanding of utterances, since they believe that to take setting into account in semantic theory would force the theorist to consider '*all* the knowledge speakers have about the world'

(1963: 489), and that would make the theory far too complex. This means that the theory really does confine itself to the explication of intralinguistic relationships. Lewis (1970/ 1983: 190) remarks in this connection:

Semantic markers are *symbols*: items of an artificial language we may call *Semantic Markerese*. Semantic interpretation by means of them amounts merely to a translation algorithm from the object language to the auxiliary language Markerese. But we can know the Markerese translation of an English sentence without knowing the first thing about the meaning of the English sentence: namely, the conditions under which it would be true. Semantics with no treatment of truth conditions is not semantics. Translation into Markerese is at best a substitute for real semantics, relying either on our tacit competence (at some future date) as speakers of Markerese or on our ability to do real semantics at least for the one language Markerese. Translation into Latin might serve as well, except insofar as the designers of Markerese may choose to build into it useful features – freedom from ambiguity, grammar based on logic – that might make it easier to do real semantics for Markerese than for Latin.

No theory which concentrates exclusively on intralinguistic relationships can serve as a theory of meaning, because it offers no way into the theory in the first place (for further information on Katz and Fodor's work, see INTERPRETIVE SEMANTICS; LEXIS AND LEXICOLOGY).

Deixis

Arguably, the most important links between language and context are interpreted by speakers through the deictic systems of languages (see Fillmore 1973, 1975, 1982). In English, the deictic systems include:

- The first and second person personal pronouns, which realize **person deixis**, through which speakers anchor what they say to the participants in the speech event.
- The tense system and temporal adverbs, which realize **temporal deixis**, through which speakers relate what they say to the time at which the speech event is taking place.
- The adverbs of location, *here* and *there* and the demonstratives *this*, *that*, *those* and *these*, which realize **spatial deixis**, through which speakers situate objects relative to their own position.
- Various devices used in written text, such as *above* and *below*, which realize **discourse deixis**, through which writers orientate other parts of a text relative to the point at which the discourse deictic terms occur.

- Some writers (e.g. Levinson 1983) consider that pronoun systems in which a distinction is drawn between familiar and more formal modes of address, as in French between *tu* and *vous*, and in German between *du* and *Sie*, and the systems of address in Asian languages, which are finely discriminated according to the relative social status of speaker and addressee, realize **social deixis**, through which speakers position themselves vis-à-vis their addressees in the social hierarchy.

The deictic systems of different languages have received a great deal of attention because of the apparently universal requirements on languages to offer their speakers the opportunity to relate themselves to the world around them. It is to be expected that the limits of language variation might be drawn by such seemingly inescapable categories and that their shared cores might be identified through their study (see, for example, the *Annual Report 1995* of the Max-Planck-Institut für Psycholinguistik, Wundtlaan 1, 6525 XD Nijmegen, Holland; also Jagger and Buba 1994; Anderson and Keenan 1985).

K.M.

Suggestions for further reading

Lyons, J. (1977b) *Semantics*, 2 vols, Cambridge: Cambridge University Press.
Palmer, F.R. (1981) *Semantics*, 2nd edition, Cambridge: Cambridge University Press.
Saeed, J.I. (1997) *Semantics*, Oxford: Blackwell Publishers.

Semiotics

Semiotics or **semiotic** is the study of signs, and linguistics can be seen as that subdiscipline of semiotics which is particularly concerned with the nature of the *linguistic* sign. What is of relevance to linguistics from the discipline of semiotics are those of its conclusions about signs in general which are applicable to linguistic signs. The process of making and using signs is called **semiosis**.

The term 'semiotic' originates with the American pragmatist philosopher Charles Sanders Peirce (1839–1914), and the discipline owes most to him, although in Europe Saussure's contribution was better known for a considerable time. Saussure called the study of the life of the sign in society **semiology**, and considered the sign relation **dyadic**, consisting in the relation between a concept and a sound (see INTRODUCTION).

According to Peirce, however, the sign relation is **irreducibly triadic**. He defines a sign as (1931–58: 2.228) 'something which stands to somebody for something in some respect or capacity', and **semiosis** as (1931–58: 5.484) 'an action, or influence, which is, or involves, an operation of *three* subjects, such as a sign, its object, and its interpretant, this trirelative influence not being in any way resolvable into an action between pairs'. The process is, furthermore, potentially infinite, because the **interpretant** (the interpreting thought) is itself a sign and will therefore stand in its own triadic rela-

tion to a further interpretant (see Hookway 1985: 121) – in other words, one thought leads to another ad infinitum. It is this third dimension, preventing **closure**, an end to interpretation, which has endeared Peirce to poststructuralist and deconstructivist thinkers.

Eco (1984: 4–7) distinguishes between specific semiotics and general semiotics. A **specific semiotics** deals with a particular sign system, while **general semiotics** presents a theory of, or search for, that which is shared by all sign systems. Peirce's writings on signs is an example of general semiotics, while Halliday's (1978) work on language as social semiotic (see SYSTEMIC-FUNCTIONAL LINGUISTICS) is an example of a specific semiotics of particular interest to linguists.

As mentioned above, a sign stands for something, its **object** ('object' does not mean 'thing' in this context – it is not confined to physical entities). Signs may stand for something *to* somebody, the interpreter. But a sign only functions as such to the interpreter in virtue of the interpreter's understanding that it does so function, and this understanding is called the **interpretant**. An example is given in the figure below (see Hookway 1985: 122–4).

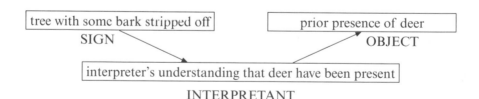

The stripped bark of the tree, which is all that the interpreter can see, gives her/him further knowledge; namely, knowledge that deer have been present, because s/he understands it as a sign of this prior presence. The sign thus brings the interpreter into cognitive contact with the deer.

Signs can be placed into three classes according to their relationship to their

object (see Peirce 1931–58: 2.249; Eco 1984: 136; Hookway 1985: 125–7):

- An **icon** is 'a sign which refers to the Object that it denotes merely by virtue of characters of its own'. Thus, because of its shape, it is conceivable that a balloon could signify a cloud; because of the configuration of the lines in it, a floor plan can signify a room; because of its colour, a colour sample can signify the colour of paint in a tin. But the balloon has its shape independently of the cloud; the floor plan has its properties independently of the room; the paint sample has its colour in and for itself. The cloud, room and paint have not actively caused the balloon, plan and colour sample to come into existence. They function as signs only because an isomorphism, a correspondence of properties, between them and their objects allows us to decide that they shall so function. In order to be able to use icons, we need to know the conventions for interpreting them, as is particularly clearly seen in the case of the floor plan, where we must know the conventions of scale, of the representation of doors and windows, and so on.

- An **index** is 'a sign which refers to the Object that it denotes by virtue of being really affected by that Object'. There is a real relation of dependency between the sign and its object, as in the case of the stripped bark and the prior presence of deer mentioned above, and in the case of illnesses and their symptoms. Less obviously, perhaps, proper names, pointing fingers and road signs are all indices – proper names because they are actively given to their bearers, pointing fingers because the placing of what they point to determine where they point, and road signs for the same reason.
- A **symbol** is 'a sign which refers to the Object that it denotes by virtue of a Law, usually an association of general ideas. . . . It is thus itself a general type.' A symbol stands in a signifying relationship with its object *only* because there exists a convention that it will be interpreted in that particular way. A flag at the beach may signify that swimming is safe; but there is neither any resemblance between the flag and the state of the tide, nor any direct causation from the tide to the flag. The only thing that qualifies the flag for signifying that swimming is safe is the general practice of using flags in this way.

Symbols are **tokens** of **types** (see Wollheim 1968: 91–3). The type itself is never encountered; only its tokens. But the type is thought of as having those properties which its tokens have *necessarily* (they may have other properties incidentally) – that is, in virtue of being tokens of that type. For instance, we have never encountered the Stars and Stripes – the type, itself – only tokens of it. These may have been made of paper, linen, painted glass, etc., and these properties would have been incidental rather than necessary for us to class the flags in question as tokens of the type Stars and Stripes. But anything that is classifiable as a token of the Stars and Stripes must necessarily have a certain set of properties: it must be red, white and blue, and must have a certain number of stripes and stars in the right spatial and colour configuration. These are the properties that we think of the type as having, and they are physical properties just as much as the tokens' incidental properties *even though the type itself is not thought of as a physical entity*.

It is useful to see linguistic items as tokens of types. Consider the linguistic item Friday. One of its tokens may look like the example just given, another may look like this: FRIDAY, yet another like this: Fríday. Or consider phonemes – we have never encountered the bilabial voiced plosive, only instances of it; yet we can say that it exists, even that it has physical properties, namely that it is bilabial, voiced and plosive. The type/token distinction is very high in explanatory value from a linguist's point of view.

Language used purposefully for communication, for **telling** (see Grice 1957), is always symbolic; but it is important to be aware that aspects of a person's language use can signify much that we would not say that s/he is actively telling others when speaking: for instance, I may become aware while listening to someone speaking that they are from Scotland, when all they are *telling* me is that they are heartily sick of linguistics. In such a case, the person's language seems to function indexically. But language also displays what appears to be iconicity: there are conventions whereby certain kinds of language are seen as appropriate to certain situations: convention plays a very large part in Halliday's theory of register, for example (see SYSTEMIC-FUNCTIONAL GRAMMAR).

K.M.

Suggestions for further reading

Eco, U. (1984) *Semiotics and the Philosophy of Language*, London and Basingstoke: Macmillan.

Hookway, C. (1985) *Peirce*, London: Routledge & Kegan Paul.

Set theory

Sets

Set theory is a branch of mathematics which studies the properties of sets. A **set** is any collection of objects, which are described as its **members**. We can specify a set by reference to a property which all members share: for example, we can speak of the set of British towns with a population over one million, or of the set of English sentences. Alternatively, a set can be specified by listing its members: for example, there is a three-membered set whose members are Margaret Thatcher, the number 7 and the city of San Francisco. As this example indicates, the members of a set need not 'belong together' in any natural fashion.

We can describe a set by listing its members within curly brackets:

{Margaret Thatcher, 7, San Francisco}

The membership relation is expressed by the lower-case epsilon. Thus:

Margaret Thatcher ∈ {Margaret Thatcher, 7, San Francisco}

This says that Margaret Thatcher is a member of the set whose members are Margaret Thatcher, the number 7 and the city of San Francisco. It is common to express the fact that some object does not belong to a set as follows:

London ∉ {Margaret Thatcher, 7, San Francisco}

i.e. London does not belong to the set whose members are Margaret Thatcher, the number 7 and the city of San Francisco. The notation for specifying a set by reference to a shared property is as follows:

{x: Fx} e.g. {x: x is an English sentence}

Hence:

'Snow is white' ∈ {x: x is an English sentence}

says that *Snow is white* belongs to the set of English sentences.

The notion of a set is **extensional**: there cannot be distinct sets with exactly the same members. For example, although . . . *is red* and . . . *is the same colour as a London bus* differ in meaning,

{x: x is red} = {x: x is the same colour as a London bus}

Although the property of being a three-sided plane figure is distinct from the property of being a three-angled plane figure, each property determines the same set.

Two special sets should be mentioned here. These are the empty set or null set and the universal set. The **null set**, **0**, has no members; everything that exists has the property of not belonging to the null set. Given the fact that set membership is extensional, it follows that there is only one null set. The **universal set**, often denoted by '**1**', contains everything: there is nothing which does not belong to the universal set. The **cardinality** of a set is the number of members it has: the cardinality of the set of letters of the English alphabet is twenty-six, for example, and the cardinality of the null set is zero. A set with just one member is referred to as a **unit set**, and it is worth making clear that an object (say, my typewriter) is distinct from the unit set to which it belongs. They are different objects. My typewriter is a concrete object – I can touch it; the unit set containing my typewriter is, like all sets, an abstract object – it cannot be touched or manipulated.

Properties of sets and operations upon sets

Set theory studies the fundamental truths about sets and various operations upon sets which, for example, construct complex sets out of others. It was developed in the late nineteenth century and the twentieth century chiefly in order to provide rigorous foundations for number theory and other branches of mathematics. Gottlob Frege, Bertrand Russell and others hoped to explain the truths of arithmetic by identifying numbers with certain sets and establishing that the whole of arithmetic could then be derived from the fundamental properties of sets and their relations.

Some of the main notions used in set theory are as follows. One set is included in another, is a **subset** of it, when all members of the first are also members of the second. Thus, the set of odd numbers is a subset of the set of natural numbers; and the set of three-word English sentences is a subset of the set of English sentences. 'S is a subset of T' is written as follows:

$$S \subseteq T$$

S is a **proper subset** of T when every member of S is a member of T, and T contains things not in S. Our two examples of the subset relation also exemplify what is involved in the relation of being a proper subset. S is a proper subset of T is written thus:

$$S \subset T$$

It will be apparent that if S is a subset of T and T is a subset of S, then S and T are the same set:

$$\text{If } S \subseteq T \text{ and } T \subseteq S \text{ then } S = T$$

The **power set** of a set S is a set which contains as a member every subset of S. For example, consider a set T which contains just three objects, a, b and c. The power set of T is

$$\{ \{a,b,c\}, \{a,b\}, \{a,c\}, \{b,c\}, \{a\}, \{b\}, \{c\}, 0 \}$$

Note that every set is a subset of itself, and that the null set is a subset of every set.

Union and **intersection** are the two principal means by which sets can be constructed out of other sets. The union of S and T is a set which contains all objects which are in S and all objects which are in T. For example, the set of positive integers is the union of the set of positive odd numbers and the set of positive even numbers; the set of students in the university is the union of the set of undergraduates and of graduates; etc. The union of S and T (S ∪ T) can thus be defined:

$$(\forall x)(x \in S \lor x \in T \leftrightarrow x \in S \cup T)$$

The intersection of S and T (S ∩ T) contains only those objects which belong both to S and T. Thus:

$$(\forall x) (x \in S \cap T \leftrightarrow x \in S \,\&\, x \in T)$$

For example, the set of third-year philosophy students in the university is the intersection of the set of third-year students and the set of philosophy students; the set of brown horses is the intersection of the set of horses and the set of brown things, etc.

Here are some other set-theoretic notions. The **difference** of S and T (S – T) contains all those objects which are in S which are not in T. If A is the set of students at the university and B is the set of physics students, then A – B is the set of students at the university who do not study physics. The **complement** of a set is the set of objects which do not belong to it: thus, the complement of the set S is 1 – S.

Sets, sequences and functions

Just as sets are to be distinguished from properties, they are to be distinguished from sequences. The expressions below specify the same sets:

{Margaret Thatcher, 7, San Francisco}
{7, San Francisco, Margaret Thatcher}

The members of a set are not placed in any particular order. In a sequence, the order matters, the sequences below being different:

(1) <1,2,3>
(2) <3,1,2>

Two- and three-membered sequences are referred to as **ordered pairs** and **ordered triples** respectively. '<' and '>' are employed when describing sequences.

Sequences can be defined in terms of the more fundamental notions of set theory. This can be done in several ways. For example, if we replace each member of the sequence by a set containing that member together with its predecessors, we ensure that the nth member of the sequence is distinguished by itself being an n-membered set. Thus, our two sequences above could be expressed set-theoretically as follows:

(3) { {1}, {{1} 2}, {{1} {{1} 2} 3} }
(4) { {3}, {{3} 1}, {{3} {{3} 1} 2} }

(3) is a three-membered set, all three members themselves being sets. The number three occurs as a member of just one of the members of (3), and this member is itself a three-membered set. The only member of (4) of which the number three is a member is a one-membered set. Hence, its different positions in the sequences (1) and (2) are reflected in the set-theoretic presentation.

Sequences are useful in studying the properties of **functions** and **relations**. Some examples will introduce the notion of a function:

4 = the square of 2
81 = the square of 9
London = the capital of the United Kingdom
Paris = the capital of France

The squaring function determines a unique number as value when applied to any number as argument: the capital function determines a unique city as value when applied to a nation as an argument, and so on. The square function yields a value when applied again to the results of an earlier application; the capital function is undefined for arguments which are not nations. Hence, while

16 = the square of the square of 2

there is not a value assigned by the capital function to

the capital of the capital of France

or, of course, to

the capital of Paris

We express that a is a function of b thus:

a = f(b)

The arguments of a function are drawn from a set which is called its **domain**. The domain of the squaring relation is the set of positive integers. The domain of the capital function is the set of nations. The values of the function for its different arguments belong to its **range** or **co-domain**: the range of the squaring function may also be the set of positive integers; that of the capital function will be a set containing cities but no nations. When the domain and range of a function are the same set, the function is called an **operation**.

Functions can have two or more arguments: for example, the addition function yields a unique value for two arguments:

$$7 = + (3,4)$$

A function can be understood as a (possibly infinite) set of sequences. For example, the capital function is a finite set of pairs, the second member of which is the capital of the first; and the addition function is an infinite set of triples, the third member of which is the sum of the first two:

{ <France, Paris>, <United Kingdom, London>, <Italy, Rome> ... }
{ <1,1,2>, <1,2,3>, <2,1,3>, <2,2,4>, <2,3,5>, <3,2,5> ... }

Relations and the properties of relations

Set theory has many applications in formal semantics (see FORMAL SEMANTICS). Corresponding to a predicate expression such as *red* or *horse* is the set of things to which it applies: this is described as its **extension**. Thus, the set of horses is the extension of *horse*, the set of red things is the extension of *red*, and so on. This can be extended to the study of relations. Corresponding to a dyadic relational expression such as ... *kills* ... is a set of ordered pairs of objects such that the first kills the second:

{ <Brutus, Caesar>, <St George, the dragon> ... }

This serves as the extension of the relational expression. Logicians often speak as if this set of pairs *is* the relation. In the same fashion, triadic relational expressions like ... *gives* ... *to* ... have extensions which are sets of ordered triples, and so on. For discussion of the application of these ideas in semantics, see FORMAL SEMANTICS.

The attempt to use these ideas in explaining semantic properties of expressions from a natural language has led some cognitive scientists to a generalization of standard set theory – **fuzzy set theory**, due (primarily) to L.A. Zadeh and his followers. Since a word like *red* is vague, the suggestion that it has a definite extension is implausible. Some objects do not obviously belong within the extension of the term, but nor do they obviously belong outside it. Fuzzy set theory exploits the idea that there can be degrees of membership of a set. A bright scarlet flower belongs to the extension of 'red' to a higher degree than a flower that is approaching pink or orange does. Zadeh and his followers have developed fuzzy set theory in some detail (see Zadeh 1975).

Logicians have developed some useful terminology for describing the properties of relations, and this is an appropriate place to present this vocabulary. A relation is **reflexive** if every object bears it to itself. For example, everything is *the same thing as* itself. If we are talking only of concrete objects, the relations of being the same size as, and being the same weight as, are reflexive. By contrast, an **irreflexive** relation is one that *nothing* bears to itself: for example, nothing is taller than itself, or the father of itself; no natural number is the result of adding 1 to itself, etc. Of course, most relations are neither reflexive nor irreflexive. For example, although there are many people who do not love themselves, it is plain that there are some who do, and so on.

In view of the claims made about relations in this section, these points can be put slightly differently:

A relation R is reflexive if, for every object x, <x,x> ∈ R
A relation R is irreflexive if, for every object x, <x,x> ∉ R

A relation is **symmetrical** when it meets the condition that if an object a bears the relation to b, then b bears the relation to a. For example,

> If John is the same height as Mary then Mary is the same height as John

A relation like 'is taller than' is **asymmetrical**: if one object is taller then another, the second cannot be taller than the first. Hence,

> A relation R is symmetrical if, whenever <a,b> ∈ R, then <b,a> ∈ R
>
> A relation R is asymmetrical if, whenever <a,b> ∈ R, then <b,a> ∉ R

Finally, a relation is **transitive** if, whenever one object bears it to a second which, in turn, bears it to a third, then the first bears it to the third. If John is taller than Jane, and Jane is taller than Peter, it follows that John is taller than Peter. Hence the relation of being taller than is transitive. On the other hand, the relation of being father of is intransitive: if John is father of Peter, and Peter is father of Jane, it follows that John is not father of Jane.

> A relation R is transitive if, whenever <a,b> ∈ R and <b,c> ∈ R, then <a,c> ∈ R
>
> A relation R is intransitive if, whenever <a,b> ∈ R and <b,c> ∈ R, then <a,c> ∉ R

If a relation is reflexive, symmetrical and transitive, then it is called an **equivalence relation**. 'Is the same object as' is an equivalence relation, as is 'is the same height as'.

C.H.

Suggestions for further reading

Halmos, P. (1960) *Naive Set Theory*, Princeton, NJ: Van Nostrand.
Suppes, P. (1960) *Axiomatic Set Theory*, Princeton, NJ: Van Nostrand.

Sign language

Introduction

By **sign language** is usually meant a visual-gestural, non-vocal language used primarily by the deaf, and one not based on the language of the surrounding hearing community. Sign language is not to be identified with signed versions of spoken languages and cannot be translated sign-for-word into speech any more than two spoken languages are word-for-word intertranslatable. Sign language is not international; most signs used in different countries are no more alike than the words used in different countries.

A sign language almost always develops among groups of deaf-born people, even groups who are being taught to communicate orally (Wright 1969). Only a minority of deaf people (about 10 per cent; Deuchar 1996/1999: 566) have the opportunity to acquire sign language from birth, because most deaf children are born to hearing parents. However, in those cases where sign language is acquired from birth, the stages of acquisition appear to be similar to those for spoken language (see LANGUAGE ACQUISITION), although the process seems to begin earlier in the case of sign language (Deuchar 1984: 161).

The first school for the deaf to receive public support taught a sign language which its founder, Abbé de l'Epée, had developed by adding French grammar to the indigenous sign language of the poor deaf of Paris. l'Epée's school was established in 1755. He taught his pupils to read and write by associating signs with pictures and written words, so that they could write down what was said to them with the help of an interpreter and thus acquire a formal education. By the time of l'Epée's death, in

1789, teachers trained by him had established twenty-one schools for the deaf in
France, and by 1791 l'Epée's own school
had become the National Institute for
Deaf-Mutes in Paris led by the grammarian Sicard. His pupil, Roch-Ambroise
Bébian, removed the imposition of the
grammar of French from the indigenous
sign language of the deaf, realizing that the
latter had its own grammar (Sacks 1989/
1990: 16–20).

Sign language exists wherever groups
of deaf people exist. Van Cleve (1987) contains descriptions of over fifty native sign
languages, but in this entry I shall concentrate on American Sign Language (ASL)
and British Sign Language (BSL). Like all
sign languages, each of these has its own
syntactic rules. However, when they are
used to accompany speech, the order of
signs may reflect the word order of the
spoken language, and incorporate special
signs for English inflectional morphology.
For example, the English words *sits* and
sitting can be represented by the sign for
SIT followed by separate sign markers
invented for the English third person present indicative and the English progressive
inflections (Klima and Bellugi 1979: 244).
In such circumstances the signed language
is referred to as **Signed English**.

Neither Signed English, nor the Paget
Gorman Sign System, nor Cued Speech
are to be identified with ASL or BSL. The
Paget Gorman Sign System (PGSS) was
developed by Sir Richard Paget and Pierre
Gorman between 1934 and 1971. Its signs
are largely iconic representations combined
with signs for affixes, and it was intended
as an aid to the teaching of English, to be
phased out as competence in English grew.
Cued Speech is designed to assist the process of lip reading by providing disambigu-
ating signs for sounds which look identical
on the lips (Deuchar 1984: 37; see further
Griffiths 1980 for details of PGSS, and
Cornett 1967 for further details of Cued
Speech).

American Sign Language

The history of ASL begins with the establishment, in 1817, of the American Asylum
for the Deaf in Hartford by Laurent
Clerc, the Reverend Thomas Gallaudet and
Mason Cogswell. Cogswell was a surgeon
whose daughter was deaf. No special educa-
tional provision was made for the deaf in
America at that time, and Cogswell and
Gallaudet wanted to establish a school
for the deaf in Hartford. Gallaudet went to
Europe to seek expert assistance. Having
been turned away by the Braidwoods in
Britain because they kept their methods
secret, he recruited Clerc, a deaf-mute
French teacher of the deaf trained in the
Sicard tradition.

The Hartford Asylum was successful,
and other schools for the deaf were established as teachers were trained at Hartford.
The French Sign Language used by Clerc
amalgamated with indigenous sign languages used in America – in particular,
the language used by the deaf of Martha's
Vineyard, where a substantial proportion
of the population was subject to heredit-
ary deafness – to become ASL. Possibly
because of the early influence on ASL by
French Sign Language, ASL appears to
be more similar to French Sign Language
than to BSL (Deuchar 1984: 2). In 1864,
the Columbia Institution for the Deaf and
the Blind in Washington became the first
college for the deaf, under the leadership
of Edward Gallaudet, Thomas Gallaudet's
son. The institution was renamed Gallaudet
College and is now **Gallaudet University**,
still the only liberal arts college for the deaf
in the world.

After its initial success, however, ASL
came under attack from members of the
oralist school, including Alexander Graham
Bell, whose influence was so great that
oralism prevailed, and the use of signs in
schools was proscribed at the International Congress of Educators of the Deaf held
in Milan in 1880. Since this resolution

necessitated that teachers of the deaf be able to speak, the proportion of deaf teachers of the deaf fell from nearly 50 per cent in 1850 to 25 per cent by the turn of the century, and further to 12 per cent by 1960.

The rationale for oralism is that deaf people who can only use sign language are excluded from spontaneous communication with hearing people, very few of whom know how to sign. Bell thought that, just as sign language held the deaf community together, it kept deaf people from integrating with the rest of society, and that the teaching of speech and lip-reading was essential if deaf people were to achieve full integration. Unfortunately, however, the price most deaf people have to pay for speech to the exclusion of sign language seems to be a dramatic reduction in their general educational achievements. Whereas pupils who had been to the Hartford Asylum and similar schools in the 1850s reached standards similar to those of their hearing counterparts, and had, effectively, achieved social integration through education, a study carried out by Gallaudet College in 1972 shows an average reading level for 18-year-old deaf high-school graduates comparable to that of fourth-grade pupils. Conrad (1979) shows a similar situation for deaf British students, with 18-year-olds having a reading age of 9 (Sacks 1989/1990: 21–9).

Because deaf people cannot hear the sounds made by other speakers, or by themselves, they cannot compare their own efforts at accompanying lip shapes with sounds to the sounds produced by hearing people. Hence, they are left to try to work out the system of speech from visual clues which are far less specific and detailed than the signs of sign language, and from instructions on how to use their vocal apparatus. But such instructions cannot make up for a deaf person's inability to monitor the sound itself: one has only to listen briefly to someone wearing headphones trying to sing along to music s/he hears through them to realize how important the ability to monitor one's own sounds is. In contrast, signed language appears naturally among groups of deaf people, for whom it provides everything that speech provides for people who can hear (including poetry, song and humour produced by play on signs: see Klima and Bellugi 1979: chapter 4) and, as Deuchar (1984: 175) points out, the recognition and use of sign language in schools would probably increase deaf people's confidence and their desire and ability to learn English, 'and would ultimately aid their integration as bilingual, bicultural adults, into both the deaf and the hearing communities'.

ASL was the first of the world's sign languages to be studied by linguists. It is the subject of Klima and Bellugi's (1979) *The Signs of Language*, in which description is strongly supported by psycholinguistic experiments. Each sign of ASL is describable in terms of three parameters on which significant contrasts are set up between signs (namely, **location**, **hand-shape** and **movement**) and a limited number of combinations are permitted within each parameter. Stokoe (1960) describes 19 handshapes, 12 locations and 24 types of movement and provides a notation for ASL comparable to phonetic notation for speech. Location is called **tab** in the notation system; the part that acts (say, the index finger) is called **dez**; and the action performed is called **sig** (Deuchar 1984: 54).

Stokoe *et al.*'s *Dictionary* (1976) lists 3000 root signs arranged according to their parts and organization and the principles of the language. The following notation is used for tab (Deuchar 1984: 59–60):

Ø	neutral space in front of body
◯	whole face
⌢	upper face
△	nose
◡	lower face

ꝫ cheek

π neck

[ ] central trunk

∧ shoulder and upper arm

⌄ forearm/elbow

Ɒ back of wrist

A one-handed finger-spelling system can be used in conjunction with ASL for spelling out names or words for which no sign exists, and is also used as a notation for dez (Deuchar 1984: 61–4):

A: closed fist; Ȧ: thumb extended from closed fist; B: flat hand, fingers together, thumb may or may not be extended; B̈: as for B, but hand bent; 5: same as for B, but fingers spread; 5̈: bent 5, 'clawed hand'; C: fingers and thumb bent to form curve as in letter 'c'; G: index finger extended from fist; O: fingers bent and all touching thumb; F: index finger and thumb touching, all other fingers extended; H: index finger and middle fingers extended from closed fist and held together; I: little finger extended from closed fist; L: index finger and thumb extended from closed fist; R: index and middle fingers extended and crossed, as in crossing one's fingers for good luck; V: index and middle finger extended from fist and held apart; V̈: as V, but with fingers bent; W: the middle three fingers extended from fist, may or may not be spread; X: index finger extended and bent; Y: thumb and little finger extended from fist; 8: middle finger bent, rest of fingers open.

The notations for sig can be divided into three categories; as shown in Table 1 (Deuchar 1984: 69, roughly following the categories set up by Brennan et al. 1980).

As mentioned above, a number of constraints operate on the combinations of formal elements into ASL sign forms. For example, Battison (1974) observes that two-handed signs (see below) are constrained by the Symmetry Constraint and the Dominance Constraint. The **Symmetry Constraint** operates in such a way that in the vast majority of cases of signs in which both hands are used, both assume the same shape, location and movement. The **Dominance Constraint** restrains the shape of the non-leading hand in two-handed signs of type 3 (in which the leading hand contacts the other but the hand-shapes are

Table 1

Direction		Manner		Interaction	
∧	up	ɑ	supinating rotation	)(	approach
∨	down	ᴅ	pronating rotation	✕	contact
∿	up and down	ɯ	twisting	ᴖ	link or grasp
>	right	@	circular	+	cross
<	left	ɳ	nodding or bending	÷	separate
⪫	side by side	□	opening	(ˌ⥾)	interchange
⊤	towards signer	#	closing	∿	alternation
⊥	away from signer	ℚ	wiggling		
⊤̱	to and fro				

different: see below) to one of six – A, B, 5, G, C and ø. These seem to be the most basic hand-shapes: they account for 70 per cent of all signs and are among the first acquired by deaf children of deaf parents (Boyes-Braem 1973; Klima and Bellugi 1989: 63–4).

As mentioned above, ASL can employ a finger spelling system to sign concepts or phenomena for which no sign exists. However, sign language exhibits the same facility as spoken language for creating new lexical items by compounding. Klima and Bellugi (1979: 198–9) mention the phenomenon STREAKER, new to the 1970s, for which a sign compounded of the signs for NUDE and ZOOM OFF was invented which became conventional throughout the deaf communities of the USA.

A compound is distinguished from the phrase consisting of the two words (BED SOFT meaning 'pillow' from BED SOFT meaning 'soft bed') by temporal compression, particularly of the first sign in the compound, by loss of repetition of movement in the second sign, by overlap between a first sign made by one hand and a second sign made by the other, and by smoothing of the transition between the two signs, for example by bringing the two signs closer together in the signing space (see below). Finally, compression may integrate the movements of the two signs into one smooth flow (1979: 202–21). Newly coined signs are constrained in the same way as established signs.

Existing signs may also be extended in meaning, but such extensions are usually accompanied by a change in the sign, so that there are very few ambiguous signs. For example, the ASL sign for QUIET, which is made by moving both hands from a position in front of the lips downwards and outwards, is modified in the derived sign for TO ACQUIESCE so that the hands move down only, but until they 'hang down' from the wrists (1979: 200–1). Nouns are derived from verbs, for example

ACQUISITION from GET, by diminishing and repeating the movement of the verb (1979: 199–201).

A number of specific changes in the form of signs, called **modulations**, correspond to specific changes in the signs' meaning. These include, among others, the **Circular Modulation**, which appears in citation signing (see below) as a superimposed circular path of movement described by the hands. The Circular Modulation adds to the meaning of the sign the notion 'is prone to be' or 'has a predisposition to be' or 'tends to be'. It is the archetypical modulation on adjectival predicates like SICK, and Klima and Bellugi (1979: 249) refer to it as **Modulation for Predispositional Aspect**. Only signs which refer to incidental or temporary states, such as ANGRY, DIRTY and SICK can undergo this modulation and, when they do, they refer to characteristics which are natural to the person, item or phenomenon of which they are predicated, for instance SICKLY. When such signs undergo a different modulation, the **Thrust Modulation**, a single thrust-like movement combining a brief tense motion with a lax hand-shape, they refer to a readiness for the state, quality or characteristic to develop, or to a sudden change to that state, so Klima and Bellugi (1979: 255) call this the Thrust Modulation for **Susceptative Aspect**. When the sign for SICK is modulated in this way, it means 'get sick easily'. Signs which stand for characteristics which are by nature inherent or long-lasting, such as PRETTY, INTELLIGENT, HARD, TALL and YOUNG cannot undergo Circular or Thrust Modulation.

Transitory state adjectival predicates and durative verbs can accept the **Elliptical Modulation for Continuative Aspect**, a slow reduplication, which adds to the sign the meaning 'for a long time'; the **Tremolo Modulation for Incessant Aspect**, a tiny, tense, uneven movement made rapidly and repeatedly, which adds to the sign the meaning 'incessantly'; and the **Marcato**

Table 2

Pairs of modulations	Reduplicated	Even	Tense	End-marked	Fast	Elongated	
Predispositional 'be characteristically sick'	+	+	−	−	+	+	transitory state
Susceptative/frequentative 'easily get sick often'	+	+	−	+	+	+	change to state
Continuative 'be sick for a long time'	+	−	+	−	−	+	transitory state
Iterative 'keep on getting sick again and again'	+	−	+	+		+	change to state
Protractive 'be sick uninterruptedly'	−		+			−	transitory state
Incessant 'seem to get sick incessantly'	+		+	+	+	−	change to state
Intensive 'be very sick'	−	+	+	+	+	+	transitory state
Resultative 'get sick'	−	−	+	+	−	+	change to state

Modulation for Frequentative Aspect, which has a tense movement, well-marked initial and final positions, and a regular beat of four to six reduplications and which means 'often occurring' (1979: 256–8).

The meanings 'very' and 'sort of' can be added to a sign by the **Tense and Lax Modulations for Intensive and Approximate Aspects**, respectively. The change in movement for the former is tension in the muscles of hand and arm, a long tense hold at the beginning of the sign, a very rapid single performance, and a final hold. The change in movement for the latter is a lax hand-shape and an extreme reduction in size and duration of each iteration of the sign (1979: 258–60).

The meaning 'to become' is conveyed by the **Accelerando Modulation for Resultative Aspect**. In this aspect, the sign for RED, which is made by a soft downward brushing motion made twice, is made only once

and with a tense motion, which starts slowly before accelerating to a long final hold (1979: 260–1).

Klima and Bellugi (1979: 269–70) point out that the many forms displayed by modulations are realizations of grammatical processes: they differ systematically on a limited number of dimensions and the differences in dimensions correlate with a network of basic semantic distinctions. They display this as in Table 2. In general, sign language morphology tends to resist sequential segmentation at the lexical level and to favour superimposed spatial and temporal contrasts in sign movement (1979: 274). For syntactic use of the signing space, see below.

British Sign Language

The first school for the deaf in Britain was established by Thomas Braidwood in

Edinburgh in 1760. Braidwood kept his methods of instruction secret, but he seems likely to have employed a combination of speech, lip-reading and signs (McLoughlin 1980). In this and similar schools opened in other parts of the country, deaf people could come together and the sign language they used among themselves could begin to become standardized. The Braidwood Academy, which was fee-paying, was moved from Edinburgh to London in 1783, and in 1792 a society was formed to provide free education for the deaf in 'asylums', the first of which, in London, was run by Braidwood's nephew, Joseph Watson. After Braidwood's death in 1806 Watson published *Instruction for the Deaf and Dumb* (1809), from which it is apparent that he knew sign language and that he thought that all teachers of the deaf should learn it and use it to introduce the deaf to speech (Deuchar 1984: 31–2).

When the last of the Braidwoods, Thomas (the younger), died in 1825, he was replaced by a Swiss, Louis du Puget (Hodgson 1953: 163). Du Puget introduced Epée's silent method (see above). But from the 1860s onward BSL experienced a period of declining status similar to, and for the same reasons as, those described above for ASL. But the system of education for the deaf was kept entirely segregated from the rest of the education system until 1944 so that, although the aim of the system was to teach the deaf to use oral language, the schools provided a meeting ground for the deaf where they could sign between themselves.

Signing was also used in the 'missions' often attached to the schools. Missions were charitable organizations concerned with the spiritual welfare of the deaf, often established on the initiative of local deaf people themselves, and they also provided space for recreational and other social activities. The missions have developed into centres for the deaf which are to be found in most large British towns, but have become largely

detached from schools for the deaf, most of which are residential. Therefore most children do not become fully integrated into their local deaf community until they leave school, and the school community and the adult community tend to use different variants of sign language. This situation bears some similarity to that which pertains to accent and dialect in spoken language – adult signers can usually tell where other signers come from and where they went to school (see further below) (Deuchar 1984: 32–5).

It was not until the 1980s that, largely as a result of action by the British Deaf Association and the National Union of the Deaf, BSL began to be perceived as a proper language, to gain a degree of official status and to find its way into some classrooms and on to the nation's television screens (Miles 1988: 19–40). BSL has therefore developed through its use in the deaf communities around Britain and it displays some regional and other types of variation, just as spoken language does.

Sign-language use necessitates a certain amount of space in front of and to the sides of the body in which to sign. This space, plus the front and sides of the body from the head to just below the waist, is known as the **signing space**. However, the signer's face remains the focus of gaze during signing, and movement of the hands is perceived by area vision (Miles 1988: 53). Signs that are supported by the face, head and the body from the waist up are called **multichannel signs**.

A forward tilt of the body indicates astonishment, interest or curiosity, while a backward tilt indicates defiance or suspicion. Hunched shoulders imply effort, rising chest shows pride, and falling chest suggests discouragement. In addition, shifts in body direction and mime-like movements can aid storytelling and the reporting of events (Miles 1988: 64–5).

Nodding and shaking the head are used to reply 'Yes' and 'No', as in speech, but also to affirm and negate propositions. Thus rubbing the clenched leading hand (see below) with the thumb pointing upwards up and down on the stomach means 'I am hungry' when accompanied by nodding, and 'I am not hungry' when accompanied by a head-shake. Nods and tilts of the head also act as punctuation between and within sentences, and head movement can be used to indicate location (Miles 1988: 63–4).

Facial expressions include standardized versions of expressions used by everyone to express emotion, such as positive and negative face. Similarly, an open mouth with clenched teeth indicates stress or effort, while a loose pout with slightly puffed cheeks suggests ease; a loose or open mouth, possibly with the tongue showing, suggests carelessness, lack of attention or ignorance. Lips pulled tight as in saying *ee*, with the teeth just showing, suggests intensity or nearness or exactness. In descriptions of sizes, volumes, etc., fully puffed cheeks mean 'a great amount' while pursed lips and sucked in cheeks mean 'a small amount'. The lip movements of words can also be used to disambiguate signs. For example, the sign for a married person can be accompanied by the lip shape for *hu-sp* to indicate that the married person in question is male (Miles 1988: 59–62).

The eyes are used to show surprise (wide eyes) and doubt (narrow eyes). Narrow eyes can also show intensity of judgements, making the difference between the signs for *far* and *very far*, *good* and *very good*, and so on. The direction of the signer's gaze can be used like pointing to indicate the location and movement of things. Raised eyebrows accompany questions (Miles 1988: 62–3).

Just as speech makes some limited use of imitation of natural sounds, **onomatopoeia**, some manual signs imitate actions, shapes, sizes, directions, and so on. Some signs, like that for *drink*, in which the hand imitates the shape and movement involved in holding a glass and putting it to one's lips, are transparent; that is, they would probably be understood even by people who do not know sign language. Other signs, in which the link between meaning and form only becomes apparent when it is explained are called **translucent**. The sign for *cheap*, for example, involves a downward movement which may suggest that something is being reduced. Signs which give no visual clues to their meaning are called **encoded**. **Iconic** or pictorial signs can be made by the fingers or the hand outlining the shape, size or action of an object. For example, the sign for *scissors* is made by the middle and index fingers performing movements similar to those of the blades of a pair of scissors. If the hand simultaneously moves across in front of the body, the sign means 'cut' (see further Miles 1988: 66–76).

There are three kinds of manual sign – one-handed, two-handed and mixed – each having different types. One-handed signs are made by the right hand if the signer is right-handed and by the left if s/he is left-handed. The hand used for one-handed signs is called the **leading hand**. One-handed signs are either made in space (type 1) or by touching a body part (though not the other hand) (type 2).

Two-handed signs are of three types. Signs of type 1 are made with both hands moving either in space or touching each other or the body. Signs of type 2 involve the leading hand contacting the other while both hand-shapes are the same. In signs of type 3, the leading hand contacts the other, but the hand-shapes are different.

A **mixed sign** is a sign which begins as one-handed and becomes two-handed, or vice versa, as in the sign for *believe*, in which the signer first touches her/his forehead just above the eye with the index finger of the leading hand and then brings that hand down in front of the chest, with the palm facing it, to make contact with the horizontal, upward-facing palm of the other hand (Miles 1988: 54–5).

Each sign of sign language can be described in isolation, but, just as words in sentences do not sound the same as their **citation forms** (the way they sound when pronounced one at a time out of context), signs adapt to context as the hands rapidly change from one shape to another. There are more than fifty hand-shapes in BSL and around twenty-five identifiable places in the signing space. The signs are described in terms of place, movement and the direction in which the palm and fingers face (Miles 1988: 56–7), and Stokoe's tab, dez and sig, developed for ASL (see above), can be applied to BSL signs too, as Deuchar (1984: 54) demonstrates: the sign for I in BSL is made by the index finger pointing to and touching the chest, and can thus be described as:

tab: chest
dez: index finger extended from closed fist
sig: contact with tab

The sign for THINK in BSL is made by the index finger pointing to the forehead, so it can be described as:

tab: forehead
dez: index finger extended from closed fist
sig: contact with tab

This shows the signs I and THINK to be **minimal pairs**: they differ only on one parameter, tab. Similarly, THINK and KNOW are minimal pairs differing only in dez, and KNOW and CLEVER are minimal pairs which contrast in sig (Deuchar 1984: 55):

	KNOW	CLEVER
tab:	forehead	forehead
dez:	thumb extended from closed fist	thumb extended from closed fist
sig:	contact with tab	movement from right to left in contact with tab

For BSL, the following symbols for tab, dez and sig have been added to Stokoe *et al.*'s (1976) (see above):

Tab

⌒̄	top of head	⊻⊻	eyes
⌣	mouth/lips	ↄ	ear
⌐¬	upper trunk	⌞⌟	lower trunk

(Deuchar 1984: 604)

Dez

⅄ middle finger extended from fist

(Deuchar 1984: 64)

Sig

⩊ crumbling action ø no movement

(Deuchar 1984: 69–70)

The signing space forms an arena in which aspects of the syntax of sign language can be displayed through spatial relations between the signs and the type and frequency of their movements. For instance, the information encapsulated in the sentence *The house is on a hill, with a path winding up to it* can be provided in sign language by establishing a hill by moving the arms with the hands flat and palms down sideways upwards, then forming the top of the hill; next making the sign for *house* by touching the tips of the fingers of each hand to each other, arms still stretched upward where the hill is; bringing down the arms and forming a path leading up the hill with the index and middle finger of both hands tracing the path; then tracing a road below the hill with both hands flat, palms facing each other, and moving together across below where the hill has been established.

Anaphora, backward reference, can be made to items already placed in the signing space by pointing to them (Miles 1988: 88–9). This means that in many cases there is no need to employ the third person pronoun. However, sign-language grammar is not dependent on linearity, since more than one sign can be made simultaneously. For example, whereas in speech the words in a sentence must follow one another linearly, as in *a small boy who was born deaf*, in BSL the left hand can sign BOY while the right is signing SMALL; the left hand can sign BORN while the right is signing DEAF (Woll 1990: 775). In addition, signs made with the hands can be accompanied by non-manual behaviour: clause connectors are made with the head and eyebrows; for example, in an *if–then* construction, the *if*-part is signed with raised brows and the head tilted slightly back, and the brows and head drop to introduce the *then*-part. The topic of a sentence is introduced first, often with raised brows and a backward head-tilt, followed by the comment, often accompanied by a nod.

A sign moves from the direction of the subject of the sentence towards the object, so that there may be no need to mark subject and object by pronouns. When pronoun signs are used, they are usually made at the beginning of a sentence and repeated at the end. In reporting the speech of others, the signer can adopt their different roles by body shift and eye gaze, and portray the different emotions of the interactants through facial expressions. As mentioned above, mood and modality can be indicated with the face, head, eyes and eyebrows.

Tense can be marked by using the signs for *will* (future), *now* (present) and *finish* (past). Tense and aspect are also marked by the use of four **timelines**, A, B, C and D:

- A, past to future, runs from just behind the signer's shoulder to 50 cm or so in front of him or her. Signs made just above or behind the shoulder indicate past time. Distant past is indicated by circling both hands backward alternately, and increasing the size, number and speed of the circles in tandem with the length of time being described. To show the passing of time, the hands circle forward.
- B, short time units, runs along the arm and hand that is not a signer's leading arm and hand. It is used to show calendar time, succession and duration.
- C, continuing time, crosses in front of the signer; the sign for *now* or *today* is made here, but timeline C generally represents continuous aspect, particularly if the sign moves from left to right.

- D, growing time, which is indicated by moving the flat hand with palm pointing down, from the position it would take to indicate the height of a hip-high child, upwards to shoulder height. The signs for *small*, *tall*, *child(ren)* and *adult* are made at points on this line, while for *grew up* and *all my life* the hand moves upward (Miles 1988: 90–105).

Plural number can be indicated by repetition of a sign. For example, the sign for CHILDREN is made by repeating the sign for CHILD. However, signs which involve the use of extended fingers can also be modified to include reference to plural number. For example, the two-finger handshape of the sign for DEAF PERSON can be replaced by one involving three fingers to indicate THREE DEAF PEOPLE, and the sign for GIRL, which involves the use of the index finger can be made to mean THREE GIRLS by the use of three fingers (Deuchar 1984: 87–8). Some one-handed signs (AEROPLANE, CUP) can be pluralized by making the sign with both hands (Woll 1990: 762).

A two-handed finger spelling system, the **British manual alphabet**, is used with BSL for spelling names and words for which no sign exists. The hands form the shapes of the letters, and some signs, for instance, for *father*, *daughter*, *bible*, *kitchen* and *government*, are made by repetition of the finger-spelled initial letter of the corresponding word (Miles 1988: 845).

There are several number systems used in BSL in different areas of Britain. They all involve a complex use of the fingers and various hand-shapes. For example, in the system used in the south of England, the sign for 3 is made with the palm towards the body and the index, middle and ring fingers of the hand pointing upwards, while the thumb and little finger are folded into the palm; the sign for 8 is made with the palm towards the body, the thumb pointing upwards, and the index and middle finger pointing across the front of the body. Each region has its own way of using the number system for indicating the time. A number sign starting near the mouth indicates that the number is a number of pounds (£); if it moves out from the nose, it indicates age (Miles 1988: 79–81).

BSL has its own discourse rules (Miles 1988: 51–3). For instance, it is considered bad manners to get someone's attention by turning their face towards you, as a child might do, to wave your hand in front of their face, or to flick the light on and off, *unless* you want to address all of a large group. Tapping a person on the arm or shoulder, and not anywhere else, is the polite means of getting their attention, but the tapping must not be too hard or too persistent. Taps can be relayed by bystanders, if one is out of physical reach of the person one wants to communicate with.

To show attention, a person is expected to keep looking at the person who is signing and s/he may nod to show comprehension, agreement or just general interest. Looking away is interpreted as an interruption of the signer.

Bidding for a turn is done by catching the eye of the other person, or by bringing one's hands up ready for signing. A person finishing a turn will drop her/his hands from the signing space and look at another participant in the conversation.

K.M.

Suggestions for further reading

Deuchar, M. (1984) *British Sign Language*, London: Routledge & Kegan Paul.

Klima, E.S. and Bellugi, U. (1979) *The Signs of Language*, Cambridge, MA and London: Harvard University Press.

Kyle, J.G. and Woll, B. (1985) *Sign Language: The Study of Deaf People and Their Language*, Cambridge: Cambridge University Press.

Miles, D. (1988) *British Sign Language: A Beginner's Guide*, London: BBC Books.

Sacks, O. (1989/1990) *Seeing Voices: A Journey into the World of the Deaf*, Berkeley and Los Angeles: University of California Press; reprinted 1990, London: Pan.

Sociolinguistics

Emphases of sociolinguistics

The most appropriate definition of modern sociolinguistics is a dual one: the study of language in its social contexts and the study of social life through linguistics. This reflects the vast array of topics and methods open to analysis in this wide and interdisciplinary field. Sociolinguistics clearly lies at the intersection of linguistics and sociology, but also, nowadays, social theory, social psychology, cultural criticism, anthropology and human communication studies.

Some of the main questions asked by sociolinguists are:

- How are forms of speech and patterns of communication distributed across time and space?
- How do individuals and social groups define themselves in and through language?
- How do communities differ in the 'ways of speaking' they have adopted?
- What are typical patterns in multilingual people's use of languages?
- How is language involved in social conflicts and tensions?
- Do our attitudes to language reflect and perpetuate social divisions and discrimination, and could a better understanding of language in society alleviate these problems?

- What are the most efficient, and defensible, ways of collecting language data?
- What are the implications of qualitative and quantitative methods of linguistic research?
- What are the relationships between researchers, their informants and language data?

Here we can only indicate some of the most general answers that sociolinguists have provided to these questions. We do this under four headings, reflecting the main sub-traditions of sociolinguistics.

Variationist sociolinguistics

William Labov pioneered ways of investigating speech variation within speech communities, and of doing so through highly systematic survey techniques, mainly in urban settings. Labov's 'department stores' study, part of an extended programme of study in the eastern USA (Labov 1966, 1972a, 1972b), was highly influential and it set in motion a wave of quantitative sociolinguistic research. The procedure used was rapid and anonymous interviewing, simply repeating the same request for information to 264 different sales assistants spread across three well-known New York City department stores: *Excuse me, where are the women's shoes?* Labov then noted the occasions when store assistants used or did not use /r/ in their pronunciation of *fourth* and *floor* (which was, conveniently, where the women's shoes were to be found). By aggregating these results, he was able to show that assistants in higher-status stores showed higher frequencies of /r/ in their speech, and also that *all* assistants used more /r/ when speaking more carefully. In the late 1960s, therefore, /r/ could be called a 'socially diagnostic' feature in the New York City speech community. It was a classic **sociolinguistic variable**, which marked social and situational differences.

Labov highlighted how this sort of survey – and the far more elaborate and extensive surveys which followed – could track dialectal sound changes in speech communities, identifying which social groups were leading these changes and which were following them (Labov 1994; Wolfram and Schiffrin 1989).

Variationist research has always stressed the importance of naturally occurring speech, especially **vernacular** (baseline dialect) speech, and objectivity in observational research methods. Labov formulated **the observer's paradox**, arguing that the speech data that was most important for sociolinguists to observe and study was *un*observed data. As a result, a system for sociolinguistic interviewing was developed where informants would be encouraged to talk about emotionally involving topics (such as when they had been in danger of dying), in an effort to distract them from monitoring their speech and rendering it 'unnatural'. Findings from this sort of research emerge as trends in statistical tables and figures, and in degrees of similarity and difference. For this reason, later sociolinguistic studies have found it important to use rigorous statistical techniques, which nowadays are often accompanied by acoustic measurements of vowel quality, to check on aural perceptions.

More recent variationist surveys include Kerswill's studies of dialect levelling and the spread of so-called 'Estuary English' in Milton Keynes and other English cities (e.g. Kerswill and Williams 2000) and Macaulay's studies of young Scottish speakers' use of 'quotative' expressions – ways of introducing quoted speech into their own utterances, such as the use of BE + LIKE and GO in *And I'm like 'Oh' and I go 'Is that where the redwoods are?'* (Macaulay 2000). Phonological features of accent and/or dialect are most commonly studied in this way because they are frequent in speech and not involved in obvious

semantic contrasts – whether /r/ is pronounced after a vowel does not affect the
referential meaning of the word or the
utterance. Still, as in the case of Macaulay's
study, non-phonological features can also
be studied distributionally.

Some of the best-documented findings
of variationist research are that, predictably, social class co-varies with dialect
'standardness' in a very systematic way
in urban communities (Chambers 1995;
Milroy and Milroy 1991; Trudgill 1983),
and that there are regular sex differences
in speech, with women tending to produce
more standard (or more 'posh') speech
variants than men do (Coates 1986/1993;
Tannen 1993). However, Eckert (2000) and
others have shown that there is a danger
of underestimating the role of subjective
and constructive processes in language
variation. Being female or male, or indeed
working class versus middle class, is a more
complex and socially negotiated role than
these terms are often taken to imply.

How people organize their lives socially,
for example their patterns of **social network-
ing** (Milroy 1980/1987), can often be better
indicators of language variation. Milroy
shows how the 'ties' between people can
be stronger or weaker, and that strong
ties working within dense networks can
explain how speech forms may remain
stable over long periods. Correspondingly,
weak ties may provide a crucial means by
which change – either linguistic or cultural
– infiltrates social networks. More radically, however, researchers are beginning
to explore the possibility that speech style
(Rickford and Eckert in press) need *not*
be linked in any simple way to group
membership. Evidence is accumulating
of how speakers can manipulate their
sociolinguistic identities creatively, *crossing*
into speech styles normally associated with
other social groups (Rampton 1995a, 1999).
Generally, variationist sociolinguistics has
been developed on principles of natural-
ism, objectivism and empiricism (Figueroa

1994), and these principles are currently
being reappraised by sociolinguists, and by
social scientists generally.

Language attitudes and social stereotypes

In social psychological research on language, facts about language use have less
intrinsic relevance than **beliefs about language**, especially where they can be shown
to be regularly and systematically held. For
example, we might be more inclined to learn
and use a minority language like Welsh if
we believe that Welsh is undergoing a significant revival, or if we believe that Welsh
is a beautiful and historic language, or that
Welsh speakers have certain sorts of status
and career opportunities in contemporary
Wales, or that they are pleasant and likable
people. In this case, our beliefs may be the
factor motivating our behaviours, whatever
the objective truths. So this form of sociolinguistics is concerned with social stereotypes (Giles and Coupland 1991; Giles and
Robinson 1990; Baker 1992).

Stereotypes are ubiquitous. They can be
positive as well as negative, accurate as
well as wrong-headed, positively functional
as well as socially dysfunctional. The core
method for studying stereotyped language
attitudes has been the **matched-guise technique**, whereby samples of speech, often performed by one speaker in different 'guises',
are played to groups of listeners, who
then evaluate the speaker or her/his speech
along predetermined social and personal
dimensions. Common dimensions include
'honesty', 'trustworthiness', 'competence',
'intelligence' and 'dynamism'. One of the
most regular findings is that speakers of
standard dialects are perceived to be more
competent, but also less socially attractive
than non-standard speakers. This pattern
suggests that there are definite advantages
and disadvantages of standard speech –
such as the accents associated with General
American English and Standard South-

ern British English (so-called 'Received Pronunciation').

A more recent development is the systematic study of **folk linguistics** (everyday, non-specialist understandings about language) and **perceptual dialectology** (see Preston 1989, 1999). Preston and others use mapping techniques to capture how language varieties are generally perceived, for example where 'the best English' is thought to be spoken in the United States, Japan or the Netherlands. Related topics include how well dialect varieties can be recognized by non-specialists and how sociolinguistic stereotypes influence important life-changing decisions – such as those made by schoolteachers, employers and other 'gatekeepers'.

The sociology of language

Discovering which languages and language varieties are spoken by members of different speech communities in different situations, and why, has been one of the primary descriptive tasks of sociolinguistics (see BILINGUALISM AND MULTILINGUALISM). When we examine the distribution and use of languages within communities (cities, regions, states, nations and the world) we are dealing with fundamental sociological concerns, and indeed often with matters of social policy, where the use of languages needs to be consciously planned and implemented. A separate, national language, for example, is often perceived as a necessary condition for a nation to exist, although the globalizing of modern work, lifestyles and politics makes this seem a dated idea in many environments.

Once again, there are both objective and subjective aspects to the sociology of language. Serbian and Croatian are good examples of languages which, until the war that broke out in the former Yugoslavia in 1991, were treated as one language, Serbo-Croat. The main difference between the two varieties was that they were written in different alphabets, Cyrillic and Roman respectively. But, after the war started, linguists and non-linguists in the former Yugoslavia went to considerable lengths to establish the varieties as separate languages by asserting how much the two codes differed structurally. Ethnic identity is often tied to a national or ethnic language, but there are important exceptions. For example, the Irish have lost Irish Gaelic but not a sense of nationhood. Many American aboriginal (or 'native') peoples have lost their indigenous languages but have not in all cases lost their ethnic identity or cultural vitality.

Much of the early intellectual impetus for the sociology of language was provided by Joshua Fishman (e.g. Fishman 1971), who exposed the political and moral questions surrounding language and ethnic identity. Generally, sociolinguists have lobbied for ethnic and linguistic diversity, not only as a universal and normal condition, but as a necessary and desirable one. A good deal of sociolinguistics has dealt with the problems suffered by **minority language groups** and threats to their survival, as for example in Dorian's research on **language obsolescence** (Dorian 1981, 1989). On the other hand, a good example of the stable coexistence of language varieties within some communities is what Ferguson (1959) called a **diglossic** situation, when 'high' and 'low' language codes or dialects exist alongside each other in a community (e.g. classical Arabic vs. a regional form of Arabic). In a diglossic community, political, religious and educational views and values are established and perpetuated.

The ethnography of speaking and interactional sociolinguistics

A different early stimulus for the development of sociolinguistics was the argument, most forcibly put by Dell Hymes and John Gumperz, for the broadening of the object of linguistic enquiry from linguistic competence to **communicative competence** (see Gumperz 1982; Gumperz and Hymes 1972/1986; Hymes 1964, 1996). This involves more than grammatical knowledge; it includes knowing the social and cultural rules for using a language. Hymes developed a checklist of dimensions of sociolinguistic awareness that are involved when speakers communicate in particular speaking situations. One version of this list is: **genre** (or type of event), **topic**, **purpose** or **function**, **setting**, **key** (or emotional tone), **participants** (their social group membership and relationships to one another), **message** form (both vocal and nonvocal), **message content**, **act sequence** (the ordering of communicative phenomena), **rules of interaction** and **norms of interpretation** (cultural expectations about how talk should proceed, and what its significance is). See also Saville-Troike (1989).

An interactional sociolinguistic perspective is committed to interpreting particular moments of language use, rather than deducing generalizations from surveys or interviews. It explores insiders' perspectives rather than trusting in researchers' own categories and questions. It aligns with **social constructivist** approaches in social science (Berger and Luckmann 1966), believing that social meaning is manufactured, at least in part, during language use.

Gumperz describes the process of **conversational inferencing** whereby speakers' culture-bound processes of perception, evaluation and interpretation are brought to bear on details of pronunciation, word choice or prosody. This is why detailed transcripts of particular episodes of social interaction have to be the focus of analysis, rather than, say, summary statistics.

Interactional approaches to sociolinguistics, which moved into the mainstream in the 1990s, overlap in many ways with approaches in pragmatics and discourse analysis (see PRAGMATICS; DISCOURSE ANALYSIS AND CONVERSATIONAL ANALYSIS).

N.C. and A.J.

Suggestions for further reading

Coulmas, F. (ed.) (1998) *The Handbook of Sociolinguistics*, Oxford: Blackwell Publishers.

Coupland, N. and Jaworski, A. (1997) *Sociolinguistics: A Reader and Coursebook*, London: Macmillan.

Fasold, R. (1984) *The Sociolinguistics of Society*, Oxford: Basil Blackwell.

——(1990) *The Sociolinguistics of Language*, Oxford: Basil Blackwell.

Hudson, R.A. (1996) *Sociolinguistics*, (2nd edition), Cambridge: Cambridge University Press.

Speech-act theory

Speech-act theory was developed by the Oxford philosopher J.L. Austin in the 1930s, and expounded in a series of William James lectures that Austin gave at Harvard University in 1955. These lectures, twelve in all, were subsequently published under the title *How to Do Things with Words* in 1962. The theory arises in reaction to what Austin (1962: 3) calls the **descriptive fallacy**, the view that a declarative sentence is always used to describe some state of affairs, some fact, which it must do truly or falsely.

Austin points out that there are many declarative sentences which do not describe, report or state anything, and of which it makes no sense to ask whether they are true or false. The utterance of such sentences is, or is part of, the doing of some action – an action which would not normally be described as simply saying something. Austin (1962: 5) gives a number of examples: *I do*, as uttered as part of a marriage ceremony; *I name this ship the Queen Elizabeth*, as uttered by the appropriate person while smashing a bottle against the stem of the ship in question; *I give and bequeath my watch to my brother*, as written in a will; *I bet you sixpence it will rain tomorrow*.

To utter such sentences in the appropriate circumstances is not to describe what you are doing: it *is* doing it, or part of doing it, and Austin calls such utterances **performatives** or **performative utterances**, distinguishing them from **constatives** or **constative utterances**, which are used to state a fact or describe a state of affairs. Only constatives can be true or false; performatives are **happy** or **unhappy**. Austin also expresses this by saying that the two types of utterance seem to have value on different dimensions; the constatives have value on the truth/falsity dimension; performatives have value on the happiness/unhappiness dimension.

The criterion for a happy, or **felicitous**, performative is that the circumstances in which it is uttered should be **appropriate**: certain **felicity conditions** must obtain. If a performative is unhappy, or **infelicitous**, something has gone wrong in the connection between the utterance and the circumstances in which it is uttered.

There are four main types of condition for the happy functioning of a performative (1962: 14–15):

1 It must be a commonly accepted convention that the uttering of particular words by particular people in particular circumstances will produce a particular effect.
2 All participants in this conventional procedure must carry out the procedure correctly and completely.
3 If the convention is that the participants in the procedure must have certain thoughts, feelings and intentions, then the participants must in fact have those thoughts, feelings and intentions.

4 If the convention is that any participant in the procedure binds her/himself to behave subsequently in a certain way, then s/he must in fact behave subsequently in that way.

If any of these criteria is unfulfilled, the performative will be unhappy in one of two ways, depending on which of the criteria is not fulfilled.

If we sin against either 1 or 2, the conventional act is *not* achieved: a person who is already married may go through another marriage ceremony, but this second marriage will be null and void because its circumstances were faulty (1). Or, a couple may go through all of the marriage ceremony except signing the register; the marriage will then be null and void because the ceremony was not carried out completely (2). Cases like these, in which the act is *not* achieved are called **misfires**.

If we sin against 3 and 4, then the conventional act *is* achieved, but the procedure will have been abused. A person may say *I congratulate you* or *I condole with you* without having the appropriate feelings of joy/sadness for the addressee; or s/he may say *I promise to be there* without having any intention of being there. In such cases, the act will be insincere (3). Or, a person may say *I welcome you* and then proceed to treat the addressee as an unwelcome intruder, in which case s/he will have breached the commitment inherent in the greeting subsequently to behave in a certain manner (4). Both types of case are called **abuses**: the act *is* achieved, but the procedure has been abused.

So the connection between performatives and constatives is that for a performance to be happy, certain constatives must be true (1962: 45): for *I congratulate you* to be happy, *I feel pleased for you* must be true.

However, Austin soon begins to question whether the distinction between the truth/falsity dimension and the happiness/unhappiness dimension is really as clear as it first seemed to be (see also Austin 1971), for it seems that not only performatives are subject to unhappiness: surely *All John's children are bald* as uttered when John has no children is just as unhappy as *I give and bequeath my watch to my brother* as written in the will of a person who does not possess a watch.

In each case, certain things are **presupposed** by the utterance; namely, in the first case, that John has children, and in the second case that the will writer owns a watch. These presuppositions fail, they are void for lack of reference. Similarly, *The cat is on the mat* as uttered by somebody who does not believe that the cat is on the mat seems to be just as much abused as *I promise to be there* as uttered by someone who has no intention of being there. Both are unhappy because their **implications** are unfulfilled: the utterance of *The cat is on the mat* has the implication that the speaker believes that the cat is on the mat just as *I promise to be there* has the implication that the speaker intends to be there. So constatives can be as unhappy as performatives, and the unhappinesses arise for the same types of reason in the case of both types of utterance. Furthermore, performatives seem to be able to be untrue just as constatives. *I advise you to do it* could be considered false in the sense of *conflicting with the facts* if my belief about what is best for you is mistaken. Similarly, *I declare you guilty* conflicts with the facts if you are innocent (at the time, a **correspondence theory of truth** was popular: a sentence was true if and only if it corresponded to the facts; cf. PHILOSOPHY OF LANGUAGE). Austin also points out that it is often difficult to decide whether a statement is strictly true or false, because the facts are vague; and if facts are vague, so is the notion of truth which depends on them. He therefore reformulates the concept of truth as a **dimension of criticism**, including, even for declarative sentences, the situation of the speaker, the purpose of speaking, the

hearers, the precision of reference, etc., and it is already beginning to look as if, as Austin indeed concludes (see below), all utterances may be performative in some sense (1962: 52):

> In order to explain what can go wrong with statements we cannot just concentrate on the proposition involved (whatever that is) as has been done traditionally. We must consider the total situation in which the utterance is issued – the total speech-act – if we are to see the parallel between statements and performative utterances, and how each can go wrong. So the total speech-act in the total speech-situation is emerging from logic piecemeal as important in special cases: and thus we are assimilating the supposed constative utterance to the performative.

However, it might still be possible to save the distinction Austin set out with; instead of concentrating on the truth/falsity– happiness/unhappiness distinction which is beginning to look unsound, perhaps we can decide whether something is or is not a performative by testing whether 'saying so makes it so'. If I say *I promise*, I thereby promise, whereas if I say *I walk*, I do not thereby walk. A possible test for performatives is therefore the **hereby-test**. In the case of performatives it is always possible to insert *hereby*: *I bequeath – I hereby bequeath*; *passengers are warned – passengers are hereby warned*. In a constative, it is not appropriate to insert *hereby*: *I walk – *I hereby walk*; *I am being watched – *I am hereby being watched*. This distinction, however, is also about to be broken down.

So far, the performatives mentioned have been clearly marked as performatives by containing within them a verb which stands for the action being performed; thus, in saying *I promise*, I am promising (*I do* looks like an exception, but Austin assumes it is short for *I do take this woman/man to be my lawful wedded wife/husband*). However, there are many performatives that do not contain these so-called **speech-act verbs** or **performative verbs**, and that are not even declarative sentences; in many cases, uttering words such as *dog*, *bull* or *fire* constitutes an action of warning just as much as uttering *I warn you that there is a dog/bull/fire*, so we would want to say that these utterances, too, are performatives.

A distinction is therefore drawn between **explicit performatives** and **implicit** or **primary** performatives. Austin believed that the explicit performatives had developed from the implicit performatives as language and society became more sophisticated. Any primary performative is expandable into a sentence with a verb in the first person singular indicative or the second or third person indicative passive, a verb which also names the action carried out by the performative. Austin estimated that a good dictionary would contain between 1000 and 9,999 of these performative or speech-act verbs, *and one of them will be 'state'*. Consequently, any constative is expandable into a performative: any utterance, *p*, can be encased in an utterance of the form *I hereby state that p*, and the distinction originally drawn between constatives and performatives has now been effectively deconstructed. *Any* utterance is part of or all of the doing of some action, and the only distinction that now remains is between performative and non-performative *verbs*. Performative verbs name actions that are performed, wholly or partly, by saying something (*state, promise*); non-performative verbs name other types of action, types of action which are independent of speech (*walk, sleep*). Because performative verbs are so numerous, Austin hoped that it might be possible to arrive at some broad classes of speech act under which large numbers of more delicately distinguished speech acts might fall. To arrive at these broad classes, he distinguished among a number of **illocutionary forces** that a speech act might have.

The illocutionary force of an utterance is distinguished from its locution and from its perlocutionary effect as follows.

Every time we direct language at some audience, we perform three simultaneous acts: a locutionary act, an illocutionary act and a perlocutionary act.

To perform a **locutionary act** is to say something in what Austin (1962: 94) calls 'the full normal sense'. It includes:

- The **phonic** act: uttering noises, **phones**.
- The **phatic** act: uttering noises *as belonging to a certain vocabulary and conforming to a certain grammar*; that is, as being part of a certain language. The noises seen from this perspective are called **phemes**.
- The **rhetic** act: using these noises with a certain sense and reference (see PHILOSOPHY OF LANGUAGE). The noises seen from this perspective are called **rhemes**.

These three simultaneous acts make up the locutionary act. However, each time one performs a locutionary act, one is also thereby performing some illocutionary act, such as stating, promising, warning, betting, etc. If a hearer, through her/his knowledge of the conventions of the language, grasps what one is doing, there is **uptake** on her/his part of the **illocutionary force** of the utterance. The effect the illocutionary act has on the hearer is called the **perlocutionary act**, such as persuading, deterring, surprising, misleading or convincing. Perlocutionary acts are performed *by* saying something rather than *in* saying it.

Austin (1962: Lecture 12) suggests that it is possible to distinguish a number of broad classes or families of speech acts, classified according to their illocutionary force. He suggests the following classes:

- **Verdictives**, typified by the giving of a verdict, estimate, reckoning or appraisal; giving a finding.
- **Excersitives**, the exercising of powers, rights or influence, exemplified by voting, ordering, urging, advising, warning, etc.

- **Commissives**, typified by promising or otherwise undertaking (1962: 151–2): 'they *commit* you to doing something, but include also declarations or announcements of intention, which are not promises, and also rather vague things which we might call espousals, as for example, siding with'.
- **Behavitives**, which have to do with social behaviour and attitudes, for example apologizing, congratulating, commending, condoling, cursing and challenging.
- **Expositives**, which make it clear how our utterances fit into the course of an argument or conversation – how we are using words. In a way, these might be classed as **metalinguistic**, as part of the language we are using about language. Examples are *I reply*; *I argue*; *I concede*; *I illustrate*; *I assume*; *I postulate*.

Austin is quite clear that there are many marginal cases, and many instances of overlap, and a very large body of research exists as a result of people's efforts to arrive at more precise classifications both of the broad classes and of the subclasses (see, for instance, Wierzbicka 1987). Here we shall follow up Searle's (1969) development of Austin's theory.

Searle (1969) describes utterances slightly differently from Austin's triad of locution, illocution and perlocution. According to Searle, a speaker typically does four things when saying something; this is because, as Searle rightly points out, not all utterances involve referring and predicating – Austin's rheme, which was part of the locutionary act. For example, *ouch* and *hurrah* do not involve rhemes. So the first of Searle's four possible elements of uttering only contains Austin's phone and pheme; that is, it only includes two of the elements of Austin's locutionary act. Searle calls this act the

- **Utterance act**: uttering words (morphemes, sentences).

Austin's rheme, the third aspect of the locutionary act, constitutes an element of its own in Searle's scheme, the

- **Propositional act**: referring and predicating. In saying

  (a) Will Peter leave the room?
  (b) Peter will leave the room
  (c) Peter, leave the room
  (d) Would that Peter left the room

a speaker will **express** the same **proposition** (symbolized as Rp, where R stands for the action of leaving the room and p stands for Peter), her/his propositional act will be the same, but s/he will be doing other radically different things too in each case. S/he will perform one of a number of possible

- **Illocutionary acts**: questioning, stating, ordering, wishing.

Many utterances contain **indicators of illocutionary force**, including word order, stress, punctuation, the mood of the verb, and Austin's performative verbs. Finally, speaking typically involves a

- **Perlocutionary act**: persuading, getting someone to do something, etc.

Having isolated the acts from each other, in particular having made it possible to separate the propositional act from the illocutionary act, Searle is able to home in on the illocutionary act. To perform illocutionary acts, he says, is to engage in rule-governed behaviour, and he draws up the rules which govern this behaviour on the basis of sets of necessary and sufficient conditions for the performance of the various illocutionary acts.

A **necessary condition** for x is a condition which must be fulfilled before x is achieved, but which cannot, by itself, necessarily guarantee the achievement of x. For example, being human is a necessary condition for becoming a lecturer at Birmingham University, but it is not a sufficient condition; other conditions must be fulfilled too.

A **sufficient condition** for x is a condition which will guarantee its achievement, but which need not be a necessary condition. For instance, the entry requirements for a course of study might state that candidates must *either* have taught English for fifteen years in Papua New Guinea, *or* have green hair. Either quality would be sufficient for admittance to the course, but neither would be necessary.

The sum of all the necessary conditions for x constitutes the necessary and sufficient conditions for it.

Searle (1969: 57–61) lists the necessary and sufficient conditions for the speech act of promising as follows:

1 Normal input and output conditions obtain (speaker and hearer both know the language, are conscious of what they are doing, are not acting under duress, have no physical impairments, are not acting, telling jokes, etc.).
2 The speaker, S, expresses that p (proposition) in making the utterance, U. This isolates the propositional content from the rest of the speech act on which we can then concentrate.
3 In expressing that p, S predicates a *future* act, A, of S. Clearly it is not possible to promise to have done something in the past; promises proper always concern the future.
4 The hearer, H, would prefer S's doing A to her/his not doing A, and S believes that H would prefer her/his doing A to not doing it. This distinguishes promises from threats.
5 It is not obvious to both S and H that S will do A in the normal course of events. If it were obvious, no promise would be necessary, of course.
6 S intends that the utterance of U will make her/him responsible for doing A.
7 S intends that the utterance of U will place her/him under an obligation to do A.

8 S intends that the utterance of U will produce in H a belief that conditions 6 and 7 obtain by means of H's recognition of S's intention to produce that belief in H; and S intends this recognition to be achieved by means of the recognition of the utterance as one conventionally used to produce such beliefs. Elucidation of this rather complexly formulated condition can be obtained through a study of Grice (1957), in which Grice sets out the necessary conditions for **telling** as opposed to **getting someone to believe**. There are many ways of getting someone to believe something; but actually to tell someone something depends on that person recognizing that you intend to get her/him to believe what you are telling her/him by your utterance.
9 The semantic rules of the dialect spoken by S and H are such that U is correctly and sincerely uttered if and only if conditions 1 to 8 obtain.

Conditions 1, 8 and 9 apply generally to all illocutionary acts, and only conditions 2–7 are peculiar to the act of promising. Conditions 2 and 3 are called the **propositional-content conditions** for promising; 4 and 5 are called the **preparatory conditions** for promising; 6 is called the **sincerity condition**; and 7 is called the **essential condition**. Condition 6 can be altered to

6a S intends that the utterance of U will make her/him responsible for intending to do A

in order to allow for insincere promises.

From this list of conditions for promising, Searle extracts a set of rules for the use of any illocutionary force indicating a device for promising. Searle believes that the semantics of a language can be regarded as a series of systems of constitutive rules and that illocutionary acts are performed in accordance with these sets of constitutive rules, so that the study of semantics boils down to the study of illocutionary acts. In discussing the question of linguistic rules, Searle mentions two positions philosophers have taken with regard to them: that knowing the meaning of any expression is simply to know the rules for its employment; this position seems untenable, since no philosopher has apparently able to say exactly what the rules are; this has led to philosophers adopting the second position – that there are no rules at all. Searle thinks that the failure of the first group of philosophers and the consequent pessimism of the second group are both consequences of a failure on the philosophers' part to distinguish between two types of rule – of thinking that there is only one kind.

In fact, Searle insists, there are two distinct kinds of rule: regulative rules and constitutive rules. But philosophers have tended to think of rules only in terms of regulative rules while, in reality, the rules for speech acts are much more like the constitutive rules.

A **regulative rule** is a rule that governs some activity which, however, exists independently of the rule in question. For instance, the rules of etiquette regulate the way in which we eat, dress and generally conduct our interpersonal relationships. However, the activities of eating and dressing exist independently of the rules; even if I shovel food into my mouth with my knife, thus breaking one of the regulative rules for eating, I am, none the less, eating.

A **constitutive rule**, on the other hand, is a rule which both regulates and *constitutes* an activity. The activity could not exist if the rule were not being followed. These are things like rules for various games such as football and chess. If you do not play football according to the rules, you are simply not playing football; if you move your king more than one square at a time, you are simply not playing chess. Similarly, if you do not use the illocutionary force indicating devices for promising according to the rules, you are simply not promising; thus,

in saying *I promise that I did it*, using the past tense, you are not, in fact, promising (you may be assuring).

The rules for the use of any illocutionary force indicator for promising, derived from conditions 2–7 above are:

1 Any illocutionary force indicating device, P, for promising is to be uttered only in the context of an utterance or larger stretch of discourse which predicates some future act, A, of the speaker, S.
2 P is to be uttered only if the hearer, H, would prefer S's doing A to her/his not doing A.
3 P is to be uttered only if it is not obvious to both S and H that S will do A in the normal course of events.
4 P is to be uttered only if S intends to do A.
5 The utterance of P counts as an undertaking of an obligation to do A.

Rule 1 is called the **propositional-content rule**; it is derived from the propositional-content conditions 2 and 3. Rules 2 and 3 are **preparatory rules** derived from the preparatory conditions 4 and 5. Rule 4 is the **sincerity rule** derived from the sincerity condition 6. Rule 5 is the **essential rule**, derived from the essential condition 7, and it is *constitutive* of P. Searle (1969: 66–7) also sets out the rules for the use of illocutionary force, indicating devices for the speech acts **request**, **assert**, **question**, **thank**, **advise**, **warn**, **greet** and **congratulate**. In a subsequent article, 'Indirect speech acts' (1975), he goes on to make a distinction between speaker meaning and sentence meaning. The distinction is drawn as part of the solution Searle offers to one of the great traditional problems in linguistic theory: how is it that speakers know when an utterance having a particular mood, say interrogative, functions as a question, and when it does not?

Normally, we expect utterances in the declarative mood to be statements, utterances in the interrogative mood to be questions, utterances in the imperative mood to be commands, and moodless utterances to be responses or announcements. Mood is an aspect of grammar, and can be read off sentences in a straightforward way:

I am studying
S   P   (S before P; mood declarative)

Is that your coat on the floor?
P   S

Am I studying?
$\begin{vmatrix} S \\ P \end{vmatrix}$ (P before S or S within P; mood interrogative)

Go away
P   (no S: mood imperative)

No
(No P: moodless)

But it is obvious that sentence mood does not stand in a one-to-one correspondence to what might be called sentence **function**. Although in many cases *I am studying* may function as a simple statement of fact, in many other cases it might function as a command or request for someone who is disturbing the speaker to go away. Although in many cases *Is that your coat on the floor?* might function as a straightforward question; in many other cases it might function as a request or command for the coat to be picked up, etc. So how do speakers know which function utterances have on various occasions?

Searle begins by drawing a distinction between the **speaker's utterance meaning** or **speaker meaning**, on the one hand, and **sentence meaning** on the other hand. In hints, insinuations, irony, metaphor, and what Searle calls indirect speech acts, these two types of meaning 'come apart' in a variety of ways (Searle 1979: 122).

- In a literal utterance, a speaker means exactly the same as the sentence means, so speaker meaning and sentence meaning coincide.
- In a simple metaphorical utterance, a speaker says that S is P, but means meta-

phorically that S is R. This utterance meaning is worked out on the basis of the sentence meaning.

- In an open-ended metaphorical utterance, a speaker says that S is P, but means metaphorically an infinite range of meanings, R_1–R_n, and, again, these meanings can be worked out on the basis of the sentence meaning.
- In a dead metaphor, the original sentence meaning is bypassed and the utterance has the meaning that used to be its metaphorical meaning.
- In an ironical utterance, a speaker means the opposite of what the sentence means. So the utterance meaning is worked out by deciding what the sentence meaning is and what its opposite is.

In an **indirect speech act**, which is what concerns us here, a speaker means what s/he says *but means something else as well*, so that the utterance meaning *includes the sentence meaning but extends beyond it*. So, in the case of an indirect speech act, the speaker means what the sentence means but something else as well. So a sentence containing an illocutionary force indicator for one particular type of illocutionary act can be used to perform that act and simultaneously, in addition, another act of a different type. Such speech acts have two illocutionary forces.

For a hearer to grasp both these forces at once, s/he must: know the rules for performing speech acts; share some background information with the speaker; exercise her/his powers of rationality and inference in general; have knowledge of certain general principles of cooperative conversation (see PRAGMATICS; see also Grice 1975).

Searle provides an example of how speakers cope with indirect speech acts:

(1) Student X: *Let's go to the movies tonight*
(2) Student Y: *I have to study for an exam*

Let's in (1) indicates that a speech act which we might call a **proposal** is being made. Example (2) is a **statement**, but in this context it is clear that it functions as the speech-act **rejection of the proposal**. Searle calls the rejection of the proposal the **primary** illocutionary act performed by Y, and says that Y performs it *by way of* the **secondary illocutionary act**, namely the statement. The secondary illocutionary act conforms to the literal meaning of the utterance, so it is a literal act; but the primary illocutionary act is **non-literal.** Given that X only actually hears the literal act, but recognizes the non-literal, primary illocutionary act, how does s/he arrive at this latter recognition on the basis of the recognition of the literal, secondary illocutionary act?

Searle proposes that X goes through the following ten steps of reasoning:

Step 1:   I have made a proposal to Y, and in response s/he has made a statement to the effect that he has to study for an exam.

Step 2:   I assume that Y is co-operating in the conversation and that therefore her/his remark is intended to be relevant.

Step 3:   A relevant response would be one of acceptance, rejection, counterproposal, further discussion, etc.

Step 4:   But her/his literal utterance was not one of these, and so was not a relevant response.

Step 5:   Therefore, s/he probably means more than s/he says. Assuming that her/his remark is relevant, her/his primary illocutionary point must differ from her/his literal one.

Step 6:   I know that studying for an exam normally takes a large amount of time relative to a single evening, and I know that going to the movies normally takes a large amount of time relative to a single evening.

Step 7:   Therefore, s/he probably cannot both go to the movies and study for an exam in one evening.

Step 8:   A preparatory condition on the acceptance of a proposal, or any other commissive, is the ability to perform the act predicated in the propositional content condition.

Step 9:   Therefore, I know that s/he has said something that has the consequence that s/he probably cannot accept the proposal.

Step 10:   Therefore her/his primary illocutionary point is probably to reject the proposal.

As step 8 indicates, knowing the rules for speech acts enables one to recognize that a literal, secondary illocutionary act somehow contains reference within it to a condition for another speech act; and this will be the speech act which is the primary, non-literal illocutionary act performed by the speaker.

For instance, the rules (derived from conditions) for the speech-act **request** are (Searle 1969: 66):

Propositional content	Future act *A* of *H*.
Preparatory	1. *H* is able to do *A*. *S* believes *H* is able to do *A*. 2. It is not obvious to both *S* and *H* that *H* will do *A* in the normal course of events of her/his own accord.
Sincerity	*S* wants *H* to do *A*.
Essential	Counts as an attempt to get *H* to do *A*.
Comment:	*Order* and *command* have the additional preparatory rule that *S* must be in a position of authority over *H* . . .

Consequently, there is a set of groups of sentences that correspond to these rules, 'that could quite standardly be used to make indirect requests and other directives such as orders' (1969: 64). The groups are (I am leaving out many of Searle's example sentences; see 1975: 65–7):

Group 1: Sentences concerning *H*'s ability to perform *A*: *Can you pass/reach the salt.*
Group 2: Sentences concerning *S*'s wish or want that *H* will do *A*: *I would like you to go now*; *I wish you wouldn't do that.*
Group 3: Sentences concerning *H*'s doing *A*: *Officers will henceforth wear ties at dinner*; *Aren't you going to eat your cereal?*
Group 4: Sentences concerning *H*'s desire or willingness to do *A*: *Would you be willing to write a letter of recommendation for me?*; *Do you want to hand me that hammer over there on the table?*
Group 5: Sentences concerning reasons for doing *A*: *It would be a good idea if you left town*; *Why don't you try it just once?*
Group 6: Sentences embedding one of these elements inside another; also sentences embedding an explicit directive illocutionary verb inside one of these contexts: *Would you mind awfully if I asked you if you could write me a letter of recommendation?*

That anyone should want to use an indirect rather than a direct speech act is due to considerations of politeness (see PRAGMATICS): by prefacing an utterance with, for example, *Can you*, as in the case of indirect requests, the speaker is not making presumptions about the hearer's capabilities, and is also clearly offering the hearer the option of refusing the request, since a Yes/No question like *Can you pass the salt?* allows for *No* as an answer.

K.M.

Suggestions for further reading

Austin, J.L. (1971) Performative-Constative', in J.R. Searle (ed.) *The Philosophy of Language*, Oxford: Oxford University Press.
Mey, J.L. (1993) *Pragmatics: An Introduction*, Oxford: Basil Blackwell.
Saeed, J.I. (1997) *Semantics*, Oxford: Blackwell Publishers.
Searle, J.R. (1971) 'What is a speech act', in J.R. Searle (ed.) *The Philosophy of Language*, Oxford: Oxford University Press.

Speech and language therapy

Definition

Speech and language therapy is the British label for the activities of members of an independent profession whose concern is with the diagnosis, assessment, treatment and management of a wide range of disorders of communication that affect people from infancy to senescence. The prime interest is with disorders of spoken language, but the profession is also concerned with disorders of written language, especially in adults. Written language in children is usually seen as the responsibility of the teaching profession, but there is often an overlap of interests, and increasingly speech and language therapists contribute to literacy programmes for young children.

Speech and language therapy is a comparatively young profession, developed in the twentieth century. Similar professions exist in a number of countries, although there are some differences in their academic backgrounds and their spheres of responsibilities, as reflected in their different titles: for example, **speech pathologists** in the USA,

Australia, New Zealand and the Republic of South Africa, and **logopedists**, **phoniatrists** and **orthophonists** in various European countries. Elsewhere in the world, e.g. Hong Kong and Malaysia, professions are developing where previously the country had relied on speech and language therapists trained abroad. Reciprocal recognition of professional qualifications is limited between countries, although there is a growing exchange of research and therapeutic techniques internationally between practitioners. The profession's international society is the **International Association of Logopedics and Phoniatrics**, founded in 1924.

Historical background

At the turn of the twentieth century there was an increase in the study, interest and knowledge of human behaviour, including speech, and a parallel expansion of knowledge in the medical sciences. For example, work by neuroanatomists such as Broca in France, Wernicke in Germany and Jackson in the United Kingdom confirmed the relationship between cortical damage and acquired language disorders (see APHASIA; LANGUAGE PATHOLOGY AND NEUROLINGUISTICS). In the early years of the twentieth century, increased sophistication in neurological studies had established a relationship between areas of cortical damage and aphasia. A framework for describing some of the components of such disorders evolved, but at that time the physicians and neurologists who were interested in speech disorders felt unable to explore methods of remediation and turned to teachers of voice, elocution and singing for help. These early interventionists, realizing their lack of scientific knowledge, sought help from eminent members of the medical and allied professions, and accumulated a relevant body of information which they were able to pass on to their own personal students. The first activities of speech and language therapists were based on contemporary studies of neurology and the developing disciplines of phonetics, psychology and a tradition of education (Quirk 1972).

Parallel to this development in medicine, there was a growing interest in speech disorders in children that arose from educationalists specializing in remedial education. The first speech therapy clinic for children was established in Manchester in 1906 and offered training for stammerers. This was followed by similar clinics elsewhere; in 1911, the first clinic for adults was established at St Bartholomew's Hospital, London, and in 1913 a second clinic opened at St Thomas's Hospital, London. In 1919 the Central School of Speech and Drama, London, in association with the clinic at St Thomas's, started a course for training speech and language therapists. Other courses were started in Scotland and in London.

During the 1930s there were two professional associations of speech and language therapists: one that represented the medical background, and one that was associated with the teachers of voice and elocution. These two associations, which reflected the two main roots of the profession, were amalgamated in 1945 to form the **College of Speech and Language Therapists**, since 1995 named the **Royal College of Speech and Language Therapists**. Speech and language therapy continues to be closely associated with medicine and education both in terms of employment and in the two main approaches to categorizing the range of disorders that are assessed and treated (see LANGUAGE PATHOLOGY AND NEUROLINGUISTICS).

Since 1975, the profession has been unified under the National Health Service. This followed the recommendations of the **Report of the Committee of Enquiry into the Speech Therapy Services** which, under the chairmanship of Randolph Quirk, was published in 1972. Prior to this time, speech and language therapists had been employed both by educational and health authorities.

Training and professional body

Since 1985, entry into the profession in the United Kingdom has been through a three- or four-year undergraduate programme or a two-year postgraduate programme. All degree programmes leading to a qualification in speech and language therapy are accredited by the Royal College of Speech and Language Therapists, which is responsible to the Secretary of State for Health and Social Services and to the Secretary of State for Scotland for ensuring that every graduate who is certified to practise as a speech and language therapist has reached the required levels of knowledge, expertise and competence. The components of each degree programme vary in emphasis, but all will contain the following subjects: neurology, anatomy, physiology, psychology, education, linguistics, phonetics, audiology, speech and language pathology and clinical studies (see LANGUAGE PATHOLOGY AND NEUROLINGUISTICS). The study of the disorders of communication is based on the study of normal speech and language from development in childhood to decay in the elderly.

Places of work

By the start of the twenty-first century, there were the equivalent of just over seven thousand full-time registered speech and language therapists working in the United Kingdom, the large majority of whom were women. In the USA there were 96,000 members of the **American Speech, Language and Hearing Association (ASHA)**, although this number includes audiologists as well as speech pathologists and speech, language and hearing scientists. As in the United Kingdom, most American speech and language therapists are women. In the United Kingdom most speech and language therapists practise in local authority health clinics, schools or hospitals. Some are employed by charitable bodies concerned with children with special needs, and an increasing number work in specialized units, for example with adults and children who have physical or cognitive impairments, or with those with hearing impairments. There are also units offering intensive rehabilitation to adults who have language problems following illness or accidents. Many education authorities offer special provision for children with specific language impairment where speech and language therapists will be employed.

Speech and language therapists work closely with a number of other professions, including medical specialists, nurses, other medical therapists, psychologists, teachers, social workers and clinical linguists. They are often part of a rehabilitation team. In all positions, the speech and language therapist remains ultimately responsible for the assessment, treatment and management of disorders of communication, although in cases which are secondary to disease or injury a doctor will usually retain overall responsibility for the patient's medical care.

Range of interest

Communicative disorders may result from abnormalities of the production or resonance of voice, the fluency of language, or language production, including the articulation of speech sounds, or they may arise from defects of the monitoring system at any level of production. Disorders at any of these levels can have a number of causes: they may be secondary to trauma, illness or degenerative processes – for example, acquired disorders of language such as aphasia and dysarthria; associated with structural abnormalities such as cleft palate; associated with abnormal developmental patterns – for example, delayed language or phonological development; secondary to or associated with other defects – for example, hearing loss or severe learning difficulties; arise from environmental damage – for example, aphonia (loss of voice) or dysphonia (abnormal voice); or they may be idiopathic, as in stuttering.

A significant number of people in the United Kingdom suffer from some type of communicative disorder. It has been estimated that approximately 800,000 people suffer from communication disorders where little or no spontaneous speech is possible, and a further 1.5 million have speech or language which is noticeably disordered (Enderby and Philipp 1986). This figure is now thought to underestimate the population with communication disorders, as a broader range of disorders and client groups are being seen by speech and language therapists. Some communication disorders can be alleviated and require remediation; others are chronic and require management and perhaps counselling. The speech and language therapist is responsible for assessing all those with communication disorders and selecting the appropriate treatment and/or management programme.

Range of disorders

Disorders of voice

Disorders of voice such as **aphonia**, total absence of sound, or **dysphonia**, abnormal sound, may arise from organic causes such as growths on (or thickening of) the vocal folds, hormonal imbalance, damage to the laryngeal nerves, or vocal abuse, or they may arise from idiopathic, unknown, causes. Cases of unknown origin are often referred to as **functional** and may be associated with stress or misuse of the vocal folds. All cases are referred to therapy through ear, nose and throat medical specialists and close contact is maintained between the speech and language therapist and the surgeon or physician. Assessment of the voice quality and assumptions about the functioning of the vocal folds are made

after listening to the voice and, depending on availability, instrumental investigations. Such investigations may include **electroglottography**, which provides information on vocal-fold activity, airflow and pressure measurements, and the use of visual displays of such information. Therapy is aimed at improving the quality of the voice through increasing the patient's awareness of the processes involved in voice production, encouraging optimal use of the voice, and increasing the patient's ability to monitor her/his own voice. Where stress is associated with the disorder, counselling techniques are added to the programme. Progress depends on the individual's physical and personal characteristics. In certain cases, additional assistance may be offered, such as amplification of the voice, or systems to augment speech.

Disorders of fluency

Disorders of fluency include **disfluency**, which is associated with neurological damage, as well as those with no known cause, termed **stammering** or **stuttering**. Stammering is characterized by one or more of the following: involuntary repetition of sounds, syllables, words and phrases; prolongation of sounds, often involving the closure phase of plosives (see ARTICULATORY PHONETICS) and associated with tension; an increase in the number of filled and unfilled pauses; and a relatively higher number of false starts, incomplete utterances and revisions than normal. The position of each disfluency can be described in terms of the phoneme (see PHONEMICS) involved and its position within the word, tone unit, phrase or clause. The speaker may also exhibit embarrassment or anxiety and fear certain words or communicative situations. The severity of disfluency can range from affecting more than 90 per cent of the utterances to less than 1 per cent.

Certain relationships have been observed between the occurrence of disfluency and the unit of speech involved. For example, there is some evidence that disfluency is more likely to be associated with open-class words and with stress and initial position in both words and clauses, but the exact relationship is far from clear. The complexity of the unit of language involved is also thought to exert an influence. There is a large amount of individual variation, and it may be that several different disorders with varying characteristics and arising from different causes are all being referred to as stammering; however, there is no agreement on where causal or symptomatic boundaries might be drawn. Many stammerers experience fluctuating periods of fluency or have fluency behaviour associated with specific situations or environments.

Most stammerers are able to increase their fluency with techniques taught by speech and language therapists, although the maintenance of fluency is often difficult. Discussion of the stammerer's perception of her/himself and her/his speech forms an important component of most programmes. The main influence on approaches to treatment are from psychology (see, for example, Ingham 1984). There has been a limited influence from linguistics, although the discipline of phonetics is becoming increasingly influential with the expanding availability of instrumental measurement of speech production.

Disorders of language

Disorders of language may be acquired as the result of disease or injury; associated with other major deficits in, for example, hearing or cognition; or, as in developmental disorders, occur when the child fails to develop language according to expectations, notwithstanding normal development in other areas. The term 'language disorder' is used as a broad category to include failure to develop, impairment or loss of any level of language production and includes understanding of language (see also LANGUAGE PATHOLOGY AND NEUROLINGUISTICS). Developmental language disorders in children will be considered first.

Language disorders in children

Children may fail to develop age-appropriate syntax, phonology, lexicon or pragmatics or may fail to develop the expected understanding of language while demonstrating other age-appropriate non-verbal cognitive skills. The extent of delay varies. For some children the delay may be slight and quickly resolved; for others the delay may also affect written language and problems with reading and/or spelling may persist for many years; while for yet other children the gap between their expected and actual linguistic abilities is so severe as to prevent them from benefiting from mainstream education. There is limited special educational provision for this small group of handicapped children in the United Kingdom, whereas in the USA these children are more likely to be integrated into mainstream education.

From time to time efforts are made to distinguish 'delayed' speech from 'deviant' speech. In practice, speech may resemble that of a younger child in terms of grammatical structures and the repertoire of sounds used, but there are very often differences that arise from the child's greater experience of the world and the influence of other aspects of development. There may also be differences in language use. Some children may produce speech that is both qualitatively and quantitatively different, for example psychiatrically disturbed children, but there seems to be little evidence that this is common for other categories of handicap, e.g. learning disability.

Although the various levels of language are interdependent and the boundaries between, for example, syntax and phonology are fuzzy, the production of speech sounds is often considered separately. Some children are slower than their peers to develop a complete repertoire of phonemes and some of this group seem to have difficulty in controlling accurate movement and timing of the supraglottal (see ARTICULATORY PHONETICS) musculature despite the lack of frank neurological impairment. Errors may be at the phonetic level and fluency and vocal quality might also be impaired, although these factors are more usually considered to be characteristic of dysarthria (see below). For this particular group of children, therapy is directed at increasing the child's muscular control and ability to sequence sounds, rather than explaining or expanding the rule-governed behaviour of phonology and syntax. These disorders are known either as **articulation disorders**, usually affecting one class of sounds, or as **articulatory dyspraxia** if there are more widespread problems. The choice of terms seems to be related to the perceived severity of the disorder, as well as to success in therapy, the first term applying to less severe disorders.

Children with frank neurological impairments involving the central nervous system frequently have disorders of speech arising from impaired muscle movement and control. These speech disorders are known as **dysarthrias** and are traditionally subdivided according to the site of the neurological lesion. Such children often have language disorders as well, either arising from damage to the cortical area (see APHASIA), or from a reduction in normal developmental stimulus and experience, or associated with learning disabilities. Abnormal vocal quality and poor control of fluency are frequent in these conditions. In addition, because the neurological and anatomical structures used in speech are the same structures involved in feeding, these children often have disordered feeding patterns. Because of the close relationship between speech and feeding, and because the speech and language therapist often has a uniquely detailed knowledge of the anatomy and neurology of this region, s/he is often involved in programmes to improve feeding skills. The role of the speech and language therapist in the management of **dysphagia** (difficulty with swallowing) has become increasingly important.

The speech and language therapist's assessment of language disorders is based on her/his knowledge of the major subjects of the qualifying degree programme, including knowledge of normal development. Medical, sociological and educational factors are considered as well as a characterization of the child's linguistic abilities. Studies in linguistics, including child language acquisition (see LANGUAGE ACQUISITION), as well as psycholinguistics (see PSYCHOLINGUISTICS) have contributed to the range of assessment procedures available and to the subsequent treatment programme that will be formulated. Three examples of assessment are **LARSP** (Crystal *et al.* 1976), which offers a description of the child's surface grammar; **TROG** (Bishop 1982), which enables the speech and language therapist to examine the child's understanding of certain grammatical structures; and the **Reynell Developmental Language Scales III** (Edwards *et al.* 1997), an assessment of production and comprehension of lexical and syntactic features of language.

Having characterized the child's speech and language, the therapist strives to teach or encourage or enhance development, often in conjunction with parents and teachers. For the child to reach age-appropriate levels of language, it is necessary for accelerated development to take place. Progress is often slow, intervention taking place over months rather than weeks.

Following the Education Act 1981, speech and language therapists have an increasing involvement with children with learning difficulties, many of whom have a language delay over and above the delay that would be predicted from their mental age. The process of characterizing their language is the same as that for normally developing children. For these children, however, it is more appropriate to aim for language that is commensurate with mental rather than chronological age.

Language disorders in adults
Disorders of language in adults arise from diseases or injury (see APHASIA) although the developmental disorders described above can persist into adulthood. Acquired disorders of language are usually considered under the two main categories of **aphasia** and **dysarthria**: **dyspraxia** or **apraxia** nearly always occurs with aphasia. Aphasia or dysphasia (see APHASIA) is a disorder of language arising from damage to the cortex of the brain. Dysarthria is a disorder of sound production which arises from damage to the central nervous system and which can affect production at all levels: air supply, vocal fold activity, supraglottal musculature including control of resonance. In addition, suprasegmental features of timing, stress and prosody are often involved.

The distinction between these two levels of language is justified in terms of focus of treatment, although theoretically (and clinically in some cases) the boundaries are less clear.

Treatment of dysarthria is aimed at helping the patient make optimal use of residual skills, increasing self-monitoring of speech, teaching strategies to enhance intelligibility, and advising and providing augmentative or alternative means of communication. Aphasia therapy is aimed at other levels of language – phonology, syntax, semantics and pragmatics – and aims to increase the patient's production and understanding of both written and spoken language. As in all speech and language therapy, intervention starts with an assessment of the patient's medical and social background as well as a full description of the language problem. Most of the patients with aphasia or dysarthria seen by the speech and language therapist will have other medical problems, which, with the language problem, are secondary to the injury or disease. Thus the speech and language therapist

working with these patients is usually part of a medical team and collaborates with other medical personnel.

Aphasia therapy reflects the major strands of aphasiology, neurology, psychology and, to a much lesser extent, linguistics. Approaches also reflect the underlying theories concerned with aphasia. For example, a **unitary** view of aphasia is associated with therapy which aims to stimulate language activity but does not select any level or process for particular attention. A more systematic approach which focuses on components of language behaviour arises from the detailed psychoneurological approach initiated in the USSR (see, for instance, Luria 1970). A more recent detailed approach has been pioneered in the United Kingdom following investigations by psychologists and speech and language therapists who, by series of individually designed tasks, seek to pinpoint which levels, using models of dynamic speech production, are most impaired by the aphasia. A third approach bases therapy on linguistic theory, usually some version of generative grammar, and aims to highlight the constituent relationships in sentences of contrasting structure. In all approaches, both written and spoken language will be used. The prime concern of the therapist will be the individual's present and future need for language; it is also appropriate to consider the patient's social and emotional needs as well as those of her/his or her carers.

Dyspraxia of speech is often interpreted as a disorder which lies between the planning processes of language and the execution of speech production (Miller 1986). In most cases it is concomitant with aphasia, which makes the extent of the linguistic influences on this disorder difficult to define. Clinically, exercises aimed at improving muscle strength and co-ordination often seem inappropriate despite the characteristic phonetic distortions which may resemble certain dysarthrias. Treatment strategies include: a detailed approach to forming individual sounds; focusing on sequencing sounds within words; using context and linguistic contrast; and supplementing spoken with written language.

A third category of language disorder in adults is that associated with dementia. The speech and language therapist is most often asked to help in the differential diagnosis of aphasia and dementia in the elderly and to advise in the subsequent management of such cases, but in a population which has an increasing number of elderly and old citizens, this category is likely to make increasingly heavy demands on speech and language therapy.

S.E.

Suggestions for further reading

Crystal, D. and Varley, R. (1993) *Introduction to Language Pathology*, 3rd edition, London: Whurr.

Van der Gaag, A. (1996) *Communicating Quality*, London: The Royal College of Speech and Language Therapists.

Stratificational linguistics

Stratificational theory

In its broadest sense, the term **stratificational linguistics** can be applied to any view which apportions language structure into two or more strata, or layers. In practice, however, the term has commonly been applied to the outgrowth of ideas originated in the late 1950s and early 1960s by Sydney M. Lamb and H.A. Gleason Jr.

Lamb's version began as an elaboration of the theory of levels in neo-Bloomfieldian linguistics first appearing in Lamb's dissertation, a grammar of the California Amerindian language Monachi (University of California, Berkeley, 1957). The initial idea was refined while Lamb was directing a machine translation project at Berkeley (1957–64).

By 1964, when Lamb moved to Yale University, he had become aware that Gleason, then at the Hartford Seminary Foundation, had been developing a broadly similar model. As a result of collaboration and interchange, their views came to a rough convergence, though they were never completely unified.

At about the time he moved to Yale, Lamb began to develop a unified notation as an adjunct to his theory. From this work he concluded that linguistic structure consists entirely of configurations of a few basic relationships. One of these was named the **AND** – the syntagmatic relation occurring, for instance, when an idiom like *kick the bucket*, 'die', is seen as a combination of smaller elements *kick*, *the* and *bucket*. Another was named the **OR** – the paradigmatic relation evident, for example, when we enumerate the alternative suffixes compatible with a verb stem like *walk*, including -*s*, -*ed* and -*ing*. Lamb soon began to use a notation depicting such basic relations for all of linguistic structure. At the same time, he realized that linguistic structure consists not of items with relationships between them, as he once believed, but of relationships alone, interconnecting in a network. Since a similar idea had been asserted in the **glossematic theory** of **Louis Hjelmslev** (see GLOSSEMATICS), Lamb came to see Hjelmslev's work as a precursor of his own.

Soon afterwards, Lamb concluded that the relational-network structure was more essential to his view than stratification, which he treated as deriving from a confrontation of the relational view with linguistic data. This notion was not shared by Gleason, however, nor by all of those who had based their work on Lamb's model. Since about 1965, the term **Relational**

Network Grammar has been applicable to the work of Lamb and some of his followers, particularly Peter A. Reich, who especially favoured this term, but also William J. Sullivan, David G. Lockwood and others. The term 'stratificational' is still needed, however, for the work of Gleason and his students, and others like Ilah Fleming, who has drawn from both Lamb and Gleason, as well as from other sources.

From the late 1960s, Lamb began a serious investigation of how his theory could be related to what is known about the structure of the brain, and this led him to begin to speak of his own version as **cognitive linguistics**. He taught and lectured on this view around that period, but published very little on it until the 1980s. His teaching at Rice University (from 1980 until his retirement in 1998) led to the ultimate publication of Lamb (1999), which presents his view of what he now calls **neuro-cognitive linguistics**. This modified name was adopted because others (led by George Lakoff and Ronald Langacker) had begun to use the similar term **cognitive grammar** for a view based on semantic considerations, but not relating to neural structure.

Unless otherwise indicated, the present discussion deals with the 'standard' model of stratificational theory. This view, based on Lamb's ideas of the 1970–1 period, was incorporated in D.G. Lockwood (1972). This model treats language as a relational network organized into four primary stratal systems and two peripheral (probably extralinguistic) systems.

Each primary stratal system has a tactic pattern specifying the arrangements of its units and a realizational portion relating these units to adjacent systems. The four stratal systems are the sememic, treating essentially the linguistic organization of meanings; the lexemic, treating the internal relations of phrases, clauses and sentences; the morphemic, treating the internal structure of grammatical words; and the phonemic, treating classical morphophonemic relations, but with a componential representation comparable to classical phonemics at its lowest level (see MORPHOLOGY; PHONEMICS).

Like the primary systems, the peripheral systems are seen as relational networks, but the organization of tactic and realizational portions appears not to be as strictly defined in these systems as in the primary ones. These systems link language proper with extralinguistic matters. Bordering on the sememic system is the gnostemic (or conceptual) system, organizing general knowledge. Some more recent views, probably more correctly, allow this system to connect to any of the primary systems, not just to semology, to handle stylistically conditioned alternation. The other peripheral system is the phonetic, correlating minimal phonological units with phonetic realizations of the classically sub-phonemic type. This system ultimately relates to both articulatory movements and auditory impressions.

Stratificational analysis of a sample sentence

The analysis of a short example on multiple strata is a good way to illustrate the workings of a stratificational analysis. An appendix to D.G. Lockwood (1972: 290–301) treated the English sentence *All the best woodpeckers were shot by Lance's friends*.

Limited space does not permit the reproduction of that example, but briefer discussion of the sentence *All Tom's compact disks were stolen [by a burglar]* is offered here as an updated form.

The semological structure of this example is shown in Figure 1. On this stratum, the structures are not presented in a linear order. Triangular nodes with all their downward lines coming from a single point are UNORDERED ANDs. This representation includes two sub-varieties of such ANDs: the shaded node is an ASSOCIATIVE AND, marking an association in no particular

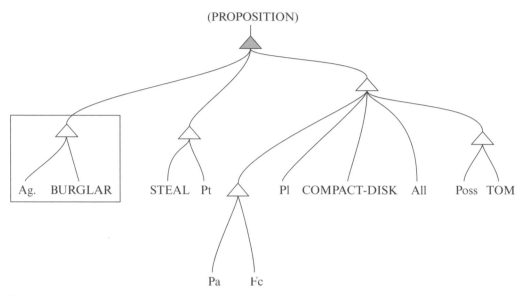

Figure 1

sequence, while the others are simply SIMULTANEOUS ANDs. The configuration inside the box is the optional part corresponding to *by the burglar*. In the view found in this theory, the relation of classes of verbs to various classes of nominals capable of serving as subjects and/or objects in the same clause with them are treated in the semology. These classes involve such distinctions as concrete/abstract, animate/inanimate and human/non-human. Then the lexology does not have to treat them, because it is controlled by the semology. In addition, provision must be made to treat these patterns essentially as norms, capable of being violated in such contexts as fantasy stories, and not as absolutes. Essentially, those 'syntactic' matters more easily handled in the semiology of a language are treated there, while others, such as the linear order of phrasal constituents, are treated in the lexology.

The corresponding structure on the lexemic stratum is shown in Figure 2. The most important task of the lexology in any language, specifically of the lexotactics, is to specify the arrangements of words into larger units: phrases, clauses and sen-

tences. On this stratum, the units (lexemes) are mostly given in linear order, which is signalled by ORDERED ANDs, depicted with their downward lines in a sequence corresponding to their order. Unordered nodes are still used, however, for the association of inflectional marks with their stems. Again the boxed portion indicates the optional part.

On the morphemic stratum, primary attention is paid to the internal structure of words distinguishing prefixes, suffixes and simulfixes, and specifying linear orders among affixes where relevant. (Any affix which is not a prefix or a suffix is treated as a simulfix, with further distinctions – as between superfixes and infixes – being left to the phonology.) Only some words are shown in Figure 3, because most of the rest have no internal morphemic structure.

Table 1 illustrates the relationships among these three strata in a different fashion, concentrating on the way sememes, lexemes and morphemes line up in various relationships. In most cases, there is a simple one-to-one-to-one correspondence between adjacent strata, as illustrated by the first three examples. The morphemic

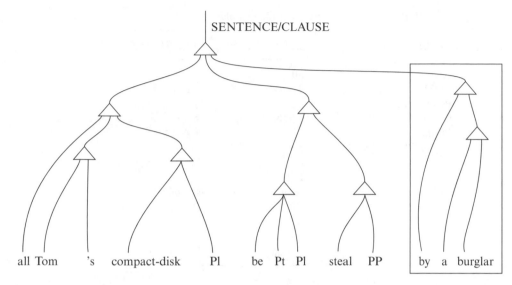

Figure 2

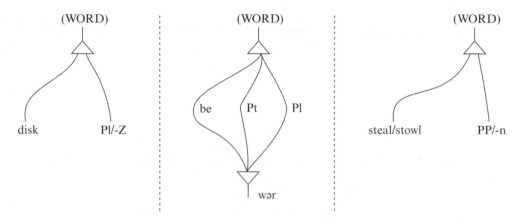

Figure 3

representation is generally given in terms of MORPHONs, which correspond to one of the classic conceptions of morphophonemes. Technically, the combinations of morphons are not morphemes proper, but MORPHEMIC SIGNs, and there can be alternative morphemic signs for the same morpheme. More complex examples have been assigned numbers and are discussed in the numbered comments below.

1 First, we note that there is a single sememe and a corresponding lexeme for compact disk, but ultimately this corresponds to a sequence of two morphemes represented here as ^{M}/k a m p æ k t/ and ^{M}/d i s k/. This is a case of COMPOSITE REALIZATION. In a fuller presentation it would be localized within the lexemic system. This is generally the case for idiomatic phrases whose meaning is different from or more than the sum of the usual meanings of their parts. It can be noted that the sememe, ^{S}/COMPACT-DISK/, is often realized by the acronymic lexeme, ^{L}/CD/, which

Table 1 Realizational relations in the sample sentence

SEMEMIC	LEXEMIC	MORPHEMIC
ALL	all	ɔ l
TOM	Tom	t a m
Poss[essive]	-'s	S
COMPACT-DISK	compact disk	k a m p æ k t d i s k (1)
Pl[ural]	s	z/Z (2)
Pa[tient] & F[o]c[us] (3)	be	⎫
P[as]t	Pt	⎬ be & Pt & Pl/wər (4)
	Pl (5)	⎭
STEAL	steal	steal/s t o w l (2)
Pa & Fc (3)	PP	PP/ən (2)
Ag[ent]	by	b a y
	a (5)	ə
BURGLAR	burglar	b ə r g l ə r

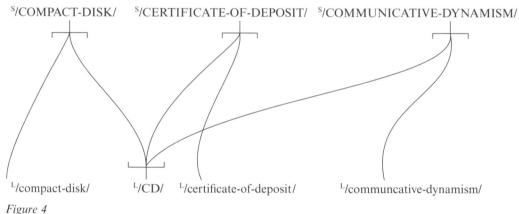

^{S}/COMPACT-DISK/ ^{S}/CERTIFICATE-OF-DEPOSIT/ ^{S}/COMMUNICATIVE-DYNAMISM/

^{L}/compact-disk/ ^{L}/CD/ ^{L}/certificate-of-deposit/ ^{L}/communcative-dynamism/

Figure 4

connects to at least two alternative sememic units: ^{S}/CERTIFICATE OF DEPOSIT/ in the financial realm, and (in the vocabulary of some linguists) ^{S}/COMMUNICATIVE DYNAMISM/ in the realm of discourse studies. The relationships connecting these are diagramed in Figure 4.

2 There are several cases where two different labels separated by a slash are shown in the morphemic column. This notation is intended to represent the occurrence of DIVERSIFICATION, also known as ALTERNATE REALIZATION. Here only the selected alternate has been shown, but the language has other pos-sible ways of manifesting the morphemes for plural, ^{M}/Pl/ and ^{M}/PP/ for the past participle and the verb ^{M}/steal/.

3 In the indication of the passive, there are several complications. Basically, the English passive here involves the mark of the Patient (Pa) (the undergoer) combined with the marked Focus (Fc). Their relationship is one of PORTMANTEAU REALIZATION within the semology. This passive element is in turn realized by two discontinuous lexemes: (1) the auxiliary verb ^{L}/be/ and the past-participle suffix ^{L}/PP/ on the main verb. (It can also be argued that a third part of the realization of passive is the selection of the

Table 2 Simplified representation of the sample in terms of phonemes and phonons

ɔ	l	+	t	a	m	z	+	k	a	m	p	æ	k	t	+	d	i	s	k	s
Vo	Ap		Cl	Vo	Ns	Sp		Cl	Vo	Ns	Cl	Vo	Cl	Cl		Cl	Vo	Sp	Cl	Sp
Lb			Ap	Lo	Lb	Rz		Do	Lo	Lb	Lb	Fr	Do	Ap		Ap	Fr	Rz	Do	Rz
Lo						Vd						Lo				Vd	Hi			

w	ə	r	s	t	o	w	l	ə	n	+	b	a	y	ə	b	ə	r	g	l	ə	r
Lb	Vo	Rz	Sp	Cl	Vo	Lb	Ap	Vo	Ns		Cl	Vo	Fr	Vo	Cl	Vo	Rz	Cl	Ap	Vo	Rz
			Rz	Ap	Lb				Ap		Lb	Lo			Lb			Do			
											Vd				Vd			Vd			

Key to symbols

Ap	=	Apical	Hi	=	High	Rz	=	Retracted
Cl	=	Closed	Lb	=	Labial	Sp	=	Spirant
Do	=	Dorsal	Lo	=	Low	Vd	=	Voiced
Fr	=	Frontal	Ns	=	Nasal	Vo	=	Vocalic

entity marked as Patient as the grammatical subject.)

4 The single word, *were*, in the morphology is here treated as another case of PORTMANTEAU REALIZATION, manifesting ᴹ/be/ ᴹ/Pt/ and ᴹ/Pl/ all in one.

5 There are two instances of what is called EMPTY REALIZATION in this data. One is the plural concord seen on the verb, and the other involves the occurrence of the indefinite article, *a*. In the first instance, the verb is required by the lexotactics to agree with its subject, so it takes on the Plural (Pl) marker. In the latter instance, some kind of determiner is required, and the lexology supplies ᴸ/a/ when no different specification (such as one for a definite article or a possessive expression) is received from the semology. A fuller account of English would need to deal with special cases when no overt determiner is found, as with mass nouns or plurals, as well as with proper names.

When it comes to the phonology, there is actually a considerable hierarchy to represent, including organization into what might be seen as intonation units, breath groups and phonological words. In the version shown here, in Table 2, most suprasegmentals have been omitted to keep the presentation fairly straightforward. What is given is a representation of each phonological word as a string of segments broken down into simultaneous phonological components termed phonons. Segmental phonemic labels have been included for ease of reference and exposition. The plus symbols separating phonological words are kinds of juncture elements, which are viewed as phonemes also. Each segment is shown to consist of between one and three phonons. This is sufficient to distinguish the phonemic segments in English, but some languages may require larger bundles depending on the complexity of their segmental phonology. Phonons are essentially singularly articulatory features. So they are present in the segments marked with them, and absent in other segments: distinctively voiced segments contain ᴾᴺ/Vd/. Others lack distinctive voicing – meaning that voicing is either distinctively absent (as with ᴾ/p t k/ among others) or predictable (as with vowels and resonants in English and many other languages).

The active example corresponding to the sample sentence is, of course, *A burglar stole all Tom's compact disks.* The sememic structure for this would differ only minimally from that given in Figure 1: it would simply lack the sememe ˢ/Fc/ marking the special focus. Its lexemic structure in relation to Figure 2 would show greater differences. The same noun phrases used as subject and prepositional 'object' in the passive example would now occur as object and subject, respectively. Further differences on the lower strata would largely parallel those found in the lexology.

Tactic patterns

As mentioned above, the sample representations at each stratum are related to a tactic pattern associated with that stratum, which has the task of specifying well-formed combinations at its level. As an illustration of the details of such a pattern, we can consider the structure of the English noun phrase on the lexemic stratum. The particular noun phrase examples *all Tom's compact disks* and *a burglar* in the sample above would be among the outputs possible from this structure.

Represented in an algebraic form the structure of this phrase (NP) can be shown as follows:

$$\text{NP/[PreD] Det [Enum] [M] H}_n \text{ [Q]}$$

This states that an NP consists of an optional predeterminer ([PreD]), an obligatory determiner (Det), an optional enumerator ([Enum]), an optional modifier ([M]), an obligatory nominal head (Hn) and an optional qualifier ([Q]), in that order. The symbol /, can be read here as 'may consist of', though more generally it means 'leads down to'. An optional constituent is enclosed in square brackets, while the space between symbols on the right-hand side of the formula indicates a linear order between the constituents involved.

The sample phrase *all Tom's compact disks* includes three of the possible constituents, predeterminer (*all*), determiner (*Tom's*) and nominal head (*compact disks*). An expansion of it incorporating the other

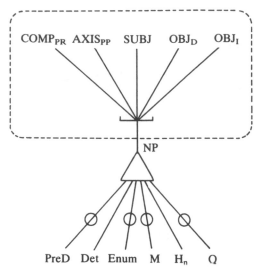

Figure 5

possibilities would be *all Tom's twenty valuable compact disks from Russia*, which adds an enumerator (*twenty*) a modifier (*valuable*) and a qualifier (*from Russia*).

Figure 5 represents the same information as the formula, translated into the relational-network notation. The fact that the NP relates to the functions at the bottom is represented by the triangular ORDERED AND node below the NP symbol. The optionality of four of these functions is shown by the small circle on the line involved. In such a case, one may either take that line or omit it. The boxed upper portion shows some further connections of the English NP: predicate complement (COMPPR), as in *These are the three men I told you about*; axis of a prepositional phrase, the traditional 'object of a preposition', (AXISpp), as in *They were in the woods*; subject (SUBJ) as in *Some dogs were there*; direct object (OBJD) as in *She gave them some new books*; and indirect object (OBJI), as in *They gave all those boys some money*. The bracket-like node is an UNORDERED OR, indicating alternatives. A given NP may be either a subject or a direct object, etc., but not more than one at the same time.

Relationship to other theories

Views of language have often been classified based on the distinction between item-and-process (IP) and item-and-arrangement (IA) models, as discussed by Hockett (1954).

From the beginning, stratificationalists have strongly rejected the IP view of much traditional grammar and early anthropological description, with its fullest elaboration in versions of the Chomskyan approach. In view of this rejection, it might be thought that stratificational theory is an IA view. While this might justly be said of the earliest versions of stratificationalism, and of the continuing practice of some stratificationalists, it has not been true of Lamb's views since the mid-1960s. Lamb has pointed out that items are not essential in his theory, so it cannot be either IA or IP.

In holding a relational view that sees such linguistic units as lexemes, sememes and morphemes not as substantive items, but merely points in a network of relationships comprising the linguistic system, Lamb allies himself with a relational tradition in linguistic theory which, through Hjelmslev's glossematics, ultimately traces back to the views of Ferdinand de Saussure.

So the IA/IP distinction, as was indicated in Hockett's discussion, is only a part of the picture. More fundamentally, relational systems differ from item-based ones, and the IA/IP distinction applies only among the latter.

Lamb's refusal to use process in linguistic description does not totally deny the relevance of processes in the language. It recognizes, rather, that true processes are relevant in certain aspects of language, but not in describing the structure of the linguistic system. Processes are essential, for instance, in characterizing language change, both in a single individual (ontogeny) and for a whole speech community (phylogeny). Language use also involves processes of encoding and decoding. The linguistic system which develops as a result of processes of the second sort is itself a relational system. The invention of pseudo-processes to describe the structure of this system merely makes it harder to deal with the real processes in the aspects of language that involve them. According to some contemporary views based on other theories, however, particularly in the Chomskyan tradition (see GENERATIVE GRAMMAR), much of what the standard stratificational model places in three stratal systems – the sememic, lexemic and morphemic – is viewed as part of syntax, including lexicon.

In more recent years, considerable attention has been focused on the distinction between formal and functional approaches to language. The formalists are those, like the Chomskyans, who rely on the supposed power of formalization to provide explanations for the facts of language, believing that formalization captures innate properties of the human brain. On the other hand, the functionalists seek to explain language by considering how it functions in actual use, and many functionalists tend to neglect formalization.

The stratificational approach resembles that of the formalists in insisting on the value of a complete and explicit formalization of linguistic structure. In line with the functionalists, however, stratificationalists seek explanations for language universals more in function, and function-related diachronic aspects, and less in formalism, which they treat as a foundation for explanation rather than a source of it. Outlines of the standard stratificational models are generally non-committal on this matter, but in practice their advocates usually favour functional explanations.

As already mentioned, Lamb's stratificational model evolved out of neo-Bloomfieldian structuralism with a strong influence from glossematics. It stands apart from the IA/IP dichotomy, since items are not essential for it, though it rejects processes in synchronic description. It is both a formal and a functional model, insisting on formalization of structures while still emphasizing the great importance of functional factors as sources of explanations. In its overall outlook, stratificationalism has a great deal in common with two other contemporary approaches: tagmemics and systemic grammar (see HISTORY OF GRAMMAR; SYSTEMIC-FUNCTIONAL GRAMMAR).

D.G.L.

Suggestions for further reading

The first book treating the approach is Lamb (1966). Lockwood (1972) is a later and more detailed presentation of the approach. The most current statement of Lamb's more recent views is found in his 1999 work, including newer versions of network diagrams and extensive discussion of the relation of the theory to research on the human brain.

Articles on various aspects of stratificational theory have most often been published in the annual Forum volumes of the Linguistic Association of Canada and the United States (LACUS) since 1974.

Stylistics

Stylistics is the study of style in spoken and written text. By **style** is meant a consistent occurrence in the text of certain items and structures, or types of items and structures, among those offered by the language as a whole.

A full stylistic analysis of a given spoken or written text would describe the text at all the traditional levels of linguistic description – i.e. sound, form, structure and meaning – but it will not typically look at patterns created by long stretches of text (see DISCOURSE ANALYSIS AND CONVERSATION ANALYSIS; TEXT LINGUISTICS). In stylistic analysis, items and structures are isolated and described using terminology and descriptive frameworks drawn from whatever school of descriptive linguistics the stylistician subscribes to or finds most useful for a given purpose. The overall purpose, of course, will also vary according to the linguistic affiliations of the stylistician. For instance, to linguists of the London School (see FUNCTIONALIST LINGUISTICS), the immediate goal of stylistic analysis 'is to show why and how the text means what it does' (Halliday 1983: x).

The texts studied may be those produced in a certain period of time (texts in medieval English), or by a certain group of language users (people who write newspaper editorials), or by individuals (Wordsworth), and the purposes of the analyses range from the purely descriptive ('the verbal groups in scientific texts tend to be in the passive voice') through the explanatory ('scientists use the passive because they are describing universal processes which are independent of the individual scientist') to the interpretive ('by using the passive, scientists absolve themselves from any responsibility for their actions').

Stylistic analysis can be used as supporting evidence in law courts ('this cannot be a verbatim report of what the accused said; it conflicts with the person's normal patterns of language use') and as an aid to deciding authorship of unascribed manuscripts. It is an important component of sociolinguistic surveys and it can be an important teaching aid (see, for instance, Widdowson 1975, 1992; Short 1989; Carter and McRae 1996; people who need to learn to write or speak in a particular style will benefit from becoming conscious of which linguistic devices realize the style in question. For instance, in the teaching of English for Specific Purposes, one of the useful things to do is to show people that particular types of texts have particular structures and conventions, and that stages of argument and evaluation as opposed to statement of fact, for example, tend to be fairly subtly signalled by linguistic devices of various sorts (see also GENRE ANALYSIS; TEXT LINGUISTICS). Knowledge of this kind can enhance understanding of the text and aid composition. Similarly, actors can benefit from becoming aware of the linguistic characteristics of those accents, dialects and styles that they may have to adopt in order to represent characters.

Stylisticians may be also be interested in discovering the defining features of different **genres** of spoken and written texts (see also GENRE ANALYSIS), and the major distinction drawn here is traditionally between literary and non-literary texts. There is a consequent major traditional division between literary and non-literary stylistics, although, as Halliday (1983: viii) among others points out, there is no feature found in a literary text which is not also found in non-literary texts. The distinction between what is literary and what is not is often questioned (see, for instance, Eagleton 1983; Carter and Nash 1990), but it is possible to maintain it in purely practical terms: there are some texts that become literature by being attended to in the special way which involves, among other things, their inclusion in courses on literature and subsequent special treatment, including special attention to their language. It can then be argued that non-literary stylistics differs from literary stylistics simply in that, in the case of the former, the texts that are being given the type of attention typically given only to literary texts are not, in fact, normally classed as literary texts. But, basically, any text is open to stylistic analysis.

The methods and aims of the non-literary stylistician are the same as those of the literary stylistician, but non-literary stylistics may be seen as derivative, in so far as modern stylistics as a whole has developed from an interest in what is special about the way language is used in literary texts and from a belief that literary language does differ from non-literary language, at least in terms of its function. For example, Sebeok (1960) is a record of an *interdisciplinary* conference on style held at Indiana University, Bloomington, USA, in 1958 in the hope that 'a clearer perception of what *literature* is and what the constituent elements of style are' might result (Sebeok 1960: v, foreword by John W. Ashton; emphasis added); Chatman (1971) arises from a symposium on literary style, which was originally intended as a follow-up to the Indiana conference, but which, in the end, concentrated on literary style alone (see further the discussion of **foregrounding** below).

Work in **narratology** has also benefited from the analysis of narrative genres. Analyses have involved exploration of speech presentation, point of view and the different modalities entailed by the stylistic choices made by narrators and characters. See, in particular, Toolan (1989), who also contrasts traditional literary narratives with courtroom, political and news media narratives.

Textual genres studied in non-literary stylistics include advertisements (Leech 1966; Vestergaard and Schröder 1986; Cook 1992), political speeches and writings (Carter 1963; Chilton 1982; Fairclough 2000), and other texts related to a particular sector of the social organization. Aspects of this type of stylistic analysis also enter into what Swales (1990) dubbed genre analysis, although here, as in discourse and conversation analysis and text linguistics, the emphasis tends to be on suprasentential structural features (see GENRE ANALYSIS).

Typically, writers on critical linguistics (see CRITICAL LINGUISTICS/CRITICAL DISCOURSE ANALYSIS) make extensive references to stylistic features of the texts they are working with. For instance, a critical linguist may make a stylistic analysis of a political pamphlet which would reveal large numbers of occurrences of questions of the form 'Why do we need x'; this much constitutes pure stylistic analysis. S/he will then bring into the analysis an explanatory element by suggesting that the choice of this question form is motivated by the writer's desire to convince readers that our need for x is a foregone conclusion. The final step which turns the work into critical linguistics might be a claim that this wish on the writer's part reflects her/his ideology (see Chilton 1982; Fairclough 1989).

Claims about the relative frequency of elements in, on the one hand, the language as a whole and, on the other, a particular text or groups of texts, clearly imply that both have been subjected to some form of statistical analysis, and the tradition of using statistical analysis in the study of text has been with us for a long time (Kenny 1982: 1):

> The beginning of the statistical study of style in modern times is commonly dated to 1851 when Augustus de Morgan suggested that disputes about the authenticity of some of the writings of St Paul might be settled by the measurement of the length, measured in letters, of the words used in the various Epistles. The first person actually to test the hypothesis that word-length might be a distinguishing characteristic of writers was the American geophysicist, T.C. Mendenhall, who published the results of an analysis of several authors' frequency distributions of word-length in the popular journal, *Science*, in 1887.

With the development of computer technology and the collection of large corpora of text (see corpora), statements about relative frequency of various linguistic items in a corpus have become very accurate, and are used for a variety of purposes, including EFL textbook writing as well as the estab-

lishment of authorship and interpretive stylistics.

The interpretive element which tends to turn non-literary stylistic analysis into critical linguistics is a major component of much literary stylistics. For, although it is clearly possible to direct the stylistic study of a literary text solely towards the establishment of those linguistic features which characterize a writer, literary genre or period, it is far more common to view literary stylistics as 'an extension of practical criticism' (Cluysenaar 1976: 7) – as an interface between literary studies and linguistics.

An interesting debate about the value of linguistics to literary study was conducted between Roger Fowler (1967, 1968) and F.W. Bateson (1967), and is reprinted in Fowler (1971). The point of view generally adopted by people favourably disposed towards stylistics is that, from the literary theorist's or critic's point of view, literary stylistics is valuable in that it affords a vocabulary for talking about those intersubjectively observable linguistic features of the text which prompt individual responses, thus providing a degree of objectivity, which literary criticism sometimes lacks (see Richards 1960; Burton 1982). From a linguist's point of view, literary stylistics is of interest because it allows the linguist to analyse texts in which language is used to create what the culture classes as art. However, the purpose of writing literature is obviously less easily defined than the purpose of writing advertising material or political pamphlets, and the fact that some features occur relatively frequently in a literary text does not by itself guarantee that they are of particular importance.

The typical way of dealing with this problem is by reference to the notion of **foregrounding** (see Van Peer 1986: 1–14). Foregrounding is Garvin's (1964) translation of the Czech term *aktualisace* used by the Prague School linguists, and its application to literature derives from an analogy with what is thought to be 'a fundamental characteristic of human perception' – namely, the ability to distinguish '*a figure against a ground*' (Van Peer 1986: 21).

The notion of foregrounding derives in the first place from the work of the Russian formalists, notably Viktor Shklovsky (or Šklovskij) (1917), according to whom the main function of art was to make people see the world in a new way through **defamiliarization** or **making strange** (in Russian, *ostranenie*). The way the world is made strange through text is by **foregrounding** certain aspects or features of it, the idea being that certain aspects of a work can be made to stand out, be foregrounded; that a form of linguistic highlighting can be achieved through breaking the norms of the standard language.

The **formalists** were so called because they tended to concentrate on certain formal aspects of literary texts (say, a rhyme scheme), in isolation from other aspects. The **structuralists**, in contrast, stressed the interdependence of the various elements of the text, According to the Prague Scholar Jan Mukarovsky (1932), although violation of the norms of the standard language is the essence of poetic language and the device whereby foregrounding is achieved, the literary work is a unified aesthetic structure 'defined by the interrelationships between those items that are foregrounded and those elements in the work that remain in the background' (Van Peer 1986: 7). This view of foregrounding as relational paves the way for Roman Jakobson's (1960) notion of **parallelism**.

Literary language, and the language of poetry in particular, tends to differ from the standard language by being highly patterned – this independently of whether it also violates rules of grammar and lexis. This patterning is what Jakobson calls parallelism, which he takes to be the defining feature of poetic language.

Jakobson sees language as having six basic functions, defined in terms of the language user's **set** towards, or emphasis on, one of the six factors involved in any successful act of communication. These factors are the **code** through which **contact** is established between the participants, **addresser** and **addressee**, in such a way that a **message** will refer to a **context**. A given set relates to a given dominant function as follows:

Set	*Dominant function*
addresser	emotive
addressee	conative
context	referential
contact	phatic
code	metalingual
message	**poetic**

According to Jakobson (1960: 358), 'the empirical linguistic criterion of the poetic function', 'the indispensable feature inherent in any piece of poetry' is that '*the poetic function projects the principle of equivalence from the axis of selection into the axis of combination.* Equivalence is promoted to the constitutive device of the sequence.'

Jakobson thinks, with Saussure, that any piece of language is mappable on two dimensions, represented schematically as two axes:

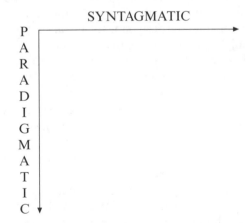

Normally, one axis, the syntagmatic, is solely concerned with structure, while equivalences are mappable downwards on the paradigmatic axis. However, in writing poetry, the syntagmatic axis comes to contain equivalences, too; in fact, a poem is constructed in terms of linearly sequenced equivalences of parallel structures at all levels (see below). To give an example, a language user may wish to report the fact that the cat was sitting on a rug. If the set is on the context so that the referential function of language dominates, the language user may simply use the words *The cat was sitting on the rug*. If, however, the set is on the message itself so that the poetic function predominates, the user will allow the principle of parallelism to predominate also and influence the word choice, which may become *The cat sat on the mat*, where there is phonological parallelism (rhyme) between the words *cat*, *sat* and *mat*. So, while normal language consists of combinations of different kinds of elements, poetic language consists of combinations of the same kinds of element, and this device of parallelism both organizes the literary work and pervades all aspects of it. In this way, parallelism is foregrounded in, and defining of, literary language.

Parallelisms may be of many types at each linguistic level of description. It is possible to provide a full linguistic description of all the levels of a text, and this would show up the parallelisms. At the level of phonemic transcription, for instance, there might be alliteration, rhyme and metre (see below). At the syntactic level, there might be parallel structures, and at the lexical level there might be various types of verbal repetition. At the level of larger stretches of text than the clause, parallelisms may operate in the structure of a whole work – some works, for example, are organized into chapters, sections or books.

But clearly the notion of foregrounding needs a finer definition than this before it can be used in a truly explanatory sense. For 'even a thorough scanning of all instances of parallelism [in a literary work] ... does not provide a framework for a justifiable interpretation of the patterns that are described, which in themselves are only neutral with regard to interpreting the text' (Van Peer 1986: 11). As Halliday (1971: 330) points out, it is necessary to distinguish between 'mere linguistic regularity, which in itself is of no interest to literary studies, and regularity which is significant for the poem or prose work in which we find it'.

As an illustration of the point at issue, compare the significance of a large number of references to the weather in, on the one hand, a weather report and, on the other hand, Hemingway's novel *A Farewell to Arms* (1929). In the case of the weather report, we would not want to claim that an unusually large number of references to the weather as compared with the language as a whole was foregrounded in the defamiliarization sense. The weather forecaster does not want to make the weather strange for us – s/he just wants to tell us about it. But if we are reading Hemingway's novel about an American in the Italian army during a war and find large numbers of references to the weather, then we might begin to think that there is some particular reason for this; that it is meant to be somehow meaningful; to add to the overall meaning of the book; that the passages about the weather have some sort of thematic importance in the work – that, in other words, Hemingway has a motive or reason for mentioning the weather so often.

Halliday (1971: 339) defines **foregrounding** as 'prominence that is motivated'. He discusses Golding's use of language in *The Inheritors* (1955), a novel about a group of Neanderthal people whose world is invaded by a tribe of more advanced people. He shows that the two groups have different grammars: in the part of the book that is about the Neanderthal people, most verbal groups are intransitive, and a large proportion of the grammatical subjects are realized by words which do not refer to people, but to plants and inanimate objects and parts of the body; where the subjects are people, frequently the clauses are not clauses of action. This creates a picture of a world 'in which people act, but they do not act on things; they move, but they move only themselves . . . the scene is one of constant movement, but movement which is as much inanimate as human and in which only the mover is affected – nothing else changes' (1971: 349–50). It is a world in which no cause and effect is perceived by its inhabitants, and this reflects their limited cognitive capacity. The predominance of the kinds of structure and grammatical category which Halliday describes in this part of the book constitutes a breaking of the norms of the standard language, statistically speaking. Halliday shows that this is a motivated phenomenon: it constitutes part of the meaning of the novel. In the case of the language of the new people, on the other hand, there is no norm-breaking – the language in the part of the book which deals with them is normal by our standards, reflecting their far greater similarity to people as they are now, their wider horizons and more complex perceptions compared to the Neanderthal people. The fact that the language here is normal while the language earlier in the book is not illustrates the important point that norms broken need not be just the norms of the idealized standard language. A norm may be set up within a work itself, and then be internally broken, as is often the case in poetry (see below).

In similar vein to Halliday (1971), Burton (1982) shows how, in *The Bell Jar*, Sylvia Plath uses transitivity patterns to write her main character into inactivity and helplessness. Both writers arrive at their conclusions through a thorough grammatical analysis of their texts. As mentioned above, the analysis of choices of lexical items, such as references to the weather, is also an important aspect of a full stylistic analysis

and, in poetry in particular, much attention will normally be focused on the level of phonology.

A distinction may be drawn between **tropes**, which are stylistic effects created by choices in grammar and vocabulary, and **schemes**, which are segmental phonemic effects (Wellek and Warren 1949 1956 1963) (see list of terms at the end of this entry). Sound patterns within syllables include alliteration, assonance, consonance, reverse rhyme, pararhyme and rhyme, all of which would be described in a full stylistic analysis of a poem. Normally, however, most attention is focused on 'the rhythmic measure, i.e., the unit of rhythmic patterning, which extends from the onset of one stressed syllable to the onset of the next' (Leech 1969: 91). In English, there may be up to four unstressed syllables between two stressed syllables and, when the pattern is regular, stylisticians talk of it in terms of **metrical** feet. A **foot** is 'the unit or span of stressed and unstressed syllables which is repeated to form a metrical pattern' (Leech 1969: 112).

There are four kinds of metre usually employed to describe English poetry; namely (Leech 1969: 112), 'Iamb x/; Anapest xx/; Trochee /x; Dactyl /xx' (x = an unstressed syllable, / = a stressed syllable). As we can see, the metrical foot does not coincide with the unit of measure, since a foot may begin with an unstressed syllable. There are a number of problems involved in applying the classical foot to English (see Leech 1969: 112–14); however, it can be instructive to use it in the case of some types of poetry, and I shall do so at this point, in order to illustrate the importance a stylistician may attach to instances in which a norm set up within a text is broken. Compared to the language as a whole, the internal norm consisting of the regular iambic metre of Byron's 'She Walks in Beauty' (*Hebrew Melodies*, 1815) is deviant. But, within the poem itself, the regularity is the norm:

She	walks	in	beauty,	like	the	night,	
x	/	x	/ x	/	x	/	
Of	cloudless	climes	and	starry	skies;		
x	/ x	/	x	/ x	/		
And	all	that's	best	of	dark	and	bright
x	/	x	/	x	/	x	/
Meet	in	her	aspect	and	her	eyes:	
x	/	x	/ x	/	x	/	
Thus	mellowed	to	that	tender	light		
x	/ x	/	x	/ x	/		
Which	heaven	to	gaudy	day	denies		
x	/	x	/ x	/	x /		

The metre here consists of four iambic feet per line; it is possible to read this poem aloud in strict iambs (provided that *heaven* is read as *heav'n*). A natural reading – that is, a reading of this text as if it were prose – would probably follow this pattern fairly closely for the first three lines – although, in line one, *like* is unlikely to receive a stress. If it does not, then the stressed *night* will gain extra emphasis by being preceded by three unstressed syllables. For the next two lines, the iambic pattern is likely to be followed, chiefly because the stresses at the level of sound coincide, at the lexicosyntactic level, with content words as opposed to the grammatical connectives, *and, of* and *that's*, which are unstressed. However, in line four, a natural reading would stress *meet*, thus breaking the iambic pattern much more starkly than in the first line; in the first line, *like*, which is stressed in the metrical reading, is made unstressed in the natural reading; here, *meet*, which is unstressed in the metrical reading, will be stressed in the natural reading. We therefore have two consecutive stressed syllables, and this may make a reader, lulled by the regularity of the previous two lines, stop and catch her/his breath in surprise. *Meet* thus becomes very strongly emphasized. We can now add to this quite obvious internal norm-breaking prominence some literary-historical knowledge which will tend to indicate that this prominence is motivated, and is consequently real foregrounding.

We know that Byron was a Romantic poet, and that the Romantics objected to the rigid opposition traditionally claimed to exist between the heavenly, good, bright regions above the moon on the one hand, and the dark, evil, earthly regions beneath it on the other hand. And we know that they objected to all the oppositions that this opposition itself was used to symbolize. Byron lets beauty, night, dark and bright meet in the woman he is describing, and the breaking of the regular metre on the very word *meet* emphasizes this meeting. The rhyme scheme gives further emphasis to the meeting of the phenomena in question: *night* rhymes with *bright* and *light* (see Cummings and Simmons 1983: 39–40).

Much more could be said about this poem by a stylistician; I have hinted at the interplay of analysis at the different levels of the poem, and Van Peer (1986: 16) adds to the notion of meaningful prominence the notion of a **nexus of foregrounding**. This is a nodal point in a text where foregrounding devices occur at several linguistic levels of a text. Fairly rigorously grounded in tests of reader reactions and text interpretations, his study is the first to show conclusively the influence of foregrounding as defined by textual analysis on these phenomena.

Sinclair (1982: 172) provides an outline of the separate stages of a stylistic analysis, emphasizing that the text must already be understood at some level before benefit can be gained from analysing it:

First . . . there is the reading and full critical understanding of the text. . . . Analysis must be interpreted through the impressions created by the work as a whole. . . .

The second stage . . . is the analysis of one area, perhaps sentence structure, rhyme or antonomy. In practice, the larger grammatical units offer the more fruitful starting-point, but there is no restriction . . .

The third stage is called *scan*. The analytical data are examined for patterns to see whether any aspect of the symbols in the display is worth following up. A decision is made: namely, a return to further analysis if no likely lead arises from the analysis, or a description of some aspect of patterning. . . .

At this point the nature of the patterning under attention should be described exactly. The next step is to consider how it relates to the unanalysed 'total meaning'.

In the analysis of the poem above, Sinclair's first step was assumed to have taken place already; an assumed analysis of rhyme and metre was drawn on; the patterning found there was followed up (though its exact description is not included here); and a beginning was made to relate this to the total meaning of the full text (there are more verses).

The type of stylistic analysis dealt with so far has been surface-structure-orientated. The approach of stylisticians using the theoretical framework and terminology of generative grammar (see GENERATIVE GRAMMAR) adds further dimensions to the stylistic analysis of text with the notion that both the deep structure itself, and the relationships between it and the surface structure are significant to a text (Closs Traugott and Pratt 1980: 167):

On the one hand, there are texts in which deep structure matches surface structure very closely. In others, there is

considerable difference between the two. In this latter case, we may find that deep structures are relatively diverse, while surface structures are relatively uniform and deceptively simple. Or we may find that surface structures are relatively diverse, whereas the deep structures are relatively uniform.

Traugott and Pratt illustrate the method employed through analyses of extracts from four texts, Donald Barthelme's short story 'Edward and Pia' (1967), Ernest Hemingway's *For Whom the Bell Tolls* (1940), Henry James' *The Portrait of a Lady* (1908), and Carl Sandburg's poem 'The Harbor' (1970); I shall quote extensively from their treatment of the first two texts, to give an indication of what is involved.

The Barthelme text consists mainly of simple sentences with few connectives between them and no subordination (Closs Traugott and Pratt 1980: 169):

One of the few exceptions is found in lines 14–15: *'What are you thinking about?' Edward asked Pia and she said she was thinking about Willie's hand.* The whole paragraph in which this occurs is coherent, and, significantly, this paragraph is about a person and events external to Edward and Pia. Others live connected lives; not so our hero and heroine except when thinking about others. This is reflected by the use of the embedded complement in *she said she was thinking about Willie's hand*, where *that* is deleted and the complement is thus more tightly related to the main clause *she said* than if it were not deleted. . . . Place expressions such as *in the mailbox, in London, at the train station* are moved out of their normal position at the end of the sentence to the beginning. This transformation takes on a significance it would not have in ordinary discourse, since place expressions are the only expressions that undergo an optional movement transformation in this passage. (Questions require movement, and therefore movement is stylistically irrelevant in such a question as *What are you thinking about*.)

The analysis of the Hemingway text contrasts two adjoining passages from chapter 13 of the novel. In the first passage, both deep and surface structures are simple and therefore match quite closely; the passage describes a character's several actions, and an uncommonly large proportion of the sentences begin with *he*, in spite of an option to delete it. This 'has the special effect of drawing attention to the person. . . . In other words, nonuse of an optional transformation may foreground and make special the scene being presented' (1980: 170). The second passage, a love scene, which precedes the first in the novel, contrasts with the first in several ways. The language is simple on the surface, but the deep structure is complex 'and contributes to the total orgasmic effect of the scene' (1980: 172). However, (1980: 174):

> What is striking again is that certain transformations have not been used, specifically not subject deletion. However, a subject deletion is used to great effect in one instance: *he held the length of her body tight to him and felt her breasts against his chest*. This allows an interpretation of simultaneity to the holding and the feeling which *and he felt her breasts* would not.

In contrast to Hemingway's simplicity of style, James' is known for its syntactic complexity – 'his surface structures are very diverse even when his underlying structures are similar. Furthermore, he will, at times, not use a transformation where use of one would aid comprehension' (1980: 174–5).

Work in stylistics in the last part of the 1990s involved continuing critical reflections on the positioning of the analyst socially and ideologically, with important texts –

for example, Mills (1995) – illustrating that different readings and different contents for analysis cannot be divorced from considerations of gender. Paul Werth's work on the cognitive components entailed by stylistic analysis (Werth 1999) takes fuller account than hitherto of the psycholinguistic processing of texts and asks fundamental questions about the ways in which everyday uses of language and their associated mental representations influence the construction of interpretations. Such work builds on the foundations of continuing work in cognitive poetics illustrated by Gibbs' (1994) work on *The Poetics of Mind*, which explores continuities between everyday and poetic metaphors, idioms and metonymies and the kinds of rhetorical figures in canonical literary texts.

List of terms which may be encountered in stylistic analyses

(From Chatman 1960; Leech 1969; Chapman 1973.) C = consonant or consonant cluster; V = vowel or diphthong.

accent: stress on a spoken syllable

alliteration: (consonant alliteration): CVC *mellow moments, flags flying;* (vowel alliteration): VC *every effort employed*

allusion: allusion may be made to religion, history, ideals, etc.

ambiguity: double or multiple meaning of a word or longer stretch of text

anacoluthon: changed or incomplete grammatical sequence: *could you just . . . , oh, it's OK, I've done it*

anadiplosis: the last part of one unit is repeated at the beginning of the next: *The children were playing on the beach. The beach was a silvery white*

anaphora: initial repetition (but see also the section on **cohesion** in the entry on TEXT LINGUISTICS)

antistrophe: inverted clause or sentence; the repetition of items in reverse order: *I love you – you love me*

antithesis: definition of something by elimination; *or* parallelism of form combined with contrast in meaning

aphaeresis: an initial V is lost, so that the C which follows it clusters with the initial sound of the next word: *it is – 'tis*

apocope: a word-final V is left out to allow the preceding C to cluster with the initial C or V of the next word: *the army – th'army*

appeal: appeal may be made to emotion

archaism: using the language of the past in a text of the present; often the result of a wish to emulate a writer or school of writers of the past, and often considered to provide **poetic heightening** (see below)

assonance: CVC *fame late*

augmentation: CC becoming CVC: *slowly and soulfully*

chiasmus: Reversed phoneme sequence /ul/:/il/::/il/:/ul/: *dupes of a deep delusion*

connotations: ideas or emotions which tend to be aroused by a linguistic item

consonance: CVC: *first and last*

dialectism: the use of features of dialect

diminution: CVC becoming CC: *silent and slow*

epanalepsis: the final part of each unit of the pattern repeats the initial part

epistrophe: final repetition

epizeuxis: repetition of a word or phrase without any break; free immediate repetition

euphuism: an artificial and ornate style of writing or speaking ('flowery' language)

eye rhyme: (written text only) identical letters representing different sounds: *blood mood*

free repetition: irregularly occurring exact repetitions of previous parts of a text

homeoteleuton: repetition of whole final unstressed syllables with preceding consonant stressed syllables: *fusion motion*

homoioteleuton: the repetition of the same derivational or inflectional ending on different words

hyperbaton: arranging syntactic elements in an unusual order: *pillows soft* instead of *soft pillows*

hyperbole: overstatement

litotes: understatement using a negation of a term with negative connotations to highlight the positive connotations of the opposite, unused term: *not bad*

meiosis: understatement

metaphor: implicit comparison (but see also METAPHOR): *You are my sunshine*

metonymy: the use of a feature closely associated with a referent to stand for it: *the **crown*** for *the **monarch***

monosyllabification or **synechphonesis** or **synizesis**: very common in everyday speech – the reduction of several syllables to a single nucleus: *be-ing* /biŋ/

neologism: an item newly introduced into the lexicon of a language

nonce-formation: a neologism used on just one occasion; that is, one that will not become a regularly used linguistic item (Lewis Carroll uses these frequently in the poem 'Jabberwocky' from *Through the Looking-Glass*, 1872)

onomatopoeia: the use of words which sound like 'natural' sounds: ***buzzing*** *bees*

pararhyme: CVC *tick tock*

ploce /plousi/: free intermittent repetition

poetic heightening: using language in a way which is perceived as particularly dignified; archaisms were often in the past considered to have this dignifying effect

polypton: the repetition of a word with varying grammatical inflections

pseudo-elision: might more logically be called syllabic expansion – 'the assumption of elision between two consonants that cannot be clustered without one of them becoming syllabic (for example, words ending in "-ism," " rhythm" etc.)' (Chatman 1960: 163)

reverse rhyme: CVC: *mope and moan*

rhyme: CVC *cat mat*; a distinction is sometimes drawn between **masculine** rhyme – repetition of final stressed V and final C if there are any (as above and *be agree*)

– and **feminine** rhyme, which is as masculine rhyme but also includes any additional unstressed identical syllables *taker maker* (Chatman 1960: 152)

simile: explicit comparison: *You are like sunshine*

stress: relative force of breath in uttering a syllable

syllepsis: one verb governing two or more nouns, at least one of which it is literally incongruous: *I bought the milk and the idea of going shopping*

symploce: initial combined with final repetition

synaeresis: 'the consonantizing of a vowel (usually into /y-/ or /w-/), or the loss of syllabicity of a syllabic consonant, such that it clusters with a following vowel rather then standing alone as a syllable (for example "many a" becomes /menyə/, "jollier" becomes /jalyər/, "title of" becomes /taytləv/)' (Chatman 1960: 162–3); a phenomenon which occurs constantly in normal speech

syncope: (consonant) the loss of a C and consequent fusion of the syllables on either side of it often involving loss of the second V: *by his – by's*; (vowel) the loss of a V which has the effect that a syllable is lost without affecting syllables on either side of it: *medicine – med'cine*

synecdoche: use of part of a referent to stand for the whole: *all **hands** on deck*

zeugma: one verb governing two or more nouns: *I saw the horses and sheep* (see also **syllepsis**)

K.M and R.A.C.

Suggestions for further reading

Bex, A.R. (1996) *Variety in Written English: Texts in Society, Society in Texts*, London: Routledge.

Bradford, R. (1997) *Stylistics*, London: Routledge.

Carter, R.A. and Nash, W. (1990) *Seeing Through Language*, Oxford: Basil Blackwell.

Short, M.H. (1996) *Exploring the Language of Poetry, Prose and Drama*, Harlow: Longman.

Systemic-functional grammar

Although systemic-functional grammar is a widely applied grammar for describing the surface structure of language, popular especially with some educationalists and translation scholars, it is much more than a descriptive, surface grammar. It is, rather, a full-blown theory of language, developed by the British linguist Michael Alexander Kirkwood Halliday (b. 1925). It began, in the late 1950s and 1960, as Scale and Category Grammar.

Scale and Category Grammar

Scale and Category Grammar built insights derived from J.R. Firth (1890–1960) into an overall theory of what language is and how it works. While Halliday's own post-1965 work has tended to move away from the scale and category model towards systemic and functional grammar, Fawcett (1974, 1975, 1976) has developed the model for use as a basis for his own version of systemic grammar.

Firth viewed meaning as the function of a linguistic item in its context of use (Butler 1985: 5):

Context of situation, though of central importance, was just one kind of context in which linguistic units could function. Other contexts were provided by the levels postulated to account for various types of linguistic patterning. Thus grammatical items could be seen as functioning in grammatical contexts, lexical items in lexical contexts, phonological items in phonological contexts, and so on.

He considered the context of situation to be of the same abstract nature as grammatical categories, and insisted that all such abstract constructs should be relatable back to textual data, a concern which has remained with Halliday.

Within each of the levels, Firth saw language as organized along two axes, the **syntagmatic** (horizontal) and the **paradigmatic** (vertical). Along the syntagmatic axis, elements formed **structures**, while on the paradigmatic axis elements were arranged in **systems**. Firth differs from Saussure (see INTRODUCTION) in that, whereas the latter saw language as one huge system, Firth thought that a large number of systems must be set up to account for the diversity of linguistic phenomena. In addition, he believed that it would not be possible to account in one fell swoop for all of language, but that linguistic descriptions should be applied, at least in the first instance, to so-called **restricted languages**, examples of which would be (Butler 1985: 5) 'the specialist languages of science, sport, narrative, political propaganda, personal reference and address, the writings of a single author, or even a single text'.

Firth's work has been criticized for lack of explicitness and for incoherence (Langendoen 1968: 37–8), but in Halliday's work Firth's categories and the relationships between them are made explicit (Butler 1985: 13). He begins (Halliday 1956, in Kress 1976: 36–51) by providing a framework within which the relationships between linguistic items can be handled in a consistent manner (Butler 1985: 14). He discusses three types of grammatical category to be established in the description – unit, element and class.

The **unit** is 'that category to which corresponds a segment of the linguistic material about which statements are to be made',

and five units are proposed at the level of grammar: **sentence**, **clause**, **group**, **word** and **character** (Halliday 1956, in Kress 1976: 36). Here, Halliday aims to provide an account of categories in modern Chinese; in later papers, dealing with English, the fifth unit, character, appears as **morpheme**. Each unit, except character, can be simple, composed of a single element, or compound, composed of two or more elements – the character is always simple.

The units are arranged hierarchically, in what is now known as a **rank scale**, the principle of the arrangement being that a unit at any rank other than morpheme/character is composed of one or more elements of the classes of units at the rank below it. A **class** is defined according to its operation at a given place in the unit next above; thus the classes of groups are defined according to the structural positions they can occupy in the clause. Classes may be either **primary**, 'when it is the unique term operating at a particular place in structure', or **secondary**, 'integral subdivisions of the primary classes and systems in other dimensions cutting across the primary classes'. The former are called **direct secondary classes**; the latter, **indirect secondary classes** (Butler 1985: 37).

The different classes of element operating at each rank form **systems**. For instance, at sentence rank, two classes of clause, **free** and **subordinate**, or **bound**, may be elements of structure (Butler 1985: 15):

> These two classes of clause form a two-term *system* of clause classes in sentence structure. We can also recognize secondary classes of clause within the primary classes 'free' and 'subordinate': 'free' clauses are either 'disjunctive' or 'conjunctive' . . . 'subordinate' clauses are either 'conditional' or 'adjectival'.

The **sentence** is defined as 'the largest unit about which grammatical statements are to be made' (Halliday 1956, in Kress 1976: 37). Any statements made about the context in which the sentence occurs would be at another level, to which we would now refer as the level of discourse or text. Halliday symbolizes the structural elements of the sentence as O and X, with free clauses operating at O and subordinate clauses operating at X. The clause classes are thus defined in terms of their occurrence in the structure of the sentence, and the definitions of all other units and the structures set up for them proceed systematically downwards through the rank scale; thus there are two basic elements of clause structure, V and N. The verbal group operates at V; the nominal group, at N. A basic structure will contain one V only, while subsidiary structures may contain two V elements. In addition, subsidiary structures may contain an element A at which adverbial groups will operate.

The 1956 paper set up the basic framework for Scale and Category Grammar, although the most comprehensive account is to be found in Halliday (1961) (Butler 1985: 15). Here, Halliday lists a number of different levels at which linguistic events should be accounted for (Halliday 1961: 243–4):

> The primary levels are 'form,' 'substance' and 'context.' The substance is the material of language: 'phonic' (audible noises) or 'graphic' (visible marks). The form is the organization of the substance into meaningful events. . . . The context is the relation of the form to non-linguistic features of the situation in which language operates, and to linguistic features other than those of the item under attention: these being together the 'extra-textual' features.

Form is further said to be, in fact, two related levels (namely, **grammar** and **lexis**), while **context** is actually an **interlevel**, which relates form to extratextual features. The meaning of a linguistic event derives from a combination of its **formal meaning** and its **contextual meaning**. 'The formal meaning

of an item is its operation in the network of formal relations', while (Halliday 1961: 245):

> the contextual meaning of an item is its relation to extratextual features; but this is not a direct relation of the item as such, but of the item in its place in linguistic form: contextual meaning is therefore logically dependent on formal meaning.

For this reason 'the statement of formal meaning logically precedes the statement of contextual meaning'; in other words, before we can relate language to situation as Firth desired, it is necessary to provide a systematic description of the linguistic systems – the systems being the networks of formal relations of which language is composed.

The systems which operate at the level of grammar are **closed systems**, that is, systems which have the following three characteristics (Halliday 1961: 247):

a the number of terms is finite: they can be listed as A B C D, and all other items E . . . are outside the system.
b each term is exclusive of all the others: a given term A cannot be identical with B or C or D.
c if a new term is added to the system this changes the meaning of all the others.

System, class, structure and unit are the fundamental, primary categories of the theory of grammar necessary for accounting for the data. All four are mutually defining, logically derivable from each other.

Unit is now defined as 'the category set up to account for the stretches that carry grammatical patterns' (Halliday 1961: 251), and, as in the 1956 paper, the units are arranged in a rank scale in such a way that 'going from top (largest) to bottom (smallest) each "consists of" one, or more than one, of the unit next below (next smaller)' (Halliday 1961: 151). The scale is the same as that set up in the earlier paper, except that, since Halliday is now concerned with describing English, the lowest rank is morpheme, rather than character.

Halliday has to allow for one type of instance in which the principle of arrangement of the rank scale appears not to apply. We can analyse a sentence like *I saw the house* quite unproblematically as consisting of one clause, consisting of three groups *I*, *saw* and *the house*; each of these groups consists of words – in the case of the third group, the words *the* and *house*. However, a sentence like *I saw the house on the corner* appears to present a problem: the third group here, *the house on the corner*, seems itself to be composed of two groups, namely *the house* and *on the corner*. But groups are supposed to be composed of words, since word is the unit next below group. To deal with this kind of problem, Halliday allows for a phenomenon, which he refers to as **downward rankshift**, 'the transfer of a (formal realization of a) given unit to a lower rank' (1961: 251), in this case the transfer of a group to the rank of word. So *on the corner*, a group, functions in this clause as a word.

The pattern carried by the unit is a **structure**, the category set up to account for likeness between events in succession; it is 'an arrangement of elements ordered in "places"' (1961: 255, 256):

> Each place and each element in the structure of a given unit is defined with reference to the unit next below. Each place is the place of operation of one member of the unit next below, considered as one occurrence. Each element represents the potentiality of operation of a member of one *grouping* of members of the unit next below, considered as one item-grouping. It follows from this that the lowest unit has no structure; if it carried structure, there would be another unit below it.

Any account of the structure of the morpheme, therefore, would have to be given in phonology, not in the grammar.

According to Halliday (1961), four elements are needed to describe the structure of the English clause, namely **subject (S)**, **predicator (P)**, **complement (C)**, and **adjunct (A)**; Berry (1975) also only operates with these four, while others, for instance Sinclair (1972), introduce a further two elements – **object direct (O^D)** and **object indirect (O^I)**. To account for the structure of the group called nominal group, Halliday (1961: 257) uses the names **modifier (M)**, **head (H)**, and **qualifier (Q)**. However, a structure described as, for instance, MHQ, cannot account in very fine detail for the structure of a nominal group, like, for instance *the house on the corner*; it accounts only for its primary structure, the structure which distinguishes 'the minimum number of elements necessary to account comprehensively for the operation in the structure of the given unit of members of the unit next below; necessary, that is, for the identification of every item at all ranks' (1961: 258); thus,

The <u>house</u> on the corner
M   H   Q

If we want to be more specific, we need to employ another type of scale of grammatical description, to which Halliday refers as a scale of **delicacy**, or depth of detail. This would, in this case, enable us to specify, for instance, that M is realized by a **deictic**, H by a **headword**, and Q by an **adverbial group**, rankshifted downward and consisting of a preposition and a nominal group, the nominal group, in turn, having the structure MH, M being a deictic and H a headword, and so on. Such subsequent more delicate differentiations are stated as **secondary structures**; at finer and finer degrees of delicacy, structural statements become more and more probabilistic.

Classes are defined, as in the 1956 paper, by their operation in the structure of the unit next above. **Primary classes** stand in one-to-one relations to elements of primary structures, while **secondary classes** are derived from secondary structures. The primary classes form the link between elements of structure and more delicate classes.

System is the category set up to account for 'the occurrence of one rather than another from among a number of like events' (1961: 264). At the ultimate level of delicacy of grammatical description, the grammar will be linked directly to the data, because the last statement made will specify which item from a given system (subsystem of a system) actually appears in the text. The notion of 'appearing in the text' is explicated in terms of a scale of **exponence**, 'which relates the categories of the theory . . . to the data' (1961: 270), although, in most cases, grammar must hand over to **lexis**, for the final statement of exponence.

The theory of the 1961 paper, and its differences from the 1956 one, may then be summed up as follows (Butler 1985: 16):

> Four categories (unit, structure, class and system) and three scales relating them (rank, exponence and delicacy) are proposed. Several differences from the 1956 version of the theory are immediately apparent: system is now one of the fundamental categories, rather than secondary to class; the concept of structure, hitherto subsidiary to that of element, is now given full recognition; and the relationships between the categories, and between these and the data, are more explicitly accounted for in terms of the three scales, which were merely implicit in the earlier work.

Halliday's scale and category model has been extensively modified by Fawcett (1974; see Butler 1985: 6). While the categories of unit and element of structure remain essentially unaltered, the notion of delicacy loses its importance. Fawcett removes the category of system to the semantics and provides a treatment of class, rank and exponence that differs from Halliday's.

The scale of exponence is split into three parts, **exponence**, **componence** and **filling** (Butler 1985: 95):

> Componence is the relation between a unit and the elements of structure of which it is composed. For example, a clause may be composed of the elements S, P, C and A. Each of these elements of structure may be . . . filled by groups. In the specification of a syntactic structure, componence and filling alternate until . . . the smallest elements of structure are not filled by any units. It is at this point that we need the concept of exponence, as used by Fawcett: the lowest elements of structure are expounded by 'items' which . . . are more or less equivalent to 'words' and 'morphemes' in Halliday's model. Exponence thus takes us out of syntax, as viewed by Fawcett.

It takes us out of syntax because Fawcett's rank scale for grammar only contains clause, group, and **cluster**, a new syntactic unit Fawcett needs to handle possessive constructions, proper names and pre-modifiers of adjectives and adverbs, because he gives up word and morpheme.

In giving up the sentence, Fawcett is following Huddleston's (1965) suggestion; he justifies giving up word and morpheme by pointing out that (1976: 50, in Butler 1985: 97)

> some elements of group structure are typically *not* filled by 'words': for instance, qualifiers in nominal groups are almost always rank shifted groups or clauses. Furthermore, when an element of group structure *can* be filled by a single word, it can equally well, in many cases, be filled by a higher unit: for example, the completive to a preposition can be a single word (as in 'in cities'), but this can be expanded into a nominal group with more than one element of structure (as in 'in all the largest cities'). Another problem is that some elements

of group structure can be filled by items which are not obviously 'words' in any meaningful sense, and yet have to be treated as 'functioning as a word' in a Hallidayan model. Examples include complex prepositions such as 'in spite of', 'because of', and complex conjunctions such as 'in order that'.

In order to resolve these problems, Fawcett removes from the theory any expectation that elements of group structure will be filled by a particular kind of unit, or indeed by any kind of unit at all. Some elements of group structure are indeed filled by units, but others may be expounded directly by items (for instance, the element p could be expounded directly by the item 'in spite of').

Fawcett's use of the notion of filling allows him to use the internal structure, or **constituency**, of units in his definition of class, instead of Halliday's criterion of function in the next highest unit of the rank scale. He points out (Fawcett 1974: 10) that there is no one-to-one relationship between unit and element of structure (Butler 1985: 96):

> Thus, for example, the Adjunct element of clause structure can be filled by adverbial groups such as 'very quickly', prepositional groups (or, as Fawcett calls them, 'prepend groups') such as 'for a month', or nominal groups such as 'last week'. Fawcett also allows the A element (as well as the S and C elements) to be filled by a clause.

Systemic grammar

By 1966, Halliday had come to view the **system** as more a single set of choices available at a particular place in structure, and this change in view marks the move to systemic grammar. Now (Butler 1985: 40):

> we find the paradigmatic patterning of language described in terms of sets of systems, or system 'networks', operating

with a particular rank of unit, and sometimes a particular class of a given rank, as their 'point of origin'. Certain system networks are selected from a clause rank, others operate at the nominal class of the unit group, and so on.

The notion of the **network** of systems obviously indicates that there are interrelations between the various systems. So choices from within one system may co-occur with choices from within other systems, in one of two ways: either the choices made are independent of each other, in which case the systems are **simultaneous** and **unordered** with respect to each other; or a choice made from within one system implies certain choices from within other systems, in which case the systems are **dependent** on each other, and **hierarchically ordered** (Halliday 1966b, in Kress 1976: 92):

> So for example the system whose terms are declarative/interrogative would be hierarchically ordered with respect to the system indicative/imperative, in that selection of either of the features declarative and interrogative implies selection of indicative.

A simplified system network for the English clause might look like Figure 1 (from Halliday 1966b, in Kress 1976: 93). The change from system of structure to paradigmatic system network is made possible in this model because the systemic relations, as well as the structural relations, are now described in terms of delicacy. A more delicate description of an indicative clause will show that it is of the type interrogative; a more delicate statement about the interrogative clause is that it is of the Yes/No type; and so on.

The description of paradigmatic patterns in terms of system networks allows Halliday to deal, in his own way, with deep grammar (Halliday 1966b, in Kress 1976: 93–4):

> Systemic description may be thought of as complementary to structural description,

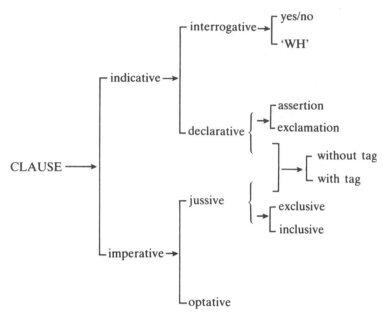

Figure 1 A simplified system network for the clause in English

the one concerned with paradigmatic and the other with syntagmatic relations. On the other hand it might be useful to consider some possible consequences of regarding systemic description as the underlying form of representation, if it turned out that the structural description could be shown to be derivable from it. In that case structure would be fully predictable, and the form of a structural representation could be considered in the light of this. It goes without saying that the concept of an explicit grammar implied by this formulation derives primarily from the work of Chomsky, and that steps taken in this direction on the basis of any grammatical notions are made possible by his fundamental contribution.

According to Halliday, the paradigmatic relations between linguistic items are more fundamental than the syntagmatic relations; the underlying grammar is 'semantically significant' grammar – the part of grammar which is 'closest to' the semantics (1966b, in Kress 1976). As Butler points out (1985: 46):

This is an extremely important statement. Halliday's work had, from the beginning always insisted on the meaningfulness of linguistic elements, building as it did on the work of Firth; but here we have an explicit claim that grammars can be written so as to reflect, at least in part, the specifically semantic meaning (to use a Firthian distinction) of formal choices, and that such a grammar can and should take the system as its most fundamental category.

This semantically significant grammar, which Halliday often (for instance, 1970: 142) refers to as the **meaning potential** of language, is, according to Halliday (for instance 1968, 1970) functionally organized. The notion of **language function** is used to answer the question: Why is language as it is? (1970: 141). A general answer is that 'the nature of language is closely related to the demands that we make on it, the functions it has to serve'. But these functions are very diverse; 'we cannot explain language by simply listing its uses, and such a list could in any case be prolonged indefinitely' (1970: 141). Generalizations such as Malinowski's distinction between pragmatic and magical functions, and Bühler's division into representational, expressive and conative functions (see FUNCTIONALIST LINGUISTICS), 'are directed towards sociological or psychological inquiries' (1970: 141). Halliday wants an account of linguistic functions which is related to an account of linguistic structure (1970: 142):

It is fairly obvious that language is used to serve a variety of different needs, but until we examine its grammar there is no clear reason for classifying its uses in a particular way. However, when we examine the meaning potential of language itself, we find that the vast numbers of options embodied in it combine into a very few relatively independent 'networks'; and these networks of options correspond to certain basic functions of language. This enables us to give an account of the different functions of language that is relevant to the general understanding of linguistic structure rather than to any particular psychological or sociological investigation.

The basic functions of language listed are: the **ideational** function, which (1970: 143) 'serves for the expression of "content": that is, of the speaker's experience of the real world, including the inner world of his own consciousness; the **interpersonal** function, the function language has of establishing and maintaining social relations – language serves (1970: 143)

for the expression of social roles, which include the communication roles created by language itself – for example the roles of questioner or respondent, which we take on by asking or answering a question; and also for getting things done, by means of the interaction between one person and another[;]

and the **textual** function, the function language has of providing links with itself

and with features of the situation in which it is used (1970: 143): 'this is what enables the speaker or writer to construct "texts", or connected passages of discourse that is situationally relevant; and enables the listener or reader to distinguish a text from a random set of sentences'.

Halliday now shows how these functions are reflected in the structure of the English clause; the functions, however, are supposed to be relevant for all cultures (1970: 141). From the basic functions derive **structural roles**, 'functional elements such as "process" and "actor"' (1970: 144). These functional elements express certain very general meanings or semantic options which are realized in the clause. Each functional component contributes to structure through the functional roles (1970: 144):

Since normally every speech act serves each of the basic functions of language, the speaker is selecting among all the types of options simultaneously. Hence the various sets of structural 'roles' are mapped onto one another, so that the actual structure-forming element in language is a complex of roles, like a chord in a fugue.

The ideational function is reflected in the expression of processes in the clause: 'the system of clause types is a general framework for the representation of processes in the grammar' (1970: 155–6). The clause in English serves to express **processes** of two kinds, **transitive** and **intransitive**, and 'associated with each type of process are a small number of functions or "roles", each representing the parts that the various persons, objects or other classes of phenomena may play in the process concerned' (1970: 146). The process itself is usually represented by a verb, for instance *built*, in the clause *Sir Christopher Wren built this gazebo*. The specific roles taken on by persons and objects involved in the process are referred to as **participant functions**, and there may also be **circumstantial functions**, 'the associated conditions and constraints such as those of time, place and manner' (1970: 146–7). The main types of transitivity role – process, participant and circumstance – correspond more or less to the word classes – verb, noun and adverb.

The participant roles are listed as (1970: 148–9):

a   actor ('logical subject'): prepositionally *by*
b   goal ('logical direct object')
c   beneficiary ('logical indirect object'): prepositionally *to/for*
d   instrument: prepositionally *with/by*

with the possibility of further subdivisions. For different types of clause, the roles are either **inherent**, 'always associated with a given clause type even if it is not necessarily expressed in the structure of all clauses of that type', or **optional**. Any clause which is concerned with actions or events has an actor as inherent role; these are called **action clauses**, and may be of two types: if there is only the one inherent participant, agent, the clause is called a **middle** clause; if there are two participants, actor and goal, one of which may not be expressed in the structure, the clause is called a **non-middle** clause. Non-middle clauses may be either in the **active** or **passive voice**; it is thus the function of the voice system to align participants in various ways, and Table 1 shows the possibilities of voices in action clauses, and the roles associated with them; roles which are inherent but not expressed are in parentheses (from Halliday 1970: 152).

In addition to action clauses, English has two further types of clause corresponding to two types of process recognized by English; namely, **mental** processes and **relations**. The roles inherent in mental process clauses, such as *I like your hairstyle*, are called **processor** and **phenomenon**. Relational clauses are of two types: attributive, such as *Marguerite is a poet* and *Marguerite looks desperate*, where Marguerite is being given membership of a class, the class of poets and the class of desperate-looking people respectively; and **equative**, such as *Templecombe is the treasurer*. Attributive clauses are irreversible: we cannot say **A poet is Marguerite*. The inherent role is **attribute**. Equative clauses are reversible, and have the inherent role **identifier**.

The interpersonal function of language is manifest in the structure of the clause through the system of **mood**, which defines the grammatical subject (as opposed to the logical subject, which is defined by the transitivity system). The options in the mood system are **declarative**, **interrogative** and **imperative**, and the system is carried by the finite element of the verb plus one nominal, which is the grammatical subject. The fact that something is a grammatical subject contributes to the meaning of the clause through the interpersonal function (1970: 160):

The function of the 'grammatical subject' is thus a meaningful function in the clause, since it defines the communication role adopted by the speaker. It is

Table 1 Voice in action clauses in English

Voice (clause)		Roles	Voice (verb)	Example
	middle	actor	active	the gazebo has collapsed
	'active'	actor, goal	active	the Council are selling the gazebo
	'active'	actor (goal)	active	the Council won't sell
non-middle	'passive'	goal	active	the gazebo won't sell
	'passive'	goal, actor	passive	the gazebo has been sold by the Council
	'passive'	goal (actor)	passive	the gazebo has been sold

present in clauses of all moods, but its significance can perhaps be seen most clearly in the imperative, where the meaning is 'I request you to . . .'; here the speaker is requiring some action on the part of the person addressed, but it is the latter who has the power to make this meaning 'come true'.

The textual function of language is manifest in the clause structure in the **thematic structure**; that is, the organization of the clause as message (1970: 161):

> The English clause consists of a 'theme' and a 'rheme'. The theme is another component in the complex notion of subject, namely the 'psychological subject'; it is as it were the peg on which the message is hung, the theme being the body of the message. The theme of a clause is the element which, in English, is put in first position.

Normally, theme, actor and modal subject are identical, as in *Sir Christopher Wren built this gazebo*. In the passive, however, the actor is dissociated from theme and modal subject, either by being placed at the end of the clause (*This gazebo was built by Sir Christopher Wren*), or by being left out completely (*This gazebo is being restored*). In interrogative structures whose theme is a request for information, the questioning element is put first so that the theme is dissociated from actor and modal subject. A final option in thematic structure is the use of nominalization to split the clause into two parts as in *The one who built this gazebo was Sir Christopher Wren*.

Often the organization of a clause as message through the theme/rheme distinction corresponds with its information structure in terms of the notions of **given** and **new**. Information structure in English is expressed by intonation (see INTONATION). The theme will typically be associated with the given, the rheme with the new.

The functional model described above formed the basis for Halliday's later work in functional grammar (see below). Other linguists, however, although operating within a general Hallidayan framework, have developed systemic grammar in other directions. Above, we saw how Fawcett developed the original scale and category version of the model; here, we shall concentrate on Hudson's (1971, 1974, 1976) version of systemic grammar. However, both developments share two fundamental assumptions not compatible with Halliday's own views. The first is that syntax and semantics are to be treated as separate linguistic levels, since otherwise it is difficult to be specific about the relationships between them. The second is that the grammar should be generative, 'should consist of rules that can be used in a completely mechanical way to decide whether or not any given object is well-formed' (Hudson 1971: 7). He differs radically from Halliday in believing that it is the goal of grammatical description to lay bare precisely what a native speaker of a language *knows*; for Halliday, the major question is always what a native speaker *can do* with language.

Hudson's grammar accounts, like all systemic grammars, for two types of patterning, syntagmatic and paradigmatic (Butler 1985: 105):

> Syntagmatic relations can be broken down into three components: constituency, sequence and dependency relations. . . . Constituency and sequence relations are shown by the tree diagrams used for structural representation. By dependency, Hudson means relations of the type exemplified by subject–verb concord, concord between demonstrative determiners and head nouns ('this plate'/'these plates'), the relationship between 'have' and the '-en' form of the succeeding verb in the English perfect construction, and so on. The discussion of such relations is one of Hudson's major contributions

to systemic theory (it is not entirely clear how Halliday would handle, for instance, subject–verb concord). . . .

Paradigmatic relations are shown by means of Systems.

The terms in the systems are classes of syntactic item, and the classes are defined by distribution and those internal constituency properties relevant to distribution. Since Halliday's units – clause, phrase (group), word and morpheme – are defined in this way, Hudson treats them all as classes, which means, in turn, that they are seen as being in paradigmatic relation; and all the classes have places in one supernetwork of systems, so that Firth's and Halliday's insistence on the multiplicity of systems in grammatical description is abandoned.

Functional grammar

Halliday's own development of the systemic version of his linguistic theory is to be found in Halliday (1985/1994). While the earlier model contained a strong functional component, and while the theory behind functional grammar remains systemic, Halliday (1985/1994) concentrates exclusively on the functional part of grammar, 'that is, the interpretation of the grammatical patterns in terms of configurations of functions' (1985/1994: x); these, according to Halliday, are particularly relevant to the analysis of text, where, by **text**, Halliday means 'everything that is said or written' (1985/1994: xiv). The focus here is on language in use and, indeed, Halliday (1985/1994: xiv) defines a **functional grammar** as 'essentially a "natural" grammar, in the sense that everything in it can be explained, ultimately, by reference to how language is used'.

Halliday's functional grammar is not a formal grammar; indeed, he opposes the term 'functional' to the term 'formal'. In this respect, it differs from the **functional grammar** developed by S.C. Dik (1978), summarized in Dik (1980), and from Kay's

(1985, 1986) **functional unification grammar**. All three types of functional grammar, however, display some influence from Prague School linguistics, and Dik's description of 'a functional view of natural language' differs from Halliday's in terminology only, if at all (1980: 46):

> A language is regarded in the first place as an instrument by means of which people can enter into communicative relations with one other [*sic*]. From this point of view language is primarily a pragmatic phenomenon – a symbolic instrument used for communicative purposes.

However, while Halliday's functional grammar begins from the premise that language has certain functions for its users as a social group, so that it is primarily sociolinguistic in nature, Dik concentrates on speakers' competence, seeing his grammar as (1980: 47) 'a theory of the grammatical component of communicative competence'. The notion of **communicative competence** derives from Hymes (1971a). It consists of **grammatical competence**, the speaker's ability to form and interpret sentences, and **pragmatic competence**, the ability to use expressions to achieve a desired communicative effect. Dik shares, in some measure, Chomsky's view of grammar as a part of cognitive psychology. Halliday makes no separation of grammatical and pragmatic competence; he sees grammar as a **meaning potential** shared by a language and its speakers.

Dik's functional grammar falls within the broad framework of contemporary generative grammar (see GENERATIVE GRAMMAR), but differs from it in that it does not allow underlying constituent order to differ from surface constituent order, and in that it does not allow constituents which are not present in surface structure to be posited at some point in the derivation (Moravcsik 1980: 11). It begins a description of a linguistic expression with the construction of an **underlying predication** consisting of **terms**, which can be used to refer to items in the world, inserted in **predicate frames**, schemata which specify a predicate and an outline of the structures in which it can occur. Dik calls the set of terms and the set of predicate frames the **fund** of the language. A predicate frame for *walk* looks like this (Dik 1980: 52):

$$walk_v \; (x_1: \text{animate}(x_1))_{Ag}$$

It says that *walk* is a verbal predicate (V), which takes one argument (x_1). The argument has the Agent function (Ag) and must be animate. In addition to predicate frames, the grammar has a lexicon consisting of **basic terms** such as *John*, which is specified as being a proper noun, animate, human and male. It is hence an appropriate term for insertion into the predicate frame for *walk*, and this insertion will result in a predication. Non-simple terms can be formed by **term formation**. The predication is mapped on to the form of the expression by means of rules which determine the form and the order of constituents.

Dik's functional grammar represents an interesting attempt at taking full account of the factors which guide speakers' use of language, their **performance**, within a framework of a formal grammatical system which was originally developed with competence alone in mind.

Halliday's functional grammar is based on the premise that language has two major functions (**metafunctions**) for its users: it is a means of reflecting on things, and a means of acting on things – though the only things it is possible to act on by means of a symbolic system such as language are humans (and some animals). Halliday calls these two functions the **ideational 'content' function** and the **interpersonal function**. Both these functions rely on a third, the **textual function**, which enables the other two to be realized and ensures that the language used is relevant. The textual function represents the language user's text-forming potential.

Halliday's systemic theory, which, as mentioned above, underlies his functional grammar, 'is a theory of *meaning as choice*' (1985/1994: xiv; emphasis added) and, for Halliday, grammar is always seen as meaningful (1985/1994: xvii):

A language . . . is a system for making meanings: a semantic system, with other systems for encoding the meanings it produces. The term 'semantics' does not simply refer to the meanings of words; it is the entire system of meanings of a language, expressed by grammar as well as by vocabulary. In fact the meanings are encoded in 'wordings': grammatical sequences, or 'syntagms', consisting of items of both kinds – lexical items such as most verbs and nouns, grammatical items like *the* and *of* and *if* as well as those of an in between type such as prepositions.

The ideational, interpersonal and textual functions are therefore functional components of the semantic system that is language. The grammar enables all three of them to come into play at every point of text: it receives meanings from each component and splices them together in the wordings, as Halliday shows through his analysis of the clause in English. The clause is chosen because it is the grammatical unit in which 'three distinct structures, each expressing one kind of semantic organization, are mapped onto one another to produce a single wording' (1985/1994: 53):

Ideational meaning is the representation of experience: our experience of the world that lies about us, and also inside us, the world of our imagination. It is meaning in the sense of 'content'. The ideational function of the **clause** is that of representing what in the broadest sense we can call 'processes': actions, events, processes of consciousness, and relations . . .

Interpersonal meaning is meaning as a form of action: the speaker or writer doing something to the listener or reader by means of language, The interpersonal function of the **clause** is that of exchanging roles in rhetorical interaction: statements, questions, offers and commands, together with accompanying modalities. . . .

Textual meaning is relevance to the context: both the preceding (and following) text, and the context of situation. The textual function of the **clause** is that of constructing a message.

The message is constructed in the English clause in terms of theme and rheme. One element of the clause is given the special status of **theme** by being put first, and it then combines with the rest of the clause to constitute the message; other languages mark theme by other means – for instance, Japanese uses the suffix -*wa* to signify that whatever it follows is the theme (1985/1994: 38). The theme is defined as 'the element which serves as the point of departure of the message; it is that with which the clause is concerned', and the rest of the message is referred to as the **rheme**, which is normally realized by nominal groups (examples (1), (2) and (3)), adverbial groups (5) or prepositional phrases (4).

	Theme	*Rheme*
(1)	Tomas	gave Sophie that Easter egg
(2)	That Easter egg	was given to Sophie by Tomas
(3)	Sophie	was given that Easter egg by Tomas
(4)	At Easter	Tomas went to see Sophie and Katie
(5)	Very soon	they were eating Easter eggs

Themes may, however, also be realized by clauses, as in the case of:

What Tomas gave to Sophie was an Easter egg.

However, in this case the clause *what Tomas gave to Sophie* functions as a nominal group in the whole clause; this phenomenon is referred to as **nominalization**. It is also possible to have cases of predicated theme having the form *it + be*, as in

It was an Easter egg that Tomas gave to Sophie.

The most usual themes in English are those realized by the grammatical subject of the clause, and these are are called **unmarked** themes. When the theme is something other than the subject, it is called **marked** theme (examples (4) and (5)).

In its interpersonal function, as an interactive event, an exchange between speakers, the clause in English is organized in terms of **mood**. Mood is the relationship between the grammatical subject of the clause and the finite element of the verbal group, with the remainder of the clause called the **residue**. So any **indicative** clause – a clause which has a subject and a finite element – will have a mood structure. Subject and finite together make up the **proposition** of the clause, the part that can be affirmed, denied, questioned and negotiated by speakers in other ways (wished about, hoped for, demanded, etc.). The grammatical subject of a declarative clause is recognizable as that element which is picked up in the pronoun of a **tag** (1985/ 1994: 73):

So in order to locate the Subject, add a tag (if one is not already present) and see which element is taken up. For example, *that teapot was given to your aunt:* here the tag would be *wasn't it?* – we cannot add *wasn't she?*. On the other hand with *that teapot your aunt got from the duke* the tag would be *didn't she?*; we cannot say *didn't he?* or *wasn't it?*

Table 2

Temporal operators

Past	Present	Future
did, was, had, used to	does, is, has	will, shall, would, should

Modal operators

Low	Median	High
can, may, could, might	will, would, should, is to, was to	must, ought to, need, has to, had to

It is that *by reference to which* the proposition is affirmed, denied, etc. The finite element further enhances the proposition as something to negotiate by giving it a **primary tense** (past, present, future) and a **modality**, an indication of the speaker's attitude in terms of certainty and obligation to what s/he is saying. Halliday represents the finite verbal operators as in Table 2 (1985/1994: 75).

There are two moods within the indicative, realized through the ordering of subject and finite (1985/1994: 74):

a The order Subject before Finite realizes 'declarative';
b The order Finite before Subject realizes 'yes/no interrogative';
c In a 'WH-interrogative' the order is:

  (i) Subject before Finite if the WH-element is the Subject;
  (ii) Finite before Subject otherwise.

Declarative

the duke	has	given that teapot away
Subject	Finite	
Mood		Residue

Yes/no interrogative

has	the duke	given that teapot away
Subject	Finite	
Mood		Residue

Examples of (c) would be
(c. i)

who	gave	you that teapot
Subject	Finite	
Mood		Residue

(c. ii)

why	were	you	given that teapot
WH	Finite	Subject	
	Mood		
Residue			

In a third mood, the **imperative**, the subject is often missing, as in *Go away!* Halliday chooses to treat this absence as a case of **ellipsis** of the subject, that is, the subject is understood to be there, but is not explicitly mentioned; the hearer supplies it mentally. Sinclair (1972: 71) recognizes a fourth mood choice, **moodless**, made in clauses which have neither subject nor finite (which Sinclair treats as part of the predicator), as in the case of announcements (*Rotunda next stop*) and responses (*yes/no*).

The clause residue consists of three kinds of functional element: one (and only one) **predicator**, one or two **complements** and up to about seven **adjuncts**. The predicator is what there is of the verbal group in addition to the finite – if there is one; some clauses, known as **non-finite clauses**, have only a predicator 'for example *eating her curds and* *whey* (following *Little Miss Muffet sat on a tuffet*)' (Halliday 1985/1994: 78). It has four functions (1985/1994: 79):

(i) It specifies time reference *other than* reference to the time of the speech event, i.e. 'secondary' tense: past, present or future relative to the primary tense. . . . (ii) It specifies various other aspects and phases like seeming, trying, hoping. . . . (iii) It specifies the voice: active or passive. . . . (iv) It specifies the process (action, event, mental process, relation) that is predicated of the Subject. These can be exemplified from the verbal group *has been trying to be heard*, where the Predicator, *been trying to be heard*, expresses (i) a complex secondary tense, *been* + *ing*; (ii) a conative phase, *try* + *to*; (iii) passive voice, *be* + *-d*; (iv) the mental process *hear*.

The **complement** is anything that could have functioned as the subject in the clause, but which does not, including, thus, nominal groups realizing what other grammarians tend to refer to as direct and indirect objects, and also what Halliday refers to as **attributive** complement: for instance, *a famous politician* in *Dick Whittington became a famous politician*.

The **adjunct**(s) include those elements which do not have the potential of being used as subjects.

In its ideational function, as representation, the clause is structured in terms of processes, participants and circumstances. These are specified through choices in the transitivity system. A process consists potentially of three components (1985/1994: 101):

(i)   the process itself;
(ii) participants in the process;
(iii) circumstances associated with the process.

Typically, these elements are realized as follows: processes by verbal groups; participants by nominal groups; and circumstances by adverbial groups or prepositional phrases.

Halliday lists three principal types of process: **material processes**, processes of doing, have an obligatory **actor**, someone who does something, and an optional **goal**, 'one to which the process is extended' (1985/ 1994: 103). When both are present, the clause is **transitive**; when only the actor is present, it is **intransitive**. **Mental processes**, of feeling, thinking and perceiving, have an obligatory **senser** and an obligatory **phenomenon**, although the phenomenon need not be present in the clause; it may only be there implicitly. Relational processes are processes of being, and there are six types of these in English (Table 3).

Any relational-process clause in the **attributive mode** contains two participants,

Table 3

type \ mode	(i) attributive	(ii) identifying
(1) intensive	Sarah is wise	Tom is the leader; the leader is Tom
(2) circumstantial	the fair is on Tuesday	tomorrow is the 10th; the 10th is tomorrow
(3) possessive	Peter has a piano	the piano is Peter's Peter's is the piano

Source: Halliday 1985, p. 113

carrier and attribute; one in the **identifying mode** contains **identified** and **identifier**. There are several further subdivisions of process and participant types (see Halliday 1985/1994: chapter 5).

The principal circumstantial elements of clauses in English are (1985/1994: 137): 'Extent and Location in time and space, including abstract Space; Manner (means, quality and comparison); Cause (reason, purpose and behalf); Accompaniment; Matter; Role'. Again these are further subdivided.

Halliday (1971), in which choices in the transitivity system (in particular) are explored, is a fine illustration of the claim that functional grammar is particularly well suited to text analysis (see STYLISTICS).

Halliday (1985/1994) further explores grammatical functions above, below and beyond the clause. Halliday (1978) relates both his grammatical theory and his theory of first-language acquisition to an account of how language relates to the world in which it is used, thus producing one of the most comprehensive theories of language as a social phenomenon.

K.M.

Suggestions for further reading

Butler, C.S. (1985) *Systemic Linguistics: Theory and Applications*, London: Batsford Academic and Educational.

Dik, S.C. (1978) *Functional Grammar* (North Holland Linguistic Series, no. 37), Amsterdam: North Holland.

Halliday, M.A.K. (1961) 'Categories of the theory of grammar', *Word* 17: 241–92.

—— (1970) 'Language structure and language function', in J. Lyons (ed.) *New Horizons in Linguistics*, Harmondsworth: Penguin.

—— (1985/1994) *An Introduction to Functional Grammar*, London: Edward Arnold; 2nd edition 1994.

T

Teaching English as a Foreign Language (TEFL)

TEFL is the term used to refer to the activity of teaching English to non-native speakers of the language. This activity is also referred to as **Teaching English as a Second Language (TESL)**. In the USA, the latter seems to be the preferred term, whereas in Britain 'TESL' is used more specifically to refer to the teaching of English in those countries where English has an official role in the educational or political system, e.g. in former British or American colonies such as India or the Philippines, where English is still used as a medium of education and is recognized as an official language alongside the national language. TESL thus contrasts with TEFL, which refers to those situations where English is not used as a medium of instruction and has no official status. In Britain itself, 'TESL' is often used to refer to the teaching of English to immigrants or non-native speakers born in Britain. Because of the possible confusion between TEFL and TESL, the more general terms **English Language Teaching (ELT)** and **English for Speakers of Other Languages (ESOL)** are often used, the former in Britain and the latter in the USA. The term ELT will be used in this entry.

ELT can be traced back to the late sixteenth century, when large numbers of French Huguenot refugees needed to learn English and the first textbooks were written (Howatt 1984). English has been taught in Europe and countries that were part of the British Empire since then, but it is undoubtedly the case that there was a huge growth in English language teaching in the twentieth century and particularly since 1945. This is largely due to the growth in use of English as the international language of science, technology, diplomacy and business. Baldauf and Jernudd (1983) and Swales (1985) have shown that the proportion of academic articles written in the areas of science, technology and economics has been increasing rapidly, and it is estimated that of the several million articles published every year at least half are published in English (Swales 1987). No corresponding figures about the proportion of business correspondence and negotiation exist, but it is reasonable to assume that growth in these areas is similar to that in the academic world.

These trends have led to the development of the teaching of **English for Specific Purposes (ESP)**, which aims to teach specific language skills related to different activities in academic or business life (see below for a fuller description of ESP). But the teaching of **General-Purpose English** has also grown considerably and the British Council and the American Information Services both run very successful institutes in many countries of the world. The British

Council, for example, stated in its annual report for 1987/8 that it was running fifty Direct Teaching Centres in thirty-one countries and was planning further centres in three more countries. It also reported that over 40 per cent of its revenue was derived from English language services.

The development of ELT has been dominated by issues of syllabus design and methodology. Howatt (1984) describes how the **grammar-translation method** developed at the end of the eighteenth century in Germany and spread throughout Europe. The method involved grammatical explanation of key structures, the teaching of selected areas of vocabulary, and exercises involving the translation of disconnected sentences into the mother tongue. The emphasis was on written text.

The **Reform Movement** developed in the late eighteenth century and was based on three fundamental points:

- the primacy of speech
- the use of connected text as opposed to disconnected sentences
- the use of an oral methodology

The syllabuses that arose from the Reform Movement still involved a graded, step-by-step approach. They thus contrasted with a parallel development in ELT, the rise of what Howatt (1984) refers to as 'natural methods of language teaching'. These have gone under the names of the **Natural Method**, the **Conversation Method** and, most notably, the **Direct Method**. The methodology of these approaches is less structured than that of the Reform Movement and is based on a theory according to which language learning is an 'intuitive process for which human beings have a natural capacity provided only that the proper conditions exist'. These conditions are 'someone to talk to, something to talk about and a desire to understand and make yourself understood' (1984: 192).

The early part of the twentieth century saw the fusion of these philosophies,

particularly in the work of H.E. Palmer and his **Oral Method**. Palmer and Palmer's *English Through Actions* (1925/1979) uses the question–answer techniques of the Direct Method but has a more systematic approach to the selection of vocabulary and the presentation of grammatical points than that favoured by the Direct Method. Subsequent courses in ELT, e.g. Eckersley's *Essential English for Foreign Students* (1938–42) and Hornby's *Oxford Progressive English for Adult Learners* (1954–6), have followed the approach used by Palmer, combining some Direct Method exercises with pattern practice, teaching the main structures of English. Even courses from the 1960s such as L.G. Alexander's *First Things First* (1967), with its extensive use of situations presented in pictures, and the courses that arose from the **Audiolingual Method** developed in the United States by Fries (see for example Fries 1952/1957), which used very controlled pattern practice, are really refinements of the basic Palmer/Hornby approach. The main emphasis is on teaching the form and vocabulary of the language, and the ways in which these forms are used in natural language are largely neglected.

In the 1970s, however, a very considerable change in emphasis arose, largely as a result of the writings of various British applied linguists, notably Widdowson (see for example Widdowson 1978). Widdowson argued that language courses should concentrate on the **use** of language rather than **usage**. He defines **usage** as 'that aspect which makes evident the extent to which the language user demonstrates his knowledge of linguistic rules'; **use** is 'another aspect of performance: that which makes evident the extent to which the language user demonstrates his ability to use his knowledge of linguistic rules for effective communication' (1978: 3).

Widdowson's ideas have had a profound influence on ELT, particularly on ESP. The striking development has been the rise of a **Communicative Approach**, which emphasizes language use rather than language form. The Communicative Approach aims to teach **communicative competence** (Hymes 1972), which is the ability to apply the rules of grammar appropriately in the correct situation.

The actual syllabuses that have arisen from attempts to put the Communicative Approach into practice have varied considerably. Many courses have followed a **functional/notional** syllabus, putting into practice the ideas expressed in Wilkins' *Notional Syllabuses* (1976). The aim of such syllabuses is to base teaching on what people do with language, such as requesting, inviting, informing, apologizing, ordering, etc. These are **communicative functions**. **Notions** – or **semantico-grammatical** categories, as Wilkins calls them – are more difficult to define; they are the basic 'building blocks' that constitute meaning, such as **location**, **time**, **duration**, **space**. The most general notions, such as **time**, are clearly too abstract to form the basis of teaching materials, but others that are more concrete, such as **quantity**, **location** or **cause** and **effect**, may be used. Most coursebooks following a functional/notional syllabus, e.g. *Strategies* (Abbs and Freebairn 1975), have concentrated on functions rather than notions, even though the very full syllabus worked out by van Ek (1975) in *The Threshold Level* does integrate both functions and notions.

Many have argued (notably Brumfit 1980) that functional/notional syllabuses have done little more than reorganize and reorder the grammatical syllabus and have failed to address the question of methodology. The basic aim of a **communicative syllabus** should be the creation of tasks in which learners have to communicate in English in order to complete them. A typical **communicative task** would be the labelling of a diagram using information from a written or spoken text. The most interesting experiment in this regard is the project directed by Prabhu in Bangalore, south India. This project arose from dissatisfaction with the previous grammatical syllabus rather than with a functional/notional syllabus, and its underlying philosophy is that grammatical form is best learned when the learner's attention is on meaning. The syllabus is thus based on a series of graded tasks for which the teacher provides necessary input and learners show their comprehension by carrying out an activity such as labelling a diagram. Grammatical points are not taught, but results of the project indicate that learners have in fact performed better on tests of grammar than learners following a traditional grammatical syllabus (Prabhu 1987).

Since the late 1980s, both applied linguists and course designers have seemed to favour an **Eclectic** Approach, which selects features from grammatical syllabuses, functional/notional syllabuses, and task-based approaches. *The Cambridge English Course*, the most widely used coursebook in Britain in the late 1980s, is a good example of this eclecticism. An interesting development, however, is the reawakening of interest in the teaching of vocabulary and the emergence of the idea of a **lexical syllabus**. *The COBUILD English Course, Level I* (Willis and Willis 1988) is designed for **false beginners** (people who have had some experience of the foreign language, and usually some tuition, but who, for one reason or another, have not progressed beyond elementary level, or have forgotten what they had once learned) and aims to teach the 700 most common words in English. The list is derived from the 20-million-word corpus built up at the University of Birmingham by the COBUILD Dictionary Project (see CORPORA).

The **English for Specific Purposes** movement has played an important and influential role in ELT since the 1960s. In ESP, the aims of the course are determined by the particular needs of the learners, and the growth of the use of English in science, technology and business has led to both research into the nature of learners' needs (**needs analysis**) and the preparation of teaching materials to meet those needs. In ESP, as in ELT in general, there have been considerable changes in approach. Early courses, such as Herbert's *The Structure of Technical English* (1965) and Ewer and Latorre's *Course in Basic Scientific English* (1969), adopted a grammatical approach concentrating largely on those structures, such as the present simple (both active and passive) and the present perfect, that register analysis has shown to be important in scientific and technical English.

The functional/notional syllabus probably worked more effectively in ESP courses than in General English courses. Allen and Widdowson's *English in Focus* series (1974 onwards), based largely on functions, and, more particularly, Bates and Dudley-Evans' *Nucleus* series (1976), based on scientific notions or concepts, have both been influential courses. Subsequent courses, e.g. *Reading and Thinking in English*, edited by Moore and Widdowson (1980) and *Skills for Learning*, which developed from a project at the University of Malaya directed by Sinclair (Sinclair 1980), have concentrated on particular study skills, particularly reading. Task-based approaches have also been very appropriate for ESP work; a course called *Interface*, written by Hutchinson and Waters (1984) and developed originally for a group of technical students preparing to study in Britain, is a good example of such an approach.

It has become common to make a distinction between two main branches of ESP: **English for Academic Purposes (EAP)** and **English for Occupational Purposes (EOP)**. In the United States, English for Occupational Purposes is usually referred to as **English for Vocational Purposes (EVP)**. EAP began as the dominant branch, but with the increased interest in business English EOP has become increasingly important. Most EOP courses, except for early courses,

have been strongly influenced by task-based syllabuses. The results of genre analysis (see GENRE ANALYSIS) are likely to have an increasing influence on both branches of ESP.

The relationship between ELT and linguistics or applied linguistics has always been interesting. At certain times, research carried out by either descriptive or applied linguists has had a strong influence on ELT materials and methodology. At other times, pioneering work done in the classroom has been ahead of applied linguistics, which has subsequently provided a theoretical framework to explain what has already been discovered in the classroom. The pattern seems to be that most new developments in ELT have been prompted by new work in linguistics or applied linguistics; the work in ELT then expands in a number of directions and leads to discoveries which feed back into applied linguistics.

Howatt (1984) describes how the Reform Movement of the late nineteenth century was closely associated with the development of phonetics and the formation of associations such as the International Phonetic Association (see INTERNATIONAL PHONETIC ALPHABET). Similarly, the professionalization of ELT in the first half of the twentieth century begins with the work of Daniel Jones in phonetics (see PHONEMICS) but was developed by the more practically orientated work of Palmer, West and Hornby. Their work in developing teaching materials and ideas for using those materials culminated in a number of books on teaching methodology published in the late 1950s and early 1960s, notably West's *Teaching English in Difficult Circumstances* (1960) and Billows' *Techniques of Language Teaching* (1962). Abercrombie's *Problems and Principles* (1956) was also influential. As noted earlier, Widdowson had a considerable influence on the emergence of the Communicative Approach to language teaching and he in turn drew on the tradition of relating language and social context that begins with Firth and continues with Halliday (see FUNCTIONALIST LINGUISTICS). But the various interpretations of a Communicative Approach in the actual classroom and discussion of the claimed successes of these approaches have played an important part in the applied linguistics literature, both in journals such as *English Language Teaching Journal* (*ELTJ*) and books such as Johnson's *Communicative Syllabus Design and Methodology* (1982).

It is interesting to note that in the USA the influence of both descriptive and applied linguistics has been more direct. Howatt (1984) reports Fries as stating that the relationship should be hierarchical, with the descriptive linguist providing the description of the target language, the applied linguist selecting and grading the structures from this description and also providing a contrastive analysis of the source and target languages. The applied linguist then prepares the materials that the teacher uses in the classroom. It is perhaps noteworthy that the main American journal concerned with ELT, *TESOL Quarterly*, has always published many more data-based empirical studies related to classroom methodology than the British *ELTJ*. It is likely that, with the increased numbers of ELT teachers following postgraduate courses in applied linguistics, the gap between the two professions will diminish and that more systematic approaches to the development and validation of teaching materials and methodology will emerge.

T.D.-E.

Suggestions for further reading

Dudley-Evans, A. and St John, M.J. (1998) *Developments in ESP: A Multidisciplinary Approach*, Cambridge: Cambridge University Press.

Howatt, A.T.R. (1984) *A History of English Language Teaching*, Oxford: Oxford University Press.

White, R. (1988) *The ELT Curriculum*, Oxford: Basil Blackwell.

Widdowson, H.G. (1983) *Learning Purpose and Language Use*, Oxford: Oxford University Press.

Text linguistics

Background

As Hoey points out (1983–4: 1),

> there is a tendency . . . to make a hard-and-fast distinction between discourse (spoken) and text (written). This is reflected even in two of the names of the discipline(s) we study, discourse analysis and text linguistics. But, though the distinction is a necessary one to maintain for some purposes . . . it may at times obscure similarities in the organisation of the spoken and written word.

The distinction Hoey mentions is made in this volume on practical, not theoretical grounds, and the overlap between text linguistics and discourse and conversation analysis should be borne in mind.

Early modern linguistics, with its emphasis on discovering and describing the minimal units of each of the linguistic levels of sound, form, syntax and semantics, made no provision for the study of long stretches of text as such; traditional grammatical analysis stops at sentence length. It is even possible to argue that 'the extraction of tiny components diverts consideration away from the important unities which bind a text together' (de Beaugrande and Dressler 1981: 21) and, although Zellig Harris (1952) had proposed to analyse whole discourses on distributional principles, employing the notion of transformations between stretches of text, this emergent interest in text and discourse study was lost at the time in Chomsky's modification of the notion of transformation to an intrasentential phenomenon.

Early large-scale enquiries into text organization remained essentially descriptive and structurally based (Pike 1967; Koch 1971; Heger 1976), with occasional expansion of the framework to include text sequences or situations of occurrence (Coseriu 1955–6; Pike 1967; Harweg 1968; Koch 1971). **Text** was defined as a unit larger than the sentence, and the research was orientated towards discovering and classifying types of text structure; these were assumed to be something given, rather than something partly construed by the reader, and dependent on context. 'We end up having classifications with various numbers of categories and degrees of elaboration, but no clear picture of how texts are utilized in social activity' (de Beaugrande and Dressler 1981: 23).

The descriptive method, however, tends to break down because the language is too complex, with too many and diverse constituents to be captured. Ironically, it was the concept of transformations, lost by Harris to Chomsky, which allowed a new outlook on text that encouraged the upsurge in text linguistics during the 1970s. In transformational grammar, the infinite set of possible sentences of a language are seen as derivable from a small set of underlying deep patterns plus a set of rules for transforming these into the more elaborate actual surface structures. It was argued, first (Katz and Fodor 1963), that a whole text could be treated as a single sentence by seeing full stops as substitutes for conjunctions like *and*. This approach, however, deliberately leaves out reference to speakers' motives and knowledge. In addition, it ignores the fact that 'factors of accent, intonation, and word-order within a sentence depend on the organization of other sentences in the vicinity' (de Beaugrande

and Dressler 1981: 24). This was noted by Heidolph (1966), who suggests 'that a feature of "mentioned" vs "not mentioned" could be inserted in the grammar to regulate these factors'. Isenberg (1968, 1971) lists other factors which could be dealt with within a single sentence, such as pronouns, articles and tense sequences, and 'appeals to coherence relations like cause, purpose, specification, and temporal proximity' (de Beaugrande and Dressler 1981: 24).

Similar approaches to text analysis may be found in the school of rhetorical structure analysis, where the emphasis is on how units of meaning (which are not necessarily sentences) relate to one another in a hierarchy, and how such devices as exemplification, summary, expansion, etc. build on core propositions to construct the finished text (Mann and Thompson 1988), an approach which in its turn owes much to the text linguistics of Longacre (1983).

The **Konstanz project**, set up at the University of Konstanz in Germany, is related to these traditions of analysis. A group of researchers, including Hannes Rieser, Peter Hartmann, János Petöfi, Teun van Dijk, Jens Ihwe, Wolfgang Köck and others, attempted to construct a grammar and lexicon which would generate a Brecht text; some of the results of this project are presented by van Dijk *et al.* (1972). The project highlighted more problems than it solved, though (de Beaugrande and Dressler 1981: 24): 'Despite a huge apparatus of rules, there emerged no criteria for judging the text "grammatical" or "well-formed". . . . The problem of common reference was not solved.' The basic assumption of the undertaking was questioned by Kummer (1972), who points out that 'the "generating" of the text is presupposed by the investigators rather than performed by the grammar' (de Beaugrande and Dressler 1981: 25).

In contrast to the grammatical method employed by the Konstanz group, Petöfi's (1971, 1974, 1978, 1980) **text-structure/**

world-structure theory (TeSWeST) operates with factors relating to text users rather than to the text as an isolated artefact, and with representational devices drawn from formal logic. His project is extremely complex (de Beaugrande and Dressler 1981: 25–6):

> In the 1980 version, components are offered for representing a text from nearly every perspective. To meet the demands of the logical basis, a 'canonic' mode (a regularized, idealized correlate) is set up alongside the 'natural language' mode in which the text is in fact expressed. Rules and algorithms are provided for such operations as 'formation', 'composition', 'construction', 'description', 'interpretation', and 'translation'. The reference of the text to objects or situations in the world is handled by a 'world-semantics' component; at least some correspondence is postulated between text-structure and world structure.

Retaining the idea of a text grammar designed to cope with features of text which a sentence grammar cannot handle, van Dijk (1972) introduces the notion of the **macrostructure**, a large-scale statement of the text's context (de Beaugrande and Dressler 1981: 27; see van Dijk 1977: chapter 5):

> Van Dijk reasoned that the generating of a text must begin with a main idea which gradually evolves into the detailed meanings that enter individual sentence-length stretches. . . . When a text is presented, there must be operations which work in the other direction to extract the main idea back out again, such as *deletion* (direct removal of material), *generalization* (recasting material in a more general way), and *construction* (creating new material to subsume the presentation). . . . Accordingly, van Dijk turned to cognitive psychology for a *process-oriented* model of the text. In collaboration with Walter Kintsch, he

investigated the operations people use to summarize texts . . . (cf. Kintsch and van Dijk 1978; van Dijk and Kintsch 1978). The typical summary for a text ought to be based on its macrostructure. . . . However, research showed that the actual outcome involves both the macro-structure of the text and previously stored macro-structures based on knowledge of the events and situations in the real world.

De Beaugrande and Dressler (1981) view their own **procedural** approach to text linguistics as evolved out of these other views, and most text linguists make some reference to both micro- and macrostructural features of the text, and to speakers' world knowledge. By a procedural approach, de Beaugrande and Dressler (1981: 31) mean an approach in which 'all the levels of language are to be described in terms of their utilization'. They (1931: 3) define text as a communicative occurrence which meets seven standards of **textuality** – namely **cohesion** and **coherence**, which are both text-centred, and **intentionality**, **acceptability**, **informativity**, **situationality** and **intertextuality**, which are all user-centred. These seven standards, described below, function as the constitutive principles which define and create communication. In addition, at least three regulative principles, also described below, control textual communication (for the distinction between constitutive and regulatory rules and principles, see SPEECH-ACT THEORY). These are **efficiency**, **effectiveness** and **appropriateness**.

The constitutive principles of communication

Cohesion

The major work on cohesion in English is Halliday and Hasan (1976/1989), but Jakobson's (1960) stress on textual parallelism created by patterning and repetition in text (see STYLISTICS) is the earliest detailed development of the idea of cohesion (see Closs Traugott and Pratt 1980: 21).

Cohesion concerns the way in which the linguistic items of which a text is composed are meaningfully connected to each other in a sequence on the basis of the grammatical rules of the language. In English, cohesion is created in four ways (Halliday 1985/1994: chapter 9): by **reference**, **ellipsis** (including **substitution**), **conjunction** and **lexical organization**.

Reference may be of several types: **exophoric**, referring out of the text to an item in the world (*look at that*); **endophoric**, referring to textual items either by **cataphora**, forward reference (as in *the house that Jack built*, where *the* refers forward to the specifying *that Jack built*); or **anaphora**, backward reference (as in *Jack built a house. It . . .* , where *it* refers back to *house*); **homophora**, self-specifying reference to an item of which there can only be one, or only one that makes sense in the context (*the sun* was shining or *She fed the cat*). Devices that refer are the personal pronouns and demonstratives, which corefer, and comparatives, which contrast.

Ellipsis works anaphorically by leaving out something mentioned earlier, as in *Help yourself* (for instance, to some apples mentioned earlier). **Substitution** works by substituting a 'holding device' in the place of a lexical item *Help yourself to one*.

Devices which create **conjunction** constitute cohesive bonds between sections of text. There are three types, according to Halliday (1985/1995: chapter 9):

- **Elaboration** by **apposition**, either **expository** (*in other words*) or **exemplifying** (*for example*); or by **clarification**: **corrective** (*or rather*), **distractive** (*incidentally*), **dismissive** (*in any case*), **particularizing** (*in particular*), **resumptive** (*as I was saying*), **summative** (*in short*) and **verifactive** (*actually*).
- **Extension**, which is either **additive** (*and, nor*), **adversative** (*but*), or a **variation** type, of which there are three – **replacive**

(*instead, on the contrary*), **subtractive** (*apart/except from/for that*) and **alternative** (*alternatively*).
- **Enhancement**, either **spatio-temporal** (*here, there, nearby, behind, in the first place*) or **manner** (comparison, reference to means), or **causal-conditional** (*so, therefore*) or **matter** (*in this respect, in other respects*).

De Beaugrande and Dressler (1981: 71–3) call these relationships **junctions**, and the devices signalling them **junctive expressions**; they distinguish four major types:

- **Conjunction**, which is an additive relation linking things which have the same status, e.g. both true in the textual world (see below, under **coherence**). Their signals are *and, moreover, also, in addition, besides, furthermore.*
- **Disjunction**, which links things that have alternative status, e.g. two things which cannot both be true in the textual world. Their signals are *or, either/or, whether or not.*
- **Contrajunction**, which links things having the same status but appearing incongruous or incompatible in the textual world, i.e. a cause and an unanticipated effect. Their signals are *but, however, yet, nevertheless.*
- **Subordination**, which links things when the status of one depends on that of the other, e.g. things true under certain conditions or for certain motives (precondition/ event, cause/effect, etc.). Their signals are *because, since, as, thus, while, therefore, on the grounds that, then, next, before, after, since, whenever, while, during, if.*

Lexical cohesion is created by **repetition**, **synonymy** and **collocation**. While reference, ellipsis and conjunction tend to link clauses which are near each other in the text, lexical cohesion tends to link much larger parts of the text (but see the discussion of patterns under 'Coherence' below).

One of the most thoughtful and prolific writers on the subject of relations between clauses is Eugene Winter (Hoey 1983: 17):

His work on clause relations can for the most part be divided into two major strands. On the one hand, he is concerned to place a sentence in the context of its adjoining sentences and show how its grammar and meaning can only be fully explained if its larger context is taken into account . . . On the other, he is concerned to reveal the clause organisation of a passage as a whole without focussing on any one sentence in particular within it.

In a similar vein, de Beaugrande and Dressler (1981: 79) distinguish between **short-range** and **long-range** stretches of surface text structures, the former set up as closely knit patterns of grammatical dependencies, the latter constituted by the reutilization of previous elements or patterns (see also van Dijk 1977: 93).

However, as Hoey (1983: 18) points out, Winter's (1971) definition of the clause relation as 'the cognitive process whereby we interpret the meaning of a sentence or group of sentences in the text in the light of its adjoining sentence or group of sentences', has the implication that 'uninterpreted grammatical cohesion is not a relation'. Most writers on cohesion (see, for instance, Halliday and Hasan 1976/1989) stress that it is created by the reader on the basis of the signalling devices, and Halliday and Hasan (1976/1989) develop their earlier work on the overt signals of cohesion by stressing that cohesion is a necessary but not sufficient condition for coherence. For this reason, their work is discussed under 'Coherence' below.

De Beaugrande and Dressler (1981: 80) include as long-range cohesive devices (compare Halliday's lexical-cohesion devices listed above):

Recurrence: the exact repetition of material.
Partial recurrence: different uses of the same basic language items (word stems).
Parallelism: reuse of structures with different material in them.

Paraphrase: approximate conceptual equivalence among outwardly different material.
Proforms: brief, empty elements used to keep the content of fuller elements current and to reuse basic syntactic structures.
Ellipsis: allows the omission of some structural component, provided a complete version is recoverable from elsewhere in the text.

Coherence

Coherence concerns the way in which the things that the text is about, called the **textual world**, are mutually accessible and relevant. The textual world is considered to consist of concepts and relations. A **concept** is defined as 'a configuration of knowledge (cognitive content) which can be recovered or activated with more or less unity and consistency in the mind', and **relations** as the links between the concepts 'which appear together in a textual world' (de Beaugrande and Dressler 1981: 4). Some of the most common relations can be classified in terms of two major notions, namely causality relations and time relations.

- Causality relations 'concern the ways in which one situation or event affects the conditions for some other one' (de Beaugrande and Dressler 1987: 4), and are of four major types:
  a **Cause**: *David hit the ball so hard that it flew over the hedge*; here the event of 'hitting the ball hard' has created the **necessary conditions** for the event of 'the ball flying over the hedge'.
  b **Enablement**: *Tabitha lay quietly in the sun and Tomas crept over and pulled her tail*; here a weaker relation obtains between the event consisting of Tabitha lying quietly in the sun, and the event consisting of Tomas creeping over and pulling her tail; the former event is a **sufficient**, but not a **necessary**, condition for the latter.

c **Reason**: *Because I've been writing about text linguistics all day I deserve a rest this evening*; in this case, the second event follows as a rational response to the first, but is not actually caused or enabled by it.

d **Purpose**: *You are reading this to find out about text linguistics*; in this case, although the first event enables the second, there is an added dimension, in so far as the second event is the **planned outcome** of the first.

- **Time** relations concern the arrangement of events in time. In the case of cause, enablement and reason, an earlier event causes, enables or provides the reason for a later one, so that we might say that **forward directionality** is involved. Purpose, however, has **backward directionality**, since a later event is the purpose for an earlier event.

Winter, for his part, divides clause relations into the two broad classes of **Logical Sequence** relations and **Matching** relations, where the most basic form of Logical Sequence relation is the time sequence (see Hoey 1983: 19). Both of these types are, however, governed by 'a still more fundamental relation, that of Situation–Evaluation, representing the two facets of world-perception "knowing" and "thinking". Indeed . . . all relations are reducible to these basic elements' (Hoey 1983: 20). De Beaugrande and Dressler (1981) do not display such an overtly reductive tendency.

- **Logical Sequence relations** 'are relations between successive events or ideas, whether actual or potential' (Hoey 1983: 19). They include:

  a **Condition–Consequence**, signalled by, e.g. *if* (*then*);

  b **Instrument–Achievement**, signalled by, e.g. *by* (*means of*);

  c **Cause–Consequence**, signalled by, e.g. *because, so*.

- **Matching relations** 'are relations where statements are "matched" against each

other in terms of identicality of description' (Hoey 1983: 20). They include:

a **Contrast**, signalled by, e.g. *however*;

b **Compatibility**, signalled by, e.g. (*and*), (*similarly*).

One of the most valuable aspects of Winter's work – and one which powerfully suggests that his (and Hoey's) work should be seen as a contribution to our understanding of coherence rather than only of cohesion – is his insistence that a clause relation cannot simply be read off from one textual surface signal. This must, of course, be obvious to anyone who peruses the various lists writers produce of signalling devices, since the same item is often listed as a signal for several relations (see, for instance, Halliday and Hasan 1976/ 1989: 242–3).

What Winter importantly stresses, however, is that *other* lexical items, in addition to junctive expressions, help readers to determine which relation a given junctive expression signals. He divides junctive expressions proper into two traditional types, namely **subordinators**, which he calls **Vocabulary 1**, and **conjuncts**, which he calls **Vocabulary 2**. But he adds to these the class of **lexical signals**, which he calls **Vocabulary 3**. The *same* clause relation may be signalled by an item from any one of these three classes, as Hoey (1983: 23), drawing on Winter (1977), demonstrates. The **Instrument–Achievement** relation is signalled in each of the following three near-paraphrases (signals in italics):

(1) *By* appealing to scientists and technologists to support his party, Mr Wilson won many middle-class votes.

(2) Mr Wilson appealed to scientists and technologists to support his party. He *thereby* won many middle-class votes.

(3) Mr Wilson's appeals to scientists and technologists to support his party *were instrumental* in winning many middle-class votes.

In (1) the relation is signalled with a Vocabulary 1 item; in (2) by a Vocabulary 2 item; and in (3) by a Vocabulary 3 item. Furthermore (Hoey 1983: 24),

> Vocabulary 3 items not only help signal the relations that hold between the sentences of a paragraph. They also signal the organisation of longer passages and whole discourses. Winter (1977) [and see also Winter (1986)] draws attention, for example, to what he terms 'items of the metastructure'; these are lexical signals which serve a larger function.

Hoey's own work is mostly concerned with this metastructural organization of the text. He discusses **Matching patterns**, **General–Particular patterns** and, in particular, the **Problem–Solution pattern**, where by 'pattern' he means 'combination of relations organising (part of) a discourse' (Hoey 1983: 31).

Both Hoey and Winter show that the stylistic device of **repetition** (see also STYLISTICS) both connects sentences and contributes to sentence and text interpretation, 'because where two sentences have material in common, it is what is changed that receives attention by the reader, while the repeated material acts as a framework for the interpretation of the new material' (Hoey 1983: 25).

Repetition typically signals Matching relations and General–Particular relations. It may take the form of **simple repetition** 'of a lexical item that has appeared earlier in a discourse, with no more alteration than is explicable by reference to grammatical paradigms' (1983: 108), e.g., *they dance – she dances*. Or it may take the form of **complex repetition**, in which a morpheme is shared by items of different word classes: *she danced* (verb) – *the dance* (noun) – *the dancing shoes* (adjective). Repetition may, however, also take the form of **substitution** in Hoey's system (in contrast with Halliday and Hasan 1976/1989, who treat substitu-tion as a subclass of ellipsis – see above). His signals of this type of repetition are the same as those listed by Halliday and Hasan (1976/1989) (see above). Finally, **paraphrase** is also classed as repetition. For further analysis of patterns of lexical repetition in both spoken and written texts, see Tannen (1989) and Hoey (1991).

Repetition is the clearest signal of the **Matching** relation (Hoey 1983: 113):

> Matching is what happens when two parts of a discourse are compared in respect of their detail. Sometimes they are matched for similarity, in which case we call the resulting relation Matching Compatibility, and sometimes for difference, in which case we call the resulting relation Matching Contrast.

The only types of text that are occasionally organized solely in terms of Matching relations are letters and poems. Normally, the Matching relation is used together with one of the General–Particular relations (see below). This is because it is usual when matching pieces of information first to provide a generalization which will make sense of the matching. In the case of letters, the reader's background knowledge may, however, supply the generalization, and, in the case of poetry, supplying it may be part of the process of interpretation.

Hoey (1983: chapter 7) discusses two types of **General–Particular** pattern, namely the **Generalization–Example** relation, and the **Preview–Detail** relation, both of which, in combination with the Matching relation, may organize whole texts, or long passages of them. He shows, for instance, how two Matching example sentences (1983: 113),

> (2) For example, a map will only contain those features which are of interest to the person using the map. (3) Similarly, architects' models will be limited to include only those features which are of interest to the person considering employing the architect

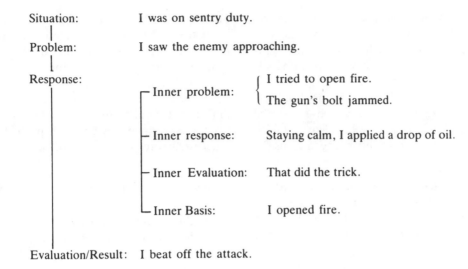

Situation: I was on sentry duty.

Problem: I saw the enemy approaching.

Response:
    Inner problem: { I tried to open fire.
                       The gun's bolt jammed.

    Inner response: Staying calm, I applied a drop of oil.

    Inner Evaluation: That did the trick.

    Inner Basis: I opened fire.

Evaluation/Result: I beat off the attack.

Figure 1

are prefaced with the generalization for which they serve as examples:

(1) It is interesting to note that iconic models only represent certain features of that portion of the real world which they simulate.

(The sentences are from Alan Jenkin, 'Simulation under focus', *Computer Management*, March 1971: 38.)

In the case of a **Preview–Detail** relation, the Detail member of the relation supplies information about the Preview member, or about a part of it, and the details may be Matched. The most typical Detail member is definition. In the following example, sentence (1) is the Preview, and sentences (2) and (3) Matched Details:

(1) The Danish word *hyggelig* is interesting, but difficult to master for foreign learners of the language. (2) On the one hand, it can be used of situations in which one is comfortable, in a warm, snug, feeling-at-home sort of way. (3) On the other hand, it can be used about a person who makes one feel comfortable and at home.

One can test for the Preview–Detail relation by seeing whether, if one asks after sentence (1), 'Can you give me more detail?', the following clauses do so.

The most typical discourse pattern is, however, the Problem–Solution pattern. Many texts can be treated as conforming to the pattern **Situation – Problem – Response – Evaluation/Result** with recursion on Response – that is, a Response may itself cause a new problem, requiring a new Response, etc. Hoey gives the example shown in Figure 1 (from Hoey 1983: 53). The pattern can be revealed by questioning. After each of the sentences in Figure 1, a reader might ask a question like: What happened then? What did you do then? Or the pattern may be revealed by paraphrase using lexical signals (1983: 53):

The *means* whereby I beat off the attack was by opening fire. The *cause* of my opening fire was that I saw the enemy approaching. The *circumstances* of my seeing the enemy approaching was that I was on sentry duty.

The lexical signals used in the paraphrase may be the terms used in the pattern itself

(1983: 53): 'My *situation* was that I was on sentry duty. I saw the enemy approaching. I *solved* this *problem* by opening fire. This *achieved* the *desired result* of beating off the attack.'

Hoey (1983: 57–8) draws up four sets of mapping conditions which show the relationship between the Problem–Solution *pattern* and the *relations* between clauses:

(1) We will assume two parts of a discourse, *a* and *b*, in a Cause–Consequence relation. *If (i) a* has been independently established as Problem *and (ii) b* contains the role of agent, then *b* is Response.

(2) We will assume three parts of a discourse, *a, b* and *c,* of which *a* and *b* are in an Instrument–Achievement or Instrument–Purpose relation (Purpose being more or less equivalent to hoped-for achievement), and of which *a* has not been independently established as a Problem.

Given these circumstances, if *(i) b* contains the role of agent *and (ii) c* prevents, reverses, avoids, avoids harm to, or seeks help in preventing, etc., some crucial aspect of *a,* then *a* is Problem and *b* is Response.

(3) We will assume two parts of a discourse, *a* and *b,* in a Cause–Consequence relation and that *a* has not been independently established as Problem.

If (i) b contains the role of agent *and (ii) b* also prevents, reverses, avoids or avoids harm to some crucial aspects of *a,* then *a* is Problem and *b* Response.

(4) We will assume the same as for mapping condition 3.

If (i) b contains the role of agent *and (ii)* b also can have attached to it a Purpose clause, *c,* which spells out a layman's understanding of what *b* means, and if *(iii)* the newly formed trio conforms to the conditions of mapping condition 2, then *a* is Problem and *b* Response.

Hoey's and Winter's approaches differ from that of de Beaugrande and Dressler (1981) and van Dijk and Kintsch (1978) in remaining fairly strictly on the surface of discourse (although making reference to such 'deep' roles as 'agent', as in the above), and in not emphasizing the psychological processes of understanding and perceiving macrostructure (Hoey 1983: 33):

Instead, the emphasis is laid on the ways in which the surface of the discourse (not necessarily to be contrasted with hidden depths) contains sufficient clues for the reader/listener to perceive accurately the discourse's organisation.

This has the advantage that the phenomena described are fairly directly observable, while the reference to concepts and relations of the textual world and to schemata remains of a hypothetical nature. However, the two approaches are best seen as complementary; surface-structure linguists have provided valuable detailed work on cohesion and coherence; nevertheless, it would be naive to think that readers' cognitive processes and knowledge of various aspects of the world are not important in text comprehension. It might even be arguable that the reason why the Problem–Solution pattern is so fruitful for text analysis is that it closely matches those cognitive writer and reader processes which de Beaugrande and Dressler (1981) refer to in discussing the remaining five conditions of textuality.

In Hoey (1991), the topic of textual patterns is pursued further with particular reference to the ways in which particular lexical patterns cluster to establish topic coherence.

Intentionality

Intentionality concerns the text producer's intention to produce a cohesive and coherent text that will attain whatever goal s/he has planned that it should attain. Text producers and receivers both rely on Grice's Co-operative Principle (see PRAGMATICS) in managing discourse, but in text linguistics the notion of conversational implicature is supplemented with the notion that language users *plan* towards a *goal* (de Beaugrande and Dressler 1981: 132–3):

> Successful communication clearly demands the ability to detect or infer other participants' goals on the basis of what they say. . . . By the same token, text producers must be able to anticipate the receiver's responses as supportive of or contrary to a plan, for example, by building an *internal model* of the receivers and their beliefs and knowledge.

Acceptability

Acceptability concerns the *receiver's* wish that the text should be cohesive and coherent and be of relevance to her/him (de Beaugrande and Dressler 1981: 7): 'This attitude is responsive to such factors as text type, social or cultural setting, and the desirability of goals.' The receiver will be *tolerant* of things, such as false starts, which interfere with coherence and cohesion and will use *inferencing*, based on her/his own general knowledge, to bring the textual world together.

Informativity

Informativity 'concerns the extent to which the occurrences of the presented text are expected vs unexpected or known vs unknown/certain' (de Beaugrande and Dressler 1981: 8–9). Hence it needs reference to the notion of **probability** (1981: 140) – the more probable in any particular context will be more expected than the less probable. When something very unexpected occurs (1981: 144),

> the text receiver must do a MOTIVA-TION SEARCH – a special case of

problem-solving – to find out what these occurrences signify, why they were selected, and how they can be integrated back into the CONTINUITY that is the basis of communication.

If no solution is forthcoming, the text will appear as nonsensical.

A receiver's expectations of what will appear in a text are powerfully affected by her/his perception of what text type s/he is currently encountering. What is unexpected in a technical report may be less unexpected in a poem, and it is interesting to observe how people faced with apparent nonsense will normally be able to give it a meaning if they are told that the text is a poem.

Most cognitive approaches to text analysis emphasize what readers bring to the text: the text is not a file full of meaning which the reader simply downloads. How sentences relate to one another and how the units of meaning combine to create a coherent extended text is the result of interaction between the reader's world and the text, with the reader making plausible interpretations.

Situationality

Situationality 'concerns the factors which make a text RELEVANT to a SITUATION of occurrence' (de Beaugrande and Dressler 1981: 9). Again, a text-receiver will typically try hard to solve any problem arising from the occurrence of apparently irrelevant items in text; that is, s/he will engage in Problem–Solution in order to make such items appear relevant.

Intertextuality

Intertextuality concerns the way in which the use of a certain text depends on knowledge of other texts. For instance, a traffic sign saying 'resume speed' only makes sense on the basis of a previous sign telling a driver to slow down. The interdependence of texts covered by the notion of inter-textuality is responsible for the evolution of *text types*, which are groups of texts displaying characteristic features and patterns. Parodies, critical reviews, reports and responses to the arguments of others are highly and obviously reliant on inter-textuality. In other cases, we are less aware of intertextuality. For instance, a novel we are reading may appear as an independent text; however, it relies on the tradition of novel-writing, and we bring our knowledge of what a novel is to the reading of it.

Regulative principles of textual communication

Efficiency

Efficiency depends on the text being used in communicating with minimum effort by the participants; that is, it 'contributes to *processing ease* . . . the running of operations with a light load on resources of attention and access' (de Beaugrande and Dressler 1981: 34).

Effectiveness

Effectiveness depends on the text leaving a strong impression and creating favourable conditions for attaining a goal. 'It elicits *processing depth*, that is, intense use of resources of attention and access on materials removed from the explicit surface representation' (de Beaugrande and Dressler 1981: 34).

Appropriateness

Appropriateness is the agreement between the setting of a text and the ways in which the standards of textuality are upheld. It determines 'the correlations between the current occasion and the standards of textuality such that reliable estimates can be made regarding ease or depth of participants' processing' (de Beaugrande and

Dressler 1981: 34). It mediates between efficiency and effectiveness which

> tend to work against each other. Plain language and trite content [efficiency] are very easy to produce and receive, but cause boredom and leave little impression behind. In contrast, creative language and bizarre content [effectiveness] can elicit a powerful effect, but may become unduly difficult to produce and receive.

Naturalness

In text linguistics, then, the links between clauses are observed across sentence boundaries, and these links can be seen to form larger patterns of text organization. In addition, however, reference to the text surrounding a given sentence may be seen to cast light on the **naturalness** of the sentence in question.

Naturalness is Sinclair's term for 'the concept of well-formedness of sentences *in text*' (1984: 203), and it is contrasted with what is normally thought of as sentence well-formedness, which is a property sentences may or may not have when seen in isolation. Sinclair argues that many well-formed sentences do not appear natural to a native speaker, and that, since these appear odd in spite of being well formed, they 'must violate some restrictions which are not among the criteria for well-formedness' (1984: 203), so that well-formedness and naturalness are independent variables.

Some of the determinants for the fulfilment of the criteria for naturalness are situated in the surrounding discourse, while those for well-formedness are all within the sentence itself. Thus *If you like* is not well formed by the traditional grammatical criteria, but is a natural response to a type of request. It contains what Sinclair calls a **rangefinder**, an indication that an item in the **co-text** (the rest of the text) or **context** (the situation in which the text is being used) will render it unproblematic, the item being (in this case) the request preceding it.

The degree to which a sentence depends for its naturalness on its co-text and/or context is called its **isolation** – one of three parameters in terms of which statements about sentence naturalness can be made. Isolation also depends on **allowables**, so called because they are features of the sentence which, although dependent on co-text or context for their specification, do not interfere with its well-formedness. Allowables include pronouns, as displayed in the sentence *I wouldn't have bought **it** if **he** hadn't been **there*** (1984: 204; allowables in bold; bold and italics added). The allowables in this sentence do not render it ill formed, but they do indicate its dependence on the surrounding discourse, since that is where we would expect to be able to discover their referents, i.e., what *it, he* and *there* refer to.

In contrast, *Prince Charles is now a husband* is well formed by traditional grammatical criteria, but is not a natural sentence, chiefly because 'there is a conflict between the mutual expectations of the equative structure, the indefinite article, and the word *husband*. Words denoting occupations (e.g. *sailor*) would not cause this conflict.' The sentence violates the second parameter in terms of which naturalness statements are made – namely, **idiomaticity**.

Had the item *husband* been preceded by the item *good*, however, the sentence would have been far more natural than it is. An item which has this effect on naturalness is called a **supporter**. The notion of support rests on the notion of collocation, the tendency which linguistic items have to occur with certain other items. When expectations about collocation are fulfilled in a sentence, it will display **neutrality**, a further parameter for statements about naturalness. Supporters also affect idiomaticity, so that in the sentence *I'm trying to rack my brains* (Sinclair 1984: 203ff.) the very low expectation of collocation between *trying* and *rack my brains* contributes considerably to its low status on the scale of idiomaticity and to its consequent non-naturalness.

Sinclair hopes that an extended study of text will establish the precise conditions for sentence naturalness (1984: 210):

> The study of allowables will lead to the specification of an abstract text framework for any sentence. The study of rangefinders will
>
> a. show how each sentence is integrated into its text
> b. establish the range of individual features.
>
> The study of supporters will tell us a lot about the resolution of textual ambiguity, and will lead to a precise specification of
>
> a. complex items, e.g. phrases
> b. permitted range of variation.
>
> The three scales of neutrality, isolation and idiomaticity will allow sentences to be compared with each other and might lead to a modern rhetoric at the rank of sentence.

It thus appears that, while a grammatical approach was found to be unhelpful to text linguistics, further study in the field of naturalness may be able to provide illumination not just of the nature of text, but also of the traditional domain of grammar, the sentence. For further discussion, see Sinclair (1991).

R.A.C. and K.M.

Suggestions for further reading

Beaugrande, R. de and Dressler, W.V. (1981) *Introduction to Text Linguistics*, London and New York: Longman.

Halliday, M.A.K. and Hasan, R. (1976/ 1989) *Language, Context and Text*, Oxford: Oxford University Press.

Hoey, M. (1983) *On the Surface of Discourse,* London: George Allen and Unwin.

—— (1991) *Patterns of Lexis in Text,* Oxford: Oxford University Press.

Tone languages

All the languages in the world use consonants and vowels to build morphemes, which in turn join together to form words. Thus the English word *me* is made up of a nasal consonant followed by a high vowel. If we change the consonant to a /b/ we would get a different word, *be*, and if we change the vowel to a low vowel, we would also get a different word, *ma*.

We may pronounce the word *ma* with various pitch patterns, depending on the occasion. We may pronounce it with a high pitch if we are emphatic; we may say it with a rising pitch in a question, etc. But these different pitch patterns do not alter the word in the way that changing a consonant or changing a vowel does. These different pitch patterns that do not change, but merely add to the basic meaning of words, are called **intonations** (see INTONATION).

Yet there are some languages in the world that use pitch patterns to build morphemes in the same way consonants and vowels are used. The best-known such language is Chinese, as illustrated in Figure 1 (Wang 1973). As the figure shows, the syllable *ma*, when pronounced with a falling pitch pattern, means 'to scold' in the **Putonghua** dialect of Chinese. (*Putonghua*, which literally means 'common speech', is the speech form sponsored by the People's Republic of China. It is a variety of Mandarin.) When pronounced with a rising pattern, the meaning is 'hemp'; when pronounced with a high level pattern, the meaning is 'mother', as in some dialects of English; and lastly, when pronounced with a low dipping pattern, the meaning is 'horse'.

When pitch patterns are used in this lexical capacity, i.e. to build words and morphemes much as consonants and vowels do,

they are called **tones**. And languages that use tones in this way are called **tone languages**. Putonghua, then, is a tone language. It has four tones, as illustrated in Figure 1.

Tones are different from consonants and vowels in a fundamental way. Whereas the latter are formed primarily in the mouth, by movement of the tongue, the velum, the jaw, etc., tones are formed primarily at the larynx – a box of cartilages situated at the top of the windpipe –which contains the vocal folds. One cycle of vibration of the vocal folds is the phonetic basis of sound in speech (see also ARTICULATORY PHONETICS).

During speech, the folds vibrate very rapidly – so rapidly, in fact, that when we look at them with the aid of a dentist's mirror, all we can see is a blur at the edges. The typical rate of vibration of the vocal folds, the fundamental frequency, abbreviated **F0**, is around 100 cycles per second (**cps**) for men and around 180 cps for women and children.

Variation in F0 is controlled by pulling the vocal folds toward the rear with different degrees of tension. As the folds are pulled more taut, somewhat in the manner of stretching a rubber band, they become thinner and vibrate at a higher frequency. The higher the frequency, the higher we perceive its pitch to be. So **frequency** is a physical concept, while **pitch** is a psychological one, i.e. the ear's response to frequency. The two scales are not identical, but they are sufficiently similar for our purposes here, so that we may interchange them for convenience.

We automatically normalize pitch for each speaker according to the pitch range we expect. When a man says *Hello*, his average F0 may be around 100 cps. When a woman says *Hello*, her average F0 may

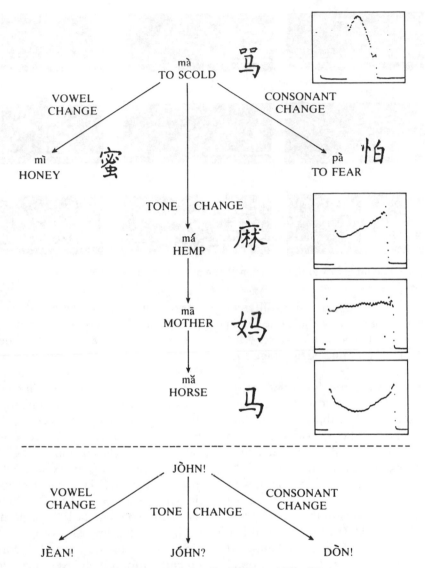

Figure 1 The four tones of Putonghua Chinese (from Wang 1982: 58)
TONES are used to alter the meaning of Chinese words. Standard Chinese has only four tones: falling (as in *mà*), rising (as in *má*), level (*mā*), and dipping, or falling and then rising, (*mǎ*). The **oscillograph** traces at the right show the fundamental frequency of the author's voice as he spoke the words. In English, on the other hand, variation in tone is used to convey different moods; the meaning of the words being spoken does not change. In Chinese, changing tone has the same kind of effect on the meaning of a word as changing a vowel or a consonant.

be around 180 cps. Yet we understand them to be saying the same linguistic thing, in spite of the great difference in the physical signal. We are able to do this by evaluating the average F0 of the utterance relative to the F0 of the speaker.

Similarly, in a tone language the F0 of a tone is evaluated relative to the F0 average and the F0 range of the speaker, as well as relative to the other tones in the system. This relative mode of perceiving F0 allows us constantly to adjust the

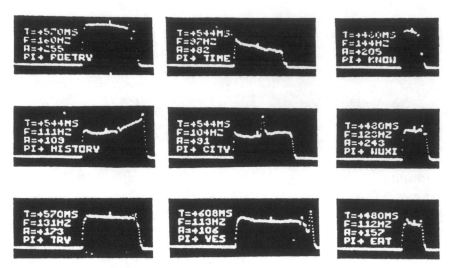

Figure 2 The nine tones of Cantonese (from Wang and Cheng 1987: 515)

baseline and range. As a result, different F0s may be linguistically the same, as in the *Hello* example above. Conversely, the same F0 may be evaluated as linguistically different.

A system of notation for tones, called **tone letters**, was proposed in 1930, which is widely used for describing the tone languages of East and Southeast Asia (Chao 1930). In this notation, a vertical line is used to represent the pitch range of the tones. The top of the line corresponds to the highest pitch, or value 5. The bottom of the line corresponds to the lowest pitch, or value 1. The middle of the vertical line corresponds to a mid pitch. A high-level tone would be represented by a horizontal line drawn from the left to the top of the vertical line. Such a tone may be described numerically as '5–5', or simply '55'.

We may now refer back to the four tones of Putonghua, as shown in Figure 1. There we see the F0 of these four syllables, as spoken by the present author and analysed by computer. The top tone, for the meaning 'to scold', may be described as '51', since the F0 starts high and falls low. (The small rise at the beginning may be explained as an effect of the consonant and is irrelevant to the basic pattern of the tone.) The next

one down may be described as '35', a rising tone. The next one down, meaning 'mother', is level enough to be described as '55'. And, lastly, the bottom one may be described as a dipping tone, '424'.

There are many different linguistic systems which use more than four tones. The dialect of Chinese spoken in Guangzhou and Hong Kong, popularly called **Cantonese**, has nine tones (Wang and Cheng 1987). In Figure 2 we see again the computer tracings of the F0 of the speaker's voice. For the six long tones in the left columns and the middle column, the syllable pronounced is /si/, as in the English word *see*.

So we see in the upper left corner the F0 pattern for a high-level tone, shown on the computer screen as 160 cps. (The 'HZ' in the figure is the abbreviation for 'hertz', which is equivalent to cps.) The meaning is 'poetry'. Compare this with the mid-level tone in the lower left corner, at 131 cps, where the meaning is 'to try'. The other four long tones in these two columns have the meanings 'history', 'time', 'city' and 'yes'.

In Cantonese, the short tones occur only on syllables that end in plosive consonants, i.e. /p/, /t/ or /k/. These tones are short because they are stopped by these con-

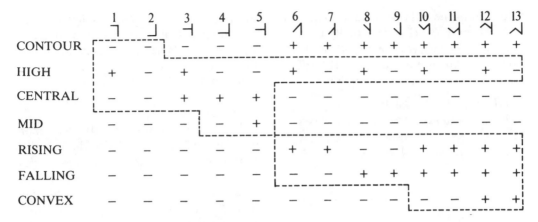

	1 ⌐	2 ⌐	3 ⌐	4 ⌐	5 ⌐	6 ⌐	7 ⌐	8 ⌐	9 ⌐	10 ⌐	11 ⌐	12 ⌐	13 ⌐
CONTOUR	–	–	–	–	–	+	+	+	+	+	+	+	+
HIGH	+	–	+	–	–	+	–	+	–	+	–	+	–
CENTRAL	–	–	+	+	+	–	–	–	–	–	–	–	–
MID	–	–	–	–	+	–	–	–	–	–	–	–	–
RISING	–	–	–	–	–	+	+	–	–	+	+	+	+
FALLING	–	–	–	–	–	–	–	+	+	+	+	+	+
CONVEX	–	–	–	–	–	–	–	–	–	–	–	+	+

Figure 3 Phonological features of tone (from Wang 1967: 103)

sonants; notice that they are less than half the duration when compared with the long tones. Strictly speaking, then, the short tones are never in minimal contrast with the long tones, because the long tones never occur on syllables that end in stop consonants. The syllable illustrated in the column to the right in Figure 2 is /sik/. Pronounced with a high tone it means 'to know', and with a low tone it means 'to eat'. Pronounced with a mid tone it occurs in the name of a Chinese city, Wuxi.

The question naturally arises as to the maximum number of tones a language can have. Is there an upper limit? A theory of tones has been proposed to answer this question (Wang 1967). This is shown in Figure 3. The theory states that the maximum number is thirteen, as shown by the tone letters in the figure. Furthermore, the theory states a maximum for each of the five categories of tones. The maximum for level tones is five. And the maximum is two for each of the other four categories: rising, falling, concave, and convex.

It is interesting to note that for the Putonghua system discussed earlier there is one level tone (55), one rising tone (35), one falling tone (51) and one concave tone (424). This is a rather typical distribution. It is as though the language selects from as many categories as possible, rather than

fills up its inventory with just one or two categories. In this respect, tones behave much like consonants and vowels in their selection process (Lindblom 1989).

Consonants, too, tend to be selected a few from many categories, rather than many from a few categories. Notice that in English, plosives, affricates, fricatives, nasals and liquids are all represented, but only a few from any one category. We can make the same observation about vowel systems. This similarity in the selection process suggests that tones too may be factored into a smaller set of phonological features, as has been done for consonants and vowels. This is the plan shown in Figure 3. The maximum set of thirteen tones can be analysed into seven binary features.

The Cantonese system illustrated in Figure 2 is an unusually complex one in terms of its tone inventory. There are tone languages all over the world, and most of them have a simpler inventory of tones. In part, this is due to the fact that the majority of morphemes in these languages are polysyllabic, as opposed to Chinese, where most morphemes are monosyllabic. A language with two tones can have eight distinct tone sequences over three syllables, i.e. 2 × 2 × 2.

Below is a set of examples from **Kikuyu**, a Bantu language spoken in Kenya, where seven out of the eight possible sequences of high (H) and low (L) are actually used to build morphemes (McCawley 1978: 127). The only sequence not used is HLL. (The phonetic notation has been simplified here.)

HHH	*hengere*	'slab'
HHL	*ngauro*	'person with shaved head'
HLH	*tingori*	'large boy not circumcised with his age-mates'
LHH	*remere*	'way of cultivating'
LHL	*bariti*	'anger'
LLH	*boboto*	'downpour'
LLL	*beredi*	'leaf-shaped spear'

Tones as a linguistic topic were discussed in China as early as 1500 years ago, by the scholar Shen Yue (441–513). It is now well known that most of the languages of China and Southeast Asia are tone languages, perhaps due to extensive mutual influence through the millennia. In Western scholarship, an early study of this topic is by Beach (1924), on the Bantu languages of East Africa. Kikuyu, exemplified above, is one such language. Another Bantu language whose tone system has been studied extensively recently is **Makua**, spoken in southern Tanzania and in Mozambique (Cheng and Kisseberth 1979–81). Numerous languages of West Africa are tone languages as well. Furthermore, these languages offer much important data for linguistic theory, as discussed by Hyman and Schuh (1974).

Among the languages of native America, many are tonal. A classic work on the study of tone languages is that by Pike (1948), which gives in-depth analyses of two Amerindian languages of Mexico, **Mazatec** and **Mixtec**. The presence of a step-up tone is an especially intriguing phenomenon of the tone system of one of the Mixtec dialects, that of the town of Acatlan in central Mexico. (This phenomenon was discovered after the publication of Pike's book.)

The effect of the step-up is to raise the pitch of the syllable one step higher than the pitch of the preceding syllable, if the preceding syllable carries a high tone or a step-up tone. When a sequence of step-up tones occurs one after another in a sentence, it sounds a bit as if the person is singing a musical scale rather than speaking (Wang 1972).

This phenomenon is all the more intriguing when we consider the so-called **terrace-level** tone languages of West Africa. In these languages, there is a **step-down tone**, which has the opposite effect of the step-up in Mixtec. Due to a complex interaction between these tones and the intonation of the sentence, the auditory effect is like going down a terrace, one step at a time.

Tone languages occur widely in Africa, Asia and among the American Indians. They occur also in Europe. Among Germanic languages, Norwegian and Swedish are tonal, in that a word can be classified according to two 'accents' differing primarily in their F0 pattern (Garding 1973). Among Slavic languages, Serbo-Croatian and Slovenian are similar in this respect. Similar observations have also been made for **Lithuanian**, a Baltic language.

There is in fact a wide spectrum of criteria for what constitutes a tone language. The criteria may rest with the tone features used in the system (e.g. does it have contour tones?), with the lexical versus morphological function of the tones, and with the degree to which the various tones may be predicted on the basis of grammatical information. Some efforts have been made to construct a typology of tone languages, e.g. Wang (1972) and McCawley (1978). However, no comprehensive framework which has gained general usage has yet been worked out.

Earlier in this entry, I indicated that, unlike consonants and vowels, tones are produced primarily at the larynx. However, the activities of the articulators above the larynx frequently have a significant influence on the F0. This influence may be manifested physiologically and acoustically.

Physiologically, different consonants and vowels are produced with different degrees of pull on laryngeal structures. This means that, everything else being equal, consonants and vowels may have distinct F0 patterns associated with them.

Acoustically, different sounds produce different degrees of opening within the mouth, which in turn influences the pattern of airflow through the larynx. Thus, a consonant may be voiced, aspirated or glottalized; this has a clear effect on the F0 of the following vowel. Such effects have been extensively documented in the phonetic literature, sometimes under the term **intrinsic variation**, to suggest that the variation in F0 is due to the mode of production of the sound itself (Mohr 1971). As a result of these physiological and acoustic factors, certain tones are favoured over others. For example, Cheng (1973), in a quantitative study of over 700 tone systems, found that high tones are used more often than low tones, and falling tones more often than rising tones.

How does a language acquire a tone system? The answer to this question may be sought in these intrinsic variations. Take, for example, the English words *bin* and *pin*. As suggested in the spelling, we consider the main distinction between them to be due to the initial consonant, i.e. /b/ versus /p/. But a careful analysis will show that the F0s of the two words are also quite different. The F0 of *bin* starts much lower and has a lower average value as well. Suppose that, at some future point in time, the distinction between /b/ and /p/ is lost; that is, suppose that /b/ changes into /p/, a rather common sound change in the languages of the world. At that point, English will become a tone language, since the two words will then be distinguished exclusively by the two F0 patterns (i.e. the two tones).

Such a scenario is very plausible. In fact, many scholars feel that this is how Chinese became a tone language several thousand years ago. Presumably, this came about precisely through the loss of consonantal distinctions. It is a two-step process: first the consonants cause the F0 to vary, then the distinction shifts over to the F0 when the consonants merge or become lost (Wang and Cheng 1987).

A tone language may also lose its tone system. This is probably the case with Swahili, a widely used language of the Bantu family. Almost all of the Bantu languages have tones, such as the Kikuyu example discussed earlier. However, because Swahili was used for a long time as a trade language in East Africa, it imported a large number of non-Bantu words, especially from Arabic languages. This importation was presumably implemented through the medium of many bilingual speakers of Arabic and Swahili. These speakers probably stopped using tonal distinctions on more and more Swahili words as they switched back and forth between the two languages, since Arabic is not a tone language. Through the decades, the tone system in Swahili was eroded, until it became lost completely.

In conclusion, a few general remarks on the nature of tone languages. Because such systems are so dependent on F0, the questions naturally arise as to what happens to intelligibility when F0 is absent (as during whispering) and when the speaker has to follow a melody line (as in singing). The answer is that intelligibility is largely preserved in both cases. Briefly put, this is because there are a number of secondary cues in the signal which accompany these tones, such as duration, loudness, contour, vowel quality, etc. These cues take on increased perceptual importance when F0 is not fully available.

Finally, the question of the relation between linguistic tones and music is often raised. It appears that speakers of tone languages have no special advantage in learning music. In fact, they may be quite tone deaf musically, and yet use tones with normal facility. At the same time, neither is there any evidence that people who are exceptionally gifted in music have any special advantage in learning tone languages.

These observations are not surprising when we note that the resemblance between music and linguistic tone is really quite a superficial one – they share only some of the raw materials each is made of. Tones can be decomposed into phonological features, as we have seen in Figure 3. In addition, tones are perceived in terms of linguistic categories (Wang 1976), as is the case with consonants and vowels. Furthermore, tones appear to be processed more in the left hemisphere, together with consonants and vowels, rather than in the right hemisphere, with music (Van Lancker and Fromkin 1973).

The evidence is quite strong, therefore, considered both from the viewpoint of internal phonological organization and from laboratory experimentation, that tones behave much like consonants and vowels in their contribution to building words. Through the chance of historical development, we find today that some languages make use of tones while other languages do not. But the pattern is a changing one, since historical development makes it possible for a tone language to lose its tones, and for a non-tone language to become one.

W.S.-Y.W.

Suggestions for further reading

Fromkin, V.A. (ed.) (1978) *Tone: A Linguistic Survey*, New York: Academic Press.

Pike, K.L. (1948) *Tone Languages*, Ann Arbor: University of Michigan Press.

Wang, W.S.-Y. (1973) 'The Chinese language', *Scientific American* 50 (March); reprinted in W.S.-Y. Wang (ed.) (1982) *Human Communication*, New York: W.H. Freeman.

Writing systems

A **writing system** (script, orthography) may be defined as a given set of written marks together with a particular set of conventions for their use (Sampson 1985: 19). The units of a writing system are known as **graphs**, and in citation (mention) of one or more graphs, angle brackets, < >, are standardly used.

While speech may not be a logically necessary prerequisite for writing, it is a historical fact that any culture which has writing has speech, and that it had speech before it had a writing system. Therefore it is common to see a writing system as a means of representing the spoken language; but this does not mean that a writing system needs to be representative of the **sounds** of a language. Those, such as alphabetic systems, which are designed with sound representation in view are known as **phonographic** systems, and they are of three types: **syllabic**, **segmental** and **featural** (see below). Systems, such as Chinese (see below), which are not based on sound representation but rather on representation of the meaningful units of the language words or morphemes – are known as **logographic** writing systems.

Early writing systems tend to be logographic, possibly because, as Sampson (1985: 36) suggests, the obvious thing to do if one wants to represent meaning in writing is to make a picture of the meaning unit one wants to represent. The terms **pictographic** and **ideographic** are frequently used to describe writing systems displaying varying degrees of **iconicity** (similarity to the entity referred to), but Sampson lists two good reasons for discarding these as technical terms for talking about writing systems: their history of use is such as to make it unclear exactly what is meant by them; and they tend to make it difficult to distinguish writing systems from **semasiographic** systems like road signs, which, although they clearly signify and are systems of visible communication, are not **glottographic**, i.e. visible representations of utterances. As Sampson (1985: 30) puts it, 'messages in the semasiographic system could be *translated* more or less faithfully into the spoken language, but it would make no sense to talk of *reading* them aloud word by word'. Semasiographic systems are forerunners of true writing, and are, according to Gelb (1963: 29), best represented among the American Indians (see 1963: 29–32 for examples).

The oldest known writing system is that of the Sumer culture, which existed from approximately 4500 to 1750 BC in lower Mesopotamia, now southern Iraq. The earliest Sumerian writing is believed to date from 3000 or 4000 BC, and consists of marks drawn on to clay tablets with a pointed reed stylus. Some of its graphs are:

< 📖 > meaning 'head',

< 〰 > meaning 'water', and

< 📖 // > meaning 'drink'.

The subject of these tablets appears to be administrative matters like tax payments and distribution of rations, and the inscriptions were brief and context-bound, like entries in a notebook. At this stage, many words of the language had no written form, and some graphs stood for two or more words. Early in the history of this writing system, the graphs were turned ninety degrees anticlockwise, thus:

< 🖐 >, < ‖ >, < 🔨 >.

Drawing on to clay, however, tends to cause clotting of the lines by small balls of clay accumulating in front of the stylus; and by around 2500 BC the pointed stylus had been replaced with a blunt one with which wedge-shaped impressions were made on the clay. Most rounded lines were thus replaced with straight lines, although some graphs still required the stylus to be dragged through the clay:

< ▣ >, < ‖ >, < ▣ >.

This script is known as **Cuneiform**, from the Latin term for 'wedge-shaped'. It was now being used for writing down myths and other types of literature, and legal judgements; it was linear, and 'capable of recording all lexical and grammatical elements of the spoken Sumerian language' (Sampson 1985: 50). By 1800 BC, there were no rounded lines left at all, and the direction of the wedges had been standardized for ease of writing:

< ▣ >, < ▣ >, < ▣ >.

The Sumerian writing system presents an interesting case of how an initially wholly logographic system may become increasingly phonographic. For example, the Sumerian word for *water* was pro-

nounced /a/; it so happened that the pronunciation of the word for *in* was the same, so the graph for *water* was used to stand for this word too, thus solving the problem of how *in*-ness might be depicted. Gradually, all grammatical morphemes and affixes came to be represented by graphs chosen chiefly on phonological grounds, and this **phonographic principle** was also employed to deal with proper names. Nevertheless, the Sumerian script remains primarily logographic, since signs were only used phonographically in cases where a logograph could not be readily created.

A writing system is not normally associated with any one language, and the Cuneiform script was adopted by the Akkadians around 2500 BC. The Akkadians were neighbours of the Sumerians, but they spoke an unrelated Semitic language. Whereas in Sumerian most root forms of words were monosyllabic so that individual graphs could easily be used to stand for syllables, Akkadian was inflecting, which meant that 'the chain of spoken sounds could not be neatly divided up into morphemic meaning-units (compare the way that English *men* collapses the idea of "man" and "plurality" into a single sound-shape)' (Sampson 1985: 56). The Akkadians were therefore forced to develop the phonographic aspects of Cuneiform. Most of the Cuneiform writing available is, in fact, Akkadian, because the Akkadians, later known as Babylonians and Assyrians, gradually became the dominant cultural group in Mesopotamia, 'eventually extinguishing Sumer as a political entity and Sumerian as a language' (Sampson 1985: 56).

It is thought that the invention of Egyptian Hieroglyphic soon after the Sumerian writing system was influenced by the latter. It developed in a similar way to the Akkadian version of Cuneiform, though the shape of the graphs was different. The Egyptian Hieroglyphic script was mainly phonographic, although it is often mistakenly thought of as logographic (or even semasiographic) because of its obvious iconicity, retained throughout the history of Egyptian civilization. It existed side by side with two non-iconic versions, Hieratic and Demotic, which were used for informal purposes. The Egyptian Hieroglyphic writing system largely followed what is known as the **acrophonic** principle, in that many Hieroglyphic graphs were iconic with some entity whose name began with the sound for which the graph stood. 'Thus the Hieroglyphic sign ᴧᴧᴧᴧᴧ, representing the rippled appearance of water, stood for /n/, the first sound of the Egyptian word for "water"' (Sampson 1985: 78). However, there were also many Hieroglyphic graphs which stood for groups of sounds, rather than for single consonants.

It is believed that the inventors of the Semitic alphabet, from which all segmental writing systems probably descend, took the very idea of writing and the agrophonic principle from the Egyptians. However, the Semitic alphabet, created sometime in the second millennium BC 'somewhere in the Palestine/Syria region' (Sampson 1985: 78), probably by the Phoenicians, 'was clearly an independent creation: many of the graph-shapes are not similar to any Hieroglyphic graphs, and (more important) the relationships between objects pictured and graph-value hold for Semitic languages but not for Egyptian' (1985: 78). Thus the Semitic letter < > /m/ looks as if it is adapted from the Hieroglyphic graph for /n/ referred to above. However, it is 'used by the Semites for /m/ because their own word for "water" [majim] began with that sound' (1985: 78).

The original Semitic alphabet had no graphs for vowel sounds and is therefore often called **consonantal**, as are those of its descendent Systems which still do not have letters for vowels, such as the modern Hebrew writing system and the modern Arabic writing system. However, it is wrong to think of consonantal writing systems and alphabetic writing systems as belonging to different categories. A consonantal system is alphabetic even though it does not have vowel letters. I therefore follow Sampson (1985: 77ff.) in referring to both the original alphabet and to those of its modern descendants which have no vowel letters as Semitic *writing Systems*. But please bear in mind that not all Semitic *languages* (see HISTORICAL LINGUISTICS) are written in the Semitic writing system (Maltese is not), and that not every language written in a Semitic script is a Semitic language (Persian is an Indo-European language, but it is written in Arabic script).

The term **alphabet** derives from the names of the first two graphs of the Greek adaptation of the Semitic alphabet, alpha and beta. The first two Semitic graphs < ⋏ > and < ꝫ > are called ʔālep and bēt and there are clear similarities between the ordering of the Semitic, Greek and Roman alphabets; it is not known why this ordering was chosen. The reason why Semitic does not contain vowel letters is simply that they are unnecessary, since vowels play a very limited role as distinctive elements in the lexis of Semitic languages (Sampson 1985: 85):

> A high proportion of the vocabulary of a Semitic language . . . consists of words derived from a root (having a verbal or adjectival meaning) which is made up purely of consonants (usually three consonants), between which different patterns of vowels, representing different grammatical inflexions, are interdigitated.

Nevertheless, it is possible to indicate vowel value in two ways: some consonant letters can be used also to indicate vowels, and these are referred to as *matres lectionis*, 'mothers of reading'; and tiny dots and dashes above, below or within the consonant letters can be used to indicate pronunciation very precisely. This is known as **pointing**, and is used in modern Israel, for instance, to assist learner readers. The Arabic version of Semitic script, which, unlike modern Hebrew, has a **cursive** form, i.e. the letter shapes have been adapted so that whole words can be written without taking the pen from the paper, can be written down almost as quickly as shorthand because of the absence of letters for vowels. Semitic scripts are written from right to left.

The Arabic and modern Hebrew alphabets descend from one of two traditions of forming Semitic letter shapes, namely the eastern or Aramaic tradition. The other is known as the western or Canaanite tradition, and this was used by the Phoenicians. It is almost certain that it was this version of the Semitic alphabet which gave rise to the Greek, since the Phoenicians were the only Semitic people who traded and hence travelled overseas, and since the Greeks (who had colonies in ancient Phoenicia) called their alphabet Phoenician letters.

The Greeks used six of the Semitic letters, <ʔh wħ jʕ>, to stand for vowels. It was important for the Greeks to be able to indicate vowels, because Greek is a European language and so vowels are used to indicate lexical contrasts. In addition, some Greek words begin with vowels and some contain sequences of two or more vowels. Of the five Semitic letters mentioned above, only one, <w>, had a value, /w/, which also existed as a phoneme in Greek. From <w>, the two Greek letters <FY> were developed to stand for /w/ and /u/ respectively. Of these, /w/ was lost in later spoken Greek so that the letter /F/ became obsolete. The Greeks used <ʔ> for /a/, <h> for /e/, <ħ> for /h/, <j> for /i/ and <ʕ> for /o/ (Sampson 1985: 100–101).

The Greeks very soon stopped writing every line from right to left; instead, they would use **boustrophedon** (ox-turning) style, writing the first line from right to left, the second from left to right, and so on, as if ploughing a field. The direction of the letters varied with the direction of the writing, so that when a convention of writing only from left to right was finally adopted, the

shapes of the Greek letters became mirror images of their original Semitic counterparts (allowing for other shape-changing developments, of course). Thus Semitic <ꓱ>, <ꓶ>, <ꓱ> became Greek <B>, <Γ>, <E> (Sampson 1985: 103).

The Etruscans, who lived in Etruria, north of Rome, borrowed the Greek alphabet, and the Romans acquired it from them in about 650 BC. It is from the Roman adaptation of the Greek alphabet that the various modern European writing styles and typefaces descend. It is also believed that the runic **futharks**, named, like the alphabet, on the basis of the sounds represented by its initial graphs (f u th a r k), descended from the Roman alphabet, because they resemble several alphabetic inscriptions, dated from between the fourth and first centuries BC, found in the North Italic Alps. However, some runic figures which predate the Alpine inscription have also been found carved into stones and rocks, so it is possible that an earlier runic script blended with the Alpine. In any case, it is certain that the Roman alphabet influenced some of the graphs of the standard Scandinavian dotted (pointed) runic futhark (see Page 1987: 8–22).

As in the case of the Hebrew version of Semitic, each graph of the Roman alphabet was written separately, but all were simplified in various ways and could be written with a single pen-stroke. When the Roman Empire dissolved, different 'national hands' (Sampson 1985: 111) developed in various parts of Europe. By the fifteenth century, there were two main rival styles, the 'Humanist' script used primarily in northern Italy in an attempt at reconstructing classical Roman handwriting, and the 'Gothic' or 'black-letter' script of France and Germany. Early printers emulated the handwritten scripts of the day, which thereby obtained a degree of permanence, although Gothic script was largely eliminated in Britain in the seventeenth century and in Germany in 1941.

Modern Hebrew, Arabic, Roman and the Russian Cyrillic alphabets are all representatives of the Semitic alphabet, 'one of the two great systems of writing which between them provide the media of most of the world's written language', and which also exemplify 'the two main typological categories of script' (Sampson 1985: 145), phonographic and logographic.

The other of the two is the Chinese logographic writing system, in which a graph does not stand for a unit of pronunciation, but for a morpheme, a minimal meaningful unit of the Chinese language. For this reason, and because written Chinese is not simply the written version of a particular dialect of Chinese, any Chinese speaker, of whichever version of Chinese (and some of these differ to such a degree that they are not mutually intelligible), is able to use virtually the same written form of the language. So two Chinese speakers who are unable to communicate with each other through speech will, nevertheless, be able to understand each other almost perfectly in writing.

There are several reasons why it is possible for the Chinese writing system to operate in this manner. First, Chinese morphemes always correspond to syllables, and the syllables are clearly demarcated from each other in speech. Second, Chinese is an isolating language; that is, 'its grammar works exclusively by stringing separate words together' (Sampson 1985: 147). If English had this characteristic, we would have to say something like *I go already* instead of *I went*, and we would not have to observe rules of agreement such as the one which demands that *go* + third person singular becomes *goes*. Finally, there is no clear distinction between compounds and collocates (see MORPHOLOGY; LEXIS AND LEXICOLOGY). For all these reasons, each Chinese word tends to correspond straightforwardly to what we would call a morpheme, and a graph of the writing system can straightforwardly represent such a meaning unit.

Since this is the case, and since Chinese, as any other language, contains thousands of meaning units, its writing system contains thousands of graphs. Of these, about 1000 are so-called 'simple' graphs of relatively easily depicted objects and concepts; for instance,

< 日 > 'sun'

(derived from < 🜊 >) and

< 東 > 'east' ('sun behind tree')

(derived from < 🜨 >).

In addition, Chinese contains complex graphs in the case of which a simple, iconic graph has been adapted to stand for a word whose pronunciation resembled it in the Old Chinese language of around 2000 to 1000 BC, when the script was developing. To distinguish among graphs which would thus otherwise be ambiguous, a further element is added, called a **signific**. This shows the semantic category of the word, while the element which has been adapted to stand for an item for reasons of pronunciation similarities is called the **phonetic**.

Since Chinese pronunciation has changed and diversified greatly since the writing system was stabilized, the relationship between morphemes and graphs is by no means transparent, and 'from the point of view of a modern speaker, the most important benefit of the phonetic/signific structure is that graphs involving many brushstrokes can be seen as groupings of familiar visual units, rather than having to be remembered stroke by stroke (Sampson 1985: 157). The graphs are composed of a number of distinct elements in various configurations, and there is no evidence whatever to support claims that Chinese is more difficult to learn to read and write than any other system (see Sampson 1985: 160–5). Each graph occupies an imaginary square, and graphs were traditionally written downwards in columns, beginning at the right. In the People's Republic of China, writing now begins at the left and it is common to write horizontally. Typing and word processing are relatively slow processes using the Chinese system – since there are too many graphs to be contained on a keyboard, typewriters have a single arm which picks up separate pieces of type, while word-processor keyboards invite users to select properties of the graph they want; several graphs with the selected properties will then appear on the screen, and the user can choose the relevant one.

The Japanese became familiar with the Chinese civilization in the first millennium AD, at which point they had no writing system of their own, and the modern Japanese writing system, which began to be developed in the seventh century AD, is wholly, though by no means straightforwardly, derived from Chinese. Some Chinese graphs are used in Japanese to stand for words whose meanings are the same, or nearly the same, as their Chinese counterparts. These graphs are said to have *kun* (instruction) reading. However, Japanese in not an isolating language, but is heavily derivational and inflectional, so that individual morphemes cannot be simply represented by individual graphs. To deal with this problem, graphs with *kun* readings were interspersed, in early Japanese writing, with graphs whose Chinese pronunciation resembled the Japanese pronunciation of the relevant grammatical item. This method of writing is known as *man'yogana*. Nor do Japanese words normally consist of one syllable only; however, the syllable structure is very simple, having either a single vowel or a single consonant followed by a single vowel. Therefore, a single Japanese word in this period, about 1000 years ago, would be represented by at least one, but mostly by more than one, Chinese graph, and a reader would simply have to work out from the context which graphs were supposed to have *kun* reading, and which to have *man'yogana* reading. To complicate matters further,

Japanese also borrowed many Chinese words, and these would continue to be written with their Chinese graphs. Such graphs are said to have *on* readings.

Gradually, the *man'yogana* system developed in two ways. First, the graphs used for *man'yogana* were standardized so that the same graph or a small set of graphs was always used for a particular Japanese syllable. Second, the forms of the graphs were simplified so that they could be written faster, and so that it became possible to tell at a glance whether a given graph was in fact *man'yogana*, or *kun* or *on*. Ultimately, two syllabaries evolved, of which one, **hirigana** (plain *kana* 'script'), consists of simplified cursive outlines of complete Chinese graphs, while the other, **katakana** (partial *kana*) consists of small distinctive elements of the original Chinese graph. Chinese graphs in their full form are called **kanji**. In modern Japanese, *kanji* are used for lexical morphemes, *hirigana* for grammatical morphemes and inflections, and *katakana* for foreign names. The Japanese writing system is **mixed**; it is partly logographic, partly phonographic (Sampson 1985: chapter 9).

In order to provide examples of a purely syllabic writing system and a featural writing system, it is necessary to look at systems which have no connection with either Semitic or Chinese. A good example of a purely **syllabic** writing system is the system known as **Linear B**, adapted in about the sixteenth century BC by the Mycenaean civilization to write an early form of Greek, from **Linear A**, which was used to write the unknown language of the Minoan civilization of the second millennium BC. The Mycenaean civil service used Linear B for record-keeping purposes until about 1250 BC, when the Minoan cities were destroyed, but a distant relative of Linear B was used to write Greek in Cyprus in the Classical period. Linear B consists of at least eighty-nine graphs, of which seventy-three have known values, and it is genuinely syllabic, in so far as each separate written mark stands arbitrarily for a distinct syllable, thus

<Ꞃ> /ta/, < ≢ > /te/, <∧> /ti/,

<ꓕ> /to/, <ꝏ> /tu/

(Sampson 1985: 65). This script was lost after the collapse of Mycenean civilization in the thirteenth century BC and was unknown to the later Greeks who adapted the Semitic alphabet used by the Phoenicians (see above).

Other scripts, often referred to as syllabic, are, in fact, **segmentally** based, in so far as the shape of the graphs is relatable to sound segments of the syllable, so that syllables beginning with the same consonantal sound are of similar shape, as in the following examples taken from the Ethiopian writing system.

<ϯ> /ta/, <ϯ> /tû/,

<ϯ> /tî/, <ϯ> /tê/

(Sampson 1985: 66). Almost all Linear B graphs stood for simple syllables consisting of one consonant followed by one vowel, while the spoken language used many other types of syllable. Consequently, the writing system did not reflect the pronunciation particularly accurately, and a reader relied on contextual clues to the meaning of any inscription. However, it is unlikely that this created many problems, given the restricted uses to which Linear B was put (Sampson 1985: 4).

More recent syllabic systems include the Cherokee script invented by the Indian Sikwayi in the early 1820s. Having given up the idea of devising a word-based script as too cumbersome, he divided the words of the spoken language into around 200 syllables, with a sign for each. Subsequently, he was able to reduce the number of signs to a more manageable eighty-five, by disregarding unimportant distinctions and by introducing a separate sign for the sound /s/, which could be prefixed to signs for syllables beginning with other consonants. Thus it would no longer be necessary to have one sign for a particular CV syllable and a separate sign for a syllable beginning with /s/, but otherwise consisting of the same CV. The sign for /s/ represents an aspect of alphabeticality in the Cherokee writing system. Otherwise it is, however, properly syllabic (Jensen 1970: 241–2). The Cree system, on the other hand, is segmentally based (see Jensen 1970: 244, for illustration), as is the System used for Inuktitut (Eskimo) in the Canadian Arctic (see Mallon 1985).

For an example of a featural writing system, let us look at the Korean **Han'gul**, a phonographic script invented by King Sejong, who ruled Korea from 1418 to 1450, and a team of scholars he had assembled. This system is **featural** in that its graphs systematically represent the distinctive phonemic features of the spoken Korean language. Vowels are represented by graphs consisting of long horizontal and vertical lines combined with small distinguishing marks – for instance, <ㅣ> stands for /i/, <ㅔ> for /e/ and <ㅐ> for /æ/. Consonants are represented by more compact, two-dimensional graphs, divided into five families according to their places of articulation (see ARTICULATORY PHONETICS). Members of each family share a basic shape – for instance, <ㅁ> stands for the bilabial /m/, <ㅂ> for /b/ and <ㅍ> for /pʰ/ (Sampson 1985: 124). In written text, the graphs are grouped into syllables, so that each group looks like a Chinese character; Han'gul thereby 'succeeds in reconciling two contradictory desiderata for a writing-system: the fewness of the basic graphic elements makes Han'gul easy to learn, while the large size of the perceptually-salient units makes it efficient to read' (Sampson 1985: 132).

K.M.

Suggestions for further reading

Campbell, G.L. (1997) *Handbook of Scripts and Alphabets*, London and New York: Routledge.

Diringer, D. (1968) *The Alphabet: A Key to the History of Mankind*, 3rd edition, 2 vols, London: Hutchinson.

Gelb, I.J. (1963) *A Study of Writing*, revised edition, Chicago and London: University of Chicago Press.

Jensen, H. (1970) *Sign, Symbol and Script: An Account of Man's Efforts to Write*, London: George Allen and Unwin.

Sampson, G. (1985) *Writing Systems*, London: Hutchinson.

Bibliography

Abbs, B. and Freebairn, I. (1975) *Strategies*, London: Longman.

Abercrombie, D. (1956) *Problems and Principles*, London: Longman.

—— (1967) *Elements of General Phonetics*, Edinburgh: Edinburgh University Press.

—— (1968) 'Paralanguage', *British Journal of Disorders of Communication* 3: 55–9.

Ackerman, F. and Webelhuth, G. (1998) *A Theory of Predicates*, Stanford, CA: CSLI Publications.

Adams, V. (1973) *An Introduction to Modern English Word Formation*, London: Longman.

Agar, M. (1980) *The Professional Stranger*, New York: Academic Press.

Aijmer, K. and Altenberg, B. (1996) 'Introduction', in K. Aijmer, B. Altenberg and M. Johansson (eds) *Languages in Contrast: Papers from a Symposium on Text-Based Cross-Linguistic Studies, Lund 4–5 March 1994*, Lund: Lund University Press.

——, —— and Johansson, M. (eds) (1996) *Languages in Contrast: Papers from a Symposium on Text-Based Cross-Linguistic Studies, Lund 4–5 March 1994*, Lund: Lund University Press.

Aitchison, J. (1987) *Words in the Mind: An Introduction to the Mental Lexicon*, Oxford: Basil Blackwell.

—— (1996/2000) *The Seeds of Speech: Language Origin and Language Evolution*, Cambridge: Cambridge University Press; 1st edition 1996, Canto edition 2000.

—— (1998) *The Articulate Mammal: An Introduction to Psycholinguistics*, 4th edition, London: Routledge.

Ajdukiewicz, K. (1935) 'Die syntaktische Konnexität', *Studia Philosophica* 1: 1–28; translated as 'Syntactic Connexion', in

S. McCall (ed.) (1967) *Polish Logic: 1920–1939*, Oxford: Oxford University Press.

Akamatsu, T. (1988) *The Theory of Neutralization and the Archiphoneme in Functional Phonology* (Amsterdam Studies in the Theory and History of Linguistic Science, series V: Current Issues in Linguistic Theory (CILT) no. 43), Amsterdam and Philadelphia: John Benjamins.

—— (1992a) *Essentials of Functional Phonology* (Série Pédagogique de l'Institut de Linguistique de Louvain (SPILL) no. 16), Louvain-la-Neuve: Peeters.

—— (1992b) 'Whither the archiphoneme?', *Revue roumaine de linguistique* 38: 380–94.

—— (2000) *Japanese Phonology: A Functional Approach*, Murich: Lincom Europa.

Alexander, L.G. (1967) *First Things First*, London: Longman.

Allen, H.B. (1973–76) *The Linguistic Atlas of the Upper Midwest*, 3 vols, Minneapolis: University of Minnesota Press.

Allen, J.F. (1987) *Natural Language Processing*, Amsterdam: John Benjamins.

—— and Perrault, C.R. (1980) 'Analysing intention in utterances', *Artificial Intelligence* 15(3): 143–78.

Allen, J.P.B. and Widdowson, H.G. (1974 onwards) *English in Focus*, Oxford: Oxford University Press.

—— (1975) 'Grammar and language teaching', in J.P.B. Allen and S. Pit Corder (eds) *The Edinburgh Course in Applied Linguistics* vol. 2, *Papers in Applied Linguistics*, London: Oxford University Press.

Allerton, D.J. (1979) *Essentials of Grammar Theory: A Consensus View of Syntax and Morphology*, London: Routledge & Kegan Paul.

Altenberg, B. (1987) *Prosodic Patterns in Spoken English* (Lund Studies in English, no. 76), Lund: Lund University Press.

Altmann, G.T.M. and Steedman, M. (1988) 'Interaction with context during human sentence processing', *Cognition* 30: 191–238.

Ambrazas, V. (ed.) (1997) *Lithuanian Grammar*, Vilnius: Baltos Lankos.

Andersen, B. (1959) *Rønnemaalet, en strukturallingvistisk analyse of udtryksplanet i en bornholmsk dialekt*, Copenhagen: Udvalg for folkemaals publikationer A.18.

Andersen, H. (ed.) (1986) *Sandhi Phenomenon in the Languages of Europe*, Amsterdam: Mouton.

Anderson, J.M. (1973) *Structural Aspects of Language Change*, London: Longman.

Anderson, J.R. and Paulson, R. (1977) 'Representation and retention of verbal information', *Journal of Verbal Learning and Verbal Behavior* 16: 439–51.

Anderson, S.R. (1982) 'Where's morphology?', *Linguistic Inquiry* 13: 571–612.

—— (1986) 'Disjunctive ordering in inflectional morphology', *Natural Language and Linguistic Theory* 4: 1–31.

—— (1988) 'Morphological theory', in F. Newmeyer (ed.) *Linguistics: The Cambridge Survey* vol. 1, Cambridge: Cambridge University Press.

—— (1992) *A-Morphous Morphology*, Cambridge: Cambridge University Press.

—— and Keenan, E.L. (1985) 'Deixis', in T. Shopen (ed.) *Language Typology and Syntactic Description* vol. 3, *Grammatical Categories and the Lexicon*, Cambridge: Cambridge University Press.

Anttila, R. (1972) *An Introduction to Historical and Comparative Linguistics*, New York: Macmillan.

Appelt, D. (1985) *Planning English Sentences*, Cambridge: Cambridge University Press.

Aristotle (*c.* 330 BC) *Rhetoric*, trans. J.H. Fries (1926), London: William Heinemann.

Arlotto, A. (1972) *Introduction to Historical Linguistics*, Boston, MA: University Press of America.

Armstrong, S.L., Gleitman, L.R. and Gleitman, H. (1983) 'What concepts might not be', *Cognition* 13: 263–308.

Aronoff, M. (1976) *Word Formation in Generative Grammar*, Cambridge, MA: MIT Press.

Arsleff, H. (1967/1983) *The Study of Language in England, 1780–1860*, Minneapolis and London: University of Minnesota Press and the Athlone Press; 1st edition 1967, Princeton: Princeton University Press.

Ascoli, G.I. (1870) *Corsi di Glottologia: Lezioni di Fonologia Comparata*, Turin and Florence: Ermanno Loescher.

Atkinson, A. (1992) 'The evolution of medical research writing from 1735 to 1985: the case of the *Edinburgh Medical Journal*', *Applied Linguistics* 13: 337–74.

Atkinson, M. (1996) 'Generative grammar', in E.K. Brown and J. Miller (eds) *A Concise Encyclopaedia of Syntactic Theories*, Oxford: Pergamon Press.

Austin, J.L. (1962) *How to Do Things with Words*, Oxford: Oxford University Press.

—— (1971) 'Performative-Constative', in J.R. Searle (ed.) *The Philosophy of Language*, Oxford: Oxford University Press.

Ayala, F.J. (1978) 'The mechanisms of evolution', *Scientific American* 239: 56–69.

Ayer, A. (1936/1971) *Language, Truth and Logic*, Harmondsworth: Penguin; 1st edition 1936, London: Victor Gollancz.

Bach, E. (1970) 'Pronominalization', *Linguistic Inquiry* 1: 121–2.

—— (1980) 'In defence of passive', *Linguistics and Philosophy* 3: 297–341.

Baddeley, A. (1990) *Human Memory: Theory and Practice*, Hillsdale, NJ: Lawrence Erlbaum Associates.

Bailey, C.-J.N. (1973) *Variation and Linguistic Theory*, Arlington, MA: Center for Applied Linguistics.

Bailey, D. (ed.) (1965) *Essays on Rhetoric*, New York: Oxford University Press.

Bailey, R.W. and Görlach, M. (eds) (1982) *English as a World Language*, Cambridge: Cambridge University Press.

Baker, C. (1992) *Attitudes and Language*, Clevedon: Multilingual Matters.

—— (1996) *Foundations of Bilingual Education and Bilingualism*, 2nd edition, Clevedon: Multilingual Matters.

—— and Jones, S.P. (1998) *The Encyclopedia of Bilingualism and Bilingual Education*, Clevedon: Multilingual Matters.

Baker, M. (1985) 'The Mirror Principle and morphosyntactic explanation', *Linguistic Inquiry* 16: 373–416.

—— (1988) *Incorporation: A Theory of Grammatical Function Changing*, Chicago: University of Chicago Press.

Baker, Mona (1993) 'Corpus Linguistics and Translation Studies: Implications and Applications', in Mona Baker, G. Francis and E. Tognini-Bonelli (eds) *Text and Technology: In Honour of John Sinclair*, Amsterdam and Philadelphia: John Benjamins.

—— (1995) 'Corpora in translation studies: an overview and some suggestions for future research', *Target* 7(2): 223–43.

—— (1996) 'Corpus-based translation Studies: the Challenges that lie ahead', in H. Somers (ed.) *Terminology, LSP and Translation: Studies in Language Engineering, in Honour of Juan C. Sager*, Amsterdam and Philadelphia: John Benjamins.

Baker, S. (1973) *The Practical Stylist*, 3rd edition, New York: Crowell.

Bakhtin, M. (1981) *The Dialogic Imagination: Four Essays*, Austin: University of Texas Press.

Baldauf, R.B. and Jernudd, J.H. (1983) 'Language use patterns in the fisheries periodical literature', *Scientometrics* 5: 245–55.

Baldwin, J. and French, J. (1990) *Forensic Phonetics*, London: Pinter.

Balota, D.A., Ferraro, F.R. and Connor, L.T. (1991) 'On the early influence of meaning on word recognition', in P.J. Schwanenflugel (ed.) *The Psychology of Word Meanings*, Hillsdale, NJ: Lawrence Erlbaum Associates.

—— Paul, S.T.P. and Spieler, D.H. (1999) 'Attentional control of lexical processing pathways during word recognition and reading', in S. Garrod and M. Pickering (eds) *Language Processing*, Hove: Psychology Press.

—— Pollatsek, A. and Rayner, K. (1985) 'The interaction of contextual constraints and parafoveal visual information in reading', *Cognitive Psychology* 17: 364–90.

Baltaxe, C.A.M. (1978) *Foundations of Distinctive Feature Theory*, Baltimore: University Park Press.

Banich, M.T. and Mack, M. (eds) (in press) *Mind, Brain and Language: Multidisciplinary Perspectives*, Mahwah, NJ: Lawrence Erlbaum Associates.

Bard, E.G., Shillcock, R.C. and Altmann, G.T.M. (1988) 'The recognition of words after their acoustic offsets in spontaneous speech:

effects of subsequent context', *Perception and Psychophysics* 44: 395–408.

Bar-Hillel, Y. (1953) 'A quasi-arithmetical notation for syntactic description', *Language* 29: 47–58.

Barley, N. (1983) *The Innocent Anthropologist: Notes from a Mud Hut*, Harmondsworth: Penguin.

Barsalou, L.W. (1982) 'Context-independent and context-dependent information in concepts', *Memory and Cognition* 10: 82–93.

—— (1985) 'Ideals, central tendency, and frequency of instantiation as determinants of graded structure in categories', *Journal of Experimental Psychology: Learning, Memory, and Cognition* 11: 629–54.

—— (1987) 'The instability of graded structure: implications for the nature of concepts', in U. Neisser (ed.) *Concepts and Conceptual Development*, Cambridge: Cambridge University Press.

Bartlett, F.C. (1932) *Remembering: A Study in Experimental and Social Psychology*, Cambridge: Cambridge University Press.

Barton, S. and Sanford, A.J. (1993) 'A case-study of pragmatic anomaly-detection: relevance-driven cohesion patterns', *Memory and Cognition* 21: 477–87.

Barwise, J. and Perry, J. (1983) *Situations and Attitudes*, Cambridge, MA: Bradford Books.

Bastiaanse, R. and Grodzinsky, Y. (eds) (2000) *Psycholinguistic Aspects of Aphasia*, London: Whurr.

—— Edwards, S. and Rispens, J. (2001) *The Verb and Sentence Test* (VAST), Bury St. Edmunds: Thames Valley Test Company.

Bates, M. and Dudley-Evans, A. (1976) *Nucleus*, London: Longman.

Bateson, F.W. (1967) 'Literature and linguistics', *Essays in Criticism* 17: 322–47.

Battison, R. (1974) 'Phonological deletion in American sign language', *Sign Language Studies* 5: 1–19.

Bauer, L. (1983) *English Word-Formation*, Cambridge: Cambridge University Press.

Baugh, A.C. and Cable, T. (1978) *A History of the English Language*, 3rd edition, London: Routledge & Kegan Paul, and Englewood Cliffs, NJ: Prentice Hall.

Bazell, C.E. (1949) 'On the problem of the morpheme', *Archivum Linguisticum* 1: 1–15.

—— Catford, J.C., Halliday, M.A.K. and Robins, R.H. (eds) (1966) *In Memory of J.R. Firth*, London: Longman.

Bazerman, C. and Paradis, J. (1991) *Textual Dynamics of the Professions*, Madison, WI: University of Wisconsin Press.

Beach, D. (1924) 'The science of tonetics and its application to Bantu languages', *Bantu Studies* 2: 75–106.

Beardsley, M.C. (1967) 'Metaphor', in P. Edwards (ed.) *Encyclopedia of Philosophy* vol. 5, New York: Macmillan.

Beaugrande, R. de (1991) *Linguistic Theory: The Discourse of Fundamental Works*, London: Longman.

—— and Dressler, W.V. (1981) *Introduction to Text Linguistics*, London and New York: Longman.

Becker, C.A. (1979) 'Semantic context and word frequency effects in visual word recognition', *Journal of Experimental Psychology: Human Perception and Performance* 5: 252–9.

Behrens, H. (1999) 'Was macht Verben zu einer besonderen Kategorie im Spracherwerb?', in J. Meibauer and M. Rothweiler (eds) *Das Lexikon im Spracherwerb*, Tübingen-Basel: A. Francke.

Béjoint, H. (2000) *Modern Lexicography: An Introduction*, Oxford: Oxford University Press.

Békésy, G. von (1960) *Experiments in Hearing*, New York: McGraw-Hill.

Belanger, M. (1982) 'A preliminary analysis of the structure of the discussion sections in ten neuroscience journal articles', mimeo.

Belin, P., Zatorre, R.J., Lafaille, P., Ahad, P. and Pike, B. (2000) 'Voice-selective areas in human auditory context', *Nature* 403: 309–12.

Bell, A. (1978) 'Language samples', in J.H. Greenberg, C.A. Ferguson and E.A. Moravcsik (eds) *Universals of Human Language*, 4 vols, Stanford, CA: Stanford University Press.

Belsey, C. (1980) *Critical Practice*, London: Methuen.

Benedict, H. (1979) 'Early lexical development: comprehension and production', *Journal of Child Language* 6: 183–200.

Benson, M., Benson, E. and Ilson, R.F. (1986) *Lexicographic Description of English*, Amsterdam and Philadelphia: John Benjamins.

Berger, P. and Luckmann, T. (1966) *The Social Construction of Reality*, Harmondsworth: Penguin.

Berkenkotter, C. and Huckin, T. (1995) *Genre Knowledge in Disciplinary Communication: Cognition/Culture/Power*, Hillsdale, NJ: Lawrence Erlbaum Associates.

Berko, J. (1958) 'The child's learning of English morphology', *Word* 14: 150–77.

Berlin, B. and Kay, P. (1969) *Basic Color Terms*, Berkeley: University of California Press.

Bernard, J. (1972) *The Sex Game*, New York: Athenaeum.

Bernstein, B. (ed.) (1971) *Class, Codes and Control* vol. 1, *Theoretical Studies Towards a Sociology of Language* (Primary Socialization, Language and Education), London: Routledge & Kegan Paul; revised edition 1973, London: Paladin.

—— (1972) 'Social class, language and socialization', in P.P. Giglioli (ed.) *Language and Social Context: Selected Readings*, Harmondsworth: Penguin.

—— (ed.) (1973) *Class, Codes and Control* vol. 2, *Applied Studies Towards a Sociology of Language*, London: Routledge & Kegan Paul.

Berry, M. (1975) *Introduction to Systemic Linguistics* vol. 1, *Structures and Systems*, London: Batsford.

—— (1981) 'Systemic linguistics and discourse analysis: a multi-layered approach to exchange structure', in M. Coulthard and M. Montgomery (eds) *Studies in Discourse Analysis*, London: Routledge & Kegan Paul.

Best, C.T. and Strange, W. (1992) 'Effects of phonological and phonetic factors on cross-language perception of approximants', *Journal of Phonetics* 20: 305–30.

Bex, A.R. (1996) *Variety in Written English: Texts in Society, Society in Texts*, London: Routledge.

Bhatia, V.K. (1981) 'Defining legal scope in statutory writing', paper given at the BAAL Annual Conference, Brighton.

—— (1993) *Analysing Genre*, London: Longman.

Biber, D., Conrad, S. and Reppen, R. (1998) *Corpus Linguistics: Investigating Language Structure and Use*, Cambridge: Cambridge University Press.

Bickerton, D. (1971) 'Inherent variability and variable rules', *Foundations of Language* 7(4): 457–92.

—— (1974) 'Creolization, linguistic universals, natural semantax and the brain', *Working Papers in Linguistics* (University of Hawaii) 6(3): 124–41.

—— (1977) 'Pidginization and creolization: language acquisition and language universals', in A. Valdman (ed.) *Pidgin and Creole Linguistics*, Bloomington: Indiana University Press.

—— (1979) 'Beginnings', in K.C. Hill (ed.) *The Genesis of Language*, Ann Arbor, MI: Karoma.

—— (1981) *Roots of Language*, Ann Arbor, MI: Karoma.

—— (1984a) 'Author's response', *Behavioral and Brain Sciences* 7(2): 212–18.

—— (1984b) 'The language bioprogram hypothesis', *Behavioral and Brain Sciences* 7(2): 173–88.

—— (1990) *Language and Species*, Chicago: University of Chicago Press.

—— (1991) 'Language origins and evolutionary plausibility', *Language and Communication* 11(1): 37–9.

—— (1998) 'Catastrophic evolution: the case for a single step from protolanguage to full human language', in J.R. Hurford, M. Studdard-Kennedy and C. Knight (eds) *Approaches to the Evolution of Language: Social and Cognitive Bases*, Cambridge: Cambridge University Press.

Bierwisch, M. and Schreuder, R. (1992) 'From concepts to lexical items', *Cognition* 42: 23–60.

Billows, L. (1962) *Techniques of Language Teaching*, London: Longman.

Birch, H.G. (1962) 'Dyslexia and the maturation of visual function', in D. Money (ed.) *Reading Disability. Progress and Research Needs in Dyslexia*, New York: Johns Hopkins Press.

Birdwhistell, R.L. (1970) *Kinesics and Context: Essays on Body Motion Communication*, Philadelphia: University of Pennsylvania Press.

Bishop, D. (1982) *Test for the Reception of Grammar*, London: Medical Research Council.

Black, M. (1979) 'More about metaphor', in A. Ortony (ed.) *Metaphor and Thought*, Cambridge: Cambridge University Press.

Blevins, J.P. (to appear) 'Feature-based grammar', in R.D. Borsley and K. Börjars (eds) *Nontransformational Grammar*, Oxford: Blackwell Publishers.

Bley-Vroman, R. (1989) 'What is the logical problem of foreign language learning?', in S. Gass and J. Schachter (eds) *Linguistic Perspectives on Second Language Acquisition*, Cambridge: Cambridge University Press.

Bloch, B. (1949) 'Leonard Bloomfield', *Language* 25: 87–98.

—— and Trager, G.L. (1942) *Outline of Linguistic Analysis*, Baltimore: Linguistic Society of America.

Bloom, L.M. (1970) *Language Development: Form and Function in Emerging Grammars*, Cambridge, MA: MIT Press.

Bloomfield, L. (1914/1983) *An Introduction to the Study of Language* (Amsterdam Studies in the Theory and History of Linguistic Science, Series II, 3, Classics in Psycholinguistics); facsimile reprint K. Koerner (ed.), introduction by J.F. Kress, Amsterdam and Philadelphia: John Benjamins; 1st edition 1914, London and New York: Bell and Holt.

—— (1923) 'Review of Ferdinand de Saussure's *Cours de Linguistique Générale*', *Modern Language Journal* 8: 317–19.

—— (1926), 'A set of postulates for a science of language', *Language*, 2: 153–64.

—— (1933/1935), *Language*, New York, Holt, Rinehart and Winston; revised edition 1935, London: George Allen and Unwin.

—— (1942) *An Outline Guide for the Practical Study of Foreign Languages*, Baltimore: Linguistic Society of America.

Blum-Kulka, S. (1983) 'Interpreting and performing speech acts in a second language: a cross-cultural study of Hebrew and English', in N. Wolfson and E. Judd (eds) *Sociolinguistics and Language Acquisition*, Rowley, MA: Newbury House.

—— (1987) 'Indirectness and politeness in requests: same or different', *Journal of Pragmatics* 11: 131–46.

Blumstein, S. and Cooper, W.E. (1974) 'Hemispheric processing of intonation contours', *Cortex* 10: 146–58.

Boas, F. (1911) *Handbook of American Indian Languages*, Washington, DC: Smithsonian Institution, Bureau of American Ethnology, Bulletin 40.

Bobrow, D.G. (1968) 'Natural language input for a computer problem-solving system', in

M. Minsky (ed.) *Semantic Information Processing*, Cambridge, MA: MIT Press.

Boden, D. and Zimmerman, D.H. (eds) (1991) *Talk and Social Structure: Studies in Ethnomethodology and Conversation Analysis*, Oxford: Polity Press.

Bolinger, D.L. (1948) 'On defining the morpheme', *Word* 4(1): 18–23.

—— (1961) *Generality, Gradience, and the All-or-None*, The Hague: Mouton.

—— (1965a) *Forms of English: Accent, Morpheme, Order*, Cambridge, MA: Harvard University Press.

—— (1965b) 'The atomization of meaning', *Language* 41(4): 555–73.

—— (1976) 'Meaning and memory', *Forum Linguisticum* 1(1): 1–14.

—— (1985) *Intonation and its Parts: Melody in Spoken English*, London: Edward Arnold.

—— and Sears, D.A. (1981) *Aspects of Language*, New York: Harcourt Brace Jovanovich.

Bolling, G.M. (1929) 'Linguistics and philology', *Language* 5(1): 27–32.

Booij, G.E. (1986) 'Form and meaning in morphology: the case of Dutch "agent nouns"', *Linguistics* 24: 503–17.

Boole, G. (1854) *The Laws of Thought*, London: Walton.

Booth, W. (1961) *The Rhetoric of Fiction*, Chicago: University of Chicago Press.

Bopp, F. (1816) *Über das Conjugationssystem der Sanskritsprache in Vergleichung mit jenem der griechischen, lateinischen, persischen und germanischen Sprache*, Frankfurt-am-Main: In der Andreaischen Buchhandlung.

Borer, H. and Wexler, K. (1987) 'The maturation of syntax', in T. Roeper and E. Williams (eds) *Parameter Setting*, Dordrecht: Foris.

Borsley, R.D. (1996) *Modern Phrase Structure Grammar*, Oxford: Blackwell Publishers.

—— and Börjars, K. (eds) (to appear) *Non-transformational Grammar*, Oxford: Blackwell Publishers.

Bowen, F. (1964) *Return to Laughter*, New York: Doubleday.

Bowerman, M. (1996) 'The origins of children's spatial semantic categories: cognitive versus linguistic determinants', in J.J. Gumperz and S.C. Levinson (eds) *Rethinking Linguistic Relativity*, Cambridge: Cambridge University Press.

Boyd, R. (1979) 'Metaphor and theory change: what is "metaphor" a metaphor for?', in A. Ortony (ed.) *Metaphor and Thought*, Cambridge: Cambridge University Press.

Boyes-Braem, P. (1973) 'The acquisition of hand-shape in American Sign Language', manuscript, Salk Institute for Biological Studies, La Jolla, CA.

Bradford, R. (1997) *Stylistics*, London: Routledge.

Bradshaw, J.L. and Nettleton, N.C. (1981) 'The nature of hemispheric specialization in man', *Behavioral and Brain Sciences* 4: 51–92.

Braine, M.D.S. (1963) 'The ontogeny of English phrase structure: the first phase', *Language* 39: 1–13.

Brame, M. (1976) *Conjectures and Refutations in Syntax and Semantics*, New York: North Holland.

Bransford, J.D., Barclay, J.R. and Franks, J.J. (1972) 'Sentence memory: a constructive versus interpretive approach', *Cognitive Psychology* 3: 193–209.

Brazil, D.C. (1985) *The Communicative Value of Intonation in English*, Birmingham (Discourse Analysis Monograph, no. 8): English Language Research, University of Birmingham.

—— (1997) *The Communicative Value of Intonation in English*, 2nd edition, Cambridge: Cambridge University Press.

Bredsdorff, J.H. (1821/1886) 'Om aarsagerne til sprogenes forandringer' ('On the causes of change in languages'), *Programme of the Roskilde Catholic School*, republished 1886, Copenhagen: Vilhelm Thomsen.

Brennan, M., Colvill, M.D. and Lawson, L. (1980) *Words in Hand*, Moray House College of Education, Edinburgh, British Sign Language Research Project.

Bresnan, J.W. (1978) 'A realistic transformational grammar', in M. Halle, J. Bresnan and G.A. Miller (eds) *Linguistic Theory and Psychological Reality*, Cambridge, MA: MIT Press.

—— (ed.) (1982a) *The Mental Representation of Grammatical Relations*, Cambridge, MA and London: MIT Press.

—— (1982b) 'The passive in lexical theory', in J. Bresnan (ed.) (1982a) *The Mental Representation of Grammatical Relations*, Cambridge, MA and London: MIT Press.

—— (1995) 'Linear order, syntactic rank and empty categories: on weak crossover', in M. Dalrymple, J.T. Maxwell III and A. Zaenen (eds) *Formal Issues in Lexical Functional Grammar*, Stanford: CSLI Publications.

—— (2000) 'Optimal syntax', in J. Dekkers, F. van der Leeuw and J. van de Weijer (eds) *Optimality Theory: Phonology, Syntax and Acquisition*, Oxford: Oxford University Press.

—— (2001) *Lexical-Functional Syntax*, Oxford: Blackwell Publishers.

—— and Kanerva, J.M. (1989) 'Locative inversion in Chichewa: a case study in factorization in grammar', *Linguistic Inquiry* 20: 1–50.

—— and Kaplan, R.M. (1982) 'Introduction: grammars as mental representations of language', in J.W. Bresnan (ed.) *The Mental Representation of Grammatical Relations*, Cambridge, MA and London: MIT Press.

——, Peters, S. and Zaenen, A. (1982) 'Cross-serial dependencies in Dutch', *Linguistic Inquiry* 13: 613–35.

Brett, P. (1994) 'A genre analysis of the Results section of sociology articles', *English for Specific Purposes* 11: 33–49.

Bridge, J. (1977) *Beginning Model Theory*, Oxford: Oxford University Press.

Briere, E. (1964/1968) 'A psycholinguistic study of phonological interference', University of Washington Ph.D. thesis and The Hague: Mouton.

Britt, A.M. (1994) 'The interaction of referential ambiguity and argument structure in the parsing of prepositional phrases', *Journal of Memory and Language* 33: 251–83.

——, Perfetti, C.A., Garrod, S. and Rayner, K. (1992) 'Parsing in discourse: context effects and their limits', *Journal of Memory and Language* 31: 293–314.

Broca, P. (1865) 'Sur la faculté du langage articulé', *Bulletin de la Société d'Anthropologie* 4: 4934.

Brown, A.S. (1991) 'A review of the tip-of-the-tongue experience', *Psychological Bulletin* 109: 204–23.

Brown, E.K. (1984) *Linguistics Today*, Glasgow: Fontana/Collins.

—— and Miller, J. (1982) *Syntax: Generative Grammar*, London: Hutchinson.

—— (1996) *A Concise Encyclopaedia of Syntactic Theories*, Oxford: Pergamon Press.

—— (1999) *A Concise Encyclopaedia of Grammatical Categories*, Oxford: Pergamon Press.

Brown, G. and Yule, G. (1983) *Discourse Analysis*, Cambridge: Cambridge University Press.

——, Malmkjær, K. and Williams, J. (eds) (1996) *Performance and Competence in Second Language Acquisition*, Cambridge: Cambridge University Press.

Brown, P. and Levinson, S. (1978/1987) 'Universals in language usage: politeness phenomena', in E.S. Goody (ed.) *Questions and Politeness: Strategies in Social Interaction*, Cambridge: Cambridge University Press; reprinted 1987 as *Politeness: Some Universals in Language Usage*, Cambridge: Cambridge University Press.

Brown, R. (1973) *A First Language: The Early Stages*, Cambridge, MA: Harvard University Press.

—— and Fraser, C. (1963) 'The acquisition of syntax', in C. Cofer and B. Musgrave (eds) *Verbal Behavior and Learning: Problems and Processes*, New York: McGraw-Hill.

Bruce, B. (1975) 'Case systems for natural language', *Artificial Intelligence* 6: 327–60.

Brumfit, C. (1980) 'Problems and principles in English teaching', Oxford: Pergamon Press.

Burton, D. (1982) 'Through glass darkly: through dark glasses', in R. Carter (ed.) *Language and Literature: An Introductory Reader in Stylistics*, London: George Allen and Unwin.

Burton, G. (1996–2001) *The Forest of Rhetoric: Silva Rhetoricae*, humanities.bya.edu/rhetoric/silva.HTM

Butler, C.S. (1985) *Systemic Linguistics: Theory and Applications*, London: Batsford Academic and Educational.

Buyssens, F. (1972a) 'Intervention', in R. Rigault and R. Charbonneau (eds) *Proceedings of the Seventh International Congress of Phonetic Sciences*, The Hague: Mouton.

—— (1972b) 'Phonème, archiphonème et pertinence', *La Linguistique* 8(2): 39–58.

Bybee, J.L. (1985) *Morphology: A Study of the Relation Between Meaning and Form*, Amsterdam: John Benjamins.

Bynon, T. (1977) *Historical Linguistics*, Cambridge: Cambridge University Press.

Cameron, D. (1992) *The Feminist Critique of Language*, London: Routledge.

Campbell, B.C. (1996/1999) 'An outline of human phylogeny', in A. Lock and C.R. Peters (eds) *Handbook of Human Symbolic Evolution*, Oxford: Blackwell Publishers; 1st edition 1996, Oxford: Oxford University Press.

Campbell, G.L. (1997) *Handbook of Scripts and Alphabets*, London and New York: Routledge.

Campbell, R. and Wales, R. (1970) 'The study of language acquisition', in J. Lyons (ed.) *New Horizons in Linguistics*, Harmondsworth: Penguin.

Candlin, C.N., Leather, J.H. and Bruton, C.J. (1978) *Doctor–Patient Communication Skills*, Chelmsford: Graves Audio-Visual Medical Foundation.

Canger, U. (1969) 'Analysis in outline of Mam, a Mayan language', unpublished Ph.D. thesis, Berkeley, CA.

Cannon, G. (1986) 'Blends in English word formation', *Linguistics* 24: 725–53.

Caputo, C. (1986) *Il segno di Giano, Studi su Louis Hjelmslev, Testi i Studi* 54, Milano: Edizioni Unicopli.

Caramazza, A., Laudanna, A. and Romani, C. (1988) 'Lexical access and inflectional morphology', *Cognition* 28(3): 297–332.

—— and Miozzo, M. (1997) 'The relation between syntactic and phonological knowledge in lexical access: evidence from the "tip-of-the-tongue" phenomenon', *Cognition* 64: 309–43.

——, Yeni-Komshian, G.H., Zurif, E.B. and Carbone, F. (1973) 'The acquisition of a new phonological contrast: the case of stop consonants in French–English bilinguals', *Journal of the Acoustical Society of America* 54: 421–8.

Cardona, G. (1990/1994) 'Indian Linguistics', in G. Lepschy (ed.) *History of Linguistics* vol 1, London: Longman.

Carlsson, F., Voutilainen, A., Heikkilä, J. and Anttila, A. (eds) (1995) *Constraint Grammar: A Language-Independent System for Parsing Unrestricted Text*, Berlin: Mouton.

Carnap, R. (1928) *Der logische Aufbau der Welt*, Berlin-Schlactensee: Weltkreis.

Carroll, J.B. (ed.) (1956) *Language, Thought and Reality: Selected Writings of Benjamin Lee Whorf*, Cambridge, MA: MIT Press.

—— (1971) 'Statistical analysis of the corpus', in J.B. Carroll, F. Davies and B. Richman (eds) *The American Heritage Word Frequency Book*, New York: American Heritage.

——, Davies, P. and Richman, B. (eds) (1971) *The American Heritage Word Frequency Book*, New York: American Heritage.

Carter, B., Jr (1963) 'President Kennedy's inaugural address', *College Composition and Communication* 14 (February): 36–40; reprinted in G.A. Love and M. Payne (eds) (1969) *Contemporary Essays on Style: Rhetoric, Linguistics, and Criticism*, Glenview, IL: Scott, Foresman and Co.

Carter, R.A. (1987) 'Is there a core vocabulary? Some implications for language teaching', *Applied Linguistics* 8(2): 178–93.

—— and McRae, J. (eds) (1996) *Literature, Language and the Learner: Creative Classroom Practice*, Harlow: Longman.

—— and Nash, W. (1990) *Seeing Through Language*, Oxford: Basil Blackwell.

Catford, J.C. (1957) 'The linguistic survey of Scotland', *Orbis* 6(1): 105–21.

Cauldwell, G. (1982) 'Anglo-Quebec on the verge of its history', *Language and Society* (Ottawa, Office of the Commissioner of Official Language no. 8): 3–6.

Cedergren, H.J. and Sankoff, D. (1974) 'Variable rules: performance as a statistical reflection of competence', *Language* 50(2): 333–55.

Chambers, J.K. (1995) *Sociolinguistic Theory: Linguistic Variation and its Social Significance*, Oxford: Blackwell Publishers.

—— and Trudgill, P.J. (1980) *Dialectology*, Cambridge: Cambridge University Press; 2nd edition 1998.

Chao, Y.R. (1930) 'A system of tone letters', *Le Maître phonétique* 30: 24–7.

Chapman, R. (1973) *Linguistics and Literature: An Introduction to Literary Stylistics*, London: Edward Arnold.

Charles, M. (1996) 'Business negotiations: interdependence between discourse and the business relationship', *English for Specific Purposes* 15: 19–36.

Charniak, F. and McDermott, D.V. (1985) *An Introduction to Artificial Intelligence*, Reading, MA: Addison Wesley.

Chase, P.G. (1999) 'Symbolism as reference and symbolism as culture', in R. Dunbar, C. Knight and C. Power (eds) *The Evolution of Culture*, Edinburgh: Edinburgh University Press.

Chater, N. and Christiansen, M.H. (1999) 'Connectionism and natural language processing', in S. Garrod and M. Pickering (eds) *Language Processing*, Hove: Psychology Press.

Chatman, S. (1960) 'Comparing metrical styles', in T.A. Sebeok (ed.) *Style in Language*, Cambridge, MA: MIT Press.

—— (ed.) (1971) *Literary Style: A Symposium*, London and New York: Oxford University Press.

Chellas, B. (1980) *Modal Logic*, Cambridge: Cambridge University Press.

Cheng, C.C. (1973) 'A quantitative study of Chinese tones', *Journal of Chinese Linguistics* 1: 93–110.

—— and Kisseberth, C.W. (1979–81) 'Ikorovere Makua tonology, parts 1, 2, 3', *Studies in the Linguistic Sciences* 9, 10, 11.

Chevalier, J.C. (1968) *Histoire de la syntaxe – naissance de la notion de compliment dans la langue française*, Geneva: Droz.

Chilton, P. (1982) 'Nukespeak: nuclear language, culture and propaganda', in C. Aubrey (ed.) *Nukespeak: The Media and the Bomb*, London: Comedia Press Group.

—— (ed.) (1985) *Language and the Nuclear Arms Debate: Nukespeak Today*, London and Dover, NH: Frances Pinter.

Chomsky, N. (1957) *Syntactic Structures*, The Hague: Mouton.

—— (1959) 'A review of B.F. Skinner's *Verbal Behavior*', *Language* 35(1): 26–58; reprinted in J. Fodor and J. Katz (eds) (1964) *The Structure of Language: Readings in the Philosophy of Language*, Englewood Cliffs, NJ: Prentice Hall, and L.A. Jakobovits and M.S. Miron (eds) (1967) *Readings in the Psychology of Language*, Englewood Cliffs, NJ: Prentice Hall.

—— (1964) *Current Issues in Linguistic Theory*, The Hague: Mouton; reprinted in J. Fodor and J.J. Katz (eds) *The Structure of Language: Readings in the Philosophy of Language*, Englewood Cliffs, NJ: Prentice Hall.

—— (1965) *Aspects of the Theory of Syntax*, Cambridge, MA: MIT Press.

—— (1966) *Cartesian Linguistics: A Chapter in the History of Rationalist Thought*, New York: Harper and Row.

—— (1967) 'The formal nature of language', in E. Lenneberg (ed.) *Biological Foundations of Language*, New York: John Wiley and Sons.

—— (1970) 'Remarks on nominalization', in R. Jacobs and P. Rosenbaum (eds) *Readings in English Transformational Grammar*, Waltham, MA: Blaisdell.

—— (1971) 'Deep structure, surface structure, and semantic interpretation', in D. Steinberg and L. Jakobovits (eds) *Semantics*, Cambridge: Cambridge University Press.

—— (1972a) *Language and Mind*, New York: Harcourt Brace Jovanovich.

—— (1972b) *Studies on Semantics in Generative Grammar*, The Hague: Mouton.

—— (1972c) 'Some empirical issues in the theory of transformational grammar', in S. Peters (ed.) *Goals of Linguistic Theory*, Englewood Cliffs, NJ: Prentice Hall.

—— (1973) 'Conditions on transformations', in S. Anderson and P. Kiparsky (eds) *A Festschrift for Morris Halle*, New York: Holt, Rinehart and Winston.

—— (1975a) *The Logical Structure of Linguistic Theory*, New York: Plenum Press.

—— (1975b) *Reflections on Language*, New York: Pantheon.

—— (1977) *Essays on Form and Interpretation*, New York: North Holland.

—— (1979) *Morphophonemics of Modern Hebrew*, New York: Garland; MA thesis, University of Pennsylvania, 1951.

—— (1981) *Lectures on Government and Binding*, Dordrecht: Foris.

—— (1982) *Some Concepts and Consequences of the Theory of Government and Binding*, Cambridge, MA: MIT Press.

—— (1986a) *Barriers*, Cambridge, MA: MIT Press.

—— (1986b) *Knowledge of Language: Its Nature, Origin and Use*, New York: Praeger.

—— (1995) *The Minimalist Program*, Cambridge, MA: MIT Press.

—— and Halle, M. (1968) *The Sound Pattern of English*, New York: Harper and Row.

——, —— and Lukoff, F. (1956) 'On accent and juncture in English', in M. Halle *et al.* (eds) *For Roman Jakobson*, The Hague: Mouton.

Chouliaraki, L. and Fairclough, N. (1999) *Discourse in Late Modernity: Rethinking Critical Discourse Analysis*, Edinburgh: Edinburgh University Press.

Clahsen, H. (1990) 'Constraints on parameter setting: a grammatical analysis of some

acquisition stages in German child language',
Language Acquisition 1: 361–91.

—— (1999) 'Lexical entries and the rules of language: a multidisciplinary study of German inflection', *Behavioral and Brain Sciences* 22: 991–1060.

—— and Featherston, S. (1999) 'Antecedent priming and trace positions: evidence from German scrambling', *Journal of Psycholinguistic Research* 28: 415–37.

——, Penke, M. and Parodi, T. (1993/1994) 'Functional categories in early child German', *Language Acquisition* 3: 395–429.

Clark, E.V. (1993) *The Lexicon in Acquisition*, Cambridge: Cambridge University Press.

Clark, H.E. and Clark, E.V. (1977) *Psychology and Language: An Introduction to Psycholinguistics*, New York: Harcourt Brace Jovanovich.

Clark, R. (1979) 'In search of Beach-la-mar: a history of Pacific Pidgin English', *Te Reo* 22: 3–64.

Clements, G.N. (1976) 'The autosegmental treatment of vowel harmony', in W. Dressler and O.E. Pfeiffer (eds) *Phonologica, 1976*, Innsbruck: Institut für Sprachwissenschaft.

—— (1985) 'The geometry of phonological features', *Phonology Yearbook* 2: 225–52.

—— and Hume, E.V. (1995) 'The internal organization of speech sounds', in J.A. Goldsmith (ed.) *The Handbook of Phonological Theory*, Oxford: Basil Blackwell.

Cloitre, M. and Bever, T.G. (1988) 'Linguistic anaphors, levels of representation, and discourse', *Language and Cognitive Processes* 3: 293–322.

Closs Traugott, F. and Pratt, M.L. (1980) *Linguistics for Students of Literature*, New York: Harcourt Brace Jovanovich.

Cluysenaar, A. (1976) *Introduction to Literary Stylistics: A Discussion of Dominant Structures in Verse and Prose*, London: Batsford.

Coates, J. (1983) *The Semantics of the Modal Auxiliaries*, London: Croom Helm.

—— (1986/1993) *Women, Men and Language: A Sociolinguistic Account of Gender Differences in Language*, London: Longman; 2nd edition 1993.

—— (1998) *Language and Gender: A Reader*, Oxford: Blackwell Publishers.

Cobley, P. (ed.) (1996) *The Communication Theory Reader*, London: Routledge.

COBUILD (1987) *Collins COBUILD English Language Dictionary*, editor-in-chief John Sinclair, London and Glasgow: Collins.

Cohen, J.L. (1979) 'The semantics of metaphor', in A. Ortony (ed.) *Metaphor and Thought*, Cambridge: Cambridge University Press.

Cohen, P.R. and Perrault, C.R. (1979) 'Elements of a plan-based theory of speech acts', *Cognitive Science* 3: 177–212.

Collinson, W.E. (1939) 'Comparative synonymics: some principles and illustrations', *Transactions of the Philological Society* 11: 54–77.

Coltheart, M. (1978) 'Lexical access in simple reading tasks', in G. Underwood (ed.) *Strategies of Information Processing*, London: Academic Press.

—— (1987) 'Functional architecture of the language-processing system', in M. Coltheart, C. Sartori and R. Job (eds) *The Cognitive Neuro-Psychology of Language*, London and Hillsdale, NJ: Lawrence Erlbaum Associates.

——, Sartori, C. and Job, R. (eds) (1987) *The Cognitive Neuro-Psychology of Language*, London and Hillsdale, NJ: Lawrence Erlbaum Associates.

——, Curtis, B., Atkins, P. and Haller, M. (1993) 'Models of reading aloud: dual-route and parallel-distributed processing approaches', *Psychological Review* 100: 589–608.

——, Materson, J., Byng, S., Prior, M. and Riddoch, J. (1983) 'Surface dyslexia', *Quarterly Journal of Experimental Psychology* 35A: 469–95.

Comrie, B. (1977) 'In defence of spontaneous demotion: the impersonal passive', in *Syntax and Semantics*, vol. 8, *Grammatical Relations*, New York: Academic Press.

—— (1981/1989) *Language Universals and Linguistic Typology: Syntax and Morphology*, Oxford: Basil Blackwell; 2nd edition 1989.

Connerton, P. (ed.) (1976) *Critical Sociology*, Harmondsworth: Penguin.

Connor, U.M. (1996) *Contrastive Rhetoric: Cross-cultural Aspects of Second Language Writing*, Cambridge: Cambridge University Press.

Conrad, R. (1979) *The Deaf Schoolchild: Language and Cognitive Function*, London and New York: Harper and Row.

Cook, G. (1992) *The Discourse of Advertising*, London: Routledge.

Cook, V.J. (1988) *Chomsky's Universal Grammar: An Introduction*, Oxford: Basil Blackwell.

—— (1992) 'Evidence for multicompetence', *Language Learning* 42(4): 557–91.

Corbett, G. (1991) *Gender*, Cambridge: Cambridge University Press.

Corder, S.P. 1973. *Introducing Applied Linguistics*, Harmondsworth: Penguin.

Cornett, R.O. (1967) 'Cued speech', *American Annals of the Deaf* 112: 3–15.

Coseriu, E. (1952) *Sistema, norma y habla*, Montevideo: Universidad de la República.

—— (1954) *Forma y substancia en los sonidos del lenguaje*, Montevideo: Universidad de la República.

—— (1955–6) 'Determinación y etorno', *Romanistische Jahrbuch* 7: 29–54.

Coulmas, F. (1979) 'Idiomaticity as a problem of pragmatics', in H. Parret, M. Sbisa and J. Verschueren (eds) *Possibilities and Limitations of Pragmatics*, Amsterdam: John Benjamins.

—— (1981) *Conversational Routine*, The Hague: Mouton.

—— (ed.) (1998) *The Handbook of Sociolinguistics*, Oxford: Blackwell Publishers.

Coulthard, M. (1977) *An Introduction to Discourse Analysis*, London, Longman; new edition 1985.

Council for the Welsh Language/Cyngor yr Iaith Gymraeg (1978) *A Future for the Welsh Language/Dyfodol i'r iaith Gymraeg*, Cardiff: HMSO.

Coupland, N. and Jaworski, A. (1997) *Sociolinguistics: A Reader and Coursebook*, London: Macmillan.

Cowie, A.P. (1981) 'The treatment of collocations and idioms in learners' dictionaries', *Applied Linguistics* 2(3): 223–35.

Critchley, M. (1964) *Developmental Dyslexia*, London: William Heinemann Medical Books.

Crocker, M.W. (1999) 'Mechanisms for sentence processing', in S. Garrod and M. Pickering (eds) *Language Processing*, Hove: Psychology Press.

Crowley, T. (1996) *Language in History: Theories and Texts*, London: Routledge.

Cruse, D.A. (1973) 'Some thoughts on agentivity', *Journal of Linguistics* 9: 1–23.

—— (1975) 'Hyponymy and lexical hierarchies', *Archivum Linguisticum* 6: 26–31.

—— (1986) *Lexical Semantics*, Cambridge: Cambridge University Press.

Cruttenden, A. (1986) *Intonation*, Cambridge: Cambridge University Press; 2nd edition 1997.

Crystal, D. (1979) *Prosodic Systems and Intonation in English*, London: Cambridge University Press.

—— (1980) *An Introduction to Language Pathology*, London: Edward Arnold.

—— (1981a) *Directions in Applied Lingusitics*, London: Academic Press.

—— (1981b) *Linguistics* revised edition, Harmondsworth: Penguin.

—— (1985) *A Dictionary of Linguistics and Phonetics*, 2nd edition, updated and enlarged, Oxford: Basil Blackwell, in association with André Deutsch.

—— and Davy, D. (1969) *Investigating English Style*, London and Harlow: Longmans, Green & Co.

—— and Varley, R. (1993) *Introduction to Language Pathology*, 3rd edition, London: Whurr.

——, Fletcher, P. and Garman, M. (1976) *The Grammatical Analysis of Language Disability*, London: Edward Arnold.

Culler, J. (1976/1986) *Saussure*, London: Fontana.

Cummings, M. and Simmons, R. (1983) *The Language of Literature: A Stylistic Introduction to the Study of Literature*, Oxford: Pergamon Press.

Cummins, J. (2000) *Language, Power and Pedagogy: Bilingual Children in the Crossfire*, Clevedon: Multilingual Matters.

Cutler, A. (1989) 'Auditory lexical access: where do we start?', in W. Marslen-Wilson (ed.) *Lexical Representation and Process*, Cambridge, MA: MIT Press.

——, Mehler, J., Norris, D. and Segui, J. (1986) 'The syllable's differing role in the segmentation of French and English', *Journal of Memory and Language* 25: 385–400.

——, ——, —— and —— (1992) 'The non-bilingual nature of speech segmentation in bilinguals', *Cognitive Psychology* 24: 381–410.

Dalrymple, M. and Kaplan, R.M. (2000) *Language* 76(4): 759–98.

——, Maxwell, J.T. III and Zaenen, A. (eds) (1995) *Formal Issues in Lexical Functional Grammar*, Stanford: CSLI Publications.

Darwin, C. (1859/1964) *On the Origin of Species*, facsimile edition, Cambridge, MA: Harvard University Press.

—— (1877) 'A biographical sketch of an infant', *Mind* 2: 252–9.

Davidsen-Nielsen, N. (1978) *Neutralization and Archiphoneme: Two Phonological Concepts and Their History*, Copenhagen: Akademisk Forlag.

Davidson, D. (1967) 'Truth and meaning', *Synthese* 17: 304–23; reprinted in D. Davidson (1984) *Inquiries into Truth and Interpretation*, Oxford: Clarendon Press.

—— (1973) 'Radical interpretation', *Dialectica*: 313–28; reprinted in D. Davidson (1984) *Inquiries into Truth and Interpretation*, Oxford: Clarendon Press.

—— (1986) 'A nice derangement of epitaphs', in E. LePore (ed.) *Truth and Interpretation: Perspectives on the Philosophy of Donald Davidson*, Oxford: Basil Blackwell.

Davies, C. (1981) 'Ysgolion Cymraig', *Education*: 3–13.

Davies, M. and Ravelli, L. (eds) (1992) *Advances in Systemic Linguistics: Recent Theory and Practice*, London and New York: Pinter.

Davis, F. (1937) *The Development of Linguistic Skills in Twins, Singletons with Siblings, and Only Children from Age Five to Ten Years* (Institute of Child Welfare Monograph Series, no. 14), Minneapolis: University of Minnesota.

Davis, G.A. (2000) *Aphasiology: Disorders and Clinical Practice*, Boston, MA: Allyn and Bacon.

Davis, T. (1994) 'ESDA and the analysis of contested contemporaneous notes of police interviews', *Forensic Linguistics* 1(1): 71–90.

Day, E. (1932) 'The development of language in twins: 1. A comparison of twins and single children; 2. The development of twins: their resemblances and differences', *Child Development* 3: 179–99.

Day, R. (ed.) (1980) *Issues in English Creoles*, Heidelberg: Julius Groos.

DeCamp, D. (1971a) 'The study of pidgins and creole languages', in D. Hymes (ed.) *Pidginization and Creolization of Languages*, proceedings of a conference, University of the West Indies, April 1968, Cambridge: Cambridge University Press.

—— (1971b) 'Towards a generative analysis of a post-creole continuum', in D. Hymes (ed.) *Pidginization and Creolization of Languages*, proceedings of a conference, University of the West Indies, April 1968, Cambridge: Cambridge University Press.

DeHouwer, A. (1995) 'Bilingual language acquisition', in P. Fletcher and B. Macwhinney (eds) *The Handbook of Child Language*, Oxford: Blackwell Publishers.

Delgutte, B. and Kiang, N.Y.S. (1984) 'Speech coding in the auditory nerve: I. Vowel-like sounds', *Journal of the Acoustical Society of America* 75: 866–78.

Dell, G.S. (1986) 'A spreading activation theory of retrieval in sentence production', *Psychological Review* 93: 283–321.

Deuchar, M. (1984) *British Sign Language*, London: Routledge & Kegan Paul.

—— (1996/1999) 'Spoken language and sign language', in A. Lock and C.R. Peters (eds) *Handbook of Human Symbolic Evolution*, Oxford: Blackwell Publishers; 1st edition 1996, Oxford: Oxford University Press.

Di Sciullo, A.M. and Williams, E. (1987) *On the Definition of Word*, Cambridge, MA: MIT Press.

Dik, S.C. (1978) *Functional Grammar* (North Holland Linguistics Series, no. 37), Amsterdam: North Holland.

—— (1980) 'Seventeen sentences: basic principles and application of functional grammar', in E.A. Moravcsik and J.R. Wirth (eds) *Syntax and Semantics* vol. 13, *Current Approaches to Syntax*, New York and London: Academic Press.

Dimond, S.J. and Beaumont, J.G. (1974) *Hemisphere Function in the Human Brain*, London: Elek Science.

Dinneen, F.P. (1967) *An Introduction to General Linguistics*, New York: Holt, Rinehart and Winston.

Dinnsen, D.A. (ed.) (1979) *Current Approaches to Phonological Theory*, Bloomington: Indiana University Press.

Diringer, D. (1968) *The Alphabet: A Key to the History of Mankind*, 3rd edition, 2 vols, London: Hutchinson.

Dirven, R. (ed.) (1989) *A User's Grammar of English: Word, Sentence, Text, Interaction*, Frankfurt-am-Main: Peter Lang.

—— (1994) *Metaphor and Nation: Metaphors Afrikaners Live by*, Frankfurt-am-Main: Peter Lang.

—— and Fried, V. (eds) (1987) *Functionalism in Linguistics*, Amsterdam and Philadelphia: John Benjamins.

—— and Radden, G. (eds) (1987) *Fillmore's Case Grammar: A Reader*, Heidelberg: Julius Groos.

—— and Vanparys, J. (eds) (1995) *Current Approaches to the Lexicon*, Frankfurt-am-Main: Peter Lang.

—— and Verspoor, M. (eds) (1998) *Cognitive Exploration of Language and Linguistics*, Amsterdam: John Benjamins.

Dominicy, M. (1984) *La Naissance de la grammaire moderne*, Brussels: Márdaga.

Donegan, P. and Stampe, D. (1979) 'The study of natural phonology', in D. Dinnsen (ed.) *Current Approaches to Phonological Theory*, Bloomington: Indiana University Press.

Donohue, C. and Sag, I.A. (1999) 'Domains in Walpiri', paper presented at HPSG-99, Edinburgh.

Donzé, R. (1971) *La Grammaire générale et raisonnée de Port Royal*, 2nd edition, Berne: A. Francke.

Dorian, N. (1981) *Language Death*, Philadelphia: University of Pennsylvania Press.

—— (1989) *Investigating Obsolence: Studies in Language Contraction and Death*, Cambridge: Cambridge University Press.

Dougherty, R. (1970) 'Recent studies on language universals', *Foundations of Language* 6: 505–61.

Dowty, D.R. (1982) 'Grammatical relations and Montague Grammar', in G.K. Pullum and P. Jacobson (eds) *The Nature of Syntactic Representation*, Dordrecht: Reidel.

——, Wall, R.E. and Peters, S. (1981) *Introduction to Montague Semantics*, Dordrecht: Reidel.

Dressler, W.U. (1985) 'On the predictiveness of natural morphology', *Journal of Linguistics* 21: 321–37.

—— (1986) 'Explanation in natural morphology, illustrated with comparative and agent-noun formation', *Linguistics* 24: 519–48.

Drew, P. and Heritage, J. (eds) (1992) *Talk at Work: Interaction in Institutional Settings*, Cambridge: Cambridge University Press.

Dudley-Evans, A. (1994) 'Genre analysis: an approach to text analysis for ESP', in M. Coulthard (ed.) *Advances in Written Text Analysis*, London: Routledge.

—— and St John, M.J. (1998) *Developments in ESP: A Multidisciplinary Approach*, Cambridge: Cambridge University Press.

Duffy, F.H. *et al.* (1980) 'Dyslexia: automated diagnosis by computerised classification of brain electrical activity', *Annals of Neurology* 7(5): 421–8.

Dulay, H. and Burt, M. (1972) 'Goofing: an indicator of children's second language learning strategies', *Language Learning* 22(2): 235–51.

—— (1973) 'Should we teach children syntax?', *Language Learning* 23(2): 245–58.

—— (1974a) 'Errors and strategies in child second language acquisition', *TESOL Quarterly* 8(2): 129–36.

—— (1974b) 'Natural sequences in child second language', *Language Learning* 24(1): 37–53.

—— (1974c) 'You can't learn without goofing: an analysis of children's second language "errors"', in J. Richards (ed.) *Error Analysis: Perspectives on Second Language Acquisition*, London: Longman.

Dummett, M. (1973) *Frege: Philosophy of Language*, London: Duckworth.

Durand, J. (1990) *Generative and Non-Linear Phonology*, London: Longman.

Durrant, J.D. and Lopovrinic, J.H. (1995) *Bases of Hearing Science*, 3rd edition, Baltimore: Lippincott, Willimas and Wilkins.

Eagleton, T. (1983) *Literary Theory: An Introduction*, Oxford: Basil Blackwell.

Eakins, B.W. and Eakins, R.G. (1978) *Sex Differences in Human Communication*, Boston, MA: M. Houghton Mifflin.

Earley, J. (1970) 'An efficient context-free parsing algorithm', *Communications ACM* 6(8): 451–5.

Eckersley, C.F. (1938–42) *Essential English for Foreign Students*, London: Longman.

Eckert, P. (2000) *Linguistic Variation as Social Practice*, Oxford: Blackwell Publishers.

Eco, U. (1984) *Semiotics and the Philosophy of Language*, London and Basingstoke: Macmillan.

Edwards, J.R. (1994) *Multilingualism*, London and New York: Routledge.

Edwards, S., Fletcher, P., Garman, M., Hughes, A., Letts, C. and Sinka, I. (1997) *The Reynell Developmental Language Scales III*, Windsor: NFER-Nelson.

Eimas, P.D., Siqueland, E.R., Jusczyk, P. and Vigorito, J. (1971) 'Speech perception in infants', *Science* 171: 303–6.

Ekman, P. and Friesen, W. (1969) 'The repertoire of non-verbal behavior: categories, origins, usage and coding', *Semiotica* 1(1): 49–98.

Ellis, A.J. (1889) *On Early English Pronunciation part 5, The Existing Phonology of English Dialects*, London: Trübner.

Ellis, R. (1994) *The Study of Second Language Acquisition*, Oxford: Oxford University Press.

Elyan, O., Smith, P., Giles, H. and Bourhis, R. (1978) 'RP-accented female speech: the voice of perceived androgyny?', in P. Trudgill (ed.) *Sociolinguistic Patterns in British English*, London: Edward Arnold.

Emonds, J.E. (1976) *A Transformational Approach to English Syntax*, New York: Academic Press.

Enderby, P. and Philipp, R. (1986) 'Speech and language handicap: towards knowing the size of the problem', *British Journal of Disorders of Communication* 21(2): 151–65.

Espir, M.L.E. and Rose, F.C. (1983) *The Basic Neurology of Speech and Language*, 3rd edition, Oxford: Blackwell Scientific.

Eubank, L. (1993/1994) 'On the transfer of parametric values in L2 development', *Language Acquisition* 3: 283–308.

—— (1996) 'Negation in early German–English interlanguage: more valueless features in the L2 initial state', *Second Language Research* 12: 73–106.

Evnine, S. (1991) *Donald Davidson*, Stanford: Stanford University Press.

Ewer, J.R. and Latorre, C. (1969) *Course in Basic Scientific English*, London: Longman.

Fabri, R., Ortman, A. and Parodi, T. (eds) (1998) *Models of Inflection*, Tübingen: Niemeyer.

Fairclough, N. (1989) *Language and Power*, Harlow: Longman.

—— (1992a) *Discourse and Social Change*, Cambridge: Polity Press.

—— (1992b) 'Introduction', in N. Fairclough (ed.) *Critical Language Awareness*, London: Longman.

—— (1995) *Critical Discourse Analysis: The Critical Study of Language*, London: Longman.

—— (2000) *New Labour, New Language*, London: Routledge.

—— and Wodak, R. (1997) 'Critical discourse analysis', in T. van Dijk (ed.) *Discourse as Social Interaction*, London: Sage.

Farrar, F.W. (1870) *Families of Speech*, London: Longmans & Green.

Fasold, R. (1984) *The Sociolinguistics of Society*, Oxford: Basil Blackwell.

—— (1990) *The Sociolinguistics of Language*, Oxford: Basil Blackwell.

Fauconnier, G. (1985/1994) *Mental Spaces: Aspects of Meaning Construction in Natural Language*, Cambridge: Cambridge University Press.

—— (1997) *Mappings in Thought and Language*, New York: Cambridge University Press.

—— and Sweetser, E. (eds) (1996) *Spaces, Worlds and Grammars*, Chicago: University of Chicago Press.

Fawcett, R.P. (1974) 'Some proposals for systemic syntax, Part 1', *MALS Journal* 1: 1–15.

—— (1975) 'Some proposals for systemic syntax, Part 2', *MALS Journal* 2(1): 43–68.

—— (1976) 'Some proposals for systemic syntax, Part 3', *MALS Journal* 2(2): 35–68.

Ferguson, C.A. (1959) 'Diglossia', *Word* 15: 325–40.

—— and Heath, S.B. (eds) (1981) *Language in the USA*, Cambridge: Cambridge University Press.

Ferreira, F. and Henderson, J.M. (1990) 'The use of verb information in syntactic parsing: evidence from eye movements and word-by-word self-paced reading', *Journal of Experimental Psychology: Language, Memory, and Cognition* 16: 555–68.

Fiez, J.A., Raichle, M.C., Balota, D.A., Tallal, P. and Petersen, S.E. (1996) 'PET activation of posterior temporal regions during auditory word presentation and verb generation', *Cerebral Cortex* 6: 1–10.

Figueroa, E. (1994) *Sociolinguistic Metatheory*, Oxford: Pergamon Press.

Fikes, R.E. and Nilsson, N. (1971) 'STRIPS: a new approach to the application of theorem proving to problem solving', *Artificial Intelligence* 2: 189–208.

Fillmore, C.J. (1966) 'A proposal concerning English prepositions', *Monograph Series on Languages and Linguistics* 19: 19–34.

—— (1968) 'The case for case', in E. Bach and R.T. Harms (eds) *Universals in Linguistic Theory*, New York: Holt, Rinehart and Winston.

—— (1969) 'Toward a modern theory of case', in D. Reibel and S. Schane (eds) *Modern Studies in English*, Englewood Cliffs, NJ: Prentice Hall.

—— (1971a) 'Some problems for case grammar', *Monograph Series on Languages and Linguistics* 24.

—— (1971b) 'Types of lexical information', in D. Steinberg and L. Jakobovits (eds) *Semantics: An Interdisciplinary Reader*, Cambridge: Cambridge University Press.

—— (1973) 'May we come in?', *Semiotica* 9: 98–115; and (1997) *Lectures on Deixis*, Stanford, CA: CSLI Publications.

—— (1975) *Santa Cruz Lectures on Deixis*, Bloomington, IN: Indiana University Linguistics Club.

—— (1977) 'The case for case reopened', in P. Cole and J.M. Sadock (eds) *Sytax and Semantics*, vol. 8, *Grammatical Relations*, New York: Academic Press.

—— (1982) 'Towards a descriptive framework for spatial deixis', in R.J. Jarvella and W. Klein (eds) *Speech, Place and Action*, New York: John Wiley and Sons.

—— (1990) *Construction Grammar: Course Reader for Linguistics 120A*, Berkeley: University of California Press.

—— and Kay, P. (in progress) *Construction Grammar*, Stanford, CA: CSLI Publications.

——, —— and O'Connor, C. (1988) 'Regularity and idiomaticity in grammatical construction: the case of *let alone*', *Language* 64: 501–38.

Firbas, J. (1992) 'On some basic problems of Functional Sentence Perspective', in M. Davies and L. Ravelli (eds) *Advances in Systemic Linguistics: Recent Theory and Practice*, London and New York: Printer.

Firth, J.R. (1930/1964) *The Tongues of Men and Speech*, London: Oxford University Press.

—— (1946/1957a) 'The English School of Phonetics', in *Papers in Linguistics 1934–1951*, London: Oxford University Press; first published in *Transactions of the Philological Society*.

—— (1950/1957b) 'Personality and language in society', in *Papers in Linguistics 1934–1951*, London: Oxford University Press; first published in *The Sociological Review* 42(2).

—— (1957c) *Papers in Linguistics 1934–1951*, London: Oxford University Press.

—— (1957d) *A Synopsis of Linguistic Theory 1930–55* (Special Volume of the Philological Society), Oxford: Basil Blackwell.

—— (1968) *Selected Papers of J.R. Firth*, ed. F.R. Palmer, London: Longman.

Fischer-Jørgensen, E. (1967a) 'Form and substance in glossematics', *Acta Linguistica Hafniensia* 10: 1–33.

—— (1967b) 'Introduction' to H.J. Uldall, *Outline of Glossematics* (Travaux du Cercle Linguistique de Copenhague, X_1), 2nd edition, Copenhagen: Nordisk Sprog-og Kulturforlag.

Fisher, M. (1934) *Language Patterns of Preschool Children* (Child Development Monographs, no. 15), New York: Teachers' College Press, Columbia University.

Fishman, J.A. (1971) *Sociolinguistics: A Brief Introduction*, Rowley, MA: Newbury House.

—— (1980) 'Bilingualism and biculturalism as individual and as societal phenomena', *Journal of Multilingual and Multicultural Development* 1: 3–15.

—— (ed.) (1999) *Handbook of Language and Ethnic Identity*, New York: Oxford University Press.

Fishman, P. (1980) 'Conversational insecurity', in H. Giles, W.P. Robinson and P.M. Smith (eds) *Language: Social Psychological Perspectives*, Oxford: Pergamon Press.

Flege, J.E. (1992) 'Speech learning in a second language', in C. Ferguson, L. Menn and C. Stoel-Garnman (eds) *Phonological Development: Models, Research and Applications*, Parkton, MD: York Press.

—— (1995) 'Second-language speech learning: theory, findings and problems', in W. Strange (ed.) *Speech Perception and Linguistic Experience: Theoretical and Methodological Issues*, Timonium, MD: York Press.

—— and Hillenbrand, J. (1986) 'Differential use of temporal cues to the /s/–/z/ contrast by native and non-native speakers of English', *Journal of the Acoustical Society of America* 79: 508–17.

——, MacKay, I.R.A. and Meador, D. (1999) 'Native Italian speakers' production and perception of English vowels', *Journal of the Acoustical Society of America* 106: 2973–87.

Fodor, J.A. (1983) *The Modularity of Mind*, Cambridge, MA: MIT Press.

—— and Katz, J. (eds) (1964) *The Structure of Language: Readings in the Philosophy of Language*, Englewood Cliffs, NJ: Prentice Hall.

Fodor, J.D. (1989) 'Empty categories in sentence processing', *Language and Cognitive Processes* 4(3/4): 155–209.

—— and Frazier, L. (1980) 'Is the human sentence parsing mechanism an ATN?', *Cognition* 8: 417–59.

Foley, W.A. (1988) 'Language birth: the processes of pidginization and creolization', in F.J. Newmeyer (ed.) *Linguistics: The Cambridge Survey* vol. 4, *Language: The Socio-Cultural Context*, Cambridge: Cambridge University Press.

Forster, K.I. (1976) 'Accessing the mental lexicon', in R.J. Wales and C.T. Walker (eds) *New Approaches to Language Mechanisms*, Amsterdam: North Holland.

—— (1979) 'Levels of processing and the structure of the language processor', in W.E. Cooper and E.C.T. Walker (eds) *Sentence Processing: Psycholinguistic Studies Presented to Merril Garrett*, Hillsdale, NJ: Lawrence Erlbaum Associates.

—— (1981) 'Priming and the effects of sentence and lexical contexts on naming time: evidence for autonomous lexical processing', *Quarterly Journal of Experimental Psychology* 33A: 465–95.

Foster, M.L. (1996/1999) 'The reconstruction of the evolution of human spoken language', in A. Lock and C.R. Peters (eds) *Handbook of Human Symbolic Evolution*, Oxford: Blackwell Publishers; first published 1996, Oxford: Oxford University Press.

Foucault, M. (1966) *Les Mots et Les Choses*, Paris: Gallimard.

—— (1972) *The Archaeology of Knowledge*, London: Tavistock.

—— (1977) *Discipline and Punish: The Birth of the Prison*, London: Allan Lane.

Fouts, R. and Rigby, R. (1977) 'Man–chimpanzee communication', in T.A. Sebeok (ed.) *How Animals Communicate*, Bloomington and London: Indiana University Press.

Fowler, C.A. (1986) 'An event approach to the study of speech perception from a direct-realist perspective', *Journal of Phonetics* 14: 3–28.

Fowler, R. (1967) 'Literature and linguistics', *Essays in Criticism* 17: 322–47.

—— (1968) 'Language and literature', *Essays in Criticism* 18: 164–82.

—— (1971) *The Languages of Literature*, London: Routledge & Kegan Paul.

—— (1977) *Linguistics and the Novel*, London: Methuen.

—— (1991) *Language in the News: Discourse and Ideology in the Press*, London: Routledge.

—— , Hodge, R., Kress, G. and Trew, T. (1979) *Language and Control*, London: Routledge & Kegan Paul.

Fox, A. (1984) *German Intonation: An Outline*, Oxford: Clarendon Press.

—— (1990) *The Structure of German*, Oxford: Clarendon Press.

—— (1995) *Linguistic Reconstruction: An Introduction to Theory and Method*, Oxford: Oxford University Press.

—— (2000) *Prosodic Features and Prosodic Structure: The Phonology of Suprasegmentals*, Oxford: Oxford University Press.

Francis, W.N. (1958) *The Structure of American English*, New York: Ronald.

—— (1983) *Dialectology*, London: Longman.

—— and Kucera, H. (1964) *A Manual of Information to Accompany a Standard Sample of Present-Day Edited American English, for Use with Digital Computers*, Providence, RI: Linguistics Department, Brown University; revised editions 1971, 1979.

Frazier, L. (1987) 'Sentence processing: a tutorial review', in M. Coltheart (ed.) *Attention and Performance XII: The Psychology of Reading*, Hove: Lawrence Erlbaum Associates, pp. 559–86.

—— (1995) 'Constraint satisfaction as a theory of sentence processing', *Psycholinguistic Research* 24(2): 437–68.

—— and Clifton, C. (1989) 'Identifying gaps in English sentences', *Language and Cognitive Processes* 4: 93–126.

Frege, G. (1891/1977a) 'Function and concept', address to the Jenaische Gesellschaft für Medizin und Naturwissenschaft, 9 January 1891; English trans. in P. Geach and M. Black (eds) (1977) *Translations from the Philosophical Writings of Gottlob Frege*, Oxford: Basil Blackwell.

—— (1892/1977b) 'On concept and object', *Vierteljahrsschrift für wissenschaftlische Philosophie* 16: 192–205; English trans. in P. Geach and M. Black (eds) (1977) *Translations from the Philosophical Writings of Gottlob Frege*, Oxford: Basil Blackwell.

—— (1892/1977c) 'On sense and reference', *Zeitschrift für Philosophie und philosophische Kritik* 100: 25–50; English trans. in P. Geach and M. Black (eds) (1977) *Translations from the Philosophical Writings of Gottlob Frege*, Oxford: Basil Blackwell.

Freidin (1996) 'Generative grammar: principles and parameters', in E.K. Brown and J. Miller (eds) *A Concise Encyclopaedia of Syntactic Theories*, Oxford: Pergamon Press.

Friedman, J (1969), 'Directed random generation of sentences', *Communications ACM* 12: 40–6.

—— (1971) *A Computer Model of Transformational Grammar*, New York: American Elsevier.

Fries, C.C. (1952/1957) *The Structure of English: An Introduction to the Construction of English Sentences*, New York: Harcourt Brace Jovanovich, and London: Longman.

—— (1961/1962) 'The Bloomfield "School"', in C. Mohrmann, A. Sommerfelt and J. Whatmough (eds) *Trends in European and American Linguistics 1930–1960*, Cambridge, MA, Ninth International Congress of Linguistics and (1962) Utrecht: Spectrum.

Frisch, K. von (1967) *The Dance Language and Orientation of Bees*, Cambridge, MA: Harvard University Press.

Fromkin, V.A. (ed.) (1978) *Tone: A Linguistic Survey*, New York: Academic Press.

Fry, D.B. (1979) *The Physics of Speech*, Cambridge: Cambridge University Press.

——, Abramson, A.S., Eimas, P.D. and Lieberman, A.M. (1962) 'The identification and discrimination of synthetic vowels', *Language and Speech* 5: 171–89.

Fudge, E. (ed.) (1973) *Phonology*, Harmondsworth: Penguin.

Funnell, E. (1983) 'Phonological processes in reading: new evidence from acquired dyslexia', *British Journal of Psychology* 74: 159–80.

Ganong, W.F. (1980) 'Phonetic categorization in auditory word perception', *Journal of Experimental Psychology: Human Perception and Performance* 6: 110–25.

Garding, E. (1973) *The Scandinavian Word Accents* (Lund University Working Papers, no. 8), Lund: Lund University Press.

Gardner, B.T. (1981) 'Project Nim: who taught whom?', *Contemporary Psychology* 26: 425–6.

Gardner, R.A. and Gardner, B.T. (1971) 'Two-way communication with an infant chimpanzee', in A.M. Schrier and F. Stollnitz (eds) *Behavior of Non-Human Primates*, New York: Academic Press.

—— (1978) 'Comparative psychology and language acquisition', *Annals of the New York Academy of Sciences* 309: 37–76.

Garfinkel, H. (1967) *Studies in Ethnomethodology*, Englewood Cliffs, NJ: Prentice Hall.

—— (1974) 'On the origins of the term "ethnomethodology"', in R. Turner (ed.) *Ethnomethodology*, Harmondsworth: Penguin.

Garnham, A. (1985) *Psycholinguistics: Central Topics*, London and New York: Methuen.

—— (1999) 'Reference and anaphora', in S. Garrod and M. Pickering (eds) *Language Processing*, Hove: Psychology Press.

—— and Oakhill, J. (1992) 'Discourse processing and text representation from a "mental models" perspective', *Language and Cognitive Processes* 7: 193–204.

Garnsey, S.M., Pearlmutter, N.J., Myers, E. and Lotocky, M.A. (1997) 'The contributions of verb bias and plausibility to the comprehension of temporarily ambiguous sentences', *Journal of Memory and Language* 37: 58–93.

Garrett, M. F. (1990) 'Sentence processing', in D.H. Osherson and H. Lasnik (eds) *An Invitation to Cognitive Science*, vol. 1, Cambridge, MA: MIT Press.

Garrod, S. and Pickering, M. (1999) *Language Processing*, Hove: Psychology Press.

—— and Sanford, A. (1990) 'Referential processes in reading: focusing on roles and individuals', in D.A. Balota, G.B. Flores d'Arcais and K. Rayner (eds) *Comprehension Processes in Reading*, Hillsdale, NJ: Lawrence Erlbaum Associates.

Garside, R. and Leech, G. (1987) 'The UCREL probabilistic parsing system', in R. Garside, G. Leech and G. Sampson (eds) *The Computational Analysis of English: A Corpus-Based Approach*, London: Longman.

——, Leech, G. and McEnery, T. (eds) (1997) *Corpus Annotation: Linguistic Information from Computer Text Corpora*, London: Longman.

Garvin, P.L. (ed.) (1964) *A Prague School Reader on Esthetics, Literary Structure and Style*, Washington, DC: Georgetown University Press.

Gathercole, S. and Baddeley, A. (1993) *Working Memory and Language*, Hove: Lawrence Erlbaum Associates.

Gazdar, G. (1981) 'Unbounded dependencies and coordinate structure', *Linguistic Inquiry* 12: 155–84.

—— (1987) 'Generative grammar', in J. Lyons, R. Coates, M. Deuchar and G. Gazdar (eds) *New Horizons in Linguistics*, vol. 2, Harmondsworth: Penguin.

——, Klein, E., Pullum, G. and Sag, I. (1985) *Generalised Phrase Structure Grammar*, Oxford: Basil Blackwell, and Cambridge, MA: Harvard University Press.

Gazzaniga, M.S. (1974) 'Cerebral dominance viewed as a decision-system', in S.J. Dimond and J.G. Beaumont (eds) *Hemisphere Function in the Human Brain*, London: Elek Science.

Geeraerts, D. (1985) *Paradigm and Paradox: Explorations into a Paradigmatic Theory of Meaning and its Epistemological Background*, Leuven: Leuven University Press.

—— (1989) 'Prospects and problems of prototype theory', *Linguistics* 27: 587–612.

Gelb, I.J. (1963) *A Study of Writing*, revised edition, Chicago and London: University of Chicago Press.

Georges, R. and Jones, M. (1980) *People Studying People*, Berkeley: University of California Press.

Gernsbacher, M.A. (1994) *Handbook of Psycholinguistics*, San Diego: Academic Press.

—— and Foertsch, J.A. (1999) 'Three models of discourse comprehension', in S. Garrod and M. Pickering (eds) *Language Processing*, Hove: Psychology Press.

Geschwind, N. (1982) 'Biological foundations of dyslexia', paper presented to BPS Cognitive Psychology Section Conference on Dyslexia, Manchester, England.

Gibbon, D., Moore, R. and Winski, R. (1998) *Handbook of Standards and Resources for Spoken Language Systems*, Berlin: Mouton de Gruyter.

Gibbons, J. (ed.) (1994) *Language and the Law*, London: Longman.

Gibbs, R. (1994) *The Poetics of Mind*, Cambridge: Cambridge University Press.

Gibson, K.R. (1988) 'Brain size and the evolution of language', in M. Landsberg (ed.) *The Genesis of Language: A Different Judgement of Evidence*, The Hague: Mouton.

—— (1996/1999) 'The ontogeny and evolution of the brain, cognition, and language', in A. Lock and C.R. Peters (eds) *Handbook of Human Symbolic Evolution*, Oxford: Blackwell Publishers; 1st edition 1996, Oxford: Oxford University Press.

Giddens, A. (1991) *Modernity and Self-Identity: Self and Society in the Late Modern Age*, Cambridge: Polity Press.

Giglioli, P.P. (1972) *Language and Social Context: Selected Readings*, Harmondsworth: Penguin.

Giles, H. and Coupland, N. (1991) *Language: Contexts and Consequences*, Buckingham: Open University Press.

—— and Robinson, W.P. (eds) (1990) *Handbook of Language and Social Psychology*, Chichester: John Wiley & Sons.

Gilliéron, J. and Edmont, E. (1902–10) *Atlas linguistique de la France*, Paris: Champion.

Gleitman, L. (1990) 'The structural sources of verb meaning', *Language Acquisition* 1: 3–55.

Glenberg, A.M., Kruley, P. and Langston, W.M. (1994) 'Analogical processes in comprehension: simulation of a mental model', in M.A. Gernsbacher (ed.) *Handbook of Psycholinguistics*, San Diego: Academic Press.

Glushko, R.J. (1979) 'The organization and activation of orthographic knowledge in reading aloud', *Journal of Experimental Psychology: Human Perception and Performance* 5: 674–91.

Goatley, A. (1997) *The Language of Metaphors*, London: Routledge.

Goffman, E. (1959) *The Presentation of Self in Everyday Life*, New York: Anchor Books.

—— (1967) *Interaction Ritual: Essays on Face-to-Face Behavior*, New York: Doubleday.

Goldberg, A.E. (1992) 'The inherent semantics of argument structure: the case of the English ditransitive construction', *Cognitive Linguistics* 3: 37–74.

—— (1995) *Construction Grammar Approach to Argument Structure*, Chicago: University of Chicago Press.

—— (ed.) (1996) *Conceptual Structure, Discourse and Language*, Stanford, CA: CSLI Publications.

Goldsmith, J. (1976) *Autosegmental Phonology*, Ph.D. MIT, distributed by Indiana University Linguistics Club.

—— (1989) *Autosegmental and Metrical Phonology*, Oxford: Blackwell Publishers.

Goldstein, U. (1979) 'Modeling children's vocal tracts', paper presented at the 97th Meeting of the Acoustical Society of America, Cambridge, MA, June.

Goodglass. H. (1993) *Understanding Aphasia*, San Diego: Academic Press.

Goodluck, H. (1991) *Language Acquisition*, Oxford: Blackwell Publishers.

Goodman, M. (1984) 'Are creole structures innate?', *The Behavioral and Brain Sciences* 7(2): 193–4.

Gosling, J.N. (198la) *Discourse Kinesics* (English Language Research Monograph, no. 10), University of Birmingham.

—— (1981b) 'Kinesics in discourse', in M. Coulthard and M. Montgomery (eds), *Studies in Discourse Analysis*, London: Routledge & Kegan Paul.

Grabe, W. (1992) 'Applied linguistics and linguistics', in W. Grabe and R.B. Kaplan (eds) *Introduction to Applied Linguistics*, Reading, MA: Addison Wesley.

—— and Kaplan, R.B. (eds) (1992) *Introduction to Applied Linguistics*, Reading, MA: Addison Wesley.

Graesser, A.C., Singer, M. and Trabasso, T. (1994) 'Constructing inferences during narrative text comprehension', *Psychological Review* 101: 371–95.

Graham, A. (1975) 'The making of a non-sexist dictionary', in B. Thorne and N. Henley (eds) *Language and Sex: Difference and Dominance*, Rowley, MA: Newbury House.

Granger, S. (1996) 'From CA to CIA and back: an integrated approach to computerized bilingual and learner corpora', in K. Aijmer, B. Altenberg and M. Johansson (eds) *Languages in Contrast: Papers from a Symposium on Text-Based Cross-Linguistic Studies, Lund 4–5 March 1994*, Lund: Lund University Press.

Grassmann, H. (1863) 'Über die Aspiranten und ihr gleichzeitiges Vorhandensein im An- und Auslaute der Wurzeln', *Zeitschrift für vergleichende Sprachforschung auf dem Gebiete des Deutschen, Griechischen und Lateinischen* 12(2): 81–138.

Grayling, A.C. (1982) *An Introduction to Philosophical Logic*, Brighton, Sussex: Harvester Press.

Greenbaum, S. (1970) *Verb Intensifiers in English: An Experimental Approach*, The Hague: Mouton.

—— (ed.) (1996) *Comparing English Worldwide: The International Corpus of English*, Oxford: Clarendon Press.

Greenberg, J.H. (1954) 'A quantitative approach to the morphological typology of language', in R.F. Spencer (ed.) *Method and Perspective in Anthropology*, Minneapolis, University of Minnesota Press; reprinted (1960) in *International Journal of American Linguistics* 26(3): 178–94.

—— (ed.) (1963/1966a) *Universals of Language*, 2nd edition, Cambridge, MA and London: MIT Press, 1966.

—— (1966b) 'Some universals of grammar with particular reference to the order of meaningful elements', in J.H. Greenberg (ed.) *Universals of Language*, 2nd edition, Cambridge, MA, and London: MIT Press.

—— (1974) *Language Typology: A Historical and Analytic Overview* (Janua Linguarum, Series Minor, no. 184), The Hague: Mouton.

——, Osgood, C.E. and Jenkins, J.J. (1966) 'Memorandum concerning language universals: presented to the Conference on Language Universals, Gould House, Dobbs Ferry, NY, 13–15 April 1961', in J.H. Greenberg (ed.) *Universals of Language*, 2nd edition, Cambridge, MA, and London: MIT Press.

Greenspan, S.L. (1986) 'Semantic flexibility and referential specificity of concrete nouns', *Journal of Memory and Language* 25: 539–57.

Greimas, A.J. (1966) *Sémantique structurale*, Paris: Librairie Larousse.

Grice, H.P. (1957) 'Meaning', *Philosophical Review* 66: 377–88.

—— (1975) Logic and conversation', in P. Cole and J.L. Morgan (eds) *Syntax and Semantics* vol. 3, *Speech Acts*, New York: Academic Press; reprinted in edited form in A. Jaworski and N. Coupland (eds) (1999) *The Discourse Reader*, London: Routledge.

Griffiths, P. (1980) 'The Paget Gorman Sign System as an educational tool', *British Deaf News* 12: 258–60.

Grimm, J. (1822/1893) *Deutsche Grammatik*, Göttingen; reprinted 1893, Gütersloh Bertelmann.

Groenendijk, J. and Stokhof, M. (1991) 'Dynamis predicate logic', *Linguistics and Philosophy* 14: 39–100.

Grosjean, F (1985) 'The bilingual as a competent but specific speaker-hearer', *Journal of Multilingual and Multicultural Development* 6: 467–77.

—— (1992) 'Another view of bilingualism', *Cognitive Processing in Bilinguals* 83: 51–62.

—— (1994) 'Individual Bilingualism', in R.E. Asher and J.M. Simpson (eds) *The Encyclopedia of Language and Linguistics*, vol. 3, Oxford: Pergamon Press.

Grosz, B.J. and Sidner, C.L. (1986) 'Attention, intentions and the structure of discourse', *Computational Linguistics* 12(3): 175–205.

——, Joshi, A. and Weinstein, S. (1995) 'Centering: a framework for modeling the local coherence of discourse', *Computational Linguistics*: 175–204.

——, Sparck Jones, K. and Webber, B.L. (1986) *Readings in Natural Language Processing*, Los Altos: Morgan Kaufman.

Gu, Y. (1990) 'Politeness phenomena in modern Chinese', *Journal of Pragmatics* 14: 237–57.

Guilfoyle, E. and Noonan, M. (1992) 'Functional categories and language acquisition', *The Canadian Journal of Linguistics* 37: 241–72.

Gumperz, J.J. (ed.) (1982) *Language and Social Identity*, Cambridge: Cambridge University Press.

—— and Hymes, D. (eds) (1972/1986) *Directions in Sociolinguistics: The Ethnography of Communication*, Oxford: Basil Blackwell, and New York: Holt, Reinhart and Winston; 2nd edition 1986.

—— and Levinson, S.C. (eds) (1996) *Rethinking Linguistic Relativity*, Cambridge: Cambridge University Press.

Guttenplan, S. (1997) *The Languages of Logic*, Oxford: Blackwell Publishers.

Haas, W. (1960) 'Linguistic structures', *Word* 16: 251–76.

Haiman, J. (1980) 'Dictionaries and encyclopedias', *Lingua* 50: 329–57.

—— (ed.) (1985) *Iconicity in Syntax*, Amsterdam: John Benjamins.

—— (1986) *Natural Syntax: Iconicity and Erosion*, Cambridge: Cambridge University Press.

Hall, R.A., Jr (1962) 'The life cycle of pidgin languages', *Lingua* 11: 151–6.

—— (1966) *Pidgin and Creole Languages*, Ithaca: Cornell University Press.

—— (1972) 'Pidgins and creoles as standard languages', in J.B. Pride and J. Holmes (eds) *Sociolinguistics*, Harmondsworth: Penguin.

Halle, M. (1959) *The Sound Pattern of Russian*, The Hague: Mouton.

—— (1962) 'Phonology in generative grammar', *Word* 18: 54–72.

—— (1973) 'Prolegomena to a theory of word formation', *Linguistic Inquiry* 4: 3–16.

—— and Marantz, A. (1993) 'Distributed Morphology and the pieces of inflection', in K. Hale and S.J. Keyser (eds) *The View from Building 20*, Cambridge, MA: MIT Press.

—— and Stevens, K. (1962) 'Speech recognition: a model and a program for research', in J. Fodor and J. Katz (eds) *The Structure of Language: Readings in the Philosophy of Language*, Englewood Cliffs, NJ: Prentice Hall.

—— and Vergnaud, J.-R. (1987) *An Essay on Stress*, Cambridge, MA: MIT Press.

Halliday, M.A.K. (1956) 'Grammatical categories in modern Chinese', in *Transactions of the Philological Society*, pp. 177–224; reprinted in part in G. Kress (ed.) (1976) *Halliday: System and Function in Language: Selected Papers*, Oxford: Oxford University Press.

—— (1961) 'Categories of the theory of grammar', *Word* 17: 241–92.

—— (1966a) 'Lexis as a linguistic level', in C.E. Bazell, J.C. Catford, M.A.K. Halliday and H.R. Robins (eds) *In Memory of J.R. Firth*, London: Longman.

—— (1966b) 'Some notes on "deep" grammar', *Journal of Linguistics* 2: 56–67; reprinted in part in G. Kress (ed.) (1976) *Halliday: System and Function in Language: Selected Papers*, Oxford: Oxford University Press.

—— (1967) *Intonation and Grammar in British English*, The Hague: Mouton.

—— (1968) 'Notes on transitivity and theme in English, part 3', *Journal of Linguistics* 4: 179–215.

—— (1970) 'Language structure and language function', in J. Lyons (ed.) *New Horizons in Linguistics*, Harmondsworth: Penguin.

—— (1971) 'Linguistic function and literary style: an inquiry into the language of William

Golding's *The Inheritors*', in S. Chatman (ed.) *Literary Style: A Symposium*, London and New York: Oxford University Press.

—— (1973) *Explorations in the Functions of Language*, London: Edward Arnold.

—— (1975) *Learning How to Mean: Explorations in the Development of Language*, London: Edward Arnold.

—— (1978) *Language as Social Semiotic*, London: Edward Arnold.

—— (1983) 'Foreword' to M. Cummings and R. Simmons, *The Language of Literature: A Stylistic Introduction to the Study of Literature*, Oxford: Pergamon Press.

—— (1985/1994) *An Introduction to Functional Grammar*, London: Edward Arnold; 2nd edition 1994.

—— and Hasan, R. (1976/1989) *Cohesion in English*, London: Longman; 2nd edition 1989.

—— and —— (1989) *Language, Context and Text*, Oxford: Oxford University Press.

Halmos, P. (1960) *Naive Set Theory*, Princeton, NJ: Van Nostrand.

Harding, E. and Riley, P. (1986) *The Bilingual Family: A Handbook for Parents*, Cambridge: Cambridge University Press.

Harley, T.A. (1995) *The Psychology of Language: From Data to Theory*, Hove: Psychology Press.

Harman, G.H. (1963) 'Generative grammars without transformational rules', *Language* 39: 567–616.

Harris, R. (1981) *The Language Myth*, London: Duckworth.

—— (1987) *Reading Saussure*, London: Duckworth.

Harris, Z. (1942) 'Morpheme alternants in linguistic analysis', *Language* 18: 169–80.

—— (1946) 'From morphene to utterance', *Language* 22: 161–83.

—— (1951) *Methods in Structural Linguistics*, Chicago: University of Chicago Press.

—— (1952) 'Discourse analysis', *Language* 28: 1–30, 474–94.

Harrison, J.M. and Howe, M.E. (1974) 'Anatomy of the afferent auditory nervous system of mammals', in W.D. Keidel and W.D. Neff (eds) *Handbook of Sensory Physiology*, vol. 5, New York: Springer.

Harweg, R. (1968) *Pronomina und Textkonstitution*, Munich: Fink.

Hasan R. (1984) 'Coherence and cohesive harmony', in J. Flood (ed.) *Understanding Reading Comprehension*, Newark, DE: International Reading Association.

Haselrud, V. and Stenström, A.-B. (1995) 'The Bergen Corpus of London Teenager Language (COLT)', in G. Leech, G. Myers and J. Thomas (eds) (1995) *Spoken English on Computer: Transcription, Mark-Up and Application*, London: Longman.

Haugen, E. (1953) *The Norwegian Language in America: A Study in Bilingual Behavior*, Philadelphia: University of Philadelphia Press.

Hausmann, F.J. (1977) *Einführung in die Benutzung der neufranzösischen Wörterbücher*, Tübingen: Max Niemeyer.

Hawkins, J.A. (1988) 'Explaining language universals', in J.A. Hawkins (ed.) *Explaining Language Universals*, Oxford: Basil Blackwell.

Hayes, B. (1989) 'Compensatory lengthening in moraic phonology', *Linguistic Inquiry* 20: 253–306.

—— (1995) *Metrical Stress Theory*, Chicago: University of Chicago Press.

Hayes, K. and Hayes, C. (1952) 'Imitation in a home-raised chimpanzee', *Journal of Comparative and Physiological Psychology* 45: 450–9.

Hayward, R.J. (ed.) (1990) *Omotic Linguistics*, London: SOAS.

Heger, K. (1976) *Monem, Wart, Satz, und Text*, Tübingen: Niemeyer.

Heidolph, K.-E. (1966) 'Kontextbeziehungen zwischen Sätzen in einer generativen Grammatik', *Kybernetika* 2: 274–81.

Helmholtz, H. (1869) *Die Mechanik der Gehorknochelchen und des Trommelfells*, Bonn: M. Cohen.

Herbert, A.J. (1965) *The Structure of Technical English*, London: Longman.

Herder, J.G. (1891/1966) 'On the origin of language', in J.H. Moran and A. Gode (eds) *On the Origin of Language*, Chicago and London: University of Chicago Press.

Heritage, J. (1984) *Garfinkel and Ethnomethodology*, Oxford: Blackwell.

Hewes, G.W. (1996/1999) 'A history of the study of language origins and the gestural primacy hypothesis', in A. Lock and C.R. Peters (eds) *Handbook of Human Symbolic Evolution*, Oxford: Blackwell Publishers; first published 1996, Oxford: Oxford University Press.

Hewitt, C. (1971) 'PLANNER: a language for proving theorems in robots', Proceedings of the 2nd International Joint Conference on Artificial Intelligence, London, UK, September 1971, Los Altos, California: William Kaufmann, Inc.

Hickok, G., Canseco-Gonzalez, E., Zurif, E. and Grimshaw, J. (1992) 'Modularity in locating gaps', Journal of Psycholinguistic Research 21: 545–61.

Hill, A.A. (1958) Introduction to Linguistic Structures: From Sound to Sentence in English, New York: Harcourt Brace Jovanovich.

Hinshelwood, J. (1917) Congenital Dyslexia, London: Levis.

Hirst, D. and Di Cristo, A. (1998) (eds) Intonation Systems: A Survey of Twenty Languages, Cambridge: Cambridge University Press.

Hjelmslev, L. (1928) Principes de grammaire générale, Det Kgl. Danske (Videnskabernes Selskab, Historistfilologisk Meddelelser XVI. 1), Copenhagen: Høst.

—— (1935) La Catégorie de cas I, Aarhus: Universitetsforlaget.

—— (1938) 'Essai d'une théorie des morphèmes', Actes du 4ème Congrés International des Linguistes: 140–51; reprinted in L. Hjelmslev (1959) Essais linguistiques: Travaux du Cercle Linguistique de Copenhague, vol. 12, Copenhagen: Nordisk Sprog-og Kulturforlag.

—— (1943a) Omkring sprogteoriens grundlæggelse, Festskrift udgivet af Københavns Universitet i anledning af Universitetets Aarsfest, Copenhagen: University of Copenhagen; reprinted 1966 and 1976 Copenhagen: Akademisk Forlag.

—— (1943b) 'Langue et parole', Cahiers Ferdinand de Saussure 2: 29–44; reprinted in L. Hjelmslev (1959) Essais linguistiques: Travaux du Cercle Linguistique de Copenhague, vol. 12, Copenhagen: Nordisk Sprog-og Kulturforlag.

—— (1948) 'Structural analysis of language', Studia Linguistica: 69–78; reprinted in L. Hjelmslev (1959) Essais linguistiques: Travaux du Cercle Linguistique de Copenhague, vol. 12, Copenhagen: Nordisk Sprog-og Kulturforlag.

—— (1951) 'Grundtræk af det danske udtrykssystem med særligt henblik på stødet', in Selskab for nordisk filologis årsberetning for 1948-49-50: 12–24; published in English as 'Outline of the Danish expression system with special reference to the stød', trans. F.J. Whitfield, in L. Hjelmslev (1973a) Essais linguistiques II: Travaux du Cercle Linguistique de Copenhague, vol. 14, Copenhagen: Nordisk Sprog-og Kulturforlag.

—— (1953) Prolegomena to a Theory of Language, trans. F.J. Whitfield, International Journal of American Linguistics 1(1): memoir no. 7; 2nd revised edition 1967, Madison: University of Wisconsin Press.

—— (1954) 'La Stratification du langage', Word 10: 163–88; reprinted in L. Hjelmslev (1959) Essais linguistiques: Travaux du Cercle Linguistique de Copenhague, vol. 12, Copenhagen: Nordisk Sprog-og Kulturforlag.

—— (1959) Essais linguistiques: Travaux du Cercle Linguistique de Copenhague, vol. 12, Copenhagen: Nordisk Sprog-og Kulturforlag; 2nd edition, 1970.

—— (1963) Sproget, en introduktion, Copenhagen: Berlingske Leksikon Bibliotek; 2nd edn 1973; published in English as An Introduction to Linguistics, trans. F. Whitfield (1970) Language, Madison: University of Wisconsin Press.

—— (1973a) Essais linguistiques II: Travaux du Cercle Linguistique de Copenhague, vol. 14, Copenhagen: Nordisk Sprog-og Kulturforlag.

—— (1973b) 'A causerie on linguistic theory', in L. Hjelmslev Essais linguistiques II: Travaux du Cercle Linguistique de Copenhague, vol. 14, trans. C. Hendriksen, Copenhagen: Nordisk Sprog-og Kulturforlag.

—— (1975) Résumé of a Theory of Language: Travaux du Cercle Linguistique de Copenhague, vol. 16, ed. and trans. with an introduction by Francis J. Whitfield Copenhagen: Nordisk Sprog-og Kulturforlag.

Hockett, C.F. (1947) 'Problems of morphemic analysis', Language 23: 321–43.

—— (1950) 'Peiping morphophonemics', Language 26: 63–85.

—— (1954) 'Two models of grammatical description', Word 10: 210–34.

—— (1955) 'A manual of phonology', International Journal of American Linguistics 21(4): memoir no. 11.

—— (1958) A Course in Modern Linguistics, New York: Macmillan.

—— (1960) 'Logical considerations in the study of animal communication', in W. Lanyon and W. Travolga (eds) Animal Sounds and

Communication, Bloomington and London: Indiana University Press.

—— and Altmann, S. (1968) 'A note on design features', in T. Sebeok (ed.) *Animal Communication*, Bloomington and London: Indiana University Press.

Hodge, R. and Kress, G. (1991) *Social Semiotics* (2nd edn 1993), Cambridge: Polity Press.

—— and —— (1993) *Language as Ideology*, 2nd edition, London: Routledge; 1st edition 1979.

Hodges, W. (1977) *Logic*, Harmondsworth: Penguin.

Hodgson, J.M. (1991) 'Informational constraints on pre-lexical priming', *Language and Cognitive Processes* 6: 169–205.

Hodgson, K.W. (1953) *The Deaf and Their Problems: A study in Special Education*, London: Franklin Watts.

Hoey, M. (1983) *On the Surface of Discourse*, London: George Allen and Unwin.

—— (1983–4) 'The place of clause relational analysis in linguistic description', *English Language Research Journal* 4: 1–32.

—— (1991) *Patterns of Lexis in Text*, Oxford: Oxford University Press.

Holloway, R.L. (1996/1999) 'Evolution of the human brain', in A. Locke and C.R. Peters (eds) *Handbook of Human Symbolic Evolution*, Oxford: Blackwell Publishers Ltd. First published by OUP, pp. 74–116.

Holm, J.A. (1988) *Pidgins and Creoles*, vol. 1, *Theory and Structure*, Cambridge: Cambridge University Press.

Holmes, J. (1984) 'Hedging your bets and sitting on the fence: some evidence for hedges as support structures', *Te Reo* 27: 47–62.

Hookway, C. (ed.) (1984) *Minds, Machines and Evolution*, Cambridge: Cambridge University Press.

—— (1985) *Peirce*, London: Routledge & Kegan Paul.

—— (1988) *Quine: Language, Experience and Reality*, Cambridge: Polity Press.

—— (1990) *Scepticism*, London: Routledge.

—— (2000) *Truth, Rationality, and Pragmatism: Themes from Peirce*, Oxford: Clarendon Press.

—— and Peterson, D. (eds) (1993) *Philosophy and Cognitive Science*, Cambridge: Cambridge University Press.

Hooper, J.B. (1976) *An Introduction to Natural Generative Phonology*, New York: Academic Press.

Hopkins, A. and Dudley-Evans, A. (1988) 'A genre-based investigation of the discussion sections in articles and dissertations', *English for Specific Purposes* 7: 113 22.

Hornby, A.S. (1954–6) *Oxford Progressive English for Adult Learners*, Oxford: Oxford University Press.

Horne, K.M. (1966) *Language Typology: 19th and 20th Century Views*, Washington, DC: Georgetown University Press.

Houghton, D. (1980) 'Contrastive rhetoric', *English Language Research Journal* 1: 79–91.

—— and Hoey, M. (1982) 'Linguistics and written discourse: contrastive rhetorics', *Annual Review of Applied Linguistics* 3: 2–22.

Hovelacque, A. (1877) *The Science of Language: Linguistics, Philology, Etymology*, trans. A.H. Keene, London: Chapman and Hall.

Howatt, A.T.R. (1984) *A History of English Language Teaching*, Oxford: Oxford University Press.

Howes, R.F. (ed.) (1961) *Historical Studies of Rhetoric and Rhetoricians*, Ithaca, NY: Cornell University Press.

Hubel, D.H. and Wiesel, T.N. (1968) 'Receptive fields and functional architecture of monkey striate cortex', *The Journal of Physiology* 195: 215–44.

Huddleston, R.D. (1965) 'Rank and depth', *Language* 41: 574–86.

—— (1970) 'Some remarks on case grammar', *Journal of Linguistics* 1: 501–10.

—— (1976) *An Introduction to Transformational Syntax*, Cambridge, MA: MIT Press.

Hudson, R.A. (1971) *English Complex Sentences: An Introduction to Systemic Grammar*, Amsterdam: North Holland.

—— (1974) 'Systemic generative grammar', *Linguistics* 139: 5–42.

—— (1976) *Arguments for a Non-Transformational Grammar*, Chicago and London: University of Chicago Press.

—— (1996) *Sociolinguistics*, (2nd edition), Cambridge: Cambridge University Press.

Hughes, G.E. and Cresswell, M.J. (1968) *An Introduction to Modal Logic*, London: Methuen.

Hurford, J.R. (1999) 'The evolution of language and languages', in R. Dunbar, C. Knight and C. Power (eds) *The Evolution of Culture*, Edinburgh: Edinburgh University Press.

Hutchby, I. and Wooffitt, R. (1998) *Conversation Analysis*, Cambridge: Polity Press.

Hutchinson, T. (1978) 'The practical demonstration', *Practical Papers in English Language Education* (University of Lancaster, no. 1).

—— and Waters, A. (1984) *Interface: English for Technical Communication*, London: Longman.

Hwang, J. (1990) '"Deference" versus "politeness" in Korean speech', *International Journal of the Sociology of Language* 82: 41–55.

Hyams, N. (1992) 'The genesis of clausal structure', in J.M. Meisel (ed.) *The Acquisition of Verb Placement: Functional Categories and V2 Phenomena in Language Development*, Dordrecht: Kluwer.

—— (1994) 'V2, Null Arguments and COMP Projections', in T. Hoekstra and B.D. Schwartz (eds) *Language Acquisition Studies in Gener-ative Grammar*, Amsterdam: John Benjamins.

—— (1996) 'The underspecification of functional categories in early grammar', in H. Clahsen (ed.) *Generative Perspectives on Language Acquisition*, Amsterdam: John Benjamins.

Hyman, L.M. (1982) 'Nasality in Gokana', in H. van der Hulst and N. Smith (eds) *The Structure of Phonological Representations*, Dordrecht: Foris.

—— and Schuh, R.G. (1974) 'Universals of tone rules: evidence from West Africa', *Linguistic Inquiry* 5: 81–115.

Hymes, D. (ed.) (1964) *Language, Culture and Society: A Reader in Linguistics and Anthropology*, New York: Harper and Row.

—— (1971a) *On Communicative Competence*, Philadelphia: University of Pennsylvania Press; extracts in J.B. Pride and J. Holmes (eds) (1972) *Sociolinguistics*, Harmondsworth: Penguin.

—— (ed.) (1971b) *Pidginization and Creolization of Languages*, proceedings of a conference, University of the West Indies, April 1968, Cambridge: Cambridge University Press.

—— (1972) *Towards Communicative Competence*, Philadelphia: University of Pennsylvania Press.

—— (1996) *Ethnography, Linguistics, Narrative Inequality: Toward an Understanding of Voice*, London: Taylor & Francis.

Ilson, R.F. (ed.) (1985) *Dictionaries, Lexicography and Language Learning*, Oxford: Pergamon Press, in association with the British Council.

Ingham, R. (1984) *Stuttering and Behavior Therapy: Current Status and Experimental Foundations*, San Diego, CA: College-Hill Press.

Ingram, D. (1985) 'The psychological reality of children's grammars and its relation to grammatical theory', *Lingua* 66: 79–103.

—— (1989) *First Language Acquisition: Methods, Description and Explanation*, Cambridge: Cambridge University Press.

Inner London Education Authority (1979) *Report on the 1978 Census of Those ILEA Pupils for Whom English Was Not a First Language*, London: ILEA.

International Phonetic Association (1949) *The Principles of the International Phonetic Association*, University College London: International Phonetic Association.

—— (1999) *Handbook of the International Phonetic Association: A Guide to the Use of the International Phonetic Alphabet*, Cambridge: Cambridge University Press.

Ireland, J. (1989) 'Ideology, myth and the maintenance of cultural identity', *ELR Journal* (new series) 3: 95–136.

Isenberg, H. (1968) 'Motivierung zur "Texttheorie"', *Replik* 2: 13–17.

—— (1971) 'Uberlegungen zur Texttheorie', in J. Ihwe (ed.) *Litteraturwissenschaft und Linguistik: Ergebnisse und Perspektiven*, Frankfurt: Athenäum.

Jaberg, K. and Judd, J. (1928–40) *Sprach- und Sachatlas Haliers und der Südschweiz*, Zofingen: Ringier.

Jackendoff, R. (1972) *Semantic Interpretation in Generative Grammar*, Cambridge, MA: MIT Press.

Jacobson, P. (1987) 'Phrase structure, grammatical relations and discontinuous constituents', in G.J. Huck and A.E. Ojeda (eds) *Syntax and Semantics* vol. 20, *Discontinuous Constituency*, New York: Academic Press.

Jagger, P. and Buba, M. (1994) 'The space and time adverbials NAN/CAN in Hausa: cracking the deictic code', *Language Sciences* 16.

Jain, M.P. (1969) 'Error analysis of an Indian English corpus', unpublished University of Edinburgh manuscript.

—— (1974) 'Error analysis: source, cause and significance' in J.C. Richards (ed.) *Error Analysis: Perspectives on Second Language Acquisition*, London: Longman.

Jakobovits, L.A. and Miron, M.S. (eds) (1967) *Readings in the Psychology of Language*, Englewood Cliffs, NJ: Prentice Hall.

Jakobson, R. (1941) *Kindersprache, Aphasie, und allgemeine Lautgesetze*, Uppsala Universitetets Aarsskrift; published in English in R. Jakobson (1968) *Child Language, Aphasia and Phonological Universals*, The Hague: Mouton, and in R. Jakobson (1962) *Selected Writings* vol. 1, The Hague: Mouton.

—— (1959) 'On linguistic aspects of translation', in R.A. Brower (ed.) *On Translation*, Cambridge, MA: Harvard University Press; reprinted in K. Pomorska and S. Rudy (eds) (1987) *Language in Literature*, Cambridge, MA and London: The Belknap Press of Harvard University Press, © 1987 The Jakobson Trust.

—— (1960) 'Closing statement: linguistics and poetics', in T.A. Sebeok (ed.) *Style in Language*, Cambridge, MA: MIT Press.

—— (1968) *Child Language, Aphasia and Phonological Universals*, The Hague: Mouton.

—— and Halle, M. (1956) *Fundamentals of Language*, The Hague: Mouton.

——, Fant, C.G.M. and Halle, M. (1951) *Preliminaries to Speech Analysis: The Distinctive Features and their Correlates*, Cambridge, MA: MIT Press.

Janssen, Th. and Redeker, G. (eds) (1999) *Cognitive Linguistics: Foundations, Scope, and Methodology* (Cognitive Linguistics Research, no. 15), Berlin and New York: Mouton.

Jared, D. (1997) 'Spelling–sound consistency affects the naming of high-frequency words', *Journal of Memory and Language* 36: 505–29.

—— and Seidenberg, M.S. (1991) 'Does word identification proceed from spelling to sound to meaning?', *Journal of Experimental Psychology: General* 120: 358–94.

——, McRae, K. and Seidenberg, M.S. (1990) 'The basis of consistency effects in word naming', *Journal of Memory and Language* 29: 687–715.

Jarvella, R.J. (1971) 'Syntactic processing of connected speech', *Journal of Verbal Learning and Verbal Behaviour* 10: 409–16.

Jaworski, A. and Coupland, N. (eds) (1999) *The Discourse Reader*, London: Routledge.

Jensen, H. (1970) *Sign, Symbol and Script: An Account of Man's Efforts to Write*, London: George Allen & Unwin.

Jescheniak, J.D. and Schreifers, H. (1997) 'Lexical access in speech production: serial or cascade processing?', *Language and Cognitive Processes* 12: 847–52.

Jespersen, O. (1922) *Language, its Nature, Development and Origin*, London: George Allen & Unwin.

—— (1924) *The Philosophy of Grammar*, London: George Allen & Unwin.

Johansson, S. and Hofland, K. (1989), *Frequency Analysis of English Vocabulary and Grammar*, 2 vols, Oxford: Clarendon Press.

—— and Oksefjell, S. (eds) (1998) *Corpora and Cross-Linguistic Research: Theory, Method, and Case Studies*, Amsterdam and Atlanta, GA: Rodopi.

——, Leech, G. and Goodluck, H. (1978) *A Manual of Information to Accompany the Lancaster–Oslo/Bergen Corpus of British English, for Use with Digital Computers*, University of Oslo, Department of English.

Johns, T. (1994) 'From printout to handout: grammar and vocabulary teaching in the context of data-driven learning', in T. Odlin (ed.) *Perspectives on Pedagogical Grammar*, Cambridge: Cambridge University Press.

Johnson, D.E. and Postal, P.M. (1980) *Arc Pair Grammar*, Princeton, NJ: Princeton University Press.

Johnson, K. (1982) *Communicative Syllabus Design and Methodology*, Oxford: Pergamon Press.

—— (1997) *Acoustic and Auditory Phonetics*, Cambridge: Blackwell Publishers.

Johnson, M. (1987) *The Body in the Mind: The Bodily Basis of Meaning, Reason and Imagination*, Chicago and London: University of Chicago Press.

Johnson, N.F. and Pugh, K.R. (1994) 'A cohort model of visual word recognition', *Cognitive Psychology* 26: 240–346.

Johnson-Laird, P.N. (1983) *Mental Models*, Cambridge: Cambridge University Press.

—— (1987) 'The mental representation of the meaning of words', *Cognition* 25: 189–211.

—— and Stevenson, R. (1970) 'Memory for syntax', *Nature* 227: 412.

Jones, D. (1932) 'The theory of phonemes, and its importance in practical linguistics', in *Proceedings of the First International Congress of Phonetic Sciences*, Amsterdam.

—— (1950) *The Phoneme: Its Nature and Use*, Cambridge: Heffer, 2nd edition 1962, 3rd edition 1967.

—— (1957) 'The history and meaning of the term "phoneme"', supplement to *Le Maître phonétique*; reprinted in F. Fudge (1973) *Phonology*, Harmondsworth: Penguin.

Jones, D. (1980) 'Gossip: notes on women's oral culture', in C. Kramarae (ed.) *The Voices and Words of Women and Men*, Oxford: Pergamon Press.

Jones, L.K. (1980) 'A synopsis of tagmemics', in E.A. Moravcsik and J.R. Wirth (eds) *Syntax and Semantics*, vol. 13, *Current Approaches to Syntax*, New York and London: Academic Press.

Joos, M. (1961) *The Five Clocks*, New York: Harcourt, Brace, and World.

Joseph, J.E. (1994) 'Twentieth-century linguistics: overview of trends', in R.E. Asher (editor-in-chief) *The Encyclopedia of Language and Linguistics*, vol. 9, Oxford: Pergamon.

Joshi, A. and Schabes, Y. (1996) 'Tree Adjoining Grammars', in G. Rosenberg and A. Salomaa (eds) *Handbook of Formal Languages*, vol. 3, Berlin: Springer Verlag.

Jusczyk, P. (1997) *The Discovery of Spoken Language*, Cambridge, MA: MIT Press.

Kager, R. (1999) *Optimality Theory*, Cambridge: Cambridge University Press.

Kahn, D. (1976) 'Syllable-based generalisations in English phonology', unpublished Ph.D. thesis, distributed by Indiana University Linguistics Club.

Kamp, H. (1984) 'A theory of truth and semantic representation', in J. Groenendijk, J. Janssen and M. Stokhof (eds) *Formal Methods in the Study of Language*, Dordrecht: Foris.

Kaplan, R.B. (ed.) (1980a) *On the Scope of Applied Linguistics*, Rowley, MA: Newbury House.

—— (1980b) 'On the scope of applied linguistics and non', in R.B. Kaplan (ed.) *On the Scope of Applied Linguistics*, Rowley, MA: Newbury House.

—— and Grabe, W. (2000) 'Applied linguistics and the *Annual Review of Applied Linguistics*', *Annual Review of Applied Linguistics* 20: 3–21.

Kaplan, R.D. (1966) 'Cultural thought patterns in intercultural education', *Language Learning* 16: 1–20.

Kaplan, R.M. and Bresnan, J.W. (1982) 'Lexical-functional grammar: a formal system for grammatical representation', in J.W. Bresnan (ed.) *The Mental Representation of Grammatical Relations*, Cambridge, MA and London: MIT Press.

—— and Maxwell, J.T., III (1995) 'Constituent coordination in Lexical Functional Grammar', in M. Dalrymple, J.T. Maxwell III and A. Zaenen (eds) (1995) *Formal Issues in Lexical Functional Grammar*, Stanford, CA: CSLI Publications.

—— and Zaenen, A. (1995) 'Formal devices for linguistic generalisations: West Germanic word order in LFG', in M. Dalrymple, J.T. Maxwell III and A. Zaenen (eds) *Formal Issues in Lexical Functional Grammar*, Stanford, CA: CSLI Publications.

Karmiloff-Smith, A. (1979) *A Functional Approach to Child Language*, Cambridge: Cambridge University Press.

—— (1987) 'Some recent issues in the study of language acquisition', in J. Lyons, R. Coates, M. Denchar and G. Gazdar (eds) *New Horizons in Linguistics*, vol. 2, Harmondsworth: Penguin.

Kasper, R. and Rounds, W. (1986) 'A logical semantics for feature structuring', in R. Kasper (ed.) *Proceedings of the 24th Annual Meeting of the ACL*, Columbia University, New York.

Kastovsky, D. (1986) 'Diachronic word-formation in a functional perspective', in D. Kastovsky and A. Szwedek (eds) *Linguistics Across Historical and Geographical Boundaries: In Honour of Jacek Fisiak on the Occasion of his Fiftieth Birthday*, Berlin and New York: Mouton de Gruyter.

Katamba, F. (1989) *An Introduction to Phonology*, London and New York: Longman.

Kathol, A. (2000) *Linear Syntax*, Oxford: Oxford University Press.

Katz, J. (1972) *Semantic Theory*, New York: Harper and Row.

—— and Fodor, J. (1963) 'The structure of a semantic theory', *Language* 39: 170–210.

—— and Postal, P. (1964) *An Integrated Theory of Linguistic Descriptions*, Cambridge, MA: MIT Press.

Kay, M. (1979) 'Functional grammar', in *Proceedings of the Fifth Annual Meeting of the Berkeley Linguistics Society*: 142–58.

—— (1985) 'Parsing in functional unification grammar', in D.R. Dowty, L. Karttunen and A.M. Zwicky (eds) *Natural Language Parsing: Psychological, Computational, and Theoretical Perspectives*, Cambridge: Cambridge University Press.

—— (1986) 'Algorithmic schemata and data structures in syntactic processing', in B.J. Grosz, K. Sparck-Jones and B.L. Webber (eds) *Readings in Natural Language Processing*, Los Altos: Morgan Kaufman.

——, Gavron, J.M. and Norvig, P. (1994) *VERMOBIL: A Translation System for Face-to-Face Dialog*, Stanford, CA: CSLI Publications.

Kay, P. and Filmore, C.J. (1999) 'Grammatical constructions and linguistic generalizations: the What's X doing Y? construction', *Language* 75: 1–33.

—— and McDaniel, C. (1978) 'The linguistic significance of the meanings of basic color terms', *Language* 54: 610–46.

Kaye, K. (1980) 'Why don't we talk "baby talk" to babies', *Journal of Child Language* 7: 489–507.

Keenan, E.L. (1979) 'On surface form and logical form', *Studies in the Linguistic Sciences* (Department of Linguistics, University of Illinois no. 8(2); reprinted in E.L. Keenan (1987) *Universal Grammar: 15 Essays*, London: Croom Helm.

—— (1987) *Universal Grammar: 15 Essays*, London: Croom Helm.

——, MacWhinney, B. and Mayhew, D. (1977) 'Pragmatics in memory: a study of natural conversation', *Journal of Verbal Learning and Verbal Behaviour* 23: 115–26.

Kellerman, E. and Sharwood Smith, M. (1986) *Cross-Linguistic Influence in Second Language Acquisition*, Elmsford, New York: Pergamon Press.

Kellogg, W. and Kellogg, L. (1967) *The Ape and the Child: A Study of Environmental Influence on Early Behavior*, New York: Haffner.

Kempen, G. and Hoenkamp, E. (1987) 'An incremantal procedural grammar for sentence formulation', *Cognitive Science* 11: 201–58.

Kempson, R. (1977) *Semantic Theory*, Cambridge: Cambridge University Press.

Kennedy, G. (1998) *An Introduction to Corpus Linguistics*, London: Longman.

Kenny, A. (1982) *The Computation of Style: An Introduction to Statistics for Students of Literature and Humanities*, Oxford: Pergamon Press.

Kenstowicz, M. (1994) *Phonology in Generative Grammar*, Oxford: Basil Blackwell.

Kenyon, J.S. (1930) 'Flat a and broad A', *American Speech* 5: 323–6.

Kershaw, J. (1974) 'People with dyslexia', *Rehab*, British Council for Rehabilitation of the Disabled.

Kerswill, P. and Williams, A. (2000) 'Creating a new town koine: children and language change in Milton Keynes', *Language in Society* 29(1): 1–64.

Kess, J.F. (1983) Introduction to L. Bloomfield (1914/1983) *An Introduction to the Study of Language* (Amsterdam Studies in the Theory and History of Linguistic Science, Series II, 3, Classics in Psycholinguistics); facsimile reprint K. Koerner (ed.), introduction by J.F. Kress, Amsterdam and Philadelphia: John Benjamins, 1st edition 1914, London and New York: Bell and Holt.

Kewley-Port, D. (1983) 'Time-varying features as correlates of place of articulation in stop consonants', *Journal of the Acoustical Society of America* 73: 322–35.

—— and Zheng, Y. (1999) 'Vowel formant discrimination: towards more ordinary listening conditions', *Journal of the Acoustical Society of America* 106: 2945–58.

Kiang, N.Y.S. (1980) 'Processing of speech by the auditory nervous system', *Journal of the Acoustical Society of America* 69: 830–5.

——, Watanabe, T., Thomas, E.C. and Clark, L.F. (1965) *Discharge Patterns of Single Fibers in the Cat's Auditory Nerve* (MIT Research Monograph no. 35), Cambridge, MA: MIT Press.

Kilbury, J. (1976) *The Development of Morphophonemic Theory*, Amsterdam: Benjamins.

Kimball, J.P. (1973) *The Formal Theory of Grammar*, Engelwood Cliffs, N.J.: Prentice Hall.

Kimura, D. (1979) 'Neuromotor mechanisms in the evolution of human communication', in H.D. Steklis and M.J. Raleigh (eds) *Neurobiology of Social Communication in Primates*, New York: Academic Press.

Kingston, J. and Diehl, R. (1994) 'Phonetic knowledge', *Language* 70: 419–54.

Kintsch, W. (1988) 'The role of knowledge in discourse comprehension: A construction-integration model', *Psychological Review* 95: 163–82.

—— and Dijk, T. van (1978) 'Toward a model of text comprehension and production', *Psycho-analytic Review* 85: 363–94.

——, Kozminsky, E., Streby, W.J., McKoon, G. and Keenan, J.M. (1975) 'Comprehension and recall of text as a function of context variable', *Journal of Verbal Learning and Verbal Behaviour* 14: 158–69.

Kiparsky, P. (1982a) *Explanation in Phonology*, Dordrecht: Foris.

—— (1982b) 'From cyclic phonology to lexical phonology', in H. van der Hulst and N. Smith (eds) *The Structure of Phonological Representations*, Dordrecht: Foris.

Klatt, D.H. (1980) 'Speech perception: a model of acoustic-phonetic analysis and lexical access', in R.A. Cole (ed.) *Perception and Production of Fluent Speech*, Hillsdale, NJ: Lawrence Erlbaum Associates.

—— (1989) 'Review of selected models of speech perception', in W. Marslen-Wilson (ed.), *Lexical Representation and Process*, Cambridge, MA: MIT Press.

Klima, E.S. (1964) 'Negation in English', in J.A. Fodor and J.J. Katz (eds) *The Structure of Language: Readings in the Philosophy of Language*, Englewood Cliffs, NJ: Prentice Hall.

—— and Bellugi, U. (1966) 'Syntactic regularities in the speech of children', in J. Lyons and R. Wales (eds) *Psycholinguistic Papers*, Edinburgh: Edinburgh University Press.

—— (1979) *The Signs of Language*, Cambridge, MA and London: Harvard University Press.

Knowles, G., Wichmann, A. and Alderson, P. (eds) (1996) *Working with Speech*, London: Longman.

Koch, W. (1971) *Taxologie des Englischen*, Munich: Fink.

Kohts, N. (1935) 'Infant ape and human child', *Scientific Memoirs of the Museum Darwinian*, Moscow.

Koutsoudas, A., Sanders, G. and Knoll, C. (1974) 'On the application of phonological rules', *Language* 50: 1–28.

Kramsch, C. (1995) 'The applied linguist and the foreign language teacher: can they talk to each other?', *Australian Review of Applied Linguistics* 18: 1–16.

Kreitman, N. (1999) *The Roots of Metaphor: A Multidisciplinary Study in Aesthetics*, Aldershot: Ashgate.

Kress, G. (ed.) (1976) *Halliday: System and Function in Language: Selected Papers*, Oxford: Oxford University Press.

—— (1985) *Linguistic Processes in Sociocultural Practice*, Geelong, Australia: Deakin University Press; 2nd edition 1989, Oxford: Oxford University Press.

Kripke, S. (1963) 'Semantical considerations on modal logic', *Acta Philosophica Fennica*: 83–94.

Kuhl, P.K. (1979) 'Speech perception in early infancy: perceptual constancy for spectrally dissimilar vowel categories', *Journal of the Acoustical Society of America* 66: 1668–79.

—— (1992) 'Psychoacoustics and speech perception: Internal standards, perceptual anchors and prototypes', in L.A. Werner and E.W. Rubel (eds) *Developmental Psychoacoustics*, Washington, DC: American Psychological Association.

—— (1994) 'Learning and representation in speech and language', *Current Opinion in Neurobiology* 4: 812–22.

—— and Miller, J.D. (1975) 'Speech perception by the chinchilla: voiced–voiceless distinction in alveolar plosive consonants', *Science* 190: 69–72.

Kummer, W. (1972) 'Versuch einer Exploration der neuentdeckten Formelwälder von der Insel Mainau', *LinguistischeBerichte* 18: 53–5.

Kurath, H. *et al.* (1939–43) *Linguistic Atlas of New England*, Providence, RI: Brown University Press.

—— and McDavid, R.I., Jr (1961) *The Pronunciation of English in the Atlantic States*, Ann Arbor: University of Michigan Press.

Kussmaul, A. (1877) 'Disturbance of speech', *Ziemssens Encyclopedia of the Practice of Medicine*, London.

Labov, W. (1966) *The Social Stratification of English in New York City*, Washington, DC: Center for Applied Linguistics, and Oxford: Basil Blackwell.

—— (1969) 'The logic of non-standard English', *Georgetown Monographs on Language and Linguistics* 22: 1–31.

—— (1971) 'Variation in language', in C.E. Reed *The Learning of Language*, New York: National Council for Teachers of English.

—— (1972a) *Language in the Inner City*, Philadelphia: University of Pennsylvania Press and Oxford: Basil Blackwell.

—— (1972b) *Sociolinguistic Patterns*, Philadelphia: University of Pennsylvania Press and Oxford: Basil Blackwell.

—— (1994) *Principles of Linguistic Change: Internal Factors*, Oxford: Blackwell Publishers.

Ladd, D.R. (1996) *Intonational Phonology*, Cambridge: Cambridge University Press.

Ladefoged, P. (1962) *Elements of Acoustic Phonetics*, Chicago: University of Chicago Press.

—— (1971) *Preliminaries to Linguistic Phonetics*, Chicago: University of Chicago Press.

—— (1975/1982), *A Course in Phonetics*, New York: Harcourt Brace Jovanovich; 2nd edition 1982.

——, DeClerk, J., Lindau, M. and Papun, G. (1972) 'An auditory-motor theory of speech production', *UCLA Working Papers in Phonetics* 22: 48–75.

Lado, R. (1957) *Linguistics Across Cultures: Applied Linguistics for Language Teachers*, Ann Arbor: University of Michigan Press.

Lakoff, G. (1970) 'Global rules', *Language* 46: 627–39.

—— (1971a) 'On generative semantics', in D. Steinberg and L. Jakobovits (eds) *Semantics*, Cambridge: Cambridge University Press.

—— (1971b) 'Presupposition and relative wellformedness', in D. Steinberg and L. Jakobovits (eds) *Semantics*, Cambridge: Cambridge University Press.

—— (1971c) 'The role of deduction in grammar', in C. Fillmore and D.T. Langendoen (eds) *Studies in Linguistic Semantics*, New York: Holt, Rinehart and Winston.

—— (1973) 'Fuzzy grammar and the performance/competence terminology game', in C. Corum, T.C. Smith-Stark and A. Weiser (eds) *Papers from the Ninth Regional Meeting of the Chicago Linguistic Society*, Chicago: Chicago Linguistic Society.

—— (1974) 'Interview with H. Parret', in *Discussing Language*, The Hague: Mouton.

—— (1977) 'Linguistic Gestalts', *CLS* 13: 236–87.

—— (1982) *Categories and Cognitive Models* (Series A, Paper 96), Trier: Linguistic Agency, University of Trier.

—— (1987a) *Women, Fire and Dangerous Things: What Categories Reveal About the Mind*, Chicago and London: University of Chicago Press.

—— (1987b) 'Cognitive models and prototype theory' in U. Neisser (ed.) *Concepts and Conceptual Development*, Cambridge: Cambridge University Press.

—— and Johnson, M. (1980) *Metaphors We Live By*, Chicago and London: University of Chicago Press.

—— (1999) *Philosophy in the Flesh: The Embodied Mind and its Challenges to Western Thought*, Chicago: University of Chicago Press.

Lakoff, R. (1975) *Language and Woman's Place*, New York: Harper and Row.

Lamb, S.M. (1966) *Outline of Stratificational Grammar*, Washington, DC: Georgetown University Press.

—— (1999) *Pathways of the Brain: The Neurological Basis of Language*, Amsterdam: John Benjamins.

Lambek, J. (1961) 'On the calculus of syntactic types', in R. Jakobson (ed.) *Structure of Language and its Mathematical Aspects*, Providence: American Mathematical Society.

Langacker, R.W. (1987/1991b) *Foundations of Cognitive Grammar*, vol. 1, *Theoretical Prerequisites*, vol. 2, *Descriptive Application*, Stanford, CA: Stanford University Press.

—— (1991a) *Concept, Image, and Symbol: The Cognitive Basis of Grammar* (Cognitive Linguistics Research no. 1), Berlin: Mouton.

—— (1995) 'Cognitive Grammar', in J. Verschueren, J.-O. Östman and J. Blommaert (eds) *Handbook of Pragmatics Manual*, Amsterdam and Philadelphia: John Benjamins.

—— (1999) *Grammar and Conceptualization* (Cognitive Linguistics Research no. 14), Berlin: Mouton.

Langendoen, D.T. (1968) *The London School of Linguistics: A Study of the Linguistic Theories of B. Malinowski and J.R. Firth* (Research Monograph no. 46), Cambridge, MA: MIT Press.

Lapointe, S., Brentari, D.K. and Farrell, P.M. (eds) (1998) *Morphology and its Relation to Phonology and Syntax*, Stanford, CA: CSLI Publications.

Large, A. (1985) *The Artificial Language Movement*, Oxford: Basil Blackwell.

Lass, R. (1984) *Phonology*, Cambridge: Cambridge University Press.

Laviosa-Braithwaite, S. (1996) 'The English Comparable Corpus (ECC): a resource and a methodology for the empirical study of translation', unpublished Ph.D. thesis, Department of Language Engineering, University of Manchester Institute of Science and Technology (UMIST).

Le Page, R.B. (ed.) (1961) *Creole Language Studies II*, proceedings of the Conference on Creole Language Studies, University of the West Indies, March–April 1959, London: Macmillan.

Lebeaux, D. (1988) 'Language acquisition and the form of the grammar', unpublished Ph.D. thesis, University of Massachusetts.

Lee, D. (1992) *Competing Discourses*, London: Longman.

Lee, M.W. and Williams, J.N. (1997) 'Why is short-term sentence recall verbatim? An evaluation of the role of lexical priming', *Memory and Cognition* 25: 156–72.

Lee, P. (1996) *The Whorf Theory Complex: A Critical Reconstruction*, Amsterdam and Philadelphia: John Benjamins.

Leech, G.N. (1966) *English in Advertising*, London: Longman.

—— (1967) *Towards a Semantic Description of English*, London: Longman.

—— (1969) *A Linguistic Guide to English Poetry*, London: Longman.

—— (1981) *Semantics: The Study of Meaning*, 2nd edition, Harmondsworth: Penguin.

—— (1983) *Principles of Pragmatics*, London and New York: Longman.

Lees, R.B. (1960/1963) *The Grammar of English Nominalizations*, Bloomington: Indiana University Press; reprinted 1963, The Hague: Mouton.

—— and Klima, E.S. (1963) 'Rules for English Pronominalization', *Language* 39: 17–28.

Lehmann, W.P. (1962) *Historical Linguistics: An Introduction*, New York: Holt, Rinehart and Winston.

—— (1967) *A Reader in Nineteenth-Century Historical Indo-European Linguistics*, Bloomington and London: Indiana University Press.

Lehnert, W.C. (1978) *The Process of Question-Answering: A Computer Simulation of Cognition*, Hillsdale, NJ: Lawrence Erlbaum Associates.

Lehrer, A. (1969) 'Semantic cuisine', *Journal of Linguistics* 5: 39–56.

—— (1974) *Semantic Fields and Lexical Structure*, Amsterdam: North Holland.

—— (1978) 'Structures of the lexicon, and transfer of meaning', *Lingua* 45: 95–123.

Lenat, D.B. and Guha, R.V. (1990) *Building Large Scale Knowledge Based Systems*, Reading, MA: Addison Wesley.

Lenneberg, E. (1964) 'The capacity for language acquisition', in J. Fodor and J. Katz (eds) *The Structure of Language: Readings in the Philosophy of Language*, Englewood Cliffs, NJ: Prentice Hall.

—— (1967) *Biological Foundations of Language*, New York: Wiley.

—— (1969) 'On explaining language', *Science* 164(3880): 635–43.

Lepschy, G.E. (1994) *The Eastern Tradition of Linguistics*, History of Linguistics vol. 1, London: Longman; first published 1990, Bologna: Il Mulino.

Lesser, R. and Milroy, L. (1993) *Linguistics and Aphasia*, London: Longman.

Levelt, W.J.M. (1989) *Speaking: From Intention to Articulation*, Cambridge, MA and London: MIT Press.

——, Roelofs, A. and Meyer, A.S. (1999) 'A theory of lexical access in speech production', *Behavioural and Brain Sciences* 22: 1–75.

Levinson, S.C. (1983) *Pragmatics*, Cambridge: Cambridge University Press.

Levy, Y. (1983) 'It's frogs all the way down', *Cognition* 15: 75–93.

Lewis, C.I. (1918) *A Survey of Symbolic Logic*, Berkeley, CA: University of California Press.

Lewis, D. (1970/1983) 'General semantics', *Synthese* 22: 18–67; reprinted 1983, in *Philosophical Papers*, vol. 1, New York and Oxford: Oxford University Press.

—— (1973) *Counterfactuals*, Oxford: Basil Blackwell.

Liberman, A.M., Delattre, P.C. and Cooper, F.S. (1952) 'The role of selected stimulus variables in the perception of the unvoiced stop consonants, *American Journal of Psychology* 65: 497–516.

——, Cooper, F.S., Schankweiler, D.P. and Studdert-Kennedy, M. (1967) 'Perception of the speech code', *Psychological Review* 74: 431–61.

Liberman, M. (1975) 'The intonational system of English', unpublished Ph.D. thesis, distributed by Indiana University Linguistics Club.

—— and Prince, A. (1977) 'On stress and linguistic rhythm', *Linguistic Inquiry* 8: 249–336.

Lieber, R. (1980) 'The Organization of the Lexicon', unpublished Ph.D. dissertation, MIT.

Lieberman, P. (1968) 'Primate vocalization and human linguistic ability', *Journal of the Acoustical Society of America* 44: 1574–84.

—— (1975) *On the Origin of Language*, New York: Macmillan.

—— (1977) 'The phylogeny of language', in T.A. Sebeok (ed.) *How Animals Communicate*, Bloomington and London: Indiana University Press.

—— (1984) *The Biology and Evolution of Language*, Cambridge, MA and London: Harvard University Press.

—— (1991a) *Uniquely Human: The Evolution of Speech, Thought, and Selfless Behavior*, Cambridge, MA: Harvard University Press.

—— (1991b) 'Preadaptation, natural selection and function', *Language and Communication* 11(1): 63–5.

—— (1998) *Eve Spoke: Human Language and Human Evolution*, New York: W.W. Norton and Company.

—— (2000) *Human Language and our Reptilian Brain: The Subcortical Bases of Speech, Syntax and Thought*, Cambridge, MA: Harvard University Press.

—— and Blumstein, S.E. (1988) *Speech Physiology, Speech Perception, and Acoustic Phonetics*, Cambridge: Cambridge University Press.

Lightfoot, D.W. (1984) 'The relative richness of triggers and the bioprogram', *Behavioral and Brain Sciences* 7(2): 198–9.

Lindblom, B. (1989) 'Models of phonetic variation and selection', *Proceedings of the International Conference on Language Change and Biological Evolution*, Turin.

Llorach, E. Alarcos (1951) *Gramática estructural según la Escuela de Copenhague y con especial atención a la Lengua española*, Madrid Biblioteca Hispánica, Editorial Gredos.

Lloyd, R.J. (1896) *Neuren Sprachen* 3(10): 615–17.

Lock, A. and Peters, C.R. (eds) (1996/1999) *Handbook of Human Symbolic Evolution*, Oxford: Blackwell Publishers; 1st edition 1996, Oxford: Oxford University Press.

Locke, J. (1960/1977) *An Essay Concerning Human Understanding*, Glasgow: Fontana Collins; 1st edition 1690.

Lockwood, D.G. (1972) *Introduction to Stratificational Linguistics*, New York: Harcourt Brace Jovanovich.

—— (1993) *Morphological Analysis and Description: A Realizational Approach*, Tokyo, Taipei, Dallas: International Language Sciences Publishers.

Lockwood, W.B. (1972) *A Panorama of Indo-European Languages*, London: Hutchinson.

Lombardi, L. and Potter, M.C. (1992) 'The regeneration of syntax in short term memory', *Journal of Memory and Language* 31: 713–33.

Long, M.H. (1990) 'Maturational constraints on language development', *Studies in Second Language Acquisition* 12(3).

Longacre, R.E. (1964) *Grammar Discovery Procedures*, The Hague: Mouton.

—— (1968–9/1970) *Discourse, Paragraph, and Sentence Structure in Selected Philippine Languages*, 3 vols, US Department of Health, Education and Welfare, Office of Education, Institute of International Studies, vols 1–2; reprinted 1970, *Philippine Languages: Discourse, Paragraph, and Sentence Structure*, Santa Ana: Summer Institute of Linguistics.

—— (1976) *An Anatomy of Speech Notions*, Lisse: de Ridder.

—— (1983) *The Grammar of Discourse*, New York and London: Plenum Press.

Love, G. and Payne, M. (eds) (1969) *Contemporary Essays on Style: Rhetoric, Linguistics, and Criticism*, Glenview, IL: Scott, Foresman and Co.

Lukatela, G. and Turvey, M.T. (1994) 'Visual lexical access is initially phonological: 1. Evidence from associative priming by words, homophones, and pseudohomophones', *Journal of Experimental Psychology: General* 123: 107–28.

Lupker, S. (1984) 'Semantic priming without associations: a second look', *Journal of Verbal Learning and Verbal Behaviour* 23: 709–33.

Luria, A.R. (1970) *Traumatic Aphasia: Its Syndromes, Psychology and Treatment*, London: Humanities Press.

Lyons, J. (1968) *Introduction to Theoretical Linguistics*, Cambridge: Cambridge University Press.

—— (1970) 'Generative syntax', in J. Lyons (ed.) *New Horizons in Linguistics*, Harmondsworth: Penguin.

—— (1977a) *Chomsky*, 2nd edition, Glasgow: Fontana Collins, 3rd edition 1991.

—— (1977b) *Semantics*, 2 vols, Cambridge: Cambridge University Press.

—— (1981) *Language and Linguistics: An Introduction*, Cambridge: Cambridge University Press.

—— (1987) 'Introduction', in J. Lyons, R. Coates, M. Deuchar and G. Gazdar (eds) *New Horizons in Linguistics*, vol. 2, Harmondsworth: Penguin.

—— (1991) *Natural Language and Universal Grammar: Essays in Linguistic Theory* vol. 1, Cambridge: Cambridge University Press.

——, Coates, R., Deuchar, M. and Gazdar, G. (eds) (1987) *New Horizons in Linguistics* vol. 2, Harmondsworth: Penguin.

McCarthur, R. (1976) *Tense Logic*, Dordrecht: Reidel.

McCarthy, D.A. (1930) *The Language Development of the Preschool Child* (Institute of Child Welfare Monograph Series no. 4), Minneapolis: University of Minnesota Press.

McCarthy, J.J. and Prince, A.S. (1993a) 'Generalized alignment', in *Yearbook of Morphology 1993*: 79–154.

—— (1993b) 'Prosodic morphology I: constraint interaction and satisfaction', manuscript, University of Massachussetts, Amherst.

McCarthy, M.J. (1987) 'Interactive lexis: prominence and paradigms', in M. Coulthard (ed.) *Discussing Discourse* (Discourse Analysis Monograph, no. 14), English Language Research, University of Birmingham.

—— (1988) 'Some vocabulary patterns in conversation', in R.A. Carter and M.J. McCarthy *Vocabulary in Language Teaching*, Harlow: Longman.

Macaulay, R.K.S. (1977) *Language, Social Class and Education*, Edinburgh: Edinburgh University Press.

—— (1978) 'Variation and consistency in Glaswegian English', in P. Trudgill (ed.) *Sociolinguistic Patterns in British English*, London: Edward Arnold.

Macaulay, R. (2000) 'You're like "why not?": The quotative expressions of Glasgow adolescents', *Journal of Sociolinguistics*.

McCawley, J.D. (1968) 'Lexical insertion in a transformational grammar without deep structure', in R.I. Binnick, A. Davison, G.M. Green and J.L. Morgan (eds) *Papers from the Fifth Regional Meeting of the Chicago Linguistic Society*, Chicago: University of Chicago Press.

—— (1976) *Grammar and Meaning*, New York: Academic Press.

—— (1978) 'What is a tone language', in V.A. Fromkin (ed) *Tone: A Linguistic Survey*, New York: Academic Press.

—— (1981) *Everything That Linguists Have Always Wanted to Know About Logic . . . But were Ashamed to Ask*, Oxford: Basil Blackwell.

McClelland, J.L. (1987) 'The case of interactionism in language processing', in M. Coltheart (ed.) *Attention and Performance*, vol. 12, *The Psychology of Reading*, London: Earlbaum.

—— and Elman, J.F. (1986) 'The Trace Model of Speech perception', *Cognitive Psychology* 18: 1–86.

—— and Rumelhart, D.E. (1981) 'An interactive model of context effects in letter perception. Part 1: An account of basic findings', *Psychological Review* 88: 375–407.

MacDonald, M.C., Perlmutter, N.J. and Seidenberg, M.S. (1994) 'Lexical nature of syntactic ambiguity resolution', *Psychological Review* 101: 676–703.

McEnery, A. and Wilson, A. (1996) *Corpus Linguistics*, Edinburgh: Edinburgh University Press.

McIntosh, A. (1961/1966) 'Patterns and ranges', *Language* 37(3): 325–37; reprinted in A. McIntosh and M.A.K. Halliday (eds) *Patterns of Language: Papers in General Descriptive and Applied Linguistics*, London: Longman.

McKeown, K. (1985) *Generating English Text*, Cambridge: Cambridge University Press.

McKoon, G. and Ratcliff, R. (1989) 'Semantic associations and elaborative inference', *Journal of Experimental Psychology: Learning, Memory and Cognition* 15: 326–38.

—— (1992) 'Inference during reading', *Psychological Review* 99: 440–66.

McLoughlin, M.G. (1980) 'History of the education of the deaf', *Teacher of the Deaf* (January).

MacMahon, M.K.C. (1996) 'Phonetic notation', in P.T. Daniels and W. Bright (eds) *The World's Writing Systems*, New York: Oxford University Press.

McRae, K., Spivey-Knowlton, M.J. and Tanenhaus, M.K. (1998) 'Modeling the influence of thematic fit (and other constraints) in on-line sentence comprehension', *Journal of Memory and Language* 38: 283–312.

Mack, M. (1982) 'Voicing-dependent vowel duration in English and French: monolingual and bilingual production', *Journal of the Acoustical Society of America* 71: 173–8.

—— (1988) 'Sentence processing by non-native speakers of English: evidence from their perception of natural and computer-generated anomalous L2 sentences', *Journal of Neurolinguistics* 2: 293–316.

—— (1992) 'How well is computer-processed speech understood?: a cross-linguistic and cross-dialectal analysis', *World Englishes* 11: 285–301.

—— (2001a) 'From the Ancients to axial slices: a historical perspective on the role of neuroscience in linguistic science', in F. Fabbro (ed.) *Brain and Mind in Bilinguals.*

—— (2001b) 'The phonetic systems of bilinguals', in M. Mack and M.T. Banich (eds) *Mind, Brain and Language: Multidisciplinary Perspectives*, Mahwah, NJ: Lawrence Erlbaum Associates.

—— and Blumstein, S.E. (1983) 'Further evidence of acoustic invariance in speech production: the stop–glide contrast', *Journal of the Acoustic Society of America* 73: 1739–50.

——, Bott, S., Trofimovich, P. and Baker, W. (in progress) 'Age-related effects upon English vowel perception among Korean–English bilinguals'.

Makkai, A. (1972) *Idiom Structure in English*, The Hague: Mouton.

—— (1978) 'Idiomaticity as a language universal', in J. Greenberg, C.A. Ferguson and E.A. Moravcsik (eds) *Universals of Human Language*, vol. 3, Stanford, CA: Stanford University Press.

Malinowski, B. (1923) 'The problem of meaning in primitive languages', supplement to C.K. Ogden and I.A. Richards, *The Meaning of Meaning: A Study of the Influence of Language Upon Thought and the Science of Symbolism*, London: Kegan Paul, Trench, Trubner.

Malkiel, Y. (1959) 'Studies in irreversible binominals', *Lingua* 8: 113–60.

—— (1978) 'Derivational categories', in J. Greenberg (ed.) *Universals of Human Language*, vol. 3, *Word Structure*, Stanford, CA: Stanford University Press.

Mallinson, G. and Blake, B.J. (1981) *Language Typology: Cross-Linguistic Studies in Syntax* (North-Holland Linguistics Series, no. 46), Amsterdam: North Holland.

Mallon, S.T. (1985) 'Six years later: the ICI dual orthography for Inuktitut', in B. Burnaby (ed.) *Promoting Native Writing Systems in Canada*, Toronto: Ontario Institute for Studies in Education.

Malmberg, B. (1964) *New Trends in Linguistics* (Bibliotheca Linguistica, no. 1), Stockholm: Bibliotheca Linguistica.

Mandelbaum, D.G. (ed.) (1949) *Selected Writings of Edward Sapir in Language, Culture and Personality*, Berkeley and Los Angeles: University of California Press, and London: Cambridge University Press.

Mann, W. and Thompson, S. (1988) 'Rhetorical structure theory: toward a functional theory of text organization', *Text* 8(3): 243–81.

Marantz, A. (1984) *On the Nature of Grammatical Relations*, Cambridge, MA: MIT Press.

Maratsos, M. (1984) 'How degenerate is the input to Creoles and where do its biases come from?', *Behavioral and Brain Sciences* 7(2): 200–1.

Marchand, H. (1969) *The Categories and Types of Present-Day English Word-Formation*, 2nd edition, Munich: C.H. Beck.

Marcus, M. (1980) *A Theory of Syntactic Recognition for Natural Language*, Cambridge, MA: MIT Press.

Marshall, J.C. and Newcombe, F. (1980) 'The conceptual status of deep dyslexia: an historical perspective', in M. Coltheart and J.C. Marshall (eds) *Deep Dyslexia*, London: Routledge & Kegan Paul.

Marslen-Wilson, W. (1987) 'Functional parallelism in spoken word recognition', *Cognition* 25: 71–102.

—— (1989) 'Access and integration: projecting sound onto meaning', in W. Marslen-Wilson (ed.) *Lexical Representation and Process*, Cambridge, MA: MIT Press.

—— (1999) 'Abstractness and combination: the morphemic lexicon', in S. Garrod and M. Pickering (eds) *Language Processing*, Hove: Psychology Press.

—— and Warren, P. (1994) 'Levels of perceptual representation and process in lexical access: words, phonemes, and features', *Psychological Review* 101: 653–75.

—— and Welsh, A. (1978) 'Processing inter-actions and lexical access during word recognition in continuous speech', *Cognitive Psychology* 10: 29–63.

——, Tyler, L.K., Waksler, R. and Older, L. (1994) 'Morphology and meaning in the English mental lexicon', *Psychological Review* 101: 3–33.

Martinet, A. (1946) 'Au Sujet des fondements de la théorie linguistique de Louis Hjelmslev', *Bulletin de la Société de Linguistique de Paris* 42(1): 19–42.

—— (1964) *Elements of General Linguistics*, London: Faber and Faber.

Mason, M. (1988) *Illuminating English*, Wigan: Trace.

Mather, J.Y. and Speitel H.H. (1975) *The Linguistic Atlas of Scotland*, London: Croom Helm.

Matsumoto, Y. (1988) 'Reexamination of the universality of face: politeness phenomena in Japanese', *Journal of Pragmatics* 12: 403–26.

—— (1989) 'Politeness and conversational universals: observations from Japanese', *Multilingua* 8: 207–21.

Matthews, P.H. (1972) *Inflectional Morphology*, Cambridge: Cambridge University Press.

—— (1974/1991) *Morphology*, Cambridge: Cambridge University Press.

—— (1984) 'Word formation and meaning', *Quadernidi Semantica* 5(1): 85–92.

—— (1993) *Grammatical Theory in the United States from Bloomfield to Chomsky*, Cambridge, Studies in Linguistics 67, Cambridge: Cambridge University Press.

—— (1994) 'Greek and Latin linguistics', in G.E. Lepschy (ed.) *Classical and Medieval Linguistics*, History of Linguistics, vol. 2, London: Longman; 1st edition 1990, Bologna: Il Mulino.

Mead, M. (1931) 'Talk-boy', *Asia* 31: 141–51.

Mehler, J., Dommergues, J. and Frauenfelder, U. (1981) 'The syllable's role in speech segmentation', *Journal of Verbal Learning and Verbal Behavior* 20: 298–305.

Meisel, J.M. (1991) 'Principles of universal grammar and strategies of language learning: some similarities and differences between first and second language acquisition', in L. Eubank (ed.) *Point Counterpoint: Universal Grammar in Second Language Acquisition*, Amsterdam: John Benjamins.

Mellema, P. (1974) 'A brief against case grammar', *Foundations of Language* 11: 39–76.

Menn, L. (1976) 'Pattern, control, and contrast in beginning speech: a case study in the development of word form and word function', unpublished Ph.D. thesis, University of Illinois.

Mey, J.L. (1993) *Pragmatics: An Introduction*, Oxford: Basil Blackwell.

Miles, D. (1988) *British Sign Language: A Beginner's Guide*, London: BBC Books.

Miles, T.R. (1983) *Dyslexia: the Pattern of Difficulties*, London: Granada.

Miller, C. and Swift, K. (1981) *The Handbook of Non-Sexist Writing for Writers, Editors and Speakers*, British edition revised by S. Dowrick, London: The Women's Press.

Miller, C.R. (1984) 'Genre as social action', *Quarterly Journal of Speech* 70: 151 67.

Miller, N. (1986) *Dyspraxia and Its Management*, London: Croom Helm.

Miller, W. and Ervin, S. (1964) 'The development of grammar in child language', in U. Bellugi and R. Brown (eds) *The Acquisition of Language* (Monographs of the Society for Research in Child Development, no. 29).

Mills, S. (1995) *Feminist Stylistics*, London: Routledge.

Milroy, J. and Milroy, L. (1991) *Authority in Language: Investigating Language Prescription and Standardisation*, 2nd edition, London: Routledge.

Milroy, L. (1980/1987) *Language and Social Networks*, 2nd edition 1980, Oxford: Basil Blackwell.

Minsky, M. and Papert, S. (1969) *Perceptrons*, Cambridge, MA: MIT Press.

Mitchell, D. (1987) 'Lexical guidance in human parsing: locus and processing characteristics', in M. Coltheart (ed.) *Attention and Performance*, vol. 12, *The Psychology of Reading*, Hove: Lawrence Erlbaum Associates.

—— (1994) 'Sentence parsing', in M.A. Gernsbacher (ed.) *Handbook of Psycholinguistics*, San Diego: Academic Press.

Mitchell, T.F. (1958) 'Syntagmatic relations in linguistic analysis', *Transactions of the Philological Society*: 101–18.

—— (1966) 'Some English phrasal types', in C.E. Bazell, J.C. Catford, M.A.K. Halliday and R.H. Robins (eds) *In Memory of J.R. Firth*, London: Longman.

—— (1971) 'Linguistic "goings on": collocations and other lexical matters arising on the syntagmatic record', *Archivum Linguisticum* 2: 35–69.

—— (1975) *Principles of Firthian Linguistics*, London: Longman.

Mitzka, W. and Schmidt, L.E. (1953–78) *Deutsche Wortatlas*, Giessen: Schmitz.

Moens, M. and Steedman, M. (1988) 'Temporal ontology and temporal reference', *Computational Linguistics* 14(2): 15–28.

Mohanan, K.P. (1986) *The Theory of Lexical Phonology*, Dordrecht: Reidel.

Mohr, B. (1971) 'Intrinsic variation in the speech signal', *Phonetica* 23: 65–93.

Molino, J. (1985) 'Où en est la morphologie?', *Langages* 78: 5–40.

Money, J. (ed.) *Reading Disability*, Baltimore: John Hopkins Press.

Moore, B.C.J. (1997) *An Introduction to the Psychology of Hearing*, 4th edition, London: Academic Press.

Moore, G.E. (1936) 'Is existence a predicate?', *Proceedings of the Aristotelean Society* (supplementary volume): 175–88.

Moore, J. and Widdowson, H.G. (eds) (1980) *Reading and Thinking in English*, Oxford: Oxford University Press.

Moortgat, M. (1988) *Categorial Investigations: Logical and Linguistic Aspects of the Lambek Calculus*, Dordrecht: Foris.

Moravcsik, E.A. (1980) 'Introduction: on syntactic approaches', in E.A. Moravcsik and J.R. Wirth (eds) *Syntax and Semantics*, vol. 13, *Current Approaches to Syntax*, New York and London: Academic Press.

Morgan, J.L. (1979), 'Observations on the pragmatics of metaphor', in A. Ortony (ed.) *Metaphor and Thought*, Cambridge: Cambridge University Press.

Morpurgo Davies, A. (1998) *Nineteenth-Century Linguistics*, G.E. Lepschy (ed.) *History of Linguistics* vol. 4, London: Longman.

Morrill, G. (1994) *Type Logical Grammar: Categorial Logic of Signs*, Dordrecht: Kluwer.

Morse, P.A. (1972) 'The discrimination of speech and nonspeech stimuli in early infancy', *Journal of Experimental Child Psychology* 14: 477–92.

Morton, J. (1969) 'The interaction of information in word recognition', *Psychological Review* 76: 165–78.

—— (1979) 'Facilitation in word recognition: experiments causing change in the logogen model', in P.A. Kolers, M.E. Wrolstad and H. Bouma (eds) *Processing of Visible Language*, vol. 1, New York: Plenum.

Moss, H.E. and Gaskell, G. (1999) 'Lexical semantic processing during speech', in S. Garrod and M. Pickering (eds) *Language Processing*, Hove: Psychology Press.

Moulton, W.H. (1960) 'The short vowel systems of northern Switzerland: a study in structural dialectology', *Word* 16: 155–82.

Mowrer, O.H. (1960) *Learning Theory and Symbolic Processes*, New York: John Wiley.

Mühlhäusler, P. (1986) *Pidgin and Creole Linguistics*, Oxford: Basil Blackwell.

Mukarovsky, J. (1932) 'Standard language and poetic language', in P.L. Garvin (ed.) (1964) *A Prague School Reader on Esthetics, Literary Structure and Style*, Washington, DC: Georgetown University Press.

Müller, F.M. (1891) *The Science of Language*, 2 vols, London: Longman, Green and Company; 1st edition 1877.

Murray, S.O. (1993) *Theory Groups and the Study of Language in North America: A Social History*, Amsterdam and Philadelphia: John Benjamins.

Myers, G. (1989) *Writing Biology: Texts in the Construction of Scientific Knowledge*, Madison, WI: University of Wisconsin Press.

Myers-Scotton, C. (1992) *Duelling Languages: Grammatical Structure in Codeswitching*, Oxford: Oxford University Press.

—— (1993) *Social Motivations for Codeswitching: Evidence from Africa*, Oxford: Clarendon Press.

—— (1998) 'Code-switching', in F. Coulmas (ed.) *The Handbook of Sociolinguistics*, Oxford: Blackwell Publishers.

Nauta, W.J.H. and Fiertag, M. (1979) 'The organization of the brain', in *The Brain (A Scientific American book)*, San Francisco: W.H. Freeman.

Nearey, T.M. (1980) 'On the physical interpretation of vowel quality: Cineflourographic and acoustic evidence', *Journal of Phonetics* 8: 213–41.

—— (1997) 'Speech perception as pattern recognition', *Journal of the Acoustical Society of America* 101: 3241–54.

Neely, J.H. (1991) 'Semantic priming effects in visual word recognition: a selective review of current findings and theories', in D. Besner and G. Humphreys (eds) *Basic Processes in Reading: Visual Word Recognition*, Hillsdale, NJ: Lawrence Erlbaum Associates.

Negus, V.E. (1949) *The Comparative Anatomy and Physiology of the Larynx*, New York: Hafner.

Nemser, W. (1961/1971) 'Experimental phonological study in the English of Hungarians', Columbia University Ph.D. thesis, and The Hague: Mouton.

Nespor, M. and Vogel, I. (1986) *Prosodic Phonology*, Dordrecht: Foris.

Newbrook, M. (1986) *Sociolinguistic Reflexes of Dialect Interference in West Wirral*, Bern and Frankfurt: Peter Lang.

—— (1987) *Aspects of the Syntax of Educated Singaporean English: Attitudes, Beliefs and Usage*, Bern and Frankfurt: Peter Lang.

—— (1991) *Exploring English Errors: Grammar, Vocabulary, Pronunciation*, 2 vols, Hong Kong: Oxford University Press.

—— (ed.) (1999) *English is an Asian Language*, Sydney: Macquarie Library.

Newmeyer, F.J. (1980/1986) *Linguistic Theory in America: The First Quarter Century of Transformational Generative Grammar*, New York and London: Academic Press; 2nd edition 1986.

—— (1988) (ed.) *Linguistics: The Cambridge Survey*, Cambridge: Cambridge University Press.

—— (1998) *Language Form and Language Function*, Cambridge, MA: MIT Press.

Newton, B. (1972) *The Generative Interpretation of Dialect*, London: Cambridge University Press.

Newton, M.J. (1977) 'Dyslexia: the problem of recognition', *Update* (April).

—— (1984) *Specific Literacy Difficulties: Dyslexia*, Birmingham: Centre for Extension Education, University of Aston in Birmingham.

——, Thompson, M.E. and Richards, I.L. (1979) *Readings in Dyslexia* (Learning Development Aids Series), Wisbech, Cambridgeshire: Bemrose.

—— et al. (1985) 'A positive approach to dyslexia: information processing and computer science', *Aston University Occasional Papers*.

Nice, M. (1925) 'Length of sentences as a criterion of child's progress in speech', *Journal of Educational Psychology* 16: 370–9.

Nida, E.A. (1946) *Morphology: The Descriptive Analysis of Words*, Ann Arbor: University of Michigan Press.

—— (1968) *A Synopsis of English Syntax*, 2nd revised edition, The Hague, Mouton.

—— (1975) *Componential Analysis of Meaning*, The Hague: Mouton.

Ning Yu (1998) *The Contemporary Theory of Metaphor: A Perspective from Chinese* (Human Cognitive Processing, vol. 1), Amsterdam and Philadelphia: Benjamins.

Noiré, L. (1877/1917) *The Origin and Philosophy of Language*, 2nd revised edition, Chicago: The Open Court Publishing Company; 1st edition 1877.

Norman, D.E., Rumelhart, D.E. and the INR Research Group (1975) *Explorations in Cognition*, San Francisco: Freeman.

Norris, D. (1993) 'Bottom-up connectionist models of "interaction"', in G. Altmann and R. Shillcock (eds) *Cognitive Models of Speech Processing: The Second Sperloga Meeting*, Hillsdale, NJ: Lawrence Erlbaum Associates.

Nygaard, L.C. and Pisoni, D.B. (1998) 'Talker-specific learning in speech production', *Perception and Psychophysics* 60: 355–76.

O'Brien, E.J., Duffy, S.A. and Myers, J.L. (1986) 'Anaphoric inference during reading', *Journal of Experimental Psychology: Learning, Memory & Cognition* 12: 346–52.

O'Connor, J.D. (1973) *Phonetics*, Harmondsworth: Penguin.

—— and Arnold, G.F. (1961/1973) *Intonation of Colloquial English*, London: Longman; 2nd edition 1973.

Oakhill, J., Garnham, A., Gernsbacher, M.A. and Cain, K. (1992) 'How natural are conceptual anaphors?', *Language and Cognitive Processes* 7: 257–80.

Ogden, C.K. and Richards, I.A. (1923) *The Meaning of Meaning: A Study of the Influence of Language Upon Thought and the Science of Symbolism*, London: Kegan Paul, Trench, Trubner.

Ohmann, R. (1959) 'Prolegomena to the analysis of prose style', in H.C. Martin (ed.) *Style in Prose Fiction: English Institute Essays*, New York: Columbia University Press.

Oller, D.K., Wieman, L.A., Doyle, W.J. and Ross, C. (1976) 'Infant babbling and speech', *Journal of Child Language* 3: 1–11.

Olu Tomori, S.H. (1977) *The Morphology and Syntax of Present-Day English: An Introduction*, London: Heinemann.

Onions, C.T. (1921) 'Henry Sweet', *Dictionary of National Biography, 1921*: 519.

Orton, H. (1962) *Survey of English Dialects: Introduction*, Leeds: Arnold.

—— and Dien, E. (1962–71) *Survey of English Dialects: Basic Material*, 4 vols, Leeds: Arnold.

——, Sanderson, S. and Widdowson, J. (1978) *Linguistic Atlas of England*, London: Croom Helm.

Orton, S.T. (1937) *Reading, Writing and Speech Problems in Children*, London: Chapman & Hall.

Ortony, A. (ed.) (1979a/1993) *Metaphor and Thought*, Cambridge: Cambridge University Press; 2nd edition 1993.

—— (1979b) 'Metaphor: a multidimensional problem', in A. Ortony (ed.) *Metaphor and Thought*, Cambridge: Cambridge University Press.

Page, R.I. (1987) *Runes*, London: British Museum Publications for the Trustees of the British Museum.

Palmer, F.R. (ed.) (1970) *Prosodic Analysis*, London: Oxford University Press.

—— (1971) *Grammar*, Harmondsworth: Penguin.

—— (1981) *Semantics*, 2nd edition, Cambridge: Cambridge University Press.

Palmer, H.E. (1917/1968) *The Scientific Study and Teaching of Language*, London: Oxford University Press.

—— and Palmer, D. (1925/1959) *English Through Actions*, Tokyo, IRET; reprinted 1959, London: Longman.

Paprotté, Wolf and Dirven, René (eds) (1985) *The Ubiquity of Metaphor: Metaphor in Language and Thought* (Amsterdam Studies in the Theory and History of Linguistic Science, series 4 – Current Issues in Linguistic Theory, no. 29), Amsterdam: John Benjamins.

Paradis, J. and Genesee, F. (1996) Syntactic Acquisition in Bilingual Children: Autonomous or Interdependent? *Studies in Second Language Acquisition* 18(1): 1–25.

Pariente, J.C. (1985) *L'Analyse du langage à Port-Royal*, Paris: Editions Minuit.

Parodi, T. (1998) *Der Erwerb funktionaler Kategorien im Deutschen*, Tübingen: Gunter Narr.

Pavlides, G.T. and Miles, T.R. (1981) *Dyslexia Research and Its Application to Education*, Chichester: John Wiley and Sons.

Pearce, D.C. (1974) *Statutory Interpretation in Australia*, Sydney: Butterworths.

Pears, D. (1971) *Wittgenstein*, Glasgow: Fontana Collins.

Pêcheux, M. (1982) *Language, Semantics and Ideology*, Basingstoke: Macmillan.

Peirce, C.S. (1868) 'Some consequences of four incapacities', *Journal of Speculative Philosophy* 2: 140–57.

—— (1931–58) *Collected Papers*, Cambridge, MA: Harvard University Press.

Penn, G. (1999) 'Linearization and WH-extraction in HPSG', in R.D. Borsley and A. Przepiórkowski (eds) *Slavic in Head-Driven Phrase Structure Grammar*, Stanford, CA: CSLI Publications.

Pereira, F.C.N. and Warren, D.H.D. (1980) 'Definite clause grammars for language analysis – a survey of the formalism and a comparison with augmented transition networks', *Artificial Intelligence* 13(3): 231–78.

Perfetti, C. and Zhang, S. (1995) 'Very early phonological activation in Chinese reading', *Journal of Experimental Psychology: Learning, Memory, and Cognition* 21: 24–33.

Perkins, W.H. and Kent, R.D. (1986) *Textbook of Functional Anatomy of Speech, Language, and Hearing*, San Diego: College-Hill.

Perlmutter, D.M. (ed.) (1983) *Studies in Relational Grammar*, vol. 1, Chicago: University of Chicago Press.

—— and Postal, P.M. (1984) 'The 7-Advancement Exclusiveness Law', D.M. Perlmutter and C.G. Rosen (eds) *Studies in Relational Grammar 2*, Chicago: University of Chicago Press.

—— and Rosen, C.G. (eds) (1984) *Studies in Relational Grammar*, vol. 2, Chicago: University of Chicago Press.

Perrig, W. and Kintsch, W. (1985) 'Propositional and situational representations of text', *Journal of Memory and Language* 24: 503–18.

Peterson, G.E. and Barney, H.L. (1952) 'Control methods used in a study of the vowels', *Journal of the Acoustical Society of America* 73: 175–84.

Peterson, R.R. and Savoy, P. (1998) 'Lexical selection and phonological encoding during language production: evidence for cascade processing', *Journal of Experimental Psychology: Learning, Memory, and Cognition* 24: 539–57.

Petöfi, J. (1971) *Transformationsgrammatiken und eine kö-textuelle Texttheorie*, Frankfurt: Athenäum.

—— (1974) 'Toward an empirically motivated grammatical theory of verbal texts', in J. Petöfi and H. Rieser (eds) *Studies in Text Grammar*, Dordrecht: Reidel.

—— (1978) 'A formal semiotic text theory as an integrated theory of natural languages', in W.U. Dressler (ed.) *Current Trends in Textlinguistics*, Berlin and New York: Walter de Gruyter.

—— (1980) 'Einige Grundfragen der pragmatisch-semantischen Interpretation von Texten', in T. Ballmer and W. Kindt (eds) *Zum Thema 'Sprache und Logik': Ergebnisse einer interdisziplinären Diskussion*, Hamburg: Buske.

Pettinari, C. (1981) 'The function of a grammatical alternation in 14 surgical reports', mimeo, University of Michigan.

Petyt, K.M. (1980) *The Study of Dialect*, London: André Deutsch.

Philips, S. (1972) 'Participant structures and communicative competence: Warm Springs children in community and classroom', in C. Cazden, V. John and D. Hymes (eds) *Functions of Language in the Classroom*, New York: Teachers' College Press.

Piaget, J. (1980), in M. Piattelli-Palmarni (ed.) *Language and Learning: The Debate Between Jean Piaget and Noam Chomsky*, Cambridge, MA: Harvard University Press.

Pickering, M.J. (1994) 'Processing local and unbounded dependencies: A unified account', *Journal of Psycholinguistic Research* 23(4): 323–52.

—— and Barry, G. (1991) 'Sentence processing without empty categories', *Language and Cognitive Processes* 6: 229–59.

Pickett, J.M. (1999) *The Acoustics of Speech Communication: Fundamentals, Speech Perception Theory, and Technology*, Boston, MA: Allyn and Bacon.

Pickford, G.R. (1956) 'American linguistic geography: a sociological appraisal', *Word* 12: 211–33.

Pike, K.L. (1945) *The Intonation of American English*, Ann Arbor: University of Michigan Press.

—— (1948) *Tone Languages*, Ann Arbor: University of Michigan Press.

—— (1967) *Language in Relation to a Unified Theory of Human Behavior*, The Hague: Mouton.

—— (1970) *Tagmemics and Matrix Linguistics Applied to Selected African Languages*, Norman, Summer Institute of Linguistics of the University of Oklahoma.

—— (1982) *Linguistic Concepts: An Introduction to Tagmemics*, Lincoln, NE and London: University of Nebraska Press.

Pinker, S. (1984) *Language Learnability and Language Development*, Cambridge, MA: Harvard University Press.

—— (1989) *Learnability and Cognition: The Acquisition of Argument Structure*, Cambridge, MA: MIT Press.

—— (1994) *The Language Instinct*, Harmondsworth: Allen Lane.

—— and Bloom, P. (1990) 'Natural language and natural selection', *Behavioral and Brain Sciences* 12: 707–84.

—— and Prince, A. (1992) 'Regular and irregular morphology and the psychological status of rules of grammar', in *Proceedings of the 17th Annual Meeting of the Berkeley Linguistics Society*. Berkeley, CA: Berkeley Linguistics Society.

Pisoni, D.B. (1973), 'Auditory and phonetic memory codes in the discrimination of consonants and vowels', *Perception and Psychophysics* 13: 253–60.

Pitt, M.A. and McQueen, J.M. (1998) 'Is compensation for coarticulation mediated by the lexicon?', *Journal of Memory and Language* 39: 347–70.

Platt, J.T. (1971) *Grammatical Form and Grammatical Meaning: A Tagmemic View of Fillmore's Deep Structure Case Concepts*, Amsterdam and London: North Holland.

Plaut, D.C. (1997) 'Structure and function in the lexical system: insights from distributed models of word reading and lexical decision', *Language and Cognitive Processes* 12: 756–805.

——, McClelland, J.L., Seidenberg, M.S. and Patterson, K.E. (1996) 'Understanding normal and impaired word reading: computational principles in quasi-regular domains', *Psychological Review* 103: 56–115.

Poeppel, D. and Wexler, K. (1993) 'The Full Competence Hypothesis of clause structure', *Language* 69: 1–33.

Polkinghorne, D.E. (1988) *Narrative Knowing and the Human Sciences*, Albany, NY: State University of New York Press.

Pollard, C. (1984) 'Generalized phrase atructure grammars, head grammars and natural language', unpublished Ph.D. thesis, Stanford University.

—— and Sag, I.A. (1987) *Information-Based Syntax and Semantics*, Stanford: CSLI.

—— (1994) *Head-Driven Phrase Structure Grammar*, Stanford, CA: University of Chicago Press and CSLI Publications.

Postal, P.M. (1970) 'On the surface verb "remind"', *Linguistic Inquiry* 1: 37–120.

—— (1986) *Studies of Passive Clauses*, Albany: SUNY Press.

—— and Joseph, B.D. (eds) (1990) *Studies in Relational Grammar*, vol. 3, Chicago: University of Chicago Press.

Potter, M.C. and Lombardi, L. (1990) 'Regeneration in the short-term recall of sentences', *Journal of Memory and Language* 29: 633–54.

Potts, G.R., Keenan, J.M. and Golding, J.M. (1988) 'Assessing the occurrence of elaborative inferences: lexical decision versus naming', *Journal of Memory and Language* 27: 399–415.

Prabhu, N.S. (1987) *Second Language Pedagogy: A Perspective*, Oxford: Oxford University Press.

Premack, A. and Premack, D. (1972) 'Teaching language to an ape', *Scientific American* 227: 92–9.

Preston, D. (1989) *Perceptual Dialectology*, Dordrecht: Foris.

—— (ed.) (1999) *Handbook of Perceptual Dialectology*, vol. 1, Amsterdam and Philadelphia: John Benjamins.

Preyer, W. (1882) *Die Seele des Kindes*, Leipzig; published in English, 1880–90 as *The Mind of the Child*, trans. H.W. Brown, 2 vols, New York: Appleton.

Prince, A. and Smolensky, P. (1993) *Optimality Theory: Constraint Interaction in Generative Grammar*, Cambridge, MA: MIT Press.

Prince, E. (1981) 'Language and the law: a case for linguistic pragmatics', *Working Papers in Sociolinguistics*, Austin, TX: Southwest Educational Development Laboratory.

Pritchett, B.L. (1992) 'Parsing with grammar: islands, heads, and garden paths', in H. Goodluck and M. Rochemont (eds) *Island Constraints: Theory, Acquisition, and Processing*, Dordrecht: Kluwer.

Propp, V. (1928/1958) *Morfologiya skazki*, Leningrad; published in English, 1958 as *Morphology of the Folktale* (Indiana University Publications in Anthropology, Folklore and Linguistics, no. 10), Bloomington, IN.

Pulleyblank, D. (1986) *Tone in Lexical Phonology*, Dordrecht: Reidel.

Pustejovsky, J. (1991) 'The generative lexicon', *Computational Linguistics* 17(4): 409–41.

Putnam, H. (1970) 'Is semantics possible?', in H. Kiefer and M. Munitz (eds) *Languages, Belief and Metaphysics* (Contemporary Philosophical Thought: The International Philosophy Year Conferences at Brockport, no. 1), New York: State University of New York Press.

Quay, S. (1994) 'Language choice in early bilingual development', unpublished Ph.D. thesis, University of Cambridge.

Quine, W.V.O. (1951/1961) 'Two dogmas of empiricism', *Philosophical Review* (January); reprinted 1961, in *From a Logical Point of View: 9 Logico-Philosophical Essays*, 2nd revised edition, New York: Harper and Row.

—— (1960) *Word and Object*, Cambridge, MA: MIT Press.

Quirk, R. (1960) 'Towards a description of English usage', *Transactions of the Philological Society*: 40–61.

—— (1972) Report of the Committee of Enquiry into the Speech Therapy Services, London: Her Majesty's Stationary Service.

—— and Svartvik, J. (1979) 'A corpus of modern English', in H. Bergenholtz and B. Schraeder (eds) *Empirische Textwissenschaft: Aufbau und Auswertung von Text-Corpora*, Königstein: Scriptor.

——, Greenbaum, S., Leech, G. and Svartvik, J. (1985) *A Comprehensive Grammar of the English Language*, London: Longman.

Radford, A. (1988) *Transformational Grammar*, Cambridge: Cambridge University Press.

—— (1990) *Syntactic Theory and the Acquisition of English Syntax*, Oxford: Basil Blackwell.

—— (1996) 'Towards a structure-building model of acquisition', in H. Clahsen (ed.) *Generative Perspectives on Language Acquisition*, Amsterdam: John Benjamins.

—— (1997) *Syntactic Theory and the Structure of English: A Minimalist Approach*, Cambridge: Cambridge University Press.

Rae, J. (1862) *The Polynesian*; reprinted as an appendix to R.A.S. Paget (1963) *Human Speech: Some Observations, Experiments and Conclusions as to the Nature, Origin, Purpose and Possible Improvement of Human Speech*, London: Routledge & Kegan Paul.

Rampton, B. (1995a) *Crossing: Language and Ethnicity Among Adolescents*, London: Longman.

—— (1995b) 'Politics and change in research in applied linguistics', *Applied Linguistics* 16: 231–56.

—— (1999) 'Socio-linguistics and cultural studies: new ethnicities, liminality and interaction', *Social Semiotics* 9(3): 355–73.

Ramsay, A.M. (1994) 'The co-operative lexicon', in H. Bunt (ed.) *Proceedings of the 1st International Workshop on Computational Semantics I*, Tilburg: University of Tilburg.

Rask, R. (1818) 'Undersøgelse om det gamle Nordiske eller Islandske Sprogs Oprindelse', Copenhagen; reprinted in R. Rask (1932) *Ausgewählte Abhandlungen*, ed. L. Hjelmslev, vol. 1, Copenhagen: Levin og Munksgaard.

Rastier, F. (1985) 'L'Œuvre de Hjelmslev aujourd'hui', *II Protagora XXV* 4(7–8): 109–25.

Ratcliff, R. and McKoon, G. (1978) 'Priming in item recognition: evidence for the propositional structure of sentences', *Journal of Verbal Learning and Verbal Behavior* 17: 403–18.

Rayner, K. and Pacht, J.M. (1994) 'Effects of prior encounter and global discourse bias on the processing of lexically ambiguous words: evidence from eye fixations', *Journal of Memory and Language* 33: 527–44.

—— and Pollatsek, A. (1989) *The Psychology of Reading*, New Jersey: Prentice Hall.

——, Carlson, M. and Frazier, L. (1983) 'The interaction of syntax and semantics during sentence processing', *Journal of Verbal Learning and Verbal Behavior* 22: 358–74.

Reape, M. (1993) 'A formal theory of word order: a case study in West Germanic',

unpublished Ph.D. thesis, University of Edinburgh.

Recherches structurales (1949) Travaux du Cercle Linguistique de Copenhague, *Interventions dans le débat glossématique, publiées à l'occasion du cinquantenaire de M. Louis Hjelmslev*, Copenhagen: Nordisk Sprog-og Kulturforlag.

Reddy, R. (1980) 'Machine models of speech perception', in R.A. Cole (ed.) *Perception and Production of Fluent Speech*, Hillsdale, NJ: Lawrence Erlbaum Associates.

Reid, G. (1999) *Dyslexia: A Practitioner's Handbook*, 2nd edition, Edinburgh: Moray House.

Reilly, R. and Sharkey, N.E. (1992) *Connectionist Approaches to Language Processing*, Howe: Lawrence Erlbaum Associates.

Rescorla, L. (1980) 'Overextensions in early language development', *Journal of Child Language* 7: 321–35.

Richards, I.A. (1936) 'Metaphor', in I.A. Richards, *The Philosophy of Rhetoric*, London: Oxford University Press.

—— (1960) 'Poetic process and literary analysis', in T.A. Sebeok (ed.) *Style in Language*, Cambridge, MA: MIT Press.

Richards, J.C. (ed.) (1974) *Error Analysis: Perspectives on Second Language Acquisition*, London: Longman.

Rickford, J.R. (1998) 'The creole origins of African-American vernacular English: evidence from copula absence', in S.S. Mufwene, J.R. Rickform, G. Bailey and J. Baugh (eds) *African-American English: Structure, History and Use*, London and New York: Routledge.

—— and Eckert, P. (eds) (2001) *Style and Sociolinguistic Variation*, Cambridge: Cambridge University Press.

Riesbeck, C.K. (1978) 'An expectation-driven production system for natural language understanding', in D.A. Waterman and R. Hayes-Roth (eds) *Pattern Directed Inference Systems*, Amsterdam: North Holland.

Ringbom, H. (1987) *The Role of the First Language in Foreign Language Learning*, Clevedon and Philadelphia: Multilingual Matters.

Rischel, J. (1976) 'The contribution of Louis Hjelmslev', *Third International Conference of Nordic and General Linguistics*, Stockholm: Almqvist and Wiksell.

Ristan, C.A. (1996/1999) 'Animal language and cognition projects', in A. Lock and

C.R. Peters (eds) *Handbook of Human Symbolic Evolution*, Oxford: Blackwell Publishers; 1st edition 1996, Oxford: Oxford University Press.

Robinett, B.W. and Schachter, J. (eds) (1983) *Second Language Learning: Contrastive Analysis and Related Aspects*, Ann Arbor: University of Michigan Press.

Robins, R.H. (1959) 'In defence of WP', *Transactions of the Philological Society*: 116–44.

—— (1964/1989) *General Linguistics: An Introductory Survey*, London: Longman; 4th edition 1989.

—— (1967) *A Short History of Linguistics*, London: Longman.

—— (1980) *General Linguistics: An Introductory Survey*, 3rd edition, London: Longman.

—— (1988) 'Leonard Bloomfield: the man and the man of science' *Transactions of the Philological Society* 86(1): 63–87.

Roca, I. (1994) *Generative Phonology*, London: Routledge.

Romaine, S. (1978) 'Postvocalic /r/ in Scottish English: sound change in progress?', in P. Trudgill (ed.) *Sociolinguistic Patterns in British English*, London: Edward Arnold.

—— (1988) *Pidgin and Creole Languages*, London and New York: Longman.

—— (1995) *Bilingualism*, 2nd edition, Oxford: Basil Blackwell.

Rondal, J. and Edwards, S. (1997) *Language in Mental Retardation*, London: Whurr.

Rosch, E. (1973) 'Natural categories', *Cognitive Psychology* 4: 328–50.

—— (1975) 'Cognitive representations of semantic categories', *Journal of Experimental Psychology: General* 104: 192–233.

—— (1977a) 'Classification of real-world objects: origins and representations in cognition', in P.N. Johnson-Laird and P.C. Wason (eds) *Thinking: Readings in Cognitive Science*, Cambridge: Cambridge University Press.

—— (1977b) 'Human categorization', in Warren, N. (ed.) *Studies in Cross-Cultural Psychology*, vol. 1, London etc.: Academic Press.

—— (1978) 'Principles of categorization', in E. Rosch and B.B. Lloyd (eds) *Cognition and Categorization*, Hillsdale, NJ: Lawrence Erlbaum Associates.

—— and Mervis, C.B. (1975) 'Family resemblances: studies in the internal structure of categories', *Cognitive Science* 7: 573–605.

——, ——, Gray, W.D., Johnson, D.M. and Boyes-Braem, O. (1976) 'Basic objects in natural categories', *Cognitive Psychology* 8: 382–439.

Ross, J.R. (1968) *Constraints on Variables in Syntax*, Bloomington, IN: Indiana University Linguistics Club.

—— (1970) 'On declarative sentences', in R. Jacobs and P. Rosenbaum (eds) *Readings in English Transformational Grammar*, Waltham, MA: Ginn.

—— (1973) 'Nouniness', in O. Fujimara (ed.) *Three Dimensions of Linguistic Theory*, Tokyo: TEC Corporation.

Rothweiler, M. and Meibauer, J. (eds) (1999a) *Das Lexikon im Spracherwerb*, Tübingen-Basel: A. Francke.

—— and —— (1999b) 'Das Lexikon im Spracherwerb – ein Überblick', in M. Rothweiler and J. Meibauer (eds) *Das Lexikon im Spracherwerb*, Tübingen-Basel: A. Francke.

Ruhlen, M. (1975) *A Guide to the Languages of the World*, Language Universals Project: Stanford University.

Rumbaugh, D., Gill, T. and von Glasersfeld, E. (1973) 'Reading and sentence completion by a chimpanzee (Pan)', *Science* 182: 731–3.

Rumelhart, D.E. (1975) 'Notes on a schema for stories', in D.G. Bobrow and A. Collins, *Representation and Understanding: Studies in Cognitive Science*, New York: Academic Press.

—— (1979) 'Some problems with the notion of literal meaning', in A. Ortony (ed.) *Metaphor and Thought*, Cambridge: Cambridge University Press.

—— and McClelland, J.L. (1986) *Parallel Distributed Processing: Explorations in the Microstructure of Cognition*, Cambridge, MA: MIT Press.

Russell, B. (1903) *The Principles of Mathematics*, Cambridge: Cambridge University Press.

Russell, K. (1997) 'Optimality Theory and morphology', in D. Archangeli and D.T. Langendoen (eds) *Optimality Theory: An Overview*, Oxford: Blackwell Publishers.

Sachs, M. and Young, E. (1979) 'Encoding of steady state vowels in the auditory-nerve: representation in terms of discharge rate', *Journal of the Acoustical Society of America* 66: 470–9.

Sacks, H., Schegloff, E.A. and Jefferson, G.A. (1974) 'A simplest systematic for the organization of turn-taking for conversation', *Language* 50: 696–735.

Sacks, O. (1989/1990) *Seeing Voices: A Journey into the World of the Deaf*, Berkeley and Los Angeles: University of California Press; reprinted 1990, London: Pan.

Sadock, J.M. (1974) *Toward a Linguistic Theory of Speech Acts*, New York: Academic Press.

—— (1979) 'Figurative speech and linguistics', in A. Ortony (ed.) *Metaphor and Thought*, Cambridge: Cambridge University Press.

Saeed, J.I. (1997) *Semantics*, Oxford: Blackwell Publishers.

Sag, I.A. (1997) 'English relative clause constructions', *Journal of Linguistics* 30: 431–83.

—— and Wasow, T. (1999) *Syntactic Theory: A Formal Introduction*, Stanford, CA: CSLI Publications.

Saifullah Kahn, V. (1980) 'The "mother-tongue" of linguistic minorities in multicultural England', *Journal of Multilingual and Multicultural Development* 1(1): 71–88.

Salager-Meyer, F. (1990) 'Discoursal flaws in medical English abstracts: a genre analysis per research- and text-type', *Text*: 365–84.

Samarin, W. (1967) *Field Linguistics*, New York: Holt, Rinehart and Winston.

Sampson, G. (1980) *Schools of Linguistics: Competition and Evolution*, London: Hutchinson.

—— (1985) *Writing Systems*, London: Hutchinson.

—— (1987) 'Probabilistic models of analysis', in R. Garside, G. Leech and G. Sampson (eds) *The Computational Analysis of English: A Corpus-Based Approach*, London: Longman.

—— (1995) *English for the Computer*, Oxford: Clarendon Press.

Samuel, A.G. (1997) 'Lexical activation produces potent phonemic percepts', *Cognitive Psychology* 32: 97–127.

Sanford, A.J. (1999) 'Word meaning and discourse processing: a tutorial review', in S. Garrod and M. Pickering (eds) *Language Processing*, Hove: Psychology Press.

—— and Garrod, S.C. (1981) *Understanding Written Language: Explorations in Comprehension Beyond the Sentence*, New York: John Wiley and Sons.

—— and —— (1994) 'Selective processes in text understanding', in M.A. Gernsbacher (ed.) *Handbook of Psycholinguistics*, San Diego: Academic Press.

Sapir, E. (1921) *Language: An Introduction to the Study of Speech*, Oxford: Oxford University Press.

—— (1927) 'The unconscious patterning of behaviour in society', in E.S. Dummer, *The Unconscious: A Symposium*, New York: Knopf; reprinted in D.G. Mandelbaum (ed.) (1949) *Selected Writings of Edward Sapir in Language, Culture and Personality*, Berkeley and Los Angeles: University of California Press, and London: Cambridge University Press.

—— (1929) 'The status of linguistics as a science', *Language* 5; reprinted in D.G. Mandelbaum (ed.) (1949) *Edward Sapir, Culture, Language, Personality: Selected Essays*, Berkeley, Los Angeles and London: University of California Press.

Šaumjan, S.K. (1962) *Problemy teoretičeskoj fonologii*; revised edition 1968, *Problems of Theoretical Phonology* (Janua Linguarum, Series Minor, no. 41), trans. A.L. Vañek, The Hague and Paris: Mouton.

Saussure, F. de (1916/1974/1983) *Cours de linguistique générale*, Lausanne and Paris: Payot, reprinted 1974 as *Course in General Linguistics*, Glasgow: Fontana/Collins; 1983, Oxford: Duckworth, annotated by R. Harris.

Savage-Rumbaugh, E.S., Murphy, J., Sevcik, R.A., Brakke, K.E., Williams, S.L. and Rumbaugh, D.M. (1993) *Language Comprehension in Ape and Child* (Monograph of the Society for Research in Child Development, Serial 233): 58.

Saville-Troike, M. (1989) *The Ethnography of Communication: An Introduction*, 2nd edition, Oxford: Basil Blackwell.

Sayce, A.H. (1880) *Introduction to the Science of Language*, 2 vols, London: Kegan Paul.

Scalise, A. (1984) *Generative Morphology*, Dordrecht: Foris.

Scalise, S. (1988) 'Inflection and derivation', *Linguistics* 26: 561–82.

Schachter, J. (1990) 'On the issue of completeness in second language acquisition', *Second Language Research* 6: 93–124.

—— (1996) 'Maturation and the issue of Universal Grammar in second language acquisition', in W.C. Ritchie and T.K. Bhatia (eds)

Handbook of Second Language Acquisition, San Diego: Academic Press.

Schane, S.A. (1968) *French Phonology and Morphology*, Cambridge, MA: MIT Press.

Schank, R.C. (1972) 'Conceptual dependency: a theory of natural language understanding', *Cognitive Psychology* 3: 552–631.

—— (1982) *Dynamic Memory: A Theory of Learning in Computers and People*, Cambridge: Cambridge University Press.

—— and Abelson, R.P. (1977) *Scripts, Plans, Goals and Understanding*, Hillsdale, NJ: Lawrence Erlbaum Associates.

Schegloff, E.A. and Sacks, H. (1973/1999) 'Opening up closings', *Semiotica* 7: 289–327; reprinted in A. Jaworski and N. Coupland (eds) (1999) *The Discourse Reader*, London: Routledge.

Scherer, A. (1868) *Die Urheimat der Indogermanen*, Darmstadt: Wissenschaftliche Buchgesellschaft.

Schiffman, H.F. (1998) 'Diglossia as a sociolinguistic solution', in F. Coulmas (ed.) *The Handbook of Sociolinguistics*, Oxford: Blackwell Publishers.

Schiffrin, D. (1994) *Approaches to Discourse*, Oxford: Blackwell Publishers.

Schlegel, F. von (1808) *Über die Sprache und Weisheit der Inder: Em Beitrag zur Begrundung der Alterthumskunde*, Heidelberg: Mohr Zimmer.

Schlick, M. (1936) 'Meaning and verification', *Philosophical Review* 45: 339–82.

Schlosser, M.J., Aoyagi, N., Fulbright, R.K., Gore, J.C. and McCarthy, G. (1998) 'Functional MRI studies of auditory comprehension', *Human Brain Mapping* 6: 1–13.

Schlyter, S. (1995) 'The weaker language in bilingual Swedish–French children', in K. Hyltenstam and Å. Viberg (eds) *Progression and Regression in Language*, Cambridge: Cambridge University Press.

Schmalhofer, F. and Glavanov, D. (1986) 'Three components of understanding a programmer's manual: verbatim, propositional, and situational representations', *Journal of Memory and Language* 25: 279–94.

Schneider, J. and Hacker, S. (1972) 'Sex role imagery and the use of the generic man', *American Sociologist* 8(1): 64–75.

Schouten, J.F. (1940) 'The residue, a new component in subjective sound analysis', *K. Akademie van Wetenschappen, Amsterdam, Afdeeling Natuur-kunde* (Proceedings) 43: 356–65.

Schouten, M.E.H. and van Hessen, A.J. (1992) 'Modeling phoneme perception', *Categorial Perception* 92: 1841–55.

Schreifers, H., Meyer, A.S. and Levelt, W.J.M. (1990) 'Exploring the time course of lexical access in speech production: picture–word interference studies', *Journal of Memory and Language* 29: 86–102.

Schuchardt, H. (1882) 'Kreolische Studien II: über das Indoportugiesische von Cochim', Vienna, Akademie der Wissenschaften, Sitzungsberichte, Philosophisch-historische Klasse 102 (II).

—— (1883) 'Kreolische Studien IV: über das Malaiospanische der Philippinen', Vienna, Akademie der Wissenschaften, Sitzungsberichte, Philosophisch-historische Klasse 105 (II).

—— (1885) *Über die Lautgesetze; gegen die Junggrammatiker*, Berlin; reprinted with English trans. in Th. Vennemann and T.H. Wilbur (1972) *Schuchardt, the Neogrammarians and the Transformational Theory of Phonological Change*, Frankfurt: Athenäum.

Schwartz, B. and Sprouse, R. (1994) 'Word order and nominative case in nonnative language acquisition: a longitudinal study of (L1 Turkish) German interlanguage', in T. Hoekstra and B. Schwartz (eds) *Language Acquisition Studies in Generative grammar: Papers in Honor of Kenneth Wexler from the GLOW 1991 Workshops*, Amsterdam: John Benjamins.

Scott, M. (1996) *WordSmith*, Oxford: Oxford University Press.

Searle, J.R. (1969) *Speech Acts: An Essay in the Philosophy of Language*, Cambridge: Cambridge University Press.

—— (1971) 'What is a speech act', in J.R. Searle (ed.) *The Philosophy of Language*, Oxford: Oxford University Press.

—— (1975) 'Indirect speech acts', in P. Cole and J. Morgan (eds) *Syntax and Semantics*, vol. 3, *Speech Acts*, New York: Academic Press.

—— (1979) 'Metaphor', in A. Ortony (ed.) *Metaphor and Thought*, Cambridge: Cambridge University Press.

Sebeok, T.A. (ed.) (1960) *Style in Language*, Cambridge, MA: MIT Press.

—— (ed.) (1977) *How Animals Communicate*, Bloomington and London: Indiana University Press.

Seidenberg, M.S. and McClelland, J.L. (1989) 'A distributed, developmental model of word recognition and naming', *Psychological Review* 96: 523–69.

——, Tanenhaus, M.K., Leiman, J.M. and Bienkowski, M. (1982) 'Automatic access of the meanings of ambiguous words in context: some limitations on knowledge-based processing', *Cognitive Psychology* 14: 489–532.

Selinker, L. (1972) 'Interlanguage', *International Review of Applied Linguistics* 10: 209–31.

—— (1992) *Rediscovering Interlanguage*, London: Longman.

—— (1996) 'On the notion of 'IL Competence' in early SLA research: an aid to understanding some baffling current issues', in G. Brown, K. Malmkjær and J. Williams (eds) *Performance and Competence in Second Language Acquisition*, Cambridge: Cambridge University Press.

Selkirk, E.O. (1982) *The Syntax of Words*, Cambridge, MA: MIT Press.

Sells, P. (1985) *Lectures on Contemporary Syntactic Theories*, Stanford: CSLI Publications.

Seyfarth, R.M. and Cheney, D.L. (1986) 'Vocal development in vervet monkeys', *Animal Behaviour* 34: 1640–58.

——, —— and Marler, P. (1980a) 'Monkey responses to three different alarm calls: evidence for predator classification and semantic communication', *Science* 210: 801–3.

——, —— and —— (1980b) 'Vervet monkey alarm calls: semantic communication in a free-ranging primate', *Animal Behaviour* 28: 1070–94.

Shamma, S.A. (1985) 'Speech processing in the auditory system, II: Lateral inhibition and the central processing of speech evoked activity in the auditory nerve', *Journal of the Acoustical Society of America* 78: 1622–32.

Shankweiler, D. and Studdert-Kennedy, M. (1967) 'Identification of consonants and vowels presented to left and right ears', *Quarterly Journal of Experimental Psychology* 19: 59–63.

Shelton, J.R. and Martin, R.C. (1992) 'How semantic is automatic semantic priming?' *Journal of Experimental Psychology: Learning, Memory, and Cognition* 18: 1191–210.

Shieber, S.M. (1986) *An Introduction to Unification-Based Approaches to Grammar*, Stanford, CA: CSLI Publications.

Shklovsky, V. (1917) 'Art as device', in L.T. Lemon and M.J. Reis (eds) (1965) *Russian Formalist Criticism: Four Essays*, Lincoln: Nebraska University Press.

Short, M.H. (ed.) (1989) *Reading, Analysing and Teaching Literature*, Harlow: Longman.

—— (1996) *Exploring the Language of Poetry, Prose and Drama*, Harlow: Longman.

—— and Leech, G. (1981) *Style in Fiction*, Harlow: Longman.

Shotter, J. (1993) *Conversational Realities*, London: Sage.

—— and Gergen, K.J. (eds) (1989) *Texts of Identity*, London: Sage.

Shuy, R.W., Wolfram, W.A. and Riley, W.K. (1968) *Linguistic Correlate of Social Stratification in Detroit Speech*, Michigan: Michigan State University Press.

Siegel, D. (1977) 'The Adjacency Condition and the theory of morphology', *NELS* 8: 189–97.

Siertsema, B. (1954) *A Study of Glossematics: Critical Survey of Its Fundamental Concepts*, The Hague: Martinus Nijhoff; 2nd edition 1965.

Sifianou, M. (1992) *Politeness Phenomena in England and Greece: A Cross-Cultural Perspective*, Oxford: Clarendon Press.

Simos, P.G., Molfese, D.L. and Brendan, R.A. (1997) 'Behavioral and electro-physiological indices of voicing-cue discrimination: laterality patterns and development', *Brain and Language* 57: 122–50.

Simpson, G.B. (1994) 'Context and the processing of ambiguous words', in M.A. Gernsbacher (ed.) *Handbook of Psycholinguistics*, San Diego: Academic Press.

Sinclair, J.McH. (1966) 'Beginning the study of lexis', in C.F. Bazell, J.C. Catford, M.A.K. Halliday and R.H. Robins (eds) *In Memory of J.R. Firth*, London: Longman.

—— (1972) *A Course in Spoken English: Grammar*, London: Oxford University Press.

—— (ed.) (1980) *Skills for Learning*, London: Nelson.

—— (1982) 'Lines about "Lines"', in R. Carter (ed.) *Language and Literature: An Introductory Reader in Stylistics*, London: George Allen and Unwin.

—— (1984) 'Naturalness in language', in J. Aarts and W. Meijs (eds) *Corpus Linguistics: Recent Developments in the Use of Computer Corpora in English Language Research*, Amsterdam: Rodopi.

—— (1987a) 'Collocation: a progress report', in R. Steele and T. Threadgold (eds) *Language Topics: Essays in Honour of Michael Halliday*, vol. 3, Amsterdam: John Benjamins.

—— (1987b) 'The nature of the evidence', in J.McH. Sinclair (ed.) *Looking Up: An Account of the COBUILD Project in Lexical Computing*, London and Glasgow: Collins.

—— (1991) *Corpus, Concordance, Collocation*, Oxford: Oxford University Press.

—— and Coulthard, M. (1975) *Towards an Analysis of Discourse: The English Used by Teachers and Pupils*, London: Oxford University Press.

Sinnott, J.M. and Brown, C.H. (1997) 'Perception of the American English liquid /ra-la/ contrast by humans and monkeys', *Journal of the Acoustical Society of America* 102: 588–602.

Skelton, J. (1994) 'Analysis of the structure of original research papers: aid to writing original papers for publication', *British Journal of Medical Practice* (October): 455–9.

Skinner, B.F. (1957) *Verbal Behavior*, New York: Appleton Crofts.

Skutnabb-Kangas, T. (1981) *Bilingualism or Not: The Education of Minorities*, Clevedon: Multilingual Matters.

Skutnabb-Kangas, T. and Toukomaa, P. (1976) 'Teaching migrant children's mother-tongue and learning the language of the host country in the context of the socio-cultural situation of the migrant family' (Tampere, Finland, UNESCO Report, Tutkimuksia Research Reports, no. 15), Department of Sociology and Social Psychology, University of Tampere.

Skwire, D. (1985) *Writing with a Thesis: A Rhetoric and Reader*, 4th edition, New York and London: Holt, Rinehart and Winston.

Skydgaard, H.B. (1942) *Den Konstituelle Dyslexi*, Copenhagen.

Skyrms, B. (1975) *Choice and Chance: An Introduction to Inductive Logic*, Enrico, CA: Dickenson.

Slobin, D.I. (1977) 'Language change in childhood and history', in J. MacNamara (ed.) *Language Learning and Thought*, New York: Academic Press.

—— (1982) 'Universal and particular in the acquisition of language', in E. Wanner and L. Gleitman (eds) *Language Acquisition: The State of the Art*, Cambridge: Cambridge University Press.

—— (1984) 'Cross-linguistic evidence for the language-making capacity', in D.I. Slobin (ed.) *The Cross-Linguistic Study of Language Acquisition*, Hillsdale, NJ: Laurence Erlbaum Associates.

—— (1996) 'From "thought and language" to "thinking for speaking"', in J.J. Gumperz and S.C. Levinson (eds) *Rethinking Linguistic Relativity*, Cambridge: Cambridge University Press.

Smart, G. (1993) 'Genre as community invention: a central bank's response to the executive's expectations as readers', in R. Spilka (ed.) *Writing in the Workplace: New Research Perspectives*, Carbondale: South Illinois University Press.

Smith, E.E. and Medin, D.L. (1981) *Categories and Concepts*, Harvard: Harvard University Press.

Smith, M. (1926) *An Investigation of the Development of the Sentence and the Extent of Vocabulary in Young Children* (University of Iowa Studies in Child Welfare, 3(5)), Iowa City.

Smith, P.M. (1985) *Language, the Sexes and Society*, Oxford: Basil Blackwell.

Smith, R.C. (1999) *The Writings of Harold Palmer: An Overview*, Tokyo: Hon-no-Tomosha.

Sowa, J.F. (1984) *Conceptual Structures: Information Processing in Mind and Machine*, Reading, MA, and London: Addison Wesley.

Sparck Jones, K. and Wilks, Y. (1983) *Automatic Natural Language Parsing*, Chichester: Ellis Horwood.

Spencer, A. (1991) *Morphological Theory: An Introduction to Word Structure in Generative Grammar*, Oxford: Basil Blackwell.

Spender, D. (1980) *Man Made Language*, London: Routledge & Kegan Paul.

Sperber, D. and Wilson, D. (1986/1995) *Relevance: Communication and Cognition*, Oxford: Basil Blackwell; 2nd edition 1995.

—— (1987) 'Précis of *Relevance*', *The Behavioral and Brain Sciences* 10(4): 697–710.

Spivey-Knowlton, M.J., Trueswell, J.C. and Tanenhaus, M.K. (1995) 'Context effects in syntactic ambiguity resolution: discourse and semantic influences in parsing reduced relative clauses', in J.M. Henderson, M. Singer and F. Ferreira (eds) *Reading and Language Processing*, Mahwah, NJ: Lawrence Erlbaum Associates.

Spolsky, B. (1980) 'Educational linguistics', in R.B. Kaplan (ed.) *On the Scope of Applied Linguistics*, Rowley, MA: Newbury House.

—— (ed.) (1999) *Concise Encyclopedia of Educational Linguistics*, Oxford: Pergamon.

Springer, S.P. and Deutsch, G. (1985/1993) *Left Brain, Right Brain*, New York: W.H. Freeman; 4th edition 1993.

Stabler, E.P., Jr (1987) 'Restricting logic grammars with government-binding theory', *Comparative Linguistics* 13(1–2): 1–10.

Stampe, D. (1969) 'The acquisition of phonetic representation', in R.I. Binnick, A. Davison, G.M. Green and J.L. Morgan (eds) *Papers from the Fifth Regional Meeting of the Chicago Linguistic Society*: 443–54.

—— (1973) 'On chapter 9', in M. Kenstowicz and C. Kisseberth (eds) *Issues in Phonological Theory*, The Hague: Mouton.

Stanley, J.P. (1973) *Paradigmatic Woman: The Prostitute*, New York: Linguistic Society of America.

—— (1977) 'Gender-marking in American English: usage and reference', in A.P. Nilsen, H. Bosmajian, H.L. Gershuny and J.P. Stanley (eds) *Sexism and Language*, Urbana, IL: National Council of Teachers of English.

Stanovich, K.E. (1990) 'Concepts in developmental theories of reading skill: cognitive resources, automaticity, and modularity', *Developmental Review* 10: 72–100.

Stati, S. (1985) 'Un ipotesi di semantica lessicale: forma–sostanza–materia', *Il Protagora XXV* 4(7–8): 91–105.

Steedman, M. (1996) *Surface Structure and Interpretation*, Cambridge, MA: MIT Press.

Steklis, H.D. and Raleigh, M.J. (1979) 'Requisites for language: interspecific and evolutionary aspects', in H.D. Steklis and M.J. Raleigh (eds) *Neurobiology of Social Communication in Primates: An Evolutionary Perspective*, New York: Academic Press.

Stern, C. and Stern, W. (1907) *Die Kindersprache*, Leipzig: Barth.

Sternberg, R.J., Tourangeau, R. and Nigro, G. (1979) 'Metaphor, induction, and social policy: the convergence of macroscopic and microscopic views', in A. Ortony (ed.) *Metaphor and Thought*, Cambridge: Cambridge University Press.

Stevens, K.N. (1960) 'Towards a model for speech-recognition', *Journal of the Acoustical Society of America* 32: 47–55.

—— (1981) 'Constraints imposed by the auditory system on the properties used to classify speech sounds: data from phonology, acoustics, and psychoacoustics', in T. Meyers, J. Laver and J. Anderson (eds) *The Cognitive Representation of Speech*, New York: North Holland.

—— and Blumstein, S.E. (1978) 'Invariant cues for place of articulation in stop consonants', *Journal of the Acoustical Society of America* 64: 358–68.

Stewart, W.A. (1962a) 'Creole languages in the Caribbean', in F.A. Rice (ed.) *Study of the Role of Second Languages in Asia, Africa and Latin America*, Washington, DC: Center for Applied Linguistics.

—— (1962b) 'An outline of linguistic typology for describing multilingualism', in F.A. Rice (ed.) *Study of the Role of Second Languages in Asia, Africa and Latin America*, Washington, DC: Center for Applied Linguistics.

Stokoe, W.C. (1960) *Sign Language Structure*, Silver Spring, M.D.: Linstok Press.

——, Casterline, D.C. and Croneberg, C.G. (1976) *A Dictionary of American Sign Language on Linguistic Principles*, revised edition, Silver Spring, MD: Linstok Press.

Stowe, L.A. (1986) 'Parsing wh-constructions: evidence for on-line gap location', *Language and Cognitive Processes* 1: 227–45.

——, Tanenhaus, M.K. and Carlson, G. (1991) 'Filling gaps on-line: use of lexical and semantic information in sentence processing', *Language and Speech* 34(4): 319–40.

Strässler (1982) *Idioms in English: A Pragmatic Analysis*, Tübingen: Gunter Narr.

Strevens, P. (1992) 'Applied linguistics: an overview', in W. Grabe and R.B. Kaplan (eds) *Introduction to Applied Linguistics*, Reading, MA: Addison Wesley.

Stringer, C. and McKie, R. (1996) *African Exodus: The Origins of Modern Humanity*, London: Cape.

Stubbs, M. (1983) *Language, Schools and Classrooms*, 2nd edition, London and New York: Methuen.

—— (1986) *Educational Linguistics*, Oxford: Basil Blackwell.

—— and Hillier, H. (eds) (1983) *Readings on Language, Schools and Classrooms*, London and New York: Methuen.

Stump, G.T. (2001) *Inflectional Morphology: A Theory of Paradigm Structure*, Cambridge: Cambridge University Press.

Suomi, K. (1993) 'An outline of a developmental model of adult phonological organization and behaviour', *Journal of Phonetics* 21: 29–60.

Suppes, P. (1960) *Axiomatic Set Theory*, Princeton, NJ: Van Nostrand.

Sutcliffe, D. (1984) 'British Black English and West Indian Creoles', in P.J. Trudgill (ed.) *Language in the British Isles*, Cambridge: Cambridge University Press.

—— with Figueroa, J. (1992) *System in Black Language*, Clevedon, Philadelphia and Adelaide: Multilingual Matters.

Svartvik, J. (1968) *The Evans Statements: A Case for Forensic Linguistics*, Göteborg: University of Gothenburg Press.

——, Eeg-Olofsson, M., Forsheden, O., Örestrom, B. and Thavenius, C. (1982) *Survey of Spoken English: Report on Research 1975–81* (Lund Studies in English, no. 63), Lund: CWK Gleerup.

Swacker, M. (1975) 'The sex of the speaker as a sociolinguistic variable', in B. Thorne and N. Henley (eds) *Language and Sex: Difference and Dominance*, Rowley, MA: Newbury House.

Swadesh, M. (1934) 'The phonemic principle', *Language* 10: 117–29.

Swales, J.M. (1981) *Aspects of Article Introductions* (Aston ESP Research Reports, no. 1), Language Studies Unit, University of Aston in Birmingham.

—— (1985) 'English language papers and authors' first language: preliminary explorations', *Scientometrics* 8: 91–101.

—— (1987) 'Utilizing the literatures in teaching the research paper', *TESOL Quarterly* 21: 41–68.

—— (1990) *Genre Analysis: English in Academic and Research Settings*, Cambridge: Cambridge University Press.

—— (1998) *Other Floors, Other Voices: A Textography of a Small University Building*, Mahwah, NJ: Lawrence Erlbaum Associates.

Sweet, H. (1877) *A Handbook of Phonetics, Including a Popular Exposition of the Principles of Spelling Reform*, Oxford: Clarendon Press.

—— (1884) 'On the practical study of language', *Transactions of the Philological Society 1882–84*: 577–99.

—— (1899/1964) *The Practical Study of Languages: A Guide for Teachers and Learners*, London: Oxford University Press; 1st edition 1899, London: Dent.

Swigart, L. (1992) 'Two codes or one? The insiders' view and the description of code-switching in Dakar', *Journal of Multilingual and Multicultural Development* 13(1–2): 83–102.

Swinney, D.A. (1979) 'Lexical access during sentence comprehension: (re)consideration of context effects', *Journal of Verbal Learning and Verbal Behaviour* 18: 654–9.

Tabossi, P. (1988) 'Accessing lexical ambiguity in different types of sentence context', *Journal of Memory and Language* 27: 324–40.

Taft, M. (1994) 'Interactive-activation as a framework for understanding morphological processing', *Language and Cognitive Processes* 9: 271–94.

Taine, H. (1877) 'On the acquisition of language by children', *Mind* 2: 252–9.

Talmy, L. (1978) 'Figure and ground in complex sentences', in J.H. Greenberg (ed.), *Universals of Human Language*, vol. 3, *Syntax*, Stanford, CA: Stanford University Press.

—— (1988a) 'Force dynamics in language and cognition', *Cognitive Science* 12(1): 49–100.

—— (1988b) 'The relation of grammar to cognition', in B. Rudzka-Ostyn (ed.) *Topics in Cognitive Linguistics*, Amsterdam: John Benjamins.

Tannen, D. (1989) *Talking Voices: Repetition, Dialogue and Imagery in Conversational Discourse*, Cambridge: Cambridge University Press.

—— (ed.) (1993) *Gender and Conversational Interaction*, New York and Oxford: Oxford University Press.

Taraban, R. and McClelland, J.L. (1988) 'Constituent attachment and thematic role assignment in sentence processing: influence of context-based expectations', *Journal of Memory and Language* 27: 597–632.

Tarnapol, M. and Tarnapol, L. (1976) 'Dyslexia: the problem of recognition', *Update*.

Taylor, D.R. (1959) 'On function words versus form in "non-traditional" languages', *Word* 15: 485–589.

—— (1960) 'Language shift or changing relationship?', *International Journal of American Linguistics* 26: 155–61.

Taylor, J.R. (1995a) *Linguistic Categorization: Prototypes in Linguistic Theory*, Oxford: Clarendon Press.

—— (1995b) 'Models of word meaning in comparison: the two-level model (Manfred Bierwisch) and the network model (Ronald Langacker)', in R. Dirven and J. Vanparys (eds) *Current Approaches to the Lexicon*, Frankfurt-am-Main: Peter Lang.

—— (1998) 'Syntactic constructions as prototype categories', in M. Thomasello (ed.), *The New Psychology of Language: Cognitive and Functional Approaches to Language Structure*, Hillsdale, N.J.: Lawrence Erlbaum.

Templin, M. (1957) *Certain Language Skills in Children* (University of Minnesota Institute of Child Welfare Monograph Series, no. 26), Minneapolis: University of Minnesota Press.

Tench, P. (1996) *The Intonation Systems of English*, London: Cassell.

Terrace, H.S. (1979) *Nim: A Chimpanzee Who Learned Sign Language*, New York: Alfred Knopf.

Thomas, C.K. (1958) *An Introduction to the Phonetics of American English*, 2nd edition, New York: Ronald Press.

Thompson, M.E. (1984) *Developmental Dyslexia*, London: Edward Arnold.

Thompson, R.W. (1961) 'A note on some possible affinities between the creole dialects of the Old World and those of the New', in R.B. Le Page (ed.) *Creole Language Studies II*, Proceedings of the Conference on Creole Language Studies, University of the West Indies, March–April 1959, London: Macmillan.

Thompson-Schill, S.L., Kurtz, K.J. and Gabrieli, J.D.E. (1998) 'Effects of semantic and associative relatedness on automatic priming', *Journal of Memory and Language* 38: 440–58.

Threadgold, T. (1986) 'Semiotics – ideology – language', in T. Threadgold, E.A. Grosz, G. Kress and M.A.K. Halliday (eds) *Semiotics,*

Ideology, Language (Sydney Studies in Society and Culture, no. 3), Sydney: Sydney Association for Studies in Society and Culture.

Tiedemann, D. (1787) *Beobachtungen über die Entwicklung der Seelenfähigkeit bei Kindern*, Altenburg; published in English in F.L. Solden (1877) *Tiedemann's Record of Infant Life*, Syracuse, NY.

Tinbergen, N. (1972) *The Animal and Its World*, 2 vols, London: George Allen and Unwin.

Todd, L. (1974), *Pidgins and Creoles*, London: Routledge and Kegan Paul.

Togeby, K. (1951) *Structure immanente de la langue française* (Travaux du Cercle Linguistique de Copenhague VI); 2nd edition 1965, Paris: Larousse.

Tomasello, M. (ed.) (1998) *The New Psychology of Language: Cognitive and Functional Approaches to Language Structure*, Hillsdale, NJ: Lawrence Erlbaum Associates.

Tomlin, R.S. (1986) *Basic Word Order: Functional Principles*, London: Croom Helm.

Toolan, M. (1989), *Narrative*. London: Routledge.

Tottie, G. and Bäcklund, I. (eds) (1986) *English in Speech and Writing: A Symposium* (Studia Anglistica Uppsaliensia Series, no. 60), Uppsala, Acta Universitatis Upsaliensis.

Toukomaa, P. and Skutnabb-Kangas, T. (1977) *The Intensive Teaching of the Mother-Tongue to Migrant Children at Pre School Age* (Tutkimuksia Research Report, no. 26), Department of Sociology and Social Psychology, University of Tampere, Finland.

Trager, G.L. and Smith, H.L., Jr (1951) *An Outline of English Structure* (Studies in Linguistics, Occasional Papers, no. 3), Norman, OK: Battenburg Press.

Travis, L. (1984) 'Parameters and effects of word order variation', unpublished Ph.D. thesis, MIT.

Traxler, M.J. and Pickering, M.J. (1996) 'Plausibility and the processing of unbounded dependencies: an eye-tracking study', *Journal of Memory and Language* 35: 454–75.

Treffers-Daller, J. (1992) 'French–Dutch code-switching in Brussels: social factors explaining its disappearance', *Journal of Multilingual and Multicultural Development* 13(1–2): 143–56.

Trubetzkoy, N.S. (1929) 'Sur la "morphophonologie"', *Travaux du Cercle Linguistique de Prague* 1: 85–8.

—— (1931) 'Gedanken über Morphophonologie', *Travaux du Cercle Linguistique de Prague* 4: 160–3.

—— (1939/1969) *Grundzüge der Phonologie: Travaux du Cercle Linguistique de Prague*; published in English 1969 as *Principles of Phonology*, trans. C.A.M. Baltaxe, Berkeley and Los Angeles: University of California Press.

Trudgill, P.J. (1972) 'Sex, covert prestige and linguistic change in the urban British English of Norwich', *Language in Society* 1: 179–95.

—— (1974a) *The Social Differentiation of English in Norwich*, London: Cambridge University Press.

—— (1974b/1983) *Sociolinguistics: An Introduction*, Harmondsworth: Penguin; 2nd, revised edition 1983.

—— (1975) *Accent, Dialect and the School*, London: Edward Arnold.

—— (1979/1983) 'Standard and non-standard dialects of English in the UK: problems and policies', *International Journal of the Sociology of Language* 21: 9–24; reprinted in M. Stubbs and H. Hillier (eds) (1983) *Readings on Language, Schools and Classrooms*, London and New York: Methuen.

—— (1983) *On Dialect: Social and Geographical Perspectives*, Oxford: Basil Blackwell.

—— (ed.) (1984) *Language in the British Isles*, Cambridge: Cambridge University Press.

—— (1990) *The Dialects of England*, Oxford: Basil Blackwell.

Trueswell, J.C. (1996) 'The role of lexical frequency in syntactic ambiguity resolution', *Journal of Memory and Language* 35: 566–85.

——, Tanenhaus, M.K. and Garnsey, S.M. (1994) 'Semantic influences on parsing: use of thematic role information in syntactic ambiguity resolution', *Journal of Memory and Language* 33: 285–318.

Turner, R. (1974) *Ethnomethodology*, Harmondsworth: Penguin.

Uldall, H.J. (1957) *Outline of Glossematics* vol. 1, *General Theory* (Travaux du Cercle Linguistique de Copenhague vol. 11); 2nd edition 1967, Copenhagen: Nordisk Sprog-og Kulturforlag.

Ullmann, S. (1962) *Semantics*, Oxford: Basil Blackwell, and New York: Barnes and Noble.

Ungerer, F. and Schmid, H.-J. (1996) *An Introduction to Cognitive Linguistics*, London: Longman.

Vachek, J. (1933) 'What is phonology?', *English Studies* 15: 81–92.

—— (ed.) (1964) *A Prague School Reader in Linguistics*, Bloomington: Indiana University Press.

—— (1966) *The Linguistic School of Prague: An Introduction to Its Theory and Practice*, Bloomington and London: Indiana University Press.

Vainikka, A. and Young-Scholten, M. (1994) 'Direct access to X-theory: Evidence from Korean and Turkish adults learning German', in T. Hoekstra and B. Schwartz (eds) *Language Acquisition Studies in Generative Grammar: Papers in Honor of Kenneth Wexler from the GLOW 1991 Workshops*, Amsterdam: John Benjamins.

Valdman, A. and Highfield, A. (eds) (1980) *Theoretical Orientations in Creole Studies*, New York: Academic Press.

Van Cleve, J.V. (ed.) (1987) *Gallaudet Encyclopedia of Deaf People and Deafness*, New York: McGraw-Hill.

Van der Gaag, A. (1996) *Communicating Quality*, London: The Royal College of Speech and Language Therapists.

van Dijk, T.A. (1972) *Some Aspects of Text Grammars*, The Hague: Mouton.

—— (1977) *Text and Context: Exploration in the Semantics and Pragmatics of Discourse*, London and New York: Routledge.

—— (1993) *Discourse and Elite Racism*, London: Sage.

—— and Kintsch, W. (1978) 'Cognitive psychology and discourse: recalling and summarizing stories', in W.U. Dressler (ed.) *Trends in Textlinguistics*, Berlin and New York: Walter de Gruyter.

——, Ihwe, J., Petöfi, J. and Rieser, H. (1972) *Zur Bestimmung narrativer Structuren auf der Grundlage von Textgrammatiken*, Hamburg: Buske.

van Ek, J.A. (1975) *The Threshold Level*, Strasbourg: Council of Europe, reprinted (1980), Oxford: Pergamom Books.

Van Lancker, D. and Fromkin, V.A. (1973) 'Hemispheric specialization for pitch and tone: evidence from Thai', *Journal of Phonetics* 1: 101–9.

Van Orden, G.C. and Goldinger, S.D. (1994) 'Interdependence of form and function in cognitive systems explains perception of printed words', *Journal of Experimental Psychology: Human Perception and Performance* 20: 1269–91.

——, Johnston, J.C. and Halle, B.L. (1988) 'Word identification in reading proceeds from spelling to meaning', *Journal of Experimental Psychology: Learning, Memory, and Cognition* 14: 371–85.

Van Peer, W. (1986) *Stylistics and Psychology: Investigations of Foregrounding*, London: Croom Helm.

Vellutino, F.R. (1979) *Dyslexia: Theory and Research*, London: MIT Press.

Vestergaard, T. and Schröder, K. (1986) *The Language of Advertising*, Oxford: Basil Blackwell.

Vigliocco, G., Antonini, T. and Garrett, M.F. (1997) 'Grammatical gender is on the tip of Italian tongues', *Psychological Science* 8(4): 314–17.

Vihman, M.M. (1996) *Phonological development*, Oxford: Blackwell Publishers.

Voegelin, C.F. (1952) 'Edward Sapir (1884–1939)', *Word Study* 27: 1–3.

Volterra, V. and Taeschner, R. (1978) 'The acquisition and development of language by bilingual children', *Journal of Child Language* 5: 311–26.

Voorhoeve, J. (1973) 'Historical and linguistic evidence in favor of the relexification theory in the formation of creoles', *Language in Society* 2: 133–45.

Wakelin, M.F. (1972) *English Dialects: An Introduction*, London: Athlone Press.

Wall, R. (1972) *Introduction to Mathematical Linguistics*, Englewood Cliffs, NJ: Prentice Hall.

Wallace, A.R. (1895) 'Expressiveness of speech: or mouth gestures as a factor in the origin of language', *Fortnightly Review* 64 ns 58: 528–43.

Wallis, S., Aarts, B. and Nelson, G. (2000) 'Parsing in reverse: exploring ICE-GB with fuzzy tree fragments and ICECUP,' in J.M. Kirk (ed.) *Corpora Galore: Analyses and Techniques in Describing English*, Amsterdam: Rodopi.

Walsh, K.W. (1978) *Neuropsychology: A Clinical Approach*, Edinburgh: Churchill Livingstone.

Wang, W.S.-Y. (1967) 'Phonological features of tone', *International Journal of American Linguistics* 33(2): 93–105.

—— (1972) 'The many uses of FO', *Papers in Linguistics and Phonetics to the Memory of Pierre Delattre*, The Hague: Mouton.

—— (1973) 'The Chinese language', *Scientific American* 50 (March); reprinted in W.S.-Y. Wang (ed.) (1982) *Human Communication*, New York: W.H. Freeman.

—— (1976) 'Language change', *Annals of the NY Academy of Science* 280: 61–72.

—— and Cheng, C.C. (1987) 'Middle Chinese tones in modern dialects', in R. Channon and L. Shockey (eds) *In Honor of Ilse Lehiste*, Dordrecht: Fans.

Wardhaugh, R. (1970) 'The contrastive analysis hypothesis', *TESOL Quarterly* 4(2): 123–30.

Warren, D.H.D. and Pereira, F.C.N. (1982) 'An efficient easily adaptable system for interpreting natural language queries', *American Journal of Computational Linguistics* 8(34): 110–22.

Warren, R.M. (1982) *Auditory Perception: A New Synthesis*, New York: Pergamon Press.

Waterhouse, V.G. (1974) *The History and Development of Tagmemics*, The Hague and Paris: Mouton.

Watson, J. (1809) *Instruction for the Deaf and Dumb: Or, a Theoretical and Practical View of the Means by Which They Are Taught*, London: Darton and Harvey.

Watson, J.B. (1924) *Behaviorism*, Chicago and New York: University of Chicago Press.

Weaver, W. (1955) 'Translation', in W.N. Locke and A.D. Booth (eds) *Machine Translation of Language*, New York: John Wiley and Sons.

Webber, B.L. (1983) 'So what can we talk about now?', in R.C. Berwick and J.M. Brady (eds) *Computational Models of Discourse*, Cambridge, MA: MIT Press.

Webster, D.B. (1995) *Neuroscience of Communication*, San Diego, CA: Singular Publishing Group, Inc.

Weinreich, U. (1953/1968) *Languages in Contact*, The Hague: Mouton; revised edition 1968.

—— (1954) 'Is a structural dialectology possible?', *Word* 10: 388–400.

—— (1969) 'Problems in the analysis of idioms', in J. Puhvel (ed.) *Substance and Structure in Language*, Los Angeles: University of California Press.

Weiss, A.P. (1925) 'Linguistics and psychology', *Language* 1(2): 52–7.

Weissenborn, J. (1990) 'Functional categories and verb movement: the acquisition of German syntax reconsidered', in M. Rothweiler (ed.) *Spracherwerb und Grammatik*, Opladen: Westdeutscher Verlag.

—— (1992) 'Null subjects in early grammars: implications for parameter-setting theories', in J.H. Weissenborn, H. Goodluck and T. Roeper (eds) *Theoretical Issues in Language Acquisition*, Hillsdale, NJ: Lawrence Erlbaum Associates.

Weizenbaum, J. (1966) 'ELIZA – a computer program for the study of natural language communication between man and machine', *Communications of the ACM* 9: 36–45.

Wellek, R. and Warren, A. (1949/1956/1963) *Theory of Literature*, Austin, TX: Harcourt Brace Jovanovich; 2nd edition 1956, New York: Harcourt Brace Jovanovich; 3rd edition 1963, Harmondsworth: Penguin.

Wellman, B.L., Case, I.M., Mengert, I.G. and Bradbury, D.E. (1931) *Speech Sounds of Young Children* (University of Iowa Studies in Child Welfare 5(2)).

Wells, R.S. (1947) 'Immediate constituents', *Language* 23: 81–117.

—— (1949) 'Automatic alternation', *Language* 25: 99–116.

Werker, J.F. (1995) 'Age-related changes in cross-language speech perception: standing at the cross-roads', in W. Strange (ed.) *Speech Perception and Linguistic Experience: Issues in Cross-Language Research*, Timonium, MD: York Press.

Werth, P. (1999) *Text Worlds: Representing Conceptual Space in Discourse*, Harlow: Longman.

West, M. (1960) *Teaching English in Difficult Circumstances*, London: Longman.

Wheeldon, L.R. and Monsell, S. (1994) 'Inhibition of spoken word production by priming a semantic competitor', *Journal of Memory and Language* 33: 332–56.

Whinnom, K. (1956) *Spanish Contact Vernaculars in the Philippine Islands*, Hong Kong: Hong Kong University Press.

Whitaker, H. and Whitaker, H.A. (eds) (1976) *Studies in Neurolingustics* (Perspectives in Neurolingustics and Psycholinguistics Series), vol. 1, New York: Academic Press.

White, L. (1989) *Universal Grammar and Second Language Acquisition*, Amsterdam: John Benjamins.

—— (1992) 'Long and short verb movement in second language acquisition', *Canadian Journal of Linguistics* 37: 273–386.

White, R. (1988) *The ELT Curriculum*, Oxford: Basil Blackwell.

Whitfield, F.J. (1954) 'Glossematics', in A. Martinet and U. Weinreich (eds) *Linguistics Today: Publication on the Occasion of Columbia University Bicentennial*, New York: Linguistic Circle of New York.

Whitney, P. (1986) 'Processing category terms in context: instantiations as inferences', *Memory and Cognition* 14: 39–48.

——, McKay, T., Kellas, G. and Emerson, W.A. (1985) 'Semantic activation of noun concepts in context', *Journal of Experimental Psychology: Learning, Memory, and Cognition* 11: 126–35.

Whitney, W.D. (1867) *Language and the Study of Language: Twelve Lectures on the Principles of Linguistic Science*, 4th, augmented edition 1884, London: Trübner.

—— (1875) *The Life and Growth of Language*, London: King.

Whorf, B.L. (1939/1941/1956/1997) 'The relation of habitual thought and behavior to language'; written in 1939, published in L. Spier (ed.) (1941) *Language, Culture and Personality*, Menasha, WI: Sapir Memorial Publication Fund; reprinted in J.B. Carroll (ed.) (1956) *Language, Thought and Reality: Selected Writings of Benjamin Lee Whorf*, Cambridge MA: MIT Press, and in N. Coupland and A. Jaworski (eds) (1997) *Sociolinguistics: A Reader and Coursebook*, London: Macmillan.

—— (1940) 'Science and linguistics', *Technological Review* 42(6): 229–31, 247–8.

—— (1950) 'An American Indian model of the universe', *International Journal of American Linguistics* 16: 67–72; reprinted in J.B. Carroll (ed.) (1956) *Language, Thought and Reality: Selected Writings of Benjamin Lee Whorf*, Cambridge, MA: MIT Press.

Wichmann, A., Fligelstone, S., McEnery, T. and Knowles, G. (eds) (1997) *Teaching and Language Corpora*, London: Longman.

Widdowson, H.G. (1975) *Stylistics and the Teaching of Literature*, London: Longman.

—— (1978) *Teaching Language as Communication*, Oxford: Oxford University Press.

—— (1980) 'Models and fictions', *Applied Linguistics* 1: 165–70.

—— (1983) *Learning Purpose and Language Use*, Oxford: Oxford University Press.

—— (1992) *Practical Stylistics*, Oxford: Oxford University Press.

—— (2000a) 'Object language and the language subject: on the mediating role of applied linguistics', *Annual Review of Applied Linguistics* 20: 21–33.

—— (2000b) 'On the limitation of linguistics applied', *Applied Linguistics* 21: 2–25.

Wierzbicka, A. (1972) *Semantic Primitives*, Linguistische Forschungen, no. 22, Frankfurt: Athenäum.

—— (1985) 'Different cultures, different languages, different speech acts: Polish vs English', *Journal of Pragmatics* 9: 145–78.

—— (1987) *English Speech Act Verbs: A Semantic Dictionary*, Sydney: Academic Press.

—— (1996) *Semantics: Primes and Universals*, Oxford and New York: Oxford University Press.

Wilensky, R. (1978) 'Why John married Mary: understanding stories involving recurring goals', *Cognitive Science* 2: 235–66.

Wilkins, D.A. (1976) *Notional Syllabuses*, Oxford: Oxford University Press.

Wilks, Y. (1978) 'Making preferences more active', *FIArtInt.* 11: 197–223.

Williams, E. (1981) 'On the notions "lexically related" and "head of a word"', *Linguistic Inquiry* 12(2): 245–74.

Williams, I. (1999) 'Results sections of medical research articles: analysis of rhetorical categories for pedagogical purposes', *English for Specific Purposes* 18: 347–66.

Williams, J.N. (1992) 'Processing polysemous words in context: evidence for interrelated meanings', *Journal of Psycholinguistic Research* 21: 193–218.

—— (1993) 'Processing of anaphoric nouns in extended texts: the role of surface information', *Language and Speech* 36: 373–91.

—— (1996) 'Is automatic priming semantic?', *European Journal of Cognitive Psychology* 8: 113–61.

Willis, J. and Willis, D. (1988) *The COBUILD English Course*, Glasgow and London: Collins.

Winograd, T. (1972) *Understanding Natural Language*, New York: Academic Press.

—— (1983) *Language as a Cognitive Process*, vol. 1, *Syntax*, Reading, MA: Addison Wesley.

Winter, E.O. (1971) 'Connections in science material: A proposition about the semantics of clause relations' (Centre for Information on Language Teaching Papers and Reports, no. 7), London: Centre for Information on Language Teaching and Research for British Association for Applied Linguistics.

—— (1977) 'A clause-relational approach to English texts: a study of some predictive lexical items in written discourse', *Instructional Science* 6(1): 1–92.

—— (1986) 'Clause relations as information structure: two basic text structures in English', in M. Coulthard (ed.) *Talking About Text: Studies Presented to David Brazil on his Retirement* (Discourse Analysis Monograph, no. 13), English Language Research, University of Birmingham.

Witmer, L. (1909) 'A monkey with a mind', *Psychological Clinic* 13(7): 189–205.

Wittgenstein, L. (1921/1974) *Tractatus Logico-Philosophicus, Annalen der Naturphilosophie*, London and Henley: Routledge & Kegan Paul; reprinted 1974.

—— (1953/1968) *Philosophical Investigations*, Oxford: Basil Blackwell; reprint of English text, with index, 1968.

Wodak, R. (1996) *Disorders of Discourse*, London: Longman.

Wolfram, W. and Schiffrin, D. (eds) (1989) *Language Change and Variation*, Amsterdam and Philadelphia: John Benjamins.

Woll, B. (1990) 'Sign language', in N.E. Collinge (ed.) *An Encyclopaedia of Language*, London and New York: Routledge.

Wollheim, R. (1968) *Art and Its Objects*, Harmondsworth: Penguin.

Wood, A.S. (1982) 'An examination of the rhetorical structures of authentic chemistry texts', *Applied Linguistics* 3: 121–43.

Woods, W.A. (1970) 'Transition network grammars for natural language analysis', *Communications of the ACM* 13: 591–606.

—— (1973) 'An experimental parsing system for transition network grammars', in R. Rustin (ed.) *Natural Language Processing*, New York: Algorithmics Press.

Woolford, E. (1984) 'Why creoles won't reveal the properties of universal grammar', *Behavioral and Brain Sciences* 7(2): 211–12.

Woolls, D. and Coulthard, R.M. (1998) 'Tools for the trade', *Forensic Linguistics: The Inter-*

national Journal of Speech Language and Law 5(1): 33–57.

Worden, F.G. (1971) 'Hearing and the neural detection of acoustic patterns', *Behavioral Science* 16: 20–30.

Wrede, F. and Mitzka, W. (1926–56) *Deutsche Sprachatlas*, Marburg: Elwert.

Wright, C. and Hale, R. (eds) (1999) *A Companion to the Philosophy of Language*, Oxford: Blackwell Publishers.

Wright, D. (1969) *Deafness*, New York: Stein and Day.

Wright, J. (ed.) (1898–1905) *English Dialect Dictionary*, London: Frowde.

—— (1905) *The English Dialect Grammar*, London: Frowde.

Wundt, W.M. (1900) *Völkerpsychologie II Die Sprache*, Leipzig: Engelmann.

Wydell, T.N., Patterson, K.E. and Humphreys, G.W. (1993) 'Phonologically mediated access to meaning for Kanji: Is *rows* still a *rose* in Japanese Kanji?', *Journal of Experimental Psychology: Learning, Memory, and Cognition* 19(3): 491–514.

York Papers in Linguistics II (1983), Proceedings of the York Creole Conference, University of York.

Yoshimura, Kimihiro (1998) 'The middle construction in English: a cognitive linguistic analysis', unpublished Ph.D. thesis, University of Otago, Dunedin, New Zealand.

Yost, W.A. and Nielsen, D.W. (1977), *Fundamentals of Hearing: An Introduction*, New York and London: Holt, Rinehart and Winston.

Young, E.D. and Sachs, M.B. (1979) 'Representation of steady-state vowels in the temporal aspects of the discharge patterns of populations of auditory-nerve fibers', *Journal of the Acoustical Society of America* 66: 1381–403.

Young, F. (1941) 'An analysis of certain variables in a developmental study of language', *Genetic Psychology Monographs* 23: 3–141.

Young, S. and Bloothooft, G. (eds) (1997) *Corpus-Based Methods in Language Speech Processing*, Dordrecht: Kluwer.

Yule, G. (1985) *The Study of Language: An Introduction*, Cambridge: Cambridge University Press.

—— (1996) *Pragmatics*, Oxford: Oxford University Press.

Zadeh, L.A. (1975) 'Fuzzy logic and approximate reasoning', *Synthese* 30(34): 407–28.

Zangwill, O.L. (1971) 'The neurology of language', in N. Minnis (ed.) *Linguistics at Large*, London: Victor Gollancz.

Zatorre, R.J., Evans, A.C., Meyer, E. and Gjedde, A. (1992) 'Lateralization of phonetic and pitch discrimination in speech processing', *Science* 256: 846–9.

Zgusta, L. (1967) 'Multiword lexical units', *Word* 23: 578–87.

Zhou, X. and Marslen-Wilson, W. (1999) 'Phonology, orthography, and semantic activation in reading Chinese', *Journal of Memory and Language* 41: 579–606.

Zimmerman, D. and West, C. (1975) 'Sex roles, interruptions and silences in conversation', in B. Thorne and N. Henley (eds) *Language and Sex: Difference and Dominance*, Rowley, MA: Newbury House.

Zwicky, A. (1986) 'The general case: basic form versus default form', Proceedings of the 12th Annual Meeting of the Berkeley Linguistics Society: 305–14.

Index